INDEX TO

LITERARY BIOGRAPHY

by

Patricia Pate Havlice

Volume I: A-K

The Scarecrow Press, Inc.
Metuchen, N.J.   1975

016.809
H 388
v.1

Library of Congress Cataloging in Publication Data

Havlice, Patricia Pate.
    Index to literary biography.

    1. Literature--Bio-bibliography--Bibliography.
2. Authors--Indexes. I. Title.
Z6511.H38   016.809   74-8315
ISBN 0-8108-0745-9

PREFACE

This work is intended as a quick reference tool for locating biographical information on approximately 68,000 authors from antiquity to the present. Each entry includes the author's real name, pseudonyms, dates of birth and death, nationality, type of writing engaged in and a letter code referring the user to a volume of the bibliography containing that author's biography. Full information for some writers is found under the real name, for others under the pseudonym. Cross references guide the user from one name to the other.

I would like to thank Jane Gray Morning and her staff at the Batavia (Illinois) Public Library for their aid and thoughtfulness. I am grateful also for the help I received from Northern Illinois University, the Newberry Library and various member libraries of the Dupage Library System in obtaining the books to be indexed.

P. P. H.

BIBLIOGRAPHY

AL   O Albrecht, Günter, et al. Deutsches Schriftstellerlexikon von den Anfängen bis zur Gegenwart. Leipzig: Veb Bibliographisches Institut, 1964.

BL   O Bleiberg, Germán y Julián Marías. Diccionario de literatura española. Tercera edición corregida y aumentada. Madrid: Revista de Occidente, 1967.

BRO O Browning, D. C., ed. Everyman's Dictionary of Literary Biography: English and American. Rev. ed. New York: Dutton, 1962.

COL R Columbia Dictionary of Modern European Literature. New York: 803 Columbia University Press, 1947. C7

COM O Commire, Anne. Something about the Author: Facts and Pictures about Contemporary Authors and Illustrators of Books for Young People. 2 vols. Detroit: Gale, 1971.

CON R Contemporary Authors: The International Bio-Bibliographical 928 Guide to Current Authors and Their Works. Vols. 1-40, indexed. C761 Detroit: Gale, 1962-73.

DI R Diccionario de la literatura latinoamericana: Ecuador. Washing- 860.3 ton, D. C.: Unión Panamericana, 1962. P187

DIC   Dictionnaire de littérature contemporaine. 3rd ed. Paris: Edi- R840.3 tions Universitaire, 1963.   Lib. has 1 st ed. B862

DIF O Dictionnaire des auteurs français. Nouvelle ed. Paris: Collection Seghers, 1961.

DIL R Dictionnaire des lettres françaises. 2 vols. Paris: Librairie 840.3 Arthéme Fayard, 1960.   Lib. has 1951 ed. D554

DOY   Doyle, Brian. The Who's Who of Children's Literature. New O York: Schocken, 1968.

FLE R Fleischmann, Wolfgang Bernard. Encyclopedia of World Litera- 803 ture in the 20th Century. 3 vols. Enl. & updated ed. of Herder E56 Lexikon der Weltliteratur im 20. Jahrhundert. New York: Ungar, 1967.

FUL R Fuller, Muriel, ed. More Junior Authors. New York: Wilson, 809 1963. F967

HAR   Hargreaves-Mawdsley, W. N. Everyman's Dictionary of European O Writers. New York: Dutton, 1968.

R
891.703 HARK Harkins, William E. *Dictionary of Russian Literature.* New
H 28 York: Philosophical Library, 1956.

HIG ○ Higginson, Alexander Henry. *British and American Sporting Authors; Their Writings and Biographies.* Berryville, Va.: Blue Ridge Press, 1949.

HIL ○ Hilbert, Rachel. *Michigan Poets; With Supplement to Michigan Authors, 1960.* Ann Arbor, Mich.: Association of School Librarians, 1964.

R
922 HO Hoehn, Matthew. *Catholic Authors: Contemporary Biographical Sketches.* Newark, N. J.: St. Mary's Abbey, 1952. Vol 2
H69 put in 1952

HOE Hoehn, Matthew, O. S. B. *Catholic Authors: Contemporary Biographical Sketches, 1930-1947.* Newark, N. J.: St. Mary's Abbey, 1948.

HOO ○ Hook, J. N., Ellen Burkhart, and Louise Lane. *Illinois Authors and a Literary Map of Illinois.* Urbana: Illinois Association of Teachers of English, 1952.

JO ○ Joint Committee of the North Carolina English Teachers Association and the North Carolina Library Association. *North Carolina Authors: A Selective Handbook.* Chapel Hill: University of North Carolina Library, 1952.

R
810.9 KAA Kunitz, Stanley J. and Howard Haycraft. *American Authors, 1600-1900: A Biographical Dictionary of American Literature.* New
K96 York: Wilson, 1938.

KAT ○ Kunitz, Stanley J. *Authors Today and Yesterday.* New York: Wilson, 1933.

R
820.9 KB Kunitz, Stanley J. and Howard Haycraft. *British Authors before 1800: A Biographical Dictionary.* New York: Wilson, 1952.
K96a

KBA R Kunitz, Stanley J. and Howard Haycraft. *British Authors of the*
820.9 Nineteenth Century. New York: Wilson, 1936.
K96

R
928 KE Kunitz, Stanley J. and Vineta Colby. *European Authors, 1000-1900: A Biographical Dictionary of European Literature.* New
K96 York: Wilson, 1967.

KJU R Kunitz, Stanley J. and Howard Haycraft. *The Junior Book of*
809 Authors. 2nd ed. rev. New York: Wilson, 1951.
K96b

KL ○ Kunitz, Stanley (pseud., Dilly Tante). *Living Authors: A Book of Biographies.* New York: Wilson, 1931.

R
809 KT Kunitz, Stanley J. and Howard Haycraft. *Twentieth Century*
K96 Authors: A Biographical Dictionary of Modern Literature. New
York: Wilson, 1942.
KTS 1st suppl., 1955. Updates biographies in main vol.

KU R Kunisch, Hermann. *Handbuch der deutschen Gegenwartsliteratur.* Munich: Nymphenburger Verlagshandlung, 1965.
830.9
K96 Lib. has v. 1-3

KUN   Kunisch, Hermann. Kleines Handbuch der deutschen Gegenwartsliteratur. Munich: Nymphenburger Verlagshandlung, 1967.

LAN   Lang, David M., ed. A Guide to Eastern Literatures. New
York: Praeger, 1971.

LEN   Lennartz, Franz. Die dichter unserer Zeit. Stuttgart: A. Krö-
ner, 1951.

MAG   Magill, Frank N. Cyclopedia of World Authors. New York:
Harper, 1958 (orig. title Masterplots Cyclopedia of World Authors).

MAL   Malignon, Jean. Dictionnaire des écrivains français. Paris:
Editions du Seuil, 1971.

MAR   Marable, Mary Hays and Elaine Boylan. A Handbook of Oklahoma
Writers. Norman: University of Oklahoma Press, 1939.

MAT   Matlaw, Myron. Modern World Drama: An Encyclopedia. New
York: Dutton, 1972.

MIN   Minchero Vilasaró, Angel. Diccionario universal de escritores.
2 vols. San Sebastian, Spain: 1957 [only vol. 2, South America,
indexed].

MUR   Murphy, Rosalie. Contemporary Poets of the English Language.
New York: St. Martin's Press, 1970.

PAC   Pacific Northwest Library Association. Reference Section. Who's
Who Among Pacific Northwest Authors. 2nd ed. Bozeman, Mont.:
1970.

PIN   Pingaud, Bernard. Ecrivains d'aujourd'hui, 1940-1960; Dictionnaire anthologique et critique. Paris: Grasset, 1960.

RIC   Richardson, Kenneth. Twentieth Century Writing: A Reader's
Guide to Contemporary Literature. New York: Newnes Books,
1969.

SA   Sainz de Robles, Federico Carlos. Diccionario de la literatura.
3 vols. 2nd ed. Madrid: Aguilar, 1956.

SCA   Scally, Sister Mary Anthony. Negro Catholic Writers, 1900-1943;
A Biobibliography. Detroit: W. Romig & Co., 1945.

SP   Spender, Stephen and Donald Hall. The Concise Encyclopedia of
English and American Poets and Poetry. New York: Hawthorn,
1963.

ST   Steinberg, S. H. Cassell's Encyclopedia of World Literature. 2
vols. New York: Funk & Wagnalls, 1954.

SY   Sylvestre, Guy. Canadian Writers: A Biographical Dictionary.
Toronto: Ryerson Press, 1964.

WA   Ward, Martha E. and Dorothy A. Marquardt. Authors of Books
for Young People. 2nd ed. Metuchen, N.J.: Scarecrow, 1971.

WAF ○ Warfel, Harry R. <u>American Novelists of Today.</u> New York: American Book Co., 1951.

'A. E.' see RUSSELL, George W.
'A. L. F.' see SNAKENBURG, Theodoor van
'A. L. O. E.' see TUCKER, Charlotte M.
'A. M. V.' see CRUICKSHANK, Helen B.
'A. N. A.' see CRUICKSHANK, Helen B.
'A. R. P. M.' see GALSWORTHY, John
'A. Riposte' see MORDAUNT, Evelyn M. C.
AA, Pierre van de, -1730, French; nonfiction DIL
AAFJES, Lambertus Jacobus Johannes, 1914- , Dutch; poetry, journalism HAR ST
AAKJAER, Jeppe, 1866-1930, Danish; poetry, fiction COL FLE HAR ST
AALL, Anathon, 1897-1943, Norwegian; nonfiction, essays SA
AANRUD, Hans, 1863- , Norwegian; fiction, plays COL SA ST
AARDEMA, Verna Norberg, 1911- , American; juveniles CON
AARESTRUP, Carl Ludvig Emil, 1800-56, Danish; poetry HAR ST
AARON, Benjamin, 1915- , American; nonfiction CON
AARON, Chester, 1923- , American; nonfiction CON
AARON, Daniel, 1912- , American; nonfiction CON
AARON, James Ethridge, 1927- , American; nonfiction CON
AARONOVITCH, Sam, 1919- , English; nonfiction CON
AARONSON, Bernard Seymour, 1924- , American; nonfiction CON
AARSLEFF, Hans, 1925- , Danish-American; nonfiction CON

AASEN, Ivar Andreas, 1813-96, Norwegian; poetry COL HAR SA ST
ABAD, Diego José, 1727-79, Mexican; poetry SA
ABAD, Pedro see ABBAT, Pero
ABAILARD, Pierre see ABELARD, Peter
ABARBANEL, Isaac ben Jehudah (Abravanel), 1437-1508, Portuguese; nonfiction HAR LAN ST
ABARBANEL, Juda (Leo Herbreo; Leo Judaeus; Leone Ebreo, Judah Leon Medigo) 1460-1535, Jewish; poetry BL HAR KE LAN SA ST
ABARCA, Pedro, 1619-92, Spanish; nonfiction SA
ABARCA de BOLEA Y PORTUGAL, Jerónimo, 16th cent., Spanish; nonfiction SA
ABARZUZA, Francisco, 1838- , Cuban; poetry MIN
ABASOLO, Jenaro, 1825/33-84, Chilean; nonfiction MIN
ABATI y DIAZ, Joaquín, 1865-1936, Spanish; plays, fiction BL SA
ABAUNZA, Pedro, 1599-1649, Spanish; nonfiction SA
ABAUZIT, Firmin, 1679-1767, French; nonfiction DIL
ABBA, Giuseppe Cesare, 1838-1910, Italian; diaries, fiction HAR SA ST
ABBAD, Abu Abd Allah, 1371- , Arab; poetry SA
ABBAGNANO, Nicola, 1901- , Italian; nonfiction CON
'ABBAS b. al-AHNAF, -808?, Arab; poetry LAN
ABBAS Effendi see ABDU'l-Bahá
ABBAT, Per, 14th cent., Spanish; poetry BL
ABBAT, Pero, 17th cent., Spanish; nonfiction SA

1

ABBATTUTIS, Gian Alesio see
BASILE, Giambattista
ABBE, Elfriede Martha, 1919- ,
American; nonfiction CON
ABBE, George Bancroft, 1911- ,
American; nonfiction, fiction
CON
ABBES, Guillaume d', -1785/95,
French; nonfiction DIL
ABBEY, Henry, 1842-1911, Amer-
ican; poetry KAA SA
ABBEY, Merrill R., 1905- ,
American; nonfiction CON
ABBOT, John, fl. 1623, English;
poetry ST
'ABBOTT, Anthony' see OURSLER,
Fulton
ABBOTT, Anthony S., 1935- ,
American; nonfiction CON
ABBOTT, Claude Colleer, 1889- ,
English; nonfiction, translations
CON
ABBOTT, Eleanor Hallowell, 1872- ,
American; fiction BRO KT SA
ABBOTT, Evelyn, 1843-1901, Brit-
ish; nonfiction KBA
ABBOTT, Freeland Knight, 1919- ,
American; nonfiction CON
ABBOTT, George, 1887- , Amer-
ican; plays MAT
ABBOTT, Jacob, 1803-79, Amer-
ican; juveniles BRO KAA SA
ABBOTT, Jane Ludlow Drake,
American; juveniles WAF
ABBOTT, John Jamison, 1930- ,
American; nonfiction CON
ABBOTT, John Stevens Cabot, 1805-
77, American; nonfiction BRO
KAA SA
ABBOTT, Lawrence, American;
poetry, juveniles HIL
ABBOTT, Lyman, 1835-1922, Amer-
ican; nonfiction KT SA
'ABBOTT, Manager Henry' see
Stratemeyer, Edward L.
ABBOTT, Margaret, American;
poetry, juveniles HIL
ABBOTT, Martin, 1922- , Amer-
ican; nonfiction CON
ABBOTT, May Laura, 1916- ,
English; fiction CON
ABBOTT, Richard Henry, 1936- ,
American; nonfiction CON
ABBOTT, Robert Tucker, 1919- ,
American; nonfiction CON
ABBOTT, Walter Matthew, 1923- ,
American; nonfiction CON
ABBOUSHI, Wasif Fahmi, 1931- ,

American; nonfiction CON
ABBT, Thomas, 1738-66, German;
nonfiction ST
ABCARIAN, Richard, 1929- ,
American; nonfiction CON
'ABD al-Hamid (al-Katib), -750,
Persian; letters LAN ST
ABD ALLAH ANSARI, Khajeh, 1006-
88, Persian; poetry ST
ABD AL-Malik Habib, 796-853,
Arab; nonfiction SA
ABDALA, fl. 1688-1710, French;
nonfiction DIL
ABDEL-MALEK, Anouar ('Ebn el-
Nil'), 1924- , Egyptian; non-
fiction CON
ABDILL, George B., American;
nonfiction PAC
ABDUL, Raoul, 1929- , American;
nonfiction CON
ABDU'l BAHA, Abbas Effendi, 1844-
1921, Persian; nonfiction ST
ABDÜLHAK, Hamid, 1852-1937,
Turkish; poetry, plays ST
ABDÜLKAK Sinasi Hisar, 1888- ,
Turkish; journalism, fiction ST
ABDULLAH, Achmed, 1881-1945,
Russian-English; fiction, poetry
HOE KT SA
ABE, Kobo, 1924- , Japanese; fic-
tion LAN
ABE, No Nahamaro, 701-70, Japan-
ese; poetry ST
ABE, Ziro, 1883- , Japanese; non-
fiction WHO
A BECKETT, Gilbert Abbott, 1811-
56, British; plays, nonfiction
BRO KBA ST
ABEELE, Charles van den ('Gode-
fridus Veramantius'), 1691-1776,
Belgian; nonfiction DIL
ABEILLE, Gaspar, 1648-1718,
French; poetry, plays SA
ABEILLE, Louis Paul, 1719-1807,
French; nonfiction DIL
ABEL, A.C., 18th cent., French;
fiction DIL
ABEL, Alan Irwin ('Julius Bristol'),
1928- , American; nonfiction
CON
ABEL, Caspar, 1676-1763, German;
poetry ST
ABEL, Jeanne ('Yetta Bronstein'),
1937- , American; fiction CON
ABEL, Lionel, 1910- , American;
poetry, plays, translations
MAT
ABEL, Theodore, 1896- , Polish-

American; nonfiction CON
ABELARD, Pierre (Abailard), 1079-
1142, French; nonfiction DIF
HAR KE MAG MAL SA ST
ABELARD of BATH, 12th cent.,
English; nonfiction SA
ABELL, George O., 1927- ,
American; nonfiction CON
ABELL, Kjeld, 1901-61, Danish;
plays COL FLE HAR MAT SA
ST
ABELLA CAPRILE, Margarita,
1902- , Argentinian; poetry
MIN SA
ABELLIO, Raymond, 1907- ,
French; fiction, essays DIC
DIF
ABEL-SMITH, Brian, 1926- ,
English; nonfiction CON
ABELSON, Ann see CAVALLARO,
Anna A.
ABELSON, Raziel A., 1921- ,
American; nonfiction CON
ABEN Guzmán see IBN Quzman
ABENALCUTIA (Abu Bakr Ben Al-
Qutiyya), -997, Arab; non-
fiction SA
'ABENAMAR' see LOPEZ PELEGRIN,
Santos
ABENARABI (Ibn Al-Arabi), 1164-
1240, Arab; nonfiction SA
ABEND, Norman Anchel, 1931- ,
American; nonfiction CON
ABEN-EZRA see EZRA, Mose Ibn
ABENHAYAN (Ibn Hayyan), 987-
1070, Arab; nonfiction SA
ABENHAZAM see IBN HAZM
ABENJALDUN see IBN Khaldun
ABENMASSARRA (Ibn Massarra),
883-931, Arab; nonfiction SA
ABENNALJATIB (Ibn Al-Jatib), 14th
cent., Arab; poetry SA
ABENSAID (Ibn Said al-Magribi),
1210?-74, Arab; poetry SA
ABENTOFAIL see IBN TUFAYL
ABENZAIDUN see IBN ZAYDUN
ABERCROMBIE, John, 1780-1844,
Scots; nonfiction BRO KBA
ABERCROMBIE, Lascelles, 1881-
1938, English; poetry, criti-
cism BRO FLE KAT KT RIC
SA ST
ABERCROMBIE, Patrick, 1656-
1716?, Scots; nonfiction BRO
ST
ABERG, Sherrill E., 1924- ,
American; nonfiction CON
ABERIGH-MACKAY, George Robert,

1848-81, Anglo-Indian; fiction
KBA
ABERLE, David Friend, 1918- ,
American; nonfiction CON
ABERLE, John Wayne, 1919- ,
American; nonfiction CON
ABERLE, Kathleen Gough, 1925- ,
English; nonfiction CON
ABERNATHY, M. Elton, 1913- ,
American; nonfiction CON
ABERNATHY, Mabra Glenn, 1921- ,
American; nonfiction CON
ABERNATHY, Thomas Perkins,
1890- , American; nonfiction
CON
ABERNETHY, Francis Edward,
1925- , American; nonfiction
CON
ABERNETHY, George Lawrence,
1910- , American; nonfiction
CON
ABERNETHY, Robert Gordon,
1927- , Swiss-American; non-
fiction CON
ABERTAZZI, Avendaño José, 1892-
, Costa Rican; journalism,
poetry MIN
ABERVAL, fl. 1778, French; plays
DIL
ABESCH, Roslyn Kroop, 1927- ,
American; nonfiction CON
ABGUERBE, Quentin Godin d',
-1765, French; nonfiction DIL
ABLESIMOV, Alexander Onisimovich,
1742-83, Russian; plays, fiction
HAR HARK ST
ABOAB, Isaac, fl. 1300, Spanish-
Jewish; nonfiction ST
ABODAHER, David J. Naiph, 1919-
, American; nonfiction CON
ABOT de BAZINGHEN, François
André, 1711-91, English-French;
nonfiction DIL
ABOUT, Edmond Francois Valentin,
1828-85, French; journalism,
fiction COL DIF HAR MAG
SA ST
ABOVIAN, Khachatur, 1805-48,
Armenian; nonfiction LAN
ABRABANEL, Judah see ABARBAN-
EL, Juda
ABRAHAM, Ben Meir Aben Ezra
see IBN EZRA, Abraham
ABRAHAM, Claude Kurt, 1931- ,
German-American; nonfiction
CON
ABRAHAM, Henry Julian, 1921- ,
German-American; nonfiction
CON

ABRAHAM, Willard, 1916- , Amer-
ican; nonfiction CON
ABRAHAM, William Israel, 1919- ,
American; nonfiction CON
ABRAHAM, Willie E., 1934- , Eng-
lish; nonfiction CON
'ABRAHAM a Sancta Clara' (Johann
Ulrich Megerle), 1644-1709,
German; nonfiction AL ST
ABRAHAM Bedersi, 1240-1300,
French-Jewish; poetry, nonfiction
ST
ABRAHAM de la BRETONNIERE,
Pierre, 1701-78, French; poetry;
DIL
ABRAHAM Ibn Hasdai,   -1240,
Spanish-Jewish; poetry ST
ABRAHAMS, Doris Caroline see
'BRAHMS, Caryl'
ABRAHAMS, Peter, 1919- , South
African; fiction, poetry RIC ST
ABRAHAMS, Raphael Garvin, 1934- ,
English; nonfiction CON
ABRAHAMS, Robert David, 1905- ,
American; juveniles CON WA
ABRAHAMS, Roger D., 1933- ,
American; nonfiction CON
ABRAHAMSON, Otto see 'Brahm,
Otto'
ABRAM, Harry Shore, 1931- ,
American; nonfiction CON
ABRAMOV, Fyodor, 1920- , Russian;
fiction RIC
ABRAMOWITZ, Jack, 1918- , Amer-
ican; nonfiction CON
ABRAMOWITZ, Shalom Jacob ('Men-
dele Mocher Seforim'; Shalom
Yaakov), 1836-1917, Jewish;
fiction COL KE LAN MAT SA
ST
ABRAMS, Charles, 1901- , Polish-
American; nonfiction CON
ABRAMS, Peter David, 1936- ,
American; nonfiction CON
ABRAMS, Richard M., 1932- ,
American; nonfiction CON
ABRAMS, Samuel, 1935- , Amer-
ican; nonfiction CON
ABRAMSON, Doris E., 1925- ,
American; nonfiction CON
ABRAMSON, Joan, 1932- , Amer-
ican; nonfiction CON
ABRANTES, Laure Saint-Martin
Permont, 1748-1838, French;
diary DIF SA
ABRASH, Merritt, 1930- , Amer-
ican; nonfiction CON
ABRASSART, Jean Joseph, 1758-

1800, French; nonfiction DIL
ABRAVANEL see ABARBANEL,
Juda
ABREU, Casimiro José, 1837-60,
Brazilian; poetry SA ST
ABREU, Guillermo Augusto de
Vasconçelos, 1842-1906,
Portuguese; nonfiction SA
ABREU, Héctor, 1856-1929?,
Spanish; fiction, journalism
SA
ABREU, Juan Capistrano de, 1853-
1927, Brazilian; nonfiction
SA
ABREU GOMEZ, Ermilo, 1894- ,
Mexican; fiction, plays, criti-
cism SA
ABREU LICAIRAC, Rafael, 1850-
1915, Dominican; nonfiction,
journalism MIN SA
ABREU LIMA, José Ignacion,
1796-1869, Brazilian; nonfic-
tion SA
ABRIL, Manuel, 1884-1940/46,
Spanish; plays poetry BL SA
ABRIL, Pedro Simón, 1530?-95?,
Spanish; nonfiction BL SA
ABROMOWITZ, Sholem Y. see
ABRAMOWITZ, Shalom J.
ABSE, Dannie, 1923- , Welsh;
poetry, plays MUR
ABSHIRE, David M., 1926- ,
American; nonfiction CON
ABT, Lawrence Edwin, 1915- ,
American; nonfiction CON
ABU Firas al-Hamdani, 932-68
Arab; poetry LAN
ABU JABER, Kamil S., 1932- ,
Jordanian-American; nonfiction
CON
ABU Nuwas, 747-813, Arab;
poetry LAN SA ST
ABU Okil Lebid Ben Rabiat see
LEBID
ABU Sa'id, Fazl Allah ibn Abi'l
Khayr, 967-1049, Persian;
poetry ST
ABU TAMMAN, 805-45, Arab;
poetry LAN ST
ABUBACER see IBN TUFAIL
ABU-L-AFIA, Todros ben
Yehuda, 1247-1300/06,
Spanish-Jewish; poetry
SA ST
ABU'l-'Ala' al-Ma'arri, 973-
1057, Arab; poetry LAN
SA ST
ABU'l-'Atahiya, 748-826, Arab;

poetry LAN ST
ABULBECA, 13th cent., Arab;
poetry SA
ABULBECA de RONDA, 13th cent.,
Arab; poetry BL
ABULFARADGE, 1226-86, Jewish;
nonfiction SA
ABU'L FAZL, 1550-1602/08, Arab;
nonfiction SA ST
ABULFEDA (Emadedin, Ismael),
1271-1331, Arab; nonfiction SA
ABUL-GHAZI-BAHADUR, 1605-64,
Arab; nonfiction SA
ABUL'l M'ALI Nasr Allah see NASR
ALLAH, Nizam
ABU-LUGHOD, Ibrahim Ali, 1929- ,
American; nonfiction CON
ABUSCH, Alexander, 1902- , Ger-
man; nonfiction AL
ABUSHADY, Ahmad Zaki, 1892- ,
Egyptian; poetry, essays, plays
ST
ABUTSU, 1233-83, Japanese; poetry
ST
ACA, Francisco Zacarias de Araujo
da Costa, 1839-1908, Portuguese;
nonfiction SA
'ACADEMIC INVESTOR' see REDDA-
WAY, William B.
AÇARQ, Jean-Pierre de, 1717-1809,
French; nonfiction DIL
ACART de HESDIN, Jean, 14th cent.,
French; poetry ST
ACCARIAS, Jean Jacques, 1751-1842,
French; nonfiction DIL
ACCARIAS de SERIONNE, Jacques,
1706-92, French nonfiction DIL
ACCIUS, Lucius (Attio), 170-85 B.C.
Roman, plays SA ST
ACCOLA, Louis Wayne, 1937- ,
American; nonfiction CON
ACCOLTI, Bernardo (Unico Aretino),
1458-1535, Italian; poetry ST
ACCOLTI, Bernardo, 1440- , Italian;
nonfiction SA
ACCOLTI, Francesco, 1416?-84/88,
Italian; poetry ST
ACCONCI, Vito, 1940- , American;
poetry MUR
ACCORAMBONI, Vittoria (Virginia),
16th cent., Italian; poetry SA
ACEBAL, Francisco, 1866-1933,
Spanish; fiction, plays BL SA
ACEVEDO, Alfonso M. de, 1550- ,
Spanish; poetry BL SA
ACEVEDO de GOMEZ, Maria Josefa,
1803-61, Colombian; poetry,
fiction MIN

ACEVEDO DIAZ, Eduard, 1851-
1921/24, Uruguayan; fiction
BL FLE SA ST
ACEVEDO DIAZ, Eduardo,
1882- , Argentinian, fiction
FLE MIN
ACEVEDO FAJARDO, Antonio,
17th cent., Spanish; plays SA
ACEVEDO GUERRA, Evaristo
('Cam'; 'Evaristóteles';
'Fernando Arrieta'), 1915- ,
Spanish; fiction SA
ACEVEDO HERNANDEZ, Antonio,
1885- , Chilean; plays, fic-
tion, essays MIN SA
ACHARD, Amédée, 1814-75,
French; fiction, criticism,
journalism DIF SA
ACHARD, Antoine, 1696/1708-72,
French; nonfiction DIL
ACHARD, Claude Francois, 1751-
1809, French; nonfiction DIL
'ACHARD, George' see TORRES,
Tereska S.
'ACHARD, Marcel' (Marcel Auguste
Ferréol), 1899- , French;
plays COL DIF FLE HAR
MAT SA ST
ACHEBE, Chinua, 1930- , Ni-
gerian; fiction CON RIC
ACHER, Nicolas, 1727-1814,
French; nonfiction DIL
ACHERY, Dom Jean Luc d', 1609-
85, French; nonfiction DIF
ACHESON, Dean Gooderham, 1893-
1971, American; nonfiction
CON
ACHESON, Patricia Castles, 1924- ,
American; nonfiction, juveniles
CON WA
ACHILLE, Louis T., 1909- ,
American; nonfiction SCA
ACHILLES Tatius, 3rd cent.,
Greek; nonfiction ST
ACHTEMEIER, Elizabeth Rice,
1926- , American; nonfiction
CON
ACHTEMEIER, Paul John, 1927- ,
American; nonfiction CON
ACHTERBERG, Gerrit, 1905-62,
Dutch; poetry FLE
'ACHYUT' see BIRLA, Lakashmi-
niwas
ACILIO CAYO, 215?-140 B.C.,
Roman; nonfiction SA
ACKER, Duane Calvin, 1931- ,
American; nonfiction CON
ACKER, Helen, , American;

juveniles WA
ACKEREE, Maria van Doolaeghe,
1802-84, Flemish; poetry ST
ACKERMAN, James S., 1919- ,
American; nonfiction CON
ACKERMAN, Nathan Ward, 1908- ,
Russian-American; nonfiction
CON
ACKERMANN, Louise, 1813-90,
French; poetry DIF SA
ACKERSON, Duane Wright, Jr.,
1942- , American; nonfiction
CON
ACKROYD, Peter Runham, 1917- ,
English; nonfiction CON
ACKWORTH, Robert Charles, 1923- ,
American; fiction CON
ACONZIO, Jacopo (Jacobus Acontius),
1500-67?, Italian; nonfiction
HAR
ACORN, Milton, 1923- , Canadian;
poetry MUR
ACOSTA, Agustin, 1886/87- , Cuban;
poetry MIN SA
ACOSTA, Cecilio, 1831-89, Venezua-
lan; poetry SA
ACOSTA, Joaquín, 1799/1800-52,
Colombian; nonfiction MIN
ACOSTA, José de, 1539-1600, Span-
ish; nonfiction SA ST
ACOSTA, Soledad, 1831-1913, Colom-
bian; nonfiction SA
ACOSTA de SEMPER, Soledad, 1833-
1903, Colombian; fiction MIN
ACOSTA TOVAR, José María, 1881-
1939, Spanish; fiction SA
ACQUARONI, José Luis, 1920- ,
Spanish; fiction BL
ACQUAYE, Alfred Allotey, 1939- ,
Ghanian; nonfiction CON
'ACRE, Stephen' see GRUBER, Frank
ACRED, Arthur, 1926- , English;
nonfiction CON
ACTON, Lord (John Emerich Edward
Dalberg), 1834-1902, British;
nonfiction BRO KBA
ACTON, C.R. ('Sydney the Standard'),
1890- , English; nonfiction HIG
ACTON, Harold Mario Mitchell,
1904- , English; nonfiction,
translations CON
ACUÑA, Carlos, 1886/89- , Chilean;
journalism, poetry MIN
ACUÑA, Hernando de, 1520-80, Span-
ish; poetry BL SA ST
ACUÑA, Manuel, 1849-73, Mexican;
poetry, plays BL SA ST

ACUÑA de FIGUEROA, Francisco,
1790-1862, Uruguayan; poetry
BL SA ST
ACUÑA y VILLANUEVA de la
IGLESIA, Rosario de, 1851-
1923, Spanish; poetry, plays
SA
ACUSILAO, 544-490 B.C., Greek;
nonfiction SA
ADAIR, Cecil see EVERETT-GREEN,
Evelyn
ADAIR, James, 1709-83, American;
nonfiction KAA
ADAIR, James R., 1923- , Amer-
ican; nonfiction CON
ADAIR, Margaret Weeks, , Amer-
ican; fiction CON
'ADAM' see LEBENSOHN, Abraham D.
ADAM, Antoine, 1705- , French;
nonfiction DIL
ADAM, Charles, -1778, French;
nonfiction DIL
ADAM, Helen, 1909- , Scots;
poetry CON MUR
ADAM, Jacques, 1663-1735, French;
nonfiction DIL
ADAM, Jean, 1710-65, Scots;
poetry BRO
ADAM, Juliette Lamber, 1836-1936,
French; nonfiction DIF SA
ADAM, Karl, 1876- , German;
nonfiction HOE
ADAM, Nicolas, 1717-92, French;
nonfiction DIL
'ADAM, Onkel' see WETTERBERGH,
Carl A.
ADAM, Paul Auguste Marie, 1862-
1920, French; fiction COL
DIF HAR KE SA ST
ADAM, Ruth Augusta, 1907- ,
English; juveniles, fiction
CON
ADAM, Thomas Ritchie, 1900- ,
Scots; nonfiction CON
ADAM Billaut, 1602-65, French;
poetry SA
ADAM de Givenchy, fl. 1230-68,
French; poetry ST
ADAM del la Bassée, -1286,
French; poetry ST
ADAM de la HALLE (Le Bossu
d'Arras), 1250?-89?, French;
poetry, plays DIF HAR MAL
SA ST
ADAM de ROSS, fl. 1200, Anglo-
Norman; poetry ST
ADAM de ST. VICTOIRE, fl. 1140,

French; poetry DIF HAR ST
ADAM of BREMEN, 1045-81/85,
German; nonfiction ST
ADAM of DRYBURGH, -1212,
German; nonfiction ST
ADAM OF USK, 1352-1430, English;
nonfiction ST
ADAMA van SCHELTEMA, Carel
Steven, 1877-1924, Dutch; poetry
COL SA
ADAMCZEWSKI, Zygmunt, 1921- ,
American; nonfiction CON
ADAME MARTINEZ, Serafín, 1901- ,
Spanish; journalism, fiction,
plays SA
ADAMEC, Warren Ludwig, 1924- ,
Austrian-American; nonfiction
CON
ADAMIC, Louis, 1899-1951, Ameri-
can; nonfiction, fiction KT SA
ADAMNAN, St., 625?-704, Irish;
nonfiction BRO ST
ADAMOV see MARKOVIC, Paja-
Adamov
ADAMOV, Arthur, 1908-70, French;
plays CON DIC DIF FLE MAL
MAT PIN
ADAMOVICH, Georgyi Viktorovich,
1894- , Russian, poetry, essays
FLE
'ADAMS, A. Don' see CLEVELAND,
Philip S.
ADAMS, A. John, 1931- , Ameri-
can; nonfiction CON
ADAMS, Abigail Smith, 1744-1818,
American; diary KAA SA
ADAMS, Agatha Boyd, 1894-1950,
American; nonfiction JO
ADAMS, Andy, 1859-1935, American;
juveniles KJU
'ADAMS, Annette' see ROWLAND,
Donald S.
ADAMS, Ansel Easton, 1902- ,
American; nonfiction CON
ADAMS, Arthur B., 1887- , Amer-
ican; nonfiction MAR
ADAMS, Arthur Eugene, 1917- ,
American; nonfiction CON
ADAMS, Arthur Henry, 1872-1936,
New Zealander, poetry, fiction
BRO RIC ST
'ADAMS, Betsy' see PITCHER, Gladys
ADAMS, Brooks, 1848-1927, Ameri-
can; nonfiction KAA SA
ADAMS, Charles Follen, 1842-1918,
American; poetry BRO KAA
ADAMS, Charles Francis, Jr., 1835-
1915, American; nonfiction KAA

ADAMS, Charles Joseph, 1924- ,
American; nonfiction CON
ADAMS, Charles Kendall, 1835-
1902, American; nonfiction
KAA
'ADAMS, Christopher' see HOP-
KINS, Kenneth
ADAMS, Cindy, American; nonfic-
tion CON
ADAMS, Clifton ('Jonathan Gant';
'Matt Kinkaid'; 'Clay Randall'),
1919- , American; fiction
CON
ADAMS, Clinton, 1918- , Amer-
ican; nonfiction CON
ADAMS, Donald Kendrick, 1925- ,
American; nonfiction CON
ADAMS, Dorothy, American; non-
fiction HO
ADAMS, Elie Maynard, 1919- ,
American; nonfiction CON
ADAMS, Elizabeth Laura, 1909- ,
American; nonfiction SCA
ADAMS, Francis William Lauder-
dale, 1862-93, Anglo-Australian;
poetry, fiction BRO KBA
ADAMS, Frank Ramsay ('Carl
Dane'), 1883-1963, American;
fiction, plays CON HOO
ADAMS, Franklin Pierce ('F.P.A.'),
1881- , American; journalism,
poetry, essays HOO KT SA
ADAMS, Frater William, 1913- ,
American; nonfiction SCA
ADAMS, Georgia Sachs, 1913- ,
American; nonfiction CON
ADAMS, Graham, Jr., 1928- ,
American; nonfiction CON
ADAMS, Hannah, 1755-1831, Amer-
ican; nonfiction KAA SA
ADAMS, Harlen Martin, 1904- ,
American; nonfiction CON
ADAMS, Harriet Stratemeyer,
('Victor Appleton II'; 'May
Hollis Barton'; 'Franklin W.
Dixon'; 'Laura Lee Hope';
'Carolyn Keene'), American
juveniles COM CON DOY
'ADAMS, Harrison' see STRATE-
MEYER, Edward L.
ADAMS, Hazard, 1926- , Amer-
ican; fiction, nonfiction CON
ADAMS, Henry Brooks, 1838-1918,
American; nonfiction, fiction
BRO KAA KAT MAG RIC SA
ST
ADAMS, Henry Hilch ('Henry
Allen'), 1917- , American;

nonfiction CON
ADAMS, Henry Mason, 1907- ,
American; nonfiction CON
'ADAMS, Henry T.' see RANSOM,
Jay Ellis
ADAMS, Herbert Baxter, 1850-1901,
American; nonfiction KAA
ADAMS, Herbert Mayow, 1893- ,
English; nonfiction CON
ADAMS, James Donald, 1891- ,
American; nonfiction CON
ADAMS, James Frederick, 1927- ,
American; nonfiction CON
ADAMS, James Truslow, 1878-1949,
American, nonfiction BRO KAT
KT
ADAMS, John, 1704-40, American;
poetry KAA
ADAMS, John, 1735-1826, American;
nonfiction; BRO MAG ST
ADAMS, John Clarke, 1910- ,
American; nonfiction CON
ADAMS, John Cranford, 1903- ,
American; nonfiction KTS
ADAMS, John Festus, 1930- ,
American; nonfiction CON
ADAMS, John R., 1900- , Ameri-
can; nonfiction CON
ADAMS, Joseph Quincy, 1881-1946,
American; nonfiction BRO ST
ADAMS, Julian, 1919- , American;
nonfiction CON
ADAMS, Katharine, American; juven-
iles KJU
ADAMS, Kramer A., 1920- , Amer-
ican; nonfiction CON
ADAMS, Léonie, 1899- , American;
poetry CON KL KTS MUR RIC
SP
'ADAMS, Lowell' see JOSEPH, James
H.
ADAMS, Michael Evelyn, 1920- ,
English; nonfiction CON
ADAMS, Nehemiah, 1806-78, Ameri-
can; nonfiction KAA
ADAMS, Nicholson B., 1895- ,
American; nonfiction BL
ADAMS, Percy Guy, 1914- , Amer-
ican; nonfiction CON
ADAMS, Perseus, 1933- , South
African; poetry MUR
ADAMS, Richard Newbold ('Stokes
Newbold'), 1924- , American;
nonfiction CON
ADAMS, Richard Perrill, 1917- ,
American; fiction CON
ADAMS, Robert Martin ('R.M. Krapp'),
1915- , American; nonfiction
CON

ADAMS, Robert P., 1910- ,
American; nonfiction CON
ADAMS, Ruth Joyce, American;
juveniles, poetry WA
ADAMS, Samuel, 1722-1803,
American; nonfiction KAA
ADAMS, Samuel Hopkins, 1871- ,
American; fiction, essays
KT SA WA WAF
ADAMS, Sarah Flower, 1805-48,
British; poetry KBA
ADAMS, Sexton, 1936- , Ameri-
can; nonfiction CON
ADAMS, Terrence Dean, 1935- ,
American; nonfiction CON
ADAMS, Theodore Floyd, 1898- ,
American; nonfiction CON
ADAMS, Thomas F., 1927- ,
American; nonfiction CON
ADAMS, Thomas William, 1933- ,
American; nonfiction CON
ADAMS, Walter, 1922- , Ameri-
can; nonfiction CON
ADAMS, William Taylor ('Oliver
Optic'), 1822-97, American;
juveniles KAA
ADAMSON, David Grant, 1927- ,
English; nonfiction CON
ADAMSON, Gareth, 1925- , Eng-
lish; juveniles CON
ADAMSON, Hans Christian, 1890-
1968, American; nonfiction
CON
ADAMSON, Margot Robert, 1898- ,
Scots; poetry, translation,
fiction, nonfiction MUR
ADAMSON, Robert, 1852-1902,
Scots; nonfiction KBA SA
ADAMSON, William Robert,
1927- , Canadian; nonfiction
CON
ADAWIYA, Rabi'a, 714-801 Arab;
poetry ST
ADBURGHAM, Alison Haig,
1912- , English; nonfiction
CON
ADCOCK, Cyril John, 1904- ,
English; nonfiction CON
ADCOCK, Kareen Fleur (Kareen
Fleur Campbell), 1934- ,
New Zealander; poetry CON
MUR
ADDAMS, Jane, 1860-1935, Amer-
ican; nonfiction HOO
ADDINGTON, Larry Holbrook,
1932- , American; nonfiction
CON
ADDISON, Joseph, 1672-1719,
English; essays, plays,

BRO KB MAG SA ST
ADDISON, William, 1905- , English; nonfiction CON
ADDONA, Angelo F., 1925- , American; nonfiction CON
ADDY, George Milton, 1927- , American; nonfiction CON
'ADDY, Ted' see WINTERBOTHAM, Russell R.
ADE, George, 1866-1944, American; plays, essays BRO HOO KAT KT MAT RIC SA ST
ADEBERG, Roy P., 1928- , American; nonfiction CON
'ADELER, Max' see CLARK, Charles H.
ADELMAN, Gary, 1935- , American; nonfiction CON
ADELMAN, Howard, 1938- , American; nonfiction CON
ADELMAN, Irena Glicman, American; nonfiction CON
ADELMAN, Irving, 1926- , American; nonfiction CON
ADELSON, Joseph Bernard, 1925- , American; nonfiction CON
ADELSON, Leone, 1908- , American; juveniles WA
ADELSTEIN, Michael E., 1922- , American; nonfiction CON
ADELUNG, Johan Gottfried, 1743-1806, German; nonfiction SA
ADENES le ROIS, 13th cent., French; poetry SA
ADENET, le Roi des Ménestrels, 1240?-97?, French; poetry DIF HAR ST
ADER, Paul Fassett, 1919- , American; fiction WAF
ADERMAN, Ralph Merl, 1919- , American; nonfiction CON
ADET, Pierre Auguste, 1763-1834, French; nonfiction DIL
ADGAR (William), 12th cent. Anglo-Norman; poetry ST
ADIB Saber of Termed,   -1143/44, Persian; poetry ST
ADIZES, Ichak, 1937- , Yugoslav-American; nonfiction CON
ADKINS, Dorothy C., 1912- , American; nonfiction CON
ADKINS, Jan, 1944- , American; nonfiction CON
ADLEMAN, Robert H., 1919- , American; nonfiction CON
ADLER, Alfred, 1870-1937, Austrian; nonfiction KT SA

ADLER, Betty, 1918- , American; nonfiction CON
ADLER, Felix, 1851-1933, American; nonfiction KT
ADLER, H.G., 1910- , Czech-English; nonfiction CON
ADLER, Helmut Ernest, 1920- , German-American; nonfiction CON
'ADLER, Irene' see STORR, Catherine C.
ADLER, Irving ('Robert Irving'; 'Robert Adler'), 1913- , American; juveniles, nonfiction COM CON WA
ADLER, Jacob, 1913- , American; nonfiction CON
ADLER, Jacob Henry, 1919- , American; nonfiction CON
ADLER, Maria Raquel, 1910- , German-Argentinian; nonfiction, poetry MIN SA
ADLER, Max Kurt, 1905- , Czech-English; nonfiction CON
ADLER, Mortimer Jerome, 1902- , American; nonfiction KTS
ADLER, Peggy, American; juveniles; WA
'ADLER, Robert' see ADLER, Irving
ADLER, Ruth, 1915-68, American; juveniles COM CON WA
ADLER, Selig, 1909- , American; nonfiction CON
ADLER, Sol, 1925- , American; nonfiction CON
ADLER, William, 1929- , American; nonfiction CON
ADLERBETH, Baron Gudmund Jöran, 1751-1818, Swedish; poetry ST
ADLERFIELD, Gustav, 1671- , Swiss; nonfiction SA
ADOFF, Arnold, American; juveniles WA
ADOLPHE, René, fl. 1743-50, French; nonfiction DIL
ADOLPHUS, John, 1768-1845, English; nonfiction ST
'ADONY, Raoul' see LAUNAY, Andre J.
ADORNO, Theodor W., 1903-69, German-American; nonfiction KU KUN
ADOUM, Jorge Enrique (Ricardo Ariel), 1923- , Ecuadoran; poetry, criticism DI

ADRET, Solomon, 1235-1310,
Spanish-Jewish; nonfiction ST
ADRIAAN, Florisz Boeyens (Pope
Adrian VI), 1459-1523, Dutch;
nonfiction ST
ADRIAN, Arthur Aleen, 1906- ,
American; nonfiction CON
ADRIAN, Charles R., 1922- ,
American; nonfiction CON
ADRIAN, Edgar Douglas, 1889- ,
British; nonfiction ST
'ADRIAN, Mary' see VENN, Mary E.
ADRIEN de CITEAUX, Dom, 18th
cent., French; nonfiction DIL
ADRIEN de NANCY, -1745, French;
nonfiction DIL
ADRY, Jean Félicissime, 1749-1819,
French; nonfiction DIL
ADSHEAD, Gladys Lucy, 1896- ,
English; juveniles CON FUL
ADY, Endre, 1877-1919, Hungarian;
poetry COL HAR RIC SA ST
'ADYTUM' see CURL, James S.
AEBY, Jacquelyn, American; juveniles
CON
AELFRED see ALFRED
AELFRIC (Grammaticus), 955?-1020?,
British; nonfiction BRO KB ST
AELIAN (Claudius Aelianus), 2nd-3rd
cent., Greek; nonfiction ST
AELRED of RIEVAULX see AILRED
AENEAS Silvius see PICCOLOMINI,
Enea S.
AENEAS Tacticus, 4th cent. B.C.,
Greek; nonfiction ST
AESCHINES, 390-314 B.C., Athenian;
nonfiction ST
AESCHINES of SPHETTUS, 4th cent.
B.C., Greek; nonfiction ST
AESCHYLUS, 525/24-456/55 B.C.,
Greek; plays MAG ST
'AESOP' see HEYSHAM, W. Nuñez
AESOP, 6th cent. B.C., Greek;
fiction DOY MAG SA ST
AFAN de RIBERA, Fulgencio, 18th
cent., Spanish; fiction BL SA
AFAN de RIBERA, Gaspar, 1617?- ,
Spanish; poetry SA
AFAN de RIVERA, Fernando, 1614-33,
Spanish; poetry SA
AFAN de RIVERA y ENRIQUEZ,
Fernando, 1584?-1637, Spanish;
poetry SA
AFAN de RIVERA y GADEA, Baltasar,
17th cent., Spanish; poetry SA
AFANASYEV, Alexander Nikolayevich,
1826-71, Russian; fiction HAR
ST

AFFLIGHEM, Willem van, 1210?-
97, Dutch; poetry HAR ST
AFFORTY, Charles Francois,
1706-86, French; nonfiction
DIL
AFFRE, Denis Auguste, 1793-1848,
French; nonfiction SA
AFFRE, Dom Nicolas, 1731-1817,
French; nonfiction DIL
AFFRON, Charles, 1935- , Amer-
ican; nonfiction CON
AFINOGENOV, Alexander Nikolaye-
vich, 1904-41, Russian; plays
COL HAR HARK MAT RIC SA
ST
AFLALO, Frederick George, 1870-
1918, English; nonfiction HIG
AFNAN, Ruhi Muhsen, 1899-1971,
Arab; nonfiction CON
AFRANIUS, Lucius, 150 B.C.- ,
Roman; plays, poetry SA ST
AFRICA, Thomas Wilson, 1927- ,
American; nonfiction CON
AFRICANO, Sexto Julio, 3rd cent.,
Greek; nonfiction SA
AFTONIO (Afthonio), 3rd-4th cent.,
Greek; fiction SA
AFZELIUS, Arvid August, 1785-
1871, Swedish; fiction HAR
ST
AGAN, Anna Tessie, 1897- ,
American; nonfiction CON
AGAN, Raymond John, 1919- ,
American; nonfiction CON
AGANOOR -POMPILI, Vittoria,
1855-1910, Italian; poetry
HAR ST
AGAPETUS the DEACON, fl. 527,
Byzantine; nonfiction ST
'AGAR, Brian' see BALLARD,
Willis T.
AGAR, Herbert, 1897- , Ameri-
can; poetry, criticism KT
AGAR, William Macdonough, 1894-
1972, American; nonfiction
HOE
AGARBICEANU, Ion, 1882- ,
Rumanian; fiction ST
AGARD, H.E. see EVANS, Hilary
AGARKAR, Gopal Ganes, 1865-95,
Indian; essays, journalism
LAN
AGARWALA, Amar N., 1917- ,
Indian; nonfiction CON
AGASSIZ, Alexander, 1835-1910,
American; nonfiction KAA
AGASSIZ, Jean Louis Rodolphe,
1807-73, American; nonfiction
KAA

AGATARQUIDES de GNIDO, 2nd cent.
B. C. , Greek; nonfiction SA
'AGATE' see REID, Whitelaw
AGATE, James Evershed, 1877-1947,
English; criticism, fiction, jour-
nalism, essays BRO KT RIC
AGATHIAS SCHOLASTICUS, 536-82,
Byzantine; poetry ST
'AGATHON' see MASSIS, Henri
AGATHON, 5th cent. B. C. , Athenian;
poetry ST
AGATIAS, 6th cent. , Greek; nonfic-
tion SA
AGATON, 445 B. C. - , Greek; plays
SA
AGATSTEIN, Mieczylslaw see
'JASTRUN, Mieczyslaw'
'AGED Eagle' see ELIOT, Thomas S.
AGEE, James, 1909-55, American;
fiction, movies, poetry KTS
RIC
AGEE, Warren Kendall, 1916- ,
American; nonfiction CON
AGETON, Arthur Ainsley, 1900-71,
American; nonfiction, fiction,
juveniles CON
AGGERTT, Otis J. , 1936- , Amer-
ican; nonfiction CON
AGGESEN, Svend, 1130- , Danish;
nonfiction ST
AGLE, Nan Hayden, 1905- , Amer-
ican; juveniles CON WA
AGNEAUX, Charles J. B. d', 1728-
92, French; nonfiction DIL
AGNESI, María Gaetana Angelica,
1718-99, Italian; nonfiction SA
AGNEW, Edith Josephine ('Marcelino'),
1897- , American; poetry CON
AGNEW, Peter Lawrence, 1901- ,
American; nonfiction CON
AGNIEL, Lucien D. , 1919- , Amer-
ican; nonfiction CON
AGNOLETTI, Fernando, 1875-1933,
Italian; nonfiction SA
AGNON, Shmuel Yosef (Tschatsky),
1888-1970, Jewish; fiction CON
FLE LAN RIC ST
AGOSTINELLI, Maria Enrica, 1929- ,
Italian; juveniles CON
AGOULT, Marie de Flavigny ('Daniel
Stern'), 1800/05-76, French;
nonfiction DIF HAR SA
AGRAMONT y TOLDEDO, Juan, 1701-
69?, Spanish; poetry, plays SA
AGRANOFF, Robert, 1936- , Amer-
ican; nonfiction CON
AGREDA, María de Jesús de (Maria
Coronel y Arana), 1602-65,

Spanish; fiction, nonfiction BL
SA ST
AGREDA y VARGAS, Diego, 1591?-
1639?, Spanish; fiction SA
AGREE, Rose H. , 1913- , Polish-
American; poetry CON
AGRELL, Alfhild Teresea Martin,
1849-1923, Swedish; fiction,
plays ST
'AGRICOLA' see CREVECOEUR,
Michel G. J. de
AGRICOLA, Johannes (Schnitter),
1494-1566, German; nonfiction
AL
AGRICOLA, Rudold (Roelof Huys-
mann), 1442-85, Dutch; non-
fiction HAR KE ST
AGRIPPA, Cornelius (Nettesheim),
1486-1535, German; nonfiction
HAR SA
AGRIPPA D'AUBIGNE see AUBIGNE,
Théodore A.
AGUADO, Pedro de, 1520-95,
Colombian; nonfiction BL MIN
AGUADO BLEYE, Pedro, 1884-
1954, Spanish; nonfiction BL
AGUADO HERNANDEZ, Emiliano,
1907- , Spanish essays,
criticism BL SA
AGUAYO, Albert de, 1469-1525,
Spanish; poetry, translation
BL SA
AGÜERO, Concepción de, 1847- ,
Cuban; plays, poetry MIN
AGUESSEAU, Henri F. d', 1668-
1751, French; nonfiction DIL
AGUIAR, Manuel Caetano Pimenta
de, 1765-1832, Portuguese;
poetry SA
AGUILAR, Gaspar de, 1561-1623,
Spanish; poetry BL SA ST
AGUILAR, Grace, 1816-47, British;
fiction BRO KBA ST
AGUILAR, Luis E. , 1926- ,
Cuban-American; nonfiction
CON
AGUILAR, Santiago, 1899- ,
Spanish; fiction, nonfiction SA
AGUILAR CATENA, Juan, 1888- ,
Spanish; fiction SA
AGUILERA, Donna Conant, Amer-
ican; nonfiction CON
AGUILERA GARCIA, Emiliano M. ,
1905- , Spanish; nonfiction,
journalism SA
AGUILERA MALTA, Demestrio,
1909- , Ecuadorian; poetry,

fiction, plays DI
AGUILO, Tomás, 1812-84, Spanish;
poetry SA
AGUILO y FUSTER, Mariano, 1825-
97, Spanish; poetry SA
AGUIRRE, Juan Bautista, 1725-86,
Ecuadorian; poetry SA
AGUIRRE, Manuel Agustin, 1904- ,
Ecuadorian; poetry DI
AGUIRRE, Nataniel, 1843-88, Bolivian;
journalism, plays, fiction, poetry
MIN SA ST
AGUIRRE BELLVER, Joaquín, 1929- ,
Spanish; fiction SA
AGUIRRE de ACHA, José, 1877- ,
Bolivian; poetry MIN
AGUS, Irving Abraham, 1910- ,
Polish-American; nonfiction CON
AGUS, Jacob Bernard, 1911- ,
Polish-American; nonfiction CON
AGUSTI, Ignacion, 1913- , Spanish;
poetry, fiction, journalism BL
SA
AGUSTIN, Antonio, 1517-86, Spanish;
nonfiction SA
AGUSTINI, Delmira, 1886?-1914,
Uruguayan; poetry BL SA ST
AGWANI, Mohammed Shafi, 1928- ,
American; nonfiction CON
'AHAD Ha-Am' (Asher Ginzbury),
1856-1927, Jewish; essays LAN
ST
AHARONI, Yohanan (Jochanan), 1919- ,
German-Israeli; nonfiction CON
AHARONSOHN see ANOCHI, Zalman
Y.
AHERN, Barnabas M., 1915- ,
American; nonfiction CON
AHERN, James see HERNE, James
A.
AHERN, Margaret McCrohan ('Peg
O'Connell), 1921- , American;
juveniles CON
'AHERNE, Owen' see CASSILL,
Ronald V.
'AHLGREN, Ernst' see BENEDICTS-
SON, Victoria, M.
AHLIN, Lars Gustav, 1915- , Swed-
ish; fiction FLE
AHLSEN, Leopold, 1927- , German
plays KU MAT
AHLSTROM, Sydney Eckman, 1919- ,
American; nonfiction CON
AHMAD, Nafis, 1913- , American;
nonfiction CON
AHMAD AL-RAZI see RASIS
AHMAD, Bey Shauki see SHAUQI,
Ahmad

AHMAD Faris Ash-Shidyaq, 1801-
87, Lebanese; fiction, essays
ST
AHMAD KHAN, Sir Syed, 1817-98,
Indian; nonfiction ST
AHMANN, Mathew Hall, 1931- ,
American; nonfiction CON
AHMED, Hamdi Tanpinar, 1901- ,
Turkish; nonfiction CON
AHMED, Hasim, 1885-1933, Turk-
ish; poetry, essays ST
AHMED Pasa, 1420?-97, Turkish;
poetry ST
AHMED SHAUKI see SHAUQI,
Ahmad
'AHMEDI' (Taceddin Ibrahim),
1334-1413, Turkish; poetry
ST
AHNEBRINK, Lars, 1915- ,
Swedish; nonfiction CON
AHNSTROM, Doris N., 1915- ,
American; juveniles CON WA
'AHO, Juhani' (Johannes Brofelt),
1861-1921, Finnish; fiction,
plays FLE HAR SA ST
AHRENBERG, Jacob, 1847-1914,
Swiss-Finnish; essays, poetry
SA
'AHRIMAN' see MARTINEZ RUIZ,
José
AHRON, Ben Josef, 17th cent.,
Jewish; poetry ST
AICARD, Jean Francois Victor,
1848-1921, French; poetry,
nonfiction, fiction DIF SA
AICARDO, José Manuel, 1860- ,
Spanish; criticism SA
AICHINGER, Helga, 1937- , Aus-
trian; nonfiction CON
AICHINGER, Ilse, 1921- , Aus-
trian; fiction, plays AL FLE
KU KUN
AICKMAN, Robert Fordyce, 1914- ,
English; nonfiction CON
AIDENOFF, Abraham, 1913- ,
American; nonfiction CON
AIDOO, Christina Ama Ata,
1940- , Ghanaian; plays RIC
AIE-IMOUKHUEDE, Frank Abiodun,
1935- , Nigerian; poetry,
plays MUR
AIGUEBERRE, Jean Dumas d'
(Aiguebert), 1692-1755, French;
plays DIL
'AIGUILLETTE' see HARGREAVES,
Reginald C.
AIGUILLON, Anne Charlotte de
Crussol-Florensac, 1700-72,

French; translations DIL
AIGUILLON, Armand Louis de
Vignerot, 1683-1750, French;
nonfiction DIL
AIKEN, Anna Letitia see BARBAULD,
Anna L.A.
AIKEN, Charles, 1901- , Ameri-
can; nonfiction CON
AIKEN, Clarissa Lorenz, 1899- ,
American; juveniles CON
AIKEN, Conrad Potter ('Samuel Jeake,
Jr.'), 1889-1973, American;
poetry, plays, fiction, journalism
BRO CON FLE KL KT MAT MUR
RIC SA SP ST WA
AIKEN, George L., 1830-76, Amer-
ican; plays KAA
AIKEN, Henry David, 1912- ,
American; nonfiction CON
AIKEN, Joan, 1924- , English;
juveniles COM CON WA
AIKEN, John Robert, 1927- , Amer-
ican; nonfiction CON
AIKEN, Lewis Roscoe, Jr., 1931- ,
American; nonfiction CON
AIKEN, Michael Thomas, 1932- ,
American; nonfiction CON
AIKHENVALD, Yuly I. see EICHEN-
WALD, Yuly I.
AIKEN, John, 1747-1822, Scots;
nonfiction BRO KBA ST
AIKIN, Lucy ('Mary Godolphin'),
1781-1864, British; nonfiction,
juveniles, poetry BRO KBA SA
ST
AIKMAN, Ann see McQUADE, Ann
A.
AILE, 18th cent., French; poetry,
plays DIL
AILLY, Pierre d', 1350-1420,
French; nonfiction, poetry ST
AILRED (Aelred of Rievaulx), 1110-
67, English; nonfiction ST
'AIMARD, Gustave' (Olivier Gloux),
1818-87, French; fiction DIF
HAR SA
AIMERIC de BELENOI, fl. 1217-42,
French; poetry SA ST
AIMERIC de PEGUILHAN, 1195?-
1228/30, French; poetry DIF
HAR KE SA ST
AIMERICH, Mateo see AYMERICH,
Mateo
AINE, Marie Jean Baptiste Nicolas
d', 1733-1804, French; transla-
tions DIL
AINGER, Alfred, 1873-1904, British;
nonfiction BRO KBA ST

AINSLEIE, Hew, 1792-1878, Amer-
ican; poetry KAA
AINSLIE, Rosalynde, 1932- ,
South African; nonfiction CON
AINSWORTH, Edward Maddin,
1902-68, American; nonfiction
CON
AINSWORTH, Katherine, 1908- ,
American; nonfiction CON
AINSWORTH, Mary Dinsmore
Salter, 1913- , American;
nonfiction CON
AINSWORTH, Norma ('Norma Paul
Ruedi'), American; fiction,
poetry CON
AINSWORTH, Ruth see GILBERT,
Ruth G.A.
AINSWORTH, William Harrison,
1805-82, English; fiction,
juveniles BRO DOY KBA
MAG SA ST
AIRAS, Joan, 18th cent., Spanish;
poetry SA
AIRAS de SANTIAGO, Joan, fl.
1250, Spanish; poetry ST
AIRAS NUNES, 13th cent., Spanish;
poetry SA
'AIRD, Catherine' see McINTOSH,
Kinn H.
AIRD, Thomas, 1802-76, Scots;
poetry, journalism BRO KBA
AIRES de GOUVEIA, Antonio, 1828-
1916, Portuguese; poetry,
criticism SA
AIRES RAMOS da SILVA de ECA,
Matías, 1705- , Brazilian;
nonfiction SA
AIRES RAMOS da SILVA de ECA,
Teresa Margarita, 1711- ,
Brazilian; fiction SA
AISSE, 1695-1733, French; diary,
poetry DIL SA
'AISTIS, Jonas' (Kossu Alexandravi-
cius), 1904- , Lithuanian;
poetry FLE
AISTROP, Jack Bentley, 1916- ,
American; juveniles, nonfiction
CON WA
AITKEN, Adam Jack, 1921- ,
Scots; nonfiction CON
AITKEN, Hugh George Jeffrey,
1922- , American; nonfiction
CON
AITKEN, Jonathan William Patrick,
1942- , Irish; nonfiction CON
AITKEN, Thomas, Jr., 1910- ,
American; nonfiction CON
AKA-GÜND ÜZ, 1884- , Turkish;

fiction, plays SA
AKAHITO see YAMABE No Akahito
AKASHI, Yoji, 1928- , Japanese-
American; nonfiction CON
AKAZOME, Emon, 11th cent., Japa-
nese; poetry ST
AKBAR of ALLAHABAD, 1846-1921,
Indian; poetry LAN
AKE, Claude, 1938- , Nigerian;
nonfiction CON
AKEHURST, Michael Barton, 1940- ,
English; nonfiction CON
AKEN, Hein van, -1330, Dutch;
poetry ST
AKENS, David S., 1921- , Ameri-
can; nonfiction CON
AKENSIDE, Mark, 1721-70, English;
poetry, essays BRO KB ST
AKERS, Charles Wesley, 1920- ,
American; nonfiction CON
AKERS, Elizabeth Chase (Allen;
'Florence Percy'), 1832-1911,
American; poetry BRO KAA
'AKERS, Floyd' see BAUM, Lyman F.
AKHA, 1615-74, Indian; poetry LAN
'AKHMATOVA, Anna' (Anna Andreyev-
na Gorenko), 1888-1966, Russian;
poetry COL CON FLE HAR
HARK RIC SA ST
AKHTAL, 640-710, Arab; poetry
LAN ST
AKIF, Mehmed, 1873-1936, Turkish;
poetry ST
AKIN, Wallace Elmus, 1923- ,
American; nonfiction CON
AKINJOGBIN, Isaac Adeagbo, 1930- ,
Nigerian; nonfiction CON
AKINS, Zoë, 1886-1958, American;
poetry, plays, fiction KT MAT
SA
AKITA, George, 1926- , American;
nonfiction CON
AKIYAMA, Kazuo, Japanese; juveniles,
WA
AKOPIAN, Akop ('Raffi'), 1866-1937,
Armenian; poetry LAN
AKRIGG, George Philip Vernon,
1913- , Canadian; nonfiction
CON
AKSAKOV, Ivan Sergeyevich, 1823-86,
Russian; journalism, poetry
HARK ST
AKSAKOV, Konstantin S., 1817-60,
Russian; nonfiction HARK ST
AKSAKOV, Sergei Timofeyevich,
1791-1859, Russian; fiction,
criticism HAR HARK KE SA ST

AKSIONOV, Vasily Parlovich,
1932- , Russian; fiction RIC
AKUTAGAWA RYUNSOKU, 1892-
1927, Japanese; fiction LAN
ST
ALABASTER, William, 1567-1640,
English; poetry SP
ALACIO see ALLACE, León
ALACOQUE, Santa Margarita María
de, 1647-90, French; nonfiction
SA
ALAGIYAVANNA, 1590-1620,
Sinhalese; poetry LAN
ALAILIMA, Fay C. ('Fay Calkins'),
1921- , American; nonfiction
CON
ALAIN see ALANUS de INSULIS
'ALAIN' (Émile Chartier), 1868-
1951, French; nonfiction,
essays FLE DIF HAR MAL
SA ST COL
ALAIN, Robert, 1660?-1720,
French; plays DIL
ALAIN de LILLE see ALANUS de
INSULIS
'ALAIN-FOURNIER' (Henri Alain
Fournier), 1886-1914, French;
fiction DIF FLE HAR KAT
KT MAG MAL RIC SA ST
ALAMAN, Lucan, 1792-1853,
Mexican; nonfiction SA
ALAMANNI, Luigi (Alemanni),
1495-1556, Italian; poetry
HAR KE SA ST
ALAMOS Barrientos, Baltasar,
1535-1624?, Spanish; nonfiction
SA
ALAN of LILLE see ALANUS de
INSULIS
ALAND, Kurt, 1915- , German;
nonfiction CON
ALANUS de INSULIS (Alain; Alan
of Lille; Alain de Lille),
1116?-1202, French; poetry
DIF KE SA ST
ALAOL, 17th cent., Indian; poetry
LAN
ALARCON, Abel, 1881- , Bolivian;
fiction, poetry, criticism
MIN SA
ALARCON, Antonia de, 17th cent.,
Spanish; poetry SA
ALARCON, Arcángel de, 16th cent.,
Spanish; poetry SA
ALARCON, Pedro Antonio de,
1833-91, Spanish; fiction,
poetry BL COL HAR KE MAG
SA ST

ALARCON y MENDOZA, Juan Ruiz
de see RUIZ de ALARCON, Juan
ALARCOS, Emilio, 1895- , Spanish;
nonfiction BL
ALARY, Pierre Joseph, 1690-1770,
French; nonfiction DIL
ALAS y UREÑA, Leopoldo ('Clarín'),
1852-1901, Spanish; fiction, criti-
cism BL COL HAR KE SA ST
ALAVI, Aqa Buzurg, 1908- , Per-
sian; fiction LAN ST
ALAYA, Flavia M., 1935- , Amer-
ican; nonfiction CON
ALAYDON, D. Jean Baptiste, 1671-
1753, French; nonfiction DIL
AL-AZM, Sadik J., 1934- , Syrian;
nonfiction CON
ALAZRAKI, Jaime, 1934- , Argen-
tinian-American; nonfiction CON
ALBA, Victor, 1916- , Spanish-
Mexican; nonfiction CON
ALBAMONTE, Luis María, 1912- ,
Argentinian; fiction, journalism
SA
ALBAREDA, Ginés de, 1908- ,
Spanish; poetry, plays, essays
SA
ALBARET, Jean, -1728, French;
nonfiction DIL
ALBAUGH, Ralph M., 1909- ,
American; nonfiction CON
ALBAUM, Gerald Sherwin, 1933- ,
American; nonfiction CON
ALBEDYLL, Gustave, -1819,
French; poetry, nonfiction DIL
ALBEE, Edward Franklin, 1928- ,
American; plays CON MAT RIC
ALBEE, Georg Sumner, 1905-64,
American; fiction CON
ALBEMARLE, Lord (George Thomas
Keppel), 1799-1891, British; non-
fiction KBA
ALBER, Mike, 1938- , American;
nonfiction CON
ALBERDI, Juan Bautista, 1810-84,
Spanish; nonfiction, poetry, plays
BL MIN SA
ALBERDINGK THIJM, Josephus
Albertus ('Pauwels Foreestier'),
1820-89, Dutch; fiction, poetry
HAR ST
ALBERDINGK THIJM, K.I.L. see
'DEYSSEL, Lodewijk van'
ALBERGATI COPACELLI, Francesco,
1728-1804, Italian; plays, fiction
SA
ALBERIC of TROIS-FONTAINES,
-1241, French; nonfiction
ST

ALBERIC von BESINZO, fl. 1120,
French; fiction ST
ALBERINI, Coriolano, 1886- ,
Argentinian; nonfiction MIN
ALBERS, Anni, German-American;
nonfiction CON
ALBERS, Henry H., 1919- ,
American; nonfiction CON
ALBERS, Josef, 1888- , German-
American; nonfiction CON
ALBERT, Saint see ALBERTUS
MAGNUS
ALBERT, Mme d., 18th cent.,
French; fiction DIF
ALBERT, Antoine, 1717-1804,
French; nonfiction DIL
ALBERT, Ethel Mary, 1918- ,
American; nonfiction CON
ALBERT, Harold A., English;
nonfiction CON
ALBERT, Heinrich, 1604-51,
German; poetry ST
ALBERT, Marvin H., American;
juveniles WA
ALBERT, Walter E., 1930- ,
American; nonfiction CON
ALBERT De LUYNES, Louis
Joseph, 1672-1758, French;
nonfiction DIF
ALBERT i PARADIS, Catalina
see 'CATALA, Victor'
ALBERT von STADE, 1200-61?,
German; poetry, diary HAR
ST
ALBERTAS, Jean Baptiste, 1716-
90, French; diary DIL
ALBERTAZZI, Adolfo, 1865-1924,
Italian; fiction, criticism SA
ST
ALBERT-BIROT, Pierre, 1885- ,
French; poetry DIF
ALBERTI, Leon Battista, 1404-72,
Italian; nonfiction KE SA ST
ALBERTI, Rafael, 1902/03- ,
Spanish; poetry BL COL FLE
HAR KTS MAT RIC SA ST
ALBERTINUS, Ägigius, 1560-1620,
German; translations, fiction
ST
ALBERTRANDY, Johan Christian,
1731-1808, Polish; nonfiction
SA
ALBERTS, David Stephen, 1942- ,
American; nonfiction CON
ALBERTS, Frances Jacobs, 1907- ,
American; juveniles CON
ALBERTS, Robert Carmen, 1907- ,
American; nonfiction CON

ALBERTS, William W., 1925- ,
American; nonfiction CON
ALBERTSON, Dean, 1920- , Amer-
ican; nonfiction CON
ALBERTUS MAGNUS, Saint, 1193/
1206-80, German; nonfiction
HAR KE SA ST
ALBERUS, Erasmus, 1500-53, Ger-
man; fiction AL ST
ALBERY, James, 1838-89, British;
plays, KBA
ALBINSKI, Henry Stephen, 1931- ,
American; nonfiction CON
ALBINUS see ALCUIN
ALBION, Robert Greenhalgh, 1896- ,
American; nonfiction CON
ALBIS de BELBEZE, Jean Francois
(Belvèze), 1730-1804, French;
nonfiction DIL
ALBISSON, Jean, 1732-1810, French;
nonfiction DIL
ALBIZZI, Rinaldo degli, 1370-1442,
Italian; nonfiction ST
ALBO, Joseph, 1380-1444, Jewish;
nonfiction KE ST
ALBON, Claude Camille Francois,
1753-89, French; nonfiction DIL
ALBORG, Juan Luis, 1914- , Span-
ish; nonfiction BL SA
ALBORNOZ y SALAS, Alvara de,
1908?- , Spanish; fiction SA
ALBOV, Mikhail Nolovich, 1851-1911,
Russian; fiction HAR HARK ST
'ALBRAND, Martha' (Heidi Huberta
Freybe Lowewngard; 'Katrin
Holland'; 'Christine Lambert'),
1913- , German-American;
fiction CON KTS WAF
ALBRECHT, Charles Milton, 1904- ,
American; nonfiction CON
ALBRECHT, Friedrich Wilhelm,
1774-1840, German; poetry ST
ALBRECHT, Lillie Vanderveer,
1894- , American; juveniles
CON
ALBRECHT, Robert Charles, 1933- ,
American; nonfiction CON
ALBRECHT, Ruth E., 1910- ,
American; nonfiction CON
ALBRECHT, William Price, 1907- ,
American; nonfiction CON
ALBRECHT von EYB, 1420-75, Ger-
man; nonfiction AL ST
ALBRECHT von HALBERSTADT, fl.
1210-50, German; nonfiction ST
ALBRECHT von JOHANNSDORF, fl.
1185-1209, Bavarian; poetry
KE ST

ALBRECHT von SCHARFENBERG,
fl. 1280, German; translations,
poetry ST
ALBRECHT-CARRIE, Rene, 1904- ,
American; nonfiction CON
ALBRIGHT, Bliss James F.,
1903- , American; nonfiction
CON
ALBRIGHT, Raymond Wolf, 1901- ,
American; nonfiction CON
ALBRIZZI, Isabel Teotochi, 1770-
1836, Italian; nonfiction SA
ALBROW, Martin, 1937- , Amer-
ican; nonfiction CON
ALBUQUERQUE, Afonso de, 1461-
1515, Portuguese; letters ST
ALBUQUERQUE, Afonso, 1500-80,
Portuguese; nonfiction SA
ALBUQUERQUE, Bràs de, 1500-
80, Portuguese; nonfiction ST
ALCAEUS, 7th-6th centuries B.C.,
Greek; poetry ST
ALCAIDE SANCHEZ, Juan, 1911-
51, Spanish; poetry SA
ALCALA, Jerónimo, 1563-1632,
Spanish; nonfiction BL
ALCALA GALIANO, Alvaro, 1886-
1936, Spanish; journalism SA
ALCALA GALIANO, Antonio, 1789-
1865, Spanish; nonfiction BL
SA ST
ALCALA y HERRERA, Alonso,
1599-1682, Spanish; fiction,
poetry BL SA
ALCALA YAÑEZ de RIBERA,
Jerónimo de, 1563-1632,
Spanish; fiction, poetry SA
ST
'ALCALDE, E.L.' see CHAIJ,
Fernando
ALCALDE VALLADARES, Antonio,
1829-94, Spanish; poetry, non-
fiction SA
ALCANTARA, Francisco José,
1922- , Spanish; fiction SA
ALCANTARA, Manuel, 1928- ,
Spanish; poetry SA
ALCAYAGA L.G. see 'MISTRAL,
Gabriela'
ALCAZAR, Baltasar del, 1530-
1606, Spanish; poetry BL
SA ST
ALCEO, 620-586 B.C., Greek?;
poetry SA
ALCIATO, Andrea, 1492-1550,
Italian; nonfiction ST
ALCIDAMAS of ELAEA, 4th cent.
B.C., Greek; nonfiction SA
ST

ALCIMO, 4th cent., Greek; nonfiction SA
ALCINOO, 1st-2nd cent., Greek; nonfiction SA
ALCIPHRON, 2nd-3rd cent., Greek; letters SA ST
ALCMAER, Heinric van, 15th cent., Dutch; poetry ST
ALCMAN, 7th cent. B.C., Greek; poetry SA ST
ALCMEON, 4th cent. B.C., Greek; nonfiction SA
ALCOBACA, Frey Bernardo, -1478, Portuguese; nonfiction SA
ALCOBRE, Manuel, 1900- , Argentinian; poetry, essays MIN SA
ALCOCER, Pedro de, 16th cent., Spanish; nonfiction BL SA
ALCOFORADO, Mariana, 1640-1723, Portuguese; letters HAR SA ST
ALCORN, Marvin D., 1902- , American; nonfiction CON
ALCORN, Robert Hayden, 1909- , American; fiction CON
ALCOTT, Amos Bronson, 1799-1888, American; poetry, nonfiction BRO KAA ST
ALCOTT, Louisa May, 1832-88, American; fiction, juveniles BRO DOY KAA MAG SA ST WA
ALCOTT, William Andrus, 1798-1859, American; nonfiction KAA
ALCOVER i MASPONS, Joan, 1854-1926, Spanish; poetry COL FLE SA ST
ALCOVER y SUREDA, Antonio María, 1862-1935?, Spanish; nonfiction SA
ALCUIN (Ealhwine; Albinus; Alkuin), 735-804, English; nonfiction AL BRO KB SA ST
ALDA TESAN, Jesús Manuel, 1910- , Spanish; nonfiction BL SA
ALDAN, Daisy, 1923- , American; poetry, nonfiction CON
ALDANA, Francisco de ('El Divino'), 1537-78, Spanish; poetry BL HAR SA ST
'ALDANOV, Mark' (Mark Alexandrovich Landau), 1886-1957, Russian; fiction, essays COL FLE HARK KT RIC SA ST
ALDAO, Martín, 1876/79- , Argentinian; fiction, essays, criticism MIN SA
ALDAO, Martín, 1907- , Argentinian; fiction, essays MIN SA
ALDCROFT, Derek H., 1936- ,

Welsh; nonfiction CON
ALDECOA, Ignacio, 1925- , Spanish; fiction BL SA
ALDEN, Henry Mills, 1836-1919, American; nonfiction KAA
'ALDEN, Jack' see BARROWS, Marjorie
ALDEN, John D., 1921- , American; nonfiction CON
ALDEN, Joseph, 1807-85, American, nonfiction KAA
ALDEN; William Livingstone, 1837-1908, American; journalism KAA
ALDERETE, Bernardo José de, 1565-1645, Spanish; nonfiction BL SA
ALDERFER, Clayton, P., 1940- , American; nonfiction CON
ALDERFER, Harold Freed, 1903- , American; nonfiction CON
ALDERMAN, Clifford Lindsey, 1902- , American; juveniles CON WA
ALDERMAN, Edwin Anderson, 1861-1931, American; nonfiction JO
ALDERSON, Arthur Stanley, 1927- , English; nonfiction CON
ALDERSON, Sir Edwin Aldred Hervey, 1859-1927, English; nonfiction HIG
ALDERSON, William Thomas, Jr., 1926- , American; nonfiction CON
ALDHELM, St., 640?-709, English; nonfiction KB ST
ALDIN, Cecil, 1870-1935, English; nonfiction HIG
ALDINGTON, Richard, 1892-1962, English; poetry, fiction, nonfiction BRO FLE KL KT MAG RIC SA ST
ALDIS, Dorothy Keeley, 1896/97-1966, American; juveniles poetry COM CON HOO KJU WA
ALDISS, Brian Wilson ('C. C. Shackleton'), 1925- , English; fiction CON RIC
'ALDON, Adair' see MEIGS, Cornelia L.
ALDOUBY, Zwy Herbert, 1931- , American; nonfiction CON
ALDRICH, Bess Streeter, 1881-1954, American; fiction KAT

KT SA WAF
ALDRICH, Clarence Knight, 1914- ,
American; nonfiction CON
ALDRICH, Frederic DeLong, 1899- ,
American; nonfiction CON
ALDRICH, Gustave B., American;
nonfiction SCA
ALDRICH, Thomas Bailey, 1836-
1906/07, American; poetry, fic-
tion BRO KAA MAG ST
ALDRIDGE, Alfred Owen, 1915- ,
American; nonfiction CON
ALDRIDGE, James, 1918- , Austral-
ian; fiction KTS
ALDRIDGE, Jeffrey, 1938- , Eng-
lish; plays CON
ALDRIDGE, John Watson, 1922- ,
American; fiction, nonfiction CON
ALDRIDGE, Josephine Haskell, Amer-
ican; juveniles WA
ALDRIDGE, Richard Boughton, 1930- ,
American; fiction CON
AL-e AHMAD, 1920- , Persian;
nonfiction LAN
ALEANDRO, Girolamo, 1480-1542,
Italian; nonfiction SA ST
ALEARDI, Aleardo, 1812-78, Italian;
poetry HAR KE SA ST
ALECIS GUILLAUME (Alexis), 1425?-
86?, French; poetry ST
ALECSANDRI, Vasile, 1821-90,
Rumanian; plays, poetry HAR
SA ST
ALEGRE, Francisco Javier, 1729-
88, Mexican; poetry SA
ALEGRIA, Ciro, 1909- , Peruvian;
fiction, poetry BL FLE KTS
MAG RIC SA ST
ALEGRIA, Fernando, 1918- , Chilean-
American; nonfiction CON
ALEGRIA, Ricardo E., 1921- ,
Puerto Rican; nonfiction CON
ALEICHEM, Sholem see SHOLEM
ALEICHEM
ALEIXANDRE, José Javier, 1924- ,
Spanish; nonfiction SA
ALEIXANDRE, Vicente, 1898/1900- ,
Spanish; poetry, nonfiction BL
COL FLE HAR RIC SA ST
ALEJANDRO, Cornelio 80 B.C.- ,
Greek nonfiction SA
'ALEJANDRO, Julio' (Julio Canstro),
20th cent., Spanish; poetry,
plays SA
ALEJANDRO de AFRODISIA, Greek;
nonfiction SA
ALEJANDRO de BERNAY, 12th

cent., French; poetry, fiction
SA
ALEJANDRO de EGEA, 1st cent.,
Greek?; poetry SA
ALEJANDRO NUMENIO, Greek;
nonfiction SA
ALEM, Leandro N., 1844-96,
Argentinian; nonfiction MIN
ALEMAN, Mateo, 1546-1613/15,
Spanish; fiction, nonfiction
BL HAR KE MAG SA ST
ALEMAN SAINZ, Francisco, 1919- ,
Spanish; nonfiction BL
ALEMANNI, Luigi see ALAMANNI,
Luigi
ALEMANY BOLUFER, José,
1866?- , Spanish; nonfiction
SA
ALEMBERT, Jean le Rond d',
1717-83, French; nonfiction
DIF DIL HAR KE MAL SA ST
ALENCAR, José Martiniano de,
1829-77, Brazilian; nonfiction,
fiction SA ST
ALENCAR, Mario Cokrane, 1871-
1925, Brazilian; poetry SA
ALDENDER, Martha Wheelock,
1941- , American; nonfiction
CON
'ALERAMO, Sibilla' (Rina Faccio),
1879- , Italian; fiction, poetry,
COL SA
ALES, Pierre Alexandre, 1715-70,
French; nonfiction DIL
ALESIUS, Alexander, 1500-65,
Scots; nonfiction BRO
ALESSANDRI, Maria Buonacorsi,
1670-1735, Italian; poetry SA
ALEWIJN, Abraham Martijnsz,
1664-1721, Dutch; poetry ST
ALEXANDER, Albert, 1914- ,
American; nonfiction CON
ALEXANDER, Anna Cooke, 1913- ,
American; juveniles COM
CON
ALEXANDER, Anne, 1913- ,
American; juveniles WA
ALEXANDER, Anthony Francis,
1920- , American; nonfiction
CON
ALEXANDER, Archibald, 1772-1851,
American; nonfiction KAA
ALEXANDER, Arthur Wilson,
1927- , Canadian; nonfiction
CON
ALEXANDER, Calvert Page, 1900- ,
American; nonfiction HOE

ALEXANDER, Cecil Frances (Cecil
Frances Humphreys), 1818/20-
95, Irish; poetry BRO KBA ST
'ALEXANDER, Charles' see HAD-
FIELD, Ellis C.
ALEXANDER, Charles Comer, 1935- ,
American; nonfiction CON
ALEXANDER, Charles Stevenson,
1916- , American; nonfiction
CON
ALEXANDER, Colin James ('Simon
Jay'), 1920- , English; fiction
CON
ALEXANDER, David, 1907- , Amer-
ican; fiction CON
ALEXANDER, Edward, 1936- ,
American; nonfiction CON
ALEXANDER, Edward Porter, 1907- ,
American; nonfiction CON
ALEXANDER, Edwin P., 1905- ,
American; nonfiction CON
ALEXANDER, Floyce, 1938- , Amer-
ican; poetry CON
ALEXANDER, Frances Laura, 1888- ,
American; poetry CON
ALEXANDER, Francisco, 1912- ,
Ecuadorian; criticism, transla-
tions DI
ALEXANDER, Franklin Osborne,
1897- , American; nonfiction
CON
ALEXANDER, Franz Gabriel, 1891-
1964, American; nonfiction CON
ALEXANDER, George Moyer, 1914- ,
American; nonfiction CON
ALEXANDER, Hubert Griggs, 1909- ,
American; nonfiction CON
ALEXANDER, Ian Welsh, 1911- ,
Scots, nonfiction CON
ALEXANDER, Jocelyn Anne Arundel
('Jocelyn Arundel'; 'Anne Arundel'),
1930- , American; juveniles
CON WA
ALEXANDER, John Aleck, 1912- ,
Greek-American; nonfiction CON
ALEXANDER, John Henry, 1812-67,
American; poetry KAA
ALEXANDER, John Thorndike, 1940- ,
American; nonfiction CON
ALEXANDER, John W., 1918- ,
American; nonfiction CON
ALEXANDER, Jon, 1940- , Ameri-
can; nonfiction CON
ALEXANDER, Jonathan James Graham,
1935- , English; nonfiction CON
'ALEXANDER, Kyle' see MARLOWE,
Alan S.
ALEXANDER, Lewis McElwain,

1921- , American; nonfiction
CON
ALEXANDER, Linda, 1935- ,
American; juveniles COM
CON
ALEXANDER, Lloyd Chudley,
1924- , American; juveniles,
translations CON WA
ALEXANDER, Marc, 1929- ,
American; juveniles, fiction
CON
'ALEXANDER, Marge' see ED-
WARDS, Roselyn
ALEXANDER, Mary Jean Mc-
Cutcheon, American; nonfic-
tion CON
ALEXANDER, Milton, 1917- ,
Polish-American; nonfiction
CON
'ALEXANDER, Ric' see LONG,
Richard A.
ALEXANDER, Robert J., 1918- ,
American; nonfiction CON
ALEXANDER, Samuel, 1859-1938,
English; essays SA
ALEXANDER, Sidney, 1912- ,
American; nonfiction, fiction,
poetry CON
ALEXANDER, Theron, 1913- ,
American; nonfiction CON
ALEXANDER, Thomas Williamson,
Jr., 1930- , American; non-
fiction CON
ALEXANDER, Sir William, 1567?-
1640, Scots; poetry KB
ALEXANDER, William Marvin,
1912- , American; nonfiction
CON
ALEXANDER de HALES, 1180-
1245, English; nonfiction SA
ALEXANDER NECKHAM see
NECKHAM, Alexander
ALEXANDER of APHRODISIAS, 3rd
cent., Greek; nonfiction ST
ALEXANDERSSON, Gunnar Vilhelm,
1922- , Swedish; nonfiction
CON
ALEXANDRAVICIUS, Kossu see
'AISTIS, Jonas'
'ALEXANDRE, Jacques' (Allexandre),
1653-1734, French; nonfiction
DIL
ALEXANDRE, Jean Baptiste Charles,
1720-85, French; nonfiction
DIL
ALEXANDRE, Dom Nicolas, 1654-
1728, French; nonfiction DIL
ALEXANDRE de BERNAI (de Paris),

fl. 1190, French; poetry ST
ALEXANDRE du PONT, 13th cent.,
French; poetry ST
ALEXANDRESCU, Grigore, 1812-85,
Wallachian; poetry SA ST
ALEXANDRI, Basil, 1821-90, Ru-
manian; poetry, plays KE SA
ALEXANDROWICZ, Charles Henry,
1902-   , Australian; nonfiction
CON
ALEXEYEV, S. A. see 'NAYDENOV,
S.'
ALEXIS, 390/80-280/70 B. C., Greek;
plays SA ST
ALEXIS, 1715-   , French; nonfiction
DIL
ALEXIS, Guillaume, 15th cent.,
French; poetry SA
ALEXIS, Paul, 1847-1901, French;
nonfiction, plays, fiction COL
DIF SA
'ALEXIS, Willibald' (Georg Wilhelm
Häring), 1798-1871, German;
fiction AL KE SA ST
ALEYN, Charles, 1602?-40, English;
poetry ST
ALFANDARY-ALEXANDER, Mark,
1923-   , American; nonfiction
CON
ALFANI, Gianni, 1260/70-1320,
Florentine; poetry ST
ALFARABI see FARABI
ALFARO, José María, 1905-   ,
Spanish; poetry BL
ALFARO, Manuel Ibo, 1828-   , Span-
ish; fiction, journalism SA
ALFARO, María, 1900?-   , Spanish;
poetry SA
ALFARO COOPER, José, M., 1861-   ,
Costa Rican; poetry MIN
ALFARO y POLANCO, José, María,
1906-   , Spanish; poetry, journal-
ism SA
ALFASI, Isaac Ben Jacob ('Rif'),
1013-1103, Jewish; poetry LAN
ST
ALFIERI, Vittorio, 1749-1803,
Italian; plays, poetry HAR KE
SA ST
ALFONSO X, 'El Sabio', 1221-84,
Spanish; poetry, nonfiction BL
KE SA ST
ALFONSO XI, 1314?-50, Spanish;
poetry BL
ALFONSO, Pedro (Pero; Moseh Sep-
hardi), 1062-1140, Jewish; transla-
tions BL SA

ALFONSO María de Ligorio, San,
1696-1787, Italian; nonfiction
SA
ALFORD, Henry, 1810-71, British;
nonfiction, poetry BRO KBA
ST
ALFORD, Normal William, 1929-   ,
English; nonfiction, fiction
CON
ALFRED (Aelfred), 849-901,
Saxon; nonfiction, translations
BRO KB ST
ALFRED, William, 1922-   , Amer-
ican; nonfiction CON
ALFVEN, Hannes Olof Goesta
('Olof Johannesson') 1908-   ,
Swedish; nonfiction CON
ALGAROTTI, Francesco, 1712-64,
Italian; poetry, nonfiction
HAR SA ST
ALGAZEL see GHAZZALI
ALGEO, John Thomas, 1930-   ,
American; nonfiction CON
ALGER, Horatio, 1834-99, Ameri-
can; juveniles BRO DOY KAA
ALGER, Leclaire G. ('Sorche Nic
Leodhas'), 1898-1971, Ameri-
can; juveniles WA
ALGREN, Nelson, 1909-   , Amer-
ican; fiction CON FLE HOO
KTS RIC WAF
ALHAIQUE, Claudio, 1913-   ,
Italian; nonfiction CON
AL-HARIZI Yehuda Ben Schlomoh
(Alcharisi), 1165-1235, Jewish;
poetry LAN SA
ALHOY, Louis François Joseph,
1756-1826, French; nonfiction
DIL
ALI, Ahmed, 1910-   , Indian; non-
fiction, translations, poetry
CON
ALI, Sir Nevai, 1441-1501, Turkish;
poetry SA ST
ALI, Tariq, 1943-   , Indian; non-
fiction CON
ALIBER, Robert Z., 1930-   ,
American; nonfiction CON
ALIBERT, François Paul, 1873-   ,
French; poetry COL SA
ALIGER, Margarita Iosifovna,
1915-   , Russian; poetry HAR
HARK RIC ST
ALIGHEIRI, Jacopo,   -1348, Ital-
ian; poetry ST
ALIGHEIRI, Pietro,   -1864, Italian;
poetry ST

ALIGHIERI, Dante, 1265-1321, Italian; poetry MAG
'ALIKI' see BRANDENBERG, Aliki L.
ALIKAN, Milla, Russian-American; nonfiction CON
ALILUNAS, Leo John, 1912- , American; nonfiction CON
ALISKY, Marvin Howard, 1923- , American; nonfiction CON
ALISON, Archibald, 1757-1839, Scots; nonfiction BRO
ALISON, Sir Archibald, 1792-1867, English; nonfiction BRO
ALISON, Sir Archibald, 1792-1867, English; nonfiction BRO KBA SA ST
ALIX, Ferdinand, 1740-1825, French; nonfiction DIL
ALIX, Guillaume, French; plays DIL
ALKAZI, Roshen Padamsee, 1923- , Indian; poetry MUR
ALKENDI, -860, Arab; nonfiction SA
ALKER, Hayward Rose, Jr., 1937- , American; nonfiction CON
ALKMAER, Heinrich von, 15th cent., German; poetry SA
ALKUIN see ALCUIN
ALLACE, León (Allatio; Alacio), 1586-1669, Greek; nonfiction SA
ALLAIN, Marcel, 1885- , French; fiction DIF
ALLAINVAL, Leónor Jean Christine Soules d', 1700-53, French; plays DIL
ALLAIS, Alphonse, 1855-1905, French; fiction DIF
ALLAMAND, François Louis, 1709-84, French; nonfiction DIL
ALLAMAND, Jean Nicolas Sébastien, 1713-87, French; nonfiction DIL
ALLAN, Alfred K., 1930- , American; nonfiction CON
ALLAN, David Guy Charles, 1925- , English; nonfiction CON
ALLAN, Harry T., 1928- , American; nonfiction CON
ALLAN, Mabel Esther ('Jean Estoril'; 'Priscilla Hagon'; 'Anne Pilgrim'), 1915- , American; juveniles, fiction CON WA
ALLAN, Mea, 1909- , Scots; nonfiction CON
ALLANA, G., Pakistani; poetry MUR
ALLAND, Alexander, Jr., 1931- , American; nonfiction CON
ALLARD, Sven, 1896- , Swedish; nonfiction CON

ALLARDYCE, Gilbert Daniel, 1932- , American; nonfiction CON
ALLART, Marie Françoise, 1765-1821, French; fiction DIL SA
ALLART, Mary Gay, 1750-1821, French; nonfiction SA
ALLATIO see ALLACE, Leon
ALLBECK, Willard Dow, 1898- , American; nonfiction CON
ALLCHIN, Arthur Macdonald, 1930- , English; nonfiction CON
ALLDRIDGE, James Charles, 1910- , English; nonfiction CON
ALLDRITT, Keith, 1935- , English; nonfiction CON
ALLEE, Marjorie Hill, 1890-1945, American; juveniles HOO KJU
ALLEGER, Daniel Eugene, 1903- , American; nonfiction CON
ALLEGRO, John Marco, 1923- , English; nonfiction CON
ALLEN, A. Dale Jr., 1935- , American; nonfiction CON
'ALLEN, Adam' see EPSTEIN, Beryl and EPSTEIN, Samuel
ALLEN, Agnes, -1959, English; juveniles DOY
ALLEN, Alexander Viets Griswold, 1841-1908, American; nonfiction KAA
'ALLEN, Allyn' see EBERLE, Irmengarde
ALLEN, Arthur Augustus, 1885-1964, American; nonfiction CON
ALLEN, Arthur Bruce ('Borough Trice'), 1903- , English; nonfiction CON
'ALLEN, Barbara' see STUART, Vivian F.
'ALLEN, Betsy' see CAVANNA, Betty
ALLEN, Cecil John ('Mercury'; 'Voyageur'), 1886- , American; nonfiction CON
ALLEN, Charles Richards, 1885- , New Zealander; poetry, fiction ST
ALLEN, Chris, 1929- , American; nonfiction CON
ALLEN, Clifford Edward, 1902- , English; fiction, nonfiction CON
ALLEN, Clinton M., 1878- ,

American; nonfiction MAR
ALLEN, David, 1925- , American;
nonfiction CON
ALLEN, David Elliston, 1932- ,
English; nonfiction CON
ALLEN, Dick, 1939- , American;
nonfiction CON
ALLEN, Diogenes, 1932- , American; nonfiction CON
ALLEN, Don Cameron, 1903- ,
American; nonfiction CON
ALLEN, Donald Merriam, 1912- ,
American; nonfiction CON
ALLEN, Dwight William, 1931- ,
American; nonfiction CON
ALLEN, Edith Beavers, 1920- ,
American; nonfiction CON
ALLEN, Edith Marion, American;
nonfiction CON
ALLEN, Edward Joseph, 1907- ,
American; nonfiction CON
ALLEN, Elizabeth A. see AKERS,
Elizabeth C.
ALLEN, F. M. see DOWNEY, Edmund
A.
ALLEN, Francis Alfred, 1919- ,
American; nonfiction CON
ALLEN, Frank Waller, 1878- ,
American; essays, poetry, fiction
HOO
ALLEN, Frederick Lewis, 1890-1954,
American; nonfiction KT
ALLEN, Gay Wilson, 1903- , American; nonfiction CON
ALLEN, Geoffrey Francis, 1902- ,
English; nonfiction CON
ALLEN, George Cyril, 1900- ,
English; nonfiction CON
ALLEN, George Francis, 1907- ,
English; nonfiction CON
ALLEN, Gina, 1918- , American;
fiction, juveniles CON
ALLEN, Grant (Charles Grant
Blairfindie Allen) 'Cecil Power',
1848-99, Canadian; fiction, nonfiction BRO KBA SY
ALLEN, Harold Byron, 1902- ,
American; nonfiction CON
ALLEN, Harry Cranbrook, 1917- ,
English; nonfiction CON
'ALEN, Hazel' see HERSHBERGER,
Hazel K.
ALLEN, Helena Gronlund ('H. Fredericka Allen'), American; nonfiction CON
ALLEN, Henry see ADAMS, Henry H.
ALLEN, Hervey, 1889-1949, American; fiction, poetry, nonfiction BRO FLE KL KT MAG
RIC ST WAF
ALLEN, Heywood (Woody), 1935- ,
American; nonfiction, plays
CON
ALLEN, Howard W., 1931- ,
American; nonfiction CON
ALLEN, Irene, 1903- , English;
nonfiction CON
ALLEN, Jack, 1914- , American;
nonfiction CON
ALLEN, James Lane, 1849-1925,
American; fiction KAA ST
ALLEN, James Lovie, Jr., ('Allen
James'), 1929- , American;
nonfiction CON
ALLEN, Jerry, 1911- , American;
nonfiction CON
ALLEN, Johannes, 1916- , Danish;
fiction CON
ALLEN, John, 1771-1843, British;
nonfiction KBA
ALLEN, John Alexander, 1922- ,
American; nonfiction CON
ALLEN, John Daniel, 1898- ,
American; nonfiction CON
ALLEN, John Jay, 1932- , American; nonfiction CON
'ALLEN, John W. Jr.' see LESLEY,
Peter
ALLEN, Joseph H.D., 1911- ,
American; nonfiction BL
ALLEN, Joseph Henry, 1820-90,
American; nonfiction KAA
ALLEN, Layman Edward, 1927- ,
American; nonfiction CON
ALLEN, Lee, 1915- , American;
nonfiction, juveniles CON WA
ALLEN, Louis A., 1917- , Canadian; nonfiction CON
ALLEN, Marie Louise, American;
juveniles WA
ALLEN, Marion C. ('Sam Allen'),
1914- , American; nonfiction
CON
ALLEN, Maury, 1932- , American;
nonfiction CON
ALLEN, Mel, 1913- , American;
juveniles WA
ALLEN, Merritt Parmelee, 1892-
1954, American; juveniles
KJU WA
ALLEN, Myron Sheppard, 1901- ,
American; nonfiction CON
ALLEN, Paul, 1775-1826, American; poetry KAA

ALLEN, R. Earl, 1922- , American; nonfiction CON
ALLEN, Ralph, 1913- , Canadian; fiction SY
ALLEN, Reginald E., 1931- , American; nonfiction CON
ALLEN, Richard C., 1926- , American; nonfiction CON
'ALLEN, Richard C.' see TAYLOR, John M.
ALLEN, Richard Hugh Sedley, 1903- , English; nonfiction CON
ALLEN, Richard J., American; juvenile WA
ALLEN, Richard Sanders, 1917- , American; nonfiction CON
ALLEN, Richard V., 1936- , American; nonfiction CON
ALLEN, Roach van, 1917- , American; nonfiction CON
'ALLEN, Robert' see GARFINKEL, Bernard
ALLEN, Robert Francis, 1928- , American; nonfiction CON
ALLEN, Robert J., 1930- , American; nonfiction CON
ALLEN, Robert Livingston, 1916- , American; nonfiction CON
ALLEN, Robert Loring, 1921- , American; nonfiction CON
ALLEN, Robert M., 1909- , American; nonfiction CON
ALLEN, Robert Porter, 1905-63, American; nonfiction CON
ALLEN, Ronald Royce, 1930- , American; nonfiction CON
ALLEN, Ross Roundy, 1928- , American; nonfiction CON
'ALLEN, Sam' see ALLEN, Marion C.
ALLEN, Shirley Walter, 1883- , American; nonfiction CON
ALLEN, Steve, 1921- , American; nonfiction, fiction, poetry CON
ALLEN, Sue P., 1913- , American; nonfiction CON
ALLEN, Sydney Earl, Jr. ('David Currie'), 1929- , American; nonfiction CON
ALLEN, Terril Diener, 1908- , American; fiction CON
ALLEN, Thomas B., 1929- , American; nonfiction CON
ALLEN, Vernon Lesley, 1933- , American; nonfiction CON
ALLEN, Walter, 1911- , English; fiction, criticism RIC
ALLEN, William, 1784-1868, Amer-

ican; nonfiction KAA
ALLEN, William Austin, 1916- , American; nonfiction CON
ALLEN, William Francis, 1830-89, American; nonfiction KAA
ALLEN, William Richard, 1924- , American; nonfiction CON
ALLEN, William Sheridan, 1932- , American; nonfiction CON
ALLEN, Woody see ALLEN, Heywood
ALLEN of HURTWOOD, Marjory, 1897- , English; nonfiction CON
ALLENDE, Juan Rafael, 1850-1905, Chilean; poetry, fiction MIN
ALLENDE IRAGORRI, Tomás, 1881- , Argentinian; poetry MIN
ALLENDOERFER, Carl Barnett, 1911- , American; nonfiction CON
ALLENTUCK, Harriet Ray, 1933- , American; nonfiction CON
ALLENTUCK, Marcia Epstein, 1928- , American; nonfiction CON
ALLERS, Rudolf, 1883- , Austrian; nonfiction HOE
'ALLERTON, Mary' see GOVEN, Christine N.
ALLEXANDER, Jacques see ALEXANDRE, Jacques
ALLEY, Louis Edward, 1914- , American; nonfiction CON
ALLEY, Rewi, 1897- , New Zealander; poetry, translations, nonfiction MUR
ALLEY, Robert S., 1932- , American; nonfiction CON
ALLFREY, Katherine, American; juveniles WA
ALLGIRE, Mildred J., 1910- , American; nonfiction CON
ALLIBONE, Samuel Austin, 1816-89, American; nonfiction KAA
'ALLID' see LANIGAN, George T.
ALLIETTE, fl. 1753-91, French; nonfiction DIL
ALLINGHAM, Margery Louise, 1904-66, English; fiction BRO CON KT RIC
ALLINGHAM, William, 1824-89, Irish; poetry BRO KBA SA ST
ALLIOT, Dominique Hyacinthe, 1705- , French; nonfiction DIL

ALLIOT, Hyacinthe, -1701, French;
nonfiction DIL
ALLIOT, Don Pierre, 1653-1715,
French; nonfiction DIL
ALLIS, Marguerite, American; fic-
tion WAF
ALLISON, Alexander Ward, 1919- ,
American; nonfiction CON
ALLISON, Anthony C., 1928- ,
South African; nonfiction CON
ALLISON, Bob, American; juveniles
WA
ALLISON, Christopher Fitzsimons,
1927- , American; nonfiction
CON
'ALLISON, Clay' see KEEVILL,
Henry J.
ALLISON, John Murray, 1889- ,
American; nonfiction CON
'ALLISON, Marian' see REID,
Frances P.
'ALLISON, Rand' see McCORMICK,
Wilfred
'ALLISON, Sam' see LOOMIS, Noel
M.
ALLITZ, Pons Augustin, 1703-85,
French; nonfiction DIL
ALLIX, Pierre, -1793, French;
poetry DIL
ALLMERS, Hermann, 1821-1902,
German; poetry ST
ALLOTT, Kenneth, 1912- , English;
poetry, fiction, play, criticism
MUR
ALLOTT, Robert, fl. 1600, English;
poetry ST
ALLOWAY, David Nelson, 1927- ,
American; nonfiction CON
ALLPORT, Gordon Willard, 1897-
1967, American; nonfiction CON
ALLRED, Gordon T., 1930- , Amer-
ican; nonfiction CON
ALLSOP, Kenneth, 1920- , English;
fiction, nonfiction CON
ALLSOPP, Harold Bruce, 1921- ,
English; nonfiction CON
ALLSTON, Washington, 1779-1843,
American; poetry, fiction BRO
KAA ST
ALLUE, SALVADOR, Miguel, 1885- ,
Spanish; nonfiction SA
ALLUE y MORER, Fernando,
1905- , Spanish; poetry, essays
SA
ALLUM, Nancy Patricia Eaton,
1920- , English; nonfiction
CON

ALLUT, Jean (L'Eclaireur'),
18th cent., French; nonfiction
DIL
ALLWARD, Maurice, 1923- ,
English; fiction CON
'ALLYN, Paul' see SCHOSBERG,
Paul A.
'ALMAFUERTE' see PALACIOS,
Pedro B.
ALMAGRO San Martín, Melchor,
1882-1947, Spanish; nonfiction,
essays BL SA
ALMAN, David ('Emily David'),
1919- , American; fiction
CON WAF
AL-MARAYATI, Abid Amin,
1931- , American; nonfiction
CON
ALMARAZ, Felix Diaz, Jr.,
1933- , American; nonfiction
CON
ALMEDINGEN, E.M. (Martha
Edith von Almedingen), 1898- ,
Russian-English; fiction, ju-
veniles, nonfiction CON
ALMEIDA, Antonio de José,
1866-1929, Portuguese; jour-
nalism SA
ALMEIDA, Guilherme de, 1890- ,
Brazilian; poetry SA
ALMEIDA, José Valentim Failho
de, 1857-1911, Portuguese;
fiction HAR ST
ALMEIDA, Doña Leanor de
(Leanor Alorna), 1750-1839,
Portuguese; poetry SA ST
ALMEIDA, Manoel Antonio de,
1830-61, Brazilian; fiction
ST
ALMEIDA, Manuel, 1580-1646,
Portuguese; nonfiction SA
ALMEIDA, Nicolau Tolentino de,
1740/45-1811, Portuguese;
poetry SA ST
ALMEIDA GARRETT, João
Baptista da Silva Leitão,
1799-1854, Portuguese; poetry,
fiction, plays HAR KE ST
ALMELA y VIVES, Francisco,
1902- , Spanish; poetry, non-
fiction, fiction SA
ALMENDROS AGUILAR, Antonio,
1825-1904, Spanish; poetry,
plays SA
ALMON, Clopper, Jr., 1934- ,
American; nonfiction CON
ALMON, John, 1738-1805, English;

essays SA
ALMORO see BARBARO, Ermolao
ALMOTAMID (Mutamid), 1040-95,
   Arab; poetry SA ST
ALMQUIST, L. Arden, 1921- ,
   American; nonfiction CON
ALMQVIST, Carl Jonas Love, 1793-
   1866, Swedish; fiction, poetry,
   plays HAR KE SA ST
ALOIAN, David, 1928- , American;
   nonfiction CON
ALOMAR, Gabriel, 1873-1941,
   Spanish; poetry, essays COL
   FLE SA ST
'ALONE' see DIAZ ARRIETA, Hernán
ALONSO, Amado, 1896/97-1952,
   Spanish; nonfiction BL COL
   MIN SA
ALONSO, Dámaso, 1898- , Spanish;
   poetry, criticism BL COL FLE
   HAR SA ST
ALONSO, Eduardo, 1898-1956, Span-
   ish; poetry SA
ALONSO, Martín, 1903- , Spanish;
   poetry, essays, fiction BL
ALONSO, William, 1933- , Amer-
   ican; nonfiction CON
ALONSO ALCALDE, Manuel, 1919- ,
   Spanish; poetry SA
ALONSO CORTES, Narciso, 1875- ,
   Spanish; nonfiction, poetry BL
   SA
ALONSO de BETANCOURT, Dora,
   1910- , Cuban; journalism,
   poetry MIN
ALONSO de HERRERA, Gabriel see
   HERRERA, Gabriel A. de
ALONSO de HERRERA, Hernando
   see HERRERA, Hernando
ALONSO FUEYO, Sabino, 1908- ,
   Spanish; essays, criticism SA
ALONSO GAMO, José María,
   1913- , Spanish; nonfiction BL
   SA
ALONSO Getino, Luis G. see GETINO,
   Luis
ALONSO, Luengo, Luis, 1909- ,
   Spanish; poetry SA
ALONSO PEDRAZ, Martín, 1903- ,
   Spanish; poetry SA
'ALONSO QUESADA' (Rafael Romero),
   1886-1925, Spanish; fiction,
   poetry SA
ALONSO TRELLES, Jose, 1860-1924,
   Uruguayan; poetry MAL
ALONSO y TRELLES, José, 1867-
   1925, Spanish; poetry SA

ALORNA, Leonor see ALMEIDA,
   Leonor de
ALPERS, Antony, 1919- , New
   Zealander; nonfiction CON
ALPERT, Hollis ('Robert Carroll'),
   1916- , American; fiction,
   nonfiction CON
'ALPHA of the PLOUGH' see
   GARDINER, Alfred G.
ALPHANUS of SALERNO,   -1085,
   Italian; poetry ST
ALPHEN, Hieronymus van, 1746-
   1803, Dutch; poetry, criticism
   ST
ALPHONSO-KARKALA, John B.,
   1923- , American; nonfiction
   CON
ALQUIE, Ferdinand, 1906- ,
   French; nonfiction DIF
ALSCHULER, Rose H., 1887- ,
   American; nonfiction CON
ALSINA, José Arturo, 1900- ,
   Argentinian; plays, poetry,
   essays SA
ALSINA COUTERET, José, 1878-
   1941, Spanish; journalism,
   criticism SA
ALSINO see BENITES VINUEZA,
   Leopoldo
ALSOP, Mary O'Hara ('Mary
   O'Hara'; 'Mary Sture-Vasa'),
   1885- , American; juveniles
   COM CON KTS HO WAF
ALSOP, Reese Fell, American;
   juveniles WA
ALSOP, Richard, 1761-1815,
   American; poetry KAA
ALSTON, Mary Niven ('Marian
   Niven'), 1918- , American;
   fiction CON
ALSTON, Patrick Lionel, 1926- ,
   American; nonfiction CON
ALSTON, William Payne, 1921- ,
   American; nonfiction CON
ALTABELLA HERNANDEZ, José,
   1921- , Spanish; journalism,
   nonfiction BL SA
ALTADILL y TEIXIDO, Antonio
   ('Antonio de Padua'), 1828-80,
   Spanish; fiction SA
ALTAMIRA y CREVEA, Rafael,
   1866-1951, Spanish; criticism
   BL COL SA ST HAR
ALTAMIRANO, Ignacio Manuel,
   1834-93, Mexican; fiction,
   poetry BL MAG SA ST
ALTBACH, Philip Geoffrey, 1941- ,

American; nonfiction CON
'ALTELING, William' see POUND,
Ezra L.
'ALTENBERG, Peter' (Richard Eng-
lander), 1859-1919, Austrian;
fiction AL COL FLE KU SA
ALTER, John Cecil, 1879-1964,
American; nonfiction CON
ALTER, Moshe Jacob see 'ROSEN-
FELD, Morris'
ALTER, Robert Edmond ('Robert
Raymond'; 'Robert Retla'), 1925-
65, American; nonfiction CON
WA
ALTERMAN, Nathan, 1910- ,
Jewish; poetry ST
ALTET PASCUAL, Francisco, 1891- ,
Spanish; poetry, plays SA
ALTET y RUATE, Benito, 1827-93,
Spanish; poetry SA
ALTHAUS, August Wilhelm Hermann
Paul, 1888- .
ALTHAUS, Clemente, 1835-81,
Peruvian; poetry, plays SA
ALTHAUS, Peter Paul, 1892- ,
German; nonfiction KU
ALTHOFF, Phillip, 1941- , Ameri-
can; nonfiction CON
ALTHOUSE, La Vonne, 1932- ,
American; nonfiction CON
ALTHOZ, Josef Lewis, 1933- ,
American; nonfiction CON
ALTHUSIUS, Johannes, 1557-1638,
German; nonfiction ST
ALTICK, Richard Daniel, 1915- ,
American; nonfiction CON
ALTIZER, Thomas Jonathan Jackson,
1927- , American; nonfiction
CON
ALTMAN, Dennis, 1943- , Austral-
ian; nonfiction CON
ALTMAN, Jack, 1938- , English;
fiction CON
ALTMAN, Robert A., 1943- ,
American; nonfiction CON
ALTMAN, Wilfred, 1927- , German-
English; nonfiction CON
ALTMANN, Johann Georg, 1695-1738,
Swiss; nonfiction DIL
ALTOLAGUIRRE, Manuel, 1904/06-
59, Spanish; poetry BL COL
FLE HAR SA ST
ALTROCCHI, Julia Cooley, 1893- ,
American; poetry, nonfiction
CON
ALTSHELER, Joseph Alexander,
1862-1919, American; juveniles
KT WA

ALTSHULER, Edward A., 1919- ,
American; nonfiction CON
ALUKO, Timothy Mofolorunsho,
1918- , Nigerian; fiction
RIC
'ALUN' (John Blackwell), 1797-
1840, Welsh; poetry ST
'AL-VAN-GAR' see RADWANSKI,
Pierre A.
ALVAR LOPEZ, Manuel, 1923- ,
Spanish; nonfiction BL
ALVARADO, Francisco, 1756-1814,
Spanish; nonfiction BL
ALVARADO, Maria de see AMA-
RILIS
ALVARADO QUIROS, Alejandro,
1875/76- , Costa Rican;
nonfiction, criticism MIN
ALVARENGA PEIXOTO, Ignácio
José, 1744-93, Brazilian;
poetry ST
ALVARES, Frei João, 15th cent.,
Portuguese; nonfiction SA
ALVARES de AZEVEDO, Manoel,
1831-52, Brazilian; poetry
SA ST
ALVARES de ORIENTE, Fernão,
1540-95, Portuguese; fiction,
poetry SA ST
ALVAREZ, Alfred, 1929- , Eng-
lish; poetry, criticism, non-
fiction CON MUR
ALVAREZ, Agustín, 1857-1914,
Argentinian; nonfiction MIN
'ALVAREZ, Alejandro Rodríguez
see 'CASONA, Alejandro'
ALVAREZ, Enrique, 1847/48-
1913, Colombian; poetry, es-
says, plays MIN
ALVAREZ, Jose Sixto ('Nemisio
Machuca'; 'Fabio Carrizo';
'Fray Mocho'), 1845-1903,
Argentinian; nonfiction, transla-
tions, fiction MIN SA
ALVAREZ, Joseph A., 1930- ,
American; nonfiction CON
ALVAREZ, Miguel de los Santos,
1817/18-92, Spanish; poetry,
fiction BL SA
ALVAREZ, Pedro, 1909- , Span-
ish; fiction BL
ALVAREZ, Valentín Andrés,
1891- , Spanish; nonfiction,
poetry, fiction BL
ALVAREZ ALTMAN, Grace De
Jesus, 1926- , American;
nonfiction CON
ALVAREZ de CIENFUEGOS see

CIENFUEGOS, Nicasio A. de
ALVAREZ de ESTRADA, Juan,
1892- , Spanish; poetry, criti-
cism SA
ALVAREZ de TOLEDO, Hernando,
1550-81, Chilean; poetry BL
MIN SA
ALVAREZ de TOLEDO y PELLICER,
Gabriel, 1662-1714, Spanish;
poetry, plays, nonfiction BL SA
ST
ALVAREZ de VELASCO y ZORRILLA,
Francisco, -1647, Colombian;
poetry MIN
ALVAREZ de VILLASANDINO, Alfonso
see VILLASANDINO, Alfonso A.
de
ALVAREZ de VILLASANDINO, Alonso,
1350-1425/30, Spanish; poetry
SA
ALVAREZ FERNANDEZ, Pedro,
1914- , Spanish; fiction SA
ALVAREZ GATO, Juan, 1433/40-
96/1509, Spanish; poetry BL SA
ST
ALVAREZ GOMEZ, Pedro, 1909- ,
Spanish; fiction, journalism SA
ALVAREZ HENAO, Enrique, 1871-
1914, Colombian; poetry MIN
ALVAREZ LENCERO, Luis, 1923- ,
Spanish; poetry SA
ALVAREZ LLERAS, Antonio Diego,
1892-1952, Colombian; poetry,
fiction, plays MIN SA ST
ALVAREZ ORTEGA, Manuel, 1923- ,
Spanish; nonfiction SA
ALVAREZ Posada, José María,
1911- , Spanish; poetry SA
ALVAREZ QUINTERO, Joaquín,
1873-1944, Spanish; plays BL
COL FLE KL KT HAR HOE
MAT RIC SA ST
ALVAREZ QUINTERO, Serafín, 1871-
1938, Spanish; plays BL COL
FLE HAR HOE KL KT MAT RIC
SA ST
ALVARO, Corrado, 1889/95-1956,
Italian; fiction, poetry, journal-
ism COL FLE SA ST
ALVARO, Franciso, 1913- , Spanish;
journalism, criticism SA
ALVARO deCORDOBA, Paulo,
-861/62, Spanish; nonfiction
SA
ALVARS, 800- , Tamil; poetry ST
ALVER, Betti, 1906- , Estonian;
poetry, fiction FLE

ALVERDES, Paul, 1897- , Ger-
man; poetry, fiction, essays
COL KT KU SA
ALVERSON, Charles, 1935- ,
American; nonfiction, juveniles
CON
ALVES, Colin, 1930- , English;
nonfiction CON
ALWORTH, E. Paul, 1918- ,
American; nonfiction CON
ALXINGER, Johann Baptist von,
1755-97, Austrian; poetry
ST
ALY, Bower, 1903- , American;
nonfiction CON
ALY, Lucile Folse, 1913- ,
American; nonfiction CON
ALYESHMERNI, Mansoor, 1943- ,
Irani-American; nonfiction
CON
ALYN, Marc, 1937- , French;
poetry, criticism DIF
'ALZEY, Korad von' see NIES,
Konrad
AMABILE, George N., 1936- ,
American; poetry CON MUR
AMABLE-TASTU, Sabinne Casimira,
1798- , French; poetry SA
AMACHER, Richard Earl, 1917- ,
American; nonfiction CON
'AMAD' see DICK, Isaac M.
AMADEO, Octavio, R., 1878- ,
Argentinian; nonfiction MIN
AMADI, Elechi Emmanuel, 1934- ,
Nigerian; fiction, plays CON
AMADO, Jorge, 1912- , Brazilian;
fiction FLE MAG RIC ST
AMADOR de los RIOS, José, 1818-
78, Spanish; poetry, nonfiction
BL SA
AMADOR de los RIOS, Rodrigo,
1843-1917, Spanish; nonfiction
SA
AMADOR FERNAN, Félix de,
1889- , Spanish; poetry,
journalism SA
AMALFI, Codtanza de Avalos,
1501-60, Italian; poetry SA
AMAMOO, Joseph Godson (Joseph
Kambu), 1931- , Ghanaian;
nonfiction CON
'AMANDA' see WYNNE-TYSON,
Esme
AMARAL, Anthony, 1930- ,
American; nonfiction CON
AMARASINHA, fl. 550, Sanskrit;
nonfiction ST

'AMARCIUS Gallus Piosistratus',
fl. 1040, German; poetry ST
'AMARILIS' (María de Alvarado),
17th cent., Spanish; poetry BL
SA
AMARU, fl. 850, Sanskrit; poetry ST
AMASEO, Romolo, 1498-1552, Italian;
nonfiction ST
AMATORA, Sister Mary ('Delphine
Fleury'), American; nonfiction
CON
AMBIRAJAN, Srinivasa, 1936- ,
Indian; nonfiction CON
AMBLER, Eric ('Eliot Reed'), 1909- ,
English; fiction CON KTS RIC
AMBOISE, Francois de, 1550-1620,
French; poetry, translations
SA
AMBRASER, Heldenbuck see THEUER-
DANK
AMBROGI, Arturo, 1878-1936,
Salvadorean; fiction, journalism
BL SA
'AMBROGINI, Angelo' see 'POLITIAN'
AMBROISE, fl. 1200, French; non-
fiction ST
AMBROISE de LOMBEZ (Jean de
Lapeyrie), 1708-78, French;
nonfiction DIL
AMBROSE, Saint, 310-97, Roman;
nonfiction SA
AMBROSE, Aurelius Ambrosius,
337-97, Italian; nonfiction ST
AMBROSE, Eric ('Christopher Ren-
nie'; 'Edgar Vance'; 'Esor B.
MacIre'), 1908- , English; non-
fiction CON
AMBROSE, Stephen Edward, 1936- ,
American; nonfiction CON
AMBROSE, W. Haydn, 1922- ,
Welsh; nonfiction CON
AMBROSETTI, Juan Bautista, 1865-
1917, Italian-Argentinian; non-
fiction MIN
AMBROSINI, Maria Luisa, Italian-
English; nonfiction CON
AMBRUS, Victor Giozo, 1935- ,
American; juveniles COM CON
DOY
AMBRUS, Zoltán, 1861-1932/33,
Hungarian; fiction, criticism,
essays COL FLE SA
AME, Antoine Rémy, 1711-82, French;
nonfiction DIL
AMECHINO, Florentino, 1854-1911,
Argentinian; nonfiction MIN
AMEILHON, Hubert Pascal, 1730-
1811, French; nonfiction DIL
SA

AMEIPSIAS, fl. 424-04 B.C.,
Greek; poetry ST
AMELIO, Ralph S., 1939- ,
American; nonfiction CON
AMELOT deCHAILLOU, Jean
Jacques, French; nonfiction
DIL
AMELOT de la HOUSSAYE,
Abraham Nicolas, 1634-1706,
French; nonfiction SA
AMEND, Victor Earl, 1916- ,
American; nonfiction CON
'AMERICAN SHIPMASTER' see
CODMAN, John
'AMERICO ELYSIO' see ANDRADE
y SILVA, Jose B.
AMERMAN, Lockhart, 1911-69,
American; nonfiction CON
WA
AMERVAL, Eloi d', 1483-1508,
French; poetry ST
AMES, Charles Edgar, 1895- ,
American; nonfiction CON
AMES, Charles Gordon, 1828-
1912, American; nonfiction
KAA
AMES, Fisher ('Camillus'), 1758-
1808, American; essays KAA
AMES, Francis Herbert ('Frank
Watson'; 'Martin Bunn'),
1900- , American; fiction
CON PAC
AMES, Jocelyn Green, American;
fiction CON
AMES, Lee Judah, 1921- , Amer-
ican; nonfiction CON WA
AMES, Louise Bates, 1908- ,
American; nonfiction CON
AMES, Nathaniel, 1708-64, Amer-
ican; nonfiction KAA
'AMES, Noel' see BARROWS,
Marjorie
AMES, Norma ('Ames Norman'),
1920- , American; nonfiction
CON
AMES, Ruth Margaret, 1918- ,
American; nonfiction CON
AMES, Van Meter, 1898- , Amer-
ican; nonfiction CON
AMES, Winslow, 1907- , Amer-
ican; nonfiction CON
AMEZAGA, Carlos Germán, 1862-
1906, Peruvian; poetry, plays,
journalism SA
AMEZUA, Augustín, G. de see
GONZALEZ de AMEZUA,
Agustín
AMFITEATROV, Alexander Valen-
tinovich, 1862-1938, Russian;

fiction HAR ST
'AMGIS' see SARGENT, Lucius M.
AMICIS, Edmundo de see DE AMICIS,
    Edmundo
AMICK, Robert Gene, 1933- ,
    American; nonfiction CON
AMIEL, Denys, 1884- , French;
    plays COL SA ST
AMIEL, Henri Frédéric, 1821-81,
    Swiss; nonfiction, poetry, diary
    COL DIF HAR KE MAL SA ST
AMIENS, Dom Jacques, 1701-84,
    French; nonfiction DIL
AMIGHETTI, Francisco, 1908- ,
    Costa Rican; poetry MIN
AMIOT, Dom Hugues, 1643-1703,
    French; nonfiction DIL
AMIOT, Jacques see AMYOT, Jacques
AMIOT, Jean Joseph Marie, 1718-
    93, French; nonfiction DIL
AMIR ALI, Sir Syed, 1844-95, Indian;
    nonfiction ST
AMIR KHUSROW see KHUSROW
    Dihlavi
AMIRI, Sadaq, 1860/61-1917, Per-
    sian; poetry, journalism ST
'AMIS, Breton' see BEST, Rayleigh
    B. A.
AMIS, Kingsley William, 1922- ,
    English; poetry, plays, fiction,
    nonfiction CON FLE MUR RIC
AMLUND, Curtis Arthur, 1927- ,
    American; nonfiction CON
AMME, Carl H., Jr., 1913- ,
    American; nonfiction CON
AMMER, Dean S., 1926- , Ameri-
    can; nonfiction CON
AMMERMAN, Leila Tremaine, 1912- ,
    American; nonfiction CON
AMMERMAN, Robert Ray, 1927- ,
    American; nonfiction CON
AMMERS-KÜLLER, Johanna van,
    1884- , Dutch; fiction FLE
    KL KT MAG SA
AMMIANUS, Marcellinus, 330-400,
    Roman; nonfiction SA ST
AMMIRATO, Scipione, 1531-1601,
    Italian; nonfiction ST
AMMONIO, fl. 480, Greek; nonfiction
    SA
AMMONIO, fl. 389, Greek; nonfiction
    SA
AMMONS, A. R., 1926- , American;
    poetry CON MUR
AMOERS, Jan, 15th cent., Dutch;
    poetry ST
'AMOR, Amos' see HARRELL, Irene
    B.

AMOR MEILLAN, Manuel, 1850?- ;
    Spanish; fiction, journalism,
    plays SA
AMORETTI, María Pellegrina,
    1756-87, Italian; nonfiction
    SA
AMORIE van der HOEVEN, Ab-
    raham des, Sr., 1798-1855,
    Dutch; poetry ST
AMORIE van der HOEVEN, Jr.,
    Abraham, 1821-48, Dutch;
    poetry ST
AMORIM, Enrique M., 1900-60,
    Uruguayan; fiction, poetry
    FLE MIN SA
AMOROS, Juan Bautista see
    'LANZA, Silverio'
AMORY, Anne Reinberg, 1931- ,
    American; nonfiction CON
AMORY, Cleveland, 1917- ,
    American; fiction KTS
AMORY, Thomas, 1691?-1788,
    British; fiction BRY KB
AMOS KOMENSKY, Jan see
    COMENIUS, Jan A.
AMOS, William E., 1926- ,
    American; nonfiction CON
AMOSS, Berthe, 1925- , Ameri-
    can; juveniles CON
AMPELIO, Luio, 3rd cent.,
    Roman; nonfiction SA
AMPERE, André-Marie, 1775-
    1836, French; nonfiction DIF
    SA
AMPERE, Jean Jacques Antoine,
    1800-64, French; nonfiction
    DIF
'AMPLEGIRTH, Antony' see DENT,
    Anthony A.
AMPRIMOZ, Alexandre, 1948- ,
    Canadian; nonfiction CON
AMPZING, Samuel, 1590-1632,
    Dutch; poetry ST
AMRAM, David Werner, III,
    1930- , American; nonfiction
    CON
AMSBARY, Wallace Bruce, 1867- ,
    American; poetry HOO
AMSTEAD, Billy Howard, 1921- ,
    American; nonfiction CON
AMSTUTZ, Arnold E., 1936- ,
    American; nonfiction CON
AMUNATEGUI ALDUNATE, Miguel
    Luis, 1828-88, Chilean; non-
    fiction MIN SA
AMUNATEGUI y REYES, Miguel
    Luis, 1863-1949, Chilean; non-
    fiction MIN

AMUNATEGUI y SOLAR, Domingo,
1860-1946, Chilean; nonfiction
MIN
AMUNATEQUI, Gregorio Victor,
1830-99, Chilean; nonfiction,
essays MIN SA
AMUNDSEN, Kirsten, 1932- ,
Norwegian; nonfiction CON
AMYOT, Jacques (Amiot), 1513-93,
French; nonfiction, translations
DIF HAR KE MAL SA ST
ANA Comneno see COMNENO, Anna
ANACARSIS (Anacharsis), 590 B.C.- ,
Greek; nonfiction SA
ANACLET du HAVRE, 18th cent.,
French; nonfiction DIL
ANACREON, 570-485 B.C., Greek;
poetry ST
ANACREONTE, 590-475 B.C.,
Greek; poetry SA
ANANIA, Michael, 1939- , Ameri-
can; poetry CON
ANANIO, 6th century B.C., Greek;
poetry SA
ANARARCO, Greek; poetry SA
ANASTAPLO, George, 1925- ,
American; nonfiction CON
ANASTASE, Louis A. Guichard,
-1739, French; nonfiction
DIL
ANASTASI, Anne, 1908- , Ameri-
can; nonfiction CON
ANASTASIO, 9th cent., Italian;
nonfiction SA
ANASTASIUS Bibliothecarius, 810-
78, Italian; nonfiction ST
ANASTASIUS of SINAI, fl. 640-700,
Byzantine; nonfiction ST
ANAU, Benjamin (Anavi degli
Mansi), 13th cent., Italian;
poetry ST
ANAXAGORAS, 500-428 B.C., Greek;
nonfiction SA ST
ANAXANDRIDES, 380-40 B.C., Greek;
poetry ST
ANAXANDRITA, Greek; poetry SA
ANAXIMANDER, 610-546 B.C.,
Greek; nonfiction SA ST
ANAXIMENES, 6th cent. B.C.,
Greek; nonfiction ST
ANAXIMENES de LAMPSACO, 4th
cent., Greek; nonfiction SA
ANAXIMENES de MILETO, 550-500
B.C., Greek; nonfiction SA
ABCEAUME, Dom François, 1652-
1729, French; nonfiction DIL
ANCELOT, Marguerite Virginie
Chardon, 1792- , French; non-

fiction, fiction SA
ANCEY, Georges Marie Edmond
Mathevon de Curnieu, 1860-
1917, French; plays DIF MAT
ANCEZONE, Françoise Félicité
Colbert, 1698-1749, French;
nonfiction DIL
ANCHELL, Melvin, 1919- ,
American; nonfiction CON
ANCHIETA, José, de, 1530-97,
Brazilian; poetry ST
ANCOLLON, Johan Peter Friedrich,
1766-1837, German; nonfiction
SA
ANCIZAR y ZABALETA, José
Francisco, 1812-82, Colombian;
nonfiction MIN
ANCKARSVARD, Karin Inez Maria,
1915/18- , Swedish; juveniles
CON WA
ANCONA, Alessandro see D'ANCONA
ANCONA, Eligio, 1836-93, Mexican;
nonfiction, fiction SA
ANCZYC, Wladyslaw Ludwik
('Kazimarierz Goralzyyk'),
1823-83, Polish; poetry, plays
ST
ANDEBEZ de MONTGAUBET, 18th
cent., French; plays DIL
ANDELSON, Robert Vernon, 1931- ,
American; nonfiction CON
ANDELY, Henri d', 18th cent.,
French; poetry DIF
'ANDEREICH, Justus' see STEINER,
Gerolf
ANDERS, Edith Mary England,
1899- , Australian; poetry,
fiction CON
ANDERS, Evelyn, 1916- , Amer-
ican; nonfiction CON
ANDERS, Leslie, 1922- , Amer-
ican; nonfiction CON
ANDERSCH, Alfred, 1914- ,
German; fiction, criticism
AL CON FLE KU KUN
ANDERSCH, Elizabeth Genevieve,
1913- , American; nonfiction
CON
ANDERSEN, Arlow W., 1906- ,
American; nonfiction CON
ANDERSEN, Doris, 1909- ,
American; fiction CON
ANDERSEN, Hans Christian, 1805-
75, Danish; juveniles, fiction
DOY HAR KE KJU MAG SA
ST WA
ANDERSEN, Kenneth Eldon, 1933- ,
American; nonfiction CON

ANDERSEN, Rudolph Clifton,
1933- , American; nonfiction
CON
'ANDERSEN, Ted' see BOYD, Waldo
T.
ANDERSEN, Tryggve, 1866-1920,
Norwegian; fiction COL HAR SA
ST
ANDERSEN, Uell Stanley, 1917- ,
American; nonfiction CON
ANDERSEN, Vilhelm Rasmus Andreas,
1864-1953, Danish; criticism ST
ANDERSEN, Wayne, V., 1928- ,
American; nonfiction CON
ANDERSEN, Wilhelm, 1911- , Ger-
man; nonfiction CON
ANDERSEN, Yvonne, 1932- , Amer-
ican; nonfiction CON
ANDERSEN NEXO, Martin see NEXÖ,
Martin A.
ANDERSON, Alan Ross, 1925- ,
American; nonfiction CON
ANDERSON, Alexander ('Surfaceman'),
1845-1909, Scots; poetry BRO
KBA
ANDERSON, Alpha E., 1914- ,
American; nonfiction CON
ANDERSON, Barbara, 1894- , Amer-
ican; fiction WAF
ANDERSON, Barry Franklin, 1935- ,
American; nonfiction CON
ANDERSON, Bern, 1900-63, Ameri-
can; nonfiction CON
ANDERSON, Bertha Moore, 1892- ,
American; poetry CON
ANDERSON, C. W., 1891- , Amer-
ican; juveniles KJU
ANDERSON, Camilla May, 1904- ,
American; nonfiction CON
ANDERSON, Carl Dicmann, 1912- ,
American; nonfiction CON
ANDERSON, Carl Leonard, 1901- ,
American; nonfiction CON
ANDERSON, Catherine Corley, 1909- ,
American; juveniles CON
ANDERSON, Charles C., 1931- ,
American; nonfiction CON
ANDERSON, Charles Roberts, 1902- ,
American; nonfiction CON
ANDERSON, Charles William, 1934- ,
American; nonfiction CON
ANDERSON, Chester Grant, 1923- ,
American; nonfiction CON
ANDERSON, Clarence W., 1891-1971,
American; juveniles WA
'ANDERSON, Clifford' see GARDNER,
Richard

ANDERSON, Coleman Michael,
1891- , American; nonfiction
CON
ANDERSON, Courtney, 1906- ,
American; nonfiction CON
ANDERSON, David Daniel, 1924- ,
American; nonfiction CON
ANDERSON, David Leonard, 1919- ,
American; nonfiction CON
ANDERSON, Dillon, 1906- ,
American; nonfiction CON
ANDERSON, Donald Kennedy, Jr.,
1922- , American; nonfiction
CON
ANDERSON, Edgar ('Edgars Ander-
sons'), 1920- , Latvian-Amer-
ican; nonfiction CON
ANDERSON, Einar, 1909- , Amer-
ican; nonfiction CON
ANDERSON, Elmo M., 1888- ,
American; nonfiction SCA
ANDERSON, Ethel Todd, American;
juveniles WA
ANDERSON, Eugene Newton, 1900- ,
American; nonfiction CON
ANDERSON, Eva Greenslit, 1889- ,
American; juveniles PAC
ANDERSON, Forrest Clayton,
1903- , American; poetry
PAC
ANDERSON, Frank John, 1919- ,
American; nonfiction CON
ANDERSON, Frederick Irving,
1877-1947, American; fiction
KT
'ANDERSON, George' see GROOM,
Arthur W.
'ANDERSON, George' see WEISS-
MAN, Jack
ANDERSON, George Christian,
1907- , English; nonfiction
CON
ANDERSON, George Kumler, 1901- ,
American; nonfiction CON
ANDERSON, George La Verne,
1905- , American; nonfiction
CON
ANDERSON, Gerald Harry, 1930- ,
American; nonfiction CON
'ANDERSON, Graham' see GROOM,
Arthur W.
ANDERSON, Harold Homer, 1897- ,
American; nonfiction CON
ANDERSON, Henry P., 1927- ,
American; nonfiction CON
ANDERSON, Hugh, 1920- , Scots-
American; nonfiction CON

ANDERSON, Jack, 1935- , American; poetry CON

ANDERSON, James Elliott, 1933- , American; nonfiction CON

ANDERSON, James George, 1936- , American; nonfiction CON

ANDERSON, James Maxwell, 1933- , American; nonfiction CON

ANDERSON, James Norman Dalrymple, 1908- , English; nonfiction CON

ANDERSON, Jessica Margaret Queale, Australian; fiction CON

ANDERSON, John Bayard, 1922- , American; nonfiction CON

ANDERSON, John Edward, 1903- , English; nonfiction, translations CON

ANDERSON, John Kinloch, 1924- , American; nonfiction CON

ANDERSON, John Lonzo, 1905- , American; juveniles COM CON

ANDERSON, John Mueller, 1914- , American; nonfiction CON

ANDERSON, John Q., 1916- , American; nonfiction CON

ANDERSON, John Richard Lane, 1911- , English; nonfiction CON

ANDERSON, Jon Victor, 1940- , American; poetry CON MUR

ANDERSON, Joy, 1928- , American; juveniles COM CON

ANDERSON, Ken, 1917- , American; nonfiction CON

ANDERSON, Lee, 1896-1972, American; poetry CON

ANDERSON, Lester William, 1918- , American; nonfiction CON

ANDERSON, M.D., 1902- , American; nonfiction CON

ANDERSON, Madeleine Paltenghi, 1899- , American; juveniles, CON

ANDERSON, Malcolm, 1934- , English; nonfiction CON

ANDERSON, Margaret Bartlett, 1922- , American; nonfiction CON

ANDERSON, Margaret Johnson, 1909- , American; juveniles, nonfiction CON

ANDERSON, Margaret Vance, 1917- , American; nonfiction CON

ANDERSON, Martin, 1936- , American; nonfiction CON

ANDERSON, Matthew Smith, 1922- , Scots; nonfiction CON

ANDERSON, Maxwell, 1888-1959, American; plays, essays, poetry

BRO FLE KL KT MAG MAT RIC SA ST

'ANDERSON, Neil' see BEIM, Jerrold

ANDERSON, Norman Dean, 1928- , American; nonfiction CON

ANDERSON, Odin Waldemar, 1914- , American; nonfiction CON

ANDERSON, Orvil Roger, 1937- , American; nonfiction CON

ANDERSON, Patrick, 1936- , American; fiction CON

ANDERSON, Patrick John McAlister, 1915- , Canadian; poetry, nonfiction MUR SY

ANDERSON, Paul E., 1925- , American; nonfiction CON

ANDERSON, Paul Seward, 1913- , American; nonfiction CON

ANDERSON, Poul William ('Winston P. Sanders'), 1926- , American; fiction CON

ANDERSON, Quentin, 1912- , American; nonfiction CON

ANDERSON, Rachel, 1943- , English; fiction CON

ANDERSON, Richard Lloyd, 1926- , American; nonfiction CON

ANDERSON, Robert, 1770-1833, British; poetry BRO KBA

ANDERSON, Robert Gordon, 1881-1950, American; nonfiction HO SA

ANDERSON, Robert Thomas, 1926- , American; nonfiction CON

ANDERSON, Robert W., 1926- , American; nonfiction CON

ANDERSON, Robert Woodruff, 1917- , American; plays CON MAT

ANDERSON, Roy, 1936- , English; nonfiction CON

ANDERSON, Roy Allen, 1895- , American; nonfiction CON

ANDERSON, Ruth Irene, 1919- , American; nonfiction CON WA

ANDERSON, Sherwood, 1876-1941, American; fiction, plays, poetry, essays BRO FLE HOO KL KT MAG RIC SA ST

ANDERSON, Stanley Edwin, 1900- , American; nonfiction CON

ANDERSON, Stanley Victor, 1928- , American; nonfiction CON

ANDERSON, Thomas, 1929- , American; fiction CON

ANDERSON, Thomas Scott, 1853- ,
English; nonfiction HIG
ANDERSON, Totton James, 1909- ,
American; nonfiction CON
ANDERSON, Verily Bruce, 1915- ,
English; fiction CON
ANDERSON, Vernon Ellsworth,
1908- , American; nonfiction
CON
ANDERSON, Violet Louise Maw,
1906- , Canadian; poetry MUR
ANDERSON, Virgil Antris, 1899- ,
American; nonfiction CON
ANDERSON, Virginia R. Cronin
('Hyacinthe Hill'), 1920- ,
American; poetry CON
ANDERSON, Vivienne, American;
nonfiction CON
ANDERSON, Wallace Ludwig, 1917- ,
American; nonfiction CON
ANDERSON, Warren De Witt, 1920- ,
American; nonfiction CON
ANDERSON, William Charles, 1920- ,
American; fiction CON
ANDERSON, William Davis, 1938- ,
American; nonfiction CON
ANDERSON, William Robert, 1921- ,
American; fiction CON
ANDERSON, Wilton Thomas, 1916- ,
American; nonfiction CON
ANDERSON IMBERT, Enrique, 1910- ,
Argentinian; fiction, essays BL
CON SA
'ANDERSONS, Edgars' see ANDERSON,
Edgar
ANDERS-RICHARDS, Donald, 1928- ,
English; nonfiction CON
ANDERSSON, Dan, 1888-1920, Swedish;
poetry, fiction COL SA ST
ANDERSSON, Theodore Murdock,
1934- , American; nonfiction
CON
ANDERSTON, Stanford, 1934- ,
American; nonfiction CON
ANDJELINOVIC, Danko, 1891- ,
Dalmatian; poetry, fiction ST
ANDLAU, Mme. du Crest de Saint
Aubin, 18th cent., French; fic-
tion DIL
'ANDO JISHO' (Ando Hachizaemon),
1658-1745, Japanese; fiction SA
ST
ANDOCIDES, 440-390? B.C., Athenian;
nonfiction SA ST
ANDONOV-POLJANSKI, Hristo, 1927- ,
Yugoslav; nonfiction CON
ANDRADE, Edward Neville Da Costa,

1887- , English; nonfiction
CON
ANDRADE, Francisco, 1540?-1614,
Portuguese; poetry SA
ANDRADE, Jacinto Freire de, 1597-
1657, Portuguese; nonfiction
SA
ANDRADE, Mário Raúl de Morais,
1892-1945, Brazilian; poetry,
fiction, essays FLE SA ST
ANDRADE, Olegario Victor, 1839/
41-82, Argentinian; poetry,
journalism MIN BL SA ST
ANDRADE, Osward de, 1890- ,
Brazilian; poetry, fiction SA
ANDRADE, Raul, 1905- , Ecua-
dorian; nonfiction, plays DI
ANDRADE y CORDERO, Cesar,
1904- , Ecuadorian; poetry,
criticism DI
ANDRADE y SILVA, José Bonifacio
de ('Americo Elysio'), 1765-
1838, Brazilian; poetry SA ST
ANDRE, Charles, 1722-85, French;
nonfiction DIL
ANDRE, Jean, 1722- , French;
nonfiction DIL
ANDRE, Jean François, 1744- ,
French; nonfiction DIL
ANDRE, Yves Marie, 1675-1764,
French; nonfiction, poetry
DIF DIL
ANDRE de GRAZAC (François
Besson de la Rochette), 18th
cent., French; nonfiction DIL
ANDRE le CHAPELAIN (Andreas
Capellanus), 12th cent., French;
poetry KE ST
ANDREÄ, Johann Valentin, 1586-
1654, German; poetry AL
KE ST
ANDREA, Monte, 13th cent.,
Florentine; poetry ST
ANDREA de NERCIAT (André
Robert), 1739-1800, French;
fiction DIL
ANDREACH, Robert J., 1930- ,
American; nonfiction CON
ANDREANO, Ralph Louis, 1929- ,
American; nonfiction CON
ANDREAS, Bernard (André), fl.
1500, French; poetry ST
ANDREAS Capellanus see ANDRE
le CHAPELAIN
ANDREAS Ratisbonensis, 1380-
1438, Bavarian; nonfiction ST
ANDREAS-SALOME, Lou, 1861-

1937, German; nonfiction, fiction KU

ANDRE-BARDON, Michel François, 1700-83, French; poetry, nonfiction DIL

ANDREE, Robert Gerald, 1912- , American; nonfiction CON

ANDREEV LEONID, N. see ANDRE-YEV, Leonid N.

ANDRE-FRANCOIS de Tournon, fl. 1690-1716, French; nonfiction DIL

ANDREINI, Isabel, 1562-1604, Italian; poetry SA

ANDRELINI, Publio Fausto, 1462-1518, Italian; poetry SA ST

'ANDRENIO' see GOMEZ de BAQUERO, Eduardo

ANDRES, Juan, 1740-1817, Spanish; nonfiction BL SA ST

ANDRES, Stefan, 1906- , German; fiction, poetry, plays AL FLE HAR KU LEN RIC ST

ANDRES, Valero, 1587-1655, Belgian; nonfiction SA

ANDRES ALVAREZ, Valentín, 1891- , Spanish; fiction, plays SA

ANDRESEN, Heinrich, 1875- , German; poetry ST

ANDRESEN, Ingeborg, 1878- , German; plays ST

ANDREW, Prudence Hastings, 1924- , English; fiction, juveniles CON

ANDREW, Warren, 1910- , American; nonfiction CON

ANDREW of CAESAREA, 6th cent., Byzantine; nonfiction ST

ANDREW of CRETE, 660-740?, Byzantine; poetry ST

ANDREWES, Christopher Howard, 1896- , English; nonfiction CON

ANDREWES, Lancelot, 1555-1626, English; nonfiction BRO KB ST

ANDREWES, Patience see BRADFORD, Patience A.

ANDREWS, Burton Allen, 1906- , American; nonfiction CON

ANDREWS, Charles McLean, 1863-1943, American; nonfiction KT

ANDREWS, Charles Robert Douglas Hardy ('Robert D. Andrews'; 'Robert Doughlas'; 'Douglas Hardy') 1908- , American; nonfiction CON ST

ANDREWS, Claire ('Keith Claire'), 1940- , English; fiction CON

ANDREWS, Clarence Adelbert

('Steven Randall'), 1912- , American; nonfiction CON

ANDREWS, Donald Hatch, 1898- , American; nonfiction CON

ANDREWS, Elisha Benjamin, 1844-1917, American; nonfiction KAA

ANDREWS, Frank Emerson, 1902- , American; nonfiction CON

ANDREWS, Frank Michael, 1916- , American; juveniles CON

ANDREWS, George Clinton, 1926- , American; nonfiction CON

ANDREWS, James Sydney, 1934- , English; nonfiction CON

ANDREWS, John, 1583- , English; poetry ST

ANDREWS, John, 1746-1813, American; nonfiction KAA

ANDREWS, Julie ('Julie Edwards'), 1935- , English; juveniles CON

ANDREWS, Keith ('Keith Claire'), 1930- , English; fiction CON

ANDREWS, Kenneth Richmond, 1916- , American; nonfiction CON

ANDREWS, Margaret Elizabeth, American; nonfiction CON

ANDREWS, Mark Edwin, 1903- , American; nonfiction CON

ANDREWS, Mary Evans, American; nonfiction CON

ANDREWS, Mary Raymond Shipman, 186?-1936, American; fiction KT

ANDREWS, Peter, 1931- , American; nonfiction CON

ANDREWS, Ralph Warren, 1897- , American; nonfiction CON PAC

'ANDREWS, Robert D.' see ANDREWS, Charles R.D.H.

ANDREWS, Robert Hardy, 1903- , American; fiction WAF

ANDREWS, Roy Chapman, 1884-1960, American; nonfiction BRO KT WA

ANDREWS, Stephen Pearl, 1812-86, American; nonfiction KAA

ANDREWS, Tom ('Gin and Beer'), 1863- , English; nonfiction HIG

ANDREWS, Wayne ('Montagu O'Reilly'), 1913- , American; nonfiction CON

ANDREWS, William George, 1930- ,
American; nonfiction CON
ANDREWS, William Lenton ('Edith
Settle'), 1886- , English; non-
fiction CON
ANDREWS, William Loring, 1837-
1920, American; nonfiction KAA
ANDREYEV, Leonid Nikolayevich
(Andreev), 1871-1919, Russian;
fiction, plays, translations COL
FLE HAR HARK KAT KT MAG
MAT RIC SA ST
'ANDREYEVICH' see SOLOVYEV,
Evgeny A.
ANDREYEVSKI, Sergey Arkadievich,
1847-1920, Russian; criticism,
poetry HARK ST
'ANDREZEL, Pierre' see 'DINESEN,
Isak'
ANDRIAN-WERBURG, Leopold, 1875-
1951, Austrian; poetry COL KU
SA
ANDRIC, Ivo, 1892- , Serbian;
poetry, fiction COL FLE HAR
RIC SA ST
ANDRIEKUS, Kazimieras, Leonardus,
1914- , Lithuanian-American;
poetry CON
ANDRIEU CONTREDIT,   -1248,
French; poetry ST
ANDRIEUX, François Guillaume Jean
Stanislaus, 1759-1833, French;
poetry, plays DIF HAR SA ST
ANDRIST, Ralph K., 1914- , Amer-
ican; juveniles CON
ANDRONICO, Calixto, 1405-78,
Greek; nonfiction SA
ANDRONICO, Marco Livoo, fl. 240
B.C., Roman; poetry SA
ANDRONICO, Marco Pompilio, 1st
cent. B.C., Roman; nonfiction
SA
ANDRUS, Hyrum Leslie, 1924- ,
American; nonfiction CON
ANDRUS, Vera, 1895- , American;
nonfiction, poetry CON
ANDRY, Claude,   -1718, French;
nonfiction DIL
ANDRZEJEWSKI, Jerzy, 1909- ,
Polish; fiction CON FLE RIC
ANDUJAR, Juan de, Spanish; poetry
BL
ANDUJAR, Manuel, 1913- , Spanish;
fiction SA
ANEAU, Barthélemy, 1500-61,
French; plays ST
ANEIRIN, fl. 600, Welsh; poetry ST

'ANET, Claude' see SCHOPFER,
Jean
ANEURIN (Aneirin), fl. 600?,
Welsh; poetry KB SA
AÑEZ, Jorge, 20th cent., Colom-
bian; criticism MIN
ANFRAY, Guillaume, 1731-1807,
French; nonfiction DIL
ANGE de SAINTE-ROSALIE,
1655-1726, French; nonfiction
DIL
ANGEL, Daniel D., 1939- ,
American; nonfiction CON
ANGEL, Marie, 1923- , English;
nonfiction CON
ANGEL MONTOYA, Alberto,
1903- , Colombian; poetry
MIN
ANGELES, Carlos A., 1921- ,
Filipino; poetry MUR
ANGELES, Jose, 1930- , Spanish-
American; nonfiction CON
ANGELES, Juan de los, 1536-
1609, Spanish; nonfiction BL
SA ST
ANGELES, Peter A., 1931- ,
American; nonfiction CON
ANGELES, Philip, 1909- ,
American; nonfiction CON
ANGELI, Pietro Angelo, 1517-96,
Italian; poetry SA ST
ANGELINI, Cesare, 1887- , Ital-
ian; poetry SA
ANGELIS, Pedro de, 1784-1859,
Argentinian; nonfiction MIN
ANGELL, Frank Joseph, 1919- ,
American; nonfiction CON
ANGELL, Sir Norman (Ralph
Norman Angel Lane), 1874- ,
English; nonfiction, journalism
BRO CON KT
ANGELL, Richard Bradshaw,
1918- , American; nonfiction
CON
ANGELLIER, Auguste Jean, 1848-
1911, French; poetry, essays
DIF
ANGELO, Valenti, 1897- , Ital-
ian-American; juveniles, fiction
HO KJU WA
ANGELOCCI, Angelo, 1926- ,
American; nonfiction CON
ANGELONI, Francesco, 1570?-
1652, Italian; nonfiction SA
'ANGELUS Silesius' (Johannes
Scheffer), 1624-77, Polish;
nonfiction AL HAR KE SA ST

ANGERS, Felicite see CONAN,
Laure
ANGEULLARA, Giovanni Andrea
della, 1517-70, Italian; poetry
SA
ANGHEL, Dimitrie, 1872-1914,
Rumanian; poetry, plays COL
FLE HAR SA ST
ANGHIERA, Pietro Mariere d' see
'MARTYR, Peter'
ANGIER, 13th cent., English; poetry
ST
ANGIER, Bradford, American; non-
fiction CON
ANGIOLETTI, Giovanni Battista,
1896- , Italian; essays, criti-
cism, journalism SA ST
ANGIOLIERI, Cecco, 1260?-1312?,
Italian; poetry HAR ST
ANGLE, Paul McClelland, 1900- ,
American; nonfiction CON HOO
KTS
ANGLERIUS see 'MARTYR, Peter'
ANGLIN, Douglas George, 1923- ,
Canadian; nonfiction CON
ANGLUND, Joan Walsh, 1926- ,
American; juveniles COM CON
WA
ANGOFF, Charles ('Richard W.
Hinton'), 1902- , American;
nonfiction CON
ANGOT, Mme., 18th cent., French;
nonfiction DIL
ANGOULEME, Charlotte Marie
Thérèse de France, 1778-1851/58;
French; diary DIL SA
ANGOULEVENT, Nicolás Joubert,
17th cent., French; poetry SA
ANGRESS, Ruth Klueger, 1931- ,
Austrian-American; translations
CON
ANGRESS, Werner Thomas, 1920- ,
German-American; nonfiction
CON
ANGRIST, Shirley Sarah, 1933- ,
Canadian; nonfiction CON
ANGRIST, Stanley Wolff, 1933- ,
American; nonfiction CON
ANGUEZA, José María, 19th cent.,
Cuban; fiction, plays MIN
ANGULO FERNANDEZ, Julio, 1902- ,
Spanish; fiction, journalism BL
SA
ANGULO GURIDI, Alejandro, 1822-
1906, Dominican; nonfiction,
poetry, fiction, essays MIN SA
ANGULO GURIDI, Javier, 1816-84,
Dominican; fiction, poetry,

plays MIN
ANGULO y HEREDIA, Antonio,
1837-73, Cuban; journalism
MIN
ANGUS, Douglas Ross, 1909- ,
Canadian-American; fiction
CON
ANGUS, Margaret, 1908- , Amer-
ican; nonfiction CON
ANGUS, Marion, 1866-1946, Scots;
poetry BRO ST
ANIANO, 15th cent., Roman;
poetry SA
ANIANTE, Antonio, 1900- , Ital-
lian; plays, fiction, poetry
SA
ANIBERT, Louis Mathieu, 1742-
82, French; poetry DIL
'ANICET' see BOURGEOIS,
Auguste
ANICHKOV, Evgeny Vasilyevich,
1866-1937, Russian; criticism
ST
ANIS, 1801-74, Indian; poetry LAN
ST
ANKENBRAND, Frank, Jr.,
1905- , American; nonfiction
CON
ANKER, Nini Magdalene Roll,
1873-1942, Norwegian; fiction,
plays ST
ANKER LARSEN, Johannes, 1874- ,
Danish; fiction, plays HAR
KAT KT SA ST
'ANMAR, Frank' see NOLAN,
William F.
ANNA, Comnena see COMNENA,
Anna
ANNE, Nicolas, fl. 1714, French;
nonfiction DIL
ANNEAU, Barthélemy, 1500?-65,
French; poetry SA
ANNENKOV, Pavel Vasilyevich,
1812-87, Russian; criticism
HARK ST
ANNENSKY, Innokenty Fyodorovich,
1855-1909, Russian; poetry
COL FLE HAR HARK KE SA
ST
ANNESS, Milford Edwin, 1918- ,
American; nonfiction CON
'ANNETT, Cora' see SCOTT, Cora
A. P.
ANNETT, John, 1930- , English;
nonfiction CON
ANNEVILLE le TORPT, Thomas
François, 1742-1828, French;
nonfiction DIL

'ANNIXTER, Jane' see STURTZEL,
Jane L.
'ANNIXTER, Paul' see STURTZEL,
Howard A.
ANNOLIED, 11th cent., German;
nonfiction AL
ANNUNZIO, Gabriele see D'ANNUN-
ZIO, Gabriele
ANOCHI, Zalman Yitzhack (Aharon-
sohn), 1876- , Jewish; fiction
ST
ANORBE Y CORREGEL, Tomás,
1686?-1741, Spanish; plays,
poetry SA
ANOUILH, Jean Marie Lucien Pierre,
1910- , French; plays CON
DIC DIF FLE HAR KTS MAG
MAL MAT SA ST
ANQUETH, Louis Pierre, 1723-1806,
French; nonfiction SA
ANQUETIL-DUPERRON, Abraham
Hyacinthe, 1731-1805, French;
nonfiction DIF DIL SA
ANQUETIL, Louis Pierre, 1723-
1806, French; nonfiction DIL
ANROOY, Frans van see VAN
ANROOY, Francine
ANSAI see YAMAZAKI ANSAI
ANSARI, Abd Allah see ABD ALLAH
A. K.
ANSART, André Joseph, 1723-90,
French; nonfiction DIL
ANSART, Jean Baptiste François,
18th cent., French; plays DIL
ANSART, Louis Joseph Auguste,
1748- , French; nonfiction DIL
ANSBACHER, Heinz Ludwig, 1904- ,
German-American; nonfiction
CON
ANSBERRY, William F., 1926- ,
American; nonfiction CON
ANSELL, Helen, 1940- , American;
fiction CON
ANSELL, Jack, 1925- , American;
fiction CON
ANSELM, St., 1033-1109, Italian;
nonfiction SA ST
'ANSELM, Felix' see POLLAK, Felix
ANSELM of BESATE, fl. 1040,
Italian; nonfiction ST
ANSELME d'ESCH Sur la Surre,
1710-83, French; nonfiction DIL
ANSELME de LAON, 1050?-1117,
French; nonfiction DIL
ANSEN, Alan, 1922- , American;
poetry, criticism CON MUR
'AN-SKI, S.' see RAPPOPORT,
Solomon

ANSLEY, Gladys Pitt, 1906- ,
American; nonfiction CON
ANSLIJN, Nicolaas, 1777-1838,
Dutch; juveniles ST
ANSLINGER, Harry Jacob, 1892- ,
American; nonfiction CON
ANSLO, Reyer, 1626-69, Dutch;
poetry, plays ST
ANSON, Peter Frederick, 1889- ,
English; nonfiction CON HOE
ANSON, Sir William Reynell,
1843-1914, British; nonfiction
KBA
ANSON OLIART, Luis María,
1935- , Spanish; essays SA
ANSPACH, Elisabeth Craven,
1750-1828, English; plays SA
ANSQUER, Henri Simon Joseph,
1730-83, French; nonfiction
DIL
ANSQUER, Theophile Ignace,
1728-73, French; nonfiction
DIL
ANSTER, John, 1789-1867, Irish;
poetry ST
ANSTEY, Christopher, 1724-1805,
English; poetry BRO KB ST
ANSTEY, Edgar, 1917- , Amer-
ican; nonfiction CON
'ANSTEY, F.' see GUTHRIE,
Thomas A.
ANSTEY, Roger Thomas, 1927- ,
English; nonfiction CON
ANSTEY, Vera Powell, 1889- ,
English; nonfiction CON
ANSTRUTHER, George Elliott,
1870- , English; journalism,
nonfiction HOE
ANTAGORAS de RHODES, 330-
250 B.C., Greek; poetry SA
ANTAR, 6th cent., Arab; poetry
SA ST
ANTCLIFFE, Herbert, Jr., 1875- ,
English; nonfiction HOE
ANTELMY, Pierre Thomas, 1730-
83, French; nonfiction DIL
ANTHEAUME, Antoine, 1644-1712,
French; nonfiction DIL
ANTHENAISE, Jean Baptiste
Prosper, 1698-1746, French;
nonfiction DIL
ANTHON, Charles, 1797-1867,
American; nonfiction KAA
'ANTHONY, C. L. see SMITH,
Dodie
ANTHONY, Edward, 1895-1971,
American; juveniles WA
'ANTHONY, Evelyn' see WARD-

THOMAS, Evelyn
ANTHONY, Frank S., 1891-1925,
New Zealander; fiction RIC
'ANTHONY, John' see ROBERTS,
John S.
'ANTHONY, John' see SABINI, John
A.
ANTHONY, Katharine Susan, 1877-
1965, American; nonfiction KAT
KT
ANTHONY, Michael, 1932- , Eng-
lish; nonfiction CON
'ANTHONY, Piers' see JACOB,
Piers A.D.
ANTHONY, Robert Newton, 1916- ,
American; nonfiction CON
ANTHONY, Susan B., 1820-90,
American; nonfiction SA
ANTHONY, William G., 1934- ,
American; nonfiction CON
ANTICO, John, 1924- , Scots; non-
fiction CON
ANTIFON, 480- , Greek; nonfiction
SA
ANTIGNAC, 18th cent., French; non-
fiction DIL
ANTIGONO de CARISTIA, 3rd cent.
B.C., Greek; nonfiction SA
ANTILL, James Macquarie, 1912- ,
Australian; nonfiction CON
'ANTILON' see DULANY, Daniel
ANTIMACHUS, 544 B.C., Greek;
poetry SA ST
ANTIN, David, 1932- , American;
poetry MUR
ANTIN, Mary, 1881-1949, American;
nonfiction KT
ANTIOCO de ASCALON, 1st cent.
B.C., Greek; nonfiction SA
ANTIPATER, 2nd cent. B.C., Greek;
epigrams ST
ANTIPATER, Lelio Celio, 1st cent.,
Roman; nonfiction SA
ANTIPHANES, 408-334 B.C., Greek;
poetry ST
ANTIPHON, 480-11 B.C., Athenian;
nonfiction ST
ANTIPHON of ATHENS, 5th cent.
B.C., Greek; nonfiction ST
ANTISTENES, 444-399 B.C., Greek;
nonfiction SA
ANTISTHENES of ATHENS, 455-
360 B.C., Greek; nonfiction ST
ANTOINE, André, 1858-1943, French;
criticism COL SA
ANTOINE, Antoine, 1744-1818, French;
nonfiction DIL

ANTOINE, Jean Baptiste, 1707-85,
French; nonfiction DIL
ANTOINE, Paul Gabriel, 1678-1743,
French; nonfiction DIL
ANTOKOLSKY, Pavel Grigoryevich,
1896- , Russian; poetry,
plays HAR SA ST
ANTON, John Peter, 1920- ,
American; nonfiction CON
ANTON, Rita Kenter, 1920- ,
American; fiction CON
ANTON de MONTORO see MONTORO,
Antón de
ANTON del OLMET, Luis, 1886-
1922, Spanish; journalism SA
ANTON ULRICH, 1633-1714,
German; poetry, fiction AL
KE ST
ANTONACCI, Robert Joseph,
1916- , American; nonfiction
CON
ANTONCICH, Betty Kennedy,
1913- , American; juveniles
CON WA
ANTONELLI, Pierre Antoine
Barthelémy, 1774-1817,
French; nonfiction DIL
ANTONELLI, Luigi, 1882-1942,
Italian; plays FLE
ANTONICK, Robert J. ('Nick
Kamin'), 1939- , American;
fiction CON
ANTONINI, Annibale, 1702-55,
Italian; nonfiction DIL
'ANTONINUS, Brother' (William
Oliver Everson), 1912- ,
American; poetry MUR ST
ANTONIO, Nicolás, 1617-84,
Spanish; nonfiction SA ST
ANTONIO da FERRARA see BEC-
CARI, Antonio
ANTONOVSKY, Aaron, 1923- ,
American; nonfiction CON
'ANTONY, John' see BECKETT,
Ronald B.
ANTONY, Jonquil, 1916- , Eng-
lish; fiction CON
'ANTONY, Peter' see SHAFFER,
Peter L.
ANTRECHARX, Jean d', 1693-
1762, French; nonfiction DIL
ANTRIM, Harry Thoms, 1936- ,
American; nonfiction CON
ANTSCHEL, Paul see 'CELAN,
Paul'
ANTTILA, Raimo Aulis, 1935- ,
Finnish-American; nonfiction
CON

ANVARI, Awhad Al-din Ali,   -1191,
Persian; poetry ST
ANVILLE, Jean Baptiste Bourguignon,
1697-1782, French; nonfiction
DIL
ANYON, George Jay, 1909- , Amer-
ican; nonfiction CON
ANYTA de TEJEO, 280-160 B.C.;
Greek; poetry SA
ANZE MATIENZO, Eduardo, 1902- ,
Argentinian; fiction MIN
ANZENGRUBER, Ludwig, 1839-89,
Austrian; plays, fiction AL COL
HAR KE SA ST
ANZOATEGUI, Ignacio B., 1905- ,
Argentinian; nonfiction, poetry,
essays MIN SA
ANZOATEGUI de CAMPERO, Lindaura,
1846-98, Bolivian; fiction, poetry,
plays MIN SA
AOUGSTIN, François, 1711- ,
French; nonfiction DIL
APARICIO, Juan, 1906- , Spanish;
journalism SA
APARISI y GUIJARRO, Antonio,
1815-72, Spanish; poetry SA
APEL, Willi, 1893- , German-
American; nonfiction CON
APELTERN, H. van' see ENGLELEN,
A.W.
APES, William, 1798- , American;
nonfiction KAA
APHTHONIUS, fl. 400, Greek; non-
fiction ST
APICIUS, Marcus Gavius, fl. 14-37
A.D., Roman; nonfiction ST
APION, 1st cent., Greek; nonfiction
SA
APITZ, Bruno, 1900- , German;
nonfiction AL
'APOLLINAIRE, Guillaume' (Wilhelm
Apollinaris de Kostrowitski),
1880-1918, French; poetry, fic-
tion, essays COL DIF FLE
HAR KAT KT MAL MAT RIC SA
ST
APOLLODORUS, 2nd cent. B.C.;
Greek; poetry SA ST
APOLLONIUS DYSCOLUS, fl. 150,
Greek; nonfiction ST
APOLLONIUS, Rhodius, 295-30 B.C.,
Greek; poetry ST SA
APOLONIO de TIANA,   -97, Greek;
nonfiction SA
APOLONIO el DISCOLO, 2nd cent.,
Greek; nonfiction SA
APOSTLE, Christos Nicholas,

1935- , American; nonfiction
CON
APP, Austin Joseph, 1902- ,
American; nonfiction HO
APPEL, Benjamin, 1907- , Amer-
ican; fiction, poetry CON KT
WAF
APPEL, David, American; juveniles,
journalism WA
APPEL, John J., 1921- , Amer-
ican; nonfiction CON
APPELMAN, Hyman Jedidiah,
1902- , American; nonfiction
CON
APPELMANS, Gheraert, fl. 1300,
Dutch; nonfiction ST
APPERLEY, Charles James ('Nim-
rod'), 1779-1843, English;
nonfiction HIG KBA
APPERLEY, Newton Wynne, 1846-
1925, British; nonfiction HIG
APPIAN, fl. 160, Greek; nonfiction
SA ST
APPLEBAUM, William, 1906- ,
Russian-American; nonfiction
CON
APPLEBY, Jon, 1948- , Ameri-
can; fiction CON
APPLEGATE, James Earl, 1923- ,
American; nonfiction CON
APPLEMAN, John Alan, 1912- ,
American; nonfiction CON
APPLEMAN, Mark Jerome ('Mark
Jerome'), 1917- , American;
nonfiction CON
APPLEMAN, Philip Dean, 1926- ,
American; poetry CON
APPLEMAN, Roy Edgar, 1907- ,
American; nonfiction CON
APPLETON, James Henry, 1919- ,
English; nonfiction CON
APPLETON, Sheldon Lee, 1933- ,
American; nonfiction CON
APPLETON, Thomas Gold, 1812-
84, American; poetry, essays
KAA
'APPLETON, Victor' see STRATE-
MEYER, Edward L.
'APPLETON, Victor II' see
ADAMS, Harriet S. and
STRATEMEYER, Edward L.
APPLEY, Mortimer Herbert
('M.H. Applezweig), 1921- ,
Canadian; nonfiction CON
APPLEYARD, Donald, 1928- ,
English; nonfiction CON
APPLEYARD, Reginald Thomas,

1927- , Australian; nonfiction
CON
APRAIZ y SAENZ del BURGO, Julián,
1848-1910, Spanish; nonfiction
SA
APRES de MANNEVILLETTE, Jean
Baptiste Nicolas Denis, 1707-80,
French; nonfiction DIL
APRILOV, Vassil, 1789-1847, Bul-
garian; nonfiction ST
APSLER, Alfred, 1907- , American;
nonfiction CON PAC
APSLEY, Lady, 1897- , English;
nonfiction HIG
APTE, Hari Narayan, 1864-1919,
Indian; fiction LAN ST
APTED, Michael R., 1919- , Eng-
lish; nonfiction CON
APTER, David Ernest, 1924- ,
American; nonfiction CON
APTER, Michael John, 1939- ,
English; nonfiction CON
APTHEKER, Bettina, 1944- , Amer-
ican; nonfiction CON
APTHEKER, Herbert, 1915- , Amer-
ican; nonfiction CON
APTHORP, William Foster, 1848-1913,
American; criticism KAA
APUKHTIN, Aleksei Nikolayevich,
1841-93, Russian; poetry COL
HARK SA ST
APULEIUS, Lucius, 125-75, Roman;
plays, nonfiction MAG SA ST
AQQAD, Abbas Mahmud, 1889- ,
Egyptian; fiction, poetry ST
'AQUARIAN' see OPPENHEIMER,
Joel L.
AQUEO, 5th cent. B.C., Greek;
poetry SA
AQUILANO, Serafino, 1466-1500,
Italian; poetry ST
AQUILES Tacio, 4th cent., Greek;
nonfiction SA
AQUIN de CHATEAU-LYON, Pierre
Louis, 1720-96, French; fiction
DIL
AQUINAS, Thomas, St., 1225-74,
Italian; nonfiction HAR KE
MAG SA ST
AQUINO, Pedro Benjamín, 1887-1935,
Argentinian; fiction MIN
ARABENA WILLIAMS, Hermelo,
1910- , Chilean; criticism,
poetry, fiction MIN
ARAGON, Louis, 1897- , French;
poetry, fiction, essays COL
DIC DIF FLE HAR KT MAL
MAT RIC SA ST

ARAGON, Don Enrique de (Villena),
1384-1434, Spanish; nonfiction
BL SA ST
ARAGONA, Tullia d', 1508/10-
56/67, Italian; poetry ST SA
ARAGONES, Juan, 1512-76,
Spanish; fiction BL SA
ARAGONES DAROCA, Juan Emilio,
1926- , Spanish; essays, fic-
tion, criticism SA
ARAGONESES URQUIJO, Encarna-
ción see 'FORTUN, Elena'
'ARAI HAKUSEKI' (Arai Kimiyoshi),
1657-1725, Japanese; nonfic-
tion SA ST
ARAIGNON, Jean Louis, fl. 1756,
French; plays DIL
ARAKI, James Tomomasa, 1925- ,
American; nonfiction CON
ARAKIDA MORITAKE, 1473-1549,
Japanese; poetry ST
ARAMBURU, Julio, 1895/98- ,
Argentinian; essays, fiction
MIN SA
ARAMBURU y MACHADO, Mariano,
1870-1941, Cuban; essays
MIN
ARANAZ CASTELLANOS, Manuel,
1875-1925, Spanish; journalism
SA
ARANGO, Rodolfo, 1896- ,
Cuban; journalism, poetry
MIN
ARANGO FERRER, Javier, 20th
century, Colombian; criticism
MIN
ARANGO y ESCANDON, Alejandro,
1821-83, Mexican; poetry,
criticism SA
ARANGO y PARREÑO, Francisco
de, 1765-1837, Cuban; nonfic-
tion MIN
ARANGUREN, José Luis L.,
1909- , Spanish; nonfiction,
essays BL SA
ARANY, Janos, 1817-82, Hungarian;
poetry, translations, plays
COL HAR KE SA ST
ARANY, Laszlo, 1844-98, Hun-
garian; poetry SA
ARAPOFF, Nancy, 1930- , Amer-
ican; nonfiction CON
ARAQUISTAIN y QUEVEDO, Luis,
1886-1959, Spanish; essays,
journalism, fiction, plays SA
ARASON, Jón, 1484-1550, Icelandic;
poetry HAR KE ST
ARASON, Steingrimur, Icelandic-

American; juveniles WA

ARATO, 270 B.C. - , Greek; poetry
SA

ARATOR, fl. 540, Roman; poetry
SA ST

ARATUS, 315-240 B.C., Greek;
poetry ST

ARAUCO, F. see SANTIBAÑEZ PUGA,
Fernando A.

ARAUJO, Joaquim de, 1858-1917,
Portuguese; poetry SA

ARAUJO, José Joaquín de, 1762-1835,
Argentinian; nonfiction MIN

ARAUJO COSTA, Luis, 1885-1956,
Spanish; essays, criticism SA

ARBAUD, Joseph d', 1874- , French;
poetry, fiction COL DIF SA

ARBAUD, L. C.G.J., 1727- ,
French; nonfiction DIL

ARBAUD de PORCHERES, François
de, 1590-1640, French; poetry
SA

ARBAUD de ROGNAC, Bruno, 1671-
1747, French; nonfiction DIL

ARBER, Edward, 1836-1912, British;
nonfiction KBA

ARBERRY, Arthur John, 1905- ,
American; nonfiction, translations
CON MUR

ARBES, Jan Jakub, 1840-1914, Czech;
fiction HAR SA ST

ARBIB, Robert Simeon, Jr., 1915- ,
American; nonfiction CON

ARBINGAST, Stanley Alan, 1910- ,
American; nonfiction CON

ARBLAY, Madam d' see BURNEY,
Fanny

ARBO, Sebastián Juan, 1902- ,
Spanish; fiction BL SA

ARBOLEDA, Julio, 1817-62, Colombian; journalism, poetry BL
MIN SA ST

ARBOLEDA RESTREPO, Gustavo,
1831-1938, Colombian; journalism,
nonfiction, essays MIN

ARBUCKLE, Dugald Sinclair, 1912- ,
Canadian; nonfiction CON

ARBUTHNOT, John, 1667-1735,
Scots; nonfiction BRO KB SA ST

ARBUTHNOT, May Hill, 1884-1969,
American; juveniles COM CON
WA

ARBUZOV, Aleksei Nikolaevich,
1908- , Russian; plays MAT

ARCE, Manuel, 1928- , Spanish;
poetry, fiction SA

ARCE de los REYES, Ambrosio,

1621?-61, Spanish; poetry,
plays BL

ARCE de VAQUEZ, Margot,
1904- , Puerto Rican; nonfiction BL

ARCE y SOLORZANO, Juan de,
1565-1620?, Spanish; nonfiction
SA

ARCERE, Louis Etienne, 1698-
1782, French; nonfiction, poetry
DIL

ARCESILAO, 318/16-241/39 B.C.,
Greek; nonfiction SA

ARCHAMBAULT, Mme., 18th cent.,
French; nonfiction DIL

'ARCHER, A.A.' see JOSCELYN,
Archie L.

ARCHER, Horace Richard, 1911- ,
American; nonfiction CON

ARCHER, Jules, 1915- , American; journalism CON WA

ARCHER, Marion Fuller, 1917- ,
American; juveniles CON

ARCHER, Peter Kingsley, 1926- ,
English; nonfiction CON

'ARCHER, Ron' see WHITE, Theodore E.

ARCHER, Sellers G., 1908- ,
American; nonfiction CON

ARCHER, Stephen Hunt, 1928- ,
American; nonfiction CON

ARCHER, William, 1856-1924,
British; plays, criticism,
journalism BRO KAT KT MAT
SA ST

ARCHEVESQUE, Hue, 13th cent.,
French; poetry SA

ARCHHENHOLTZ, Johan Wilhelm,
1741-1812, German; nonfiction
SA

ARCHIBALD, John J., 1925- ,
American; nonfiction CON

ARCHIBALD, Joseph Stopford,
1898- , American; fiction,
juveniles CON WA

ARCHILOCHUS, 7th cent. B.C.,
Greek; poetry SA ST

ARCHIMBAUD, Abbé (Archimbault),
18th cent., French; nonfiction
DIL

ARCHIMEDES, 287-12 B.C., Greek;
nonfiction ST

ARCHPOET, fl. 1160, German;
poetry AL ST

ARCINIEGA, Rosa, 1909- , Peruvian; fiction, nonfiction SA

ARCINIEGAS, Germán, 1900- ,

Italian; poetry SA
ARGELLATI, Filippo, 1685-1735,
   Italian; nonfiction SA
ARGENCE, François Archard-
   Joumard Tison, 18th cent.,
   French; nonfiction DIL
ARGENS, Jean Baptiste de Boyer,
   1704-71, French; nonfiction DIL
   SA
ARGENSOLA, Bartolomé Leonardo de
   Villahermosa, 1562-1631, Spanish;
   poetry BL HAR SA
ARGENSOLA, Lupercio Leonardo de,
   1559-1613, Spanish; poetry,
   translations BL HAR SA ST
ARGENSON, Marc Pierre de Voyer,
   1696-1764, French; nonfiction
   DIL
ARGENSON, Marc René de Voyer,
   1652-1721, French; nonfiction
   DIL
ARGENSON, René Louis de Voyer de
   Paulmy, 1694-1757, French;
   nonfiction DIF DIL
'ARGENT, Isaac Etienne' (J.E.D.
   Phylarèthe), 18th cent., French;
   nonfiction DIL
ARGENTAL, Charles Augustin de
   Ferreol, 1705-88, French; non-
   fiction DIL
ARGENTRE, Charles du Plessis,
   1673-1740, French; nonfiction
   DIL
ARGENVILLE, Antoine J. see
   DEZALLIER D'ARGENVILLE,
   Antoine J.
ARGERICH, Juan Antonio, 1862- ,
   Argentinian; fiction MIN
'ARGHEZI, Tudor' (I.N. Teodorescu),
   1880- , Rumanian; poetry FLE
   ST
ARGIRO, Larry, 1909- , American;
   nonfiction CON
ARGNIES, Louis Michel d', 18th
   cent., French; nonfiction DIL
ARGOTE de MOLINA, Gonzalo,
   1548-98, Spanish; nonfiction,
   poetry BL SA
ARGOW, Waldemar, 1916- , Amer-
   ican; nonfiction CON
ARGUEDAS, Alcides, 1879-1946,
   Bolivian; nonfiction, fiction BL
   FLE MIN SA ST
ARGÜELLES, Agustín, 1776-1844,
   Spanish; nonfiction BL
ARGÜELLO, Santiago, 1872-1940,
   Nicaraguan; poetry BL SA

ARGUIJO, Juan de, 1560-1623,
   Spanish; poetry BL SA ST
'ARGUS' see PHILLIPS-BIRT,
   Douglas
ARGYLE, Aubrey William, 1910- ,
   English; nonfiction CON
ARGYLE, Michael, 1925- , Eng-
   lish; nonfiction CON
ARGYLL, Duke of (George Douglas
   Campbell), 1823-1900, Scots;
   nonfiction BRO KBA ST
ARGYRIS, Chris, 1923- , Amer-
   ican; nonfiction CON
ARGYROPOULOS, Juan, 1410-86,
   Byzantine; nonfiction SA
ARI see LURIA, Isaac, B.S.
ARI, Thorgilsson, Frooi, 1067/
   68-1148, Icelandic; nonfiction
   KE
ARIAN, Edward, 1921- , Amer-
   ican; nonfiction CON
ARIAS, Augusto (Gracian), 1903- ,
   Ecuadorian; poetry, criticism
   DI SA
ARIAS, Pedro G., 1892- ,
   Spanish; poetry SA
ARIAS ARGAEZ, Daniel, 1890- ,
   Colombian; poetry, fiction
   MIN
ARIAS MONTANO, Benito, 1527-
   98, Spanish; poetry BL SA
   ST
ARIAS SUAREZ, Eduardo (Con-
   stantino Pla), 1896/97- ,
   Colombian; fiction MIN
ARIAS VARGAS, Leopoldo, 1832/
   33-84, Colombian; plays,
   poetry MIN
ARIBAU, Bonaventura Carles,
   1798-1862, Spanish; poetry,
   nonfiction BL HAR SA ST
ARICHA, Yoseph, 1907- , Jewish;
   fiction ST
'ARIEL' see MORAES, Frank R.
ARIEL, Ricardo see ADOUM,
   Jorge E.
ARIENTI, Giovanni Sabadino,
   -1540, Italian; nonfiction
   ST
ARIETI, Silvano, 1914- , Italian-
   American; nonfiction CON
ARIF, Abul Qasim, 1882-1933,
   Persian; poetry ST
ARIHARA No Narihara, 825-80,
   Japanese; fiction MAG
ARINOS, Afonso, 1868- , Brazil-
   ian; nonfiction SA

ARION, 7th cent., Greek; poetry SA
ST
ARIOSTO, Ludovico, 1474-1533,
Italian; poetry, plays BL HAR
KE MAG SA ST
ARISHIMA TAKEO, 1878-1923,
Japanese; plays, essays, fiction
LAN ST
ARISTAENETUS, 5th cent., Greek;
letters ST
ARISTARCHUS, 216-144 B.C., Greek;
nonfiction ST
ARISTARCHUS, 160-90 B.C., Greek;
nonfiction SA
ARISTARCHUS of SAMOS, 300-230
B.C., Greek; nonfiction ST
ARISTENETES, 300- B.C., Greek;
nonfiction SA
ARISTEO, 9th cent. B.C., Greek;
poetry SA
ARISTIAS, Constantino, 1798-1884,
Greek-Rumanian; poetry SA
ARISTIDES, Aelius, 120-189, German;
nonfiction ST
ARISTIDES, Elio, 117/29-89, Greek;
nonfiction SA
ARISTIDES, San, 2nd cent., Greek;
nonfiction SA
ARISTIDES de MILETO, 2nd cent.,
Greek; fiction SA
ARISTIPO, 430- B.C., Greek;
nonfiction SA
ARISTOBULO, 150- B.C., Jewish;
nonfiction SA
ARISTOBULO de CASANDREA, Greek;
nonfiction SA
ARISTOCLES, 230-140 B.C., Greek;
nonfiction SA
ARISTOCLES of PERGAMON, 2nd
cent., Greek; nonfiction SA
ARISTOCLES of RHODES, Greek;
nonfiction SA
ARISTOGENES, 4th cent. B.C.,
Greek; nonfiction SA
ARISTON de CEOS, 3rd cent. B.C.,
Greek; nonfiction SA
ARISTON de QUIOS, Greek; nonfiction
SA
ARISTON of ALEXANDRIA, 1st cent.
B.C., Greek; nonfiction SA
ARISTOPHANES, 448-385 B.C.,
Greek; plays MAG SA ST
ARISTOPHANES of BYZANTIUM,
257-180 B.C., Greek; nonfiction
SA ST
ARISTOTLE, 384-22 B.C., Greek;
nonfiction MAG SA ST

ARISTOXENUS, 370- , Greek;
nonfiction ST
ARISTOXENUS de TARENTO, 4th
cent., Greek; nonfiction SA
ARIWARA No Narihira, 825-80,
Japanese; poetry ST
ARIYOSH SAWAKO, 1931- ,
Japanese; fiction LAN
ARIZA, Juan, 1816-76, Spanish;
plays, fiction, poetry BL
SA
ARJONA, J.H., 1906- , Amer-
ican; nonfiction BL
ARJONA, Juan de, 1560-1603?,
Spanish; poetry BL SA
ARJONA y de CUBAS, Manuel
María de, 1771-1820, Spanish;
poetry BL SA ST
ARJUN (Arjan Mal), 1563-1606,
Indian; poetry LAN ST
'ARKEL, Frank Floriszoon van'
see HALL, Maurits C. van
ARKHURST, Frederick Seigfried,
1920- , American; nonfiction
CON
ARKHURST, Joyce Cooper, 1921- ,
American; fiction CON
ARKIN, David, 1906- , Ameri-
can; nonfiction CON
ARKIN, Herbert, 1906- , Amer-
ican; nonfiction CON
ARKIN, Joseph, 1922- , Amer-
ican; nonfiction CON
ARLAND, Marcel, 1899- ,
French; essays, fiction,
criticism DIC DIF FLE MAL
ST
ARLANDSON, Leone ('Lee Ryland'),
1917- , American; juveniles
CON
'ARLEN, Michael' (Dikran
Kouyoumdjian), 1895-1956,
Armenian-English; fiction
BRO KL KT RIC ST
ARLEO, Joseph, 1933- , Amer-
ican; fiction CON
'ARLES, Henri d' ' (Henri Beaudet),
1870-1930, Canadian; fiction
SY
ARLOTT, Leslie Thomas John,
1914- , English; fiction CON
ARLOTTO, Anthony Thomas,
1939- , American; nonfiction
CON
ARLT, Roberto, 1900-42, Argen-
tinian; fiction, plays MIN SA
'ARMAND' see STRUBBERG,

Friedrich
ARMAND, fl. 1759, French; plays
DIL
ARMAND, Huguet, 1699-1765, French;
plays DIL
ARMAND, Louis, 1905- , French;
nonfiction CON
ARMANDO, Dante see GATTI, Armand
ARMAS, Augusto de, 1869-93, Cuban;
journalism MIN
ARMAS, Juan Ignacio, 1842-70, Cuban;
nonfiction MIN
ARMAS y CARDENAS, Jose de ('Justo
de Lara'), 1866-1919, Cuban;
journalism MIN
ARMBRUSTER, Carl J., 1929- ,
American; nonfiction CON
ARMBRUSTER, Francis Edward
(Frank), 1923- , American;
nonfiction CON
'ARMBRUSTER, Johann' see HAUSEN-
STEIN, Wilhelm
ARMBRUSTER, Maxim Ethan, 1902- ,
American; nonfiction CON
ARMENDARIZ, Julian, 1585?-1614,
Spanish; poetry, plays SA
ARMENTIA, Nicolás, 1845- ,
Bolivian; nonfiction MIN
ARMENS, Sven, 1921- , American;
nonfiction CON
ARMENTROUT, William Winfield,
1918- , American; nonfiction
CON
ARMER, Alberta Roller, 1904- ,
American; juveniles CON
ARMER, Laura Adams, 1874- ,
American; juveniles KAT KJU
WA
ARMERDING, Hudson Taylor, 1918- ,
American; nonfiction CON
ARMIGER, Charles, 1800- , Eng-
lish; nonfiction HIG
ARMIN, Robert, 1568-1615, English;
poetry ST
ARMIÑAN ODRIOZOLA, Luis de,
1899- , Spanish; journalism,
plays, fiction SA
ARMIÑAN PEREZ, Luis de, 1873- ,
Spanish; journalism, nonfiction
SA
ARMITAGE, Angus, 1902- , English;
nonfiction CON
ARMITAGE, Edward Liddall, 1887- ,
English; nonfiction CON
ARMOUR, George Denholm, 1864-
1949, English; nonfiction HIG
ARMOUR, Lloyd R., 1922- , Amer-
ican; nonfiction CON

ARMOUR, Richard, 1906- ,
American; nonfiction, poetry,
juveniles CON WA
ARMOUR, Rollin Stely, 1929- ,
American; nonfiction CON
ARMS, George Warren, 1912- ,
American; nonfiction CON
ARMSTRONG, A. James, 1924- ,
American; nonfiction CON
ARMSTRONG, Ann Siedel, 1917- ,
American; fiction CON
ARMSTRONG, Annette, 1924- ,
American; nonfiction CON
ARMSTRONG, Annette Elizabeth
('A. E. Tyler'), 1917- ,
English; nonfiction CON
'ARMSTRONG, Anthony' see WILLIS,
George A. A.
ARMSTRONG, Charlotte ('Jo
Valentine'), 1905-69, Ameri-
can; fiction CON
ARMSTRONG, David Malet, 1926- ,
Australian; nonfiction CON
ARMSTRONG, Douglas Albert
('Albert Douglas'; 'Rex Windsor';
'Tribune'), 1920- , English;
nonfiction CON
ARMSTRONG, Edward Allworthy,
1900- , Irish; nonfiction CON
ARMSTRONG, Frederick Henry,
1926- , Canadian; nonfiction
CON
ARMSTRONG, Gerry Breen,
1929- , American; juveniles
CON
ARMSTRONG, Gregory Timon,
1933- , American; nonfiction
CON
ARMSTRONG, Hamilton Fish,
1893- , American; nonfiction
KT
ARMSTRONG, John, 1709?-79,
English; poetry BRO KB ST
ARMSTRONG, John Alexander, Jr.,
1922- , American; nonfiction
CON
ARMSTRONG, John Borden,
1926- , American; nonfiction
CON
ARMSTRONG, John Byron ('John
Byron'; 'Charles Willard'),
1917- , American; nonfiction
CON
ARMSTRONG, Keith Francis Whit-
field ('Carm Mac'; 'Keith X.'),
1950- , South African; poetry
CON
ARMSTRONG, Laurence, 1926- ,

American; nonfiction CON

ARMSTRONG, Margaret Neilson,
1867-1944, American; nonfiction
KT

ARMSTRONG, Martin Donisthorpe,
1882- , English; fiction, poetry
KAT KT

ARMSTRONG, Paul, 1869-1915,
American; plays KT

ARMSTRONG, Raymond Paul, 1912- ,
American; nonfiction CON

ARMSTRONG, Richard, 1903- ,
English; juveniles DOY WA

ARMSTRONG, Roger D., 1939- ,
American; nonfiction CON

ARMSTRONG, Ruth Gallup, 1891- ,
American; fiction CON

ARMSTRONG, Terence Ian Tytton
('John Gawsworth'), 1912-70,
English; poetry, criticism BRO
CON MUR

ARMSTRONG, Thomas, 1899- ,
American; nonfiction CON

ARMSTRONG, William Alexander
('Alexander Hazelton'), 1912- ,
Scots; nonfiction CON

ARMSTRONG, William Arthur,
1915- , English; nonfiction
CON

ARMSTRONG, William H., 1914- ,
American; juveniles CON WA

ARMSTRONG, William Martin, 1919- ,
American; nonfiction CON

ARMYTAGE, Walter Harry Green,
1915- , English; nonfiction
CON

ARNADE, Charles Wolfgang ('Julius
Giersch'), 1927- , German-
American; nonfiction CON

ARNALDO de MARVEIL, 12th cent.,
French; poetry SA

ARNAO, Antonio, 1828-89, Spanish;
poetry BL SA

'ARNARSON, Orn' (Magnús Stefánsson),
1884-1942, Icelandic; poetry FLE
ST

ARNASON, Jón, 1819-88, Icelandic;
nonfiction KE ST

ARNAU de VILANOVA, 1238-1311,
Spanish; nonfiction SA

ARNAUD, Archie W., American;
nonfiction SCA

ARNAUD, François, 1721-84, French;
nonfiction DIL

ARNAUD, François Thomas Marie de
Baculard d', 1718-1805, French;
plays, fiction DIF DIL

ARNAUD, Georges, 1918- ,
French; fiction DIC DIF

ARNAUD de Saint Maurice, 18th
cent., French; poetry DIL

ARNAULD, Antoine, 1612-94,
French; nonfiction DIF SA ST

ARNAULD, Marie Angelique,
1591- , French; nonfiction
SA

ARNAULD d'ANDILLY, Robert,
1589-1674, French; translations, nonfiction DIF

ARNAULT, Antoine Vincent, 1766-
1834, French; poetry, plays,
nonfiction DIF HAR SA

ARNAULT LA PIE, Maurice,
1707- , French; nonfiction
DIL

ARNAUT, Daniel, 1180-1210,
French; poetry DIF KE SA
ST

ARNAUT de MAREUIL, 17th cent.,
French; poetry DIF KE ST

ARNAY, Jean Rodolphe, 1710-65,
French; nonfiction DIL

ARNAY, Simon Auguste (Arnex),
1750- , French; nonfiction
DIL

ARNDT, Ernst Heinrich Daniel,
1899- , American; nonfiction
CON

ARNDT, Ernst Moritz, 1769-1860,
German; poetry AL HAR KE
SA ST

ARNDT, Johann, 1555-1621, German; nonfiction AL HAR

ARNDT, Karl John Richard,
1903- , American; nonfiction
CON

ARNDT, Walter Werner, 1916- ,
American; nonfiction CON

ARNETT, Carroll, 1927- , American; poetry CON

ARNETT, Harold Edward, 1931- ,
American; nonfiction CON

ARNEZ, Nancy Levi, 1928- ,
American; nonfiction CON

ARNHEIM, Daniel David, 1930- ,
American; nonfiction CON

ARNHEIM, Rudolf, 1904- , German-American; nonfiction CON

ARNICHES y BARRERA, Carlos,
1866-1943, Spanish; plays BL
COL FLE HAR SA ST

ARNIM, Bettina von Brentano
(Elisabeth), 1785-1859, German; nonfiction AL HAR ST

ARNIM, Ludwig Joachim (Achim von), 1781-1831, German; poetry, fiction AL HAR KE SA ST

ARNIMAL, 18th cent., Indian; poetry LAN

ARNOBIUS, fl. 300, Roman?, nonfiction SA ST

ARNOLD, Adlai Franklin ('A. Franklin'), 1914- , American; nonfiction CON

ARNOLD, Alan, 1922- , English; nonfiction CON

ARNOLD, Armin H., 1931- , Swiss-Canadian; nonfiction CON

ARNOLD, Arnold Ferdinand, 1921- , German-American; nonfiction CON

ARNOLD, Sir Arthur, 1833-1902, British; nonfiction KBA

ARNOLD, Denis Midgely, 1926- , American; nonfiction CON

ARNOLD, Djuro, 1854-1948, Croatian; nonfiction ST

ARNOLD, Edmund, Clarence, 1913- , American; nonfiction CON

ARNOLD, Sir Edwin, 1832-1904, British; poetry, journalism BRO KBA ST

ARNOLD, Elliott, 1912- , American; juveniles, fiction CON KTS WA WAF

ARNOLD, Emmy von Hollander, 1884- , Latvian-American; nonfiction CON

ARNOLD, Francena Harriet Long, 1888- , American; fiction CON

ARNOLD, George ('McArone'), 1834-65, American; poetry KAA

ARNOLD, Gottfried, 1666-1714, German; nonfiction AL

ARNOLD, Guy, 1932- , English; nonfiction CON

ARNOLD, Harry John Philip, 1932- , American; nonfiction CON

ARNOLD, Herbert, 1935- , Czech-American; nonfiction CON

ARNOLD, Isaac Newton, 1815-84, American; nonfiction KAA

'ARNOLD, Joseph H.' see HAYES, Joseph

ARNOLD, June Davis, 1926- , American; fiction CON

'ARNOLD, L.J.' see CAMERON, Lou

ARNOLD, Lloyd R., 1906-70, American; nonfiction CON

ARNOLD, Magda Blondiau, 1903- , Austrian-American; nonfiction CON

ARNOLD, Matthew, 1822-80/88, English; poetry, essays BRO KBA MAG SP SA ST

ARNOLD, Oren, 1900- , American; fiction, nonfiction CON

ARNOLD, Pauline, 1894- , American; nonfiction CON

ARNOLD, Ralph, English; juveniles WA

ARNOLD, Ray Henry, 1895- , American; nonfiction CON

ARNOLD, Richard ('Coch-y-Bonddhu), 1912- , Scots; nonfiction CON

ARNOLD, Richard Eugene, 1908- , American; nonfiction CON

ARNOLD, Rollo Davis, 1926- , New Zealander, nonfiction CON

ARNOLD, Thomas, 1795-1842, British; nonfiction BRO KBA ST

ARNOLD, Thurman Wesley, 1891- , American; nonfiction CON KTS

ARNOLD, William Robert, 1933- , American; nonfiction CON

ARNOLD, William Thomas, 1852-1904, British; nonfiction KBA

ARNOLD-BAKER, Charles, 1918- , American; nonfiction CON

ARNOLD von IMMESSEN, 15th cent., German; plays ST

ARNOLDUS GEILHOVEN (Gheiloven), -1442, Dutch; nonfiction ST

'ARNOLDY, Julie' see BISCHOFF, Julia B.

ARNOTT, Peter Douglas, 1931- , Anglo-American; nonfiction, fiction CON

ARNOULD, Joseph, 1729-72, French; nonfiction DIL

ARNOULD, Sophie Madeleine, 1740-1802, French; plays DIL

ARNOULT, Ambr. M., 1757-1812, French; nonfiction DIL

ARNOULT, Charles, 1750-93/96, French; nonfiction DIL

ARNOULT, J.B., 1689-1753, French; nonfiction DIL

ARNOULX, C.B., 1708-78, French; nonfiction DIL

ARNOUX, Paul Alexandre, 1884-1973, French; poetry, fiction, plays, nonfiction DIF HAR ST

ARNOV, Boris, Jr., 1926- , American; nonfiction, juveniles CON WA

ARNOW, Harriette Simpson, 1908- , American; fiction

CON WAF
ARNSTEIN, Flora Jacobi, 1885- ,
American; poetry CON
ARNSTEIN, Walter Leonard, 1930- ,
American; nonfiction CON
ARNTSON, Herbert Edward, 1911- ,
American; nonfiction CON PAC
ARNULF of LISIEUX, -1184,
French; nonfiction ST
AROGONESES URQUIJO, Encarnación
see 'FORTUN, Elena'
AROLAS, Juan, 1805-40/49, Spanish;
poetry BL SA ST
ARON, Raymond, 1905- , French;
nonfiction DIF
ARONFREED, Justin, 1930- ,
American; nonfiction CON
ARONSON, Alvin, 1928- , American;
plays CON
ARONSON, Elliot, 1932- , American;
nonfiction CON
ARONSON, James, 1915- , American;
nonfiction CON
ARONSON, Joseph, 1898- , Amer-
ican; nonfiction CON
ARONSON, Theo, 1930- , South
African; nonfiction CON
ARORA, Shirley Lease, 1930- ,
American; juveniles, nonfiction
COM CON
AROUET, François Marie see
'VOLTAIRE, Françoise M. A. de'
AROZAMENA BERASATEGUI, Jesús
María, 1918- , Spanish; plays
SA
AROZARENA, Marcelino, 1912- ,
Cuban; poetry MIN
'ARP, Bill' see SMITH, Charles
Henry
ARP, Hans (Jean), 1887-1966,
French; poetry CON FLE KU
ARP, Jan van, 17th cent., Dutch;
plays ST
ARPE, Pedro Federico, 1682-1748,
Danish; essays SA
ARQUELAO, 4th cent., Greek;
poetry SA
ARQUELAO, 5th cent. B.C., Greek;
nonfiction SA
ARQUELAO, 5th cent., Greek;
poetry SA
ARQUETTE, Lois Steinmetz (Cardozzo;
'Lois Duncan'; 'Lois Kerry'),
1934- , American; juveniles
COM CON WA
ARQUIAS, 4th cent., Greek; plays
SA

ARQUIAS, Aulo Licinio, 2nd cent.,
Greek; poetry SA
ARQUITAS, 440-360 B.C., Greek;
nonfiction SA
ARQUSTRATO, 4th cent., Greek;
poetry SA
'ARRABAL' (Fernando Arrabal
Téran), 1932- , Spanish;
plays CON MAT RIC
ARRAIS, Amador, 1530?-1600,
Portuguese; nonfiction ST
ARRAS, Jean de, 14th cent.,
French; poetry SA
ARRATE, José Martín, 1697-1766,
Cuban; nonfiction MIN
ARRAULT, Charles, 1643- ,
French; nonfiction DIL
'ARRE, Helen' see ROSS, Zola H.
'ARRE, John' see HOLT, John R.
ARREBO, Anders Christensen,
1587-1637, Danish; poetry SA
ST
ARRESO, José Luis de, 1907- ,
Spanish; poetry, nonfiction SA
ARRHENIUS, Claudius, 1627-85,
Swedish; nonfiction SA
ARRIAN (Flavius Arrianus), 95-
175, Greek; nonfiction SA ST
ARRIAS, Frei Amador, 1530-1600,
Portuguese; nonfiction SA
ARRIAZA, Armando see 'NAHUEL,
Hermes'
ARRIAZA y SUPERVIELA, Juan
Bautista, 1770-1837, Spanish;
poetry BL HAR SA ST
ARRIETA, Diógenes, 1848/49-98,
Colombian; poetry MIN
'ARRIETA, Fernando' see ACEVEDO
GUERRA, Evaristo
ARRIETA, Rafael Alberto, 1889- ,
Argentinian; nonfiction, poetry,
criticism BL FLE MIN SA ST
ARRIGHI, Cletto see RIGHETTI,
Carlo
ARRINGTON, Alfred W. ('Charles
Summerfield'), 1810-67, Amer-
ican; nonfiction, poetry KAA
ARRINGTON, Leonard James,
1917- , American; nonfiction
CON
ARRIO, 256-336, Greek; nonfiction
SA
ARROM, Juan José, 1910- ,
Cuban; nonfiction BL
ARROW, Kenneth J., 1921- ,
American; nonfiction CON
ARROWSMITH, William Ayres,

1924-   , American; translations,
nonfiction CON
ARROYO, César A., 1890-   , Ecua-
dorian; fiction, plays, journalism
SA
ARTAIZE, M. de Feucher, 18th cent.,
French; nonfiction DIL
ARTAL, Jorge, 1909-   , Colombian;
poetry MIN
ARTAUD, Antonin, 1896-1948, French;
poetry DIF FLE HAR MAL MAT
RIC ST
ARTAUD, Jean Baptiste, 1732-96,
French; plays, essays DIL
ARTAVAZD II, fl. 55-43 B.C.,
Armenian; plays LAN
ARTEAGA, Esteban de, 1747-98/99,
Spanish; nonfiction BL SA ST
ARTEAGA ALEMPARTE, Domingo,
1835-80, Chilean; journalism
MIN
'ARTEFEUIL' (Louis Ventre), 1706-
67, French; nonfiction DIL
ARTEFIO, 1130-   , Arab; nonfiction
SA
ARTHOS, John, 1908-   , American;
nonfiction CON
'ARTHUR, Burt' see SHAPPIRO,
Herbert A.
ARTHUR, Donald Ramsay, 1917-   ,
Welsh; nonfiction CON
'ARTHUR, Frank' see EBERT, Arthur
F.
'ARTHUR, Gladys' see OSBORNE,
Dorothy G. Y.
'ARTHUR, Herbert' see SHAPPIRO,
Herbert A.
ARTHUR, Percy C., 1910-   , Amer-
ican; nonfiction CON
ARTHUR, Richard O., 1928-   ,
American; nonfiction CON
ARTHUR, Ruth M., 1905-   , Scots,
juveniles CON
'ARTHUR, Tiffany' see PELTON,
Robert W.
ARTHUR, Timothy Shay, 1809-85,
American; fiction KAA SA
'ARTHUR, William' see NEUBAUER,
William A.
ARTHUYS, Pierre Joseph, 1682-1721,
French; nonfiction DIL
'ARTIFEX' see GREEN, Peter M.
ARTIGAS FERRANDO, Miguel, 1887-
1947, Spanish; nonfiction BL SA
ARTIGNY, Antoine Gachet d', 1704-
78, French; nonfiction DIL
ARTIQUES see CASTERA, Jean H.

ARTILES, Jenaro J., 20th cent.,
Spanish; nonfiction BL
ARTIS y BALAGUER, Avelino,
1881-   , Spanish; plays SA
ARTMANN, Hans Carl, 1921-   ,
German; nonfiction KU
ARTOM, Guido, 1906-   , Italian;
nonfiction CON
ARTSYBASHEV, Mikhail Petrovich,
1878-1927, Russian; plays,
fiction COL FLE HAR KT
MAG SA ST HARK KAT MAT
ARTURO, Aurelio, 1909-   ,
Colombian; poetry MIN
ARTZ, Frederick, B., 1894-   ,
American; nonfiction CON
ARTZYBASHEFF, Boris, 1899-
1965, Russian-American;
juveniles KJU WA
ARUEGO, Jose, 1932-   , Filipino;
juveniles CON
'ARUNDEL, Anne' see ALEXANDER,
Jocelyn
ARUNDEL, Honor Morfydd, 1919-   ,
Welsh; plays, juveniles CON
'ARUNDEL, Jocelyn' see ALEXAN-
DER, Jocelyn
ARUNDELL, George Edmund Milnes
Monckton, 1844-1931, English;
nonfiction HIG
ARVERS, Alexis Félix, 1806-50,
French; poetry, plays HAR
SA ST
ARVIN, Newton, 1900-   , Ameri-
can; criticism, nonfiction KT
ARY, Sheila Mary Littleboy,
1929-   , English; nonfiction
CON
ARYASURA, fl. 500, Sanskrit;
fiction ST
ARZAK, Nikolay see DANIEL, Yuri
ARZENGRUBER, Ludwig, 1839-
89, Austrian; plays SA
ASADI, Ali Ibn-i Tusi, 11th cent.,
Persian; poetry ST
ASAI RYOI, 1610?-90, Japanese;
nonfiction, fiction ST
ASAKI, Ghiorghe, 1788-1869/71,
Moldavian; poetry, plays, fic-
tion ST
ASALACHE, Khadambi, Kenyan;
poetry, fiction MUR
ASBAJE, Juana see CRUZ, Sor
Juana I. de la
ASBJORNSEN, Peter Christian,
1821-85, Norwegian; juveniles,
nonfiction DOY HAR KE SA
ST

ASBURY, Herbert, 1891- , Ameri-
can; nonfiction KT
ASCASUBI, Hilario, 1807-75, Argen-
tinian; poetry BL MIN ST
ASCENSIO SEGURA, Manuel, 1805-
71, Peruvian; poetry, plays SA
ASCENSIUS see BADE, Josse
ASCH, Nathan, 1902- , American;
fiction KT
ASCH, Sholem, 1880-1957, Polish;
fiction, plays COL FLE KAT KT
LAN MAG RIC SA MAT WAF ST
ASCHAM, Roger, 1515-68, English;
nonfiction BRO KB ST
ASCHERSON, Neal, 1932- , Scots;
nonfiction CON
ASCHMANN, Helen Tann, American;
juveniles CON
ASCLEPIADES, 600 B.C., Greek;
poetry SA
ASCLEPIADES of MYRLEA
('Ampameo'), 1st cent. B.C.,
Greek; nonfiction SA
ASCLEPIADES of SAMOS, 3rd cent.,
Greek; poetry SA ST
ASCLEPIDDES, 200 B.C., Greek;
nonfiction SA
ASCLEPIDES, 5th cent., Greek;
nonfiction SA
ASCLEPIO, 6th cent. B.C., Greek;
nonfiction SA
ASCOLI, Guido Isaia, 1829-1902,
Italian; nonfiction ST
ASCONIUS PEDIANUS, 9 B.C.-76
A.D., Roman; nonfiction SA ST
ASCOSUBI, Hilario, 1807-75, Argen-
tinian; poetry SA
ASENJ BARBIERI, Francisco, 1823-
94, Spanish; plays BL
ASENJO, Antonio, 1879-1940, Spanish;
journalism, plays SA
ASENJO BARBIERI see BARBIERI,
Francesco
ASENSIO, Eugenio, 1902- , Spanish;
nonfiction BL
ASENSIO y TOLEDO, José María,
1829-1905, Spanish; nonfiction
SA
ASEYEV, Nikolay Nikolayevich, 1889-
1963, Russian; poetry COL FLE
HARK RIC SA ST
ASFILD, Jacques Vincent Bidal,
1664-1745, French; nonfiction
DIL
ASGILL, John, 1659-1738, English;
nonfiction BRO ST
ASGRIMSSON, Eysteinn see EY-

STEINN ASGRIMSSON
ASH, Bernard, 1910- , English;
fiction CON
ASH, Christopher Edward, 1914- ,
English; nonfiction CON
ASH, David Wilfred, 1923- ,
American; nonfiction CON
ASH, Douglas, 1914- , English;
nonfiction CON
ASH, Sarah Leeds, 1904- ,
American; poetry CON
ASH, William Franklin, 1917- ,
American; nonfiction CON
A'SHA, 6th-7th cent., Arab;
poetry ST
ASHABRANNER, Brent Kenneth,
1921- , American; juveniles
COM CON
ASHBERY, John Lawrence (Ash-
berry), 1927- , American;
poetry, fiction, plays CON
MUR
ASHBROOK, James Barbour,
1925- , American; nonfiction
CON
ASHBROOK, William Sinclair,
1922- , American; nonfiction
CON
ASHBURNE, Jim G., 1912- ,
American; nonfiction CON
ASHBY, Cliff, 1919- , English;
poetry, fiction CON
ASHBY, Darrel Le Roy, 1938- ,
American; nonfiction CON
ASHBY, Gwynneth, 1922- , Eng-
lish; fiction CON
ASHBY, LaVerne, 1922- , Amer-
ican; nonfiction CON
ASHBY, Philip Harrison, 1916- ,
American; nonfiction CON
ASHCOM, Benjamin, B., 1903- ,
American; nonfiction BL
ASHCRAFT, Allan Coleman,
1928- , American; nonfiction
CON
ASHE, Geoffrey Thomas, 1923- ,
English; nonfiction CON
'ASHE, Gordon' see CREASEY,
John
ASHE, Samuel A'Court, 1840-
1938, English; nonfiction JO
ASHE, Thomas, 1836-89, English;
poetry KBA
ASHEIM, Lester Eugene, 1914- ,
American; nonfiction CON
ASHER, Harry, 1909- , English;
nonfiction, translations CON

ASHER, John Alexander, 1921- ,
New Zealander; nonfiction CON
ASHER ben Yehiel (Asheri; Rosh),
1250-1327, Spanish; nonfiction
ST
ASHFORD, Daisy, 1881-1972, Eng-
lish; juveniles BRO DOY
'ASHFORD, Jeffrey' see JEFFRIES,
Roderic G.
ASHI, 352-427, Iraqui; nonfiction
SA ST
ASHIQ of ISFAHAN,   -1767/68,
Persian; poetry ST
ASHKENAZI, Jacob ben Yitzchok,
1550-1628, Jewish; nonfiction
ST
ASHLEY, Arthur Ernest ('Francis
Vivian'), 1906- , American;
fiction CON
'ASHLEY, Graham' see ORGAN, John
ASHLEY, Leonard R.N., 1929- ,
American; nonfiction CON
'ASHLEY, Mary' see TOWNSEND,
Mary A.
ASHLEY, Paul Pritchard, 1895- ,
American; nonfiction CON
ASHLEY, Robert Paul, Jr., 1915- ,
American; juveniles; CON WA
ASHLIN, John see CUTFORTH,
John A.
ASHLOCK, Robert B., 1930- ,
American; nonfiction CON
ASHMEAD, Gordon, American;
juveniles WA
ASHMEAD, John, Jr., 1917- ,
American; fiction, nonfiction
CON
ASHMOLE, Elias, 1617-92, English;
nonfiction BRO ST
ASHMORE, Harry Scott, 1916- ,
American; nonfiction CON
ASHMORE, Jerome, 1901- , Amer-
ican; nonfiction CON
ASHMUN, Margaret, American;
juveniles KJU
ASHTON, Dore, 1928- , American;
nonfiction CON
ASHTON, Helen Rosaline Jordan,
1891- , English; fiction, non-
fiction KAT KT
ASHTON, Robert, 1924- , English;
nonfiction CON
ASHTON, Winifred ('Clemence Dane'),
1888-1965, English; fiction,
plays BRO KL KT MAT RIC
SA ST
ASHTON-WARNER, Sylvia, New

Zealander; fiction RIC
ASHWORTH, John, 1813-75,
American; fiction KBA
ASHWORTH, Mary Wells Knight,
1903- , American; nonfiction
CON
ASHWORTH, Wilfred, 1912- ,
English; nonfiction CON
ASHWORTH, William, 1920- ,
English; nonfiction CON
ASIMOV, Isaac ('Paul French'),
1920- , Russian-American;
fiction, nonfiction COM CON
RIC WA
ASIN y PALACIOS, Miguel, 1871-
1944, Spanish; nonfiction BL
COL SA ST
ASINIUS POLLIO see POLLIO,
Gaius A.
ASINOF, Eliot, 1919- , Ameri-
can; fiction CON
ASIO, 5th cent. B.C., Greek;
poetry SA
ASJADI, Abu Nazar Abd Al-Aziz,
11th cent., Persian; poetry
ST
'ASKARI, Hussaini M.' see
PEREIRA, Harold B.
ASKELÖF, Johan Christoffer,
1787-1848, Swedish; journalism,
ST
ASKENAZY, Syzmon, 1867-1935,
Polish; nonfiction ST
'ASKHAM, Francis' see GREEN-
WOOD, Julia
ASLANAPA, Oktay, 1914- ,
Turkish; nonfiction CON
ASMODI, Herbert, 1923- , Ger-
man; nonfiction KU
ASNYK, Adam Prot, 1838-97,
Polish; poetry COL HAR SA
ST
ASPASIA, 480 B.C., Greek; non-
fiction SA
'ASPAZIJAN' (Elia Rozenberga),
1868-1943, Latvian; nonfiction
poetry ST
ASPELL, Patrick Joseph, 1930- ,
American; nonfiction CON
ASPIAZU, Augustín, 1827-97,
Bolivian; nonfiction MIN SA
'ASPIN, Jehoshaphat', fl. 1825- ,
English; nonfiction HIG
ASPINALL, Honor Ruth Alastair,
1922- , English; fiction
CON
ASPLUND, Karl, 1890- , Swedish;

poetry ST
ASPREY, Robert B., 1923- ,
American; nonfiction CON
ASQUERINO, Eduardo, 1826-92,
Spanish; poetry, plays SA
ASQUERINO, Eusebio, 1822-92,
Spanish; plays SA
ASQUITH, Emma Alice Margaret,
1864-1945, Scots; nonfiction
BRO
ASQUITH, Glenn Hackney, 1904- ,
American; nonfiction CON
ASSELIJN, Thomas, 1620-1701,
Dutch; plays ST
ASSELIN, E.B., 1735-93, French;
nonfiction DIL
ASSELIN, E. Donald, 1903- , Amer-
ican; nonfiction CON
ASSELIN, Gilles Thomas, 1682-1767,
French; poetry DIL
ASSELIN, Joseph François Olivar,
1874-1937, Canadian; nonfiction
ST SY
ASSELIN, D. Nicolas, 1638-1724,
French; nonfiction DIL
ASSELINE, Jean René, 1742-1807,
French; nonfiction DIL
ASSENEDE, Diederic, 13th cent.,
Dutch; poetry ST
ASSER (Asserius Menevensis) -909?,
English; nonfiction BRO KB ST
'ASSIAC' see FRAENKEL, Heinrich
ASSING, Ludmila (Grimelli), 1827-80,
German; nonfiction SA
ASSOLANT, Alfred, 1827-86, French;
fiction DIF
ASSOUCI, Charles Coypeau d', 1605-
-79, French; poetry ST
ASTEROPHERUS, Magnus Olai,
-1647, Swedish; plays ST
ASTIN, Alexander William, 1932- ,
American; nonfiction CON
ASTIN, Helen Stavridou, 1932- ,
American; nonfiction CON
ASTIZ, Carlos A., 1933- , Argen-
tinian; nonfiction CON
ASTLEY, Joan Bright, 1910- ,
English; nonfiction CON
ASTLEY, Sir John Dugdale ('The
Mate'), 1829-94, English; non-
fiction HIG
ASTOR, Mary, 1906- , American;
fiction CON
ASTOR, William Waldorf, 1848-1919,
American; fiction KAA
ASTORQUIZA, Eliodoro, 1884- ,
Chilean; nonfiction MIN

ASTRADA, Carlos, 1894- ,
Argentinian; nonfiction MIN
ATRANA MARIN, Luis, 1889-1960,
Spanish; translations BI SA
ASTRO, Richard, 1941- , Amer-
ican; nonfiction CON
ASTRUC, Jean, 1684-1766, French;
nonfiction DIL
ASTURIAS, Miguel Angel, 1899- ,
Spanish; fiction BL CON
FLE RIC SA
ASTYDAMAS, Greek; poetry ST
ASVAGHOSHA, 2nd cent., Indian;
plays ST
'ASWIN' see NANDAKUMAR,
Prema
ASZENDORF, Israel, 1909- ,
Jewish; poetry ST
ATA Malik-i Juvayni, Ala al-din,
1226-83, Persian; nonfiction
SA ST
'ASTLL, Peter, Jr.' see WALN,
Robert
ATANACKOVIC, Bogoboj, 1826-
58, Serbian; poetry, fiction
ST
ATAVA, S. see TERPIGOREV,
Sergey N.
ATCHESON, Richard ('Charles
Tressilian'), 1934- , Amer-
ican; nonfiction CON
ATCHISON, Sandra Dallas, 1939- ,
American; fiction CON
ATHANASIUS, 295/300-73, Greek;
nonfiction SA ST
ATHANASSIADIS, Nikos, 1924- ,
Greek; fiction, plays CON
ATHAS, Daphne, 1923- , Amer-
can; fiction, poetry, plays
CON
ATHAY, Robert E., 1925- , Amer-
ican; nonfiction CON
ATHEAAEUS, fl. 200, Greek; non-
fiction ST
ATHEARN, Robert Greenleaf,
1914- , American; nonfiction
CON PAC
ATHENAGORAS, 2nd cent., Greek;
nonfiction SA
ATHENEO, 2nd cent., Greek; non-
fiction SA
ATHENODORO CANANITA, 1st
cent., Greek; nonfiction SA
ATHENODORO CORDILION, 1st
cent., Greek; nonfiction SA
ATHENODORO de RODAS, Greek;
nonfiction SA

ATHERSTONE, Edwin, 1788-1872,
English; poetry, fiction BRO
KBA ST
ATHERTON, Alexine, 1930- , Amer-
ican; nonfiction CON
ATHERTON, Gertrude Franklin Horn,
1857-1948, American; fiction
BRO KL KT RIC SA
ATHERTON, James Stephen, 1910- ,
English; fiction CON
ATHERTON, Lewis E., 1905- ,
American; nonfiction CON
ATHERTON, Maxine, American; non-
fiction CON
ATHILL, Diana, 1917- , English;
fiction CON
'ATHOS' see WALKERLEY, Rodney L.
ATHOS, Anthony George, 1934- ,
American; nonfiction CON
ATICO, Tito Pomponio, 110-33 B.C.,
Roman; nonfiction SA
ATILIO, 2nd cent., Roman; poetry
SA
ATIYA, Aziz S., 1898- , Egyptian-
American; nonfiction CON
ATIYAH, Patrick Selim, 1931- ,
English; nonfiction CON
ATKINS, George Pope, 1934- ,
American; nonfiction CON
ATKINS, Harry, 1933- , American;
fiction CON
'ATKINS, Jack' see HARRIS, Mark
ATKINS, James G., 1932- , Amer-
ican; nonfiction CON
ATKINS, John Alfred, 1916- , Eng-
lish; fiction, nonfiction CON
ATKINS, Stewart, 1913- , American;
poetry JO
ATKINS, Stuart Pratt, 1914- ,
American; nonfiction CON
ATKINSON, Basil Ferris Campbell,
1895- , English; nonfiction CON
ATKINSON, Brooks see ATKINSON,
J.B.
ATKINSON, Carroll Holloway, 1896- ,
American; nonfiction CON
ATKINSON, Mrs. Dean see 'FIFE,
Duncan'
ATKINSON, Edward, 1827-1905,
American; nonfiction KAA
ATKINSON, Eleanor Stackhouse,
1863-1942, American; fiction KT
ATKINSON, George Francis, 1854-
1918, American; nonfiction KAA
ATKINSON, James, 1914- , English;
nonfiction CON
ATKINSON, John William, 1923- ,

American; nonfiction CON
ATKINSON, Justin Brooks (Brooks
Atkinson), 1894- , American;
criticism, essays KT
'ATKINSON, M.E.' see FRANKAU,
Mary E.A.
ATKINSON, Margaret Fleming,
American; juveniles WA
ATKINSON, Mary Evelyn, 1899- ,
English; juveniles DOY
ATKINSON, Philip, S., 1921- ,
American; nonfiction CON
ATKINSON, Richard Chatham,
1929- , American; nonfiction
CON
ATKINSON, Ronald Field, 1928- ,
English; nonfiction CON
ATKINSON, William C., 1902- ,
Scots; nonfiction BL
ATLAS, Martin, 1914- , Amer-
ican; nonfiction CON
ATMORE, Anthony, 1932- ,
South African; nonfiction CON
'ATTAR' (Shaykh Farid al Din),
-1230, Persian; poetry
LAN SA ST
ATTENBOROUGH, David Frederick,
1926- , English; nonfiction
CON
ATTERBOM, Per Daniel Amadeus,
1790-1855, Swedish; poetry
HAR KE SA ST
ATTERBURY, Francis, 1663-1732,
English; nonfiction BRO KB
ST
ATTICUS, Titus Pomponius, 109-
32 B.C., Roman; letters ST
ATTIO, Lucio see ACCIUS, Lucius
ATTIRET, Jean Denis, 1702- ,
French; nonfiction DIL
ATTWATER, Donald, 1892- ,
English; nonfiction HOE
ATTWELL, Mabel Lucie, 1879-
1964, English; juveniles DOY
ATTWOOD, William, 1919- ,
American; nonfiction CON
ATWATER, Constance Elizabeth
Sullivan; 1923- , American;
nonfiction CON
ATWATER, Florence Hasseltine
Carroll, American; juveniles
FUL
ATWATER, Montgomery Meigs,
1904- , American; juveniles,
nonfiction FUL PAC WA
ATWATER, Richard Tupper, 1892-
1948, American; juveniles FUL

'ATWOOD, Drucy' see MORRISON,
Atwood E.
ATWOOD, Margaret Eleanor, 1939- ,
Canadian; poetry, fiction MUR
AUB, Max, 1902/03- , Spanish;
plays, fiction, criticism BL
RIC SA
AUBANEL, Antoine, 1724-1804,
French; nonfiction DIL
AUBANEL, Théodore, 1829-86,
French; poetry COL DIF HAR
KE SA ST
AUBER, Guillaume François, 1745-
1803, French; nonfiction DIL
AUBERRY, Pierre, 1920- , French;
nonfiction CON
AUBERT, 18th cent., French; poetry
DIL
AUBERT, Don Bonaventure, 1678-
1744, French; nonfiction DIL
AUBERT, Georges Bernard, 1614-
1702, French; nonfiction DIL
AUBERT, Jean Louis, 1731-1814,
French; nonfiction DIL
AUBERT, Joseph, 1676-1749, French;
nonfiction DIL
AUBERT de GASPE, 1786-1871,
Canadian; nonfiction SY
AUBEY, Robert Thaddeus, 1930- ,
American; nonfiction CON
AUBIAS, Charles de Baschi, 1868-
1777, French; nonfiction DIL
AUBIGNAC, François Hédelin,
1604-76, French; plays DIF ST
AUBIGNE, Théodore Agrippa d',
1551/52-1630, French; poetry,
nonfiction DIF HAR KE MAL SA
ST
AUBIN, 1655- , French; nonfiction
DIL
AUBIN, Jean Charles Joseph, 1747-
1829, French; nonfiction DIL
AUBLET de MAUBAY, Jean Zorobabel,
18th cent., French; fiction DIL
AUBREI, Guillaume, 1648-1730,
French; nonfiction DIL
AUBREY, John, 1626-97, English;
nonfiction BRO KB ST
AUBRUN, Charles Vincent, 1906- ,
French; nonfiction BL
AUBRY, Jean Baptiste Benoit, 1736-
1809, French; nonfiction DIL
AUBRY, Marie Olimpye, 1755-93,
French; nonfiction SA
AUBRY, Octave, 1881-1946, French;
fiction, nonfiction DIF HAR KT
SA

AUCHINCLOSS, Louis Stanton
('Andrew Lee'), 1917- ,
American; fiction, nonfiction,
plays CON RIC
AUCHTERLONIE, Dorothy Green,
1915- , Australian; poetry,
criticism MUR
AUCLERT, Humbertina, 1851- ,
French; nonfiction SA
AUDEFROI le BASTART, 13th
cent., French; poetry HAR
ST
AUDELAY, John (Awdelay), 15th
cent., English; poetry ST
AUDEMARS, Pierre, 1909- ,
English; fiction CON
AUDEN, J.E., 1860-1946, English;
nonfiction HIG
AUDEN, Wystan Hugh, 1907-73,
American; poetry, plays,
criticism BRO CON FLE KT
MAG MAT MUR RIC SA SP ST
AUDIBERTI, Jacques, 1899-1965,
French; plays, poetry, fiction
COL CON DIC DIF FLE HAR
MAL MAT SA
AUDIERNE, Jacques, 1710?-85,
French; nonfiction DIL
AUDINOT, Nicolas Médard, 1732-
1801, French; plays DIL
AUDISIO, Gabriel, 1900- , French;
fiction, poetry DIF
AUDORF, Jakob, 1835-98, German;
nonfiction AL
AUDOUX, Marguerite, 1863-1937,
French; fiction DIF
AUDRA, Joseph, 1713-71, French;
nonfiction DIL
AUDREN de KERDREL, Jean Muir,
1651-1725, French; nonfiction
DIL
AUDUBON, John James, 1785-
1851, American; nonfiction
KAA
AUE, Hartmann see HARTMANN
von AUE
AUER, J. Jeffery, 1913- ,
American; nonfiction CON
AUERBACH, Arnold M., 1912- ,
American; fiction CON
'AUERBACH, Berthold' (Moses
Baruche), 1812-82, German;
fiction AL HAR KE SA ST
AUERBACH, Erich, 1892-1957,
German; criticism FLE
AUERBACH, Jerold S., 1936- ,
American; nonfiction CON

AUERBACH, Marjorie Hoffberg,
American; juveniles CON
AUERSPERG, A.A. see 'GRÜN,
Anastasius'
AUFRESNE, Mlle. E., 18th cent.,
French; plays DIL
AUGELLI, John Patsy, 1921- ,
American; nonfiction CON
AUGER, Athanase, 1734-92, French;
translations DIL
AUGER, Edmond, 1530-91, French;
nonfiction SA
AUGER, Louis, 1674-1759, French;
nonfiction DIL
AUGHTRY, Charles Edward, 1925- ,
American; nonfiction CON
AUGIER, Emile, 1820-89, French;
plays DIF MAL
AUGIER, Guillaume Victor Emile,
1820-89, French; plays HAR KE
SA ST
AUGSBERGER, David W., 1938- ,
American; nonfiction CON
AUGSBURGER, A. Don, 1925- ,
American; nonfiction CON
AUGSBURGER, Myron, S., 1929- ,
American; nonfiction CON
AUGUSTIJNKEN van dordt, 14th cent.,
Dutch; poetry ST
AUGUSTIN, Pius, 1934- , American;
nonfiction CON
AUGUSTIN, Ernst, 1927- , German;
nonfiction KU
AUGUSTINE, St., 354-430, Roman;
nonfiction MAG SA ST
AUGUSTO de la Inmaculada, Fray,
1922- , Spanish; poetry SA
AUKERMAN, Robert C., 1910- ,
American; nonfiction CON
AUKRUST, Olav, 1883-1929, Norwe-
gian; poetry COL FLE SA ST
AULAIRE, Edgar Parin d', Norwegian-
American; juveniles KJU WA
AULAIRE, Ingri Mortenson d', 1904- ,
Norwegian-American; juveniles
KJU WA
AULARD, François Victor Alphonse,
1849-1928, French; nonfiction,
journalism DIF
AULETA, Michael S., 1909- , Amer-
ican; nonfiction CON
AULICK, June L., 1906- , Amer-
ican; nonfiction CON
AULIO Gelio, 2nd cent., Roman;
criticism SA
AULNOY, Marie Catherine le Jumel
de Barneville, 1650-1705,

French; nonfiction DIF ST
AULTMAN, Donald S., 1930- ,
American; nonfiction CON
AUMALE, Marie Jeanne, 1683-
1756, French; nonfiction DIL
AUMONIER, Stacy, 1887-1928,
English; fiction BRO KT
AUMONT, Jean Pierre, 1913- ,
French; plays CON
'AUNBRY, Alan' see BAYLEY,
Barrington J.
AUNG, Maung Htin ('The Fourth
Brother'), 1909- , Burmese;
nonfiction CON
AUNGERVILLE, Richard (Richard
de Bury) 1281?-1345, English;
nonfiction BRO DIL KB SA ST
AUNILLON, P.C. Fabiot, 1684-
1760, French; fiction DIL
AUNOS PEREZ, Eduardo, 1894- ,
Spanish; fiction, essays SA
'AUNT Fanny' see GAGE, Frances
D.B.
AURELIUS, Marcus, 121-180,
Roman; nonfiction ST
AURELIUS VICTOR, fl. 360,
Roman; nonfiction SA ST
AURELL, Tage, 1895- , Swedish;
fiction ST
'AURISPA, Giovanni' (G. Pichume-
rio), 1375?-1459, Italian; non-
fiction ST
AURNER, Robert Ray, 1898- ,
American; nonfiction CON
AUSLANDER, Joseph, 1897- ,
American; poetry KL KT
AUSONIUS, Decimus Magnus, 310-
95, Latin; poetry SA ST
AUSTEN, Jane, 1775-1817, Eng-
lish; fiction BRO KBA MAG
SA ST
AUSTEN, Ralph A., 1937- ,
German-American; nonfiction
CON
AUSTGEN, Robert Joseph, 1932- ,
American; nonfiction CON
AUSTIN, Alfred, 1835-1913, Eng-
lish; poetry BRO KBA RIC
SA
AUSTIN, Allen, 1922- , Amer-
ican; nonfiction CON
AUSTIN, Anthony, 1919- , Amer-
ican; nonfiction CON
'AUSTIN, Barbara Leslie' see
LINTON, Barbara L.
'AUSTIN, Brett' see FLOREN, Lee
AUSTIN, David Edwards, 1926- ,

American; nonfiction CON
AUSTIN, Elizabeth S., 1907- ,
American; nonfiction CON
'AUSTIN, Harry' see McINERNY,
Ralph
AUSTIN, Henry, fl. 1613, English;
poetry ST
AUSTIN, James, Clayton, 1923- ,
American; nonfiction CON
AUSTIN, Jane Goodwin, 1831-94,
American; juveniles, fiction KAA
AUSTIN, John, 1790-1859, English;
nonfiction BRO KBA ST
AUSTIN, Linda ('Tom Austin'; 'Claire
Blackburn'; 'Lloyd Blackburn'),
1943- , American; nonfiction
CON
AUSTIN, Lloyd, James, 1915- ,
Australian; nonfiction CON
AUSTIN, Margot, American; juveniles
CON FUL WA
AUSTIN, Mary Carrington, 1915- ,
American; nonfiction CON
AUSTIN, Mary Hunter, 1868-1934,
American; fiction, essays, non-
fiction HOO KL KT
AUSTIN, Neal Fuller, 1926- , Amer-
ican; nonfiction CON
'AUSTIN, Tom' see AUSTIN, Linda
AUSTIN, William, 1584-1634, Eng-
lish; nonfiction ST
AUSTIN, William, fl. 1662, English;
poetry ST
AUSTIN, William, 1778-1841, Amer-
ican; fiction, essays KAA
AUSTIN, William Weaver, 1920- ,
American; nonfiction CON
'AUSTWICK, John' see LEE, Austin
AUSUBEL, Herman, 1920- , Amer-
ican; nonfiction CON
AUTON, Jean d', 1465-1528, French;
nonfiction ST
AUTRAN, Joseph, 1813-77, French;
poetry, plays ST
AUTRAN DOURADO, Waldomiro see
DOURADO, Autran
AUTREAU, Jacques, 1657-1745,
French; plays DIL
AUTREPE,   -1787, French; plays
DIL
AUTREY, C.E., 1904- , American;
nonfiction CON
AUTREY, Henri Jean Baptiste Fabri
de Moncaut, 1723-77, French;
nonfiction DIL
AUTRY, Ewart Arthur, 1900- ,
American; fiction CON

AUTY, Phyllis ('Phyllis Richards'),
1910- , English; nonfiction
CON
AUVERGNE, Antoine, 1713-96,
French; plays DIL
AUVERGNE, Martial d', 1430?-
1508, French; poetry, fiction
HAR ST
AUVERT-EASON, Elizabeth,
1917- , Venezuelan; nonfic-
tion CON
AUVIL, Kenneth William, 1925- ,
American; nonfiction CON
AUVRY, Claude, 17th cent.,
French; nonfiction DIL
AUZIERES, Pierre, 1650-1734,
French; nonfiction DIL
AVA, fl. 1130, German; poetry
AL ST
AVALLE-ARCE, Juan Bautista
('Luis Galvez de Montalvo';
'Gabriel Goyeneche'), 1927- ,
Argentinian-American; non-
fiction BL CON
AVALLONE, Michael Angleo, Jr.
('Priscilla Dalton'; 'Mark
Dane'; 'Steve Michaels';
'Dorothea Nile'; 'Edwina Noone';
'John Patrick'; 'Sidney Stuart'),
1924- , American; fiction
CON
'AVALON' see BLASER, Robin
AVALOS, Costanza de, 1501-60,
Italian; poetry SA
AVANCINI, Nicolaus von, 1612-
86, Austrian; plays ST
AVEBURY, Lord (Sir John Lubbock),
1834-1913, English; nonfiction
BRO KBA
AVED de LOIZEROLLES, Jean
Simon, 1723-94, French; fic-
tion DIL
AVELINE, Claude, 1901- ,
French; fiction CON DIF
AVELLANEDA, Alonso F. see
FERNANDEZ de AVELLANEDA,
Alonso
AVELLANEDA, Gertrudis G. de
see GOMEZ de AVELLANEDA,
Gertrudis
AVELLANEDA, Marcos Manuel,
1813-41, Argentinian; poetry
MIN
AVELLANEDA, Nicolás, 1837-85,
Argentinian; journalism MIN
AVELLANEDA y de la CUEVA,
Francisco, 1622?-75?,

Spanish; nonfiction BL SA
AVELLONI, Francesco Antonio,
1756-1837, Italian; plays SA
AVEMPACE see IBN-BAJJA
AVENARIUS, Richard, 1843-96,
French; nonfiction SA
AVENDAÑO, Francisco de, 1551- ,
Spanish; plays BL SA
AVENTINUS, Johannes (Johannes
Thuramayr), 1477-1534, Ger-
man; nonfiction HAR SA ST
AVERBACH, Albert, 1902- ,
American; nonfiction CON
AVERBAKH, Leopold Leonidovich,
1903- , Russian; criticism
HARK
AVERCHENKO, Arkady Timofeyevich,
1881-1925, Russian; fiction COL
HAR HARK SA ST
AVERILL, Esther Holden, 1902- ,
American; juveniles COM CON
KJU WA
AVERILL, Lloyd James, 1923- ,
American; nonfiction CON
AVERITT, Robert T., 1931- ,
American; nonfiction CON
AVERROES (Ibn-Rushd), 1126-98,
Spanish-Arab; nonfiction HAR
KE SA ST
'AVERY, Al' see MONTGOMERY,
Rutherford G.
AVERY, Benhamin Parke, 1828-75,
American; journalism KAA
AVERY, George Costas, 1926- ,
American; nonfiction CON
AVERY, Gillian Elise, 1926- ,
English; juveniles, fiction CON
DOY WA
AVERY, Harold, 1867-1943, English;
juveniles DOY
AVERY, Isaac Erwin, 1871-1904,
American; nonfiction JO
AVERY, Kay, 1908- , American;
juveniles CON
AVERY, Laurence Green, 1934- ,
American; nonfiction CON
'AVERY, Lynn' see COLE, Lois D.
AVERY, Mary Williamson, 1907- ,
American; nonfiction PAC
AVERY, Peter, 1923- , English;
nonfiction, translations CON
AVERY, Robert Sterling, 1917- ,
American; nonfiction CON
AVEY, Albert Edwin, 1886- ,
American; nonfiction CON
AVIANUS, fl. 400, Roman; fiction
SA ST

AVICEBRON see IBN GABIROL
AVICENNA see IBN-SINA
AVIENUS, Rufius Festus, 4th
cent., Roman; poetry SA ST
AVILA, Beato Juan de, 1500-69,
Spanish; nonfiction BL SA
ST
AVILA, Julio Enrique, 1890- ,
Salvadorian; poetry BL SA
AVILA y ZUÑIGA, Luis de,
1503?-73, Spanish; plays,
nonfiction BL SA
AVILES RAMIREZ, Eduardo,
1896- , Nicaraguan; nonfic-
tion BL
AVINERI, Shlomo, 1933- ,
Israeli; nonfiction CON
'AVINOAM' (Reuben Grossmann),
1905- , American; poetry
ST
AVISON, Margaret Kirkland,
1918- , Canadian; poetry,
fiction CON MUR SY
AVISON, Neville Howard, 1934- ,
American; nonfiction CON
AVISSE, Etienne, 1694-1747,
French; poetry, plays DIL
AVISSE, J.B., 1771-1802, French;
nonfiction DIL
AVITO, Sexto Alcimo Ecolicio,
-525, Roman; poetry SA
'AVI-YONAH, Michael' (Michael
Buchstab), 1904- , Austrian;
nonfiction CON
AVNI, Abraham Albert, 1921- ,
Czech-American; nonfiction
CON
AVRETT, Robert, 1901- , Amer-
ican; poetry, nonfiction, juven-
iles CON
AVRICOURT, 18th cent., French;
plays DIL
AVRIGNY, P. Hyacinthe Rebillard,
1675-1719, French; nonfiction
DIL
AVRIL, Louis, 1722- , French;
nonfiction, poetry DIL
AVRIL, Pierre, 1930- , French;
nonfiction CON
AVRILLON, Jean Baptiste, 1652-
1729, French; nonfiction DIL
AVSEYENKO, Vasily Grigoryevich,
1842-1913, Russian; nonfiction
ST
AVVAKUM, Petrovich (Archpriest),
1620/21-82, Russian; nonfic-
tion HARK KE SA ST

AWA, Eme Onuoha, 1921- , Nigerian; nonfiction CON

AWAD, Elias M., 1934- , Syrian-American; nonfiction CON

AWDELAY, John see AUDELAY, John

AWDRY, Rev. Wilbert Vere, 1911- , English; juveniles DOY

AWE, Chulho, 1927- , Korean-American; nonfiction CON

AWFI, Muhammad, 13th cent., Persian; nonfiction ST

A WOOD, Anthony see WOOD, Anthony

AWOONOR, Kofi ('George Awoonor-Williams'), 1935- , Ghanaian; poetry CON MUR RIC

AXELROD, Joseph, 1918- , American; nonfiction CON

AXELROD, Robert, 1943- , American; nonfiction CON

AXELSON, Eric, 1913- , English; nonfiction CON

AXFORD, H. William, 1925- , American; nonfiction CON

AXFORD, Joseph Mack, 1879- , American; nonfiction CON

AXFORD, Lavonne Brady, 1928- , American; nonfiction CON

AXFORD, Roger William, 1920- , American; nonfiction CON

AXLINE, W. Andrew, 1940- , American; nonfiction CON

AXTON, William Fitch, 1926- , American; nonfiction CON

AYAL, Igal, 1942- , American; nonfiction CON

AYALA see LOPEZ de AYALA

AYALA, Francisco, 1906- , Spanish; fiction, nonfiction, translations BL RIC SA

AYALA, Ramon see PEREZ de AYALA, Ramón

AYALA VIGUERA, Félin, 1908- , Spanish; fiction SA

AYANDELE, Emmanuel Ayankanmi, 1936- , Nigerian; nonfiction CON

AYARRAGARAY, Lucas, 1861-1944, Argentinian; nonfiction MIN

AYARS, Albert Lee, 1917- , American; nonfiction CON

AYARS, James Sterling, 1898- , American; juveniles CON WA

AYATEY, Siegfried B.Y., 1934- , Ghanaian-American; nonfiction CON

AYBAR, Andrejulio, 1893- , Dominican; poetry MIN

AYCKBOURN, Alan, 1939- , English; plays CON

AYDELOTTE, Dora, 1878- , American; fiction HOO MAR

AYEARST, Morley, 1899- , American; nonfiction CON

AYER, Alfred Jules, 1910- , American; nonfiction CON

AYER, Margaret, American; juveniles FUL

AYERS, Donald Murray, 1923- , American; nonfiction CON

AYERS, Michael Richard, 1935- , English; nonfiction CON

AYGUALS de IZCO, Wenceslao, 1801-73, Spanish; fiction BL SA

AYLESWORTH, Thomas Gibbons, 1927- , American; nonfiction CON

AYLETT, Robert, 1583-1655?, English; poetry ST

AYLMAR, Felix see JONES, Felix E.A.

AYLMER, Gerald Edward, 1926- , American; nonfiction CON

AYLMER, Isabella, 1837-1908, English; fiction ST

AYMAR, Brandt, 1911- , American; nonfiction CON

AYMAR, Gordon Christian, 1893- , American; nonfiction CON

AYME, Marcel, 1902-67, French; fiction, plays, essays COL DIC DIF FLE HAR KTS MAL MAT RIC SA ST

AYMERICH, Mateo see AIMERICH, Mateo

AYMES, Sister Maria de la Cruz, American; fiction, juveniles CON

AYRAULT, Evelyn W., 1922- , American; nonfiction CON

AYRE, Robert Hugh, 1900- , Canadian; fiction, nonfiction, juveniles CON WA

AYRENHOFF, Kornelius Hermann von, 1733-1819, Austrian; plays ST

AYRER, Jacob, 1543?-1605, German; plays AL KE ST

AYRES, Philip, 1638-1712, English; translations ST

AYRES, Ruby Mildred, 1883-1955, English; fiction RIC

AYRTON, Elisabeth Walshe, English; nonfiction CON

AYRTON, Michael ('Michael Gould'),
1921- , English; fiction CON
AYSCOUGH, Florence Wheelock,
1878-1942, American; poetry,
translations HOO KT
AYSCOUGH, John see BICKESTAFFE-
DREW, F.B.D.
AYTON, Sir Robert (Aytoun), 1570-
1638, Scots; poetry BRO KB ST
AYTOUN, William Edmonstoune,
1813-65, Scots; poetry, fiction
BRO KBA ST
AYUB KHAN, Mohammad, 1907- ,
Pakistani; nonfiction CON
AYUSO, Francisco G. see GARCIA
AYUSO, Francisco
AZA, Vital, 1851-1912, Spanish;
plays BL SA ST
AZAD, Muhammad Husain, 1827-1910,
Indian; criticism, essays, poetry
LAN
AZAÑA y DIAZ, Manuel, 1880-1940,
Spanish; nonfiction BL COL HAR
SA ST
AZARA, José Nicolás de, 1730-1803,
Spanish; nonfiction BL
AZCARATE, Gumersindo de, 1840-
1917, Spanish; nonfiction BL SA
AZCARATE, Patricio de, 1800-86,
Spanish; nonfiction BL SA
AZCARRAGA, Gonzalo, 1907- ,
Spanish; plays SA
AZCOAGA IBAS, Enrique, 1912- ,
Spanish; poetry, essays, criti-
cism BL SA
AZCONA, Rafael, 1926- , Spanish;
fiction SA
AZCUENAGA, Domingo, 1758-1821,
Argentinian; poetry MIN
AZEGLIO, Massimo T. see
D'AZEGLIO, Massimo T.
AZEMAR, Louis Guérin, 18th cent.,
French; plays DIL
AZEVEDO, Aluizio de, 1857-1913,
Brazilian; fiction SA ST
AZEVEDO, Artur, 1855-1908,
Brazilian; plays SA
AZEVEDO, Guilherme de, 1839-82,
Portuguese; journalism, plays
SA
AZEVEDO, Joao de, 1811-54,
Portuguese; nonfiction SA
AZEVEDO, Joao Lucio, de, 1855-
1933, Portuguese; nonfiction SA
AZHAYEV, Vasili Nikolayevich,
1915- , Russian; fiction HARK
AZNAR, Manuel, 1894- , Spanish;

journalism SA
AZNEER, J. Leonard, 1921- ,
Rumanian-American; nonfiction
CON
'AZORIN' see MARTINEZ RUIZ,
José
AZOY, Anastasio C.M., 1891- ,
American; nonfiction CON
AZUCENA, Adolfo de la see
ZENEA, José C.
AZUELA, Mariano, 1873-1952,
Mexican; fiction BL FLE
MAG RIC SA ST
AZUMAMARO see KADA AZUMA-
MARO
AZUMI, Koya, 1930- , Japanese-
American; nonfiction CON
AZUOLA, Eduardo, 1892- ,
Costa Rican; nonfiction MIN
AZURRA, Gomes Eannes de, 15th
cent., Portuguese; nonfiction SA
AZZY, Faustina de los, 1660-
1721, Italian; nonfiction SA

B

'B, Rev.' see EISNER, Betty G.
'B.B.' see WATKINS-PITCHFORD,
D.J.
'B.L.T.' see TAYLOR, Bert L.
'B.V.' see THOMSON, James
BA'AL SHEM Tov, Israel, 1700-
60, Russian; nonfiction SA ST
BAAL-TESHUVA, Jacob, 1929- ,
Israel; nonfiction CON
BAAR, Jindrich Simon, 1869-1925,
Czech; fiction ST
BAAST, B., 1921- , Mongolian;
poetry, fiction LAN
BAATH, Albert Ulrik, 1853-1918,
Swedish; poetry COL SA ST
BAB, Siyyid Ali Muhammad, 1819-
50, Persian; nonfiction ST
BABA TAHIR-I, Hamadani ('Uryan'),
11th cent., Persian; poetry ST
BABAYEVSKI, Semyon Petrovich,
1909- , Russian; fiction
HARK
BABB, Howard S., 1924- ,
American; nonfiction CON
BABB, Hugh Webster, 1887- ,
American; nonfiction CON
BABB, Janice Barbara, 1933- ,
American; nonfiction CON
BABB, Lawrence, 1902- , Amer-
ican; nonfiction CON

BABB, Sanora, 1907- , American;
CON
BABBAGE, Charles, 1792-1871,
English; nonfiction KBA
BABBAGE, Stuart Barton, 1916- ,
New Zealander; nonfiction CON
'BABBIS, Eleanor' see FRIIS-
BAASTAD, Babbis E.
BABBITT, Irving, 1865-1933, Amer-
ican; nonfiction KL KT ST
'BABBLER' see LLOYD, John I.
BABCOCK, Clarence Merton, 1908- ,
American; nonfiction CON
BABCOCK, Frederic ('Matthew
Mark'), 1896- , American; non-
fiction CON
BABCOCK, Robert Joseph, 1928- ,
American; nonfiction CON
BABEL, Isaak Emmanuilovich,
1894-1941?, Russian; fiction
COL FLE HAR HARK KL KT
MAT RIC SA ST
BABELON, Jea, 1889- , French-
Spanish; nonfiction BL
BABER, Asa, 1936- , American;
nonfiction CON
BABIC, Ljubo see GJALSKI, Ksaver
S.
BABIN, David E., 1925- , Ameri-
can; nonfiction CON
BABIN, François, 1651-1734, French;
nonfiction DIL
BABINGTON, John, 1820- , English;
nonfiction HIG
BABINI, José, 1897- , Argentinian;
nonfiction MIN
BABITS, Mihály, 1883-1941, Hungar-
ian; fiction, poetry, criticism
COL FLE HAR SA ST
BABLADELIS, Georgia, 1931- ,
American; nonfiction CON
'BABLI, Hillel' (Hillel Raschgolski),
1893- , Jewish; poetry ST
BABLOT, Louis Nicolas, 1754-1802,
French; nonfiction DIL
BABOIS, Margueriet Victoire, 1760- ,
French; poetry SA
BABRIS, Peter J., 1917- , Latvian-
American; nonfiction CON
BABRIUS, 2nd cent., Greek; fiction
ST
BABSON, Naomi Lane, 1895- ,
American; fiction PAC WAF
BABST, Diederich George, 1741-
1800, German; poetry ST
BABUR, Zahiruddin Muhammed,
1483-1530, Turkish; poetry SA
ST

BACALLAR y SANNA, Vicente,
1669-1728, Spanish; nonfiction
SA
BACARDI, Emilio, 1844-1922,
Cuban; fiction MIN
BACARISSE, Mauricio, 1895-
1931, Spanish; poetry, fiction
BL HAR SA ST
BACCHELLI, Riccardo, 1891- ,
Italian; fiction, poetry COL
CON FLE HAR MAG RIC SA
ST
BACCHINI, Benedetto, 1651-1721,
Italian; nonfiction SA
BACCHYLIDES, 522 B.C., Greek;
poetry ST
BACCINI, Ida, 1850-1915?, Italian;
nonfiction CON
BACH, Bert Coates, 1936- ,
American; nonfiction CON
BACH, George Leland, 1915- ,
American; nonfiction CON
BACH, Richard David, 1936- ,
American; nonfiction CON
BACHARACH, Alfred Louis,
1891- , English; nonfiction
CON
BACHAUMONT, François le
Coigneux, 1624-1702, French;
nonfiction DIF
BACHAUMONT, Louis Petit de,
1690-1771, French; nonfiction
DIF DIL HAR
BACHE, William B., 1922- ,
American; nonfiction CON
BACHELARD, Gaston, 1884-1962,
French; nonfiction DIF MAL
ST
BACHELIER, Jean Jacques, 1724-
1806, French; nonfiction DIL
BACHELIN, Henri, 1879-1941,
French; fiction DIF
BACHELLER, Irving, 1859-1950,
American; fiction KL KT
BACHET de MEGIRIAC, Claude
Gaspar, 1581-1638, French;
nonfiction SA
BACHI, Amurath see WOENSEL,
Pieter van
'BACHILLER, Juan P. de M.'
see LARRA y SANCHEZ de
CASTRO, J. de
BACHILLER MORALES, Antonio,
1812-89, Cuban; nonfiction
MIN
BACHINI, Antonio, 1860- ,
Uruguayan; journalism SA

BACHMAN, John, 1790-1874, American; nonfiction KAA

BACHMAN, John Walter, 1916- , American; nonfiction CON

BACHMANN, Ingeborg, 1926- , Austrian; poetry AL FLE KU KUN RIC

BACHOFEN, Johann Jacob, 1815-87, Swiss; nonfiction KE ST

BACHUR, Elijah ('Germanus'; 'Levita'; 'Tishbi'), 1468-1549, Jewish; nonfiction, translations ST

BACK, Joe W., 1899, American; fiction CON

BACK, Kurt Wolfgang, 1919- , American; nonfiction CON

BACK, Philip, 1858- , English; nonfiction HIG

BACKER, John H., 1902- , Austrian-American; nonfiction CON

BACKER, Morton, 1918- , American; nonfiction CON

BACKHOUSE, Sally, 1927- , English; nonfiction CON

BACKMAN, Carl W., 1923- , American; nonfiction CON

BACKMAN, Jules, 1910- , American; nonfiction CON

BACKMAN, Melvin Abraham, 1919- , American; nonfiction CON

BACKMAN, Milton V., Jr., 1927- , American; nonfiction CON

BACKSTROM, Charles Herbert, 1926- , American; nonfiction CON

BACKUS, Jean Louise ('David Montross'), 1914- , American; fiction CON

BACKUS, Oswald Prentiss III, 1921-72, American; nonfiction CON

BACMEISTER, Ernst, 1874- , German; poetry, plays, essays FLE

BACMEISTER, Rhoda Warner, 1893- , American; nonfiction CON

BACON, Anne, 1528- , English; nonfiction SA

BACON, Delia Salter, 1811-59, American; criticism, fiction KAA SA

BACON, Edward ('Francis Boon'), 1906- , English; nonfiction CON

BACON, Edwin Munroe, 1844-1916, American; journalism KAA

BACON, Elizabeth ('Betty Morrow'), 1914- , American; juveniles CON

BACON, Elizabeth Emaline, 1904- , American; nonfiction CON

BACON, Frances Atchinson, 1903- , American; juveniles CON

BACON, Sir Francis, 1561-1626, English; essays BRO KB MAG SA ST

BACON, Frank, 1864-1922, American; plays MAT

BACON, Jean Pierre Baptiste, 18th cent., French; nonfiction DIL

BACON, Josephine Dodge Daskam, 1876- , American; juveniles, fiction KT

BACON, Leonard, 1887-1954, American; poetry, criticism KT

BACON, Margaret Hope, 1921- , American; nonfiction CON

BACON, Paul, 1913- , American; juveniles WA

BACON, Peggy, 1895- , American; juveniles COM CON

BACON, Roger, 1214?-94, English; nonfiction BRO KB SA ST

BACON, Wallace Alger, 1914- , American; nonfiction CON

BACOTE, Clarence Albert, 1906- , American; nonfiction CON

'BACOVIA, Gheorghe' (Gheorghe Vasiliu), 1881-1957, Rumanian; poetry FLE ST

BACQUEVILLE de la POTERIE, Claude Charles, 1663-1736, French; nonfiction DIL

BACQUIE, Sophie, French; nonfiction DIL

BACQUILIDES see BAQUILIDES

BACQUOI-GUEDON, Alexis, fl. 1766-97, French; nonfiction DIL

BACULARD d'ARNAUD, François Thomas de, 1718-1805, French; plays, fiction HAR ST

BADAJENA, Brajanath, 1730-95, Indian; poetry LAN

BADALIC, Hugo, 1851-1900, Croatian; poetry ST

BADAONI, Abdul Kadir, 1540- , Indian; nonfiction ST

BADASH, Lawrence, 1934- , American; nonfiction CON

BADE, Josse (Ascensius), 1462-

1535, Belgian; nonfiction ST
BADEN-POWELL, Lord Robert,
1857-1941, English; juveniles
DOY
BADGER, Ralph Eastman, 1890- ,
American; nonfiction CON
BADGLEY, John, 1930, American;
nonfiction CON
BADIA, Antonio M., 1920- ,
Spanish; nonfiction BL
BADIAN, Ernst, 1925- , American;
nonfiction CON
BADRI-AZ-ZAMAN see HAMADHANI
BADIER, Jean Etienne, 1650-1719,
French; nonfiction DIL
BADIO, Iodoco (Joseph), 1462-1535,
Belgian; poetry SA
BADON, Jean Isaac, 1719- , French;
nonfiction DIL
BADONICUS see GILDAS
BADOS, Jean Placide, 1711-68,
French; translations DIL
BADOSA, Enrique, 1927- , Spanish;
poetry, translations SA
BADURA-SKODA, Eva, 1929- ,
German-American; nonfiction
CON
BÄCKSTRÖM, Per Johan Edvard,
1841-86, Swedish; poetry, criti-
cism, plays ST
BAEDA see BEDE
BAEKELMANS, Lode, 1879- ,
Flemish; fiction, essays, plays
ST
BAENA, Antonio Ladislao Monteiro,
-1859, Portuguese; nonfiction
SA
BAENA, Juan Alfonso de, fl. 1410-
45, Spanish; anthologist, poetry
BL HAR SA ST
BAER, Daniel Joseph, 1929- ,
American; nonfiction CON
BAER, Eleanora Agnes, 1907- ,
American; nonfiction CON
BAER, Frédéric Charles, 1719-97,
French; nonfiction DIL
BAER, Gabriel, 1919- , German;
nonfiction CON
BAER, George Webster, 1935- ,
American; nonfiction CON
BAIER, Jean L., American; fiction
CON
BAER, Max Frank, 1912- , Amer-
ican; nonfiction CON
BAER, Werner, 1931- , German;
nonfiction CON
BAERG, Harry John, 1909- ,

American; fiction CON
BAERLE, Kasper van, 1584-1648,
Dutch; poetry HAR ST
BAERMANN, Jürgen Niklas,
1785-1850, German; plays
ST
BAERT, François, 1651-1719,
French; nonfiction DIL
BAERT du HOLLAND, Alexandre
Balthasar, 1750-1825, French;
nonfiction DIL
'BAERTMAEKER, Jan de' see
SMEKEN, Jan
BAERWALD, Hans Herman,
1927- , American; nonfiction
CON
BÄTE, Ludwig, 1892- , German;
nonfiction AL
BAETZHOLD, Howard George,
1923- , American; nonfiction
CON
BÄUMER, Gertrud, 1873- ,
German; nonfiction KU
BAEZ, Cecilio, 1862- , Para-
guayan; nonfiction SA
BAEZ, Joan, 1941- , American;
nonfiction CON
BAEZ, Nolo see OTERO VERTIZ,
Gustavo A.
BAEZ, Pulino G., 1895- ,
Cuban; journalism MIN
BAEZA, Fernando, 1920- ,
Spanish; fiction BL
BAEZA, Ricardo, 1890-1956,
Cuban; journalism, translations
BL MIN SA
'BAGARAG, Shibli' see LAWLOR,
Patrick A.
BAGARD, Henry, 1663-1709,
French; nonfiction DIL
'BAGATELLE' see BAGOT, A.G.
'BAGBY, George' see STEIN,
Aaron M.
BAGBY, George William, 1828-
83, American; fiction KAA
BAGBY, Wesley Marvin, 1922- ,
American; nonfiction CON
BAGDIKIAN, Ben Haig, 1920- ,
American; nonfiction CON
BAGE, Robert, 1728-1801, Eng-
lish; fiction BRO KB ST
BAGEHOT, Walter, 1826-77, Eng-
lish; nonfiction, criticism
BRO KBA ST
BAGGALEY, Andrew Robert,
1923- , American; nonfiction
CON

BAGGER, Carl Christian, 1807-46,
Danish; poetry, fiction ST
BAGGER, Eugene, 1892- , Hungar-
ian; nonfiction HOE
BAGGESEN, Jens Immanuel, 1764-
1826, Danish; poetry, nonfiction
HAR KE SA ST
BAGLEY, Desmond, 1923- , Eng-
lish; fiction CON
BAGLEY, John Joseph, 1908- ,
English; nonfiction CON
BAGNO, Pannuccio del, 1250-1300,
Italian; poetry ST
BAGNOLD, Enid ('Lady of Quality'),
1889- , English; juveniles,
plays, fiction BRO COM CON
DOY KT MAT RIC WA
BAGOT A.G. ('Bagatelle'), 1830- ,
English; nonfiction HIG
BAGREIEV SPERANSKY, Isabel de,
1799-1857, Russian; nonfiction
SA
BAGRIANA, Eliaveta, 1893- ,
Bulgarian; poetry ST
'BAGRITSKY, Eduard' (Eduard
Dzyubin; Dzhubin), 1897-1934,
Russian; poetry COL FLE HAR
HARK SA ST
'BAGRYNOWSKI, Sirko O.' see
SIEROSZEWSKI, W.
'BAGSTER, Hubert' see TRUMPER,
Hubert B.
BAGWELL, Philip Sidney, 1914- ,
English; nonfiction CON
BAGWELL, William Francis, Jr.,
1923- , American; nonfiction
CON
BAHA u'llah, Mirza Husain Ali,
1817-92, Persian; nonfiction SA
ST
BAHADUR Shah II, 1837-58, Persian;
poetry ST
'BAHAR, Muhammed Taqi' (Malik al-
Shu'Ara), 1886-1951, Persian;
poetry LAN SA ST
BAHDANOVICH, Maxim (Bogdanovich),
1891-1917, Russian; poetry
HARK
BAHITHAT-al-BADIYAH see HIFNI
NASIF, Malak
BAHL, Roy W., Jr., 1939- ,
American; nonfiction CON
BAHLKE, George Wilbon, 1934- ,
American; nonfiction CON
BAHM, Archie John, 1907- , Amer-
ican; nonfiction CON
BAHN, Eugene, 1906- , American;

nonfiction CON
BAHN, Margaret Elizabeth Linton,
1907-69, Scots; juveniles
CON
BAHR, Erhard, 1932- , German-
American; nonfiction CON
BAHR, Hermann, 1863-1934,
Austrian; plays, criticism,
nonfiction AL COL FLE HAR
KU MAT SA ST
BAHR, Howard M., 1938- ,
American; nonfiction CON
BAHR, Jerome, 1909- , Ameri-
can; fiction CON
BAHREY, fl. 1565-97, Ethiopian;
nonfiction LAN
BAHYA, Ibn Paquda (Bahya ben
Joseph), fl. 1040, Spanish-
Jewish; poetry HAR KE ST
BAIA, Jerónimo, 17th cent.,
Portuguese; poetry ST
BAÏF, Jean Antoine de, 1532-89,
French; poetry DIF HAR KE
MAL SA ST
BAÏF, Lazare de, 1496-1547,
French; translations ST
BAIERL, Helmut, 1926- , Ger-
man; nonfiction AL
BAIG BAÑOS, Aurelio, 1873-
1933?, Cuban; journalism,
poetry SA
BAILEY, Alfred Goldsworthy ('Susan
Clayton'), 1905- , Canadian;
nonfiction CON MUR SY
BAILEY, Alice Cooper, 1890- ,
American; nonfiction CON
BAILEY, Anthony, 1933- ,
American; nonfiction CON
BAILEY, Bernadine Freeman,
1901- , American; juveniles
CON HOO WA
BAILEY, Carolyn Sherwin, 1875- ,
American; juveniles KJU WA
BAILEY, Charles Waldo II,
1929- , American; nonfiction,
fiction CON
BAILEY, David Roy Shackleton
('D.R. Shackleton Bailey'),
1917- , English; nonfiction
CON
BAILEY, Derrick Sherwin, 1910- ,
English; nonfiction CON
BAILEY, Dudley, 1918- , Amer-
ican; nonfiction CON
BAILEY, Ebenezer, 1795-1839,
American; nonfiction KAA
BAILEY, Eric, 1933- , English;

fiction CON

BAILEY, Flora, American; juveniles
WA

BAILEY, Frederick George, 1924- ,
English; nonfiction CON

BAILEY, Frederick Marshman,
1882- , English; nonfiction
CON

BAILEY, George, 1919- , American; nonfiction CON

BAILEY, Gerald Earl, 1929- ,
American; fiction CON

BAILEY, Harry Augustine, Jr.,
1932- , American; nonfiction
CON

BAILEY, Helen Miller, 1909- ,
American; nonfiction CON

BAILEY, Henry Christopher, 1878-
1961, English; fiction BRO KT

BAILEY, Hugh Coleman, 1929- ,
American; nonfiction CON

BAILEY, James Montgomery, 1841-
94, American; fiction KAA

BAILEY, James Osler, 1903- ,
American; nonfiction CON

BAILEY, Joan Hauser, 1922- ,
American; nonfiction CON

BAILEY, Joe Allen, 1929- , American; nonfiction CON

BAILEY, John, American; juveniles
WA

BAILEY, John Amedee, 1929- ,
American; nonfiction CON

BAILEY, Kenneth Kyle, 1923- ,
American; nonfiction CON

'BAILEY, Matilda' see RADFORD,
Ruby L.

BAILEY, Nathan (Nathaniel), -1742,
English; nonfiction KB

BAILEY, Norman Alishan, 1931- ,
American; nonfiction CON

BAILEY, Paul, 1937- , English;
fiction CON

BAILEY, Paul Dayton, 1906- ,
American; fiction, nonfiction
CON

BAILEY, Philip James, 1816-1902,
English; poetry BRO KBA ST

BAILEY, Ralph Edgar, 1893- ,
American; nonfiction, juveniles
CON

BAILEY, Richard Weld, 1939- ,
American; nonfiction CON

BAILEY, Stephen Kemp, 1916- ,
American; nonfiction CON

BAILEY, Temple, 188?-1953, American; fiction KT

BAILEY, Thomas Andrew, 1902- ,
American; nonfiction CON

BAILIE, Victoria Worley, 1894- ,
American; nonfiction CON

BAILKEY, Nels Martin, 1911- ,
American; nonfiction CON

BAILLARGEON, Pierre, 1916- ,
Canadian; fiction, poetry SY

BAILLET, Adrien, 1649-1706,
French; criticism HAR

BAILLET, Louis Guillaume, 18th
cent., French; nonfiction DIL

BAILLEY, Pierre, 1680-1762,
French; nonfiction DIL

BAILLIE, Lady Grisell (Grizel),
1665-1746, English; poetry
BRO KB ST

BAILLIE, Joanna, 1762-1851,
Scots; plays, poetry BRO
KBA SA ST

BAILLIE, Robert, 1599-1622, English; nonfiction, diary BRO
KB

BAILLIE-GROHMAN, William A.,
1851-1921, English; nonfiction
HIG

BAILLIVET, Jean see BALLIVET,
Jean

BAILLON, André, 1875-1932,
Belgian; fiction DIF

BAILLY, Jaques, 1701-69, French;
plays DIL

BAILLY, Jean Sylvain, 1736-93,
French; nonfiction DIL SA

BAILLY, Louis, 1730-1808,
French; nonfiction DIL

BAILLY, Nicolas (Baillif), 1726-
81, French; nonfiction DIL

BAILLY du ROLLET see DUROLLET

BAILY, Leslie, 1906- , English;
nonfiction CON

BAILY, Nathan A., 1920- ,
American; nonfiction CON

BAILY, Samuel Longstreth, 1936- ,
American; nonfiction CON

BAIN, Alexander, 1818-1903, Scots;
nonfiction BRO KBA SA ST

BAIN, Chester Arthur, 1912- ,
American; nonfiction CON

BAIN, Edward Ustick, American;
juveniles WA

BAIN, Joe S., 1912- , American;
nonfiction CON

BAIN, Willard S., Jr., 1938- ,
American; fiction CON

BAINBRIDGE, Beryl, 1933- ,
English; nonfiction CON

BAINBRIDGE, Geoffrey, 1923- ,
English; fiction CON
BAINBRIDGE, John, 1913- ,
American; nonfiction CON
BAINES, Anthony Cuthbert, 1912- ,
English; nonfiction CON
BAINTON, Roland H., 1894- ,
English-American; nonfiction,
translations CON
BAINVILLE, Charles, -1745,
French; poetry DIL
BAINVILLE, Jacques, 1879-1936,
French; nonfiction COL DIF SA
BAIRD, Albert Craig, 1883- ,
American; nonfiction CON
BAIRD, Alexander John, 1925- ,
English; fiction, nonfiction,
poetry CON MUR
BAIRD, Forrest J., 1905- , Amer-
ican; nonfiction CON
BAIRD, Henry Martin, 1832-1906,
American; nonfiction KAA
BAIRD, Jesse Hays, 1889- , Amer-
ican; nonfiction CON
BAIRD, John Edward, 1922- ,
American; nonfiction CON
BAIRD, Joseph Armstrong, Jr.,
1922- , American; nonfiction
CON
BAIRD, Joseph Arthur, 1922- ,
American; nonfiction CON
BAIRD, Russell N., 1922- , Amer-
ican; nonfiction CON
BAIRD, William Robb, 1924- ,
American; nonfiction CON
BAITELLI, Angélica, 1600-70,
Italian; nonfiction SA
BAITY, Elizabeth Chesley, 1907- ,
American; juveniles, nonfiction
COM CON FUL JO
BAJANSKY, Svetozar Hurban, 1847-
1916, Slovak; journalism, poetry,
fiction SA
BAJARLIA, Juan Jacobo, 1914- ,
Argentinian; poetry, criticism,
essays MIN SA
BAJEMA, Carl Jay, 1937- ,
American; nonfiction CON
BAJOV, Pavel, 1883- , Russian;
essays, fiction SA
BAJZA, Jóssef Ignac, 1755-1836,
Slovak; fiction HAR ST
BAKAL, Carl, 1918- , American;
nonfiction CON
BAKALOV see TSERKOVSKI, Tsanko
BAKAN, David, 1921- , American;
nonfiction CON

BAKAN, Paul, 1928- , Ameri-
can; nonfiction CON
BAKELESS, John Edwin, 1894- ,
American; nonfiction, juven-
iles CON KT WA
BAKELESS, Katherine Little,
1895- , American; nonfiction,
plays CON
BAKER, Alton Wesley, 1912- ,
American; nonfiction CON
BAKER, Augusta, 1911- , Amer-
ican; nonfiction CON
BAKER, Benjamin, 1818-90,
American; plays KAA
BAKER, Benjamin, 1915- ,
American; nonfiction CON
'BAKER, Betty' see VENTURO,
Betty L. B.
BAKER, Betty Doreen Flock
('Elizabeth Renier'), 1916- ,
English; fiction CON
BAKER, Carlos Heard, 1909- ,
American; nonfiction CON
BAKER, Charlotte, 1910- ,
American; juveniles, fiction
COM CON WA
BAKER, Denys Val, 1917- ,
English; fiction, nonfiction
CON
BAKER, Donald Gene, 1932- ,
American; nonfiction CON
BAKER, Donald Noel, 1936- ,
Canadian; nonfiction CON
BAKER, Dorothy Dodds, 1907-68,
American; fiction CON KT
WAF
BAKER, Elizabeth Faulkner,
American; nonfiction CON
BAKER, Elsworth, F., 1903- ,
American; nonfiction CON
BAKER, Frank, 1908- , English;
fiction, plays KTS
BAKER, Frank Shaeffer, 1910- ,
American; nonfiction CON
BAKER, Gary, G., 1939- ,
American; nonfiction CON
BAKER, George Pierce, 1866-
1935, American; nonfiction
KT
BAKER, George Walter, 1915- ,
American; nonfiction CON
BAKER, Gladys, American; non-
fiction HO
BAKER, Gordon Pratt, 1910- ,
American; nonfiction CON
BAKER, Howard Wilson, 1905- ,
American; poetry, plays,

fiction CON MUR
BAKER, Hugh D.R., 1937- , English; nonfiction CON
BAKER, James Rupert, 1925- , American; nonfiction CON
BAKER, Jehu, 1822-1901, American; nonfiction HOO
BAKER, John Alec, 1926- , English; fiction CON
BAKER, John Henry, 1936- , American; nonfiction CON
BAKER, John Roger, 1934- , English; nonfiction CON
BAKER, Joseph Ellis, 1905- , American; nonfiction CON
BAKER, Laura Nelson, 1911- , American; juveniles, fiction CON WA
BAKER, Lawrence Manning, 1907- , American; nonfiction CON
BAKER, Leonard, 1931- , American; nonfiction CON
BAKER, Letha Elizabeth Mitts, 1913- , American; fiction CON
BAKER, Liva, 1930- , American; juveniles CON
BAKER, Louise Maxwell, 1909- , American; fiction WAF
BAKER, Margaret, 1890- , English; juveniles CON KJU
BAKER, Margaret J., 1918- , English; juveniles CON FUL WA
BAKER, Mary, 1897- , English; juveniles KJU
BAKER, Mary Elizabeth Gillette, 1923- , American; juveniles CON
BAKER, Mary Gladys ('Sheila Stuart'), 1892- , Scots; juveniles CON
BAKER, Nelson Blaisdell, 1905- , American; nonfiction CON
BAKER, Nina Brown, 1888-1957, American; juveniles KJU WA
BAKER, Olaf, English; juveniles KJU
BAKER, Paul R., 1927- , American; nonfiction CON
BAKER, Paul Thornell, 1927- , American; nonfiction CON
BAKER, Pearl Biddlecome, 1907- , American; nonfiction CON
BAKER, Peter Gordon, 1928- , English; fiction CON
BAKER, Rachel Mininberg, 1903/04- , American; juveniles COM CON FUL WA
BAKER, Ray Stannard ('David Grayson'), 1870-1946, American;

journalism, nonfiction, essays BRO KAT KT RIC
BAKER, Sir Richard, 1568?-1645, English; nonfiction BRO ST
BAKER, Richard M., Jr., 1924- , American; nonfiction CON
BAKER, Richard St. Barbe, 1889- , English; nonfiction CON
BAKER, Richard Terrill, 1913- , American; nonfiction CON
BAKER, Robert Michael Graham, 1938- , English; fiction CON
BAKER, Robin Campbell, 1941- , English; nonfiction CON
BAKER, Ronald James, 1924- , English; nonfiction CON
BAKER, Ross Kenneth, 1938- , American; nonfiction CON
BAKER, Samm Sinclair, 1909- , American; nonfiction CON
BAKER, Sir Samuel White, 1821-93, English; nonfiction BRO KBA
BAKER, Sheridan Warner, Jr., 1918- , American; nonfiction CON
BAKER, Stephen, 1921- , American; nonfiction CON
BAKER, Thomas, 1656-1740, English; nonfiction ST
BAKER, Thomas Francis Timothy, 1935- , English; nonfiction CON
BAKER, Thomas Harrison, 1933- , American; nonfiction CON
BAKER, Wesley C., American; nonfiction CON
BAKER, William Avery, 1911- , American; nonfiction CON
BAKER, William C., 1891- , American; juveniles WA
BAKER, William Edwin, 1935- , American; nonfiction CON
'BAKER, William Howard' see McNEILLY, Wilfred G.
BAKER, William Mumford ('George F. Harrington'), 1825-83, American; nonfiction KAA
BAKEWELL, Paul, Jr., 1889- , American; nonfiction CON
BAKHUIZEN van den BRINK, Reinier Cornelis, 1810-65, Dutch; criticism ST
BAKI, 1526-1600, Turkish; poetry LAN SA ST
BAKIN KYOKUTEI' (Takizawa

Okikuni; Takizawa Tokuru),
1767-1848, Japanese; fiction
LAN SA ST
BAKKE, Mary Sterling, 1904- ,
American; nonfiction CON
BAKKER, Nina Dikeman, American;
poetry HIL
BAKLANOFF, Eric N., 1925- ,
Austrian-American; nonfiction
CON
BAKUNIN, Mikail Aleksandrovich,
1814-76, Russian; nonfiction
HARK KE ST
BAKWIN, Harry, 1894- , American;
nonfiction CON
BAKWIN, Ruth Morris, 1898- ,
American; nonfiction CON
BALABKINS, Nicholas, 1926- ,
American; nonfiction CON
'BALAGUER, Joaquín', 1906- ,
Dominican; poetry, journalism,
criticism SA
BALAGUER, Victor, 1824-1901,
Spanish; plays, poetry BL HAR
SA ST
BALAMI, Muhammad, Abu Ali,
-974?, Persian; nonfiction
ST
BALARAM, Das, 16th cent., Indian;
poetry LAN
BALARD, Albi, 1760- , French;
poetry SA
BALART, Federico, 1831-1905,
Spanish; poetry, criticism BL
COL SA
BALAS, David Laszlo, 1929- ,
Hungarian-American; fiction CON
BALASSA, Bálint, 1554-94, Hungarian;
poetry HAR ST
BALASSA, Bela, 1928- , Hungarian-
American; nonfiction CON
BALBI, Girolamo, 1451?-1535,
Italian; nonfiction SA ST
BALBIN, Bohuslav, 1621-88, Czech;
poetry ST
BALBIN LUCAS, Rafael de, 1910- ,
Spanish; fiction, poetry BL SA
BALBO, Cesare, 1789-1853, Italian;
nonfiction ST
BALBO, Lucio Cornelio, 1st cent.,
Roman; nonfiction SA
BALBONTIN, José Antonio, 1895- ,
Spanish-English; poetry, plays
CON
BALBUENA, Bernardo de (Valbuena),
1568-1627, Spanish; poetry,
fiction BL HAR SA ST

BALBULUS, N. see NOTKER
d. der STAMMLER
'BALBUS' see HUXLEY, Sir Julian
S.
BALCARCE, Florencio, 1818-39,
Argentinian; poetry MIN SA
BALCESCU, Niculai, 1819-52,
Rumanian; nonfiction SA ST
BALCH, Glenn, 1902- , American;
juveniles, fiction CON
FUL PAC WA
BALCHIN, Nigel Marlin ('Mark
Spade'), 1908-70, English;
fiction BRO KTS RIC
BALCOMB, Raymond, E., 1923- ,
American; nonfiction CON
BALD, Frederick Clever, 1897- ,
American; nonfiction CON
BALD, Robert Cecil, 1901-65,
Australian; nonfiction CON
BALDANZA, Frank, 1924- ,
American; nonfiction CON
BALDE, Jakob, 1604-68, German;
poetry, plays AL HAR ST
BALDENSPERGER, Fernand
('Fernand Baldenne'), 1871- ,
French; nonfiction COL SA
BALDERICO, 1097-1112, French;
nonfiction SA
BALDERSON, Margaret, Australian;
juveniles CON
BALDERSTON, John Lloyd, 1889-
1954, American; plays MAT
BALDI, Bernardino, 1553-1617,
Italian; poetry HAR ST
BALDINGER, Stanley, 1932- ,
American; nonfiction CON
BALDINGER, Wallace Spencer,
1905- , American; nonfiction
CON
BALDINI, Antonio, 1889-1962,
Italian; fiction, criticism
COL FLE SA ST
BALDRIDGE, Letitia Katherine,
American; nonfiction CON
BALDRY, Harold Caparne,
1907- , American; nonfiction
CON
BALDUCCI, Carolyn, 1946- ,
American; nonfiction CON
BALDUCCI, Ernesto, 1922- ,
Italian; nonfiction CON
BALDUINO, Jean, 1590-1650,
French; nonfiction SA
BALDUINO de CONDE, 13th cent.,
French; poetry SA
BALDWIN, Anne Norris, 1938- ,

American; juveniles CON

BALDWIN, Arthur H., American;
juveniles WA

'BALDWIN, Bates' see JENNINGS,
John E., Jr.

BALDWIN, Charles Sears, 1867-
1935, American; nonfiction HOE

BALDWIN, David, A., 1936- ,
American; nonfiction CON

BALDWIN, Ewart Merlin, 1915- ,
American; nonfiction PAC

BALDWIN, Faith, 1893- , American; fiction CON KT WAF

BALDWIN, Gordon C. ('Gordo
Baldwin'; 'Lew Gordon'), 1908- ,
American; nonfiction CON

BALDWIN, Hanson Weightman, 1903- ,
American; journalism KTS

BALDWIN, James, 1841-1925, American; juveniles KJU WA

BALDWIN, James Arthur, 1924- ,
American; plays, fiction, nonfiction CON FLE MAT RIC

BALDWIN, Joseph Glover, 1815-64,
American; nonfiction KAA

BALDWIN, Michael ('Michael Jesse'),
1930- , English; poetry, nonfiction CON

BALDWIN, William, fl. 1547-60,
English; poetry ST

BALDWIN, William Lee, 1928- ,
American; nonfiction CON

BALE, John, 1495-1563, English;
plays BRO KB MAG ST

BALE, Robert Osborne, 1912- ,
American; nonfiction CON

BALES, James David, 1915- ,
American; nonfiction CON

BALES, William Alan, 1917- ,
American; nonfiction CON

BALESTIER, Charles Wolcott, 1861-
91, American; nonfiction KAA

BALET, Jan B., 1913- , German-
American; juveniles WA

BALETTI, Hélèn Virginie Riccoboni,
1686-1771, French; plays DIL

BALEXERT, Jacques (Ballexserd),
1726-74, French; nonfiction DIL

BALEY, James A., 1918- , American; nonfiction CON

BALFOUR, Arthur James, 1848-
1930, English; nonfiction BRO
KT SA ST

BALFOUR, Francis Maitland, 1851-
82, Scots; nonfiction KBA

BALFOUR, James, 1925- , English;
fiction CON

BALFOUR, Michael Leonard
Graham, 1908- , English;
nonfiction CON

'BALFOUR, Patrick' see KINROSS,
Patrick

BALFOUR-KINNEAR, George
Purvis Russell, 1888- ,
Scots; nonfiction CON

BALIGH, Helmy H., 1931- ,
Egyptian-American; nonfiction
CON

BALIKCI, Asen, 1929- , Turkish-
Canadian; nonfiction CON

BALINKY, Alexander, 1919- ,
American; nonfiction CON

BALINSKI, Stanislaw, 1898- ,
Polish; poetry COL SA ST

BALINT, Michael, 1896- , English; nonfiction CON

BALK, Alfred, 1930- , American; nonfiction CON

BALL, Brian Neville ('Brian
Kinsey-Jones'), 1932- ,
English; fiction, juveniles CON

BALL, DORIS Bell Collier
('Josephine Bell'), 1897- ,
English; fiction, nonfiction
CON

BALL, F. Carlton, 1911- ,
American; nonfiction CON

BALL, George Wildman, 1909- ,
American; nonfiction CON

BALL, Howard, 1937- , American;
nonfiction CON

BALL, Hugo, 1886-1927, German;
plays, fiction, essays FLE
KU

BALL, Jane Eklund, 1921- ,
American; fiction CON

BALL, John Dudley, Jr., 1911- ,
American; nonfiction, fiction,
juveniles CON WA

BALL, John C., 1924- , American; nonfiction CON

BALL, John Miller, 1923- ,
American; nonfiction CON

BALL, Joseph H., 1905- ,
American; nonfiction CON

BALL, Kurt Herwarth ('Jochim
Dreetz'), 1903- , German;
fiction AL

BALL, Mary Margaret, 1909- ,
American; nonfiction CON

BALL, Nelson, 1942- , Canadian;
poetry MUR

BALL, Richard Francis, 1860- ,
English; nonfiction HIG

BALL, Robert Hamilton, 1902- ,
American; nonfiction CON
BALL, Sir Robert Stawell, 1840-
1913, Irish; nonfiction BRO KBA
'BALL, Zachary' see MASTERS,
Kelly R.
BALLAGAS, Emilio, 1908/10-54,
Cuban; poetry MIN SA
BALLANCHE, Pierre Simon, 1776-
1847, French; nonfiction DIF
SA
BALLANTINE, James, 1808-77,
Scots; poetry, nonfiction BRO
KBA
BALLANTYNE, David Watt, 1924- ,
New Zealander; fiction RIC ST
BALLANTYNE, Dorothy Joan Smith,
1922- , English; nonfiction
CON
BALLANTYNE, Robert Michael,
1825-94, English; juveniles BRO
DOY ST
BALLARD, Charles Martin, 1929- ,
English; juveniles COM CON
'BALLARD, Dean' see WILKES-
HUNTER, Richard
BALLARD, Edward Goodwin, 1910- ,
American; nonfiction CON
BALLARD, James Graham, 1930- ,
English; fiction CON RIC
BALLARD, Joan Kadey, 1928- ,
American; juveniles CON
BALLARD, Lowell Clyne, 1904- ,
American; nonfiction CON
'BALLARD, K.G.' see ROTH, Holly
BALLARD, Willis Todhunter ('Brian
Agar'; 'P.D. Ballard'; 'Parker
Bonner'; 'Sam Bowie'; 'Hunter
Allard'; 'Harrison Hunt'; 'John
Hunter'; 'Neil MacNeil'; 'John
Shepherd'), 1903- , American;
fiction CON
BALLARD d' INVILLIERS, Charles
François, 1711-71, French; non-
fiction DIL
BALLENGER, Raymond, A., 1907- ,
American; nonfiction CON
BALLESTER NICOLAS, José, 1891- ,
Spanish; poetry, fiction SA
BALLESTEROS GAIBROIS, Manuel,
1911- , Spanish; criticism,
essays SA
BALLESTEROS, Mercedes, 1913- ,
Spanish; plays BL SA
BALLESTEROS BERETTA, Antonio,
1880-1949, Spanish; nonfiction
BL SA

BALLESTEROS LARRAIN, Juan,
Chilean; poetry MIN
BALLET, François, 1702- ,
French; nonfiction DIL
BALLEXSERD see BALEXERT,
Jacques
BALL-HENNINGS, Emmy, 1885-
1948, German; fiction KU
BALLIERE de LAISEMENT,
Charles Louis Denis, 1729-
1800, French; fiction DIL
BALLIETT, Whitney, 1926- ,
American; nonfiction CON
BALLIN, Caroline, American;
fiction CON
BALLINGER, Harry Russell,
1892- , American; nonfiction
CON
BALLINGER, James Lawrence,
1919- , American; nonfiction
CON
BALLINGER, Louis Bowen,
1909- , American; nonfiction
CON
'BALLINGER, William A.' see
McNEILLY, Wilfred G.
BALLINGER, William Sanborn
(Bill S. Ballinger, 'Frederic
Freyer'; 'B.X. Sanborn'),
1912- , American; fiction,
movies CON
BALLIVET, Jean (Baillivet), 1652-
1734, French; nonfiction DIL
BALLIVIAN, Manuel Vicente, 1848-
1921, Bolivian; nonfiction MIN
BALLIVIAN, Rafael, 1897- ,
Bolivian; nonfiction, poetry
MIN
BALLON, Louise Blanche Thérèse
Perrucard de, 1591-1668,
French; nonfiction SA
BALLOU, Adin, 1803-90, American;
nonfiction KAA
BALLOU, Arthur W., 1915- ,
American; fiction CON
BALLOU, Ellen Bartlett, 1905- ,
American; nonfiction CON
BALLOU, Maturin Murray ('Lieut.
Murray'), 1820-95, American;
journalism, nonfiction KAA
BALLOWE, James, 1933- ,
American; nonfiction CON
BALMA, Michael James, 1930- ,
American; nonfiction CON
BALMASEDA, Francisco Javier,
1833-1907, Cuban; journalism,
fiction, plays MIN

BALMES URPIA, Jaime Luciano, 1810-48, Spanish; nonfiction BL HAR KE SA ST

BALMONT, Konstantin Dmitrievich, 1867-1943, Russian; poetry, essays COL FLE HAR HARK SA ST

BALOGH, Penelope, 1916- , English; juveniles COM CON

BALOT de SOVOT, -1761, French; plays DIL

BALSDON, John Percy Vyvian Dacre ('Dacre Balsdon'), 1901- , English; nonfiction, fiction CON

BALSEIRO, José Agustín, 1900- , Puerto Rican; poetry, fiction, criticism BL SA

BALSLEY, Howard Lloyd, 1913- , American; nonfiction CON

BALSLEY, Irol Whitmore, 1912- , American; nonfiction CON

BALTAZAR, Eulalio R., 1925- , American; nonfiction CON

BALTEFERRI AMMANNATI, Luisa, 1513-89, Italian; poetry SA

BALTERMAN, Marcia Ridlon, 1942- , American; juveniles, poetry CON

'BALTRUSHAITIS, Jurgis' (Yuri Kazimirovich), 1893-1945, Russian; poetry FLE HARK ST

BALTUS, Jean François, 1667-1742, French; nonfiction DIL

BALTZ, Howard Burl, 1930- , American; nonfiction CON

BALTZELL, Edward Digby, 1915- , American; nonfiction CON

BALUCKI, Michal ('Elpidon'; 'Zalega'), 1837-1901, Polish; plays, fiction COL MAT SA ST

BALUZE, Etienne, 1631-1718, French; nonfiction SA

BALY, Alfred Denis, 1913- , English; nonfiction CON

BALZAC, Honoré de, 1799-1850, French; fiction, plays DIF HAR KE MAG MAL SA ST

BALZAC, Jean Louis Guez de, 1595/97-1654, French; nonfiction, poetry DIF HAR SA ST

BALZANO, Jeanne Koppel ('Gina Bell'; 'Gina Bell-Zano'), 1912- , American; juveniles CON

BALZE, J. (Nicolas?), 1733/35-92, French; poetry DIL

BAMBARA, Toni Cade, American; nonfiction CON

BAMBERGER, Bernard Jacob, 1904- , American; nonfiction CON

BAMBERGER, Carl, 1902- , Austrian-American; nonfiction CON

'BAMM, Peter' (Curt Emmrich), 1897- , German; essays, criticism CON FLE KU

BAMMAN, Henry A., 1918- , American; nonfiction CON

BAN, Joseph Daniel, 1926- , American; nonfiction CON

BAN, Matija, 1818-1903, Serbian; poetry, plays SA ST

BAN, Thomas A., 1929- , Hungarian-Canadian; nonfiction CON

BANA, Sanskrit; nonfiction ST

BANANI, Amin, 1926- , Irani-American; nonfiction CON

BANCES CANDAMO, Francisco Antonio de, 1662-1704/09, Spanish; poetry, plays BL HAR SA ST

BANCHS, Enrique, 1888- , Argentinian; poetry BL FLE MIN SA ST

BANCROFT, Caroline, 1900- , American; nonfiction CON

'BANCROFT, F.' (Frances Charlotte Slater), -1947, South African; fiction ST

BANCROFT, George, 1800-91, American; nonfiction BRO KAA SA ST

BANCROFT, Griffing, 1907- , American; nonfiction CON WA

BANCROFT, Hubert Howe, 1832- , American; nonfiction SA

BANCROFT, John, -1696, English; plays ST

'BANCROFT, Robert' see KIRSCH, Robert R.

BANCROFT, Thomas, -1658, English; poetry ST

BANDARANAIKE, Dias see GOONERATNE, Yasmine

BANDARRA, Gonzalo Aunes, 1500-56, Portuguese; poetry, plays SA

BANDAS, Rudolph G., 1896- , American; nonfiction HOE

BANDEIRA FILHO, Manuel Carneiro de Sousa, 1886-1968, Brazilian; poetry, essays, criticism, translations FLE RIC

BANDELIER, Adolph Francis Alphonse,
1840-1914, American; nonfiction
KAA
BANDELLO, Mateo, 1480?-1562,
Spanish; nonfiction BL HAR KE
SA ST
BANDER, Edward J., 1923- ,
American; nonfiction CON
BANDERA, Volodimir Nicholas,
1932- , Russian-American;
nonfiction CON
BANDETTINI-LANDUCCI, Teresa,
1756- , Italian; poetry SA
BANDIERA, Manuel, 1886- ,
Brazilian; poetry, criticism SA
ST
BANDINI, Albert R., 1882- , Italian-
American; nonfiction HOE
BANDMAN, Bertram, 1930- , Amer-
ican; nonfiction CON
BANDROWSKI, Juljusz (Kaden), 1885-
1945, Polish; fiction COL FLE
SA ST
BANDURA, Albert, 1925- , Amer-
ican; nonfiction CON
BANDURI, Anselme, 1671-1743,
French; nonfiction DIL
BANDY, Eugene Franklin, Jr.,
('Eugene Franklin'), 1914- ,
American; fiction CON
BANDY, William Thomas, 1903- ,
American; nonfiction CON
BANDYOPADHYAY, Bhabani Caran,
1787-1848, Indian; nonfiction
LAN
BANDYOPADHYAY, Krsnamohan,
1813-85, Indian; nonfiction, plays
LAN
BANER, Shulda Vanadis, 1897-1964,
American; fiction CON
BANERJI, Bibhuti Bhusan, 1894-
1950, Indian; fiction LAN
BANERJI, Ranan Bihari, 1928- ,
American; nonfiction CON
BANET, Doris Beatrice Robinson,
1925- , American; juveniles
CON
BAÑEZ, Domingo, 1528-1604, Spanish;
nonfiction BL
BANG, Herman Joachim, 1857-1912,
Danish; fiction, poetry, criticism
COL FLE HAR KT SA ST
BANGHAM, Mary Dickerson, 1896- ,
American; nonfiction CON
BANGS, Carl Oliver, 1922- , Amer-
ican; nonfiction CON
BANGS, John Kendrick, 1862-1922,

American; fiction KT
BANGS, Robert Babbit, 1914- ,
American; nonfiction CON
BANHAM, Peter Reyner, 1922- ,
English; nonfiction CON
BANIER, Antoine, 1673-1741,
French; nonfiction, translations
DIL
BANIM, John, 1798-1842/44,
Irish; fiction BRO KBA SA
ST
BANIM, Michael, 1796-1874,
Irish; fiction BRO KBA ST
'BANK-JENSEN, Thea' see
OTTESEN, Thea T.
BANKOWSKY, Richard James,
1928- , American; fiction
CON
BANKS, Arthur S., 1926- ,
American; nonfiction CON
BANKS, Fillmore, 1934- ,
American; nonfiction CON
BANKS, John Houston, 1911- ,
American; nonfiction CON
BANKS, James Albert, 1941- ,
American; nonfiction CON
BANKS, Lynne Reid, English;
fiction RIC
BANKS, Richard L., 1920- ,
American; nonfiction CON
BANKWITZ, Philip Charles Farwell,
1924- , American; nonfiction
CON
BANNATYNE, George, 1545-1608?,
Scots; nonfiction BRO
BANNATYNE, Richard -1605,
English; nonfiction BRO
BANNER, Hubert Stewart ('Vexil-
lum'), 1891-1964, English;
fiction, poetry CON
BANNERMAN, Helen Brodie Cowan,
1863-1946, Scots; juveniles
DOY
BANNERMAN, Helen Watson,
English; juveniles KJU
BANNING, Evelyn I., 1903- ,
American; nonfiction CON
BANNING, Margaret Culkin,
1891- , American; fiction
CON KT WAF
BANNISTER, Nathaniel Harrington,
-1847?, American; plays
KAA
BANNISTER, Robert Corwin, Jr.,
1935- , American; nonfiction
CON
BANNOCK, Graham, 1932- ,

English; nonfiction CON

BANNON, John Francis, 1905- ,
American; nonfiction, tv CON
HO

BANNON, Laura May -1963, American; juveniles CON FUL HIL
WA

'BANNON, Peter' see DURST, Paul

BANTA, Richard Elwell, 1904- ,
American; nonfiction CON

BANTLEMAN, Lawrence ('Lingam'),
1942- , Indian; poetry MUR

BANTOCK, Gavin Marcus August,
1939- , British; poetry CON
MUR

BANTOCK, Geoffrey Herman, 1914- ,
English; nonfiction CON

'BANTON, Cy' see NORWOOD, Victor
G.C.

BANTON, Michael Parker, 1926- ,
English; nonfiction CON

BANVILLE, Théodore de, 1823-91,
French; poetry COL DIF HAR
KE SA ST

BANY, Mary A., 1913- , American;
nonfiction CON

BANZ, George, 1928- , Swiss; nonfiction CON

BANZAN see KUMAZAWA BANZAN

BAOUR, Jean Florent, fl. 1767,
French; nonfiction, poetry DIL

BAOUR LORMIAN, Pierre Marie,
1770-1854, French; poetry,
plays HAR SA ST

BAPTISTA, Mariano, 1830/32-1907,
Bolivian; nonfiction MIN

BAPTISTE, Sister Mary of Good
Cousel, 1906- , American; nonfiction SCA

'BAPU' see KHARE, Narayan B.

BAQUERO, Gastón, 1916- , Cuban;
journalism, essays, poetry
MIN

BAQUERO GOYANES, Mariano,
1923- , Spanish; criticism BL
SA

BAQUILIDES (Bacquilides), 5th cent.
B.C., Greek; poetry SA

BAR, Hilarion de, 1643-1715, French;
nonfiction DIL

BAR, Jean de, 1700-67, French;
nonfiction DIL

BAR, Pierre Gabriel, 1752-90,
French; nonfiction DIL

BARA, Nicostrat, 1673-1720, French;
nonfiction DIL

BARABAS, Steven, 1904- , American; nonfiction CON

BARACK, Nathan A., 1913- ,
American; juveniles CON

BARACKMAN, Paul Freeman,
1894- , American; nonfiction
CON

BARAGUE, -1755, French;
poetry DIL

BARAHONA de SOTO, Luis,
1548-95, Spanish; poetry BL
HAR SA ST

BARAHONA VEGA, Clemente,
1863- , Chilean; journalism
MIN

BARAKOVIC, Juraj, 1549-1628,
Dalmatian; poetry HAR ST

BARAL, Robert, 1910- , American; nonfiction CON

BARALT, Luis A., 1892- ,
Cuban; plays, nonfiction SA

BARALT, Rafael María, 1810/19-
60, Venezuelan; poetry, nonfiction BL SA

BARANAUSKAS, Antanas (Baronas),
1835-1902, Lithuanian; poetry
SA ST

BARANOVICH, Lazar, 1620-93,
Russian; nonfiction ST

BARANTE, Aimable Guillaume
Prosper, 1782-1866, French;
nonfiction DIF

BARANTSEVICH, Kazimir
Stanislavovich, 1851-1927,
Russian; fiction HARK ST

BARANY, George, 1922- ,
Hungarian-American; nonfiction
CON

BARASCH, Frances K., 1928- ,
American; nonfiction CON

BARASH, Asher, 1889-1952,
Jewish; fiction LAN ST

BARASH, Meyer, 1916- ,
American; nonfiction CON

BARATASHVILI, Prince Nikoloz,
1817-45, Russian; poetry LAN

BARATTE, Jean, 1669-1753,
French; nonfiction DIL

BARATYN SKY, Evgeny Abramo-
vich (Boratynsky), 1800-44,
Russian; poetry HAR HARK
KE SA ST

BARAVI, 5th cent., Indian; poetry
SA

BARBA, Harry (Baron Mikan,
Ohon), 1922- , American;
fiction CON

BARBA, Jacob see OSORIO, Miguel
A.

'BARBADIÑO' (Luis Antonio de

Verney), 1713-92, Portuguese;
nonfiction BL ST
BARBARO, Dominick A., 1914- ,
American; nonfiction CON
BARBARO, Ermolao (Almoró), 1453-
93, Italian; nonfiction ST
BARBARO, Francesco, 1390-1454,
Italian; nonfiction ST
'BARBARY, James' see BEECHING,
Amy and Jack
BARBASH, Jack, 1910- , American;
nonfiction CON
BARBAULD, Anna Letitia Aikin,
1743-1825, English; juveniles,
poetry, criticism, fiction BRO
KBA SA ST
BARBAULT-ROYER, P.F., 18th
cent., French; nonfiction DIL
BARBAZ, Abraham Louis, 1770-
1833, Dutch; poetry, criticism,
plays, translations ST
BARBAZAN, Etienne, 1696-1770,
French; nonfiction DIL SA
BARBE, P. Philippe, 1723-92,
French; nonfiction DIL
BARBE, Walter Burke, 1926- ,
American; nonfiction CON
BARBE, Wren, 1913- , American;
nonfiction CON
BARBEAU, Charles Marius, 1883- ,
Canadian; nonfiction ST
BARBEAU, Victor, 1896- , Canadian;
nonfiction SY
BARBEAU de BOURG, Jacques, 1709-
79, French; nonfiction DIL
BARBEAU de la BRUYERE, Jean
Louis, 1710-81, French; non-
fiction DIL
BARBEGIERE, Jean Baptiste, 1723-
97, French; nonfiction DIL
'BARBELLION, W.N.P.' see CUM-
MINGS, Bruce
BARBER, Benjamin R., 1939- ,
American; nonfiction CON
BARBER, Charles Laurence, 1915- ,
English; nonfiction CON
BARBER, Elsie Oakes, 1914- ,
American; fiction WAF
BARBER, James David, 1930- ,
American; nonfiction CON
BARBER, John Warner, 1798-1885,
American; nonfiction KAA
BARBER, Margaret Fairless
('Michael Fairless'), 1869-1901,
English; nonfiction, essays BRO
KT
BARBER, Richard J., 1932- ,

American; nonfiction CON
BARBER, Richard William,
1941- , English; nonfiction
CON
BARBER, Willard Foster, 1909- ,
American; nonfiction CON
BARBER, William Henry, 1918- ,
English; translations, non-
fiction CON
BARBERA, Carmen, 1927- ,
Spanish; fiction SA
BARBERENA, Santiago Ignacio,
1850-1916, Salvadoran; non-
fiction, essays BL SA
BARBERINO, Andrea de, 1370?-
1430?, Italian; fiction HAR
ST
BARBERIS, Franco, 1905- ,
Swiss; nonfiction CON
BARBEY d'AUREVILLY, Jules
Amedee, 1808-89, French;
fiction COL DIF HAR KE
MAL SA ST
BARBEYRAC, Jean, 1674-1744,
French; nonfiction DIL
BARBI, Michele, 1867-1941,
Italian; criticism ST
BARBIER, Alexandre, 1741-1819,
French; nonfiction DIL
BARBIER, Edmond Jean François,
1689-1771, French; nonfiction
DIL
BARBIER, Henri Auguste, 1805-
82, French; poetry DIF HAR
KE SA ST
BARBIER, Marie Anne, 1670-1742,
French; nonfiction DIL SA
BARBIER d'AUCOUR, Jean, 1641-
94, French; nonfiction DIF
SA
BARBIERI, Francisco (Asenjo),
1823-94, Spanish; nonfiction
SA ST
BARBIERI, Giovanni Maria, 1519-
74, Italian; nonfiction HAR ST
BARBIERI, Vicente, 1903- ,
Argentinian; poetry, fiction,
journalism SA
BARBILIAN, Dan see 'BARBU,
Ion'
BARBLAN, Gudench, 1860-1916,
Raeto-Romansch; poetry ST
BARBOSA, Duarte,   -1521,
Portuguese, nonfiction SA
BARBOSA-BACELLAR, Antonio,
1610-63, Portuguese; poetry
SA

BARBOSA du BOCAGE, Manuel M.
see BOCAGE, Manuel M.
BARBOSA MACHADO, Diego, 1682-
1770, Portuguese; nonfiction SA
BARBOUR, Frances Martha, 1895- ,
American; nonfiction CON
BARBOUR, Hugh Stewart, 1921- ,
American; nonfiction CON
BARBOUR, Ian Graeme, 1923- ,
American; nonfiction CON
BARBOUR, James Murray, 1897- ,
American; nonfiction CON
BARBOUR, John, 1316/20-95, Scots;
poetry BRO KB ST
BARBOUR, Kenneth Michael, 1921- ,
American; nonfiction CON
BARBOUR, Nevill, 1895- , English;
nonfiction CON
BARBOUR, Philip Lemont, 1898- ,
American; nonfiction CON
BARBOUR, Ralph Henry, 1870-1944,
American; juveniles KJU WA
BARBOUR, Russell B., 1906- ,
American; nonfiction CON
'BARBU, Ion' (Dan Barbilian), 1895-
1961, Rumanian; poetry FLE ST
BARBUSSE, Henri, 1873-1935,
French; fiction, poetry COL
DIF FLE HAR KL KT MAG MAL
RIC SA ST
BARCHILON, Jacques, 1923- ,
American; nonfiction CON
BARC-IVAN, Július, Slovak; plays
ST
BARCK, Oscar Theodore, Jr.,
1912- , American; nonfiction
CON
BARCLAY, Alexander, 1475?-1552,
Scots; poetry BRO KB SA ST
BARCLAY, Barbara, 1938- , Amer-
ican; nonfiction CON
BARCLAY, Cyril Nelson, 1896- ,
English; nonfiction CON
BARCLAY, Florence Louisa Charles-
worth, 1862-1921, English;
fiction BRO KT RIC SA
BARCLAY, Harold B., 1924- ,
American; nonfiction CON
BARCLAY, Isobel see DOBELL,
Isabel M. B.
BARCLAY, John, 1582-1621, Eng-
lish; poetry, fiction BRO KB
MAG SA ST
BARCLAY, Major Maurice Edward,
1886- , English; nonfiction
HIG
BARCLAY, Robert, 1648-90, Scots;
nonfiction BRO

BARCLAY, Vera, 1893- ,
American; juveniles HO
BARCO CENTENERA, Martín de,
1536-1605, Argentinian;
poetry MIN SA
BARCOS, Arthus Timoléon, 18th
cent., French; nonfiction DIL
BARCUS, James Edgar, 1938- ,
American; nonfiction CON
BARD, Bernard, 1927- , Ameri-
can; nonfiction, juveniles
CON
BARD, Harry, 1906- , American;
nonfiction CON
BARD, Patti, 1935- , American;
nonfiction CON
BARDALOI, Rajanikant, 1867-1939,
Indian; fiction LAN
BARDE, Frederich Samuel, 1869-
1916, American; nonfiction
MAR
BARDECHE, Maurice, 1909- ,
French; essays, criticism
DIF
BARDEN, Leonard William,
1929- , American; nonfiction
CON
BARDENS, Dennis Conrad ('Conrad
Farel'; 'Julian Roberts'),
1911- , American; nonfiction
CON
BARDILI, Christoph Gottfried,
1761-1808, German; nonfiction
SA
BARDINET de BINTAR, 18th cent.,
French; plays DIL
BARDIS, Panos Demetrios, 1924- ,
Greek-American; fiction CON
'BARDO', Celtic; Poetry BL
BARDOS, Marie Dupuis, 1935- ,
American; fiction CON
BARDOU, Jean, 1729-1803, French;
nonfiction DIL
BARDOU-DUHAMEL, Charles
Louis, 18th cent., French;
nonfiction DIL
BARDSLEY, Cuthbert Killick
Norman, 1907- , English;
nonfiction CON
BARDWELL, George Eldred,
1924- , American; nonfiction
CON
BARDY, Rev. Gustave, 1881- ,
American; nonfiction HO
BAREA, Arturo, 1897-1957,
Spanish; fiction, criticism
BL HAR KTS RIC SA ST
BAREA, Juan Bautista, 1742-89,

Cuban; translations MIN
BARET, Paul, -1795, French;
plays, fiction DIL
BARETTI, Giuseppe Marc' Antonio,
1719-89, Anglo-Italian; nonfiction
HAR KE SA ST
BARFIELD, Owen ('G.A.L. Burgeon'),
1898- , English; nonfiction
CON
BARFOOT, Audrey Ilma, 1918-64,
English; nonfiction CON
BARGA, Andrés García de la see
'CORPUS BARGA'
BARGAR, Bradley Duffee, 1924- ,
American; nonfiction CON
BARGEBUHR, Frederick Perez,
1904- , German-American; non-
fiction CON
BARGELLINI, Piero, 1897- ,
Italian-American; nonfiction HO
SA
BARGEO, Pietro A. see ANGELI,
Pietro A.
BARGER, Harold, 1907- , American;
nonfiction CON
BARGONE, Charles see 'FARRERE,
Claude'
BARHAM, Richard Harris, 1788-
1845, English; fiction, poetry
BRO KBA SA ST
BARILE, Angelo, 1888- , Italian;
poetry, criticism SA
BARILLI, Bruno, 1880- , Italian;
nonfiction SA
BARING, Maurice, 1874-1945, Eng-
lish; fiction, essays, poetry
BRO FLE HOE KL KT RIC SA
ST
BARINGER, William Eldon, 1909- ,
American; nonfiction CON HOO
BARING-GOULD, Sabine, 1834-1924,
English; fiction, essays, hymns
BRO KBA
BARISH, Jonas A., 1922- , Amer-
ican; nonfiction CON
BARITZ, Loren, 1928- , American;
nonfiction CON
BARJA, César, 1892-1952, Spanish;
nonfiction BL SA
BARJAVEL, René, 1911- , French;
fiction DIC
BARK, William Carroll, 1908- ,
American; nonfiction CON
BARKAN, Elliott Robert, 1940- ,
American; nonfiction CON
BARKER, Arthur James ('Muskateer'),
1918- , English; nonfiction CON

BARKER, Audrey Lillian, 1818- ,
English; fiction CON KTS
BARKER, Charles M. Jr.,
1926- , American; nonfiction
CON
BARKER, Dennis Malcolm, 1929- ,
English; fiction CON
BARKER, Derek Roland, 1930- ,
American; nonfiction CON
BARKER, Dudley ('Lionel Black'),
1910- , English; fiction, non-
fiction CON
BARKER, Elsa McCormick,
1906- , American; fiction
CON
BARKER, Elver A. ('Carl B.
Harding'), 1920- , American;
nonfiction CON
BARKER, Eric, 1905- , Anglo-
American; poetry, nonfiction
CON MUR
BARKER, Sir Ernest, 1874-1960,
English; nonfiction BRO KTS
BARKER, Frank Granville,
1923- , English; nonfiction
CON
BARKER, George, 1913- , Eng-
lish; poetry, plays, fiction
FLE MUR RIC SP
BARKER, George Granville,
1913- , English; poetry, non-
fiction CON KTS
BARKER, Granville see GRAN-
VILLE-BARKER, Harley
BARKER, James Nelson, 1784-
1858, American; plays KAA
ST
BARKER, John Walton, Jr.,
1933- , American; nonfiction
CON
BARKER, Kathleen F., 1901- ,
English; nonfiction HIG
BARKER, Lillian, American; non-
fiction HOE
BARKER, Mary Anne, 1831-1911,
New Zealander, fiction ST
BARKER, Melvern, 1907- ,
American; nonfiction, juveniles
CON
BARKER, Myrtie Lillian, 1910- ,
American; nonfiction CON
BARKER, Ralph, 1917- , Eng-
lish; nonfiction CON
BARKER, Robert Lee, 1937- ,
American; nonfiction CON
BARKER, Roger Garlock, 1903- ,
American; nonfiction CON

BARKER, S. Omar ('Jose Canusi';
'Phil Squires'; 'Dan Scott'),
1894- , American; fiction CON
BARKER, Shirley Frances, 1911-65,
American; nonfiction, fiction,
poetry CON KTS
BARKER, Theodore Cardwell, 1923- ,
English; nonfiction CON
BARKER, Thomas M., 1929- ,
American; nonfiction CON
BARKER, Will ('Doug Demarest'),
1913- , American; nonfiction
CON WA
BARKER, William Alan, 1923- ,
English; nonfiction CON
BARKER, William P., 1927- ,
American; nonfiction CON
BARKIN, David Peter, 1942- ,
American; nonfiction CON
BARKIN, Solomon, 1907- , Amer-
ican; nonfiction CON
BARKINS, Evelyn Warner, 1919- ,
American; poetry CON
BARKMAN, Paul Friesen, 1921- ,
American; nonfiction CON
BARKS, Coleman Bryan, 1937- ,
American; nonfiction CON
BARKSDALE, Hiram Collier,
1921- , American; nonfiction
CON
BARKSDALE, Lena, American;
juveniles WA
BARKSTED, William, fl. 1611, Eng-
lish; poetry ST
BARLACH, Ernst, 1870-1938, Ger-
man; plays, fiction AL COL FLE
HAR KU KUN LEN MAT SA ST
'BARLAY, Bennett' see CROSSEN,
Kendell F.
BARLAY, Stephen, 1930- , Hungarian-
English; juveniles CON
BARLETTA, Leónidas, 1900/02- ,
Argentinian; poetry, plays,
criticism MIN SA
BARLETTI de SAINT PAUL, François
Paul, 1734-1809, French; non-
fiction DIL
BARLING, Muriel Vere Mant ('Charles
Barling'; 'P.V. Barrington';
'Pamela Barrington'), 1904- ,
English; fiction CON
BARLOW, Claude Willis, 1907- ,
American; nonfiction CON
BARLOW, Emma Nora, 1885- ,
English; nonfiction CON
BARLOW, Frank, 1911- , English;
nonfiction CON

BARLOW, Genevieve, 1910- ,
American; nonfiction CON
BARLOW, James, 1921-73, Eng-
lish; nonfiction CON
BARLOW, Jane, 1857-1917,
Irish; poetry, criticism KT
SA ST
BARLOW, Joel, 1754-1812, Amer-
ican; poetry BRO KAA SA ST
BARLOW, John Alfred, 1924- ,
American; nonfiction CON
'BARLOW, Roger' see LECKIE,
Robert H.
BARLOWE, Raleigh, 1914- ,
American; nonfiction CON
BARMANN, Laurence Francis,
1932- , American; nonfiction
CON
BARNA, Marika Robert, Czech-
American; fiction CON
BARNABY, Charles Frank, 1927- ,
English; nonfiction CON
BARNARD, Lady Anne Lindsay,
1750-1825, English; poetry
BRO KB ST
BARNARD, Charlotte Allington
('Claribel'), 1830-69, English;
poetry KBA
BARNARD, Ellsworth, 1907- ,
American; nonfiction CON
BARNARD, Frederick Mechner,
1921- , Czech-Canadian;
nonfiction CON
BARNARD, Harry, 1906- , Amer-
ican; nonfiction CON
BARNARD, Henry, 1811-1900,
American; nonfiction KAA
BARNARD, James Alan, 1928- ,
Australian; nonfiction CON
BARNARD, John Darrell, 1906- ,
American; nonfiction CON
BARNARD, Leslie Gordon, 1890-
1961, Canadian; fiction SY
BARNARD, Marjorie see 'ELDER-
SHAW, Barnard'
BARNARD, Mary, 1909- , Amer-
ican; poetry MUR
BARNARD, Mary Ethel, 1909- ,
American; nonfiction CON
BARNARD, Virgil John, 1932- ,
American; nonfiction CON
BARNAVE, Antoine Pierre Joseph
Marie, 1761-93, French; non-
fiction DIF DIL
BARNE, Kitty, 1883-1957, English;
juveniles, plays DOY KJU
BARNES, Arthur Stapylton, 1861-

1936, English; nonfiction HOE
BARNES, Barnabe, 1569?-1609,
English; poetry BRO KB ST
BARNES, Carmen, 1912- , American; fiction WAF
BARNES, Charlotte Mary Sanford,
1818-63, American; plays KAA
SA
BARNES, Chesley Virginia see
YOUNG, Chesley V.
BARNES, Clara Ernst (Clara Ernst),
1895- , German-American;
nonfiction CON
BARNES, Djuna ('Lydia Steptoe'),
1892- , American; poetry,
plays CON FLE KT RIC ST
BARNES, Eric Wollencott, 1907- ,
American; juveniles WA
BARNES, Gregory Allen, 1934- ,
American; juveniles CON
BARNES, Harry Al, American; nonfiction HIL
BARNES, Harry Elmer, 1889- ,
American; nonfiction CON KT
BARNES, Hazel Estelle, 1915- ,
American; nonfiction CON
BARNES, Henry A., 1906- , American; nonfiction CON
BARNES, James Anderson, 1898- ,
American; nonfiction CON
BARNES, James J., 1931- , American; nonfiction CON
BARNES, John Bertram, 1924- ,
American; nonfiction CON
BARNES, Juliana see BERNERS,
Juliana
BARNES, Leonard John, 1895- ,
English; nonfiction CON
BARNES, Margaret Ayer, 1886-
1967, American; fiction, plays
HOO KAT KT
BARNES, Phoebe, 1908- , American; nonfiction CON
BARNES, Ralph Mosser, 1900- ,
American; nonfiction CON
BARNES, Richard Gordon, 1932- ,
American; plays, nonfiction
CON
BARNES, Robert Jay, 1925- ,
American; nonfiction CON
BARNES, Samuel Gill, 1913- ,
American; nonfiction CON
BARNES, Samuel Henry, 1931- ,
American; nonfiction CON
BARNES, Thomas Garden, 1930- ,
American; nonfiction CON
BARNES, Viola Florence, 1885- ,

American; nonfiction CON
BARNES, William, 1800/01-86,
British; poetry BRO KBA
SP ST
BARNET, Richard J., American;
nonfiction CON
BARNET, Sylvan, 1926- , American; nonfiction CON
BARNETT, A. Doak, 1921- ,
American; nonfiction CON
'BARNETT, Adam' see FAST,
Julius
BARNETT, Correlli, 1927- ,
English; nonfiction CON
BARNETT, George Leonard,
1915- , American; nonfiction
CON
BARNETT, Grace Treleven,
1899- , American; juveniles
PAC
BARNETT, Homer Garner,
1906- , American; nonfiction
PAC
'BARNETT, L. David' see
LASCHEVER, Barnett D.
BARNETT, Leo, 1925- , American; nonfiction CON
BARNETT, Leonard, 1919- ,
English; nonfiction CON
BARNETT, Nicolas Guy, 1928- ,
English; nonfiction CON
BARNETT, Richard Chambers,
1932- , American; nonfiction
CON
BARNETT, Samuel Anthony,
1915- , English; nonfiction
CON
BARNETTE, W. Leslie, Jr.,
1910- , American; nonfiction
CON
BARNEY, Le Roy, 1930- ,
American; nonfiction CON
BARNFIELD, Richard, 1574-1627,
English; poetry BRO KB SP
ST
BARNHART, Clarence Lewis,
1900- , American; nonfiction
CON
BARNHILL, Myrtle Fait, 1896- ,
American; poetry CON
BARNITZ, Harry W., 1920- ,
American; nonfiction CON
BARNOUW, Adriaan Jacob,
1877- , Dutch-American;
juveniles WA
BARNOUW, Erik, 1908- , Dutch-American; nonfiction CON

BARNSLEY, Alan Gabriel ('Gabriel
Fielding'), 1916- , English;
nonfiction, fiction CON

BARNSTONE, Willis, 1927- ,
American; nonfiction CON

BARNUM, Jay Hyde, American;
juveniles WA

'BARNUM, Richard' see STRATE-
MEYER, Edward L.

BARNUM, William Paul ('Jon
O'Bryant'; 'Eric O'Neil'), 1933- ,
American; poetry CON

BARNUTIU, Simion, 1808-64, Transyl-
vanian; nonfiction ST

BARNWELL, D. Robinson, 1915- ,
American; fiction CON

BARO, Gene, 1924- , American;
poetry MUR

BAROJA y NESSI, Pio, 1872-1956,
Spanish; fiction, essays BL COL
FLE HAR KAT KT MAG RIC SA
ST

BAROJA y NESSI, Ricardo, 1871-1953,
Spanish; nonfiction, plays BL SA

BAROLINI, Antonio, 1910- , Italian-
American; poetry CON

BARON, Alexander, 1917- , British;
fiction KTS

BARON, Charles, 1655-1730, French;
poetry DIL

'BARON, David' see PINTER, Harold

BARON, Devorah, 1887- , Jewish;
nonfiction ST

BARON, Hans, 1900, German-American; nonfiction CON

BARON, Jean Léonore, 1720-85,
French; fiction DIL

'BARON, Joseph Alexandre' (Alec
Bernstein), 1917- , American;
fiction CON

BARON, Robert, fl. 1645, English;
plays, poetry ST

BARON, Samuel H., 1921- , American; nonfiction CON

BARON, V., 1761-90, French; nonfiction DIL

BARON, Virginia Olsen, 1931- ,
American; nonfiction CON

BARON CASTRO, Rodolfo, 1909- ,
Salvadoran; nonfiction BL

BARONAS, Atanas see BARANAUSKAS,
Antanas

BARONDESS, Sue Kaufman (Sue
Kaufman), 1926- , American;
fiction CON

BARONI, P. Luigi, fl. 1770-80,
Italian; nonfiction DIL

BARONIO, Cesare, 1538-1607,
Italian; nonfiction HAR SA ST

BAROTO, Jean Pierre Nicolas
Baroteau, 1743-1800, French;
plays DIL

BARR, Amelia Edith Huddleston,
1831-1919, American; fiction
KAA

BARR, Chester Alwyn, Jr.,
1938- , American; nonfiction
CON

BARR, Donald, 1921- , American;
juveniles CON

BARR, Doris Wilson, 1923- ,
American; nonfiction CON

BARR, George, 1907- , American;
nonfiction, juveniles COM
CON WA

BARR, Gladys Hutchison, 1904- ,
American; fiction CON

BARR, Isabel Harriss, American;
poetry MAR

BARR, James, 1924- , American;
nonfiction CON

BARR, Jene, 1900- , American;
juveniles CON WA

BARR, Orlando Sydney, 1919- ,
American; nonfiction CON

BARR, Patricia Miriam ('Laurence
Hazard'), 1934- , English;
nonfiction CON

BARR, Robert ('Luke Sharp'),
1850-1912, Anglo-American;
fiction, journalism BRO KT

BARR, Stephen, 1904- , English;
nonfiction CON

BARR, Stringfellow, 1897- ,
American; nonfiction CON KTS

'BARRA, Casimiro de la' see
SOTO BORDA, C.

BARRA, Eduardo de la, 1839-1900,
Chilean; nonfiction, poetry
MIN SA

BARRA, Emma de la see 'DUAYEN,
Cesár'

BARRA, Mary Margaret, 1909- ,
American; nonfiction SCA

BARRAL, Mary Rose, 1925- ,
American; nonfiction CON

BARRAL, Pierre, -1772, French;
nonfiction DIL

BARRANGER, Milly Slater,
1937- , American; nonfiction
CON

BARRANTES, Pedro, 1850- ,
Spanish; poetry, journalism
SA

BARRANTES y MORENO, Vicente,
1829-98, Spanish; poetry, nonfiction, poetry SA

BARRAU DIHIGO, Luis, 1876- ,
French; nonfiction BL

BARRE, Pierre Ives, 1749-1832,
French; plays SA

BARREDA, Ernest Mario, 1883/90- ,
Argentinian; journalism, poetry,
fiction, essays MIN SA

BARREDA, Luis, 1874- , Spanish;
poetry SA

BARREGA, Juan Agustín, 1853- ,
Chilean; journalism MIN

BARREIROS, Gaspar, 1496?-1574,
Portuguese; nonfiction SA

BARREME, Jean Nicolas, 1687-
1742/56, French; nonfiction DIL

BARREN, Charles ('Thomas Rainham'),
1913- , English; fiction CON

BARRENCCHEA, Julio, 1906- ,
Chilean; poetry MIN SA

BARRENECHEA, Mariano Antonio,
1884- , Argentinian; essays,
journalism MIN

BARRENECHEA y ALBIS, Juan de,
1669- , Chilean; nonfiction
MIN

BARRERA, Cayetano Alberto de la,
1815-72, Spanish; nonfiction BL
SA

BARRERA, Isaac J. (Juan de Cuesta),
1884- , Ecuadorian; nonfiction
DI

BARRES, Augustin Maurice, 1862-
1923, French; fiction, essays,
nonfiction COL DIF HAR KAT
KT MAL SA ST

BARRES, Oliver, 1921- , American;
nonfiction CON

BARRET, Rafael, 1877-1910, Argentinian; nonfiction SA

BARRET, Robert, fl. 1603-06, English; poetry ST

BARRETO de RESENDE, Pedro,
1590-1651, Portuguese; nonfiction
SA

BARRETT, Alfred J., 1906- ,
American; nonfiction, poetry HOE

BARRETT, Anne Mainwaring Gillett,
1911- , English; juveniles CON

BARRETT, Charles Kingsley, 1917- ,
English; nonfiction CON

BARRETT, Donald Neil, 1920- ,
American; nonfiction CON

BARRETT, Eaton Stannard, 1786-
1820, Irish; poetry BRO

BARRETT, Edward Louis, Jr.,
1917- , American; nonfiction
CON

BARRETT, George West, 1908- ,
American; nonfiction CON

BARRETT, Gerald Van, 1936- ,
American; nonfiction CON

BARRETT, James Francis, 1888-
1934, American; fiction HOE

BARRETT, James Henry, 1906- ,
American; nonfiction CON

BARRETT, Jean Jacques, 1717-92,
French; translations DIL

BARRETT, John Edward, 1932- ,
American; nonfiction CON

BARRETT, John Gilchrist, 1921- ,
American; nonfiction CON

BARRETT, Laurence I., 1935- ,
American; nonfiction CON

BARRETT, Linton Lomas, 1904- ,
American; nonfiction CON

BARRETT, Mary Ellin, 1927- ,
American; fiction CON

BARRETT, Nancy Smith, 1942- ,
American; nonfiction CON

BARRETT, Nathan Noble, 1933- ,
American; fiction CON

BARRETT, Patricia, 1914- ,
American; nonfiction CON

BARRETT, Russell Hunter, 1919- ,
American; nonfiction CON

BARRETT, Stephen Melvil, 1865- ,
American; nonfiction MAR

BARRETT, Sylvia, 1914- , English; nonfiction CON

BARRETT, Ward J., 1927- ,
American; nonfiction CON

BARRETT, William, 1913- ,
American; nonfiction CON

BARRETT, William Edmund,
1900- , American; fiction
CON HO

BARRETT, Wilson, 1846-1904,
British; plays KBA

BARRETTO, Larry (Laurence
Brevoort), 1890-1971, American; fiction KL KT SA WAF

BARRI, Giraldus de see GIRALDUS
de BARRI

BARRI, Joseph, 1692?-1764,
French; nonfiction DIL

BARRICK, Mac Eugene, 1933- ,
American; nonfiction CON

BARRIE, Alexander, 1923- ,
English; tv, nonfiction CON

BARRIE, Donald Conway, 1905- ,
American; juveniles CON

BARRIE, Sir James Matthew ('Gavin
Ogilvy'), 1860-1937, English
poetry, fiction, juveniles, plays
BRO DOY KL FLE KT MAG MAT
RIC SA ST
BARRIERE, Théodore, 1823-77,
French; plays DIF HAR SA
BARRILI, Antonio Giulio, 1836-1908,
Italian; fiction COL HAR ST
'BARRINGTON, E.' see BECK, Lil
M.A.
'BARRINGTON, John' see BROWNJOHN,
Alan
'BARRINGTON, Maurice' see BROGAN
Denis W.
'BARRINGTON, P.V.' see BARLING,
Murcel V.M.
'BARRINGTON, Pamela' see BARL-
ING, Murcel V.M.
BARRIO (Barrios), 2nd cent., Greek;
fiction SA
BARRIO, Raymond, 1921- , Ameri-
can; nonfiction CON
BARRIOBERO y HERRAN, Eduardo,
1880-1939?, Spanish; fiction,
journalism SA
BARRIONUEVO, Jerónimo de, 1587-
1671, Spanish; nonfiction, poetry,
plays BL SA
BARRIOS, Eduardo, 1884-1963,
Chilean; fiction, plays BL FLE
MIN RIC SA ST
BARRIOS, Miguel de ('Daniel Levi
de Barrios'), 1625?-1701?,
Spanish; poetry BL HAR SA ST
BARRITI, Anton Giulio, 1836-1908,
Italian; fiction SA
BARRITT, Denis Phillips, 1914- ,
Irish; nonfiction CON
BARROIS, Jacques Marie, 1707-69,
French; nonfiction DIL
BARRON, Frank, 1922- , American;
nonfiction CON
BARRON, Milton L., 1918- , Amer-
ican; nonfiction CON
BARROS, Alonso de, 1552-98,
Spanish; poetry, nonfiction SA
BARROS, João de, 16th cent.,
Portuguese; nonfiction SA
BARROS, João de, 1496-1570,
Portuguese; nonfiction HAR SA
ST
BARROS ARANA, Diego, 1830-1907,
Chilean; nonfiction BL MIN SA
BARROS GREZ, Daniel, 1834-1904,
Chilean; plays, fiction MIN SA
BARROS JARPA, Ernesto, 1894- ,

Chilean; nonfiction MIN
BARROS y GOMEZ, Bernardo G.,
1890-1922, Cuban; journalism
MIN
BARROSEE, Thomas, 1926- ,
American; nonfiction CON
BARROT, Joseph Marie, 18th cent.,
French; nonfiction DIL
BARROW, Geoffrey Wallis Steuart,
1924- , English; nonfiction
CON
BARROW, Isaac, 1630-77, English;
nonfiction BRO KB ST
BARROW, Sir John, 1764-1848,
British; nonfiction KBA
BARROW, Raymond, 1920- ,
West Indian; poetry MUR
BARROW, Rhoda Catharine Kitto,
1910- , English; nonfiction
CON
BARROW, Thomas Churchill,
1929- , American; nonfiction
CON
BARROWS, Marjorie ('Jack Alden';
'Noel Ames'; 'Ruth Barrows';
'Ruth Dixon'; 'Hugh Graham'),
American; fiction, juveniles
CON HOO WA
BARRUEL, Augustin, 1741-1820,
French; nonfiction DIL
'BARRY, Charles' see BRYSON,
Charles
BARRY, Colman J., 1921- ,
American; nonfiction CON
BARRY, Herbert III, 1930- ,
American; nonfiction CON
BARRY, Jackson Granville,
1926- , American; nonfiction
CON
BARRY, James Donald, 1926- ,
American; nonfiction CON
BARRY, James Patrick, 1915- ,
American; nonfiction CON
BARRY, Jane Powell, 1925- ,
American; fiction CON
BARRY, Jerome Benedict, 1894- ,
American; fiction, radio, tv
CON
BARRY, John Vincent William,
1903- , American; nonfiction
CON
BARRY, Katharina Watjen, 1936- ,
German-American; juveniles
CON WA
BARRY, Lord (Lording), 1580-1629,
English; plays ST
BARRY, Lucy Brown, 1934- ,

American; fiction CON

BARRY, Marie Jeanne Gomart de
Vaubernier, 1743-93, French;
nonfiction SA

BARRY, Noëlline Buttress, 1915- ,
British-Rhodesian; poetry, fiction MUR

BARRY, Philip, 1896-1949, American; plays BRO HOE KL KT
MAT RIC SA ST

BARRY, Raymond Walker, 1894- ,
American; nonfiction CON

BARRY, Robert Everett, 1931- ,
American; juveniles CON WA

'BARRY, Spranger' see KAUFFMANN,
Stanley

BARRY, William F., 1849-1930,
Irish; nonfiction HOE

BARSNESS, Larry, 1919- , American; nonfiction PAC

BARSTOW, Charles Murray ('An Old
Sportsman'), 1810- , English;
nonfiction HIG

BARSTOW, Stanley, 1928- , Anglo-
American; fiction, tv, radio CON
RIC

BART, Benjamin Franklin, 1917- ,
American; nonfiction CON

BARTAS, Guillaume de Salluste du
see DU BARTAS, Guillaume
de S.

BART-CISINSKI, Jakub see CISINSKI,
Jakub

BARTEK, Edward John, 1921- ,
American; nonfiction CON

BARTEL, Roland, 1919- , American; nonfiction CON

BARTELL, Ernest, 1932- , American; nonfiction CON

BARTELS, Robert, 1913- , American; nonfiction CON

BARTELS, Robert A., 1923- ,
American; nonfiction CON

BARTEN, Harvey Harold, 1933- ,
American; nonfiction CON

BARTH, Alan, 1906- , American;
nonfiction CON

BARTH, Charles P. ('Buffalo Chuck'),
1895- , American; fiction CON

BARTH, Christoph F., 1917- ,
Swiss; nonfiction CON

BARTH, Emil, 1900-58, German;
poetry FLE KU LEN

BARTH, John Robert, 1931- ,
American; nonfiction CON

BARTH, John Simmons, 1930- ,
American; fiction CON RIC

BARTH, Karl, 1886-1968, Swiss;
nonfiction KTS KU KUN SA

'BARTH, Lois' see FREIHOFER,
Lois D.

BARTH, Markus Karl, 1915- ,
Swiss-American; nonfiction
CON

BARTHE, Nicolas Thomas,
1734-85, French; poetry,
plays DIL

BARTHEL, Kurt see 'KUBA'

BARTHELEMY, Auguste Marseille,
1796-1867, French; poetry
HAR SA

BARTHELEMY, Jean Jacques,
1716-95, French; nonfiction
DIF DIL HAR SA

BARTHELEMY, Louis, 1759-
1815, French; nonfiction DIL

BARTHELEMY, Nicolas, 1478-
1540, French; poetry ST

BARTHELEMY, Nicolas Michel,
1730-94, French; nonfiction
DIL

BARTHELME, Donald, 1931- ,
American; fiction CON

BARTHES, Roland, 1915- ,
French; criticism DIC PIN

BARTHEY, Paul Joseph, 1734-
1806, French; nonfiction DIL

BARTHEZ de MARMORIERES,
Antoine, 1736- , French;
nonfiction DIL

BARTHOLOMAEUS, Anglicus
(Bartholomew de Glanville),
fl. 1230-50, English; nonfiction ST

BARTHOLOMEW, Cecilia, 1907- ,
Canadian; fiction CON

BARTHOLOMEW, Edward Ells-
worth ('Jesse Ed Rascoe'),
1914- , American; fiction
CON

BARTHOLOMEW, Paul Charles,
1907- , American; nonfiction
CON

BARTIER, Pierre ('Peter Pan'),
1945- , Belgian; nonfiction
CON

'BARTLETT, Billie' see BART-
LETT, Marie S.

BARTLETT, Charles Leffingwell,
1921- , American; nonfiction
CON

BARTLETT, Christopher John,
1931- , English; nonfiction
CON

'BARTLETT, David' see MASON, Madeline

BARTLETT, Elizabeth Winters, 1911- , American; poetry CON

BARTLETT, Elsa Jaffe, 1935- , American; nonfiction CON

BARTLETT, Eric George, 1920- , Welsh; fiction, nonfiction CON

BARTLETT, Gerald Robert, 1935- , English; nonfiction CON

BARTLETT, Irving Henry, 1923- , American; nonfiction CON

BARTLETT, John, 1820-1905, American; nonfiction BRO KAA

BARTLETT, John Russell, 1805-86, American; nonfiction KAA

BARTLETT, Margaret Farrington, 1896- , American; juveniles CON

BARTLETT, Marie Swan ('Billie Bartlett'; 'Rowena Lee'; 'Sara Linden'; 'Valerie Rift'; 'Marie Swan'), 1910- , English; fiction CON

BARTLETT, Nancy W., 1913- , American; fiction CON

BARTLETT, Paul, 1909- , American; fiction CON

'BARTLETT, Philip A.' see STRATEMEYER, Edward L.

BARTLETT, Richard Adams, 1920- , American; nonfiction CON

BARTLETT, Robert Merrill, 1899- , American; juveniles, nonfiction CON

BARTLETT, Ruhl J., 1897- , American; nonfiction CON

BARTLETT, Ruth, American; fiction, juveniles CON

BARTLETT, Vernon, 1894- , English; journalism, fiction KL KT

BARTLEY, William Warren III, 1934- , American; nonfiction CON

BARTOCCI, Gianni, 1925- , Italian-Canadian; nonfiction CON

BARTOL, Vladimir, 1903- , Slovene; fiction, criticism ST

BARTOLI, Adolfo, 1833-94, Italian; nonfiction SA

BARTOLI, Daniello, 1608-85, Italian; nonfiction ST

BARTOLINI, Luigi, 1892- , Italian; poetry FLE SA

'BARTOLITO' see MITRE y VEDIA, Bartolomé

BARTOLOME COSSIO, Manuel, 1857-1935, Spanish; criticism ST

BARTOLOME de las CASAS see LAS CASAS, Bartolome de

BARTOLOMEO da SAN CONCOR-DIO, 1262-1347, Italian; nonfiction ST

BARTON, Allen Hoisington, 1924- , American; nonfiction CON

BARTON, Benjamin Smith, 1766-1815, American; nonfiction KAA

BARTON, Bernard, 1784-1849, British; poetry BRO KBA ST

BARTON, Frank Townend, 1864- , English; nonfiction HIG

BARTON, George, 1866-1940, American; fiction, journalism HOE

BARTON, Humphrey Douglas Elliott, 1900- , English; nonfiction CON

BARTON, John Mackintosh Tilney, 1898- , English; nonfiction CON HOE

BARTON, Margaret Dover, 1902- , American; nonfiction CON

BARTON, Mary Neill, 1899- , American; nonfiction CON

'BARTON, May Hollis' see ADAMS, Harriet S. and STRATEMEYER, Edward L.

'BARTON, R. Rush' see BRAV, Stanley R.

BARTON, Vernon Wayne, American; nonfiction CON

BARTON, Weldon, V., 1938- , American; nonfiction CON

BARTON, William Eleazer, 1861-1930, American; nonfiction, fiction HOO

BARTOS-HOEPPNER, Barbara, 1923- , German; juveniles CON

BARTRAM, John, 1699-1777, American; nonfiction KAA

BARTRAM, William, 1739-1823, American; nonfiction KAA ST

BARTRAN, Margaret, 1913- , American; nonfiction CON

BARTRINA, Joaquín María, 1850-80, Spanish; poetry BL COL HAR SA ST

BARTRINA y de AIXEMUS, Francisco,
1846-94?, Spanish; poetry SA
BARTRUM, Douglas Albert, 1907- ,
English; nonfiction CON
BARTSCH, Rudolf Hans, 1873-1952,
Austrian; fiction AL HAR ST
BARTULOVIC, Niko, 1890-1946,
Dalmatian; fiction ST
BART-WILLIAMS, Gaston, 1938- ,
Sierra Leonese; poetry MUR
BARTZ, Albert Edward, 1933- ,
American; nonfiction CON
BARUA, Hemcandra, 1837-96,
Indian; plays, essays LAN
BARUCH, Löb see 'BÖRNE, Ludwig'
BARUCH, Ruth Marion, 1922- ,
American; nonfiction CON
BARUCHE, Moses see 'AUERBACH,
Berthold'
BARWICK, Stephen, 1921- , Amer-
ican; nonfiction CON
BARYKA, Piotr, 1600- , Polish;
plays ST
BAR-YOSEF-YEHOSHUA, 1912- ,
Jewish; fiction, plays ST
BARZANTI, Sergio, 1925- , Italian-
American; nonfiction CON
BARZINI, Luigi, 1908- , American;
nonfiction CON
BAR-ZOHAR, Michael, 1938- ,
Bulgarian; nonfiction CON
BARZUN, Jacques Martin, 1907- ,
French-American; nonfiction
KT
BAS, William see BASSE, William
BASA, 3rd-4th cent., Hindu; plays
SA
BASAN, Pierre François, 1723-97,
French; nonfiction DIL
BASAN, Walter, 1920- , German;
fiction AL
BASANAVICIUS, Jonas, 1851-1927,
Lithuanian; nonfiction ST
BASART, Ann Phillips, 1931- ,
American; nonfiction CON
BASCHE, James, 1926- , American;
nonfiction CON
BASCOM, John, 1827-1911, American;
nonfiction KAA
BASCOM, Willard N., 1916- ,
American; nonfiction, movies
CON
BASCOM, William, Russel, 1912- ,
American; nonfiction CON
BASDEKIS, Demetrios, 1930- ,
American; nonfiction CON
'BASHEVIS, Isaac' see SINGER, Isaac
B.

BASHKIRTSEFF, Maria Konstanti-
nova (Bashkirtseva), 1860-84,
Russian; diary, nonfiction
DIF HAR KE ST
BASHO, Matsuo, 1644-94, Japanese;
poetry, diary LAN MAG SA
ST
BASHSHAR ben BURD, 714-83/84,
Arab; poetry LAN ST
BASIL, 330-79, Greek; nonfiction
ST
BASILE, Giambattista ('Gian Alesio
Abbattutis'), 1575-1632, Italian;
poetry, fiction HAR KE ST
BASILE, Joseph, 1912- , Belgian;
nonfiction CON
BASILIO, San, 329-79, Greek;
nonfiction SA
BASILIUS, Harold A., 1905- ,
American; translations, non-
fiction CON
BASIN, Thomas, 1412-91, French;
nonfiction DIF
BASKERVILLE, Barnet, 1916- ,
American; nonfiction CON
BASKETTE, Floyd Kenneth,
1910- , American; nonfiction
CON
BASKIN, Samuel, 1921- ,
Lithuanian-American; nonfiction
CON
BASKIN, Wade, 1924- , American;
nonfiction CON
BASLER, Roy Prentice, 1906- ,
American; nonfiction CON
BASO, Lolio (Bassus), 1st cent.,
Greek; poetry SA
BASON, Frederick Thomas ('The
Gallerite'), 1907- , American;
nonfiction CON
BASS, Altha Leah ('Althea BASS'),
1892- , American; poetry
CON HOO MAR
BASS, Bernard Morris, 1925- ,
American; nonfiction CON
BASS, Clarence Beaty, 1922- ,
American; nonfiction CON
'BASS, Eduard' (Eduard Schmidt),
1888-1946, Czech; fiction HAR
RIC ST
BASS, Herbert Jacob, 1929- ,
American; nonfiction CON
BASS, Howard, 1923- , English;
nonfiction CON
BASS, Jack, 1934- , American;
nonfiction CON
BASS, Milton R., 1923- , Amer-
ican; fiction CON

BASS, Samuel, 1906-49, Jewish;
poetry, essays, fiction ST
BASSAN, Maurice, 1929- , Amer-
ican; nonfiction CON
BASSANI, Giorgio, 1916- , Italian;
poetry, fiction HAR RIC
BASSARABESCU, Ion A., 1870- ,
Russian; fiction ST
BASSE, William (Bas), 1583?-1653?,
English; poetry BRO ST
BASSELIN, Olivier, 1375?-1419,
French; poetry HAR SA
'BASSERMANN, Lujo' see SCHREIBER,
Hermann
BASSET, Rev. Bernard, S.J.,
1909- , American; fiction CON
HO
BASSET de la MARELLE, Louis,
1730-94, French; nonfiction DIL
BASSET des ROSIERS, Gilles, 18th
cent., French; nonfiction DIL
BASSETT, Edward Eryl, 1940- ,
Welsh; nonfiction CON
BASSETT, Glen Arthur, 1930- ,
American; nonfiction CON
'BASSETT, Jack' see ROWLAND,
Donald S.
'BASSETT, John Keith' see KEATING,
Lawrence A.
BASSETT, John Spencer, 1867-1928,
American; nonfiction KT
BASSETT, Richard, 1900- , Amer-
ican; nonfiction CON
BASSETT, Sara Ware, 1872- ,
American; fiction WAF
BASSETT, Thomas Day Seymour,
1913- , American; nonfiction
CON
BASSETT, William B.K. ('Peter
Darien'), 1908- , American;
fiction CON
BASSETT, William Travis, 1923- ,
American; nonfiction CON
BASSETT, William W., 1932- ,
American; nonfiction CON
BASSEVILLE, Nicolas Jean Hugon
(Basville), 1753-93, French;
fiction DIL
BASSHE, Emjo (Emmanul Jo Bashe),
1900-39, Russian-American;
plays KT SA
BASSI, Laura Maria Catalina Veratti,
1711-78, Italian; nonfiction SA
BASSIOUNI, M. Cherif, 1937- ,
Egyptian-American; nonfiction
CON
BASSO, Hamilton, 1904- , American;

fiction KT WAF
BASSUS see BASO, Lolio
BASTARD, Lucien see 'ESTANG,
Luc'
BASTERRA, Ramón de, 1888-
1928, Spanish; poetry BL
COL FLE HAR SA ST
BASTIAT, Claude Frédéric,
1801-50, French; nonfiction
DIF
BASTIDE, François Regis, 1926- ,
French; fiction DIF PIN
BASTIDE, Jean Baptiste, 1747-
1810, French; nonfiction DIL
BASTIDE, Jean François, 1724-
98, French; nonfiction DIL
BASTIN, John Sturgus, 1927- ,
Australian; nonfiction CON
BASTLUND, Knud, 1925- ,
Danish; nonfiction CON
BASTON, Guillaume André René,
1741-1825, French; nonfiction
DIL
BASTOS, Augusto Roa, 1917- ,
Paraguayan, fiction RIC
BASURTO, Luis G., 1921- ,
Mexican; plays SA
BASVILLE, Nicolas see BASSE-
VILLE, Nicolas J.H.
BATAILLE, Georges, 1897-1963/65,
French; fiction, essays, poetry
DIF FLE MAL
BATAILLE, Henri Félix, 1872-
1922, French; plays, poetry
COL DIF HAR KE MAT SA ST
BATAILLON, Marcel, 1895- ,
French; nonfiction BL
BATBEDAT, Jean ('Michel
Larneuil'), 1926- , French;
fiction CON
BATCHELDER, Alan Bruce,
1931- , American; nonfiction
CON
BATCHELDER, Howard Timothy,
1909- , American; nonfiction
CON
BATE, Hendrik, 1246-1310, Dutch;
nonfiction ST
BATE, Norman Arthur, 1916- ,
American; juveniles CON WA
BATE, Walter Jackson, 1918- ,
American; nonfiction CON
BATEMAN, Robert Moyes Car-
ruthers, 1922- , American;
nonfiction, juveniles CON
BATEMAN, Sidney Francis Cowlle,
1823-81, American; plays KAA

BATEMAN, Walter Lewis, 1916- ,
American; nonfiction CON
BATES, Alan Lawrence, 1923- ,
American; nonfiction CON
BATES, Arlo ('Eleanor Putnam';
'Harriet L. Vose'), 1850-1918,
American; fiction, poetry KAA
BATES, Barbara Snedeker ('Stephen
Cuyler'; 'Jim Roberts'), 1919- ,
American; juveniles CON
BATES, Darrell, 1913- , English;
nonfiction CON
BATES, Ernest Sutherland, 1879-
1939, American; nonfiction KT
BATES, Henry Walter, 1825-92, Brit-
ish; nonfiction KBA
BATES, Herbert Ernest, 1905-74,
English; fiction BRO FLE KL
KT RIC
BATES, James Leonard, 1919- ,
American; nonfiction CON
BATES, Jerome E., 1917- ,
American; nonfiction CON
BATES, Katharine Lee, 1859-1929,
American; poetry, juveniles,
hymns BRO KT RIC SA
BATES, Kenneth Francis, 1904- ,
American; nonfiction CON
BATES, Margaret Jane, 1918- ,
American; nonfiction CON
BATES, Marston, 1906- , Amer-
ican; nonfiction CON
BATES, Paul Allen, 1920- ,
American; nonfiction CON
BATH, Philip Ernest, 1898- ,
English; nonfiction CON
BATES, Ralph, 1899- , English;
fiction KT RIC
BATES, Ralph Samuel, 1906- ,
American; nonfiction CON
BATES, Ronald Gordon Nudell,
1924- , Canadian; poetry CON
MUR SY
BATES, Sylvia Chatfield, American;
fiction WAF
BATESON, Frederick Wilse, 1901- ,
English; nonfiction CON
BATEY, Richard Alexander, 1933- ,
American; nonfiction CON
BATHO, Edith Clara, 1895- , Eng-
lish; nonfiction CON
BATHURST, Earl, 1864-1943, Eng-
lish; nonfiction HIG
BATI, 5th cent., Hindu; poetry SA
BATLLORI, Miquel, 20th cent.,
Spanish; translations BL
BAT-MIRIAM, Yocheved, 1901- ,

Jewish; poetry ST
BATON, Charles, -1728, French;
nonfiction DIL
BATRES y MONTUFAR, José,
1809-44, Guatamalan; poetry
BL SA
BATSON, George Donald, 1918- ,
American; plays CON
BATTAGLIA, Elio Lee, 1928- ,
American; nonfiction CON
BATTAN, Louis Joseph, 1923- ,
American; nonfiction CON
BATTCOCK, Gregory, 1937- ,
American; nonfiction CON
BATTEN, Harold Mortimer,
1888- , English; juveniles
DOY
BATTEN, James William, 1919- ,
American; nonfiction CON
BATTEN, Joyce Mortimer see
MANKOWSKA, Joyce K.B.
BATTEN, Thomas Reginald,
1904- , English; nonfiction
CON
BATTENHOUSE, Roy Wesley,
1912- , American; nonfiction
CON
BATTERSBY, William John,
1904- , American; nonfiction
CON
BATTESTIN, Martin Carey,
1930- , American; nonfiction
CON
BATTEUX, Charles, 1713-80,
French; criticism DIF DIL
BATTIFERRI, Laura, 1525-89,
Italian; poetry SA
BATTIN, Rosabell Ray, 1925- ,
American; nonfiction CON
BATTIS, Emery John, 1915- ,
American; nonfiction CON
BATTISCOMBE, Esther Georgina
Harwood ('Gina Harwood'),
1905- , American; nonfiction
CON
BATTISTA, Orlando Aloysius,
1917- , Canadian; nonfiction
CON
BATTISTA MANTOVANO see
MANTOVANO, Battista
BATTISTESSA, Angel José, 1902- ,
Argentinian; criticism SA
BATTISTI, Eugenio ('Angiolo
Rinaldini'), 1924- , Italian-
American; nonfiction CON
BATTLE, Jean Allen, 1914- ,
American; nonfiction CON

BATTLE, Kemp Plummer, 1831-1919,
American; nonfiction JO

BATTLE, Sol, 1934- , American;
nonfiction CON

BATTLES, Ford Lewis, 1915- ,
American; nonfiction CON

BATTY, Charles David, 1932- ,
English; fiction CON

BATTY, Joyce Dorothea, 1919- ,
Australian; nonfiction CON

BATTYE, Louis Neville, 1923- ,
English; fiction CON

BATY, Gaston, 1885- , French;
criticism, plays COL SA

BATY, Wayne, 1925- , American;
nonfiction CON

BATYUSHKOV, Konstantin Nikolayevich, 1787-1855, Russian; poetry
HAR HARK KE ST

BAUCHANT, Jacques, -1396,
French; translations ST

BAUDART, Willem, 1565-1640,
Dutch; nonfiction ST

BAUDE, Henri, 1430?-96, French;
poetry DIF ST

BAUDEAU, 18th cent., French;
plays DIL

BAUDELAIRE, Charles Pierre,
1821-67, French; poetry, essays
COL DIF HAR KE MAG MAL SA
ST

BAUDET, Herenc, 15th cent., French;
nonfiction DIF

BAUDHAYANA, fl. 400, Sanskrit;
nonfiction ST

BAUDIER, Dominique ('Baudius';
'Julianus Robecius'; 'Latinus
Pacatus'), 1561-1613, Dutch;
nonfiction SA

BAUDIN des ARDENNES, Pierre
Charles Louis, 1748-99, French;
nonfiction DIL

BAUDISSIN, Wolf Heinrich von, 1789-
1878, German; translations HAR

BAUDOT de JUILLY, Nicolas, 1678-
1759, French; plays DIL

'BAUDOUIN, Charles Pierre' see
PEGUY, Charles P.

BAUDOUIN, Etienne, 18th cent.,
French; nonfiction DIL

BAUDOUIN de GUEDMADEUC, 1734-
1817, French; nonfiction DIL

BAUDOUY, Michel Aime, 1909- ,
French; juveniles CON

BAUDOUX, Ferdinand, 1755-1815,
French; plays DIL

BAUDRAIS, Jean, 1749-1832, French;
plays, poetry DIL

BAUDRILLART, Henri Marie
Alfred, 1859-1942, French;
nonfiction HOE

BAUDRY, Pierre -1752, French;
nonfiction DIL

BAUDRY de BOURGUEIL, 1046-
1130, French; nonfiction,
poetry HAR ST

BÄUMER, Gertrud, 1873-1954,
German; essays FLE LEN

BAUER, Bruno, 1809-82, German;
criticism SA

BAUER, E. Charles, 1916- ,
American; nonfiction CON

BAUER, Erwin A. ('Ken Bourbon';
'Tom Hardin'; 'Charles W.
North'), 1919- , American;
nonfiction CON

BAUER, Florence Marvyne,
American; fiction CON HOO
WAF

BAUER, Fred, 1934- , American;
nonfiction CON

BAUER, George Howard, 1933- ,
American; nonfiction CON

BAUER, Gérard, 1888- , French;
essays, journalism, criticism
SA

BAUER, Harry Charles, 1902- ,
American; nonfiction CON

BAUER, Helen, 1900- , American;
juveniles COM CON

BAUER, Josef Martin, 1901- ,
German; nonfiction, plays,
poetry, fiction CON FLE KU
LEN

BAUER, Karl Jack, 1926- ,
American; nonfiction CON

BAUER, Royal Daniel Michael,
1889- , American; nonfiction
CON

BAUER, Walter, 1904- , German;
poetry, essays, fiction AL
FLE KU LEN

BAUER, Werner, 1925- , German; nonfiction AL

BAUER, William Waldo, 1892- ,
American; nonfiction CON

BAUER, Wolfgang Leander,
1930- , German; nonfiction
CON

BAUER, Yehuda, 1926- , Czech-
Israeli; nonfiction CON

BAUERNFEIND, Harry B., 1904- ,
American; nonfiction CON

BAUERNFELD, Eduard von, 1802-

90, Austrian; plays AL ST
BAUGHAN, Blanche Edith, 1870- ,
New Zealander; fiction ST
BAUGHER, Ruby Dell, American;
poetry HOO
BAUGHMAN, Ernest Warren,
1916- , American; nonfiction
CON
BAUGHMAN, James Porter, 1936- ,
American; nonfiction CON
BAUGHMAN, Ray Edward, 1925- ,
American; nonfiction CON
BAUGHN, William Hubert, 1918- ,
American; nonfiction CON
BAUGIN, Pierre François Cantien,
-1829, French; plays DIL
BAULACRE, Léonard, 1670-1760,
French; nonfiction DIL
BAULAND, Peter, 1932- , Amer-
ican; nonfiction CON
BAULCH, Lawrence, 1926- , Amer-
ican; nonfiction CON
BAUM, Allyn Zelton, 1924- , Amer-
ican; nonfiction CON
BAUM, Bernard Helmut, 1926- ,
German-American; nonfiction
CON
BAUM, Betty, American; juveniles
WA
BAUM, Daniel Jay, 1934- , Amer-
ican; nonfiction CON
BAUM, Gregory, German-Canadian;
nonfiction CON
BAUM, Kurt, 1876- , German-
American; poetry ST
BAUM, Lyman Frank ('Floyd Akers';
'Schuyler Stanton'; 'Edith Van
Dyne'), 1856-1919, English; juven-
iles, plays DOY KT WA
BAUM, Paull Franklin, 1886- ,
American; nonfiction CON
BAUM, Richard Fitzgerald, 1913- ,
American; nonfiction CON
BAUM, Vicki, 1888/96-1960, Aus-
trian-American; fiction HAR KAT
KT LEN MAG RIC SA ST WAF
BAUM, Willi, 1931- , Swiss-Amer-
ican; nonfiction CON
BAUMAN, Herman Carl, 1913- ,
American; nonfiction CON
BAUMANN, Carol Edler, 1932- ,
American; nonfiction CON
BAUMANN, Emile, 1868-1941/42,
French; fiction DIF HOE
BAUMANN, Hans, 1914- , German;
juveniles COM CON
BAUMANN, Nicolas, 18th cent.,

French; nonfiction DIL
BAUMANN, Walter, 1935- ,
Swiss; nonfiction CON
BAUMBACH, Jonathan, 1933- ,
American; nonfiction CON
BAUMBACH, Rudolf, 1840-1905,
German; nonfiction AL
BAUME, Michael, 1930- , Aus-
tralian; nonfiction CON
BAUMER, William Henry, 1909- ,
American; nonfiction CON
HOE
BAUMGARD, Herbert Mark,
1920- , American; nonfiction
CON
BAUMGARDT, David, 1890- ,
German-American; nonfiction
CON
BAUMGART, Reinhard, 1929- ,
German; nonfiction KU
BAUMGARTEN, Alexander
Gottlieb, 1714-62, German;
nonfiction HAR SA
BAUMGARTNER, John Stanley,
1924- , American; nonfiction
CON
BAUMIER, French; poetry DIL
BAUMOL, William Jack, 1922- ,
American; nonfiction CON
BAUMRIN, Bernard Herbert
('Stefan Baumrin'; 'Stefan
Bernard'), 1934- , American;
nonfiction CON
BAUR, John Edward, 1922- ,
American; nonfiction CON
BAURANS, Pierre, 1710-64,
French; plays DIL
BAUS, Herbert Michael, 1914- ,
American; nonfiction CON
BAUSCH, William J., 1929- ,
American; nonfiction CON
BAUSSONNET, Jean Baptiste,
1700-80, French; nonfiction
DIL
BAUVIN, Jean Gregoire, 1714-76,
French; nonfiction DIL
BAUZA, Francisco, 1849-99,
Uruguayan; nonfiction SA
BAVEREL, Jean Pierre, 1744-
1822, French; nonfiction DIL
BAVIERE, Elisabeth Charlotte,
1652-1722, French; letters
DIL
'BAWDEN, Nina' see KARK, Nina
M. M.
'BAWN, Mary' see WRIGHT, Mary
P. G.

BAWR, Alexandrinne Sophie Coury,
1776-   , French; plays, fiction
SA

'BAX, Roger' see WINTERTON, Paul

BAXT, George, 1923-   , American;
fiction CON

BAXTER, Annette Kar, 1926-   ,
American; nonfiction CON

BAXTER, Batsell Barrett, 1916-   ,
American; nonfiction CON

BAXTER, Craig, 1929-   , American;
nonfiction CON

BAXTER, Edna May, 1890-   , American; nonfiction CON

BAXTER, Eric George, 1918-   ,
English; nonfiction CON

BAXTER, Eric Peter, 1913-   ,
English; nonfiction CON

'BAXTER, Hazel' see ROWLAND,
Donald S.

BAXTER, Ian F.G., Canadian; nonfiction CON

BAXTER, James Keir, 1926-   , New
Zealander; poetry, criticism
MUR RIC ST

BAXTER, James Phinney III, 1893-   ,
American; nonfiction KTS

BAXTER, John ('Martin Loran'),
1939-   , Australian; nonfiction
CON

BAXTER, Maurice Glen, 1920-   ,
American; nonfiction CON

BAXTER, Richard, 1615-91, English;
nonfiction BRO KB ST

'BAXTER, Shane V.' see NORWOOD,
Victor G.C.

BAXTER, Stephen Bartow, 1929-   ,
American; nonfiction CON

BAY, Christian, 1921-   , Norwegian-
Canadian; nonfiction CON

BAYARD, Jean François Alfred,
1769-   , French; plays SA

BAYBARS, Taner ('Timothy Bayliss'),
1936-   , British; poetry, fiction
MUR

BAYEN, Pierre, 1725-98, French;
nonfiction DIL

BAYER, William ('Leonie St. John'),
1939-   , American; fiction, plays
CON

BAYES, Ronald Homer, 1932-   ,
American; nonfiction, poetry
CON

BAYEUX, Georges Louis, 1752-92,
French; nonfiction DIL

BAYHAQI, Muhammad Abu'l Fazl,
995-1077, Persian; nonfiction
ST

BAYLE, Pierre, 1647-1706, French;
nonfiction, criticism DIF DIL
HAR KE MAL SA ST

BAYLEBRIDGE, William, 1883-
1942, Australian; poetry ST

BAYLEN, Joseph Oscar, 1920-   ,
American; nonfiction CON

BAYLES, Ernest Edward, 1897-   ,
American; nonfiction CON

BAYLEY, Barrington John ('Alan
Aumbry'; 'P.F. Woods'),
1937-   , English; fiction CON

BAYLEY, Charles Calvert, 1907-   ,
English; nonfiction CON

BAYLEY, David Hume, 1933-   ,
American; nonfiction CON

BAYLEY, Viola Powles, 1911-   ,
English; fiction, juveniles
CON

BAYLISS, John Clifford ('John
Clifford'), 1919-   , British;
poetry CON MUR

BAYLISS, Marguerite Farleigh,
1895-   , American; fiction
WAF

'BAYLISS, Timothy' see BAYBARS,
Taner

BAYNES, Ernest Harold, 1868-
1925, English; juveniles KJU

BAYLOR, Frances Courtenay, 1848-
1920, American; fiction KAA

BAYLOR, Robert, 1925-   , American; fiction CON

BAYLY, Ada Ellen ('Edna Lyall'),
1857-1903, English; fiction
BRO

BAYLY, Joseph Tate, 1920-   ,
American; nonfiction CON

BAYLY, Thomas Haynes, 1797-
1839, British; songs, fiction
plays BRO KBA

BAUNE-JARDINE, Colin Charles,
1932-   , Scots; juveniles CON

BAYNES, John Christopher Malcolm, 1928-   , English; nonfiction CON

BAYNES, Pauline Diana, 1922-   ,
English; juveniles DOY

BAYNES, Thomas Spencer, 1823-
87, British; nonfiction BRO
KBA ST

BAYNHAM, Henry W.F., 1933-   ,
Welsh; nonfiction CON

BAYO y SEGUROLA, Ciro, 1860-
1939, Spanish; fiction BL SA

BAYR, Rudolf, 1919-   , German;
plays, poetry, essays KU

BAYS, Gwendolyn McKee, Ameri-

can; nonfiction CON
BAZAN, Emilia Pardo see PARDO
BAZAN, Emilia
BAZAN de la CAMARA, Rosa, 1895- ,
Argentinian; essays MIN
BAZANI-CAVOZZONI, Virginia,
1681-1715, Italian; poetry SA
BAZELON, David T., 1923- ,
American; nonfiction CON
BAZHOV, Pavel Petrovich, 1879- ,
Russian; fiction ST
BAZIL, Osvaldo, 1884-1946, Domini-
can; poetry MIN SA
BAZIN, Germain Rene, 1907- ,
French; nonfiction CON
BAZIN, Gilbert Auguste, -1754,
French; nonfiction DIL
BAZIN, Jean Hervé, 1911- ,
French; fiction, poetry, essays
DIC DIF FLE MAL PIN RIC
BAZIN, René, 1853-1932, French;
fiction COL DIF HAR HOE KAT
KT SA
BAZINCOURT, Mlle. Thomas, French;
nonfiction DIL
BAZINGHEN, François André Abot,
1711-91, French; nonfiction DIL
BAZOLLE, 18th cent., French;
poetry DIL
BEACH, Belle, 1875- , American;
nonfiction HIG
'BEACH, Charles Amory' see STRATE-
MEYER, Edward L.
BEACH, Dale S., 1923- , American;
nonfiction CON
BEACH, Earl Francis, 1912- ,
American; nonfiction CON
BEACH, Edward Latimer, 1918- ,
American; nonfiction CON
BEACH, Joseph Warren, 1880- ,
American; criticism, poetry
KTS
BEACH, Rex Ellingwood, 1877-1949,
American; fiction, plays BRO
KT MAG RIC
BEACH, Stewart, 1899- , American;
juveniles WA
BEACH, Vincent Woodrow, 1917- ,
American; nonfiction CON
BEACHCROFT, Thomas Owen,
1902- , English; fiction CON
BEACONSFIELD, Lord see DISRAELI,
Benjamin
BEADLE, Muriel, American; nonfic-
tion CON
BEADLES, William Thomas, 1902- ,
American; nonfiction CON

BEAGLE, Peter S., 1939- ,
American; fiction CON
BEAGLHOLE, John Cawte,
1901-71, New Zealander;
nonfiction CON ST
BEAL, Anthony Ridley, 1925- ,
English; nonfiction CON
BEAL, George Melvin, 1917- ,
American; nonfiction CON
BEAL, Merrill D. ('Samuel M.
Beal'), 1898- , American;
nonfiction CON PAC
BEALE, Calvin Lunsford,
1923- , American; nonfiction
CON
BEALES, Arthur Charles
Frederick, 1905- , English;
nonfiction HOE
BEALEY, Frank William, 1922- ,
English; nonfiction CON
BEALS, Alan Robin, 1928- ,
American; nonfiction CON
BEALS, Carleton, 1893- ,
American; nonfiction, transla-
tions CON KAT KT WA
BEALS, Frank Lee, 1881- ,
American; nonfiction CON
BEALS, Ralph Leon, 1901- ,
American; nonfiction CON
BEALU, Marcel, 1908- , French;
poetry DIF
BEAMAN, Joyce Proctor, 1931- ,
American; nonfiction CON
BEAMAN, S.G. Hulme, 20th cent.,
English; juveniles DOY
BEAMISH, Annie O'Meara de Vic
('Noel de Vic Beamish'),
1883- , Irish; fiction CON
BEAMISH, Huldine V., 1904- ,
Irish; nonfiction CON
BEAN, George Ewart, 1903- ,
English; nonfiction CON
BEAN, Keith Fenwick ('Kay Fen-
wick'; 'K. Harrington'),
1911- , Australian; plays,
nonfiction CON
BEAN, Walton Elbert, 1914- ,
American; nonfiction CON
BEAR, James Adam, Jr., 1919- ,
American; nonfiction CON
BEAR, Roberta Meyer, 1942- ,
American; nonfiction CON
BEARCE, George D., 1922- ,
American; nonfiction CON
BEARD, Charles Austin, 1874-
1848, American; nonfiction
BRO KT ST

BEARD, Daniel Carter, 1850-1941,
American; juveniles KT
BEARD, James Franklin, 1919- ,
American; nonfiction CON
BEARD, John, 1760- , English;
nonfiction HIG
BEARD, Mary Ritter, 1876-1958,
American; nonfiction KT
BEARD, Peter H., 1938- , Amer-
ican; fiction CON
BEARDE de L'ABBAYE, 18th cent.,
French; nonfiction DIL
BEARDEN, James Hudson, 1933- ,
American; nonfiction CON
BEARDSLEE, John Walter III,
1914- , American; nonfiction
CON
BEARDSLEY, Aubrey Vincent, 1872-
98, British; poetry KBA SA
BEARDSLEY, Charles Noel, 1914- ,
American; fiction, nonfiction
CON
BEARDSLEY, Elizabeth Lane, Amer-
ican; nonfiction CON
BEARDSLEY, Monroe Curtis, 1915- ,
American; nonfiction CON
BEARDSLEY, Richard King, 1918- ,
American; nonfiction CON
BEARDSLEY, Theodore Sterling, Jr.,
1930- , American; nonfiction
CON
BEARDWOOD, Valerie Fairfield,
American; fiction CON
BEARE, Francis Wright, 1902- ,
Canadian; nonfiction CON
BEARE, M.A. Nikki, 1928- ,
American; nonfiction CON
BEARN, Pierre, 1902- , French;
poetry, fiction DIF
BEARSS, Edwin Cole, 1923- ,
American; nonfiction CON
BEAS, Diego Luque de, 1828-90,
Spanish; journalism, fiction,
plays SA
BEASLAI, Piaras, 1883- , Irish;
nonfiction HOE
BEASLEY, Jerry Carr, 1940- ,
American; nonfiction CON
BEASLEY, M. Robert, 1918- ,
American; nonfiction CON
BEASLEY, Rex, 1925- , American;
nonfiction, plays CON
BEATH, Paul Robert, 1905- ,
American; nonfiction CON
'BEATON, Anne' see WASHINGTON,
Marguerite B.
BEATO, Donald Leonard, 1929-71,

Canadian; nonfiction CON
BEATON, George see BRENAN,
Gerald
BEATON-JONES, Cynon, 1921- ,
Welsh; juveniles CON
BEATRICE de DIE, fl. 1160?,
French; poetry DIF HAR ST
BEATTIE, Carol, 1918- , Amer-
ican; nonfiction CON
BEATTIE, James, 1735-1803, Eng-
lish; poetry BRO KB SA ST
BEATTIE, Jessie Louise, 1896- ,
Canadian; poetry, nonfiction,
fiction CON
BEATTIE, John Hugh Marshall,
1915- , English; nonfiction
CON
BEATTIE, Lisa Redfield, 1924- ,
American; nonfiction CON
BEATTY, Charles Clinton, 1715-
72, American; nonfiction KAA
'BEATTY, Elizabeth' see HOLLO-
WAY, Teresa B.
BEATTY, Hetty Burlingame, 1907- ,
American; juveniles, nonfiction
CON FUL WA
BEATTY, Jerome, Jr. ('Aaron W.
Stookey'), 1918- , American;
fiction, juveniles CON WA
BEATTY, John Louis, 1922- ,
American; fiction CON
BEATTY, Patricia Robbins,
1922- , American; juveniles,
nonfiction COM CON WA
BEATTY, William Alfred, 1912- ,
Australian; nonfiction CON
BEATUS RHENANUS (Bild aus
Rheinai), 1485-1547, Alsation;
nonfiction ST
BEATY, David, 1919- , English;
fiction CON
BEATY, Janice Janowski, 1930- ,
American; nonfiction CON
BEATY, John Yocum, 1884- ,
American; juveniles HOO WA
BEAUBENS, Guillaume, 1718-78,
French; nonfiction DIL
BEAUCHAMP, Kenneth Lloyd,
1939- , American; nonfiction
CON
BEAUCHAMP, Mary Annette see
RUSSELL, Mary A.B.
BEAUCHAMP, Kathleen M. see
MANSFIELD, Katherine
'BEAUCHAMP, Pat' see WASHING-
TON, Marguerite B.
BEAUCHAMPS, Pierre François

Godard, 1689-1761, French; non-
fiction DIL
BEAUCHEMIN, Neree, 1850-1931,
Canadian; poetry SY
BEAUCLAIR, P. L., 1735-1804,
French; nonfiction DIL
BEAUCLERK, Helen de Vere, 1892- ,
English; fiction KT
BEAUCOUSIN, François Jean, 1692-
1723, French; poetry DIL
BEAUDEAU, Nicolas, 1730-92,
French; nonfiction DIL
BEAUDET, Henri see 'ARLES, Henri
d' '
BEAUDOIN, Kenneth Lawrence ('Victor
de Chatillrault'; 'James de
Todany'), 1913- , American; non-
fiction CON
BEAUFILS, Guillaume, 1674-1757,
French; nonfiction DIL
BEAUFORT, Louis, 18th cent.,
French; nonfiction DIL
BEAUFORT, Margaret, 1441-1509,
English; nonfiction SA
BEAUGENDRE, Antoine, 1628-1708,
French; nonfiction DIL
BEAUHARNAIS, Marie Françoise,
1737-1813, French; poetry DIL
SA
BEAULAC, Willard L., 1899- ,
American; nonfiction CON
BEAULIEU, Charles Gilloton, 18th
cent., French; nonfiction DIL
BEAUMAN, Eric Bentley, English;
nonfiction CON
BEAUMANOIR, Philippe de Remi,
1250?-96, French; poetry DIF
BEAUMARCHAIS, Pierre Augustin
Caronde, 1732-99, French; plays,
nonfiction DIF DIL HAR KE
MAG MAL SA ST
BEAUMER, Mme. de,   -1766,
French; fiction DIL
BEAUMONT, Anne Louise Morin,
1729-83, French; nonfiction DIL
BEAUMONT, Charles ('Keith Grant-
land'; 'C. B. Lovehill'; 'S. M.
Tenneshaw'), 1929- , American;
fiction CON
BEAUMONT, Charles Allen, 1926- ,
American; nonfiction CON
BEAUMONT, Christophe de, 1703-
81, French; nonfiction DIL
BEAUMONT, Cyril William, 1891- ,
English; juveniles, nonfiction
CON
BEAUMONT, Francis, 1584/85-1616,

English; plays BRO KB MAG
SA SP ST
BEAUMONT, Guillaume Robert
Philippe,   -1761, French;
nonfiction DIL
BEAUMONT, Jean François Albani,
1753-1811, French; nonfiction
DIL
BEAUMONT, Jeanne, 1711-80,
French; nonfiction SA
BEAUMONT, Sir John, 1582-1627,
English; poetry BRO ST
BEAUMONT, Joseph, 1616-99,
English; poetry BRO ST
BEAUMONT, Simon van, 1574-
1654, Dutch; poetry ST
BEAUNIER, Charles, 1676-1737,
French; nonfiction DIL
BEAUNOIR, Alexandre Louis
Bertrand, 1746-1823, French;
plays DIL
BEAURAIN, Jean, 1696-1771,
French; nonfiction DIL
BEAUREGARD, Bernard, 1735- ,
French; poetry DIL
BEAUREGARD, Jean Nicolas,
1733-1804, French; nonfiction
DIL
BEAURIEU, Gaspard Guillard,
1728-95, French; nonfiction
DIL
BEAURLINE, Lester Albert, 1927- ,
American; nonfiction CON
BEAUSAY, Florence Edith, 1911- ,
American; nonfiction CON
BEAUSOBRE, Isaac, 1659-1738,
French; nonfiction DIL
BEAUSOBRE, Louis, 1730-83,
French; nonfiction DIL
BEAUVAIS, Gilles François, 1693-
1733, French; nonfiction DIL
BEAUVAIS, Guillaume, 1698-1773,
French; nonfiction DIL
BEAUVAIS, Jean B. Charles,
1731-90, French; nonfiction
DIL
BEAUVAU, Charles Just, 1720-93,
French; nonfiction DIL
BEAUVILLIER, 1610-87, French;
nonfiction DIL
BEAUVOIR, Edouard Roger de,
1806-66, French; fiction HAR
BEAUVOIR, Simone de, 1908- ,
French; fiction, essays, plays,
nonfiction CON DIC DIF FLE
HAR KTS MAL PIN RIC ST
BEAVER, Bruce Victor, 1928- ,

Australian; poetry, fiction MUR
BEAVER, Harold, Lothar, 1929- ,
German-English; nonfiction CON
BEAVER, Jack Patrick ('John Billing-
ton'), 1923- , English; nonfiction
CON
BEAVER, Robert Pierce, 1906- ,
American; nonfiction CON
BEAUZEE, Nicolas, 1717-89, French;
nonfiction DIL
BEBEL, Heinrich (Augustin Tünger),
1472-1518, German; fiction AL
HAR ST
BEBELL, Mildred Hoyt, 1909- ,
American; juveniles CON
BEC, Uruch see 'PERSIA, Juan de'
BECCADELLI, Antonio ('Panormita'),
1394-1471, Italian; nonfiction
ST
BECCARI, Mme., 18th cent., French;
fiction DIL
BECCARI, Antonio ('Antonio da Fer-
rara'), 1315-70, Italian; poetry
ST
BECCARI, Gilberto, 1085?- ,
Italian; fiction SA
BECCARIA, Cesare, 1738-94, Italian;
nonfiction HAR ST
BECERRA, Ricardo, 1836-1905,
Colombian; nonfiction MIN
BECHER, Emilio, 1882-1921,
Argentinian; journalism MIN
BECHER, Johannes Robert, 1891-
1958, German; poetry, nonfiction
AL FLE HAR KU ST
BECHER, Ulrich, 1910- , German;
nonfiction KU
BECHERVAISE, John Mayston, 1910-
Australian; poetry, fiction CON
BECHHOEFER, Bernhard G., 1904- ,
American; nonfiction CON
BECHSTEIN, Ludwig, 1801-60,
German; poetry, fiction AL
HAR ST
BECHT, J. Edwin, 1918- , Amer-
ican; nonfiction CON
BECHTEL, Louise Seaman, 1894- ,
American; nonfiction, juveniles
CON
BECHTLE, Wolfgang see 'DURIAN,
Wolf'
BECIC, Ferdo, 1844-1916, Croatian;
fiction ST
BECK, Aaron Temkin, 1921- ,
American; nonfiction CON
BECK, Barbara L., 1927- ,
American; juveniles CON

BECK, Carl, 1930- , American;
nonfiction CON
BECK, Charles, 1798-1866,
American; nonfiction KAA
BECK, Christian Daniel, 1757-
1832, German; nonfiction SA
'BECK, Christopher' see BRIDGES,
Thomas C.
BECK, Earl Ray, 1916- , Amer-
ican; nonfiction CON
BECK, Evelyn Torton, 1933- ,
Australian-American; nonfiction
CON
BECK, Henry Gabriel Justin,
1914- , American; nonfiction
CON
BECK, Hubert F., 1931- , Amer-
ican; nonfiction CON
BECK, Karl, 1817-79, Hungarian;
poetry, plays AL HAR ST
BECK, Lewis White, 1913- ,
American; nonfiction CON
BECK, Lil Moresby Adams ('E.
Barrington'; 'Louis Moresby'),
-1931, English; fiction KL
KT
'BECK, Phineas' see CHAMBER-
LAIN, Samuel
BECK, Robert Holmes, 1918- ,
American; nonfiction CON
BECK, Robert Nelson, 1924- ,
American; nonfiction CON
BECK, Victor Emmanuel, 1894-
1963, American; essays, non-
fiction, poetry CON
BECK, Warren Albert, 1918- ,
American; nonfiction CON
BECKE, George Lewis, 1855-
1913, Australian; fiction BRO
BECKEL, Graham, 1913- ,
American; nonfiction CON
BECKELHYMER, Paul Hunter,
1919- , American; nonfiction
CON
BECKER, Abraham Samuel, 1927- ,
American; nonfiction CON
BECKER, Albert B., 1903- ,
American; nonfiction CON
BECKER, Arthur Peter, 1918- ,
American; nonfiction CON
BECKER, Beril, 1901- , Russian-
American; nonfiction CON
BECKER, Carl Lotus, 1873-1945,
American; nonfiction KTS
BECKER, Ethel Anderson, 1893- ,
American; nonfiction PAC
BECKER, George Joseph, 1908- ,

American; nonfiction CON
BECKER, Harold K., 1933- ,
American; nonfiction CON
BECKER, Johannes Robert, 1891-
1958, German; poetry, fiction,
plays COL KUN LEN MAT SA
BECKER, John Leonard, 1901- ,
American; juveniles, nonfiction
CON WA
BECKER, Joseph M., 1908- ,
American; nonfiction CON
BECKER, Knuth, 1891/93- ,
Danish; fiction, poetry FLE ST
BECKER, Lucien, 1911- , French;
poetry DIF
BECKER, Lucille Frackman, 1929- ,
American; nonfiction CON
BECKER, Manning H., 1922- ,
American; nonfiction CON
BECKER, Marion Rombauer, 1903- ,
American; nonfiction CON
BECKER, May Lamberton, 1873- ,
American; criticism KAT KT
BECKER, Nikolaus, 1809-45, Ger-
man; poetry HAR ST
BECKER, Paula Lee, 1941- ,
American; juveniles CON
BECKER, Ruby Wirt, 1915- ,
American; juveniles CON
BECKER, Russell James, 1923- ,
American; nonfiction CON
BECKER, Samuel Leo, 1923- ,
American; nonfiction CON
BECKER, Seymour, 1934- , Amer-
ican; nonfiction CON
BECKER, Stephen David ('Steve
Dodge'), 1927- , American;
fiction, nonfiction, translations
CON
BECKER, Thomas William, 1933- ,
American; nonfiction CON
BECKER, Ulrich, 1910- , German;
fiction, plays, poetry AL
BECKER, Wesley Clemence, 1928- ,
American; nonfiction CON
BECKERMAN, Bernard, 1921- ,
American; nonfiction CON
BECKERMAN, Wilfred, 1925- ,
English; nonfiction CON
BECKETT, John Angus, 1916- ,
American; nonfiction CON
BECKETT, Ralph Lawrence, 1923- ,
American; nonfiction CON
BECKETT, Ronald Brymer ('John
Anthony'), 1891- , American;
nonfiction, fiction CON
BECKETT, Samuel Barclay, 1906- ,

Irish-French; plays, fiction,
poetry CON DIC DIF FLE
HAR KTS MAG MAL MUR
MAT PIN RIC ST
BECKEY, Fred W., 1921- ,
German-American; nonfiction
PAC
BECKFORD, 1740-1811, English;
nonfiction HIG
BECKFORD, William, 1759/60-
1844, English; fiction, non-
fiction BRO DIL KBA MAG
ST
BECKHAM, Barry, 1944- ,
American; fiction CON
BECKHARD, Arthur J., American;
juveniles WA
BECKINSALE, Robert Percy,
1908- , English; nonfiction
CON
BECKLER, Marion Floyd, 1889- ,
American; nonfiction CON
BECKMAN, Gunnel, 1910- ,
Swedish; fiction CON
BECKMANN, George Michael,
1926- , American; nonfiction
CON
BECKMANN, Martin Josef, 1924- ,
German; nonfiction CON
BECKNER, Welden Earnest,
1933- , American; nonfiction
CON
BECKOVIC, Matija, 1939- ,
Yugoslav; nonfiction, poetry
CON
BECKSON, Karl, 1926- , Amer-
ican; nonfiction CON
BECKWITH, Burnham Putnam
('John Burnham'; 'John Put-
nam'), 1904- , American;
nonfiction CON
BECKWITH, Charles Emilio,
1917- , American; nonfiction
CON
BECKWITH, John Gordon, 1918- ,
English; nonfiction CON
'BECKWITH, Lillian' see COMBER,
Lillian
BECMANN, B. L., 1694-1760,
German; nonfiction DIL
BECOMBES, 18th cent., French;
plays DIL
BECQUE, Henri François, 1837-
99, French; plays COL DIF
HAR KE MAL MAT SA ST
BECQUER, Gustavo Adolfo, 1836-
70, Spanish; poetry, fiction

BL COL HAR KE SA ST
BECQUET, Antoine, -1730,
French; nonfiction DIL
BEDAU, Hugo Adam, 1926- ,
American; nonfiction CON
BEDDALL, Barbara Gould, 1919- ,
American; nonfiction CON
BEDDALL-SMITH, Charles John,
1916- , English; nonfiction
CON
'BEDDOE, Ellaruth' see ELKINS,
Ella R.
BEDDOES, Richard Herbert, 1926- ,
Canadian; nonfiction CON
BEDDOES, Thomas Lovell, 1803-49,
British; poetry, plays BRO
KBA SA SP ST
BEDE (Baeda; Beda), 673-735, Eng-
lish; nonfiction BRO KB SA ST
'BEDE, Andrew' see BEHA, Ernest
'BEDE, Cuthbert' see BRADLEY,
Edward
BEDELL, L. Frank, 1888- , Amer-
ican; nonfiction CON
BEDELL, Maurice, 1884-1954,
French; fiction, essays DIF
FLE KT SA
BEDERSI, Abraham see ABRAHAM
BEDERSI
BEDERSI, Jeremiah see JEDAIAH
Ha-Penini Bedersi
'BEDFORD, A.N.' see WATSON,
Jane W.
'BEDFORD, Annie North' see WAT-
SON, Jane W.
BEDFORD, Francis Donkin, 1864-
1950?, English; juveniles DOY
BEDFORD, Henry Frederick, 1931- ,
American; nonfiction CON
'BEDFORD, John' see HASTINGS,
Phyllis D.H.
BEDFORD, Norton Moore, 1916- ,
American; nonfiction CON
BEDFORD, Sybille, 1911- , English;
nonfiction CON
BEDFORD-JONES, Henry, 1887- ,
American; fiction, translations
KT
BEDIER, Joseph Charles Marie,
1864-1938, French; nonfiction,
fiction COL DIF KTS SA
'BEDIAKO, K.A.' see KONADU,
Samuel A.
BEDIGIS, François Nicolas, 1738-
1802, French; poetry DIL
BEDINI, Silvio A., 1917- , Amer-
ican; nonfiction CON

'BEDNY, Demian' see PRIDVOROV,
Yefim A.
BEDOS de CELLES, Jean François,
1706- , French; nonfiction
DIL
'BEDOTT, Widow' see WHITCHER,
Frances M.B.
BEDOUIL, Jean (Bedoisch), 1683-
1755, French; nonfiction DIL
BEDOYA, Javier M. de see
MARTINEZ de BEDOYA,
Javier
BEDREGAL, Juan Francisco,
1883-1945, Bolivian; poetry,
fiction MIN SA
BEDREGAL, Yolanda, 1910- ,
Bolivian; poetry MIN
BEDSOLE, Adolph, 1914- ,
American; nonfiction CON
BEE, Clair Francis, 1900- ,
American; juveniles, nonfiction
CON WA
BEE, John David Ashford, 1931- ,
South African; fiction CON
BEEBE, Burdetta Faye, 1920- ,
American; juveniles COM
CON
BEEBE, Catherine, 1899- , Amer-
ican; juveniles HOE
BEEBE, H. Keith, 1921- , Amer-
ican; nonfiction CON
BEEBE, Maurice Laverne, 1926- ,
American; nonfiction CON
BEEBE, Ralph Kenneth, 1932- ,
American; nonfiction CON
BEEBE, Robb, 1891- , American;
juveniles HOE
BEEBE, William, 1877- , Amer-
ican; nonfiction BRO KL KT
BEECH, George T., 1931- ,
American; nonfiction CON
BEECH, Harold Reginald, 1925- ,
English; nonfiction CON
BEECH, Keyes, 1913- , Amer-
ican; nonfiction CON
BEECH, Robert Paul, 1940- ,
American; nonfiction CON
'BEECH, Webb' see BUTTER-
WORTH, William E.
BEECHER, Catherine Esther,
1800-78, American; nonfiction
KAA
BEECHER, Henry Ward, 1813-87,
American; nonfiction BRO
KAA ST
BEECHER, John, 1904- , Amer-
ican; poetry, fiction CON MUR

BEECHER, Lyman, 1775-1863,
American; nonfiction KAA
BEECHHOLD, Henry Frank ('Annraoi
O'Doire'), 1928- , American;
nonfiction CON
BEECHING, Amy Brown ('Alexis
Brown'; 'James Barbary'),
1922- , English; fiction CON
BEECHING, Jack 'James Barbary'),
English; fiction, juveniles CON
BEECROFT, John William Richard,
1902-66, American; fiction, non-
fiction CON WA
'BEEDING, Francis' ('David Pilgrim'),
Hilary St. G. Saunders, 1898-
1951; John Leslie Palmer, 1885-
1944; English; fiction BRO HOE
KT RIC
BEEGLE, Dewey Maurice, 1919- ,
American; nonfiction CON
BEEK, Martin A., 1909- , Dutch;
nonfiction CON
BEEKMAN, Allan, 1913- , Ameri-
can; fiction CON
BEEKMAN, Eric Montague, 1939- ,
Dutch; nonfiction CON
BEELER, Nelson Frederick, 1910- ,
American; juveniles FUL WA
BEELO, Andrianus, 1798-1878,
Dutch; poetry, plays ST
BEER, Eloise C.S. ('Lisl Beer';
'Lisl Drake'), 1903- , Ameri-
can; poetry, fiction CON
BEER, Ethel S., 1897- , American;
nonfiction CON
BEER, Francis Anthony, 1939- ,
American; nonfiction CON
BEER, Johann ('Daniel Speer'),
1655-1700, German; fiction
AL HAR ST
BEER, John Bernard, 1926- ,
English; nonfiction CON
BEER, Kathleen Costello, 1926- ,
American; juveniles CON
BEER, Lawrence Ward, 1932- ,
American; nonfiction CON
'BEER, Lisl' see BEER, Eloise C.S.
BEER, Michael, 1800-33, German;
plays ST
BEER, Patricia Parsons, 1924- ,
British; poetry MUR
BEER, Thomas, 1889-1940,
American; essays, fiction,
criticism BRO KL KT
BEERBOHM, Sir Max, 1872-1956,
English; essays, fiction BRO
FLE KL KT MAG MAT RIC SA
ST

BEER-HOFMANN, Richard, 1866-
1945, Austrian; fiction, poetry,
plays FLE KU MAT SA
BEERS, Burton Floyd, 1927- ,
American; nonfiction CON
BEERS, Ethel Lynn, 1827-79,
American; poetry, fiction
BRO KAA
BEERS, Henry Augustin, 1847-
1926, American; nonfiction
KAA
BEERS, Henry Putney, 1907- ,
American; nonfiction CON
BEERS, Jan van, 1821-88,
Flemish; poetry ST
BEERY, Mary, 1907- , Ameri-
can; nonfiction CON
BEETON, Isabella Mary Mayson,
1836-65, English; nonfiction
BRO
BEETS, Nicolaas ('Hildebrand'),
1814-1903, Dutch; nonfiction
KE SA ST
BEEZLEY, Paul C., 1895- ,
American; nonfiction CON
BEFFROY de REIGNEY, Louis
Abel, 1757-1811, French;
plays, fiction DIL HAR SA
BEGG, Howard Bolton, 1896- ,
American; nonfiction CON
BEGGS, David Whiteford III,
1931- , American; nonfiction
CON
BEGGS, Donald Lee, 1941- ,
American; nonfiction CON
BEGLEY, James, 1929- , Amer-
ican; nonfiction CON
BEGNER, Edith P., American;
fiction CON
BEGOVIC, Milan ('Xeres de la
Maraja'; 'Stanko Dusic'),
1876-1948, Croatian; poetry,
fiction, plays FLE ST
BEGUELIN, Nicolas de, 1714-89,
Swiss; nonfiction DIL
BEGUILLET, Edme, -1786,
French; nonfiction DIL
BEGUIN, Albert, 1901-57, Swiss;
criticism DIF
BEGUIN, Nicolas, 18th cent.,
French; nonfiction DIL
BEHA, Ernest ('Andrew Bede';
'Drake Elvin'), 1908- ,
English; nonfiction CON
BEHA, Sister Helen Marie, 1926- ,
American; nonfiction CON
BEHAN, Brendan, 1923-64, Irish;
fiction, plays, essays FLE

MAT RIC
'BEHAN, Leslie' see GOTTFRIED,
Theodore M.
BEHEIM, Michael (Behaim; Beham),
1416-74, German; poetry AL
HAR ST
BEHEIM-SCHWARZBACH, Martin,
1900- , German; fiction KU LEN
BEHLE, William Harroun, 1909- ,
American; nonfiction CON
BEHM, William Herman, Jr.,
1922- , American; juveniles
CON
BEHMEN, Jakob see BÖHME, Jakob
BEHN, Aphra Amis, 1649-89, Eng-
lish; plays, fiction BRO KB
MAG SA ST
BEHN, Harry, 1898- , American;
juveniles, poetry, plays COM
CON FUL WA
BEHNKE, Charles Albert, 1891- ,
American; nonfiction CON
BEHNKE, Frances L., American;
juveniles CON
BEHNKEN, Heinrich, 1880- , Ger-
man; plays, fiction ST
BEHR, Edward, 1926- , French;
fiction, nonfiction CON
BEHREND, Jeanne, 1911- , Amer-
ican; nonfiction CON
BEHRENS, Ernst, 1878- , German;
poetry, plays ST
BEHRENS, Herman Daniel, 1901- ,
American; nonfiction CON
BEHRENS, John C., 1933- , Amer-
ican; nonfiction CON
BEHRENS, June York, 1925- , Amer-
ican; juveniles CON WA
BEHRMAN, Jack Newton, 1922- ,
American; nonfiction CON
BEHRMAN, Lucy C., 1940- ,
American; nonfiction CON
BEHRMAN, Samuel Nathaniel, 1893-
1973, American; plays CON
KAT KT MAT ST
BEHETY, Matías, 1848/49-85,
Argentinian; journalism MIN
BEICHNER, Paul Edward, 1912- ,
American; nonfiction CON
BEIER, Ernst Gunter, 1916- ,
German-American; nonfiction
CON
BEIER, Ulli, 1922- , German;
translations CON RIC
BEIGEL, Hugo George, 1897- ,
American; nonfiction CON
BEIK, Paul Harold, 1915- , Amer-
can; nonfiction CON

BEILENSON, Lawrence, W.,
1899- , American; nonfiction
CON
BEILER, Edna, 1923- , Ameri-
can; juveniles, nonfiction CON
BEILHARZ, Edwin Alanson, 1907- ,
American; nonfiction CON
BEIM, Jerrold ('Neil Anderson'),
1910-57, American; juveniles
KJU WA
BEIM, Lorraine Levey, 1909- ,
American; juveniles KJU WA
BEIN, Albert, 1902- , American;
fiction, plays MAT
BEIRNE, Brother Kilian, 1896- ,
Irish; nonfiction CON
BEISER, Arthur, American;
juveniles WA
BEISER, Germaine, American;
juveniles WA
BEISNER, Robert Lee, 1936- ,
American; nonfiction CON
BEISSEL, Henry Eric, 1929- ,
Canadian; poetry MUR
BEISSEL, Johann Conrad, 1690-
1768, German-American;
nonfiction ST
BEISSER, Arnold Ray, 1925- ,
American; nonfiction CON
BEITH, Sir John Hay ('Ian Hay'),
1876-1952, English; fiction,
plays BRO KT RIC
BEITLER, Ethel Jane Heinkel,
1906- , American; nonfiction
CON
BEITLER, Stanley Samuel, 1924- ,
American; nonfiction, juveniles
CON WA
BEJA, Morris, 1935- , American;
nonfiction CON
BEJEROT, Nils, 1921- , Swedish;
nonfiction CON
'BEJLA, J.' see RZEWUSKI,
Henryk
BEJOT, François, 1718-87,
French; nonfiction DIL
BEKESSY, Jean see 'HABE, Hans'
BEKKER, Balthasar, 1634-98,
Dutch; nonfiction ST
BEKKER, Elizabeth Wolff, 1738-
1804, Dutch; poetry, fiction
SA
BEKKER-NIELSEN, Hans, 1933- ,
Danish; nonfiction CON
BEKLEMISHEV, Yuri Solomonovich
('Yuri Krymov'), 1908-41,
Russian; fiction HARK RIC
BEL, Jean Jacques, 1693-1738,

French; nonfiction DIL
BELAIR, Richard L., 1934- ,
American; fiction CON
BELANEY, Archie see 'GREY OWL'
BELANEY, George Stanfeld ('Grey
Owl'), 1888-1938, Canadian;
fiction ST SY
BELASCO, David, 1859-1931, Amer-
ican; plays BRO KT MAT RIC
ST
BELAUNDE, Victor Andrés, 1883- ,
Peruvian; nonfiction SA
BELCARI, Feo, 1410-84, Italian;
poetry ST
BELCASTRO, Joseph, 1910- ,
Italian-American; nonfiction CON
BELDA, Joaquin, 1880?-1937,
Spanish; fiction, journalism SA
BELDEBUSCH, Charles Leopold
(Belderbusch), 1749-1826,
French; nonfiction DIL
BELDEN, Shirley, American;
juveniles WA
BELDING, Robert Edward, 1911- ,
American; nonfiction CON
BELEW, M. Wendell, 1922- ,
American; nonfiction CON
BELFIELD, Eversley Michael Galli-
more, 1918- , English; nonfic-
tion CON
BELFORD, Lee Archer, 1913- ,
American; nonfiction CON
BELFRAGE, Cedric, 1904- ,
British; journalism, fiction CON
KT WAF
BELGION, Harold Montgomery, 1892- ,
Franco-English; nonfiction CON
BELGRANO, Manuel, 1800-40, Argen-
tinian; plays MIN
BELGRANO, Mario, 1884- , Argen-
tinian; nonfiction MIN
BELGUM, David, 1922- , Ameri-
can; nonfiction CON
BELHOMME, Humbert, 1653-1727,
French; nonfiction DIL
BELHUMAU (Belle-Humeur), 18th
cent., French; poetry DIL
BELIARD, François, 18th cent.,
French; plays DIL
BELIN, François, 1672-1732, French;
plays DIL
BELIN, Jacques Nicolas, 18th cent.,
French; nonfiction DIL
BELINDE BELLU, Jacques Nicolas,
1753-1815, French; nonfiction
DIL
BELINSKI, Maxim see YASINSKI,
Yeronim Y.

BELINSKY, Vissarion Grigoryevich,
1811-48, Russian; plays,
journalism HAR HARK KE
SA ST
BELITSKY, Abraham Harvey,
1929- , American; nonfiction
CON
BELITT, Ben, 1911- , American;
poetry CON KTS MUR
BELKIN, Samuel, 1911- , Polish-
American; nonfiction CON
BELKIND, Allen, 1927- , Amer-
ican; nonfiction CON
BELKNAP, Ivan Carl, 1916- ,
American; nonfiction CON
BELKNAP, Jeremy, 1744-98,
American; nonfiction KAA
BELKNAP, Robert Lamont, 1929- ,
American; nonfiction CON
BELKNAP, Sally Yancey, 1895- ,
American; nonfiction CON
BELL, Adrian Hanbury, 1901- ,
English; fiction, nonfiction,
poetry BRO KT
BELL, Alan Paul, 1932- , Amer-
ican; nonfiction CON
BELL, Arthur Donald, 1920- ,
American; nonfiction CON
BELL, Aubrey P.G. Fitzgerald,
1881-1950, English; nonfiction
BL SA
BELL, Bernard Iddings, 1886- ,
American; nonfiction KTS
BELL, Caroline Rose Buchanan,
1939- , English; nonfiction
CON
BELL, Carolyn Shaw, 1920- ,
American; nonfiction CON
BELL, Charles G., 1929- ,
American; nonfiction CON
BELL, Charles Greenleaf, 1916- ,
American; poetry, fiction, non-
fiction CON MUR
BELL, Charles Wentworth ('Earl
of Killreynard'), 1858-1929,
English; nonfiction HIG
BELL, Clive, 1881-1964, English;
criticism KT
BELL, Colin, 1938- , English;
nonfiction CON
BELL, Corydon White, 1894- ,
American; juveniles, fiction,
nonfiction CON JO WA
BELL, Daniel, 1919- , American;
nonfiction CON
BELL, Earl Hoyt, 1903-63, Amer-
ican; nonfiction CON
BELL, Eileen, English; juveniles

CON
'BELL, Emily Mary' see CASON,
Mabel E.
BELL, Eric Temple ('John Taine'),
1883- , Anglo-American; non-
fiction KTS
BELL, Gertrude Margave Lowthian,
1868-1926, English; nonfiction
BRO ST
BELL, Gertrude Wood, 1911- ,
American; fiction CON
'BELL, Gina' see BALZANO, Jeanne
K.
BELL, Harold Idris, 1879- , Eng-
lish; nonfiction CON
BELL, Harry, 1899- , Scots; non-
fiction CON
BELL, Henry Glassford, 1803-74,
Scots; poetry, nonfiction BRO
KBA
BELL, Herbert Clifford Francis,
1881- , Canadian; nonfiction
HOE
BELL, Isaac, 1878- , American;
nonfiction HIG
BELL, J. Bowyer, 1931- , Amer-
ican; fiction CON
BELL, Jack L., 1904- , American;
nonfiction CON
BELL, James Edward, 1941- ,
American; nonfiction CON
BELL, James Kenton, 1937- ,
American; nonfiction CON
BELL, James Madison, 1826-1902,
American; poetry KAA
BELL, John Joy, 1871-1934, Scots;
fiction BRO
BELL, Joseph N., 1921- , Amer-
ican; juveniles CON WA
BELL, Josephine see BALL, Doris B.
BELL, Joyce Denebrink, 1936- ,
American; nonfiction CON
BELL, Kensil, 1907- , American;
juveniles WA
BELL, L. Nelson, 1894- , Amer-
ican; nonfiction CON
BELL, Louise Price ('Lita Bronson';
'Ruth Jeffrey'), American; non-
fiction CON
BELL, Mackenzie, 1856-1930, Eng-
lish; poetry, nonfiction KT
BELL, Margaret Elizabeth, 1898- ,
American; fiction, nonfiction,
juveniles COM CON FUL WA
BELL, Martin ('Titus Oates'), 1918- ,
English; poetry MUR
BELL, Marvin Hartley, 1937- ,

American; poetry CON MUR
BELL, Mary H. see HAYLEY BELL,
Mary
'BELL, Neil' see SOUTHWOLD,
Stephen
BELL, Norman W., 1928- ,
Canadian-American; nonfiction
CON
'BELL, Paul' see CHORLEY, Henry
F.
BELL, Philip Wilkes, 1924- ,
American; nonfiction CON
BELL, Raymond Martin, 1907- ,
American; nonfiction CON
BELL, Robert Charles, 1917- ,
American; nonfiction CON
BELL, Robert Eugene, 1914- ,
American; nonfiction CON
BELL, Robert Roy, American;
nonfiction CON
BELL, Robert Stanley Warren,
1871-1921, English; juveniles
DOY
BELL, Sallie Lee Riley, American;
juveniles, fiction CON
BELL, Thelma Harrington, 1896- ,
American; juveniles CON WA
BELL, Vicars Walker, 1904- ,
English; juveniles CON
BELL, Wendell, 1924- , Ameri-
can; nonfiction CON
BELL, William Stewart, 1921- ,
American; nonfiction CON
BELL, Winifred, 1914- , Amer-
ican; nonfiction CON
BELLAH, James Warner, 1899- ,
American; fiction CON KT
WAF
BELLAH, Robert Neelly, 1927- ,
American; nonfiction CON
BELLAIRS, John, 1938- , Amer-
ican; juveniles COM CON
BELLAISE, Julien, 1645-1711,
French; nonfiction DIL
BELLAMANN, Henry, 1882-1945,
American; fiction, poetry KT
MAG
BELLAMY, Edward, 1850-98,
American; fiction BRO KAA
MAG ST
BELLAMY, Elizabeth Whitfield
Croom ('Kamba Thorpe'),
1837-1900, American; fiction
KAA
BELLAMY, Francis Rufus, 1886-
1972, American; fiction WAF
BELLAMY, Jacobus (Zelandiss),

1757-86, Dutch; poetry HAR SA
ST
BELLAN, José Pedro, 1889-1930,
Uruguayan; plays SA
BELLAN, Ruben C., 1918- ,
Canadian; nonfiction CON
BELLANGER-DESFRENEAUX, 18th
cent., French; nonfiction DIL
BELLARMINE, Robert, 1542-1621,
Italian; nonfiction HAR SA
BELLASIS, Margaret ('Francesca
Marton'), English; fiction HO
BELLAY, Joachim du see DU BEL-
LAY, Joachim
BELLEAU, Rémy (Remi), 1527/28-
77, French; poetry DIF HAR KE
SA ST
BELLECOUR, Jean Claude Gilles,
1725-78, French; plays DIL
BELLE-HUMEUR see BEHHUMAU
BELLE-ISLE, François Marie,
1676-1763, French; nonfiction
DIL
BELLEMANS, Daniel, 1642-74,
Flemish; poetry ST
BELLEMERE see 'SARMENT, Jean'
BELLENDEN, John, 1492?-1587?,
English; translations BRO ST
BELLENGER, François, 1688-1749,
French; nonfiction DIL
BELLER, Jacob, 1896- , Canadian;
fiction CON
BELLER, William Stern, 1919- ,
American; nonfiction CON
BELLERBY, Frances Parker,
1899- , British; poetry, fic-
tion MUR
BELLERIVE, Jules Alexis Bernard,
1690-1770, French; nonfiction
DIL
BELLET, Isaac, -1778, French;
nonfiction DIL
BELLEY, Augustin, 1697-1771,
French; nonfiction DIL
BELLI, Angela, 1935- , American;
nonfiction CON
BELLI, Gioacchino Giuseppe, 1791-
1863, Italian; poetry HAR KE
ST
BELLICARD, Jerome Charles,
1726-86, French; nonfiction DIL
BELLIDO CORMENZANA, José
María, 1922- , Spanish; plays
MAT
BELLINCIONI, Bernardo, 1452-92,
Italian; poetry HAR ST
BELLMAN, Carl Michael, 1740-95,

Swedish; poetry HAR KE SA
ST
BELLMAN, Samuel Irving,
1926- , American; nonfiction
CON
BELLO, Andrés, 1781-1865,
Venezuelan; poetry, nonfiction
BL MIN SA ST
BELLO, Carlos, 1815-54, Vene-
zuelan; fiction MIN
BELLO, Francesco ('Il Cieco di
Ferrara'), -1505, Italian;
poetry ST
BELLO, Luis, 1872-1935, Spanish;
journalism BL SA
BELLOC, Hilaire, 1870-1953,
English; essays, fiction, poetry,
nonfiction, juveniles BRO
DOY HOE KL KT MAG RIC
SA SP ST WA
BELLOC LOWNDES see LOWNDES,
Marie A. B.
'BELLOCQ, Louise' see BOUDAT,
Marie L.
BELLOW, Saul, 1915- , Amer-
ican; fiction CON FLE KTS
RIC WAF
BELLOWS, Roger Marion, 1905- ,
American; nonfiction CON
BELLOY, Dormont de ('Pierre
Laurent Buirette'), 1727-75,
French; plays DIF DIL HAR ST
'BELL-ZANO, Gina' see BALZANO,
Jeanne K.
BELMONT, Georges, 1909- ,
French; poetry, plays CON
BELMONTE BERMUDEZ, Luis, de,
1587?-1650?, Spanish; plays,
poetry BL HAR SA ST
BELOFF, Max, 1913- , Ameri-
can; nonfiction CON
BELOFF, Michael, 1942- , Eng-
lish; nonfiction CON
BELOFF, Robert Lawrence,
1923- , American; poetry
CON MUR
BELOK, Michael Victor, 1923- ,
American; nonfiction CON
BELOT, Adolphe, 1829-90,
French; fiction, plays CON
BELOT, Octavia Guichard, 1719-
1804, French; nonfiction SA
BELOTE, James Hine, 1922- ,
American; nonfiction CON
BELOUS, Russell E., 1925- ,
American; nonfiction CON
BELOWSELSKY BELOZERKI,

Alexandre, 1756-1809, Russian;
nonfiction DIL
BELPRE, Pura, American; juveniles
WA
BELSHAW, Cyril S., 1921- , New
Zealander; nonfiction CON
BELSHAW, Michael Horace, 1928- ,
New Zealander-American; non-
fiction CON
BELSLEY, David Alan, 1939- ,
American; nonfiction CON
BELTING, Natalia Maree, 1915- ,
American; nonfiction, fiction
CON WA
BELTRAMELLI, Antonio, 1879-
1930, Italian; fiction COL SA
BELTRAN, Miriam, 1914- , Amer-
ican; nonfiction CON
BELTRAN AVILA, Marcos, 1881- ,
Bolivian; fiction, plays, nonfic-
tion MIN
BELTRAN GUERRERO, Luis,
1914- , Venezuelan; journalism,
poetry SA
BELVEAL, Lorenzo Dee, 1918- ,
American; nonfiction CON
BELVO, Mme. de, 18th cent.,
French; letters DIL
'BELY, Andrey' (Boris Nikolayevich
Bugayev; Belyi), 1880-1934,
Russian; fiction, poetry COL
FLE HAR HARK RIC SA ST
BELY, Jeanette Lobach, 1916- ,
American; nonfiction CON
BELYAYEV, Yury Dmitrievich,
1876-1917, Russian; fiction ST
BELZ, Carl, 1937- , American;
nonfiction CON
BELZNER, Emil, 1901- , German;
nonfiction KU LEN
BELZONI, Giovanni Baptista, 1778-
1823, Italian; nonfiction KBA
BELZU de DORADO, Mercedes,
1835-79, Bolivian; poetry MIN
BEMBO, Pietro, 1470-1547, Italian;
nonfiction HAR KE SA ST
BEMELMANS, Ludwig, 1898-1962,
Belgian-American; juveniles
DOY FLE FUL KT RIC WA
WAF
BEMETZRIEDER, Antoine, 1743-
1817, French; nonfiction DIL
BEMIS, Samuel Flagg, 1891-1973,
American; nonfiction CON KT
'BEN AMI' (M. Rabinovich), 1858-
1932, Russian; nonfiction ST
BEN AMITAI, Levi, 1901- ,
Jewish; poetry ST

BEN EZRA see IBN EZRA
BEN HIDJDJA, 1366-1434, Arab;
poetry SA
BEN YEHUDA, Eliezer (Perelman;
Jehudah), 1858-1922, Jewish;
essays KE LAN ST
BEÑA, Cristóbal, de, 1777?-
1833?, Spanish; poetry BL
SA
BENAMOU, Michel Jean, 1929- ,
French; nonfiction CON
BENANTE, Joseph Philip, 1936- ,
American; fiction CON
BENARD, Edmond Darvil, 1914- ,
American; nonfiction HOE
BENARDE, Melvin Albert, 1923- ,
American; nonfiction CON
BENARIO, Herbert W., 1929- ,
American; nonfiction CON
BENARY-ISBERT, Margot, 1889- ,
German-American; juveniles
COM CON FUL WA
BENASUTTI, Marion, 1908- ,
American; fiction CON
BENAVENTE, Fray Toribio de,
16th cent., Spanish; nonfic-
tion SA
BENAVENTE y MARTINEZ,
Jacinto, 1866-1954, Spanish;
plays BL COL FLE HAR
HOE KL KT MAG MAT RIC
SA ST
BENAVIDES, Manuel D., 1895-
1947, Spanish; fiction, journa-
lism SA
'BEN-AVIGDOR' (Arieh Leib
Shalkovitz), 1866-1921,
Jewish; fiction ST
BENCE-JONES, Mark, 1930- ,
English; fiction CON
BENCHLEY, Nathaniel Goddard,
1915- , American; nonfiction,
fiction, movies CON
BENCHLEY, Peter Bradford,
1940- , American; fiction,
juveniles CON
BENCHLEY, Robert Charles,
1889-1945, American; fiction
BRO KT RIC
BENCUR, Matej see 'KUKUCIN,
Martin'
BENDA, Harry J., 1919- ,
Czech-American; nonfiction
CON
BENDA, Julien, 1867-1956,
French; nonfiction, essays
COL DIF HAR KL KT SA ST
BENDER, Coleman C., 1921- ,

American; nonfiction CON
'BENDER, Eando' see BINDER, Otto
O.
BENDER, Hans, 1919- , German;
nonfiction KU
BENDER, Henry Edwin, Jr.,
1937- , American; nonfiction
CON
BENDER, James Frederick, 1905- ,
American; nonfiction CON
'BENDER, Jay' see DEINDORFER,
Robert G.
BENDER, Louis W., 1927- ,
American; nonfiction CON
BENDER, Lucy Ellen, 1942- ,
American; juveniles CON
BENDER, Marylin, 1925- , Amer-
ican; nonfiction CON
BENDER, Robert M., 1936- ,
American; nonfiction CON
BENDER, Todd K., 1936- , Amer-
ican; nonfiction CON
BENDICK, Jean, 1919- , American;
juveniles COM CON FUL WA
BENDICK, Robert, 1917- , Ameri-
can; juveniles FUL WA
BENDINER, Marvin Robert, 1909- ,
American; nonfiction CON
BENDIT, Gladys Williams ('John
Presland'), 1885- , Australian;
fiction CON
BENDIT, Laurence John, 1898- ,
English; nonfiction CON
BENDIX, Reinhard, 1916- , Amer-
ican; nonfiction CON
'BEN-DOV, Meir' see BERNET,
Michael M.
BENDRE, Dattatray Ramcandra,
1896- , Indian; poetry LAN
BENEDEIZ, fl. 1125?, Anglo-
Norman; fiction HAR ST
BENEDETTI, Arrigo, 1910- ,
Italian; fiction SA
BENEDETTI, Robert Lawrence,
1939- , American; nonfiction
CON
BENEDETTO, Arnold Joseph,
1916-66, American; nonfiction
CON
BENEDICT, Dorothy Potter, 1889- ,
American; fiction CON
'BENEDICT, Joseph' see DOLLEN,
Charles J.
'BENEDICT, Leopold' see 'WINT-
SCHEWSKI, Morris'
BENEDICT, Lois Trimble, 1902-
67, American; juveniles CON

BENEDICT, Rex, 1920- ,
American; fiction CON
BENEDICT, Ruth Fulton, 1887-
1948, American; nonfiction
KTS
BENEDICT, Stewart Hurd, 1924- ,
American; fiction CON
BENEDICTSSON, Victoria Maria
('Ernst Ahlgren') 1850-88,
Swedish; fiction, plays, COL
HAR KE SA ST
BENEDIKT, Michael, 1937- ,
American; poetry, criticism
CON MUR
BENEDIKTOV, Vladimir Grigorye-
vich, 1807-73, Russian;
poetry HAR HARK ST
BENEDIKTSSON, Einar, 1864-1940,
Icelandic; poetry COL FLE
SA ST
BENEDIX, Roderick, 1811-73,
German; play ST
BENEFIELD, Barry, 1877- ,
American; fiction KT WAF
BENEGASI y LUJAN, Francisco,
1656-1742, Spanish; poetry,
plays BL SA
BENEGASI y LUJAN, José Joaquín,
1707-70, Spanish; poetry, plays
SA
BENEIT, 12th cent., Anglo-Norman;
poetry ST
BENELL, Florence Belle, 1912- ,
American; nonfiction CON
BENELLI, Sem, 1877-1949,
Italian; plays COL MAT SA
ST
BENELLO, C. George, 1926- ,
American; nonfiction CON
BENES, Jan ('Milan Stepka'),
1936- , Czech-American;
nonfiction CON
'BENES, Václav' see 'TREBIZSKY,
Vaclav B.
BENESIC, Ante, 1864-1916,
Croatian; poetry ST
BENESON, Lawrence A., Ameri-
can; juveniles WA
BENESOVA, Bozena (Zapleto Lová),
1873-1936, Czech; fiction FLE
ST
'BENET, Edouard' see EDWARDS,
William B.
BENET, Laura, 1884- , Ameri-
can; poetry, juveniles CON
KJU WA
BENET, Stephen Vincent, 1898-

1943, American; poetry, fiction
BRO FLE KL KT MAG RIC SA
SP ST

BENET, Sula, 1903- , American;
juveniles WA

BENET, William Rose, 1886-1950,
American; poetry, fiction KL
KT

BENETEVIC, Martin, -1607,
Dalmatian; poetry, plays ST

BENETON de MORANGE de PEYRINS,
Etienne Claude, -1752, French;
nonfiction DIL

BENEYTO, María, 1925- , Spanish;
poetry BL SA

BENEYTO PEREZ, Juan, 1907- ,
Spanish; nonfiction SA

BENEZET, Antoine, 1713-84, French;
nonfiction DIL

BENEZRA, Barbara Beardsley, 1921- ,
American; juveniles CON

BENFIELD, Derek, 1926- , English;
plays CON

BEN-GAVRIEL, Moscheh Ya-akov
(Eugen Hoeflich), 1891- , Austrian; nonfiction KU

BENGOECHEA, Javier de, 1919- ,
Spanish; poetry, criticism BL
SA

BENGSCH, Gerhard, 1928- , German; nonfiction AL

BENGTSSON, Arvid, 1916- ,
Swedish; nonfiction CON

BENGTSSON, Frans Gunnar, 1894-
1954, Swedish; fiction, essays,
nonfiction COL FLE HAR SA ST

BENHAM, Leslie, 1922- , Canadian;
juveniles CON

BENHAM, Lois Dakin, 1924- ,
Canadian; nonfiction CON

BENHAM, Sir William Gurney,
1859-1944, English; nonfiction
BRO

BEN-HORIN, Meir, 1918- , American; nonfiction CON

BENIAK, Valentín, 1894- , Slovak;
poetry ST

BENIGNUS, Wilhelm, 1861-1931,
German-American; poetry ST

BENINGTON, John Elson, 1921- ,
American; nonfiction CON

BEN-ISRAEL-KIDRON, Hedva,
Israeli; nonfiction CON

BENITES VINUEZA, Leopoldo (Alsino),
1906- , Ecuadoran; poetry,
essays DI

BENITEZ, Justo Pastor, 20th cent.,

Spanish; nonfiction SA

BENITEZ CARRASCO, Manuel,
1924- , Spanish; poetry SA

BENITEZ CLAROS, Rafael, 1919- ,
Spanish; criticism SA

BENITEZ de CASTRO, Cecilio,
1917- , Spanish; fiction SA

BENITSKY, Alexander Petrovich,
1780-1809, Russian; fiction,
poetry ST

BENIUSEVICIUTE-ZIMANTIENE,
Julija see ZEMAITE, Julija

BENIVIENI, Girolamo, 1483-1542,
Italian; poetry KE

BENJAMIN, Annette Francis,
1928- , American; nonfiction
CON

BENJAMIN, Bry, 1924- , American; nonfiction CON

BENJAMIN, Claude Max Edward
Pohlman ('Max Edwards';
'Marion E. George'), 1911- ,
American; nonfiction, plays
CON

BENJAMIN, Harry, 1885- ,
American; nonfiction CON

BENJAMIN, Herbert Stanley,
1922- , American; juveniles,
nonfiction CON

BENJAMIN, Park, 1809-64, American; poetry KAA

BENJAMI, Philip Robert, 1922-66,
American; fiction CON

BENJAMIN, René, 1885-1948,
French; fiction COL DIF SA

BENJAMIN, Roger W., 1942- ,
American; nonfiction CON

BENJAMIN, Samuel Greene
Wheeler, 1837-1914, American;
nonfiction KAA

BENJAMIN, Walter ('Detlev Holz';
'C. Conrad'), 1892-1940,
German; essays, nonfiction
FLE KU KUN

BENJAMIN, William Earl, 1942- ,
American; nonfiction CON

BENJAMIN ben JONAH, of
Tudela, -1173, Spanish-
Jewish; nonfiction HAR SA ST

BENKO, Stephen, 1924- , Hungarian-American; nonfiction
CON

BENKOVITZ, Miriam, J., 1911- ,
American; nonfiction CON

BENLLIURE y TUERO, Mariano,
1888- , Spanish; journalism,
fiction SA

BENLOWES, Edward, 1603?-76,
English; poetry KB ST
BENN, Caroline Decamp Wedgwood,
1926- , American; fiction,
tv, radio CON
BENN, Gottfried, 1886-1956, Ger-
man; poetry, nonfiction AL
COL FLE HAR KU KUN LEN
SA ST
BENNE, Kenneth Dean, 1908- ,
American; nonfiction CON
BENNER, Ralph Eugene, Jr.,
1932- , American; nonfiction
CON
BENNETT, Addison C., 1918- ,
American; nonfiction CON
BENNETT, Anna Elizabeth, 1914- ,
American; juveniles CON
BENNETT, Archibald, F., 1896- ,
American; nonfiction CON
BENNETT, Arnold, 1867-1931, Eng-
lish; fiction, plays BRO FLE
KL KT MAG MAT RIC SA ST
BENNETT, Bruce Lanyon, 1917- ,
American; nonfiction CON
BENNETT, Charles, 1901- , Amer-
ican; nonfiction CON
BENNETT, Charles, 1932- , Amer-
ican; nonfiction CON
BENNETT, Charles Edward, 1910- ,
American; nonfiction CON
'BENNETT, Christine' see NEU-
BAUER, William A.
BENNETT, D.M., 1818-82, Amer-
ican; nonfiction KAA
BENNETT, David H., 1935- ,
American; nonfiction CON
'BENNETT, Dwight' see NEWTON,
Dwight B.
BENNETT, Edward Martin, 1924- ,
American; nonfiction CON
BENNETT, Edward Moore, 1927- ,
American; nonfiction CON
BENNETT, Emerson, 1822-1905,
American; poetry, fiction KAA
BENNETT, Ethel M. Granger,
1891- , English; fiction, juven-
iles CON
BENNETT, Eve, American; juveniles
WA
BENNETT, Frances Grant, 1899- ,
American; nonfiction CON
BENNETT, Fredna Willis, 1906- ,
American; nonfiction CON
BENNETT, Geoffrey Martin ('Sea-
Lion'), 1909- , English; fiction
CON

BENNETT, George, 1920- ,
English; nonfiction CON
BENNETT, Gordon Anderson,
1940- , American; nonfiction
CON
BENNETT, Gordon C., 1935- ,
American; nonfiction CON
'BENNETT, Hall' see HALL,
Bennie C.H.
BENNETT, Howard Franklin,
1911- , American; nonfiction
CON
BENNETT, Jack Arthur Walter,
1911- , English; nonfiction
CON
BENNETT, James Richard, 1932- ,
American; nonfiction CON
'BENNETT, Jeremy' see BENNETT,
John J.N.
BENNETT, John, 1865- , Amer-
ican; juveniles, fiction KJU
KL
BENNETT, John Frederic,
1920- , American; poetry
CON
BENNETT, John Jerome Nelson
('Jeremy Bennett'), 1939- ,
English; nonfiction CON
BENNETT, John William, 1915- ,
American; nonfiction CON
BENNETT, Joseph, 1922- ,
American; nonfiction, fiction,
poetry CON
BENNETT, Josephine Waters,
1899- , American; nonfiction
CON
BENNETT, Kay Curley, 1922- ,
American; juveniles CON
BENNETT, Louise Coverley,
Jamaican; poetry MUR
BENNETT, Margaret Elaine,
1893- , American; nonfiction
CON
BENNETT, Marion Tinsley,
1914- , American; nonfiction
CON
BENNETT, Melba Berry, 1901- ,
American; nonfiction CON
BENNETT, Meridan, 1927- ,
American; nonfiction CON
BENNETT, Mildred R., 1909- ,
American; nonfiction CON
BENNETT, Norman Robert,
1932- , American; nonfiction
CON
BENNETT, Paul Lewis, 1921- ,
American; nonfiction CON

BENNETT, Penelope Agnes, 1938- ,
English; nonfiction CON
'BENNETT, Rachel' see HILL,
Margaret O.
BENNETT, Richard, 1899- , Irish-
American; juveniles KJU
BENNETT, Robert Andrew, 1927- ,
American; nonfiction CON
BENNETT, Scott Boyce, 1939- ,
American; nonfiction CON
BENNETT, Victor, 1919- , Amer-
ican; nonfiction CON
BENNETT, William Cox, 1820-95,
British; songs KBA
BENNETT, William L., 1924- ,
American; fiction CON
BENNETT, William Robert, 1921- ,
South African; fiction CON
BENNETTS, Pamela, 1922- , Eng-
lish; fiction CON
BENOIS, Alexander Nikolayevich,
1870- , Russian; criticism
ST
BENOIST, 12th cent., Anglo-Norman;
poetry, fiction SA
BENOIST, Michel, 1715- , French;
nonfiction DIL
BENOIT, fl. 1175, French; nonfiction
ST
BENOIT, Emile, 1910- , American;
nonfiction CON
BENOIT, Françoise Albine, 1724- ,
French; fiction, plays DIL
BENOIT, Leroy James, 1913- ,
American; nonfiction CON
BENOIT, Pierre, 1886-1962, French;
poetry, fiction COL DIF FLE
HAR KT SA
BENOIT de SAINTE MAURE (More),
fl. 1160?, French; poetry DIF
HAR KE SA ST
BENOIT de TOUL, P., 1663- ,
French; nonfiction DIL
BENOT y RODRIGUEZ, Eduardo,
1822-1907, Spanish; nonfiction
BL SA
BENOZZI, Zanetta Rosa (Silvia),
1701- , French; plays DIL
'BENRATH, Henry' (Albert Heinrich
Rausch), 1882- , German;
nonfiction KU LEN
BENSE, Max, 1910- , German;
nonfiction KU
BENSEN, Donald R., 1927- ,
American; nonfiction CON
BENSERADE, Isaac de, 1613-91,
French; poetry, plays DIF
HAR SA ST
BENSMAN, Joseph ('Jay Bentham';

'Ian Lewis'), 1922- , Ameri-
can; nonfiction CON
BENSON, Arthur Christopher,
1862-1925, English; essays,
poetry, nonfiction BRO KAT
KT SA
BENSON, C. Randolph, 1923- ,
American; nonfiction CON
BENSON, Charles Scott, 1922- ,
American; nonfiction CON
BENSON, Dennis Carroll, 1936- ,
American; nonfiction CON
BENSON, Edward Frederic, 1867-
1940, English; fiction, essays,
nonfiction BRO KL KT RIC
SA
BENSON, Frederick R., 1934- ,
American; nonfiction CON
BENSON, Godfrey R. see CHARN-
WOOD, Godfrey R.B.
BENSON, Jackson J., 1930- ,
American; nonfiction CON
BENSON, Larry Dean, 1929- ,
American; nonfiction CON
BENSON, Margaret H. Benson,
1899- , American; nonfiction
CON
BENSON, Mildred W., American;
juveniles WA
'BENSON, Richard' see COOPER,
Saul
BENSON, Robert Green, American;
nonfiction CON
BENSON, Robert Hugh, 1871-1914,
English; fiction BRO KT SA
BENSON, Robert Slater, 1942- ,
American; nonfiction CON
BENSON, Sally, 1900-72, Ameri-
can; juveniles COM CON KTS
BENSON, Stella, 1892-1933, Eng-
lish; fiction BRO KL KT RIC
SA ST
BENSON, Stephana Vere, 1909- ,
English; nonfiction, juveniles
CON
BENSON, Thomas Godfrey,
1899- , English; nonfiction
CON
BENSON, Thomas Walter, 1937- ,
American; nonfiction CON
BENSON, William Howard,
1902- , American; nonfiction
CON
BENSTED-SMITH, Richard Brian,
1929- , English; nonfiction
CON
BENSTOCK, Bernard, 1930- ,
American; nonfiction CON
BENT, Charles N., 1935- ,

American; nonfiction CON

BENT, James Theodore, 1852-97,
British; nonfiction KBA

BENT, Rudyard Kipling, 1901- ,
American; nonfiction CON

BENT, Silas, 1882- , American;
nonfiction KT

BENTEL, Pearl Bucklen, 1901- ,
American; nonfiction, juveniles
CON WA

BENTHAM, George, 1800-84,
British; nonfiction KBA

'BENTHAM, Jay' see BENSMAN,
Joseph

BENTHAM, Jeremy, 1748-1832,
English; nonfiction BRO KBA
SA ST

BENTHUL, Herman Forrest, 1911- ,
American; nonfiction CON

BENTINCK, Lord Charles Cavendish,
1868- , English; nonfiction
HIG

BENTINCK, Lord Henry, 1804-70,
English; nonfiction HIG

BENTIVOGLIO, Ercole, 1507-73,
Italian; poetry, plays, criticism
HAR ST

BENTIVOGLIO, Guido, 1579-1644,
Italian; nonfiction HAR ST

BENTIVOGLIO, Hercules, 1506-73,
Italian; nonfiction SA

BENTIVOGLIO, Matilde, 18th cent.,
Italian; poetry SA

BENTKOWSKI, Félix, 1781-1852,
Polish; nonfiction SA

BENTLAGE, Margarete, 1891- ,
German; nonfiction KU LEN

BENTLEY, Edmund Clerihew, 1875-
1956, English; journalism, fiction BRO KT RIC

BENTLEY, Eric Russell, 1916- ,
Anglo-American; nonfiction CON
KTS

BENTLEY, George Nelson, Jr.,
1918- , American; poetry PAC

BENTLEY, Gerald Eades, Jr.,
1930- , American; nonfiction
CON

BENTLEY, Howard Beebe, 1925- ,
American; nonfiction CON

BENTLEY, Phyllis Eleanor,
1894- , English; nonfiction,
tv, fiction BRO CON KAT KT
RIC SA

BENTLEY, Richard, 1662-1742, English; nonfiction, criticism BRO
KB SA ST

BENTLEY, William, 1759-1819,
American; diary KAA

BENTON, Joel, 1832-1911, American; journalism, poetry KAA

BENTON, John W., 1933- ,
American; juveniles CON

BENTON, Josephine Moffett,
1905- , American; nonfiction
CON

BENTON, Lewis Robert, 1920- ,
American; nonfiction CON

BENTON, Patricia, 1907- ,
American; juveniles CON

BENTON, Robert Douglass,
1932- , American; nonfiction
CON

BENTON, Wilbourn Eugene,
1917- , American; nonfiction
CON

BENTON, William, 1900- ,
American; fiction CON

BENVENISTI, James Lincoln,
1890- , American; nonfiction
HOE

BENWARD, Bruce Charles,
1921- , American; nonfiction
CON

BENY, Wilfred Roy ('Roloff Beny'),
1924- , Canadian; nonfiction
CON

BEN-YOSEF, Avraham Chaim,
1917- , English; nonfiction
CON

BENZ, Ernst, 1907- , German;
nonfiction CON

BENZ, Francis E., 1899- ,
American; nonfiction, juveniles
HOE

BENZIE, William, 1930- , Scots;
nonfiction CON

BENZIGER, James, 1914- ,
American; nonfiction CON

'BEN-ZION, Sh' (Simcha Alter
Gutmann), 1870-1932, Jewish;
fiction ST

BENZON, Carl Otto Valdemar,
1856-1927, Danish; plays ST

BEOLCO, Angelo ('Il Ruzzante'),
1502-42, Italian; plays HAR
ST

BERAL, Claude (Bérat; Béras),
1674-1734, French; nonfiction
DIL

BERANEK, Leo Leroy, 1914- ,
American; nonfiction CON

BERANEK, William, 1922- ,
American; nonfiction CON

BERANGER, Pierre Jean de, 1780-
1857, French; poetry DIF HAR
KE SA ST

BERARD, Jules Aram, 1933- ,
American; nonfiction CON

BERARDIER, Denis, 1729-92,
French; nonfiction DIL

BERARDIER, de BATAOT, François
Joseph, 1720-94, French; nonfiction DIL

BERAT, Claude see BERAL, Claude

BERAUD, Henri, 1885-1958, French;
fiction, criticism, journalism
DIF SA

BERAUD, Paul Emilien, 1751-1836,
French; nonfiction DIL

BERAULT-BERCASTEL, Antoine,
Henry, 1722-94, French; nonfiction, poetry DIL

BERBEROVA, Nina Nikolaevna,
1901- , Russian-American;
nonfiction CON

BERBRICH, Joan D., 1925- , American; nonfiction CON

BERBUSSE, Edward Joseph, 1912- ,
American; nonfiction CON

BERCEO, Gonzalo de, 1198?-1246/74,
Spanish; poetry BL SA ST

'BERCH, William O.' see COYNE,
Joseph E.

BERCHET, Giovanni, 1783-1851,
Italian; poetry, criticism, translations HAR KE SA ST

BERCKMAN, Evelyn Domenica ('Joanna
Wade'), 1900- , American; fiction, nonfiction CON

BERCOVICI, Konrad, 1882- ,
Rumanian-American; fiction, plays
KL KT SA WAF

BERCZELLER, Richard, 1902- ,
Hungarian-American; nonfiction
CON

BERDES, George R., 1931- ,
American; nonfiction CON

BERDIALES, German, 1896- ,
Argentinian; poetry, nonfiction
SA

BERDICHEWSKI, Micah Joseph
(Berdichevsky; 'Micha Yoseph
Bin Girion'), 1865-1921, Jewish;
fiction, essays KE LAN ST

BERDIE, Ralph Freimuth, 1916- ,
American; nonfiction CON

BERDING, Andrew Henry, 1902- ,
American; nonfiction CON

BERDYAYEV, Nikolay Alexandrovich
(Berdyaev), 1874-1948, Russian;
nonfiction COL FLE HAR HARK

KT SA ST

BEREDAY, George Z.F., 1920- ,
Polish-American; nonfiction
CON

'BEREFORD, Russell' see
ROBERTS, Cecil

BERELSON, Bernard, R.,
1912- , American; nonfiction
CON

BERELSON, David, 1943- ,
American; fiction CON

BERENDSOHN, Walter Arthur,
1884- , American; nonfiction
CON

BERENGER, Jean Pierre, 1740-
1807, Swiss; nonfiction DIL

BERENGUER CARISOMO, Arturo,
1905- , Argentinian; essays,
criticism, plays SA

BERENSON, Bernhard, 1865- ,
American; criticism KT ST

BERENSON, Conrad, 1930- ,
American; nonfiction CON

BERENSTAIN, Janice, American;
juveniles, nonfiction CON WA

BERENSTAIN, Stanley, 1923- ,
American; nonfiction, juveniles
CON WA

BERENS-TOTENOHL, Josefa see
GRIESE, Friedrich

'BERENT, Waclaw' (Waclaw
Rawicz), 1873-1940, Polish;
fiction COL FLE HAR SA ST

'BERESFORD, Anne' (Anne Ellen
File Hamburger), 1930- ,
British; poetry MUR

BERESFORD, James, 1764-1840,
English; nonfiction, fiction
BRO ST

BERESFORD, John Davys, 1873-
1947, English; fiction BRO
KL KT RIC

BERESFORD, Maurice Warwick,
1920- , English; nonfiction
CON

BERESFORD-HOWE, Constance,
1922- , Canadian; fiction SY

BERETTA, Lia, 1934- , Italian;
nonfiction CON

BERG, Darrel E., 1920- , American; fiction CON

BERG, David, 1920- , American;
nonfiction CON

BERG, Fred Anderson, 1948- ,
American; nonfiction CON

BERG, Irwin August, 1913- ,
American; nonfiction CON

BERG, Ivar Elis, Jr., 1929- ,

American; nonfiction CON
BERG, Jean Lutz, 1913- , Amer-
ican; juveniles CON
BERG, Orley M., 1918- , Amer-
ican; nonfiction CON
BERG, Paul Conrad, 1921- , Amer-
ican; nonfiction CON
BERG, Stephen, 1934- , American;
poetry CON MUR
BERGALLI, Liugia, 1703-60, Italian;
poetry SA
BERGAMEN, José, 1894/97- , Span-
ish; essays, plays COL BL SA ST
BERGAMINI, David Howland, 1928- ,
American; nonfiction, fiction
CON
BERGAMO, Andrea da see NELLI,
Pietro
BERGAUST, Erik, Norwegian-Amer-
ican; juveniles WA
BERGE, Carol ('Laura Keel'),
1928- , American; nonfiction
CON
BERGE, Carol Peppis, American;
poetry, fiction MUR
BERGEL, Egon Ernst, 1894- ,
Austrian-American; nonfiction
CON
BERGELSON, David, 1884-1952,
Jewish; fiction, plays FLE LAN
ST
BERGENDOFF, Conrad John Immanuel,
1895- , American; nonfiction
CON
BERGENGRUEN, Werner, 1892-1964,
German; poetry, fiction AL
FLE HAR KU KUN LEN RIC ST
BERGER, Arthur A., 1933- , Amer-
ican; nonfiction CON
BERGER, Bennett Maurice, 1926- ,
American; nonfiction CON
BERGER, Carl, 1925- , American;
nonfiction CON
BERGER, Evelyn Miller, 1896- ,
American; nonfiction CON
BERGER, H. Jean, 1924- , Amer-
ican; nonfiction CON
BERGER, Johan Henning, 1872-1924,
Swedish; fiction, plays COL SA
BERGER, Josef ('Jeremiah Digges'),
1903-71, American; juveniles
CON
BERGER, Klaus, 1901- , German-
American; nonfiction CON
BERGER, Marjorie Sue, 1916- ,
American; nonfiction CON
BERGER, Melvin H., 1927- ,

American; nonfiction CON
WA
BERGER, Morroe, 1917- , Amer-
ican; nonfiction CON
BERGER, Peter Ludwig, 1929- ,
American; nonfiction CON
BERGER, Rainer, 1930- , Aus-
trian-American; nonfiction
CON
BERGER, Terry, 1933- , Amer-
ican; juveniles CON
BERGER, Thomas Louis, 1924- ,
American; fiction CON
BERGER, Uwe, 1928- , German;
poetry AL
BERGER, Yves, 1933- , French;
fiction RIC
BERGERAC, Savinien Cyrano de
see CYRANO de BERGERAC,
Hector S.
BERGERAT, 18th cent., French;
plays DIL
BERGERAT, Emile, 1845-1922,
French; poetry, plays SA
BERGERE, Thea, American;
juveniles WA
BERGEVIN, Paul Emile, 1906- ,
American; nonfiction CON
BERGEY, Alyce Mae, 1934- ,
American; juveniles CON
BERGH, Henry, 1811-88, American;
nonfiction KAA
BERGH, Pieter Theodoor Helvetius
van den, 1799-1873, Dutch;
plays, poetry ST
BERGH, Samuel Johannes van den,
1814-68, Dutch; poetry, transla-
tions ST
BERGHE, Jan van den, 1360-1449,
Dutch; nonfiction ST
BERGHE, Jan van den ('Jan van
Diest'), -1559, Dutch; poetry
ST
BERGHOLZ, Olga Fyodorovna,
1910- , Russian; poetry
HARK
BERGIER, Claude François, 1721-
84, French; nonfiction, transla-
tions DIL
BERGIER, Nicolas Sylvestre, 1718-
90, French; nonfiction DIL
BERGIN, Thomas Goddard, 1904- ,
American; nonfiction, transla-
tions CON
BERGK, Theodor, 1812-81, Ger-
man; criticism SA
BERGMAN, Bo Hjalmar, 1869-

1967, Swedish; poetry, fiction
COL FLE ST

BERGMAN, Hjalmar Fredrik Elgerus,
1883-1930/40, Swedish; fiction,
plays, radio COL FLE HAR
MAT SA ST

BERGMANN, Anton (Tony), 1835-74,
Flemish; fiction HAR ST

BERGMANN, Peter Gabriel, 1915- ,
American; nonfiction CON

BERGNER, Herz, 1913- , Jewish;
fiction ST

BERGNER, Edith Müller-Beeck,
1917- , German; juveniles AL

BERGOLTS, Olga Fëdorovna, 1910- ,
Russian; poetry ST

BERGONZI, Bernard, 1929- , English; nonfiction CON

BERGONZO, Jean Louis, 1939- ,
French; fiction CON

BERGSOE, Jorgen Vilhelm, 1835-
1911, Danish; fiction HAR ST

BERGSON, Abram, 1914- , American; nonfiction CON

BERGSON, Henri, 1859-1941, French;
nonfiction COL DIF FLE HAR
KL KT RIC SA ST

'BERGSON, Leo' see STEBEL, Sidney
L.

BERGSTEDT, Harald Alfred (Peter-
sen), 1877- , Danish; poetry,
fiction ST

BERGSTROM, Louise, 1914- ,
American; fiction CON

BERGUA, Juan Bautista, 1892- ,
Spanish; fiction SA

BERIMONT, Luc, 1915- , French;
poetry, fiction DIF

BERINGAUSE, Arthur F., 1919- ,
American; nonfiction CON

BERISSO, Emilio, 1878-1922,
Argentinian; journalism MIN

BERKEBILE, Fred Donovan ('William
Donovan'; 'William Ernest'; 'Don
Stauffer'), 1900- , American;
juveniles, fiction CON

'BERKELEY, Anthony' see COX,
Anthony B.

BERKELEY, George, 1685-1753,
Irish; nonfiction BRO KB SA
ST

BERKELEY, Grantley, 1800-81,
English; nonfiction HIG

BERKEMEYER, William C., 1908- ,
American; nonfiction CON

BERKEY, Helen, 1898- , American;
nonfiction, juveniles CON

BERKHEY, Johannes le Francq
van, 1729-1812, Dutch; poetry
ST

BERKHOFER, Robert Frederick,
Jr., 1931- , American; nonfiction CON

'BERKLEY, Helen' see MOWATT,
Anna C. O. R.

BERKOVITS, Eliezer, 1908- ,
American; nonfiction CON

BERKOVITZ, Yitzchak, 1885- ,
Jewish; fiction, plays ST

BERKOWITZ, David Sandler,
1913- , American; nonfiction
CON

BERKOWITZ, Freda Pastor,
1910- , American; juveniles
CON WA

BERKOWITZ, Luci, 1938- ,
American; nonfiction CON

BERKOWITZ, Marvin, 1938- ,
American; nonfiction CON

BERKOWITZ, Pearl Henriette,
1921- , American; nonfiction
CON

BERKSON, William C., 1939- ,
American; poetry CON MUR

BERLAK, Harold, 1932- , American; nonfiction CON

BERLAND, Theodore, 1929- ,
American; nonfiction CON

BERLE, Adolf Augustus, 1895-
1971, American; nonfiction
CON

BERLEANT, Arnold, 1932- ,
American; nonfiction CON

BERLICHINGEN, Götz (Gottfried)
von, 1480-1562, German;
nonfiction HAR ST

BERLIN, Ellin, 1903- , American; fiction WAF

BERLIN, Irving N., 1917- ,
American; nonfiction CON

BERLIND, Bruce, 1926- , American; poetry CON

BERLINER, Franz, 1930- ,
Danish; fiction CON

BERLITZ, Charles L. Frambach,
1913- , American; nonfiction
CON

BERLYN, Phillippa Mary, 1923- ,
Rhodesian; poetry MUR

BERLYNE, Daniel Ellis, 1924- ,
English; nonfiction CON

BERMAN, Claire, 1936- , American; nonfiction CON

BERMAN, Daniel Marvin, 1928- ,

American; nonfiction CON
BERMAN, Louise Marguerite,
1928- , American; nonfiction
CON
BERMAN, Marshall, 1940- , Amer-
ican; nonfiction CON
BERMAN, Milton, 1924- , Ameri-
can; nonfiction CON
BERMAN, Morton, 1924- , Amer-
ican; nonfiction CON
BERMAN, Ronald, 1930- , Ameri-
can; nonfiction CON
BERMAN, Sanford, 1933- , Ameri-
can; nonfiction CON
BERMANN, Mlle. de, 18th cent.,
French; nonfiction DIL
BERMEJO, Ildefonso, 1820-92,
Spanish; plays, journalism SA
BERMONT, Hubert Ingram, 1924- ,
American; nonfiction CON
BERMOSK, Loretta Sue, 1918- ,
American; nonfiction CON
BERMUDEZ, Anacleto, 1806-52,
Cuban; poetry MIN
BERMUDEZ, Jerónimo, 1530?-99,
Spanish; poetry, plays BL SA
BERMUDEZ de CASTRO y DIEZ,
Salvador, 1817-83, Spanish;
essays, nonfiction BL HAR SA
ST
BERNA, Paul, 1913- , French;
juveniles WA
BERNAGIE, Pieter, 1656-99, Dutch;
plays HAR ST
BERNAL, Calixto, 1804-86, Cuban;
fiction MIN
BERNAL, Emilia, 1888- , Cuban;
poetry MIN SA
BERNAL de BONAVAL, 18th cent.,
Spanish; poetry SA
BERNAL y GARCIA y PIMENTAL,
Ignacio, 1910- , Mexican;
nonfiction CON
BERNALDEZ, Andrés, -1513,
Spanish; nonfiction BL SA
BERNANOS, Georges, 1888-1948,
French; fiction, essays COL
DIF FLE HAR HOE KT MAG
MAL MAT RIC SA ST
'BERNARD, A.' see KURELLA,
Alfred
BERNARD, Catherine, 1662-1712,
French; poetry SA
BERNARD, Charles, 1804-50,
French; fiction SA
BERNARD, Claude, 1813-78, French;
nonfiction DIF
BERNARD, Harold W., 1908- ,

American; nonfiction CON
BERNARD, Harry, 1896- ,
Canadian; nonfiction SY
BERNARD, Hugh Yancey, Jr.,
1919- , American; nonfiction
CON
BERNARD, Jack F., 1930- ,
American; nonfiction CON
BERNARD, Jacqueline de Sieyes,
1921- , Franco-American;
nonfiction CON
BERNARD, Jean Frédéric,
-1752, French; nonfiction
DIL
BERNARD, Jean Jacques, 1888-
1972, French; play, fiction,
essays COL DIF FLE MAT
SA ST
BERNARD, Kenneth Anderson,
1906- , American; nonfiction
CON
BERNARD, Laureat Joseph,
1922- , American; nonfiction
CON
BERNARD, Oliver, 1925- ,
British; poetry, translations
CON MUR
BERNARD, Paul ('Tristan'), 1866-
1957, French; plays, fiction
COL DIF HAR MAT SA
'BERNARD, Robert' see MARTIN,
Robert B.
BERNARD, Shirley, 1918- ,
American; nonfiction CON
'BERNARD, Stefan' see BAUMRIN,
Bernard H.
BERNARD, Tristan, 1866-1947,
French; fiction, plays ST
BERNARD, Valère, 1860-1936,
French; poetry DIF
BERNARD, William Bayle, 1807-
75, British; plays, fiction
KAA KBA
BERNARD d'ARRAS, 1757- ,
French; nonfiction DIL
BERNARD de CLAIRVAUX, 1090-
1153, French; poetry, nonfic-
tion DIF HAR KE SA ST
BERNARD de MORLAIX (Morlas),
fl. 1140, Anglo-French;
poetry HAR ST
BERNARD de VENTADOUR,
-1200?, French; poetry
DIF
BERNARD of CHARTRES, -1124/
30, French; nonfiction SA
BERNARD SILVESTER (Silvestris),
fl. 1150, French; poetry, non-

fiction DIF HAR ST
BERNARDES, Diogo, 1530/32-97/
1605, Portuguese; poetry HAR
KE SA ST
BERNARDES, Manuel, 1644-1710,
Portuguese; nonfiction HAR SA
ST
BERNARDEZ, Francisco Luis,
1900- , Argentinian; poetry BL
MIN SA
BERNARDIN de PICQUIGNY, 1633-
1709, French; nonfiction DIL
BERNARDIN de SAINT PIERRE,
Jacques Henri, 1737-1814,
French; nonfiction DIF HAR KE
MAL SA ST
BERNARDINO da SIENA, 1380-1444,
Italian; nonfiction ST
BERNARDO, Aldo Sisto, 1920- ,
American; nonfiction CON
BERNARDO, James V., 1913- ,
American; nonfiction CON
BERNARDO del CARPIO, 17th cent.,
Spanish; nonfiction BL
BERNARDONE, Giovanni see
FRANCIS of ASSISI
'BERNARN, Terrave' see BURNETT,
David
BERNART de VENTADOUR (Ventadorn),
fl. 1150-95, French; poetry HAR
KE ST
BERNART MARTI (Le Pintor), fl.
1170, French; poetry HAR ST
BERNASCONI, Ugo, 1874- , Italian;
nonfiction SA
'BERNASEK, Antonin' see 'TOMAN,
Karel'
BERNAT y BALDOVI, José, 1810-
64, Spanish; poetry, plays,
journalism SA
BERNATOWICZ, Feliks Aleksander
Gasztowt, 1786-1836, Polish;
fiction, plays ST
BERNAUER, George F., 1941- ,
American; nonfiction CON
BERNAY, Alexandre de, 12th cent.,
French; poetry DIF
BERNAYS, Anne see KAPLAN, Anne
B.
BERNAYS, Edward L., 1891- ,
Austrian-American; nonfiction
CON
BERNAZZA, Ann Marie see HAASE,
Ann M.B.
BERND, Joseph Laurence, 1923- ,
American; nonfiction CON
BERNDT, Ronald Murray, 1916- ,

Australian; nonfiction CON
BERNE, Eric Lennard ('Lennard
Gandalac'; 'Ramsbottom
Horsely'; 'Peter Pinto';
'Cyprian St. Cyr'), 1910-70,
Canadian-American; nonfiction
CON
'BERNE, Leo' see DAVIES, Leslie
P.
BERNERS, Lord, 16th cent., Eng-
lish; nonfiction BL
BERNERS, Gerald Hugh Trywhitt-
Wilson, 1883-1950, English;
fiction BRO
BERNERS, John Bourchier
(Bouchier; Bourcher), 1467-
1553, English; translations,
nonfiction BRO KB ST
BERNERS, Juliana (Bernes;
Barnes), 1388?- , English;
nonfiction BRO HIG ST
BERNET, Michael M. ('Meir Ben-
Dov'), 1930- , American;
nonfiction CON
BERNHARD, Thomas, 1931- ,
German; nonfiction KU
BERNHARDSEN, Einar Christian
Rosenvinge, 1923- , Norwe-
gian; fiction CON
BERNHARDT, Karl S., 1901- ,
Canadian; nonfiction CON
BERNHART, Joseph, 1881- ,
German; nonfiction HO
BERNHEIM, Evelyne, 1935- ,
Austrian-American; nonfiction
CON
BERNHEIM, Marc, 1924- ,
Franco-American; nonfiction
CON
BERNI, Francesco, 1497?-1535/36,
Italian; poetry HAR SA ST
BERNIER, François, 1620-88,
French; nonfiction DIF
BERNIER, Jovette, 1900- ,
Canadian; nonfiction SY
BERNIS, François Joachim de
Pierres, 1715-94, French;
nonfiction DIL SA
BERNOLAK, Anton, 1762-1813,
Slovak; nonfiction ST
BERNOU, Etienne, 1662-1714,
French; nonfiction DIL
BERNSTEIN, Alec see 'BARON,
Joseph A.'
BERNSTEIN, Aline, 1880- , Amer-
ican; fiction WAF
BERNSTEIN, Arnold, 1920- ,

American; nonfiction CON

BERNSTEIN, Barton Jannen, 1936- ,
American; nonfiction CON

BERNSTEIN, Burton, 1932- ,
American; nonfiction, fiction,
tv CON

BERNSTEIN, Harry, 1909- , American; nonfiction CON

BERNSTEIN, Henry Léon Gustave
Charles, 1876-1953, French;
plays COL DIF HAR KT MAT
SA ST

BERNSTEIN, Jeremy, 1929- ,
American; nonfiction CON

BERNSTEIN, Jerome Straus, 1936- ,
American; nonfiction CON

BERNSTEIN, Jerry Marx ('Jerry
Marx'), 1908-69, American;
fiction CON

BERNSTEIN, Leonard, 1918- ,
American; nonfiction, tv CON

BERNSTEIN, Lewis, 1915- , American; nonfiction CON

BERNSTEIN, Marilyn, 1929- ,
American; nonfiction CON

BERNSTEIN, Marver H., 1919- ,
American; nonfiction CON

BERNSTEIN, Merton Clay, 1923- ,
American; nonfiction CON

BERNSTEIN, Morey, 1919- , American; nonfiction CON

BERNSTEIN, Norman R., 1927- ,
American; nonfiction CON

BERNSTEIN, Ralph, 1921- , American; juveniles WA

BERNSTEIN, Theodore Menline,
1904- , American; nonfiction
CON

BERNUS, Alexander von, 1880- ,
German; poetry, plays FLE
KU LEN ST

BERNZWEIG, Eli P., 1927- ,
American; nonfiction CON

BEROALDE de VERVILLE, François
Vatable (Brouart), 1556/58-
1623/31, French; fiction DIF
HAR SA ST

BEROALDO, Filippo, 1453-1505,
Italian; nonfiction ST

BERON, Petar, 1797-1871, Bulgarian;
nonfiction ST

BEROSO (Berosio), 3rd cent. B.C.,
Chaldean; nonfiction SA

BEROUL, fl. 1180-1200, French;
poetry HAR SA ST

BERQUIN, Arnaud, 1750-91, French;
nonfiction, fiction DIL

BERQUIST, Goodwin Fauntleroy,
1930- , American; nonfiction
CON

BERRIAN, Albert H., 1925- ,
American; nonfiction CON

BERRIDGE, Percy Stuart Attwood,
1901- , English; nonfiction
CON

'BERRIEN' see HEAL, Edith

BERRIEN, F. Kenneth, 1909-71,
American; nonfiction CON

BERRIGAN, Daniel J., 1921- ,
American; poetry, nonfiction
CON MUR

BERRIGAN, Philip F., 1923- ,
American; essays CON

BERRIGAN, Ted (Edmund J.
Berrigan, Jr.), 1934- ,
American; poetry MUR

BERRILL, Jacquelyn Batsel,
1905- , American; juveniles
CON WA

BERRILL, Norman John, 1903- ,
English; nonfiction CON

BERRIO, Gonzalo Mateo de,
1554-1630, Spanish; poetry,
plays SA

BERRIOS, José David, 1849- ,
Bolivian; journalism, plays
MIN

BERRISFORD, Judith Mary,
1921- , English; juveniles
WA

BERRUTI, Alejandro E. (Berrutti),
1888- , Argentinian; journalism, plays MIN SA

BERRUTTI, José J., 1871- ,
Argentinian; plays, essays
MIN

BERRUYER, Isaac Joseph, 1681-
1758, French; nonfiction DIL

BERRY, André, 1902- , French;
poetry, fiction DIF

BERRY, Barbara J., 1937- ,
American; fiction CON

BERRY, Brewton, 1901- , American; nonfiction CON

BERRY, Brian Joe Lobley,
1934- , English; nonfiction
CON

BERRY, David Ronald, 1942- ,
English; nonfiction CON

BERRY, Edmund Grindlay, 1915- ,
American; nonfiction CON

'BERRY, Erick' see BEST, Evangel
A. C.

BERRY, Francis, 1915- , British;

poetry, criticism CON MUR
'BERRY, Helen' see ROWLAND,
Donald S.
BERRY, Jack, 1918- , English;
nonfiction CON
BERRY, James, 1932- , Ameri-
can; nonfiction CON
BERRY, Julia Elizabeth, 1920- ,
American; nonfiction CON
BERRY, Katherine Fiske, 1877- ,
American; nonfiction CON
BERRY, Lloyd Eason, 1935- ,
American; nonfiction CON
BERRY, Mary, 1763-1852, English;
diary, nonfiction KBA SA
BERRY, Mary Frances, 1938- ,
American; nonfiction CON
BERRY, Michael F., 1906- , Eng-
lish; nonfiction HIG
BERRY, Ronald Anthony, 1920- ,
Welsh; fiction CON
BERRY, Thomas, 1914- , Ameri-
can; nonfiction CON
BERRY, Thomas Elliott, 1917- ,
American; nonfiction CON
BERRY, Wallace Taft, 1928- ,
American; nonfiction CON
BERRY, Wendell, 1934- , Ameri-
can; poetry, fiction MUR
BERRY, William D., American;
juveniles WA
BERRY, William Turner, 1888- ,
English; nonfiction CON
BERRYMAN, John, 1914-72, Ameri-
can; poetry CON KTS MUR SP
'BERSCHADSKY, Isaiah' (Isaiah
Domaschevitsky), 1872-1910,
Polish; fiction ST
BERSCHEID, Ellen, 1936- , Ameri-
can; nonfiction CON
BERSEZIO, Vittorio, 1828-1900,
Italian; plays, fiction SA ST
BERSON, Harold, 1926- , American;
nonfiction, juveniles CON
BERSUIRE, Pierre, 1290?-1362,
French; translations ST
BERTAUT, Jean, 1552-1611, French;
poetry DIF HAR SA ST
BERTELSON, David Earl, 1934- ,
American; nonfiction CON
BERTHELET, Grégoire, 1680-1754,
French; nonfiction DIL
BERTHELOT, Joseph A., 1927- ,
American; nonfiction CON
BERTHELOT, Marcelin, 1827-1907,
French; nonfiction DIF
BERTHEREAU, François Georges,

1732-94, French; nonfiction
DIL
BERTHERS, Ray, 1902- , Amer-
ican; nonfiction CON
BERTHIER, Guillaume François,
1704-82, French; nonfiction
DIL
BERTHOD, Anselme, 1733-88,
French; nonfiction DIL
BERTHOFF, Rowland Tappan,
1921- , American; nonfiction
CON
BERTHOFF, Warner Bement,
1925- , American; nonfiction
CON
BERTHOLD von HOLLE, fl.
1250-60, German; poetry ST
BERTHOLD von REGENSBURG,
1210-72, German; nonfiction
ST
BERTHOLET, Jean, 1688-1755,
French; nonfiction DIL
BERTHOUD, Jacques Alexandre,
1935- , Swiss-English; non-
fiction CON
BERTIN, 1752-90, French; fiction
DIF
BERTIN, Antoine de, 1752-90,
French; nonfiction DIL
BERTIN, Célia, French; fiction
DIC DIF
BERTIN, Charles, 1919- ,
Belgian; fiction, poetry, plays
MAT
BERTIN, Leonard M., 1918- ,
English; nonfiction, juveniles
CON
BERTIN, Louise Angelique, 1805-
77, French; poetry SA
BERTIN d'ANTILLY, Louis
Auguste, 1760-1804, French;
plays DIL
BERTINAZZI, 1710-83, Italian;
plays DIL
BERTINI, Giovanni María, 1900- ,
Spanish; nonfiction BL
BERTINORO, Obadiah di, 1450-
1500, Italian; poetry ST
BERTKIN, Suster, 1427-1514,
Dutch; poetry ST
BERTO, Giuseppe, 1914- ,
Italian; fiction HAR KTS ST
BERTOCCI, Peter Anthony,
1910- , American; nonfiction
CON
BERTOLA de' GIORGI, Aurelio,
1753-98, Italian; poetry ST

BERTOLE, Emilia, 20th cent.,
Argentinian; poetry MIN
BERTOLINO, James, 1942- , Amer-
ican; poetry MUR
BERTOLOME ZORZI, 1230?-90,
French; poetry HAR ST
BERTOLUCCI, Attilio, 1911- ,
Italian; poetry, criticism SA
BERTON, Pierre, 1920- , American;
fiction, nonfiction CON SY
BERTOUX, Guillaume, 1723- ,
French; nonfiction DIL
BERTRAM, Ernst, 1884-1957, Ger-
man; poetry FLE HAR KU ST
BERTRAM, George Colin Lawder,
1911- , English; nonfiction
CON
BERTRAM, James Munro, 1910- ,
Australian; journalism, criticism
ST
BERTRAN, Juan Bautista, 1911- ,
Spanish; poetry SA
BERTRAN de BAR-SUR-AUBE, fl.
1200, French; poetry ST DIF
HAR
BERTRAN de BORN (Bertrand),
1140?-1215?, French; poetry
DIF HAR KE SA ST
BERTRAN y PIJOAN, Luis, 1893- ,
Spanish; poetry, essays SA
BERTRANA y CAMPTE, Prudencio,
1867-1941, Spanish; fiction,
plays SA COL
BERTRAND, Adrien, 1888-1917,
French; poetry, fiction SA
BERTRAND, Alexandre,   -1740,
French; nonfiction DIL
BERTRAND, Aloysius (Jacques
Louis Napoléon), 1807-41,
French; poetry DIF HAR KE
MAL SA ST
BERTRAND, Elie, 1712- , Swiss;
nonfiction DIL
BERTRAND, Jean, 1737-79, French;
nonfiction DIL
BERTRAND, Jean Joseph Aquiles,
1884- , French; criticism SA
BERTRAND, Louis, 1866-1941,
French; nonfiction, criticism,
fiction HOE SA
BERTSCH, Hugo, 1851-1935, German-
American; fiction ST
BERTUCH, Friedrich Justin, 1747/
48-1822/31, German; nonfiction
BL SA
BERWANGER, Eugene H., 1929- ,
American; nonfiction CON

BERWICK, Jacques Fitz-James,
1670- , French; nonfiction
DIL
BERWICK, Jean Shepherd, 1929- ,
American; juveniles CON
BERWICK, Keith Bennet, 1928- ,
Canadian; nonfiction CON
BERWINSKI, Ryszard Wincenty,
1819-79, Polish; poetry HAR
ST
BERZSENYI, Daniel, 1776-1836,
Hungarian; poetry, essays ST
BESANT, Annie Wood, 1847-1933,
English; nonfiction BRO KT
SA
BESANT, Sir Walter, 1836-1901,
British; fiction BRO KBA ST
BESCHEFER, Louis François
Xavier, 1708-93, French;
nonfiction DIL
BESCHI, Constantinus, 1680-1746,
Indian; poetry LAN
BESELER, Horst, 1925- , Ger-
man; nonfiction AL
BESENOAL, Pierre Joseph Victor,
1722-94, Swiss; nonfiction DIL
BESHERS, James Monahan,
1931- , American; nonfiction
CON
BESIER, Rudolf, 1878-1942, Eng-
lish; play BRO KT MAT
BESKOW, Bernard von, 1796-
1868, Swedish; plays HAR ST
BESKOW, Elsa Martman, 1874- ,
Norwegian-Swedish; juveniles
KJU KL
BESOIGNE, Jerome, 1686-1763,
French; nonfiction DIL
BESPLAS, Joseph Marie Anne
Gros, 1734-83, French; non-
fiction DIL
BESSARION, John, 1395-1472,
Byzantine; nonfiction ST
BESSENYEI, György, 1747-1811,
Hungarian; nonfiction, poetry
SA ST
BESSER, Johann von, 1654-1729,
German; poetry HAR ST
BESSET de la CHAPELLE, N.P.,
18th cent., French; transla-
tions DIL
BESSETTE, Gerard, 1920- ,
Canadian; poetry CON SY
BESSIE, Alvah Cecil, 1904- ,
American; fiction, essays
CON KT WAF
BESSIN, Alexandre Jacques, 1734-

1810, French; nonfiction DIL

BESSIN, Guillaume, 1654-1726,
French; nonfiction DIL

BESSINGER, Jess Balsor, Jr.,
1921- , American; nonfiction
CON

'BEST, Adam' see CARMICHAEL,
William E.

BEST, Edward, M.D., 1887- ,
American; nonfiction, fiction
SCA

BEST, Evangel Allena Champlin
('Erick Berry'; 'Anne Maxon'),
1892- , American; juveniles
COM CON KJU WA

BEST, Gary Allen, 1939- , American; nonfiction CON

BEST, Herbert, 1894- , English;
fiction, juveniles COM KJU WA
WAF

BEST, James Joseph, 1938- ,
American; nonfiction CON

BEST, John Wesley, 1909- , American; nonfiction CON

BEST, Michael Robert, 1939- ,
Australian; nonfiction CON

BEST, Oswald Herbert, 1894- ,
English; fiction CON

BEST, Rayleigh Breton Amis ('Breton
Amis'), 1905- , English; fiction
CON

BEST, Thomas Waring, 1939- ,
American; nonfiction CON

BESTE, Konrad, 1890- , German;
fiction LEN ST

BESTE, Raymond Vernon, 1908- ,
Anglo-American; plays tv,
radio, nonfiction CON

BESTER, Alfred, 1913- , American;
fiction CON

BESTIC, Alan Kent, 1922- , English;
fiction CON

BESTON, Henry Sheahan, 1888-1968,
American; juveniles, nonfiction
KJU KT

BESTOR, Arthur Eugene, Jr.,
1908- , American; nonfiction
CON

BESTUZHEV, Alexander Alexandrovich
('A. Marlinski'), 1797-1837,
Russian; fiction, poetry HARK ST

BESUCHET, Elisabeth, 1704-84,
French; poetry DIL

BESUS, Roger, 1915- , French;
fiction, plays, essays DIC FLE

BESZF, Teodoro de see BEZE,
Teodoro de

BETANCOURT, José Ramón, 1801-

57, Cuban; nonfiction MIN

BETANCOURT, José Victoriano,
1813-75, Cuban; nonfiction
MIN

BETANCOURT, Luis Victorino,
1842-85, Cuban; poetry MIN

BETANCOURT y CISNEROS,
Gaspart ('El Lugareno'), 1803-
66, Cuban; journalism MIN

BETENCOURT, Pierre Louis
Joseph, 1745-1829, French;
nonfiction DIL

BETH, Loren Peter, 1920- ,
American; nonfiction CON

BETHAM-EDWARDS, Matilda
Barbara, 1836-1919, English;
fiction KBA

BETHEL, Dell, 1929- , American; nonfiction CON

BETHEL, Paul Duane, 1919- ,
American; nonfiction CON

BETHELL, Jean Frankenberry,
1922- , American; juveniles
CON

BETHELL, Mary Ursula ('Evelyn
Hayes'), 1874-1945, New
Zealander; poetry RIC ST

BETHERS, Ray, 1902- , American; juveniles CON WA

BETHGE, Hans, 1876-1946, German; poetry, fiction, essays,
translations FLE

BETHMANN, Erick Waldemar,
1904- , American; nonfiction
CON

BETHUNE, Alexander, 1804-43,
Scots; poetry KBA

BETHUNE d'ORVAL, Anne Leonore
de, 1657-1733, French; nonfiction SA

BETHURUM, Frances Dorothy,
1897- , American; nonfiction
CON

'BETI, Mongo' (Alexandre Biyidi),
1932- , Camerounian; fiction
RIC

BETJEMAN, John, Sir, 1906- ,
British; poetry BRO CON
KTS MUR RIC SP

BETOCCHI, Carlo, 1899- ,
Italian; nonfiction, poetry
CON SA

BETSHCLA, Andrea see BEZZOLA,
Andrea

BETT, Walter Reginald, 1903- ,
British; nonfiction, poetry
CON

BETTELONI, Vittorio, 1840-1910,

Italian; poetry, translations COL
HAR SA ST
BETTEN, Francis Salesius, 1861-
1942, German; nonfiction HOE
BETTENSON, Henry Scowcroft,
1908- , English; nonfiction
CON
'BETTERIDGE, Anne' see POTTER,
Margaret M.
BETTERIDGE, Harold Thomas,
1910- , English; nonfiction
CON
BETTERSWORTH, John Knox, 1909- ,
American; nonfiction CON
BETTERTON, Thomas, 1635?-1710,
English; plays KB ST
BETTI, Ugo, 1892-1953, Italian;
plays, poetry, fiction COL FLE
HAR MAT RIC SA ST
'BETTINA' see EHRLICH, Bettina
BETTINA von ARNIM see ARNIM,
Elisabeth
BETTINELLI, Saverio, 1718-1808,
Italian; plays, criticism, nonfic-
tion HAR ST
BETTIS, Joseph Dabney, 1936- ,
American; nonfiction CON
BETTMANN, Otto Ludwig, 1903- ,
German-American; nonfiction
CON
BETTS, Doris Waugh, 1932- ,
American; fiction CON
BETTS, Emmett Albert, 1903- ,
American; nonfiction CON
BETTS, Raymond F., 1925- ,
American; nonfiction CON
BETTS, William Wilson, Jr.,
1926- , American; nonfiction
CON
BETZ, Betty, 1920- , American;
juveniles, nonfiction CON FUL
WA
BETZ, Eva Kelly ('Caroline Peters'),
American; fiction, juveniles
CON
BETZNER, Anton, 1895- , German;
nonfiction LEN
BEUM, Robert, 1929- , American;
poetry, nonfiction CON
BEUMELBURG, Werner see DWINGER,
Edwin E.
BEUTHIEN, Angelicus Erich Wilhelm,
1834-1926, German; poetry, plays
ST
'BEVAN, Alistair' see ROBERTS,
Keith J. K.
BEVAN, Bryan, 1913- , English;

nonfiction CON
BEVAN, E. Dean, 1938- ,
American; nonfiction CON
BEVAN, Jack, 1920- , English;
poetry, nonfiction CON
BEVAN, Tom, 1868- , English;
juveniles DOY
BEVANS, Margaret, American;
juveniles WA
BEVANS, Michael H., American;
juveniles WA
BEVERIDGE, Albert Jeremiah,
1862-1927, American; nonfic-
tion KT
BEVERIDGE, Oscar Maltman,
1913- , American; nonfiction
CON
BEVERLEY, Robert, 1673-1722,
American; nonfiction KAA
BEVERLEY-GIDDINGS, Arthur
Raymond, Anglo-American;
fiction WAF
BEVILACQUA, Alberto, 1934- ,
Italian; nonfiction, poetry
CON
BEVILLE, 18th cent., French;
plays DIL
BEVINGTON, David Martin,
1931- , American; nonfiction
CON
BEVINGTON, Helen, 1906- ,
American; poetry CON JO
BEVIS, Herbert Urlin, 1902- ,
American; fiction CON
BEVK, France, 1890- , Slovene;
poetry, fiction FLE ST
BEVLIN, Marjorie Elliot, 1917- ,
American; nonfiction CON
BEVY, Charles Joseph, 1738-
1830, French; nonfiction DIL
BEWICK, Thomas, 1753-1828,
English; juveniles DOY
BEWKES, Eugene Garrett, 1895- ,
American; nonfiction CON
BEWLEY, Charles Henry, 1888- ,
Irish; nonfiction CON
BEWLEY, Marius, 1918- , Amer-
ican; nonfiction CON
BEXON, Gabriel Leópold Charles
Aimé, 1748-84, French;
nonfiction DIL
BEYER, Audrey White, 1916- ,
American; juveniles CON
BEYER, Evelyn M., 1907- ,
American; juveniles CON
BEYER, Glenn H., 1913- ,
American; nonfiction CON

BEYER, Werner William, 1911- ,
 American; nonfiction CON
BEYERLE, Jean Pierre Louis,
 1740- , French; nonfiction
 DIL
BEYLE, Marie Henri see 'STENDHAL'
BEYLE, Thad L., 1934- , Ameri-
 can; nonfiction CON
BEZBARUA, Laksminath, 1868-1938,
 Indian; translations, plays, fic-
 tion LAN
BEZE, Théodore de Beszf (Beza),
 1519-1605, French; poetry, plays,
 nonfiction DIF HAR SA ST
BEZIERS, Michel, 1721-82, French;
 nonfiction DIL
BEZRUC, Petr' (Vladimir Vasek),
 1867-1958, Czech; poetry COL
 FLE SA ST
BEZWODA, Eva Susanne, 1942- ,
 South African; poetry MUR
BEZYMENSKI, Alexander Ilyich,
 1898-1973, Russian; poetry,
 plays COL HARK SA ST
BEZZOLA, Andrea (Betschla), 1840-
 97, Swiss-Romansch; poetry
 HAR ST
BEZZOLA, Eduard ('N.U. Spigna'),
 1875-1948, Raeto-Romansch;
 poetry ST
BHAGAT, Goberdham, 1928- ,
 Indian; nonfiction CON
BHAGAVATULA, Murty S., 1921- ,
 Indian; nonfiction CON
BHAGWATI, Jagdish N., 1934- ,
 Indian; nonfiction CON
BHALAN, 1426-1500, Indian; poetry
 LAN
BHANJA, Upendra, 1670-1720, Indian;
 poetry LAN
BHARATA, fl. 200, Sanskrit; nonfic-
 tion ST
BHARATI, Agehananda (Leopold
 Fischer), 1923- , Austrian-Amer-
 ican; nonfiction CON
BHARATI, C. Subrahmanya, 1882- ,
 Indian; poetry LAN
BHARAWI, 7th century, Indian;
 poetry ST
BHARTRHARI,   -651, Indian;
 poetry, nonfiction LAN ST
BHASA, 350- , Indian; plays LAN
 ST
BHASKARAN, M.P., 1921- , Indian;
 poetry MUR
BHATTA NARAYANA, 800- ,
 Sanskrit; plays ST

BHATTACHARJI, Sukumari, 1921- ,
 Indian; nonfiction CON
BHATTACHARYA, Bhabani, 1906- ,
 Indian; fiction, translations
 CON
BHAVABHUTI, 8th cent., Indian;
 plays LAN ST
BHOJA, 1008-60, Indian; fiction
 ST
BIALEK, Hayyim Nahman (Chaim),
 1873-1934, Jewish; poetry
 FLE LAN ST
BIALK, Elisa (Krautter), 1912- ,
 American; juveniles COM
 CON FUL
BIALY, Harvey, 1945- , Ameri-
 can; poetry MUR
BIANCHI, Alfred, 1882-1942,
 Argentinian; nonfiction MIN
BIANCHI, Edmundo, 1880- ,
 Uruguayan; poetry, plays,
 journalism SA
BIANCHI, Eugene Carl, 1930- ,
 American; nonfiction CON
BIANCO, José, 20th cent.,
 Argentinian; fiction MIN
BIANCO, Margery Williams
 ('Pamela Bianco'), 1881-1944,
 English; juveniles DOY KJU
 KL WA
BIANCO, Pamela, 1906- , Eng-
 lish; juveniles WA
BIANCO di SANTI da SIENA,
 1350- , Italian; poetry HAR
 ST
BIANCOLELLI, Pierre François,
 1680-1734, French; nonfiction
 DIL
BIANKI, Vitali, Russian-American;
 juveniles WA
BIASCIOLI, Niccolo Josafat,
 1768-1830, Italian; nonfiction
 SA
BIASIN, Gian-Paolo, 1933- ,
 Italian-American; nonfiction
 CON
BIBACULO, M. Furio, 103 B.C.- ,
 Roman; poetry SA
BIBAUD, Michel, 1782-1857,
 Canadian; nonfiction SY
'BIBBIENA, Il' see DOVIZI,
 Bernardo
BIBBIENA, Jean Golli, 1709-79,
 French; fiction DIL
BIBBY, Cyril, 1914- , English;
 nonfiction CON
BIBBY, Thomas Geoffrey, 1917- ,

English; nonfiction CON
BIBERMAN, Herbert, 1900-71,
American; fiction CON
BIBESCO, Princesse Marthe Lucie
Lahovary ('Lucile Decaux'),
1887- , Rumanian; fiction, es-
says FLE HO KT SA
BICE, Clare, Canadian; juveniles
WA
BICKEL, Alexander Mordecai,
1924- , Rumanian-American;
nonfiction CON
BICKERMAN, Elias Joseph, 1897- ,
Russian-American; nonfiction
CON
BICKERSTAFFE, Isaac, 1745?-1812?,
English; plays BRO KB ST
BICKERSTAFFE-DREW, Francis
Browning Drew, Count ('John
Ayscough'), 1858-1928, English;
essays, fiction KT
BICKET, Zenas Johan, 1932- ,
American; nonfiction CON
BICKHAM, Jack Miles ('Jeff Clinton';
'John Miles'), 1930- , Amer-
ican; fiction CON
BICKLE, Judith Brundrett ('J.
Tweedale'), English; fiction,
poetry CON
BIDAULT de MONTIGNY, Charles
François Jean, 18th cent.,
French; poetry DIL
BIDDLE, Bruce Jesse, 1928- ,
American; nonfiction CON
BIDDLE, Francis, 1886- , Ameri-
can; nonfiction CON
BIDDLE, Nicholas, 1786-1844, Amer-
ican; nonfiction KAA
BIDDLE, Phillips R., 1933- ,
American; nonfiction CON
BIDDLE, William Wishart, 1900- ,
American; nonfiction CON
BIDERMAN, Albert D., 1923- ,
American; nonfiction CON
BIDERMAN, Sol, 1936- , American;
fiction CON
BIDERMANN, Jakob, 1578-1639,
German; plays, fiction AL HAR
ST
BIDLOO, Govert, 1649-1713, Dutch;
poetry, plays HAR ST
BIDLOO, Lambert, 1638-1724, Dutch;
poetry ST
BIDNEY, David, 1908- , American;
nonfiction CON
BIDWELL, Percy Wells, 1888- ,

American; nonfiction CON
BIE, Cornelis de, 1627-1715,
Flemish; poetry, plays ST
BIEBER, Margarete, 1879- ,
American; nonfiction CON
BIEBUYCK, Daniel P., 1925- ,
Belgian-American; nonfiction
CON
BIEDMA, Juan José, -1931,
Argentinian; nonfiction MIN
BIEDMA, Nicasio, 19th cent.,
Argentinian; plays MIN
BIEHL, Carlota Dorotea, 1731-88,
Danish; poetry SA
BIEHLER, Robert Frederick,
1927- , American; nonfiction
CON
BIELENBERG, Christabel, 1909- ,
English; nonfiction CON
BIELER, Ludwig, 1906- ,
Austrian; nonfiction CON
BIELER, Manfred, 1934- ,
German; poetry AL
BIELFELD, Jacques Frédéric,
1717-70, German-French;
nonfiction DIL
BIELINSKY, Besarion (Visarion),
1810-48, Russian; criticism
SA
BIELOWSKI, August, 1806-76,
Polish; poetry SA
BIELSKI, Alison Joy Prosser,
1925- , British; poetry MUR
'BIELSKI, Feliks' see GIERGIELE-
WICZ, Mieczysław
BIELSKI, Joaquín, 1540-99,
Polish; poetry SA
BIELSKI, Marcin (Martin), 1495?-
1575, Polish; plays, diary
HAR SA ST
'BIELY, Andrei' see BELY, Andrey
'BIELYI, Sergei' see HOLLO,
Anselm
BIELYJ, Andrei, 1880- , Russian;
poetry, fiction, criticism SA
BIEMILLER, Ruth Cobbett, 1914- ,
American; nonfiction CON
BIEN, David Duckworth, 1930- ,
American; nonfiction CON
BIEN, Peter, 1930- , American;
nonfiction, translations CON
BIENEK, Horst, 1930- , German;
nonfiction KU
BIENSTOCK, Myron Joseph,
1922- , American; nonfiction
CON

BIENVENU, Bernard J., 1925- ,
American; nonfiction CON
BIER, Jesse, 1925- , American;
nonfiction, poetry CON PAC
BIER, William Christian, 1911- ,
American; nonfiction CON
BIERBAUM, Margaret, 1916- ,
American; nonfiction CON
BIERBAUM, Otto Julius, 1865-1910,
German; poetry, fiction, criticism
AL COL HAR SA ST
BIERCE, Ambrose Gwinett, 1842-
1914?, American; essays, fic-
tion, journalism BRO KAA MAG
ST
BIERHORST, John William, 1936- ,
American; nonfiction CON
BIERMAN, Harold, Jr., 1924- ,
American; nonfiction CON
BIERMAN, Mildred Thornton,
1912- , American; fiction CON
BIERSTEDT, Robert, 1913- , Amer-
ican; nonfiction CON
BIESANZ, Mavis Hiltunen, 1919- ,
American; nonfiction CON
BIESTER, Ernesto, 1829-80,
Portuguese; plays SA
BIESTERVELD, Betty Parsons,
1923- , American; juveniles
CON
BIEVRE, Georges Mareschal, 1747-
89, French; nonfiction DIL
BIEZANEK, Anne Campbell, 1927- ,
English; juveniles CON
BIFFI, Alcibiades, 1874- , Italian-
Argentinian; plays MIN
BIFRUN, Jocham e Tuetschét, 1506-
72, Swiss; translations ST
BIGART, Robert James, 1947- ,
American; nonfiction CON
BIGELOW, John, 1817-1911, Ameri-
can; nonfiction KAA
BIGELOW, Marybelle Schmidt,
1923- , American; nonfiction
CON
BIGG, John Stanyan, 1828-65, Eng-
lish; poetry, journalism KBA
BIGGE, Morris L., 1908- , Amer-
ican; nonfiction CON
BIGGERS, Earl Derr, 1884-1933,
American; fiction BRO KAT KT
RIC SA
BIGGERS, John Thomas, 1924- ,
American; nonfiction CON
BIGGLE, Lloyd, Jr., 1923- ,
American; fiction CON
BIGGS, Anselm G., 1914- , Ameri-
can; nonfiction CON

'BIGGS, Peter' see RIMEL, Duane
W.
BIGGS-DAVISON, John Alec,
1918- , English; nonfiction
CON
BIGIARETTI, Libero, 1906- ,
Italian; nonfiction CON
BIGLER, Vernon, 1922- , Amer-
ican; nonfiction CON
BIGNE, Gace de la, 14th cent.,
French; poetry ST
BIGNICOURT, Simon de, 1709-75,
French; nonfiction, poetry DIL
BIGONGIARI, Pietro, 1914- ,
Italian; nonfiction SA
BIGSBY, Christopher William
Edgar, 1941- , American;
nonfiction CON
BIHARI LAL, 1603-63, Indian;
poetry LAN ST
BIHRUZ, Zabih, 1890- , Persian;
fiction ST
BIJNS, Anna, 1493-1575, Dutch;
poetry ST
BIJOU, Sidney William, 1908- ,
American; nonfiction CON
BIKEL, Theodore, 1924- ,
Austrian-American; nonfiction
CON
BIKELAS, Demetrio, 1835-1908,
Greek; poetry, fiction SA
BILAC, Olavo Braz Martinos dos
Guimarães, 1865-1918,
Brazilian; poetry, essays,
journalism FLE SA ST
BILBAO, Bernardino, 1788-1844,
Chilean; nonfiction MIN
BILBAO, Francisco, 1823-64/65,
Chilean; nonfiction MIN
BILBAO, Manuel, 1827-95,
Chilean; nonfiction MIN
BILBOW, Antony, 1932- , Eng-
lish; nonfiction CON
BILD aues RHEINAE see BEATUS
RHENANUS
BILDERDIJK, Willem (Catalina),
1756-1831, Dutch; poetry,
plays HAR SA ST
BILENCHI, Romano, 1909- ,
Italian; nonfiction SA
BILHANA, 1100- , Indian; poetry
ST
BILINSKY, Yaroslav, 1932- ,
Ukranian-American; nonfiction
CON
BILKEY, Warren Joseph, 1920- ,
American; nonfiction CON
BILL, Alfred H., 1879- , Amer-

ican; juveniles KJU

BILL, Valentine T., Russian-American; nonfiction CON

BILLARD, Etienne, -1785, French; plays DIL

BILLARDON de SAUVIGNY, Etienne Louis, 1734-1807, French; nonfiction DIL

BILLARDON de SAUVIGNY, Louis Edme, 1736-1812, French; nonfiction DIL

BILL-BELOTSERKOVSKY, Vladimir Naumovich, 1884- , Russian; plays MAT

BILLECOQ, 18th cent., French; nonfiction DIL

BILLEMAZ, François, 1750-93, French; plays DIL

BILLET de FAVIERE, Martin, 1675-1727, French; nonfiction DIL

BILLETDOUX, François, 1927- , French; plays, fiction CON DIC MAT

BILLETT, Roy Oren, 1891- , American; nonfiction CON

BILLIAS, George Athan, 1919- , American; nonfiction CON

BILLINGER, Richard, 1893-1965, Austrian; poetry, plays AL COL FLE KU LEN MAT

BILLINGS, Harold Wayne, 1931- , American; nonfiction CON

BILLINGS, Henry, 1901- , American; juveniles FUL

'BILLINGS, Josh' see SHAW, Henry W.

BILLINGS, Peggy, 1928- , American; nonfiction CON

BILLINGSLEY, Edward Baxter, 1910- , American; nonfiction CON

BILLINGTON, Dora May, 1890- , English; nonfiction CON

'BILLINGTON, John' see BEAVER, Jack P.

BILLINGTON, Monroe Lee, 1928- , American; nonfiction CON

BILLINGTON, Rachel, 1942- , English; fiction CON

BILLINGTON, Ray Allen, 1903- , American; nonfiction CON

BILLINI, Francisco Gregorio, 1844-98, Dominican; journalism MIN

BILLOUET, Jacques Philippe, 1684-1720, French; nonfiction DIL

BILLUART, Charles René, 1685-1757, French; nonfiction DIL

BILLY, André, 1882-1971, French;

fiction, essays, journalism DIF SA ST

BILLY, Catherine, 1682-1758, French; nonfiction DIL

BILLY, René Toustain, -1709, French; nonfiction DIL

BIMARD, Joseph, 1703-42, French; nonfiction DIL

BIMYO see YAMADA BIMYO

'BIN GORION, M.Y.' see BERDECHEVSKY, Mikhah Y.

BINAYAN, Narciso, 1896- , Chilean; nonfiction CON

BINCHY, Daniel, 1899- , Irish; nonfiction HOE

'BINDER, Eando' see BINDER, Otto O.

BINDER, Frederick Melvin, 1931- , American; nonfiction CON

BINDER, Otto Oscar ('Eando Binder'; 'John Coleridge'; 'Gordon A. Giles'; 'Dean D. O'Brien'), 1911- , American; fiction, nonfiction CON WA

BINDING, Rudolf Georg (Arthur Moeller van der Breck), 1867-1938, German; nonfiction, poetry, fiction AL COL FLE HAR KU LEN SA ST

BINDLEY, Charles ('Harry Hiover'), 1795-1859, English; nonfiction HIG

BINDLOSS, Harold, 1866-1945, English; fiction KT

BINET-VALMER, Gustave, 1875- , French; fiction SA

BINGLE, Horst, 1933- , German; nonfiction KU

BINGER, Norman Henry, 1914- , American; nonfiction CON

BINGHAM, Alfred Mitchell, 1905- , American; nonfiction KT

'BINGHAM, Carson' see CASSIDAY, Bruce B.

BINGHAM, Edwin Ralph, 1920- , American; fiction CON

BINGHAM, Hiram, 1789-1869, American; nonfiction KAA

BINGHAM, Hiram, 1831-1908, American; translations KAA

BINGHAM, John Michael Ward, 1908- , English; fiction CON

BINGHAM, Jonathan Brewster, 1914- , American; nonfiction CON

BINGHAM, June Rossbach, 1919- ,
American; nonfiction CON

BINGHAM, Madeleine ('Julia Man-
nering'), 1912- , English;
fiction, plays CON

BINGHAM, Robert Charles, 1927- ,
American; nonfiction CON

BINGHAM, Robert E., 1925- ,
American; nonfiction CON

BINGHAM, Sallie see ELLSWORTH,
Sallie B.

BINGLEY, Clive Hamilton, 1936- ,
South African; nonfiction CON

BINGIE, Francisco Joaquín, 1763-
1856, Portuguese; poetry SA

BINION, Rudolph, 1927- , American; nonfiction CON

BINKLEY, Luther John, 1925- ,
American; nonfiction CON

'BINKS, Sarah' see HIEBERT, Paul
G.

BINNS, Archie, 1899- , American;
fiction, nonfiction KT PAC WAF

BINYON, Laurence, 1869-1943, English; poetry, plays, criticism
BRO KL KT RIC SA SP ST

BIOM, 3rd cent. B.C., Greek;
poetry ST

BION, Greek; nonfiction SA

BIONDO, Flavio, 1392-1463, Italian;
nonfiction ST

BIOT, François, 1923- , French;
nonfiction CON

BIOY-CASARES, Adolfo ('Martin
Sacastrú'; 'Javier Miranda';
'Honorio Bustos Domecq'; 'B.
Suarez Lynch'), 1914- ,
Argentinian; fiction CON MIN SA

BIRCBEAU, André, 1890- , French;
plays MAT

BIRCH, Anthony Harold, 1924- ,
English; nonfiction CON

BIRCH, David L., 1937- , American; nonfiction CON

BIRCH, Leo Bedrich, 1902- , Czech-
American; poetry, nonfiction
CON

BIRCH, Reginald, 1856-1943, English;
juveniles KJU

BIRCH-PFEIFFER, Charlotte Katharina,
1800-68, German; plays, fiction
AL HAR ST

BIRCK, Sixt see BIRK, Sixt

BIRD, Annie Laurie, 1893- ,
American; nonfiction PAC

BIRD, Anthony Cole, 1917- , English; nonfiction CON

'BIRD, Branden' see EVANS, Kay
H.

BIRD, Caroline, 1915- , American; nonfiction CON

BIRD, Cyril Kenneth ('Fougasse'),
1887- , English; fiction CON

BIRD, Dorothy Maywood, 1899- ,
American; fiction CON

BIRD, George Lloyd, 1900- ,
American; nonfiction, juveniles
CON

BIRD, Isabella see BISHOP,
Isabella B.

BIRD, Maria, 20th cent., English;
juveniles DOY

BIRD, Richard Miller, 1938- ,
Canadian; nonfiction CON

BIRD, Robert Montgomery, 1806-
54, American; fiction, plays
BRO KAA MAG SA ST

BIRD, Will R., 1891- , Canadian;
fiction CON SY

BIRD, William Ernest, 1890- ,
American; nonfiction CON

BIRENBAUM, William M.,
1923- , American; nonfiction
CON

BIRK, Sixt (Birck), 1500-54,
German; plays AL HAR ST

BIRKBECK, Morris, 1764-1825,
American; nonfiction HOO

BIRKELAND, Torger, Norwegian-
American; nonfiction PAC

BIRKEN, Siegmund von, 1626-81,
German; poetry, plays AL ST

BIRKENFELD, Günther, 1901- ,
German; nonfiction LEN

BIRKENMAYER, Sigmund Stanley,
1923- , American; nonfiction
CON

BIRKET-SMITH, Kaj, 1893- ,
Danish; nonfiction CON

BIRKOS, Alexander Sergei,
1936- , American; nonfiction
CON

BIRLA, Lakshminiwas ('Achyut'),
1909- , Indian; translations
CON

BIRLEY, Julia Davies, 1928- ,
English; fiction CON

BIRMELIN, John, 1873-1950,
American; poetry ST

BIRMINGHAM, David Bevis,
1938- , English; nonfiction
CON

BIRMINGHAM, Frances Atherton,
1920- , American; fiction CON

BIRMINGHAM, Frederic Alexander,
1911- , American; nonfiction
CON
'BIRMINGHAM, George A.' see
HANNAY, James O.
BIRMINGHAM, Walter Barr, 1913- ,
English; nonfiction CON
BIRNBACH, Martin, 1929- , Amer-
ican; nonfiction CON
BIRNBAUM, Eleazar, 1929- , Ger-
man; nonfiction CON
BIRNBAUM, Milton, 1919- , Polish-
American; nonfiction CON
BIRNE, Henry, 1921- , American;
fiction CON
BIRNEY, Alfred Earle, 1904- ,
Canadian; poetry, nonfiction,
criticism, fiction CON MUR
RIC ST SY
BIRNEY, Alice Lotvin, 1938- ,
American; nonfiction CON
BIRO, Balint Stephen ('Val Biro'),
1921- , Hungarian-English;
juveniles COM CON
BIROT, Pierre Albert, 1885-1967,
French; poetry, plays MAL
BIROTEAU, Jean Baptiste, 1758-93,
French; nonfiction DIL
BIRRELL, Augustine, 1850-1933, Eng-
lish; essays BRO KAT KT RIC
BIRREN, Faber ('GregorLang';
'Martin Lang'), 1900- , Amer-
ican; nonfiction, fiction CON
BIRREN, James Emmett, 1918- ,
American; nonfiction CON
BIRSE, Arthur Herbert, 1889- ,
American; nonfiction CON
BIRSTEIN, Ann, American; fiction
CON
BIRYUKOV, Pavel Ivanovich, 1860-
1931, Russian; nonfiction ST
BISCHOF, Ledford Julius, 1914- ,
American; nonfiction CON
BISCHOFF, Friedrich, 1896- ,
German; poetry AL KU LEN
BISCHOFF, Ilse Marthe, 1903- ,
American; juveniles FUL WA
BISCHOFF, Julia Bristol ('Julie
Arnoldy'), 1909- , American;
juveniles CON WA
BISGOOD, Margaret see MARIE
THERESE, Mother
BISHAI, Wilson B., 1923- , Amer-
ican; nonfiction CON
BISHER, James Furman, 1918- ,
American; fiction CON
BISHOP, Claire Huchet, Franco-

American; juveniles, fiction
HO KJU WA
BISHOP, Crawford M., 1885- ,
American; nonfiction CON
BISHOP, Curtis Kent ('Curt
Brandon'; 'Curt Carroll'),
1912- , American; juveniles
CON WA
BISHOP, Donald G., 1907- ,
American; nonfiction CON
BISHOP, Elizabeth, 1911- ,
American; poetry CON FLE
KTS MUR RIC SP
'BISHOP, Evelyn Morchard' see
STONOR, Oliver
BISHOP, Ferman, 1922- , Amer-
ican; nonfiction CON
BISHOP, George Wesley, Jr.,
1910- , American; nonfiction
CON
BISHOP, Grace, American;
juveniles WA
BISHOP, Isabella Bird, 1831-1904,
English; nonfiction KBA
'BISHOP, Jack' see DORMAN,
Michael
BISHOP, James Alonzo, 1907- ,
American; nonfiction CON
BISHOP, John Lyman, 1913- ,
American; nonfiction CON
BISHOP, John Peale, 1892-1944,
American; poetry, essays
FLE KTS SA SP
BISHOP, Joseph Warren, Jr.,
1915- , American; nonfiction
CON
BISHOP, Leonard, 1922- , Amer-
ican; fiction CON
BISHOP, Maxine H., 1919- ,
American; nonfiction CON
'BISHOP, Morchard' see STONOR,
Oliver
BISHOP, Morris Gilbert ('W. Boling-
broke Johnson'), 1893-1973,
American; nonfiction, transla-
tions CON KTS
BISHOP, Robert Lee, 1931- ,
American; nonfiction CON
BISHOP, Samuel, 1731-95, English;
poetry BRO ST
BISHOP, Tania Kroitor ('Tetiana
Shevchuck'; 'Virlyana Semkiw'),
1906- , Canadian-American;
nonfiction CON
BISHOP, Thomas Walter, 1929- ,
Austrian-American; nonfiction
CON

BISHOP, William Arthur, 1923- ,
English; nonfiction CON
BISHOP, William Warner, Jr.,
1906- , American; nonfiction
CON
BISKIN, Miriam, 1920- , American;
nonfiction CON
'BISQUE, Anatole' see BOSQUET,
Alain
BISSELL, Claude T., 1916- ,
Canadian; nonfiction SY
BISSELL, Richard Pike, 1913- ,
American; nonfiction, fiction,
plays CON
BISSETT, Bill, 1939- , Canadian;
poetry MUR
BISSET, Donald, 1910- , English;
juveniles CON
BISSON, Alexandre, 1848-1912,
French; plays DIF
BISSOONDOYAL, Basdeo, 1906- ,
Mauritian; nonfiction CON
BISTICCI, Vespasiano, da, 1421-98,
Italian; nonfiction ST
BISTRIZKI, Nathan, 1895- , Russian;
fiction, plays ST
BITAUBE, Paul Jérémie, 1732-1808,
French; translations, poetry, non-
fiction DIL SA
'BITE, Ben' see SCHNECK, Stephen
BITTEL, Lester Robert, 1918- ,
American; nonfiction CON
BITTERMAN, Henry John, 1904- ,
American; nonfiction CON
BITTINGER, Desmond Wright, 1905- ,
American; nonfiction CON
BITTINGER, Emmert Foster, 1925- ,
American; nonfiction CON
BITTLE, Rev. Celestine, 1884- ,
American; nonfiction HO
BITTNER, William Robert, 1921- ,
American; nonfiction CON
BITTON, Davis, 1930- , American;
nonfiction CON
BITZIUS, Albert see 'GOTTHELF,
Jeremias'
BIVEN, William Carl, 1925- ,
American; nonfiction CON
BIXBY, Jerome Lewis ('Jay B.
Drexel'; 'Emerson Jans'; 'D.B.
Lewis'; 'Harry Neal'; 'Albert
Russell'; 'J. Russell'; 'M. St.
Vivant'), 1923- , American;
fiction CON
'BIXBY, Ray Z.' see TRALINS, S.
Robert
BIXBY, William Courtney, 1920- ,

American; nonfiction CON WA
BIXLER, William Allen, 1876- ,
American; juveniles, nonfiction
HOO
BIYIDI, Alexandre see 'BETI,
Mongo'
BIZZELL, William Bennett,
1876- , American; nonfiction
MAR
BJAERREGARD, Henrik Anker,
1792-1848, Norwegian; poetry,
plays SA ST
BJARKLIND, Unnur B. see
'HULDA'
BJERKE, Jarl André ('Bernhard
Borge'), 1918- , Norwegian;
poetry, translations, fiction
FLE
BJERRE, Jens, 1921- , American;
nonfiction CON
BJÖRKMAN, Edwin August, 1866- ,
Swedish-American; fiction, crit-
icism KT
BJÖRLING, Gunnar Olof, 1887-
1960, Finnish; poetry FLE
BJOERN, Jousson de Skardsá,
1574-1655, Icelandic; poetry
SA
BJORKMAN, Gorna, 1860-1923,
Swedish; nonfiction SA
BJORN, Thyra Ferre, 1905- ,
Swedish; fiction CON
BJORNARD, Reidar Bernhard,
1917- , Norwegian-American;
nonfiction CON
BJORNSON, Bjornstjerne Martinus,
1832-1910, Norwegian; plays,
fiction, poetry, nonfiction COL
HAR KE MAG MAT SA ST
BJORNSTAD, James, 1940- ,
American; nonfiction CON
BJURSTEN, Anders Herman,
1825-66, Swedish; nonfiction
SA
BLACAM, Hugh Aodh de, 1890?- ,
Irish; juveniles, fiction, non-
fiction HOE
BLACHFORD, George, 1913- ,
English; nonfiction CON
BLACHLY, Frederick Frank,
1880- , American; nonfiction
MAR
BLACHLY, Lou, 1889- , Ameri-
can; nonfiction CON
BLACK, Algernon David, 1900- ,
American; nonfiction CON
BLACK, Angus, 1943- , American;

nonfiction CON

BLACK, Charles Lund, Jr., 1915- ,
American; nonfiction, poetry
CON

BLACK, Cyril Edwin, 1915- ,
American; nonfiction CON

BLACK, David Macleod, 1941- ,
Scots; poetry CON MUR

BLACK, Duncan, 1908- , English;
nonfiction CON

BLACK, Edward Loring, 1915- ,
English; nonfiction CON

BLACK, Eugene Charlton, 1927- ,
American; nonfiction CON

BLACK, Eugene Robert, 1898- ,
American; nonfiction CON

'BLACK, Gavin' see WYND, Oswald
M.

BLACK, Hugh Cleon, 1920- , American; nonfiction CON

BLACK, Ian Stuart, 1915- , English;
fiction, plays CON

BLACK, Irma Simonton, 1906-72,
American; juveniles, nonfiction
COM CON WA

'BLACK, Ivory' see JANVIER,
Thomas A.

BLACK, James Menzies, 1913- ,
American; nonfiction CON

BLACK, John Nicholson, 1922- ,
English; nonfiction CON

BLACK, John Wilson, 1906- , American; nonfiction CON

BLACK, Joseph E., 1921- , American; nonfiction CON

BLACK, Kenneth, Jr., 1925- ,
American; nonfiction CON

'BLACK, Lionel' see BARKER, Dudley

'BLACK, Mansell' see TREVOR,
Elleston

BLACK, Margaret Katherine ('M.K.
Howorth'), 1921- , English;
fiction CON

BLACK, Martha Ellen, 1901- ,
American; nonfiction CON

BLACK, Mary Childs, 1922- ,
American; nonfiction CON

BLACK, Matthew Wilson, 1895- ,
American; nonfiction CON

BLACK, Millard H., 1912- , American; nonfiction CON

BLACK, Misha, 1910- , Russian-
English; nonfiction CON

BLACK, Percy, 1922- , Canadian;
nonfiction CON

BLACK, Stephen William, 1881-1931,
South African; fiction, plays ST

'BLACK, Veronica' see PETERS,
Maureen

'BLACK, Vince' see CERNY,
James J.

BLACK, William, 1841-98, Scots;
fiction BRO KBA ST

'BLACKBURN, Claire' see AUSTIN,
Linda

BLACKBURN, Douglas, 1857-1916,
South African; fiction, journalism ST

BLACKBURN, Edith H., American;
juveniles WA

BLACKBURN, John Fenwick,
1923- , American; fiction
CON

BLACKBURN, Joyce Knight,
1920- , American; juveniles
CON

'BLACKBURN, Lloyd' see AUSTIN,
Linda

BLACKBURN, Paul, 1926-71,
American; poetry, translations
MUR

BLACKBURN, Thomas, 1916- ,
English; poetry MUR RIC

BLACKER, Carmen Elizabeth,
1924- , English; nonfiction
CON

BLACKER, Irwin Robert, 1919- ,
American; fiction, nonfiction,
tv, movies CON

BLACKHALL, David Scott, 1910- ,
English; poetry, fiction CON

BLACKHAM, Garth J., 1926- ,
American; nonfiction CON

BLACKHAM, Harold John, 1903- ,
English; nonfiction CON

BLACKIE, John Stuart, 1809-95,
Scots; nonfiction BRO KBA
ST

BLACKING, John Anthony Randoll,
1928- , English; nonfiction
CON

BLACKLEDGE, Ethel H., 1920- ,
American; nonfiction CON

BLACKLOCK, Thomas, 1721-91,
Scots; poetry BRO

BLACKMAN, Sheldon, 1935- ,
American; nonfiction CON

'BLACKMANTLE, Bernard' see
WESTMACOTT, Charles M.

BLACKMER, Donald L.M., 1929- ,
American; nonfiction CON

BLACKMON, Charles Robert,
1925- , American; nonfiction
CON

BLACKMORE, Peter, 1909- , English; plays, fiction CON

BLACKMORE, Sir Richard, 1653-1729, English; poetry BRO KB ST

BLACKMORE, Richard Doddridge, 1825-1900, English; fiction, translations, poetry BRO KBA MAG

BLACKMUR, Richard P., 1904-65, Scots-American; poetry, criticism BRO CON FLE KT RIC ST

BLACKOFF, Edward M., 1934- , American; nonfiction CON

BLACKSHEAR, Helen Friedman, 1911- , American; nonfiction CON

'BLACKSTOCK, Charity' (Ursula Torday), 1888- , English; fiction RIC

BLACKSTOCK, Paul William, 1913- , American; nonfiction CON

BLACKSTOCK, Walter, 1917- , American; poetry CON

BLACKSTONE, Geoffrey Vaughan, 1910- , English; fiction, nonfiction CON

BLACKSTONE, Sir William, 1723-80, English; nonfiction BRO KB ST

BLACKSTONE, William Thomas, 1931- , American; nonfiction CON

BLACKWELDER, Bernice Fowler, 1902- , American; nonfiction CON

BLACKWELDER, Boyce W., 1913- , American; nonfiction CON

BLACKWELL, Alice Stone, 1857-1950, American; translations KT

BLACKWELL, Annie Louise, 1919- , American; nonfiction CON

BLACKWELL, Antonieta Louise Brown, 1825-80, American; nonfiction SA

BLACKWELL, John see 'ALUN'

BLACKWELL, Leslie, 1885- , American; nonfiction CON

BLACKWELL, Richard Joseph, 1929- , American; nonfiction CON

BLACKWELL, William L., 1929- , American; nonfiction CON

BLACKWOOD, Algernon Henry, 1869-1951, English; fiction BRO KL KT RIC

BLACKWOOD, Andrew W. Jr., 1915- , American; nonfiction CON

BLACKWOOD, Andrew Watterson, 1882- , American; nonfiction CON

BLACKWOOD, Frederick, H. T. see DUFFERIN, Lord

BLACKWOOD, George Douglas, 1919- , Canadian; nonfiction CON

BLACKWOOD, Helen Selina see DUFFERIN, Lady

BLACKWOOD, James R., 1918- , American; nonfiction CON

BLAGA, Lucien, 1895-1961, Rumanian; poetry, plays FLE ST

BLAGDEN, Cyprian, 1906-62, English; nonfiction CON

BLAGG, Charles John, 1832-1915, English; nonfiction HIG

BLAHER, Damian Joseph, 1913- , American; nonfiction CON

BLAHOSLAV, Jan, 1523-71, Czech; nonfiction ST

BLAICH, Hans Erich see 'OWL-GLASS, Dr.'

BLAICH, Theodore Paul, 1902- , American; nonfiction CON

BLAIKIE, Robert J., 1923- , New Zealander; nonfiction CON

BLAIKLOCK, Edward Musgrave ('Grammaticus'), 1903- , English; nonfiction CON

BLAINE, Delabere P., fl. 1800, English; nonfiction HIG

'BLAINE, John' see GOODWIN, Harold L. and HARKINS, Philip

BLAINEY, Ann Warriner, 1935- , American; nonfiction CON

BLAINEY, Geoffrey Norman, 1930- , Australian; nonfiction CON

BLAINVILLE, Charles Henri, 1711-69, French; nonfiction DIL

BLAIR, Calvin Patton, 1924- , American; nonfiction CON

BLAIR, Charles E., 1920- , American; nonfiction CON

BLAIR, Claude, 1922- , English; nonfiction CON

BLAIR, Edward H., 1938- , American; nonfiction CON

BLAIR, Edward Payson, 1910- ,
American; nonfiction CON
BLAIR, Eric see 'ORWELL, George'
BLAIR, Everette Love, 1907- ,
American; nonfiction CON
BLAIR, George Simms, 1924- ,
American; nonfiction CON
BLAIR, Glenn Myers, 1908- ,
American; nonfiction CON
BLAIR, Hugh, 1718-1800, Scots;
nonfiction BRO KB SA ST
BLAIR, James, 1655-1743, American;
nonfiction KAA
BLAIR, John George, 1934- ,
American; nonfiction CON
BLAIR, Kay Reynolds, 1942- ,
American; nonfiction CON
BLAIR, Leon Borden, 1917- ,
American; nonfiction CON
'BLAIR, Lucile' see YEAKLEY,
Marjory H.
BLAIR, Robert, 1699-1746, Scots;
poetry BRO KB ST
BLAIR, Robert Dike, 1919- ,
American; nonfiction CON
BLAIR, Ruth Van Ness, 1912- ,
American; juveniles CON
BLAIR, Walter, 1900- , American;
juveniles, nonfiction CON WA
BLAIR-FISH, Wallace Wilfred ('Blair',
'Wilfrid Blair'), 1889-1968, Eng-
lish; poetry CON
BLAIS, Marie Claire, 1939- ,
Canadian; fiction CON
'BLAISDELL Anne' see LININGTON,
Elizabeth
BLAISDELL, Donald C., 1899- ,
American; nonfiction CON
BLAJOT PENA, José, 1921- ,
Spanish; poetry, criticism BL
SA
'BLAKE, Andrew' see JANIFER,
Laurence M.
BLAKE, George, 1893-1961, English;
fiction BRO KT RIC ST
BLAKE, Harlan Morse, 1923- ,
American; nonfiction CON
BLAKE, Harrison Gray Otis, 1816-98,
American; nonfiction KAA
BLAKE, Israel George, 1902- ,
American; nonfiction CON
BLAKE, John Lauris, 1788-1857,
American; nonfiction KAA
BLAKE, Judith Kincade, 1926- ,
American; nonfiction CON
'BLAKE, Katherine' see WALTER,
Dorothy B.

'BLAKE, Kay' see WALTER,
Dorothy B.
BLAKE, Leslie James ('James
Lester'; 'Peter Tabard'),
1913- , Australian; nonfic-
tion CON
BLAKE, Lillie Devereux ('Tiger
Lily'), 1835-1913, American;
fiction KAA SA
BLAKE, Mary Elizabeth McGrath,
1840-1907, American; poetry
KAA
'BLAKE, Monica' see MUIR,
Marie
BLAKE, Nelson Manfred, 1908- ,
American; nonfiction CON
'BLAKE, Nicholas' see LEWIS,
Cecil Day
BLAKE, Paul C., 1916- ,
American; nonfiction CON
BLAKE, Quentin, 1932- , Eng-
lish; juveniles CON
'BLAKE, Robert' see DAVIES,
Leslie P.
BLAKE, Robert Norman William,
1916- , English; nonfiction
CON
BLAKE, Robert Rogers, 1918- ,
American; nonfiction CON
BLAKE, Robert William, 1930- ,
American; nonfiction CON
BLAKE, Sally Mirliss ('Sara'),
1925- , American; fiction
CON
BLAKE, W. H., 1861-1924,
Canadian; translations SY
'BLAKE, Walker E.' see BUTTER-
WORTH, William E.
BLAKE, William, 1757-1827,
English; poetry, essays BRO
KBA MAG SA SP ST
BLAKE, William James, 1894-
1968, American; fiction, non-
fiction CON
'BLAKE, Wilton' see PARRY,
David H.
BLAKELEY, Thomas John, 1931- ,
American; nonfiction CON
BLAKELY, Paul Lindrum, 1880-
1943, American; journalism
HOE
BLAKELY, Robert John, 1915- ,
American; nonfiction CON
BLAKENEY, Lena Whittaker,
1882- , American; poetry
MAR
BLAKER, Richard, 1893-1940,

English; fiction KT
BLAKOSLAV, Jan, 1528- , Czech;
nonfiction SA
BLALOCK, Hubert Morse, Jr.,
1926- , American; nonfiction
CON
'BLAMAN, Anna' (J. P. Vrugt),
1905-60, Dutch; fiction FLE
BLAMIRE, Susanna, 1747-94, English;
poetry BRO ST
BLAMIRES, Harry, 1916- , English;
nonfiction CON
BLANC, 18th cent., French; poetry
DIL
BLANC, Auguste Alexandre Philippe,
1813-82, French; criticism SA
BLANC, Felicidad, 1914- , Spanish;
journalism BL
BLANC, Jean Joseph Louis, 1811-82,
French; nonfiction DIF SA
BLANC, Suzanne, American; fiction
PAC
BLANCH, Robert J., 1938- , Amer-
ican; nonfiction CON
BLANCHARD, Carroll Henry, Jr.,
1928- , American; nonfiction
CON
BLANCHARD, Edward Litt Laman,
1820-89, English; plays KBA
BLANCHARD, Elie, 1672-1755, French;
nonfiction DIL
BLANCHARD, Fessenden Seaver,
1888-1963, American; nonfiction
CON
BLANCHARD, Howard Lawrence,
1909- , American; nonfiction
CON
BLANCHARD, Maurice, 1890- ,
French; poetry DIF
BLANCHARD, Ralph Harrub, 1890- ,
American; nonfiction CON
BLANCHARD, Samuel Laman,
1804-45, English; poetry, essays,
journalism KBA
BLANCHARD, William Henry, 1922- ,
American; nonfiction CON
BLANCHE, August Theodor, 1811-68,
Swedish; plays HAR ST
BLANCHE, Pierre, 1927- , French;
nonfiction CON
BLANCHET, Emilio, 1829-1915,
Cuban; poetry, plays, essays
MIN
BLANCHET, François, 1707-84,
French; nonfiction DIL
BLANCHET, Jean, 1724-78, French;
nonfiction DIL

BLANCHOT, Maurice, 1907- ,
French; essays, fiction,
criticism DIC DIF FLE MAL
PIN
BLANCK, Jacob Nathaniel, 1936- ,
American; nonfiction CON
BLANCK, Rubin, 1914- , Ameri-
can; nonfiction CON
BLANCO, Andrés Eloy, 1897-1955,
Venezuelan; poetry SA
BLANCO, Benjamín ('Juan de la
Encina'), 1832-1902, Bolivian;
nonfiction MIN
BLANCO, Eduardo, 1839-1912,
Venezuelan; nonfiction SA
BLANCO, White see WHITE,
Joseph B.
BLANCO AGUINAGA, Carlos,
1926- , Spanish; nonfiction
BL
BLANCO-AMOR, Eduardo, 1905- ,
Spanish; fiction, essays,
criticism SA
BLANCO AMOR, José, 1910- ,
Spanish; fiction SA
BLANCO BELMONTE, Marcos
Rafael, 1871- , Spanish;
poetry, fiction, journalism
SA
BLANCO CUARTIN, Manuel, 1822-
90, Chilean; journalism,
juveniles, poetry MIN
BLANCO ENCALADA, Ventura,
1782-1856, Bolivian; poetry
MIN
BLANCO FOMBONA, Horacio,
1889- , Venezuelan; poetry,
journalism SA ST
BLANCO FOMBONA, Rufino,
1874-1944, Venezuelan; poetry,
fiction, essays BL SA
BLANCO, García, Francisco,
1864- , Spanish; nonfiction
SA
BLANCO GARCIA, Vicente,
1906- , Spanish; nonfiction
SA
BLANCO PLAZA, Conrado,
1910- , Spanish; poetry,
plays SA
BLANCO SOLER, Carlos, 1894-
1962, Spanish; journalism,
nonfiction BL SA
BLANCPAIN, Marc, 1909- ,
French; fiction DIC DIF
BLAND, Edith Nesbit see NESBIT,
Edith

BLAND, Peter, 1934- , British;
poetry, plays MUR
BLANDFORD, Percy William, 1912- ,
English; nonfiction CON
BLANDIN, Louis Ambroise, 1760-
1848, French; poetry DIL
BLANDING, Don, 1894- , American;
poetry MAR
BLANDINO, Giovanni, 1923- ,
Italian; nonfiction CON
BLANE, Howard Thomas, 1926- ,
American; nonfiction CON
BLANE, William, fl. 1750- , Eng-
lish; nonfiction HIG
BLANES, Henri Barthélemy, 1707-
54, French; fiction DIL
BLANFORD, James T., 1917- ,
American; nonfiction CON
BLANK, Leonard, 1927- , Ameri-
can; nonfiction CON
BLANK, S. L., 1883- , Jewish;
fiction ST
BLANK, Sheldon Haas, 1896- ,
American; nonfiction CON
BLANKENSHIP, Albert B., 1914- ,
American; nonfiction CON
BLANKENSHIP, Lila McDowell,
1886- , American; nonfiction
CON
BLANKENSHIP, William Douglas,
1934- , American; nonfiction
CON
BLANKFORT, Michael, 1907- ,
American; fiction CON WAF
BLANKSTEN, George Irving, 1917- ,
American; nonfiction CON
BLANQ-des-ISLES, 18th cent.,
French; plays DIL
BLANSHARD, Brand, 1892- ,
American; nonfiction CON
BLANSHARD, Paul, 1892- , Amer-
ican; journalism, nonfiction
KTS
BLANTON, Martha Catherine, 1907- ,
American; plays, fiction CON
WA
BLANZACO, Andre C., 1934- ,
American; nonfiction CON
BLANZAT, Jean, 1906- , French;
fiction, criticism DIF
BLAS y UBIDE, Juan, 19th cent.,
Spanish; fiction SA
BLASCO, Eusebio, 1844-1903,
Spanish; journalism, plays,
poetry BL SA
BLASCO, Ricardo Juan, 1921- ,
Spanish; poetry SA

BLASCO IBAÑEZ, Vicente,
1867-1928, Spanish; fiction
BL COL FLE HAR KAT KT
MAG RIC SA ST
BLASE, Melvin George, 1933- ,
American; nonfiction CON
BLASER, Robin ('Avalon'),
1925- , American; poetry
MUR
BLASIER, Stewart Cole, 1925- ,
American; nonfiction CON
BLASKOV, Iliya, 1839-1913,
Bulgarian; fiction ST
BLASS, Birgit Annelise, 1940- ,
Danish-American; nonfiction
CON
BLASS, Ernst, 1890- , German;
nonfiction KU
BLASSINGAME, Wyatt Rainey,
1909- , American; nonfiction,
juveniles, fiction COM CON
WA
BLATT, Sidney Jules, 1928- ,
American; nonfiction CON
BLATTER, Dorothy, 1901- ,
American; nonfiction, fiction
CON
BLATTY, William Peter ('Terence
Clyne'), 1928- , American;
fiction CON
BLAU, Joseph, 1919- , Rumanian-
Israeli; nonfiction CON
BLAU, Joseph Leon, 1909- ,
American; nonfiction CON
BLAU, Peter Michael, 1918- ,
American; nonfiction CON
'BLAU, Sebastian' see EBERLE,
Josef
BLAUG, Mark, 1927- , Dutch-
English; nonfiction CON
BLAUMANIS, Rudolfs, 1863-1908,
Latvian; fiction SA ST
BLAUNER, Robert, 1929- ,
American; nonfiction CON
BLAUSHIELD, Babette, 1927- ,
American; nonfiction CON
BLAUSTEIN, Albert Paul, 1921- ,
American; nonfiction CON
BLAUSTEIN, Arthur I., 1933- ,
American; nonfiction CON
BLAUW, Johannes, 1912- , Dutch;
nonfiction CON
BLAVET, Jean Louis, 1719-1809,
French; nonfiction DIL
BLAXLAND, John, 1917- , Amer-
ican; nonfiction CON
BLAXLAND, William Gregory,

1918- , English; nonfiction
CON
BLAYDS, Charles Stuart see
CALVERLY, Charles S.
BLAZEK, Douglas, 1941- , Amer-
ican; poetry CON
BLECHMAN, Burt, 1932- , Ameri-
can; fiction CON
BLECUA y TEIXEIRO, José Manuel,
1913- , Spanish; nonfiction,
poetry BL SA
'BLEDLOW, John' see VALE, Henry
E.T.
BLEDSOE, Albert Taylor, 1809-77,
American; nonfiction KAA
BLEDWOE, Joseph Cullie, 1918- ,
American; nonfiction CON
BLEDSOE, Thomas Alexander,
1914- , American; nonfiction
CON
'BLEECK, Oliver' see THOMAS,
Ross
BLEECKER, Anna Eliza, 1752-83,
American; poetry KAA
BLEEKER, Sonia (Zim), 1909-71,
American; juveniles COM CON
FUL
BLEES, Robert Arthur, 1922- ,
American; nonfiction CON
BLEGEN, Theodore C., 1891- ,
American; nonfiction CON
BLEHERIS see BRERI
BLEHL, Vincent Ferrer, 1921- ,
American; nonfiction CON
BLEI, Franz, 1871- , German;
nonfiction KU
BLEIBERG, Germán, 1915- ,
Spanish; poetry, journalism,
translations BL SA
BLEIBTREU, Karl, 1859-1928,
German; criticism, fiction,
plays COL SA
BLEICH, Alan R., 1913- , Ameri-
can; nonfiction CON
BLEICHER, Michael Nathaniel, 1935- ,
American; nonfiction CON
BLEMUR, Sor Marie Jacqueline
Boutte de, 1618-96, French;
nonfiction SA
BLENCH, John Wheatley, 1926- ,
English; nonfiction CON
BLEND, Charles Daniels, 1918- ,
American; nonfiction CON
BLENERHASSET, fl. 550?-64,
English; poetry ST
BLENKINSOPP, Joseph, 1927- ,
English; nonfiction CON

BLESH, Rudolph Pickett, 1899- ,
American; nonfiction CON
BLESSINGTON, Lady (Marguerite
Power Farmer Gardiner),
1789-1849, English; diary,
fiction BRO KBA SA ST
BLEST GANA, Alberto, 1830-1920,
Chilean; fiction, poetry BL
MIN SA ST
BLEST GANA, Guillermo, 1829-
1905, Chilean; poetry, fiction
MIN SA
BLEVINS, William L., 1937- ,
American; nonfiction CON
BLEW, William Charles Arlington,
19th cent., English; nonfiction
HIG
BLEZNICK, Donald Williams,
1924- , American; nonfiction
CON
BLICHER, Steen Steensen, 1782-
1848, Danish; poetry, fiction
HAR KE SA ST
BLICK, Elsa see 'TRIOLET, Elsa'
BLICQ, Anthony, 1926- , English;
fiction CON
BLIGGER von STEINACH, fl.
1190-1200, German; poetry ST
'BLIGH, Aurora' see FABILI,
Mary
'BLIGH, Norman' see NEUBAUER,
William A.
BLIGHT, John, 1913- , American;
poetry MUR
BLIN de SAINMORE, Adrien
Michel Hyacinthe, 1733-1807,
French; plays DIL
BLIND, Mathilde Cohen, 1841-96,
German-English; poetry BRO
KBA
'BLIND HARRY' see HENRY the
MINSTREL
BLISH, James Benjamin, 1921- ,
American; fiction, poetry, tv,
novels CON
BLISHEN, Bernard Russell,
1919- , English-Canadian;
nonfiction CON
BLISHEN, Edward, 1920- , Eng-
lish; juveniles CON
BLISTEIN, Elmer Milton, 1920- ,
American; poetry, nonfiction
CON
BLITCH, Fleming Lee, 1933- ,
American; nonfiction CON
BLITZSTEIN, Marc, 1905-64,
American; plays MAT

BLIVEN, Bruce Ormsby, 1889- ,
American; criticism CON KT WA
BLIVEN, Bruce, Jr., 1916- , Amer-
ican; juveniles COM CON
BLIVEN, Naomi, 1925- , American;
nonfiction CON
BLIX, Elias, 1836-1902, Norwegian;
hymns COL SA ST
BLIXEN, Samuel, 1869-1909,
Uruguayan; criticism, journalism
SA
BLIXEN-FINECKE, Karen see
'DINESEN, Isak'
BLIZINSKI, Józef Franciszek, 1827-
93, Polish; plays ST
BLO-BZANG Chos-Kyi Nyi-Ma,
1737-1802, Tibetan; nonfiction
LAN
BLOCH, E. Maurice, American;
nonfiction CON
BLOCH, Ernst, 1885- , German;
nonfiction CON KU KUN
BLOCH, Herman David, 1914- ,
American; nonfiction CON
BLOCH, Herbert A., 1904- ,
American; nonfiction CON
BLOCH, Jean Richard, 1884-1947,
French; nonfiction, fiction, plays,
poetry, criticism DIF HAR KL KT
ST
BLOCH, Marc, 1886-1944, French;
nonfiction DIF
BLOCH, Marie Halun, 1910- ,
Russian-American; juveniles
CON WA
BLOCH, Robert, 1917- , American;
fiction CON
BLOCHMAN, Lawrence Goldtree,
1900- , American; fiction CON
BLOCK, Eugene B., 1890- , Amer-
ican; fiction CON
BLOCK, Jack, 1921- , American;
nonfiction CON
BLOCK, Irvin, 1917- , American;
juveniles CON
BLOCK, Jean Libman, American;
fiction CON
BLOCK, Lawrence, 1938- , Amer-
ican; fiction CON
BLOCKER, Clyde Edward, 1918- ,
American; nonfiction CON
BLOCKLINGER, Peggy O'More
('Peggy O'More'; 'Betty Block-
inger'; 'Jeanne Bowman'),
1895- , American; fiction CON
BLODGETT, Geoffrey Thomas, 1931- ,
American; nonfiction CON

BLODGETT, Harold William,
1900- , American; nonfiction
CON
BLODGETT, Harriett Eleanor,
1919- , American; nonfiction
CON
BLOEM, Jakobus Cornelis, 1887- ,
Dutch; poetry, essays FLE
BLOEMARDINNE van BRUSSEL,
Heilwijch,   -1336, Dutch;
nonfiction ST
BLOESCH, Donald G., 1928- ,
American; nonfiction CON
BLOESSER, Robert, 1930- ,
American; nonfiction CON
BLO-IDAN Snying-po, 14th cent.,
Tibetan; nonfiction LAN
BLOK, Alexander Alexandrovich,
1880-1921, Russian; poetry,
criticism, plays COL FLE
HAR KAT HARK KT RIC MAT
SA ST
BLOM, Gaston E., 1920- ,
American; nonfiction CON
BLOMBERG, Erik Axel, 1894-
1965, Swedish; poetry, essays,
criticism, translations COL
FLE SA ST
BLOMBERG, Harry, 1893- ,
Swedish; poetry, fiction COL
SA
BLOMBERG, Héctor Pedro,
1890-1955, Argentinian;
journalism, poetry, plays BL
MIN SA
BLOM-COOPER, Louis Jacques,
1926- , English; nonfiction
CON
BLOME, Richard, 1650-1705,
English; nonfiction HIG
BLONDE, André, 1734-94, French;
nonfiction DIL
BLONDEAU de CHARNAGE, Claude
François, 1710-76, French;
nonfiction DIL
BLONDEL, Jacques François,
1705-74, French; nonfiction
DIL
BLONDEL, Maurice, 1861-1949,
French; nonfiction DIF HO
SA
BLONDEL, Pierre Jacques, 1674-
1730, French; journalism DIL
BLONDEL, Robert, 1390-1461,
French; poetry SA
BLONDEL De NESLE, fl. 1190- ,
French; poetry HAR KE SA ST

BLONDIN, Antoine, 1922- , French;
fiction DIC DIF PIN
BLONDIN, Charles, 1681-1738,
French; nonfiction DIL
BLONDIN, Pierre, 1682-1713,
French; nonfiction DIL
BLOOD, Benjamin Paul, 1832-1919,
American; poetry, nonfiction
KAA
BLOOD, Jerome W., 1926- ,
American; nonfiction CON
BLOOD, Robert Oscar, 1921- ,
American; nonfiction CON
BLOOM, Alan Hubert Vawser, 1906- ,
English; nonfiction CON
BLOOM, Edward Alan, 1914- ,
American; nonfiction CON
BLOOM, Gordon F., 1918- ,
American; nonfiction CON
BLOOM, Harold, 1930- , Ameri-
can; nonfiction CON
BLOOM, Harry, 1913- , South
African; fiction RIC
BLOOM, John, 1921- , English;
nonfiction CON
BLOOM, Lillian D., 1920- , Amer-
ican; nonfiction CON
BLOOM, Lynn Marie Zimmerman,
1934- , American; nonfiction
CON
BLOOM, Murray Teigh, 1916- ,
American; nonfiction CON
BLOOM, Robert, 1930- , American;
nonfiction CON
BLOOM, Samuel William, 1921- ,
American; nonfiction CON
BLOOM, Ursula ('Sheil Burns';
'Mary Essex'; 'Rachel Harvey';
'Deborah Mann'; 'Sara Sloane';
'Lozania Prole'), English; fiction
CON RIC
BLOOMAN, Percy A. ('Pab'), 1906- ,
English; nonfiction CON
BLOOMFIELD, Anthony John West-
gate, 1922- , English; tv, non-
fiction CON
BLOOMFIELD, Barry Cambray,
1931- , English; nonfiction
CON
BLOOMFIELD, Lincoln Palmer,
1920- , American; nonfiction
CON
BLOOMFIELD, Morton Wilfred,
1913- , American; nonfiction
CON
BLOOMFIELD, Robert (Richard),
1766-1823, English; poetry BRO
KBA SA ST

BLOOMGARTEN, Solomon see
'YEHOASH'
BLOOMQUIST, Edward R.,
1924- , American; nonfiction
CON
BLOOMSTEIN, Morris J., 1928- ,
American; nonfiction CON
BLOSSEVILLE, Hugues de Saint
Mardt, fl. 1470, French;
diary DIF
BLOSSOM, Thomas, 1912- ,
American; nonfiction CON
BLOTNER, Joseph Leo, 1923- ,
American; nonfiction CON
BLOUET, Jean François Nicolas,
1745-1809, French; nonfiction
DIL
BLOUGH, Glenn Orlando, 1907- ,
American; juveniles, fiction,
nonfiction COM CON FUL HIL
WA
BLOUNT, Charles, 1654-93, Eng-
lish; nonfiction KB ST
BLOUNT, Charles Harold Clavell,
1913- , English; nonfiction
CON
BLOUNT, Melesina Mackenzie
('Mrs. George Norman'),
English; fiction HOE
BLOY, Léon, 1846-1917, French;
fiction COL FLE HAR MAL
SA ST
BLOY, Marie Joseph Cain, 1846-
1917, French; journalism,
nonfiction, fiction, essays
DIF KE
'BLUE, Wallace' see KRAENZEL,
Margaret P.
BLUEFARB, Samuel, 1919- ,
English; nonfiction CON
BLUEMLE, Andrew Waltz,
1929- , American; nonfiction
CON
BLUESTONE, George, 1928- ,
American; movies, fiction,
poetry CON
BLUESTONE, Max, 1926- ,
American; nonfiction CON
BLUHM, Heinz, 1907- , German-
American; nonfiction CON
BLUHM, William Theodore,
1923- , American; nonfiction
CON
BLUM, Albert Alexander, 1924- ,
American; nonfiction CON
BLUM, Eleanor, 1914- , Amer-
ican; nonfiction CON
BLUM, Fred, 1932- , American;

nonfiction CON

BLUM, Henrik L., 1915- , American; nonfiction CON

BLUM, Jerome, 1913- , American; nonfiction CON

BLUM, John Morton, 1921- , American; nonfiction CON

BLUM, Klara, 1904- , German; nonfiction AL

BLUM, Léon, 1872-1950, French; nonfiction COL DIF SA

BLUM, Richard Hosmer Adams, 1927- , American; nonfiction CON

BLUM, Shirley Neilsen, 1932- , American; nonfiction CON

BLUM, Virgil Clarence, 1913- , American; nonfiction CON

BLUMAUER, Johannes Aloys, 1755-98, Austrian; poetry, plays AL HAR ST

BLUMBERG, Arnold, 1925- , American; nonfiction CON

BLUMBERG, Dorothy Rose, 1904- , American; nonfiction CON

BLUMBERG, Harry, 1903- , American; nonfiction CON

BLUMBERG, Myrna, 1932- , South African; nonfiction, fiction CON

BLUME, Bernhard, 1901- , German; plays MAT

BLUME, Judy Sussman, 1928- , American; juveniles COM CON

BLUMENFELD, F. Yorick, 1932- , Dutch-American; fiction CON

BLUMENFELD, Gerry, 1906- , American; nonfiction CON

BLUMENFELD, Hans, 1892- , American; nonfiction CON

BLUMENSON, Martin, 1918- , American; nonfiction CON

BLUMENTHAL, Arthur L., 1936- , American; nonfiction CON

BLUMENTHAL, Gerda Renee, 1923- , German-American; nonfiction CON

BLUMENTHAL, Henry, 1911- , American; nonfiction CON

BLUMENTHAL, Lassor Agoos, 1926- , American; nonfiction CON

BLUMENTHAL, Walter Hart, 1883- , American; nonfiction CON

BLUNCK, Hans Friedrich, 1880- , German; fiction, poetry COL SA

BLUNDEN, Edmund Charles, 1896- , British; poetry, nonfiction, criticism BRO CON FLE KAT KT MUR RIC SP ST

BLUNDEN, Margaret Anne, 1939- , English; nonfiction CON

BLUNDSON, Norman Victor Charles, 1915- , English; nonfiction CON

'BLUNT, Don' see BOOTH, Edwin

BLUNT, Hugh Francis, 1877- , American; nonfiction, poetry HOE

BLUNT, Wilfrid Jasper Walter, 1901- , English; nonfiction CON

BLUNT, Wilfrid Scawen, 1840-1922, English; poetry, nonfiction BRO KBA

'BLUPHOCKS, Lucien' see SELDES, Gilbert V.

'BLUTIG, Eduard' see GOREY, Edward St. J.

BLUVSTEIN, Rahel, 1890-1931, Jewish; poetry LAN

'BLY, Nellie' see SEAMAN, Elizabeth C.

BLY, Robert, 1926- , American; poetry, translations CON MUR

BLYN, George, 1919- , American; nonfiction CON

BLYTH, Harry ('Hal Meredith'), 1852-98, Scots; juveniles DOY

BLYTH, Henry, 1910- , English; nonfiction CON

BLYTHE, Ronald George, 1922- , English; nonfiction, fiction CON

BLYTHE, William Le Gette, 1900- , American; nonfiction, fiction CON JO

BLYTON, Enid Mary, 1900-68, Anglo-American; juveniles DOY WA

BLYTON, William Joseph, 1887-1944, English; nonfiction HOE

BO, Carlo, 1911- , Italian; fiction, nonfiction BL SA

BOAK, Arthur Edward Romilly, 1888-1962, American; nonfiction CON

BOAK, Charles Denis, 1932- , English; nonfiction CON

BOALCH, Donald Howard, 1914- , English; nonfiction CON

BOARD, Joseph Breckinridge, Jr.,
1931- , American; nonfiction
CON
BOARDMAN, Charles C., 1932- ,
American; nonfiction CON
BOARDMAN, Eunice, 1926- ,
American; nonfiction CON
BOARDMAN, Fon Wyman, Jr.,
1911- , American; nonfiction
CON
BOARDMAN, Neil Servis, 1907- ,
American; fiction CON
BOARINO, Gerald Louis, 1931- ,
American; nonfiction CON
BOARMAN, Patrick Madigan,
1922- , American; nonfiction
CON
BOAS, Franz, 1858-1942, German-
American; nonfiction KTS
BOAS, Guy Herman Sidney ('G.B.'),
1896- , English; nonfiction
CON
BOAS, Louise Schutz, 1885- ,
American; nonfiction CON
BOAS, Marie see HALL, Marie B.
BOAS, Maurits Ignatius, 1892- ,
Dutch-American; nonfiction CON
BOASE, Alan Martin, 1902- ,
Scots; nonfiction CON
BOASE, Paul Henshaw, 1915- ,
American; nonfiction CON
BOASE, Thomas Sherrer Ross,
1898- , American; nonfiction
CON
BOATENG, Ernest Amano, 1920- ,
Ghanaian; nonfiction CON
BOATMAN, Don Earl, 1913- ,
American; nonfiction CON
BOATNER, Mark Mayo, III, 1921- ,
American; nonfiction CON
BOATON, Pierre François de,
1734-94, Swiss; nonfiction DIL
BOATRIGHT, Mody Coggin, 1896- ,
American; nonfiction CON
BOAZ, Martha, American; nonfiction
CON
BOB, Brother see BUELL, Robert
K.
BOBADILLA, Emilio ('Fray Candil'),
1862-1920/21, Cuban; poetry,
fiction, essays MIN SA
BOBB, Bernard Earl, 1917- ,
American; nonfiction CON
BOBBE, Dorothie, 1905- , Anglo-
American; juveniles COM CON
BOBER, Stanley, 1932- , American;
nonfiction CON

BOBINSKI, George Sylvan, 1929- ,
American; nonfiction CON
BOBORYKIN, Peter Dmitrievich,
1836-1921, Russian; fiction
COL HAR HARK SA ST
BOBROFF, Edith, 1924- ,
American; nonfiction CON
BOBROV, Semyon Sergeyevich,
1767?-1810, Russian; poetry
HARK ST
BOBROW, Edwin E., 1928- ,
American; nonfiction CON
BOBROWSKI, Johannes, 1917-65,
East German; poetry, fiction
AL FLE KU RIC
BOCAGE, Louis Jacques Collin du
see 'VERNEUIL, Louis'
BOCAGE, Manuel Maria Barbosa
du, 1765-1805, Portuguese;
poetry, plays HAR KE ST SA
BOCANGEL y UNZUETA, Gabriel,
1608?-58, Spanish; poetry,
plays BL SA ST
BOCAYUVA, Quintino, 1836-1912,
Brazilian; journalism SA
'BOCCA, Al' see WINTER, Bevis
BOCCACCIO, Giovanni, 1313-75,
Italian; fiction, poetry, non-
fiction BL HAR KE MAG SA
ST
BOCCAGE, Marie Anne Fiquet du,
1710-1802, French; poetry
HAR SA
BOCCALINI, Traiano, 1556-1613,
Italian; fiction, nonfiction
HAR SA ST
BOCHAT, Charles Guillaume Loys
de, 1695-1753, Swiss; nonfic-
tion DIL
BOCHENSKI, Joseph M. ('Innocen-
tius M. Bochenski'; 'Giuseppe
Miche'), 1902- , American;
nonfiction CON
BOCK, Carl Heinz, 1930- ,
American; nonfiction CON
BOCK, Fred ('Jason Richards'),
1939- , American; nonfiction
CON
BOCK, Frederick, 1916- , Amer-
ican; poetry CON
BOCK, Harold I., 1939- , Amer-
ican; nonfiction CON
BOCK, Jean Nicolas, 1747-1809,
French; nonfiction DIL
BOCK, Peter Gidon, 1934- ,
Czech-American; nonfiction
CON

BOCK, Philip K., 1934- , American;
nonfiction CON
BOCK, Vera, Russian-American;
juveniles FUL
BOCKELMAN, Wilfred, 1920- ,
American; nonfiction CON
BOCKMON, Guy Alan, 1926- ,
American; nonfiction CON
BOCQUET, León Joseph, 1876-1954,
French; poetry DIF
BOCZEK, Boleslaw Adam, 1922- ,
Polish-American; nonfiction
CON
BODARD de TEZAY, Nicolas Marie
Félix, 1757-1823, French;
plays DIL
BODART, Roger, 1910- , French;
poetry, essays DIC
BODDAERT, Marie Agathe, 1844-
1914, Dutch; poetry, fiction
HAR ST
BODDAERT, Pieter, 1694-1760,
Dutch; poetry ST
BODDEWYN, Jean, 1929- , Amer-
ican; nonfiction CON
BODE, Carl, 1911- , American;
nonfiction CON
BODE, Elroy, 1931- , American;
nonfiction CON
BODECHEER BENNINGH, Johan,
1606-42, Dutch; poetry, plays
ST
BODEEN, DeWitt, 1908- , American;
plays CON
BODEL D'ARRAS, Jean, 13th cent.,
French; poetry, plays DIF HAR
ST
BODELL, Mary see PECSOK, Mary
B.
BODENHAM, Hilda Morris ('Hilden
Boden'; 'Pauline Welch'), 1901- ,
English; fiction, juveniles CON
BODENHAM, John, 1558-1600, Eng-
lish; nonfiction BRO ST
BODENHEIM, Maxwell, 1893-1954,
American; poetry, fiction KT
BODENHEIMER, Edgar, 1908- ,
American; nonfiction CON
BODENSTEDT, Freidrich Martin von,
1819-92, German; poetry, transla-
tions AL HAR ST
'BODFAN' see ANWYL, John B.
BODIN, Jean, 1530-96, French; non-
fiction DIF HAR KE SA ST
BODIN, Robert, 1731-1803, French;
nonfiction DIL
BODIN de BOISMORTIER, Suzanne,

1691-1765, French; nonfiction
DIL
BODINI, Vittorio, 1914- ,
Italian; poetry FLE
BODKIN, Maud, 1875- , English;
nonfiction CON KTS
BODKIN, Ronald George, 1936- ,
American; nonfiction CON
BODKIN, Thomas, 1887- , Irish;
nonfiction HIG HO
BIDLE, Yvonne Gallegos, 1939- ,
American; nonfiction CON
BODLEY, Sir Thomas, 1545-1613,
English; nonfiction BRO ST
BODMER, Johann Jakob, 1698-
1783, Swiss; poetry AL HAR
KE SA ST
BODMERSHOF, Imma von, 1895- ,
German; nonfiction KU
BO-DONG Phyogs-Las Rnam-
Rgyal, 1306-86, Tibetan; non-
fiction LAN
BODSWORTH, Charles Frederick
1918- , American; fiction, non-
fiction CON
BODTCHER, Ludvig Adolph, 1793-
1874, Danish; poetry ST
BOE, Jacques see 'JASMIN'
BOECE, Hector ('Boethius'),
1456?-1536, English; non-
fiction BRO KB ST
BÖCKH, Philipp August, 1785-
1867, German; nonfiction ST
BOECKMAN, Charles, 1920- ,
American; fiction CON
BOECKX, Bertolmeus, fl. 1600,
Dutch; poetry ST
BOEX, Justin see ROSNY, J.H.
BOEGEHOLD, Betty, American;
juveniles WA
BÖHL de FABER, Cecilia see
'CABALLERO, Fernán'
BÖHL de FABER, Juan Nicolas,
1770-1863, Spanish; nonfiction
plays BL SA
BÖHLAU, Helene Arndt, 1859-
1940, German; fiction AL
COL
BOEHLKE, Frederick John, Jr.,
1926- , American; nonfiction
CON
BOEHLKE, Robert Richard,
1925- , American; nonfiction
CON
BOEHM, Eric H., 1918- , Ger-
man-American; nonfiction CON
BÖHME, Jakob (Behmen), 1575-

1624, German; nonfiction AL
HAR KE SA ST
BOEHME, Lillian Rodberg, 1936- ,
American; nonfiction CON
BÖLL, Heinrich, 1917- , German;
fiction, essays, plays AL CON
FLE HAR KU KUN LEN RIC
BOELSCHE, Wilhelm, 1861-1939,
German; criticism, fiction COL
SA
BOENDALE, Jan van, 1280-1352,
Dutch; poetry ST
BÖÖK, Martin Fredrik, 1883- ,
Swedish; criticism ST
BOER, Charles, 1939- , American;
poetry MUR
BOER, Harry Reinier, 1913- ,
Dutch; nonfiction CON
BÖRJESSON, Johan, 1790-1866,
Swedish; poetry, plays ST
BÖRNE, Ludwig ('Löb Baruch'),
1786-1837, German; journalism
AL HAR SA ST
BOERNER, Klaus Erich, 1915- ,
German; nonfiction LEN
BOERNSTEIN, Heinrich, 1805-92,
German-American; journalism,
fiction ST
BOESCH, Mark Joseph, 1917- ,
American; juveniles, nonfiction
CON PAC
BOESEN, Victor ('Jesse Hall'; 'Eric
Harald'), 1908- , American;
nonfiction CON
BOETHIUS, Anicius Manlias Severinus,
480-524, Italian; nonfiction MAG
SA ST
BOETHIUS, Hector see BOECE, Hec-
tor
BOETIUS à BOLSWERT, 1580-1633,
Dutch; nonfiction ST
BOETTCHER, Henry J., 1893- ,
American; nonfiction CON
BOETTIGER, Carl August, 1760-
1835, German; nonfiction SA
BÖTTIGER, Carl Vilhelm, 1807-78,
Swedish; poetry ST
BOEVE, Edgar G., 1929- , Amer-
ican; nonfiction CON
BOEWE, Charles Ernst, 1924- ,
American; nonfiction CON
BOFARULL y de BROCA, Antonio de,
1821-92, Spanish; nonfiction SA
BOFILL i MATES, Jaume see
GUERAN de LIOST
'BOGADUCK' see LINDSAY, Harold
A.

BOGAN, Louise, 1897-1970,
American; poetry, criticism
FLE KL KT MUR RIC SP WA
BOGAERS, Adriano, 1795-1870,
Dutch; poetry SA ST
BOGAERT, Abraham, 1663-1727,
Dutch; poetry, plays ST
BOGAERTS, Félix, 1805-51,
Flemish; poetry SA
BOGART, William H. ('Sentinel'),
1870- , English; nonfiction
HIG
'BOGDANOV, A.' (Alexander
Alexandrovich Malinovski),
1873-1928, Russian; nonfiction
HARK ST
BOGDANOVICH, Ippolit Fyedoro-
vich, 1743-1802/03, Russian;
poetry HAR HARK SA ST
BOGDANOVICH, Maxim see
BAHDANOVICH, Maxim
BOGDANOVICH, Peter, 1939- ,
American; nonfiction CON
'BOGEN, Alexander' see SCHOLTIS,
August
BOGERT, L., Jean, 1885- ,
Scots-America; nonfiction CON
BOGGS, Ralph Steele, 1901- ,
American; juveniles CON WA
BOGGS, Wade Hamilton, Jr.,
1916- , American; nonfiction
CON
BOGGS, Wilmot Arthur, 1916- ,
American; nonfiction, poetry
CON
BOGISLAO, León, Luis see
GREIFF, Leon de
BOGNER, Norman, 1935- ,
American; nonfiction CON
BOGOMIL, Pop, 10th cent.,
Bulgarian; nonfiction ST
BOGOROV, Ivan, 1818-69, Bul-
garian; journalism ST
BOGOVIC, Mirko, 1816-93,
Croatian; poetry, plays ST
BOGUE, Lucile Maxfield ('Lucy
Max'), 1911- , American;
plays CON
BOGUSLAWSKI, Wofciech, 1757/
60-1829, Polish; poetry,
plays ST
BOHAN, Peter, American; non-
fiction CON
BOHANNAN, Paul James, 1920- ,
American; nonfiction CON
BOHEN, Sister Marian, 1930- ,
American; nonfiction CON

BOHI, M. Janette, 1927- , American; nonfiction CON
BOHLANDER, Jill, 1936- , American; nonfiction CON
BOHLAU, Helene, 1859- , German; fiction SA
BOHLE, Bruce, 1918- , American; nonfiction CON
BOHLE, Edgar Henry, 1909- , American; fiction CON
BOHLEN, Joe Merl, 1919- , American; nonfiction CON
BOHLMAN, Edna McCaull ('M. E. McCaull'), 1897- , American; nonfiction CON
BOHLMAN, Herbert William, 1896- , American; nonfiction CON
BOHME, Jakob, 1575-1624, German; nonfiction SA
BOHN, Henry George, 1796-1884, English; publisher KBA
BOHN, Ralph C., 1930- , American; nonfiction CON
BOHNSTEDT, John Wolfgang, 1927- , German-American; nonfiction CON
BOHOMOLEC, Franciszek, 1720-84, Polish; plays, essays HAR ST
BOHR, Russell LeRoi Riis, 1916- , American; nonfiction CON
BOHRNSTEDT, George William, 1938- , American; nonfiction CON
BOHROD, Aaron, 1907- , American; nonfiction CON
BOIARDO, Matteo Maria, 1440/41-94, Italian; poetry HAR KE MAG ST
BOICE, James Montgomery, 1938- , American; nonfiction CON
BOIE, Heinrich Christian, 1744-1806, German; journalism HAR ST
BOILEAU, Ethel Mary Young, 1882?-1942, English; fiction BRO KT
BOILEAU-DESPREAUX, Nicolas, 1636-1711, French; poetry, criticism DIF HAR KE MAG MAL SA ST
BOINDIN, Nicolas, 1676-1751, French; plays DIL SA
BOINE, Giovanni, 1887- , Italian; nonfiction SA
BOIS, Joseph Samuel, 1892- , Canadian; nonfiction CON
BOIS MESLE, Jean Baptiste Torchet, 18th cent., French; fiction DIL
BOISARD, Jean Jacques François,

1744-1833, French; poetry DIL
BOISARD de PONTEAU, Claude Florimond, -1742, French; plays DIL
BOIS GELIN de CUIE, Jean de Dieu, 1732-1804, French; nonfiction DIL
'BOISGOBEY, Fortuné de' (Castille), 1824-91, French; fiction HAR
BOISMONT, Nicolas de Thyrel de, 1715-86, French; nonfiction DIL
BOISNIER de L'ORME, 18th cent., French; nonfiction DIL
BOISROBERT François le Metel de, 1592-1662, French; poetry, plays DIF HAR ST
BOISSIER, Marie Louis Antoine Gaston, 1823-1908, French; nonfiction DIF
BOISSONADE, Jean François, 1774-1857, French; nonfiction SA
BOISSONNAS, Edith, Swiss-French; poetry PIN
BOISSY, Louis de, 1694-1758, French; plays DIL
BOISTARD de PREMAGNY, Etienne François, 1708-67, French; nonfiction DIL
BOITO, Arrigo ('Tobia Gorri'), 1842-1918, Italian; poetry COL HAR KE SA ST
BOIVIN, Louis, 1649-1724, French; nonfiction DIL
BOIVIN de VILLENEUVE, Jean, 1663-1726, French; nonfiction DIL
BOIX y RICARTE, Vicente, 1813-80, Spanish; poetry, plays SA
'BOJ, Silverio' (Walter Guido Weyland), 20th cent., Argentinian; fiction MIN
BOJARDO, Matteo M. see BOYARDO, Matteo M.
BOJER, Johan (John), 1872-1959, Norwegian; fiction COL HAR KL KT MAG SA ST
BOK, Edward William, 1863-1930, Dutch-American; essays, nonfiction KT
BOKENHAM, Osbern (Bokenam), 1392?-1447, English; translations ST
BOKER, George Henry, 1823-90,

American; poetry, plays BRO
KAA ST

BOKUM, Fanny Butcher, 1888- ,
American; nonfiction CON

BOLAND, Bertram, John, 1913- ,
American; fiction, nonfiction
CON

BOLAND, Charles Michael, 1917- ,
American; nonfiction CON

BOLAND, Daniel, 1891- , Irish;
nonfiction CON

BOLAND, Eavan Aisling, 1944- ,
Irish; poetry MUR

BOLAND, Lillian Canon, 1919- ,
American; nonfiction CON

BOLAÑOS, Luis de, 1539-1629,
Argentinian; nonfiction MIN

BOLD, Alan, 1943- , Scots; poetry,
fiction CON MUR

BOLDING, Amy, 1910- , American;
nonfiction CON

'BOLDREWOOD, Ralph' see BROWNE,
Thomas A.

BOLEMIR, Nebesky, 1818-82, Czech;
poetry, criticism SA

BOLES, Donald Edward, 1926- ,
American; nonfiction CON

BOLES, Harold Wilson, 1915- ,
American; nonfiction CON

BOLES, John B., 1943- , American;
nonfiction CON

BOLES, Paul Darcy, 1919- , American; nonfiction CON

'BOLESLAWITA, B.' see KRASZEW-
SKI, Józef I.

BOLET PERAZA, Nicanor, 1838-
1906, Venezuelan; journalism,
nonfiction SA

BOLEY, Jean, 1914- , American;
fiction WAF

BOLGAR, Boyan, 1910- , Bulgarian;
essays, fiction ST

BOLIAN, Polly, 1925- , American;
juveniles CON

BOLIN, Luis A., 1894-1969,
Spanish-American; nonfiction
CON

BOLINGBROKE, Henry St. John,
1678-1751, English; nonfiction
BRO KB SA ST

BOLINGER, Dwight L., 1907- ,
American; nonfiction BL CON

BOLINO, August Constantino, 1922- ,
American; nonfiction CON

'BOLINTINEANU, Dimitrie' (Dimitrie
Cosmand), 1819-72, Rumanian;
poetry HAR ST

BOLITHO, Axchie Ardella, 1886- ,
American; nonfiction CON

BOLITHO, Henry Hector, 1898- ,
Australian; nonfiction BRO
CON KT

BOLITHO, William (William B.
Ryall), 1890-193?, English;
journalism KT

BOLIVAR, Simón, 1783-1830,
Venezuelan; nonfiction ST

BOLL, Carl R., 1894- ,
German-American; nonfiction
CON

BOLL, David, 1931- , English;
fiction CON

BOLL, Theophilus Ernest Martin,
1902- , American; nonfiction
CON

BOLLAND, G. I. P. J., 1854-1922,
Dutch; nonfiction SA

BOLLAND, Jean, 1596-1665,
Flemish; nonfiction ST

BOLLE, Kees W. (Cornelius),
1927- , Dutch-American;
nonfiction CON

BOLLENS, John Constantinus,
1920- , American; nonfiction
CON

BOLLER, Paul Franklin, Jr.,
1916- , American; nonfiction
CON

BOLLES, Edmund Blair, 1911- ,
American; nonfiction CON

BOLLES, Robert Charles, 1928- ,
American; nonfiction CON

BOLLIGER, Max, 1929- , American; poetry, fiction, juveniles
CON

BOLLING, Richard Walker,
1916- , American; fiction
CON

BOLLIOUD-MERMED, Louis,
1709-93, French; nonfiction
DIL

BOLLO, Sarah, 1908?- ,
Uruguayan; poetry SA

'BOLO, Solomon' see GOLDSTEIN,
William I.

'BOLO, Solomon' see WHITON,
James N.

BOLOGNE, Pierre de, 1706-89,
French; poetry DIL

BOLT, David Michael Langstone,
1927- , English; fiction CON

BOLT, Robert, 1924- , English;
plays CON MAT RIC

BOLTEN, Steven E., 1941- ,

American; nonfiction CON

BOLTON, Edmund, 1575-1633, English; poetry, translations ST

BOLTON, Guy Reginald, 1884-86, English; plays, fiction CON MAT

'BOLTON, Isabel' see MILLER, Mary B.

BOLTON, Ivy Mary, 1879- , English; juveniles WA

BOLTON, Kenneth Ewart, 1914- , English; nonfiction CON

BOLTON, Maisie Sharman ('Stratford Davis'), 1915- , Scots; fiction, plays CON

BOLTON, Margaret, 1873-1943, American; juveniles HOE

BOLTON, Rosemary de B. see DOBSON, Rosemary

BOLTON, Sarah Knowles, 1841-1916, American; poetry KAA

BOLTON, Sarah Tittle Barrett, 1814-93, American; poetry KAA

BOLTON, Whitney French, 1930-69, American; nonfiction CON

BOLU-HJALMAR see JONSSON, Hjálmar

BOLZANO, Bernhard, 1781-1848, Austrian; nonfiction SA

BOMAN, Thorleif, Gustav, 1894- , Norwegian; nonfiction CON

'BOMBA, Gerwazy' see SZTYRMER, Ludwik

BOMBAL, María Luisa, 1910- , Chilean; fiction MIN

BOMBECK, Erma, 1927- , American; nonfiction CON

BOMBELLES, Joseph T., 1930- , Yugoslav-American; nonfiction CON

BOMELI, Edwin Clarence, 1920- , American; nonfiction CON

BONAFOUX y QUINTERO, Luis, 1855-1918, Spanish; journalism, nonfiction BL SA

BONAGUINTA ORBICCIANI, 1220-1300, Tuscan; poetry ST

BONALD, Louis Gabriel Ambroise, 1754-1840, French; nonfiction DIF SA

BONAMY, Pierre Nicolas, 1694-1770, French; nonfiction DIL

BONANCA João, 1836-1924, Portuguese; nonfiction SA

BONAR, Horatius, 1808-89, Scots; hymns BRO ST

BONARELLI, Guidobaldo della

Rovere, 1563-1608, Italian; poetry HAR SA ST

BONARELLI della Rovere, Próspero, 1590-1659, Italian; poetry SA

'BONAVENTURA' (Giovanni di Fidanza; Buenaventura), 1221/22-74, Italian; nonfiction HAR KE SA ST

'BONAVENTURA' (Freidrich Gottlob Wetzel), 1799-1819, German; nonfiction ST

BONAVENTURE de LUXEMBOURG, Henri Remi, 1691-1756, French; nonfiction DIL

BONAVENTURE de SISTERON, 18th cent., French; nonfiction DIL

BONAVIA-HUNT, Noel Aubrey, 1882- , English; nonfiction CON

BONBRIGHT, James Cummings, 1891- , American; nonfiction CON

BONCERF, Claude Joseph, 1724-1811, French; nonfiction DIL

BOND, Donald Frederic, 1898- , American; nonfiction CON

BOND, Edward, 1934- , English; plays CON

BOND, Geoffrey, 1924- , English; juveniles CON

BOND, Gladys Baker ('Jo Mendal'), 1912- , American; juveniles CON PAC

BOND, Horace Mann, 1904-72, American; nonfiction CON

'BOND, Ian' see WILLETT, Brother Franciscus

'BOND, J. Harvey' see WINTERBOTHAM, Russell R.

'BOND, Mrs. James' see BOND, Mary F.

BOND, Marshall, Jr., 1908- , American; nonfiction CON

BOND, Mary Fanning Wickham ('Mrs. James Bond'; 'Mary F. W. Lewis'; 'Mary F. Wickham Porcher'; 'Mary Fanning Wickham'), 1898- , American; fiction, poetry CON

BOND, Michael, 1926- , English; juveniles DOY

BOND, Nelson Slade, 1908- , American; fiction, plays CON

BOND, Otto Ferdinand, 1885- , American; nonfiction CON

BOND, Richmond Pugh, 1899- ,
American; nonfiction CON
BOND, Ruskin, 1934- , English;
fiction CON
BOND, Thomas Michael, 1926- ,
English; juveniles CON
BONDI, Joseph C., 1936- , Ameri-
can; nonfiction CON
BONE, Sir David William, 1874-1959,
Scots; fiction, nonfiction BRO KT
BONE, Hugh Alvin, 1909- , Ameri-
can; nonfiction CON PAC
BONE, Robert Clarke, 1917- ,
American; nonfiction CON
'BONEHILL, Capt. Ralph' see
STRATEMEYER, Edward L.
BONELLY, J. Alexandre, 1738- ,
French; nonfiction DIL
BONER, John Henry, 1845-1903,
American; poetry JO KAA
BONER, Ulrich, fl. 1324-49, Swiss;
fiction AL HAR ST
BONESS, A. James, 1928- , Amer-
ican; nonfiction CON
BONET, Carmelo Militón, 1886- ,
Uruguayan; criticism, essays
MIN
BONET, Honoré, 1345?-1406?,
French; poetry, nonfiction HAR
ST
'BONETT, Emery' see COULSON,
Felicity C.
'BONETT, John' see COULSON, John
H. A.
BONEY, Mary Lily, 1918- , Amer-
ican; nonfiction CON
BONEY, William Jerry, 1930- ,
American; nonfiction CON
BONFANTE, Giuliano, 1904- ,
Spanish; nonfiction BL
BONFINI, Antonio, 1427-1502/05,
Italian; nonfiction ST
BONGAR, Emmet Wald, 1919- ,
American; nonfiction CON
BONGARTZ, Roy, 1924- , Ameri-
can; nonfiction CON
BONGHI, Ruggero, 1826-95, Italian;
journalism, criticism ST
BONHAM, Barbara Thomas, 1926- ,
American; juveniles CON
BONHAM, Frank, 1914- , American;
juveniles, tv, COM CON WA
BONHAM CARTER, Helen Violet
Asquith, 1887- , English; non-
fiction CON
BONHAM CARTER, Victor, 1913- ,
English; nonfiction CON

BONHEIM, Helmut, 1930- ,
American; nonfiction, poetry,
translations CON
BONIFACE, 675-764, English;
nonfiction ST
BONIFACE, J.X. see 'SAINTINE,
Xavier B.'
BONIFACIO, Calvo, fl. 1250-70?,
Italian; poetry HAR ST
BONIFACIO, Juan, 1538-1606,
Spanish; nonfiction SA
BONILLA Alonso de, 16th cent.,
Spanish; poetry BL SA
BONILLA y SAN MARTIN, Adolfo,
1875-1926, Spanish; criticism
BL COL SA
BONIME, Walter, 1909- , Amer-
ican; nonfiction CON
BONINE, Gladys Nichols, 1907- ,
American; nonfiction CON
BONINI, Charles Pius, 1933- ,
American; nonfiction CON
BONJOUR, Casimir, 1795-1856,
French; plays SA
BONK, Wallace J., 1923- ,
American; nonfiction CON
BONAMTI de CODECIDO, Fran-
cisco, 1901- , Spanish; non-
fiction SA
BONN, John Louis, 1906- ,
American; nonfiction HOE
BONNAIRE, Louis de, 1680- ,
French; nonfiction DIL
BONNAR, Alphonsus, 1895- ,
American; nonfiction CON
BONNARD, Bernard de, 1744-84,
French; poetry DIL
BONNARUD, Jean Baptiste, 1684-
1758, French; nonfiction DIL
BONNAT, Agustín R., 1873-1925,
Spanish; journalism, fiction
SA
BONNAUD, Bienheureux Jacques
Jules, 1740-92, French; non-
fiction DIL
BONNAY, Charles François, 1750-
1825, French; nonfiction DIL
BONNE CARRERE, Guillaume,
1754-1825, French; nonfiction
DIL
BONNEFOY, Yves, 1923- ,
French; poetry, essays, trans-
lations DIC PIN
BONNELL, Dorothy Haworth,
1914- , American; fiction,
nonfiction CON
BONNELL, John Sutherland,

1893-   , Canadian; nonfiction
CON
BONNELYCKE, Emil Christian Theo-
dor, 1893-   , Danish; poetry,
fiction ST
BONNER, Charles, 1896-   , Ameri-
can; fiction WAF
BONNER, Gerald, 1926-   , English;
nonfiction CON
BONNER, James Calvin, 1904-   ,
American; nonfiction CON
BONNER, Mary Graham, 1890-1974,
Canadian; juveniles WA
'BONNER, Michael' see GLASSCOCK,
Anne B.
'BONNER, Parker' see BALLARD,
Willis T.
BONNER, Paul Hyde, 1893-   , Amer-
ican; fiction, nonfiction CON
'BONNER, Sherwood' see MacDOWELL,
Katherine S. B.
BONNER, Thomas N., 1923-   ,
American; nonfiction CON
BONNET, Charles, 1720-93, Swiss;
nonfiction DIF DIL
BONNET, Joseph,   -1738, French;
nonfiction DIL
'BONNETTE, Victor' see ROY,
Ewell P.
BONNEVAL, Jean Jacques Gimat,
18th cent., French; fiction DIL
BONNEVAL, Michel de, 1766-   ,
French; plays DIL
BONNEVAL, René de, 1700-60,
French; nonfiction DIL
BONNEVILLE, Douglas Alan, 1931-   ,
American; nonfiction CON
BONNEVILLE, Nicolas de, 1760-
1828, French; nonfiction DIL
'BONNEY, Bill' see KEEVILL, Henry
J.
BONNEY, Hanning Orrin, 1903-   ,
American; nonfiction CON
BONNEY, Merl Edwin, 1902-   ,
American; nonfiction CON
BONNIER, Ange Elisabeth Louis,
1749-99, French; nonfiction DIL
BONNIN-ARMSTRONG, Ana Inés,
20th cent., Spanish; poetry SA
BONNOR, William Bowen, 1920-   ,
English; nonfiction CON
BONSAL, Stephen, 1865-1951, Amer-
ican; nonfiction, journalism KTS
BONSANTI, Alessandro, 1904-   ,
Italian; nonfiction SA
BONSELS, Waldemar, 1881-1952,
German; nonfiction AL COL

KAT KT KU LEN SA
BONSTETTEN, Karl Viktor von,
1745-1832, Swiss; nonfiction
DIF HAR SA ST
BONTEKOE, Willem Ijsbrandsz,
1587-1630, Dutch; nonfiction
ST
BONTEMPELLI, Massimo, 1878-
1960, Italian; poetry, plays,
fiction, journalism, criticism
COL FLE MAT SA ST
BONTEMPS, Arna Wendell, 1902-
73, American; fiction, nonfic-
tion, plays, juveniles, poetry
COM CON KJU MUR WA WAF
BOMTEMPS, Marie Jeannet de
Chatillon, 1718-68, French;
nonfiction DIL
BONTEMPS, Roger see 'COL-
LERYE, Roger de'
BONVALLET de BROSSES,
French; nonfiction DIL
BONVESIN de la RIVA, 1240-1315,
Italian; poetry ST
BONZON, Paul Jacques, 1908-   ,
French; juveniles WA
BOODMAN, David M., 1923-   ,
American; nonfiction CON
BOOG WATSON, Elspeth Janet,
1900-   , Scots; fiction,
juveniles CON
BOOKER, Simeon Saunders,
1918-   , American; nonfiction
CON
BOOLE, George, 1815-64, English;
nonfiction KBA
BOOM, Alfred B., 1928-   ,
American; nonfiction CON
'BOON, Francis' see BACON, Ed-
ward
BOONE, Daniel R., 1927-   ,
American; nonfiction CON
BOONE, Pat, 1934-   , American;
nonfiction CON
BOORDE, Andrew (Borde), 1490?-
1549, English; nonfiction BRO
ST
BOORE, Walter Hugh, 1904-   ,
Welsh; poetry, fiction CON
BOORMAN, Scott Archer, 1949-   ,
American; nonfiction CON
BOORSTIN, Daniel Joseph, 1914-   ,
American; nonfiction CON
BOOS, Frank Holgate, 1893-1968,
American; nonfiction CON
BOOT, John C.G., 1936-   ,
American; nonfiction CON

BOOTH, Charles, 1840-1916, English; nonfiction KBA
BOOTH, Charles Orrell, 1918- , English; nonfiction CON
BOOTH, Edwin ('Don Blunt'; 'Jack Hazard'), American; fiction CON
BOOTH, George Clive, 1901- , American; nonfiction CON
'BOOTH, Irwin' see HOCH, Edward D.
BOOTH, John E., 1919- , American; nonfiction CON
BOOTH, Miriam, 1944- , English; poetry MUR
BOOTH, Patrick John, 1929- , New Zealander; juveniles CON
BOOTH, Philip, 1925- , American; poetry, fiction CON MUR
BOOTH, Wayne C., 1921- , American; nonfiction CON
BOOTHBY, Guy Newell, 1867-1905, Australian; fiction BRO KBA
BOOTHE, Clare (Luce), 1903- , American; plays HOE KT MAT
BOOTHROYD, John Basil, 1910- , English; nonfiction CON
'BOOZ, Mateo' see CORREA, Miguel A.
BOPP, Franz, 1791-1867, German; nonfiction SA
BOPP, Raúl, 1898- , Brazilian; poetry SA
'BOR, Matei' (Vladimir Pavsíc), 1913- , Slovene; poetry, plays FLE
BOR, Pieter, 1559-1635, Dutch; nonfiction ST
BORAAS, Roger Stuart, 1926- , American; nonfiction CON
BORAGHINI, Vittorio, 1902- , Italian; criticism SA
'BORAH, Timm' see ZECH, Paul
BORAH, Woodrow Wilson, 1912- , American; nonfiction CON
BORAISCHA, Menahem (Goldberg), 1888-1949, Jewish; poetry LAN
BORAO y CLEMENTE, Jerónimo, 1821-78, Spanish; nonfiction SA
BORATYNSKI see BARATYNSKI
BORBERG, Svend, 1888-1947, Danish; plays HAR ST
BORCH, Michel Jean, 1751-1810, French; nonfiction DIL
'BORCH, Ted' see LUND, A. Morten
BORCHARD, Ruth Berendsohn ('Iqua'; 'Anne Medley'), 1910- , German-English; nonfiction CON

BORCHARDT, Dietrich Hans, 1916- , German-Australian; nonfiction CON
BORXHARDT, Frank Louis, 1938- , American; nonfiction CON
BORCHARDT, George H. see 'HERMANN, Georg'
BORCHARDT, Hermann, 1888-1951, German-American; fiction HO
BORCHARDT, Rudolf, 1877-1945, German; poetry, essays, translations AL COL FLE KU KUN SA ST
BORCHERS, Gladys, L., 1891- , American; nonfiction CON
BORCHERT, Gerald Leo, 1932- , American; nonfiction CON
BORCHERT, Wolfgang, 1921-47, German; poetry, fiction, plays AL FLE KU KUN LEN MAT
BORCHGRAVE, Peter Joost de, 1758-1817, Flemish; poetry, plays ST
BORCK, Caspar Wilhelm von, 1704-47, German; translations ST
BORDA, José Joaquín, 1835-78, Colombian; poetry, fiction, essays, translations MIN
BORDALO, Francisco María, 1821-61, Portuguese; fiction SA
BORDE, Andrew see BOORDE, Andrew
BORDE, Charles (Bordes), 1711-81, French; poetry DIL
BORDEAUX, Henri, 1870-1963, French; fiction, nonfiction COL DIF FLE HAR HOE KT SA ST
BORDEN, Charles A., 1912- , American; juveniles WA
'BORDEN, Lee' see DEAL, Borden
BORDEN, Lucille Papin, 1873- , American; fiction HOE
'BORDEN, M.' see SAXON, Gladys R.
BORDEN, Mary ('Bridget Maclagen'), 1886/87-1968, Anglo-American; fiction, poetry BRO CON KL KT
BORDEN, Morton, 1925- , American; nonfiction CON
BORDEN, Neil Hopper, 1895- , American; nonfiction CON

BORDEN, Norman Easton, 1907- ,
American; juveniles CON
BORDEN, Richard Carman, 1900- ,
American; nonfiction CON
BORDEN, William Vickers, 1938- ,
American; fiction CON
'BORDERER' see GREEN-PRICE,
Sir Richard D.
BORDES, Charles see BORDE,
Charles
BORDEU, Théophile, 1722-76,
French; nonfiction DIL
BORDEWIJK, Ferdinand ('Ton Ven'),
1884- , Dutch; poetry, fiction
FLE ST
BORDIER, L.C., French; nonfiction
DIL
BORDIN, Ruth Brigitta, 1917- ,
American; nonfiction CON
BORDING, Anders Christensen,
1619-77, Danish; poetry ST
BORDON, Charles A., 1912-68,
American; nonfiction CON
BORDONOVE, Georges, 1920- ,
French; fiction, essays DIC
BOREA, Phyllis Gilbert, 1924- ,
American; juveniles CON
BOREE, Karl Friedrich, 1886- ,
German; fiction, essays KU
LEN
BOREL, Jacques, 1925- , French;
nonfiction CON
BOREL, Joseph Pierre Borel d'Haute-
rive (Petrus), 1809-59, French;
poetry, fiction DIF HAR KE ST
BOREL, Pierre, French; poetry,
DIL
BORELLI, Jean Marie, 1723-1808,
French; nonfiction DIL
BOREMAN, Jean, 1909- , American;
juveniles CON
BOREN, Henry Charles, 1921- ,
American; nonfiction CON
BORER, Mary Cathcart, 1906- ,
English; juveniles, nonfiction,
plays CON
BORG, Dorothy, 1902- , American;
nonfiction CON
BORG, Ina, Swedish; juveniles WA
BORG, Walter Raymond, 1921- ,
American; nonfiction CON
'BORGE, Bernhard' see BJERKE,
Jarl A.
BORGEN, Johan, 1902- , Norwegian;
fiction, plays, criticism FLE
BORGER, Elias Anne, 1784-1820,
Dutch; nonfiction, poetry ST

BORGES, Jorge Luis ('Honorio
Bustos Domecq'; 'B. Suarez
Lynch'), 1899- , Argentinian;
criticism, poetry, essays,
fiction BL CON FLE MIN RIC
SA ST
BORGESE, Giuseppe Antonio, 1882-
1952, Italian-American; fiction,
criticism COL FLE KT SA
ST
BORGGESS, Louise Bradford,
1912- , American; nonfiction
CON
BORGHI, Giuseppe, 1790-1847,
Italian; poetry HAR ST
BORGHINI, Raffaello, 1541-88?,
Italian; plays HAR ST
BORGHINI, Vincenzo, 1515-80,
Italian; criticism ST
BORGMANN, Dimitri Alfred ('El
Uqsor'), 1927- , German-
American; nonfiction CON
BORGSTROM, George Arne, 1912- ,
American; nonfiction CON
BORHEGYI, Suzanne Catherine
Sims, 1926- , American;
juveniles WA
BORING, Edwin Garrigues, 1886- ,
American; nonfiction CON
BORJA, Arturo Cesar, 1892/94-
1912/15, Ecuadoran; poetry
DI SA
BORJA, Cesar, 1847/52-1910,
Ecuadoran; poetry, nonfiction
DI SA
BORJA, Don Franciso de, 1851- ,
Spanish; poetry SA
'BORJA, N.A.' see VIRAY, Manuel
BORK, Alfred M., 1926- ,
American; nonfiction CON
BORKLUND, Carl Wilbur, 1930- ,
American; nonfiction CON
BORKO, Harold, 1922- , Amer-
ican; nonfiction CON
BORLAND, Barbara Dodge, Amer-
ican; fiction, poetry CON
BORLAND, Hal ('Ward West'),
1900- , American; poetry,
nonfiction, fiction, juveniles
CON
BORMANN, Ernest Gordon,
1925- , American; nonfiction
CON
BORMEESTER, Abraham, 1618-45,
Dutch; plays ST
BORN, Bertran de see BERTRAN
de BORN

BORN, Max, 1882-1970, German-
English; nonfiction CON

BORNE, Alain, 1915-62, French;
poetry DIF

BORNEMAN, Ernest ('Cameron Mc-
Cabe'), 1915- , German; nonfiction, plays CON

'BORNEMAN, H.' see GOTTSCHALL,
Franklin H.

BORNEMANN, Alfred H., 1908- ,
American; nonfiction CON

BORNEMANN, Wilhelm, 1766-1851,
German; poetry ST

BORNET, Vaughn Davis, 1917- ,
American; nonfiction CON

BORNIER, Henri de, 1825-1901,
French; plays DIF

BORNING, Bernard Carl, 1913- ,
American; nonfiction CON

BORNSTEIN, George Jay, 1941- ,
American; nonfiction CON

BORNSTEIN, Morris, 1927- ,
American; nonfiction CON

BOROCHOV, Dov-Ber, 1881-1917,
Russian; fiction ST

BORODIN, Sergey Petrovich (Amir
Sargedzhan), 1902- , Russian;
fiction ST

BOROFF, David, 1917-65, American;
nonfiction CON

BOROSON, Warren ('Warren Brown'),
1935- , American; nonfiction
CON

BOROVSKI, Conrad, 1930- , American; nonfiction CON

BORQUEZ SOLAR, Antonio, 1873/74-
1938, Chilean; poetry, fiction
MIN

BORRAS, Tomás, 1891- , Spanish;
fiction, plays, criticism SA

BORREGAARD, Ebbe, 1933- ,
American; poetry MUR

BORRELL, Dorothy Elizabeth
('Dorothea E. Finn'), Rhodesian;
poetry MUR

BORRELLO, Alfred, 1931- , American; nonfiction CON

BORRERO, Juana, 1877/78-96,
Cuban; poetry MIN SA

BORRERO de LUJAN, Dulce María,
1883-1945, Cuban; journalism,
poetry MIN SA

BORRERO ECHEVARRIA, Esteban,
1849-1906, Cuban; poetry MIN
SA

BORROFF, Marie, 1923- , American; nonfiction CON

BORROR, Donald Joyce, 1907- ,
American; nonfiction CON

BORROW, George Henry, 1803-
81, English; nonfiction, translations BL BRO KBA MAG SA
ST

BORSCH, Frederick Houk, 1935- ,
American; nonfiction CON

BORSI, Giosue Francesco, 1888-
1915, Italian; journalism,
poetry, essays COL HAR SA
ST

BORSSELEN, Philibert van, 1575-
1627, Dutch; poetry ST

BORTEN, Helen Jacobson, 1930- ,
American; juveniles CON WA

BORTNER, Doyle McLean,
1915- , American; nonfiction
CON

BORTNER, Morton, 1925- ,
American; nonfiction CON

BORTON, Elizabeth see TREVINO,
Elizabeth B. de

BORTON, John C., Jr. (Terry),
1938- , American; nonfiction
CON

BORTSTEIN, Larry, 1942- ,
American; nonfiction CON

BORTZ, Edward Le Roy, 1896- ,
American; nonfiction CON

BORUP, Morten, 1446?-1526,
Danish; poetry HAR ST

BORUS, Michael Eliot, 1938- ,
American; nonfiction CON

BORUWKASKI, Joseph, 1739-1837,
French; nonfiction DIL

BORY, Gabriel de, 1720-1801,
French; nonfiction DIL

BORZA, Eugene Nicholas, 1935- ,
American; nonfiction CON

BOS, Charles du, 1882-1939,
French; essays, diary HAR
ST

BOS, Lambert, van den, 1620-
98, Dutch; poetry, plays,
translations ST

BOSANQUET, Bernard, 1848-
1923, English; nonfiction ST

BOSBOOM-TOUISSANT, Anna
Louise Geertruida, 1812-86,
Dutch; fiction KE HAR SA ST

BOSC, Louis Charles Paul,
-1800, French; nonfiction
DIL

BOSCAN ALMUGAVER, Juan,
1493?-1542, Spanish; poetry,
translations BL HAR SA ST

BOSCH, Bernardus, 1746-1803,
Dutch; poetry ST
BOSCH, Jeronimo de, 1740-1811,
Dutch; poetry ST
BOSCH, Mariano G., 20th cent.,
Argentinian; criticism, essays
MIN
BOSCH, William Joseph, 1928- ,
American; nonfiction CON
BOSCHERE, Jean de, 1878-1953,
French; poetry DIF
BOSCHERON, 18th cent., French;
nonfiction DIL
BOSCO Antoinette Oppedisano,
1928- , American; nonfiction
CON
BOSCO, Ferdinand Marius Joseph
Henri, 1888- , French; fiction,
poetry DIF FLE HAR ST
'BOSCO, Jack' see HOLLIDAY,
Joseph
BOSCOVICH, Roger Joseph, 1711- ,
French; nonfiction DIL
BOSE, Nirmal Kumar ('Mirmala-
Kumara Vasu'), 1901- , Indian;
nonfiction CON
BOSKIN, Joseph, 1929- , American;
nonfiction CON
BOSKINSKI, Blanch, 1922- , Amer-
ican; juveniles CON
BOSIS, Adolfo y Lauro de see DE
BOSIS, Adolf and Lauro
BOSKOFF, Alvin, 1924- , Ameri-
can; nonfiction CON
BOSLAND, Chelcie Clayton, 1901- ,
American; nonfiction CON
BOSMAJIAN, Haig Aram, 1928- ,
American; nonfiction CON
BOSMAN, Herman Charles, 1905-51,
South African; fiction, poetry,
essays RIC ST
BOSQUET, Alain ('Anatole Bisque'),
1919- , Russian-American;
poetry, fiction, essays CON
DIC DIF
BOSSDORF, Hermann, 1877-1921,
German; plays ST
BOSSELMAN de BELLEMONT, 18th
cent., French; nonfiction DIL
BOSSHART, Jakob, 1862-1924,
German; nonfiction AL
BOSSONE, Richard M., 1924- ,
American; nonfiction CON
BOSSU, French; nonfiction DIL
BOSSUET, Jacques Bénigne, 1627-
1704, French; nonfiction DIF
HAR MAL SA ST

'BOSTON, Charles K.' see
GRUBER, Frank
BOSTON, Lucy Maria, 1892- ,
English; juveniles DOY WA
BOSTON, Noel, 1910- , English;
nonfiction CON
BOSTON, Thomas, 1677-1732,
Scots; nonfiction BRO ST
BOSTROEM, Annemarie, 1922- ,
German; poetry, plays AL
BOSTRÖM, Christopher Jacob,
1797-1866, Swedish; nonfiction
ST
BOSWELL, Sir Alexander, 1775-
1822, Scots; nonfiction, poetry
BRO KBA ST
BOSWELL, Charles Meigs, Jr.,
1909- , American; nonfiction
CON
BOSWELL, James, 1740-95,
Scots; diary, nonfiction BRO
KB MAG SA ST
BOSWORTH, Allan Rucker ('Alamo
Boyd'), 1901- , American;
nonfiction CON
BOSWORTH, Clifford Edmund,
1928- , English; nonfiction
CON
BOSWORTH, J. Allen, American;
juveniles WA
BOSWORTH, William, -1650?,
English; poetry ST
BOSWORTH SMITH, Reginald,
1839-1908, English; nonfiction
KBA
BOTE, Hermann, -1520, Ger-
man; poetry ST
BOTELHO, Abel Acácio de Almeida,
1854-1917, Portuguese; fiction
COL SA ST
BOTELHO de OLIVEIRA, Manuel,
1636-1711, Brazilian; poetry,
plays SA
BOTELHO GOSALVEZ, Raúl,
1917- , Bolivian; fiction,
criticism, essays MIN
BOTERO, Giovanni, 1543/44-1617,
Italian; nonfiction ST
BOTEV, Christo, 1847-76, Bul-
garian; poetry HAR SA ST
BOTEZ, Demostene, 1893- ,
Rumanian; poetry ST
BOTHWELL, Jean, American;
juveniles, fiction COM CON
KJU WA
BOTIN POLANCO, Antonio, 1898-
1956, Spanish; fiction BL SA

BOTKIN, Benjamin Albert, 1901- ,
American; nonfiction CON KTS
MAR

BOTO, Antonio Tomás, 1900- ,
Portuguese; poetry ST

BOTSFORD, Keith, 1928- , Belgian-
American; nonfiction CON

BOTTA, Anne Charlotte Lynch, 1815-
91, American; poetry KAA SA

BOTTA, Carlo, 1766-1837, Italian;
nonfiction HAR SA ST

BOTTEL, Helen, 1914- , American;
nonfiction CON

BOTTI, Regino E., 1878- , Cuban;
poetry, essays MIN

BOTTICHER, Hans see 'RINGELNATZ,
Joachim'

BOTTIGLIA, William Filbert, 1912- ,
American; nonfiction CON

BOTTO, Ján, 1829-81, Slovak;
poetry ST

BOTTO, Ján ('Ivan Krasko'; 'Bond J.
Potokinová'), 1876-1958, Slovak;
poetry FLE ST

BOTTOM, Raymond, 1927- , American; nonfiction CON

BOTTOME, Edgar M., 1937- ,
American; nonfiction CON

BOTTOME, Phyllis, 1884-1963, English; fiction BRO KL KT RIC

BOTTOMLEY, Gordon, 1874-1948,
English; poetry, plays BRO
KAT KT RIC ST

BOTTOMORE, Thomas Burton,
1920- , English; nonfiction
CON

BOTTRALL, Francis James Ronald,
1906- , British; poetry, criticism MUR SP

BOUBE, 18th cent., French; plays
DIL

BOUCHARD, Lois Kalb, 1938- ,
American; juveniles CON

BOUCHARD, Robert H., 1923- ,
American; nonfiction CON

BOUCHAUD, Mathieu Antoine,
1719-1904, French; nonfiction
DIL

BOUCHER, Alan Estcourt, 1918- ,
English; nonfiction CON

'BOUCHER, Anthony' (William
Anthony Parker White; 'H. H.
Holmes'; 'Herman W. Mudgett'),
1911- , American; fiction, nonfiction CON KTS

BOUCHER, Elie Marcoul, 1680-1754,
French; nonfiction DIL

BOUCHER, John Gregory, 1930- ,
American; nonfiction CON

BOUCHER, Paul Edward, 1893- ,
American; nonfiction CON

BOUCHER, Philippe, 1691-1768,
French; nonfiction DIL

BOUCHER D'ARGIS, Antoine
Gospard, 1708-91, French;
nonfiction DIL

BOUCHER de CREVECOEUR de
PERTHES, Jacques, 1788-
1868, French; nonfiction DIF

BOUCHER de la RICHARDERIE,
Gilles, 1733-1810, French;
nonfiction DIL

BOUCHERVILLE, Georges Boucher
de, 1814-94, Canadian; nonfiction SY

BOUCHET, André du, 1924- ,
French; poetry PIN

BOUCHET, Guillaume, 1514-94,
French; fiction ST

BOUCHET, Jean, 1476-1557,
French; poetry HAR ST

BOUCHET de BROCOURT,
Guillaume, 1514?-94, French;
fiction HAR

BOUCHIER, John see BERNERS,
John B.

BOUCHOR, Maurice, 1855-1929,
French; poetry, plays HAR
SA

BOUCICAULT, Dionysius Lardner,
1820?-90, Anglo-Irish; plays
BRO KBA ST

BOUDAT, Marie Louise ('Louise
Bellocq'), 1909- , French;
nonfiction CON

BOUDET, Claude, -1774, French;
nonfiction DIL

BOUDET, Teodoro José (Conde de
Puymaigre), 1816-98, Spanish;
nonfiction BL

BOUDEWIJNS, Katharina, 1520-
1603, Dutch; poetry ST

BOUDIER, Pierre François, 1704-
87, French; nonfiction DIL

BOUDIER de VILLERMET, Pierre
Joseph, 1716- , French; nonfiction DIL

BOUDIN, Pierre, 18th cent.,
French; plays DIL

BOUDINOT, Elias, 1803-39, American; nonfiction KAA

BOUDREAUX, Patricia Duncan,
1941- , American; nonfiction
CON

BOUELLES, Charles de see
BOUVELLES, Charles de
BOUFFLERS, Marie Charlotte,
1725-1800, French; nonfiction
DIL
BOUFFLERS, Stanislas Jean, 1738-
1815, French; nonfiction DIL
BOUGAINVILLE, Jean Pierre, 1722-
63, French; nonfiction DIL SA
BOUGAINVILLE, Louis Antoine,
1729-1811, French; nonfiction
DIL
BOUGEANT, Guillaume Hyacinthe,
1690-1743, French; nonfiction
DIL
BOUGEREL, Joseph, 1681-1733,
French; nonfiction DIL
BOUGHNER, Daniel Cliness, 1909- ,
American; nonfiction CON
BOUHILIER, Saint Georges de, 1876-
1947, French; plays, poetry ST
BOUHOURS, Père Dominique, 1628-
1702, French; nonfiction DIF
BOUILHET, Louis Hyacinthe, 1821/
22-63/69, French; plays, poetry
DIF HAR SA ST
BOUILLART, Jacques, 1669- ,
French; nonfiction DIL
BOUILLET, Jean, 1690-1777,
French; nonfiction DIL
BOUILLY, Jean Nicolas, 1763-1842,
French; nonfiction HAR
BOULAINVILLIERS, Henri, 1658-1722,
French; nonfiction DIF DIL
BOULANGER, Nicolas Antoine, 1722-
59, French; nonfiction DIL
BOULANGER de RIVERY, Claude,
François Félix, 1725-58, French;
nonfiction DIL
BOULARAN, Jacques see 'DEVAL,
Jacques'
BOULBY, Mark, 1929- , English;
nonfiction CON
BOULDING, Elise Biorn-Hansen,
1920- , Norwegian-American;
nonfiction CON
BOULDING, Kenneth Ewart, 1910- ,
Anglo-American; nonfiction CON
BOULLE, Pierre, 1912- , French;
fiction CON DIC RIC
BOULLEMIER, Charles, 1725-1803,
French; nonfiction DIL
BOULLENOIS, Louis, 1680-1762,
French; nonfiction DIL
BOULLIER, David Renaud, 1699-
1759, Dutch; nonfiction DIL
BOULTING, Sydney see 'COTES,
Peter'

BOULTON, David, 1935- ,
English; nonfiction CON
BOULTON, James Thompson,
1924- , American; nonfiction
CON
BOUMAN, Pieter Marinus, 1938- ,
Belgian; nonfiction CON
BOUMAN, Walter Richard, 1929- ,
American; nonfiction CON
BOUQUET, Martin, 1685-1754,
French; nonfiction DIL
BOUQUET, Pierre, 1715-81,
French; nonfiction DIL
BOUQUIER, Gabriel, 1750-1811,
French; nonfiction DIL
BOURADOUE, Louis, 1632-1704,
French; nonfiction SA
BOURASSA, Henri, 1868-1952,
Canadian; nonfiction ST SY
'BOURBON, Ken' see BAUER,
Erwin A.
BOURBON, Nicolas, 1502-53?,
French; poetry HAR SA ST
BOURBON, Nicolas, 1574-1644,
French; poetry ST
BOURBON BUSSET, Jacques de,
1912- , French; fiction, es-
says DIC
BOURBON PARME, Isabelle de,
18th cent., French; nonfiction
DIL
BOURCHER, John see BERNERS,
John B.
BOURCIER, Jean Léonard, 1749-
1826, French; nonfiction DIL
BOURCIER, Jean Louis, 1687-
1749, French; nonfiction DIL
BOURDALOUE, Louis, 1632-1704,
French; nonfiction DIF
BOURDEAUX, Michael, 1934- ,
English; nonfiction CON
BOURDET, Edouard, 1887-1944/45,
French; plays COL DIF HAR
MAT SA ST
BOURDIC VIOT, Marie Anne,
1746-1802, French; poetry
DIL SA
BOURDON, David, 1934- , Amer-
ican; nonfiction CON
BOURDON, Louis Gabriel, 1741-
95, French; nonfiction DIL
BOURET, Pierre, 1710-77, French;
poetry DIL
BOURETTE, Charlotte Reynier,
1714-84, French; poetry DIL
SA
BOURGEOIS, Auguste ('Anicet'),
1806-71, French; plays DIF

BOURGEOIS, Nicolas, 1710-76,
French; nonfiction DIL
BOURGES, Elémir, 1852-1925,
French; fiction, journalism DIF
SA
BOURGET, Jean, 1724-76, French;
nonfiction DIL
BOURGET, Paul Charles Joseph,
1852-1935, French; fiction,
poetry, plays, essays COL DIF
HAR HOE FLE KAT KT MAG
MAL SA ST
BOURGEZ, Jean, 18th cent., French;
fiction DIL
BOURGHOLTZER, Frank, 1919- ,
American; fiction CON
BOURGOINE de VILLEFORE, Joseph
François, 1652-1737, French;
nonfiction DIL
BOURGUEVILLE, Charles de, 1504-
93, French; nonfiction SA
BOURIGNON, François Marie, 1752-
93, French; nonfiction DIL
BOURILLON, Pierre see 'HAMP,
Pierre'
BOURINOT, Arthur Stanley, 1893- ,
Canadian; nonfiction, poetry SY
BOURINOT, Sir John George, 1837-
1902, Canadian; nonfiction KBA
BOURJAILY, Vance Nye, 1922- ,
American; fiction, nonfiction
CON
BOURKE, Dermot Robert Wyndham,
1851-1939, Irish; nonfiction HIG
BOURKE, John Gregory, 1846-96,
American; nonfiction KAA
BOURKE, Vernon Joseph, 1907- ,
Canadian-American; nonfiction
CON
BOURKE-WHITE, Margaret, 1904- ,
American; nonfiction CON
BOURLET de VAUXCELLES, Simon
Jacques, 1733-1802, French;
nonfiction DIL
BOURNE, Charles P., 1931- ,
American; nonfiction CON
BOURNE, Dorothy Dulles, 1893- ,
American; nonfiction CON
BOURNE, Edward Gaylord, 1860-
1908, American; nonfiction KAA
BOURNE, Frank Card, 1914- ,
American; nonfiction CON
BOURNE, Geoffrey Howard, 1909- ,
Australian; nonfiction CON
BOURNE, James R., 1897- ,
American; nonfiction CON
BOURNE, Kenneth, 1930- , English;

nonfiction CON
BOURNE, Larry Stuart, 1939- ,
Canadian; nonfiction CON
'BOURNE, Lesley' see MARSHALL,
Evelyn
BOURNE, Miriam Anne, 1931- ,
American; juveniles CON
BOURNE, Randolph Silliman, 1886-
1918, American; essays KAT
KT
BOURNE, Ruth M., American;
nonfiction CON
BOURNE, Vincent, 1695-1747,
English; poetry ST
BOUROTTE, Nicolas, 1710-84,
French; nonfiction DIL
BOURRICAUD, François, 1922- ,
American; nonfiction CON
BOURRIT, Marc Théodore, 1735-
1815, French; nonfiction DIL
BOURSAULT, Edme, 1638-1701,
French; plays DIF HAR ST
BOUSCAREN, Anthony Trawick,
1920- , American; nonfiction
CON
BOUSCAREN, Timothy Lincoln,
1884- , American; nonfiction
CON
BOURSIER, Laurent François,
1679-1749, French; nonfiction
DIL
BOUSOÑO, Carlos, 1923- ,
Spanish; nonfiction, poetry
BL SA
BOUSQUET, Joë, 1897-1950,
French; poetry DIF
BOUSSANELLE, Louis de, -1796,
French; nonfiction DIL
BOUSSARD, Jacques Marie,
1910- , French; nonfiction
CON
BOUSSENARD, Louis, 1847-1910,
French; fiction DIF
BOUSSU, Gilles Joseph de, 1681-
1755, French; plays DIL
BOUSSUET, Jacques Bénigne,
1627-1704, French; nonfiction
KE
BOUTARIC, François de, 1672-
1733, French; nonfiction DIL
BOUTELLEAU, Jacques see
'CHARDONNE, Jacques'
BOUTENS, Peter Cornelis, 1870-
1943, Dutch; poetry COL FLE
HAR SA ST
BOUTERWECK, Friedrich, 1766-
1828, German; poetry, criti-

cism SA
BOUTET de MONVEL, 1850-1913,
French; juveniles KJU
BOUTIER, Pierre (Jean Le Verrier),
15th cent., French; nonfiction
ST
BOUTILLIER, Maximilien Jean,
1745-1811, French; plays DIL
BOUTON, John Bell, 1830-1902,
American; journalism KAA
BOUTROUX, Etienne Emile Marie,
1845-1921, French; nonfiction
COL DIF SA
BOUVARD, Marguerite Anne,
1937- , American; nonfiction
CON
BOUVELLES, Charles de (Bouelles;
Bovillus), 1480-1533, French;
nonfiction DIF SA
BOUVET, Marie Marguerite, 1865-
1915, American; juveniles KAA
BOUVIER, Emile, 1906- , Canadian;
nonfiction CON
BOUVIT, Joachim, 1656-1730, French;
nonfiction DIL
BOUZONIE, Jean, 1645-1726, French;
poetry DIL
BOVA, Benjamin William, 1932- ,
American; nonfiction, juveniles,
fiction CON
BOVASSO, Julie, 1930- , American;
plays CON
BOVEDA, Xavier, 1898-1963, Argen-
tinian; poetry, journalism MIN
SA
BOVIER, Gaspard, 1733-1836,
French; nonfiction DIL
BOVILLUS see BOUVELLES, Charles
de
BOVIS, Henry Eugene, 1928- ,
American; nonfiction CON
BOW, Russell, 1925- , American;
nonfiction CON
BOWDEN, Edwin Turner, 1924- ,
American; nonfiction CON
BOWDEN, Jocelyn Jean, 1927- ,
American; nonfiction CON
BOWDEN, John William, 1798-1844,
English; poetry, essays, nonfic-
tion KBA
BOWDEN, Leonard Walter, 1933- ,
American; nonfiction CON
BOWDITCH, Nathaniel, 1773-1838,
American; nonfiction KAA
BOWDLER, Thomas, 1754-1825,
English; editor BRO KB ST
BOWE, Gabriel Paul, 1923- ,

Irish-American; nonfiction
CON
BOWEN, Barbara Cherry, 1937- ,
English; nonfiction CON
'BOWEN, Betty Morgan' see WEST,
Betty
BOWEN, Catherine Shober Drinker,
1897-1973, American; nonfic-
tion CON KTS
BOWEN, Desmond, 1921- ,
Canadian; nonfiction CON
BOWEN, Earl Kenneth, 1918- ,
American; nonfiction CON
BOWEN, Edward Ernest, 1836-
1901, English; poetry BRO
BOWEN, Elbert Russell, 1918- ,
American; nonfiction CON
BOWEN, Elizabeth Dorothea Cole,
1899-1973, Irish; fiction BRO
CON FLE KAT KT MAG RIC
ST WA
BOWEN, Francis, 1811-90, Amer-
ican; nonfiction KAA
BOWEN, Howard Rothmann, 1908- ,
American; nonfiction CON
BOWEN, Irene, American; juveniles
WA
BOWEN, James Keith, 1932- ,
American; nonfiction CON
BOWEN, Jean Donald, 1922- ,
American; nonfiction CON
BOWEN, John Griffith, 1924- ,
English; fiction, plays CON
RIC
BOWEN, Joshua David, 1930- ,
American; juveniles WA
'BOWEN, Marjorie' see LONG,
Margaret
BOWEN, Mary, 1932- , American;
nonfiction CON
BOWEN, Olwen, 20th cent., Eng-
lish; juveniles DOY
BOWEN, Richard M., 1928- ,
American; juveniles CON
BOWEN, Robert O., 1920- ,
American; fiction, nonfiction
CON
BOWEN, Robert Sidney, 1900- ,
American; juveniles WA
BOWEN, Zack Phollie, 1934- ,
American; nonfiction CON
BOWEN-JUDD, Sara Hutton ('Sara
Woods'), 1922- , English;
fiction CON
BOWER, Archibald, 1686-1766,
Scots; nonfiction BRO
BOWER, Bertha Muzzy Sinclair,

1871-1940, American; fiction KT
BOWER, David Allan, 1945- , American; nonfiction CON
BOWER, Gordon Howard, 1932- , American; nonfiction CON
BOWER, Louise, 1900- , American; juveniles CON
BOWER, Walter (Bowmaker), 1385-1449, Scots; nonfiction BRO
BOWER, William Clayton, 1878- , American; nonfiction CON
BOWERING, George ('The Panavision Kid'), 1935- , Canadian; fiction CON MUR
BOWERS, C. A., 1935- , American; nonfiction CON
BOWERS, Claude Gernade, 1879- , American; journalism, nonfiction KT
BOWERS, Edgar, 1924- , American; poetry CON MUR
BOWERS, Faubion, 1917- , American; nonfiction CON
BOWERS, Fredson Thayer, 1905- , American; nonfiction CON
BOWERS, George K., 1916- , American; nonfiction CON
BOWERS, Georgina, 1830- , English; fiction HIG
BOWERS, John, 1928- , American; fiction CON
BOWERS, Joseph O., 1910- , American; nonfiction, fiction SCA
BOWERS, Margaretta Keller, 1908- , American; nonfiction CON
BOWERS, Peter Meiere, American; nonfiction PAC
BOWERS, Santha Rama Rau, 1928- , Indian; fiction, nonfiction, plays CON RIC
BOWETT, Derek William, 1927- , English; nonfiction CON
'BOWIE, Jim' see NORWOOD, Victor G. C.
'BOWIE, Jim' see STRATEMEYER, Edward L.
BOWIE, Norman E., 1942- , American; fiction NON
BOWIE, Robert Richardson, 1909- , American; nonfiction CON
'BOWIE, Sam' see BALLARD, Willis T.
BOWIE, Walter Russell, 1882- , American; nonfiction CON
BOWKER, John Westerdale, 1935- , English; nonfiction CON

BOWKER, Margaret, 1936- , American; nonfiction CON
BOWLE, John, 1725-88, English; nonfiction BL
BOWLE, John Edward, 1905- , Anglo-American; nonfiction CON
BOWLES, Caroline Anne see SOUTHEY, Caroline B.
BOWLES, Delbert Richard, 1910- , American; nonfiction CON
BOWLES, Edmund Addison, 1925- , American; nonfiction CON
BOWLES, Frank Hamilton, 1907- , American; nonfiction CON
BOWLES, Gordon Townsend, 1904- , American; nonfiction CON
BOWLES, Jane Sydney, 1917-73, American; fiction CON
BOWLES, Paul Frederick, 1910- , American; fiction, translations, nonfiction CON KTS RIC
BOWLES, William Lisle, 1762-1850, English; poetry, criticism BRO KBA SA ST
BOWLING, Jackson Michael, 1934- , American; fiction CON
BOWMAKER, Walter see BOWER, Walter
BOWMAN, David J., 1919- , American; nonfiction CON
BOWMAN, Frank Paul, 1927- , American; nonfiction CON
BOWMAN, Henry Adelbert, 1903- , American; nonfiction CON
BOWMAN, James Cloyd, 1880- , American; juveniles KJU WA
'BOWMAN, Jeanne' see BLOCK-LINGER, Peggy O'M.
BOWMAN, John Stewart, 1931- , American; fiction CON
BOWMAN, Captain John Walter, 1908- , American; fiction SCA
BOWMAN, John Wick, 1894- , American; nonfiction CON
BOWMAN, Locke E., Jr., 1927- , American; nonfiction CON
BOWMAN, Marcelle, 1914- , American; juveniles CON
BOWMAN, Mary D., 1924- , American; juveniles CON
BOWMAN, Mary Jean, 1908- , American; nonfiction CON
BOWMAN, Paul Hoover, 1914- ,

American; nonfiction CON

BOWMAN, Robert, 1928- , Scots; fiction CON

BOWMAN, Sylvia Edmonia, 1914- , American; nonfiction CON

BOWMANS, Godfried Jan Arnold, 1913- , Dutch; nonfiction, fiction CON

BOWNE, Borden Parker, 1847-1910, American; nonfiction KAA

'BOWOOD, Richard' see DANIELL, Albert S.

BOWRA, Cecil Maurice, 1898-1971, English; nonfiction BRO CON KTS

BOWRING, Sir John, 1792-1872, English; nonfiction, translations BRO KBA ST

BOWSER, Pearl Joan, 1931- , American; nonfiction CON

BOWYER, John W., 1921- , American; nonfiction CON

BOWYER, Mathew Justice, 1926- , American; nonfiction CON

BOWYER, William, 1699-1777, English; nonfiction KB

'BOX, Edgar' see VIDAL, Gore

BOXER, Devorah, American; juveniles WA

'BOY' see ZELENSKI, Tadeusz

BOYARDO, Matteo Maria (Bojardo), 1434-94, Italian; poetry BL SA

BOYARS, Arthur, 1925- , British; poetry, translations MUR

BOYARSKY, Bill, 1934- , American; nonfiction CON

BOYCE, Burke, 1901- , American; fiction WAF

BOYCE, Gray Cowan, 1899- , American; nonfiction CON

BOYCE, Hector see BOECE, Hector

BOYCE, Neith see HAPGOOD, Mrs. Hutchins

BOYCE, Ronald Reed, 1931- , American; nonfiction CON

'BOYD, Alams' see BOSWORTH, Allan R.

BOYD, Andrew Kennedy Hutchinson, 1825-99, Scots; essays, nonfiction BRO KBA ST

BOYD, Andrew Kirk Henry, 1920- , English; nonfiction CON

BOYD, Dean Wallace, American; nonfiction CON

BOYD, Ernest Augustus, 1887-1946, Irish-American; criticism, essays KL KT ST

'BOYD, Frank' see KANE, Frank

BOYD, Harper White, Jr., 1917- , American; nonfiction CON

BOYD, James, 1888-1944, American; fiction, poetry JO KL KT MAG

BOYD, James Moore, 1919- , American; nonfiction CON

'BOYD, John' see UPCHURCH, Boyd

BOYD, John D., 1916- , American; nonfiction CON

BOYD, John Francis, 1910- , English; nonfiction CON

BOYD, Malcolm, 1923- , American; nonfiction CON

BOYD, Martin a Beckett, 1893- , Swiss-English; fiction CON RIC

BOYD, Maurice, 1921- , American; nonfiction CON

BOYD, Mildred Worthy, 1921- , American; nonfiction CON

BOYD, Robert S., 1928- , American; fiction CON

BOYD, Robin, 1919- , Australian; nonfiction CON

BOYD, Thomas, 1898-1935, American; fiction KT

BOYD, Waldo T. ('Ted Andersen'; 'Robert Parker'), 1918- , American; nonfiction CON

BOYD, William Kenneth, 1879-1938, English; nonfiction JO

BOYD, Zachary, 1585?-1653, Scots; nonfiction BRO ST

BOYDSTON, Jo Ann, 1924- , American; fiction CON

BOYE, Karin Maria, 1900-41, Swedish; poetry, fiction, criticism COL FLE SA ST

BOYER, Abel, 1667-1729, English; nonfiction DIL KB

BOYER, Claude, 1618?-98, French; plays HAR ST

BOYER, François, 1677-1755, French; nonfiction DIL

BOYER, Harold W., 1908- , American; nonfiction CON

BOYER, Jacques, 18th cent., French; nonfiction DIL

BOYER, Richard Edwin, 1932- , American; nonfiction CON

BOYER, William W., Jr., 1923- , American; nonfiction CON

BOYESEN, Hjalmar Hjorth, 1848-95, American; juveniles KAA

BOYKIN, James Handy, 1914- ,
American; nonfiction CON
BOYL VIVES de CANESMA, Carlos,
1577-1618, Spanish; plays BL
SA ST
'BOYLAN, Boyd' see WHITON,
James N.
BOYLAN, Rev. Eugene, 1904- ,
Irish; nonfiction HO
BOYLAN, James Richard, 1927- ,
American; nonfiction CON
BOYLAN, Lucile, 1906- , Ameri-
can; nonfiction CON
BOYLAN, Patrick, Irish; nonfiction
HOE
BOYLE, Andrew, 1923- , Scots;
nonfiction CON
BOYLE, Ann Peters, 1916- ,
American; juveniles CON
BOYLE, Emily Joyce, 1901- ,
Canadian; juveniles CON
BOYLE, Harry Joseph, 1915- ,
Canadian; nonfiction CON
BOYLE, Kay, 1903- , American;
fiction, poetry, essays CON
FLE KAT KT MUR ST WAF
BOYLE, Robert, 1627-91, Irish;
nonfiction BRO ST
BOYLE, Robert, 1915- , American;
nonfiction CON
BOYLE, Robert H., 1928- , Amer-
ican; nonfiction CON
BOYLE, Roger see ORERY, Robert
B.
BOYLE, Sarah Patton, 1906- ,
American; nonfiction CON
BOYLE, Ted Eugene, 1933- ,
American; nonfiction CON
BOYLEN, Margaret Currier, 1921- ,
American; fiction CON
BOYLES, Clarence Scott, Jr. (Will
C. Brown), 1905- , American;
fiction CON
'BOYLESTON, Peter' see CURTIS,
George T.
BOYLESVE, Joseph François, 1692-
1769, French; nonfiction DIL
'BOYLESVE, René' (René Marie
Auguste Fardiveau), 1867-1926,
French; fiction COL DIF HAR
KT SA ST
BOYLSTON, Helen Dore, 1895- ,
American; juveniles DOY KJU
WA
BOYNTON, Lewis Delano, 1909- ,
American; nonfiction CON
BOYNTON, Percy Holmes, 1875-

1946, American; criticism,
nonfiction KT
BOYSEN, Johann Wilhelm, 1834-
70, German; poetry ST
BOYTON, Neil, 1884- , Ameri-
can; juveniles HOE WA
BOYUM, Joy Gould, 1934- ,
American; nonfiction CON
BOYVE, Jonas, 1654-1739, Swiss;
nonfiction DIL
BOZE, Claude Groa, 1680-1753,
French; nonfiction DIL
BOZEMAN, Adda Bruemamer,
1908- , Latvian-American;
nonfiction CON
BOZVELI, Neofit, 1785-1848,
Bulgarian; nonfiction ST
BRAAK, Ivo, 1906- , German;
plays ST
BRAAK, Menno ter, 1902-40,
Dutch; essays, plays ST
BRAASCH, William Frederick,
1878- , American; nonfiction
CON
BRAATEN, Oskar Alexander,
1881-1939, Norwegian; fiction,
plays ST
BRABANT, Jan, 1268-94, German;
poetry ST
BRABOURNE, Lord see KNATCH-
BULL-HUGESSEN, Edward H.
BRABSON, George Dana, 1900- ,
American; nonfiction CON
BRACCESI, Alessandro (Bracci),
1445-1503, Italian; poetry ST
BRACCIALARGHE, C. see
TESTENA, Folco
BRACCIOLINI-POGGIO, Gian
Francesco see POGGIO BRAC-
CIOLINI, Gian F.
BRACCO, Roberto, 1862-1943,
Italian; plays, essays, criti-
cism, poetry, fiction COL
FLE MAT SA
BRACE, Gerald Warner, 1901- ,
American; fiction CON KTS
WAF
BRACE, Richard Munthe, 1915- ,
American; nonfiction CON
'BRACE, Timothy' see PRATT,
Theodore
BRACEWELL-MILNES, John Barry,
1931- , English; nonfiction
CON
BRACEY, Howard Edwin, 1905- ,
English; nonfiction CON
BRACEY, John Henry, Jr.,

1941-   , American; nonfiction
CON
BRACHER, Marjory Louise, 1906- ,
American; nonfiction CON
BRACHMANN, Louise C., 1777- ,
German; poetry SA
BRACHVOGEL, Albert Emil, 1824-
78, German; plays, fiction
HAR ST
BRACHVOGEL, Udo, 1835-1913,
German-American; journalism,
poetry ST
BRACK, Harold Arthur, 1923- ,
American; nonfiction CON
BRACKBILL, Yvonne, 1928- ,
American; nonfiction CON
BRACKEN, Dorothy Kendall, Amer-
ican; nonfiction CON
BRACKEN, Joseph Andrew, 1930- ,
American; nonfiction CON
BRACKEN, Peg, 1920- , American;
nonfiction CON
BRACKEN, Thomas, 1843-98, New
Zealander; journalism, poetry
ST
BRACKENRIDGE, Henry Marie,
1786-1871, American; nonfiction
KAA
BRACKENRIDGE, Hugh Henry,
1748-1816, American; fiction,
plays KAA MAG ST
BRACKER, Jon, 1936- , American;
nonfiction CON
BRACKETT, Leigh Douglass, 1915- ,
American; fiction, tv CON
BRACKMAN, Arnold Charles,
1923- , American; nonfiction
CON
BRACLAVER, Nachman, 1772-1811,
Jewish; fiction ST
BRACONNIER,   -1716, French;
nonfiction DIL
BRACTON, Henry de (Bratton;
Bretton),   -1268, English;
nonfiction KB
BRADBROOK, Muriel Clara, 1909- ,
English; nonfiction CON
BRADBURN, Norman M., 1933- ,
American; nonfiction CON
BRADBURNE, Elizabeth S. ('E. S.
Lawrence'), 1915- , English;
fiction CON
BRADBURY, Bianca, 1908- ,
American; juveniles, fiction,
poetry CON WA
BRADBURY, John Mason, 1908- ,
American; nonfiction CON

BRADBURY, Malcolm Stanley,
1932- , British; poetry,
fiction, criticism CON MUR
RIC
BRADBURY, Parnell, 1904- ,
English; juveniles, plays CON
BRADBURY, Ray Douglas ('Leonard
Spaulding'), 1920- , Ameri-
can; fiction CON KTS RIC
BRADDOCK, Richard Reed, 1920- ,
American; nonfiction CON
BRADDON, Mary Elizabeth Max-
well, 1837-1915, English;
fiction BRO KBA ST
BRADDON, Russell Reading,
1921- , English; fiction, tv,
radio CON
BRADDY, Haldeen, 1908- ,
American; nonfiction CON
BRADDY, Nella, 1894- , Ameri-
can; juveniles WA
BRADE-BIRKS, Stanley Graham,
1887- , English; nonfiction
CON
BRADEN, Charles Samuel, 1887- ,
American; nonfiction CON
BRADEN, Waldo Warder, 1911- ,
American; nonfiction CON
BRADEN, William, 1930- ,
American; nonfiction CON
BRADFIELD, James McComb,
1917- , American; nonfiction
CON
BRADFIELD, Nancy, 1913- ,
English; nonfiction CON
BRADFIELD, Richard, 1896- ,
American; nonfiction CON
BRADFIELD, Roger, 1924- ,
American; juveniles CON
'BRADFORD, Adam, M. D.' see
WASSERSUG, Joseph D.
BRADFORD, Gamaliel, 1863-1932,
American; nonfiction, poetry
KL KT ST
BRADFORD, George Partridge,
1807-90, American; nonfiction
KAA
'BRADFORD, Joseph' (William
Randolph Hunter; 'Jay Bee'),
1843-86, American; poetry,
plays, journalism KAA
BRADFORD, Leland Powers,
1905- , American; nonfiction
CON
BRADFORD, Patience Andrewes,
1918- , English; nonfiction
CON

BRADFORD, Roark Whitney Wickliffe, 1896-1948, American; fiction KL KT

BRADFORD, Saxton, 1907-66, American; nonfiction CON

BRADFORD, William, 1589/90-1657, American; nonfiction BRO KAA ST

BRADFORD, William C., 1910- , American; nonfiction CON

BRADLEE, Frederic, 1920- , American; fiction CON

BRADLEY, Andrew Cecil, 1851-1935, English; nonfiction BRO KT ST

BRADLEY, Brigitte Looke, 1924- , Polish-American; nonfiction CON

BRADLEY, Cuthbert, 1860-1941, English; nonfiction HIG

BRADLEY, David G., 1916- , American; nonfiction CON

'BRADLEY, Duane' see SANBORN, Duane

BRADLEY, Edward ('Cuthbert Bede'), 1827-89, English; fiction, poetry BRO KBA ST

BRADLEY, Erwin Stanley, 1906- , American; nonfiction CON

BRADLEY, Francis Herbert, 1846-1924, English; nonfiction BRO KBA ST

BRADLEY, Harold Whitman, 1903- , American; nonfiction CON

BRADLEY, Henry, 1845-1923, English; nonfiction BRO

BRADLEY, James Vandiver, 1924- , American; nonfiction CON

BRADLEY, John Francis Nejez, 1930- , Czech-English; nonfiction CON

BRADLEY, John Hodgdon, Jr., 1898- , American; nonfiction KT

BRADLEY, John Lewis, 1917- , English; nonfiction CON

BRADLEY, Joseph Francis, 1917- , American; nonfiction CON

BRADLEY, Katharine Harris ('Michael Field'), 1848-1914, English; poetry BRO

BRADLEY, Kenneth Granville, 1904- , English; nonfiction CON

BRADLEY, Marjorie D., 1931- , English; nonfiction CON

BRADLEY, Mary Hastings, American; fiction HOO

BRADLEY, R.C., 1929- , American; nonfiction CON

BRADLEY, Robert Austin, 1917- , American; nonfiction CON

BRADLEY, Samuel McKee, 1917- , American; poetry CON MUR

BRADLEY, Van Allen, 1913- , American; nonfiction CON

BRADLEY, William Lee, 1918- , American; nonfiction CON

BRADLOW, Edna Rom, South African; nonfiction CON

BRADLOW, Frank Rosslyn, 1913- , South African; nonfiction CON

'BRADLY, Mr.' see BURROUGHS, William S.

BRADSTREET, Anne, 1612?-72, American; poetry BRO KAA SA SP ST

BRADWARDINE, Thomas, 1290?-1349, English; nonfiction BRO ST

BRADWAY, John Saeger, 1890- , American; nonfiction CON

BRADY, Charles Andrew, 1912- , American; criticism CON HO

BRADY, Frank, 1924- , American; nonfiction CON

BRADY, Gerald Peter, 1929- , American; nonfiction CON

BRADY, Irene, 1943- , American; juveniles CON

BRADY, John Paul, 1928- , American; nonfiction CON

BRADY, Leo, 1917- , American; fiction HO

BRADY, Nicholas, 1659-1726, English; poetry BRO

BRADY, Rita G., American; juveniles WA

BRÄKER, Ulrich, 1735-98, German; nonfiction AL ST

BRAENNE, Berit, 1918- , Norwegian; nonfiction CON

BRAGA, Alberto, 1851-1911, Portuguese; plays, fiction COL SA

'BRAGA, Teófilo' (Joaquim Teófilo Fernandes), 1843-1924, Portuguese; criticism, nonfiction, poetry COL HAR SA ST

BRAGDON, Elspeth MacDuffie, 1897- , American; poetry, juveniles CON

BRAGDON, Henry Wilkinson, 1906- , American; nonfiction CON

BRAGDON, Lillian Jacot, Amer-

ican; juveniles WA
BRAGG, Arthur Norris, 1897- ,
American; nonfiction CON
BRAHAM, Randolph Lewis, 1922- ,
Rumanian-American; nonfiction
CON
'BRAHM, Otto' (Otto Abrahamson),
1856-1912, German; journalism
COL SA
'BRAHMS, Caryl' (Doris Caroline
Abrahams), 1901- , English;
fiction RIC
BRAIDER, Donald, 1923- , Amer-
ican; nonfiction CON
BRAILSFORD, Frances, 1917- ,
American; juveniles CON
BRAILSFORD, Henry Noel, 1873- ,
British; journalism KT
BRAIN, Joseph J., 1920- , Amer-
ican; nonfiction CON
BRAINARD, Harry Guy, 1907- ,
American; nonfiction CON
BRAINARD, John Gardiner Calkins,
1796-1828, American; poetry
KAA
BRAINE, John Gerard, 1922- ,
English; fiction CON RIC
BRAINERD, Barron, 1928- ,
Canadian; nonfiction CON
BRAINERD, David, 1718-47, Ameri-
can; nonfiction KAA
BRAININ, Reuben, 1862-1939, Jewish;
fiction LAN ST
BRAITHWAITE, Eustace Edward
Ricardo, 1920- , West Indian;
fiction RIC
BRAITHWAITE, Richard (Brathwaite),
1588-1673, English; poetry BRO
ST
BRAITHWAITE, William Stanley
Beaumont, 1878- , American;
poetry KT
BRAKEL, Samuel Johannes, 1943- ,
Dutch-American; nonfiction CON
BRAKELANS, Jocelin of, fl. 1170-
1200, English; nonfiction ST
BRALY, Malcolm ('Ray Lorning'),
1925- , American; fiction CON
'BRAMAH, Ernest' see SMITH,
Ernest B.
BRAMALL, Eric, 1927- , English;
nonfiction CON
'BRAMBEUS, Baron' see SENKOV-
SKI, Osip I.
BRAMBILLA, M., 18th cent., Swiss;
nonfiction DIL
BRAMELD, Theodore, 1904- ,

American; nonfiction CON
BRAMER, Jennie Perkins ('Faith
Perkins'), 1900- , American;
nonfiction CON
BRAMER, John Conrad, Jr.,
1924- , American; nonfiction
CON
BRAMMER, Lawrence M., 1922- ,
American; nonfiction CON
BRAMS, Stanley Howard, 1910- ,
American; nonfiction CON
BRAMSON, Leon, 1930- ,
American; nonfiction CON
BRAMSTON, James, 1674?-
1744, English; poetry BRO ST
BRAMWELL, James Guy ('James
Byrom'), 1911- , English;
nonfiction CON
BRANCA, Albert A., 1916- ,
American; nonfiction CON
BRANCAFORTE, Benito, 1934- ,
Italian-American; nonfiction
CON
BRANCATI, Vitaliano, 1907-54,
Italian; fiction, plays, essays
FLE HAR ST
BRANCH, Anna Hempstead, 1875-
1937, American; poetry KAT
KT
BRANCH, Daniel Paulk, 1931- ,
American; nonfiction CON
BRANCH, Edgar Marquess,
1913- , American; nonfiction
CON
BRANCH, Harold Francis, 1894-
1966, American; nonfiction
CON
BRANCH, Houston, 1903- ,
American; fiction WAF
BRANCH, Mary, 1910- , Ameri-
can; nonfiction CON
BRAND, Carl Fremont, 1892- ,
American; nonfiction CON
BRAND, Charles Peter, 1923- ,
English; nonfiction CON
BRAND, Clarence Eugene, 1895- ,
American; nonfiction CON
BRAND, Charles Macy, 1932- ,
American; nonfiction CON
'BRAND, Clay' see NORWOOD,
Victor G.C.
'BRAND, Hedwig' see COURTHS-
MAHLER, Hedwig
BRAND, Jeanne Laurel, 1919- ,
American; nonfiction CON
'BRAND, Max' (Frederick Faust),
1892-1944, American; fiction
KT

BRAND, Millen, 1906- , American;
fiction CON KT WAF
BRAND, Myles, 1942- , American;
nonfiction CON
BRAND, Oscar, 1920- , American;
nonfiction, juveniles CON WA
'BRAND, Peter' see LARSEN, Erling
BRANDAN CARAFFA, Alfredo,
1898/1900- , Argentinian;
poetry MIN
BRANDÃO, Antonio, 1584-1637,
Portuguese; nonfiction ST
BRANDÃO, Raúl Germano, 1867-
1930, Portuguese; fiction, plays,
essays FLE SA ST
BRANDE, Dorothea Thompson, 1893-
1948, American; fiction KT
BRANDE, Ralph T., 1921- , Amer-
ican; nonfiction CON
BRANDEL, Marc, 1919- , American;
fiction WAF
BRANDEN, Nathaniel, 1930- ,
American; nonfiction CON
BRANDENBERG, Aliki Liacouras
('Aliki'), 1929- , American;
juveniles COM CON WA
BRANDENBERG, Franz, 1932- ,
American; fiction CON
BRANDENBURG, Frank Ralph,
1926- , American; nonfiction
CON
BRANDENBURG, Hans, 1885- ,
German; nonfiction KU
BRANDES, Carl Edvard Cohen,
1847-1931, Danish; plays, fic-
tion, criticism ST
BRANDES, Georg Morris Cohen,
1842-1927, Danish; criticism
COL FLE HAR KAT KT RIC
SA ST
BRANDES, Joseph, 1928- , Ameri-
can; nonfiction CON
BRANDHORST, Carl Theodore, 1898- ,
American; juveniles CON
'BRANDON, Curt' see BISHOP,
Curtis K.
BRANDON, Dick H., Dutch-Ameri-
can; nonfiction CON
BRANDON, Frances Sweeney,
1916- , American; juveniles
CON
'BRANDON, Joe' see DAVIS, Robert
P.
BRANDON, Samuel, fl. 1598, Eng-
lish; plays ST
'BRANDON, Sheila' see RAYNER,
Claire

BRANDSTAEDER, Morcechai
David, 1844-1928, Jewish;
fiction ST
BRANDSTAETTER, Roman,
1906- , Polish; plays MAT
BRANDT, Adolf see 'STILLFRIED,
Felix'
BRANDT, Alvin G., 1922- ,
American; nonfiction CON
BRANDT, Floyd Stanley, 1930- ,
American; nonfiction CON
BRANDT, Geeraerdt, 1626-85,
Dutch; nonfiction HAR ST
'BRANDT, Harvey' see EDWARDS,
William B.
'BRANDT, Harvey' see SELL,
Francis E.
BRANDT, Joseph A., 1899- ,
American; nonfiction MAR
'BRANDT, Kaspar' see WINKLER
PRINS, Jacob
BRANDT, Leslie F., 1919- ,
American; nonfiction CON
BRANDT, Rexford Elson, 1914- ,
American; nonfiction CON
BRANDT, Richard Martin, 1922- ,
American; nonfiction CON
BRANDT, Sue Reading, 1916- ,
American; juveniles CON
'BRANDT, Tom' see DEWEY,
Thomas B.
BRANDT, Vincent S. R., 1924- ,
American; nonfiction CON
BRANDT, William Edward,
1920- , American; nonfiction
CON
BRANDWEIN, Chaim Naftali ('Ch.
Naftali'), 1920- , Israeli-
American; nonfiction CON
BRANDYS, Kazimierz, 1916- ,
Polish; fiction FLE
BRANLEY, Franklyn Mansfield,
1915- , American; juveniles
CON FUL WA
BRANN, Esther, American;
juveniles KJU WA
BRANN, William Cowper, 1855-
98, American; nonfiction KAA
BRANNAN, Robert Louis, 1927- ,
American; nonfiction CON
BRANNEN, Noah Samuel, 1924- ,
American; nonfiction CON
BRANNEN, Ted R., 1924- ,
American; nonfiction CON
BRANNER, Hans Christian, 1903-
66, Danish; fiction, plays FLE
HAR RIC ST

BRANNER, Robert, 1927- , American; nonfiction CON

BRANNON, William T. ('Lawrence Gardner'; 'Jack Hamilton'; 'Peter Hermanns'; 'Dwight Mc-Glinn'; 'Peter Oberholtzer'; 'S. T. Peters'; 'William Tibbetts'), 1906- , American; nonfiction CON

BRANSOM, Paul, 1885- , American; juveniles FUL

BRANT, Charles Sanford, 1919- , American; nonfiction CON

BRANT, Irving Newton, 1885- , American; nonfiction CON KTS

'BRANT, Lewis' see ROWLAND, Donald S.

BRANT, Sebastian, 1458?-1521, German; poetry AL HAR KE SA ST

BRANTOME, Pierre de Bourdeille, 1535?-1614, French; nonfiction DIF HAR KE MAL SA ST

BRARD, A. J., 18th cent., French; nonfiction DIL

BRASCH, Charles, 1909- , New Zealander; poetry MUR RIC ST

BRASCH, Rudolph, 1912- , German-Australian; nonfiction CON

BRASHER, Christopher William, 1928- , English; fiction CON

BRASHER, Norman Henry, 1922- , English; nonfiction CON

BRASHERS, Howard Charles, 1930- , American; nonfiction CON

'BRASIER-CREAGH, Patrick' see CREAGH, Patrick

BRASILLACH, Robert, 1909-45, French; fiction, essays, juveniles DIC DIF FLE MAL

BRASS, Paul Richard, 1936- , American; nonfiction CON

BRASSEY, Anna (Annie, Braoness Brassey), 1839-87, English; nonfiction KBA

BRASSEY, Robert Bingham, 1875- , English; nonfiction HIG

BRATESCU-VOINESTI, Ion Alexandre, 1868-1944, Rumanian; fiction SA ST

BRATHWAITE, L. Edward, 1930- , Barbadian; poetry, plays CON MUR

BRATHWAITE, Sheila R., 1914- , English; juveniles CON

BRATHWAITE, Richard see BRAITH-WAITE, Richard

BRATLI, Carlos, 1871-1957, Danish; nonfiction BL

BRATT, Elmer Clark, 1901- , American; nonfiction CON

BRATT, John Harold, 1909- , American; nonfiction CON

BRATTGARG, Helge Axel Kristian, 1920- , Swedish; nonfiction CON

BRATTON, Fred Gladstone, 1896- , American; nonfiction CON

BRATTON, Helen, 1899- , American; fiction CON

BRATTON, Henry de see BRACTON, Henry de

BRATTON, Karl H., 1906- , American; juveniles WA

BRAUDE, Jacob Morton, 1896- , American; nonfiction CON

BRAUDE, Michael, 1936- , American; juveniles CON

BRAUDE, William Gordon, 1907- , Lithuanian-American; nonfiction CON

BRAUDES, Avraham, 1907- , Jewish; poetry ST

BRAUDES, Reuben Asher, 1851-1902, Jewish; fiction ST

BRAUDY, Leo, 1941- , American; nonfiction CON

BRAUER, Jerald Carl, 1921- , American; nonfiction CON

BRAUER, Kinley, Jules, 1935- , American; nonfiction CON

BRAUER, Theodor, 1880-1942, German; nonfiction HO

BRAULIO de ZAROGOZA, San, 585-651, Spanish; nonfiction SA ST

BRAULT, Gerard Joseph, 1929- , American; nonfiction CON

BRAUN, Felix, 1885- , Austrian; poetry, fiction plays, essays AL FLE KU LEN

BRAUN, Günter, 1928- , German; nonfiction AL

BRAUN, Henry, 1930- , American; poetry CON MUR

BRAUN, Hugh, 1902- , English; nonfiction CON

BRAUN, John Richard, 1928- , American; nonfiction CON

BRAUN, Kathy, American; juveniles WA

BRAUN, Johanna, 1929- , German; nonfiction AL

BRAUN, Richard Emil, 1934- ,
American; poetry CON
BRAUN, Saul M., American;
juveniles WA
BRAUN, Theodore E.D., 1933- ,
American; nonfiction CON
BRAUN, Thomas, 1876- , Belgian;
poetry ST
BRAUN, Werner von, 1912- ,
German-American; juveniles
WA
BRAUN MENENDEZ, Armando,
1898- , Argentinian; nonfiction
MIN
BRAUNE, Rudolf, 1907-32, German;
nonfiction AL
BRAUNSCHWEIG-LÜNEBURG, Anton
Ulrich see ANTON ULRICH v.
Braunschweig-Lüneberg
BRAUNTHAL, Gerard, 1923- ,
German-American; nonfiction
CON
BRAUNTHAL, Julius, 1891- ,
American; nonfiction CON
BRAUQUIER, Louis, 1900- ,
French; poetry DIF
BRAUTIGAN, Richard, 1935- ,
American; poetry, fiction MUR
BRAUTLACHT, Erich, 1902- ,
German; nonfiction KU LEN
BRAV, Stanley Rosembaum ('R. Rush
Barton'), 1908- , American;
nonfiction CON
BRAVO, Mario, 1882-1942/43,
Argentinian; journalism, poetry
MIN
BRAVO Fray Nicolas, 1587?-1648,
Spanish; nonfiction SA
BRAVO-VILLASANTE, Carmen,
Spanish; nonfiction BL
BRAWER, Florence Blum, 1922- ,
American; nonfiction CON
BRAWLEY, Benjamin Griffith,
1882-1929, American; nonfiction
KT
BRAWN, Dympna, 1931- , Irish;
fiction CON
BRAXATORIS, Ondrij see 'SLAD-
KOVIC, Andrej'
'BRAY, Alison' see ROWLAND,
Donald S.
BRAY, Allen Farris, III, 1926- ,
American; nonfiction CON
BRAY, Anna Eliza Kempe Stothard,
1790-1883, English; fiction,
juveniles BRO KBA ST
BRAY, Douglas W., 1918- ,

American; nonfiction CON
BRAY, Warwick, 1936- , English;
nonfiction CON
BRAYBROOKE, David, 1924- ,
American; nonfiction CON
BRAYBROOKE, Neville Patrick
Bellairs, 1925- , American;
nonfiction CON
'BRAYCE, William' see ROWLAND,
Donald S.
BRAYMAN, Harold, 1900- ,
American; nonfiction CON
'BRAYMER, Marguerite' see
DODD, Marguerite
BRAYMER, Marjorie Elizabeth,
1911- , American; nonfiction
CON
BRAYNARD, Frank O., 1916- ,
American; nonfiction CON
BRAZA, Jacque see McKEAG,
Ernest L.
BRAZIL, Angela, 1868-1947,
English; juveniles BRO DOY
'BRAZIL, Felix' see KLEMM,
Wilhelm
BREACH, Robert Walter, 1927- ,
English; nonfiction CON
BREANT, Jacques Philippe, 1710-
72, French; poetry DIL
BREARLEY, Denis, 1940- ,
Canadian; nonfiction CON
BREASTED, James Henry, 1865-
1935, American; nonfiction
BRO HOO KT
BREATHETT, George, 1925- ,
American; nonfiction CON
BREBEUF, Georges de, 1618-61,
French; poetry, DIF ST
BRECHER, Edward Moritz,
1911- , American; nonfiction
CON
BRECHER, Michael, 1925- ,
Canadian; nonfiction CON
BRECHER, Ruth Anestine, 1911- ,
American; nonfiction CON
BRECHT, Bertolt, 1898-1956,
German; plays, fiction, poetry
AL COL FLE HAR KT KU
KUN LEN MAG MAT RIC SA
ST
BRECHT, Edith, 1895- , Amer-
ican; juveniles CON
BRECK, Allen du Pont, 1914- ,
American; nonfiction CON
BRECKENFIELD, Vivian Gurney
('Vivian Breck'), 1895- ,
American; juveniles COM
CON FUL WA

BRECKENRIDGE, Adam Carlyle,
1916- , American; nonfiction
CON
BRECOURT, 18th cent., French;
nonfiction DIL
'BREDA, Tjalmar see DeJong,
David C.
BREDAHL, Christian Hviid, 1784-
1860, Danish; poetry ST
BREDEL, Willi, 1901- , German;
nonfiction AL KU
BREDEMEIER, Harry Charles,
1920- , American; nonfiction
CON
BREDEN, Christiane von see
'CHRISTEN, Ada'
BREDERO, Gerbrand Adriaenszoon
(Brederode), 1585-1618, Dutch;
poetry, plays HAR KE SA ST
BREDOOW, Gabreil Gottfried, 1773-
1814, German; nonfiction SA
BREDOW, Miriam see WOLF, Miriam
B.
BREDSDORFF, Elian Lunn, 1912- ,
Danish-English; nonfiction CON
BREDSDORFF, Jan, 1942- , Danish-
English; fiction CON
BREDVOLD, Louis Ignatius, 1888- ,
American; nonfiction CON
BREE, Germaine, 1907- , Ameri-
can; nonfiction CON
BREED, Paul F., 1916- , Ameri-
can; nonfiction CON
BREEN, Quirinus, 1896- , Ameri-
can; nonfiction CON
BREESKIN, Adelyn Dohme, 1896- ,
American; nonfiction CON
BREETVELD, Jim Patrick ('Avery
Mann'), 1925- , American;
nonfiction CON WA
BREGENDAHL, Maria, 1867-1940,
Danish; fiction COL FLE ST
BREGY, Katherine Marie Cornelia,
1888- , American; poetry HOE
BREHIER, Emile, 1876-1952, French;
nonfiction DIF SA
BREHM, Bruno, 1892- , Austrian;
fiction ST
BREIDJÖRD, Sigurdur Eiriksson,
1798-1846, Icelandic; poetry
KE SA ST
BREIG, Joseph Anthony, 1905- ,
American; journalism CON HO
BREIHAN, Carl William, 1916- ,
American; nonfiction CON
BREILLAT, Catherine, 1950- ,
French; fiction CON

BREIMYER, Harold Frederick,
1914- , American; nonfiction
CON
BREISACH, Ernst Adolf, 1923- ,
Austrian-American; nonfiction
CON
BREIT, Harvey, 1913-68, Ameri-
can; nonfiction CON
BREIT, William Leo, 1933- ,
American; nonfiction CON
BREITBACH, Joseph, 1903- ,
German; nonfiction KU
BREITENKAMP, Edward Carlton,
1913- , American; nonfiction
CON
BREITINGER, Johann Jakob,
1701-76, Swiss; criticism
AL HAR KE SA ST
'BREITMANN, Hans' see LELAND,
Charles G.
BREITMEYER, Lois, 1923- ,
American; nonfiction HIL
BREKKAN, Fredrik Asmundsson,
1888- , Icelandic; fiction,
poetry ST
BRELAND, Osmond Philip, 1910- ,
American; nonfiction CON
BRELIS, Dean, 1924- , American;
nonfiction CON
BRELIS, Nancy Burns, 1929- ,
South African; fiction CON
BRELSFORD, William Vernon,
1907- , English; nonfiction
CON
BREMAN, Paul, 1931- , Dutch-
English; nonfiction CON
BREMBATI, Isotta, 15th cent.,
Italian; poetry SA
BREMER, Fredrika, 1801-65,
Swedish; fiction HAR KE SA
ST
BREMNER, Robert Hamlett,
1917- , American; nonfiction
CON
BREMOND, André, 1872- ,
French; nonfiction HOE
BREMOND, Antonin, 1692-1755,
French; nonfiction DIL
BREMOND, Abbé, Henri, 1865-
1933, French; criticism COL
DIF HOE SA ST
BREMS, Hans, 1915- , Danish-
American; nonfiction CON
BREMSER, Ray, 1934- , Amer-
ican; poetry CON MUR
BRENAN, Gerald (George Beaton),
1894- , English; nonfiction,

fiction BL CON KTS
BRENDER à BRANDIS, Gerrit, 1751-
1802, Dutch; poetry, plays ST
BRENDTRO, Lawrence K., 1940- ,
American; nonfiction CON
BRENER, Milton E., 1930- ,
American; nonfiction CON
BRENES ARGÜELLO de RIZO,
Carlota, 1905- , Costa Rican;
poetry MIN
BRENGELMANN, Johannes Clemens,
1920- , American; nonfiction
CON
BRENNAN, Bernard Patrick, 1918- ,
American; nonfiction CON
BRENNAN, Christopher John, 1870-
1932, Australian; poetry RIC
ST
BRENNAN, Elizabeth, 1922- ,
Irish; fiction HO
BRENNAN, Rev. Gerald Thomas,
1898- , American; juveniles
HO
BRENNAN, John Needham Huggard
('John Welcome'), 1914- ,
Irish; fiction CON
BRENNAN, Joseph Gerard, Ameri-
can; nonfiction CON WA
BRENNAN, Joseph Lomas ('Steve
Lomas'), 1903- , American;
fiction CON
BRENNAN, Joseph Payne, 1918- ,
American; poetry, nonfiction,
fiction CON
BRENNAN, Lawrence David, 1915- ,
American; fiction, nonfiction
CON
BRENNAN, Louis Arthur, 1911- ,
American; fiction CON
BRENNAN, Maynard J., 1921- ,
American; nonfiction CON
BRENNAN, Michael Joseph, Jr.,
1928- , American; nonfiction
CON
BRENNAN, Neil Francis, 1923- ,
American; nonfiction CON
BRENNAN, Niall, 1918- , Austral-
ian; nonfiction CON
BRENNAN, Robert Edward, 1897- ,
American; nonfiction HOE
'BRENNAN, Tim' see CONROY,
John W.
'BRENNAND, Frank' see LAMBERT,
Eric
BRENNECKE, Bert, 1898- , Ger-
man; nonfiction AL
BRENNECKE, John Henry, 1934- ,

American; nonfiction CON
BRENNECKE, Wolf D., 1922- ,
German; nonfiction AL
BRENNEMAN, Helen Good,
1925- , American; nonfiction,
fiction CON
BRENNER, Barbara Johnes,
1925- , American; juveniles
CON WA
BRENNER, Hans George, 1903- ,
German; nonfiction LEN
BRENNER, Joseph Hayyim, 1881-
1921, Jewish; fiction LAN
ST
BRENNER, Sofia Elisabet Weber,
1659-1730, Swedish; poetry
HAR ST
BRENNER, Yehojachin Simon,
1926- , German; nonfiction
CON
'BRENNGLASS' see GLASSBRENNER,
Adolf
BRENSES MESEN, Roberto, 1874-
1947, Costa Rican; poetry,
essays MIN
BRENT, Harold Patrick, 1943- ,
American; nonfiction CON
BRENT, Stuart, American; juven-
iles WA
'BRENT of BIN BIN' see FRANK-
LIN, Miles
BRENTANO, Bernhard von,
1901- , German; nonfiction
KU LEN
BRENTANO, Clemens Maria,
1778-1842, German; poetry
AL HAR KE SA ST
BRENTANO, Elisabeth, 1785-1859,
German; nonfiction SA
BRENTANO, Franz, 1838-1917,
German; nonfiction SA
BRANTANO, Robert, 1926- ,
American; nonfiction CON
BRENTANO, Sophie, 1761-1806,
German; fiction SA
BRENT-DYER, Elinor Mary, 20th
cent., English; juveniles
DOY
BREQUIGNY, Louis Georges Oudard
Feudrix, 1714-94, French;
nonfiction DIL
BRERETON, Captain Frederick
Sadleir, 1872-1957, English;
juveniles DOY
BRERETON, Geoffrey, 1906- ,
English; nonfiction CON
BRERI (Bleheris), French?;

fiction ST
BRESLAUER, George W., 1946- ,
American; nonfiction CON
BRESLIN, James E., 1935- ,
American; nonfiction CON
BRESLOVE, David, 1891- ,
Canadian; nonfiction CON
BRET, Antoine, 1717-92, French;
plays, poetry DIL
BRETEL, Jacques, fl. 1285, French;
poetry HAR ST
BRETEL, Jean, -1272, French;
poetry ST
BRETON, André, 1896-1966, French;
poetry, essays COL CON DIC
DIF FLE HAR KTS MAL MAT
RIC SA ST
BRETON, Nicholas, 1545?-1626?,
English; poetry, essays BRO
KB SP ST
BRETON de los HERREROS, Manuel,
1796-1873, Spanish; plays,
poetry BL HAR SA ST
BRETONNEAU, François, 1660-1741,
French; nonfiction DIL
BRETSCHER, Paul Gerhardt, 1921- ,
American; nonfiction CON
'BRETT, David' see CAMPBELL,
Will D.
BRETT, Grace Neff, 1900- ,
American; juveniles CON
BRETT, Mary Elizabeth ('Molly
Brett'), English; juveniles CON
'BRETT, Michael' see TRIPP, Miles
BRETT, Raymond Laurence, 1917- ,
English; nonfiction CON
BRETT YOUNG see YOUNG, Frances
B.
BRETTELL, Noel Harry, 1908- ,
Rhodesian; poetry MUR
BRETT-JAMES, Eliot Antony,
1920- , American; fiction CON
BRETTON, Henry De see BRACTON,
Henry de
BRETTON, Henry L., 1916- ,
German; nonfiction CON
BRETTSCHNEIDER, Bertram Donald,
1924- , American; nonfiction
CON
BRETT-SMITH, Richard, 1923- ,
English; nonfiction CON
BRETT-YOUNG, Jessica Hankinson,
1883- , English; nonfiction
CON
BREUER, Elizabeth, 1892/93- ,
American; fiction CON KT
BREUER, Ernest Henry, 1902- ,

American; nonfiction CON
BREUER, Marcel, 1902- ,
Hungarian-American; nonfic-
tion CON
BREUGHEL, Gerris Hendricksz
van, 1573-1635, Dutch;
poetry ST
BREUNIG, Jerome Edward,
1917- , American; nonfiction
CON
BREVOORT, Laurence see BAR-
RETTO, Larry
BREW, O.H. Kwesi, 1928- ,
Ghanaian; poetry MUR
BREWER, Anthony, -1624?,
English; plays ST
BREWER, Derek Stanley, 1923- ,
English; nonfiction CON
BREWER, Ebenezer Cobham,
1810-97, English; nonfiction
BRO
BREWER, Edward Samuel, 1933- ,
Canadian; nonfiction CON
BREWER, Frances Joan, 1913- ,
Austrian-American; nonfiction
CON
BREWER, Fred Aldwyn ('Aldred
Wynn'), 1921- , American;
nonfiction CON
BREWER, Garry Dwight, 1941- ,
American; nonfiction CON
BREWER, Jack A., 1933- ,
American; nonfiction CON
BREWER, James H. Fitzgerald,
1916- , American; nonfiction
CON
BREWER, John Mason, 1896- ,
American; poetry, nonfiction
CON
BREWER, John Sherren, 1810-79,
English; nonfiction KBA
BREWER, Margaret L., 1929- ,
American; nonfiction CON
BREWER, Thomas, fl. 1624,
English; nonfiction ST
BREWER, Thomas B., 1932- ,
American; nonfiction CON
BREWER, Wilmon, 1895- ,
American; nonfiction CON
BREWINGTON, Marion Vernon,
1902- , American; nonfiction
CON
'BREWSTER, Benjamin' see
ELTING, Mary
'BREWSTER, Benjamin' see
FOLSOM, Franklin B.
BREWSTER, Sir David, 1781-1868,

Scots; nonfiction BRO KBA ST
BREWSTER, Dorothy, 1883- ,
American; nonfiction CON
BREWSTER, Elizabeth, 1922- ,
Canadian; poetry CON MUR
BREWSTER, William, 1851-1919,
American; nonfiction KAA
BREWTON, John Edmund, 1898- ,
American; fiction, nonfiction
CON
BREYE, François Xavier, 1694-
1736, French; nonfiction DIL
BREYER, Rémy, 1669-1749, French;
nonfiction DIL
BREZAN, Jurij ('Dusan Switz'),
1916- , German; fiction, poetry
AL
BREZILLAC, Jean François, 1710-
80, French; nonfiction DIL
BREZINA, Ján, 1917- , Slovak;
poetry ST
'BREZINA, Otokar' (Václav Ignac
Jebavy), 1868-1929, Czech;
poetry, essays COL FLE SA
ST
BREZOVIC, Titus, 1757-1804,
Croatian; poetry ST
BRIAL, Michel Jean Joseph, 18th
cent., French; nonfiction DIL
'BRIAN' see POWELL, Brian
BRIAN, Denis, 1923- , Welsh;
fiction CON
BRIAND, Paul L., Jr., 1920- ,
American; nonfiction CON
BRIAND, Rena, 1935- , Australian;
nonfiction CON
BRIATTE, Jean Baptiste, 18th cent.,
French; nonfiction DIL
BRICE, Douglas, 1916- , English;
nonfiction CON
BRICE, Etienne, 1697-1755, French;
nonfiction DIL
BRICE, Germain (Brixius), 1500-38,
French; poetry ST
BRICE, Marshall Moore, 1898- ,
American; nonfiction CON
BRICEÑO, Ramón, 1814-82, Chilean;
nonfiction MIN
BRICHANT, Colette Dubois, 1926- ,
French-American; nonfiction
CON
'BRICK' see POMEROY, Marcus M.
BRICK, John, 1922- , American;
juveniles CON WA
BRICK, Michael, 1922- , American;
nonfiction CON
BRICKHILL, Paul Chester Jerome,

1916- , Australian; journal-
ism BRO CON RIC
BRICKMAN, William Wolfgang,
1913- , American; nonfiction
CON
BRICKNER, Richard Pilpel,
1933- , American; fiction
CON
BRIDAINE, Jacques (Brydaine),
1701-67, French; nonfiction
DIL
BRIDARD de la GARDE, Philippe,
18th cent., French; nonfiction
DIL
BRIDAULT, Jean Pierre, -1761,
French; nonfiction DIL
BRIDEL, Bedrich, 1619-80,
Croatian; poetry ST
BRIDEL, J. P. L., 18th cent.,
Swiss; nonfiction DIL
BRIDEL, Philippe, 1757-1845,
Swiss; poetry DIL HAR ST
BRIDENBAUGH, Carl, 1903- ,
American; nonfiction CON
'BRIDGE, Ann' (Mary Dolling
Sanders O'Malley), English;
fiction HO KT
BRIDGE, Horatio, 1806-93, Amer-
ican; diary KAA
'BRIDGEMAN, Richard' see
DAVIES, Leslie P.
BRIDGEMAN, William Barton,
1916- , American; fiction
CON
BRIDGES, Ann Preston, 1891- ,
American; fiction JO
BRIDGES, Hal, 1918- , American;
nonfiction CON
BRIDGES, John Henry, 1832-1906,
English; nonfiction KBA
BRIDGES, Robert Seymour, 1844-
1930, English; poetry FLE
BRO KAT KT RIC SA SP ST
BRIDGES, Roy, 1885- , Australian;
journalism, fiction BRO
BRIDGES, Thomas Charles
('Christopher Beck'), 1868-
1944, English; juveniles DOY
BRIDGES, William, 1901- ,
American; juveniles WA
BRIDGES, William, 1933- , Amer-
ican; nonfiction CON
BRIDGES, William Andrew,
1901- , American; nonfiction
CON
BRIDGES-ADAMS, William, 1889- ,
English; nonfiction CON

BRIDGET, Saint (Brigitta), 1303-
73, Swedish; nonfiction HAR KE
SA ST
BRIDGWATER, William Patrick,
1931- , American; nonfiction
CON
'BRIDIE, James' see MAVOR,
Osborne H.
BRIDOUX y MAZZINI, Victorina,
1835-62, Spanish; poetry BL
BRIDWELL, Norman, 1928- ,
American; juveniles CON
BRIEBA, Liborio, E. , 1841-97,
Chilean; fiction MIN
BRIEFS, Goetz Antony, 1889- ,
German-American; nonfiction
CON HO
BRIEGEL, Ann Carrick, 1915- ,
American; nonfiction CON
BRIEN, Roger, 1910- , Canadian;
poetry SY
BRIENNE, John, 1148?-1237, French;
poetry ST
BRIER, Howard Maxwell, 1903-69,
American; fiction CON FUL
PAC WA
BRIER, Warren Judson, 1931- ,
American; nonfiction CON
BRIEUX, Eugène, 1858-1932, French;
plays COL DIF HAR KAT KT
MAT SA ST
BRIFAUT, Charles, 1781-1857,
French; poetry SA
BRIFFAULT, Robert, 1876-1948,
English; fiction, nonfiction KT
BRIGADERE, Anna, 1869-1933,
Latvian; poetry, plays FLE ST
BRIGGS, Asa, 1921- , English;
nonfiction CON
BRIGGS, Austin Eugene, Jr., 1931- ,
American; nonfiction CON
BRIGGS, Barbara, American; juven-
iles WA
BRIGGS, Charles Frederick ('Harry
Franco'), 1804-77, American;
fiction, journalism KAA
BRIGGS, Dorothy Corkille, 1924- ,
American; nonfiction CON
BRIGGS, Rev. Everett Francis,
1908- , American; nonfiction
HO
BRIGGS, Fred Allen, 1916- , Amer-
ican; nonfiction CON
BRIGGS, George McSpadden, 1919- ,
American; nonfiction CON
BRIGGS, Katharine Mary, 1898- ,
English; plays, juveniles CON

BRIGGS, Kenneth R. , 1934- ,
American; nonfiction CON
BRIGGS, Lloyd Cabot, 1909- ,
American; nonfiction CON
BRIGGS, Peter, 1921- , Ameri-
can; juveniles CON
BRIGGS, Raymond, 1934- ,
English; juveniles DOY
BRIGGS, Robert Cook, 1915- ,
American; nonfiction CON
BRIGHAM, Besmilr, 1923- ,
American; nonfiction CON
BRIGHOUSE, Harold, 1882-1958,
English; fiction, plays KT
MAT RIC
BRIGHT, John, 1908- , Ameri-
can; nonfiction CON
BRIGHT, Mary Chavelita ('George
Egerton'), 1860-1945, English;
fiction, plays, translations
BRO KT
BRIGHT, Robert, 1902- , Amer-
ican; fiction, juveniles FUL
WAF
BRIGHT, Verne, 1893- , Amer-
ican; poetry PAC
BRIGHT, William, 1824-1901,
English; nonfiction KBA
BRIGHT, William, 1928- ,
American; nonfiction CON
BRIGHTBILL, Charles Kestner,
1910- , American; nonfiction
CON
BRIGHTWEN, Eliza, 1830-1906,
English; nonfiction KBA
BRIGNON, Jean, 1626-1712,
French; nonfiction, translations
DIL
BRIK, Osip Maximovich, 1888- ,
Russian; fiction ST
BRILHART, John K., 1929- ,
American; nonfiction CON
BRILL, Abraham Arden, 1874-
1948, American; nonfiction
KTS
BRILL, Earl Hubert, 1925- ,
American; nonfiction CON
BRILLAT-SAVARIN, Anthelme,
1755-1826, French; nonfiction
DIF HAR KE SA ST
BRILLIANT, Alan, 1936- ,
American; poetry MUR
BRILLIANT, Richard, 1929- ,
American; nonfiction CON
BRILLON, P., 1693- , French;
nonfiction DIL
BRIM, Orville Gilbert, Jr.,

1923- , American; nonfiction
CON
BRIMLEY, George, 1819-57, English;
criticism KBA
BRIN, Ruth Firestone, 1921- ,
American; fiction CON
BRINCKERINCK, Johannes, 1359-
1419, Dutch; nonfiction ST
BRINCKMAN, John, 1814-70, Ger-
man; poetry AL KE SA ST
BRINDLEY, James, 1860- , Eng-
lish; nonfiction HIG
BRINDZE, Ruth, 1903- , American;
juveniles FUL WA
BRINIG, Myron, 1900- , American;
fiction KT WAF
BRINITZER, Carl ('Usikota'),
1907- , Russian-English; non-
fiction CON
BRINK, Carol Ryrie, 1895- , Amer-
ican; juveniles, fiction COM
CON KJU PAC WA
BRINK, Jan ten, 1834-1901, Dutch;
nonfiction ST
BRINKER, Paul A., 1919- ,
American; nonfiction CON
BRINKLEY, George A., Jr.,
1931- , American; nonfiction
CON
BRINKLEY, William Clark, 1917- ,
American; fiction CON
BRINKS, Herbert John, 1935- ,
American; nonfiction CON
BRINLEY, Bertrand Russell, 1917- ,
American; nonfiction, juveniles
CON
BRINNIN, John Malcolm, 1916- ,
American; poetry, critics, non-
fiction CON MUR KTS
BRINSMEAD, Hesba Fay ('Pixie
Hungerford'), 1922- , Australian;
fiction, juveniles CON
BRINTON, Clarence Crane, 1898-
1968, American; nonfiction CON
KT
BRINTON, Daniel Garrison, 1837-
99, American; nonfiction KAA
BRINTON, Henry ('Alex Fraser'),
1901- , English; fiction, juven-
iles CON
BRINTON, Howard Haines, 1884- ,
American; nonfiction CON
'BRION, Guy' see MADSEN, Axel
BRION, John M., 1922- , Ameri-
can; nonfiction CON
BRIQUET,   -1748, French; nonfic-
tion DIL

BRIQUET, Margueriet Ursuel
Bernier, 1782-1815, French;
poetry SA
BRISBANE, Albert, 1809-90,
American; nonfiction KAA
BRISBANE, Arthur, 1864-1936,
American; journalism KT
BRISBANE, Holly E., 1927- ,
American; nonfiction CON
BRISCO, Patricia, 1927- ,
American; fiction, juveniles
CON
BRISCOE, David Stuart, 1930- ,
English; nonfiction CON
BRISKIN, Jacqueline, 1927- ,
English; fiction CON
BRISOUT de BARENVILLE,
Nicolas Denis François,
1759-1842, French; nonfiction
DIL
BRISSENDEN, Paul Frederick,
1885- , American; nonfiction
CON
BRISSENDEN, Robert Francis,
1928- , Australian; nonfiction
CON
BRISSON, 18th cent., French;
nonfiction DIL
BRISSON, Mathurin Jacques, 1723-
1806, French; nonfiction DIL
BRISSOT, Jean Pierre, 1754-93,
French; nonfiction DIL
BRISTED, Joan, 1778-1855, Amer-
ican; nonfiction KAA
BRISTER, Commodore Webster,
1926- , American; nonfiction
CON
BRISTER, Richard ('Will O. Grove';
'C. L. Lewin'; 'George Rich-
mond'), 1915- , American;
fiction CON
BRISTOL, George Digby, 1612-77,
English; plays, translations
KB ST
'BRISTOL, Julius' see ABEL,
Alan I.
BRISTOL, Lee H., Jr., 1923- ,
American; nonfiction CON
BRISTOW, Allen P., 1929- ,
American; nonfiction CON
BRISTOW, Gwen, 1903- , Amer-
ican; fiction CON KT WAF
BRISTOW, Robert O'Neil, 1926- ,
American; fiction CON
BRISTOWE, Anthony Lynn, 1921- ,
English; nonfiction CON
'BRITAIN, Dan' see PENDLETON,

Donald E.
BRITO, Bernardo de, 1568-1617,
Portuguese; nonfiction SA ST
BRITO, Duarte de, fl. 1490,
Portuguese; poetry ST
BRITO ARANHA, Pedro Venceslau
de, 1833-1914, Portuguese,
journalism SA
BRITO LETELIER, Ercilia see
'MONVEL, Maria'
BRITT, Albert, 1874- , American;
fiction, juveniles CON
BRITT, Dell, 1934- , American;
juveniles COM CON
BRITT, Rev. Matthew, 1872- ,
American; nonfiction HO
BRITT, Steuart Henderson, 1907- ,
American; nonfiction CON
BRITTAIN, Frederick, English;
translations, nonfiction CON
BRITTAIN, Joan Tucker, 1928- ,
American; nonfiction CON
BRITTAIN, Robert, 1908- , Amer-
ican; poetry MAR
BRITTAIN, Vera Mary, 1896?-1970,
English; essays, fiction BRO
CON KT RIC
BRITTAN, Samuel, 1933- , English;
nonfiction CON
BRITTEN AUSTIN, Paul, 1922- ,
English; juveniles CON
BRITTIN, Norman Aylsworth,
1906- , American; nonfiction
CON
BRITTING, Georg, 1891/92-1964,
German; poetry, fiction AL FLE
KU KUN LEN
BRITTON, Karl William, 1909- ,
English; nonfiction CON
BRITTON, Mattie Lula Cooper (Mattie
Lula Cooper; 'Jane Patterson'),
1914- , American; nonfiction
CON
BRIUSOV, Valery Y. see BRYUSOV,
Valery Y.
BRIX, Hans Nicolaus, 1870- ,
Danish; nonfiction ST
BRIZARD, Gabriel, 18th cent.,
French; nonfiction DIL
BRIZE, Blondel de, 18th cent.,
French; plays DIL
BRIZEUX, Auguste Julien Pélage,
1803-58, French; poetry DIF
HAR ST
BRO, Harmon Hartzell, 1919- ,
American; nonfiction CON
BRO, Margueritte, 1894- , Amer-
ican; juveniles FUL

BROAD, Charles Lewis, 1900- ,
English; nonfiction CON
BROADDUS, John Morgan, Jr.,
1929- , American; nonfiction
CON
BROADHURST, Allan R., 1932- ,
American; nonfiction CON
BROADHURST, George Howells,
1866-1952, Anglo-American;
journalism, plays KT MAT
BROADHURST, Ronald Joseph
Callender, 1906- , English;
nonfiction CON
BROADUS, Catherine, 1929- ,
American; nonfiction CON
BROADUS, Loren, Jr., 1928- ,
American; nonfiction CON
BROBY-JOHANSEN, Rudolf,
1900- , Danish; poetry CON
'BROCENSE, El' see SANCHEZ
de las BROZAS, Francisco
BROCH, Hermann, 1886-1951,
Austrian-American; fiction
AL COL FLE KT KU KUN
LEN MAG RIC SA
BROCK, Betty, 1923- , American;
juveniles CON
BROCK, Charles Edmond (H. M.
Brock), 1870-1938, English;
juveniles DOY KJU
BROCK, Clutton see CLUTTON-
BROCK, Arthur
BROCK, David William Errington,
1907- , English; nonfiction
HIG
BROCK, Dewey Clifton, Jr.,
1930- , American; nonfiction
CON
BROCK, Edwin, 1927- , British;
poetry MUR
BROCK, Emma Lilian, 1886- ,
American; juveniles CON KJU
PAC WA
'BROCK, Gavin' see LINDSAY,
John M.
BROCK, H. M. see BROCK, C. E.
BROCK, Henry Matthew, 1875-
1960, English; juveniles DOY
BROCK, Peter, 1920- , English;
nonfiction CON
'BROCK, Rose' see HANSEN,
Joseph
'BROCK, Stuart' see TRIMBLE,
Louis P.
BROCK, William Hodson, 1936- ,
English; nonfiction CON
BROCK, William Ranulf, 1916- ,
English; nonfiction CON

BROCKBANK, Reed, 1923- ,
American; nonfiction CON
BROCKES, Barthold Heinrich, 1680-
1747, German; poetry AL HAR
ST
BROCKETT, Eleanor Hall, 1913- ,
English; translations, nonfiction
CON
BROCKETT, Oscar Gross, 1923- ,
American; nonfiction CON
BROCKMAN, Christian Frank, 1902- ,
American; nonfiction CON PAC
BROCKMAN, Zoe Kincaid, American;
fiction, poetry JO
BROCKRIEDE, Wayne Elmer, 1922- ,
American; nonfiction CON
BROCKWAY, Allan Reitz, 1932- ,
American; nonfiction CON
BROCKWAY, Archibald Fenner,
1888- , English; nonfiction CON
BROCKWAY, Edith E., 1914- ,
American; fiction CON
BROCKWAY, Thomas Parmelee,
1898- , American; nonfiction
CON
BROD, Max, 1884-1968, German;
fiction, poetry, plays, essays
AL CON FLE HAR KT KU ST
BRODEAU, Jean, 18th cent., French;
nonfiction DIL
BRODER, Berl, 19th cent., Jewish;
poetry ST
BRODERICK, Carlfred Bartholomew,
1932- , American; nonfiction
CON
BRODERICK, Dorothy M., 1929- ,
American; juveniles CON WA
BRODERICK, Henry, 1880- ,
American; nonfiction PAC
BRODERICK, James, 1891- , Irish;
nonfiction HOE
BRODERICK, John Caruthers, 1926- ,
American; nonfiction CON
BRODERICK, John F., 1909- ,
American; nonfiction CON
BRODERICK, Robert Carlton, 1913- ,
American; nonfiction CON HO
BRODEUR, Paul Adrian, Jr.,
1931- , American; fiction CON
BRODEY, James Miles ('Ann Taylor';
'Femora'), 1942- , American;
poetry MUR
BRODHEAD, John, Romeyn, 1814-
73, American; nonfiction KAA
BRODIE, Bernard, 1910- , Ameri-
can; nonfiction CON
BRODIE, Fawn McKay, 1915- ,

American; nonfiction CON
BRODIE, John ('John Guthrie'),
1905- , New Zealander;
fiction, journalism ST
BRODSKY, Stanley L., 1939- ,
American; nonfiction CON
BRODY, Baruch Alter, 1943- ,
American; nonfiction CON
BRODY, David, 1930- , Ameri-
can; nonfiction CON
BRODY, Elaine, 1923- , Ameri-
can; nonfiction CON
BRODY, Jules, 1928- , Ameri-
can; nonfiction CON
'BRODY, Marc' see WILKES-
HUNTER, Richard
BRODY, Sándor, 1863-1924,
Hungarian; fiction, plays COL
SA ST
BRODZINSKI, Kazimierz Maciej
Jozef, 1791-1835, Polish;
poetry, criticism, translations
HAR SA ST
BROECKAERT, Karel, 1767-1826,
Flemish; essays ST
BROEG, Bob, 1918- , American;
nonfiction CON
BRÖGER, Karl, 1886- , German;
poetry, fiction COL SA
BROEHL, Wayne Gottlieb, Jr.,
1922- , American; nonfiction
CON
BROEK, Jan Otto Marius, 1904- ,
Dutch-American; nonfiction
CON
BROEK, Lambrecht van den,
1805-63, Dutch; poetry ST
BROEKEL, Ray, 1923- , Ameri-
can; nonfiction, juveniles CON
BROEKHUIZEN, Joan van, 1649-
1704, Dutch; poetry ST
BROER, Marion Ruth, 1910- ,
American; nonfiction CON
BROF, Janet, 1929- , American;
nonfiction CON
BROFELT, Johannes see 'AHO,
Juhani'
BROFFERIO, Angelo, 1802-66,
Italian; plays, poetry, criti-
cism HAR SA ST
BROGAN, Colm, 1902- , Scots;
nonfiction HO
BROGAN, Denis William ('Maurice
Barrington'), 1900-74, Irish;
nonfiction BRO KTS
BROGAN, Gerald Edward, 1924- ,
American; nonfiction CON

BROGAN, Philip Francis, 1896- ,
American; nonfiction CON
BROGLIE, Aquiles Charles Victor,
1785-1870, French; criticism
SA
BROGLIE, Louis Victor, 1892- ,
French; nonfiction DIF
BROHON, Jacqueline Aimée, 1718-
78, French; nonfiction DIL
BROKE, Arthur (Brooke), -1563,
English; translations BRO ST
BROKE, Lord Willoughby de, 1843-
1902, English; nonfiction HIG
BROKE, Lord Willoughby de, 1869-
1923, English; nonfiction HIG
BROKENSHA, David Warwick, 1923- ,
American; nonfiction CON
BROMAGE, Mary Cogan, 1906- ,
American; nonfiction CON
BROMBERGER, Serge Paul, 1912- ,
French; nonfiction CON
BROMBERT, Victor H., 1923- ,
German-American; nonfiction
CON
BROME, Alexander, 1620-66, Eng-
lish; poetry ST
BROME, Richard, -1652/53,
English; plays BRO KB MAG
ST
BROMFIELD, Louis, 1896-1956,
American; fiction BRO FLE KL
KT MAG RIC SA ST WAF
BROMHALL, Winifred, Anglo-Ameri-
can; juvenile FUL
BROMIGE, David Mansfield, 1935- ,
English; poetry, plays CON
MUR
BROMILEY, Geoffrey William,
1915- , English; nonfiction
CON
BROMKE, Adam, 1928- , Polish-
Canadian; nonfiction CON
BROMLEY, John Carter, 1937- ,
American; nonfiction CON
BROMYARDE, John de, fl. 1390- ,
English; nonfiction ST
BRONDSTED, Holger, 1889- ,
Danish; nonfiction BL
BRONER, Esther Masserman, Ameri-
can; plays CON
BRONFENBRENNER, Martin,
1914- , American; nonfiction
CON
BRONIEWSKI, Wladyslaw, 1898-1962,
Polish; poetry FLE ST
BRONNEN, Arnolt (Bronner), 1895-
1959, Austrian; plays AL KU
MAT

BRONNER, Edwin Blaine, 1920- ,
American; nonfiction CON
BRONWOSKI, Jacob, 1908- ,
Polish-American; nonfiction
CON
BRONSEN, David, 1926- , Amer-
ican; nonfiction CON
'BRONSON, Lita' see BELL,
Louise P.
'BRONSON, Lynn' see LAMPMAN,
Evelyn S.
'BRONSON, Oliver' see ROWLAND,
Donald S.
BRONSON, Wilfrid S., 1894- ,
American; juveniles KJU WA
BRONSTEIN, Arthur J., 1914- ,
American; nonfiction CON
BRONSTEIN, Lev Davidovich see
'TROTSKI, Leon'
'BRONSTEIN, Yetta' see ABEL,
Jeanne
BRONTE, Anne, 1820-49, English;
fiction, poetry BRO KBA
MAG SA ST
BRONTE, Charlotte, 1816-55,
English; fiction BRO KBA
MAG SA ST
BRONTE, Emily Jane, 1818-48,
English; fiction, poetry BRO
KBA MAG SA SP ST
BRONWELL, Arthur B., 1909- ,
American; nonfiction CON
BROOK, Barry Shelley, 1918- ,
American; nonfiction CON
BROOK, David, 1932- , Ameri-
can; nonfiction CON
BROOK, George Leslie, 1910- ,
English; nonfiction CON
BROOK, Victor John Knight,
1887- , English; nonfiction
CON
BROOKE, A.B. see JENNINGS,
Leslie N.
BROOKE, Arthur see BROKE,
Arthur
BROOKE, Bernard Jocelyn,
1908- , English; poetry,
fiction, nonfiction CON
'BROOKE, Carol' see RAMSKILL,
Valerie P.R.
BROOKE, Charles Frederick
Tucker, 1883-1946, American;
nonfiction KTS
BROOKE, Charlotte, 1740-93,
English; nonfiction BRO ST
BROOKE, Christopher, 1619-27/28,
English; poetry ST
BROOKE, Christopher Nugent

Lawrence, 1927- , English;
nonfiction CON
BROOKE, Frances, 1724-89, Canadian;
fiction SY
BROOKE, Fulke Greville, 1554-1628,
English; poetry BRO KB ST
BROOKE, Geoffrey, 1884- , Irish;
nonfiction HIG
BROOKE, Henry, 1703-83, Irish;
fiction, plays, poetry BRO KB
MAG SA ST
BROOKE, Jocelyn, 1908- , British;
fiction KTS
BROOKE, Leonard Leslie, 1862-1940,
Irish-American; juveniles DOY
KJU
BROOKE, Maxey, 1913- , American;
nonfiction CON
BROOKE, Nicholas Stanton, 1924- ,
English; nonfiction CON
BROOKE, Rupert Chawner, 1887-
1915, English; poetry BRO FLE
KAT KT RIC SA SP ST
BROOKE, Stopford Augustus, 1832-
1916, Anglo-Irish; essays, criti-
cism BRO KBA ST
BROOKE-LITTLE, John, 1927- ,
English; nonfiction CON
BROOKE-ROSE, Christine, 1926- ,
English; fiction CON RIC
'BROOKER, Clark' see FOWLER,
Kenneth A.
BROOKES, Edgar Harry, 1897- ,
American; nonfiction CON
BROOKES, Pamela, 1922- , English;
nonfiction CON
BROOKHOUSE, John Christopher,
1938- , American; nonfiction
CON
BROOKHOUSER, Frank, American;
nonfiction, fiction CON
BROOKMAN, Denise Cass, 1921- ,
American; juveniles CON
BROOKOVER, Wilbur Bone, 1911- ,
American; nonfiction CON
BROOKS, Alfred Russell, 1906- ,
American; nonfiction CON
BROOKS, Anita, 1914- , American;
juveniles CON WA
BROOKS, Anne Tedlock ('Anne
Carter'; 'Cynthia Millburn'),
1905- , American; fiction CON
BROOKS, Charles Benton, 1921- ,
American; nonfiction CON
BROOKS, Charles Stephen, 1878-
1934, American; essays, non-
fiction KT

BROOKS, Charles Timothy, 1813-
83, American; translations,
poetry KAA
BROOKS, Charles William Shirley
('Epicurus Rotundus'), 1816-
74/80, English; fiction, plays
BRO KBA ST
BROOKS, Charlotte, American;
juvenile WA
BROOKS, Clarence Carlyle,
1888- , American; nonfiction
CON
BROOKS, Cleanth, 1906- ,
American; nonfiction CON KTS
ST
BROOKS, David P., 1915- ,
American; nonfiction CON
BROOKS, Edwy Searles, 1889-
1965, English; juveniles DOY
BROOKS, Elbridge Streeter, 1846-
1902, American; juveniles KAA
BROOKS, Frank Leonard, 1911- ,
English; nonfiction CON
BROOKS, George Edward, Jr.,
1933- , American; nonfiction
CON
BROOKS, Glenn Ellis, Jr.,
1931- , American; nonfiction
CON
BROOKS, Gwendolyn, 1917/18- ,
American; poetry, fiction
CON HOO KTS MUR
BROOKS, Harvey, 1915- , Amer-
ican; nonfiction CON
BROOKS, Hugh C., 1922- , Amer-
ican; nonfiction CON
BROOKS, James Gordon, 1801-41,
American; poetry KAA
BROOKS, Jeremy ('Clive Meikle'),
1926- , English; nonfiction,
fiction CON
BROOKS, John, 1892- , American;
nonfiction BL
BROOKS, John Nixon, 1920- ,
American; fiction CON
BROOKS, Keith, 1923- , Ameri-
can; nonfiction CON
BROOKS, Lester, 1924- , Ameri-
can; nonfiction CON
BROOKS, Maria Gowen, 1794-1845,
American; poetry BRO KAA
SA
BROOKS, Noah, 1830-1903, Amer-
ican; journalism, juveniles
KAA
BROOKS, Patricia, 1926- ,
American; nonfiction CON

BROOKS, Paul, 1909- , American; fiction CON

BROOKS, Peter Wright, 1920- , American; nonfiction CON

BROOKS, Polly Schoyer, 1912- , American; nonfiction CON

BROOKS, Richard, 1912- , American; fiction WAF

BROOKS, Stewart M., 1923- , American; nonfiction CON

BROOKS, Van Wyck, 1886-1963, American; nonfiction, translations, criticism BRO CON KL KT RIC ST

BROOKS, Walter R., 1886- , American; juveniles KJU

BROOKS, William Dean, 1929- , American; nonfiction CON

'BROOKSBY' see PENNELL-ELMHIRST, Edward

BROOK-SHEPHERD, Gordon, 1918- , English; nonfiction CON

BROOM, Leonard, 1911- , American; nonfiction CON

BROOME, William, 1689-1745, English; poetry, translations BRO ST

BROOMELL, Myron Henry, 1906- , American; poetry CON

BROOMFIELD, Gerald Webb, 1895- , English; nonfiction CON

BROOMFIELD, John Hindle, 1935- , New Zealander; nonfiction CON

BROOMSNODDER, Bradley MacKinley, 1940- , American; nonfiction, juveniles CON

BROPHY, Brigid Antonia, 1929- , English; fiction, essays CON RIC

BROPHY, Donald Francis, 1934- , American; nonfiction CON

BROPHY, James David, Jr., 1926- , American; nonfiction CON

BROPHY, Jean, 1899- , English; fiction CON

BROPHY, John, 1899- , English; fiction BRO KT RIC

BROPHY, Liam, 1910- , Irish; fiction, poetry CON

BRORSON, Hans Adolph, 1694-1764, Danish; poetry ST

'BROSBOLL, Johan Carl Christian' (Carit Etlar), 1816-1900, Dutch; fiction HAR ST

BROSNAHAN, Katherine Mary (Sr. Mary Eleanore), 1890-1940, American; nonfiction HOE

BROSNAN, James Patrick, 1929- , American; fiction, juveniles CON

BROSS, Irwin Dudley Jackson, 1921- , American; nonfiction CON

BROSSES, Charles de, 1709-77, French; nonfiction DIF DIL HAR SA

BROSSETTE, Claude, 1671-1743, French; nonfiction DIL

BROSTER, Dorothy Kathleen, 1878-1950, English; fiction, juveniles KJU RIC

BROSTERHUYSEN, Johan van, 1596-1650, Dutch; nonfiction ST

BROSTOWIN, Patrick Ronald, 1931- , American; nonfiction CON

BROSZKEIWICZ, Jerzy, 1922- , Polish; fiction, criticism, plays MAT

'BROTHER, Bob' see BUELL, Robert K.

BROTHERS, Joyce Diane Bauer, 1927- , American; nonfiction CON

BROTHERSTON, Gordon, 1939- , English; translation, nonfiction CON

BROTIER, André Charles, 1751-98, French; nonfiction DIL

BROTIER, Gabriel, 1723-89, French; nonfiction DIL

BROUDY, Harry Samuel, 1905- , Polish-American; nonfiction CON

BROUGHAM, Lord Henry Peter, 1778-1868, Scots; nonfiction BRO KBS ST

BROUGHAM, John, 1810-80, American; plays KAA

BROUGHTON, Bradford B., 1926- , American; nonfiction CON

BROUGHTON, James, 1913- , American; poetry, plays, movies MUR

BROUGHTON, John Cam Hobhouse, 1786-1869, English; nonfiction BRO ST

BROUGHTON, Rhoda, 1840-1920, English; fiction BRO KBA ST

BROUILLETTE, Jeanne S., American; nonfiction CON

'BROUN, Emily' see STERNE, Emma G.

BROUN, Heywood Campbell, 1888-1939, American; journalism, essays, fiction HOE KT

BROUN, Heywood Hale, 1918- , American; nonfiction CON

BROUSSARD, Louis, 1922- , American; nonfiction CON

BROUSSONNET, Pierre Marie Auguste, 1761-1807, French; nonfiction DIL

'BROUWER, A. see LOOY, Jacobus van

BROW, Robert, 1924- , American; nonfiction CON

'BROWARD, Donn' see HALLERAN, Eugene E.

BROWER, Brock Henrickson, 1931- , American; nonfiction CON

BROWER, Kenneth David, 1944- , American; nonfiction CON

BROWER, Linda A. ('Linda A. Meeks'), 1945- , American; nonfiction CON

BROWER, Reuben Arthur, 1908- , American; nonfiction CON

BROWIN, Frances Williams, 1898- , American; nonfiction CON WA

BROWN, Abbie Farwell, 1872-1927, American; juveniles KT

BROWN, Alan A., 1929- , Yugoslav-American; nonfiction CON

BROWN, Alberta Louise, 1894- , American; nonfiction CON

BROWN, Alexander Crosby, 1905- , American; nonfiction CON

'BROWN, Alexis' see BEECHING, Amy B.

BROWN, Alfred J., 1894- , English; nonfiction HOE

BROWN, Alice ('Martin Redfield'), 1857-1948, Anglo-American; fiction, plays BRO KAT KT

BROWN, Allen, 1926- , American; nonfiction CON

BROWN, Anne Seddon Kinsolving, 1906- , American; nonfiction CON

BROWN, Arthur Wayne, 1917- , American; nonfiction CON

BROWN, Ashley, 1923- , American; nonfiction CON

BROWN, Audrey Alexandra, 1904- , Canadian; fiction, poetry ST SY

BROWN, B. Frank, 1917- ,

American; nonfiction CON

BROWN, Beatrice Bradshaw ('Michael Kent'), American; juveniles, fiction HO

BROWN, Beatrice C. see CURTIS BROWN, Beatrice

BROWN, Bernard Edward, 1925- , American; nonfiction CON

BROWN, Bessie Katherine Taylor, 1917- , American; nonfiction CON

BROWN, Beth ('Beth A. Retner'), American; fiction CON

BROWN, Blanche R. Levine, 1915- , American; nonfiction CON

BROWN, Bob see BROWN, Robert J.

BROWN, Bob Burton, 1925- , American; nonfiction CON

BROWN, Camille, 1917- , American; nonfiction CON

'BROWN, Carter' see YATES; Alan G.

BROWN, Charles Brockden, 1771-1810, American; fiction BRO KAA MAG SA ST

BROWN, Charles H., 1910- , American; nonfiction CON

BROWN, Clark, 1935- , American; fiction CON

BROWN, Conrad, 1922- , American; juveniles WA

BROWN, Constantine, 1889- , American; nonfiction CON

BROWN, Dale W., 1926- , American; nonfiction CON

BROWN, David, 1916- , American; nonfiction CON

BROWN, David Grant, 1936- , American; nonfiction CON

BROWN, David Springer, 1915- , American; nonfiction CON

BROWN, Dee Alexander, 1908- , American; fiction, nonfiction CON

BROWN, Donald Eugene, 1909- , American; nonfiction CON

BROWN, Douglas Frank Lambert, 1907- , English; nonfiction CON

BROWN, Duane, 1937- , American; nonfiction CON

BROWN, Edgar S., Jr., 1922- , American; nonfiction CON

BROWN, Edna A., 1875-1944, American; juveniles KJU

BROWN, Edward James, 1909- ,
American; nonfiction CON
BROWN, Edward Kelloran, 1905-51,
Canadian; nonfiction ST SY
BROWN, Eleanor Frances, 1908- ,
American; juveniles CON WA
BROWN, Evelyn M., 1911- ,
Canadian; nonfiction CON
BROWN, Frederick, 1934- ,
American; nonfiction CON
BROWN, Frederick Gramm, 1932- ,
American; nonfiction CON
BROWN, George Douglas ('George
Douglas'; 'Kennedy King'), 1869-
1902, Scots; fiction BRO KBA
MAG ST
BROWN, George Earl, 1883-1964,
American; juveniles CON
BROWN, George Mackay, 1921- ,
British; poetry CON MUR
BROWN, George Neville, 1932- ,
American; nonfiction CON
BROWN, Gerald Saxon, 1911- ,
American; nonfiction CON
BROWN, Gerald William, 1916- ,
American; nonfiction CON
BROWN, Giles Tyler, 1916- ,
American; nonfiction CON
BROWN, Ginny see BROWN, Virginia
S.
BROWN, Gwilym Slater, 1928- ,
American; fiction CON
BROWN, Harold Ogden Joseph,
1933- , American; nonfiction
CON
BROWN, Harriett M., 1897- ,
American; juveniles CON
BROWN, Harry ('Peter M. Nab'),
1917- , American; fiction,
poetry, plays KTS WAF
BROWN, Harry Matthew, 1921- ,
American; nonfiction CON
BROWN, Helen Evans, American;
juveniles WA
BROWN, Helen Gurley, 1922- ,
American; nonfiction CON
BROWN, Herbert Ross, 1902- ,
American; nonfiction CON
BROWN, Howard Mayer, 1930- ,
American; nonfiction CON
BROWN, Huntington, 1899- , Amer-
ican; nonfiction CON
BROWN, Ida Mae, American; juven-
iles CON
BROWN, Ina Corinne, American;
nonfiction CON
BROWN, Ina Ladd, 1903- , Ameri-

can; poetry, plays CON
BROWN, Ira Vernon, 1922- ,
American; nonfiction CON
BROWN, Irene Bennett, 1932- ,
American; juveniles CON
BROWN, Ivor John Carnegie,
1891- , English; journalism
BRO CON KTS
BROWN, James Cooke, 1921- ,
American; nonfiction CON
BROWN, James Isaac, 1908- ,
American; nonfiction CON
BROWN, James Montgomery,
1921- , American; nonfiction
CON
BROWN, James Patrick, 1948- ,
American; nonfiction CON
BROWN, Jeff, American; juveniles
WA
BROWN, Jerry Wayne, 1936- ,
American; nonfiction CON
BROWN, Joe David, 1915- ,
American; fiction CON WAF
BROWN, John, 1715-66, English;
poetry, plays, essays BRO
KB
BROWN, Dr. John, 1810-82,
Scots; essays BRO KBA ST
BROWN, John, 1887- , English;
nonfiction CON
BROWN, John, 1920- , American;
nonfiction CON
BROWN, John Arthur, 1914- ,
American; nonfiction CON
BROWN, John E., 1934- , Amer-
ican; juveniles CON
BROWN, John H. ('Boris Shera-
shevski'), 1916- , Canadian;
nonfiction CON
BROWN, John Mason, 1900-69,
American; criticism CON KT
BROWN, John Pairman, 1923- ,
American; nonfiction CON
BROWN, John Russell, 1923- ,
English; nonfiction CON
BROWN, Judith Gwyn, American;
juveniles WA
BROWN, Katherine Holland,
-1931, American; fiction
HOO
BROWN, Kenneth H., 1936- ,
American; plays CON
BROWN, Leland, 1914- , Amer-
ican; nonfiction CON
BROWN, LeRoy Chester, 1908- ,
American; nonfiction CON
BROWN, Leslie Hilton, 1917- ,

English; nonfiction CON

BROWN, Leslie Wilfrid, 1912- ,
English; nonfiction CON

BROWN, Lester L., 1928- ,
American; nonfiction CON

BROWN, Lloyd Arnold, 1907- ,
American; juveniles CON WA

BROWN, Marcia, 1918- , American;
juveniles FUL WA

BROWN, Margaret Wise ('Golden
MacDonald'), 1910-52, American;
juveniles KJU WA

BROWN, Margery, American; juveniles CON

BROWN, Marion Marsh, 1908- ,
American; juveniles CON WA

BROWN, Mark Herbert, 1900- ,
American; nonfiction CON

BROWN, Marshall L., 1924- ,
American; nonfiction CON

BROWN, Mary L.T., American;
juveniles CON

BROWN, Michael, 1931- , American; juveniles CON

BROWN, Michael John, 1932- ,
Anglo-American; nonfiction CON

BROWN, Milton Perry, Jr., 1928- ,
American; nonfiction CON

BROWN, Morna Doris ('Elizabeth
Ferrars'; 'E.X. Ferrars'),
1907- , English; fiction CON

BROWN, Morris Cecil ('Marianne
Goslovich'), 1943- , American;
nonfiction CON

BROWN, Muriel Whitbeck, 1892- ,
American; nonfiction CON

BROWN, Murray, 1929- , American;
nonfiction CON

'BROWN, Myra' see COOK, Myra B.

BROWN, Myra Berry, 1918- , American; juveniles CON WA

BROWN, Neville George, 1932- ,
English; nonfiction CON

BROWN, Norman Oliver, 1913- ,
American; nonfiction CON

BROWN, Oliver Madox, 1855-74,
English; fiction KBA

BROWN, Pamela, 1924- , English;
juveniles CON DOY WA

BROWN, Paul, 1893- , American;
juveniles, nonfiction HIG KJU
WA

BROWN, Peter Douglas, 1925- ,
English; fiction CON

BROWN, Peter Robert Lamont,
1935- , American; nonfiction
CON

BROWN, Philip S., American;
juveniles WA

BROWN, Ralph Adams, 1908- ,
American; nonfiction CON

BROWN, Raymond Bryan, 1923- ,
American; nonfiction CON

BROWN, Regina Margaret, American; juveniles WA

BROWN, Reginald Allen, 1924- ,
English; nonfiction CON

BROWN, Richard Carl, 1919- ,
American; nonfiction CON

BROWN, Richard Holbrook,
1927- , American; nonfiction
CON

BROWN, Richard Maxwell, 1927- ,
American; nonfiction CON

BROWN, Robert, 1773-1858, Scots;
nonfiction KBA

BROWN, Robert Eldon, 1907- ,
American; nonfiction CON

BROWN, Robert Goodell, 1923- ,
American; nonfiction CON

BROWN, Robert Joseph, 1907- ,
American; nonfiction CON

BROWN, Robert L., 1921- ,
American; nonfiction CON

BROWN, Robert Mc Afee, 1920- ,
American; nonfiction CON

BROWN, Roger H., 1931- ,
American; nonfiction CON

BROWN, Roger William, 1925- ,
American; nonfiction CON

BROWN, Rollo Walter, 1880- ,
American; fiction, essays KT

BROWN, Ronald Gordon Sclater,
1929- , Scots; nonfiction CON

BROWN, Rosalie Gertrude Moore
('Rosalie Moore'), 1910- ,
American; juveniles, poetry
CON WA

BROWN, Sanborn Conner, 1913- ,
American; nonfiction CON

BROWN, Sidney De Vere, 1925- ,
American; nonfiction CON

BROWN, Solyman, 1790-1876,
American; poetry KAA

BROWN, Stephen J., 1881- ,
Irish; nonfiction HOE

BROWN, Stephen W., 1940- ,
American; nonfiction CON

BROWN, Stuart C., 1938- ,
Scots; nonfiction CON

BROWN, Stuart Gerry, 1912- ,
American; nonfiction CON

BROWN, Theodore Lawrence,
1928- , American; nonfiction
CON

BROWN, Theodore Morey, 1925- ,
American; nonfiction CON
BROWN, Theophilus, 1811-79?,
American; nonfiction KAA
BROWN, Thomas, 1663-1704, English;
fiction BRO KB ST
BROWN, Thomas, 1778-1820, Scots;
nonfiction, poetry BRO KBA SA
BROWN, Thomas Edward, 1830-97,
English; poetry BRO KBA ST
BROWN, Truesdell Sparhawk,
1906- , American; nonfiction
CON
BROWN, Vinson, 1912- , American;
nonfiction, juveniles CON WA
BROWN, Virginia Sharpe (Ginny),
1916- , American; nonfiction
CON
BROWN, Wallace, 1933- , Canadian;
fiction CON
BROWN, Walter Lee, 1924- , Amer-
ican; nonfiction CON
BROWN, Wenzell, American; nonfic-
tion, fiction CON
BROWN, Wilfred Banks Duncan,
1908- , Scots; nonfiction CON
'BROWN, Will C.' see BOYLES,
Clarence S., Jr.
BROWN, William English, 1907- ,
American; nonfiction CON
BROWN, William Ferdinand, 1928- ,
American; nonfiction, juveniles
CON
BROWN, William Frank, 1920- ,
American; nonfiction CON
BROWN, William Hill, 1865-93,
American; fiction, poetry, plays
JO KAA
BROWN, William James, 1889- ,
American; nonfiction CON
BROWN, William Louis, 1910-64,
American; juveniles, nonfiction
CON WA
BROWN, William Wells, 1816-84,
American; nonfiction KAA
BROWN, Yeats see YEATS-BROWN,
Francis C. C. P.
BROWN, Zenith Jones ('Leslie Ford';
'David Frome'), 1898- , Amer-
ican; fiction CON KT
BROWN AZAROWICZ, Marjory F.,
1922- , Canadian; nonfiction
CON
BROWNE, Charles Farrar ('Artemus
Ward'), 1834-67, American; fic-
tion BRO KAA ST
BROWNE, Courtney, 1915- , Eng-

lish; fiction CON
BROWNE, Elliott Martin, 1900- ,
English; nonfiction CON
BROWNE, Frances, 1816-79?,
Irish; juveniles, poetry DOY
KBA
BROWNE, Francis Fisher, 1843-
1913, American; editor, non-
fiction, poetry HOO KAA
BROWNE, George Stephenson,
1890- , Australian; nonfiction
CON
BROWNE, Gerald Peter, 1930- ,
Canadian; nonfiction CON
BROWNE, Gordon, 1858-1932,
English; juveniles DOY
BROWNE, Henry J., 1853-1941,
Irish; nonfiction HOE
BROWNE, Isaac Hawkins, 1705-
60, English; poetry BRO ST
BROWNE, Lewis, 1897-1949,
Anglo-American; nonfiction
KT
BROWNE, Louis, 1897- , Amer-
ican; nonfiction KAT
BROWNE, Malcolm Wilde, 1931- ,
American; nonfiction CON
BROWNE, Maurice, 1881-1955,
English; plays MAT
BROWNE, Michael Dennis, 1940- ,
British; poetry CON MUR
BROWNE, Ray B., 1922- , Amer-
ican; nonfiction CON
BROWNE, Robert Span, 1924- ,
American; nonfiction CON
'BROWNE, Sam' see SMITH, Ronald
G.
BROWNE, Sir Thomas, 1605-82,
English; nonfiction BRO KB ST
BROWNE, Thomas Alexander
('Rolf Boldrewood'), 1826-1915,
Australian, fiction BRO KBA
ST
BROWNE, Tom, 1872-1910, Eng-
lish; juveniles DOY
BROWNE, Walter Anderson,
1895- , American; nonfiction
CON
'BROWN, Warren' see BOROSON,
Warren
BROWNE, William, 1590/91-1643/
45?, English; poetry BRO KB
SP ST
BROWNELL, Baker, 1887- ,
American; poetry, nonfiction
HOO KTS
BROWNELL, Henry Howard,

1820-72, American; poetry, non-
fiction KAA
BROWNELL, John Arnold, 1924- ,
American; nonfiction CON
BROWNELL, William Crary, 1851-
1928, American; criticism KT
ST
BROWNING, David George, 1938- ,
English; nonfiction CON
BROWNING, Douglas, 1929- ,
American; nonfiction CON
BROWNING, Elizabeth Barrett
Moulton, 1806-61, English;
poetry BRO KBA MAG SP SA ST
BROWNING, Gordon, 1938- , Amer-
ican; nonfiction CON
'BROWNING, Henry C.' see MOWATT,
Anna C.O.R.
BROWNING, Mary, 1887- , Amer-
ican; nonfiction CON
BROWNING, Oscar, 1837-1923,
English; nonfiction BRO KBA
BROWNING, Robert, 1812-89,
English; poetry, plays BRO
KBA MAG SA ST
BROWNING, Robert, 1914- , Scots;
nonfiction CON
BROWNING, Wilfrid Robert Francis,
1918- , English; nonfiction
CON
BROWNJOHN, Alan Charles ('Barring-
ton, John'), 1931- , British;
poetry CON MUR
BROWNLEE, Frank, 1875- , South
African; fiction ST
BROWNLEE, William Hugh, 1917- ,
American; nonfiction CON
BROWNLEY, Ava, 1926- , Yugoslav-
American; nonfiction CON
BROWNLIE, Ian, 1932- , English;
nonfiction CON
BROWNLOW, David Timothy, 1941- ,
Irish; poetry MUR
BROWNLOW, Kevin, 1938- , Eng-
lish; nonfiction CON
BROWNLOW, William Gannaway ('Par-
son Brownlow'), 1805-77, Amer-
ican; nonfiction KAA
BROWN-OLF, Lillian, 1880- ,
American; nonfiction HOE
BROWNSON, Josephine Van Dyke,
-1942, American; nonfiction
HOE
BROWNSON, Orestes Augustus,
1803-76, American; nonfiction
KAA ST
BROWNSTEIN, Michael, 1943- ,

American; poetry CON MUR
BROWNSTEIN, Samuel C., 1909- ,
American; nonfiction CON
BROYLES, John Allen, 1934- ,
American; nonfiction CON
BRUBACHER, John Seiler, 1898- ,
American; nonfiction CON
BRUBAKER, Sterling, 1924- ,
American; nonfiction CON
BRUCCOLI, Matthew J., 1931- ,
American; nonfiction CON
BRUCE, Ben F., Jr., 1920- ,
American; nonfiction CON
BRUCE, C.D., 1862-1934, Eng-
lish; nonfiction HIG
BRUCE, Charles Tory, 1906- ,
American; poetry, fiction
MUR ST SY
BRUCE, Donald James, 1930- ,
English; nonfiction CON
BRUCE, Frederick Fyvie, 1910- ,
Scots; nonfiction CON
BRUCE, George, 1909- , Scots;
poetry, criticism MUR ST
BRUCE, Harry J., 1931- ,
American; nonfiction CON
BRUCE, James, 1730-94, Scots;
nonfiction BRO KB ST
BRUCE, Jeanette M., 1922- ,
American; nonfiction CON
BRUCE, Lennart, 1919- ,
Swedish-American; poetry
CON
BRUCE, Lenny, 1925-66, Ameri-
can; nonfiction CON
BRUCE, Lockhart Robin, 1920- ,
English; nonfiction CON
BRUCE, Mary, 1927- , American;
juveniles COM CON
BRUCE, Michael, 1746-67, English;
poetry BRO ST
'BRUCE, Monica' see MELARO,
Constance L.
BRUCE, Robert, 1927- , English;
nonfiction CON
BRUCE, Sylvia Valerie, 1936- ,
English; fiction CON
BRUCE, Violet Rose, English;
nonfiction CON
BRUCE, William Cabell, 1860-1946,
American; nonfiction KT
BRUCHAC, Joseph III, 1942- ,
American; nonfiction, poetry
CON
BRUCHESI, Jean, 1901- ,
Canadian; nonfiction HOE ST
SY

BRUCHEY, Stuart Weems, 1917- ,
American; nonfiction CON
BRUCKBERGER, Rev. Raymond
Leopold, 1907- , French; fic-
tion HO
BRUCKER, Herbert, 1898- , Amer-
ican; nonfiction CON
'BRUCKNER, Ferdinand' (Theodor
Tagger), 1891-1953, German;
plays AL KU LEN MAT
BRÜES, Otto, 1897- , German;
nonfiction KU
BRUEHL, Charles, 1876- , Ameri-
can; nonfiction HOE
BRÜHL, Gustav see 'KARA GIORG'
BRÜLOW, Caspar, 1585-1627, Ger-
man; plays ST
BRÜNING, Elfriede, 1910- , Ger-
man; fiction AL
BRUES, Otto, 1897-1967, German;
plays MAT
BRUESS, Clint E., 1941- , Amer-
ican; nonfiction CON
BRUEYS, David Augustin, 1640-1723,
French; plays SA
BRUFEE, Kenneth A., 1934- ,
American; nonfiction CON
BRUFF, Nancy, American; fiction
WAF
BRUGGEN, Carolina Lea Carry van
de Haan, 1881-1932, Dutch; fic-
tion, essays ST
BRUGGINK, Donald J., 1929- ,
American; nonfiction CON
BRUGHETTI, Romualdo, 1907?- ,
Argentinian; essays, poetry,
criticism SA
BRUGMAN, Johannes, 1400-73,
Dutch; poetry ST
BRUTHIER d' ABLAINCOURT, Jacques
Jean,   -1756, French; nonfiction,
poetry, translations DIL
BRUIN, Claas, 1671-1732, Dutch;
nonfiction ST
BRUIX, 1728-80, French; nonfiction
DIL
BRULEZ, Raymond, 1895- ,
Flemish; fiction, essays, criti-
cism FLE
BRULL, Mariano, 1891-1956, Cuban;
poetry MIN
BRULLER, Jean see 'VERCORS'
BRUMBAUGH, Robert Sherrick,
1918- , American; nonfiction
CON
BRUMM, Ursula, 1919- , German;
nonfiction CON

BRUMMET, R. Lee, 1921- ,
American; nonfiction CON
BRUMMITT, Wyatt B., 1897- ,
American; nonfiction CON
BRUMOY, Pierre, 1688-1742,
French; nonfiction DIL
BRUN, André, 1881-1926, Portu-
guese; fiction SA
BRUN, Federica Sofia Cristian,
1765-1835, Danish; poetry
SA
BRUN, Johan Nordal, 1745-1816,
Norwegian; plays, poetry SA
ST
BRUN von SCHÖNBECK, 13th
cent., German; poetry ST
BRUNCK, Richard François
Philippe, 1729-1803, French;
nonfiction DIL
BRUNDAGE, James Arthur,
1929- , American; nonfiction
CON
BRUNE, Joan de, 1588-1658,
Dutch; poetry ST
BRUNE, Joan de, 1618-49, Dutch;
poetry ST
BRUNE, Lester Hugo, 1926- ,
American; nonfiction CON
BRUNER, Margaret E. Baggerley,
1886- , American; poetry
CON
BRUNET, Berthelot, 1901-48,
Canadian; fiction SY
BRUNET, Domingo, 1890- ,
Argentinian; poetry, essays
MIN
BRUNET, Jean Louis, 1688-1747,
French; nonfiction DIL
BRUNET, Marta, 1901- , Chilean;
fiction MIN SA
BRUNET, Pierre Nicolas, 1733-71,
French; nonfiction DIL
BRUNETIERE, Ferdinand Vincent
de Paul Marie, 1849-1906,
French; criticism COL DIF
HAR KE SA ST
BRUNETTI, Cledo, 1910- ,
American; nonfiction CON
BRUNETTO LATINI see LATINI,
Brunetto
BRUNHOFF, Jean de, 1899-1937,
French; juveniles DOY KJU
WA
BRUNHOFF, Laurent de, 1925- ,
Franco-American; juveniles
DOY FUL WA
BRUNI, Leonardo (Aretino), 1374?-

1444, Italian; nonfiction ST
BRUNINI, John Gilland, 1899- ,
American; poetry HOE
BRUNIUS, Bernardus, 18th cent.,
Dutch; translations ST
BRUNN, Harry Otis, Jr., 1919- ,
American; nonfiction, radio,
tv CON
BRUNNE, Robert of see MANNYNG,
Robert
BRUNNER, Edmund de Schweinitz,
1889- , American; nonfiction
CON
BRUNNER, Heinrich Emil, 1889- ,
Swiss; nonfiction KTS
BRUNNER, James Albertus, 1923- ,
American; nonfiction CON
BRUNNER, John Kilian Houston
('Keith Woodcott'), 1934- ,
English; fiction CON
BRUNNER, Theodore Friedrich,
1934- , American; nonfiction
CON
BRUNNGRABER, Rudolf, 1900/01- ,
Austrian; fiction KT LEN
BRUNO see SAMPAIO, José P. de
'BRUNO, Frank' see ST. BRUNO,
Albert F.
BRUNO, Giordano, 1548/50-1600,
Italian; poetry, plays, nonfiction
HAR KE SA ST
BRUNO, José, 1898- , Spanish;
journalism SA
BRUNO, Michael, 1921- , American;
nonfiction CON
BRUNOT, Ferdinand, 1860-1938,
French; nonfiction DIF
BRUNS, James Edgar, 1923- ,
American; nonfiction CON
BRUNS, Marianne, 1897- , German;
fiction AL
BRUNS, William John, Jr., 1935- ,
American; nonfiction CON
BRUNSCHVIGG, León (Brunschwich),
1869-1944, French; nonfiction
DIF SA
BRUNTON, Mary, 1778-1818, Scots;
fiction BRO KBA SA
BRUNTZ, George G., 1901- ,
American; nonfiction CON
BRUNY, 18th cent., French; fiction
DIL
BRUSH, Craig, Balcombe, 1930- ,
American; nonfiction CON
BRUSH, John Edwin, 1919- ,
American; nonfiction CON
BRUSH, Katharine Ingham, 1902-52,

American; fiction KAT KT
WAF
BRUSHWOOD, John Stubbs,
1920- , American; nonfiction
CON
BRUSSEL, James Arnold, 1905- ,
American; fiction, nonfiction
CON
BRUSSEL, Pierre, -1780/81,
French; nonfiction DIL
BRUST, Alfred, 1891-1934, Ger-
man; plays KU MAT
BRUSTEIN, Robert S., 1927- ,
American; nonfiction CON
BRUSTLEIN, Janice Tworkov
('Janice'), American; juveniles
CON WA
BRUTE de LOIRELLE, -1783,
French; plays DIL
BRUTON, Eric Moore, English;
fiction, nonfiction CON
BRUTON, Henry Jackson, 1921- ,
American; nonfiction CON
BRUTON, Jack Gordon, 1914- ,
English; nonfiction CON
BRUTTEN, Gene J., 1928- ,
American; nonfiction CON
'BRUTUS' see SIMPSON, Stephen
BRUTUS, Dennis Vincent, 1924- ,
British; poetry MUR RIC
BRUUN, Arthur Geoffrey, 1898- ,
Canadian; nonfiction CON KTS
BRUUN, Mathe Conrad, 1775-1826,
Danish; poetry ST
BRUYERE, Jean de la see LA
BRUYERE, Jean de
BRUYN, Kathleen, 1903- , Amer-
ican; nonfiction CON
BRUYS, François, 1708-38,
French; nonfiction DIL
BRY, Adelaide, 1920- , American;
nonfiction CON
BRYAN, Carter Royston, 1911- ,
American; nonfiction CON
BRYAN, Dorothy M., American;
juveniles HO
BRYAN, George McLeod, 1920- ,
American; nonfiction CON
BRYAN, Jack Yeaman, 1907- ,
American; fiction CON
BRYAN, Joseph, 1904- , Ameri-
can; juveniles WA
BRYAN, Martin, 1908- , Ameri-
can; nonfiction CON
BRYAN, Mary Edwards, 1842-1913,
American; journalism, fiction
KAA

BRYAN, William Jennings, 1860-1925,
American; nonfiction HOO
BRYANS, Robert Harbinson ('Robin
Bryans'; 'Robert Harbinson'),
1928- , American; fiction CON
BRYANT, Sir Arthur, 1899- , Eng-
lish; nonfiction KTS RIC
BRYANT, Arthur Herbert, 1917- ,
American; fiction WAF
BRYANT, Sir Arthur Wynne Morgan,
1899- , English; nonfiction
BRO
BRYANT, Bernice Morgan, 1908- ,
American; juveniles CON
BRYANT, Beth Elaine, 1936- ,
American; nonfiction CON
BRYANT, Donald Cross, 1905- ,
American; nonfiction CON
BRYANT, Edward, 1928- , Ameri-
can; nonfiction CON
BRYANT, Gertrude Thomson, Amer-
ican; juveniles WA
BRYANT, Jacob, 1715-1804, English;
nonfiction BRO
BRYANT, Jerry Holt, 1928- ,
American; nonfiction CON
BRYANT, John, 1807-1902, Ameri-
can; poetry HOO
BRYANT, Joseph Allen, Jr., 1919- ,
American; nonfiction CON
BRYANT, Margaret M., 1900- ,
American; nonfiction CON
BRYANT, Robert Harry, 1925- ,
American; nonfiction CON
BRYANT, Thomas Alton, 1926- ,
American; nonfiction CON
BRYANT, Verda E., 1910- ,
American; nonfiction CON
BRYANT, William Cullen, 1794-
1878, American; poetry, essays
BRO KAA MAG SP ST
BRYANT, Willis Rooks, 1892- ,
American; nonfiction CON
BRYANT-JONES, Mildred, American;
nonfiction SCA
BRYCE, James (Viscount Bryce of
Deckmont), 1838-1922, Scots;
nonfiction BRO KBA
BRYCE, Murray Davidson, 1917- ,
Canadian; nonfiction CON
BRYDAINE, Jacques see BRIDAINE,
Jacques
BRYDE, John Francis, 1920- ,
American; nonfiction CON
BRYDEN, Henry Anderson, 1854-
1937, English; nonfiction HIG
BRYDEN, John Rennie, 1913- ,

American; nonfiction CON
BRYDGES, Sir Samuel Egerton,
1762-1837, English; nonfiction,
fiction, poetry BRO ST
BRYER, Jackson Robert, 1937- ,
American; nonfiction CON
BRYHER, Winifred, 1894- ,
English; fiction KTS
BRYNJULFSSON, Gísli, 1827-88,
Icelandic; poetry HAR KE ST
BRYNOLF, Algotsson, 1250-1317,
Swedish; hymns ST
BRYSON, Charles ('Charles Barry'),
1887/88- , Irish; fiction
HOE KTS
BRYUSOV, Valery Yakovevich
(Briusov), 1873-1924, Russian;
poetry, fiction COL FLE
HARK KT RIC SA ST
BRZEZINSKI, Zbigniew K., 1928- ,
Polish-American; nonfiction
CON
BRZOVIC, Franco, Chilean; fiction,
essays MIN
BRZOZOWSKI, Leopold Stanislaw,
Leon ('Adam Czepiel'), 1878-
1911, Polish; criticism, fiction
ST
BUBE, Richard H., 1927- ,
American; nonfiction CON
BUBER, Martin, 1878-1965,
Australian; nonfiction AL FLE
KTS KU KUN
BUCCHIERI, Theresa F., 1908- ,
American; fiction CON
BUCCO, Martin, 1929- , Ameri-
can; poetry CON
BUCHAN, Anna ('Olive Douglas'),
-1948, English; fiction
BRO
BUCHAN, John (Lord Tweedsmuir),
1875-1940, Scots; fiction, non-
fiction BRO KL KT MAG RIC
SA ST
BUCHAN, Perdita, 1940- , Eng-
lish; nonfiction CON
BUCHAN, Thomas Buchanan,
1931- , Scots-American; non-
fiction CON MUR
BUCHANAN, Albert Russell,
1906- , American; nonfiction
CON
'BUCHANAN, Chuck' see BOWLAND,
Donald S.
BUCHANAN, Colin Ogilvie, 1934- ,
American; nonfiction CON
BUCHANAN, Cynthia Dee, 1937- ,

American; juveniles CON
BUCHANAN, Daniel Crump, 1892- ,
American; nonfiction CON
BUCHANAN, Donald W., 1908- ,
Canadian; nonfiction CON
BUCHANAN, George, 1506-82, Scots;
nonfiction, poetry BRO KB SA
ST
BUCHANAN, George Henry Perrott,
1904- , British; poetry, plays,
fiction, nonfiction CON MUR
BUCHANAN, George Wesley, 1921- ,
American; nonfiction CON
BUCHANAN, James Junkin, 1925- ,
American; nonfiction CON
BUCHANAN, James McGill, 1919- ,
American; nonfiction CON
BUCHANAN, James Shannon, 1864-
1921, American; nonfiction MAR
BUCHANAN, Keith, 1919- , English;
nonfiction CON
BUCHANAN, Milton Alexander, 1878-
1952, Canadian; nonfiction BL
BUCHANAN, Pegasus, 1920- ,
American; nonfiction CON
BUCHANAN, Robert Angus, 1930- ,
English; nonfiction CON
BUCHANAN, Robert William, 1841-
1901, Scots; poetry, fiction,
plays BRO KBA ST
BUCHANAN, Thomas Gittings, 1919- ,
American; nonfiction CON
BUCHANAN, William see BUCK,
William R.
BUCHANAN-JARDINE, Sir John,
1900- , English; nonfiction HIG
BUCHARD, Robert, 1931- , Swiss;
nonfiction CON
BUCHEN, Irving H., 1930- , Amer-
ican; nonfiction CON
BUCHER, Bradley, 1932- , Ameri-
can; nonfiction CON
BUCHER, Charles A., 1912- ,
American; nonfiction CON
BUCHER, François, 1927- , Swiss-
American; nonfiction CON
BUCHET, Pierre François, 1679-
1721, French; nonfiction DIL
BUCHHEIMER, Naomi Barnett,
1927- , American; juveniles
CON
BUCHHOLTZ, Andreas Heinrich,
1607-71, German; poetry, fiction
AL HAR ST
BUCHHOLTZ, Johannes, 1882-1940,
Danish; fiction FLE HAR KT
ST
BUCHINSKAYA, Nadezhda Alexandrov-

na ('Teffi'), 1876-1952, Rus-
sian; poetry, fiction HARK
ST
BUCHLER, Justus, 1914- ,
American; nonfiction CON
BUCHNER, Augustus, 1591-1661,
German; poetry ST
BUCHSTAB, Michael see 'AVI-
YONAH, Michael'
BUCHWALD, Arthur, 1925- ,
American; nonfiction CON
BUCK, Alan Michael, Irish-Amer-
ican; fiction HOE
BUCK, Charles Henry, Jr.,
1915- , American; nonfiction
CON
BUCK, Frederick Silas, American;
nonfiction CON
BUCK, Harry Merwyn, Jr.,
1921- , American; nonfiction
CON
BUCK, John Nelson, 1906- ,
American; nonfiction CON
BUCK, Margaret Waring, 1910- ,
American; juveniles CON WA
BUCK, Marion Ashby, 1909- ,
American; nonfiction CON
BUCK, Paul Herman, 1899- ,
American; nonfiction KT
BUCK, Pearl Sydenstricker ('John
Sedges'), 1892- , American;
fiction, nonfiction, juveniles,
plays BRO COM CON FLE
KAT KT MAG RIC SA ST WA
WAF
BUCK, Stratton, 1906- , Ameri-
can; nonfiction CON
BUCK, Vernon Ellis, 1934- ,
American; nonfiction CON
BUCK, William Ray (William
Buchanan), 1930- , American;
fiction, juveniles CON WA
BUCKE, Richard Maurice, 1837-
1902, Canadian; poetry SY
BUCKERIDGE, Anthony Malcolm,
1912- , English; juveniles
DOY
BUCKINGHAM, Clyde Edwin,
1907- , American; nonfiction
CON
BUCKINGHAM, George Villiers,
Duke of, 1628-87, English;
plays BRO KB
BUCKINGHAM, James Silk,
1786-1855, English; nonfiction
BRO KBA
BUCKINGHAM, James William,
1932- , American; nonfiction
CON

BUCKINGHAM, Walter Samuel, Jr.,
1924- , American; nonfiction
CON
BUCKINGHAM, Willis John, 1938- ,
American; nonfiction CON
BUCKINGHAM AND NORMANDY,
Duke of see SHEFFIELD, James
BUCKINGHAM AND NORMANDY,
John Sheffield, 1648-1721, Eng-
lish; nonfiction BRO KB ST
BUCKLAND, Francis Trevelyan,
1826-80, English; nonfiction BRO
KBA
BUCKLE, Henry Thomas, 1821-62,
English; nonfiction BRO KBA
ST
BUCKLER, Ernest, 1908- ,
Canadian; fiction, poetry CON
RIC SY
BUCKLER, William Earl, 1924- ,
American; nonfiction CON
BUCKLEY, Fergus Reid ('Peter
Crumpet'), 1930- , American;
nonfiction CON
BUCKLEY, Francis Joseph, 1928- ,
American; nonfiction CON
BUCKLEY, Helen Elizabeth, 1918- ,
American; juveniles COM CON
BUCKLEY, Jerome Hamilton, 1917- ,
American; nonfiction CON
BUCKLEY, Nancy, American; poetry
HOE
BUCKLEY, Thomas Hugh, 1932- ,
American; nonfiction CON
BUCKLEY, Vincent Thomas, 1925- ,
Australian; poetry, criticism
MUR
BUCKLEY, William Frank, Jr.,
1925- , American; nonfiction
CON
BUCKMASTER, Henrietta, American;
fiction CON WAF
BUCKMINSTER, Joseph Stevens,
1784-1812, American; nonfiction
KAA
BUCKNALL, Barbara Jane, 1933- ,
English; nonfiction CON
BUCKNER, Robert Henry, 1906- ,
American; movies, fiction, tv
CON
BUCKSTONE, John Baldwin, 1802-79,
English; plays KBA
BUCQUOY, Jean Albert, 1650-1740,
French; nonfiction DIL
BUCUTA, Emanoil, 1887-1942,
Rumanian; nonfiction, poetry ST
BUDAEUS see BUDE, Guillaume

BUDAI-DELEANU, Ion, 1760-1820,
Rumanian; poetry ST
BUDAK, Mile, 1889-1946, Croatian;
poetry, fiction ST
BUDANTSEV, Sergey Fyodorovich,
1896- , Russian; fiction,
plays COL HARK SA ST
BUDD, Edward Carhart, 1920- ,
American; nonfiction CON
BUDD, Kenneth George, 1904- ,
English; nonfiction CON
BUDD, Lillian Peterson, 1897- ,
American; fiction, juveniles
CON WA
BUDD, Louis John, 1921- ,
American; nonfiction CON
BUDD, Richard W., 1934- ,
American; nonfiction CON
BUDDEN, John, 1884- , English;
nonfiction HIG
BUDDEN, Laura Madeline, 1894- ,
English; nonfiction CON
BUDDHAGHOSA, fl. 413, Indian;
poetry ST
BUDE, Guillaume (Budaeus), 1468-
1540, French; nonfiction DIF
HAR KE SA ST
BUDENZ, Louis Francis, 1891- ,
American; nonfiction HO
BUDGE, Ian, 1936- , English;
nonfiction CON
BUDGELL, Eustace, 1686-1737,
English; essays BRO ST
BUDGETT, Hubert Maitland,
1882- , English; nonfiction
HIG
BUDI Pjetër, 1566-1623, Albanian;
poetry HAR
BUDICH, Carl, 1904- , German;
poetry, plays ST
BUDICK, Sanford, 1942- , Amer-
ican; nonfiction CON
BUDRY, Paul, 1883-1949, Swiss;
criticism ST
BUDRYS, Algirdas Jonas, 1931- ,
American; fiction CON
BUDUROWYCZ, Bohdan Basil,
1921- , Polish-Canadian; non-
fiction CON
BUDZIK, Janet K. Sims, 1942- ,
American; nonfiction CON
BÜCHLER, Franz, 1904- , Ger-
man; nonfiction KU
BUEHNER, Andrew John, 1905- ,
American; nonfiction CON
BUECHNER, Carl Frederick,
1926- , American; fiction CON

BUECHNER, Frederick, 1926- ,
American; fiction RIC
BÜCHNER, Georg Karl, 1813-37,
German; plays AL HAR KE
MAG SA ST
BUECHNER, John Charles, 1934- ,
American; nonfiction CON
'BUEHNAU, Ludwig' see SCHREIBER,
Hermann
BUEHR, Walter Franklin, 1897-1971,
American; juveniles CON WA
BUEHRIG, Edward Henry, 1910- ,
American; nonfiction CON
BUEL, James William, 1849-1920,
American; journalism, nonfiction
HOO
BUELER, William Merwin, 1934- ,
American; nonfiction CON
BUELL, Ellen Lewis, American;
juveniles WA
BUELL, Frederick Henderson,
1942- , American; poetry CON
BUELL, John Edward, 1927- ,
Canadian; fiction CON
BUELL, Robert Kingery ('Brother
Bob'), 1908- , American;
poetry CON
BUELL, Victor Paul, 1914- ,
American; nonfiction CON
BUELOW, George J., 1929- ,
American; nonfiction CON
BUENAVENTURA, Giovanni di
Fidenza see BONAVENTURA
BUENDIA, Rogelio, 1891- , Spanish;
poetry BL
BUENDIA ABREU, Rogelio, 1872- ,
Spanish; poetry, fiction SA
BUENDIA MANZANO, Rogelio,
1891- , Spanish; poetry, non-
fiction SA
BUENO, Lillian de la Torre see
McCUE, Lillian B.
BUENO, Manuel, 1874-1936, Spanish;
fiction, journalism BL SA
BUENO y LEROUX, Juan José,
1820-81, Spanish; poetry, non-
fiction SA
BÜRGEL, Bruno Hans, 1875-1948,
German; nonfiction AL
BUERGENTHAL, Thomas, 1934- ,
Czech-American; nonfiction CON
BÜRGER, Gottfried August, 1747-
94, German; poetry AL HAR KE
ST
BUERO VALLEJO, Antonio, 1916- ,
Spanish; plays BL MAT RIC SA
BUESA, José Angel, 1910- , Cuban;

poetry MIN
BUESCHEL, Richard M., 1926- ,
American; nonfiction CON
BUFALARI, Giuseppe, 1927- ,
Italian; nonfiction CON
BUFANO, Alfredo R., 1895- ,
Argentinian; poetry, fiction
MIN SA
BUFANO, Remo, 1894-1948,
American; juveniles WA
BUFF, Conrad, 1886- , Swiss-
American; juveniles KJU WA
BUFF, Mary Marsh, 1890- ,
American; juveniles KJU WA
'BUFFALO, Chuck' see BARTH,
Charles P.
BUFFIER, Claude, 1661-1737,
French; nonfiction DIF DIL
BUFFINGTON, Albert Franklin,
1905- , American; nonfiction
CON
BUFFINGTON, Robert Ray, 1933- ,
American; nonfiction CON
BUFFON, Georges Louis Leclerc,
1707-88, French; nonfiction
DIF HAR KE MAL SA ST
BUFORD, Thomas Oliver, 1932- ,
American; nonfiction CON
BUGAYEV, Boris Nikolayevich
see 'BELY, Andrey'
BUGBEE, Emma, American;
juveniles WA
BUGBEE, Ruth Carson, 1903- ,
American; nonfiction CON
BUGENTAL, James Frederick
Thomas, 1915- , American;
nonfiction CON
BUGG, James Luckin, Jr.,
1920- , American; nonfiction
CON
BUGGE, Eliseus Sophus, 1833-1907,
Norwegian; fiction SA
BUGIANI, Arrigo, 1897- , Italian;
nonfiction SA
BUGLASS, Leslie J., 1917- ,
English; nonfiction CON
BUGNET, Georges, 1879- ,
Canadian; poetry SY
BUGNYON, Philibert, 1530-87,
French; poetry SA
BUHLER, Charlotte B., 1893- ,
German-American; nonfiction
CON
BUHLER, Curt Ferdinand, 1905- ,
American; nonfiction CON
BUHTURI, 821-97, Syrian; nonfic-
tion ST

BUIES, Arthur, 1840-1901, French-
Canadian; nonfiction ST SY
'BUIRETTE, Pierre Laurent' see
BELLOY, Dormont de
BUIST, Charlotte, 1942- , Ameri-
can; nonfiction CON
BUITENHUIS, Peter Martinus,
1925- , English; nonfiction CON
BUKHARI, 810-70, Arab; poetry
LAN
BUKKI Ben Yogli see 'KATZNELSON,
Jehuda L.'
BUKOWSKI, Charles, 1920- ,
American; poetry CON MUR
BUKTENICA, Norman August,
1930- , American; nonfiction
CON
BULATKIN, Eleanor Webster,
1913- , American; nonfiction
CON
BULATOVIC, Modrag, 1930- ,
Yugoslav; fiction CON RIC
BULEY, Roscoe Carlyle, 1893-1968,
American; nonfiction CON KTS
BULFINCH, Thomas, 1796-1867,
American; nonfiction KAA
BULGAKOV, Mikhail Afanasievich,
1891-1940, Russian; fiction,
plays COL HAR HARK MAT
RIC SA ST
BULGAKOV, Sergey Nikolayevich,
1871-1944, Russian; nonfiction
HARK ST
BULGARIN, Faddey Venediktovich,
1789-1859, Russian; fiction,
journalism HAR HARK ST
BULHÃO PATO, Raimundo Antonio,
de, 1829-1912, Portuguese;
poetry SA
BULIARD, Rev. Roger, 1909- ,
French; nonfiction HO
BULKEY SHAH, 1680-1758, Indian;
poetry LAN
BULL, Angela Mary, 1936- ,
English; juveniles CON
BULL, Francis, 1887- , Norwegian;
nonfiction ST
BULL, Geoffrey Taylor, 1921- ,
English; nonfiction CON
BULL, George, 1634-1710, English;
nonfiction BRO
BULL, Guyon Boys Garrett, 1912- ,
English; nonfiction CON
BULL, Hedley Norman, 1932- ,
Australian; nonfiction CON
BULL, Olaf Jacob Martin Luther,
1883-1933, Norwegian; poetry,

plays, fiction COL FLE SA
ST
BULL, Peter Cecil, 1912- ,
English; nonfiction CON
BULL, Storm, 1913- , American;
nonfiction CON
BULL, William Emerson, 1909- ,
American; nonfiction CON
BULLA, Clyde Robert, 1914- ,
American; juveniles COM
CON FUL WA
BULLARD, Edgar John III, 1942- ,
American; nonfiction CON
BULLARD, Fred Mason, 1901- ,
American; nonfiction CON
BULLARD, Helen, 1902- ,
American; nonfiction CON
BULLARD, Roger Aubrey, 1937- ,
American; nonfiction CON
BULLEID, H. A. V. ('D. Collins'),
1912- , English; nonfiction
CON
BULLEN, Arthur Henry, 1857-
1920, English; poetry, essays
KBA
BULLEN, Frank Thomas, 1857-
1915, English; nonfiction, fic-
tion BRO KT MAG
BULLET, Jean Baptiste, 1699-
1775, French; nonfiction DIL
BULLETT, Gerald William, 1893-
1958, English; poetry, fiction
BRO KAT KT RIC
BULLINGER, Heinrich, 1504-75,
Swiss; plays ST
'BULLINGHAM, Rodney' see
SLADEN, Norman St. B.
BULLIOUD, 1741-63, French; non-
fiction DIL
BULLIS, Harry Amos, 1890- ,
American; nonfiction CON
BULLITT, Orville Horwitz,
1894- , American; nonfiction
CON
BULLIVANT, Garland, 1920- ,
English; nonfiction HIG
BULLOCK, Alan Louis Charles,
1914- , English; nonfiction
CON
BULLOCK, Charles Spencer, III,
1942- , American; nonfiction
CON
BULLOCK, Frederick William
Bagshawe, 1903- , English;
nonfiction CON
BULLOCK, L. G. , English; juveniles
WA

BULLOCK, Michael ('Michael Hale'),
1918- , English; poetry, translations CON MUR

BULLOCK, Paul, 1924- , American;
nonfiction CON

BULLOCK, Shan, 1865-1935, Irish;
fiction ST

BULLOUGH, Geoffrey, 1901- , English; nonfiction CON

BULLOUGH, Vern LeRoy, 1928- ,
American; nonfiction CON

BULLRICH de PALENQUE, Sylvina,
1915- , Argentinian; poetry,
fiction, essays MIN SA

BULMER, Henry Kenneth ('Ernest
Corley'; 'Philip Kent'; 'Karl
Maras'; 'Kenneth Johns'), 1921- ,
English; fiction CON

BULMER-THOMAS, Ivor, 1903- ,
English; nonfiction CON

BULNES, Gonzalo, 1851-1936,
Chilean; nonfiction MIN

BULOSAN, Carlos, 1914- , Filipino;
poetry KTS

BULPIN, Thomas Victor, 1918- ,
South African; nonfiction, fiction
CON

BULTEEL, John, -1683, English;
translations ST

BULTMANN, Rudolf Karl, 1884- ,
German; nonfiction CON KU

BULWER, Edward G. E. L. see
BULWER-LYTTON, Edward
G. E. L.

BULWER, Sir Henry, 1801-72, English; nonfiction KBA

BULWER William H. L. E. see
DALLING and BULWER, William
H. L. E. W.

BULWER-LYTTON, Edward George
Earle, 1803-73, English; fiction,
plays, poetry, translations
BRO KBA MAG SA

BULYGA, A. A. see 'FADAYEV,
Alexandr'

BUNAO, Godofredo Burce ('Oscar
del Mundo'), 1926- , Filipino;
poetry MUR

BUNBURY, Sir William Henry
('Geoffrey Gambado'), 1750-1811,
English; nonfiction HIG

BUNCE, Frank David, 1907- ,
American; fiction CON

BUNCE, Oliver Bell, 1828-90, American; essays KAA

BUNCE, William Harvey, American;
juveniles WA

BUNCH, David R. ('Darryl R.
Groupe'), American; fiction
CON

'BUNDUKHARI, El' see DENT,
Anthony A.

BUNGE, Carlos Octavio, 1875-
1918, Argentinian; poetry,
fiction, plays MIN SA

BUNGE, Mario Augusto, 1919- ,
Argentinian; nonfiction CON

BUNGE, Walter Richard, 1911- ,
American; nonfiction CON

BUNGE de GALVEZ, Delfina,
1890-1953, Argentinian; fiction MIN SA

BUNI, Andrew, 1931- , American;
nonfiction CON

BUNIC-VUCICEVIC, Ivan, 1594-
1658, Dalmatian; poetry ST

BUNIN, Ivan Alexeyevich, 1870-
1953, Russian; fiction, poetry
COL FLE HAR HARK KAT KT
MAG RIC SA ST

BUNING, Johan Willem Frederik
Werumeus, 1891- , Dutch;
poetry ST

BUNKE, Harvey Charles, 1922- ,
American; nonfiction CON

BUNKER, Gerald Edward, 1938- ,
American; nonfiction CON

BUNKER, John, 1884- , American; nonfiction, poetry HOE

BUNN, John Thomas, 1924- ,
American; nonfiction CON

BUNN, John W., 1898- , American; nonfiction CON

'BUNN, Martin' see AMES,
Francis H.

BUNN, Ronald Freeze, 1929- ,
American; nonfiction CON

BUNNELL, Peter Curtis, 1937- ,
American; nonfiction CON

BUNNELL, William Stanley,
1925- , English; nonfiction
CON

BUNNER, Henry Cuyler, 1855-96,
American; poetry, fiction
BRO KAA

BUNSEN, Christian Karl Josías,
1791-1860, German; nonfiction
SA

BUNSTER TAGLE, Enrique,
Chilean; fiction, plays MIN

BUNTAIN, Ruth Jaeger, American;
juveniles WA

BUNTING, Basil, 1900- , British;
poetry MUR

'BUNTLINE, Ned' see JUDSON, Edward Z. C.
BUNCIAN, Josefina Santiago, 1935- , Filipino; nonfiction CON
BUNYA NO YASUHIDE see FUNYA NO YASUHIDE
BUNYAN, John, 1628-88, English; fiction, nonfiction BRO KB MAG SA ST
BUNZEL, John Harvey, 1924- , American; nonfiction CON
BUONAROTTI, Michelangelo, 1475-1564, Italian; poetry HAR KE ST
BUONAROTTI, Michelangelo, 1568-1642, Italian; plays ST
BUONCOMPAGNO da SEGNA, -1240, Italian; nonfiction ST
BURACK, Abraham Saul, 1908- , American; nonfiction, plays CON
BURACK, Elmer Howard, 1927- , American; nonfiction CON
BURACK, Sylvia ('Sylvia E. Kamerman'), 1916- , American; nonfiction CON
BURANELLI, Vincent, 1919- , American; nonfiction CON
BURBANK, Addison, 1895- , American; juveniles HOE
BURBANK, Natt Bryant, 1903- , American; nonfiction CON
BURBANK, Nelson L., 1898- , American; nonfiction CON
BURBANK, Rex James, 1925- , American; nonfiction CON
BURBY, William Edward, 1893- , American; nonfiction CON
BURCH, Francis Floyd, 1932- , American; nonfiction CON
BURCH, Gladys, 1899- , American; juveniles WA
BURCH, Robert Joseph, 1925- , American; juveniles COM CON WA
BURCHARD, John Ely, 1898- , American; nonfiction CON
BURCHARD, Max Norman, 1925- , American; nonfiction CON
BURCHARD, Peter Duncan, 1921- , American; juveniles, fiction CON WA
BURCHARD, Rachael Caroline, 1921- , American; nonfiction CON
BURCHARDT, Nellie, 1921- , American; juveniles CON
BURCHETT, Randall E., American;

nonfiction CON
BURCHIELLO, Domenico da Giovanni, 1404-49, Italian; poetry HAR ST
BURCKHARDT, Carl Jacob, 1891- , Swiss; nonfiction, essays FLE KU
BURCKHARDT, Jakob Christoph, 1818-97, Swiss; criticism HAR KE SA ST
BURCKHARDT, John Lewis, 1784-1817, Swiss-English; nonfiction BRO KBA ST
BURDEN, Jean Prussing, 1914- , American; poetry CON MUR
BURDETT, Winston, 1913- , American; nonfiction CON
BURDETTE, Robert Jones, 1844-1914, American; fiction KAA
BURDICK, Eric, 1934- , Canadian; fiction CON
BURDICK, Eugene Leonard, 1918-65, American; fiction CON RIC
BURDON, Randal Mathews, 1896- , New Zealander; nonfiction CON ST
BURELL, Consuelo, 1913- , Spanish; nonfiction BL
BUREN, Martha Margareta Elisabet, 1910- , Swedish; nonfiction CON
BURENIN, Viktor Petrovich, 1841-1926, Russian; fiction ST
BURETTE, Pierre Jean, 1665-1747, French; nonfiction DIL
BURFORD, Eleanor see HIBBERT, Eleanor
BURFORD, William Skelly, 1927- , American; poetry CON MUR
BURG, David, 1933- , Russian-English; nonfiction CON
BURGAN, John D., 1913- , American; fiction WAF
'BURGEON, G. A. L.' see BARFIELD, Owen
BURGER, Albert E., 1941- , American; nonfiction CON
BURGER, Carl, 1888- , American; nonfiction CON
BURGER, Chester, 1921- , American; nonfiction CON
BURGER, Gottfried August, 1747-94, German; poetry SA
'BURGER, John' see MARQUARD, Leopold
BURGER, Nash Kerr, 1908- ,

American; nonfiction CON
BURGER, Robert S., 1913- , Amer-
ican; nonfiction CON
BURGER, Ruth Pazen, 1917- ,
American; nonfiction CON
BURGERSDIJK, Leendert Alexander
Johannes, 1828-1900, Dutch;
translations, nonfiction ST
BURGESS, Anthony ('Joseph Kell';
'John Burgess Wilson'), 1917- ,
American; nonfiction, fiction
CON RIC
BURGESS, Charles Orville, 1932- ,
American; nonfiction CON
BURGESS, Chester Francis, 1922- ,
American; nonfiction CON
BURGESS, Christopher Victor,
1921- , Irish; plays, juveniles
CON
BURGESS, Eric, 1920- , English;
nonfiction CON
BURGESS, Frank Gelett, 1866-1951,
American; juveniles, poetry,
fiction BRO KT RIC
BURGESS, Jackson Visscher, 1927- ,
American; fiction CON
BURGESS, John Henry, 1923- ,
American; nonfiction CON
BURGESS, Margaret Elaine, Ameri-
can; nonfiction CON
BURGESS, Norman, 1923- , English;
nonfiction CON
BURGESS, Perry, 1886- , American;
fiction KTS
BURGESS, Philip Mark, 1939- ,
American; nonfiction CON
BURGESS, Robert Forrest, 1927- ,
American; nonfiction CON
BURGESS, Robert Herrmann, 1913- ,
American; nonfiction CON
BURGESS, Robert L., 1938- , Amer-
ican; nonfiction CON
BURGESS, Thornton Waldo, 1874-
1965, American; juveniles, fic-
tion DOY KJU KL WA
'BURGESS, Trevor' see TREVOR,
Elleston
BURGESS, Warren Randolph, 1889- ,
American; nonfiction CON
BURGETT, Donald Robert, 1925- ,
American; fiction CON
BURGH, Jacob van der, 1690-59,
Dutch; poetry ST
BURGHARD, August, 1901- , Amer-
ican; nonfiction CON
BURGHARDT, Andrew Frank,
1924- , American; nonfiction
CON

BURGHARDT, Walter John, 1914- ,
American; nonfiction CON
BURGHI, Juan, 1895- , Argen-
tinian; poetry MIN
BURGIN, Weston Richard, 1947- ,
American; fiction CON
BURGLON, Nora, American;
juveniles KJU
BURGON, John William, 1813-
88, English; nonfiction BRO
KBA
BURGOS, Fausto, 1888-1952,
Argentinian; nonfiction MIN
BURGOS, Francisco Javier de,
1778-1848/49, Spanish; poetry,
plays BL SA
BURGOS, Francisco Javier de,
1842-1902, Spanish; journalism,
plays BL HAR ST
BURGOS, Julia de, 1916- ,
Puerto Rican; poetry SA
BURGOS IZQUIERDO, Fausto,
1929- , Spanish; poetry SA
BURGOS RIZZOLE, Javier, de,
1885- , Spanish; poetry,
plays SA
BURGOS SARRAGOITI, Javier de,
1842-1902, Spanish; poetry
SA
BURGOS SEGUI, Carmen de
('Colombine'), 1879-1932,
Spanish; nonfiction, fiction
BL SA
'BURGOYNE, Elizabeth' see
PICKLES, Mabel E.
BURGOYNE, John, 1722-92, Eng-
lish; plays KB
BURGOYNE, Leon E., 1916- ,
American; juveniles WA
'BURGUILLOS, Tomé' see VEGA
CARPIO, Lope Félix
BURGWYN, Mebane Holoman,
1914- , American; fiction,
juveniles JO
BURHOE, Ralph Wendell, 1911- ,
American; nonfiction CON
BURI, Fritz, 1907- , Swiss;
nonfiction CON
BURIAN, Jarka Marsano, 1927- ,
American; nonfiction CON
BURICH, Nancy Jane, 1943- ,
American; nonfiction CON
BURIDAN, Jean, 1300-58/68,
French; nonfiction DIF SA ST
BURK, John Daly, 1775-1808,
American; plays KAA
BURKARD, Wallis, 1495?-1555,
German; fiction SA

BURKE, Arvid J., 1906- , American; nonfiction CON
BURKE, Carl Francis, 1917- , American; nonfiction CON
BURKE, Edmund, 1729-97, Irish; essays BRO KB MAG SA ST
BURKE, Edmund, M., 1928- , American; nonfiction CON
'BURKE, Fielding' see DARGAN, Olive T.
BURKE, Fred George 1926- , American; nonfiction CON
BURKE, James Lee, 1936- , American; fiction CON
'BURKE, John' see THEINER, George
BURKE, John Bruce, 1933- , American; nonfiction CON
BURKE, John Emmett, 1908- , American; nonfiction CON
BURKE, John Frederick ('Jonathan Burke'; 'Joanna Jones'; 'Sara Morris'), 1922- , English; fiction, juveniles, plays CON
BURKE, Kenneth Duva, 1897- , American; poetry, fiction, criticism BRO CON KT MUR ST
'BURKE, Leda' see GARNETT, David
BURKE, Lynn, American; juveniles WA
BURKE, Pauline Wilcox, 1884- , American; nonfiction HOE
BURKE, Robert Eugene, 1921- , American; nonfiction CON
BURKE, Russell, 1946- , American; nonfiction CON
BURKE, Thomas, 1886/87-1945, English; fiction, essays BRO KAT KT
BURKE, Ulick Peter, 1937- , English; nonfiction CON
BURKE, W. Warner, 1935- , American; nonfiction CON
BURKETT, Eva Mae, 1903- , American; nonfiction CON
BURKHALTER, Barton R., 1938- , American; nonfiction CON
BURKHARD von HOHENFELS, fl. 1225, Swiss; poetry, nonfiction ST
BURKHARDT, Richard Wellington, 1918- , American; nonfiction CON
BURKHART, Charles, 1924- , American; nonfiction CON
BURKHART, James Austin, 1914- ,

American; nonfiction CON
BURKHART, Robert Edward, 1937- , American; nonfiction CON
BURKHEAD, Jesse, 1916- , American; nonfiction CON
BURKHOLTZ, Herbert, 1932- , American; fiction CON
BURKILL, Tom Alec, 1912- , English; nonfiction CON
BURKMAN, Katherine H., 1934- , American; nonfiction CON
BURKOWSKY, Mitchell Roy, 1931- , American; nonfiction CON
BURKS, David D., 1924- , American; nonfiction CON
BURKS, Gordon Engledon, 1904- , American; nonfiction CON
BURLA, Yehuda, 1888- , Jewish; fiction ST
BURLAMAQUI, Jean Jacques, 1694-1748, Swiss; nonfiction DIF DIL
BURLAND, Brian Berkeley, 1931- , English; juveniles CON WA
BURLAND, Cottie Arthur, 1905- , English; juveniles CON WA
BURLE, Balthazar de Real de, 1701-74, French; nonfiction DIL
BURLEIGH, Anne Husted, 1941- , American; nonfiction CON
BURLEIGH, David Robert, 1907- , American; nonfiction CON
BURLEIGH, George Shepard, 1821-1903, American; poetry KAA
BURLEIGH, William Henry, 1812-71, American; journalism KAA
BURLEY, Walter, 1275-1345, English; nonfiction ST
BURLEY, William John, 1914- , English; fiction CON
BURLING, Robbins, 1926- , American; nonfiction CON
BURLINGAME, Merrill Gildea, 1901- , American; nonfiction PAC
BURLINGAME, Virginia Struble, 1900- , American; nonfiction CON
BURLINGAME, William Roger, 1889-1967, American; juveniles COM CON KT

BURLYUK, David Davidovich, 1882- ,
Russian; poetry HARK

BURMA, John Harmon, 1913- ,
American; nonfiction CON

BURMAN, Ben Lucien, 1895- ,
American; fiction CON KT WAF

BURMAN, Petrus, Jr. , 1713-78,
Dutch; nonfiction, poetry ST

BURMEISTER, Edwin, 1939- ,
American; nonfiction CON

BURMEISTER, Eva, 1899- , American; fiction CON

BURMEISTER, Jon, 1933- , American; fiction CON

BURMESTER, Heinrich, 1839-89,
German; fiction ST

BURN, Andrew Robert, 1902- ,
English; nonfiction CON

BURN, Doris, 1923- , American;
juveniles COM CON PAC

BURN, Joshua Harold, 1892- ,
American; nonfiction CON

BURNABY, John, 1891- , English;
nonfiction CON

BURNABY, William, 1672/73-1706,
English; plays, translations
ST

BURNAND, Sir Francis Cowley, 1836-
1917, English; plays BRO KBA

'BURNE, Clendennin, Jr.' see
HAWKES, John

BURNE, Glenn S. , 1921- , American; nonfiction CON

BURNE, Kevin G. , 1925- , American; nonfiction CON

BURNER, David B. , 1937- , American; nonfiction CON

BURNES, John Horne, 1916-53,
American; fiction BRO

BURNET, George Bain, 1894- ,
American; nonfiction CON

BURNET, Gilbert, 1643-1715, English; nonfiction BRO KB ST

BURNET, Thomas, 1635-1715, English; nonfiction BRO KB ST

BURNETT, Ben G. , 1924- , American; nonfiction CON

BURNETT, Calvin, 1921- , American; nonfiction CON

BURNETT, Collins W. , 1914- ,
American; nonfiction CON

BURNETT, Constance Buel, 1893- ,
American; juveniles CON WA

BURNETT, David ('Terrave Bernarn';
'Peter Pace'), 1931- , Austrian-
American; fiction CON

BURNETT, Dorothy Kirk, 1924- ,

American; nonfiction CON

BURNETT, Frances Eliza Hodgson,
1849-1924, English; juveniles,
fiction BRO DOY KT KAT ST
WA

BURNETT, Hallie Southgate,
American; nonfiction CON

'BURNETT, James' see MONBODDO,
James B.

BURNETT, Joe Ray, 1928- ,
American; nonfiction CON

BURNETT, Whit, 1899- ,
American; fiction CON KT

BURNETT, William Riley ('James
Updyke'), 1899- , American;
fiction CON KAT KT WAF

BURNETT, William Rodgers,
1899- , American; fiction
RIC

BURNETTE, Ollen Lawrence, Jr. ,
1927- , American; nonfiction
CON

'BURNEY, Anton' see HOPKINS,
Kenneth

BURNEY, Charles, 1726-1814,
English; nonfiction ST

BURNEY, Elizabeth Mary, 1934- ,
English; nonfiction CON

BURNEY, Eugenia, 1913- ,
American; nonfiction CON

BURNEY, Fanny (Madam D'Arblay),
1752-1840, English; fiction,
diary BRO KBA MAG SA ST

BURNEY, James, 1750-1821,
English; nonfiction KBA

BURNFORD, Sheila ('Philip
Cochrane'; 'S.D. Burnford';
'Philip Cochrane Every'),
1918- , American; nonfiction
CON WA

BURNHAM, Alan, 1913- , American; nonfiction CON

BURNHAM, Clara Louise Root,
1854-1927, American; fiction
KT

BURNHAM, David, 1907- ,
American; fiction HO

BURNHAM, James, 1905- ,
American; nonfiction KTS

'BURNHAM, John' see BECKWITH,
Burnham P.

BURNHAM, John Chynoweth,
1929- , American; nonfiction
CON

BURNHAM, Robert Ward, 1913- ,
American; nonfiction CON

BURNIM, Kalman Aaron, 1928- ,

American; nonfiction CON

BURNINGHAM, John, 1935- , English; juveniles DOY

BURNS, Alan, 1929- , English; fiction CON

BURNS, Arthur F., 1904- , Austrian-American; nonfiction CON

BURNS, Betty, 1909- , American; nonfiction CON

BURNS, Carol, 1934- , English; fiction CON

BURNS, Clair, American; plays MUR

BURNS, Edward Bradford, 1932- , American; nonfiction CON

BURNS, Edward McNall, 1897- , American; nonfiction CON

BURNS, Eedson Louis Millard ('Arlington B. Conway'), 1897- , Canadian; nonfiction CON

BURNS, Gerald P., 1918- , American; nonfiction CON

BURNS, Hobert Warren, 1925- , American; nonfiction CON

BURNS, James MacGregor, 1918- , American; nonfiction CON

BURNS, James William, 1937- , American; nonfiction CON

BURNS, Jim, 1936- , English; poetry MUR

BURNS, John Horne, 1916-53, American; fiction BRO KTS RIC WAF

BURNS, John V., 1907- , American; nonfiction CON

BURNS, Paul C., American; nonfiction CON

BURNS, Ralph J. ('Ralph Byrne'), 1901- , American; fiction CON

BURNS, Richard Dean, 1929- , American; nonfiction CON

BURNS, Robert, 1759-96, Scots; poetry BRO KB MAG SA SP ST

BURNS, Robert Grant, 1938- , American; nonfiction CON

BURNS, Robert Ignatius, 1921- , American; nonfiction CON

'BURNS, Sheila' see BLOOM, Ursula

'BURNS, Tex' see L'AMOUR, Louis D.

BURNS, Tom, 1913- , English; nonfiction CON

BURNS, Wayne, 1918- , American; nonfiction CON

BURNS, William A., 1909- , American; nonfiction CON

BURNS, Zed Houston, 1903- , American; nonfiction CON

BURNSHAW, Stanley, 1906- , American; poetry, fiction CON MUR

BUROW, Daniel Robert, 1931- , American; nonfiction CON

BURR, Alfred Gray, 1919- , American; poetry CON

BURR, Anna Robeson Brown, 1872-1941, American; essays, fiction, nonfiction KT

BURR, Anne, 1937- , American; plays CON

BURR, Wesley Ray, 1936- , American; nonfiction CON

BURRELL, Berkeley G., 1919- , American; nonfiction CON

BURRELL, David Bakewell, 1933- , American; nonfiction CON

BURRELL, Martin, 1858-1938, Canadian; essays SY

BURRELL, Orin Kay, 1899-1964, America; nonfiction PAC

BURRELL, Roy E.C., 1923- , English; juveniles CON

BURRIEL, Andrés Marcos, 1719-62, Spanish; nonfiction SA

BURRIN, Frank K., 1920- , American; nonfiction CON

BURRIS, B. Cullen, 1924- , American; nonfiction CON

BURRITT, Elihu, 1810-79, American; nonfiction KAA

BURROUGHS, Edgar Rice, 1875-1950, American; fiction BRO KT RIC SA

BURROUGHS, John, 1837-1921, American; essays BRO KAA

BURROUGHS, Margaret Taylor, 1917- , American; juveniles CON

BURROUGHS, Polly, 1925- , American; juveniles COM CON

BURROUGHS, William Seward ('Mr. Bradly'; 'William Lee'; 'Mr. Martin'), 1914- , American; fiction CON RIC

BURROW, James Gordon, 1922- , American; nonfiction CON

BURROW, John Wyon, 1935- , English; nonfiction CON

BURROWAY, Janet Gay, 1936- , American; fiction CON

BURROWS, Abe, 1910- , American; plays MAT

BURROWS, Rev. Eric Norman

Bromley, 1882-1938, English;
nonfiction HO
BURROWS, James C., 1944- ,
Argentinian; nonfiction CON
BURROWS, Miles James, 1936- ,
British; poetry CON MUR
BURRUP, Percy E., 1910- ,
American; nonfiction CON
BURSAY, L. -1802, French; plays
DIL
BURSK, Edward Collins, 1907- ,
American; nonfiction CON
BURSTYN, Harold Lewis, 1930- ,
American; nonfiction CON
BURT, Alfred LeRoy, 1888- ,
Canadian; nonfiction CON
BURT, Alvin Victor, Jr., 1927- ,
American; nonfiction CON
BURT, Cyril Lodowic, 1883-1971,
English; nonfiction CON
BURT, Jesse Clifton, 1921- ,
American; nonfiction CON
BURT, John J., 1934- , American;
nonfiction CON
BURT, Katharine Newlin, 1882- ,
American; fiction JO KT WAF
BURT, Maxwell Struthers, 1882-
1954, American; fiction, poetry,
plays JO KL KT WAF
BURT, Michael, 1900- , English;
fiction, radio, criticism HOE
BURT, Nathaniel, 1913- , American;
juveniles CON WA
BURT, Olive Woolley, 1894- ,
American; nonfiction, juveniles,
fiction CON WA
BURT, Samuel Mathew, 1915- ,
American; nonfiction CON
BURTCHAELL, James Tunstead,
1934- , American; nonfiction
CON
'BURTE Hermann' (Hermann Strübe),
1879-1960, German; plays, fic-
tion, poetry COL KU MAT SA
BURTIN, Paul Denis, 1694-1755,
French; nonfiction DIL
BURTNESS, Paul Sidney, 1923- ,
American; nonfiction CON
'BURTON, Alfred' see MITFORD,
John
BURTON, Arthur, 1914- , Ameri-
can; nonfiction CON
BURTON, Carl D., 1913- , Amer-
ican; nonfiction CON
BURTON, Charles Pierce, 1862-
1947, American; juveniles HOO
BURTON, Dolores Marie, 1932- ,

American; nonfiction CON
BURTON, Doris, English; nonfic-
tion HO
BURTON, Edward J. ('Michael
Carey'), 1917- , American;
fiction CON
BURTON, Elizabeth, English;
juveniles WA
BURTON, Genevieve, 1912- ,
American; nonfiction CON
BURTON, Hester Wood-Hill,
1913- , English; nonfiction,
juveniles CON DOY
BURTON, Ian, 1935- , English;
nonfiction CON
BURTON, John Hill, 1809-81,
Scots; nonfiction BRO KBA
ST
BURTON, Katherine Kurz, 1884/
90- , American; nonfiction,
juveniles HOE WA
BURTON, Lindy, 1937- , English;
nonfiction CON
BURTON, Philip, 1904- , Welsh;
nonfiction CON
BURTON, Sir Richard Francis,
1821-90, English; translations,
nonfiction BRO KBA ST
BURTON, Robert, 1577-1640,
English; essays, nonfiction
BRO KB MAG ST
BURTON, Robert Henderson,
1939- , American; nonfiction
CON
'BURTON, Thomas' see LONG-
STREET, Stephen
BURTON, Virginia Lee, 1909-68,
American; juveniles COM
CON KJU WA
BURTON, William Evans, 1804-60,
American; nonfiction, plays
KAA
BURTON, William Henry, 1890-
1964, American; nonfiction,
juveniles CON
BURTON, William Lester, 1928- ,
American; nonfiction CON
BURTSCHI, Mary, 1911- , Amer-
ican; nonfiction CON
BURTT, Edwin A., 1892- , Amer-
ican; nonfiction CON
BURTT, Everett Johnson, Jr.,
1914- , American; nonfiction
CON
BURTT, Harold Ernest, 1890- ,
American; nonfiction CON
BURY, Lady Charlotte Susan Maria,

1775-1861, English; diary, fiction,
poetry BRO KBA
'BURY, Jan' see WASYLEWSKI, S.
BURY, John Bagnell, 1861-1927,
Irish; nonfiction BRO KT SA
BURY, John Patrick Tuer, 1908- ,
English; nonfiction CON
BURY, Richard de see AUNGER-
VILLE, Richard
BUS, Gervais de, fl. 1310-39,
French; poetry HAR ST
BUSBY, Edith, American; juveniles
WA
BUSCH, Briton Cooper, 1936- ,
American; nonfiction CON
BUSCH, Francis X., 1879- ,
American; nonfiction CON
BUSCH, Frederick, 1941- , Amer-
ican; fiction CON
BUSCH, Niven, 1903- , American;
fiction CON KTS WAF
BUSCH, Wilhelm, 1832-1908, Ger-
man; poetry AL COL HAR KE
SA ST
BUSCHE, Hermann von dem, 1468-
1534, German; nonfiction ST
BUSEY, James L., 1916- , Ameri-
can; nonfiction CON
BUSH, Clifford Lewis, 1915- ,
American; nonfiction CON
BUSH, Douglas, 1896- , Canadian;
nonfiction SY
BUSH, George Pollock, 1892- ,
American; nonfiction CON
BUSH, John Nash Douglas, 1896- ,
Canadian-American; nonfiction
CON KTS
BUSH, John William, 1917- ,
American; nonfiction CON
BUSH, Martin Harry, 1930- ,
American; nonfiction CON
BUSH, Ted J., 1922- , American;
nonfiction CON
BUSH, William Shirley, Jr., 1929- ,
American; nonfiction CON
BUSHAQ ABU Ishaq i At'ameh,
Ahmed,   -1724/27, Persian;
poetry ST
BUSH-BROWN, James, 1892- ,
American; nonfiction CON
BUSH-BROWN, Louise, American;
juveniles WA
BUSHELL, Raymond, 1910- , Amer-
ican; nonfiction CON
BUSHMAN, Richard Lyman, 1931- ,
American; nonfiction CON
BUSHMILLER, Ernest Paul, 1905- ,

American; nonfiction CON
BUSHNELL, Adelyn, 1894- ,
American; fiction WAF
BUSHRUI, Suheil Badi, 1929- ,
Jordanian; nonfiction CON
BUSIRI, 1213-96, Arab; poetry
ST
BUSKE, Morris Roger, 1912- ,
American; nonfiction CON
BUSKEN HUET, Coenraad see
HUET, Coenraad B.
BUSKIRK, Richard Hobart,
1927- , American; nonfiction
CON
BUSLAYEV, Tëodr Ivanovich,
1818-97, Russian; nonfiction
ST
'BUSON' (Taniguchi Tora; 'Yosa
Buson'), 1716-84, Japanese;
poetry ST
BUSONI, Rafaello, 1900- ,
Italian-American; juveniles
KJU WA
BUSS, Arnold, H., 1924- , Amer-
ican; nonfiction CON
BUSS, Martin John, 1930- ,
American; nonfiction CON
BUSSARD, Paul, 1904- , Ameri-
can; nonfiction HOE
BUSSCHE, Henri Omer Antoine
Van den, 1920- , Belgian;
nonfiction CON
BUSSE, Carl, 1872-1918, German;
fiction, criticism, poetry COL
SA
BUSSIERES, Arthur de, 1877-1913,
Canadian; nonfiction SY
BUSSY-RABUTIN, Roger de Rabutin,
1618-193, French; nonfiction
HAR DIF
'BUSTA, Christine' (Christine Dimt),
1915- , Austrian; poetry FLE
KU
BUSTAMANTE, Agustin Jose,
1938- , Mexican; nonfiction
CON
BUSTAMANTE, Antonio Sánchez
de, 1865-1951, Cuban; essays
MIN
BUSTAMANTE, Calixto Carlos
('Concolorcovo'; 'Alonso Carrio
de la Vandera'), 18th cent.,
Peruvian; nonfiction BL SA ST
BUSTAMANTE, Carlos, 1774-1848,
Mexican; nonfiction SA
BUSTAMANTE, José Luis, 1857- ,
Argentinian; journalism MIN

BUSTAMANTE, Jose Rafael, 1881-
1961, Ecuadorian; essays, fiction
DI
BUSTAMANTE, Ricardo José, 1821-
84, Bolivian; fiction, poetry
MIN SA
BUSTILLO, Eduardo, 1836-1900,
Spanish; poetry, plays, journalism
SA
BUSTILLO, Ignacio Prudencio, 20th
cent., Bolivian; poetry, criticism
SA
BU-STON, 1290-1364, Tibetan; non-
fiction LAN
BUSTOS DOMECQ, Honorio see
BIOY CASARES, Adolfo ‾‾
BUSWELL James Oliver, Jr.,
1895- , American; nonfiction
CON
BUTCHER, Charles Philip, 1918- ,
American; nonfiction CON
BUTCHER, Harold John, 1920- ,
English; nonfiction CON
BUTCHER, James Neal, 1933- ,
American; nonfiction CON
BUTCHER, Grace, 1934- , Ameri-
can; nonfiction CON
BUTCHER, Samuel Henry, 1850-
1910, Irish; nonfiction KBA
BUTCHER, Thomas Kennedy, 1914- ,
English; nonfiction CON
BUTCHVAROV, Panayot K., 1933- ,
Bulgarian-American; nonfiction
CON
BUTEL DUMONT, Georges Marie,
1725-88, French; nonfiction DIL
BUTERA, Mary C., 1925- , Amer-
ican; nonfiction CON
BUTKOV, Yakov Petrovich, 1815-
56, Russian; fiction HARK ST
BUTLAND, Gilbert James, 1910- ,
English; nonfiction CON
BUTLER, Albert, 1923- , American;
fiction CON
BUTLER, Annie Louise, 1920- ,
American; nonfiction CON
BUTLER, Arthur D., 1923- , Amer-
ican; nonfiction CON
BUTLER, Arthur John, 1844-1910,
English; nonfiction KBA
BUTLER, Basil Christopher, 1902- ,
English; nonfiction CON
BUTLER, Beverly Kathleen, 1923/
32- , American; fiction, juveniles
CON WA
BUTLER, Bill see BUTLER, Ernest
A.

BUTLER, Charles Edward, 1909- ,
American; nonfiction, fiction
HO
BUTLER, Charles Henry, 1894- ,
American; nonfiction CON
BUTLER, David Edgeworth,
1924- , English; nonfiction
CON
BUTLER, Edward Cuthbert, 1858-
1934, Irish; nonfiction HOE
BUTLER, Edward Harry, 1913- ,
English; nonfiction CON
BUTLER, Eliza Marian, 1885- ,
British; nonfiction KTS
BUTLER, Ellis Parker, 1869-
1937, American; fiction KAT
KT
BUTLER, Erica Bracher, 1905- ,
American; nonfiction CON
BUTLER, Ernest Alton (Bill),
1926- , American; nonfiction
CON
BUTLER, Francelia McWilliams,
1913- , American; nonfiction
CON
BUTLER, Frances Anne see KEM-
BLE, Frances A.
BUTLER, Frederick Guy, 1918- ,
South African; poetry, plays,
criticism MUR
BUTLER, George D., 1893- ,
American; nonfiction CON
BUTLER, George Paul, 1900- ,
American; nonfiction CON
BUTLER, Gwendoline Williams,
1922- , English; fiction CON
BUTLER, Gwy, 1918- , South
African; plays, poetry, criti-
cism RIC
BUTLER, Hal, American; juveniles
WA
BUTLER, Iris, 1905- , English;
nonfiction CON
BUTLER, J. Donald, 1908- ,
American; nonfiction CON
BUTLER, James, 1904- , English;
nonfiction CON
BUTLER, James Ramsay Montagu,
1889- , English; nonfiction
CON
BUTLER, Jean Campbell Mac-
Laurin, 1918- , Canadian;
nonfiction CON
BUTLER, John Alfred Valentine,
1899- , English; nonfiction
CON
BUTLER, Joseph, 1692-1752,

English; nonfiction BRO KB ST
BUTLER, Joseph Thomas, 1932- ,
American; nonfiction CON
BUTLER, Josephine Grey de, 1830-
1906, English; nonfiction SA
BUTLER, Mildred Allen, 1897- ,
American; juveniles CON PAC
BUTLER, Patrick Trevor, 1929- ,
English; nonfiction CON
BUTLER, Samuel, 1612-80, English;
poetry, nonfiction BRO KB MAG
SA SP ST
BUTLER, Samuel, 1835-1902, Eng-
lish; fiction, essays, translations,
nonfiction BRO KBA MAG SA ST
BUTLER, Walter Ernest, 1898- ,
English; nonfiction CON
BUTLER, William Allen, 1825-1902,
American; nonfiction KAA
BUTLER, William Elliott II, 1939- ,
American; nonfiction CON
BUTLER, Sir William Francis,
1838-1910, Irish; nonfiction KBA
BUTLIN, Martin Richard Fletcher,
1929- , English; nonfiction
CON
BUTOR, Michel, 1926- , French;
fiction, essays CON DIC DIF
FLE HAR PIN RIC
BUTOW, Robert J. C., 1924- ,
American; nonfiction CON
BUTTER, Peter Herbert, 1921- ,
Scots; nonfiction CON
BUTTERFIELD, Herbert, 1900- ,
English; nonfiction CON KTS
BUTTERFIELD, Roger, 1907- ,
American; nonfiction CON
BUTTERS, Dorothy Gilman, 1923- ,
American; fiction, juveniles
CON WA
BUTTERWORTH, Frank Edward, Jr.,
1917- , American; nonfiction
CON
BUTTERWORTH, Hezekiah, 1839-
1905, American; journalism,
juveniles KAA
BUTTERWORTH, Michael, 1924- ,
English; fiction CON
BUTTERWORTH, Oliver, 1915- ,
American; juveniles COM CON
BUTTERWORTH, William Edmund,
III ('Webb Beech'; 'Walker E.
Blake'; 'Edmund O. Scholefield'),
1929- , American; fiction, non-
fiction CON
BUTTET, Marc Claude de, 1530-86,
French; poetry HAR SA ST

BUTTI, Enrico Annibale, 1863-
1912, Italian; plays, fiction,
poetry, criticism COL HAR
SA ST
BUTTIMER, Anne ('Sister Mary
Annette'), 1938- , Irish-
American; nonfiction CON
BUTTINGER, Joseph, 1906- ,
Austrian-American; nonfiction
CON
'BUTTLE, Myra' see PURCELL,
Victor
BUTTON, Dick, 1929- , Ameri-
can; nonfiction CON
BUTTRESS, Frederick Arthur,
1908- , English; nonfiction
CON
BUTTRESS, Noëlene E. B. see
BARRY, Noëlene E.
BUTTS, David P., 1932- ,
American; nonfiction CON
BUTTS, R. Freeman, 1910- ,
American; nonfiction CON
BUTZ, Caspar, 1825-85, German-
American; poetry ST
BUTZER, Karl Wilhelm, 1934- ,
German-Canadian; nonfiction
CON
BUXBAUM, Edith, 1902- ,
Austrian-American; nonfiction
CON
BUXBAUM, Martin ('Martin Noll'),
1913- , American; poetry
CON
BUXTON, Edward John Mawby,
1912- , English; nonfiction
CON
BUYANNEMEKH, S., 1902-37,
Mongolian; poetry LAN
BUYSERO, Dirck, 1644-1707/08,
Dutch; poetry ST
BUYSSE, Cyriel, 1859-1932,
Flemish; fiction, plays, criti-
cism COL FLE MAT SA ST
BUZOT, François Leónard Nicolas,
1760-93, French; nonfiction
DIL
'BUZZATI, Dino' (Dino Buzzati
Traverso), 1906-72, Italian;
fiction FLE RIC ST
BUZZOTTA, V. Ralph, 1931- ,
American; nonfiction CON
'BY, Carl Larsson i' see LARS-
SON, Carl F.
BYARS, Betsy, 1928- , American;
nonfiction, juveniles CON WA
BYATT, Antonia Susan Drabble,

1936- , English; fiction CON
BYE, Raymond Taylor, 1892- ,
American; nonfiction CON
BYERLY, Kenneth Rhodes, 1908- ,
American; nonfiction CON
BYERS, Amy Irene, 1906- , Eng-
lish; poetry, fiction, juveniles
CON
BYERS, Andrew L., 1869- , Amer-
ican; nonfiction HOO
BYERS, Edward E., 1921- , Amer-
ican; nonfiction CON
BYFIELD, Barbara Ninde, 1930- ,
American; nonfiction CON
BYHAM, William C., 1936- ,
American; nonfiction CON
BYLES, Mather, 1706/07-88, Amer-
ican; poetry KAA
BYNNER, Witter ('Edmund Morgan'),
1881-1968, American; poetry,
plays CON KL KT SP ST
BYNUM, David Eliab, 1936- ,
American; nonfiction CON
BYNS, Anna van, 14th cent., Ger-
man; poetry SA
BYRD, Cecil Kash, 1913- , Amer-
ican; nonfiction CON
BYRD, Elizabeth, 1912- , Ameri-
can; fiction CON
BYRD, Richard Evelyn, 1888-1957,
American; nonfiction KT
BYRD, Sam, American; fiction JO
BYRD, William, 1538?-1623, Eng-
lish; songs KB
BYRD, William, 1674-1744, Ameri-
can; nonfiction, diary BRO KAA
ST
BYRNE, Bonifacio, 1861-1936/37,
Cuban; journalism MIN
BYRNE, Donn (Brian Oswald Donn-
Byrne), 1889-1928, Irish-Amer-
ican; fiction BRO CON KAT KT
MAG RIC ST
BYRNE, Edmund Francis, 1933- ,
American; nonfiction CON
BYRNE, Edward M., 1935- ,
American; nonfiction CON
BYRNE, Frank Loyola, 1928- ,
American; nonfiction CON
BYRNE, Herbert Winston, 1917- ,
American; nonfiction CON
BYRNE, Muriel St. Clare, 1895- ,
English; nonfiction CON
'BYRNE, Ralph' see BURNS, Ralph
J.
BYRNE, Richard Hill, 1915- ,
American; nonfiction CON

BYRNES, Robert F., 1917- ,
American; nonfiction CON
BYRNES, Thomas Edmund, 1911- ,
American; nonfiction, plays
CON
'BYROM, James' see BRAMWELL,
James G.
BYROM, John, 1692-1763, English;
poetry, diary BRO KB
BYROM, Robert Michael, 1925- ,
English; nonfiction CON
BYRON, Lord (George Gordon
Noel Byron), 1788-1824, Eng-
lish; poetry BRO KBA MAG
SA SP ST
BYRON, Gilbert, 1903- , Amer-
ican; nonfiction CON
BYRON, Henry James, 1834-84,
English; plays BRO KBA
'BYRON, John' see ARMSTRONG,
John B.
BYRON, Robert, 1905-41, English;
nonfiction BRO
BYWATER, Ingram, 1840-1914,
English; nonfiction KBA

'C.E.E.' see CRUICKSHANK,
Helen B.
CABA LANDA, Carlos, 1899- ,
Spanish; nonfiction, fiction
SA
CABA LANDA, Pedro, 1903- ,
Spanish; essays, fiction,
criticism BL SA
CABAL, Constantino, 1885?- ,
Spanish; journalism, plays
SA
CABALLERO, Ann Mallory,
1928- , American; fiction
CON
CABALLERO, Fermín, 1800-76,
Spanish; nonfiction, journalism
BL
'CABALLERO, Fernán' (Cecilia
Böhl de Faber), 1796-1877,
Spanish; fiction BL HAR KE
SA ST
CABALLERO, José Agustín,
1762-1835, Cuban; nonfiction
MIN
CABALLERO, José della Luz,
1800-62, Cuban; nonfiction
MIN SA
CABALLERO, Manuel María,
1819-66, Bolivian; fiction MIN
'CABALLERO AUDAZ, El' see

CARRETERO NOVILLO, José
M.
CABALLERO BONALD, José Manuel,
1926- , Spanish; poetry, fiction
BL
CABALLERO CALDERON, Eduardo,
1910/11- , Colombian; journal-
ism, fiction, essays MIN
CABALLERO y MORGAY, Fermín,
1800-76, Spanish; nonfiction SA
CABAÑAS, Pablo, 1923- , Spanish;
nonfiction BL SA
CABANELLAS, Ramón, 1885-1954?,
Spanish; poetry SA
CABAÑERO, Eladio, 1930- , Spanish;
poetry SA
CABANES, Jean de, 1653-1717,
French; poetry DIL
CABANIS, José, 1922- , French;
fiction, essays DIC
CABANIS, Pierre Jean Georges,
1757-1808, French; nonfiction
DIF DIL SA
CABANISS, J. Allen, 1911- ,
American; nonfiction CON
CABANYES, Manuel de, 1808-38,
Spanish; poetry BL SA
CABARET d'ORVILLE, Jean, 15th
cent., French; nonfiction ST
CABEEN, David Clark, 1886- ,
American; nonfiction CON
CABELL, James Branch, 1879-1958,
American; fiction, essays BRO
FLE KL KT MAG RIC SA ST WAF
CABET, Etienne, 1788-1856, Amer-
ican; nonfiction HOO
CABEZA de VACA see NUÑEZ
CABEZA de VACA, Alvar
CABEZAS CANTELI, Juan Antonio,
1900- , Spanish; fiction SA
CABESTANY, Guillaume, 1212- ,
French; poetry SA
CABEZAS, Juan Antonio, 1900- ,
Spanish; journalism BL
CABLE, George Washington, 1844-
1925, American; fiction, nonfic-
tion BRO KAA MAG SA ST
CABLE, Mary, 1920- , American;
nonfiction CON
CABOT, Robert Moors, 1924- ,
American; fiction CON
CABRAL, Manuel del, 1907- ,
Spanish; poetry MIN SA
CABRAL, Olga, 1909- , English;
juveniles, poetry CON
CABRERA, Fray Alonso de, 1549?-
98, Spanish; nonfiction BL SA
ST

CABRERA, Juan ('Jacobo Danke'),
1905- , Chilian; poetry, fic-
tion MIN
CABRERA, Raimundo, 1852-1923,
Cuban; nonfiction MIN
CABRERA, Ramón, 1754-1833,
Spanish; nonfiction BL SA
CABRERA de CORDOBA, Luis,
1559-1623, Spanish; nonfiction
BL SA ST
CABRERA GUERRA, Marcial,
Chilian; fiction MIN
CABRISAS, Hilarión, 1883-1939,
Cuban; poetry MIN
CABRISSEAU, Nicolas, 1680-1750,
French; nonfiction DIL
CABROL, Fernand, 1855-1937,
French; nonfiction HOE
CACCIA-DOMINIONI, Paolo,
1896- , Italian; nonfiction
CON
CACCIATORE, Vera Signorelli,
1911- , Italian-American;
fiction CON
CACELLA, Rev. Joseph, 1882- ,
Portuguese; nonfiction HO
CACERES, Esther, 1910- ,
Uruguayan; poetry SA
CACERES y ESPINOSA, Pedro de,
1540?-1600?, Spanish; poetry
SA
CACHIA, Pierre J.E., 1921- ,
English; nonfiction CON
CADALSO, José see 'VALLE,
Juan del'
CADALSO y VAZQUEZ, José,
de, 1741-82, Spanish; poetry,
plays, fiction BL HAR KE
SA ST
CADBURY, Henry Joel, 1883- ,
American; nonfiction CON
CADELLA, Carmen Alicia, 1908- ,
Puerto Rican; poetry SA
CADELLA de MARTINEZ, María,
1886-1951, Puerto Rican; non-
fiction, poetry SA
CADENAS, José Juan, 1872-1947,
Spanish; poetry, plays SA
CADERAS, Gian Fadri, 1830-91,
Raeto-Romansch; poetry ST
CADIZ, Fray Diego José de, 1743-
1801, Spanish; nonfiction BL
SA
CADLE, Dean, 1920- , American;
nonfiction CON
CADMUN, 7th cent., English;
poetry SA
'CADMUS' see ZACHOS, John C.

CADMUS of MILETO, 540 B.C.,
Greek; nonfiction SA
CADOU, René Guy, 1920-51, French;
poetry DIC DIF SA
CADRY, Jean Baptiste, 1680-1756,
French; nonfiction DIL
CADWALLADER, Clyde Thomas,
1898- , American; nonfiction
CON
CADY, Edwin Harrison, 1917- ,
American; nonfiction CON
CADY, John Frank, 1901- , Amer-
ican; nonfiction CON
CAECILLIUS, Quintus Caecilius
Statius, 220-168 B.C., Roman;
plays ST
CAEDMON (Cedmon), -1680?,
English; poetry, hymns BRO
KB ST
CAEDMON, Father see WAHL,
Caedmon T.
CAEFER, Raymond John, 1926- ,
American; nonfiction CON
CAEMMERER, Richard Rudolph,
1904- , American; nonfiction
CON
CAEN, Herb Eugene, 1916- ,
American; nonfiction CON
CAESAR, Eugene Lee ('Johnny
Laredo'; 'Anthony Sterling'),
1927- , American; fiction
CON
CAESAR, Gaius Julius, 102/100-44
B.C., Roman; nonfiction MAG
SA ST
CAESAR, Gene, 1927- , American;
nonfiction HIL
CAESARIUS von HEISTERBACH,
1180-1240, German; nonfiction
ST
CAFFARO, Paulus, 1080-1164, Italian;
nonfiction SA
CAFFIAUX, Philippe, 1712-77, French;
nonfiction DIL
CAFFREY, John Gordon, 1922- ,
American; nonfiction CON
CAFFREY, Nancy, American; juven-
iles WA
CAGAN, Phillip David, 1927- ,
American; nonfiction CON
CAGE, John Milton, Jr., 1912- ,
American; nonfiction CON
'CAGNEY, Peter' see WINTER,
Bevis
CAHALANE, Victor Harrison, 1901- ,
American; nonfiction CON
CAHAN, Abraham, 1860-1951, Rus-

sian-American; fiction KT
CAHEN, Alfred B., 1932- ,
American; poetry CON
CAHID SIDKI Taranci, 1911- ,
Turkish; poetry ST
CAHILL, Audrey Fawcett, 1929- ,
South African; nonfiction CON
CAHILL, Holger, 1893- , Amer-
ican; fiction WAF
CAHILL, James Francis, 1926- ,
American; nonfiction CON
CAHILL, Jane Miller, 1901- ,
American; nonfiction CON
CAHILL, Robert S., 1933- ,
American; nonfiction CON
CAHILL, Susan Neunzig, 1940- ,
American; nonfiction CON
CAHN, Edgar S., 1935- , Amer-
ican; nonfiction CON
CAHN, Steven M., 1942- ,
American; nonfiction CON
CAHN, William, 1912- , Ameri-
can; nonfiction CON
CAHN, Zvi ('Harry C. Laurie'),
1896- , Polish-American;
nonfiction CON
CAHUZAC, Louis de, 1706-59,
French; plays DIL
CAIADO, Henrique (Cayado),
-1508?, Portuguese;
poetry ST
CAICEDO ROJAS, José, 1816-97/
98, Colombian; journalism,
poetry MIN SA
CAIDEN, Gerald Elliot, 1936- ,
English; nonfiction CON
CAIDIN, Martin, 1927- , Amer-
ican; nonfiction, fiction CON
CAIGER-SMITH, Alan, 1930- ,
English; nonfiction CON
CAIGNIEZ, Louis Charles, 1762-
1842, French; plays DIF ST
CAILHAVA de L'ESTANDOUX,
Jean François, 1731-1813,
French; plays DIL
CAILLAVET, Gaston Arman de,
1869-1915, French; journalism,
plays COL DIF HAR ST
CAILLEAU, André Charles, 1731-
98, French; plays DIL
CAILLET, Joseph, fl. 1707,
French; nonfiction DIL
CAILLET-BOIS, Julio, 1910- ,
Argentinian; criticism SA
CAILLEUX, Roland, 1908- ,
French; fiction DIC
CAILLIEU, Colijn, -1484?,

Dutch; poetry ST
CAILLOIS, Roger, 1913- , French;
  essays, criticism CON DIC DIF
  FLE
CAIN, Arthur Homer ('Arthur King'),
  1913- , American; fiction CON
'CAIN, Christopher' see FLEMING,
  Thomas J.
CAIN, Glen G., 1933- , American;
  nonfiction CON
CAIN, James Mallahan, 1892- ,
  American; fiction CON KT RIC
  WAF
'CAINE, Mark' see RAPHAEL,
  Frederic M.
CAINE, Sydney, 1902- , English;
  nonfiction CON
CAINE, Sir Thomas Henry Hall,
  1853-1931, English; fiction,
  plays BRO KAT KT RIC ST
CAIRD, Edward, 1835-1908, Scots;
  nonfiction BRO KBA ST
CAIRD, John, 1820-98, Scots; non-
  fiction BRO KBA
CAIRD, Mona Hector, 1858-1932,
  English; fiction KBA
CAIRNES, John Elliot, 1823-75,
  Irish; nonfiction KBA
CAIRNS, Earle Edwin, 1910- ,
  American; nonfiction CON
CAIRNS, Grace Edith, 1907- ,
  American; nonfiction CON
CAIRNS, John Campbell, 1924- ,
  Canadian; nonfiction CON
CAIRNS, Thomas William, 1931- ,
  American; nonfiction CON
CAIRNS, Trevor, 1922- , English;
  nonfiction CON
'CAIRO, Jon' see ROMANO, Deane
  L.
'CAISSA' see FRAENKEL, Heinrich
CAITANYA, 1486-1533, Indian; non-
  fiction LAN
CAJADE, Ramón, 1914- , Spanish;
  fiction SA
ĆAJAK, Ján, 1863-1943, Slovak;
  fiction ST
CAJAL, Rosa María, 1920- ,
  Spanish; fiction, journalism BL
  SA
CAJAL, Santiago R. see RAMON y
  CAJAL, Santiago
CAJANDER, Paavo Eemil, 1843-1913,
  Finnish; poetry SA
CAJETAN, Maria (Cajetanus), 1658?-
  1746, Italian; nonfiction SA
CAJOT, Charles, 1731- , French;

nonfiction DIL
CAJOT, Joseph, 1726-79, French;
  nonfiction DIL
CALABRESE, Hayyim Vital see
  VITAL, Hayyim
CALAGES, Marie Pech, 17th cent.,
  French; poetry SA
CALAMARI, John Daniel, 1921- ,
  American; nonfiction CON
CALAME, Romain, 17th cent.,
  French; nonfiction DIL
CALAMY, Edmund (Smectymnuus),
  1599-1666, English; nonfiction
  BRO ST
CALANCHA, Antonio de la, 1584-
  1654, Bolivian; nonfiction MIN
  SA
CALAVERA, Fernán Sánchez de
  (Talavera), 14th-15th cent.,
  Spanish; poetry BL SA ST
CALCAGNINI, Celio, 1479-1541,
  Italian; nonfiction ST
CALCAGNO, Francesco, 1827-
  1903, Cuban; nonfiction MIN
CALCAÑO, José, Antonio, 1827-
  97, Venezuelan; poetry ST
CALCAÑO, Julio, 1840-1918,
  Venezuelan; fiction, criticism
  SA
CALCAR, Elisa Carolina Ferdinanda
  van, 1822-1904, Dutch; fiction
  ST
CALDAS, Francisco José, 1770-
  1816, Colombian; nonfiction
  MIN ST
CALDAS BARBOSA, Domingo,
  1740-1800, Brazilian; poetry
  SA
CALDAS PEREIRA de SOUZA,
  Antonio, 1762-1814, Brazilian;
  poetry SA
CALDECOTT, Randolph, 1846-86,
  English; juveniles DOY KJU
CALDER, Angus, 1942- , English;
  nonfiction CON
CALDER, Nigel David Ritchie,
  1931- , American; nonfiction
  CON
CALDER, Peter Ritchie, 1906- ,
  Scots; nonfiction CON
CALDERA, Daniel (Calderón),
  1852-96, Chilean; plays MIN
CALDERON, Fernando, 1809-45,
  Mexican; poetry, fiction, plays
  BL SA
CALDERON, Serafín Estébanez
  ('El Solitario'), 1799-1867,

Spanish; nonfiction BL HAR KE SA ST

CALDERON de la BARCA, Pedro, 1600-81, Spanish; plays BL HAR KE MAG SA ST

CALDERWOOD, David, 1575-1650, Scots; nonfiction BRO ST

CALDERWOOD, James Dixon, 1917- , Anglo-American; nonfiction CON

CALDERWOOD, James Lee, 1930- , American; nonfiction CON

CALDWELL, Anne Marsh, 1791-1874, English; fiction KBA

CALDWELL, Charles Edson, 1909- , American; nonfiction CON

CALDWELL, Erskine, 1903- , American; fiction, nonfiction BRO CON FLE KAT KT MAG RIC SA ST WAF

CALDWELL, Gaylon Loray, 1920- , American; nonfiction CON

CALDWELL, Harry Boynton, 1935- , American; fiction CON

CALDWELL, Irene Smith, 1908- , American; nonfiction CON

CALDWELL, James Alexander Malcolm, 1931- , Scots; nonfiction CON

CALDWELL, John Cope, 1913- , American; juveniles CON WA

CALDWELL, Joseph Herman, 1934- , American; nonfiction CON

CALDWELL, Lynton Keith, 1913- , American; nonfiction CON

CALDWELL, Oliver Johnson, 1904- , American; nonfiction CON

CALDWELL, Richard M., 1904- , American; nonfiction MAR

CALDWELL, Robert Graham, 1904- , American; nonfiction CON

CALDWELL, Taylor ('Max Reiner'), 1900- , English; fiction CON KT WAF

CALEF, Robert, 1648-1719, American; nonfiction KAA

CALEF, Wesley Carr, 1914- , American; nonfiction CON

CALENDRE (Cualendro), 13th cent., French; poetry SA

CALEPINO, Ambrosio (Calepio), 1440-1511, Italian; nonfiction SA ST

CALET, Henri, 1903-55, French; fiction DIF

'CALEY, Rod' see ROWLAND, Donald S.

CALFISCH, Arthur, 1893- , Raeto-Romansch; poetry ST

CALHOUN, Calfrey C., 1928- , American; nonfiction CON

CALHOUN, John Caldwell, 1782-1850, American; nonfiction KAA

CALHOUN, Mary Huiskamp, 1926- , American; poetry COM CON WA

CALHOUN, Richard James, 1926- , American; nonfiction CON

CALIAN, Carnegie Samuel, 1933- , American; nonfiction CON

'CALIBAN' see REID, John C.

CALIDASA see KALIDASA

CALIMACO, 310?-240 B.C., Greek; nonfiction SA

CALIN, William Compaine, 1936- , American; nonfiction CON

CALINICO (Sutorius), fl. 259-68, Arab; nonfiction SA

CALINO de EPHESUS, 8th cent. B.C., Greek; poetry SA

CALISHER, Hortense, 1911- , American; fiction CON RIC

CALISTENES, 380-28 B.C., Greek; nonfiction SA

CALITRI, Charles Joseph, 1916- , American; juveniles, fiction CON

CALITRI, Princene, American; plays CON

'CALKINS, Fay' see ALAILIMA, Fay C.

'CALKINS, Franklin' see STRATEMEYER, Edward L.

CALKINS, Norman Allison, 1822-95, American; nonfiction KAA

CALL, Alice Elizabeth La Plant, 1914- , American; nonfiction CON

CALL, Hughie Florence, 1890-1969, American; juveniles COM CON PAC

CALL, Wathen Mark Wilks, 1817-90, English; poetry KBA

CALLAERT, Vrancke, 14th cent., Dutch; translations ST

CALLAGHAN, Catherine A., 1931- , American; nonfiction CON

CALLAGHAN, Gertrude, American;

poetry HOE
CALLAGHAN, Morley, 1903- ,
    Canadian; fiction CON HOE KL
    KT RIC ST SY
CALLAHAN, Adalbert John, 1905- ,
    American; nonfiction HOE
CALLAHAN, Charles Clifford,
    1910- , American; nonfiction
    CON
CALLAHAN, Claire Wallis ('Ann
    Kilborn Cole'; 'Nancy Hartwell'),
    1890- , American; juveniles,
    fiction, nonfiction CON WA
CALLAHAN, Daniel, 1930- , Amer-
    ican; nonfiction CON
CALLAHAN, Dorothy, American;
    juveniles WA
CALLAHAN, John Francis, 1912- ,
    American; nonfiction CON
CALLAHAN, Nelson J., 1927- ,
    American; nonfiction CON
CALLAHAN, North, 1908- , Amer-
    ican; nonfiction CON
CALLAHAN, Sidney Cornelia, 1933- ,
    American; nonfiction CON
CALLAHAN, Sterling G., 1916- ,
    American; nonfiction CON
CALLAN, Charles Jerome, 1877- ,
    American; nonfiction HOE
CALLAN, Edward T., 1917- ,
    American; nonfiction CON
CALLANAN, James, 1795-1829,
    Irish; poetry ST
CALLARD, Maurice Frederick
    Thomas, 1912- , English;
    fiction CON
CALLARD, Thomas Henry ('Suther-
    land Ross'), 1912- , English;
    fiction CON
'CALLAS, Theo' see McCARTHY,
    Shaun
CALLCOTT, George Hardy, 1929- ,
    American; nonfiction CON
CALLE, Manuel J. (Ernesto Mora),
    1866-1918, Ecuadorian; fiction,
    nonfiction DI SA
CALLE ITURRINO, Esteban, 1892- ,
    Spanish; poetry SA
CALLEJA GUTIERREZ, Rafael,
    1888- , Spanish; nonfiction SA
CALLEJAS, Félix, 1878-1936, Cuban;
    nonfiction MIN
CALLEN, William B., 1930- ,
    American; nonfiction CON
'CALLENDER, Julian' see LEE,
    Austin
CALLENDER, Wesley Payne, Jr.,

1923- , American; nonfiction,
    juveniles CON
CALLEO, David Patrick, 1934- ,
    American; nonfiction CON
CALLIHAN, Elmer Lee, 1903- ,
    American; nonfiction CON
CALLIMACHUS, 305-240 B.C.,
    Greek; poetry ST
CALLINUS, 7th cent. B.C., Greek;
    poetry ST
CALLIS, Robert, 1920- , Ameri-
    can; nonfiction CON
CALLISON, Brian, 1934- , Eng-
    lish; nonfiction CON
CALLISTER, Frank, 1916- ,
    English; nonfiction CON
CALLOT, François Joseph, 1690-
    1773, French; nonfiction DIL
CALLOW, Alexander B., Jr.,
    1925- , American; nonfiction
    CON
CALLOW, Philip Kenneth, 1924- ,
    English; fiction CON
CALLOWAY, Doris Howes,
    1923- , American; nonfiction
    CON
CALLUM, Myles, 1934- , Amer-
    ican; nonfiction CON
CALMANN, John, 1935- , Ger-
    man-English; nonfiction CON
CALMET, Augustin, 1672-1757,
    French; nonfiction DIL SA
CALMO, Andrea, 1510-71, Italian;
    plays ST
CALNAN, Thomas Daniel, 1915- ,
    English; nonfiction CON
CALOGERO, Lorenzo, 1910-61,
    Italian; poetry FLE
CALOU, Juan Pedro, 1890-1923,
    Argentinian; journalism, poetry,
    plays MIN
CALPIN, Barthélemy see GALPIN,
    Barthélemy
CALPRENEDE, Gautier des Costes
    de la, 1614-63, French; fiction
    DIF HAR ST
CALPURNIO FLACO, Roman; non-
    fiction SA
CALPURNIUS SECULUS, Titus,
    fl. 50, Roman; poetry SA ST
CALSAMIGLIA, Eduardo, -1918,
    Costa Rican; poetry, plays
    MIN
CALVERLEY, Charles Stuart
    (Blayds), 1831-84, English;
    poetry, translations BRO KBA
    ST

CALVERT, Elinor H. ('Fen H. Lasell'), 1929- , German-American; juveniles CON WA

CALVERT, George Henry, 1803-89, American; essays KAA

CALVERT, James, American; juveniles WA

CALVERT, Laura D., 1922- , American; nonfiction CON

CALVERT, Maude Richman, 1892- , American; nonfiction MAR

CALVERT, Monte Alan, 1938- , American; nonfiction CON

CALVERT, Peter Anthony Richard, 1936- , American; nonfiction CON

CALVERT, Robert, Jr., 1922- , American; nonfiction CON

CALVERTON, Victor Francis ('George Goetz), 1900-40, American; criticism KT

CALVET, Augustín ('Gaziel'), 1887- , Spanish; essays, journalism SA

CALVETE de ESTRELLA, Juan Cristóbal, 1525?-93, Spanish; nonfiction BL SA

CALVIERE, Charles François, 1693-1777, French; fiction DIL

'CALVIN, Henry' see HANLEY, Clifford

CALVIN, Jean, 1509-64, French; nonfiction DIF HAR KE MAL SA ST

CALVINO, Italo, 1923- , Italian; fiction RIC

CALVO, C. Licinio, 82-47 B.C., Roman; poetry SA

CALVO, Daniel, 1832/35-80, Bolivian; journalism, poetry MIN

CALVO, Luis, 1900- , Spanish; journalism SA

CALVO ASENSO, Pedro, 1821-63, Spanish; plays BL SA

CALVO NAVA, Gloria, 1922- , Spanish; nonfiction SA

CALVO Serer, Rafael, 1916- , Spanish; essays BL SA

CALVO SOTELO, Joaquin, 1904/95- , Spanish; plays BL MAT SA

CALVO SOTELO, Leopoldo, 1894-1930?, Spanish; nonfiction SA

CALVO y ROSALES, Joaquín Bernardo, 1799-1965, Costa Rican; nonfiction MIN

CALVUS, Gaius Licinus Macer, 82-47 B.C., Roman; poetry ST

CALZABIGI, Ranieri de', 1714-95, Italian; poetry, criticism HAR ST

'CAM' see ACEVEDO GUERRA, Evaristo

CAM, Helen Maud, 1885- , English; nonfiction CON

CAMACHO, Diogo, 17th cent., Portuguese; poetry ST

CAMACHO, Pedro, 1679?-1743?, Spanish; poetry, plays SA

CAMACHO RAMIREZ, Arturo, 1909/10- , Colombian; poetry, plays MIN

CAMACHO ROLDAN, Salvador, 1827-1900, Colombian; nonfiction MIN

CÂMARA, João de, 1852-1908, Portuguese; plays, fiction COL SA

CAMARA, Juan R. see RODRIGUEZ de la CAMARA, Juan

CAMARGO, Rafael (Fermín de Pimental y Vargas), 1858-1926, Colombian; fiction MIN

CAMARILLO, María Enriqueta see 'MARIA ENRIQUETA'

CAMATHIAS, Flurin, 1871-1946, Raeto-Romansch; poetry ST

CAMBA, Francisco, 1882-1947, Spanish; fiction, journalism BL SA

CAMBA, Julio, 1882-1962, Spanish; nonfiction, fiction BL COL HAR SA ST

CAMBACERES, Etienne François, -1802, French; nonfiction DIL

CAMBACERES, Eugenio, 1843-88/90, Argentinian; fiction MIN SA ST

CAMBIS-VELLERON, Joseph Louis Dominique, 1766-72, French; nonfiction DIL

CAMBLAK, Grigorij, 1364- , Serbian; nonfiction ST

CAMBON, Glauco Gianlorenzo, 1921- , Italian-American; nonfiction CON

CAMBRIDGE, Ada, 1844-1926, English; fiction KBA

'CAMBRIDGE, Elizabeth' see HODGES, Barbara K. W.

CAMBRIDGE, Richard Owen, 1717-1802, English; poetry BRO

CAMBRONERO y MARTINEZ, Carlos, 1849-1913, Spanish;

nonfiction SA

CAMDEN, William, 1551-1623, English; nonfiction BRO KB SA ST

CAMERON, Allan William, 1930- , American; nonfiction CON

CAMERON, Donald Allan, 1937- , Canadian; nonfiction CON

CAMERON, Edna M., 1905- , American; nonfiction CON

CAMERON, Eleanor Butler, 1912- , Canadian-American; juveniles COM CON WA

CAMERON, Elizabeth see ROBINSON, Elizabeth

CAMERON, Elizabeth Jane ('Jane Duncan'), 1910- , Scots-American; fiction CON

CAMERON, Frank T., 1909- , American; nonfiction CON

CAMERON, George Frederick, 1854-85, Canadian; poetry SY

'CAMERON, Ian' see PAYNE, Donald G.

CAMERON, Jack Bruce, 1913- , American; fiction CON

CAMERON, James, 1911- , English; fiction, nonfiction CON

CAMERON, James Munro, 1910- , English; nonfiction CON

CAMERON, James Reese, 1929- , American; nonfiction CON

CAMERON, John, 1914- , Scots; nonfiction CON

CAMERON, Kenneth Neill ('Warren Madden'), 1908- , English; nonfiction CON

CAMERON, Kenneth Walter, 1908- , American; nonfiction CON

CAMERON, Lou ('L. J. Arnold'; 'Steve Cartier'; 'W. R. Marvin'), 1924- , American; fiction CON

CAMERON, Ludovick Charles Richard, 1866- , English; nonfiction HIG

CAMERON, Mary Owen, 1915- , American; nonfiction CON

CAMERON, Meribeth Elliott, 1905- , American; nonfiction CON

CAMERON, Norman, 1905-53, English; poetry, translations RIC SP

CAMERON, Polly, 1928- , American; juveniles COM CON WA

CAMERON, Rondo Emmett, 1925- , American; nonfiction CON

CAMERON, William Bruce, 1920- , American; nonfiction CON

'CAMILLO' see CASTELLO BRANCO, Camillo

'CAMILLUS' see AMES, Fisher

'CAMILO, Don' see CELA, Camilo J.

CAMIN, Alfonso, 1890- , Spanish; poetry, fiction, journalism BL SA

CAMINER-TURRA, Isabel, 1751-96, Italian; nonfiction SA

CAMINHA, Pedro de Andrade, 1520?-89, Portuguese; poetry SA ST

CAMINO, León Felipe ('León-Felipe'), 1884- , Spanish; poetry COL HAR SA ST

CAMINO, Miguel Andrés, 1877-1944, Argentinian; journalism, poetry, plays MIN SA

CAMINO NESSI, José, 1890- , Spanish; poetry SA

CAMM, Bede, 1864-1942, English; nonfiction HOE

CAMMACK, Floyd McKee, 1933- , American; nonfiction CON

CAMMAERTS, Emile León, 1878-1953, Belgian; poetry, plays, essays HAR KTS SA ST

CAMMANN, Schuyler van Rensselaer, 1912- , American; nonfiction CON

CAMMERMEYER WELHAVEN, Yan S., 1807-73, Norwegian; poetry, fiction SA

CAMO, Pierre, 1877- , French; poetry SA

CAMOËNS, Luis de (Camões), 1524-80?, Portuguese; poetry BL HAR KE MAG SA ST

CAMON AZNAR, José, 1899- , Spanish; nonfiction BL SA

CAMP, James, 1923- , American; nonfiction CON

CAMP, Thomas Edward, 1929- , American; nonfiction CON

CAMP, Walter, 1859-1925, American; juveniles KJU

CAMP, Wesley Douglass, 1915- , American; nonfiction CON

CAMPA, Arthur Leon, 1905- , Mexican-American; nonfiction CON

CAMPAIGNE, Jameson Gilbert, 1914- , American; nonfiction CON

CAMPANA, Dino, 1885-1932, Italian; poetry COL FLE SA

CAMPANELLA, Tommaso, 1568-1639, Italian; poetry, nonfiction HAR KE SA ST

CAMPANILE, Achille, 1900- , Italian; fiction COL SA

CAMPANO, Giannatonino, 1429-77, Italian; poetry ST

CAMPBELL, Alan K., 1923- , American; nonfiction CON

CAMPBELL, Alistair, 1907- , English; nonfiction CON

CAMPBELL, Alistair Te Ariki, 1925- , New Zealander; poetry MUR

CAMPBELL, Ann R., 1925- , American; nonfiction CON

CAMPBELL, Anne, American; poetry HIL

CAMPBELL, Archibald Bruce, 1881- , English; nonfiction CON

CAMPBELL, Arthur Andrews, 1924- , American; nonfiction CON

CAMPBELL, Bartley, 1843-88, American; plays KAA

'CAMPBELL, Beatrice M.' see MURPHY, Beatrice M.

CAMPBELL, Bernard Grant, 1930- , English; nonfiction CON

CAMPBELL, Blanche ('Julian Fish'), 1902- , American; nonfiction CON

'CAMPBELL, Bruce' see EPSTEIN, Samuel

CAMPBELL, Camilla, 1905- , American; nonfiction CON

CAMPBELL, Charles, 1807-76, American; nonfiction KAA

'CAMPBELL, Clive' see MacRAE, Donald G.

CAMPBELL, Colin Dearborn, 1917- , American; nonfiction CON

CAMPBELL, David, 1915- , Australian; poetry MUR

CAMPBELL, David Aitken, 1927- , Scots; nonfiction CON

CAMPBELL, David P., 1934- , American; nonfiction CON

'CAMPBELL, Donald' see GILFORD, Charles B.

CAMPBELL, Donald Guy, 1922- , American; nonfiction CON

CAMPBELL, Edward Fay, Jr., 1932- , American; nonfiction CON

CAMPBELL, Elizabeth A., American; juveniles WA

CAMPBELL, Elizabeth McClure,

1891- , American; nonfiction CON

CAMPBELL, Ernest Queener, 1926- , American; nonfiction CON

CAMPBELL, Eugene Edward, 1915- , American; nonfiction CON

'CAMPBELL, Francis Stuart' see KUEHNELT-LEDDIHN, Erik

CAMPBELL, George, Jamaican; poetry MUR

CAMPBELL, George, 1719-96, Scots; nonfiction BRO

CAMPBELL, George Douglas see ARGYLL, Duke of

CAMPBELL, Grace, 1895-1963, Canadian; fiction SY

CAMPBELL, Hannah ('Elizabeth Franklin'), American; nonfiction CON

CAMPBELL, Isabel Jones, 1895- , American; poetry MAR

CAMPBELL, Jack Kenagy, 1927- , American; nonfiction CON

CAMPBELL, James Dykes, 1838-95, Scots; nonfiction KBA

CAMPBELL, Lord John, 1779-1861, English; nonfiction BRO KBA ST

CAMPBELL, John Coert, 1911- , American; nonfiction CON

CAMPBELL, John Francis, 1822-85, Scots; essays, fiction, nonfiction BRO KBA

CAMPBELL, John Lorne ('Fear Chanaidh'), 1906- , Socts; nonfiction CON

CAMPBELL, John Ramsey, 1946- , English; fiction CON

CAMPBELL, John Wood ('Arthur McCann'; 'Don A. Stuart'; 'Karl Van Campen'), 1910-71, American; nonfiction CON

CAMPBELL, Joseph ('Ultach'), 1879-1944, Irish; poetry, plays BRO HOE ST

CAMPBELL, Joseph, 1904- , American; nonfiction CON KTS

'CAMPBELL, Judith' see PARES, Marion S.

CAMPBELL, Kareen Fleur see ADCOCK, Fleur

CAMPBELL, Lewis, 1830-1908, Scots; nonfiction BRO KBA

CAMPBELL, Litta Belle, 1886- , American; nonfiction, fiction CON

'CAMPBELL, Margaret' see LONG, Gabrielle M.

CAMPBELL, Marie, 1907- , American; fiction HOO

CAMPBELL, Patricia Piatt, 1901- , American; fiction CON PAC

CAMPBELL, Paul N., 1923- , American; nonfiction CON

CAMPBELL, Penelope, 1935- , American; nonfiction CON

CAMPBELL, Peter Anthony, 1935- , American; nonfiction CON

CAMPBELL, Peter Walter, 1926- , English; nonfiction CON

CAMPBELL, Robert Dale, 1914- , American; nonfiction CON

CAMPBELL, Robert Wellington, 1926- , American; nonfiction CON

CAMPBELL, Rosemae Wells ('R. W. Campbell'), 1909- , American; juveniles COM CON WA

CAMPBELL, Roy, 1901-57, South African; poetry BRO FLE HOE KAT KT RIC SA SP ST

CAMPBELL, Sam, 1895- , American; juveniles HOO

CAMPBELL, Thomas, 1777-1844, Scots; poetry, nonfiction BRO KBA SA ST

CAMPBELL, Thomas F. ('Cross-country'), 1924- , Irish; nonfiction CON

CAMPBELL, Walter Stanley ('Stanley Vestal'), 1887- , American; fiction, nonfiction KT MAR

CAMPBELL, Wanda Jay, American; juveniles WA

CAMPBELL, Wayne, American; nonfiction MAR

CAMPBELL, Wilfred, 1858-1918, Canadian; poetry SY

CAMPBELL, Will Davis ('David Brett'), 1924- , American; nonfiction CON

CAMPBELL, William Edward, 1875- , English; nonfiction HO

CAMPBELL, William Edward March ('William March') 1893-1954, American; fiction KTS

CAMPBELL, William Parker, 1843-1924, American; nonfiction MAR

CAMPBELL, William Wilfred, 1861-1918, Canadian; poetry BRO KBA ST

CAMPBELL-PURDIE, Wendy, 1925- , New Zealander; nonfiction CON

CAMPE, Joachim Heinrich, 1746-1818, German; poetry, fiction AL ST

CAMPENON, François Nicholus Vincent, 1772-1843, French; poetry SA

'CAMPER, Shirley' see SOMAN, Shirley

CAMPERO, Narciso, 1813/15-96, Bolivian; nonfiction MIN

CAMPHUYSEN, Dirk Rafaëlszoon, 1586-1627, Dutch; poetry KE ST

CAMPIGNEULLES, Charles Claude Florent, 1737-1809, French; nonfiction DIL

CAMPILLO y CORREA, Narciso, 1835-1900, Spanish; poetry, criticism BL SA

CAMPION, Nardi Reeder, 1917- , American; fiction, nonfiction CON WA

CAMPION, Sidney Rona ('Geoffrey Swayne'), 1891- , English; fiction CON

CAMPION, Thomas, 1567-1619, English; poetry BRO KB SA SP ST

CAMPION JAIMEBON, Arturo, 1834- , Spanish; nonfiction SA

CAMPISTRON, Jean Galbert, 1656?-1723?, French; plays DIF HAR SA ST

CAMPO, Angel de, 1868-1908, Mexican; fiction SA

CAMPO, Estanislao del, 1835-88, Argentinian; poetry BL MIN SA ST

'CAMPO, Flora del' see VERBEL, Eva

CAMPO-ALANGE, Condesa de, 1802- , Spanish; fiction, essays BL

CAMPOAMOR y CAMPOSORIO, Ramón, 1817-1901, Spanish; poetry, epigrams BL COL HAR KE SA ST

CAMPOMANES, Pedro Rodriguez, 1723-1803, Spanish; nonfiction BL SA

CAMPOS, Jorge, 1916- , Spanish; criticism, fiction BL SA

CAMPOS, Jose Antonio ('Jack the Ripper'), 1868-1939, Ecuadorian; nonfiction DI

CAMPOS CERVERA, Herib, 1900-

53, Paraguayan; poetry, criticism SA

CAMPOS MENENDEZ, Enrique,
Chilean; essays MIN

CAMPOS MONTIERO, Abilio Adriano
de, 1876-1933, Portuguese;
poetry, journalism SA

CAMPOY, Antonio Manuel, 1924- ,
Spanish; essays, fiction, criticism, journalism SA

CAMPRODON y LAFONT, Francisco,
1816-70, Spanish; poetry, plays
BL SA

CAMPS, François de, 1643-1723,
French; nonfiction DIL

CAMPTON, David, 1924- , English;
plays CON

CAMUS, Albert, 1913-60, French;
fiction, poetry, essays, plays
COL DIC DIF FLE HAR KTS
MAG MAL MAT PIN RIC SA ST

CAMUS, Jean Pierre, 1584-1652,
French; fiction HAR ST

CAMUSAT, Dionis François, 1695-
1732, French; nonfiction SA

CANADAY, John Edwin ('Matthew
Head'), 1907- , American; nonfiction CON

CANAL, José de la, 1768-1845,
Spanish; nonfiction SA

CANAL FEIJOO, Bernardo, 1897- ,
Argentinian; plays, essays, poetry
MIN SA

CANALES, Alfonso, 1923- , Spanish;
nonfiction BL

CANARY, Robert Hughes, 1939- ,
American; nonfiction CON

CANBY, Henry Seidel, 1878- ,
American; criticism KL KT

CANCELA, Arturo, 1892- , Argentinian; journalism, plays, fiction
MIN SA

CANCER y VELASCO, Jerónimo de,
1599?-1655, Spanish; poetry,
plays BL SA ST

CANCOI, Jesús, 1885-1961, Spanish;
poetry BL SA

CAND BARDA, 12th cent., Indian;
poetry LAN

CANDAMO, Francisco A. see BANCES
CANDAMO, Francisco

CANDEILLE, Juliette, French; nonfiction SA

CANDEL, Francisco, 1925- , Spanish;
fiction SA

CANDELARIA, Frederich Henry,
1929- , American; nonfiction
CON

'CANDIDA' see HOFFMAN, Lisa

CANDIDAS, 15th cent., Indian;
poetry LAN

'CANDIL, Fray' see BOBADILLA,
Emilio

CANDILIS, Wray O., 1927- ,
English; nonfiction CON

CANDLAND, Douglas Keith,
1934- , American; nonfiction
CON

'CANDY, Edward' see NEVILLE,
Barbara A.B.

CANDY, Robert, 1920- , American; juveniles WA

CANE, Luis, 1897- , Argentinian;
poetry MIN

CANE, Melville, 1879- , American; poetry, fiction CON

CANE, Miguel, 1812-63, Argentinian; journalism, fiction, poetry
MIN SA

CAÑE, Miguel, 1851-1905, Argentinian; nonfiction MIN SA ST

CANEDO REYES, Jorge, 20th cent.,
Bolivian; journalism, poetry
MIN SA

CANELAS, Demetrio, 1881- ,
Bolivian; journalism MIN

CANELLADA, María Josefa,
1913- , Spanish; nonfiction
essays BL

CANER, Mary Pual, 1893- ,
American; nonfiction CON

CAÑETE, Manuel, 1822-91,
Spanish; nonfiction BL SA

CANETTI, Elias, 1905- , German-
English; fiction, plays, essays
CON FLE KU RIC

CANFIELD, Delos Lincoln, 1903- ,
American; nonfiction CON

CANFIELD, Dorothy see FISHER,
Dorothea F.C.

CANFIELD, James Keith, 1925- ,
American; nonfiction CON

CANFIELD, John Alan, 1941- ,
American; nonfiction CON

CANFIELD, Kenneth French;
1909- , American; nonfiction
CON

CANFIELD, Leon Hardy, 1886- ,
American; nonfiction CON

CANG, Joel, 1899- , Polish-
English; nonfiction CON

CANGEMI, Sister Marie Lucita,
1920- , American; nonfiction
CON

CANHAM, Erwin Dain, 1904- ,
American; nonfiction CON

CANITZ, Friedrich Rudolf, 1654-
99, German; poetry AL ST
CAÑIZARES, José, de, 1676-1750,
Spanish; plays BL HAR SA ST
CANKAR, Ivan, 1876-1918, Slovene;
fiction, poetry, plays COL FLE
HAR KE SA ST
CANNAM, Peggie, 1925-   , English;
juveniles CON WA
CANNAN, Gilbert, 1884-1953, Eng-
lish; fiction, plays, criticism
BRO KAT KT SA
CANNAN, Joanna Maxwell, 1898- ,
English; fiction KAT KT
CANNING, George, 1770-1827, Eng-
lish; nonfiction BRO KBA ST
CANNING, Victor, 1911-   , English;
fiction CON
'CANNON, Brenda' see MOORE,
Bertha
CANNON, Charles James (Granfather
Greenway), 1800-60, American;
poetry, fiction, plays KAA
CANNON, Cornelia James, 1876- ,
American; fiction, essays, juven-
iles KT
CANNON, Garland Hampton, 1924- ,
American; nonfiction CON
CANNON, James Monroe III, 1918- ,
American; journalism, nonfiction
CON
CANNON, Legrand, Jr., 1899- ,
American; fiction KTS WAF
CANNON, Louis S., 1933- , Amer-
ican; nonfiction CON
CANNON, Mark Wilcox, 1928- ,
American; nonfiction CON
CANNON, William Ragsdale, 1916- ,
American; nonfiction CON
CANNON, William S., 1918- ,
American; nonfiction, fiction
CON
CANO, Fidel, 1854- , Colombian;
poetry MIN
CANO, José Luis, 1912- , Spanish;
poetry, criticism BL SA
CANO, Leopoldo, 1844-1934, Spanish;
poetry, plays BL
CANO, Melchor, 1509-60, Spanish;
nonfiction BL SA
CANO y CUETO, Manuel, 1849-1916,
Spanish; plays, journalism,
poetry SA
CANO y MASAS, Leopoldo, 1844-1934,
Spanish; poetry, plays SA
CANOVAS del CASTILLO, Antonio,
1828-97, Spanish; journalism,

fiction, nonfiction BL SA ST
CANSDALE, George Soper, 1909- ,
English; nonfiction CON
CANSINOS ASSENS, Rafael, 1883-
1964, Spanish; criticism, fic-
tion BL COL SA
CANSTRO, Julio see 'ALIJANDRO,
Julio'
CANTOCUZINO, Constantin Stolnic,
1650-1716, German; nonfiction
ST
CANTALICIO, Giovanni Battista,
1450?-1515, Italian; poetry
ST
CANTELON, John Edward, 1924- ,
American; nonfiction CON
CANTEMIR, Antioch see KANTE-
MIR, Antioch
CANTEMIR, Dimitrie see KANTE-
MIR, Dimitrie
CANTERA BURGOS, Francisco,
1901- , Spanish; nonfiction
BL SA
CANTH, Minna (Ulrika Vilhelmina
Johnsson), 1844-97, Finnish;
fiction, plays HAR SA ST
CANTILLANA, Juana Ines de
Asbaje y Ramírez de see
CRUZ, Sor Juana
CANTILO, José María, 1816-72
Argentinian; poetry MIN
CANTILO, José María, 1840-91,
Argentinian; journalism,
poetry MIN
CANTINAT, Jean, 1902- , French;
nonfiction CON
CANTONI, Alberto, 1841-1904,
Italian; fiction COL HAR SA ST
CANTONI, Louis J., American;
poetry HIL
CANTOR, Arthur, 1920- , Amer-
ican; plays CON
CANTOR, Louis, 1934- , Ameri-
can; nonfiction CON
CANTOR, Muriel G., 1923- ,
American; nonfiction CON
CANTORI, Louis J., 1934- ,
American; nonfiction CON
CABTROT y MARIÑO, Prudencio,
1882-1913, Spanish; journalism,
fiction SA
CANTU, Cesare, 1804?-95,
Italian; fiction, poetry HAR
KE SA ST
CANTWELL, Robert Emmett,
1908- , American; fiction
CON KT RIC

CANTZLAAR, George La Fond,
1906- , American; nonfiction
CON
CANUCK, Janey see MURPHY, Emily
G.
'CANUSI, José' see BARKER, S.
Omar
CANZONERI, Robert Wilburn, 1925- ,
American; nonfiction CON
CANZONI, Ariel D., 1928- , Ar-
gentinian; poetry, nonfiction SA
CAPALDI, Nicholas, 1939- , Amer-
ican; nonfiction CON
CAPARROSO, Carlos Arturo, 1908- ,
Colombian; nonfiction, poetry
MIN SA
CAPDEVILA, Arturo, 1889- ,
Argentinian; poetry, fiction,
plays, essays BL FLE MIN SA
CAPDEVILA, Luis, 1892- ,
Spanish; fiction, plays SA
'CAPE, Judith' see PAGE, P.K.
CAPE, William Henry, 1920- ,
American; nonfiction CON
CAPEK, Josef, 1887-1945, Czech;
fiction, criticism COL SA ST
ČAPEK, Karl, 1890-1938, Czech;
essays, plays, fiction COL FLE
KL KT HAR MAG MAT RIC SA
ST
CAPEK, Milic, 1909- , Czech-
American; nonfiction CON
ČAPEK-CHOD, Karel Matěj, 1860-
1927, Czech; fiction COL HAR
SA ST
'CAPEL, Roger' see SHEPPARD,
Lancelot C.
CAPELLA, Luis, 1838- , Colombian;
nonfiction, poetry MIN
CAPELLA, Marciano Mineo Félix,
5th cent., Roman; nonfiction
SA
CAPELLANUS, Andreas see ANDRE
LE CHAPELAIN
CAPELLANUS, Johannes see WALTON,
John
CAPELLE, Russell Beckett, 1917- ,
American; nonfiction CON
CAPELLEN tot den POL, Joan Derk
van der, 1741-84, Dutch; non-
fiction ST
CAPEN, Nahum, 1804-86, American;
nonfiction KAA
CAPERS, Gerald Mortimer, Jr.,
1909- , American; nonfiction
CON
CAPGRAVE, John, 1393-1464, Eng-

lish; nonfiction BRO KB ST
CAPITAN, William Harry, 1933- ,
American; nonfiction CON
CAPLAN, Gerald, 1917- , Eng-
lish; nonfiction CON
CAPLAN, Harry, 1896- , Amer-
ican; nonfiction CON
CAPLAN, Lionel, Canadian; non-
fiction CON
CAPLAN, Ralph, 1925- , Amer-
ican; fiction CON
CAPLES, John, 1900- , Ameri-
can; nonfiction CON
CAPLOW, Theodore, 1920- ,
American; nonfiction CON
CAPMANY SURIS y de MONTPALAU,
Antonio, 1742-1813, Spanish;
nonfiction BL SA
CAPMARTIN de CHAUPY, Ber-
trand, 1720-98, French; non-
fiction DIL
CHAPMARTIN de XAUPY, 18th
cent., French; nonfiction DIL
CAPON, Harry Paul, 1912- ,
English; fiction, nonfiction
CON
'CAPON, Peter' see OAKLEY,
Eric G.
CAPONIGRI, Aloysius Robert,
1915- , American; nonfiction
CON
CAPORALE, Rocco, 1927- ,
American; nonfiction CON
CAPORALI, Cesare, 1531-1601,
Italian; poetry ST
CAPOTE, Truman, 1925- ,
American; fiction CON FLE
KTS MAT RIC WAF
CAPP, Glenn Richard, 1910- ,
American; nonfiction CON
CAPPER, Douglas Parode, Aus-
tralian; nonfiction CON
CAPPERONNIER, Claude, 1671-
96, French; nonfiction DIL
CAPPERONNIER, Jean, 1716-75,
French; nonfiction DIL
CAPPERONNIER, Jean Augustin,
1745-1820, French; nonfiction
DIL
CAPPON, Daniel, 1921- , English;
nonfiction CON
CAPPON, James, 1854-1939,
Canadian; nonfiction ST SY
CAPPONI, Gino, 1350?-1421,
Italian; nonfiction ST
CAPPONI, Gino Marchese, 1792-
1876, Italian; criticism KT ST

CAPPS, Benjamin Franklin, 1922- ,
American; fiction CON
CAPPS, Clifford Lucille Sheats,
1902- , American; nonfiction
CON
CAPPS, Donald Eric, 1939- ,
American; nonfiction CON
CAPPS, Jack Lee, 1926- , Ameri-
can; nonfiction CON
CAPPS, Walter Holden, 1934- ,
American; nonfiction CON
CAPRETTA, Patrick John, 1929- ,
American; nonfiction CON
CAPRON, Jean F., 1924- , Amer-
ican; nonfiction, juveniles CON
CAPRON, Louis Bishop, 1891- ,
American; nonfiction, juveniles
CON
CAPRON, Walter Clark, 1904- ,
American; nonfiction CON
CAPRON, William Mosher, 1920- ,
American; nonfiction CON
CAPRONI, Giorgio, 1912- , Italian;
nonfiction SA
'CAPTAIN Jack' see CRAWFORD,
John W.
CAPUA, Juan de, Jewish-Spanish;
nonfiction BL
CAPUANA, Luigi, 1839-1915, Italian;
fiction, criticism, plays COL
HAR KE SA ST
CAPUS, Alfred, 1858-1922, French;
plays COL DIF HAR MAT SA
CAPUTI, Anthony Francis, 1924- ,
American; nonfiction CON
CAR, Victor Emin, 1870- , Croatian;
poetry, fiction ST
CARABAJAL y SAAVEDRA, Mariana,
17th cent., Spanish; fiction SA
CARABALLO, Gustavo, 1885- ,
Argentinian; journalism, poetry,
plays MIN
CARABIAS, Josefina, 1908- ,
Spanish; journalism, nonfiction
SA
CARACCIOLI, Louis Antoine, 1719-
1803, French; nonfiction DIL
CARAGIALE, Ion Luca, 1852-1912,
Rumanian; plays, fiction COL
FLE HAR KE SA ST
CARAMAN, Philip, 1911- , English;
nonfiction, translations CON
CARAMUEL de LOBLOKOWITZ, Juan,
1606-82, Spanish; nonfiction
SA
CARANO, Paul, 1919- , American;
nonfiction CON

CARAS, Roger Andrew, 1928- ,
American; nonfiction, juveniles
CON
CARAVAJAL y SAAVEDRA, Mariana
see CARABAJAL y SAAVEDRA,
Mariana
CARAWAN, Carolanne M. (Candie),
1939- , American; nonfiction
CON
CARAWAN, Guy H., Jr., 1927- ,
American; nonfiction CON
CARBALLIDO, Emilio, 1925- ,
Mexican; plays CON
'CARBERY, Eithne' (Anna Johnston),
1886-1902, Irish; poetry ST
CARBERRY, H.D., 1921- ,
Jamaican; poetry MUR
CARBERRY, Thomas F., 1925- ,
Scots; nonfiction CON
CARBIA, Rómulo D., 1885-1944,
Argentinian; nonfiction MIN
CARBIO y GONZALEZ, Juan
Francisco, 1822-46, Spanish;
poetry, nonfiction SA
CARBONEL y RIVERO, José
Manuel, 1880- , Cuban; poetry,
fiction, essays, journalism
MIN
CARBONELL, Pedro Miguel, 1434-
1517, Spanish; poetry, fiction
SA
CARBONELL, Reyes, 1917- ,
Spanish-American; nonfiction
CON
CARBONELL y RIVERO, Miguel
Angel, 1894- , Cuban; essays
MIN
CARBONNIER, Jeanne, French;
nonfiction CON
CARBOTTE, Gabrielle see ROY,
Gabrielle
CARCANO, Giulio, 1812-82,
Italian; fiction, poetry HAR
ST
CARCANO, Ramón José, 1860-
1946, Argentinian; nonfiction
MIN
CARCINUS, Greek; poetry ST
'CARCO, Francis' (Francis
Carcopino-Tussoli), 1886-1958,
French; poetry, fiction, plays,
essays COL FLE DIF HAR
KAT KT MAL SA ST
CARDAN, Girolamo (Cardano),
1501-76, Italian; nonfiction
SA
'CARDARELLI, Vincenzo' (Nazarene

Caldrelli), 1887-1959, Italian;
poetry, fiction, journalism, es-
says COL FLE HAR SA ST
CARDEN, Priscilla, American;
juveniles WA
CARDENAL, Ernesto, 1925- ,
Nicaraguan; poetry, criticism
SA
CARDENAL IRACHETA, Manuel,
1898- , Spanish; nonfiction,
translations BL SA
CARDENAS y CHAVEZ, Miguel de,
1808- , Cuban; poetry MIN
CARDENAS y RODRIGUEZ, José
Marí (Jeremias Docaranza),
1812-82, Cuban; journalism,
poetry, fiction MIN
CARDERERA, Alfonso, 1912- ,
Spanish; nonfiction BL
CARDIJN, Josef see 'MEERSCH,
Maxence van der'
CARDILLO de VILLALPANDO,
Gaspar, 1527-81, Spanish; non-
fiction BL SA
CARDINAL see PEDRO CARDINAL
CARDONA, Rafael, 1893- , Costa
Rican; poetry MIN
CARDONA, Rodolfo, 1924- ,
Spanish; nonfiction BL
CARDONA-HINE, Alvaro, 1926- ,
American; poetry CON
CARDONA y VALVERDE, Jenaro,
1863-1930, Costa Rican; poetry,
fiction MIN
CARDONE, Samuel S., 1938- ,
American; nonfiction CON
CARDONNE, Denis Dominique,
1720-83, French; nonfiction DIL
SA
CARDOSO, Efain, 20th cent., Para-
guayan; nonfiction SA
CARDOZO, Lois Steinmetz see
ARQUETTE, Lois S.
CARDOZO, Michael H., 1910- ,
American; nonfiction CON
CARDUCCI, Giosuè, 1835-1907,
Italian; poetry, criticism COL
HAR KE MAG SA ST
'CARDUI, Van' see WAYMAN, Tony
R.
'CARDUI, Vanessa' see WAYMAN,
Tony R.
CARDWELL Guy Adams, 1905- ,
American; nonfiction CON
CARE, Norman S., 1937- , Amer-
ican; nonfiction CON
CAREL de SAINTE GARDE, Jaume,

1620-84, French; poetry SA
CARES, Paul B., 1911- , Amer-
ican; nonfiction CON
CARETTI, Louis see 'MARCEAU,
Félicien'
CAREW, John Mohun ('Tim Carew'),
1921- , English; fiction CON
CAREW, Richard, 1555-1620, Eng-
lish; translations BRO ST
CAREW, Rivers Vervain, 1935- ,
British; poetry MUR
CAREW, Thomas, 1595/98-1639/
40, English; poetry BRO KB
SP ST
'CAREW, Tim' see CAREW, John
M.
CAREY, Ernestine Gilbreth,
1908- , American; juvenile
COM CON
CAREY, Henry, 1687?-1743,
English; poetry BRO KB ST
CAREY, Henry Charles, 1793-1879,
American; nonfiction KAA
CAREY, James Charles, 1915- ,
American; nonfiction CON
CAREY, Mother Marie Aimee,
1931- , American; nonfiction
CON
CAREY, Matthew, 1760-1839, Amer-
ican; nonfiction KAA
'CAREY, Michael' see BURTON,
Edward J.
CAREY, Omer L., 1929- ,
American; nonfiction CON
CAREY-JONES, Norman Stewart,
1911- , Welsh; nonfiction
CON
'CARFAGNE, Cyril' see JENNINGS,
Leslie N.
CARGAS, Harry J., 1932- ,
American; nonfiction CON
CARGILL, Oscar, 1898-1972,
American; nonfiction CON
CARGILL, Robert L., 1929- ,
American; nonfiction CON
'CARGOE, Richard' see PAYNE,
Pierre S.R.
CARHART, Arthur Hawthorne
('Hart Thorne'; 'V.A. Van
Sickle'), 1892- , American;
fiction CON
'CARIBE, El' see PADILLA, Juan
G.
CARIDI, Ronald J., 1941- ,
American; nonfiction CON
CARIN, Arthur A., 1928- ,
American; nonfiction CON

CARIOLA, Carlos, Chilean; plays
MIN
CARITEO, Gareth Benedetto, 1450-
1514, Italian; poetry ST
CARITON de AFRONDISIA, 1st cent.
B.C., Greek; nonfiction SA
CARLE, Eric, 1929- , American;
juvenile CON
CARLELL, Lodowick, 1602-75,
English; plays KB
CARLEN, Emilie F. see FLYGARE-
CARLEN, Emilie
CARLET, Louis François, 1733-
1808, French; nonfiction DIL
'CARLETON' see COFFIN, Charles
C.
CARLETON, Barbee Oliver, 1917- ,
American; juveniles CON
CARLETON, Henry (Henry Carleton
Cox), 1785-1863, American;
essays KAA
CARLETON, Henry Guy, 1856-1910,
American; plays KAA
CARLETON, John William ('Craven'),
fl. 1800, English; nonfiction
HIG
CARLETON, Mark T., 1935- ,
American; nonfiction CON
CARLETON, Will, 1845-1912, Amer-
ican; fiction, poetry BRO HIL
KAA
CARLETON, William, 1794-1869,
Irish; fiction, journalism BRO
KBA MAG ST
CARLETON, William Graves, 1903- ,
American; nonfiction CON
CARLEY, Van Ness Royal, 1906- ,
American; juveniles CON
CARLILE, Henry, American; poetry
CON
CARLILE, Richard, 1790-1843, Eng-
lish; nonfiction KBA
'CARLIN, Francis' (James McDonnell),
1881-1945, American; poetry
HOE
CARLIN, Gabriel S., 1921- , Amer-
ican; nonfiction CON
CARLIN, Thomas Willard, 1918- ,
American; nonfiction CON
CARLING, Francis, 1945- ,
American; nonfiction CON
CARLINO, Carlos, 1910- , Argen-
tinian; poetry MIN
CARLINSKY, Dan, 1944- , Ameri-
can; nonfiction CON
CARLISLE, Carol Jones, 1919- ,
American; nonfiction CON

'CARLISLE, Clark' see HOLDING,
James C.C., Jr.
CARLISLE, Frederick Howard
('Howard Frederick'), 1748-
1825, English; plays, poetry
KB
CARLISLE, Henry Coffin, 1926- ,
American; nonfiction CON
CARLISLE, Olga Andreyev, 1930- ,
American; fiction CON
CARLISLE, R.H. ('HAWK Eye'),
1865- , English; nonfiction
HIG
CARLOCK, John Robert, 1921- ,
American; nonfiction CON
CARLON, Patricia Bernardette,
Australian; fiction CON
CARLOS, Luiz, 1880-1932, Bra-
zilian; poetry SA
CARLOVA, Vasile, 1809-31,
Rumanian; poetry ST
CARLOWITZ, Louise Christine,
1797-1863, German; nonfiction,
translations SA
CARLQUIST, Sherwin, 1920- ,
American; nonfiction CON
CARLS, John Norman, 1907- ,
American; nonfiction CON
CARLSEN, George Robert,
1917- , American; nonfiction
CON
CARLSEN, James Caldwell,
1927- , American; nonfiction
CON
CARLSEN, Ruth Christoffer,
1918- , American; juveniles
COM CON
CARLSON, Andrew Raymond,
1934- , American; nonfiction
CON
CARLSON, Arthur Eugene, 1923- ,
American; nonfiction CON
CARLSON, Bernice Wells, 1910- ,
American; juveniles CON WA
CARLSON, Betty, 1919- , Amer-
ican; nonfiction, juveniles
CON
CARLSON, Dale Bick, 1935- ,
American; juveniles, fiction
CON COM
CARLSON, Eric Walter, 1910- ,
Swedish-American; nonfiction
CON
CARLSON, Esther Elisabeth,
1920- , American; juveniles,
fiction CON WA
CARLSON, John Allyn, 1933- ,

American; nonfiction CON
'CARLSON, John Ray' see DEROUNIAN,
Avodis A.
CARLSON, Natalie Savage, 1906- ,
American; juveniles COM CON
FUL WA
CARLSON, Leland Henry, 1908- ,
American; nonfiction CON
CARLSON, Loraine, 1923- , Amer-
ican; nonfiction CON
CARLSON, Marvin, 1935- , Amer-
ican; nonfiction CON
CARLSON, Reynold Edgar, 1901- ,
American; nonfiction CON
CARLSON, Ronald L., 1934- ,
American; nonfiction CON
CARLSON, Ruth Elizabeth Kearney,
1911- , American; nonfiction
CON
CARLSON, Vada F. ('Florella Rose'),
1897- , American; nonfiction,
poetry, fiction, juveniles CON
CARLSON, William Hugh, 1898- ,
American; nonfiction CON PAC
CARLSON, William Samuel, 1905- ,
American; nonfiction CON HIL
CARLSTON, Kenneth S., 1904- ,
American; nonfiction CON
CARLTON, Robert Goodrich, 1927- ,
American; nonfiction CON
CARLYLE, Alexander, 1722-1805,
Scots; nonfiction BRO
CARLYLE, Thomas, 1795-1881,
Scots; nonfiction, essays BRO
KBA MAG SA ST
CARLYLE, Thomas, 1803-55, Scots;
nonfiction ST
CARMAN, Bliss, 1861-1929, Canadian;
poetry BRO KAT KT ST SY
CARMAN, Dulce see DRUMMOND,
Edith M.D.C.
CARMAN, Justice Neale, 1897- ,
American; nonfiction CON
CARMAN, William Young, 1909- ,
Canadian; nonfiction CON
'CARMEN, Felix' see SHERMAN,
Frank D.
CARMEN, Sister M. Joann, 1941- ,
American; nonfiction CON
'CARMEN SYLVA' see ELISABETH
of RUMANIA
CARMENES, Fray Juan Alberto de
los, 1915- , Cuban; nonfiction,
poetry MIN SA
CARMER, Carl Lamson, 1893- ,
American; essays, poetry,
juveniles CON KT WA

CARMER, Elizabeth Black,
1904- , American; juveniles
WA
'CARMI, T.' see CHARNY, Carmi
'CARMICHAEL, Ann' see Mac-
Alpine, Margaret H.M.
CARMICHAEL, Douglas Roy,
1941- , American; nonfiction
CON
CARMICHAEL, Fred, 1924- ,
American; plays CON
'CARMICHAEL, Harry' see OG-
NALL, Leopold H.
CARMICHAEL, Joel, 1915- ,
American; translations, non-
fiction CON
CARMICHAEL, Montgomery, 1857-
1936, English; fiction HOE
CARMICHAEL, Oliver Cromwell,
1891- , American; nonfiction
CON
CARMICHAEL, Peter Archibald,
1897- , American; nonfiction
CON
CARMICHAEL, Thomas Nichols,
1919- , American; nonfiction
CON
CARMICHAEL, William Edward
('Adam Best'), 1922- , Amer-
ican; nonfiction CON
CARMINA BURANA, 1803- ,
German; nonfiction AL
CARMONTEL, Louis Carrogis
(Carmontelle), 1717-1806,
French; nonfiction DIL
CARNAHAN, Marjorie, R., Amer-
ican; juveniles WA
CARNAHAN, Walter Hervey,
1891- , American; nonfiction
CON
CARNALL, Geoffrey, 1927- ,
English; nonfiction CON
CARNAP, Rudolf P., 1891-1970,
German-American; nonfiction
CON
CARNEADES, 213-129 B.C.,
Greek; nonfiction SA
CARNEGIE, Raymond Alexander
('Sacha Carnegie'), 1920- ,
Scots; fiction CON
CARNEIRO, Mário de Sá, 1890-
1916, Portuguese; poetry, fic-
tion HAR ST
CARNELL, Edward John, 1912- ,
English; nonfiction CON
CARNER, Josep (José), 1884- ,
Spanish; poetry, fiction, non-

fiction COL FLE HAR SA ST

CARNER, Mosco, 1904- , English; nonfiction CON

CARNES, Luisa, 1908?-64, Spanish; fiction, plays SA

CARNES, Ralph Lee, 1931- , American; nonfiction CON

CARNES, Valerie Bohanan, 1940- , American; nonfiction CON

CARNEY, James Patrick ('Seuman O Ceithearnaigh), 1914- , Irish; nonfiction CON

CARNEY, John Otis, 1922- , American; journalism, fiction CON

CARNEY, Richard Edward, 1929- , American; nonfiction CON

CARNEY, William Alderman, 1922- , American; fiction CON

CARNI, 18th cent., French; fiction DIL

CARNOCHAN, Walter Bliss, 1930- , American; nonfiction CON

CARNOT, Rev. Maurus, 1865-1935, Swiss; poetry, fiction, plays HO ST

CARO, Annibale, 1507-66, Italian; poetry SA ST

CARO, José Eusebio, 1817-53, Colombian; nonfiction, poetry BL MIN SA ST

CARO, Joseph (Karo), 1488-1575, Jewish; nonfiction KE ST

CARO, Miguel Antonio, 1843-1909, Colombian; poetry, translations, essays BL MIN SA ST

CARO, Rodrigo, 1573-1647, Spanish; poetry, nonfiction BL SA ST

CARO BAROJA, Julio, 1915- , Spanish; nonfiction BL

CARO MALLEN de SOTO, Ana, 17th cent., Spanish; poetry SA

CAROCCI, Alberto, 1904- , Italian; journalism SA

'CAROL, Bell J.' see KNOTT, William C., Jr.

CAROLET, Denis, 1696-1739, French; nonfiction DIL

CARON, Julie, 1735- , French; nonfiction DIL

CARON, Nicolas, 1719-68, French; nonfiction DIL

CARON de CHANSET, J.B.P., 1740- , French; plays DIL

CARON de LAMPSACO, 5th cent. B.C., Greek; nonfiction SA

CARONA, Philip Ben, 1925- , American; juveniles CON WA

CARONDAS, 7th cent. B.C., Greek; nonfiction SA

CAROSSA, Hans, 1878-1956, German; fiction, poetry AL COL FLE HAR HO KAT KT KU KUN LEN RIC SA ST

CAROSSO, Vincent P., 1922- , American; nonfiction CON

CARP, Frances Merchant, 1918- , American; nonfiction CON

CARPENTER, Alexander, fl. 1429, English; nonfiction ST

CARPENTER, Allan, 1917- , American; nonfiction CON

CARPENTER, Charles A., Jr., 1929- , American; nonfiction CON

CARPENTER, Frances, 1890-1972, American; juveniles CON FUL WA

CARPENTER, Frederic Ives, Jr., 1903- , American; nonfiction CON

CARPENTER, George H., American; nonfiction SCA

CARPENTER, James A., 1928- , American; nonfiction CON

CARPENTER, John A., 1921- , American; nonfiction CON

CARPENTER, Joyce Frances, English; nonfiction CON

CARPENTER, Margaret Haley, American; poetry, nonfiction CON

CARPENTER, Nan Cooke, 1912- , American; nonfiction CON

CARPENTER, Patricia Healy Evans, 1920- , American; juveniles, nonfiction CON

CARPENTER, Peter, 1922- , German-English; nonfiction CON

CARPENTER, Richard Coles, 1916- , American; nonfiction CON

CARPENTIER, 1739-78, French; nonfiction DIL

CARPENTIER, Alejo, 1904- , Cuban; fiction, poetry BL FLE MIN RIC SA

CARPENTIER, Pierre, 1697-1767, French; nonfiction DIL

CARPER, Jean Elinor, 1932- , American; juveniles CON

CARPETER, Edward, 1844-1929, English; poetry, essays BRO KAT KBA ST

CARPINTERO, Heliodoro, 1900- ,
Spanish; nonfiction BL
CARPIO, Manuel, 1791-1861, Mexi-
can; poetry, nonfiction BL SA
CARPOZI, George, Jr., 1920- ,
American; nonfiction CON
CARR, Albert Zolotkoff ('A. H. Z.
Carr'), 1902-71, American; non-
fiction, fiction CON
CARR, Archie Fairly, Jr., 1919- ,
American; nonfiction CON
CARR, Arthur Charles, 1918- ,
American; nonfiction CON
CARR, Bettye Jo Crisler, 1926- ,
American; nonfiction CON
'CARR, Catharine' see WADE,
Rosaline H.
CARR, David William, 1911- ,
Canadian; nonfiction CON
CARR, Donald Eaton, 1903- ,
American; nonfiction CON
CARR, Dorothy Stevenson Laird,
1912- , English; fiction CON
CARR, Edward Hallett, 1892- ,
British; nonfiction KTS
CARR, Emily, 1871-1945, Canadian;
fiction ST SY
'CARR, Glyn' see STYLES, Frank S.
CARR, Harriett Helen, 1899- ,
American; juveniles CON FUL
WA
CARR, Jesse Crowe, Jr., 1930- ,
American; nonfiction CON
CARR, Rev. John, 1878- , Irish;
nonfiction HO
CARR, John Dickson ('Carter Dick-
son'; 'Carr Dickson'), 1905/06- ,
English; fiction BRO KT RIC
CARR, Mary Jane, 1899- , Ameri-
can; juveniles COM CON HO
KJU WA
CARR, Raymond, 1919- , English;
nonfiction CON
CARR, Robert Spencer, 1909- ,
American; fiction WAF
'CARR, Roberta' see ROBERTS,
Irene
CARR, Warren Tyree, 1917- ,
American; nonfiction CON
CARR, William Henry Alexander,
1924- , American; nonfiction
CON
CARRA, Jean Louis, 1742-93, French;
nonfiction DIL
CARRANQUE de RIOS, Andrés,
1902-36, Spanish; fiction SA
CARRANZA, Adolfo F., 1857-1914,

Argentinian; nonfiction MIN
CARRANZA, Angel Justiniano,
1834-99, Argentinian; nonfic-
tion MIN
CARRANZA, Eduardo, 1913- ,
Colombian; nonfiction MIN
CARRASCO ALBANO, Manuel,
1834-73, Chilean; nonfiction
MIN
CARRASQUILLA, Francisco de
Paula, 1855-97, Colombian;
epigrams MIN
CARRASQUILLA, Rafael María,
1857-1930, Colombian; nonfic-
tion MIN
CARRASQUILLA, Ricardo, 1827-
86, Colombian; poetry MIN
CARRASQUILLA, Tomás, 1858-
1940, Colombian; fiction
BL MIN SA ST
CARRASQUILLA MALLARINO,
Eduardo, 1887- , Colombian;
fiction, poetry MIN
CARRE, Jean Baptiste Louis,
1749-1835, French; nonfiction
DIL
CARRE, Rémy, 1702-73, French;
nonfiction DIL
CARREDANO, Vicente, 1920- ,
Spanish; journalism BL
CARRELET, Louis, 1698-1781,
French; nonfiction DIL
CARRELET de ROSAY, Pierre
Barthélemy, 1695-1770,
French; nonfiction DIL
CARRELL Alexis, 1873-1944,
Franco-American; nonfiction
DIF HOE KT SA
CARRELL, Norman Gerald,
1905- , American; nonfiction
CON
CARRER, Luigi, 1801-50, Italian;
poetry HAR
CARRERA ANDRADE, Jorge,
1903- , Ecuadorian; poetry,
essays BL FLE DI KTS SA
ST
CARRERA del CASTILLO, Nicolás,
1907- , Spanish; journalism
SA
CARRERE, Emilio, 1880-1947,
Spanish; poetry HAR ST
CARRERE MORENO, Emilio,
1881-1947, Spanish; poetry,
fiction, journalism BL SA
CARRETERO NOVILLO, José Marí
('El Caballero Audaz'), 1890-

1951, Spanish; fiction, journalism
SA
CARRETTO, Galeotto, 1455-1530,
Italian; poetry, plays ST
'CARRICK A.B.' see LINDSAY,
Harold A.
'CARRICK, Edward' see CRAIG, Ed-
ward A.
'CARRICK, John' see CROSBIE, Hugh
P.
CARRICK, Valery, 1869- , Russian-
Norwegian; juveniles KJU
CARRIEDO, Gabino Alejandro,
1923- , Spanish; journalism,
poetry SA
CARRIEGO, Evaristo, 1883-1912,
Argentinian; journalism, poetry
MIN SA
CARRIER, Constance, 1908- ,
American; poetry, translations
CON MUR
CARRIER, Esther Jane, 1925- ,
American; nonfiction CON
CARRIER, Warren, 1918- , Ameri-
can; poetry, fiction CON MUR
CARRIERE-DOISIN, A., 18th cent.,
French; poetry, plays DIL
CARRIGAN, David Owen, 1933- ,
Canadian; nonfiction CON
CARRILLO, Lawrence Wilbert,
1920- , American; nonfiction
CON
CARRILLO de SOTOMAYOR, Luis,
1583-1610, Spanish; poetry BL
SA ST
CARRILLO y O'FARRILL, Isaac,
1844-1901, Cuban; poetry MIN
CARRINGTON, Charles Edmund
('Charles Edmonds'), 1897- ,
English; nonfiction CON
CARRINGTON, Henry Beebee, 1824-
1912, American; nonfiction KAA
'CARRINGTON, Molly' see MATTHEWS,
Constance M.
CARRINGTON, Paul Dewitt, 1931- ,
American; nonfiction CON
CARRINGTON, Richard, 1921- ,
English; nonfiction CON
CARRINGTON, William Langley,
1900- , Australian; nonfiction
CON
CARRIO de la VANDERA, Alonso
see BUSTAMANTE, Calixto
CARRION, Alejandro ('Juan Sin
Cielo'), 1915- , Ecuadorian;
poetry DI
CARRION, Benjamin, 1897- ,

Ecuadorian; criticism, essays
DI
CARRION y CARDENAS, Miguel,
1875-1929, Cuban; fiction,
journalism MIN
CARRISON, Daniel J., 1917- ,
American; nonfiction CON
CARRITHERS, Wallace Maxwell,
1911- , American; nonfiction
CON
CARRIZO, César, 1889-1950,
Argentinian; poetry, plays,
journalism MIN SA
'CARRIZO, Fabio' see ALVAREZ,
José S.
CARRIZO, Juan Alfonso, 1875- ,
Argentinian; fiction, poetry
SA
CARROLL, Carmal Edward,
1923- , American; nonfiction
CON
'CARROLL, Consolata' (Sister Mary
Consolata), 1892- , American;
fiction HO WAF
'CARROLL, Curt' see BISHOP,
Curtis K.
CARROLL, Donald Kingery, 1909- ,
American; nonfiction CON
CARROLL, Faye, 1937- , Amer-
ican; nonfiction CON
CARROLL, Gladys Hasty, 1904- ,
American; fiction CON KT
WAF
CARROLL, Herbert, 1897- ,
American; nonfiction CON
CARROLL, John Bissell, 1916- ,
American; nonfiction CON
CARROLL, John Joseph, 1924- ,
American; nonfiction CON
CARROLL, John Melvin, 1928- ,
American; nonfiction CON
CARROLL, John Millar, 1925- ,
American; nonfiction CON
CARROLL, Kenneth Lane, 1924- ,
American; nonfiction CON
CARROLL, Latrobe, 1894- ,
American; juveniles, fiction,
translations CON FUL JO
'CARROLL, Laura' see PARR,
Lucy
'CARROLL, Lewis' (Charles Lut-
widge Dodgson), 1832-98,
English; poetry, nonfiction,
juveniles BRO DOY KBA MAG
SP SA ST WA
CARROLL, Mother Mary Gerald,
1913- , American; nonfiction
CON

CARROLL, Patrick Joseph, 1876- ,
Irish; poetry, nonfiction, fiction
HOE
CARROLL, Paul, 1927- , Ameri-
can; poetry, criticism CON
MUR
CARROLL, Paul Vincent, 1900-68,
Irish; plays, fiction CON FLE
HOE KT MAT SA ST
CARROLL, Phil, 1895- , American;
nonfiction CON
'CARROLL, Robert' see ALPERT,
Hollis
CARROLL, Ruth Robinson, 1899- ,
American; juveniles CON FUL
JO
CARROLL, Thomas J., 1909- ,
American; nonfiction CON
CARROLL, Thomas Theodore, Jr.,
(Ted) 1925- , American; fic-
tion CON
CARROW, Milton Michael, 1912- ,
American; nonfiction CON
CARR-SAUNDERS, Alexander,
1886- , English; nonfiction
CON
CARRUTH, Estelle, 1910- , Ameri-
can; fiction CON
CARRUTH, Hayden, 1921- , Ameri-
can; poetry CON MUR
CARRUTHERS, Robert, 1799-1878,
Scots; nonfiction BRO KBA
CARRYL, Charles Edward, 1841-1920,
American; juveniles BRO KAA
CARSBERG, Bryan Victor, 1939- ,
English; nonfiction CON
CARSE, James Pearce, 1932- ,
American; nonfiction CON
CARSE, Robert, 1902-71, American;
fiction, nonfiction, juveniles
CON
CARSILLIER, Jean Baptiste, 1705-60,
French; poetry DIL
CARSON, Franklin John, 1920- ,
American; fiction CON
CARSON, Gerald Hewes, 1899- ,
American; nonfiction CON
CARSON, Hampton Lawrence,
1914- , American; nonfiction
CON
CARSON, Herbert, American; poetry
HIL
CARSON, Herbert Lee, 1929- ,
American; nonfiction CON
'CARSON, Capt. James' see STRATE-
MEYER, Edward L.
CARSON, John F., 1920- , Ameri-

can; juveniles COM CON WA
CARSON, Julia Margaret Hicks,
1899- , American; juveniles
WA
CARSON, Rachel Louise, 1907-64,
American; nonfiction BRO KTS
RIC
CARSON, Robert, 1909- , Ameri-
can; plays, fiction CON
CARSON, Robert Charles, 1930- ,
American; nonfiction CON
CARSON, Ruth see BUGBEE, Ruth
C.
CARSON, William Glasgow Bruce,
1891- , American; nonfiction
CON
CARSTEN, Francis Ludwig, 1911- ,
German-English; nonfiction
CON
CARSTENS, Grace Pearse, Amer-
ican; fiction CON
CARSTENSEN, Roger Norwood,
1920- , American; nonfiction
CON
CARSWELL, Catherine Roxbaugh
McFarlane, 1879-1946, Scots;
fiction, criticism, nonfiction
BRO KAT KT SA
CARSWELL, Evelyn, American;
juveniles WA
CARSWELL, John Patrick, 1918- ,
American; nonfiction CON
CARTAGENA, Alfonso de Santa
María de, 1384-1456, Spanish;
poetry, nonfiction BL SA
CARTAGENA, Teresa de, 1420-80,
Spanish; nonfiction BL SA
CARTAGENA PORTALATIN, Aida,
20th cent., Dominican; poetry
MIN SA
CARTAUD de la VILLATE, Fran-
çois, 1700-37, French; non-
fiction DIL
CARTE, Thomas, 1686-1754, Eng-
lish; nonfiction BRO DIL SA
ST
CARTER, Alan, 1936- , English;
nonfiction CON
CARTER, Albert Howard, 1913- ,
American; nonfiction CON
CARTER, Alfred Edward, 1914- ,
Canadian; nonfiction CON
'CARTER, Anne' see BROOKS,
Anne T.
CARTER, Barbara Barclay, Amer-
ican; nonfiction, translations
HOE

CARTER, Boyd George, 1908- ,
American; nonfiction CON
'CARTER, Bruce' see HOUGH,
Richard A.
CARTER, Byron L., 1924- , Amer-
ican; nonfiction CON
CARTER, Charles Frederick, 1919- ,
English; nonfiction CON
CARTER, Charles Howard, 1927- ,
American; nonfiction CON
CARTER, Charles Webb, 1905- ,
American; nonfiction CON
CARTER, E. Lawrence, 1910- ,
American; nonfiction CON
CARTER, Edward, 1902- , South
African; nonfiction CON
CARTER, Elizabeth, 1717-1806,
English; poetry, nonfiction BRO
KB ST
CARTER, Everett, 1919- , Ameri-
can; nonfiction CON
CARTER, Frances Tunnell, 1922- ,
American; juveniles CON
CARTER, George Francis, 1912- ,
American; nonfiction CON
CARTER, Gwendolyn Margaret,
1906- , Canadian; nonfiction
CON
CARTER, Harold, 1925- , American;
nonfiction CON
CARTER, Harvey Lewis, 1904- ,
American; nonfiction CON
CARTER, Henry H., 1905- ,
American; nonfiction BL
CARTER, Hugh, 1895- , American;
nonfiction CON
'CARTER, James' see MAYNE,
William
CARTER, John, 1905- , English;
nonfiction CON
CARTER, John Franklin ('Jay Frank-
lin'), 1897-1967, American; fic-
tion, journalism KT
CARTER, John Stewart, 1912- ,
American; fiction CON
CARTER, Helene, 1887-1960,
Canadian; juveniles FUL
CARTER, James Puckette, 1933- ,
American; nonfiction CON
CARTER, James Richard, 1940- ,
American; nonfiction CON
CARTER, John Thomas, 1921- ,
American; juveniles CON
CARTER, Katharine Jones, 1905- ,
American; juveniles COM CON
CARTER, Margaret Louise, 1948- ,
American; fiction CON

CARTER, Martin Wylde, 1927- ,
Guyanan; poetry MUR
CARTER, Mary Arkley, 1923- ,
American; fiction CON
CARTER, Mary Ellen, 1923- ,
American; nonfiction CON
CARTER, Neil, 1913- , Ameri-
can; nonfiction CON
CARTER, Paul Allen, 1926- ,
American; nonfiction CON
CARTER, Paul Jefferson, Jr.,
1912- , American; nonfiction
CON
'CARTER, Phyllis Ann' see
EBERLE, Irmengarde
'CARTER, Ralph' see NEUBAUER,
William A.
CARTER, Robert, 1819-79, Amer-
ican; editor KAA
CARTER, Robert Ayres, 1923- ,
American; fiction, plays CON
CARTER, Robert Mack, 1925- ,
American; nonfiction CON
CARTER, Victor Albert, 1902- ,
American; nonfiction CON
CARTER, William, 1934- , Amer-
ican; nonfiction CON
CARTER, William Ambrose,
1899- , American; nonfiction
CON
CARTER, William E., 1927- ,
American; juveniles COM CON
WA
CARTER, William Hodding, 1907-
72, American; juveniles COM
CON KTS WA
CARTER, William Lee, 1925- ,
American; nonfiction CON
'CARTERMACO' see FORTEQUERRI,
Escipión
CARTHY, Mother Mary Peter,
1911- , American; nonfiction
CON
'CARTIER, Steve' see CAMERON,
Lou
CARTLAND, Barbara ('Barbara
McCorquodale'), 1904- ,
English; fiction CON RIC
CARTLEDGE, Samuel Antoine,
1903- , American; nonfiction
CON
CARTOSIO, Emma de, 1920?- ,
Argentinian; poetry, fiction SA
CARTTER, Allan Murray, 1922- ,
American; nonfiction CON
'CARTUJANO, El' see PADILLA,
Juan de

'CARTWRIGHT, Jame Mc G.' see
  JENNINGS, Leslie N.
CARTWRIGHT, Peter, 1785-1872,
  American; nonfiction HOO
CARTWRIGHT, William, 1611-43,
  English; plays, poetry BRO ST
CARTWRIGHT, William H., 1915- ,
  American; nonfiction CON
CARUS, Paul, 1852-1919, German-
  American; nonfiction KT SA ST
CARUSO, John Anthony, 1907- ,
  American; nonfiction CON
CARUS-WILSON, Eleanora Mary,
  1897- , Canadian; nonfiction
  CON
CARUTH, Donald Lewis, 1935- ,
  American; nonfiction CON
CARUTHERS, William Alexander,
  1800?-46, American; fiction
  KAA
CARVAJAL (Carvajales), 15th cent.,
  Spanish; poetry BL SA ST
CARVAJAL, Alberto, 1882- ,
  Colombian; journalism, nonfiction
  MIN
CARVAJAL, María Isabel ('Carmen
  Lira'), 1888-1949, Costa Rican;
  fiction MIN
CARVAJAL, Mario V., 1896- ,
  Colombian; poetry MIN
CARVAJAL, Micael de, 1480-1530/75?,
  Spanish; plays BL SA ST
CARVAJAL, Ricardo see MENESES,
  Enrique
CARVAJAL y MENDOZA, Louisa de,
  1566-1614, Spanish; poetry ST
CARVAJAL y ROBLES, Rodrigo de,
  1589?-1635, Spanish; poetry SA
CARVAJALES see CARVAJAL
CARVALHAIS, Alfredo Pinto de
  Almeida, 1851-90, Portuguese;
  poetry SA
CARVALHO, Ronald de, 1893-1935,
  Brazilian; poetry, criticism SA
CARVALHO e ARAYO, Alexandre
  H. see HERCULANO de
  CARVALHO e Araújo, Alexandre
CARVALHO RODRIQUES dos ANJOS,
  Augusto, 1884-1914, Brazilian;
  poetry SA
CARVELL, Fred John, 1934- ,
  American; nonfiction CON
CARVER, Fred Donald, 1936- ,
  American; nonfiction CON
CARVER, George, 1888- , American;
  nonfiction HOE
'CARVER, John' see GARDNER,
  Richard

CARVER, Jonathan, 1710-80,
  American; nonfiction, diary
  KAA
CARVER, Raymond, 1938- ,
  American; poetry CON
CARVER, Saxon Rowe, 1905- ,
  American; nonfiction CON
CARY, Alice ('Patty Lee'), 1820-
  71, American; poetry, fiction
  BRO KAA SA
CARY, Elizabeth, 1585?-1639,
  English; poetry, translations
  ST
CARY, Harold Whiting, 1903- ,
  American; nonfiction CON
CARY, Henry Francis, 1772-1844,
  English; poetry, translations
  BRO KBA ST
CARY, James Donald, 1919- ,
  American; nonfiction CON
CARY, John H., 1926- , Amer-
  ican; nonfiction CON
CARY, Joyce, 1888-1957, English;
  fiction BRO FLE KTS MAG
  RIC
CARY, Lee James, 1925- ,
  American; nonfiction CON
CARY, Lucius, 1609/10-43, Eng-
  lish; poetry ST
CARY, Patrick, 1624-56, English;
  poetry ST
CARY, Phoebe, 1824-71, Ameri-
  can; poetry BRO KAA
CARY, Richard, 1909- , Ameri-
  can; nonfiction CON
CARYAPADAS, 1050-1200, Indian;
  hymns LAN
CARY-ELWES, Rev. Columba,
  1903- , English; nonfiction
  HO
'CARYL, Jean' see KAPLAN, Jean
  C.K.
CARYL, Warren ('Moss Tadrack'),
  1920- , American; fiction
  CON
CARYLL, John, 1625-1711, Eng-
  lish; poetry, plays KB
CASA, Giovanni della, 1503-56,
  Italian; nonfiction, poetry SA
  ST
CASADY, Donald Rex, 1926- ,
  American; nonfiction CON
CASAL, Julián del, 1863-93,
  Cuban; poetry BL MIN SA ST
CASAL, Julio J., 1889- ,
  Uruguayan; poetry SA
CASALANDRA, Estelle see ES-
  TELLE, Sister Mary

CASALDUERO, Joaquín, 1903- ,
Spanish; criticism BL SA
CASAÑAL SHAKERY, Alberto,
1874- , Spanish; poetry, plays
SA
CASANOVA, Giacomo, 1725-98,
Italian; nonfiction DIL
CASANOVA de LUTOSLAWSKI, Sofía,
1862-1959?, Spanish; poetry,
fiction, journalism SA
CASANOVA de SEINGALT, Giovanni
Jacopo, 1725-98, Italian; fiction,
diary HAR KE MAG MAL SA ST
CASARES, Julio, 1877-1964, Spanish;
criticism BL COL SA
CASAS, Bartolomé de las see LAS
CASAS, Bartolomé de
CASAS, José Joaquín, 1865/66-1951,
Colombian; journalism, poetry,
criticism BL MIN SA
CASASSUS, Carlos, Chilean; poetry,
journalism MIN
CASAUBON, Isaac, 1559-1614, Swiss;
nonfiction SA
CASAUX, Charls, 1727-96, French;
nonfiction DIL
CASBOIS, Nicolas, 1728- , French;
nonfiction DIL
CASCALES, Francisco, 1564-1642,
Spanish; nonfiction BL SA ST
CASCELLA, Armando, 1900- ,
Argentinian; fiction SA
CASE, Brian David, 1937- , English;
fiction CON
CASE, Elinor Rutt, 1914- , Ameri-
can; juveniles CON WA
CASE, Fred E., 1918- , American;
nonfiction CON
CASE, Josephine Young, 1907- ,
American; fiction CON
'CASE, Justin' see GLEADOW, Rupert
S.
CASE, Leland Davidson, 1900- ,
American; nonfiction CON
CASE, Lynn Marshall, 1903- ,
American; nonfiction CON
CASE, Maurice, 1910- , Franco-
American; nonfiction CON
'CASE, Michael' see HOWARD,
Robert W.
CASE, Victoria, 1897-1972, Ameri-
can; nonfiction, fiction CON
PAC
CASELEYR, Camille Auguste Marie
('Jack Danvers'), 1909- ,
Belgian-English; fiction CON
CASELLAS, Ramón, 1855-1910,

Spanish; criticism, fiction
SA
CASERO y BARRANCO, Antonio,
1874-1936, Spanish; poetry,
plays SA
'CASEWELL, Anne' see DENHAM,
Mary O.
CASEWITT, Curtis ('D. Green';
'D. Vernor'; 'K. Werner'),
1922- , German-American;
nonfiction CON
CASEY, Bill H., 1930- , Amer-
ican; nonfiction CON
CASEY, Gavin S., 1907- ,
Australian; fiction RIC
CASEY, Kevin, 1940- , Irish;
fiction CON
CASEY, Michael T. (Mart), 1922- ,
American; nonfiction CON
CASEY, Robert Joseph, 1890- ,
American; journalism HOE
CASEY, Rosemary Alice Christ-
mann, 1922- , American;
fiction CON
CASEY, Thomas Francis, 1923- ,
American; nonfiction CON
CASGRAIN, Henri Raymond, 1831-
1904, Franco-American; fic-
tion ST SY
CASH, Grace ('Grady Cash'),
1915- , American; fiction
CON
CASH, James Allen, 1901- ,
English; nonfiction CON
'CASH, Sebastian' see SMITHELS,
Roger W.
CASH, Wilbur Joseph, 1901-41,
American; nonfiction JO
CASHIN, Edward L., 1927- ,
American; nonfiction CON
CASHIN, James A., 1911- ,
American; nonfiction CON
CASHMAN, Paul Harrison, 1924- ,
American; nonfiction CON
CASIO, Girolamo da, 1464-1533,
Italian; poetry ST
CASIO HERMINA, Lucio, 146 B.C.,
Roman; nonfiction SA
CASIO PARMENSIS, Tito, -36
B.C., Roman; poetry SA
CASIO SEVERO Longulano, Tito,
50-33 B.C., Roman; nonfiction
SA
CASIODORO, Magno Aurelio, 480-
542, Roman; nonfiction SA
CASKEY, John L., 1908- , Amer-
ican; nonfiction CON

CASMIER, Adam Anthony, 1934- ,
American; nonfiction CON
CASMIR, Fred L., 1928- , German-
American; nonfiction CON
CASNER, Andrew James, 1907- ,
American; nonfiction CON
CASO, Antonio, 1883-1946, Mexican;
essays, nonfiction SA
CASO y ANDRADE, Alfonso,
1892- , Mexican; nonfiction
SA
CASON, Mabel Earp ('Emily Mary
Bell'), 1892- , American;
juveniles CON
'CASONA, Alejandro' (Alejandro
Rodríguez Alvarezo, 1903-65,
Spanish; plays, poetry, movies
BL FLE HAR MAT RIC SA ST
CASPARY, Vera, 1904- , American;
fiction CON KTS
CASPER, Henry W., 1909- ,
American; nonfiction CON
CASPER, Leonard Ralph, 1923- ,
American; nonfiction, fiction,
poetry CON
CASPER von LOHENSTEIN see
LOHENSTEIN, Daniel C. van
'CASQUE, Sammy' see DAVIS,
Sydney C. H.
CASRIEL, Harold Daniel, 1924- ,
American; nonfiction CON
CASS, Carl Bartholomew, 1901- ,
American; nonfiction CON
CASS, Joan Evelyn, English; juveniles
COM CON WA
CASSADY, Ralph, Jr., 1900- ,
American; nonfiction CON
CASSCANO, Ricardo, 1895- ,
Brazilian; poetry SA
CASSEDY, James Higgins, 1919- ,
American; nonfiction CON
CASSEL, Russell N., 1911- ,
American; nonfiction CON
CASSELL, Frank Allan, 1941- ,
American; nonfiction CON
CASSELL, Frank Hyde, 1916- ,
American; nonfiction CON
CASSELL, Richard Allan, 1921- ,
American; nonfiction CON
CASSELL, Sylvia, 1924- , Amer-
ican; nonfiction CON
'CASSELLS, John' see DUNCAN,
William M.
CASSELS, Alan, 1929- , English;
nonfiction CON
CASSELS, Louis, 1922- , American;
nonfiction CON

CASSERES see DE CASSERES
CASSERLEY, Julian Victor Lang-
mead, 1909- , Anglo-Amer-
ican; nonfiction CON
CASSERLY, Anne, American;
juveniles KJU
CASSIDAY, Bruce Bingham
('Carson Bingham'; 'Max Day'),
1920- , American; fiction,
nonfiction CON
CASSIDY, Frederic Gomes,
1907- , West Indian-Ameri-
can; nonfiction CON
CASSIDY, Harold Gomes, 1906- ,
Cuban-American; nonfiction
CON
CASSIDY, John A., 1908- ,
American; nonfiction CON
CASSIDY, Vincent H., 1923- ,
American; nonfiction CON
CASSIER, François, 1721-72,
French; poetry DIL
CASSILL, Ronald Verlin ('Owen
Aherne'; 'Jesse Webster'),
1919- , American; nonfiction
CON
'CASSILS, Peter' see KEELE,
Kenneth D.
CASSINELLI, Charles William,
Jr., 1925- , American; non-
fiction CON
CASSINI, Jacques, 1667-1756,
French; nonfiction DIL
CASSINI, Jacques Dominique,
1747-1845, French; nonfiction
DIL
CASSINI, Jean Dominique, 1625-
1712, Franco-Italian; nonfiction
DIL
CASSINI de THIERY, Cesar Fran-
çois, 1714-84, French; nonfic-
tion DIL
CASSIODORUS, Flavius Magnus
Aurelius, 480-580, Roman;
nonfiction ST
CASSIRER, Ernst, 1874-1945,
German; nonfiction KTS
CASSITY, Allen Turner, 1929- ,
American; poetry CON
CASSIUS DIO Coccieanus, 155-
235, Greek; nonfiction ST
CASSOLA, Albert Maria, 1915- ,
English; plays, nonfiction, fic-
tion CON
CASSOLA, Carlo, 1917- , Italian;
fiction RIC
CASSON, Lionel, 1914- , Ameri-

ican; nonfiction CON
CASSOU, Jean ('Jean Noir'), 1897- ,
French; fiction BL DIF FLE
HAR ST
CASSTEVENS, Thomas William,
1937- , American; nonfiction
CON
CASSYERE, Jacob Jacobsoon, 16th
cent., Dutch; poetry ST
CASTAGNA, Edwin, 1909- , Amer-
ican; nonfiction CON
CASTAGNOLA, Lawrence, A. , 1933- ,
American; nonfiction CON
CASTAHEDA, Fernando López de,
-1559, Portuguese, nonfiction
SA
CASTAING, -1800, French; plays
DIL
CASTAN PALOMAR, Fernando, 1898-
1962, Spanish; fiction SA
CASTANEDA, Carlos, 1931- ,
Brazilian; nonfiction CON
CASTAÑEDA, Francisco, 1776-1832,
Argentinian; journalism, diary
MIN
CASTANEDA, Hector Neri, 1924- ,
Guatemalan; nonfiction CON
CASTAÑEDA ARAGON, Gregorio,
1886-87, Colombian; poetry,
fiction MIN
CASTANHEDA, Fernão Lopes de,
1500?-59, Portuguese; nonfiction
ST
CASTANIER d'AURIAC, Guillaume,
1702-64, French; nonfiction DIL
CASTAÑON, de la PEÑA, José
Manuel, 1920- , Spanish; fiction
SA
CASTEL, Albert, 1928- , American;
nonfiction CON
CASTEL, Jean Gabriel, 1928- ,
French-Canadian; nonfiction CON
CASTEL, Louis Bertrand, 1688-
1757, French; nonfiction DIL
CASTELAR y RIPOLL, Emilio, 1832-
99, Spanish; nonfiction BL COL
KE SA ST
CASTELEIN, Matthys de, 1485-1550,
Dutch; poetry ST
CASTELHUN, Friedrich Karl, 1828-
1905, German-American; poetry
ST
CASTELLAN, Norman John, Jr. ,
1939- , American; nonfiction
CON
CASTELLANETA, Carlo, 1930- ,
Italian; fiction CON

CASTELLANOS, Jane Mollie
Robinson, 1913- , American;
nonfiction CON
CASTELLANOS, Jesús, 1878/79-
1912, Cuban; journalism, fic-
tion MIN SA
CASTELLANOS, Joaquín, 1860/61-
1932, Argentinian; poetry,
journalism MIN
CASTELLANOS, Juan de, 1522-
1605/07, Spanish; poetry
BL MIN SA ST
CASTELLANOS y LOSADA, Basitio
Sebastián, 1807-91, Spanish;
nonfiction SA
CASTELLANOS y VELASCO,
Julián see 'ESCAMILLA,
Pedro'
CASTELLET, José María,
Spanish; fiction, criticism BL
CASTELLION, Sebastien (Chateillon;
Castalion), 1515-63, French;
nonfiction DIF
CASTELLO, Branco, Camillo
('Camillo'), 1825-90, Portu-
guese; fiction COL HAR KE
SA ST
CASTELLOZE, Dama de, 13th
cent., French; poetry SA
CASTELLTORT, Ramón, 1915- ,
Spanish; poetry, plays, criti-
cism, essays SA
CASTELNUOVO-TEDESCO, Pietro,
1925- , Italian; nonfiction
CON
CASTELVETRO, Lodovico, 1505-
71, Italian; criticism KE ST
CASTERA, Jean Henry (Artigues),
1749-1838, French; nonfiction
DIL
CASTETTER, William Benjamin,
1914- , American; nonfiction
CON
CASTI, Giambattista, 1724-1803,
Italian; poetry HAR SA ST
CASTIGLIONE, Baldassare, 1478-
1529, Italian; nonfiction BL
HAR KE SA ST
CASTILHO, Antonio Feliciano de,
1800-75, Portuguese; poetry
SA ST
CASTILLE see 'BOIS GOBEY,
Fortuné de'
CASTILLEJO, Cristóbal de,
1490?-1550, Spanish; poetry
BL SA ST
CASTILLO, Andrés del, 1615?-80,

Spanish; fiction SA

CASTILLO, Edmund Luis, 1924- ,
American; juveniles COM CON
WA

CASTILLO, Eduardo del, 1889-1939,
Colombian; poetry, criticism
MIN

CASTILLO, Fernando del (Hernando),
16th cent., Spanish; poetry SA

CASTILLO, Florencio de, 1760-1834,
Costa Rican; fiction MIN

CASTILLO, Francisca Josefa del,
1671-1742, Spanish; nonfiction
BL

CASTILLO, Homero, 1918- ,
Chilean; nonfiction BL

CASTILLO, Michel del, 1933- ,
Spanish; fiction DIC RIC

CASTILLO de GONZALEZ, Amelia
(Aurelia), 1842-1920, Cuban;
poetry MIN

CASTILLO ELEJABEYTIA, Dietinio
de, 1906- , Spanish; nonfiction
BL SA

CASTILLO NAVARRO, José María,
1927- , Spanish; fiction SA

CASTILLO PUCHE, José Luis,
1919- , Spanish; fiction, journalism BL SA

CASTILLO SOLORZANO, Alonso del,
1584-1647?, Spanish; poetry, fiction, plays BL SA ST

CASTILLO y AYENSA, José del,
1795-1861, Spanish; nonfiction
SA

CASTILLO y CASTILLO, Abel Romeo,
1904- , Ecuadoran; poetry, nonfiction DI

CASTILLO y GUEVARA, Francisca
Josefa de, 1671-1742, Colombian;
fiction, poetry MIN SA ST

CASTILLO y LANZAS, Joaquín del,
1781-1878, Mexican; poetry SA

CASTILLO y SORIANO, José del,
1849- , Spanish; plays SA

CASTILLON, Jean de, 1708-91,
French; nonfiction DIL

CASTLE, Charles, 1939- , English;
nonfiction CON

CASTLE, Egerton, 1858-1920, English; fiction BRO KT

CASTLE, Emery Neal, 1923- ,
American; nonfiction CON

CASTLE, Marian Johnson, American;
fiction CON

CASTLE, Robert W., Jr., 1929- ,
American; nonfiction CON

'CASTLEMON, Harry' see FOS-
DICK, Charles A.

CASTLES, Francis G., 1943- ,
Australian; nonfiction CON

CASTLES, Lance, 1937- ,
Australian; nonfiction CON

CASTOR, 1st cent., Greek; nonfiction SA

CASTOR, Grahame Douglas,
1932- , English; nonfiction
CON

CASTOR, Henry, 1909- , American; juveniles, fiction CON
WA

CASTOR de RODA, 1st cent.,
Greek; nonfiction SA

CASTRESANA, Luis de, 1925- ,
Spanish; fiction BL SA

CASTRO, Alfonso, 1878- ,
Colombian; nonfiction MIN

CASTRO, Américo, 1885-1972,
Spanish; criticism COL SA

CASTRO, Baltasar, Chilean;
nonfiction MIN

CASTRO, Carmen, 1911- ,
Spanish; essays BL

CASTRO, Cristóbal de, 1878- ,
Spanish; journalism, poetry
BL

CASTRO, Eugénio de, 1869-1944,
Portuguese; poetry, plays
COL FLE HAR SA ST

CASTRO, Fernando Guillermo de,
1927- , Spanish; fiction BL

CASTRO, Gabriel Pereira de,
1571-1632, Portuguese; poetry
SA

CASTRO, Guillén, de, 1565-1631,
Spanish; nonfiction BL

CASTRO, José María Ferreira de
see FERREIRA de CASTRO,
José M.

CASTRO, Josue de see DE CASTRO,
Josue

CASTRO, Juan Modesto, 1943- ,
Chilean; fiction MIN

CASTRO, Manuel, 1898- , Argentinian; nonfiction SA

CASTRO, Oscar, 1910-52, Chilean;
journalism, poetry MIN

CASTRO, Rosalía de, 1837-85,
Spanish; poetry BL COL HAR
KE SA ST

CASTRO ALVES, Antonio de, 1847-
71, Brazilian; poetry SA ST

CASTRO CALVO, José María,
1903- , Spanish; essays,

criticism BL SA
CASTRO QUESADA, Américo,
1885- , Spanish; nonfiction
BL HAR ST
CASTRO VILLACAÑAS, Demetrio,
1919- , Spanish; nonfiction
SA
CASTRO y ANAYA, Pedro de,
1603?-59?, Spanish; poetry SA
CASTRO y BELLVIS, Guillén de,
1569-1631, Spanish; plays HAR
KE SA ST
CASTRO y GUTIERREZ, Cristóbal
de, 1880-1953, Spanish; poetry,
journalism, criticism, fiction
SA
CASTRO y OROZCO, José de,
1808-69, Spanish; poetry, plays
SA
CASTRO y ROSI, Adolfo de, 1823-98,
Spanish; nonfiction BL SA
CASTRO y SERRANO, José de,
1829-96, Spanish; nonfiction
BL SA
CASTROVIDO y SANZ, Roberto,
1864-1939, Spanish; journalism
SA
CASTROVIEJO, Concha, 1918?- ,
Spanish; fiction, criticism SA
CASTROVIEJO, José María, 1909- ,
Spanish; poetry SA
CASTY, Alan Howard, 1929- ,
American; nonfiction CON
CASWELL, Helen Rayburn, 1923- ,
American; nonfiction CON
'CATALA, Victor' (Catalina Albert
i Paradis), 1873- , Spanish;
fiction COL SA ST
CATALA RIVES, Ramón A., 1896-
1941, Cuban; nonfiction MIN
CASTALAN MENENDEZ-PIDAL,
Diego, Spanish; nonfiction BL
'CATALINA, Juan' see GARCIA
LOPEZ, Juan C.
CATALINA y COBO, Mariano, 1842-
1913, Spanish; nonfiction SA
CATALINA y del AMO, Severo,
1832-71, Spanish; nonfiction SA
CATARINEU, Dolores, 1916- ,
Spanish; poetry SA
CATARINEU, Ricardo J., 1868-1915,
Spanish; poetry, plays journalism
SA
CATANESE, Anthony James, Jr.,
1942- , American; fiction CON
CATANIA, Anthony Charles, 1936- ,
American; nonfiction CON

CATE, William Burke, 1924- ,
American; nonfiction CON
CATELINOT, Ildefonse, 1671-
1756, French; nonfiction DIL
CATELLAN de la MASQUERE,
Clara Priscila Margarita,
1662-1745, French; poetry
SA
CATEORA, Philip Rene, 1932- ,
American; nonfiction CON
CATER, Silas Douglass, 1923- ,
American; nonfiction CON
CATERINA da SIENA, Saint,
1347-80, Italian; nonfiction
HAR KE ST SA
CATES, Ray A., Jr., 1940- ,
American; nonfiction CON
CATHALAN, Jacques, 1671-1757,
French; nonfiction DIL
CATHCART, Helen, English; non-
fiction CON
CATHER, Willa Sibert, 1873-1947,
American; fiction, poetry,
essays BRO FLE KL KT
MAG RIC SA ST
CATHERALL, Arthur ('A. R.
Channel'; 'Dan Corby'),
1906- , American; fiction,
juveniles CON WA
CATHERINE de RICCI, Sainte,
1535-90, Italian; nonfiction
SA
CATHERINE of BOLOGNA,
Sainte, 1413-63, Italian; non-
fiction SA
CATHERINE of GENOA, Saint,
1448?- , Italian; nonfiction
SA
CATHERINE the GREAT, 1729-96,
German-Russian; plays, essays
DIL HAR ST
CATHERWOOD, Mary Hartwell,
1847-1902, American; fiction,
juveniles HOO KAA
CATHEY, Cornelius Oliver,
1908- , American; nonfiction
CON
CATHON, Laura Elizabeth,
1908- , American; nonfiction,
juveniles CON
CATLIN, George, 1857-1934,
American; nonfiction HIL ST
CATLIN, George, 1796-1872,
American; nonfiction BRO
KAA
CATLIN, George Edward Gordon,
1896- , English; nonfiction
CON

CATLIN, Warren Benjamin, 1881- ,
American; nonfiction CON
CATLING, Darrel Charles, 1909- ,
English; nonfiction CON
CATO, Dionysius, 3rd cent.,
Roman?, nonfiction ST SA
CATO, Nancy Fotheringham ('Nancy
Norman'), 1917- , Australian;
poetry, fiction CON MUR RIC
CATO the ELDER, Marcus Porcius,
234-149 B.C., Roman; nonfic-
tion ST SA
CATO the YOUNGER, Marcus
Porcius, 95-46 B.C., Roman;
nonfiction ST
CATOIR, John T., 1931- , Ameri-
can; nonfiction CON
CATON, Charles E., 1928- , Amer-
ican; nonfiction CON
CATON, Valerio, 1st cent., Roman;
poetry SA
CATROU, François, 1569-1737,
French; nonfiction DIL
CATS, Jacob, 1577-1660, Dutch;
poetry HAR KE SA ST
CATTAN, Henry, 1906- , Israeli;
nonfiction CON
CATTAUI, Georges ('Michel Francis'),
1896- , French; nonfiction CON
CATTELL, Everette Lewis, 1905- ,
American; nonfiction CON
CATTELL, Raymond Bernard, 1905- ,
English; nonfiction CON
CATTON, Bruce, 1899- , American;
juveniles, nonfiction COM CON
HIL KTS
CATULLUS, Gaius Valerius, 84/87-
54 B.C., Roman; poetry MAG
SA ST
'CATZ, Max' see GLASER, Milton
CAU, Jean, 1925- , French; fiction,
plays RIC
CAUDILL, Harry Monroe, 1922- ,
American; nonfiction CON
CAUDILL, Rebecca, 1899- , Amer-
ican; juveniles COM CON FUL
HOO WA
'CAUDWELL, Christopher' see
SPRIGG, Christopher St. J.
'CAUDWELL, Frank' see KING,
Francis H.
CAULET, Jean de, 1693-1771,
French; nonfiction DIL
CAULEY, Troy Jesse ('Terry Cauley'),
1902- , American; nonfiction
CON
CAULFIELD, Peggy F., 1926- ,

American; nonfiction CON
'CAULIFLOWER, Sebastian' see
SELDES, Gilbert V.
CAULIN, Antonio, 1718- ,
Colombian; nonfiction MIN
CAUMAN, Sam, 1910- , Ameri-
can; nonfiction CON
CAUSLEY, Charles Stanley,
1917- , British; poetry,
fiction CON MUR SP WA
CAUSSADE, Jean Pierre de,
1675-1751, French; nonfiction
DIL
CAUSSIA de PERCEVAL, Armand
Pierre, 1795-1871, French;
nonfiction SA
CAUSSIN de PERCEVAL, Jean
Jacques Atoine, 1759-1835,
French; nonfiction SA
'CAUSTIC, Christopher' see
FESSENDEN, Thomas G.
CAUTE, David, 1936- , Ameri-
can; nonfiction, plays CON
CAUTHEN, Wilfred Kenneth,
1930- , American; nonfiction
CON
CAUVIN, French; nonfiction DIL
CAUX de CAPPEVAL, -1774,
French; nonfiction DIL
CAVA, Esther Laden, 1916- ,
American; nonfiction CON
CAVAFY, Constantine (Konstantinos
P. Kavaphes), 1863-1933,
Greek; poetry FLE HAR KTS
RIC ST
CAVALCA, Domenico, 1270-1342,
Italian; nonfiction ST
CAVALCANTI, Bartolomeo, 1503-
62, Italian; nonfiction ST
CAVALCANTI, Giovanni, 15th
cent., Italian; nonfiction ST
CAVALCANTI, Guido, 1255-1300,
Italian; poetry HAR KE SA
ST
CAVALLARI, Alberto, 1927- ,
Italian; nonfiction CON
CAVALLARO, Ann Abelson,
1918- , American; fiction
CON
CAVALLO, Diana, 1931- , Amer-
ican; fiction CON
CAVALLOTTI, Félix, 1842-98,
Italian; nonfiction SA
CAVAN, Sherri, 1938- , Ameri-
can; nonfiction CON
CAVANAGH, John Richard, 1904- ,
American; nonfiction CON

CAVANAH, Frances, 1899- ,
American; juveniles COM CON
FUL HOO WA
CAVANAUGH, Arthur, 1926- ,
American; nonfiction CON
CAVANILLES, Antonio, 1805-64,
Spanish; nonfiction SA
CAVANNA, Betty ('Betsy Allen';
'Elizabeth Headley'), 1909- ,
American; juveniles COM CON
FUL WA
CAVASSICO, Bartolomeo, 1480?-
1555, Italian; plays, poetry ST
CAVE, Alfred, A., 1935- , Ameri-
can; nonfiction CON
CAVE, Edward ('Sylvanus Urbanus'),
1691-1754, English; printer BRO
ST
CAVE, Hugh Barnett, 1910- , Eng-
lish; juveniles CON
CAVE, Roderick George James
Munro ('James Munro'), 1935- ,
English; nonfiction CON
CAVEIRAC, Jean Nove de, 1713-82,
French; nonfiction DIL
CAVELIER, Louise see LEVESQUE,
Louise
CAVELLIER (Cuvellier), 14th cent.,
French; poetry SA
CAVENDISH, George, 1500-61, Eng-
lish; nonfiction, poetry BRO KB
ST
CAVENDISH, Margaret see NEW-
CASTLE, Margaret
CAVENDISH, Richard ('Martin Corn-
wall'), 1930- , English; fiction
CON
CAVENDISH, William Newcastle,
1592-1676, English; plays, poetry
KB ST
CAVENDISH-BENTINCK, John William
Arthur James, 1857-1943, English;
nonfiction HIG
CAVERS, David Farquhar, 1902- ,
American; nonfiction CON
CAVERT, Samuel Mc Crea, 1888- ,
American; nonfiction CON
CAVERT, Walter Dudley, 1891- ,
American; nonfiction CON
CAVES, Richard Earl, 1931- ,
American; nonfiction CON
CAVESTANY, Juan Antonio, 1861-
1924, Spanish; poetry, plays
BL SA
CAVESTANY, Pablo, 1886- ,
Spanish; poetry, fiction BL
CAVIA, Mariano de, 1855-1920,

Spanish; journalism BL SA
CAVICEO, Jacopo, 1443-1511,
Italian; fiction ST
CAVITCH, David, 1933- , Amer-
ican; nonfiction CON
CAVNES, Max P., 1922- , Amer-
ican; nonfiction CON
CAVUNDARAYA, 10th cent.,
Indian; nonfiction LAN
CAWELTI, John George, 1929- ,
American; nonfiction CON
CAWLEY, Robert Ralston,
1893- , American; nonfiction
CON
CAWOOD, John W., 1931- ,
American; nonfiction CON
CAWS, Mary Ann, 1933- , Amer-
ican; nonfiction CON
CAWS, Peter James, 1931- ,
English; nonfiction CON
CAXTON, William, 1422?-91,
English; translations, printer
BRO KB ST
CAYADO, Henrique see CAIADO,
Henrique
CAYANKONTAN, fl. 1100, Indian;
poetry LAN
CAYCE, Edgar Evans, 1918- ,
American; nonfiction CON
CAYCE, Hugh Lynn, 1907- ,
American; nonfiction CON
CAYET, Pierre Victor Palma,
1545-1610, French; nonfiction
SA
CAYLUS, Anne Claude Philippe,
1692-1765, French; poetry,
plays DIL
CAYLUS, Marthe Marguerite,
1673-1729, French; nonfiction
DIF DIL SA
CAYROL, Jean, 1911- , French;
poetry, fiction, essays DIC
DIF FLE MAL
CAYTON, Horace, R., 1903-70,
American; nonfiction CON
CAZALET-KEIR, Thelma, English;
nonfiction CON
CAZAMIAN, Louis François,
1877- , French; criticism
KT
CAZDEN, Norman, 1914- , Amer-
ican; nonfiction CON
CAZDEN, Robert E., 1930- ,
American; nonfiction CON
CAZEL, Fred Augustus, Jr.,
1921- , American; nonfiction
CON

'CAZIMIR, Ottilia' (Alexandrina
Gavrilescu), Rumanian; poetry
ST
CAZIN, Hubert Martin, 1724-95,
French; nonfiction DIL
CAZOTTE, Jacques, 1720-92,
French; plays, poetry DIF DIL
MAL SA
CEARD, Henri, 1851-1924, French;
fiction DIF ST
CEBES, 5th cent. B.C., Greek;
nonfiction SA
CEBULASH, Mel ('Ben Farrell';
'Glen Harlan'; 'Jared Jansen'),
1937- , American; fiction CON
CECAUMENUS, fl. 1071-78, By-
zantine, nonfiction ST
CECCARDI ROCCALAGLIATA,
Ceccardo, 1871-1919, Italian;
poetry SA
CECCHI, Emilio ('Il Tarlo'), 1884-
1966, Italian; poetry, essays,
criticism COL FLE HAR SA ST
CECCHI, Giommaria, 1518-87,
Italian; poetry, plays HAR ST
'CECCO d' ASCOLI' see STABILI,
Francesco
CECH, Svatopluk, 1846-1908, Czech;
poetry, fiction COL KE SA ST
'CECIL' see TONGUE, Cornelius
CECIL, Algernon, 1879- , English;
nonfiction HOE
CECIL, Lord Edward Christian
David Gascoyne, 1902- , Eng-
lish; criticism BRO KT RIC ST
CECIL, Henry, 1907- , English;
fiction RIC
CECIL, Lamar John Ryan, Jr.,
1932- , American; nonfiction
CON
CEDER, Georgiana Dorcas ('Ana
Dor'), American; juveniles CON
CEDERBORGH, Frederik, 1784-1835,
Swedish; fiction, plays ST
CEDMON see CAEDMON
CEFALAS, Constantino, 5th cent.,
Greek; poetry SA
CEFKIN, J. Leo, 1916- , Ameri-
can; nonfiction CON
CEGIELKA, Francis Anthony, 1908- ,
Polish-American; nonfiction
CON
CEI, Francesco, 1471-1505, Italian;
poetry ST
CEILLIER, Rémi (Cellier), 1688-
1761, French; nonfiction DIL
'CEIRIOG' (John Ceiriog Hughes),

1832-87, Welsh; poetry ST
CEJADOR y FRAUCA, Julio,
1864-1927, Spanish; nonfiction
BL COL SA
CELA, Camilo José ('Don Camilo';
'Matilde Verdu'), 1916- ,
Spanish; fiction BL CON FLE
HAR RIC SA ST
CELA TRULOCK, Jorge, 1932- ,
Spanish; fiction BL
CELAKOVSKI, Frantisek Ladislaw,
1799-1952, Czech; poetry
SA ST KE
'CELAN, Paul' (Paul Antschel),
1920- , Austrian; poetry
AL FLE KU KUN RIC
CELAYA, Gabriel see MUGICA,
Rafael
CELE, Joan, 1345-1417, Dutch;
nonfiction ST
CELEBI, Mustafa see 'NAILI'
CELEDON, Rafael, 1831-1903,
Colombian; nonfiction MIN
'CELINE' (Louis Ferdinand
Destouches), 1894-1961,
French; fiction, essays COL
DIC DIF FLE HAR MAG MAL
RIC SA
CELIO, Antipatro, 140-90 B.C.,
Roman; nonfiction SA
CELL, Edward Charles, 1928- ,
American; nonfiction CON
CELLARIO, Cristiano, 15th-16th
cent., Flemish; nonfiction
SA
CELLARIUS, Christofer Keller,
1638-1707, German; nonfiction
SA
CELLE, Giovanni dalle, 1310?-
96?, Italian; nonfiction ST
CELLIER, Rémi see CEILLIER,
Rémi
CELLIERS, Jan F.E., 1865-1940,
South African; poetry, plays
ST
CELLINI, Benvenuto, 1500-71,
Italian; diary HAR KE MAG
SA ST
CELNART, Isabel Felicia, 1796-
1860, French; nonfiction SA
CELNIK, Max, 1933- , German-
American; nonfiction CON
CELOSSE, Jacobus, 1560-1631,
Dutch; poetry ST
CELSO, 2nd cent., Greek; non-
fiction SA
CELSUS, Aulus Cornelius, Roman;

nonfiction ST
CELTES, Conrad (Celtis), 1459-1508,
German; poetry AL ST
CENA, Giovanni, 1870-1917, Italian;
poetry, fiction COL HAR SA
CENCI, Louis, 1918- , American;
nonfiction CON
'CENDRARS, Blaise' (Frédéric
Sauser-Hall), 1887-1961, French;
poetry, fiction DIF FLE KAT KT
HAR MAL RIC SA ST
CENSORINO, 3rd cent., Roman; non-
fiction SA
CENTER, Allen Harry, 1912- ,
American; nonfiction CON
CENTLIVRE, Susanna Freeman,
1667-1723, English; plays, fic-
tion BRO KB SA ST
CENTORE, F.F., 1938- , American;
nonfiction CON
CEP, Jan, 1902- , Czech; fiction
COL FLE SA
CEPEDA y AHUMADA, Teresa de
see TERESA de JESUS
CEPELOS, Bautista, 1868-1915,
Brazilian; poetry SA
CEPPEDE, Jean de la, 1550-1622,
French; poetry SA
'CERAM, C.W.' see MAREK, Kurt
W.
CERAVOLO, Joseph, 1934- , Amer-
ican; poetry MUR
CERCIDAS, 290-20 B.C., Greek;
poetry SA ST
CERDA, Bernardino Ferreira de la,
1595-1650, Portuguese; poetry
SA
CERDA y RICO, Francisco, 1730-92/
1800, Spanish; nonfiction BL
SA
CERF, Bennett Alfred, 1898-1971,
American; juveniles COM CON
WA
CERF, Christopher Bennett, 1941- ,
American; nonfiction CON
CERF, Jay Henry, 1923- , Ameri-
can; nonfiction CON
CERFVOL, de, 18th cent., French;
nonfiction DIL
CERISIER, Antoine Marie, 1749-
1828, French; nonfiction DIL
CERMINARA, Gina, American;
nonfiction CON
'CERNA, Panait' (Panait Stancioff),
1881-1913, Rumanian; poetry ST
CERNADAS, Remigio, 1779-1859,
Cuban; nonfiction MIN

CERNEY, James Vincent ('Vince
Black'), 1914- , American;
nonfiction CON
CERNUDA, Luis, 1902/04-63,
Spanish; poetry BL COL FLE
HAR RIC SA ST
CEROU, Pierre, 1708-98, French;
plays DIL
'CERRO, Gordo' see KELLY,
Jonathan F.
CERUTTI, Jean Antoine Joachim,
1738-92, French; nonfiction
DIL SA
CERRUTO, Oscar, 1907- ,
Bolivian; poetry, fiction MIN
CERUTI, Maria Antonietta (Toni),
1932- , Italian; nonfiction
CON
CERUTTY, Percy Wells, 1895- ,
Australian; nonfiction CON
CERVANTES, Lucius F., 1914- ,
American; nonfiction CON
CERVANTES de SAAVEDRA,
Miguel de, 1547-1616, Spanish;
fiction, poetry, plays BL
HAR KE MAG SA ST
CERVANTES de SALAZAR,
Francisco, 1514-75, Spanish;
nonfiction, fiction BL SA ST
CERVEAU, René, 1700-80,
French; nonfiction DIL
CERVERI de GIRONA, 18th cent.,
Spanish; nonfiction, poetry SA
CERYCH, Ladislaw, 1925- ,
Czech-French; nonfiction CON
CESAIRE, Aimé, 1912/13- ,
French; poetry DIC DIF FLE
MAL PIN RIC
CESALPINO, Andreas, 1519-1603,
Italian; nonfiction SA
CESAREC, August, 1896-1941,
Croatian; poetry, fiction, es-
says ST
CESARI, Antonio, 1760-1828,
Italian; nonfiction ST
CESAROTTI, Melchiorre, 1730-
1808, Italian; nonfiction, poetry,
criticism HAR ST
CESBRON, Gilbert, 1913- ,
French; fiction, essays, plays
DIC DIF FLE
CESPED, Manuel see CESPEDES,
Manuel
CESPEDES, Angel María, 1892/93-
1956, Colombian; nonfiction,
poetry MIN
CESPEDES, Augusto, 1904- ,

Bolivian; plays MIN SA

CESPEDES, Julian, 1888- ,
Bolivian; journalism, fiction,
plays, essays MIN

CESPEDES, Manuel ('Manuel Césped'),
1878-1936, Bolivian; journalism,
poetry MIN SA

CESPEDES, Pablo, 1538-1603,
Spanish; nonfiction BL SA

CESPEDES de ESCANAVERINO,
Ursula, 1832-74, Cuban; journalism MIN

CESPEDES y MENESES, Gonzalo de,
1585?-1638, Spanish; fiction BL
HAR SA ST

CESTERO, Tulio A. Manuel, 1877-
1955, Dominican; poetry, journalism BL MIN SA

CESTRE, Charles, 1871- , French;
nonfiction KT

CETIN, Frank Stanley, 1921- ,
American; juveniles, nonfiction
COM CON

CETINA, Gutierre see GUTIERRE
de CETINA

CETURION, Carlos R. , 20th cent. ,
Paraguayan; nonfiction SA

CEU, Violante do, 1601-39, Portuguese; poetry SA ST

CEVALLOS, Pedro Fermin, 1812-93,
Ecaudorian; nonfiction DI

CEVASCO, George Anthony, 1924- ,
American; nonfiction CON

CHAADAYEV, Pyotr Yakovlevich,
1793-1856, Russian; nonfiction,
fiction HAR HARK KE ST

CHABANEIX, Philippe, 1898- ,
French; poetry DIF

CHABANON, Michel Paul, 1730-92,
French; plays DIL

CHACKO, Kadankavil C. , 1915- ,
Indian; nonfiction HO

CHABAS MARTI, Juan, 1898-1954,
Spanish; poetry, fiction, criticism
BL SA

'CHABER, M.E.' see CROSSEN,
Kendell F.

CHABOT, Cecile, 1907- ,
Canadian; fiction SY

CHACE, James Clarke, 1931- ,
American; fiction CON

CHACEL, Rosa, 1898- , Spanish;
fiction, poetry BL SA

CHACON, Gonzalo,   -1517, Spanish;
nonfiction BL

CHACON, Jacinto, 1822- , Chilian;
nonfiction, poetry MIN

CHACON y CALVO, José María,
1893- , Cuban; journalism
MIN SA

CHACONAS, Doris J. , 1938- ,
American; juveniles CON

CHADBOURNE, Richard McClain,
1922- , American; nonfiction
CON

CHADWICK, Gerald William St.
John, 1915- , English; nonfiction CON

CHADWICK, Henry, 1920- ,
American; nonfiction CON

CHADWICK, John, 1920- ,
English; nonfiction CON

'CHADWICK, Lester' see STRATE-
MEYER, Edward L.

CHADWICK, Nora Kershaw,
1891- , English; nonfiction
CON

CHADWICK, William Owen,
1916- , English; nonfiction
CON

CHADWIN, Mark Lincoln, 1939- ,
American; nonfiction CON

CHAFE, Wallace L. , 1927- ,
American; nonfiction CON

CHAFETZ, Henry, 1916- ,
American; juveniles, fiction
CON WA

CHAFETZ, Morris E. , 1924- ,
American; nonfiction CON

CHAFFEE, Allen, American; fiction, juveniles CON

CHAFFIN, Lillie Dorton, 1925- ,
American; juveniles CON

CHAFFIN, Yule M. , 1914- ,
American; nonfiction CON

CHAGALL, David, 1930- , American; fiction CON

'CHAGAS, Antonio das' (Antonio da
Fonseca Soares), 1631-82,
Portuguese; nonfiction ST

CHAI, Chen Kang, 1916- ,
Chinese-American; nonfiction
CON

CHAI, Ch'u, 1906- , Chinese-
American; nonfiction CON

CHAI, Hon-chan, 1931- , American; nonfiction CON

CHAI, Winberg, 1934- , American; nonfiction CON

CHAIJ, Fernando ('E.L. Alcalde'),
1909- , Argentinian-American;
nonfiction CON

CHAITANYA, 1486-1534, Bengali;
nonfiction ST

CHAKOUR, Charles M., 1929- ,
American; nonfiction CON
CHAKRAVARTY, Amiya, 1901- ,
Indian; nonfiction CON
CHALCOCONDYLAS, Laonicus,
1432?-90?, Greek; nonfiction
HAR SA ST
CHALCONDILAS, Demetrios, 15th
cent., Greek; nonfiction SA
CHALKHILL, John, fl. 1600, English;
poetry BRO KB ST
CHALL, Jeanne Sternlicht, 1921- ,
Polish-American; nonfiction CON
CHALLANS, Mary see 'RENAULT,
Mary'
CHALLES, Robert, 1659-1725,
French; nonfiction DIF DIL
CHALLIS, Cecil Gordon, 1932- ,
British; poetry MUR
CHALMERS, Audrey, 1899- ,
Canadian; juveniles WA
CHALMERS, David Mark, 1927- ,
American; nonfiction CON
CHALMERS, Floyd Sherman ('John
Duke'), 1898- , American;
nonfiction CON
CHALMERS, George, 1742-1825,
Scots; nonfiction BRO SA ST
CHALMERS, Mary Eileen, 1927- ,
American; juveniles CON WA
CHALMERS, Patrick Reginald,
1872-1942, Scots; nonfiction HIG
CHALMERS, Thomas, 1780-1847,
Scots; nonfiction BRO KBA
CHALONER, Sir Thomas, 1521-65,
English; poetry, translations
ST
CHALUPKA, Jan, 1791-1871, Slovak;
plays ST
CHALUPKA, Samo, 1812-83, Slovak;
poetry ST
CHALVET, Pierre Vincent, 1767-
1807, French; nonfiction DIL
CHAMBERLAIN, Betty, 1908- ,
American; nonfiction CON
CHAMBERLAIN, Brenda Irene,
1912- , British; poetry MUR
CHAMBERLAIN, Elinor, 1901- ,
American; juvenile CON WA
CHAMBERLAIN, Hope Summerell,
1870- , American; nonfiction
JO
CHAMBERLAIN, John Rensselaer,
1903- , American; criticism
KT
CHAMBERLAIN, Julian Ingersoll,
1873- , American; nonfiction
HIG

CHAMBERLAIN, Mellen, 1821-
1900, American; nonfiction
KAA
CHAMBERLAIN, Narcisse, 1924- ,
Franco-American; nonfiction
CON
CHAMBERLAIN, Neil Wolverton,
1915- , American; nonfiction
CON
CHAMBERLAIN, Robert, 1607-60,
English; poetry ST
CHAMBERLAIN, Robert Lyall,
1923- , American; nonfiction
CON
CHAMBERLAIN, Samuel ('Phineas
Beck'), 1895- , American;
nonfiction CON
'CHAMBERLAIN, Theodor' see
JOHNSON, Ronald and WIL-
LIAMS, Jonathan C.
CHAMBERLAN, Antoine (Chamber-
land), 1732-1803, French; non-
fiction DIL
CHAMBERLAYNE, Edward, 1616-
1703, English; nonfiction KB
CHAMBERLAYNE, William, 1619-
89, English; poetry, plays
BRO KB ST
CHAMBERLIN, Harry D., 1887-
1944, American; nonfiction
HIG
CHAMBERLIN, Jo Hubbard, Amer-
ican; juvenile WA
CHAMBERLIN, John Gordon,
1914- , American; nonfiction
CON
CHAMBERLIN, William Henry,
1897- , American; nonfiction
CON KT
CHAMBERS, Aidan, 1934- , Eng-
lish; juveniles COM CON
CHAMBERS, Dewey W., 1929- ,
American; nonfiction CON
CHAMBERS, Charles Haddon,
1860-1921, Australian; plays,
journalism BRO KT
CHAMBERS, Sir Edmund Kerchever,
1866-1954, English; nonfiction
BRO KT ST
CHAMBERS, Edward James,
1925- , Canadian; nonfiction
CON
CHAMBERS, Ephraim, -1740,
English; nonfiction KB
CHAMBERS, Frank Pentland,
1900- , English; nonfiction
CON
CHAMBERS, Henry T., 1903- ,

American; poetry MAR

CHAMBERS, Jonathan David,
1898- , English; nonfiction
CON

CHAMBERS, Margaret Ada (Peggy)
Eastwood, 1911- , English;
juveniles COM CON

CHAMBERS, Maria Cristina,
Mexican-American; fiction HOE

CHAMBERS, Merritt Madison,
1899- , American; nonfiction
CON

CHAMBERS, Mortimer Hardin, Jr.,
1927- , American; nonfiction
CON

CHAMBERS, Peggy see CHAMBERS
Margaret

'CHAMBERS, Peter' see PHILLIPS,
Dennis J. A.

CHAMBERS, Raymond John, 1917- ,
Australian; nonfiction CON

CHAMBERS, Robert, 1802-71, English; poetry, essays, fiction
BRO KBA ST

CHAMBERS, Robert Warner, American; juvenile WA

CHAMBERS, Robert William, 1865-
1933, American; fiction KAT KT

CHAMBERS, William, 1800-83, English; nonfiction BRO ST

CHAMBERS, William Nisbet, 1916- ,
American; nonfiction CON

CHAMBERS, William Trout, 1896- ,
American; nonfiction CON

CHAMBERS, William Walker,
1913- , Scots; nonfiction CON

CHAMBLISS, William Jones, 1923- ,
American; nonfiction CON

'CHAMEATUS' see NICHOLAS
CABASILAS

CHAMETZKY, Jules, 1928- , American; nonfiction CON

CHAMFORT, Nicolas Sebastien Roch,
1741-94, French; nonfiction
DIF DIL HAR KE MAL SA ST

CHAMICO see ROXLO, C. Nalé

CHAMIER, Frederick, 1796-1870,
English; fiction BRO KBA ST

CHAMIER, George, 1842-1915, English; fiction ST

CHAMISSO, Adelbert von (Louis
Charls Adélaide de), 1781-1838,
German; poetry AL HAR KE SA
ST

CHAMIZO, Luis, 1899-1944, Spanish;
poetry BL SA

CHAMOUSSET, Claude Humbert

Piarron, 1717-73, French;
nonfiction DIL

CHAMPAGNE, Marian, 1915- ,
American; fiction CON

CHAMPFLEURY, Jules François
Félix Husson, 1821-89,
French; fiction DIF HAR ST

CHAMPIER, Symphorien, 1472-1539,
French; poetry SA ST

CHAMPIGNY, Jean Bochart, 1712-
87, French; translations DIL

CHAMPIGNY, Robert Jean, 1922- ,
Franco-American; poetry CON

CHAMPION, Carr John, 1923- ,
American; fiction CON

CHAMPION, John Elmer, 1922- ,
American; nonfiction CON

CHAMPION, Larry Stephen,
1932- , American; nonfiction
CON

CHAMPION, Richard Annells,
1925- , Australian; nonfiction
CON

CHAMPION de NILON, Charles,
-1795, French; nonfiction
DIL

CHAMPKIN, Peter, 1918- ,
English; poetry CON

CHAMPLIN, James Raymond,
1928- , American; nonfiction
CON

CHAMPNEY, Freeman, 1911- ,
American; nonfiction CON

CHAMPOLLION, Jean François,
1790-1832, French; nonfiction
SA

CHAMPOLLION FIGEAC, Juan
Jacques, 1778-1867, French;
nonfiction SA

CHAMPOURCIN, Ernestina de,
1905-60, Spanish; poetry,
fiction BL SA

CHAMPSAUR, Félicien, 1859-1934,
French; fiction DIF

CHAMSON, André, 1900- ,
French; fiction, essays COL
CON DIF FLE KAT KT SA ST

'CHAMUDOT, Daniel Yish' see
LIEBERMANN, Ahron S.

'CHANAIDH, Fear' see CAMPBELL,
John L.

CHANAKIA, Indian; nonfiction SA

'CHANAKYA' see PANIKKAR,
Kavalam M.

CHANCELLOR, John, 1900- ,
American; fiction CON

CHAND BARDAL (Bardai), 12th

cent., Indian; poetry SA ST
CHANDA, Asok Kumar, 1902- ,
   Indian; nonfiction CON
CHANDI DAS, fl. 1589, Indian;
   poetry ST
CHANDLER, A. Bertram ('Andrew
   Dunstan'; 'George Whitley'),
   1912- , English; fiction CON
CHANDLER, Alfred Dupont, Jr.,
   1918- , American; nonfiction
   CON
CHANDLER, Allison, 1906- ,
   American; nonfiction CON
CHANDLER, B.J., 1921- , Amer-
   ican; nonfiction CON
CHANDLER, Caroline Augusta,
   1906- , American; nonfiction,
   juveniles CON HOE WA
CHANDLER, David Geoffrey, 1934- ,
   English; nonfiction CON
CHANDLER, Edna Walker, 1908- ,
   American; juveniles CON WA
CHANDLER, Elizabeth Margaret,
   1807-34, American; poetry KAA
CHANDLER, George, 1915- , Amer-
   ican; nonfiction CON
CHANDLER, John, 1806-76, English;
   translations BRO
CHANDLER, Margaret Kueffner,
   1922- , American; nonfiction
   CON
CHANDLER, Raymond, 1888-1959,
   American; fiction KTS RIC ST
CHANDLER, Richard Eugene,
   1916- , American; nonfiction
   CON
CHANDLER, Ruth Forbes, 1894- ,
   American; juveniles COM CON
   WA
CHANDLER, Stanley Bernard, 1921- ,
   English; nonfiction CON
CHANDLER, Thomas, 1911- ,
   American; juveniles WA
CHANDOLA, Anoop C., 1937- ,
   Indian-American; nonfiction
   CON
CHANDOR, Peter John Anthony,
   1932- , English; nonfiction CON
'CHANDOS, Fay' see SWATRIDGE,
   Irene M. M.
CHANDRAKA, Chandragomin, fl.
   600, Sanskrit; nonfiction ST
CHANEY, Jill, 1932- , English;
   juveniles CON
CHANEY, Otto Preston, Jr., 1931- ,
   American; nonfiction CON
CHANEY, William Albert, 1922- ,

American; nonfiction CON
CHANG CHI, 765-830, Chinese;
   poetry ST
CHANG, Chin Isabelle, 1924- ,
   American; nonfiction CON
CHANG CHOU see CHUANG-TZU
CHANG HENG, 78-139, Chinese;
   poetry ST
CHANG, Hsin-hai, 1900- ,
   Chinese; nonfiction CON
CHANG HUA, 232-300, Chinese;
   poetry ST
CHANG Hui-yen, 1761-1802,
   Chinese; essays, poetry ST
CHANG, Jen-chi, 1903- ,
   Chinese-American; nonfiction
   CON
CHANG, Kia-ngau, 1889- ,
   Chinese; nonfiction CON
CHANG Ping-ling, 1868-1936,
   Chinese; nonfiction ST
CHANG Shih-chao, 1886- ,
   Chinese; nonfiction ST
CHANG Tsai, 1020-77, Chinese;
   nonfiction ST
CHANG Wen-ming see ICHING
CH'ANG-Ch'um, 1148-1227,
   Chinese; nonfiction ST
CHANG-RODRIQUEZ, Eugenio,
   1924- , Peruvian-American;
   nonfiction CON
CHANGUION, François, 1695-
   1777, French; nonfiction DIL
CHANLER, Margaret, 1862- ,
   American; nonfiction HOE
'CHANNEL, A. R.' see CATHERALL,
   Arthur
CHANNING, Edward, 1856-1931,
   American; nonfiction KT
CHANNING, Edward Tyrrell,
   1790-1856, American; nonfic-
   tion KAA
CHANNING, John, fl. 1800, Eng-
   lish; nonfiction HIG
CHANNING, Steven A., 1940- ,
   American; nonfiction CON
CHANNING, William Ellery, 1780-
   1842, American; nonfiction
   BRO KAA ST
CHANNING, William Ellery,
   1818-1901, American; poetry,
   essays KAA
CHANNING, William Henry,
   1810-84, American; essays
   KAA
CHANOVER, Edmond Pierre,
   1932- , Franco-American;

nonfiction CON

CHANSKY, Norman Morton, 1929- ,
American; nonfiction CON

CHANTEREYNE, Victor Avoine de,
1762-1834, French; nonfiction
DIL

CHANTRAINE de VAN PRAAG,
Jacqueline, Belgian; nonfiction
BL

CHANTREAU, Pierre Nicolas, 1741-
1808, French; nonfiction DIL

CHANVALLON, Jean Baptiste Thibaut,
1725-88, French; nonfiction
DIL

CHAO Chih Hsin, 1662-1744, Chinese;
poetry ST

CHAO I, 1727-1814, Chinese; poetry
ST

CHAO, Kang, 1929- , Chinese-
American; nonfiction CON

CHAO Meng-fu, 1254-1322, Chinese;
poetry ST

CH'AO, Ts'o, -154 B.C., Chinese;
nonfiction ST

CHAO, Yuen Ren, 1892- , American; nonfiction CON

CHAPAIS, Sir Joseph Amable Thomas,
1858-1946, Canadian; nonfiction
ST SY

CHAPEL, Paul, 1926- , Dutch; nonfiction CON

CHAPELAIN, Jean, 1595-1674,
French; poetry, criticism DIF
HAR KE SA ST

CHAPELLE, Claude Emmanuel
Lhuillier, 1626-86, French;
nonfiction DIF

CHAPELLE, Howard Irving, 1901- ,
American; nonfiction CON

CHAPELLE, L., 1733-89, French;
nonfiction DIL

CHAPIN, Francis Stuart, Jr., 1916- ,
American; nonfiction CON

CHAPIN, Harold, 1886-1915, English;
plays MAT

CHAPIN, Henry, American; juveniles
WA

CHAPIN, June Roediger, 1931- ,
American; nonfiction CON

CHAPIN, Katherine Garrison,
1890- , American; fiction CON

CHAPIN, Ned, 1927- , American;
nonfiction CON

CHAPIN, William, 1918- , American; nonfiction CON

CHAPLIN, James Patrick, 1919- ,
American; nonfiction CON

CHAPLIN, Sidney, 1916- , English;

fiction, juveniles CON

'CHAPMAN, Allen' see STRATE-
MEYER, Edward L.

CHAPMAN, Arthur Harry,
1924- , American; nonfiction
CON

CHAPMAN, Brian, 1923- , English; nonfiction CON

CHAPMAN, Charles Henry,
1879- , English; juveniles
DOY

CHAPMAN, Colin, 1937- ,
English; nonfiction CON

CHAPMAN, Constance Elizabeth
Mann, 1919- , English;
juveniles CON

CHAPMAN, Edmund Haupt,
1906- , American; nonfiction
CON

CHAPMAN, Elwood N., 1916- ,
American; nonfiction CON

CHAPMAN, Frank Michler, 1864-
1945, American; nonfiction
KT

CHAPMAN, George, 1559-1634,
English; plays, poetry, trans-
lations BRO KB MAG SA SP
ST

CHAPMAN, George Warren Vernon
('Warren Vernon'), 1925- ,
English; fiction CON

CHAPMAN, Hester Wolferstan,
1899- , English; fiction CON

CHAPMAN, J. Dudley ('Jay
Dudley'), 1928- , American;
nonfiction CON

CHAPMAN, John Henry Palmer,
1865-1933, English; nonfiction
HOE

CHAPMAN, John Jay, 1862-1933,
American; poetry, plays, nonfiction KT

CHAPMAN, John Leslie, 1920- ,
American; nonfiction CON

CHAPMAN, John Stanton H. see
'CHAPMAN, Maristan'

CHAPMAN, June Ramey, 1918- ,
American; fiction CON

CHAPMAN, Kenneth Francis,
1910- , English; nonfiction
CON

CHAPMAN, Kenneth G., 1927- ,
American; nonfiction CON

'CHAPMAN, Maristan' (John
Stanton Higham Chapman),
1895/96- , and Mary Hamilton
Ilsley Chapman, 1895- , English; fiction, juveniles KL

WA WAF
CHAPMAN, Michael Andrew, 1884- ,
American; nonfiction HOE
CHAPMAN, Raymond ('Simon Nash'),
1924- , American; nonfiction
CON
CHAPMAN, Robert William, 1881-
1960, Scots; editor BRO
CHAPMAN, Roger Eddington, 1916- ,
American; nonfiction CON
CHAPMAN, Ronald George, 1917- ,
English; nonfiction CON
CHAPMAN, Samuel Greeley, 1929- ,
American; nonfiction CON
CHAPMAN, Stanley David, 1935- ,
English; nonfiction CON
CHAPMAN, William, 1850-1917,
Canadian; poetry SY
CHAPMAN-MORTIMER, William
Charles ('Chapman Mortimer'),
1907- , Scots; fiction CON
CHAPONE, Hester Mulso, 1727-1801,
English; nonfiction BRO KB ST
CHAPPELL, Fred, 1936- , Ameri-
can; nonfiction, fiction, poetry
CON
CHAPPELL, Vere Claiborne,
1930- , American; nonfiction
CON
CHAPPELL, Warren, 1904- , Amer-
ican; nonfiction CON
CHAPPLE, John Alfred Victor,
1928- , English; nonfiction CON
CHAPPOTIN de SAINT-LAURENT,
Michel, -1775, French; criti-
cism DIL
CHAPYGIN, Alexey Pavlovich, 1870-
1937, Russian; fiction COL HAR
HARK ST
CHAR, René, 1907- , French;
poetry, essays CON DIC DIF
FLE HAR MAL RIC SA ST
CHARANIS, Peter, 1908- , Greek-
American; nonfiction CON
CHARBONNEAU, Jean, 1875-1960,
Canadian; poetry SY
CHARBONNEAU, Robert, 1911- ,
Canadian; essays ST SY
CHARBUY, François Nicolas,
1715-86/88, French; poetry
DIL
CHARD, Leslie F., II, 1934- ,
American; nonfiction CON
CHARDON, Charles, 1695-1771,
French; nonfiction DIL
CHARDON de CROISILLES (de Reims),
fl. 1235, French; poetry ST

'CHARDONNE, Jacques' (Jacques
Boutelleau), 1884-1968, French;
fiction, essays COL DIC DIF
HAR KT FLE MAL SA ST
CHARDRY, 13th cent., Anglo-
Norman; poetry ST
CHARENTZ, Eglishe, 1897-1938,
Armenian; poetry LAN
CHARHADI, Driss ben Hamed,
Indian; fiction CON
CHARI, V. Krishna, 1924- ,
American; nonfiction CON
CHARINHO, Payo Gomes, 13th
cent., Galician; poetry ST
CHARITON de AFRODISIA, 4th-
5th cent., Greek; fiction SA
CHARLES IV, 1316-78, Bohemian;
nonfiction ST
CHARLES, Claude Aimé, 1718-68,
French; nonfiction DIL
CHARLES, Don Claude, 1918- ,
American; nonfiction CON
CHARLES, Fulgence J. B.,
1752- , French; nonfiction
DIL
CHARLES, Gerda, English; fiction
CON
CHARLES, Joan, 1914- , Ameri-
can; fiction WAF
'CHARLES, Louis' see STRATE-
MEYER, Edward L.
CHARLES, Rev. Pierre, 1883- ,
Belgian; nonfiction HO
CHARLES, Searle Franklin,
1923- , American; nonfiction
CON
'CHARLES, Theresa' see SWAT-
RIDGE, Charles and SWAT-
RIDGE, Irene
'CHARLES, Will' see WILLEFORD,
Charles R.
CHARLES d' ORLEANS, 1394-1465,
French; poetry DIF HAR KE
MAL SA ST
CHARLESWORTH, James Clyde,
1900- , American; nonfiction
CON
CHARLESWORTH, John Kaye,
1889- , English; nonfiction
CON
CHARLESWORTH, Marie Louise,
1819-80, English; juveniles
DOY
CHARLESWORTH, Maxwell John,
1925- , Australian; nonfiction
CON
CHARLEVOIX, Pierre François

Xavier de, 1682-1761, French;
nonfiction DIL
CHARLIER, Patricia Mary Simonet,
1923- , American; nonfiction
CON
CHARLIER, Roger Henri ('Henri
Rochard'), 1921- , Belgian-
American; nonfiction CON
CHARLIP, Remy, 1929- , Ameri-
can; nonfiction CON WA
CHARLOT, Jean, 1898- , French;
nonfiction CON FUL HO
'CHARLSON, David' see HOLMES,
David C.
CHARLETON, Walter, 1619-1707,
English; nonfiction BRO
CHARLTON, Donald Geoffrey,
1925- , English; nonfiction CON
CHARLTON, John, 1840- , English;
nonfiction HIG
'CHARLTON, John' see WOODHOUSE,
Martin
CHARLWOOD, Donald Ernest, 1915- ,
Australian; nonfiction, fiction
CON
CHARMATZ, Bill, 1925- , Ameri-
can; juveniles CON
CHARNEY, Maurice Myron, 1929- ,
American; nonfiction CON
CHARNEY, Shmuel see 'NIGER,
Shmuel'
CHARNOCK, Joan ('Joan Thomson'),
1903- , American; juveniles
CON
CHARNWOOD, Godfrey Rathbone
Benson, 1864-1945, English;
fiction, nonfiction KT
CHARNY, Carmi ('T. Carmi'),
1925- , American; poetry CON
CHARNY, Israel Wolf, 1931- ,
American; nonfiction CON
CHAROSH, Mannis, 1906- , Amer-
ican; nonfiction CON
'CHAROT, Mikhas' (M. Kudzolko),
1896- , Russian; fiction HARK
CHARPIER, Jacques, 1926- ,
French; poetry DIF PIN
CHARRIERE, Isabelle de van Tuyll
Zuylen, 1740-1805, Swiss-Dutch;
fiction, letters HAR SA ST
CHARRON, Etienne Leonard, 1696-
1765, French; nonfiction DIL
CHARRON, Pierre, 1541-1603,
French; nonfiction DIF SA ST
CHARROYER, Henry, -1709,
French; nonfiction DIL
'CHARTERIS, Leslie' (Leslie Charles

Bowyer Yin), 1907- , Eng-
lish; fiction BRO CON KT
RIC
CHARTERS, Ann Danberg, 1936- ,
American; nonfiction CON
CHARTERS, Samuel, 1929- ,
American; nonfiction CON
CHARTIER, Alain, 1385/95-
1429/33, French; poetry DIF
HAR KE MAL SA ST
CHARTIER, Emile see 'ALAIN'
CHARTIER, Jean, -1464, French;
nonfiction ST
CHARVAT, Frank John, 1918- ,
American; nonfiction CON
CHARVEL, Charles, 1742-79,
French; nonfiction DIL
CHARUEL d'ANTRIN, 18th cent.,
French; nonfiction DIL
CHARUEL d'ANTRIN, 18th cent.,
French; nonfiction DIL
CHARYN, Jerome, 1937- , Amer-
ican; nonfiction CON
'CHASAN, Bela' see HORWITZ,
Bela
CHASAN, Daniel Jack, 1943- ,
American; nonfiction CON
CHASCA, Edmund V. de, 1903- ,
Guatamalan; nonfiction BL
CHASE, Alan Louis, 1929- ,
American; fiction CON
'CHASE, Alice' see McHARGUE,
Georgess
CHASE, Alice Elizabeth, 1906- ,
American; juveniles CON WA
CHASE, Alston Hurd, 1906- ,
American; nonfiction CON
'CHASE, Beatrice' see PARR,
Katharine O.
CHASE, Borden, American; fic-
tion WAF
CHASE, Gilbert, 1906- , Amer-
ican; nonfiction CON
CHASE, Harold Williams, 1922- ,
American; nonfiction CON
CHASE, James Hadley, 1906- ,
English; fiction RIC
CHASE, Loring D., 1916- ,
American; nonfiction CON
CHASE, Mary Coyle, 1907- ,
American; juveniles, plays
KTS MAT WA
CHASE, Mary Ellen, 1887-1973,
American; fiction CON KT WA
WAF
CHASE, Richard, 1904- , Amer-
ican; juveniles FUL

CHASE, Richard Volney, 1914- ,
American; nonfiction KTS
CHASE, Samuel Brown, Jr., 1932- ,
American; nonfiction CON
CHASE, Stuart, 1888- , American;
nonfiction KAT KT
CHASE, Virginia Lowell see PERKINS,
Virginia C.
CHASIN, Helen, American; poetry
MUR
CHASINS, Abram, 1903- , Ameri-
can; nonfiction CON
CHASLES, Victor Euphémion
Philarête, 1798-1873, French;
criticism DIF
CHASSAING, Juan, 1838-64, Ar-
gentinian; journalism MIN
CHASSEGNET, Albert, -1714,
French; nonfiction DIL
CHASSIGNET, Jean Baptiste, 1570/78,
1620/35, French; poetry DIF
MAL
CHASTAIN, Madye Lee, 1908- ,
American; juveniles CON FUL
CHASTEEN, Edgar Ray, 1935- ,
American; nonfiction CON
CHASTELAIN, Georges (Chastellain),
1405-75, French; nonfiction,
poetry DIF SA ST
CHASTELIAN de COUCI, -1203,
French; poetry ST
CHASTELLAIN, Pierre (Vaillant),
-1408, French; poetry ST
CHASTELLUX, François Jean, 1734-
88, French; nonfiction DIL
CHATEAUBRIAND, François René
de, 1768-1848, French; fiction,
nonfiction DIF HAR KE MAG
MAL SA ST
CHATEAUBRIANT, Alphonse, de,
1877-1951, French; fiction COL
DIF
CHATEAUBRUN, Jean Baptiste Vivien
de, 1686-1775, French; nonfiction
DIL
CHATEAUROUX, Marie Anne De
Mailly, 1717-44, French; nonfic-
tion SA
CHATEILLON see CASTELLION,
Sebastien
CHATELET, Albert, 1928- , French;
nonfiction CON
CHATELET, Gabrielle Emilie Le
Tonnellier, 1706-49, French;
nonfiction SA
'CHATELLRAULT, Victor de' see
BEAUDOIN, Kenneth L.

CHATFIELD, Earl Charles, Jr.,
1934- , American; nonfiction
CON
CHATFIELD, Hale, 1936- , Amer-
ican; nonfiction, poetry CON
CHATFIELD, Michael, 1934- ,
American; nonfiction CON
CHATHAM, James Ray, 1931- ,
American; nonfiction CON
CHÂTILLON, Walter of, 1135-
84?, French; poetry ST
CHATILLON, DE see GAUTIER de
LILA, Philippe
CHATMAN, Seymour Benjamin,
1928- , American; nonfiction
CON
CHATRAIN, Alexandre see ERCK-
MANN, Chatrain
CHATRIK, Dhani Ram, 1876-1954,
Indian; poetry LAN
CHATTERJEE, Margaret Gantzer,
1925- , English; nonfiction
CON
CHATTERJI, Bankim Candra,
1838-94, Indian; fiction LAN
ST
CHATTERJI, Saratcandra, 1876-
1938, Indian; fiction LAN
CHATTERTON, Edward Keble,
1878-1944, English; nonfiction
BRO
CHATTERTON, Thomas (Thomas
Rowley), 1752-70, English;
poetry BRO KB SA SP ST
CHATTERTON, Wayne, 1921- ,
American; nonfiction CON
CHAUCER, Geoffrey, 1343-1400,
English; poetry BRO KB MAG
SA SP ST
CHAUDHURI, Haridas, 1913- ,
Indian; nonfiction CON
CHAUDHURI, Sukanta, 1950- ,
Indian; poetry MUR
CHAULOT, Paul, 1914- , French;
poetry DIF
CHAUMETTE, Pierre Gaspard,
1763-94, French; nonfiction
DIL
CHAUNCY, Charles, 1705-87,
American; nonfiction KAA
CHAUNCY, Nan Masterman,
Australian; juveniles WA CON
CHAUNDLER, Christine ('Peter
Martin'), 1887- , English;
juveniles, fiction COM CON
DOY
CHAUNDLER, Thomas, 1418-90,

English; nonfiction ST
CHAUVEAU, 18th cent., French;
  plays DIL
CHAUVEAU, Pierre Joseph Olivier,
  1820-90, Canadian; fiction SY
CHAUVELIN, Henri Philippe de,
  1716-70, French; nonfiction DIL
CHAVARRIA, Lisímaco, 1877-1913,
  Costa Rican; poetry MIN
CHAVCHAVADZE, Prince Ilia, 1837-
  1907, Russian; poetry LAN
CHAVCHAVADZE, Paul, 1899-1971,
  Russian-American; fiction, non-
  fiction CON
CHAVES, Fernando, 1902- ,
  Ecuadorian; fiction, essays DI
CHAVEZ, Angelico, 1910- , Amer-
  ican; poetry HOE
CHAYEFSKY, Paddy, 1923- , Amer-
  ican; plays CON MAT
CHAYER, Christophe, fl. 1723- ,
  French; nonfiction DIL
CHAZAL, Malcolm de, 1902- ,
  French; poetry DIC DIF
CHAZANOFF, William, 1915- ,
  American; nonfiction CON
CHEADLE, Walter Butler, 1835-1910,
  English; nonfiction KBA
CHEAVENS, Sam Frank, 1905- ,
  American; fiction, nonfiction
  CON
CHECKLAND, Sydney George,
  1916- , Canadian; nonfiction
  CON
CHEETHAM, James, 1772-1810,
  American; journalism KAA
CHEEVER, Ezekiel, 1614-1708,
  American; nonfiction KAA
CHEEVER, John, 1912- , American;
  fiction CON RIC
CHEJNE, Anwar George, 1923- ,
  American; nonfiction CON
CHEKE, Sir John, 1514-57, English;
  nonfiction BRO KB ST
CHEKHOV, Anton, 1860-1904, Rus-
  sian; plays, fiction COL FLE
  HAR HARK KE MAG MAT SA ST
CHELCHIKY, Petr, 1390-1460,
  Czech; nonfiction SA ST
CHELF, Carl P., 1937- , American;
  nonfiction CON
'CHELTON, John' see DURST, Paul
CHEMNITZER, Ivan I. see KHEMNIT-
  SER, Ivan I.
'CHEN Fek-cheung' see CHENG Chu-
  Yuan
'CHEN Hwei' see STEVENSON,
  William

CH'EN, Jerome, 1921- , Chinese-
  English; poetry CON
CHEN, Joseph Tao, 1925- ,
  Chinese-American; nonfiction
  CON
CHEN, Kenneth Kuan Sheng,
  1907- , American; nonfiction
  CON
CH'ÊN, Mêng-liu, 1651- , Chinese;
  nonfiction ST
CHEN, Nai-ruenn, 1927- , Chi-
  nese-American; nonfiction CON
CHEN, Philip Stanley, 1903- ,
  Chinese-American; nonfiction
  CON
CH'ÊN, Shih-tao, 1053-1101,
  Chinese; poetry ST
CHÊN Tê-hsiu, 1178-1235,
  Chinese; nonfiction ST
CHEN, Theodore Hsi-En, 1902- ,
  Chinese-American; nonfiction
  CON
CHEN, Tony, 1929- , American;
  juveniles CON
CH'EN, Tu-hsiu, 1879-1942, Chi-
  nese; essays ST
CH'ÊN Tzǔ-ang, 1656-98?, Chi-
  nese; poetry, essays ST
CHEN, Vincent, 1917- , Ameri-
  can; nonfiction CON
CHENAULT, Lawrence Royce,
  1897- , American; nonfiction
  CON
'CHENAULT, Nell' see SMITH,
  Linell N.
CHENEDOLLE, Charles Julien
  Lioult de, 1769-1833, French;
  poetry ST
CHENEVIERE, Jacques, 1886- ,
  Swiss; fiction ST
CHENEVIX TRENCH, Charles
  Pocklington, 1914- , English;
  juveniles CON
CHENEY, Brainard Bartwell,
  1900- , American; fiction
  CON
CHENEY, Cora, 1916- , Ameri-
  can; juveniles CON WA
CHENEY, Ednah Dow Littlehall,
  1824-1904, American; nonfic-
  tion KAA
CHENEY, Frances Neel, 1906- ,
  American; nonfiction CON
CHENEY, John Vance, 1848-1922,
  American; poetry, essays KAA
CHENEY, Lois A., 1931- , Amer-
  ican; nonfiction CON
CHENEY, Sheldon Warren, 1886- ,

American; nonfiction KL KT

CHÊNG, Ch'iao, 1104-62, Chinese;
nonfiction ST

CHENG, Chu-yuan ('Chen Fek-cheung'),
1927- , Chinese-American; nonfiction CON

CH'ÊNG HAO, 1032-85, Chinese; nonfiction ST

CHÊNG Hsiao-hsü, 1859-1938, Chinese; poetry ST

CHÊNG Hsüan, 127-200, Chinese;
nonfiction ST

CH'ÊNG I, 1033-1107, Chinese;
nonfiction ST

CHENG, James Chester, 1926- ,
American; nonfiction CON

CHENG, James Kuo Chiang, 1936- ,
Chinese-American; fiction CON

CHENIER, André Marie, 1762-94,
French; poetry DIF DIL HAR
KE MAL SA ST

CHENIER, Marie Joseph, 1764-1811,
French; poetry, plays DIF HAR
SA ST

'CHENNEVIERE, Daniel' see
RUDHYAR, Dane

CHENOWETH, Vida S., 1928- ,
American; nonfiction CON

CHERAU, Gaston, 1874-1937, French;
fiction DIF

CHERBULIEZ, Victor, 1829-99,
French; fiction DIF HAR KE SA
ST

CHERBURY, Lord see HERBERT,
Edward

CHERINGTON, Paul Whiton, 1918- ,
American; nonfiction CON

CHERITON, Odo of, -1247, English; fiction ST

CHERMAYEFF, Serge, 1900- ,
American; nonfiction CON

CHERNISS, Michael David, 1940- ,
American; nonfiction CON

CHERNOFF, Goldie Taub, 1909- ,
Austrian-American; juveniles
CON

'CHERNY, Sasha' see GLÜCKBERG,
Alexander M.

CHERNYSHEVSKY, Nikolay Gavrilo-
vich, 1828-89/98, Russian;
fiction, criticism HARK KE SA
ST

CHERRIER, Sebastien, 1699-1780,
French; nonfiction DIL

CHERRINGTON, Ernest Hurst, Jr.,
1909- , American; nonfiction
CON

CHERRINGTON, Leon G., 1926- ,
American; nonfiction CON

CHERRY, Andrew, 1762-1812,
Irish; plays BRO ST

CHERRY, C. Conrad, 1937- ,
American; nonfiction CON

CHERRY, George Loy, 1905- ,
American; nonfiction CON

'CHERRYHOLMES, Anne' see
PRICE, Olive M.

CHERWINSKI, Joseph, 1915- ,
American; poetry, fiction
CON HIL

CHESEBROUGH, Caroline, 1825-
73, American; fiction KAA

CHESEN, Eli, S., 1944- , American; fiction CON

CHESHAM, Sallie, American; nonfiction CON

CHESHIRE, Geoffrey Leonard,
1917- , English; nonfiction
CON

CHESHIRE, Gifford Paul ('Paul
Craig'; 'Chad Merriman';
'Ford Pendleton'), 1905- ,
American; fiction PAC

CHESHIRE, Joseph Blount, 1850-
1932, American; nonfiction
JO

CHESKIN, Louis, 1909- , American; nonfiction CON

CHESLER, Bernice, 1932- ,
American; nonfiction CON

CHESLOCK, Louis, 1899- ,
American; nonfiction CON

CHESNAYE, DESBOIS, François
Alexandre Aubert de la, 1699-
1784, French; nonfiction DIL

CHESNEY, Sir George Tomkins,
1830-95, English; fiction KBA

CHESNEY, Kellow Robert, 1914- ,
American; nonfiction CON

CHESNOFF, Richard Z., 1937- ,
American; nonfiction CON

CHESNUT, James Stanley, 1926- ,
American; nonfiction CON

CHESNUTT, Charles Waddell, 1858-
1932, American; fiction JO
KT MAG ST

CHESSER, Eustace, 1902- ,
Scots; nonfiction CON

CHESSMAN, George Wallace,
1919- , American; nonfiction
CON

CHESSMAN, Ruth Green, 1910- ,
American; fiction CON

CHESTE, Conde de see GONZALEZ

de la PEZUELA y CEBALLOS,
Juan
CHESTER, Edward William, 1935- ,
American; nonfiction CON
CHESTER, George Randolph, 1869-
1924, American; fiction KT
CHESTER, Michael Arthur, 1928- ,
American; juveniles CON WA
'CHESTER, Peter' see PHILLIPS,
Dennis J. A.
CHESTER, Robert, 1566-1640, Eng-
lish; poetry ST
CHESTERFIELD, Lord (Philip Dormer
Stanhope), 1694-1773, English;
essays, diary BRO KB MAG SA
ST
CHESTERTON, Arthur Kenneth,
1899- , English; nonfiction CON
CHESTERTON, Gilbert Keith, 1874-
1936, English; essays, fiction,
poetry BRO FLE HOE KL KT
MAG RIC SA SP ST
'CHESTOR, Rui' see COURTIER,
Sidney H.
CHETHAM-STRODE, Warren ('Michael
Hamilton'), 1896- , English;
fiction, plays CON
CHETHIMATTAM, John Britto,
1922- , American; nonfiction
CON
CHETIN, Helen, 1922- , American;
nonfiction CON
CHETTLE, Henry, 1565-1607?, Eng-
lish; plays BRO KB ST
CHETWOOD, Knightly, 1660-1720,
English; poetry, translations
ST
'CHETWYND, Berry' see RAYNER,
Claire
CHEUNG, Steven Ng Sheong, 1935- ,
Chinese-American; nonfiction
CON
CHEVAL, Estelle Agnes, 1910- ,
American; nonfiction SCA
CHEVALIER, 18th cent., French;
plays DIL
CHEVALIER, Elizabeth Pickett,
1896- , American; fiction WAF
CHEVALLIER, Gabriel, 1895- ,
French; fiction DIF HAR RIC
ST
CHEVASSU, Joseph, 1674-1752,
French; nonfiction DIL
CHEVIGNY, Hector, 1904- ,
American; radio, nonfiction
HOE KTS
CHEVRIER, François Antoine, 1700-

62, French; plays DIL
CHEW, Allen F., 1924- , Amer-
ican; nonfiction CON
CHEYNE, Thomas Kelly, 1841-
1915, English; criticism KBA
CHEYNEY, Arnold B., 1926- ,
American; nonfiction CON
'CHEYNEY, Peter' see SOUTHOUSE-
CHEYNEY, Reginald
CHI, Richard Hu See-Yee ('Chuan-
Chin'; 'Ernest Moncrieff'),
1918- , Chinese-American;
nonfiction CON
CHI, Wen-shun, 1910- , Chinese-
American; nonfiction CON
CHI Yün, 1724-1805, Chinese;
editor LAN ST
CHIA I, 198?-165 B.C., Chinese;
poetry ST
CHIABRERA, Gabriello, 1552-
1638, Italian; poetry HAR KE
SA ST
CHIADO Antonio Ribeiro,   -1591,
Portuguese; poetry, plays SA
ST
CHIAMPEL, Durich, 1510-82,
Raeto-Romansch; poetry ST
CHIANCA, Rui, 1891-1931, Portu-
guese; poetry, plays SA
CHIANG, K'uei, 1158?-1231?,
Chinese; poetry ST
CHIANG Lee, 1903- , American;
nonfiction KTS
CHIANG Ping-Chih see 'TING-
LING'
CHIANG Shih Ch'üan, 1725-85,
Chinese; poetry, plays ST
CHIARA, Pietro, 1913- , Italian;
nonfiction SA
CHIARELLI, Luigi, 1884-1947,
Italian; plays COL MAT SA
CHIARI, Joseph, 1911- , French;
nonfiction, translations CON
CHIARI, Pietro, 1714-85/88,
Italian; poetry, fiction, plays
SA ST
CHIARINI, Giuseppe, 1833-1908,
Italian; criticism, poetry ST
CHIBNALL, Marjorie McCallum
('Marjorie Morgan'), 1915- ,
English; nonfiction CON
CHICHARRO BRIONES, Eduardo,
1905- , Spanish; poetry BL
CHICHESTER, Francis Charles,
1901-72, English; nonfiction
CON
CHICHESTER, Jane see LONG-

RIGG, Jane C.
CHICK, Edson Marland, 1924- ,
American; nonfiction CON
CHICKERING, Arthur W., 1927- ,
American; nonfiction CON
CHIDESTER, Ann, 1919- , Amer-
ican; fiction KTS WAF
CHIDSEY, Donald Barr, 1902- ,
American; fiction CON KTS WAF
CHIDZERO, Bernard Thomas Gibson,
1927- , South African; nonfiction
CON
CH'IEN Ch'ien-i, 1582-1664, Chi-
nese; poetry ST
CH'IEN-LUNG, 1711-99, Chinese;
poetry ST
CH'IEN Ts'un-hsun see TSIEN, Tsuen-
hsuin
CHIESA, Francesco, 1871- , Italian;
poetry, fiction COL FLE HAR
SA ST
'CHIEVRE, La see ROBERT de
REIMS
'CHIGNON, Niles' see LINGEMAN,
Richard R.
'CHIKAMATSU, Hanji', 1725-83,
Japanese; plays ST
CHIKAMATSU MONZAEMON, 1653-
1725, Japanese; plays, poetry
LAN MAG SA ST
CHILCOTE, Ronald H., 1935- ,
American; nonfiction CON
CHILD, Francis James, 1825-96,
American; nonfiction BRO KAA
CHILD, Heather, 1912- , English;
nonfiction CON
CHILD, Lydia Maria Francis,
1802-80, American; nonfiction,
fiction BRO KAA SA
CHILD, Philip Albert Gillett, 1898- ,
Canadian; poetry, fiction CON
MUR ST SY
CHILD, Roderick, 1948- , English;
nonfiction CON
CHILDE, Vere Gordon, 1892- ,
British; nonfiction KTS
CHILDE, Wilfred Rowland Mary,
1890- , English; poetry HOE
CHILDERS, Robert Erskine, 1870-
1922, Anglo-Irish; fiction, non-
fiction BRO KT RIC SA
CHILDERS, Thomas Allen, 1940- ,
American; nonfiction CON
CHILDS, Barney, 1926- , Ameri-
can; nonfiction CON
'CHILDS, C. Sands' see CHILDS,
Maryanna

CHILDS, David Haslam, 1933- ,
American; nonfiction CON
CHILDS, Halla Fay Cochrane,
1890- , American; juveniles
COM CON
CHILDS, Harwood Lawrence,
1898-1972, American; nonfic-
tion CON
CHILDS, John Farnsworth,
American; juveniles WA
CHILDS, Marilyn Grace Carlson,
1923- , American; nonfiction
CON
CHILDS, Marquis William, 1903- ,
American; journalism, fiction
KTS
CHILDS, Maryanna ('C. Sands
Childs'), 1910- , American;
juveniles CON
CHILES, Robert Eugene, 1923- ,
American; nonfiction CON
CHILINGIROV, Stilian, 1881- ,
Bulgarian; nonfiction ST
CHILLINGWORTH, William, 1602-
44, English; nonfiction BRO
KB
CHILTON, Eleanor Carroll, 1898-
1949, American; fiction, poetry
KT
CHILVER, Peter, 1933- , Amer-
ican; nonfiction CON
'CHIMAERA' see FARJEON,
Eleanor
CHIN, Frank Chew, Jr. ('Fran-
cisco de Menton'), 1940- ,
American; plays, fiction CON
CHING, James C., 1926- , Amer-
ican; nonfiction CON
CHINITZ, Benjamin, 1924- ,
American; nonfiction CON
CHINN, Lawrence Chambers,
1902- , American; fiction
CON
CHINN, William G., 1919- ,
American; nonfiction CON
CHINOY, Ely, 1921- , American;
nonfiction CON
CHINOY, Helen Irish, 1920- ,
American; nonfiction CON
CHIPLUNKAR, Vishnu Shastri,
1850-82, Indian; nonfiction ST
CHIPMAN, Bruce Lewis, 1946- ,
American; nonfiction CON
CHIPMAN, Daniel, 1765-1850,
American; nonfiction KAA
CHIPMAN, Donald Eugene, 1928- ,
American; nonfiction CON

CHIPP, Herschel Browning, 1913- ,
American; nonfiction CON
CHIPPERFIELD, Joseph Eugene
('John Eland Craig'), 1909/12- ,
English; juveniles COM CON
FUL WA
CHIRIKOV, Yevgeni Nikolayevich,
1864-1932, Russian; fiction COL
HARK SA ST
CHIRVECHES ARROSPIDE, Armando,
1883-1926, Argentinian; transla-
tions, fiction MIN SA
CHISHOLM, Alan Rowland, 1888- ,
American; nonfiction CON
CHISHOLM, Mary Kathleen, 1924- ,
Scots; nonfiction CON
CHISHOLM, Michael Donald Inglis,
1931- , English; nonfiction
CON
CHISHOLM, Robert Ferguson, 1904- ,
Canadian; nonfiction CON
CHISHOLM, Roger K., 1937- ,
American; nonfiction CON
CHISHOLM, Samuel Whitten, 1919- ,
American; nonfiction CON
CHISHOLM, Shirley Anita St. Hill,
1924- , American; nonfiction
CON
CHISOLM, Lawrence Washington,
1929- , American; nonfiction
CON
CHITTUM, Ida, 1918- , American;
juveniles CON
CHITTY, Susan Elspeth, 1929- ,
English; nonfiction CON
CHITTY, Sir Thomas Willes ('Thomas
Hinde'), 1926- , English; fic-
tion CON RIC
CHITWOOD, Marie Downs, 1918- ,
American; fiction CON
CHITWOOD, Oliver Perry, 1874- ,
American; nonfiction CON
CHIU, Hungdah, 1936- , Chinese-
American; nonfiction CON
CHIVERS, Thomas Holley, 1807/09-
58, American; poetry KAA ST
'CHI-WEI' see SHU, Austin C.
'CHIYONI' see KAGA NO CHIYO
CHLUMBERG, Hans, 1897-1930,
Austrian; plays MAT
CHMELNIZKI, Nicolai Ivanovich,
1789-1846, Russian; poetry,
plays SA
CHMIELEWSKI, Edward, 1928- ,
American; nonfiction CON
CHO, Yong Sam, 1925- , Korean-
American; nonfiction CON

CHOATE, Gwen Peterson ('R.G.
Choate'), 1922- , American;
fiction CON
CHOATE, Julian Ernest, Jr.,
1916- , American; nonfiction
CON
CHOATE, Rufus, 1799-1859,
American; nonfiction KAA
CHOCANO, José Santos, 1875-
1934, Peruvian; poetry BL
FLE SA ST
'CHOCHLIK' see RADWANSKI,
Pierre A.
CHOCHOLUSEK, Prokop, 1819-
64, Czech; poetry, fiction,
journalism SA
CHODERLOS de LACLOS see
LACLOS, Pierre A.F.C. de
CHODOROV, Edward, 1904- ,
American; plays MAT
CHODOROV, Jerome, 1911- ,
American; plays MAT
CHODOROV, Stephan, 1934- ,
American; nonfiction CON
CHODZIESNER, Gertrud see
'KOLMAR, Gertrud'
CHODZKO, Ignacy ('Wirszajtis'),
1794-1861, Polish; essays ST
CHOGYU see TAKAYAMA, Chogyu
CHOISEUL, Etienne François,
1719-85, French; nonfiction
DIL
CHOISEUL, Louise Honorine
Crozat du Chatel, 1734-1801,
French; letters DIL
CHOISEUL-GOUFFIER, Marie
Gabreil Florent, 1752-1817,
French; nonfiction DIL SA
CHOISNET, Pierre, 1411?-83?,
French; nonfiction ST
CHOISY, François Temolión,
1644-1724, French; nonfiction
SA
'CHOLERIC, Brother' see VAN
ZELLER, Hubert
CHOLMONDELEY, Mary ('Pax'),
1859-1925, English; fiction
BRO KT
CHOMEL, Jean Baptiste, 1700-
65, French; nonfiction DIL
CHOMMIE, John Campbell,
1914- , American; nonfiction
CON
CHOMSKY, Avram Noam, 1928- ,
American; nonfiction CON
CHONG CHOL, 1536-93, Korean;
poetry LAN

'CHONG, Kyong-Jo' see CHUNG,
  Kyung C.
CHONG, Peng-Khuan, Chinese-Amer-
  ican; nonfiction CON
CHOPER, Jesse Herbert, 1935- ,
  American; nonfiction CON
CHOPIN, J.B. Charles Dieudonné,
  1726-72, French; plays DIL
CHOPIN, Kate O'Flaherty, 1851-1904,
  American; fiction KAA SA
CHOPIN, René, 1885-1953, Canadian;
  poetry SY
CHOQUETTE, Adrienne, 1915- ,
  Canadian; nonfiction SY
CHOQUETTE, Guy Robert, 1905- ,
  Canadian; poetry, fiction ST
  SY
CHORAFAS, Dimitris N., 1926- ,
  Greek-French; nonfiction CON
CHORLEY, Henry Fothergill ('Paul
  Bell'), 1808-72, English; criti-
  cism, poetry, fiction BRO KBA
'CHORNY, Fedya' see KOJUHAROV,
  Todor
CHOROMANSKI, Michal, 1904- ,
  Polish-Canadian; fiction, plays
  FLE HAR RIC ST
CHORON, Jacques, 1904- , Russian-
  American; juvenile CON WA
CHOU Shu-Jen see 'LUSIN'
CHOUDHURY, G.W., 1926- , Indian;
  nonfiction CON
CHOUKAS, Michael Eugene, 1901- ,
  American; nonfiction CON
CHOU-TSE, 1017-73, Chinese; non-
  fiction SA
CHOU Tso-jen, 1885-1958?, Chinese;
  essays, translations LAN ST
CHOU TUN-I, 1017-73, Chinese; non-
  fiction ST
CHOW, Gregory C., 1929- , Chinese-
  American; nonfiction CON
CHOW, Yung-Teh, 1916- , Chinese-
  American; nonfiction CON
CHOWDHARY, Savitri Devi Dumra,
  1907- , Indian; nonfiction CON
CHOYNOWSKI, Pyotr, 1885-1935, Pol-
  ish; fiction HAR ST
CHRETIEN de TROYES, 1150-90,
  French; poetry DIF HAR KE
  MAG MAL SA ST
CHRETIEN li GOIS, 13th cent.,
  French; poetry, translations
  ST
CHRIMES, Stanley Bertram, 1907- ,
  English; nonfiction CON
CHRISMAN, Arthur Bowie, 1889-

1953, American; juvenile
  KJU KL WA
CHRISMAN, Harry E., 1906- ,
  American; fiction CON
CHRIST, Carl Finley, 1923- ,
  American; nonfiction CON
CHRIST, Henry Irvine, 1915- ,
  American; nonfiction CON
CHRIST, Lena, 1881- , German;
  nonfiction LEN
CHRIST, Ronald, 1936- , Amer-
  ican; nonfiction CON
CHRISTALLER, Helene, 1872- ,
  German; nonfiction LEN
'CHRISTEN, Ada' (Christiane von
  Breden), 1844-1901, Austrian;
  poetry AL HAR ST
CHRISTENSEN, David Emun,
  1921- , American; nonfiction
  CON
CHRISTENSEN, Edward L., 1913- ,
  American; nonfiction CON
CHRISTENSEN, Erwin Ottomar,
  1890- , American; nonfiction
  CON
CHRISTENSEN, Francis, 1902- ,
  American; nonfiction CON
CHRISTENSEN, Gardell Dano,
  1907- , American; juveniles
  COM CON WA
CHRISTENSEN, Hjalmar, 1869-
  1925, Norwegian; fiction, plays,
  essays ST
CHRISTENSEN, Otto Henry, 1898- ,
  American; nonfiction CON
CHRISTENSON, Cornelia Vos,
  1903- , American; nonfiction
  CON
CHRISTENSON, Reo M., 1918- ,
  American; nonfiction CON
CHRISTESEN, Clement Byrne,
  1911- , Australian; poetry
  MUR
CHRISTGAU, Alice Erickson,
  1902- , American; fiction
  CON
CHRISTIAN, 10th? cent., Czech;
  nonfiction ST
CHRISTIAN, Curtis Wallace,
  1927- , American; nonfiction
  CON
'CHRISTIAN, Frederick' see
  GEHMAN, Richard B.
CHRISTIAN, Garth Hood, 1921- ,
  English; juveniles CON
CHRISTIAN, Henry Arthur,
  1931- , American; nonfiction
  CON

CHRISTIAN, Reginald Frank, 1924- ,
English; nonfiction CON
CHRISTIANI, Donnia Bunis, 1913- ,
Russian-American; nonfiction
CON
CHRISTIANSEN, Arne Einar, 1861-
1939, Danish; plays, poetry,
fiction ST
CHRISTIANSEN, Arthur, 1904-63,
English; nonfiction CON
CHRISTIANSEN, Sigurd Wesley,
1891-1947, Norwegian; fiction,
plays FLE HAR KT SA ST
CHRISTIANSON, John Robert,
1934- , American; nonfiction
CON
CHRISTIE, Agatha Miller Mallowan
('Mary Westmacott'), 1891- ,
English; fiction BRO CON KAT
KT RIC SA ST WA
CHRISTIE, George Custis, 1934- ,
American; nonfiction CON
CHRISTIE, Ian Ralph, 1919- ,
English; nonfiction CON
'CHRISTIE, Keith' see HAYNES,
Alfred H.
CHRISTIE, Milton, 1921- , Ameri-
can; nonfiction CON
CHRISTIE, Trevor L., 1905- ,
American; nonfiction CON
CHRISTINE, Charles Thornton,
1936- , American; nonfiction
CON
CHRISTINE, Dorothy Weaver,
1934- , American; nonfiction
CON
CHRISTINE de PISAN, 1364-1431?,
French; poetry DIF HAR KE
MAL SA ST
CHRIST-JANER, Albert W., 1910- ,
American; nonfiction CON
CHRISTMAN, Donald R., 1919- ,
American; nonfiction CON
CHRISTOFFEL, Hermanus Kühn see
'MIRKO'
CHRISTOL, Carl Quimby, 1914- ,
American; nonfiction CON
CHRISTOPH, James Bernard,
1928- , American; nonfiction
CON
CHRISTOPHE, Georges Colomb,
1856-1945, French; poetry DIF
CHRISTOPHER, John B., 1914- ,
American; nonfiction CON
'CHRISTOPHER, Louise' see HALE,
Arlene
CHRISTOPHER, Matthew F. ('Fredric

Martin'), 1917- , American;
juveniles COM CON WA
CHRISTOPHER of MYTELENE,
11th cent., Byzantine; poetry
ST
CHRISTY, George, American;
fiction CON
CHRISTY, Joseph M., 1919- ,
American; nonfiction CON
CHROUST, Anton Hermann,
1907- , German-American;
nonfiction CON
CHRUDEN, Herbert Jefferson,
1918- , American; nonfiction
CON
CHRYSIPPUS of SOLI in Cilicia,
280-07 B.C., Greek; nonfiction
ST
CHRYSOLOGUE de GY, R.P.,
1728- , French; nonfiction
DIL
CHRYSOLORAS see CRISOLORA,
Manuel
CHRYSTIE, Francis Nicholson,
1904- , American; juvenile
WA
CHTCHETEDRIN, Miguel, 1826-
88, Russian; poetry, fiction
SA
CHU, Daniel, 1933- , Chinese-
American; nonfiction CON
CHU, Grace Zia, 1899- , Chinese-
American; nonfiction CON
CHU HSI, 1130-1200, Chinese;
nonfiction ST
CHU I-tsun, 1629-1709, Chinese;
poetry ST
CHU, Louis H., 1915- , Chinese-
American; fiction CON
CH'U, Tung-tsu, 1910- , Chinese-
American; nonfiction CON
CHU, Valentin Yuan-ling, 1919- ,
Chinese-American; nonfiction
CON
'CHUAN-CHIN' see CHI, Richard
H.
CHUANG TZU, 365-290? B.C.,
Chinese; nonfiction LAN SA
ST
CHUBAK, 1916- , Persian; fic-
tion LAN
CHUBB, Thomas Caldecot, 1899-
1972, American; poetry, trans-
lations CON
CHUDOBA, Bohdan, 1909- ,
Czech; nonfiction HO
CH'Ü YÜAN, 340?-278? B.C.,

Chinese; poetry LAN ST
CHUECA y GOITIA, Fernando,
1911- , Spanish; nonfiction BL
SA
CHU-HI, 1130- , Chinese; nonfiction
SA
CHUKOVSKY, Kornei Ivanovich,
1882-1969, Russian-American;
juveniles, translations CON ST
WA
CHULKOV, Georgy Ivanovich, 1879- ,
Russian; poetry ST
CHULKOV, Mikhail Dmitrievich,
1440/43-92/93, Russian; fiction
HAR HARK ST
CHUNG, Kyung Cho ('Kyong-Jo Chung'),
1921- , Korean-American; non-
fiction CON
CHURCH, Alfred John, 1829-1912,
English; juveniles KJU WA
CHURCH, Benjamin, 1734-76, Amer-
ican; essays, poetry KAA
'CHURCH, Jeffrey' see KIRK, Richard
E.
CHURCH, Joseph, 1918- , Ameri-
can; nonfiction CON
CHURCH, Margaret, 1920- , Amer-
ican; nonfiction CON
'CHURCH, Peter' see NUTTALL,
Jeff
CHURCH, Ralph Bruce, 1927- ,
American; nonfiction CON
CHURCH, Richard ('Eccles'), 1893-
1972, English; juveniles, poetry,
fiction, criticism BRO CON
DOY FUL KT MUR RIC
CHURCH, Richard William, 1815-90,
English; essays, nonfiction BRO
KBA ST
CHURCH, Ronald James Harrison,
1915- , English; nonfiction
CON
CHURCH, Ruth Ellen Lovrien ('Mary
Meade'), American; nonfiction
CON
CHURCHILL, Charles, 1731-64,
English; poetry BRO KB SP ST
CHURCHILL, Elmer Richard,
1937- , American; nonfiction
CON
CHURCHILL, Guy E., 1926- ,
English; nonfiction CON
CHURCHILL, Linda R., 1938- ,
American; nonfiction CON
CHURCHILL, Reginald Charles,
1916- , English; nonfiction
CON

CHURCHILL, Rhona Adelaide,
1913- , English; nonfiction
CON
CHURCHILL, Samuel, 1911- ,
American; nonfiction CON
PAC
CHURCHILL, Winston, 1871-1947,
American; fiction, plays BRO
KAT KT MAG RIC ST
CHURCHILL, Sir Winston Leonard
Spencer, 1874-1965, English;
nonfiction BRO KT MAG RIC
SA ST
CHURCHMAN, Charles West,
1913- , American; nonfiction
CON
CHURCHMAN, Michael, 1929- ,
American; nonfiction CON
CHURCHYARD, Thomas, 1520?-
1604, English; poetry BRO
KB ST
'CHURTON, Henry' see TOURGEE,
Albion W.
CHUTE, Beatrice Joy, 1913- ,
American; juveniles, fiction
COM CON FUL
CHUTE, Marchette Gaylord,
1909- , American; juveniles,
nonfiction BRO COM CON
FUL KTS WA
'CHUTE, Rupert' see CLEVELAND,
Philip J.
CHUTE, William Joseph, 1914- ,
American; nonfiction CON
CHWALEK, Henryka C., 1918- ,
American; nonfiction CON
CHYET, Stanley F., 1931- ,
American; nonfiction CON
CIALENTE, Fausta, 1900- ,
Italian; fiction RIC
CIANCOLO, Patricia Jean, 1929- ,
American; nonfiction CON
CIARDI, John Anthony, 1916- ,
American; poetry, juveniles,
criticism, translations COM
CON KTS MUR WA
CIBBER, Colley, 1671-1757, Eng-
lish; plays, poetry BRO KB
MAG ST
CIBOT, Pierre, 1727-80, French;
nonfiction DIL
CIBULKA, Hanns, 1920- , Ger-
man; poetry AL
CICCI, María Luisa, 1760-94,
Italian; poetry SA
CICELLIS, Catherine Mathilda,
1926- , French-English;

fiction CON
CICERO, Marcus Tullius, 106-43
B.C., Roman; nonfiction MAG
SA ST
CICOGNANI, Amleto Giovanni,
1883- , Italian; nonfiction HOE
CICOGNANI, Bruno, 1879- , Italian;
fiction COL SA ST
CID, Miguel del, 1549?-1617, Spanish;
poetry SA
CID PEREZ, José, 1906- , Cuban;
fiction, criticism, plays SA
'CIECO de FERRARA, Il' see BELLO,
Francesco
'CIELO, Juan Sin' see CARRION,
Alejandro
CIENFUEGOS, Nicasio Alvarez de,
1764-1809, Spanish; poetry,
plays BL HAR SA ST
CIESZKOWSKI, August, 1814-94,
Polish; nonfiction ST
CIEZA de LEON, Pedro, 1518?-60,
Spanish; nonfiction BL SA ST
CIFUENTES SEPULVEDA, Jaquin,
1900-29, Chilean; poetry MIN
CIGES APARICIO, Manuel, 1873-
1936, Spanish; fiction BL SA
CIHLAR, Milutin see 'NEHAJEV,
Milutin'
CILLIERS, Charl Jean François,
1941- , South African; poetry
MUR
CIMORRA, Clemente, 1900-58,
Spanish; fiction, journalism SA
CINETO, 7th-6th cent. B.C., Greek;
poetry SA
CINGRIA, Charles Albert, 1883-1954,
Swiss; nonfiction DIF
'CINNA' see FRAENKEL, Heinrich
CINNA, Gaius Helvius, 102-44? B.C.,
Roman; poetry SA ST
CINNEMO, Juan, 12th cent., Byzan-
tine; nonfiction SA
CINO de PISTOIA (Guittocino dei
Sighibuldi), 1270-1337, Italian;
poetry KE SA HAR ST
CINTHIO see GIRALDI, Giovanni B.
CINZIO see GIRALDI, Giovanni B.
CIOFFARI, Vincenzo, 1905- , Amer-
ican; nonfiction CON
CIORAN, Emil M., 1911- , Ruma-
nian-French; essays CON DIC
DIF PIN
CIPALUNKAR, Visnusastri, 1850-82,
Indian; essays LAN
CIPARIU, Timoteiu, 1805-87, Ru-
manian; nonfiction ST

CIPICO, Ino, 1869-1933, Serbian;
fiction FLE
CIPIS, Robert M., 1930- ,
American; nonfiction CON
CIPLIJAUSKAITE, Birute,
1929- , Lithuanian-American;
nonfiction CON
CIPOLLA, Carlo Manlio, 1922- ,
Italian-American; nonfiction
CON
CIPPICO, Antonio, 1877-1935,
Italian; nonfiction ST
'CIRCUS, Jim' see ROSEVEAR,
John
'CIRE' see HAYDEN, Eric W.
CIRIA y ESCALANTE, José, 1903-
24, Spanish; poetry BL
CIRIACO d'ANCON (Pizzicolli),
1391-1452, Italian; nonfiction
ST
CIRIQUIAIN GAEZTARRO, Mariano,
1898- , Spanish; nonfiction,
fiction SA
CIRLOT, Juan Eduardo, 1916- ,
Spanish; poetry BL SA
CIRRE, José Francisco, 1905- ,
Spanish; nonfiction BL
CIRUELO, Pedro, 1470?-1554,
Spanish; nonfiction SA
CIŠINSKI, Jakub (Bart), 1856-
1909, German; nonfiction AL
CISNEROS, Cardenal see JIMENEZ
de CISNEROS, Francisco
CISNEROS, Luis Benjamín, 1837-
1904, Peruvian; poetry, plays,
fiction SA
CISZEK, Walter, 1904- , Ameri-
can; fiction CON
'CIVASQUI, José' (Sosuke Shibasaki),
1916- , Japanese; poetry
MUR
CIVININI, Guelfo, 1873- , Italian;
fiction, plays SA
CIZERON-RIVAL, François Louis,
1726-95, French; plays, nonfic-
tion DIL
CLAASEN, Harold ('Hubbard
Pomeroy'), 1905- , American;
nonfiction CON
CLACK, Robert Wood, 1886- ,
American; poetry, translations
HIL
CLADEL, Léon, 1835-92, French;
fiction DIF
CLADERA, Cristóbal, 1760-1816,
Spanish; poetry SA
CLADET, Léon, 1835-92, French;

fiction HAR
CLAES, Ernest André Jozef, 1885- ,
    Flemish; fiction FLE ST
CLAISTRE, André de, 18th cent.,
    French; nonfiction DIL
CLAFFEY, William J., 1925- ,
    American; nonfiction CON
CLAGETT, John Henry, 1916- ,
    American; juveniles, fiction
    CON WA
CLAGETT, Marshall, 1916- ,
    American; nonfiction CON
CLAGUE, Edward, 1896- , Amer-
    ican; nonfiction CON
CLAIBORNE, Craig, 1920- , Amer-
    ican; nonfiction CON
CLAIBORNE, Robert Watson, Jr.
    ('R. Armstrong McKenney'),
    1919- , English; nonfiction CON
'CLAIN, Samuil' (Miculu Maniu),
    1745-1806, Transylvanian; non-
    fiction ST
CLAIR, Andree, French; juveniles
    CON
CLAIRAMBAULT, Pierre, 1651-1740,
    French; nonfiction DIL
'CLAIRE, Keith' see ANDREWS,
    Claire and Keith
CLAIUS see KLAS, Johan
CLANCIER, Georges Emmanuel,
    1914- , French; poetry, criti-
    cism, fiction DIF
CLANCY, John Gregory, 1922- ,
    American; nonfiction CON
CLANCY, Thomas Hanley, 1923- ,
    American; nonfiction CON
CLANVOWE, Sir Thomas,   -1410,
    English; fiction ST
CLAPASSON, André ('Paul Rivière
    De Brinais'), 1708-70, French;
    nonfiction DIL
CLAPHAM, John, 1908- , English;
    nonfiction CON
CLAPHAM, Richard, 1878- , Eng-
    lish; nonfiction HIG
CLAPP, Henry, Jr. ('Figaro'),
    1814-75, American; journalism
    KAA
CLAPP, Henry Austin, 1841-1904,
    American; criticism KAA
CLAPP, James Gordon, 1909- ,
    American; nonfiction CON
CLAPP, Margaret Antoinette, 1910- ,
    American; nonfiction KTS
CLAPP, Patricia, 1912- , Amer-
    ican; plays CON
CLAPPERTON, Richard, 1934- ,

Scots; fiction CON
CLAR, Charles Raymond, 1903- ,
    American; nonfiction CON
CLARAMONTE y CORROY, Andrés,
    -1630?, Spanish; plays
    SA
CLARASO, Noel, 1902- , Spanish;
    fiction, plays, essays BL SA
CLARDY, Jesse V., 1929- ,
    American; nonfiction CON
CLARE, Francis D. see MARY
    FRANCIS, Mother
'CLARE, Helen' see HUNTER
    BLAIR, Pauline C.
CLARE, John, 1793-1864, English;
    poetry BRO KBA SA SP ST
'CLARE, Margaret' see MAISON,
    Margaret M. B.
CLARENDON, Edward Hyde,
    1608-74, English; nonfiction
    BRO KB SA ST
CLARENO, Angelo, 1247-1337,
    Italian; nonfiction ST
CLARENS, Carlos Figueredo y,
    1936- , Cuban-American;
    nonfiction CON
CLARESON, Thomas Dean, 1926- ,
    American; nonfiction CON
CLARETIE, Jules Arsène Arnaud,
    1840-1913, French; nonfiction,
    fiction SA HAR
CLARETIE, Leo Eugene Héctor,
    1862-1924, French; nonfiction
    SA
CLARI, Robert de,   -1217?,
    French; nonfiction ST
'CLARIBEL' see BARNARD, Mrs.
    Charles
CLARIDGE, Gordon S., 1932- ,
    American; nonfiction CON
CLARIMON, Carlos, 1920- ,
    Spanish; fiction BL
'CLARIN' see ALAS y UREÑA,
    Leopoldo
CLARIZIO, Harvey Frank, 1934- ,
    American; nonfiction CON
CLARK, Alan, 1928- , English;
    nonfiction CON
CLARK, Andrew Hill, 1911- ,
    Canadian; nonfiction CON
CLARK, Ann Livesey, 1913- ,
    American; nonfiction CON
CLARK, Anna Nolan, 1898- ,
    American; juveniles CON KJU
    WA
CLARK, Anne, 1909- , American;
    nonfiction CON

CLARK, Arthur Melville, 1895- ,
English; nonfiction CON
CLARK, Barrett Harper, 1890-1953,
American; criticism KT
CLARK, Billy C., 1928- , Amer-
ican; fiction CON
CLARK, C.G. Frazer, Jr., 1925- ,
American; nonfiction CON
CLARK, C.H. Douglas, 1890- ,
English; nonfiction CON
CLARK, Catherine Anthony Smith,
1892- , English; juveniles CON
CLARK, Charles Edwin, 1929- ,
American; nonfiction CON
CLARK, Charles Heber ('Max
Adeler'), 1847-1915, American;
fiction BRO KAA
CLARK, Charles Manning Hope,
1915- , Australian; nonfiction
CON
CLARK, Charles T., 1917- , Amer-
ican; nonfiction CON
CLARK, David Ridgley, 1920- ,
American; fiction, poetry CON
CLARK, Denis, -1950?, American;
juveniles WA
CLARK, Dennis E., 1916- , Eng-
lish; nonfiction CON
CLARK, Dennis J., 1927- , Amer-
ican; nonfiction CON
CLARK, Donald E., 1933- , Amer-
ican; nonfiction CON
CLARK, Donald Henry, 1930- ,
American; nonfiction CON
CLARK, Dorothy Park ('Clark
McMeekin'), 1899- , American;
fiction CON
CLARK, Eleanor, 1913- , American;
fiction, essays CON KTS
CLARK, Eleanor Grace, 1895- ,
American; nonfiction HOE
CLARK, Ella Elizabeth, 1896- ,
American; nonfiction PAC
CLARK, Elmer Talmage, 1886-1966,
American; nonfiction CON
CLARK, Eric, 1911- , Irish; non-
fiction CON
CLARK, Dr. Eugene A., 1883- ,
American; nonfiction SCA
CLARK, Francis, 1919- , South
African; nonfiction CON
CLARK, Frank James, 1922- ,
American; juveniles CON WA
CLARK, Frederick Stephen ('Clive
Dalton'), 1908- , English; non-
fiction CON
CLARK, Gerald, 1918- , Canadian;

nonfiction CON
CLARK, Gordon Haddon, 1902- ,
American; nonfiction CON
CLARK, Harry Hayden, 1901- ,
American; nonfiction CON
CLARK, Henry Balsley, II,
1930- , American; nonfiction,
translations CON
CLARK, Henry James, 1826-73,
American; nonfiction KAA
'CLARK, Howard' see HASKIN,
Dorothy C.
CLARK, James Milford, 1930- ,
American; nonfiction CON
CLARK, James Vaughan, 1927- ,
American; nonfiction CON
CLARK, Jere Walton, 1922- ,
American; nonfiction CON
CLARK, Jerome L., 1928- ,
American; nonfiction CON
CLARK, John Drury, 1907- ,
American; nonfiction CON
CLARK, John Garretson, 1932- ,
American; nonfiction CON
CLARK, John Grahame Douglas,
1907- , American; nonfiction
CON
CLARK, John Maurice, 1884-1963,
American; nonfiction CON
CLARK, John Pepper, 1935- ,
Nigerian; poetry, plays MAT
MUR RIC
CLARK, John Richard, 1930- ,
American; nonfiction CON
CLARK, John Williams, 1907- ,
American; nonfiction CON
CLARK, Joseph Deadrick, 1893- ,
American; nonfiction CON
CLARK, Joseph James, 1893-1971,
American; nonfiction CON
CLARK, Joseph Lynn, 1881- ,
American; nonfiction CON
CLARK, Sir Kenneth, 1903- ,
English; nonfiction KTS
CLARK, Kenneth Bancroft, 1914- ,
American; nonfiction CON
CLARK, L.D., 1922- , Ameri-
can; nonfiction CON
CLARK, Laurence Walter, 1914- ,
English; fiction, poetry CON
CLARK, La Verne Harrell, 1929- ,
American; nonfiction CON
CLARK, Leonard, 1905- , British;
poetry CON MUR
CLARK, Lewis Gaylord, 1808-73,
American; nonfiction KAA
CLARK, Margaret Goff, 1913- ,

American; poetry, juveniles
CON WA

CLARK, Maria Louisa Guidish, 1926- , American; nonfiction, juveniles CON

CLARK, Marjorie A., 1911- , English; nonfiction CON

CLARK, Mary T., American; nonfiction CON

'CLARK, Merle' see GESSNER, Lynne

CLARK, Miles Morton, 1920- , American; nonfiction CON

CLARK, Neil McCullough, 1890- , American; nonfiction CON

CLARK, Norman H., 1925- , American; nonfiction PAC

CLARK, Patricia Finrow, 1929- , American; nonfiction, juveniles CON

CLARK, Peter Wellington, 1914- , American; poetry, fiction SCA

CLARK, Robert, 1911- , Australian; poetry MUR

CLARK, Robert Edward David, 1906- , English; nonfiction CON

CLARK, Romane Lewis, 1925- , American; nonfiction CON

CLARK, Ronald William, 1916- , English; juveniles COM CON WA

CLARK, Samuel Delbert, 1910- , Canadian; nonfiction CON

CLARK, Septima Poinsette, 1898- , American; nonfiction CON

CLARK, Sydney Aylmer, 1890- , American; nonfiction CON

CLARK, Terry Nichols, 1940- , American; nonfiction CON

CLARK, Thomas A., 1944- , Scots; poetry MUR

CLARK, Thomas Curtis, 1877- , American; poetry HOO

CLARK, Thomas Dionysius, 1903- , American; nonfiction CON

CLARK, Tom, 1941- , American; poetry, plays MUR

CLARK, Van Deusen, 1909- , American; juveniles COM CON

CLARK, Walter Houston, 1902- , American; nonfiction CON

CLARK, Walter van Tilburg, 1909-71, American; fiction CON KTS MAG ST WAF

CLARK, Willis Gaylord, 1808-41, American; poetry, journalism KAA

CLARK, William Arthur, 1931- , American; fiction CON

CLARK, William Donaldson, 1916- , English; nonfiction CON

CLARK, William Ramsey, 1927- , American; nonfiction CON

CLARK, William Smith, II, 1900-69, American; nonfiction CON

CLARKE, Arthur Charles, 1917- , English; fiction, nonfiction BRO CON KTS RIC WA

CLARKE, Arthur Gladstone, 1887- , English; nonfiction CON

CLARKE, Austin, 1896-1974, Irish; poetry, plays, fiction, criticism CON KTS MUR RIC ST

CLARKE, Austin Chesterfield, 1934- , American; fiction CON

CLARKE, Basil Fulford Lowther, 1908- , American; nonfiction CON

CLARKE, Charles Cowden, 1787-1877, English; criticism BRO ST

CLARKE, Clorinda, 1917- , American; juvenile CON

CLARKE, David Egerton, 1920- , English; nonfiction CON

CLARKE, David Waldo ('Dave Waldo'), 1907- , Welsh; nonfiction CON

CLARKE, Donald Henderson, 1887- , American; fiction WAF

CLARKE, Dorothy Clotelle, 1908- , American; nonfiction CON

CLARKE, Dudley Wrangel, 1899- , South African; fiction CON

CLARKE, Dwight Lancelot, 1885- , American; nonfiction, fiction, poetry CON

CLARKE, Edward Daniel, 1769-1822, English; nonfiction KBA

CLARKE, Egerton, 1899-1944, American; poetry HOE

CLARKE, George Timothy, American; nonfiction CON

CLARKE, H. Harrison, 1902- , American; nonfiction CON

CLARKE, Harry Eugene, Jr., 1921- , American; nonfiction CON

CLARKE, Henry Butler, 1863-1904, English; nonfiction KBA

CLARKE, Howard William, 1929- ,

American; nonfiction CON

CLARKE, Isabel Constance, English; nonfiction HOE

CLARKE, Jack Alden, 1924- , American; nonfiction CON

'CLARKE, Capt. Jafah' see NESMITH, Robert L.

CLARKE, James Freeman, 1810-88, American; nonfiction KAA

CLARKE, Joan Dorn, 1924- , American; nonfiction CON

'CLARKE, John' see LAUGHLIN, Virginia C.

'CLARKE, John' see SONTUP, Daniel

CLARKE, John Campbell ('Hugh Cleland'; 'Robert Kingsley'), 1913- , English; fiction CON

CLARKE, John Frederick Gates, 1905- , Canadian; nonfiction CON

CLARKE, John Joseph, 1879- , English; nonfiction CON

CLARKE, Kenneth Wendell, 1917- , American; fiction CON

CLARKE, MacDonald, 1798-1842, American; poetry KAA

CLARKE, Marcus ('Andrew Hislop'), 1846-81, English; fiction, plays BRO KBA ST

CLARKE, Martin Lowther, 1909- , English; nonfiction CON

CLARKE, Mary Bayard Devereux ('Tenella'), 1827-66, American; poetry JO KAA

CLARKE, Mary Stetson, 1911- , American; nonfiction CON

CLARKE, Mary Washington, 1913- , American; nonfiction CON

CLARKE, Mary Whatley, 1899- , American; nonfiction CON

CLARKE, Pauline see HUNTER BLAIR, Pauline C.

CLARKE, Peter ('Peter Kumalo'), South African; poetry MUR

CLARKE, Rebecca Sophia ('Sophie May'), 1833-1906, American; juveniles KAA

CLARKE, Robin Harwood, 1937- , English; nonfiction CON

CLARKE, Ronald Francis, 1933- , English; nonfiction CON

CLARKE, Samuel, 1599-1683, English; nonfiction SA ST

CLARKE, Samuel, 1675-1729, English; nonfiction BRO KB ST

CLARKE, Tom, American; nonfiction PAC

CLARKE, Tom Eugene, 1915- , American; nonfiction CON

CLARKE, William Dixon, 1927- , American; nonfiction CON

CLARKSON, Edith Margaret, 1915- , Canadian; juveniles CON

CLARKSON, Geoffrey P.E., 1934- , English; nonfiction CON

CLARKSON, Evan, 1929- , American; nonfiction CON

CLARKSON, Jesse Dunsmore, 1897- , American; nonfiction CON

CLARKSON, Paul Stephen, 1905- , American; nonfiction CON

CLARKSON, Thomas, 1760-1846, English; nonfiction KBA

CLASPER, Paul Dudley, 1923- , American; nonfiction CON

CLASTER, Daniel Stuart, 1932- , American; nonfiction CON

CLAUDE, Richard P., 1934- , American; nonfiction CON

CLAUDEL, Paul, 1868-1955, French; poetry, plays COL DIF FLE HAR HOE KL KT MAL MAT RIC SA ST

CLAUDET, 18th cent., French; plays DIL

CLAUDIA, Sister Mary, 1906- , American; nonfiction CON

CLAUDIAN (Claudius Claudianus), -408?, Roman; poetry SA ST

'CLAUDIUS, Eduard' (Schmidt), 1911- , German; fiction AL

CLAUDIUS, Hermann, 1878- , German; poetry AL ST

CLAUDIUS, Matthias, 1740-1815, German; poetry AL HAR KE SA ST

CLAUDIUS AELIANUS see AELIAN

CLAUDIUS QUADRIGARIUS, fl. 80 B.C., Roman; nonfiction ST

CLAUS, Hugo Maurice Julius, 1929- , Flemish; poetry, plays, criticism FLE MAT

CLAUS, Marshall R., 1936-70, American; nonfiction CON

CLAUSEN, Connie, 1923- , American; nonfiction CON

CLAUSEN, Sven, 1893-1921, Danish; essays, poetry, plays ST

CLAUSER, Suzanne P., 1929- , American; fiction CON

CLAUSSEN, Sophus Niels Christen,
1865-1931, Danish; poetry, fic-
tion, translations COL FLE HAR
SA ST
CLAUVOLGEER, Ursina see 'GIRUN,
Gian'
CLAVELL, James du Maresq,
1924- , Anglo-American; fic-
tion CON
CLAVERING, Emile see 'HANKIN,
St. John'
'CLAVERS, Mary' see KIRKLAND,
Caroline M. S.
CLAVERIA, Carlos, 1909- ,
Spanish; nonfiction BL SA
CLAVIJERO, Francisco Javier,
1731-87, Mexican; nonfiction SA
CLAVIJO, Ruy Gonzalez de see
GONZALEZ de CLAVIJO, Ruy
CLAVIJO y FAJARDO, José, 1726/
30-1806, Spanish; nonfiction BL
SA ST
'CLAY, Duncan' see DIEHL, William
W.
CLAY, Henry, 1777-1852, American;
nonfiction KAA ST
CLAY, James, 1924- , American;
fiction CON
CLAY, Roberta, 1900- , American;
nonfiction CON
CLAYES, Stanley Arnold, 1922- ,
American; nonfiction CON
CLAYRE, Alasdair, 1935- , British;
poetry, fiction MUR
CLAYS VERBRECHTENSONE, 13th
cent., Dutch; poetry ST
'CLAYTON, Barbara' see PLUFF,
Barbara L.
CLAYTON, Charles Curtis, 1902- ,
American; nonfiction CON
CLAYTON, Francis Howard, 1918- ,
Canadian; nonfiction CON
CLAYTON, James Edwin, 1929- ,
American; nonfiction CON
CLAYTON, James L., 1931- ,
American; nonfiction CON
CLAYTON, John, 1892- , American;
nonfiction CON
CLAYTON, John Jacob, 1935- ,
American; nonfiction CON
CLAYTON, Joseph, 1868-1943,
English; nonfiction HOE
CLAYTON, Keith M., 1928- , Eng-
lish; nonfiction CON
CLAYTON, Richard Henry Michael
('William Haggard'), 1907- ,
English; fiction CON RIC

'CLAYTON, Susan' see BAILEY,
Alfred G.
CLEALL, Charles, 1927- , Amer-
ican; nonfiction CON
CLEANTHES of ASSOS, 331-232
B.C., Greek; nonfiction SA
ST
CLEARY, Beverley Bunn, 1916- ,
American; juveniles COM
CON FUL WA
CLEARY, James William, 1927- ,
American; nonfiction CON
CLEARY, Jon, 1917- , Australian;
fiction CON
CLEAVER, Dale G., 1928- ,
American; nonfiction CON
CLEAVER, Eldridge, 1935- ,
American; nonfiction CON
CLEAVER, Hylton, 1891-1961,
English; juveniles DOY
'CLEAVER, Nancy' see MATHEWS,
Evelyn C.
CLEAVER, Vera William, Amer-
ican; juveniles WA
CLEAVES, Emery Nudd, 1902- ,
American; nonfiction CON
CLEAVES, Freeman, 1904- ,
American; nonfiction CON
CLEBSCH, William Anthony,
1923- , American; nonfiction
CON
CLEGG, Charles Myron, Jr.,
1916- , American; nonfiction
CON
CLEGG, Reed K., 1907- , Amer-
ican; nonfiction CON
CLEGHORN, Reese, 1930- ,
American; nonfiction CON
CLEGHORN, Sarah Norcliffe,
1876- , American; poetry
KT
CLELAND, David I., 1926- ,
American; nonfiction CON
'CLELAND, Hugh' see CLARKE,
John C.
'CLELAND, Morton' see RENNIE,
James A.
CLELLAND, Richard Cook,
1921- , American; nonfiction
CON
CLEM, Alan Leland, 1929- ,
American; nonfiction CON
CLEMEN, Wolfgang Hermann,
1909- , German; nonfiction
CON
CLEMENCE, Joseph Guillaume,
1717-92, French; nonfiction

poetry DIL
CLEMENCE, Richard Vernon,
1910- , American; nonfiction
CON
CLEMENCEAU, Georges, 1841-1929,
French; nonfiction COL
CLEMENCET, Charles, -1721,
French; nonfiction DIL
CLEMENCIA, Isaura, 1450-1512,
French; nonfiction SA
CLEMENCIN, Diego, 1765-1834,
Spanish; nonfiction BL SA
CLEMENS, Cyril, 1902- , Ameri-
can; nonfiction HOE
CLEMENS, Diane Shaver, 1936- ,
American; nonfiction CON
CLEMENS, Jeremiah, 1814-65,
American; fiction KAA
CLEMENS, Samuel Langhorne see
'TWAIN, Mark'
CLEMENS, Walter C., Jr., 1933- ,
American; nonfiction CON
CLEMENT, Alfred John, 1915- ,
English; nonfiction CON
CLEMENT, Augustin Jean Charles,
1717-1804, French; nonfiction
DIL
CLEMENT, Charles François,
1720- , French; plays DIL
CLEMENT, Denys Xavier, 1706-71,
French; nonfiction DIL
CLEMENT, François, 1714-93,
French; nonfiction DIL
CLEMENT, George H. ('G. Henri'),
1909- , American; nonfiction
CON
'CLEMENT, Hal' see STUBBS, Harry
C.
CLEMENT, Jane Tyson, 1917- ,
American; fiction CON
CLEMENT, Pierre, 1707-67,
French; plays DIL
CLEMENT, Titus Flavius, 150-212,
Greek; nonfiction ST SA
CLEMENT de BIZON, Augustin Jean
Charles, 1717-1804, French;
nonfiction DIL
CLEMENT SMOLYATICH see KLI-
MENT SMOLYATICH
CLEMENTE ROMEO, Esteban,
1887- , Spanish; poetry ST
'CLEMENTIA' (Agnes M. Feehan),
1878- , American; juveniles
HOE
'CLEMENTIA' see MARY EDWARDS,
Sister
CLEMENTS, Arthur Leo, 1932- ,

American; nonfiction CON
CLEMENTS, Eileen Helen, 1905- ,
English; fiction CON
CLEMENTS, Ellen Catherine Scott,
1920- , English; nonfiction
CON
CLEMENTS, Frank, English;
juveniles WA
CLEMENTS, Julia, 1906- , Eng-
lish; nonfiction CON
CLEMENTS, Robert John, 1912- ,
American; nonfiction CON
CLEMENTS, Ronald Ernest,
1929- , English; nonfiction
CON
CLEMENTS, Tad S., 1922- ,
American; nonfiction CON
CLEMMER, Mary, 1839-84, Amer-
ican; fiction, journalism KAA
CLEMMONS, Robert Starr, 1910- ,
American; nonfiction CON
CLEMO, Jack (Reginald John
Clemo), 1916- , British;
poetry CON MUR RIC
'CLEMONS, Elizabeth' see ROBIN-
SON, Elizabeth C.
CLEMONS, Harry, 1879- , Amer-
ican; nonfiction CON
CLEMONS, Walter, Jr., 1929- ,
American; fiction CON
CLENDENEN, Clarence Clemens,
1899- , American; nonfiction
CON
CLENDENIN, John Cameron, 1903-,
American; nonfiction CON
CLENDENIN, William Ritchie,
1917- , American; nonfiction
CON
CLENDENING, Logan, 1884-1945,
American; nonfiction KT
CLENDENNING, Sheila T., 1939- ,
American; nonfiction CON
CLEOBURY, Frank Harold, 1892- ,
English; nonfiction CON
CLEPHANE, Irene Amy, English;
nonfiction CON
CLERC, Charles, 1926- , Amer-
ican; nonfiction CON
CLERC, Nicolas Gabriel (Leclerc),
1726-98, French; nonfiction
DIL
CLERIC, Pierre, 1662-1740,
French; nonfiction DIL
CLERKE, Agnes Mary, 1842-1907,
Irish; nonfiction KBA
CLERMONT, Emile, 1880-1916,
French; fiction DIF

CLERMONT, Louis de Bourbon,
1709-71, French; nonfiction DIL
CLERQ, René de, 1877-1932,
Flemish; poetry ST
CLEUGH, Mary Frances, 1913- ,
English; nonfiction CON
CLEUGH, Sophia, 1887?- , English;
fiction KT
CLEVELAND, Harold van Buren,
1916- , American; nonfiction
CON
CLEVELAND, Henry Russell, 1808-
43, American; nonfiction KAA
CLEVELAND, James Harlan, 1918- ,
American; nonfiction CON
'CLEVELAND, John' see McELFRESH,
Elizabeth A.
CLEVELAND, John, 1613-58, Eng-
lish; poetry BRO KB SP ST
CLEVELAND, Philip Jerome ('A.
Don Adams'; 'Rupert Chute'),
1903- , American; nonfiction,
fiction CON
CLEVELAND, Ray Le Roy, 1929- ,
American; nonfiction CON
CLEVELAND, Sidney Earl, 1919- ,
American; nonfiction CON
CLEVEN, Kathryn Seward ('Cathrine
Cleven'), American; juveniles,
fiction COM CON
CLEVERDON, Thomas Douglas
James, 1903- , English; non-
fiction CON
CLEVERLEY FORD, Douglas William,
1914- , English; nonfiction
CON
CLEVIN, Joergen, 1920- , Ameri-
can; juveniles CON
CLEWES, Dorothy Mary, 1907- ,
English; juveniles, fiction COM
CON WA
CLEWES, Winston David Armstrong,
1906- , British; fiction KTS
CLICQUOT de BLERVACHE, Simon,
1723-96, French; nonfiction DIL
CLIFFORD, Cornelius C., 1859-
1938, American; nonfiction HOE
CLIFFORD, Derek Plint, 1915- ,
English; nonfiction, poetry, fic-
tion CON
CLIFFORD, Harold B. ('Burt Farn-
ham'), 1893- , American; non-
fiction CON
CLIFFORD, Henry Dalton, 1911- ,
English; nonfiction CON
CLIFFORD, Sir Hugh, 1866-1941,
English; nonfiction HOE

CLIFFORD, James Lowry,
1901- , American; nonfiction
CON
'CLIFFORD, John' see BAYLISS,
John C.
CLIFFORD, John Edward, 1935- ,
American; nonfiction CON
CLIFFORD, John William, 1918- ,
American; nonfiction CON
CLIFFORD, Lucy Lane, 1854-1929,
English; fiction, plays KT SA
CLIFFORD, Margaret (Peggy;
'M. C. Cort'), 1929- , Amer-
ican; juveniles COM CON
CLIFFORD, Martin ('Paul Roger
Kenian'), 1910- , Polish-
American; nonfiction CON
CLIFFORD, Mary Louise Beneway,
1926- , American; nonfiction
CON
CLIFFORD, Nicholas Rowland,
1930- , American; nonfiction
CON
CLIFFORD, Peggy see CLIFFORD,
Margaret C.
CLIFFORD, Sarah, 1916- ,
American; nonfiction CON
CLIFFORD, William Kingdon,
1845-79, English; nonfiction
KBA
CLIFFTON, Katherine Potter,
1912- , American; nonfiction
CON
CLIFT, Virgil Alfred, 1912- ,
American; nonfiction CON
CLIFTON, Bernice Marie, Amer-
ican; nonfiction CON
CLIFTON, James Alfred, 1927- ,
American; nonfiction CON
CLIFTON, Marguerite Ann,
1925- , American; nonfiction
CON
CLIFTON, Violet Mary Beauclerk,
1883- , English; plays, non-
fiction HOE
CLIFTON, William, 1772-99,
American; poetry KAA
CLINARD, Dorothy Long, 1909- ,
American; fiction CON
CLINARD, Marshall Barron,
1911- , American; nonfiction
CON
CLINARD, Turner Norman, 1917- ,
American; nonfiction CON
CLINCH, Charles Powell, 1797-
1880, American; plays, criti-
cism KAA

CLINE, Catherine Ann, 1927- ,
American; nonfiction CON
CLINE, Denzel Cecil, 1903- ,
American; nonfiction CON
CLINE, Gloria Griffen, 1929- ,
American; nonfiction CON
CLINEBELL, Howard J., Jr.,
1922- , American; nonfiction
CON
CLINTON, Henry Fynes, 1781-1852,
English; nonfiction BRO ST
CLINTO, Iris A. Corbin, 1901- ,
English; fiction CON
'CLINTON, Jeff' see BICKHAM, Jack
M.
CLITARCO, fl. 304 B.C., Greek;
nonfiction SA
CLITHERO, Myrtle Ely (Sally),
1906- , American; poetry CON
CLIVE, Caroline Archer, 1801-73,
English; poetry, fiction KBA
CLIVE, Geoffry, 1927- , German-
American; nonfiction CON
CLIVE, Mary, 1907- , English;
nonfiction CON
CLOETE, Stuart, 1897- , South
African; fiction CON FLE KT
RIC ST
CLOETTA, Gian Gianet, 1874- ,
Raeto-Romansch; poetry ST
CLOGAN, Paul Maurice, 1934- ,
American; nonfiction CON
CLORE, Gerald Lewis, Jr., 1939- ,
American; nonfiction CON
CLOSE, Henry Thompson, 1928- ,
American; nonfiction CON
CLOSE, John ('Poet Close'), 1816-
91, English; poetry KBA
CLOSE, Reginald Arthur, 1909- ,
English; nonfiction CON
'CLOSE, Upton' see HALL, Josef
W.
CLOSS, August, 1898- , English;
nonfiction CON
CLOSSON, Herman, 1901- ,
Belgian; plays MAT
CLOSTERMANN, Pierre, 1921- ,
French; nonfiction RIC
CLOUD, Joseph Fred, Jr., 1925- ,
American; nonfiction CON
CLOUDSLEY-THOMPSON, John
Leonard, 1921- , American;
nonfiction CON
CLOUET, Pierre Romain, 1748-
1810, French; nonfiction, transla-
tions DIL
CLOUGH, Arthur Hugh, 1819-61,

English; poetry BRO KBA SA
SP ST
CLOUGH, Francis Frederick,
1912- , English; nonfiction
CON
CLOUGH, Rosa Trillo, 1906- ,
American; nonfiction CON
CLOUGH, Shepard Bancroft,
1901- , American; nonfiction
CON
CLOUGH, William A., 1899- ,
American; nonfiction CON
CLOUGH, Wilson Ober, 1894- ,
American; nonfiction CON
CLOUSE, Robert Gordon, 1931- ,
American; nonfiction CON
CLOUSTON, Joseph Storer, 1870-
1944, English; fiction BRO
CLOUTS, Sydney David, 1926- ,
South African; poetry MUR
CLOW, Martha de Mey, 1932- ,
American; fiction CON
CLOWNEY, Edmund Prosper,
1917- , American; nonfiction
CON
CLUBB, Oliver C., Jr., 1929- ,
American; nonfiction CON
CLUBB, Oliver Edmund, 1901- ,
American; nonfiction CON
CLUBBE, John, 1938- , Amer-
ican; nonfiction CON
CLUNE, Francis Patrick (Frank),
1893-1971, Australian; nonfic-
tion CON
CLUNE, Henry W., 1890- ,
American; nonfiction, fiction
CON
CLURMAN, Harold, 1901- ,
American; nonfiction CON
CLUTE, Morrel J., 1912- ,
American; nonfiction CON
CLUTHA, Janet Paterson Frame
('Janet Frame'), 1924- ,
American; fiction CON RIC
CLUTTERBUCK, Richard ('Richard
Jocelyn'), 1917- , English;
nonfiction CON
CLUTTON-BROCK, Arthur, 1868-
1924, English; journalism,
criticism, essays BRO KT
CLUVER, Eustace Henry, 1894- ,
American; nonfiction CON
CLUYSENAAR, Anne Alice Andrée,
1936- , Irish; poetry MUR
CLYMER, Eleanor Lowenton,
1906- , American; juveniles
WA

CLYMER, Reuben Swinburne, 1878- ,
American; nonfiction CON
CLYMER, Theodore William, 1927- ,
American; nonfiction CON
'CLYNDER, Monica' see MUIR,
Marie
'CLYNE, Terence' see BLATTY,
William P.
CLYTUS, John ('Monongo'), 1929- ,
American; nonfiction CON
CNUDDE, Charles F., 1938- ,
American; nonfiction CON
COADY, Moses Michael, 1882- ,
Canadian; nonfiction HOE
COAKLEY, Mary Lewis, American;
juveniles, nonfiction CON
COALES, Geoffrey Edward, 1917- ,
English; nonfiction CON
COAN, Otis Welton, 1895- , Amer-
ican; nonfiction, fiction CON
COAN, Titus, 1801-82, American;
nonfiction KAA
COATEN, Arthur W., 1872-1939,
English; nonfiction HIG
COATES, Belle, 1896- , American;
juveniles COM CON
COATES, Robert Myron, 1897- ,
American; fiction CON KL KT
WAF
COATES, William Ames, 1916- ,
American; nonfiction CON
COATES, Willson Havelock, 1899- ,
American; nonfiction CON
COATS, George W., 1936- , Amer-
ican; nonfiction CON
COATSWORTH, Elizabeth Jane,
1893- , American; juveniles
COM CON DOY KJU KL KT WA
WAF
COBB, Alice, 1909- , American;
nonfiction CON
COBB, Carl Wesley, 1926- ,
American; nonfiction CON
COBB, Faye Davis, 1932- , Amer-
ican; nonfiction CON
COBB, Humphrey, 1899-1944, Amer-
ican; fiction KT
COBB, Irvin Shrewsbury, 1876-1944,
American; fiction BRO KL KT
RIC
'COBB, John' (John C. Cooper III),
1921- , American; fiction WAF
COBB, John Boswell, Jr., 1925- ,
American; nonfiction CON
COBB, Lucy Maria, American; plays
JO
COBB, Lyman, 1800-64, American;

nonfiction KAA
COBB, M. C., 1932- , American;
nonfiction CON
COBB, Samuel, 1675-1713, Eng-
lish; translations ST
COBB, Sylvanus, Jr., 1823-87,
American; fiction KAA
COBB, Vicki, 1938- , American;
juveniles CON
COBBE, Frances Power, 1822-
1904, Irish; nonfiction BRO
KBA
'COBBETT' see LUDOVICI, Anthony
M.
COBBETT, Richard see PLUCK-
ROSE, Henry A.
COBBETT, William ('Peter
Porcupine'), 1762-1835, Eng-
lish; journalism, essays BRO
KBA SA ST
COBBING, Bob, 1920- , British;
poetry MUR
COBBS, Price M., 1928- ,
American; nonfiction CON
COBDEN, Richard, 1804-65, Eng-
lish; nonfiction KBA
COBLE, John Lawrence, 1924- ,
American; fiction CON
'COBLENTZ, Carl' see SCHNOG,
Karl
COBLENTZ, Catherine Cate,
1897-1951, American; juveniles
KJU
COBLENTZ, Stanton Arthur, 1896- ,
American; poetry, nonfiction
CON
COBLEY, John, 1914- , Aus-
tralian; nonfiction CON
COBRIN, Harry Aaron, 1902- ,
American; nonfiction CON
COBURN, John Bowen, 1914- ,
American; nonfiction CON
COBURN, Walter John, 1889- ,
American; fiction CON PAC
COCAGNAC, Augustin Maurice
Jean ('J. M. Warbler'),
1924- , French; nonfiction
CON
COCCIO, Marcantonio see SABE-
LICO, Marco A. C.
COCCIOLI, Carlo, 1920- ,
Italian; fiction, essays CON
FLE RIC
'COCH-y-BONDDHU' see ARNOLD,
Richard
COCHIN, Charles Nicolas, 1715-
90, French; nonfiction DIL

COCHON, Pierre, 1390?-1456?,
French; nonfiction ST
COCHRAN, Hamilton, 1898- ,
American; fiction CON WAF
'COCHRAN, Jeff' see DURST, Paul
COCHRANE, Arthur Caspersz,
1909- , Canadian; nonfiction
CON
COCHRANE, Charles Norriss, 1889-
1945, Canadian; nonfiction SY
COCHRANE, Elizabeth see SEAMAN,
Elizabeth C.
COCHRANE, James David, 1938- ,
American; nonfiction CON
COCHRANE, James L., 1942- ,
American; nonfiction CON
COCHRANE, Louise Morley, 1918- ,
American; nonfiction, fiction
CON
'COCHRANE, Philip' see BURNFORD,
Sheila
COCHRANE, Thomas see DUNDONALD,
Lord
COCHRANE, Willard Wesley, 1914- ,
American; nonfiction CON
COCHRANE de ALENCAR, Gertrude
E. L. (Gertrude von Schwarzen-
feld), 1906- , American; nonfic-
tion CON
COCKAINE, Sir Thomas, 1519-92,
English; nonfiction HIG
COCKBURN, Alicia (Alison), 1713-
94, Scots; poetry BRO KB
COCKBURN, Catherine Trotter,
1679-1749, English; nonfiction
SA
COCKBURN, Lord Henry Thomas,
1767/79-1854, Scots; nonfiction
BRO KBA ST
COCKBURN, Thomas Aiden, 1912- ,
American; nonfiction CON
COCKCROFT, John Douglas, 1897-
1967, English; nonfiction CON
COCKCROFT, James Donald,
1935- , American; nonfiction
CON
COCKETT, Mary, English; juveniles
CON
COCKER, Edward, 1631-75, English;
nonfiction KB
COCKERELL, Hugh Anthony Lewis,
1909- , English; nonfiction
CON
COCKRELL, Marian Brown, 1909- ,
American; fiction CON WAF
COCKSHUT, Anthony Oliver John,
1927- , English; nonfiction CON

COCKTON, Henry, 1807-52/53,
English; juveniles, fiction
DOY KBA
COCOZZELLA, Peter, 1937- ,
Italian-American; nonfiction
CON
COCQUARD, François Bernard,
1700-42, French; poetry DIL
COCTEAU, Jean, 1891-1963,
French; poetry, plays, fiction,
essays COL CON DIC DIF
HAR KT MAG MAL MAT FLE
KL RIC SA ST
CODAX, Martim, 13th cent.,
Galician; poetry ST
CODDING, George Arthur, Jr.,
1923- , American; nonfiction
CON
CODE, Joseph Bernard, 1899- ,
American; nonfiction HOE
CODER, Samuel Maxwell, 1902- ,
American; nonfiction CON
CODERA ZAIDIN, Francisco,
1836-1917, Spanish; nonfiction
BL SA
CODERRE, Emile ('Jean Narrache'),
1893- , Canadian; poetry,
nonfiction SY
CODINUS see GEORGE CODINUS
CODMAN, John ('American; Ship-
master'; 'Capt. Ringbolt'),
1814-1900, American; nonfic-
tion KAA
CODREANU, Mihail, 1876- ,
Rumanian; poetry ST
CODRESCU, Andrei ('Tristan
Tzara'; 'Betty Laredo'),
1946- , Rumanian-American;
nonfiction, poetry CON
CODRINGTON, Robert, -1665,
English; translations ST
'CODY, Al' see JOSCELYN,
Archie L.
CODY, John J., 1930- , Ameri-
can; nonfiction CON
'CODY, Walt' see NORWOOD,
Victor G. C.
COE, Ada M., 1890- , American;
nonfiction BL
COE, Charles Norton, 1915- ,
American; nonfiction CON
'COE, Douglas' see EPSTEIN,
Beryl and Samuel
COE, Michael Douglas, 1929- ,
American; nonfiction CON
COE, Ralph Tracy, 1929- ,
American; nonfiction CON

COE, Richard Nelson, 1923- ,
English; nonfiction CON
COE, William Charles, 1935- ,
American; nonfiction CON
COELHO, Francisco Adolfo, 1847-
1921, Portuguese; nonfiction
HAR
'COELHO, Joaquim Guilherme
Gomes' see 'DINIS, Júlio'
COELHO, José F. de T. see
TRINDADE COELHO, José
COELHO NETTO, Henrique
Maximiano, 1864-1934, Brazilian;
fiction, plays ST
COELIUS ANTIPATER, fl. 121 B.C.,
Roman; nonfiction ST
COELLO, Antonio, 1611-82, Spanish;
plays BL HAR
COELLO de PORTUGAL y PACHECO,
Carlos, 1850-88, Spanish; plays
SA
COELLO y OCHOA, Antonio, 1600-
53, Spanish; poetry, plays SA
ST
COEN, Rena Neumann, 1925- ,
American; nonfiction CON
COENS, Sister Mary Xavier, 1918- ,
American; nonfiction CON
COERR, Eleanor ('Eleanor B. Hicks';
'Eleanor Page'), 1922- ,
Canadian-American; juveniles
COM CON
COFER, Charles Norval, 1916- ,
American; nonfiction CON
COFFEY, Alan R., 1931- , Amer-
ican; nonfiction CON
COFFEY, Helen Dairine, 1933- ,
American; nonfiction CON
COFFIN, Arthur B., 1929- , Amer-
ican; nonfiction CON
COFFIN, Berton, 1910- , American;
nonfiction CON
COFFIN, Charles, 1676-1749, French;
poetry ST
COFFIN, Charles Carleton, 1823-
96, American; journalism, fiction
KAA
COFFIN, David Robbins, 1918- ,
American; nonfiction CON
COFFIN, Dean, 1911- , American;
fiction CON
COFFIN, Frank M., 1919- , Amer-
ican; nonfiction CON
'COFFIN, Geoffrey' see MASON,
Frank W.
COFFIN, George Sturgis, 1903- ,
American; nonfiction CON

COFFIN, Patricia, 1912- ,
American; nonfiction CON
COFFIN, Robert Peter Tristram,
1892-1955, American; poetry
KT SA
COFFIN, Tristram, 1912- ,
American; nonfiction CON
COFFIN, Tristram Potter, 1922- ,
American; nonfiction CON
COFFMAN, Barbara Frances,
1907- , Canadian; nonfiction
CON
COFFMAN, Edward M., 1929- ,
American; nonfiction CON
COFFMAN, Paul Brown, 1900- ,
American; nonfiction CON
COFFMAN, Ramon Peyton ('Uncle
Ray'), 1896- , American;
juveniles CON
COGER, François Marie, 1723-80,
French; nonfiction DIL
COGER, Leslie Irene, 1912- ,
American; nonfiction CON
COGGAN, Blanche B., 1895- ,
American; poetry, plays, fic-
tion HIL
COGGAN, Frederick Donald,
1909- , English; nonfiction
CON
COGGESHALL, George, 1784-1861,
American; nonfiction KAA
COGGESHALL, Ralph de, fl. 1200,
English; nonfiction ST
COGGESHALL, William Turner,
1824-67, American; journalism
KAA
COGGINS, Herbert, American;
juveniles WA
COGGINS, Jack Banham, 1911- ,
Anglo-American; juveniles
COM CON FUL WA
COGGINS, Ross, 1927- , Ameri-
can; nonfiction CON
COGHILL, Nevill Henry Kendall
Aylmer, 1899- , English; non-
fiction CON
COGHILL, Rhoda, 1903- , Irish;
poetry MUR ST
COGHLAN, Brian Laurence Dillon,
1926- , English; nonfiction
CON
COGOLIN, Joseph de Cuers de,
1702-60, French; nonfiction DIL
COGSWELL, Coralie Norris
('Coralie Howard'), 1930- ,
American; nonfiction CON
COGSWELL, Frederic William,

1917- , Canadian; poetry,
criticism, translations CON
MUR SY

COGSWELL, James Arthur, 1922- ,
American; nonfiction CON

COGSWELL, Theodore R., 1918- ,
American; nonfiction, fiction
CON

COHAN, George Michael, 1878-1942,
American; plays MAT

COHANE, Tim, 1912- , American;
nonfiction CON

COHEN, Albert Kircidel, 1918- ,
American; nonfiction CON

COHEN, Allan Y., 1939- , American; nonfiction CON

COHEN, Arthur Allen, 1928- ,
American; nonfiction CON

COHEN, Arthur M., 1927- , American; nonfiction CON

COHEN, Benjamin Bernard, 1922- ,
American; nonfiction CON

COHEN, Benjamin Victor, 1894- ,
American; nonfiction CON

COHEN, Bernard Lande, 1902- ,
Canadian; nonfiction CON

COHEN, Carl, 1931- , American;
nonfiction CON

COHEN, Edgar H., 1913- ,
Canadian; nonfiction CON

COHEN, Edward M., 1936- ,
American; fiction CON

COHEN, Florence Chanock, 1927- ,
American; fiction CON

COHEN, Gustave David, 1879-1958,
French; nonfiction DIF

COHEN, Harry, 1933- , American;
nonfiction CON

COHEN, Henry Hennig, 1919- ,
American; nonfiction CON

COHEN, Hermann, 1842-1918, German; nonfiction SA

COHEN, Ira Sheldon, 1924- ,
American; nonfiction CON

COHEN, Jerome Bernard, 1915- ,
American; nonfiction CON

COHEN, Joan Lebold, 1932- ,
American; juveniles CON

COHEN, John, 1911- , English;
nonfiction CON

COHEN, John Michael, 1903- ,
English; nonfiction, translations
CON

COHEN, Jozef, 1921- , American;
nonfiction CON

COHEN, Kalman Joseph, 1931- ,
American; nonfiction CON

COHEN, Leonard Norman, 1934- ,
American; poetry, fiction
CON MUR SY

COHEN, Lester, 1901- , American; fiction WAF

COHEN, Marvin, 1931- , American; nonfiction, fiction CON

COHEN, Morris (Mike), 1912- ,
American; fiction CON

COHEN, Morris Raphael, 1880-
1947, American; nonfiction
KT

COHEN, Morton Norton ('John
Moreton'), 1921- , Canadian-
American; nonfiction CON

COHEN, Octavius Roy, 1891- ,
American; fiction KT

COHEN, Peter Zachary, 1931- ,
American; juveniles CON

COHEN, Robert, 1938- , American; nonfiction CON

COHEN, Ronald, 1930- , American; nonfiction CON

COHEN, S. Alan, 1933- , American; nonfiction CON

COHEN, Sanford, 1920- , American; nonfiction CON

COHEN, Selma Jeanne, 1920- ,
American; nonfiction CON

COHEN, Seymour Jay, 1922- ,
American; nonfiction CON

COHEN, Sheldon S., 1931- ,
American; nonfiction CON

COHEN, Sidney, 1910- , American; nonfiction CON

COHEN, Stanley, 1928- , American; fiction CON

COHEN, Stanley Harold, 1922- ,
American; nonfiction CON

COHEN, Stephen S., 1941- ,
American; nonfiction CON

COHEN, Warren I., 1934- ,
American; nonfiction CON

COHEN, Wilbur Joseph, 1913- ,
American; nonfiction CON

COHEN, William Benjamin,
1941- , American; nonfiction
CON

COHEN, William Howard, 1927- ,
American; poetry CON

COHEN, Yaacov, 1881- , Jewish;
poetry ST

COHN, Adrian A., 1922- ,
American; nonfiction CON

COHN, Angelo, 1914- , Rumanian-
American; nonfiction CON

COHN, Clara Viebig see VIEBIG,
Clara

COHN, Jules, 1932- , American; nonfiction CON

COHN, Robert Greer, 1921- , American; nonfiction CON

COHON, Baruch Joseph (Barry), 1926- , American; nonfiction, fiction CON

COHON, Beryl David, American; nonfiction CON

COIGNARD, Gabrielle de, -1594, French; poetry ST

COIMBRA, Leonardo, 1884-1936, Portuguese; essays SA

COINTREAU, fl. 1756, French; plays COL

COISLIN, Henri Charles du Cambout, 1664-1732, French; nonfiction DIL

COIT, Margaret Louise, 1919/22- , American; juveniles COM CON WA KTS

COJEEN, Robert H., 1920- , American; nonfiction CON

COKAYNE, Sir Aston, 1608-83/84, English; poetry ST

COKE, Desmond, 1879-1940?, English; juveniles DOY

COKE, Sir Edward, 1552-1634, English; nonfiction KB

COKE, Van Deren, 1921- , American; nonfiction CON

COKER, Jerry, 1932- , American; nonfiction CON

COKER, Robert Ervin, 1876- , American; fiction JO

COL, Gontier, 1354?-1418, French; nonfiction ST

COLACCI, Mario, 1910- , American; nonfiction CON

COLADARCI, Arthur Paul, 1917- , American; nonfiction CON

COLARDEAU, Charles Pierre, 1732-76, French; plays DIL SA

COLAW, Emerson S., 1921- , American; nonfiction CON

COLBECK, Maurice, 1925- , English; fiction CON

COLBERG, Marshall Rudolph, 1913- , American; nonfiction CON

COLBERT d' ESTOUTEVILLE, -1780, French; translations DIL

COLBOURN, Harold Trevor, 1927- , Australian; nonfiction CON

COLBURN, Clyde William, 1939- , American; nonfiction CON

COLBY, Carroll Burleigh, 1904- , American; juveniles CON FUL WA

COLBY, Elbridge, 1891- , American; nonfiction CON HOE

COLBY, Frank Moore, 1865-1925, American; essays KT

COLBY, Jean Poindexter, 1909- , American; juveniles, nonfiction CON

COLBY, Merle, 1902- , American; fiction WAF

COLBY, Roy Edward, 1910- , American; nonfiction CON

COLBY, Vineta Blumoff, 1922- , American; nonfiction CON

COLDEN, Cadwallader, 1688-1776, American; nonfiction KAA

COLDIRON, Daisy Lemar, American; poetry MAR

COLDWELL, David Frederick Clarke, 1923- , Canadian; nonfiction CON

COLE, Andrew Thomas, Jr., 1933- , American; nonfiction CON

'COLE, Ann Kilborn' see CALLAHAN, Claire W.

COLE, Barry, 1936- , British; poetry, fiction CON MUR

COLE, Clifford A., 1915- , American; nonfiction CON

COLE, Dandridge MacFarlan, 1921- , American; nonfiction CON

'COLE, Davis' see ELTING, Mary

COLE, Donald Barnard, 1922- , American; nonfiction CON

COLE, Douglas, 1934- , American; nonfiction CON

COLE, Edward Cyrus, 1904- , American; nonfiction CON

COLE, George Douglas Howard, 1889- , English; fiction BRO KT SA

COLE, Sir Henry ('Felix Summerley'), 1808-82, English; juveniles KBA

COLE, Hubert Archibald Noel, 1908- , English; nonfiction CON

'COLE, Jack' see STEWART, John W.

COLE, John Alfred, 1905- , English; fiction CON

COLE, John Peter, 1928- , English; nonfiction CON

COLE, John Reece, 1916- , New
Zealander; fiction ST
COLE, Lois Dwight ('Lynn Avery';
'Nancy Dudley'; 'Allan Dwight';
'Anne Eliot'), 1902- , Ameri-
can; juveniles CON WA
COLE, Luella Winifred, 1893- ,
American; nonfiction CON
COLE, Margaret Alice ('Rosemary
Manning'; 'Julia Renton'; 'Ione
Saunders'), English; fiction,
juveniles CON
COLE, Margaret Isabel, 1893- ,
English; nonfiction CON
COLE, Michelle, 1940- , Ameri-
can; nonfiction CON
COLE, Monica Mary, 1922- ,
English; nonfiction CON
COLE, Robert H., 1918- , Ameri-
can; nonfiction CON
COLE, Roger L., 1933- , Ameri-
can; nonfiction CON
'COLE, Stephen see WEBBE, Gale
D.
COLE, Stephen, 1941- , American;
nonfiction CON
COLE, Wayne S., 1922- , Ameri-
can; nonfiction CON
COLE, Wendell, 1914- , American;
nonfiction CON
COLE, William Earl, 1904- , Amer-
ican; nonfiction CON
COLE, William Graham, 1917- ,
American; nonfiction CON
COLE, William Rossa, 1919- ,
American; juvenile CON WA
COLEAN, Miles Lanier, 1898- ,
American; nonfiction CON
COLEBURT, James Russell, 1920- ,
English; nonfiction CON
COLEGATE, Isabel, 1931- , Eng-
lish; fiction CON
COLEGROVE, Kenneth, 1886- ,
American; nonfiction CON
COLEMAN, Almand Rouse, 1905- ,
American; nonfiction CON
COLEMAN, Bernard David, 1919- ,
English; nonfiction CON
COLEMAN, Bruce Pumphrey, 1931- ,
American; nonfiction CON
COLEMAN, Clayton Webster ('Web-
ster Smith'), 1901- , American;
fiction CON
COLEMAN, Donald Cuthbert, 1920- ,
English; nonfiction CON
COLEMAN, Elliott, 1906- , Ameri-
can; poetry, translations CON

MUR
COLEMAN, Evelyn Scherabon,
1932- , Austrian-American;
nonfiction CON
COLEMAN, James Andrew,
1921- , American; nonfiction
CON
COLEMAN, James Covington,
1914- , American; nonfiction
CON
COLEMAN, James Samuel, 1926- ,
American; nonfiction CON
COLEMAN, James Smoot, 1919- ,
American; nonfiction CON
COLEMAN, John Royston, 1921- ,
Canadian-American; nonfiction
CON
COLEMAN, Kenneth, 1916- ,
American; nonfiction CON
COLEMAN, Lonnie William,
1920- , American; fiction
WAF
COLEMAN, Marion Reeves Moore,
1900- , American; nonfiction
CON
COLEMAN, Pauline Hodgkinson,
American; juveniles WA
COLEMAN, Peter Jarrett, 1926- ,
American; nonfiction CON
COLEMAN, Richard Patrick,
1927- , American; nonfiction
CON
COLEMAN, Robert Emerson,
1928- , American; nonfiction
CON
COLEMAN, Robert William Alfred
('James Insight'), 1916- ,
English; nonfiction CON
COLEMAN, Terry, 1931- ,
English; nonfiction, fiction
CON
COLENSO, John William, 1814-83,
English; criticism BRO KBA
ST
COLERIDGE, David Hartley,
1796-1849, English; poetry
KBA BRO ST
COLERIDGE, Ernest Hartley,
1846-1920, English; editor
KBA
'COLERIDGE, John' see BINDER,
Otto O.
COLERIDGE, Mary Elizabeth,
1861-1907, English; poetry,
fiction, criticism BRO KBA
SA ST
COLERIDGE, Samuel Taylor, 1772-

1834, English; poetry, plays, translations, essays, criticism BRO KBA MAG SA SP ST

COLERIDGE, Sara, 1802-52, English; poetry, translations BRO KBA SA ST

COLERIDGE, William Emanuel, 1931- , English; nonfiction CON

COLES, Cyril Henry ('Manning Coles' 'Francis Gaite'), 1899- , English; fiction CON KTS

COLES, Harry Lewis, 1920- , American; nonfiction CON

COLES, John Morton, 1930- , Canadian; nonfiction CON

COLES, Kaines Adlard, 1901- , English; nonfiction CON

'COLES, Manning' see COLES, Cyril H.

COLES, Sydney Frederick Arthur, 1896- , English; nonfiction CON

COLES, William Allan, 1930- , American; nonfiction CON

COLET, John, 1467-1519, English; nonfiction BRO ST

'COLET, Louise Revoil' (Luisa Revoil), 1810- , French; nonfiction SA

COLETTE, Gabrielle Claudine de Jouvenel Sidonie, 1873-1954, French; fiction COL DIF FLE HAR KAT KT MAG MAL RIC SA ST

COLFORD, William Edward, 1908-71, American; nonfiction CON

COLGRAVE, Bertram, 1888-1968, English; nonfiction CON

COLIMORE, Vincent Jerome, 1904- , American; nonfiction CON

COLIN, Ambroise, 1710- , French; poetry DIL

COLIN MUSET, 13th cent., French; poetry HAR ST

COLING, Tessa Patterson, 1915- , American; juveniles CON

COLISH, Marcia L., 1937- , American; nonfiction CON

COLL, Pedro Emilio, 1872-1947, Venezuelan; journalism, fiction BL SA

COLL y VEHI, José, 1823-76, Spanish; criticism, poetry BL SA

COLLADO, Casimiro del, 1822-98,

Spanish; poetry SA

COLLANTES, Alejandro, 1901-33, Spanish; journalism, poetry SA

COLLANTES, José María, 1877-1943, Cuban; journalism, poetry MIN

COLLAS, Jean Paul Louis, 1735-81, French; nonfiction DIL

COLLAZO, Francisco Emilio, 1888- , Argentinian; plays MIN

COLLE, Charles, 1709-83, French; plays DIL SA

COLLEDGE, Malcolm Andrew Richard, 1939- , English; nonfiction CON

'COLLEN, Neil' see LEE, Lincoln

COLLENS, Thomas Wharton, 1812-79, American; nonfiction KAA

COLLENUCCIO, Pandolfo, 1444-1504, Italian; nonfiction ST

'COLLERYE, Roger de' (Roger Bontemps), 1470-1538, French; poetry DIF ST

COLLET, Pierre, 1693-1770, French; nonfiction DIL

COLLETET, Guillaume, 1598-1659, French; poetry SA

COLLETT, Jacobine Camilla Wergeland, 1813-95, Norwegian; fiction COL HAR KE SA ST

COLLETTE, Henri Joseph, 18th cent., French; nonfiction DIL

COLLIE, Michael, 1929- , British; poetry MUR

COLLIER, Alan Graham, 1923- , English; nonfiction CON

COLLIER, Calhoun Crofford, 1916- , American; nonfiction CON

COLLIER, Christopher, 1930- , American; nonfiction CON

COLLIER, David Swanson, 1923- , American; nonfiction CON

'COLLIER, Douglas' see FEL-LOWES-GORDON, Ian D.

COLLIER, Edmund, American; juveniles WA

COLLIER, Ethel, American; juveniles WA

COLLIER, Gaylan Jane, 1924- , American; nonfiction CON

COLLIER, James Lincoln, 1928- , American; fiction CON

'COLLIER, Jane' see SHUMSKY, Zena F.

COLLIER, Jeremy, 1650-1726, English; nonfiction BRO ST

COLLIER, John, 1901- , English; fiction KAT KT

COLLIER, John Basil, 1908- , English; nonfiction, fiction, translations CON

COLLIER, Leonard Dawson, 1908- , English; nonfiction CON

COLLIER, Richard, 1924- , Anglo-American; fiction CON

COLLIER, Simon, 1938- , English; nonfiction CON

'COLLIER, Zena' see SHUMSKY, Zena F.

COLLIGAN, Francis James, 1908- , American; nonfiction CON

COLLIGNON, Jean Henri, 1918- , American; nonfiction CON

COLLIN, Hedvig, Danish; juveniles WA

COLLIN, Heinrich Joseph von, 1772-1811, Austrian; plays, poetry HAR ST

COLLIN, Marion Cripps, 1928- , English; fiction CON

COLLIN, William Edwin, 1893- , Canadian; nonfiction SY

'COLLIN D'HARLEVILLE, Jean Francois' (J.F. Collin), 1755-1806, French; plays DIF DIL HAR SA ST

COLLIN de PLANCY, Jacques Albine Simon, 1793-1881, French; nonfiction SA

COLLINGS, Ellsworth, 1887- , American; nonfiction MAR WA

COLLINGWOOD, Charles Cummings, 1917- , American; fiction CON

'COLLINGWOOD, Harry' (W.J.C. Lancaster), 1851-1920?, English; juveniles DOY

COLLINGWOOD, Robin George, 1889-1943, British; nonfiction KTS ST

COLLINS, Anthony, 1676-1729, English; nonfiction SA

COLLINS, Barry Emerson, 1937- , American; nonfiction CON

COLLINS, Carvel, 1912- , American; nonfiction CON

COLLINS, Charles Allston, 1828-73, English; fiction, essays KBA

COLLINS, Charles C., 1919- , American; nonfiction CON

COLLINS, Cuthbert Dale, 1897- , Australian; fiction, nonfiction BRO KT

'COLLINS, D.' see BULLEID, H.A.V.

COLLINS, Dale, 1897- , Australian; fiction KL

COLLINS, David, 1940- , American; juveniles CON

COLLINS, David Almon, 1931- , American; nonfiction CON

COLLINS, Frederica Joan Hale ('Freda Collins'), 1904- , English; juveniles, fiction, plays CON

COLLINS, Frederick Herbert, 1890- , English; nonfiction CON

COLLINS, George Edwin ('Nimrod Junior'), 1867- , English; nonfiction HIG

COLLINS, George Rosebrough, 1917- , American; nonfiction CON

COLLINS, Harold Reeves, 1915- , American; nonfiction CON

COLLINS, Henry, 1917- , English; nonfiction CON

COLLINS, Henry Hill, 1907-61, American; juveniles WA

'COLLINS, Hunt' see HUNTER, Evan

COLLINS, James Daniel, 1917- , American; nonfiction CON

'COLLINS, Jeffrey' see WILCOX, Colin

COLLINS, John, 1742?-1808, English; poetry BRO

COLLINS, John Churton, 1848-1908, English; essays, nonfiction, criticism BRO KBA ST

COLLINS, John H., 1893- , American; nonfiction CON

'COLLINS, June' see WEATHERSTONE, June I.

COLLINS, Lewis John, 1905- , English; nonfiction CON

COLLINS, Mortimer, 1827-76, English; fiction, poetry BRO KBA ST

COLLINS, Myron Dean, 1901- , American; nonfiction CON

COLLINS, Norman Richard, 1907- , English; fiction BRO KTS

COLLINS, Philip Arthur William, 1923- , English; nonfiction CON

COLLINS, Robert Oakley, 1933- , American; nonfiction CON

COLLINS, Rowland Lee, 1934- ,
American; nonfiction CON

COLLINS, Ruth Philpott, 1890- ,
Canadian; juveniles CON

'COLLINS, Tom' see FURPHY,
Joseph

COLLINS, William, 1721-59, English;
poetry BRO KB ST

COLLINS, Wilkie, 1824-89, English;
fiction, plays BRO KBA MAG
SA ST

COLLINS, William Bernard, 1913- ,
Welsh; nonfiction CON

COLLINS, William Robert Fitzgerald,
1900- , American; plays, fiction
CON

COLLINSON, Laurence Henry, 1925- ,
Australian; poetry, plays MUR

COLLIS, Louise, 1925- , English;
fiction CON

COLLIS, Maurice, 1889- , British;
nonfiction CON KTS

COLLISON, Robert Lewis Wright,
1914- , American; nonfiction
CON

COLLESS, Gertrude Florence Mary
Jones, 1908- , American; nonfiction CON

'COLLODI, Carlo' (Carlo Lorenzini),
1826-90, Italian; juveniles DOY
HAR KE KJU SA ST WA

COLLOMB, Adalbert, 1730-89,
French; nonfiction DIL

COLLOREDO, Hermes, 1622-92,
Raeto-Romansch; poetry ST

COLLOT d' HERBOIS, Jean Marie,
1750-96, French; nonfiction SA

COLLYMORE, Frank Appleton,
1893- , Barbadian; poetry MUR

COLLYNS, Charles Palk, 1765-1864,
English; nonfiction HIG

COLM, Gerhard, 1897- , German-
American; nonfiction CON

COLM, Jan S., 1575-1637, Dutch;
plays ST

COLMAN, Arthur D., 1937- ,
American; nonfiction CON

'COLMAN, George' see GLASSCO,
John S.

COLMAN, George, 1732-94, English;
plays, poetry BRO KB SA ST

COLMAN, George ('The Younger'),
1762-1836, English; plays BRO
KBA ST

COLMAN, Hila ('Teresa Crayder'),
American; juveniles COM CON
WA

COLMAN, John E., 1923- ,
American; nonfiction CON

COLMAN, Libby Lee, 1940- ,
American; nonfiction CON

COLMAN, Narciso Ramón, 20th
cent., Paraguayan; poetry
SA

COLMENARES, Diego de, 1586-
1651, Spanish; nonfiction BL
SA

COLOANE, Francisco A., 1910- ,
Chilean; fiction MIN

COLODNY, Robert G., 1915- ,
American; nonfiction CON

COLODRERO de VILLALOBOS,
Miguel, 1611-60?, Spanish;
poetry SA

COLOMA, Carlos, 1566-1637,
Spanish; nonfiction BL SA ST

COLOMA y ROLDAN, Luis,
1851-1914, Spanish; fiction
BL COL SA ST

COLOMB, Jean, 1688-1774,
French; nonfiction DIL

'COLOMBINE' see BURGOS SEGUI,
Carmen de

COLOMBINI, Giovanni, 1304?-67,
Italian; nonfiction ST

'COLOMBO, Dale' see MONROE,
Keith

COLOMBO, John Robert, 1936- ,
Canadian; poetry CON MUR

COLON, Cristobal see COLUMBUS,
Christopher

COLONIA, Dominique de, 1658-
1741, French; nonfiction DIL

COLONIUS, Lillian, 1911- , American; juveniles CON

COLONNA, Francesco, 1432?-
1527?, Italian; nonfiction HAR
ST

COLONNA, Vittoria, 1490-1525/49,
Italian; poetry HAR KE SA ST

COLONNE, Guido Delle, 1215-90,
Italian; poetry ST

COLONY, Horatio, 1900- , American; poetry CON

COLORADO CAPELLA, Antonio
Julio, 1903- , American; nonfiction CON

COLQUHOUN, Ithell, 1906- ,
English; fiction CON

COLQUHOUN, John, 1805-85,
Scots; nonfiction KBA

COLSON, Elizabeth F., 1917- ,
American; nonfiction CON

COLSON, Greta Scotchmur,

1913- , English; nonfiction
CON
COLSON, Howard Paul, 1910- ,
American; nonfiction CON
COLSON, Romain, -1712, French;
poetry DIL
'COLSON-HAIG, S.' see GLASSCO,
John S.
'COLT, Clem' see NYE, Nelson C.
'COLT, Martin' see EPSTEIN,
Samuel
'COLTER, Shayne' see NORWOOD,
Victor G. C.
COLTHARP, Lurline Hughes,
1913- , American; nonfiction
CON
'COLTMAN, Ernest Vivian' see
DUDLEY, Ernest
COLTMAN, Paul Curtis, 1917- ,
British; poetry MUR
COLTON, Calvin, 1789-1857, Ameri-
can; journalism KAA
COLTON, Charles Caleb, 1780-1832,
English; poetry, essays BRO
KBA ST
COLTON, Clarence Eugene, 1914- ,
American; nonfiction CON
COLTON, Harold Sellers, 1881- ,
American; nonfiction CON
'COLTON, James' see HANSEN,
Joseph
COLTON, James Byers, II, 1908- ,
American; nonfiction CON
COLTON, Joel, 1918- , American;
nonfiction CON
COLTON, Walter, 1797-1851, Amer-
ican; journalism KAA
COLUM, Mary Gunning Maguire,
188?- , Irish-American; criti-
cism HOE KT ST
COLUM, Padraic, 1881-1972, Irish-
American; juveniles, poetry,
plays BRO FLE HOE KJU KL
KT MAT MUR RIC SA ST WA
COLUMBA, 521-97, Irish; nonfiction
ST
COLUMBANUS, St., 540-615, Irish;
nonfiction ST
COLUMBUS, Christopher (Cristóbal
Colón), 1447/51-1506, Italian;
nonfiction BL HAR ST
COLUMBUS, Samuel Jonae, 1642-79,
Swedish; poetry ST
COLUMELLA, L. Junius Moderatus,
fl. 60, Roman; nonfiction SA ST
COLVER, Alice Mary Rosa, 1892- ,
American; nonfiction, juveniles

WA WAF
COLVER, Anne, 1908- , Ameri-
can; juveniles WA
COLVILLE, Robert, 1909- ,
English; nonfiction HIG
COLVIN, Sir Dorothy, 1845-1927,
British; criticism KT
COLVIN, Ian G., 1912- , English;
nonfiction CON
COLVIN, Sir Sidney, 1845-1927,
English; criticism BRO SA
COLWELL, Eileen Hilda, 1904- ,
English; juveniles COM CON
DOY
COLWELL, Ernest Cadman, 1901- ,
American; nonfiction CON
COLWELL, Robert, 1931- ,
Canadian; nonfiction CON
COMAN, Edwin Truman, 1903- ,
American; nonfiction CON
COMBAULT, N., -1785, French;
poetry DIL
COMBE, George, 1788-1858, Scots;
nonfiction BRO KBA ST
COMBE, William, 1741-1823/28,
English; poetry BRO KBA SA
ST
COMBER, Elizabeth K. C. see
'HAN Suyin'
COMBER, Lillian ('Lillian Beck-
with'), 1916- , English; fiction
CON
COMBES, Rev. André, 1899- ,
French; nonfiction HO
COMBS, Arthur Wright, 1912- ,
American; nonfiction CON
COMBS, Elisha Trammell, Jr.,
1924- , American; nonfiction
CON
COMBS, Richard Earl, 1934- ,
American; nonfiction CON
'COMBS, Robert' see MURRAY,
John
COMELLA y VILLAMITJAN,
Luciano Francisco, 1751-1812,
Spanish; plays BL SA ST
COMENIUS, Jan Amos (Komensky;
Amos Komensky), 1592-1670,
Czech; nonfiction HAR KE SA
ST
COMFORT, Alexander, 1920- ,
British; poetry, fiction, criti-
cism, essays BRO CON FLE
KTS MUR
COMFORT, Howard, 1904- ,
American; nonfiction CON
COMFORT, Iris Tracy, American;

nonfiction CON

'COMFORT, Jane Livingston' see STURTZEL, Jane L.

COMFORT, Mildred Houghton, 1886- , American; juveniles CON

COMFORT, Richard Allen, 1933- , American; nonfiction CON

COMFORT, Will Levington, 1878-1932, American; fiction, journalism HIL KT

COMISSO, Giovanni, 1895- , Italian; poetry, essays COL FLE SA ST

COMMAGER, Henry Steele, 1902- , American; nonfiction, juveniles CON KTS WA

COMMELERAN y GOMEZ, Francisco Andrés, 1848-1919, Spanish; nonfiction SA

COMMINS, Dorothy Berliner, American; juveniles WA

COMMIRE, Jean, 1625-1702, French; poetry ST

COMMODIANUS, 3rd-5th cent. ?, Roman; poetry ST

COMMYNES, Philippe de (Comines), 1447?-1511, French; nonfiction DIF HAR KE SA ST

COMNENA, Anna, 1083-1148, Byzantine; nonfiction KE SA ST

COMODIANO de GOZA, 3rd cent., Roman; poetry SA

COMPAGNI, Dino, 1255?-1324, Italian; nonfiction HAR ST

COMPAN, Charles, 1740- , French; fiction DIL

COMPARETTI, Alice, 1907- , American; nonfiction CON

COMPARETTI, Domenico, 1835-1927, Italian; criticism ST

'COMPERE, Mickie' see DAVIDSON, Mickie C.

COMPIUTA DONZELLA, 13th cent., Florentine; poetry ST

'COMPTON, Ann' see PREBBLE, Marjorie M. C.

COMPTON, David Guy, 1930- , English; fiction CON

COMPTON, Sir Edward Montagu see 'MACKENZIE, Sir Compton'

COMPTON, Henry Pasfield, 1909- , English; poetry CON

COMPTON, James Vincent, 1928- , American; nonfiction CON

COMPTON-BURNETT, Ivy, 1892-1969, English; fiction BRO CON FLE KTS RIC ST

COMSTOCK, Helen, 1893- , American; nonfiction CON

COMSTOCK, Henry B., 1908- , American; nonfiction CON

COMTE, Auguste Isidore Marie François Xavier, 1798-1857, French; nonfiction DIF HAR KE SA ST

COMYNS-CARR, Barbara Irene Veronica, 1912- , English; fiction CON

CONACHER, Desmond John, 1918- , Canadian; nonfiction CON

CONACHER, James Blennerhasset, 1916- , Canadian; nonfiction CON

CONAN, Laure (Felicite Angers), 1845-1924, Canadian; fiction SY

CONAN DOYLE see DOYLE, Sir Arthur C.

CONAN DOYLE, Adrian Malcolm, 1910-70, English; fiction CON

CONANT, Howard Somers, 1921- , American; nonfiction CON

CONANT, James Bryant, 1893- , American; nonfiction CON

CONANT, Kenneth John, 1894- , American; nonfiction CON

CONANT, Ralph Wendell, 1926- , American; nonfiction CON

CONARD, Alfred E., 1911- , American; nonfiction CON

CONARD, Joseph W., 1911- , American; nonfiction CON

CONARROE, Joel Osborne, 1934- , American; nonfiction CON

CONAWAY, James Alley, 1941- , American; fiction CON

CONCANNON, Helena Walsh, 1878- , Irish; nonfiction HOE

CONCHA, Marcia de S. see SANTIAGO CONCHA, Manuel de

CONCHA CASTILLO, Francisco A., 1855/56-1928, Chilean; poetry MIN

CONCHA RIFFO, Gilberto see 'VALLE, Juvencio'

CONCHALE, Inocencio see RIQUELME, D.

'CONCOLORCORVO' see BUSTA-MANTE, Calixto C.

CONDE, Carmen, 1907- , Spanish; poetry BL SA

CONDE, Francisco Javier, 1908- ,
Spanish; nonfiction BL SA
CONDE, José Antonio, 1765-1820,
Spanish; nonfiction BL SA
CONDEE, Ralph Waterbury, 1916- ,
American; nonfiction CON
CONDILLAC, Etienne Bonnet de,
1715-80, French; nonfiction DIF
DIL HAR KE SA ST
CONDIT, Carl Wilbur, 1914- ,
American; nonfiction CON
CONDLIFFE, John Bell, 1891- ,
Australian; nonfiction CON
CONDON, John Carl, 1938- , Amer-
ican; nonfiction CON
CONDON, Richard Thomas, 1915- ,
American; fiction, nonfiction
CON
'CONDOR, Gladyn' see DAVISON,
Gladys P.
CONDORCET, Marie Jean Antoine
Nicolas Caritot, 1743-94,
French; nonfiction DIF DIL HAR
KE SA ST
CONE, Carl B., 1916- , American;
nonfiction CON
CONE, James H., 1938- , Amer-
ican; nonfiction CON
CONE, John Frederick, 1926- ,
American; nonfiction CON
CONE, Molly Lamken ('Caroline
More'), 1918- , American;
juveniles COM CON PAC WA
CONE, Orello, 1835-1905, American;
nonfiction KAA
CONEGLIANO, Emanuele see 'DA
PONTE, Lorenzo'
CONERLY, Perian Collier, 1926- ,
American; nonfiction CON
CONFER, Vincent, 1913- , Ameri-
can; nonfiction CON
CONFORD, Ellen, 1942- , Ameri-
can; juveniles CON
CONFREY, Burton, 1898- , Ameri-
can; fiction, nonfiction HOE
CONFUCIUS (K'ung Ch'iu), 551-479
B.C., Chinese; essays LAN SA
ST
CONGDON, Charles Taber ('Paul
Potter'), 1821-91, American;
poetry KAA
CONGDON, Herbert Wheaton, 1876-
1965, American; nonfiction CON
CONGDON, Kirby, 1924- , Ameri-
can; nonfiction CON
CONGDON, William Grosvenor,
1912- , American; nonfiction
CON

CONGER, John Janeway, 1921- ,
American; nonfiction CON
'CONGER, Lesley' see SUTTLES,
Shirley S.
CONGER, Marion, American;
juveniles WA
CONGREVE, Richard, 1818-99,
English; essays KBA
CONGREVE, William, 1670-1729,
English; plays, fiction BRO
KB MAG SA ST
CONIAC, Hippolyte Augustin de,
1731-1802, French; nonfiction
DIL
CONIL, Jean, 1917- , French;
nonfiction CON
CONINGTON, John, 1825-69,
English; translations, nonfic-
tion BRO KBA ST
CONKIN, Paul Keith, 1929- ,
American; nonfiction CON
CONKLE, Ellsworth Prouty,
1899- , American; plays
MAT
CONKLIN, Gladys Plemon, 1903- ,
American; juveniles COM
CON WA
CONKLIN, Groff, 1904- , Amer-
ican; nonfiction CON
CONKLIN, John Evan, 1943- ,
American; nonfiction CON
CONKLING, Fleur, American;
juveniles WA
CONKLING, Grace Walcott
Hazard, 1878- , American;
poetry KT
CONLAY, Iris, 1910- , English;
nonfiction CON
CONLIN, David A., 1897- ,
American; nonfiction CON
CONLON, Denis J., 1932- ,
English; nonfiction CON
CONN, Charles William, 1920- ,
American; nonfiction CON
CONN, Frances G., 1925- ,
American; nonfiction CON
CONN, John Stewart, 1936- ,
Scots; poetry, plays MUR
CONN, Peter J., 1942- , Amer-
ican; nonfiction CON
CONN, Stetson, 1908- , Ameri-
can; nonfiction CON
CONNELL, Brian Reginald,
1916- , English; nonfiction,
translations CON
CONNELL, Evan Shelby, Jr.,
1924- , American; nonfiction
CON

CONNELL, F. Norreys see
O'RIORDAN, Conal
CONNELL, Francis J., 1888- ,
American; nonfiction CON HOE
CONNELL, Kenneth Hugh, 1917- ,
English; nonfiction CON
CONNELL, Richard Edward, 1893-
1949, American; fiction KT
CONNELLY, Marcus Cook, 1890- ,
American; plays KL KT MAT SA
CONNELLY, Merval Hannah, 1914- ,
Australian; poetry MUR
CONNELLY, Owen Sergeson, Jr.,
1924- , American; nonfiction
CON
CONNELLY, Thomas Lawrence,
1938- , American; nonfiction
CON
CONNELLY, Willard, 1888- , Eng-
lish; nonfiction CON
CONNER, Paul Willard, 1937- ,
American; nonfiction CON
CONNER, Patrick Reardon ('Readen
Conner'; 'Peter Malin'), 1907- ,
Irish; fiction CON
CONNERS, Kenneth Wray, 1909- ,
American; nonfiction CON
CONNETT, Eugene Virginius III,
1891- , American; nonfiction
CON HIG
CONNETTE, Earle, 1910- , Ameri-
can; nonfiction CON
CONNICK, Charles Milo, 1917- ,
American; nonfiction CON
CONNIFF, James Clifford Gregory
('John Coolwater' 'Anthropo-
phagus Minor'), 1920- , Amer-
ican; nonfiction CON
'CONNINGTON, J.J.' see STEWART,
Alfred W.
CONNOLLY, Cyril Vernon ('Vercors';
'Palinurus'), 1903- , English;
criticism BRO CON FLE KTS
RIC
CONNOLLY, Francis Xavier, 1909- ,
American; nonfiction, poetry
CON HO
CONNOLLY, James Brendan, 1868- ,
American; fiction HOE KT
CONNOLLY, Margaret E. see IRVIN,
Margaret E.
CONNOLLY, Terence L., 1888- ,
American; nonfiction HOE
CONNOLLY, Thomas Edmund, 1918- ,
American; nonfiction CON
CONNOR, John Anthony ('Tony
Connor'; 'Adam Hardwick'),

1930- , English; poetry CON
CONNOR, Patricia, 1943- , Eng-
lish; fiction CON
'CONNOR, Ralph' see GORDON,
Charles W.
CONNOR, Robert Digges Wimberley,
1878-1956, American; nonfiction
JO
'CONNOR, Tony' see CONNOR,
John A.
CONNOR, Tony ('Bino Spear'),
1930- , British; poetry MUR
'CONNORS, Bruton' (Edward Rohen),
1931- , Welsh; poetry, fiction
MUR
CONON, 1st cent. B.C., Greek;
nonfiction SA
CONON de BETHUNE, 1150-1219/
20, French; poetry DIF ST
'CONOR, Glen' see COONEY,
Michael
CONOVER, Charles Eugene, 1903- ,
American; nonfiction CON
CONOVER, Hobart H., 1914- ,
American; nonfiction CON
CONQUEST, Edwin Parker, Jr.
(Ned), 1931- , American;
nonfiction CON
CONQUEST, George Robert Ac-
worth ('J.E.M. Arden'),
1917- , English; nonfiction
CON
CONQUEST, Robert, 1917- ,
British; poetry, fiction MUR
RIC
CONRAD, Andree ('L.K. Conrad'),
1945- , American; nonfiction
CON
CONRAD, Barnaby, 1922- , Amer-
ican; fiction CON
'CONRAD, C.' see BENJAMIN,
Walter
CONRAD, David Eugene, 1928- ,
American; nonfiction CON
CONRAD, Earl, 1912- , American;
nonfiction CON
CONRAD, Edna G., 1893- ,
American; nonfiction CON
CONRAD, Jack Randolph, 1923- ,
American; nonfiction CON
CONRAD, Joseph (Jozef Teodor
Konrad Nalicz Korzeniowski),
1857-1924, Polish-English;
fiction, plays BRO FLE KAT
KT MAG MAT RIC SA ST
'CONRAD, L.K.' see CONRAD,
Andree

CONRAD, Michael Georg, 1846-1927,
German; criticism, fiction COL
SA

CONRAD, Robert Taylor, 1810-58,
American; plays KAA

CONRAD, Sybil, 1921- , American;
nonfiction, juveniles CON WA

'CONRAD, Tod' see WILKES-HUNTER,
Richard

CONRAD, Will C., 1882- , American; nonfiction CON

CONRAD of WÜRZBURG,   -1287,
German; poetry HAR

CONRADI, Hermann, 1862-90, German; poetry, fiction AL COL
SA ST

CONRADIS, Heinz, 1907- , German;
nonfiction CON

CONRADS, Ulrich, 1923- , American; nonfiction CON

CONRAN, Anthony, 1931- , British;
poetry MUR

CONRART, Valentin, 1603-75, French;
nonfiction SA ST

CONRON, Alfred Brandon, 1919- ,
Canadian; nonfiction CON

CONROY, Charles W., 1922- ,
American; nonfiction CON

CONROY, Jack, 1899- , American;
fiction WAF

CONROY, John Wesley ('Tim Brennan'; 'John Norcross'), 1899- ,
American; poetry, nonfiction,
fiction CON

CONSCIENCE, Hendrik, 1812-83,
Belgian; fiction COL HAR KE
MAG SA ST

CONSCIENCE, J.B., 1749-84,
French; nonfiction DIL

CONSIDINE, John Joseph, 1897- ,
American; nonfiction CON HOE

CONSIDINE, Robert Bernard, 1906- ,
American; nonfiction, fiction
HOE

CONSOLATO, Sister Mary see
CARROLL, Consolata

CONSOLO, Dominick Peter, 1923- ,
American; nonfiction CON

CONSTABLE, Henry, 1562-1613,
English; poetry BRO KB ST

CONSTABLE, John, fl. 1520, English; poetry ST

CONSTABLE, William George,
1887- , English; nonfiction CON

CONSTANT, Alberta Wilson, 1908- ,
American; nonfiction CON

CONSTANT, Rev Gustave León

Marie, 1869-1940, French;
nonfiction HO

CONSTANT de REBECQUE,
Benjamin, 1767-1830, Swiss;
nonfiction DIF HAR KE MAG
MAL SA ST

CONSTANTELOS, Demetrios J.
('Dimitris Stachys'), 1927- ,
American; nonfiction CON

CONSTANTIN, James A., 1922- ,
American; nonfiction CON

CONSTANTIN, Robert Wilfrid,
1937- , American; nonfiction
CON

CONSTANTINE, 15th cent., Bulgarian; nonfiction ST

CONSTANTINE, Grand Duke see
ROMANOV, Grand Duke
Konstantin K.

CONSTANTINE VII, PORPHYRO-
GENITUS, 905-59, Byzantine;
nonfiction ST

CONSTANTINE MANASSES,   -1187,
Byzantine; poetry ST

CONSTANTIN-WEYER, Maurice,
1881- , French; fiction DIF
KL KT SA

CONTANT d'ORVILLE, André
Guillaume, 1730- , French;
plays, fiction DIL

CONTARDO, Luis Felipe, 1880-
1921, Chilean; poetry MIN SA

CONTI, Anonio, 1677-1749, Italian;
poetry, plays HAR ST

CONTI, Giusto de, 1389?-1449,
Italian; poetry ST

CONTO, César, 1836-91/92,
Colombian; poetry MIN

CONTON, William, 1925- , American; fiction CON

CONTOSKI, Victor, 1936- , American; nonfiction CON

'CONTRADUC, A.' see HOEN,
Pieter

CONTRERA, Jerónimo de, 16th
cent., Spanish; fiction BL

CONTRERAS, Alonso, de, 1582-
1640?, Spanish; nonfiction SA
ST

CONTRERAS, Francisco, 1877-
1932, Chilean; poetry MIN SA

CONTRERAS, Heles, 1933- ,
Chilean-American; nonfiction
CON

CONTRERAS, Jerónimo de, 16th
cent., Spanish; fiction SA ST

CONTRERAS, Raúl, 1896- ,

Salvadoran; poetry, criticism
BL SA
CONTRERAS CAMARGO, Enrique,
1872- , Spanish; journalism,
fiction SA
CONTRERAS PAZO, Francisco,
1909?- , Spanish; fiction, poetry,
essays SA
CONTRERAS y LOPEZ de AYALA,
Juan de (Lozoya), 1893- ,
Spanish; poetry BL SA
CONVERSE, Paul Dulaney, 1889- ,
American; nonfiction CON
CONVERSE, Philip E., 1928- ,
American; nonfiction CON
CONWAY, Alan Arthur, 1920- ,
English; nonfiction CON
'CONWAY, Arlington B.' see BURNS,
Eedson L. M.
CONWAY, Bertrand, 1872- , Amer-
ican; nonfiction HOE
'CONWAY, Denise' see PREBBLE,
Marjorie M. C.
CONWAY, Freda, 1911- , English;
nonfiction CON
CONWAY, Helene, American; juven-
iles WA
'CONWAY, Hugh' see FARGUS,
Frederick J.
CONWAY, John Donald, 1905- ,
American; nonfiction CON
CONWAY, John Seymour, 1929- ,
English; nonfiction CON
CONWAY, Mary Margaret, 1935- ,
American; nonfiction CON
CONWAY, Moncure Daniel, 1832-1907,
American; nonfiction, essays
KAA
CONWAY, Thomas Daniel, 1934- ,
American; nonfiction CON
'CONWAY, Ward' see WESTMORE-
LAND, Reginald C.
CONYBEARE, William Daniel, 1787-
1857, English; nonfiction KBA
CONYERS, Dorothea, 1873- , English;
nonfiction HIG
CONZE, Edward J.D., 1904- , Eng-
lish; nonfiction CON
COOGAN, Daniel, 1915- , Ameri-
can; nonfiction, translations
CON
COOGAN, Joseph Patrick, 1925- ,
American; fiction CON
COOK, Albert Spaulding, 1925- ,
American; nonfiction, translations,
poetry, fiction CON
COOK, Beverly Blair, 1926- ,

American; nonfiction CON
COOK, Bruce, 1932- , American;
nonfiction CON
COOK, Clarence Chatham, 1828-
1900, American; criticism
KAA
COOK, Daniel, 1914- , American;
nonfiction CON
COOK, Donald Paul, 1920- ,
American; nonfiction CON
COOK, Eliza, 1818-89, English;
poetry BRO KBA
COOK, Fannie, American; fiction
WAF
COOK, Flavius Josephus ('Joseph
Cook'), 1838-1901, American;
nonfiction KAA
COOK, Fred James, 1911- ,
American; juveniles, fiction
COM CON WA
COOK, George Allan, 1916- ,
American; nonfiction CON
COOK, George Cram, 1873-1924,
American; fiction, plays,
poetry KT MAT
COOK, Gladys Emerson, 1899- ,
American; juveniles CON WA
COOK, Gladys Moon, 1907- ,
American; nonfiction, juveniles
CON
COOK, Glenn J., 1913- , Ameri-
can; nonfiction CON
COOK, Harold Reed, 1902- ,
American; nonfiction CON
COOK, James, 1728-79, English;
nonfiction KB
COOK, James Gordon, 1916- ,
English; nonfiction CON
COOK, James Graham, 1925- ,
American; nonfiction CON
COOK, Colonel John, 1773-1829,
English; nonfiction HIG
COOK, Joseph see COOK, Flavius
J.
COOK, Joseph Jay, 1924- ,
American; nonfiction CON WA
COOK, Margaret Gerry, 1903- ,
American; nonfiction CON
COOK, Marion Belden, American;
juveniles WA
COOK, Mark, 1942- , English;
nonfiction CON
COOK, Melva Janice, 1919- ,
American; nonfiction CON
COOK, Mercer, 1903- , American;
nonfiction SCA
COOK, Myra B. ('Myra Brown'),

1933-   , American; nonfiction, poetry CON

COOK, Olive, 1916-   , English; nonfiction CON

COOK, Olive Rambo, 1892-   , American; juveniles CON WA

COOK, Pauline Lesley, 1922-   , English; nonfiction CON

COOK, Ramona Graham, American; poetry CON

COOK, Richard Irving, 1927-   , American; nonfiction CON

COOK, Robert L., 1920-   , American; nonfiction CON

COOK, Robert (Robin), William Arthur, 1931-   , English; fiction CON

COOK, Roderick, 1932-   , English; nonfiction CON

COOK, Sherman, R., American; juveniles WA

COOK, Stuart Wellford, 1913-   , American; nonfiction CON

COOK, Sir Theodore Andrea, 1867-1928, English; nonfiction HIG

COOK, Warren L., 1925-   , American; nonfiction CON

COOK, William Jesse, Jr., 1938-   , American; nonfiction CON

COOK, William Wallace, 1867-1933, American; nonfiction HIL

COOKE, Alfred Alistair, 1908-   , British; essays, journalism KTS

COOKE, Barbara, American; juveniles WA

COOKE, Bernard J., 1922-   , American; nonfiction CON

COOKE, David Coxe, 1917-   , American; juveniles, nonfiction COM CON WA

COOKE, Donald Ewin, 1916-   , American; juveniles, nonfiction COM CON WA

COOKE, Gerald, 1925-   , American; nonfiction CON

COOKE, Gilbert William, 1899-   , American; nonfiction CON

COOKE, Greville Vaughan Turner, 1894-   , English; nonfiction CON

COOKE, Hereward Lester, 1916-   , American; nonfiction CON

COOKE, Jacob Ernest, 1924-   , American; nonfiction CON

COOKE, John, fl. 1614, English; plays ST

COOKE, John Esten, 1830-86, American; fiction, essays BRO KAA MAG ST

COOKE, Philip Pendleton, 1816-50, American; poetry, fiction KAA

COOKE, Philip St. George, 1809-95, American; nonfiction KAA

COOKE, Rose Terry, 1837-92, American; poetry, fiction KAA

COOKE, William, 1942-   , English; nonfiction CON

COOKE, Croft see CROFT-COOKE, Rupert

COOKRIDGE, Edward Henry, 1908-   , Austrian-American; nonfiction CON

COOKSON, Catherine McMullen ('Catherine Marchant'), 1906-   , English; fiction CON

COOLBRITH, Ina Donna, 1842-1928, American; poetry KAA

'COOLE, W.W.' see KULSKI, Wladslaw W.

COOLEY, John Kent, 1927-   , American; nonfiction CON

COOLEY, Lee Morrison, 1919-   , American; nonfiction CON

COOLEY, Leland Frederick, 1909-   , American; fiction CON

COOLEY, Richard, Allen, 1925-   , American; nonfiction CON

COOLIDGE, Archibald Cory, Jr., 1928-   , English; nonfiction CON

COOLIDGE, Clark, 1939-   , American; poetry CON MUR

COOLIDGE, Olivia Ensor, 1908-   , English; juveniles, nonfiction COM CON FUL WA

'COOLIDGE, Susan' see WOOLSEY, Sarah C.

COOLUS, Romain ('René Weil'), 1868-1952, French; plays HAR

'COOLWATER, John' see CONNIFF, James C.G.

COOMARASWAMY, Ananda Kentish, 1877-1947, Indian; criticism ST

COOMBE, Thomas, 1747-1822, American; poetry KAA

COOMBS, Charles Ira, 1914-   , American; juveniles CON WA

COOMBS, Douglas Stafford, 1924-   , English; nonfiction CON

COOMBS, Patricia, 1926-   ,

American; juveniles, poetry WA

COOMBS, Philip Hall, 1915- , American; nonfiction CON

COON, Carleton Stevens, 1904- , American; nonfiction CON

COON, Gene Lee, 1924- , American; nonfiction CON

COON, Martha Sutherland, 1884- , American; juveniles CON

COONEY, Barbara, 1917- , American; juveniles CON FUL WA

COONEY, David Martin, 1930- , American; nonfiction CON

COONEY, Michael ('Glen Conor'), 1921- , Irish; fiction CON

COONS, Frederica Bertha Safley, 1910- , American; nonfiction CON

COOP, Howard, 1928- , American; poetry CON

COOPER, Alfred Duff (Viscount Norwich), 1890-1954, English; nonfiction BRO

COOPER, Alfred Morton ('Morley Cooper'), 1890- , American; nonfiction CON

COOPER, Anthony Ashley see SHAFTESBURY, Anthony A.

COOPER, Arnold Cook, 1933- , American; nonfiction CON

COOPER, Barbara Ann, 1929- , Welsh; nonfiction CON

COOPER, Brian Newman, 1919- , English; fiction CON

COOPER, Bruce M. , 1925- , English; nonfiction CON

COOPER, Bryan Robert Wright, 1932- , English; nonfiction CON

COOPER, Charles William, 1904- , American; plays, nonfiction CON

COOPER, Chester L. , 1917- , American; nonfiction CON

COOPER, Christopher Donald Huntington, 1942- , Australian; nonfiction CON

COOPER, Courtney Ryley, 1886-1948, American; fiction KT

COOPER, Edith Emma ('Michael Field'), 1862-1913, English; poetry BRO

COOPER, Edmund, 1926- , American; fiction CON

COOPER, Elizabeth Ann, 1927- , American; fiction CON

COOPER, Elizabeth Keyser, 1910- , American; nonfiction CON

'COOPER, Esther' see KELLNER, Esther

COOPER, Frank Edward, 1910-68, American; nonfiction CON

COOPER, James Fenimore, 1789-1851, American; fiction, juveniles BRO DOY KAA MAG SA ST WA

'COOPER, James R.' see STRATEMEYER, Edward L.

COOPER, Jamie Lee, American; juveniles CON

COOPER, Jane Marvel, 1924- , American; poetry CON MUR

'COOPER, Jefferson' see FOX, Gardner F.

COOPER, John ('Venator'), fl. 1825- , English; nonfiction HIG

COOPER, John C. III see 'COBB, John'

COOPER, John Charles, 1933- , American; nonfiction CON

COOPER, John Cobb, 1887- , American; nonfiction CON

COOPER, John Ellsworth, 1922- , American; nonfiction CON

COOPER, John L. , 1936- , American; fiction CON

COOPER, John M. , 1912- , American; nonfiction CON

COOPER, John Montgomery, 1881- , American; nonfiction HOE

'COOPER, John R.' see STRATEMEYER, Edward L.

COOPER, Joseph Bonar, 1912- , American; nonfiction CON

COOPER, Joseph David, 1917- , American; nonfiction CON

COOPER, Kenneth, Schaaf, 1918- , American; nonfiction CON

COOPER, Lee Pelham, 1926- , American; nonfiction, juveniles CON WA

COOPER, Lettice, 1897- , English; fiction CON

COOPER, Louise Field, 1905- , American; fiction CON KTS WAF

COOPER, Mae Klein ('Nina Farewell'), American; fiction CON

COOPER, Mario, 1905- , American; nonfiction CON

COOPER, Sister Mary Ursula, 1925- , American; nonfiction CON

COOPER, Michael John, 1930- , English; nonfiction CON

COOPER, Paulette, 1944- ,

Belgian-American; nonfiction CON
COOPER, Philip J., 1926- , American; nonfiction CON
COOPER, Richard Newell, 1934- , American; nonfiction CON
COOPER, Saul ('Richard Benson'; 'Michael Milner'), 1934- , American; fiction CON
COOPER, Susan, 1935- , English; nonfiction CON
COOPER, Susan Fenimore, 1813-94, American; nonfiction KAA
COOPER, Sylvia ('Sylvia Paul Jerman'), 1903- , American; fiction CON
COOPER, Thomas, 1759-1839, American; nonfiction KAA
COOPER, Thomas, 1805-92, English; poetry, essays, fiction BRO KBA ST
COOPER, Wendy Lowe, 1919- , English; nonfiction CON
'COOPER, William' see HOFF, Henry S.
COOPER, William Wager, 1914- , American; nonfiction CON
COOPERMAN, Hasye, 1909- , American; nonfiction CON
COOPERMAN, Stanley, 1929- , American; nonfiction, poetry CON
COOPERSMITH, Harry, 1903- , American; nonfiction CON
COOPERSMITH, Stanley, 1926- , American; nonfiction CON
'COOPLANDT, A.' see PRINS, Ary
COORNHERT, Dirk Vokkertszoon, 1522-90, Dutch; poetry, plays KE ST
COORSI see KORSI, Demetrio
COOTNER, Paul Harold, 1930- , American; nonfiction CON
COOX, Alvin David, 1924- , American; nonfiction CON
COP, Matija, 1797-1835, Slovene; criticism ST
COPE, David, 1941- , American; nonfiction CON
COPE, Irving Marmer, 1917- , American; nonfiction CON
COPE, Robert Knox ('Jack Cope'), 1913- , American; nonfiction, plays, fiction CON MUR RIC
COPE, Vincent Zachary ('Zeta'), 1881- , English; nonfiction CON
COPEAU, Jacques, 1879-1949, French; plays COL DIF MAT SA

COPEE, Henry, 1821-95, American; nonfiction KAA
COPEL, Jean François, 1726-83, French; nonfiction DIL
COPEL, Sidney Leroy, 1930- , American; nonfiction CON
COPELAND, Edwin Luther, 1916- , American; nonfiction CON
COPELAND, Frances Virginia, American; juveniles WA
COPELAND, Helen, 1920- , American; juveniles CON
COPELAND, Melvin T., 1884- , American; nonfiction CON
COPELAND, Miles, 1916- , American; nonfiction CON
COPELAND, Morris Albert, 1895- , American; nonfiction CON
COPELAND, Paul William, 1917- , American; fiction CON
COPELAND, Paul Worthington, American; nonfiction, juveniles PAC WA
COPELAND, Ross H., 1930- , American; nonfiction CON
COPELAND, Thomas Wellsted, 1907- , American; nonfiction CON
COPEMAN, Fred, 1907- , English; nonfiction HO
COPEMAN, George Henry, 1922- , Australian; nonfiction CON
COPER, Rudolf, 1904- , German-American; nonfiction CON
COPERNICUS, Nicolaus (Mikolaj Kopernik), 1473-1543, Polish; nonfiction ST
COPLAN, Kate Mildred, 1901- , American; nonfiction CON
COPLAND, Aaron, 1900- , American; nonfiction CON
COPLAND, Robert, -1547?, English; nonfiction, translations CON
COPLESTON, Edward, 1776-1849, English; nonfiction KBA
COPLESTON, Rev. Frederick Charles, 1907- , English; nonfiction CON HO
COPLEY, Anthony, 1567-1607?, English; poetry ST
COPLIN, William David, 1939- , American; nonfiction CON
COPP, James III, 1916- , American; juveniles CON

COPPA, Frank John, 1937- ,
American; nonfiction CON
COPPARD, Alfred Edgar, 1878-1957,
English; juveniles, fiction,
poetry BRO DOY KL KT RIC
COPPARD, Audrey, 1931- , English;
fiction CON
COPPEE, Francis Joachim Edouard
François, 1842-1907/08, French;
poetry, plays COL DIF HAR KE
MAT SA ST
COPPEL, Alfred, 1921- , Ameri-
can; juveniles CON
COPPERUD, Roy H., 1915- ,
American; nonfiction CON
COPPIER, 18th cent., French; plays
DIL
COPPOCK, Charles, 1906- , Amer-
ican; juveniles WA
COPPOCK, John Oates, 1914- ,
American; nonfiction CON
COQUELET, Louis, 1676-1754,
French; fiction DIL
COQUELEY de CHAISSEPIERRE,
Charles Georges, 1711-91,
French; plays, poetry DIL
COQUELIN, Jerome, 1690-1771,
French; nonfiction DIL
COQUILLART, Guillaume, 1450?-
1510, French; poetry, plays ST
CORABIAS, Dimas, 1925- , Chilean;
poetry, fiction SA
CORAES see KORAËS, Adamantios
CORANCEZ, Olivier de, -1810,
French; nonfiction DIL
CORAX de SYRACUSE, 5th cent.
B.C., Greek; nonfiction SA
CORAY, Adamancio see KORAËS,
Adamtios
CORAZZINI, Sergio, 1887-1907,
Italian; poetry COL SA ST
CORBALLY, John Edward, Jr.,
1924- , American; nonfiction
CON
CORBECHON, Jean, 14th cent.,
French; translations ST
CORBERON NAMPDEVILLE, 18th
cent., French; nonfiction DIL
CORBET, Richard, 1582-1635, Eng-
lish; poetry BRO SP ST
CORBETT, Edward Patrick Joseph,
1919- , American; nonfiction
CON
CORBETT, Elizabeth Frances,
1887- , American; fiction,
essays, nonfiction CON HOO
KT WAF

CORBETT, Harry, 20th cent.,
English; juveniles DOY
CORBETT, Jack Elliott, 1920- ,
American; nonfiction CON
CORBETT, James Edward, 1875- ,
American; juveniles WA
CORBETT, Janice M., 1935- ,
American; nonfiction CON
CORBETT, John Patrick, 1916- ,
English; nonfiction CON
CORBETT, Pearson Harris,
1900- , American; nonfiction
CON
CORBETT, Richmond McLain,
1922- , American; nonfiction
CON
CORBETT, Ruth, 1912- , Amer-
ican; nonfiction CON
CORBETT, Scott, 1913- , Ameri-
can; nonfiction, juveniles
COM CON WA
CORBIERE, Edouard Joachim
('Tristan'), 1845-75, French;
poetry COL DIF HAR KE MAL
SA ST
CORBIN, Arnold, 1911- , Ameri-
can; nonfiction CON
CORBIN, Charles B., 1940- ,
American; nonfiction CON
CORBIN, Donald Alvin, 1920- ,
American; nonfiction CON
CORBIN, Richard, 1911- , Amer-
ican; nonfiction CON
'CORBIN, William' see McGRAW,
William C.
CORBISHLEY, Thomas, 1903- ,
English; nonfiction CON
CORBITT, Helen Lucy, 1906- ,
American; nonfiction CON
CORBOULD, A.C., 1870- ,
English; nonfiction HIG
'CORBY, Dan' see CATHERALL,
Arthur
CORCORAN, Barbara, 1911- ,
American; juveniles CON
CORCORAN, Gertrude Beatty,
1922- , American; nonfiction
CON
CORCORAN, Jean Kennedy,
1926- , American; fiction
CON
CORCOS, Lucille, 1908- , Amer-
ican; juveniles CON WA
CORD, Robert L., 1935- , Amer-
ican; nonfiction CON
CORD, Steven Benson, 1928- ,
American; nonfiction CON

CORD, William O., 1921- , Ameri-
can; nonfiction CON
CORDASCO, Francesco, 1920- ,
American; nonfiction CON
'CORDELL, Alexander' see GRABER,
Alexander
CORDELL, Richard Albert, 1896- ,
American; nonfiction CON
CORDEMOY, Gérard de, 1620-84,
French; nonfiction SA
CORDEN, Warner Max, 1927- ,
German-English; nonfiction CON
CORDER, Jimmy Wayne, 1929- ,
American; nonfiction CON
CORDERO, Aurelia, 1874-1922,
Ecuadorian; poetry DI
CORDERO, Luis, 1833-1912,
Ecuadorian; poetry, nonfiction
DI
CORDIER, Mathurin, 1479-1564,
French; nonfiction ST
CORDIER, Ralph Waldo, 1902- ,
American; nonfiction CON
CORDOBA, Alvaro de, 19th cent.,
Spanish; poetry BL
CORDOBA, Fernando de, 1422-86,
Spanish; nonfiction SA
CORDOBA, Martín Alfonso de, 15th
cent., Spanish; nonfiction BL
SA
CORDOBA, Matías, de, 1774?-1829,
Guatemalan; poetry SA
CORDOBA, Sebastian de, 1545?-
1604?, Spanish; poetry BL SA
CORDOBA y FIGUEROA, Pedro
Pascual de, 1692-1770, Chilean;
nonfiction MIN
CORDONE, Rogelio, 1898- , Ar-
gentinian; plays MIN
CORDOVA ITURBURA, Cayetano,
1902- , Argentinian; poetry,
criticism MIN SA
CORDUS, Eriricius, 1486-1535,
German; poetry ST
'CORELLI, Marie' see MACKAY,
Mary
CORESI, Târgoviste, 16th cent.,
Rumanian; nonfiction ST
COREY, Lewis, 1894-1953, Ameri-
can; nonfiction KT
COREY, Paul Frederick, 1903- ,
American; fiction CON KT WAF
CORICIO, 6th cent., Greek; poetry
SA
CORILA OLIMPICA, 1728-91, Italian;
poetry SA
CORINAAN, 6th cent. B.C., Greek;

poetry SA ST
CORIO, Bernardino, 1459-1512?,
Italian; nonfiction ST
CORIPPUS, Falvius Cresconius,
6th cent., African; nonfiction
SA ST
CORKE, Helen, 1882- , English;
nonfiction CON
CORKE, Hilary, 1921- , British;
poetry MUR
CORKERY, Daniel, 1878- , Irish;
fiction, plays HOE KTS ST
CORKEY, Robert, 1881- , Irish;
nonfiction CON
CORKRAN, David Hudson, Jr.,
1902- , American; nonfiction
CON
CORKRAN, Herbert, Jr., 1924- ,
American; nonfiction CON
CORLE, Edwin, 1906- , Ameri-
can; fiction KTS
CORLEY, Donald, American; fiction
KL
CORLEY, Edwin, 1931- , Ameri-
can; fiction CON
'CORLEY, Ernest' see BULMER,
Henry K.
CORLEY, Robert N., 1930- ,
American; nonfiction CON
CORLEY, Thomas Anthony Buchanan,
1923- , English; juveniles
CON
CORMACK, James Maxwell Ross,
1909- , Scots; nonfiction CON
CORMACK, Margaret Grant,
1913- , Irish; juveniles, poetry
CON
CORMACK, Margaret Lawson,
1912- , American; nonfiction
CON
CORMACK, Maribelle, 1902- ,
American; juveniles KJU WA
CORMAN, Cid (Sidney), 1924- ,
American; poetry MUR
CORMIER, Frank, 1927- , Amer-
ican; nonfiction CON
CORMIER, Robert Edmund,
1925- , American; fiction
CON
CORNARO de LUSIÑAN, Catalina,
1454-1510, Italian; nonfiction
SA
CORNAROS, Vicente, 16th cent.,
Greek; poetry SA
CORNAZZANO, Antonio, 1429-84,
Italian; poetry ST.
CORNEILLE, Pierre, 1606-84,

French; plays DIF HAR KE MAG
MAL SA ST

CORNEILLE, Thomas, 1625-1709,
French; poetry, plays DIF HAR
KE SA ST

CORNELISEN, Ann, 1926- , American; nonfiction CON

CORNELIUS, Peter, 1824-74, German;
plays, poetry HAR ST

CORNELIUS, Temple, H., 1891-
1964, American; nonfiction CON

CORNELIUS GALLUS see GALLUS,
Gaius

CORNELIUS NEPOS, 100-25 B.C.,
Roman; nonfiction SA ST

CORNELL, Frederick Carruthers,
1867-1921, South African; fiction,
poetry ST

CORNELL, George W., 1920- ,
American; nonfiction CON

CORNER, Philip, 1933- , American;
nonfiction CON

CORNFELD, Gaalyahu, 1902- ,
Israeli; nonfiction CON

CORNFORD, Frances Crofts, 1866-
1960, English; poetry BRO RIC

CORNFORD, Francis MacDonald,
1874-1943, British; nonfiction
KTS

CORNFORTH, Maurice, 1909- ,
English; nonfiction CON

CORNGOLD, Stanley Alan, 1934- ,
American; nonfiction CON

CORNELLON, John Raymond, 1941- ,
American; nonfiction, poetry
CON

CORNING, Howard McKinley, 1896- ,
American; poetry, fiction PAC

CORNISH, Dudley Taylor, 1915- ,
American; nonfiction CON

CORNISH, John Buckley, 1914- ,
Canadian; fiction CON

CORNISH, Samuel James, 1935- ,
American; poetry, juveniles
MUR

CORNISH, William Roldoph, 1937- ,
Australian; nonfiction CON

CORNOCK, John Stroud, 1938- ,
English; nonfiction CON

CORNUELLE, Richard C., 1927- ,
American; nonfiction CON

CORNUTO, Lucio Anneo, 15-54,
Roman; nonfiction SA

'CORNWALL, Barry' see PROCTOR
Bryan W.

CORNWALL, Ian Wolfran, 1909- ,
English; nonfiction CON

'CORNWALL, Jim' see RIKHOFF,
James C.

'CORNWALL, Martin' see CAVEN-
DISH, Richard

CORNWALLIS, Kinahan, 1839-1917,
American; nonfiction, fiction
KAA

CORNWELL, David John Moore
('John Le Carre'), 1931- ,
English; fiction CON RIC

COROMINAS, Joan, 1905- ,
Spanish; nonfiction BL

COROMINAS y MONTAÑA, Pedro,
1870-1939, Spanish; nonfiction,
poetry, essays COL SA

CORONADO, Carolina, 1823-1911,
Spanish; poetry BL SA

CORONADO, Guillermo de la Cruz,
1921- , Spanish; poetry SA

CORONADO, Martín, 1850-1917,
Argentinian; poetry, plays,
fiction MIN SA

CORONEL URTECHO, José, 1906- ,
Nicaraguan; poetry SA

CORONEL y ARANA, María see
AGREDA, María de J.

'CORONET' see FABER, Walter

CORPANCHO, Manuel Nicolás,
1830-63, Peruvian; poetry,
plays, criticism SA

'CORPUS BARGA' (Andriés García
de la Barga), 1888- , Spanish;
journalism, criticism SA

CORRADI, Gemma, 1939- , American; nonfiction CON

CORRADINI, Enrico, 1865-1931,
Italian; plays, fiction COL SA

CORRAL, Andrés del, 1784-1818,
Spanish; poetry SA

CORRAL, Gabriel del, 1588-1652?,
Spanish; poetry, plays SA

CORRAL, Pedro, fl. 1403, Spanish;
fiction BL HAR SA ST

CORRALES EGEA, José, 1909- ,
Spanish; fiction BL SA

CORRALL, Alice Enid ('Justine
C. Glass'), 1916- , English;
nonfiction CON

CORRE, Alan D., 1931- , American; nonfiction CON

'CORREA' see GALBRAITH, Jean

CORREA, Gustavo, 1914- ,
Colombian; nonfiction BL

CORREA, Julio, 20th cent.,
Paraguayan; plays SA

CORREA, Miguel Angel ('Mateo
Booz'), 1881-1943, Argentinian;

fiction MIN
CORREA, Raimundo de Mota de
Azevedo, 1860-1911, Brazilian;
poetry SA ST
CORREA CALDERON, Evaristo,
1899- , Spanish; poetry, nonfic-
tion, fiction BL SA
CORREA LUNA, Carlos, 1874-1936,
Argentinian; journalism, nonfiction
MIN
CORREA PASTENE, Misael, 1870- ,
Chilean; journalism MIN
CORREAS, Gonzalo, Spanish; nonfic-
tion BL
CORREDOR MATEOS, José, 1929- ,
Spanish; translations, poetry
SA
CORREGGIO, Niccolò da, 1450-1508,
Italian; poetry ST
CORREIA, Afonso John, 1924- ,
Italian; nonfiction CON
CORREIA, Gaspar, 1496-1561,
Portuguese; nonfiction SA ST
CORREIA de OLIVEIRA, Antonio,
1879- , Portuguese; poetry
COL SA
CORREIA de SERRA, José Francisco,
1750-1823, Portuguese; nonfiction
SA
'CORREN, Grace' see HOSKINS,
Robert
CORRIGAN, Francis Joseph, 1919- ,
American; nonfiction CON
CORRIGAN, Ralph Lawrence, Jr.,
1937- , American; nonfiction
CON
CORRIGAN, Robert Anthony, 1935- ,
American; nonfiction CON
CORRIGAN, Robert Willoughby,
1927- , American; nonfiction
CON
CORRINGTON, John William, 1932- ,
American; poetry, fiction CON
MUR
CORROL, Jesús del, 1871-1931,
Colombian; journalism MIN
CORSA, Helen Storm, 1915- ,
American; nonfiction CON
'CORSARI Willy' (Wilhelmina Angela
Schnidt), 1897- , Dutch; fiction
ST
CORSEL, Ralph, 1920- , American;
fiction CON
CORSINI, Raymond J., 1914- , Amer-
ican; nonfiction CON
CORSO, Gregory Nunzia, 1930- ,
American; poetry CON MUR RIC

CORSON, Fred Pierce, 1896- ,
American; nonfiction CON
CORSON, Hazel W., 1906- ,
American; juveniles CON
CORSON, Hiram, 1828-1911,
American; nonfiction KAA
CORSON, John Jay, 1905- ,
American; nonfiction CON
CORT, David, American; nonfiction
CON
CORT, Frans de, 1834-78, Flemish;
poetry ST
'CORT, M. C.' see CLIFFORD,
Margaret C.
CORTADA y SALA, Juan, 1805-68,
Spanish; fiction, nonfiction SA
CORTAZAR, Julio, 1914- ,
Argentinian; fiction CON RIC
CORTE REAL, Jerónimo, 1533?-
88?, Portuguese; poetry SA
ST
'CORTEEN, Wes' see NORWOOD,
Victor G. C.
CORTEJON y LUCAS, Clemente,
1842-1911, Spanish; nonfiction
BL SA
CORTES, Alfonso, 19th cent.,
Nicaraguan; poetry SA
CORTES, Hernán, 1485-1547,
Spanish; nonfiction, letters
BL SA ST
CORTES, Juan Bautista, 1925- ,
Spanish-American; nonfiction
CON
CORTES, Manuel Jose, 1811-65,
Bolivian; nonfiction, poetry
MIN
CORTES de TOLOSA, Juan, 1590-
1640, Spanish; nonfiction SA
CORTINA, José Manuel, 1880- ,
Cuban; nonfiction MIN
CORTINES y MURUBE, Felipe,
1886?- , Spanish; poetry SA
CORTISSOZ, Royal, 1869-1948,
American; criticism, journalism
KT
CORTY, Floyd Louis, 1916- ,
American; nonfiction CON
CORVALAN, Stella, Chilean;
poetry MIN
CORVER, Marten, 1727-94, Dutch;
plays ST
'CORNINUS, Jakob' see RAABE,
Wilhelm K.
CORVINUS, Laurentius, 1465-1527,
Silesian; nonfiction ST
'CORVO, Baron' see ROLFE,

Frederick
CORWIN, Norman Lewis, 1910- ,
    American; radio, fiction CON
    KTS
CORWIN, Ronald Gary, 1932- ,
    American; nonfiction CON
CORY, Charles Barney, 1857-1921,
    American; nonfiction CON
'CORY, Desmond' see McCARTHY,
    Shaun
CORY, Herbert Ellsworth, 1883-1947,
    American; nonfiction HOE
'CORY, Howard L.' see JARDINE,
    Jack
'CORY, Ray' see MARSHALL, Melvin
CORY, William Johnson, 1823-92,
    English; poetry BRO KBA ST
CORYATE, Thomas (Coryatt), 1577-
    1617, English; nonfiction BRO
    KB ST
COSBUA, Gdeorghe, 1866-1918,
    Rumanian; poetry SA ST
COSER, Lewis A., 1913- , Ameri-
    can; nonfiction CON
COSER, Rose Laub, 1916- , Ameri-
    can; nonfiction CON
COSGRAVE, John O'Hara II, 1908- ,
    American; juveniles, nonfiction
    CON FUL
COSGRAVE, Patrick, 1941- , Irish;
    nonfiction CON
COSGROVE, Carol Ann, 1943- ,
    English; nonfiction CON
COSGROVE, Margaret Leota, 1926- ,
    American; juvenile CON WA
COSH, Ethel Eleanor Mary, 1921- ,
    English; nonfiction CON
COSMAND, Dimitrie see 'BOLINTI-
    NEANU, Dimitrie'
COSMAS see KOZMA, Presbyter
COSMAS INDICOPLAUSTES, 6th cent.,
    Byzantine?; nonfiction ST
COSMAS of Jerusalem, 8th cent.,
    Byzantine; poetry ST
COSMAS of PRAGUE, 1045-1125,
    Czech; nonfiction ST
COSME de VILLIERS (Sainte Etienne),
    1680-1758, French; nonfiction
    DIL
COSS, Thurman L., 1926- , Ameri-
    can; nonfiction CON
COSSA, Pietro, 1830-81, Italian;
    poetry, plays HAR SA ST
COSSIGNY, Jean Françoise Charpentier,
    1693-1780, French; nonfiction
    DIL
COSSIO, Francisco, 1887- , Spanish;

journalism, fiction, plays BL
    SA
COSSIO, José María de, 1893/95- ,
    Spanish; criticism BL COL
    SA
COSSIO, Manuel Bartolomé, 1858-
    1935, Spanish; nonfiction BL
    COL SA
COSSMAN, Eli Joseph, 1918- ,
    American; nonfiction CON
COSSON, Pierre Charles, 1740-
    1801, French; nonfiction DIL
COSSON, Charlotte Catherine,
    1740-1813, French; poetry
    DIL SA
COSTA, Albert Bernard, 1929- ,
    American; nonfiction CON
COSTA, Claudio Manuel da, 1720-
    90, Brazilian; poetry SA ST
COSTA, Gustavo, 1930- , Italian-
    American; nonfiction CON
COSTA, Isaac de see DA COSTA,
    Isaac de
COSTA, Joaquín, 1846-1911,
    Spanish; nonfiction BL COL
COSTA, Margarita, 1600-82,
    Italian; poetry SA
COSTA, Pablo della, 1884- ,
    Argentinian; poetry MIN
COSTA, Paolo, 1771-1836, Italian;
    criticism, plays ST
COSTA, Richard Hauer, 1921- ,
    American; nonfiction CON
COSTA, Uriel, A., 1585-1640,
    Portuguese; nonfiction SA
COSTA du RELS, Adolfo, 1891- ,
    Bolivian; poetry, plays, fic-
    tion MIN SA
COSTA i LLOBERA, Miquel, 1854-
    1922, Spanish; poetry COL
    HAR SA ST
COSTA y MARTINEZ, Joaquin,
    1844/46-1911, Spanish; nonfic-
    tion HAR SA ST
COSTA y SILVA, José María de
    la, 1788-1854, Portuguese;
    poetry, criticism SA
COSTADAU, Alphon, 17th cent.,
    French; nonfiction DIL
COSTAFREDA, Alfonso, 1927- ,
    Spanish; poetry SA
COSTAIN, Thomas Bertram, 1885-
    1965, American; fiction CON
    KTS RIC SY WA WAF
COSTANA, 15th cent., Spanish;
    poetry SA
COSTANZO, Angelo, 1507-91?,

Italian; poetry ST
COSTAR, Pierre, 1603-60, French;
nonfiction SA
COSTE, Louis, 18th cent., French;
nonfiction DIL
COSTE D'ARNOBAT, Charles Pierre,
1732-1808/10, French; nonfiction
DIL
COSTELLO, David Francis, 1904- ,
American; nonfiction CON PAC
COSTELLO, Donald Paul, 1931- ,
American; nonfiction CON
COSTELLO, Louisa Stuart, 1799-
1870, English; poetry, fiction,
essays BRO KBA SA
'COSTELLO, Michael' see DETZER,
Karl
COSTELLO, William Aloysius, 1904- ,
American; nonfiction CON
COSTER, Charles de see DE COSTER,
Charles
COSTER, Dirk, 1887-1956, Dutch;
nonfiction, plays HAR SA ST
COSTER, Jean Louis, 1728-80,
French; nonfiction DIL
COSTER, Samuel, 1579-1665, Dutch;
plays ST
'COSTERE, Jan de' see STROOSNYDER,
Jan
COSTIGAN, Daniel M., 1929- ,
American; nonfiction CON
COSTIGAN, Giovanni, 1903- , Ameri-
can; nonfiction CON PAC
COSTIKYAN, Edward N., 1924- ,
American; nonfiction CON
COSTIL, Pierre, 1669-1749, French;
nonfiction DIL
COSTIN, Miron, 1633-92, Rumanian;
nonfiction ST
COSTOBADIE F. Palliser de, 1855- ,
English; nonfiction HIG
COTA, Rodrigo de, 1405?-70,
Spanish; poetry BL SA ST
COTARELO Y MORI, Emilio, 1857-
1935, Spanish; nonfiction BL
SA
COTARELO y VALLEDOR, Armando,
1880-1950, Spanish; nonfiction
BL SA
'COTES, Peter' (Sydney Boulting),
1912- , American; nonfiction
CON
COTGRAVE, John, fl. 1644-55,
English; nonfiction ST
COTHERN, Fayly Hardcastle, 1926- ,
American; nonfiction CON
COTHRAN, Joseph Guy, 1897- ,

American; nonfiction CON
COTIN, Charles, 1604-80, French;
nonfiction SA
COTLER, Gordon ('Alex Gordon'),
1923- , American; nonfiction
CON
COTNER, Robert Crawford,
1906- , American; nonfiction
CON
COTNER, Thomas Ewing, 1916- ,
American; nonfiction CON
COTRUS, Aron, 1891- , Rumanian;
poetry ST
COTTA, Giovanni, 1480-1510,
Italian; poetry ST
COTTAM, Walter Pace, 1894- ,
American; nonfiction CON
COTTEN, Nellie Wyllie, 1908- ,
American; juveniles CON
COTTEN, Sallie Southall, 1846-
1929, English; nonfiction JO
COTTER, Charles Henry, 1919- ,
Welsh; nonfiction CON
COTTER, Cornelius Philip, 1924- ,
American; nonfiction CON
COTTER, Edward Francis, 1917- ,
American; nonfiction CON
COTTER, James Finn, 1929- ,
American; nonfiction CON
COTTEREAU du COUDRAY, Jean
Baptiste Armand, 1697-1770,
French; nonfiction DIL
COTTEREL, Geoffrey, 1919- ,
American; nonfiction CON
COTTERL, Alexandre François,
-1775, French; nonfiction
DIL
COTTIN, Sophie Ristaud, 1773-1807,
French; fiction HAR SA
COTTLE, Thomas J., 1937- ,
American; nonfiction CON
COTTLER, Joseph, 1899- , Amer-
ican; juveniles CON
COTTON, Bartholomew de,
-1298?, English; nonfiction
ST
COTTON, Charles, 1630-86/87,
English; poetry, translations
BRO KB SA SP ST
COTTON, Frederick, 1848- ,
English; nonfiction HIG
COTTON, John, 1584-1652, Ameri-
can; nonfiction KAA ST
COTTON, John Whealdon, 1925- ,
American; nonfiction, poetry
CON MUR
COTTON, Nathaniel, 1705-88, Eng-

lish; poetry BRO KB

COTTON, Sir Robert Bruce, 1571-
1631, English; nonfiction BRO
ST

COTTON des HOUSSAYES, Jean
Baptiste, 1727-83, French;
nonfiction DIL

COTTRELL, Ida Dorothy Ottley,
1902- , Australian; fiction
BRO

COTTRELL, Leonard, 1913- , English; nonfiction CON RIC WA

COTTRELL, William Frederick,
1903- , American; nonfiction
CON

COUBIER, Heinz, 1905- , German;
nonfiction KU

COUCH, Arthur see QUILLER-COUCH,
Sir Arthur T.

COUCH, Helen Fox, 1907- , American; nonfiction CON

COUCHE, 18th cent., French; nonfiction DIL

COUCHE, Marc, 1683-1753, French;
nonfiction DIL

COUCY, Renaud de, 12th cent.,
French; poetry SA

COUDENHOVE, Ida Friedrike,
1901- , Austrian; nonfiction
HOE

COUDERET, Georges, 1713-90,
French; nonfiction DIL

COUDERT, Jo, 1923- , American;
nonfiction CON

COUDRETTE, Christophe, 1701-74,
French; nonfiction DIL

COUFFER, Jack, 1924- , American;
fiction CON

COUGHLAN, John W., 1927- ,
Canadian; nonfiction CON

COUGHLIN, Bernard J., 1922- ,
American; nonfiction CON

COUGHLIN, Joseph Welter, 1919- ,
American; juvenile CON

COUGHRAN, Larry C. ('Larry Craig'),
1925- , American; nonfiction
CON

COULANGES, Marie Angelique, 1641-
1723, French; nonfiction SA

COULDERY, Frederick Alan James,
1928- , English; nonfiction CON

COULETTE, Henri, 1927- , American; poetry MUR

COULON, Hilaire, 1678-1741, French;
nonfiction DIL

COULOUMBIS, Theodore, A., 1935- ,
American; nonfiction CON

COULSON, Charles Alfred,
1910- , English; nonfiction
CON

COULSON, Felicity Carter ('Emery
Bonett'), 1907- , English;
fiction CON

COULSON, John Hubert Arthur
('John Bonett'), 1906- ,
English; fiction CON

COULSON Juanita ('John Jay
Wells'), 1933- , American;
nonfiction CON

COULSON, Robert S. ('Thomas
Stratton'), 1928- , American;
nonfiction CON

COULTER, Ellis Merton, 1890- ,
American; nonfiction CON KTS

COULTER, John William, 1888- ,
Irish; nonfiction CON

COULTON, George Gordon, 1858-
1947, English; nonfiction BRO
KTS

'COULTON, James' see HANSEN,
Joseph

COUND, John James, 1928- ,
American; nonfiction CON

COUNT, Earl Wendel, 1899- ,
American; nonfiction CON

COUNTER, Kenneth Norman
Samuel, 1930- , English; nonfiction CON

'A COUNTRY SQUIRE', fl. 1690,
English; nonfiction HIG

COUNTRYMAN, Vern, 1912- ,
American; nonfiction CON

COUNTS, George Sylvester,
1889- , American; nonfiction
CON KTS

COUPER, John Mill, 1914- ,
Scots; poetry MUR

COUPERUS, Louis Marie Anne,
1863-1923, Dutch; fiction,
essays COL FLE HAR KAT
KT MAG RIC SA ST

COUPEY, Pierre, 1942- , Canadian;
poetry MUR

'COUPLING, J.J.' see PIERCE,
John Robinson

COUR, Paul Arvid Dornonville de
la, 1902- , Danish; poetry,
essays ST

COURAGE, James Francis, 1903/
05-63, New Zealander; fiction
RIC ST

COURCELLES, Marie Sidonia de
Lénoncourt, 1651-85, German;
nonfiction SA

COURCELLOS, 18th cent., French;
nonfiction DIL

COURCHETET d'ESNANS, Luc,
1695- , French; nonfiction
DIL

COURCY, Jean de, -1431, French;
nonfiction ST

COURCY-PARRY, Charles Norman
de ('Dalesman'), 1899- , English; nonfiction HIG

COURIER de MERE, Paul Louis,
1772-1825, French; nonfiction
DIF HAR SA ST

COURLANDER, Harold, 1908- ,
American; juvenile CON FUL
WA

COURNOS, John ('John Courtney';
'Mark Gault'), 1881- , Russian-
American; nonfiction, fiction
CON KAT KT

COUROUBLE, Léopold, 1861-1937,
Belgian; fiction HAR ST

COUROUCLI, Jennifer, 1922- ,
English; poetry CON

COURSE, Alfred George, 1895- ,
English; nonfiction CON

COURSEY, Oscar William, 1873- ,
American; fiction, nonfiction
HOO

COURT de GEBELIN, Antoine, 1728-
84, French; nonfiction DIL

COURTALON-DELAISTRE, Jean
Charles, 1735-86, French; nonfiction DIL

'COURTELINE, Georges' (Georges
Moineaux), 1858-1929, French;
plays, poetry, fiction DIF FLE
HAR MAL MAT SA ST

COURTENAY, William James, 1935- ,
American; nonfiction CON

COURTHOPE, William John, 1842-
1917, English; criticism, nonfiction, poetry BRO KBA KT

COURTHS-MAHLER, Hedwig ('Relham';
'Hedwig Brand'; 'Anna E. M.
Alzer'), 1867-1950, German; non-
fiction AL

COURTIAL, 18th cent., French;
poetry, plays DIL

COURTIER, Paul Louis, 1772-1825,
French; nonfiction MAL

COURTIER, Sidney Hebson ('Rui
Chestor'), 1904- , Australian;
fiction CON

COURTILZ de SANDRAS, Gatien,
1646?-1712, French; nonfiction
DIF

'COURTLAND, Roberta' see DERN,
Peggy G.

COURTMANNS-BERCHMANS,
Johanna Desideria, 1811-90,
Flemish; fiction ST

'COURTNEY, John' see COURNOS,
John

'COURTNEY, John' see JUDD,
Frederick C.

COURTNEY, Gwendoline, English;
fiction CON

COURTOIS, Jean Louis, 1712-72,
French; poetry DIL

COUSE, Harold C., 1925- ,
American; nonfiction CON

COUSIN, Anne Ross, 1824-1906,
English; hymns BRO

COUSIN, Victor, 1792-1867,
French; nonfiction DIF HAR
KE SA ST

'COUSIN, Virginia' see JOHNSON,
Virginia W.

'COUSIN ALICE' see HAVEN,
Emily B.N.

COUSIN de GRANVILLE, Jean
Baptiste François Xavier, 1746-
1805, French; nonfiction DIL

COUSIN-DESPREAUX, Louis, 1743-
1818, French; nonfiction DIL

COUSINS, Geoffrey Esmond,
1900- , English; nonfiction
CON

COUSINS, James, 1873- , Irish;
poetry ST

COUSINS, Margaret ('Avery Johns';
'William Masters'; 'Mary Par-
rish'), 1905- , American;
juveniles, fiction COM CON
WA

COUSINS, Norman, 1912- ,
American; essays CON KTS

COUSTANT, Pierre, 17th cent.,
French; nonfiction DIL

COUSTEAU, Philippe Pierre,
1940- , French; nonfiction
CON

COUSTELIER, Antoine Urbain,
-1763, French; nonfiction
DIL

COUTINHO, Manuel de Sousa see
SOUSA, Frei Luis de

COUTO, Diogo de, 1542-1616,
Portuguese; nonfiction SA ST

COUTO, Félix Luis de, 1642-1713,
Portuguese; poetry SA

COUTOUMANOS, George, 1877- ,
Greek-American; poetry HIL

COUTURAT, Louis Alexander, 1686-1914, French; nonfiction DIF
COUVARRUBIAS y HOROZCO, Sebastián de ('Benito R. Noydens'), 1539-1613, Spanish; nonfiction BL SA ST
COUVIGNY Jean Charles de, 1680-1745, French; nonfiction DIL
'COVENTRY, John' see PALMER, John W.
COVENTRY, Rev. John, 1915- , English; nonfiction HO
COVERDALE, Miles, 1488-1568, English; translations BRO KB ST
COVERLEY, Louise see BENNETT, Louise
COVERT, James Thayne, 1932- , American; nonfiction CON
COVEY, Cyclone, 1922- , American; nonfiction CON
COVEY, Stephen R., 1932- , American; nonfiction CON
COVICI, Pascal Jr., 1930- , American; nonfiction CON
COVILLE, Walter Joseph, 1914- , American; nonfiction CON
COVINGTON, James W., 1917- , American; nonfiction CON
COVINGTON, Martin Vaden, 1936- , American; nonfiction CON
'COWAN, Alan' see GILCHRIST, Alan W.
COWAN, George Hamilton, 1917- , Scots; nonfiction CON
COWAN, Gordan, 1937- , English; nonfiction CON
COWAN, James Costello, 1927- , American; nonfiction CON
COWAN, Joseph Lloyd, 1929- , American; nonfiction CON
COWAN, Louise Shillingburg, 1916- , American; nonfiction CON
COWAN, Michael Heath, 1937- , American; nonfiction CON
COWAN, Peter Walkinshaw, 1914- , Australian; fiction CON
COWAN, Robert Granniss, 1895- , American; nonfiction CON
COWAN, Sister St. Michael (Rosalia Cowan), 1886- , Irish; nonfiction HO
COWARD, Noel Pierce ('Hernia Whittleboat'), 1899-1973, English; plays BRO CON FLE KL KT MAG MAT RIC ST
COWASTEEL, Saros, 1931- , Indian; nonfiction CON

COWDREY, Albert Edward, 1933- , American; nonfiction CON
COWELL, Cyril, 1888- , English; nonfiction CON
COWELL, Frank Richard, American; juveniles WA
COWEN, David Laurence, 1909- , American; nonfiction CON
'COWEN, Frances' see MUNTHE, Frances
COWEN, Roy Chadwell, 1930- , American; nonfiction CON
COWEN, Robert Churchill, 1927- , American; nonfiction CON
COWEN, Zelman, 1919- , Australian; nonfiction CON
COWGILL, Donald Olen, 1911- , American; nonfiction CON
COWIE, Alexander, 1896- , American; nonfiction CON
COWIE, Evelyn Elizabeth, 1924- , English; nonfiction CON
COWIE, Leonard Wallace, 1919- , English; nonfiction CON
COWIE, Mervyn Hugh, 1909- , English; nonfiction CON
COWLER, Rosemary Elizabeth, 1925- , American; nonfiction CON
COWLES, Fleur, American; nonfiction CON
COWLES, Frederick, 1900- , English; nonfiction, fiction, essays, juvenile HOE
COWLES, Samuel Macon, Jr., 1916- , American; nonfiction CON
COWLEY, Abraham, 1618-67, English; poetry, essays BRO KB MAG SA SP ST
COWLEY, Anne Parkhouse, 1743-1809, English; plays SA
COWLEY, Cassia Joy, 1936- , New Zealander; fiction, juveniles CON
COWLEY, Hannah, 1743-1809, English; plays, poetry BRO KB
COWLEY, Malcolm, 1898- , American; criticism, poetry, translations CON FLE KL KT MUR SA
'COWLIN, Dorothy' see WHALLEY, Dorothy
COWLING, Ellis, 1905- , American; nonfiction CON

COWLING, Maurice John, 1926- ,
English; nonfiction CON
COWLISHAW, Ranson ('R. A. Wood-
rook'), 1894- , English; nonfic-
tion CON
'COWPER, Richard' see MURRY,
John M.
COWPER, William, 1731-1800,
English; poetry BRO KB MAG
SA ST
COX, Alva I. , Jr. , 1925- , Ameri-
can; nonfiction CON
COX, Anthony Berkeley ('Anthony
Berkeley'; 'Francis Iles'),
1893- , English; fiction KT
COX, Bertha Mae Hill, 1901- ,
American; nonfiction CON
COX, Bill, 1910- , English; nonfic-
tion CON
COX, Charles Brian, 1928- , Eng-
lish; nonfiction CON
COX, Claire, 1919- , American;
nonfiction CON
COX, Constance, 1915- , English;
plays CON
COX, Donald William, 1921- ,
American; nonfiction CON
COX, Edward Finch, 1946- , Ameri-
can; nonfiction CON
COX, Edward Franklin, 1925- ,
American; nonfiction CON
COX, Edwin Burk, 1930- , Ameri-
can; nonfiction CON
COX, Eugene L. , 1931- , Ameri-
can; nonfiction CON
COX, Frank D. , 1933- , American;
nonfiction CON
COX, Sir George William, 1827-1902,
English; nonfiction KBA
COX, Harding, 1854- , English; non-
fiction HIG
COX, Hebe, 1909- , English; nonfic-
tion CON
COX, Henry Carleton see CARLETON,
Henry
COX, Henry Hamilton, 1769-1821,
American; poetry KAA
COX, Hugh Stowell, 1874- , Amer-
ican; nonfiction CON
COX, Jack, 1915- , English; juven-
iles DOY
COX, James Milville, 1925- , Amer-
ican; nonfiction CON
COX, James William, 1923- , Amer-
ican; nonfiction CON
COX, John Roberts ('David Roberts';
'John Havenhand'), 1915- ,

American; nonfiction, fiction
CON
COX, Kevin B. , 1939- , Ameri-
can; nonfiction CON
COX, La Wanda Fenlason, 1909- ,
American; nonfiction CON
COX, Lee Sheridan, 1916- ,
American; nonfiction, juveniles
CON
COX, Martha Heasley, 1919- ,
American; nonfiction CON
COX, Maxwell E. , 1922- ,
American; fiction CON
COX, Miriam Stewart, American;
juveniles CON
COX, Oliver Cromwell, 1901- ,
American; nonfiction CON
COX, Palmer, 1840-1924, Ameri-
can; juveniles KAA
COX, Rachel Dunaway, 1904- ,
American; nonfiction CON
COX, Ralph Merritt, 1939- ,
American; nonfiction CON
COX, Reavis, 1900- , American;
nonfiction CON
COX, Richard, 1931- , English;
nonfiction CON
COX, Richard Howard, 1925- ,
American; nonfiction CON
COX, Robert David, 1937- ,
American; poetry, plays CON
COX, Samuel Sullivan, 1824-89,
American; nonfiction KAA
COX, Warren Earle, 1895- ,
American; nonfiction CON
COX, William R. ('Joel Reeve'),
1901- , American; fiction,
juveniles CON WA
COX, William Trevor ('William
Trevor'), 1928- , American;
fiction CON RIC
COXE, Louise Osborne, 1918- ,
American; poetry, plays CON
MUR
COXE, Nicholas, 1625?- , Eng-
lish; nonfiction HIG
COXE, Richard Smith, 1792-1865,
American; nonfiction KAA
COXE, William, 1747-1828, English;
nonfiction BRO KBA
COX-GEORGE, Noah Arthur William,
1915- , English; nonfiction
CON
COY, Harold, 1902- , American;
juveniles CON WA
COYER, Gabriel François, 1707-82,
French; nonfiction DIL

COYLE, David Cushman, 1887- ,
American; nonfiction CON
COYLE, Kathleen, 1886-1952, Irish;
fiction KAT KT
COYLE, William, 1917- , American;
nonfiction CON
COYNE, John Richard, Jr., 1935- ,
American; nonfiction CON
COYNE, Joseph E. ('William O.
Berch'), 1918- , American;
fiction CON
COYNE, Joseph Sterling, 1803-68,
Irish; plays KBA
COYPEL, Charles Antoine, 1694-
1732, French; nonfiction, plays,
poetry DIL
COZZANI, Ettore, 1884- , Italian;
poetry, fiction ST
COZZENS, Frederick Swartout
('Richard Hayward'), 1818-69,
American; fiction KAA
COZZENS, James Gould, 1903- ,
American; fiction CON FLE
HOO KAT KT MAG RIC WAF
CRABB, Alfred Leland, 1884- ,
American; fiction CON WAF
CRABB, Cecil V., Jr., 1924- ,
American; nonfiction CON
CRABB, Edmund William, 1912- ,
American; nonfiction CON
CRABB, Richard, 1911- , American;
nonfiction CON
CRABBE, George, 1754-1832, Eng-
lish; poetry BRO KBA MAG SA
SP ST
CRABITES, Pierre, 1877-1943,
American; nonfiction HOE
'CRABSHAW, Timothy' see LONG-
STREET, Augustus B.
CRABTREE, Arthur Bamford, 1910- ,
English; nonfiction CON
CRABTREE, Thomas Tavron, 1924- ,
American; nonfiction CON
CRACHEL, Theodore Joseph, 1938- ,
American; nonfiction CON
CRACKANTHORPE, Hubert Montague,
1870-96, English; fiction KBA
'CRADDOCK, Charles Egbert' see
MURFREE, Mary N.
CRADOCK, Mrs. H.C., 20th cent.,
English; juveniles DOY
CRAFT, Michael, 1928- , English;
nonfiction CON
CRAFT, Robert, 1923- , American;
nonfiction CON
CRAFTS, Glenn Alty, 1918- ,
American; nonfiction CON

CRAFTS, William, 1787-1826,
American; poetry KAA
CRAGG, Albert Kenneth, 1913- ,
English; nonfiction CON
CRAGO, Thomas Howard, 1907- ,
Australian; nonfiction CON
CRAIG, Albert Morton, 1927- ,
American; nonfiction CON
CRAIG, Alexander, 1923- ,
Australian; poetry MUR
CRAIG, Alexander George ('Arthur
Craik'), 1897- , English;
fiction, poetry CON
CRAIG, Barbara Mary St. George,
1914- , Canadian; nonfiction
CON
CRAIG, Bill, 1930- , American;
fiction CON
'CRAIG, David' see TUCKER,
Allan J.
'CRAIG, Denys' see STOLL, Dennis
G.
CRAIG, Edward A. ('Edward
Carrick'), 1905- , English;
nonfiction CON
CRAIG, Edward Gordon, 1872- ,
English; nonfiction KL KT ST
CRAIG, Elizabeth Josephine,
1883- , Scots; nonfiction CON
'CRAIG, Georgia' see DERN, Peggy
G.
CRAIG, Gerald Marquis, 1916- ,
Canadian; nonfiction CON
CRAIG, Gordon Alexander, 1913- ,
Scots-American; nonfiction
CON
CRAIG, Hardin, 1875- , American;
nonfiction KTS
CRAIG, Hazel Thompson, 1904- ,
American; juveniles CON
CRAIG, Isa (Isa Knox), 1831-1903,
Scots; poetry KBA
CRAIG, Jean T., 1936- , Ameri-
can; juveniles CON
CRAIG, John David, 1903- ,
American; fiction CON
'CRAIG, John Eland' see CHIPPER-
FIELD, Joseph
CRAIG, John Herbert, 1885- ,
English; nonfiction CON
'CRAIG, Larry' see COUGHRAN,
Larry C.
'CRAIG, Lee' see SANDS, Leo G.
CRAIG, M. Jean, American;
juvenile WA
CRAIG, Margaret Maze, 1911-64,
American; juveniles CON FUL

CRAIG, Mary Francis ('Mary
Francis Shura'), 1923- ,
American; juveniles, fiction
CON

'CRAIG, Paul' see CHESHIRE, Gifford P.

'CRAIG, Peggy' see KREIG, Margaret
B. B.

CRAIG, Philip R., 1933- , American;
fiction CON

CRAIG, Robert Charles, 1921- ,
American; nonfiction CON

CRAIGIE, Edward Horne, 1894- ,
Scots-Canadian; nonfiction CON

CRAIGIE, Pearl Mary Teresa ('John
Oliver Hobbes'), 1867-1906,
Anglo-American; fiction, plays
BRO KBA SA

CRAIGIE, Sir William Alexander,
1867-1957, Scots; nonfiction BRO

'CRAIK, Arthur' see CRAIG, Alexander G.

CRAIK, Dinah Maria Mulock, 1826-
87, English; fiction, juveniles,
poetry BRO DOY KBA MAG
ST

CRAIK, George Lillie, 1798-1866,
Scots; nonfiction, criticism BRO
KBA

CRAIK, Sir Henry, 1846-1927, Scots;
nonfiction KBA

CRAIK, Wendy Ann, 1934- , English;
nonfiction CON

'CRAILLE, Wesley' see ROWLAND,
Donald S.

'CRAIN, Jeff' see MENESES, Enrique

CRAIN, Robert Lee, 1934- , American; nonfiction CON

CRAINE, Eugene Richard, 1919- ,
American; nonfiction CON

'CRAINEC, Nichifor' (Ion Dobre),
1889- , Rumanian; essays,
poetry ST

CRAMER, Carl Gottlieb, 1758-1817,
German; fiction SA

CRAMER, Clarence Henley, 1905- ,
American; nonfiction CON

CRAMER, George H., 1913- ,
American; nonfiction CON

CRAMER, Harold, 1927- , American;
nonfiction CON

CRAMER, Heinz von, 1924- , German; nonfiction KU

CRAMER, James, 1915- , English;
nonfiction CON

CRAMER, Jan Solomon, 1928- ,
Dutch; nonfiction CON

CRAMER, John Francis, 1899- ,
American; nonfiction CON

CRAMER, Richard Seldon,
1928- , American; juveniles
CON

CRAMER, Stanley H., 1933- ,
American; nonfiction CON

CRAMEZEL, 1772- , French;
nonfiction DIL

CRAMPTON, Charles Gregory,
1911- , American; nonfiction
CON

CRAMTON, Roger C., 1929- ,
American; nonfiction CON

'CRANBROOK, James L.' see
EDWARDS, William B.

CRANCH, Christopher Pearse,
1813-92, American; criticism,
poetry KAA

CRANE, Alan, 1901- , American;
juveniles WA

'CRANE, Alex' see WILKES-
HUNTER, Richard

CRANE, Anne Moncure, 1838-72,
American; fiction KAA

CRANE, Caroline, 1930- , American; nonfiction, juvenile CON

CRANE, Clarkson, 1894- , American; fiction WAF

'CRANE, Edna T.' see EICHER,
Ethel E.

CRANE, Florence, American;
juveniles WA

CRANE, Frances Kirkwood, American; fiction HOO

CRANE, Hart, 1899-1932, American; poetry BRO FLE KL KT
MAG RIC SA SP ST

CRANE, Irving, American; juveniles
WA

CRANE, James Gordon, 1927- ,
American; fiction CON

CRANE, Lauren Edgar, 1917- ,
American; nonfiction CON

CRANE, Philip Miller, 1930- ,
American; nonfiction CON

CRANE, Ralph, 1589?- , English;
poetry ST

'CRANE, Robert' see ROBERTSON,
Frank C.

CRANE, Stephen ('Johnston Smith'),
1871-1900, American; fiction,
poetry BRO KAA MAG SA SP
ST

CRANE, Sylvia Engel, 1918- ,
American; nonfiction CON

CRANE, Walter, 1845-1915, English;

juveniles DOY KJU
CRANE, William Dwight, 1892- ,
American; juvenile COM CON
CRANFIELD, Charles Ernest Burland,
1915- , English; nonfiction CON
CRANFIELD, Geoffrey Alan, 1920- ,
English; nonfiction CON
CRANFORD, Clarence William,
1906- , American; nonfiction
CON
CRANFORD, Robert Joshua, 1908- ,
American; nonfiction CON
CRANKSHAW, Edward, 1909- ,
English; criticism, fiction CON
KTS
CRANMER, Thomas, 1489-1556,
English; nonfiction BRO KB ST
CRANNY, Titus ('Daniel Francis')
1921- , American; nonfiction
CON
CRANSTON, Maurice William,
1920- , English; nonfiction CON
CRANTOR, 4th cent. B.C., Greek;
nonfiction SA
CRAON, Amauri, 13th cent., French;
poetry ST
CRAPSEY, Adelaide, 1878-1914, Amer-
ican; poetry KAT KT SA
CRARY, Catherine S., 1909- ,
American; nonfiction CON
CRARY, Margaret Coleman, 1906- ,
American; juveniles CON WA
CRASHAW, Richard, 1613?-49,
English; poetry BRO KB SP ST
CRASSWELLER, Robert D., 1915- ,
American; nonfiction CON
CRATES, fl. 450-25 B.C., Greek;
plays SA ST
CRATE of MALLES, 2nd cent. B.C.,
Greek; nonfiction SA
CRATES of THEBES, 365-285 B.C.,
Greek; nonfiction SA ST
CRATILO, 5th cent. B.C., Greek;
nonfiction SA
CRATINO de ATHENS, 519-422 B.C.,
Greek; poetry SA
CRATINUS, 490-23 B.C., Greek;
plays ST
CRATIPO, 5th-4th cent. B.C., Greek;
nonfiction SA
CRATIPO de MITILENE, fl. 44 B.C.,
Greek; nonfiction SA
CRATTY, Bryant J., 1929- , Ameri-
can; nonfiction CON
'CRAVEN' see CARLTON, John W.
CRAVEN, Thomas, 1889- , Ameri-
can; nonfiction KT WA

CRAVERI, Marcello, 1914- ,
Italian; fiction CON
CRAWFORD, Ann Fears, 1932- ,
American; nonfiction CON
CRAWFORD, Charles Olen,
1934- , American; nonfiction
CON
CRAWFORD, Everett ('Anole
Hunter'), 1879- , English;
nonfiction HIG
CRAWFORD, Francis Marion,
1854-1909, American; fiction
BRO KAA SA ST
CRAWFORD, Iain Padruig, 1922- ,
English; nonfiction, fiction
CON
CRAWFORD, Isabella Valacy,
1850-87, Canadian; poetry,
fiction KBA ST SY
CRAWFORD, J. P. Wickersham,
1882-1939, American; nonfic-
tion BL
CRAWFORD, Joanna, 1941- ,
American; fiction CON
CRAWFORD, John Edmund, 1904- ,
American; nonfiction CON
CRAWFORD, John Wallace ('Captain
Jack'), 1847-1917, American;
nonfiction, poetry KAA
CRAWFORD, John William, 1914- ,
American; nonfiction CON
CRAWFORD, Joyce, 1931- ,
American; fiction CON
CRAWFORD, Matsu Wofford,
1902- , American; fiction
CON
CRAWFORD, Phyllis, 1899- ,
American; juveniles KJU
CRAWFORD, Robert, -1732,
Scots; songs KB
CRAWFORD, Robert Platt,
1893- , American; nonfiction
CON
CRAWFORD, Terence Gordon
Sharman, 1945- , English;
nonfiction CON
CRAWFORD, Thelmar Wyche,
1905- , American; juveniles,
nonfiction CON WA
CRAWFORD, William Elbert,
1929- , American; nonfiction
CON
CRAYDER, Dorothy, 1906- ,
American; juveniles CON
'CRAYDER, Teresa' see COLMAN,
Hila
CRAYENCOUR see YOURCENAR,

Marguerite
CRAZ, Albert G., 1926- , American; juveniles CON WA
CREAGER, Alfred Leon, 1910- , American; nonfiction CON
CREAGH, Patrick ('Patrick Brasier-Creagh), 1930- , English; poetry CON
CREAGH-OSBORNE, Richard, 1928- , English; nonfiction CON
CREAMER, Robert, 1922- , American; nonfiction CON
CREANGA, Ioan, 1837-89/90, Rumanian; fiction COL HAR SA ST
CREASEY, John ('Gordon Ashe'; 'Norman Deane'; 'Michael Halliday'; 'Kyle Hunt'; 'Peter Manton'; 'J.J. Marric'; 'Richard Martin'; 'Anthony Morton'; 'Ken Ranger'; 'William K. Reilly'; 'Tex Riley'; 'Jeremy York'), 1908-73, English; fiction CON RIC
CREASY, Sir Edward Shepherd, 1812-78, English; nonfiction BRO KBA ST
CREBILLON, Claude Prosper Jolyot de, 1707-77, French; fiction DIF DIL HAR KE MAL SA ST
CREBILLON, Prosper Jolyot de, 1674-1762, French; plays DIF DIL HAR KE MAG MAL SA ST
CRECHALES, Anthony George ('Tony Kent'; 'Tony Trelos'), 1926- , American; fiction CON
'CRECY, Jeanne' see WILLIAMS, Jeanne
CREDLE, Ellis, 1902- , American; juveniles COM CON JO KJU WA
CREECH, Thomas, 1659-1700, English; translations BRO
CREECY, Richard Benbury, 1818-1908, English; nonfiction JO
'CREED, David' see GUTHRIE, James S.
CREEKMORE, Hubert, 1907- , American; poetry, fiction KTS WAF
CREELEY, Robert White, 1926- , American; poetry, fiction, nonfiction CON MUR
CREELMAN, Marjorie Broer, 1908- , American; nonfiction CON
CREESE, Bethea, English; juveniles CON
CREEVEY, Thomas, 1768-1838, English; diary, nonfiction BRO KBA
CREGAN, Mairin, Irish; fiction HOE

CREGER, Ralph Clinton, 1914- , American; nonfiction CON
CREHAN, Thomas, 1919- , Scots; nonfiction CON
'CREIGHTON, Don' see DRURY, Maxine C.
CREIGHTON, Donald, 1902- , Canadian; nonfiction SY
CREIGHTON, Helen Evelyn, 1914- , American; nonfiction CON
CREIGHTON, Luella Bruce, 1901- , Canadian; nonfiction CON
CREIGHTON, Mandell, 1843-1901, English; nonfiction BRO KBA
CREIGHTON, Thomas Hawk, 1904- , American; nonfiction CON
CREMAZIE, Octave, 1827-79, Canadian; poetry SA ST SY
CREMEANS, Charles Davis, 1915- , American; nonfiction CON
CREMER ALONSO, Victoriano, 1910- , Spanish; poetry, plays SA BL
CREMER, Jacobus Jan, 1827-89, Dutch; fiction ST
CREMER, Jan, 1940- , American; nonfiction CON
CREMIN, Lawrence Arthur, 1925- , American; nonfiction CON
CRENA de IONGH, Daniel, 1888-1970, Dutch-American; nonfiction CON
CRENNE, Hélisenne de, fl. 1540- , French; fiction ST
CRENNER, James, 1938- , American; poetry CON MUR
CRENSHAW, James L., 1934- , American; nonfiction CON
CREQUY, Louis Marie, 1705-81, French; nonfiction DIL
CREQUY, Renée Caroline Victoire de Froulay, 1714-1803, French; letters DIL
CRESCAS, Hasdai, 1340-1410, Spanish-Jewish; nonfiction KE ST
CRESCIMBENI, Giovanni Maria, 1663-1728, Italian; poetry SA
CRESPI, Pachita, 1900- , Costa Rican-American; juveniles WA
CRESPIGNY, Sir Claude Champion de, 1847-1935, English; nonfiction HIG
CRESPO, Angel, 1926- , Spanish;

poetry BL SA

'CRESPO, Blanco' see WHITE, Joseph B.

CRESPO, Rafael José, 1800-58, Spanish; poetry SA

CRESPO TROAL, Remigio, 1860-1939, Ecuadoran; poetry, criticism DI SA

CRESSEY, Donald Ray, 1919- , American; nonfiction CON

CRESSEY, William W., 1939- , American; nonfiction CON

CRESSWELL, Helen, 1934- , English; juveniles COM CON WA

CRESSWELL, Walter D'Arcy, 1896- , New Zealander; poetry ST

CRESWELL, Keppel Archibald Cameron, 1879- , American; nonfiction CON

CRETAN, Gladys Yessayan, 1921- , American; juveniles COM CON

CRETIN, Guillauem Dubois (Crestin), 1461?-1525, French; poetry DIF SA ST

CRETZMEYER, Francis Xavier, Jr., 1913- , American; nonfiction CON

CREUTZ, Gustaf Filip, 1731-85, Swedish; nonfiction HAR ST

CREUZER, Georg Friedrich, 1771-1858, German; nonfiction SA

CREVECOEUR, Michel-Guillaume Jean de ('Agricola', 'Hector St. Johns'), 1735-1813, French; essays BRO DIL KAA MAG ST

CREVEDIA, N., 1914- , Rumanian; poetry ST

CREVEL, Jacques, 1692-1764, French; nonfiction DIL

CREVEL, René, 1900-35, French; poetry DIF MAL

CREVIER, Jean Baptiste Louis, 1693-1765, French; nonfiction DIL

CREW, Fleming H., American; juveniles KJU

CREW, Francis Albert Eley, 1888- , English; nonfiction CON

CREW, Helen Coale, 1866-1941, American; juveniles KJU

CREWS, Freiderick Campbell, 1933- , American; nonfiction CON

CREWS, Harry, 1935- , American; fiction CON

CREWS, Judson Campbell, 1917- ,

American; nonfiction CON MUR

CREWS, William J., 1931- , American; nonfiction CON

'CREYTON, Paul' see TROWBRIDGE, John T.

CRIADO del VAL, MANUEL, Spanish; nonfiction BL

CRIAPPORI, Atilio, 1880-1947, Argentinian; fiction, essays MIN

CRIBBET, John Edward, 1918- , American; nonfiction CON

'CRICHTON, Clarke, Jr.' see SCHMOE, Floyd W.

CRICHTON, J. Michael ('Jeffery Hudson'; 'John Lange'), 1942- , American; fiction CON

CRICHTON, James, 1560-83/85, Scots; poetry KB

CRICHTON, James Dunlop, 1907- , English; nonfiction CON

CRICHTON, John, 1916- , American; nonfiction CON

CRICHTON, Kyle Samuel ('Robert Forsythe'), 1896- , American; journalism KT

CRICHTON, Robert, 1925- , American; fiction CON

CRICIUS, Andrzej (Krzycki), 1482-1537, Polish; poetry ST

CRICK, Bernard Rowland, 1929- , English; nonfiction CON

CRIGHTON, John Clark, 1903- , American; nonfiction CON

CRIM, Keith Renn ('Casey Renn'), 1924- , American; fiction CON

CRIMMINS, James Custis, 1935- , American; juveniles CON

CRINKLEY, Richmond, 1940- , American; nonfiction CON

CRIPPS, Arthur Sheuly, 1869- , Rhodesian; poetry, fiction ST

CRIPPS, Matthew Anthony Leonard, 1913- , English; nonfiction CON

CRISIPO, 280-07/200 B.C., Greek; nonfiction SA

CRISLER, Lois Brown, American; nonfiction PAC

CRISOLORA, Manuele (Chrysoloras), 1350?-1415, Italian; nonfiction, translations SA ST

CRISP, Colin Godrey, 1936- , New Zealander; nonfiction CON

CRISP, Frank Robson, 1915- ,
English; fiction CON
CRISP, Lucy Cherry, American;
poetry JO
CRISP, Robert James, English;
fiction CON
CRISPO, John, 1933- , Canadian;
nonfiction CON
CRISS, Mildred, 1890- , American;
nonfiction HOE WA
CRISSEY, Elwell, 1899- , Ameri-
can; nonfiction CON
CRIST, Eda Szecskay, 1909- ,
American; juveniles WA
CRIST, Richard Harrison, 1909- ,
American; juveniles WA
'CRISTOBAL, Manuel' see GRANELL,
Manuel
CRISTOL, Vivian, Irish-American;
fiction CON
CRISTOPOLOUS, Atanasio, 1772-1847,
Greek; poetry SA
CRISWELL, Cloyd M., 1908- ,
American; nonfiction, poetry
CON
CRISWELL, Wallie Amos, 1909- ,
American; nonfiction CON
CRITCHLEY, Edmund Michael Rhys,
1931- , English; nonfiction
CON
CRITCHLEY, Thomas Alan, 1919- ,
English; nonfiction CON
CRITIAS E Mayor, 450 B.C., Greek;
poetry SA
CRITIAS of ATHENS, 5th cent. B.C.,
Greek; nonfiction ST
'CRITIC' see MARTIN, Basil K.
'CRITICUS' see HARCOURT, Melville
'CRITICUS' see ROE, Frederic G.
CRITOLAO, 2nd cent. B.C., Greek;
nonfiction SA
CRITON, Greek; nonfiction SA
CRNJANSKI, Milos ('C.R. Mill'),
1893- , Hungarian-English; non-
fiction, poetry CON
CROCCHIOLA, Rev. Francis Stanley
('Francis Stanley'), 1908- ,
American; nonfiction HO
CROCE, Benedetto, 1866-1952,
Italian; nonfiction, criticism BL
COL FLE HAR KL KT RIC SA
ST
CROCK, Clement H., 1890- ,
American; nonfiction HOE
CROCKER, Lester Gilbert, 1912- ,
American; nonfiction CON
CROCKER, Lionel George, 1897- ,

American; nonfiction CON
CROCKER, Walter Russell,
1902- , Australian; nonfiction
CON
CROCKETT, David, 1786-1836,
American; nonfiction MAG
CROCKETT, George Ronald,
1906- , Irish; nonfiction CON
CROCKETT, James Underwood,
1915- , American; nonfiction
CON
CROCKETT, Samuel Rutherford,
1860-1914, English; juveniles,
fiction, poetry BRO DOY KBA
KT ST
CROCOMBE, Ronald Gordon,
1929- , New Zealander; non-
fiction CON
CROCUS, Cornelius, 1500-50,
Dutch; plays ST
CROFFORD, Lena Henrichson,
1908- , American; nonfiction
CON
CROFT-COOKE, Rupert, 1903/04- ,
English; fiction, poetry CON
HO KT
CROFTS, Freeman Wills, 1879-
1957, Anglo-Irish; fiction BRO
KT RIC
CROFTS, John Ernest Victor,
1887- , English; nonfiction
CON
CROFUT, William E., III,
1934- , American; nonfiction
CON
'CROISE, Jacques' see SCHAKOV-
SKY, Zinaida
CROISSET, Franz Wiener, 1877-
1937, French; plays COL
HAR DIF SA ST
CROIXMARRE, Julien de, 1672-
1731, French; nonfiction, plays
DIL
CROKER, John Wilson, 1780-1857,
Anglo-Irish; nonfiction BRO
KBA ST
CROKER, Thomas Crofton, 1798-
1854, Irish; fiction BRO KBA
ST
CROLY, David Goodman, 1829-
89, American; journalism, non-
fiction KAA
CROLY, George, 1780-1860, Irish;
poetry, fiction, essays BRO
KBA ST
CROLY, Herbert David, 1869-1930,
American; journalism KT

CROLY, Jane Cunningham ('Jenny
June'), 1829-1901, American;
journalism KAA
CROMEK, Robert Hartley, 1770-1812,
English; nonfiction KBA
CROMER, Martin, 1512-89, Polish;
nonfiction SA
CROMIE, Alice Hamilton ('Vivian
Mort'), 1914- , American;
nonfiction CON
CROMIE, Robert Allen, 1909- ,
American; journalism, nonfiction,
poetry CON
CROMIE, William Joseph, 1930- ,
American; nonfiction CON
CROMMELYNCK, Fernand, 1886/88-
1970, Belgian; plays COL DIF
FLE HAR MAL MAT SA ST
CROMPTON, Anne Eliot, 1930- ,
American; nonfiction CON
CROMPTON, Henry, 1836-1904,
English; nonfiction KBA
CROMPTON, Hugh, fl. 1657, English;
poetry ST
'CROMPTON, John' see LAMBURN,
John B. C.
CROMPTON, Louis William, 1925- ,
American; nonfiction CON
CROMPTON, Margaret Norah Mair,
1901- , English; fiction CON
'CROMPTON, Richmal L.', see
LAMBURN, Richmal C.
CROMWELL, Harvey, 1907- , Amer-
ican; nonfiction CON
CRONAU, Rudolf, 1855-1939, German-
American; journalism ST
CRONBACH, Abraham, 1882-1965,
American; nonfiction CON
CRONE, Hans Rainer, 1942- ,
German; nonfiction CON
CRONE, Ruth, 1919- , American;
juveniles CON WA
CRONEGK, Johann Freidrich
Reichsfreiherr, 1731-58, Ger-
man; plays SA ST
CRONIN, Anthony, 1926- , Irish;
poetry, fiction, criticism MUR
CRONIN, Archibald Joseph, 1896- ,
English; fiction BRO FLE CON
HOE KAT KT RIC SA ST
CRONIN, John Francis, 1908- ,
American; nonfiction CON HOE
CRONIN, Vincent, 1924- , Welsh;
nonfiction CON
CRONON, Edmund David, 1924- ,
American; nonfiction CON
'CRONUS, Diodorus' see TAYLOR,
Richard

CROOK, John Anthony, 1921- ,
English; nonfiction CON
CROOK, Margaret Brackenbury,
1886- , English; nonfiction
CON
CROOK, Roger Hawley, 1921- ,
American; nonfiction CON
CROOKALL, Robert, 1890- ,
English; nonfiction CON
CROOKS, James Benedict, 1933- ,
American; nonfiction CON
CROPP, Benjamin, 1936- , Amer-
ican; nonfiction, juvenile CON
CROS, Charles Hortensius Emile,
1842-88, French; poetry DIF
HAR KE MAL ST
CROSBIE, Hugh Provan ('John
Carrick'), 1912- , English;
fiction CON
CROSBY, Alexander L., 1906- ,
American; juvenile COM CON
WA
CROSBY, Alfred W., Jr., 1931- ,
American; nonfiction CON
CROSBY, Harry Herbert, 1919- ,
American; nonfiction CON
CROSBY, James, 1924- , Ameri-
can; nonfiction BL
CROSBY, Jeremiah, 1940- ,
American; nonfiction CON
CROSBY, John Campbell, 1912- ,
American; nonfiction CON
CROSBY, John F., 1931- ,
American; nonfiction CON
CROSBY, Muriel Estelle, 1908- ,
American; nonfiction CON
CROSBY, Phoebe, American; juven-
iles WA
CROSBY, Sumner McKnight,
1909- , American; nonfiction
CON
CROSS, Anthony Glenn, 1936- ,
English; nonfiction CON
CROSS, Aleene Ann, 1922- ,
American; nonfiction CON
CROSS, Claire, 1932- , American;
nonfiction CON
CROSS, Colin John ('John Weir'),
1928- , Welsh; nonfiction CON
CROSS, Ian, 1925- , New Zea-
lander; fiction RIC
'CROSS, James' see PARRY, Hugh
J.
CROSS, Jennifer, 1932- , English;
juveniles CON
CROSS, John Keir ('Stephen Mac-
Farlane'), 1914-67, English;
juveniles DOY WA

CROSS, Kathryn Patricia, 1926- ,
American; nonfiction CON
CROSS, Kenneth Gustav Walter, 1927- ,
English; nonfiction CON
CROSS, Mary Ann see 'ELIOT,
George'
CROSS, Richard Keith, 1940- ,
American; nonfiction CON
CROSS, Robert Brandt, 1914- ,
American; nonfiction CON
CROSS, Robert Dougherty, 1924- ,
American; nonfiction CON
CROSS, Robert Singlehurst, 1925- ,
English; nonfiction CON
CROSS, Wilbur Lucius, 1862- ,
American; nonfiction KT
CROSS, Wilbur Lucius III, 1918- ,
American; juveniles, nonfiction
COM CON
'CROSSCOUNTRY' see CAMPBELL,
Thomas F.
CROSSEN, Kendell Foster ('Bennet
Barlay'; 'M.E. Chaber'; 'Richard
Foster'; 'Christopher Monig';
'Clay Richards'), 1910- , Amer-
ican; fiction CON
CROSSER, Paul K., 1902- , Ameri-
can; nonfiction CON
CROSSLEY-HOLLAND, Kevin John
William, 1941- , British; poetry,
translations, juveniles MUR
CROSSMAN, Samuel, 1624?-84,
English; poetry ST
CROTEAU, John Tougas, 1910- ,
American; nonfiction CON
CROTHER, George, D., 1929- ,
American; nonfiction CON
CROTHERS, Jessie Frances ('Frances
J. Wright'), 1913- , American;
nonfiction CON
CROTHERS, Rachel, 1878-1958,
American; plays HOO KAT KT
MAT SA
CROTHERS, Samuel McChord, 1857-
1927, American; essays KT
CROTTY, William Joseph, 1936- ,
American; nonfiction CON
CROTUS, Rubeanus (Rubianus) Johann
Jäger), 1480-1539?, German;
nonfiction ST
CROUCH, Marcus, 1913- , English;
juveniles CON DOY
CROUCH, William George Alfred,
1903- , English; nonfiction CON
CROUDACE, Glynn ('Peter Monnow'),
1917- , English; fiction CON
CROUSAZ, Jean Pierre de, 1663-

1740, Swiss; nonfiction SA
CROUSE, Anna Erskine, American;
juveniles WA
CROUSE, Russel, 1893-1966,
American; nonfiction, plays
KTS MAR MAT WA
CROUSE, William Harry, 1907- ,
American; juveniles CON WA
CROUT, George Clement, 1917- ,
American; juveniles CON
CROUZET, François Marie Joseph,
1922- , French; nonfiction
CON
CROUVITZ, Herbert Floyd,
1932- , American; nonfiction
CON
CROW, Alice von Bauer, 1894-1966,
American; nonfiction CON
CROW, Carl, 1883- , American;
journalism, nonfiction KT
CROW, John Armstrong, 1906- ,
American; nonfiction CON
CROW, Lester Donald, 1897- ,
American; nonfiction CON
CROW, Martin Michael, 1901- ,
American; nonfiction CON
CROW, William Bernard, 1895- ,
English; nonfiction CON
CROWDER, Michael, 1934- ,
English; nonfiction CON
CROWCROFT, Andrew, 1923- ,
English; nonfiction CON
CROWDER, Richard Henry,
1909- , American; nonfiction
CON
CROWDY, E. Percy, 1850-1912,
English; nonfiction HIG
CROWE, Bettina Lum ('Peter Lum'),
1911- , English; fiction CON
WA
CROWE, Catherine Stevens, 1800-
76, English; fiction, plays,
juveniles, translations BRO
KBA
CROWE, Charles, 1928- , Amer-
ican; nonfiction CON
CROWE, Charles Monroe, 1902- ,
American; nonfiction CON
CROWE, Eyre Evans, 1799-1868,
English; fiction, nonfiction
BRO ST
CROWE, John, 1906- , American;
nonfiction CON
CROWE, Sir Joseph Archer, 1825-
96, English; journalism, non-
fiction BRO ST
CROWE, Sylvia, 1901- , English;

nonfiction CON
CROWE, William, 1745-1829, English;
poetry BRO KBA
CROWELL, George H., 1931- ,
American; nonfiction CON
CROWELL, Norton B., 1914- ,
American; nonfiction CON
CROWELL, Pers, 1910- , American;
juveniles, fiction COM CON FUL
PAC
CROWLEY, Daniel John, 1921- ,
American; nonfiction CON
CROWLEY, James B., 1929- ,
American; nonfiction CON
CROWN, David A., 1928- , Ameri-
can; nonfiction CON
CROWN, Paul, 1928- , American;
nonfiction CON
CROWNE, John, 1640?-1703?, Eng-
lish; plays BRO KB SA
CROWNFIELD, Gertrude, 1867-1945,
American; juveniles KJU WA
CROWTHER, Duane Swofford, 1934- ,
American; nonfiction CON
CROWTHER, James Gerald, American;
juveniles WA
CROWTHER, Wilma ('Wilma George'),
1918- , English; nonfiction CON
CROXTON, Frederick Emory, 1899- ,
American; nonfiction CON
CROY, Homer, 1883- , American;
fiction KT WAF
CROZET, Charlotte, 1926- ,
French-English; nonfiction CON
CROZIER, Brian, 1918- , Australian;
nonfiction CON
CROZIER, John Beattie, 1849-1921,
Anglo-Canadian; nonfiction KT
CRUCHAGA SANTA MARIA, Angel,
1893-1948, Chilean; poetry, non-
fiction MIN SA
CRUCHAGA TOCORNAL, Miguel,
1869-1949, Chilean; nonfiction
MIN
CRUDEN, Alexander, 1701-70, Eng-
lish; nonfiction BRO KB
CRUDEN, Robert, 1910- , Scots;
nonfiction CON
CRUICKSHANK, Charles Greig,
1914- , Scots; nonfiction CON
CRUICKSHANK, Helen Burness ('A.
M. V.'; 'A. N. A.'; 'C. E. E.'),
1886- , Scots; poetry MUR
CRUICKSHANK, Helen Gere, 1907- ,
American; juveniles CON WA
CRUICKSHANK, John, 1924- ,
Irish; nonfiction CON

CRUL, Cornelius, 1500-50, Dutch;
poetry ST
CRUMBAUGH, James Charles,
1912- , American; nonfiction
CON
CRUMBLEY, D. Larry, 1941- ,
American; nonfiction CON
CRUMMEY, Robert O., 1936- ,
American; nonfiction CON
CRUMP, Barry John, 1935- ,
New Zealander; fiction CON
CRUMP, Fred, Jr., 1931- ,
American; juveniles CON
CRUMP, Geoffrey Herbert,
1891- , English; nonfiction
CON
CRUMP, Irving, 1887- , Ameri-
can; juveniles KJU WA
CRUMP, Kenneth Gordon, Jr.,
1931- , American; nonfiction
CON
CRUMP, Spencer M., Jr., 1923- ,
American; nonfiction CON
'CRUMPET, Peter' see BUCKLEY,
Fergus R.
CRUMRINE, Norman Ross, II,
1934- , American; nonfiction
CON
CRUNDEN, Robert M., 1940- ,
American; nonfiction CON
CRUSAT, Paulina, 1900- ,
Spanish; journalism, poetry,
fiction SA
CRUSE, Heloise ('Heloise'),
1919- , American; nonfiction
CON
CRUSENSTOLPE, Magnus Jacob,
1795-1865, Swedish; journalism,
fiction, nonfiction ST
CRUSET, José, 1912- , Spanish;
poetry SA
CRUSIUS, Christian August, 1715-
75, German; nonfiction SA
CRUZ, Agostinho da, 1540-1619,
Portuguese; poetry SA ST
CRUZ, Juan de la see JUAN de la
CRUZ
CRUZ, Sor Juana Ines de la (Juana
Ines de Asbaje y Ramírez de
Cantillana), 1651-95, Spanish;
poetry, plays BL SA ST
CRUZ, Manuel de la, 1861-96,
Cuban; criticism, journalism
MIN SA
CRUZ, Pedro Nolasco, Chilean;
fiction MIN
CRUZ, Ramón de la, 1731-94,

Spanish; nonfiction BL
CRUZ, Victor Hernandez, 1949- ,
    American; poetry MUR
CRUZ CANO y OLMEDILLA, Ramón,
    Francisco de la, 1731-94,
    Spanish; plays HAR KE SA ST
CRUZ e SILVA, Antonio Dinis da,
    1731-99, Portuguese; poetry SA
    ST
CRUZ MAGALHÃES, Artur Ernesto
    Santa, 1864-1928, Portuguese;
    poetry, criticism SA
CRUZ RUEDA, Angel, 1888-1957?,
    Spanish; essays, criticism,
    fiction BL SA
CRUZ VARELA, Juan, 1794-1839,
    Argentinian; poetry, plays BL
    SA
CRUZ y SOUSA, Juan de, 1862-98,
    Brazilian; poetry SA
CRYSTAL, David, 1941- , Irish;
    nonfiction CON
CSEZMICZEY, János (Janus Pan-
    nonius), 1434-72, Hungarian;
    poetry ST
CSICSERY-RONAY, Istvan, 1917- ,
    Hungarian; nonfiction CON
CSIKY, Gregory, 1842-91, Hungarian;
    plays SA
CSOKONAI VITEZ, Mihálay, 1773-
    1805, Hungarian; poetry, plays
    SA ST
CSOKOR, Franz Theodor, 1885-1969,
    Czech; plays, poetry, essays
    AL FLE HOE KU LEN MAT
CTESIAS, 400 B.C., Greek; nonfiction
    SA ST
CUA, Antonio S., 1932- , Filipino;
    nonfiction CON
CUADRA, Jose da le, 1903-41,
    Ecuadoran; poetry, fiction DI
    SA
CUADRA, Pablo Antonio, 1912- ,
    Nicaraguan; poetry, plays, fic-
    tion, criticism SA
CUALENDRO see CALENDRE
CUARTERO CIFUENTES, José,
    1869-1946, Spanish; journalism
    SA
CUBAN, Larry, 1934- , American;
    nonfiction CON
'CUBAS, Braz' see DAWES, Robyn M.
CUBER, John Frank, 1911- , Amer-
    ican; nonfiction CON
CUBETA, Paul Marsden, 1925- ,
    American; nonfiction CON
CUBIERES, Marie Buffaut de,

1794- , French; nonfiction
    SA
CUBIERES, Michel, 1752-1820,
    French; nonfiction DIL
CUBILLO de ARAGON, Alvaro,
    1596?-1661, Spanish; poetry,
    plays BL SA ST
CUBRANOVIC, Andrija, 1480-
    1520, Dalmatian; poetry ST
'CUCALEMBE, El' see NAPOLES
    FAJARDO, Juan C.
CUDDON, John Anthony, 1928- ,
    English; fiction CON
CUDLIPP, Edythe ('Jane Horatio';
    'G.F. Van Zandt'), 1929- ,
    American; nonfiction CON
CUDWORTH, Ralph, 1617-88,
    English; nonfiction BRO KB
    SA ST
CUELLAR, Jerónimo de, 1608-69,
    Spanish; poetry SA
CUELLAR, Jerónimo de, 1622-65,
    Spanish; plays BL
CUELLAR, José Tomás, 1830-94,
    Mexican; fiction SA
CUENCA, Carlos Luis de, 1849-
    1927, Spanish; journalism,
    poetry, plays BL SA
CUENCA, Cluadio Mamerto, 1812-
    52, Argentinian; poetry MIN
CUERVO, Angel, 1838-96/98,
    Colombian; poetry, journalism
    MIN
CUERVO, Rufino José, 1844-1911,
    Spanish; nonfiction BL MIN
    SA
CUERVO MARQUEZ, Emilio,
    1873/79-1937, Colombian;
    fiction MIN
CUESTA, Juan de see BARRERA,
    Isaac J.
CUESTA y CUESTA, Alfonso,
    1912- , Ecuadoran; fiction
    DI
CUETO, Leopoldo Augusto
    ('Marqués de Valmar), 1815-
    1901, Spanish; nonfiction BL
    SA
CUEVA, Jorge de la, 1884-1958,
    Spanish; journalism, criticism,
    plays SA
CUEVA, José de la, 1887-1955,
    Spanish; journalism, criticism,
    plays SA
CUEVA, Juan de la, 1550?-1610,
    Spanish; plays, poetry BL
    HAR KE ST

CUEVA DE GAROZA, Juan de la, 1543?-1610, Spanish; poetry, plays SA

'CUEVAS, Francisco de las' (Francisco de Quintana), 1595?-1658, Spanish; nonfiction SA

CUEVAS, José, 1918- , Spanish; nonfiction SA

CUEVAS, Jesús de las, 1920- , Spanish; nonfiction SA

CUEVAS, Mariano, 1879- , Mexican; nonfiction SA

CUEVAS GARCIA, Mariano de las, 1876- , Spanish; poetry SA

CULANT-CIRE, Rene Alexandre, 1718-99, French; nonfiction DIL

CULBERTSON, Don Stuart, 1927- , American; nonfiction CON

CULBERTSON, John Mathew, 1921- , American; nonfiction CON

CULBERTSON, Paul Thomas, 1905- , American; nonfiction CON

CULKIN, Ann Marie, 1918- , American; nonfiction CON

CULLEN, Countée, 1903-46, American; fiction KL SA

CULLEN, Patrick Colborn, 1940- , American; nonfiction CON

CULLER, Arthur Dwight, 1917- , American; nonfiction CON

CULLEY, Thomas Robert, 1931- , American; nonfiction CON

CULLINAN, Elizabeth, 1933- , American; fiction CON

CULLINAN, Gerald, 1916- , American; nonfiction CON

CULLINGFORD, Cecil Howard Dunstan, 1904- , English; nonfiction CON

CULLINGWORTH, John Barry, 1929- , English; nonfiction CON

CULLMAN, Marguerite Wagner, 1908- , American; fiction CON

CULLOP, Charles P., 1927- , American; nonfiction CON

CULLUM, Ridgwell, 1867-1943, English; fiction BRO KT SA

CULLY, Iris Virginia Arnold, 1914- , American; nonfiction CON

CULLY, Kendig Brubaker, 1913- , American; nonfiction CON

CULP, Delos Poe, 1911- , American; nonfiction CON

CULP, John Hewett, Jr., 1907- , American; nonfiction CON

CULP, Louanna McNary, 1901-65, American; juveniles COM CON

CULPEPER, Nicholas, 1616-54,

English; nonfiction KB

CULROSS, Michael Gerard, 1942- , American; nonfiction, poetry CON

CULSHAW, John Royds, 1924- , English; nonfiction CON

CULVER, Dwight W., 1921- , American; nonfiction CON

CULVER, Elsie Thomas, 1898- , American; nonfiction CON

CULVERWEL, Nathanael, -1651?, English; nonfiction KB

CUMBERLAND, Charles Curtis, 1914- , American; nonfiction CON

CUMBERLAND, Marten ('R. Laugier'; 'Kevin O'Hara'), 1892- , English; fiction CON

CUMBERLAND, Richard, 1732-1811, English; plays, fiction, translations BRO KB ST

CUMBERLAND, William Henry, 1929- , American; nonfiction CON

CUMBERLEGE, Marcus Crossley, 1938- , British; poetry MUR

CUMING, Geoffrey John, 1917- , English; nonfiction CON

CUMING, Edward William Dirom, 1862- , English; nonfiction HIG

CUMMING, Primrose Amy, 1915- , English; juveniles CON

CUMMING, William Patterson, 1900- , American; nonfiction CON

CUMMINGS, Bruce Frederick ('W.N.P. Barbellion'), 1889-1919, English; essays, diary BRO KT

CUMMINGS, Edward Estlin, 1894-1962, American; poetry, plays, fiction BRO FLE KL KT MAG MAT RIC SP SA ST WA

CUMMINGS, Jean, 1930- , American; nonfiction CON

CUMMINGS, Milton Curtis, Jr., 1933- , American; nonfiction CON

CUMMINGS, Parke, 1902- , American; juvenile, nonfiction COM CON

CUMMINGS, Paul, 1933- , American; nonfiction CON

CUMMINGS, Richard, American; juveniles WA

'CUMMINGS, Richard' see GARDNER,
Richard
CUMMINGS, Walter Thies, 1933- ,
American; fiction CON
CUMMINS, D. Duane, 1935- ,
American; nonfiction CON
CUMMINS, Geraldine, 1890- , Irish;
fiction, plays CON
CUMMINS, Maria Susanna, 1827-66,
American; juveniles, fiction BRO
DOY KAA
CUMMINS, Rev. Patrick, 1880- ,
American; nonfiction HO
CUMMINS, Paul F., 1937- , Amer-
ican; nonfiction CON
CUMMINS, Scott, 1846-1928, Ameri-
can; poetry MAR
CUNDIFF, Edward William, 1919- ,
American; nonfiction CON
CUNDY, Henry Martyn, 1913- ,
English; nonfiction CON
CUNEO VIDAL, Rómulo, 1876?- ,
Peruvian; nonfiction SA
CUNHA, Euclides da, 1866-1909,
Brazilian; fiction SA ST
CUNHA, George Martin, 1911- ,
American; nonfiction CON
CUNHA, José Anastácio da, 1744-87,
Portuguese; poetry SA ST
CUNHA BARBOSA, Jenaro, 1780-
1846, Brazilian; poetry, plays
SA
CUNLIFFE, Elaine, English; nonfic-
tion CON
CUNLIFFE, John William, 1865- ,
Anglo-American; criticism KT
CUNLIFFE, Marcus, 1922- , Eng-
lish; nonfiction CON
CUNLIFFE, William Gordon, 1929- ,
English; nonfiction CON
CUNNINGHAM, Albert A. see 'HALE,
Garth'
CUNNINGHAM, Allan, 1784-1842,
Scots; poetry, nonfiction, fiction
BRO KBA SA ST
CUNNINGHAM, Dale Speers, 1932- ,
American; nonfiction CON
'CUNNINGHAM, E.V.' see FAST,
Howard M.
CUNNINGHAM, Floyd Franklin,
1899- , American; nonfiction
CON
'CUNNINGHAM, Capt. Frank' see
GLICK, Carl C.
CUNNINGHAM, Horace Herndon,
1913- , American; nonfiction
CON

CUNNINGHAM, James F., 1901- ,
American; nonfiction CON
CUNNINGHAM, James Vincent,
1911- , American; poetry,
criticism, fiction CON MUR
CUNNINGHAM, John, 1729-73,
Scots; plays, poetry KB
CUNNINGHAM, Julia Woolfolk,
1916- , American; juvenile
COM CON WA
CUNNINGHAM, Louis Arthur,
1900- , Canadian; fiction
SY
CUNNINGHAM, Lyda Sue Martin,
1938- , American; nonfiction
CON
CUNNINGHAM, Margaret E. see
DANNER, Margaret E.
CUNNINGHAM, Mary see PIERCE,
Mary C.F.
CUNNINGHAM, Rosemary, 1916- ,
American; fiction CON
CUNNINGHAM, Thomas Mounsey,
1776-1834, Scots; poetry KBA
CUNNINGHAM, Virginia, 1909- ,
American; juvenile WA
CUNNINGHAM, William, 1849-
1919, Scots; nonfiction KBA
CUNNINGHAM, William, 1901- ,
American; fiction MAR
CUNNINGHAME-GRAHAM, Robert
see GRAHAM, Robert B.C.
CUNZ, Dieter, 1910- , German-
American; nonfiction CON
CUNQUEIRO, Alvaro, 1912- ,
Spanish; poetry SA
CUNY, Louis, 1700-55, French;
nonfiction DIL
CUOCO, Vincenzo, 1770-1823,
Italian; nonfiction HAR ST
CUOMO, George Michael, 1929- ,
American; nonfiction, fiction,
poetry CON
CUPPY, William Jacob, 1884- ,
American; fiction KAT KT
CUREL, François de, 1854-1928,
French; plays, fiction COL
DIF HAR MAT SA ST
CURIE, Eve, 1904- , Franco-
American; juveniles COM CON
CURL, Donald Walter, 1935- ,
American; nonfiction CON
CURL, James Stevens ('Adytum';
'E.B. Keeling'; 'Parsifal'),
1937- , American; nonfiction
CON
CURLE, Adam, 1916- , Franco-

American; nonfiction CON

CURLEY, Arthur, 1938- , American;
nonfiction CON

CURLEY, Daniel, 1918- , American;
fiction CON

CURLEY, Dorothy Nyren, 1927- ,
American; nonfiction CON

CURLL, Edmund, 1675-1747, English;
nonfiction KB

CURNOW, Allen, 1911- , New
Zealander; poetry, plays, criticism MUR RIC ST

CURRAN, Charles Arthur, 1913- ,
American; nonfiction CON

CURRAN, Charles E., 1934- ,
American; nonfiction CON

CURRAN, Dale, 1898- , American;
fiction WAF

CURRAN, Francis X., 1914- ,
American; nonfiction CON

CURRAN, Mona Elisa ('Giles Merton';
'Adrian Murray'; 'Mervyn
Thomas'), English; nonfiction
CON

CURRAN, Stuart Alan, 1940- ,
American; nonfiction CON

CURREN, Polly, 1917- , American;
juveniles CON

CURRENT, Richard Nelson, 1912- ,
American; nonfiction CON

CURRENT-GARCIA, Eugene, 1908- ,
American; nonfiction CON

CURREY, Cecil B., 1932- , American; nonfiction CON

CURREY, Ralph Nixon, 1907- ,
British; poetry MUR

CURREY, Ronald Fairbridge, 1894- ,
English; nonfiction CON

'CURRIE, David' see ALLEN, Sydney
E. Jr.

CURRIE, Lauchlin, 1902- , Canadian;
nonfiction CON

CURRIE, Lady Mary Montgomerie
Lamb ('Violet Fane'; 'Mary M.
Singleton'), 1843-1905, English;
poetry, fiction, essays KBA

CURRIER, Alvin, C., 1932- ,
American; nonfiction CON

CURRO, Evelyn Malone, 1907- ,
American; nonfiction CON

CURROS ENRIQUEZ, Manuel, 1851-
1908, Spanish; poetry, journalism
COL SA

CURRY, Estell H., 1907- , American; nonfiction CON

CURRY, Gladys Joseph, 1931- ,
American; nonfiction CON

CURRY, Jane Louise, 1932- ,
American; juveniles COM
CON WA

CURRY, Kenneth, 1910- , American; nonfiction CON

CURRY, Leonard Preston,
1929- , American; nonfiction
CON

CURRY, Lerond Loving, 1930- ,
American; nonfiction CON

CURRY, Peggy Simson, 1911- ,
Scots; fiction, poetry CON

CURRY, Richard Orr, 1931- ,
American; nonfiction CON

CURSAY, Jean Marie Joseph
Thomasseau, 1705-81, French;
nonfiction DIL

CURTAYNE, Alice, Irish; translations, essays, fiction HOE

CURTI, Merle, 1897- , American;
nonfiction CON KTS

CURTIN, James R., 1922- ,
American; nonfiction CON

CURTIN, Jeremiah, 1840?-1906,
American; nonfiction KAA

CURTIN, Philip D., 1922- ,
American; nonfiction CON

CURTIS, Alice Bertha, American;
juveniles WA

CURTIS, Alice Turner, 1860-1958,
American; juveniles WA

CURTIS, Charles John, 1921- ,
American; nonfiction CON

CURTIS, Charles Ralph, 1899- ,
American; nonfiction CON

CURTIS, Charlotte, American; nonfiction CON

CURTIS, David, 1942- , American; nonfiction CON

CURTIS, Edith Roelker, 1893- ,
American; nonfiction, fiction,
poetry CON

CURTIS, George Ticknor ('Peter
Boyleston'), 1812-94, American;
fiction, nonfiction KAA

CURTIS, George William ('Howadji'),
1824-92, American; essays,
journalism BRO KAA SA ST

CURTIS, Harriot see FARLEY,
Harriet

CURTIS, Hubert Arnold, 1917- ,
English; juveniles CON

CURTIS, Jean Louis, 1917- ,
French; fiction, essays DIC
DIF FLE PIN

'CURTIS, John' see PREBBLE,
John E. C.

CURTIS, Louis Perry, 1900- ,
American; nonfiction CON
CURTIS, Margaret James, 1897- ,
English; fiction CON
'CURTIS, Marjorie' see PREBBLE,
Marjorie
CURTIS, Mark Hubert, 1920- ,
American; nonfiction CON
'CURTIS, Peter' see LOFTS, Norah
R.
CURTIS, Richard Kenneth, 1924- ,
American; nonfiction CON
CURTIS, Rosemary Ann Stevens,
1935- , English; juveniles CON
'CURTIS, Tom' see PENDOWER,
Jacques
'CURTIS, Will' see NUNN, William
C.
CURTIS BROWN, Beatrice, 1901- ,
English; nonfiction CON
CURTISS, Frederic H., 1869- ,
American; nonfiction HIG
CURTISS, John Shelton, 1899- ,
American; nonfiction CON
CURTISS, Ursula Reilly, 1923- ,
American; fiction CON
CURTIUS, Ernst Robert, 1814-96,
German; nonfiction SA
CURTIUS, Ernst Robert, 1886-1956,
German; criticism, essays BL
FLE KU
CURTIUS RUFUS, Quintus, 1st cent.,
Roman; nonfiction ST
CURTO, Josephine, J., 1927- ,
American; nonfiction CON
CURVERS, Alexis, 1906- , French;
fiction DIC
CURWEN, Henry, 1845-92, English;
fiction KBA
CURWOOD, James Oliver, 1878-1927,
American; fiction KT SA
CURZON, Robert (Lord De La Zouche),
1810-73, English; nonfiction KBA
'CURZON, Sam' see KRASNEY,
Samuel A.
'CURZON, Virginia' see HAWTON,
Hector
CURZON of KEDLESTON, George
Nathaniel, 1859-1925, English;
nonfiction KT
'CUSA, Nicolás de' (Nikolas Krebs),
1401-64, German; nonfiction
SA
CUSAC, Marian Hollingsworth,
1932- , American; nonfiction
CON
CUSACK, Dymphna, Australian;

fiction RIC CON
CUSACK, Lawrence Xavier,
1919- , American; nonfiction
CON
CUSHING, Caleb, 1800-79, Amer-
ican; nonfiction KAA
CUSHING, Frank Hamilton, 1857-
1900, American; nonfiction
KAA
CUSHING, Jane, 1922- , Ameri-
can; nonfiction CON
CUSHING, Luther Stearns, 1803-
56, American; nonfiction KAA
'CUSHMAN, Clara' see HAVEN,
Emily B.N.
CUSHMAN, Dan ('Sumner Davis'),
1909- , American; fiction
CON PAC
CUSHMAN, Jerome, American;
juveniles, nonfiction CON
COM
CUSHMAN, Rebecca, American;
poetry JO
CUSKELLY, Eugene James, 1924- ,
Australian; nonfiction CON
CUSTANCE, Harry, 1842-1908,
English; nonfiction HIG
CUSTIS, George Washington Parke,
1781-1857, American; plays
KAA
CUTFORTH, John Ashlin ('John
Ashlin'), 1911- , English;
nonfiction CON
'CUTHBERT, Fr.' (Anthony Hess),
1866-1939, English; nonfiction
HOE
CUTHBERT, Clifton, 1907- ,
American; fiction CON
CUTHBERT, Diana Daphne Holman-
Hunt, 1913- , English; fiction,
nonfiction CON
CUTHBERT, Eleanora Isabel Mc-
Kenzie, 1902- , Australian;
nonfiction CON
'CUTHBERT, Mary' see HELLWIG,
Monika K.
CUTLER, Ann, American; juveniles
WA
CUTLER, Bruce, 1930- , Ameri-
can; nonfiction CON
CUTLER, Carl Custer, 1878- ,
American; nonfiction CON
CUTLER, Donald R., 1930- ,
American; nonfiction CON
CUTLER, Irving, H., 1923- ,
American; nonfiction CON
CUTLER, Ivor ('Knifesmith'),

1923- , American; fiction,
poetry CON MUR
CUTLER, Katherine Noble, 1905- ,
American; nonfiction CON
CUTLER, Lizzie Petit, 1831-1902,
American; fiction KAA
'CUTLER, Samuel' see FOLSOM,
Franklin B.
CUTLIP, Scott M., 1915- , Ameri-
can; nonfiction CON
CUTRIGHT, Phillips, 1930- ,
American; nonfiction CON
CUTSHALL, Alden, 1911- , Ameri-
can; nonfiction CON
CUTTER, Donald Colgett, 1922- ,
American; nonfiction CON
CUTTER, George Washington, 1801-
65, American; poetry KAA
CUTTINO, George Peddy, 1914- ,
American; nonfiction CON
CUTTLER, Charles David, 1913- ,
American; nonfiction CON
CUTTS, Richard, 1923- , American;
nonfiction CON
CUVELLIER see CAVELLIER
CUVIER, Georges Léopold Chrétien
Frédéric Dagobert, 1769-1832,
French; nonfiction DIF
CUYLER, Louise E., 1908- ,
American; nonfiction CON
'CUYLER, Stephen' see BATES,
Barbara S.
CVETAEVA, Marina I. see TSVETA-
YEVA, Marina I.
CWOJDZINSKI, Antoni, 1896- ,
Polish; plays MAT
CYKLER, Edmund Albert, 1903- ,
American; nonfiction CON
'CYNAN' see EVANS-JONES, Albert
CYNDDELW BRYDYDD MAWR,
1155-1200, Welsh; poetry ST
CYNEWULF, 8th cent., English;
poetry BRO KB SA ST
CYNTHIUS, see GIRALDI, Giovanni B.
'CYPHER, Angela' see SEIFFERT,
Marjorie A.
CYPRIAN, Caecilius Cyprianus,
200-58, Roman; nonfiction SA
ST
CYRANO de BERGERAC, Hector
Savinien, 1619-55, French; fic-
tion DIF HAR KE MAL SA ST
CYRIL, Saint, 372-444, Greek; non-
fiction SA
CYRIL, Saint, 826/27-69, Byzantine;
nonfiction ST
CYRIL, Bishop of Turov, fl. 1150,

Russian; nonfiction ST
CYRIL of ALEXANDRIA, -444,
Greek; nonfiction ST
CYRIL of JERUSALEM, 313-86,
Greek; nonfiction ST
CYRIL of SCYTHOPOLIS, 6th cent.,
Greek; nonfiction ST
CZAJKOWSKI, Michal, 1804-86,
Polish; fiction ST
CZARTORYSKI, Adam Jerzy,
1770-1861, Polish; poetry
ST
CZASZKA, Tomasz see RITTNER,
Tadeusz
'CZEPIEL, Adam' see BRZOZOW-
SKI, Leopold S. L.
CZEPKO von REIGERSFELD,
Daniel, 1605-60, German;
nonfiction AL ST
CZERNIAWSKI, Adam, 1934- ,
Polish-English; nonfiction
CON
CZIBULKA, Alfons Freiherr von,
1888- , German; nonfiction
LEN
CZOBAR, Agnes, 1920- , Hun-
garian; nonfiction CON

D

'D. W. N.', English; poetry HIG
'DAALBERG, Bruno' (Petrus de
Wakker van Zon), 1758-1818,
Dutch; fiction, essays ST
DAANE, James, 1914- , Ameri-
can; nonfiction CON
DAARMASENA, fl. 1250, Sinhalese;
poetry LAN
DABBS, Jack Autrey, 1914- ,
American; nonfiction CON
DABBS, James McBride, 1896- ,
American; nonfiction CON
DABIR, 1803-75, Indian; poetry
ST
DABIT, Eugène, 1898-1936,
French; fiction COL DIF FLE
HAR SA ST
DABNEY, Richard, 1787-1825,
American; poetry KAA
DABNEY, Ross H., 1934- ,
American; nonfiction CON
DABNEY, Virginius, 1835-94,
American; fiction KAA
DABNEY, Virginus, 1901- ,
American; nonfiction, journal-
ism KTS

DABNEY, William Minor, 1919- ,
American; nonfiction CON

DABOVE, Santiago, 1889- , Argentinian; fiction MIN

D'ABREU, Gerald Joseph, 1916- ,
American; nonfiction CON

DABROWSKA, Marja Szumska, 1892-
1966, Polish; fiction, plays COL
FLE SA ST

DA CAL, Ernesto Guerra, 1911- ,
Spanish; poetry BL CON

DACEY, Norman Franklyn, 1908- ,
American; nonfiction CON

DACEY, Philip, 1939- , American;
poetry CON

DACH, Simon, 1605-59, German;
poetry AL ST

DACIER, André, 1651-1722, French;
nonfiction DIL

DACIER, Anne Tanneguy Lefebvre,
1647-1720, French; translations
DIF DIL HAR SA

DACIER, Bon Joseph, 1742-1833,
French; nonfiction SA

DA COSTA, Isaac, 1798-1860, Dutch;
poetry HAR KE SA ST

DACHKOVA, Catalina Romanov, 1743-
1810, Russian; nonfiction SA

DA CRUZ, Daniel, Jr., 1921- ,
American; nonfiction CON

DADIE, Bernard Binlin, 1916- ,
African; nonfiction, poetry CON

DAEHLIN, Reidar A., 1910- ,
American; nonfiction CON

DAEM, Thelma Mary Bannerman,
1914- , Canadian; juveniles
CON

DAEMS, Servaas, 1838-1903, Flemish;
poetry, plays ST

DAETEN, Pieter see DATHENUS,
Petrus

DÄUBLER, Theodor, 1876-1934, Austrian; poetry AL COL FLE KU
KUN

DAFOE, John Wesley, 1866-1944,
Canadian; journalism ST

DAFYDD AB EDMWND, fl. 1450-
80, Welsh; poetry ST

DAFYDD AP GWILYM, fl. 1340-70,
Welsh; poetry SA ST

DAFYDD NANMOR, fl. 1450-80,
Welsh; poetry ST

DAGAN, Avigdor ('Viktor Fischl'),
1912- , Czech-Norwegian;
poetry CON

DAGERMAN, Stig Halvard, 1923-54,
Swedish; fiction, plays FLE

HAR MAT ST

'DAGONET' see SIMS, George R.

D'AGOSTINO, Angelo, 1926- ,
American; nonfiction CON

D'AGOSTINO, Guido, 1906- ,
American; fiction WAF

DAGUET, Pierre Antoine Alexandre,
1707-75, French; nonfiction
DIL

DAHL, Borghild, 1890- , American; juveniles, nonfiction, fiction CON WA

DAHL, Curtis, 1920- , American;
nonfiction CON

DAHL, Murdoch Edgcumbe, 1914- ,
English; nonfiction CON

DAHL, Roald, 1916- , Welsh;
juveniles COM CON WA

DAHL, Ronald Albin, 1938- ,
American; poetry MUR

DAHL, Vladimir Ivanovich ('Kazak
Lugansky'), 1801-72, Russian;
nonfiction, fiction HARK ST

DAHLBERG, Edward, 1900- ,
American; fiction CON KTS
RIC

DAHLBERG, Edwin, 1892- ,
American; nonfiction CON

DAHLBERG, Jane S., 1923- ,
American; nonfiction CON

DAHLGREN, Frederik August,
1816-95, Swedish; nonfiction
ST

DAHLGREN, Sarah Madeleine
Vinton, 1825-98, American;
nonfiction KAA

DAHLSTIERNA, Gunno, 1661-
1707, Swedish; poetry ST

DAHLSTROM, Earl Carl, 1914- ,
American; nonfiction CON

DAHMUS, Joseph Henry, 1909- ,
American; nonfiction CON

DAHN, Julius Sophus Felix, 1834-
1912, German; fiction, poetry
AL HAR ST

DAHOOD, Mitchell, 1920- ,
American; translations CON

DAHRENDORF, Ralf, 1929- ,
American; nonfiction CON

DAICHES, David, 1912- , English;
nonfiction, criticism BRO
CON KTS

DAIGON, Arthur, 1928- , American; nonfiction CON

DAIKEN, Leslie Herbert, 1912- ,
Irish; nonfiction CON

DAILY, Jay Elwood, 1923- ,

American; nonfiction CON

DAIN, Martin J., 1924- , American;
nonfiction CON

DAIN, Norman, 1925- , American;
nonfiction CON

'DAINI NO SAMMI' (Fujiwara No
Kataho), 1000-50, Japanese;
poetry ST

DAINTON, William Courtney, 1920- ,
English; nonfiction CON

DAIRE, Louis François, 1713-92,
French; nonfiction DIL

DAIREAUX, Godofredo, 1839-1916,
Argentinian; fiction MIN

'DAISNE, Johan' (Herman Thiery),
1912- , Belgian; poetry, fiction,
essays, criticism, translations
FLE MAT ST

DAIUTE, Robert James, 1926- ,
American; nonfiction CON

DAK, Indian; essays LAN

DAKHOW see DIHKHODA, Ali A.

DAKIN, David Julian, 1939- ,
English; nonfiction CON

DALAND, Robert Theodore, 1919- ,
American; nonfiction CON

DALBERG, John E.E. see ACTON,
Lord

DALBOR, John Bronislaw, 1929- ,
American; nonfiction CON

D'ALCAMO, Cielo, 13th cent.,
Italian; poetry ST

DALCOURT, Gerald J., 1927- ,
American; nonfiction CON

DALE, Celia Marjorie, 1912- ,
English; nonfiction CON

DALE, Dion Murray Crosbie,
1930- , American; nonfiction
CON

DALE, Edward Everett, 1879- ,
American; nonfiction CON MAR

DALE, Ernest, 1917- , American;
nonfiction CON

'DALE, Jack' see HOLLIDAY, Jack

DALE, James, 1886- , English;
plays CON

DALE, Jan van den, 1460-1522,
Dutch; poetry ST

DALE, John B., 1905- , American;
nonfiction CON

DALE, Magdalene Larsen, 1904- ,
American; nonfiction CON

DALE, Margaret Jessy Miller
('Margaret J. Miller'), 1911- ,
Scots; fiction, nonfiction CON

DALE, Paul Worthen, 1923- , American; nonfiction CON

DALE, Peter, 1938- , English;
poetry MUR

DALE, Reginald R., 1907- ,
English; nonfiction CON

DALE, Richard, 1932- , American; nonfiction CON

DALE, Ruth Bluestone, American;
juveniles WA

DALE, Thomas F., 1923- ,
English; nonfiction HIG

D'ALELIO, Ellen F., 1938- ,
American; nonfiction CON

D'ALEMBERT, Jean L. see ALEM-
BERT, Jean L. D'

DALENCE, Sebastián, 19th cent.,
Bolivian; fiction MIN

DALESKI, Hillel Matthew, 1926- ,
South African; nonfiction CON

'DALESMAN' see COURCY-PARRY,
Charles N. de

DALEY, Arthur John, 1904- ,
American; nonfiction CON

DALEY, Robert, 1930- , American; nonfiction CON

DALEY, Victor James William
Patrick, 1858-1905, Australian;
poetry ST

DAL FABRO, Beniamino, 1910- ,
Italian; criticism SA

DALFIN d'ALVERNHA (Dauphin
D'Auvergne), 1167-1235,
French; poetry ST

D'ALFONSO, John, 1918- ,
American; nonfiction CON

DALFIUME, Richard Myron,
1936- , American; nonfiction
CON

DALGADO, Sebastian Rodolfo,
1855-1922, Portuguese; nonfiction SA

DALGLIESH, Alice, 1893- ,
English; juveniles KJU WA

DALGLISH, Edward Russell,
1913- , American; nonfiction
CON

DALIBARD, Thomas François,
1703-79, French; translations
DIL

'DALIMIL', 14th cent., Czech;
nonfiction ST

DALIN, Olof von, 1703/08-63,
Swedish; poetry, plays HAR
KE SA ST

'D'ALLARD, Hunter' see BALLARD,
Willis T.

DALLAS, Eneas Sweetland, 1828-
79, English; nonfiction KBA

DALLAS, Ruth, 1919- , New
Zealander; poetry MUR
DALLAS, Sandra see ATCHISON,
Sandra D.
'DALLAS, Vincent' see WERNER,
Victor
DALLEK, Robert, 1934- , Ameri-
can; nonfiction CON
DALLIN, Alexander, 1924- ,
German-American; nonfiction
CON
DALLIN, David Julievich, 1889- ,
Russian-American; nonfiction
KTS
DALLIN, Leon, 1918- , American;
nonfiction CON
DALLING and BULWER, William
Henry Lytton Earle Bulwer,
1801-72, English; nonfiction
BRO ST
DALLMANN, Martha Elsie, 1904- ,
American; nonfiction CON
DALL'ONGARO, Francesco, 1808-73,
Italian; poetry, plays HAR ST
DALLY, Ann Mullins, 1926- ,
English; nonfiction CON
DALMAS, Henry see DELMAS, Henry
DALPATRAM DAHYABHAI, 1820-98,
Indian; poetry LAN
DALRYMPLE, Sir David see HAILES
DALRYMPLE, Jean, 1910- , Amer-
ican; fiction, plays CON
DALRYMPLE, Willard, 1921- ,
American; nonfiction CON
D'ALTENHEYM, Gabrielle, 1814-
86, French; poetry SA
'DALTON, Clive' see CLARK,
Frederick S.
DALTON, Dorothy see KUEHN,
Dorothy D.
DALTON, Gene Wray, 1928- ,
American; nonfiction CON
DALTON, John, 1766-1844, English;
nonfiction KBA ST
D'ALTON, Rev. John, 1882- ,
Irish; nonfiction HO
'DALTON, Priscilla' see AVALLONE,
Michael A., Jr.
DALVEN, Rae, 1904- , Greek-
American; nonfiction, plays CON
DALY, Anne, 1896- , Irish; juven-
iles, plays CON
DALY, Augustin see DALY, John A.
DALY, Charles Patrick, 1816-99,
American; nonfiction KAA
DALY, Elizabeth, 1878-1967, Amer-
ican; fiction CON KTS

DALY, Emily Joseph, 1913- ,
American; nonfiction CON
DALY, James, J., 1872- ,
American; nonfiction, poetry
HOE
'DALY, Jim' see STRATEMEYER,
Edward L.
DALY, John Augustin, 1838-99,
American; plays KAA MAT
DALY, Lowrie John, 1914- ,
American; nonfiction CON
DALY, Martin see MacKENNA,
Stephen
DALY, Mary, 1928- , American;
nonfiction CON
DALY, Sister Mary Virgene,
1925- , American; nonfiction
CON
DALY, Maureen McGivern,
1921- , American; juveniles
COM CON FUL HOE WA WAF
DALY, Robert Welter, 1916- ,
American; nonfiction, fiction
CON
DALY, Sheila John, 1927- ,
American; fiction, nonfiction
HO WA
DALY, Thomas Augustine, 1871- ,
1948, American; journalism,
poetry HOE
DALZEL, Job, Patrick ('Peter
Dalzel'), 1913- , English;
fiction CON
'DAM, J. van' see PRESSER,
Gerrit J.
DAMA HENARD, Juan Jose, 1805-
70, Spanish; translations BL
DAMACIO, 480/90- , Greek;
nonfiction SA
DAMARADAGUPTA, 8th cent.,
Indian; poetry SA
DAMASO, San,   -384, Spanish;
poetry SA
D'AMATO, Anthony A., 1937- ,
American; nonfiction CON
DAMAZ, Paul F., 1917- ,
American; nonfiction CON
DAMBADORJ, Ts., 1899-1934,
Mongolian; fiction LAN
DAMBINSÜREN, Ts., 1908- ,
Mongolian; fiction LAN
D'AMBRA, Francesco, 1499-1558,
Italian; plays ST
'D'AMBRA, Lucio' (Renato Eduardo
Manganella), 1880-1940,
Italian; fiction, plays, journal-
ism HAR SA ST

D'AMBROSIO, Charles., 1932- ,
American; nonfiction CON
DAME, Lawrence ('Baron Pomfret'),
1898- , American; nonfiction,
fiction CON
DAMEL, Carlos, 1890- , Argentinian;
nonfiction MIN
D'AMELIO, Dan, 1927- , Italian-
American; nonfiction CON
DAMIRON, Jean Philibert, 1794-1862,
French; nonfiction SA
DAMERON, Rafael, 1882- , Domini-
can; poetry, fiction, plays MIN
SA
DAMERST, William A., 1923- ,
American; nonfiction CON
DAMIANO, Laila see ROSENKRANTZ,
Linda
DAMLE, Indian; poetry LAN
DAMM, Christian Tobias, 1699-1778,
German; nonfiction SA
DAMM, John S., 1926- , American;
nonfiction CON
DAMON, Samuel Foster, 1893- ,
American; poetry, nonfiction KL
SA
DAMON, Virgil Green, 1895-1972,
American; nonfiction CON
DAMPIER, William, 1652-1715,
English; nonfiction BRO KB
DAMPIER, Sir William Cecil, 1867-
1952, British; nonfiction KTS
DANA, Barbara, 1940- , American;
juvenile CON
DANA, Charles Anderson, 1819-97,
American; nonfiction KAA
DANA, James Dwight, 1813-95,
American; nonfiction KAA
DANA, Marshall Newport, 1885-
1966, American; journalism,
nonfiction PAC
DANA, Richard Henry, 1787-1879,
American; poetry, criticism
BRO KAA SA ST
DANA, Richard Henry, 1815-82,
American; nonfiction BRO KAA
MAG SA ST
DANA, Robert, 1929- , American;
poetry CON MUR
DANACHAIR, Caoimhin O. see
DANAHER, Kevin
DANAGHER, Edward F., 1919- ,
American; fiction CON
DANAHER, Kevin ('Caoimhin O
Danachair'), 1913- , Irish;
nonfiction CON
DANBY, Hope Smedley, 1899- ,

English; nonfiction CON
DANBY, Miles William, 1925- ,
English; nonfiction CON
DANCE, Edward Herbert,
1894- , English; nonfiction
CON
DANCE, Francis Esburn Xavier
(Frank), 1929- , American;
nonfiction CON
DANCE, Stanley Frank, 1910- ,
English; nonfiction CON
DANCER, John, fl. 1675, Irish;
translations, plays ST
DANCHET, Antoine, 1671-1748,
French; nonfiction DIL
D'ANCONA, Alessandro, 1835-
1914, Italian; nonfiction SA
ST
DANCOURT, Florent Carton,
1661-1725, French; plays DIF
DIL HAR KE ST
DANCOURT, L.H., 1725-1801,
French; plays DIL
DANDIN, 7th cent., Indian; poetry,
fiction LAN SA ST
DANDRE-BARDON, Michel
François, 1700-78, French;
nonfiction DIL
'DANE, Carl' see ADAMS, Frank
R.
'DANE, Clemence' see ASHTON,
Winifred
'DANE, Mark' see AVALLONE,
Michael A., Jr.
DANELSKI, David J., 1930- ,
American; nonfiction CON
DANFORD, Howard G., 1904- ,
American; nonfiction CON
DANGEAU, Philippe de Courcillon,
1628-1720, French; nonfiction
DIF SA
D'ANGELO, Edward, 1932- ,
American; nonfiction CON
D'ANGELO, Luciano (Lou),
1932- , American; nonfiction,
fiction CON
'DANGERFIELD, Balfour' see
McCLOSKEY, Robert
'DANGERFIELD, Clint' see
NORWOOD, Victor G.C.
DANGERFIELD, George Bubb,
1904- , Anglo-American;
fiction CON
'DANGERFIELD, Harlan' see
GALLUP, Richard
'DANGERFIELD, Harlan' see
PADGETT, Ron

DANGERFIELD, Royden J., 1902- ,
American; nonfiction MAR

DANGEVILLE, Marie Anne Botot,
1714-96, French; plays DIL

DANHOF, Clarence Henry, 1911- ,
American; nonfiction CON

DANI, Ahmad Hasan, 1920- ,
Indian; nonfiction CON

DANIEL, 12th cent., Russian; nonfiction ST

DANIEL, Anita, Rumanian-American;
juveniles WA

DANIEL, Arnaut see ARNAUT,
Daniel

DANIEL, Elna Worrell, American;
nonfiction CON

DANIEL, Gabriel, 1649-1728,
French; nonfiction DIF

DANIEL, George, 1616-57, English;
poetry ST

DANIEL, George Bernard, Jr.,
1927- , American; nonfiction
CON

DANIEL, Glyn, 1914- , English;
nonfiction, fiction RIC

DANIEL, Hawthorne, 1890- ,
American; juveniles, fiction
CON KJU

DANIEL, Jerry Clayton, 1937- ,
American; nonfiction CON

DANIEL, Pete, 1938- , American;
nonfiction CON

DANIEL, Robert Leslie, 1923- ,
American; nonfiction CON

DANIEL, Robert Woodham, 1915- ,
American; poetry CON

DANIEL, Samuel, 1562-1619, English; poetry, plays, criticism
BRO KB SP SA ST

DANIEL, William Barker, 1753-
1833, English; nonfiction HIG

DANIEL, Yuri (Nikolay Arzak),
1926- , Russian; fiction RIC

DANIEL, Adam Z.V. see VELESLA-
VIN, Daniel A. Z.

DANIEL de PARIS,   -1746, French;
nonfiction DIL

'DANIEL von SOEST', fl. 1534-39,
German; nonfiction ST

DANIELL, Albert Scott ('David
Scott Daniell; 'Richard Bowood';
'John Lewesdon'), 1906-65,
English; fiction CON

DANIELL, Jere Rogers, 1932- ,
American; nonfiction CON

DANIELLS, Roy, 1902- , Canadian;
poetry, nonfiction MUR SY

DANIELOU, Jean, 1905- ,
French; nonfiction CON HO

'DANIEL-ROPS, Henry'
(Henry J. Petiot), 1901- ,
French; nonfiction, fiction
DIF FLE HO

DANIELS, Arlene Kaplan, 1930- ,
American; nonfiction CON

DANIELS, Elizabeth Adams,
1920- , American; nonfiction
CON

DANIELS, Farrington, 1889-1972,
American; nonfiction CON

DANIELS, George H., 1935- ,
American; nonfiction CON

DANIELS, George Morris,
1927- , American; nonfiction
CON

DANIELS, Guy, 1919- , American; juveniles, nonfiction CON

DANIELS, Harold, R., 1919- ,
American; nonfiction CON

DANIELS, John Clifford, 1915- ,
English; nonfiction CON

DANIELS, Jonathan, 1902- ,
American; nonfiction, journalism JO KT WA

DANIELS, Josephus, 1862-1948,
American; nonfiction JO

DANIELS, Robert Vincent,
1926- , American; nonfiction
CON

DANIELS, Roger, 1927- ,
American; nonfiction CON

DANIELS, Sally, 1931- , American; nonfiction CON

DANIELS, Steven Lloyd, 1945- ,
American; nonfiction CON

'DANIELS, Wayne' see OVER-
HOLSER, Wayne D.

DANIELSON, Michael Nils,
1934- , American; nonfiction
CON

DANIELSON, Richard Ely,
1885- , American; nonfiction
HIG

DANIERE, Andre Lucien, 1926- ,
American; nonfiction CON

DANIIL the Pilgrim, fl. 1106-08,
Russian; nonfiction HARK

DANIIL the Prisoner, 13th cent.,
Russian; nonfiction HARK

DANILEVSKY, Grigory Petrovich
('A. Skavronski'), 1829-90,
Russian; fiction HAR HARK
ST

DANILEVSKI, Nikolay Yakovlevich,

1822-85, Russian; nonfiction
HARK ST
DANILOV, Kirsha, 18th cent.,
Russian; poetry ST
DANILOV, Victor Joseph, 1924- ,
American; nonfiction CON
DANILOWSKI, Gustaw ('Wladyslaw
Orwid'), 1872-1927, Polish;
fiction, poetry ST
DANINOS, Pierre, 1913- , French;
fiction DIC DIF RIC
'DANKE, Jacobo' see CABRERA,
Juan
DANKER, Frederich William,
1920- , American; nonfiction
CON
DANKER, William John, 1914- ,
American; nonfiction CON
DANN, Uriel, 1920- , German-
Israeli; nonfiction CON
DANNAY, Frederic ('Ellery Queen';
'Barnaby Ross'; 'Daniel Nathan'),
1905- , American; fiction BRO
CON KT RIC WA
DANNEMILLER, Lawrence, 1925- ,
American; nonfiction CON
DANNENBERGER, Hermann see
'REGER, Erik'
DANNENFELDT, Karl Henry,
1916- , American; nonfiction
CON
DANNER, Margaret Essie (Cunning-
ham), 1915- , American;
poetry CON MUR
DANNETT, Sylvia G. L., 1909- ,
American; nonfiction, fiction
CON
DANNUNZIO, Gabrielo, 1863-1938,
Italian; poetry, fiction, plays
COL FLE HAR KL KT MAG
MAT RIC SA ST
DANOU, Pierre Claude François,
1761-1840, French; nonfiction
SA
DANOWSKI, Thaddeus, S., 1914- ,
American; nonfiction CON
DANSKA, Herbert, 1928- , Ameri-
can; juveniles, plays CON
DANTAS, Júlio, 1876-1962, Portu-
guese; plays, poetry, journalism
COL FLE HAR SA ST
DANTE ALIGHIERI, 1265-1321,
Italian; poetry HAR KE SA ST
DANTE da MAIANO, 13th cent.,
Italian; poetry ST
DANTIN, Louis, 1865-1945, Canadian;
nonfiction SY

DANTINE, Maur François,
1688- , French; nonfiction
DIL
'DANTISCUS, Joannes de Curiis'
(Flachsbinder), 1485-1548,
Polish; poetry ST
DANTO, Arthur Coleman, 1924- ,
American; nonfiction CON
DANTON, Georges Jacques,
1759-94, French; nonfiction
DIL
DANTON, Joseph Periam, 1908- ,
American; nonfiction CON
'DANVERS, Jack' see CASELEYR,
Camille A. M.
DANVILA, Alfonso, 1876/79- ,
Spanish; fiction BL COL SA
DANZIG, Allison, 1898- ,
American; nonfiction CON
DANZIGER, Marlies Kallmann,
1926- , American; nonfiction
CON
DAON, Roger François, 1678-
1749, French; nonfiction DIL
DAPHNE, Greek; poetry SA
'DA PONTE, Lorenzo' (Emanuele
Conegliano), 1749-1838,
Italian; poetry HAR ST
DA PORTO, Luigi, 1485-1529,
Italian; poetry HAR ST
DAPPER, Gloria, 1922- , Ameri-
can; nonfiction CON
D'APRIX, Roger M., 1932- ,
American; nonfiction CON
DAQIQI, -975, Persian; poetry
LAN
DAQIQI of TUS, Abu Mansur
Muhammad, -952, Persian;
poetry ST
DARANAS ROMERO, Mariano,
1897- , Spanish; essays,
journalism SA
DARBELNET, Jean Louis,
1904- , French; nonfiction
CON
D'ARBLAY, Frances see BURNEY,
Frances
DARBY, Ada Claire, 1883- ,
American; juveniles WA
DARBY, Gene Kegley, 1921- ,
American; nonfiction CON
DARBY, Henry Clifford, 1909- ,
Welsh; nonfiction CON
'DARBY, J. N.' see GOVAN,
Christine N.
DARBY, Patricia Paulsen, Amer-
ican; juveniles WA

DARBY, Raymond, 1912- ,
American; juveniles CON WA

DARBY, William, 1775-1854,
American; nonfiction KAA

DARCET, Jean (d'Arcet), 1725-1801,
French; nonfiction DIL

D'ARCH SMITH, Timothy, 1936- ,
English; nonfiction CON

D'ARCY, G. Minot, 1930- , American; nonfiction CON

D'ARCY, Martin, Cyril, 1888- ,
English; nonfiction CON HOE

D'ARCY, Paul Francis, 1921- ,
American; nonfiction CON

DAREAU, François, 1736-83/84,
French; poetry DIL

DAREFF, Hal, American; juveniles
WA

DAREGRAND,   -1771, French;
fiction DIL

DARES PHRYGIUS, Greek; nonfiction ST

DARESTE de la CHAVANNE, Antoine
Elisabeth Cléophas, 1820-82,
French; nonfiction DIF

'D'ARFY, William' see PLOMER,
William C. F.

DARGAN, Olive Tilford ('Fielding
Burke'), American; poetry,
fiction, plays JO KT WAF

'DARIEN, Peter' see BASSETT,
William B. K.

'DARING, Hope' (Anna Johnson),
1860-1943, American; fiction
HIL

DARINGER, Helen Fern, 1892- ,
American; juveniles COM CON
FUL

DARIO, Rubén, 1867-1916, Nicaraguan; poetry BL FLE KT KAT
RIC SA ST

DARK, Eleanor O'Reilly, 1901- ,
Australian; fiction KTS RIC ST

'DARK, Johnny' see NORWOOD,
Victor G. C.

DARLEY, George, 1795-1846, Irish;
poetry, fiction, criticism BRO
KBA SA SP ST

DARLING, Arthur Burr, 1892-1971,
American; nonfiction CON

DARLING, Frank Clayton, 1925- ,
American; nonfiction CON

DARLING, Lois MacIntyre, 1917- ,
American; juvenile CON WA

DARLING, Louis, 1916-70, American; juveniles CON FUL WA

DARLING, Richard Lewis, 1925- ,

American; nonfiction CON

DARLINGTON, Alice Benning,
1906- , American; nonfiction
CON

DARLINGTON, Charles F.,
1904- , American; nonfiction
CON

DARLINGTON, Cyril Dean,
1903- , English; nonfiction
CON

DARLINGTON, George E.,   -1901,
American; nonfiction HIG

DARLINGTON, William Aubrey
Cecil, 1890- , English; fiction CON

'DARLTON, Clark' see ERNSTING,
Walter

DARROCH, Maurice A., 1903- ,
American; nonfiction CON

DARROW, Clarence Seward, 1857-
1938, American; nonfiction
HOO KT

DARROW, Richard William,
1915- , American; nonfiction
CON

DART, Raymond Arthur, 1893- ,
Australian; nonfiction CON

DARTHES, Camilo, 1889- ,
Argentinian; plays MIN

DARUWALLA, Keki Nasserwanji,
1937- , Indian; poetry MUR

DARWIN, Charles, 1809-82,
English; nonfiction BRO KBA
MAG SA ST

DARWEIN, Erasmus, 1731-1802,
English; poetry BRO KB SA
ST

DARY, David A., 1934- ,
American; nonfiction CON

DAS, Deb Kumar, 1935- , Indian;
poetry MUR

DAS, Durga, 1900- , Indian; nonfiction CON

DAS, Gurcharan, 1943- , Indian;
plays CON

DAS, Kamala ('Madhavikutty'),
1934- , Indian; poetry, fiction MUR

DAS, Manmath Nath, 1926- ,
Indian; nonfiction CON

DASENT, Sir George Webbe,
1817-96, English; juveniles,
nonfiction, translations BRO
DOY KBA ST

DASH, Tony, 1945- , English;
nonfiction CON

DASHKOVA, Ekaterina Romanovna

(Daschkova), 1743-1810, Russian;
plays HAR SA ST
DASHTI, 1895- , Persian; nonfiction
LAN
DASHWOOD, Robert Julian ('Julian
Hillas'), 1899- , English; fic-
tion CON
DASMANN, Raymond Frederic,
1919- , American; nonfiction
CON
DASS, Petter, 1647-1707/08,
Norwegian; poetry, hymns HAR
KE ST
DATHENUS, Petrus (Pieter Daeten;
Daets), 1531/32-88, Dutch;
poetry ST
DATHORNE, Oscar Ronald, 1934- ,
British; poetry, fiction MUR
DATI, Agostino, 1420-78, Italian;
nonfiction SA
DATI, Carlo Huberti, 1619-76,
Italian; nonfiction SA
DATI, Gregorio, 1362-1435, Italian;
nonfiction SA ST
DATI, Guluano, 1445-1524, Italian;
poetry ST
DATI, Leonardo di Piero, 1408-72,
Italian; poetry ST
DATTA, Michael Madhusudan, 1824-
73, Indian; poetry, plays LAN
DAUBE, David, 1909- , American;
nonfiction CON
DAUBENTON, Guillaume, 1648-1723,
French; nonfiction DIL
DAUBENTON, Louis Jean Marie,
1716-1800, French; nonfiction
DIL
D'AUBIGNE see AUBIGNE
DAUD, Mautana, 14th cent., Indian;
poetry LAN
DAUDE, Pierre, 1654-1733, French;
nonfiction DIL
DAUDET, Alphonse, 1840-97, French;
fiction, poetry, plays COL DIF
HAR KE MAG MAL SA
DAUDET, Ernest, 1837-1921, French;
fiction, nonfiction, poetry SA
DAUDET, Léon, 1867-1942, French;
fiction, journalism COL DIF
FLE HAR SA ST
DAUDET, Louis, 1840-97, French;
fiction ST
DAUER, Dorothea, 1917- , German-
American; nonfiction CON
DAUER, Victor Paul, 1909- ,
American; nonfiction CON
DAUGERT, Matthew Stanley, 1918- ,

American; nonfiction CON
DAUGHEN, Joseph Robert,
1935- , American; nonfiction
CON
DAUGHERTY, Anne Scott, 1920- ,
American; nonfiction CON
DAUGHERTY, Charles Michael,
1914- , American; juveniles
WA
DAUGHERTY, James Henry,
1889- , American; juveniles
KJU WA
D'AULAIRE, Edgar Parin see
AULAIRE, Edgar P.
DAULAT, Kazi, 17th cent.,
Indian; poetry LAN
D'AULNOY, Countess, 1649-1705,
French; juveniles DOY
DAUMAL, René, 1908-44, French;
poetry DIF FLE MAL
DAUMANN, Rudolf H., 1896-
1957, German; nonfiction
AL
DAUPHINE, Rev. John W.,
1910- , American; nonfiction
SCA
DAURAT, Jean see DORAT, Jean
D'AUREVILLY, Jules A. B. see
BARBEY, D'Aurevilly, Jules
A.
DAUTEN, Carl Anton, 1913- ,
American; nonfiction CON
DAUTHENDEY, Maximilian, 1867-
1918, German; poetry, fiction,
plays AL COL FLE HAR SA
DAUTZENBERG, Johan Michel,
1808-69, Flemish; poetry ST
D'AUVERGNE, Dauphin see DAFFIN
D'ALVERNHA
DAVALOS, Juan Carlos, 1887- ,
Argentinian; poetry, plays
MIN SA
DAVANZATI, Bernardo, 1529-
1606, Italian; poetry ST
DAVANZATI, Chiaro, 123/40-80?,
Florentine; poetry SA ST
DAVANZATI BOSTICHI, Bernardo,
1562-1606, Italian; nonfiction
SA
DAVELUY, Paule Cloutier, 1919- ,
Canadian; nonfiction, fiction
CON
DAVENANT, Sir William, 1606-
68, English; plays, poetry
BRO KB MAG SA SP ST
'DAVENPORT, Francine' see
TATE, Velma

DAVENPORT, Gene Looney, 1935- ,
American; nonfiction CON
DAVENPORT, Guy Mattison Jr.
('Max Montgomery'), 1927- ,
American; nonfiction CON
DAVENPORT, Gwen, 1910- , Amer-
ican; juveniles, fiction CON
DAVENPORT, Marcia, 1903- , Amer-
ican; fiction, juvenile CON KTS
WA WAF
DAVENPORT, Robert, fl. 1623,
English; plays, poetry KB
'DAVENPORT, Spencer' see STRATE-
MEYER, Edward L.
DAVENPORT, William Bromley,
1821-84, English; nonfiction HIG
DAVENPORT, William H., 1908- ,
American; nonfiction CON
DAVENTRY, Leonard John, 1915- ,
English; fiction CON
DAVES, Michael, 1938- , American;
nonfiction CON
DAVESNE, Bertin, 18th cent., French;
plays DIL
DAVEY, Cyril James, 1911- ,
English; nonfiction, plays CON
DAVEY, Frank, 1940- , Canadian;
poetry MUR
DAVEY, Gilbert Walter, 1913- ,
English; nonfiction CON
DAVIAULT, Pierre, 1899- ,
Canadian; nonfiction SY
DAVID, Anne, 1924- , American;
nonfiction CON
DAVID, Claude, 1664-1705, French;
nonfiction DIL
'DAVID, Emily' see ALMAN, David
DAVID, Eugene, American; juveniles
WA
DAVID, Heather MacKinnon, 1937- ,
American; nonfiction CON
DAVID, Henry P., 1923- , German-
American; nonfiction CON
DAVID, Jakob Julius, 1859-1906,
German; nonfiction AL
DAVID, Kurt, 1924- , German;
nonfiction AL
DAVID, Lester, 1914- , American;
nonfiction CON
DAVID, Martin Heidenheim, 1935- ,
Dutch-American; nonfiction CON
'DAVID, Nicholas' see MORGAN,
Thomas B.
DAVID, Paul Theodore, 1906- ,
American; nonfiction CON
DAVID, Stephen Mark, 1934- ,
American; nonfiction CON

'DAVID, William' see SANDMAN,
Peter M.
DAVID de DINANT, -1215,
French; nonfiction SA
DAVID KIMCHI see KIMCHI, David
DAVID of AUGSBURG, -1272,
German; nonfiction ST
DAVIDESCU, Neculai, 1888- ,
Rumanian; poetry ST
DAVIDOV, Dionisio Vassilievitch;
1784-1839, Russian; poetry
SA
DAVIDS, Jennifer, 1945- , South
African; poetry MUR
DAVIDS, Lewis Edmund, 1917- ,
American; nonfiction CON
DAVIDSOHN, Hans see 'HODDIS,
Jakob van'
DAVIDSON, Alastair, 1939- ,
Australian; nonfiction CON
DAVIDSON, Andrew Bruce, 1831-
1902, Scots; nonfiction KBA
DAVIDSON, Angus Henry Gordon,
1898- , English; nonfiction
CON
DAVIDSON, Avram, 1923- ,
American; fiction CON
DAVIDSON, Basil, 1914- , Eng-
lish; fiction, nonfiction CON
DAVIDSON, Bill, American; juven-
iles WA
DAVIDSON, Chalmers Gaston,
1907- , American; nonfiction
CON JO
DAVIDSON, David Albert, 1908- ,
American; fiction KTS WAF
DAVIDSON, Diane, 1924- , Amer-
ican; fiction CON
DAVIDSON, Donald Grady, 1893-
1968, American; nonfiction,
poetry, essays CON KT
DAVIDSON, Ephraim Edward,
1923- , American; nonfiction
DAVIDSON, Eugene Arthur, 1902- ,
American; nonfiction CON
DAVIDSON, Frank Geoffrey, 1920- ,
English; nonfiction CON
DAVIDSON, Herbert A., 1932- ,
American; nonfiction CON
DAVIDSON, Hilda Roderick Ellis,
1914- , English; nonfiction
CON
DAVIDSON, James Wood, 1827-1905,
American; nonfiction KAA
DAVIDSON, John, 1549?-1603,
Scots; poetry KB

DAVIDSON, John, 1857-1909, Scots;
poetry, plays, fiction BRO
KBA SP ST
DAVIDSON, Lionel, 1922- , Eng-
lish; nonfiction, fiction, movies
CON
DAVIDSON, Lucrece Mary, 1808- ,
American; poetry SA
DAVIDSON, Margaret, 1936- ,
American; juveniles CON
DAVIDSON, Marshall Bowman,
1907- , American; nonfiction
CON
DAVIDSON, Mary R., 1885- ,
American; nonfiction CON
DAVIDSON, Michael Childers, 1896- ,
English; nonfiction CON
DAVIDSON, Mickie Compere, 1936- ,
American; nonfiction CON
DAVIDSON, Paul, 1930- , American;
nonfiction CON
DAVIDSON, Roger Harry, 1936- ,
American; nonfiction CON
DAVIDSON, Sol M., 1924- ,
American; nonfiction CON
DAVIDSON, Thomas, 1840-1900,
Scots; nonfiction KBA KAA
DAVIDSON, William Robert, 1919- ,
American; nonfiction CON
DAVIDSON-HAUSTON, James Vivian,
1901-65, Irish; nonfiction CON
DAVIE, Donald Alfred, 1922- ,
British; poetry, criticism CON
MUR RIC
DAVIE, Maurice Rea, 1893-1964,
American; nonfiction CON
DAVIED, Camille see ROSE,
Camille D.
DAVIES, Ada Hilton, 1893- ,
American; poetry CON
DAVIES, Alan Trewartha, 1933- ,
Canadian; nonfiction CON
DAVIES, Alfred Mervyn, 1899- ,
English; nonfiction CON
DAVIES, Alfred Thomas, 1930- ,
American; nonfiction CON
DAVIES, Daniel R., 1911- ,
American; nonfiction CON
DAVIES, David ('Ivor Novello'),
1893-1951, English; plays
BRO KTS MAT RIC
DAVIES, David Ioan, 1936- ,
English; nonfiction CON
DAVIES, David Jacob, 1916- ,
American; nonfiction CON
DAVIES, David Margerison ('David
Margerison'), 1923- , Welsh;

nonfiction CON
DAVIES, David William, 1908- ,
Canadian; nonfiction CON
DAVIES, E. W. L., 1840- ,
English; nonfiction HIG
DAVIES, Ebenezer Thomas,
1903- , Welsh; nonfiction
CON
DAVIES, Edward Tegla, 1880- ,
Welsh; fiction, essays ST
DAVIES, Eileen Winifred ('Eileen
Elias'), 1910- , English;
nonfiction CON
DAVIES, George Colliss Board-
man, 1912- , American; non-
fiction CON
DAVIES, Horton Marlais, 1916- ,
Welsh; nonfiction CON
DAVIES, J. Clarence III, 1937- ,
American; nonfiction CON
DAVIES, Sir John, 1569-1626,
English; poetry KB SP ST
DAVIES, John Gordon, 1919- ,
English; nonfiction CON
DAVIES, John of Hereford, 1565?-
1618, English; poetry BRO
KB ST
DAVIES, John Paton, Jr., 1908- ,
American; nonfiction CON
DAVIES, Leslie Purnell ('Leo
Berne'; 'Robert Blake';
'Richard Bridgeman'; 'Morgan
Evans'; 'Ian Jefferson';
'Lawrence Peters'; 'Thomas
Philips'; 'G. K. Thomas';
'Leslie Vardre'; 'Rowland
Welch'), 1914- , American;
fiction CON
DAVIES, Mansel Morris, 1913- ,
Welsh; nonfiction CON
DAVIES, Margaret Constance
Brown, 1923- , English;
fiction CON
DAVIES, Morton Rees, 1939- ,
Welsh; nonfiction CON
DAVIES, Oliver, 1905- , English;
nonfiction CON
DAVIES, Pennar, 1911- , Welsh;
poetry, fiction CON
DAVIES, Reginald Thorne, 1923- ,
English; nonfiction CON
DAVIES, Rhys, 1903- , Welsh;
fiction BRO CON KTS ST
DAVIES, Richard O., 1937- ,
American; nonfiction CON
DAVIES, Robert William, 1925- ,
English; nonfiction CON

DAVIES, Robertson, 1913- ,
Canadian; fiction, plays, essays
CON RIC ST SY
DAVIES, Ronald E.G., 1921- ,
English; nonfiction CON
DAVIES, Rupert Eric, 1909- ,
American; nonfiction CON
DAVIES, Ruth Ann, 1915- , Ameri-
can; nonfiction CON
DAVIES, Sarah Emily, 1830-1921,
English; nonfiction KBA
DAVIES, Trefor Rendall, 1913- ,
Welsh; nonfiction CON
DAVIES, Valentine, 1905- , Ameri-
can; fiction WAF
DAVIES, William David, 1911- ,
Welsh-American; nonfiction CON
DAVIES, William Henry, 1871-1940,
English; poetry BRO FLE KL
KT RIC SA SP ST
DAVIES, Wyndham Roy, 1926- ,
English; nonfiction CON
'DAVIGNON, Grace' see GLASSCO,
John S.
DAVILA, Alexandru, 1860-1929,
Rumainian; plays ST
DAVILA, Enrico Caterino, 1576-1631,
Italian; nonfiction HAR SA ST
DAVILA, Juan Bautista, 1604/ -64,
Spanish; nonfiction, poetry SA
DAVILA ANDRADE, Cesar, 1918- ,
Ecuadorian; poetry, fiction DI
DAVILA de PONCE, Waldina, 19th
cent., Colombian; fiction MIN
DAVIN, Daniel Marcus, 1913- ,
New Zealander; fiction CON RIC
ST
DAVINSON, Donald Edward, 1932- ,
American; nonfiction CON
'DAVIOT, Gordon' see MACKINTOSH,
Elizabeth
DAVIS, Adelle ('Jane Dunlap'),
1904- , American; nonfiction
CON
DAVIS, Allen Freeman, 1931- ,
American; nonfiction CON
DAVIS, Arthur G., 1915- , Ameri-
can; nonfiction CON
DAVIS, Arthur Hoey see 'RUDD,
Steele'
DAVIS, Arthur Kennard, 1910- ,
English; juveniles CON
DAVIS, Arthur Kyle, Jr., 1897- ,
American; nonfiction CON
DAVIS, Benton Vincent, Jr.,
1930- , American; nonfiction
CON

DAVIS, Bertram Hylton, 1918- ,
American; nonfiction CON
DAVIS, Burke, 1913- , American;
fiction CON JO WA
DAVIS, Calvin DeArmond, 1927- ,
American; nonfiction CON
DAVIS, Charles, 1923- , English;
nonfiction CON
DAVIS, Charles Henry Stanley,
1840-1917, American; nonfic-
tion KAA
DAVIS, Charles Till, 1929- ,
American; nonfiction CON
DAVIS, Christopher, 1928- ,
American; fiction CON
DAVIS, Clive Edward, 1914- ,
American; juveniles CON WA
DAVIS, Clyde Brion, 1894-1962,
American; fiction CON KT
WAF
DAVIS, Curtis Carroll, 1916- ,
American; nonfiction CON
DAVIS, David Brion, 1927- ,
American; nonfiction CON
DAVIS, David Charles L., 1928- ,
American; nonfiction CON
DAVIS, Donald Evan, 1923- ,
American; nonfiction CON
DAVIS, Dorothy Salisbury,
1916- , American; fiction
CON
DAVIS, Edwin Adams, 1904- ,
American; nonfiction CON
DAVIS, Elmer Holmes, 1890- ,
American; essays, fiction KT
DAVIS, Elwood Craig, 1896- ,
American; nonfiction CON
DAVIS, Floyd James, 1920- ,
American; nonfiction CON
DAVIS, Francis, 1810-85, Irish;
poetry KBA
DAVIS, Frank Marshall, 1905- ,
American; poetry HOO
DAVIS, Franklin Milton, Jr.,
1918- , American; fiction
CON
DAVIS, Fred, 1925- , American;
nonfiction CON
DAVIS, Frederick Barton, 1909- ,
American; nonfiction CON
DAVIS, George, 1906- , American;
fiction KAT
'DAVIS, Gil' see GILMORE, Don
'DAVIS, Gordon' see DIETRICK,
Robert S.
DAVIS, Grant Miller, 1937- ,
American; nonfiction CON

DAVIS, Gwen ('Brat Fink'), 1936- ,
American; fiction CON
DAVIS, Harold Eugene, 1902- ,
American; nonfiction CON
DAVIS, Harold Lenoir, 1896-1960,
American; poetry, fiction KT
MAG WAF
DAVIS, Harry Rex, 1921- , Ameri-
can; nonfiction CON
DAVIS, Rev. Henry, 1866-1952,
English; nonfiction HO
DAVIS, Henry Grady, 1890- ,
American; nonfiction CON
DAVIS, Herbert John, 1893-1967,
English; nonfiction CON
DAVIS, Hope Hale, American; fic-
tion CON
DAVIS, Horace Bancroft ('Bryan
Green'; 'Jan Reling'; 'Lowell
E. Willis'), 1898- , American;
nonfiction CON
DAVIS, Howard Vaughn, 1915- ,
American; nonfiction CON
DAVIS, James, 1721-85, American;
nonfiction JO
DAVIS, James Allen, 1929- ,
American; nonfiction CON
DAVIS, James Warren, Jr., 1935- ,
American; nonfiction CON
DAVIS, Jean Walton, 1909- , Amer-
ican; nonfiction, fiction CON
PAC
DAVIS, Jed Horace, Jr., 1921- ,
American; nonfiction CON
DAVIS, Jerome, 1891- , American;
nonfiction CON
DAVIS, Joe Lee, 1906- , American;
poetry, nonfiction CON
DAVIS, John (Davys), 1550-1605,
English; nonfiction BRO
DAVIS, Sir John, 1569-1626, English;
poetry BRO
DAVIS, John David, 1937- , English;
nonfiction CON
DAVIS, John H., 1929- , American;
nonfiction CON
DAVIS, John Herbert, 1904- , Amer-
ican; nonfiction CON
DAVIS, John James, 1936- , Amer-
ican; nonfiction CON
DAVIS, John King, 1884- , English;
nonfiction CON
DAVIS, John Michael, 1940- ,
American; nonfiction CON
DAVIS, Julia, 1900- , American;
juveniles KJU
DAVIS, Julia ('F. Draco'), 1904- ,

American; nonfiction, fiction
CON
DAVIS, Keith, 1918- , American;
nonfiction CON
DAVIS, Kenneth Rexton, 1921- ,
American; nonfiction CON
DAVIS, Kenneth S., 1912- ,
American; fiction CON WAF
DAVIS, Kingsley, 1908- , Ameri-
can; nonfiction CON
DAVIS, Lavinia Riker ('Wendell
Farmer'), 1909- , American;
juveniles KJU WA
DAVIS, Lawrence James, 1940- ,
American; fiction CON
DAVIS, Lenwood C., 1939- ,
American; nonfiction CON
DAVIS, Lew Arter, 1930- ,
American; nonfiction CON
DAVIS, Maggie Hill, American;
fiction CON
'DAVIS, Maralee G.' see THI-
BAULT, Maralee G.
DAVIS, Marc, 1934- , American;
fiction CON
DAVIS, Margaret Banfield, 1903- ,
American; nonfiction CON
DAVIS, Marilyn Kornreich, 1928- ,
American; nonfiction CON
DAVIS, Mary Evelyn Moore,
1852-1909, American; nonfic-
tion KAA
DAVIS, Mary Gould, 1882- ,
American; juveniles KJU WA
DAVIS, Mary Octavia ('Dutz'),
1901- , American; nonfiction,
juveniles CON
DAVIS, Mildred Ann Campbell,
1916- , American; fiction,
poetry CON
DAVIS, Morris Edward, 1899- ,
American; nonfiction CON
DAVIS, Moshe, 1916- , Ameri-
can; nonfiction CON
DAVIS, Nuel Pharr, 1915- ,
American; nonfiction CON
DAVIS, Owen, 1874-1956, Ameri-
can; plays KL KT MAT
DAVIS, Paxton, 1925- , Ameri-
can; fiction CON
DAVIS, Ralph Currier, 1894- ,
American; nonfiction CON
DAVIS, Ralph Henry Carless,
1918- , English; nonfiction
CON
DAVIS, Rebecca Blaine Harding,
1831-1910, American; fiction
KAA

DAVIS, Reda, American; juveniles
WA

DAVIS, Rex, D., 1924- , American;
nonfiction CON

DAVIS, Richard Beale, 1907- ,
American; nonfiction CON

DAVIS, Richard Harding, 1864-
1916, American; journalism,
fiction KAT KT BRO

DAVIS, Richard W., 1935- , American; nonfiction CON

DAVIS, Robert, 1881-1949, American;
juveniles KJU

DAVIS, Robert Murray, 1934- ,
American; nonfiction CON

DAVIS, Robert P. ('Joe Brandon'),
1929- , American; nonfiction
CON

DAVIS, Robert Ralph, Jr., 1941- ,
American; nonfiction CON

DAVIS, Ronald Leroy, 1936- ,
American; nonfiction CON

DAVIS, Rosemary, English; nonfiction CON

DAVIS, Roy Eugene, 1931- , American; nonfiction CON

DAVIS, Russell Gerard, 1922- ,
American; nonfiction CON

DAVIS, Samuel, 1930- , American;
nonfiction CON

'DAVIS, Stratford' see BOLTCN,
Maisie S.

'DAVIS, Sumner' see CUSHMAN,
Dan

DAVIS, Sydney Charles Houghton
('Sammy Casque'), 1887- ,
English; nonfiction CON

DAVIS, Terence, 1924- , English;
nonfiction CON

DAVIS, Thomas Osborne, 1814-15,
English; poetry, nonfiction BRO
KBA ST

DAVIS, Verne Theodore, 1889- ,
American; juveniles CON

DAVIS, Warren Jefferson, 1885- ,
American; nonfiction CON

DAVIS, Wayne Harry, 1930- , American; nonfiction CON

DAVIS, Willy H., 1913- , American;
nonfiction CON

DAVIS, William Hatcher, 1939- ,
American; nonfiction CON

DAVIS, William Stearns, 1877-1930,
American; fiction KT

DAVISON, Francis, fl. 1602- ,
English; poetry KB

DAVISON, Frank Dalby, 1893- ,

Australian; fiction RIC ST

DAVISON, Gladys Patton ('Gladyn
Condor'), 1905- , American;
nonfiction CON

DAVISON, Peter, 1928- , American; poetry CON MUR

DAVISON, Roderic Hollett,
1916- , American; nonfiction
CON

DAVY, Francis Xavier, 1916- ,
American; nonfiction CON

DAVY, Sir Humphrey, 1778-1829,
English; nonfiction BRO KBA
ST

DAVYDOV, Denis Vasilyevich,
1784-1839, Russian; poetry
HARK ST

DAVISON, Kenneth Edwin, 1924- ,
American; nonfiction CON

DAVISSON, Charles Nelson,
1917- , American; nonfiction
CON

DAVISSON, William I., 1929- ,
American; nonfiction CON

DAVITT, Thomas Edward, 1904- ,
American; nonfiction CON

DAVYS, John see DAVIS, John

DAWE, Bruce, 1930- , Australian;
poetry MUR

DAWE, Donald G., 1926- ,
American; nonfiction CON

DAWE, Roger David, 1934- ,
English; nonfiction CON

DAWES, Neville, 1926- ,
Jamaican; poetry, fiction CON
MUR

DAWES, Robyn Mason ('Braz
Cubas'), 1936- , American;
nonfiction CON

DAWIDOWICZ, Lucy S., American; nonfiction CON

DAWKINS, Cecil, 1927- , American; plays, fiction CON

DAWLATSHAH of SAMARKAND,
Amir, 15th cent., Persian;
nonfiction ST

DAWSON, A.J., 1872-1951,
English; juveniles DOY

DAWSON, Christopher Henry,
1889-1970, English; nonfiction
CON HOE KTS

DAWSON, Coningsby William,
1883-1959, Anglo-American;
fiction KT

'DAWSON, Elmer A.' see STRATE-
MEYER, Edward L.

DAWSON, George Glenn, 1925- ,

American; nonfiction CON

DAWSON, Giles Edwin, 1903- ,
American; nonfiction CON

DAWSON, Grace Strickler, 1891- ,
American; juvenile CON

DAWSON, Jerry F., 1933- , American; nonfiction CON

DAWSON, John Brant, 1915- ,
New Zealander; nonfiction CON

DAWSON, John Philip, 1928- ,
American; nonfiction CON

DAWSON, Lionel, 1885- , English;
nonfiction HIG

DAWSON, Mary, 1919- , English;
nonfiction CON

DAWSON, Mildred A., 1897- ,
American; nonfiction CON

DAWSON, Mitchell, 1890- , American; juveniles WA

DAWSON, Robert Merrill, 1941- ,
American; poetry CON

DAY, Alan Charles Lynn, 1924- ,
American; nonfiction CON

DAY, Albert Edward, 1884- ,
American; nonfiction CON

DAY, Alice Taylor, 1928- , American; nonfiction CON

DAY, Arthur Grove, 1904- ,
American; nonfiction CON

DAY, Beth Feagles ('Elizabeth
Feagles'), 1924- , American;
juveniles CON

DAY, Clarence Shepherd, 1874-1835,
American; essays, fiction BRO
KT MAG RIC

DAY, Dorothy, 1897- , American;
nonfiction HOE

DAY, Douglas, 1932- , American;
nonfiction CON

DAY, George Harold ('Peter Quince'),
1900- , English; nonfiction CON

DAY, Gwynn McLendon, 1908- ,
American; poetry CON

DAY, Henry, 1865- , English; nonfiction HOE

DAY, Holman Francis, 1865-1935,
American; fiction, poetry KT

DAY, James Edward, 1914- ,
American; fiction CON

DAY, James Francis, 1917- , American; nonfiction CON

DAY, James Wentworth, 1899- ,
English; nonfiction CON

DAY, John, 1574-1640, English;
plays BRO KB ST

DAY, John Arthur, 1913- , American; nonfiction CON

DAY, John Patrick, English;
nonfiction CON

DAY, John Robert, 1917- , English; nonfiction CON

DAY, Kenneth, 1912- , English;
nonfiction CON

DAY, LeRoy Judson, 1917- ,
American; nonfiction CON

DAY, Lincoln Hubert, 1928- ,
American; nonfiction CON

DAY, Martin Steele, 1917- ,
American; nonfiction CON

'DAY, Max' see CASSIDAY, Bruce
B.

'DAY, Michael' see DEMPEWOLFF,
Richard F.

DAY, Paul Woodford, 1916- ,
New Zealander; nonfiction CON

DAY, Peter Morton, 1914- ,
American; nonfiction CON

DAY, Ralph Lewis, 1926- ,
American; nonfiction CON

DAY, Richard E., 1929- ,
American; nonfiction CON

DAY, Ross Henry, 1927- ,
Australian; nonfiction CON

DAY, Stacey Biswas, 1927- ,
English; nonfiction, poetry,
fiction CON

DAY, Thomas, 1748-89, English;
poetry, fiction, nonfiction,
juveniles BRO DOY KB MAG
ST

DAY LEWIS, Cecil see LEWIS,
Cecil D.

DAYAN, Moshe, 1915- , Israeli;
nonfiction CON

DAYARAM, 1767-1852, Indian;
poetry LAN

DAYTON, Dorothy,   -1938,
American; nonfiction MAR

'DAZAI, Shundai' (Dazai Jun),
1680-1747, Japanese; nonfiction
ST

DAZAN, Mario, 1929- , Chilean;
nonfiction, poetry SA

D'AZEGLIO, Massimo Taparelli,
1798-1866, Italian; fiction HAR
SA ST

DAZEY, Agnes Johnston, American;
juveniles CON CON

DAZEY, Charles Turner, 1855-
1938, American; plays, movies
HOO

DAZEY, Frank M., American;
juveniles COM CON

DEACON, William Arthur, 1890- ,

Canadian; essays, journalism
SY

DEAK, Istvan, 1926- , Hungarian-
American; nonfiction CON

DEAKIN, Frederick William, 1913- ,
English; nonfiction CON

DEAKIN, James, 1929- , American;
nonfiction CON

DEAL, Babs Hodges, 1929- ,
American; fiction CON

DEAL, Borden ('Lee Borden'),
1922- , American; fiction CON

DEAL, William Sanford, 1910- ,
American; nonfiction CON

DEALE, Kenneth Edwin Lee ('Paul
Martin'), 1907- , Irish; nonfiction, plays, translations CON

DEALEY, Edward Musgrov (Ted),
1892- , American; fiction CON

DE AMICIS, Edmondo, 1846-1908,
Italian; essays, fiction COL
HAR KE MAG SA ST

DEAN, Amber, 1902- , American;
fiction CON

DEAN, Anabel, 1915- , American;
juveniles CON

DEAN, Basil, 1888- , English;
plays MAT

DEAN, Beryl, 1911- , English;
nonfiction CON

DEAN, Dwight Gantz, 1918- ,
American; nonfiction CON

DEAN, Edwin Robinson, 1933- ,
American; nonfiction CON

DEAN, Graham M., 1904- ,
American; juveniles WA

DEAN, Jeffrey S., 1939- , American; nonfiction CON

DEAN, Joel, 1906- , American;
nonfiction CON

DEAN, Nell Marr ('Virginia
Roberts'), 1910- , American;
fiction CON WA

DEAN, Vera Michells, 1903-72,
American; nonfiction KTS

DEAN, Warren, 1932- , American;
nonfiction CON

DEAN, William Denard, 1937- ,
American; nonfiction CON

DEAN, Yetive Hornor, 1909- ,
American; juveniles, fiction
CON

DEANE, Herbert Andrew, 1921- ,
American; nonfiction CON

'DEANE, Lorna' see WILKINSON,
Lorna H. K.

DEANE, Nancy Hilts, 1939- ,
American; nonfiction CON

'DEANE, Norman' see CREASEY,
John

DEANE, Samuel, 1733-1814,
American; nonfiction KAA

DEANE, Shirley Joan, 1920- ,
American; nonfiction CON

DE ANGELI, Marguerite, 1889- ,
American; juvenile COM
CON HIL KJU WA

DE ANGELIS, Raoul Maria,
1908- , Italian; fiction,
journalism SA

DEARDEN, James Arthur, 1924- ,
English; nonfiction CON

DEARDEN, James Shackley,
1931- , English; nonfiction
CON

DEARDEN, John, 1919- , Anglo-
American; nonfiction CON

DE ARMAND, Frances Ullmann,
American; juveniles CON WA

DE ARMAS, Frederick Alfred,
1945- , American; nonfiction
CON

DEARMER, Geoffrey, 1893- ,
English; poetry, fiction CON

DEARMIN, Jennie Tarascou,
1924- , American; nonfiction
CON

DEASE, Edmund F., 1856- ,
English; nonfiction HIG

DEASON, Hilary John, 1903- ,
American; nonfiction CON

DEASY, Mary Margaret, 1914- ,
American; fiction CON

DEATS, Paul Kindred, Jr.,
1918- , American; nonfiction
CON

DEATS, Richard Louis, 1932- ,
American; nonfiction CON

'DEAUVILLE, Max' (Maurice
Duwez), 1881- , Belgian;
fiction, plays COL SA

DEAUX, George, 1931- , American; nonfiction CON

DE AYALA see PEREZ de AYALA

DE BANKE, Cecile, 1889-1965,
English; nonfiction CON

DE BEDTS, Ralph Fortes, 1914- ,
American; nonfiction CON

DE BEER, Esmond Samuel,
1895- , New Zealander; nonfiction CON

DE BEER, Gavin Rylands, 1899- ,
English; nonfiction CON

DEBELJANOV, Dimco, 1887-1916,
Bulgarian; poetry FLE ST

DEBICKI, Andrew Peter, 1934- ,

Polish-American; nonfiction CON
DEBICKI, Roman, 1896- , Polish-
American; nonfiction CON
DE BLANK, Joost, 1908- , Dutch;
fiction CON
DE BLIJ, Harm Jan, 1935- , Dutch-
American; nonfiction CON
DEBO, Angie, American; nonfiction
MAR
DE BOER, John Charles, 1923- ,
American; nonfiction CON
DE BOER, John James, American;
nonfiction CON
DE BOIS, Wilhelmina J.E., 1923- ,
Dutch; nonfiction CON
DE BOLD, Richard C., 1927- ,
American; nonfiction CON
DE BONO, Edward, 1933- , Amer-
ican; nonfiction CON
DE BORHEGYI, Suzanne Sims,
1926- , American; nonfiction
CON
DE BORN, Edith, 1901- , Austrian;
fiction CON
DE BOSIS, Adolfo, 1863-1924,
Italian; poetry COL SA ST
DE BOSIS, Lauro, 1901-31?, Italian;
poetry COL SA
DEBRAY, Jules Regis, 1942- ,
American; nonfiction CON
DEBRECZENY, Paul, 1932- ,
American; nonfiction CON
DEBREU, Gerard, 1921- , Franco-
American; nonfiction CON
DEBUS, Allen George, 1926- ,
American; nonfiction CON
DE CAMP, Catherine Crook, 1907- ,
American; nonfiction CON
DE CAMP, Lyon Sprague ('Lyman R.
Lyon'; 'J. Wellington Wells'),
1907- , American; nonfiction,
juveniles, fiction CON WA
DE CAPITE, Michael, 1915- ,
American; fiction WAF
DE CAPITE, Raymond Anthony,
1924- , American; fiction CON
DE CASSERES, Benjamin, 1873- ,
American; essays KT
DE CASTRO, Josue, 1908-73,
Brazilian; nonfiction CON
DECAUNES, Luc, 1913- , French;
poetry DIF
DE CAUX, Leonard Howard, 1899- ,
New Zealander; nonfiction CON
'DECAUX, Lucile' see BIBESCO,
Princess Marthe
DE CECCO, John Paul, 1925- ,
American; nonfiction CON

DE CERVERA, Alejo, 1919- ,
Spanish; nonfiction CON
DECHANT, Emerald V., 1926- ,
American; nonfiction CON
DE CHANT, John Aloysius, 1917- ,
American; nonfiction CON
DECHERT, Charles Richard,
1927- , American; nonfiction
CON
DE CHIRICO, Andrea see 'SAVINIO,
Alberto'
DECIANO, 14- , Roman; poetry
SA
DECKER, Donald Milton, 1923- ,
American; nonfiction CON
DECKER, Duane Walter ('Richard
Wayne'), 1910-64, American;
juveniles CON WA
DECKER, Jeremy (Jeremias de),
1609-66, Dutch; poetry SA
ST
DECKER, Leslie Edward, 1930- ,
American; nonfiction CON
DECKERT, Alice Mae, Canadian;
fiction CON
DE CLEYRE, Voltairine, 1866-
1912, American; poetry, es-
says KAA SA
DE CONDE, Alexander, 1920- ,
American; nonfiction CON
DE COSTE, Fredrick, 1910- ,
American; nonfiction CON
DECCOSTER, Charles, 1827-79,
Belgian; fiction COL DIF HAR
KE MAG SA ST
DECOUD, José, Segundo, 1849-
1909, Paraguayan; nonfiction
SA
DECOURCELLE, Pierre, 1856-
1926, French; fiction DIF SA
DE COY, Robert Harold, Jr.,
1920- , American; nonfiction
CON
DE CRISTOFORO, R. J. ('R. J.
Cristy'; 'Cris Williams'),
1917- , American; nonfiction
CON
DE CROW, Karen, 1937- ,
American; nonfiction CON
DEDEK, John, F., 1929- ,
American; nonfiction CON
DEDEKIND, Friedrich, 1525-98,
German; poetry AL ST
DEDERICK, Robert, 1919- ,
British; poetry MUR
DEDIJER, Vladimir, 1914- ,
Yugoslav-English; nonfiction
CON

DEDING, Michel, 1933- , Franco-
American; fiction CON
DEDMON, Emmett, 1918- , Ameri-
can; nonfiction CON
'DEE HENRY' see TORBETT, Harvey
D. L.
DEE, Dr. John, 1527-1608, English;
nonfiction KB
DEE, Sylvia, 1914- , American;
fiction WAF
DEEBLE, Russell John, Australian;
poetry MUR
DEEDY, John, 1923- , American;
nonfiction CON
DEELMAN, Christian Felling, 1937-
64, English; nonfiction CON
DEEMER, Bill, 1945- , American;
poetry CON MUR
DEEN, Edith Alderman, 1905- ,
American; nonfiction CON
DEENER, David Russell, 1920- ,
American; nonfiction CON
DEEPING, George Warwick, 1877-
1950, English; fiction BRO KL
KT RIC SA
DEER, Irving, 1924- , American;
nonfiction CON
DEERING, Nathaniel, 1791-1881,
American; plays KAA
DEESE, James Earle, 1921- , Amer-
ican; nonfiction CON
DEEVY, Teresa, 1894- , Irish;
plays HO ST
DE FALCO, Joseph Michael, 1931- ,
American; nonfiction CON
DEFERRARI, Roy Joseph, 1890- ,
American; nonfiction HOE
DE FARRARI, Sister Teresa Mary,
1930- , American; nonfiction
CON
DE FERRARIIS, Antonio ('Il Galateo'),
1444-1517, Italian; nonfiction ST
DEFFANT, Marie de Vichy Chambond,
1677-1780, French; nonfiction SA
DEFFNER, Donald Louis, 1924- ,
American; nonfiction CON
DEFILIPPIS NOVOA, Francisco,
1890-1930, Argentinian; plays
MIN
DE FILIPPO, Eduardo, 1900- ,
Italian; plays MAT
DEFOE, Daniel, 1660-1731, English;
juveniles, fiction BRO DOY KB
MAG SA ST
DE FONTAINE, Felix Gregory, 1834-
96, American; journalism KAA
DE FONTAINE, Wade Hampton,
1893- , American; nonfiction
CON

'DE FORBES' see FORBES, De
Loris S.
DEFORD, Frank, 1938- , Ameri-
can; nonfiction CON
DE FORD, Miriam Allen, 1888-
1950, American; nonfiction
CON KT
DE FORD, Sara Whitcraft, 1916- ,
American; poetry CON
DE FOREST, Charlotte B., 1879- ,
American; nonfiction CON
DE FOREST, John William, 1826-
1906, American; fiction BRO
KAA MAG ST
DEFORIS, Jean Pierre, 1732-94,
French; nonfiction DIL
DEFOURNEAUX, Marcelin,
1910- , Spanish; nonfiction
BL
DE FREES, Mary Madeline (Sister
Mary Gilbert), 1919- , Amer-
ican; poetry, fiction CON MUR
PAC
DEFRY, Frank, 1938- , American;
poetry MUR
DE FUNIAK, William Quinby,
1901- , American; nonfiction
CON
DE GAVRY, Gerald, 1897- ,
American; nonfiction CON
DEGEE, Olivier see 'TOUSSEUL,
Jean'
DE GENNARO, Angelo Anthony,
1919- , American; nonfiction
CON
DE GEORGE, Richard Thomas,
1933- , American; nonfiction
CON
DE GERING, Etta Fowler, 1898- ,
American; juveniles CON WA
DEGHY, Guy ('Herald Froy'; 'Lee
Bigg'), 1912- , Hungarian-
English; fiction CON
DEGLER, Carl Neumann, 1921- ,
American; nonfiction CON
DEGLER, Stanley, E., 1929- ,
American; nonfiction CON
DE GOURMONT, Remy see
GOURMONT, Remy
DE GRAFT-JOHNSON, John Cole-
man, 1919- , Dutch; nonfic-
tion CON
DE GRAZIA, Alfred, 1919- ,
American; nonfiction CON
DE GRE, Muriel Harris, 1914- ,
American; fiction CON
DE GREEN, Kenyon Brenton,
American; nonfiction CON
DE GREGORI, Thomas Roger,

1935- , American; nonfiction
CON
DE GROOD, David H., 1937- ,
American; nonfiction CON
DE GROOT, Alfred Thomas, 1903- ,
American; nonfiction CON
'DE GROS, J.H.' see VILLIARD,
Paul
DE GRUMMOND, Lena Young,
American; juveniles, nonfiction
CON WA
DE GRUNWALD, Constantine, Rus-
sian-French; nonfiction CON
DEGUERLE, Jean Marie Nicolas,
1766-1824, French; nonfiction
SA
DE HAAN, Richard W., 1923- ,
American; nonfiction CON
'DEHAN, Richard' (Clotilde Graves),
1863-1932, Irish; plays, journal-
ism, fiction HOE
DEHARME, Lise, 20th cent., French;
fiction DIF
DE HARTOG, Jan ('F.R. Eckmar'),
1914- , Dutch-American; non-
fiction, fiction, plays CON
DEHENNIN, Elsa, Belgian; nonfiction
BL
DE HENRICO, 10th cent., German;
nonfiction AL
DEHKHODA, 1879-1956, Persian;
journalism LAN
DEHMEL, Richard, 1863-1920,
German; poetry, essays, plays
AL COL FLE HAR KE SA ST
DEHMEL, Walter, 1903-60, German;
poetry AL
DEHN, Paul Edward, 1912- ,
British; poetry MUR
DEHONY, William Wayne, 1918- ,
American; nonfiction CON
DEHR, Dorothy, 1915- , American;
nonfiction CON
DEI, Benedetto, 1418-92, Italian;
nonfiction ST
DEI-ANANG, Michael F., 1909- ,
Ghanaian; poetry, plays MUR
DEICKE, Günther, 1922- , German;
nonfiction AL
DEIGHTON, Len, 1929- , English;
fiction CON RIC
DEINDORFER, Robert Greene ('Jay
Bender'; 'Jay Dender'; 'Robert
Greene'), 1922- , American;
fiction CON
DEINZER, Harvey T., 1908- ,
American; nonfiction CON
DEISS, Joseph Jay, 1915- , Amer-

ican; fiction CON
DE JAEGHER, Raymond Joseph
('Lee Chen Yuan'), 1925- ,
Belgian; nonfiction CON
'DEJEAN' see HORNOT, Antoine
DE JONG, David Cornel ('Tjalmar
Breda'), 1906-67, Dutch-
American; fiction CON KT WA
WAF
DE JONG, Dola, 1911- , Dutch-
American; juveniles CON FUL
WA
DE JONG, Gerrit Jr., 1892- ,
American; nonfiction CON
DEJONG, Gordon Frederick,
1935- , American; nonfiction
CON
DEJONG, Meindert, 1906- ,
Dutch-American; juveniles
COM CON FUL WA
DE JOUVENEL see COLETTE,
Gabrielle
DE JOVINE, Felix Anthony,
1927- , American; nonfiction
CON
DE KAY, James Tertius, 1930- ,
American; juveniles CON
DEKEN, Agatha, 1741-1804, Dutch;
fiction SA ST
DE KIRILINE, Louise see LAW-
RENCE, Louis de K.
DEKKER, Eduard Douwes see
'MULTATULI'
DEKKER, Mairits Rudolph Jöell,
1896- , Dutch; fiction, plays
ST
DEKKER, Thomas, 1572-1632?,
English; plays BRO KB MAG
SA SP ST
DEKLE, Bernard, 1905- , Amer-
ican; fiction CON
DEKMEJIAN, Richard Hrair,
1933- , Syrian-American;
nonfiction CON
DEKOBRA, Maurice, 1885- ,
French; fiction CON SA
DEKOSTER, Lester Ronald,
1915- , American; nonfiction
CON
DE DRUIF, Paul Henry, 1890-
1971, American; nonfiction
CON KAT KT
DE KUN, Nicolas, 1923- ,
Hungarian-American; nonfiction
CON
DE LA BEDOYERE, Michael,
1900- , English; nonfiction
HOE

DE LACRETELLE, Jacques see
LACRETELLE, Jacques de
DELACROIX, Henri, 1873-1937,
French; nonfiction DIF
DE LA CROIX, Robert, French;
poetry, journalism, juveniles
WA
DE LA CUADRA, Jose see CUADRA,
Jose de la
DE LAET, Sigfried Jan, 1914- ,
Belgian; nonfiction CON
'DELAFIELD, E.M.' see de la
PASTURE, Elizabeth and Edmée
'DE LA GLANNEGE, Roger Maxe'
see LEGMAN, Gershon
DE LAGUNA, Frederica Annis,
1906- , American; nonfiction
CON
DE LAGUNA, Grace Andrus, 1878- ,
American; nonfiction CON
DELAHAY, Eileen Avril, 1915- ,
English; fiction CON
DELAHAYE, Guy, 1888- , Canadian;
poetry SY
DE LA IGLESIA, Maria Elena,
1936- , Spanish; juveniles CON
DE LA MARE, Albinia Catherine,
1932- , English; nonfiction CON
DELAMARE, Nicolas, 1639-1723,
French; nonfiction DIL
De LA MARE, Walter John ('Walter
Ramal'), 1873-1956, English;
juveniles BRO DOY FLE KJU KL
KT MAG RIC SA SP ST WA
DELAND, Margaret Wade Campbell,
1857- , American; fiction KL
KT
DELANEY, Cornelius F., 1938- ,
American; nonfiction CON
'DELANEY, Denis' see GREEN,
Peter M.
DELANEY, Edmund T., 1914- ,
American; nonfiction CON
'DELANEY, Franey' see O'HARA,
John H.
DELANEY, Harry, 1932- , English;
fiction CON
DELANEY, Jack J., 1921- ,
American; nonfiction CON
DELANEY, John Joseph, 1910- ,
American; nonfiction CON
DELANEY, Norman Conrad, 1932- ,
American; nonfiction CON
DELANEY, Robert Finley, 1925- ,
American; nonfiction CON
DELANEY, Shelagh, 1939- , Eng-
lish; plays CON MAT RIC
DELANO, Alonzo ('Old Block'),

1802/06-74, American; nonfic-
tion, poetry KAA
DELANO, Isaac O., 1904- ,
English; juveniles, fiction
CON
DELANO, Lucile K., American;
nonfiction BL
DELANO, Luis Enrique, 1907- ,
Chilean; journalism, poetry,
fiction MIN
DE LAURENTIS, Louise Budde,
1920- , American; poetry
CON
DELANY, Martin Robinson,
1812-85, American; nonfiction
KAA
DELANY, Mary Granville
Pendarves, 1700-88, English;
letters KB
DELANY, Paul, 1937- , English;
nonfiction CON
DELANY, Selden Peabody, 1874-
1935, American; nonfiction
HOE
DE LA PASTURE, Edmée Elizabeth
Monica ('E. M. Delafield'),
1890-1943, English; fiction
BRO KT
DE LA PASTURE, Elizabeth Lydia
Rosabelle Bonham ('E. M.
Delafield'), 1866-1943/45,
English; fiction BRO KL KT
RIC
DELAPLANE, Stanton Hill, 1907- ,
American; nonfiction CON
'DELAPORTE, Theophile' see
GREEN, Julien
DE LA RAMEE, Louise see
RAMEE, Louise de la
DE LA ROCHE, Mazo, 1885-1961,
Canadian; fiction, plays BRO
KL KT MAG RIC SA ST SY
DELARUE-MARDRUS, Lucie,
1880-1945, French; poetry,
fiction HAR SA ST
DELASANTA, Rodney, 1932- ,
American; nonfiction CON
DE LAS CUEVAS, Ramon see
HARRINGTON, Mark R.
DE LA SERNA see GOMEZ de la
SERNA
DE LA TAILLE, Rev. Maurice,
1872-1933, French; nonfiction
HO
DE LA TORRE, Lillian, see
McCUE, Lillian B.
DE LAUNAY, Jacques Forment,
1924- , French; nonfiction
CON

DELAUNE, Jewel Lynn de Grummond, American; juveniles, nonfiction CON WA

DE LAURA, David Joseph, 1930- , American; nonfiction CON

DELAVIGNE, Casimir Jean François, 1793-1843, French; poetry, plays DIF HAR KE SA ST

DELAVIGNE, German, 1790-1868, French; nonfiction SA

'DELAVRANCEA, Barbu' see STEFANESCU, Barbu

DE LA WARR, George, 1904- , English; nonfiction CON

DE LA ZOUCHE, Lord see CURZON, Robert

DELBANCO, Nicholas Franklin, 1942- , English; fiction CON

DEL BARCO, Lucy Salamanca, English; nonfiction CON

DEL BENE, Bartolomeo, 1514-87, Italian; poetry ST

DEL BOCA, Angelo, 1925- , Italian; nonfiction CON

DEL COLLE, Gherardo, 1920- , Italian; poetry, criticism SA

DELEAU, Frank J., 1914- , American; nonfiction CON

DELDERFIELD, Ronald Frederick, 1912-72, English; juveniles, fiction DOY

DELEDDA, Grazia, 1873/75-1936, Italian; fiction COL FLE HAR KL KT MAG RIC SA ST

DE LEEUW, Adèle Louise, 1899- , American; juveniles, poetry, fiction, nonfiction COM CON KJU WA

DE LEEUW, Cateau ('Kay Hamilton'; 'Jessica Lyon'), 1903- , American; fiction CON WA

DELEHAYE, Hippolyte, 1859-1941, Belgian; nonfiction HOE

DELEITO y PIÑUELA, Jose, 1879-1957, Spanish; nonfiction BL SA

DE LEON, Thomas Cooper, 1839-1914, American; plays, nonfiction, fiction KAA

DELESSERT, Etienne, 1941- , Swiss; nonfiction CON

DE LEY, Herbert Clemone, Jr., 1936- , American; nonfiction CON

DELEYRE, Alexandre, 1726-97, French; nonfiction DIL

DELFAUD, Beinheureux Guillaume, 1733- , French; nonfiction DIL

DELFGAAUW, Bernardus Maria Ignatius, 1912- , Dutch; nonfiction CON

DELGADO, Alan George, 1909- , English; nonfiction CON

DELGADO, Francisco see DELI-CADO, Francisco

DELGADO, Jose Manuel Rodriguez, 1915- , Spanish; nonfiction CON

DELGADO, Rafael, 1853-1914, Mexican; fiction SA

DELGADO, Sinesio, 1859-1928, Spanish; poetry, plays, journalism BL SA

DELGADO BENAVENTE, Luis, 1915- , Spanish; plays BL SA

DELGADO VALHONDO, Jesús, 1911- , Spanish; nonfiction SA

'DELIBERATE PENDANT' see ELIOT, Thomas S.

DE LIBERO, Libero, 1906- , Italian; poetry SA

DELIBES, Miguel, 1920- , Spanish; fiction, journalism BL FLE RIC SA

DELICADO, Francisco (Delgado), 16th cent., Spanish; nonfiction BL SA ST

DELIGNE, Gastón Fernando, 1861-1913, Dominican; poetry MIN SA

DELIGNE, Rafael Alfredo, 1863-1902, Dominican; nonfiction, plays, poetry MIN SA

DELILLE, Jacques, 1738-1813, French; poetry, fiction DIF DIL HAR SA ST

DE LIMA, Sigrid, 1921- , American; fiction CON

'DELIO' see ITURRONDO, Francisco

DELISLE, Joseph, 1688-1711, French; nonfiction DIL

DELILLE de la DREVETIERE, Louis François, 1682-1756, French; plays, poetry DIL

DELIUS, Anthony Ronald St. Martin, 1916- , South African; poetry, fiction CON MUR RIC

DELL, Edward Thomas, Jr., 1923- , American; nonfiction CON

DELL, Ethel Mary, 1881-1939, English; fiction BRO RIC

DELL, Floyd, 1887- , American; fiction, plays, essays HOO

KL KT
DELL, Sidney, 1918- , English;
  nonfiction CON
DELLA PORTA, Giambattista, 1535-
  1615, Italian; plays ST
DELLOFF, Irving Arthur, 1920- ,
  American; nonfiction CON
DELMAR, Viña Croter, 1905- ,
  American; fiction KL KT
DELMAS, Henry (Dalmas), 1712- ,
  French; poetry DIL
DELMER, Denis Sefton, 1904- ,
  German; fiction CON
'DELMONICO, Andrea' see MORRI-
  SON, Atwood E.
DELMONTE, Félix M. see MONTE,
  Félix M. del
DELMONTE y APONTE, Domingo,
  1804-53, Cuban; journalism MIN
  SA
DE LOACH, Charles F., 1927- ,
  American; nonfiction CON
'DELOIRE, Pierre' see PEGUY,
  Charles P.
DE LOLME, John Louis, 1740?-
  1806/07, Swiss; nonfiction BRO
  HAR ST
DELONEY, Thomas, 1543-1600?,
  English; fiction, poetry BRO
  KB MAG ST
DE LONGCHAMPS, Joanne Cutten,
  1923- , American; poetry CON
DELOUGHERY, Grace L., 1933- ,
  American; nonfiction CON
DELPRAIAN, Abbe, 18th cent.,
  French; nonfiction DIL
DELPY, G., 1897-1952, French;
  nonfiction BL
DEL RAY, Lester, 1915- , Ameri-
  can; juveniles WA
DELRUE, Emiel see STRAETEN,
  Emiel van der
'DELTA' see DENNETT, Herbert V.
'DELTA' see MOIR, David M.
DELTEIL, Joseph, 1894- , French;
  nonfiction DIF
DELLUCA, A. Michael, 1912- ,
  American; nonfiction CON
DELVIG, Anton Antonovich, Baron,
  1798-1831, Russian; poetry KE
  HARK ST
DELZELL, Charles Floyd, 1920- ,
  American; nonfiction CON
DEMACHY, Jacques François, 1728-
  1803, French; nonfiction DIL
DEMADES, fl. 1350-19 B.C., Greek;
  nonfiction ST
'DEMAINE, Don' see DRINKALL,

Gordon D.
DEMANDRE, Célestin, -1811,
  French; nonfiction DIL
DEMARAY, Donald Eugene,
  1926- , American; nonfiction
  CON
DE MARCHI, Emilio, 1851-1901,
  Italian; fiction COL HAR KE
  SA ST
DE MARCO, Angelus A., 1916- ,
  American; nonfiction CON
DE MARE, Eric Samuel, 1910- ,
  English; nonfiction CON
DE MARE, George, 1912- ,
  American; fiction CON
'DEMAREST, Doug' see BERKER,
  Will
DEMARIA, Bernabe, 1827- ,
  Argentinian; nonfiction MIN
DE MARIA, Robert, 1928- ,
  American; nonfiction, fiction
  CON
'DEMARIS, Ovid' see DESMARAIS,
  Ovide E.
DE MATTEO, Donna, 1941- ,
  American; plays CON
DE MAUNY, Erik, 1920- ,
  New Zealander; fiction CON
  ST
DEMBO, Lawrence Sanford,
  1929- , American; nonfiction
  CON
'DEMBRY, R. Emmett' see
  MURFREE, Mary N.
DE MENTE, Boye, 1928- ,
  American; nonfiction CON
'DE MENTON, Francisco' see
  CHIN, Frank C., Jr.
DEMETER, Dimitrije, 1811-72,
  Croatian; poetry, plays ST
DEMETILLO, Ricaredo D., 1920- ,
  Filipino; poetry, criticism
  MUR
DEMETRIUS, James Kleon,
  1920- , American; nonfiction
  CON
DEMETRIUS, fl. 350 B.C., Greek;
  nonfiction ST
DEMETRIUS CYDONES, -1400,
  Byzantine; nonfiction ST
DEMETRIUS of PHALERUM,
  150- , Greek; nonfiction ST
DEMETRIUS of ROSTOV see
  DMITRY ROSTOVSKY
DE MICHELIS, Curialo, 1904- ,
  Italian; poetry SA
'DEMIJOHN, Thom' see DISCH,
  Thomas M.

'DEMIJOHN, Thom' see SLADEK,
John
DE MILLE, Henry Churchill, 1853-
93, American; plays KAA
DE MILLE, James, 1836/37-80,
Canadian; fiction KBA SY
DE MILLE, Richard, 1922- , Amer-
ican; nonfiction CON
DEMING, Dorothy, 1893- , American;
juveniles WA
DEMING, Richard ('Max Franklin'),
1915- , American; fiction, ju-
veniles CON
DEMING, Robert H., 1937- , Amer-
ican; nonfiction CON
DEMOCRITUS, 460-370 B.C., Greek;
nonfiction SA ST
DEMOLDER, Eugene, 1862-1919,
Belgian; fiction, criticism COL
SA ST
DEMONACTE de CHIPRE, 15th cent.,
Greek; nonfiction SA
DEMONE, Harold Wellington, Jr.,
1924- , American; nonfiction
CON
DE MORDAUNT, Walter Julius,
1925- , American; nonfiction
CON
DEMOREST, Jean Jacques, 1920- ,
French; nonfiction, translations
CON
DE MORGAN, Augustus, 1806-71,
English; nonfiction BRO KBA
DE MORGAN, William Frend, 1839-
1917, English; fiction BRO KAT
KT MAG RIC ST
DEMOSTHENES, 384-22 B.C., Greek;
orator MAG SA ST
DE MOTT, Benjamin, 1924- , Amer-
ican; fiction, essays CON
DE MOURGUES, Odette Marie Helene
Louise, 1914- , French; non-
fiction, fiction CON
DEMPEWOLFF, Richard Frederic
('Michael Day'; 'Dick Frederick';
'Frederick Wolf'), 1914- ,
American; juveniles CON
DEMPSEY, David Knapp, 1914- ,
American; nonfiction CON
DEMPSEY, Rev. Martin, 1903- ,
Irish; nonfiction HO
DEMPSEY, Paul K., 1935- ,
American; nonfiction CON
DEMPSTER, Derek David, 1924- ,
English; nonfiction CON
DEMSKE, James Michael, 1922- ,
American; nonfiction CON
DEMUTH, Norman Frank, 1898- ,

American; nonfiction CON
'DENALI, Peter' see HOLM,
Donald R.
DENBEAUX, Fred J., 1914- ,
American; nonfiction CON
DEN BOER, James D., 1936/37- ,
American; poetry CON MUR
DENBY, Edwin Orr, 1903- ,
American; poetry MUR
DENDY, Marshall Coleman,
1902- , American; nonfiction
CON
DENE, Edewaerd de, 1505-78,
Dutch; poetry ST
DENENBERG, Herbert Sidney
('Humpty S. Dumpty'),
1929- , American; nonfiction
CON
DE NEVERS, Noel Howard,
1932- , American; nonfiction
CON
DE NEVI, Donald P., 1937- ,
American; nonfiction CON
DENG, William, 1929- , English;
nonfiction CON
DENHAM, Alice, 1933- , Ameri-
can; fiction CON
DENHAM, Sir John, 1615-59/69,
Irish; poetry, plays BRO KB
SA SP ST
DENHAM, Mary Orr ('Mary Orr';
'Anne Caswell'), American;
fiction CON
DENHAM, Reginald, 1894- ,
Anglo-American; plays CON
DENHOLM, Therese Mary Zita
White (Zita White), 1933- ,
Austrian; juvenile CON
DENIFLE, Heinrich, 1844-1905,
Austrian; nonfiction SA
DENINA, Jacopo Maria Carlo,
1731-1813, Italian; nonfiction
SA
DENIS, Jean Ferdinand, 1798-1890,
French; nonfiction SA
DENIS, Michaela Holdsworth,
English; juvenile CON
DENIS, Paul, 1909- , American;
nonfiction CON
DENIS PIRAMUS, 12th cent.,
Anglo-Norman; poetry ST
DENISOFF, R. Serge, 1939- ,
American; nonfiction CON
DENISON, Barbara, 1926- ,
American; nonfiction CON
DENISON, Carol, American;
juveniles WA
DENISON, Edward Fulton, 1915- ,

American; nonfiction CON

DENISON, Merrill, 1873- , Canadian; plays SY

DENISON, Muriel Goggin, Canadian; juveniles WA

DENISOT, Nicolas, 1515-59, French; poetry ST

DENKER, Henry, 1912- , American; fiction, plays CON WAF

DENMAN, Frank, American; juveniles WA

DENNERY, Adolphe Philippe (D'Ennery), 1811-99, French; plays DIF HAR

DENNETT, Herbert Victor ('Delta'; 'John Syntax'; 'Ned Tent'), 1893- , English; nonfiction CON

DENNETT, Tyler, 1883- , American; nonfiction KT

DENNEY, Reuel Nicholas, 1913- , American; poetry, plays CON MUR

DENNIE, Joseph ('Lay Preacher'; 'Oliver Oldschool'), 1768-1812, American; journalism, essays KAA ST

DENNING, Basil W., 1928- , English; nonfiction CON

'DENNING, Patricia' see WILLIS, Corinne D.

DENNIS, Clarence Michael James, 1876-1938, Australian; poetry, journalism BRO RIC ST

DENNIS, Geoffrey Pomeroy, 1892- , English; fiction, essays KAT KT

DENNIS, John, 1657-1734, English; criticism, plays, poetry BRO KB ST

DENNIS, Morgan, 1893-1960, American; juveniles FUL WA

DENNIS, Nigel Forbes, 1912- , English; criticism, plays, fiction CON MAT RIC

DENNIS, Suzanne Easton, 1922- , American; juveniles CON

DENNIS, Wayne, 1905- , American; nonfiction CON

DENNIS, Wesley, 1903- , American; juveniles FUL WA

DENNY, Grace Goldena, American; nonfiction PAC

DENNY, John Howard, 1920- , English; nonfiction CON

DENOMME, Robert T., 1930- , American; nonfiction CON

DE NORONHA, Lesley, 1926- ,

English; poetry, fiction MUR

DE NOVO, John A., 1916- , American; nonfiction CON

DENSEN-GERBER, Judianne, 1934- , American; nonfiction CON

DENSUSIANU, Ovid, 1873-1938, Rumanian; fiction ST

DENT, Alan Holmes, 1905- , Scots; criticism CON

DENT, Anthony Austin ('Antony Amplegirth'; 'El Bundukhari'; 'Malaby Garthwaite'), 1915- , English; fiction CON

DENT, Colin, 1921- , English; nonfiction CON

DENT, Harold Collett, 1894- , American; nonfiction CON

DENT, Lester, American; fiction MAR

DENTAN, Robert Claude, 1907- , American; nonfiction CON

'DENTINGER, Stephen' see HOCH, Edward D.

DENTLER, Robert Arnold, 1928- , American; nonfiction CON

DENTON, Charles Frederick, 1942- , Canadian-American; nonfiction CON

DENTON, Daniel, fl. 1670, American; nonfiction KAA

DENTON, Harry M., 1882- , American; fiction CON

DENTON, Wallace, 1928- , American; nonfiction CON

'DENVER, Boone' see RENNIE, James A.

'DENVER, Drake' see NYE, Nelson C.

'DENVER, Rod' see EDSON, John T.

DENZER, Peter Worthington, 1921- , American; nonfiction CON

DENZIN, Norman Kent, 1941- , American; nonfiction CON

DEON, Michel, 1919- , French; fiction CON DIC DIF

DE OSMA, Lupe, American; juveniles WA

'DE PAOR, Risteard' see POWER, Richard

DE PAUW, Linda Grant, 1940- , American; nonfiction CON

DE PEREDA, Prudencio, 1912- , American; fiction, nonfiction CON WAF

DEPERTHES, Jean Louis Hubert

Simon, 1730-92, French; nonfiction DIL

DEPEW, Walter Westerfield, 1924- , American; fiction CON

DE PEYSTER, John Watts, 1821-1907, American; nonfiction KAA

'DE POLMAN, Willem' see NICHOLAS, Dale W.

DE POLNAY, Peter, 1906- , British; fiction KTS

DE QUINCEY, Thomas, 1785-1859, English; essays, fiction BRO KBA MAG SA ST

DERBY, Lord (Edward George Geoffrey Smith Stanley), 1799-1869, English; poetry KBA

DERBY, George Horatio ('John Phoenix'; 'Squibob'), 1823-61, American; fiction KAA

DE REGIBUS, Luca, 1895- , Italian; nonfiction SA

DE REGNIERS, Beatrice Schenk, 1914- , American; juveniles COM CON FUL WA

'DEREME Tristan' (Philippe Huc), 1889-1941/42, French; nonfiction DIF SA

DE RENEVILLE, Mary Margaret Motley, Sheridan (Mary Motley), 1912- , English; fiction CON

DERFLER, Arnold Leslie, 1933- , American; nonfiction CON

DERHAM, Arthur Morgan, 1915- , English; nonfiction CON

DE RHAM, Edith, 1933- , American; nonfiction CON

DERIC, Anthony J., 1926- , American; nonfiction CON

DERIN, P.I. see 'LANSEL, Peider'

DERING, Joan Rosalind Cordelia, 1917- , English; juveniles CON

DERLETH, August William ('Stephen Grendon'; 'Tally Mason'), 1909-71, American; fiction, juveniles, nonfiction CON KT WA WAF

DERLETH, Ludwig, 1870-1948, German; poetry FLE KU

DERMONDY, Thomas, 1775-1802, Irish; poetry BRO ST

DERMOÛT, Maria, 1888-1962, Dutch; fiction FLE

DERN, Peggy Gaddis ('Robert Courtland'; 'Peggy Gaddis'; 'Georgia Craig'; 'Gail Jordan'; 'Carolina Lee'; 'Perry Lindsay'; Joan Sherman'), 1895-1966, American; fiction CON

DERNBURG, Thomas Frederick,

1930- , German-American; nonfiction CON

DE ROBECK, Nesta, 1886- , English; nonfiction CON

DE ROBERTO, Federico, 1866-1927, Italian; fiction, criticism COL HAR SA ST

DE ROMASZKAN, Gregor, 1894- , Polish-French; nonfiction CON

DE ROOS, Robert, 1912- , American; nonfiction CON

DE ROPP, Robert Sylvester, 1913- , English; fiction CON

DEROR, Yehezkel see DROR, Yehezkel

DE ROSA, Peter, 1932- , American; nonfiction CON

DEROSIER, Arthur Henry, Jr., 1931- , American; nonfiction CON

DE ROSSI, Azariah (Min Ha-Adummim), 1513-78, Italian; poetry ST

DE ROUDEDE, Paul, 1846-1914, French; poetry, plays DIF HAR SA ST

DEROUNIAN, Avodis Arthur ('John Roy Carlson'), 1909- , American; journalism KTS

DERRETT, John Duncan Martin, 1922- , English; nonfiction CON

DERRICK, John Michael, 1915- , English; nonfiction HO

DERRICK, Paul, 1916- , English; nonfiction CON HO

DERRY, John Wesley, 1933- , English; nonfiction CON

DERRY, Thomas Kingston, 1905- , Scots; nonfiction CON

DERSHOWITZ, Alan M., 1938- , American; nonfiction CON

DERTOUZOS, Michael L., 1936- , Greek-American; nonfiction CON

DERUM, James Patrick, 1893- , American; nonfiction CON

DERUTH, Jan, 1922- , Czech-American; nonfiction CON

DERVIN, Brenda, 1938- , American; nonfiction CON

DERWIN, Jordan, 1931- , American; nonfiction CON

DERY, Tibor, 1894- , Hungarian; fiction FLE RIC

DERZHAVIN, Gavrila Romanovich (Dierjavine), 1743-1816,

Russian; poetry HAR HARK
KT SA ST
DESAI, Prasannavadan Bhagwanji,
1924- , Indian; nonfiction
CON
DESAI, Ram, 1926- , Indian; non-
fiction CON
DESAI, Rashmi Harilal, 1928- ,
Indian; nonfiction CON
DE SAINT PHALLE, Therese,
1930- , American; nonfiction,
fiction CON
DE SALES, Raoul de Roussy, 1896-
1942, Franco-American; nonfic-
tion HOE
DE SANCTIS, Francesco, 1817-83,
Italian; criticism COL HAR KE
SA ST
DE SANTILLANA, Giorgio Diaz,
1902- , Italian-American; non-
fiction CON
DE SANTIS, Mary Allen Carpe,
1930- , American; juveniles
CON
DE SANTIS, Vincent P., 1916- ,
American; nonfiction CON
DESAUGIERS, Marc Antoine, 1772-
1827, French; plays SA
DESAULNIERS, Gonzalve, 1863-1934,
Canadian; poetry SY
DESAULX, Pierre, 1698-1761, French;
nonfiction DIL
DE SAUSMAREZ, Maurice, 1915- ,
Australian; nonfiction CON
DES AUTELS, Guillaume, 1529-
81?, French; poetry ST
DESBARATS, Peter, 1933- ,
Canadian; nonfiction CON
'DESBERRY, Lawrence H.' see
MÜHLEN, Hermynia
DESBILLONS, François Joseph
Terrasse, 1711-89, French;
nonfiction DIL
DESBORDES, Nicolas,   -1713,
French; nonfiction DIL
DESBORDES-VALMORE, Marceline
Félicité Josephe, 1786-1859,
French; poetry HAR DIF KE SA
ST
DESBOULMIERS, Jean Auguste Jul-
lien, 1731-71, French; fiction
DIL
DESCALZO, Giovanni, 1902- ,
Italian; poetry, fiction, criticism
SA
DESCALZO, Martín see MARTIN
DESCALZA, Ignacio
DESCAMPS, Jean Baptiste, 1714-91,

French; nonfiction DIL
DESCARGUES, Pierre, 1925- ,
French; nonfiction CON
DESCARTES, Catherine, 1627-
1706, French; nonfiction SA
DESCARTES, René, 1596-1650,
French; nonfiction DIF HAR
KE MAL SA ST
DESCAVES, Lucien Alexandre,
1861-1949, French; fiction
COL DIF HAR SA ST
DESCHAMPS, Antoine François
Marie, 1800-69, French;
poetry, translations HAR SA
DESCHAMPS, Emile, 1791-1871,
French; nonfiction HAR KE SA
ST
DESCHAMPS, Enrique, 1872-1933,
Dominican; nonfiction MIN
DESCHAMPS, Eugenio, 1862-1919,
Dominican; nonfiction MIN
DESCHAMPS, Eustache ('Morel'),
1346?-1407/15, French; poetry
DIF HAR KE SA ST
DESCHAMPS, Jacques, 1677-1759,
French; nonfiction DIL
DESCHAMPS, Jean, 1708-67,
French; nonfiction DIL
DESCHAMPS, Léger Marie, 1716-
74, French; nonfiction DIL
DESCHAMPSNEUFS, Henry Pierre
Bernard, 1911- , English;
nonfiction CON
DESCHANEL, Emile Auguste
Etienne, 1819-1904, French;
essays, journalism, criticism
SA
DESCHNER, Donald Anthony,
1933- , American; nonfiction
CON
DESCLOT, Bernat, 13th cent.,
Spanish; nonfiction ST SA
DE SELINCOURT, Aubrey,
1894- , English; juveniles
DOY
DE SELINCOURT, Ernest, 1870-
1943, English; criticism BRO
KT
DESESSARTS, 1737-93, French;
nonfiction DIL
DESESSARTZ, Jean Charles, 1729-
1811, French; nonfiction DIL
DE SEYN, Donna E., 1933- ,
American; nonfiction CON
DESFONTAINES, Guillaume
François Fouques-Deshays,
1733-1825, French; plays
DIL

DESFONTAINES, Pierre François
Guyot, 1685- , French; criti-
cism, translations DIL
DESFORGES, Pierre J. B. Choudart,
1746-1803, French; plays, fic-
tion SA
DESFORGES MAILLARD, Paul, 1699-
1772, French; poetry SA
DE SHAZO, Elmer Anthony, 1924- ,
American; nonfiction CON
DESHOULIERES, Antoinette de Ligier,
1634/38-94, French; poetry SA
ST
DESHPANDE, Gavri Karve, 1942- ,
Indian; poetry MUR
DESIDERATO, Otello, 1926- ,
Italian-American; nonfiction CON
DE SIMONE, Daniel V., 1930- ,
American; nonfiction CON
DESJARDINS, Paul, 1859-1940,
French; criticism COL
DESLANDES, André François
Boueau, 1690-1757, French;
nonfiction, fiction DIL
DESMAISEAUX, Pierre, 1666-1745,
French; nonfiction DIL
DESMARAIS, Barbara G. T., 1942- ,
American; nonfiction CON
DESMARAIS, Ovide E. ('Ovid
Demaris'), 1919- , American;
nonfiction CON
DESMAREST, Nicolas, 1725-1815,
French; nonfiction DIL
DESMARETS, de SAINT-SORLIN,
Jean, 1596-1676, French; poetry
DIF HAR ST
DESMARQUEST, Jean Antoine Sam-
son, 1722-1809, French; nonfic-
tion DIL
DES MASURES, Louis, 1515?-74,
French; plays, poetry HAR ST
DESMOLETS, Pierre Nicolas, 1678-
1760, French; nonfiction DIL
DESMOND, Alice Curtis, 1897- ,
American; juveniles CON WA
DESMOND, Claire Joanne Patrick
Scholes, 1910- , American;
nonfiction CON
DESMONDE, William Herbert,
1921- , American; nonfiction
CON
DESMONTS, Premy, 1703-87,
French; nonfiction DIL
DESMOULINS, Camille, 1760-94,
French; journalism, nonfiction
DIL HAR SA
DESMOULINS, Laurent, fl. 1511,
French; poetry ST

DES NOIRES TERRES, Hyacinthe
Jean, 1712-26, French;
poetry DIL
DESNOS, Robert, 1900-45, French;
poetry, fiction DIF FLE MAL
SA
DESNOYERS, Etienne, 1722- ,
French; nonfiction DIL
DESORMEAUX, Joseph Louis
Ripault, 1724-93, French;
nonfiction DIL
DES PERIERS, Bonaventure,
1510?-1544/54, French;
poetry, nonfiction DIF HAR
SA ST
DESPLACES, Laurent Benoît, 18th
cent., French; nonfiction DIL
'DESPLAINES, Baroness Julie' see
JENNINGS, Leslie N.
DESPORTES, Philippe, 1546/47-
1606, French; poetry DIF
HAR KE SA ST
DESPRADEL, Lorenzo, 1872-1927,
Dominican; nonfiction MIN
DESPREAUX, Nicolas see
BOILEAU-DESPREAUX, Nicolas
DESPRESS, Leo Arthur, 1932- ,
American; nonfiction CON
DESROCHERS, Alfred, 1901- ,
Canadian; poetry SY
DES ROCHES, Catherine Fradon-
net, 1547-87, French; poetry
KE ST
DES ROCHES, Madeleine Neven,
1520/30-97, French; poetry
KE SA ST
DESROSIERS, Leo Paul, 1896- ,
Canadian; fiction SY
DESSAU, Moses see MENDELS-
SOHN, Moses
DES THUILLERIES, Claude de
Moulinet, 1661-1728, French;
nonfiction DIL
DESTLER, Chester McArthur,
1904- , American; nonfiction
CON
DESTOUCHES, Louis Ferdinand
see 'CELINE'
DESTOUCHES, Philippe Néricault,
1680-1754, French; plays DIF
DIL HAR KT SA ST
DESTREE, Jules, 1863-1936,
Belgian; fiction, criticism,
diary ST
DESTREES, Jacques, 18th cent.,
French; criticism DIL
'DESTRY, Vince' see NORWOOD,
Victor G. C.

DESTUTT de TRACY, Antoine Louis
Claude, 1754-1836, French; nonfiction DIF

DE SUA, William Joseph, 1930- ,
American; nonfiction CON

DE TABLEY, John Byron Leicester
Warren, 1835-95, English;
poetry BRO KBA

DE TARR, Francis, 1926- , American; nonfiction CON

DETERLINE, William Alexander,
1927- , American; nonfiction
CON

DE TERRA, Rhoda Hoff, 1901- ,
American; juveniles, fiction
CON

DETHERAGE, May, 1908- , American; nonfiction CON

DETHLOFF, Henry Clay, 1934- ,
American; nonfiction CON

DETJEN, Ervin Winfred, American;
nonfiction CON

DETJEN, Mary Elizabeth Ford,
1904- , American; nonfiction
CON

'DETLEV von L.' see LILIENCRON,
Friedrich A. A.

DETMOLD, Johann Hermann, 1807-
56, German; nonfiction AL

DE TOURNEMIR see SALIAS de
TOURNEMIR

DETWEILER, Robert, 1932- ,
American; nonfiction CON

DETWILER, Donald Scaife, 1933- ,
American; nonfiction CON

DETZ, Phyllis, 1911- , American;
poetry CON

DETZER, Karl ('Michael Costello'),
1891- , American; nonfiction
CON

DETZLER, Jack J., 1922- , American; nonfiction CON

DEUBEL, Léon, 1879-1913, French;
poetry DIF

DEUCHER, Sybil, American; juveniles
FUL

DEUS, João de see RAMOS, João
de D. N.

'DEUTIERRE, Marie' see ENNETIE-
RES, Marie

DEUTRICH, Mabel E., 1915- ,
American; nonfiction CON

DEUTSCH, Babette, 1895- , American; juveniles, poetry, fiction,
criticism BRO COM CON FUL
KL KT MUR RIC

DEUTSCH, Bernard Francis, 1925- ,
American; nonfiction CON

DEUTSCH, Harold Charles,
1904- , American; nonfiction
CON

DEUTSCH, Morton, 1920- ,
American; nonfiction CON

DEUTSCH, Ronald Martin,
1928- , American; nonfiction
CON

DEUTSCHER, Irwin, 1923- ,
American; nonfiction CON

DEUTSCHER, Isaac, 1907-67,
Polish-English; nonfiction
CON

DEUTSCHKRON, Inge, 1922- ,
German; nonfiction CON

DEVADUTT, Vinjamuri Everett,
1908- , Indian-American;
nonfiction CON

DE VAERE, Ulric Josef, 1932- ,
American; nonfiction CON

DEVAISNE, Jean, 1753-1803,
French; nonfiction DIL

'DEVAL, Jacques' (Jacques
Boularan), 1890/94-1972,
French; plays, fiction HAR
KT MAT ST

DE VALERA, Sinead O'Flanagan,
Irish; fiction, translations
HO

'DEVON, John Anthony' see PAYNE,
Pierre S. R.

DEVANEY, John, 1926- , American; nonfiction CON

DEVANNEY, Jean Crooks, 1896- ,
New Zealander; fiction ST

DEVAS, Nicolette Macnamara,
1911- , English; fiction CON

DE VAULT, Marion Vere, 1922- ,
American; juveniles CON

DEVAULX, Noël, 1905- , French;
fiction DIF PIN

D'EVELYN, Katherine Edith,
1899- , American; nonfiction
CON

DEVER, Joseph, 1919-70, American; nonfiction, fiction CON
HO

DE VERE, Sir Aubrey, 1788-1846,
Irish; poetry, plays KBA ST

DE VERE, Aubrey Thomas,
1814-1902, Irish; poetry BRO
KBA ST

DE VERE, Edward see VERE
Edward de

DEVEREUX, Hilary, 1919- ,
English; nonfiction CON

DEVEREUX, Robert, 1566-1600/
01- , English; poetry ST

DEVEREUX, Robert Essex, 1922- ,
American; nonfiction CON
DEVEREUX, Walter, 1541-76, Eng-
lish; poetry ST
DEVI, Indra, 1899- , Russian-
Mexican; nonfiction CON
DE VINCK, Baron Jose M.G.A.,
1912- , Belgian-American;
poetry, translations CON
DEVINE, David McDonald, 1920- ,
Scots; fiction CON
DEVINE, Thomas G., 1928- ,
American; nonfiction CON
DE VINNE, Theodore Low, 1828-
1914, American; nonfiction KAA
DEVINS, Joseph Herbert, Jr.,
1930- , American; nonfiction
CON
DE VITO, Joseph Anthony, 1938- ,
American; nonfiction CON
DEVLIN, Denis, 1908- , Irish;
poetry ST
DEVLIN, John Joseph, Jr., 1920- ,
American; nonfiction CON
DEVORE, Irven, 1934- , American;
nonfiction CON
DEVOR, John Wesley, 1901- ,
American; nonfiction CON
DE VORSEY, Louis, Jr., 1929- ,
American; nonfiction CON
DEVOS, Alphonse George, 1922- ,
American; nonfiction CON
DE VOSJOLI, Philippe L. Thyraud,
1920- , American; nonfiction
CON
DE VOTO, Bernard Augustine, 1897-
1955, American; fiction FLE
KT WAF
DEVOTO, Daniel, 1916- , Argentinian;
poetry BL
DEVOTO, Juan Bautista, 1916- ,
Argentinian; nonfiction, plays
MIN
DE VRIES, Herbert H., 1917- ,
American; nonfiction CON
DE VRIES, Peter, 1907/10- ,
American; poetry, fiction CON
HOO
DEW, Charles Burgess, 1937- ,
American; nonfiction CON
DE WAAL, Ronald Burt, 1932- ,
American; nonfiction CON
DE WAAL, Victor Alexander,
1929- , Dutch-English; nonfic-
tion CON
DEWALD, Paul A., 1920- , Ameri-
can; nonfiction CON
DEWAR, Mary Williamson, 1921- ,

English; nonfiction CON
DEWART, Leslie, 1922- , Spanish-
Canadian; nonfiction CON
DE WEERD, Harvey A., 1902- ,
American; nonfiction CON
DE WELT, Don Finch, 1919- ,
American; nonfiction CON
DEWEY, Bradley R., 1934- ,
American; nonfiction CON
DEWEY, Donald Odell, 1930- ,
American; nonfiction CON
DEWEY, Godfrey, 1887- , Ameri-
can; nonfiction CON
DEWEY, Irene Sargent, 1896- ,
American; poetry CON
DEWEY, John, 1859-1952, Ameri-
can; nonfiction BRO KAT KT
SA ST
DEWEY, Robert Dyckman, 1923- ,
American; nonfiction CON
DEWEY, Robert Eugene, 1923- ,
American; nonfiction CON
DEWEY, Thomas Blanchard ('Tom
Brandt'; 'Cord Wainer'),
1915- , American; fiction
CON
DEWHURST, James Frederic,
1895- , American; nonfiction
CON
DEWHURST, Kenneth, 1919- ,
English; nonfiction CON
'DE WITT, James' see LEWIS,
Mildred D.
DEWLEN, Al, 1921- , American;
fiction CON
DE WOHL, Louis, 1903- , Ger-
man; fiction HO
DE WOLF, L. Harold, 1905- ,
American; nonfiction CON
DEWOLF, Rose, 1934- , Ameri-
can; fiction CON
DE WULF, Maurice, 1867-1947,
Belgian; nonfiction HO
DEXIPO, 4th cent., Greek; non-
fiction SA
DEXTER, Franklin Bowditch,
1842-1920, American; nonfic-
tion KAA
'DEXTER, John' see KANTO,
Peter
DEXTER, Lewis Anthony, 1915- ,
American; nonfiction CON
DEXTER, Timothy, 1747-1806,
American; fiction KAA
DEY, Joseph Charles, Jr.,
1907- , American; nonfiction
CON
DEYERMOND, Alan David, 1932- ,

American; nonfiction CON
'DEYSSEL, Lodewijk van' (Karl
Joan Lodewijk Alberdingk
Thijm), 1864-1952, Dutch; fic-
tion, criticism COL FLE SA
ST
DEZALLIER d'ARGENVILLE, Antoine
Joseph, 1680-1765, French;
nonfiction DIL
DEZALLIER d'ARGENVILLE, Antoine
Nicolas, 1732-96, French;
nonfiction DIL
DEZELIC, Djuro, 1838-1907,
Croatian; fiction SA ST
DEZMAN, Ivan, 1841-73, Croatian;
poetry SA ST
DHALLA, Nariman K., 1925- ,
Indian; nonfiction CON
'D'HALMAR, Augusto', 1882-1950,
Chilean; fiction, essays MIN SA
'd'HANNETAIRE' see SERVANDONI,
Jean N.
DHAVAMONY, Mariasusai, 1925- ,
American; nonfiction CON
'DHEORSA, MacIain' see HAY,
George C.
DHLOMO, Herbert E., 1905-57,
South African; poetry, plays
RIC
DHÔTEL, André, 1900- , French;
fiction DIF FLE MAL
DHRYMES, Phoebus James, 1932- ,
American; nonfiction CON
DIACK, Hunter, 1908- , Scots;
nonfiction CON
DIAGORA, el ATEO, 5th cent. B.C.,
Greek; nonfiction SA
DIAMANT, Lincoln ('Stan McDougal'),
1923- , American; nonfiction
CON
DIAMANTE, Juan Bautista, 1625?-
87, Spanish; plays BL HAR SA
ST
DIAMOND, Arthur Sigismund,
1897- , English; nonfiction
CON
DIAMOND, Edwin, 1925- , Ameri-
can; nonfiction CON
DIAMOND, Malcolm Luria, 1924- ,
American; nonfiction CON
DIAMOND, Robert Mack, 1930- ,
American; nonfiction CON
DIAMOND, Sigmund, 1920- , Amer-
ican; nonfiction CON
DIANA, Manuel Juan, 1814-81,
Spanish; fiction, plays BL SA
'DIANA de LIZ' (Maria Eugenia
Haas da Costa Ramos), 1892-

1930, Portuguese; nonfiction
SA
DIAPER, William, 1685-1717,
English; poetry SP
DIAS, Baltasar, 16th cent.,
Portuguese; plays SA
DIAS, Carlos Malheiro, 1875-
1941, Portuguese; fiction,
journalism ST
DIAS, Earl Joseph, 1916- ,
American; nonfiction CON
DIAZ, Abby Morton, 1821-1904,
American; fiction, essays
KAA
DIAZ, Eugenio, 1803/04-65,
Colombian; nonfiction, fiction
MIN SA
DIAZ, José María, 1800-88,
Spanish; plays SA
DIAZ, Leopoldo, 1862/68-1947,
Argentinian; poetry BL MIN
SA
DIAZ, Sebastián, 18th cent.,
Chilean; nonfiction MIN
DIAZ ARRIETA, Hernán ('Alone'),
1891- , Chilean; criticism,
fiction MIN SA
DIAZ CALLECERRADA, Marcelo,
17th cent., Spanish; poetry
BL SA
DIAZ CAÑABATE, Antonio,
1898- , Spanish; nonfiction
BL SA
DIAZ CANEJA, Guillermo, 1876-
1933, Spanish; fiction BL SA
DIAZ CANEJA, Juan, 1880- ,
Spanish; nonfiction SA
DIAZ CASANUEVA, Humberto,
1905- , Chilean; poetry, es-
says SA ST
DIAZ de ESCOVAR, Narciso,
1860-1935, Spanish; poetry,
plays, journalism BL SA
DIAZ de GAMEZ, Gutierre, 1378-
1448, Spanish; nonfiction SA
DIAZ de GUZMAN, Ruy, 1558-
1629, Argentinian; nonfiction
MIN
DIAZ de LEGUIZAMON, Héctor,
1892-1938, Argentinian; poetry
MIN
DIAZ del CASTILLO, Bernal,
1492?-1581?, Spanish; nonfic-
tion BL HAR KE SA ST
DIAZ FERNANDEZ, José, 1898-
1940, Spanish; journalism,
essays, fiction SA
DIAZ GANA, Pedro, 19th cent.,

Chilean; poetry MIN

DIAZ GARCES, Joaquín ('Angel
Pino'), 1878-1921, Chilean;
journalism, essays, fiction MIN
SA

DIAZ LOYOLA, Carlos see ROKHA,
Pablo de

DIAZ MACHICO, Porfirio, 20th cent.,
Bolivian; journalism MIN

DIAZ MEZA, Aurelio, 1879-1932,
Chilean; fiction, plays MIN

DIAZ MIRON, Salvador, 1853-1928,
Mexican; poetry BL FLE SA ST

DIAZ ORDOÑEZ, Virgilio ('Ligio
Vizardi'), 1895- , Dominican;
nonfiction, poetry MIN SA

DIAZ PEREZ, Nicolás, 1841-91,
Spanish; journalism SA

DIAZ PLAJA, Fernando, 1918- ,
Spanish; journalism, essays BL
SA

DIAZ PLAJA, Guillermo, 1909- ,
Spanish; essays, poetry, criticism BL SA

DIAZ RODRIGUEZ, Manuel, 1864-
1927/28, Venezuelan; criticism,
fiction, essays, journalism BL
FLE SA ST

DIAZ ROMERO, Eugenio, 1877-1927,
Argentinian; journalism, poetry,
essays MIN

DIAZ SANCHEZ, Ramón, 1903- ,
Venezuelan; essays, fiction SA

DIAZ SILVEIRA, Francisco, 1871-
1924, Cuban; poetry MIN

DIAZ TANCO de FREGENAL, Vasco,
1514-70, Spanish; poetry, plays
BL SA

DIB, Mohammed, 1920- , Algerian;
poetry FLE

DIBDIN, Charles, 1745-1814, English; plays, poetry, BRO KB ST

DIBDIN, Thomas John, 1771-1841,
English; songs BRO

DIBBLE, James Birney, 1925- ,
American; nonfiction CON

DICEARCO, 4th-3rd cent. B.C.,
Greek; nonfiction SA

DICENTA, Joaquín, 1863-1917,
Spanish; plays BL COL HAR
SA ST

DICENTA, Joaquín, 1893- , Spanish;
poetry, plays BL SA

DI CERTO, Joseph John, 1933- ,
American; nonfiction CON

DI CESARE, Mario Anthony, 1928- ,
American; nonfiction CON

DICHTER, Ernest, 1907- , Austrian-

American; nonfiction CON

DICK, Bernard Francis, 1935- ,
American; nonfiction CON

DICK, Everett, 1898- , American; nonfiction CON

DICK, Ignace, 1926- , Syrian;
nonfiction CON

DICK, Isaac Meyer ('Amod'),
1807-93, Jewish; fiction ST

DICK, Kay, 1915- , English;
fiction CON

DICK, Robert C., 1938- , American; nonfiction CON

DICK, Trella Lamson, 1889- ,
American; juveniles, fiction
CON WA

DICKASON, David Howard,
1907- , American; nonfiction
CON

DICKEN, Eric William Trueman,
1919- , English; nonfiction
CON

DICKEN, Samuel Newton, 1901- ,
American; nonfiction PAC

DICKENS, Charles, 1812-70, English; juveniles, fiction BRO
DOY KBA MAG SA ST WA

DICKENS, Milton, 1908- , American; nonfiction CON

DICKENS, Monica Enid, 1915- ,
English; fiction BRO CON
HOE RIC

DICKENSON, John, fl. 1594, English; poetry, fiction ST

DICKERSON, Frederick Reed,
1909- , American; nonfiction
CON

DICKERSON, Grace Leslie,
1911- , American; juveniles
CON

DICKERSON, Roy Ernest, 1886- ,
American; nonfiction CON

DICKERSON, William Eugene,
1897- , American; nonfiction
CON

DICKEY, Franklin Miller, 1921- ,
American; nonfiction CON

DICKEY, James Lafayette, 1923- ,
American; fiction, poetry
CON FLE MUR

DICKEY, Robert Preston, 1936- ,
American; poetry CON MUR

DICKEY, William, 1928- ,
American; poetry CON MUR

DICKIE, Edgar Primrose, 1897- ,
Scots; nonfiction, translations
CON

DICKIE, George Thomas, 1926- ,

American; nonfiction CON

DICKIE, John, 1923- , Scots; non-fiction CON

DICKIE-CLARK, Hamion Findlay, 1922- , South African; nonfiction CON

DICKINSON, Arthur Taylor, Jr., 1925- , American; nonfiction CON

DICKINSON, Donald C., 1927- , American; nonfiction CON

DICKINSON, Emily Elizabeth, 1830-86, American; poetry BRO KAA MAG SA SP ST

DICKINSON, Goldsworthy Lowes, 1862-1932, English; nonfiction BRO KT ST

DICKINSON, Harry Thomas, 1939- , English; nonfiction CON

DICKINSON, John ('Fabius'), 1732-1808, American; nonfiction KAA ST

DICKINSON, John Kellogg, 1918- , American; nonfiction CON

DICKINSON, Leon T., 1912- , American; nonfiction CON

DICKINSON, Maude Elizabeth, American; nonfiction PAC

DICKINSON, Patric Thomas, 1914- , British; poetry, plays CON MUR

DICKINSON, Robert Eric, 1905- , English; nonfiction CON

DICKINSON, Ruth Frankenstein, 1933- , American; nonfiction CON

DICKINSON, Thomas Herbert, 1877- , American; nonfiction KT

DICKINSON, William Croft, 1897-1964, English; juveniles, nonfiction DOY CON

DICKINSON, William Stirling, 1909- , American; nonfiction CON

DICKLER, Gerald, 1912- , American; fiction CON

DICKMANN, Max, 1902- , Argentinian; fiction, journalism, criticism, essays MIN

DICKS, Russell Leslie, 1906-65, American; nonfiction CON

'DICKSON, Carr' see CARR, John D.

'DICKSON, Carter' see CARR, John D.

DICKSON, Charles W., Jr., 1926- , American; nonfiction CON

DICKSON, Gordon Rupert, 1923- , Canadian; fiction CON

'DICKSON, Helen' see REYNOLDS, Helen M.G.

DICKSON, Horatio Henry Lovat, 1902- , Australian; fiction CON

DICKSON, Marguerite Stockman, 1873-1953, American; juveniles FUL WA

DICKSON, Mora Hope-Robertson, 1918- , Scots; nonfiction CON

DICKSON, Naida ('Grace Lee Richardson'), 1916- , American; juveniles CON

DICKSON, Paul, 1939- , American; nonfiction CON

DICKSON, Peter George Muir, 1929- , English; nonfiction CON

DICKSON, Robert James, 1919- , Irish; nonfiction CON

DICTIS de CRETA (Dictys Cretensis), Greek; nonfiction SA ST

DICUIL, -825, Irish; poetry ST

DI CYAN, Erwin, 1908- , American; nonfiction CON

DIDELOT, Benoît Joseph, 1736- , French; nonfiction DIL

DIDEROT, Denis, 1713-84, French; essays, plays DIF DIL HAR KE MAG MAL SA ST

DIDIER, Eugene Lemoine, 1838-1913, American; nonfiction KAA

DIDIMO, 1st cent. B.C., Greek; criticism SA

DIDIMO de ALEXANDRIA, 309-96, Greek; nonfiction SA

DIDION, Joan, 1934- , American; fiction, essays CON

DI DONATO, Pietro, 1911- , American; fiction KT

DIDRING, Ernst, 1868-1931, Swedish; plays, fiction COL SA

DIDYMUS, 1st cent. B.C., Greek; nonfiction ST

DIE, Beatriz Alix, 12th cent., Dutch?, poetry SA

DIEBOLD, William, Jr., 1918- , American; nonfiction CON

DIECKELMANN, Heinrich, 1898- , German; poetry,

plays ST
DIEGO, José de, 1866-1918, (Puerto
Rican; poetry, nonfiction
SA
DIEGO, Luis de, 1919- , Spanish;
fiction BL
DIEGO CENDOYA, Gerardo, 1896- ,
Spanish; poetry BL COL FLE
HAR SA ST
DIEGO PADRO, J.I. de, 1896- ,
Puerto Rican; poetry SA
DIEGUEZ OLAVERRI, Juan, 1822-
82, Guatamalan; poetry SA
DIEHL, Katharine Smith, 1906- ,
American; nonfiction CON
DIEHL, William Wells ('Duncan
Clay'), 1916- , American;
nonfiction CON
DIEKHOFF, John Siemon, 1905- ,
American; nonfiction CON
DIEKMANN, Godfrey, 1908- ,
American; nonfiction CON
DIENSTEIN, William, 1909- ,
American; nonfiction CON
DIERENFIELD, Richard Bruce,
1922- , American; nonfiction
CON
DIERJAVINE, G. R. see DERZHAVIN,
Gavrila R.
DIERKS, Jack Cameron, 1930- ,
American; nonfiction CON
DIERS, Carol Jean, 1933- ,
American; nonfiction CON
DIERX, Marais Victor Léon, 1838-
1912, French; poetry DIF HAR
KE SA ST
DIESBACH, Nicola de, 1732-98,
French; nonfiction DIL
DIESING, Paul R., 1922- , Ameri-
can; nonfiction CON
DIESKA L. Joseph, 1913- , Czech-
American; nonfiction CON
DIESPECKER, Richard E. Alan,
1907- , Canadian; journalism,
nonfiction SY
'DIEST, Jan van' see BERGHE, Jan
van den
DIESTE, Eduardo, 1893-1954,
Uruguayan; criticism, essays
SA
DIESTE, Rafael, 1899- , Spanish;
plays, essays SA
DIETL, Kirsten Ulla, 1940- ,
Danish; juveniles CON
DIETMAR von EIST (Aist),   -1171,
German; poetry AL ST
DIETRICH, John Erb, 1913- ,
American; nonfiction CON

DIETRICH, Richard Farr, 1936- ,
American; nonfiction CON
DIETRICH, Robert Salisbury
('Gordon Davis'), 1928- ,
American; fiction CON
DIETRICH, Wilson G., 1916- ,
American; juveniles CON
DIETTRICH, Fritz, 1902- ,
German; nonfiction KU
DIETZ, Betty Warner, American;
juveniles WA
DIETZ, David Henry, 1897- ,
American; nonfiction, juveniles
CON
DIETZ, Elisabeth H., 1908- ,
American; nonfiction CON
DIETZ, Gertrud see 'FUSSEGGER,
Gertrud'
DIETZ, Howard, 1896- , Ameri-
can; plays MAT
DIETZ, Lew, 1907- , American;
juveniles, fiction CON WA
DIETZ, Norman D., 1930- ,
American; nonfiction, plays
CON
DIETZ, Peter Owen, 1935- ,
American; nonfiction CON
DIETZE, Gottfried, 1922- ,
American; nonfiction CON
DIETZEL, Paul Franklin, 1924- ,
American; nonfiction CON
DIEUDONNE, Sébastien,   -1776,
French; nonfiction DIL
DIEULAFLOY, Jeanne Paulette
Henriette, 1851-1916, French;
nonfiction SA
DIEZ, Antonio, 16th cent., Spanish;
plays BL
DIEZ, Friedrich, 1794-1876, Ger-
man; nonfiction SA
DIEZ CANEDO, Enrique, 1879-
1944, Spanish; poetry, criti-
cism BL COL FLE HAR SA
ST
DIEZ CRESPO, Manuel, 1911- ,
Spanish; poetry, criticism
BL SA
DIEZ de CORRAL, Luis, 1911- ,
Spanish; nonfiction, transla-
tions BL CON
DIEZ de GAMEZ, Gutierre,
1378?-1446, Spanish; nonfiction
BL ST
DIEZ de MEDINA, Eduardo,
1881/82- , Bolivian; essays,
poetry, fiction MIN SA
DIEZ de MEDINA, Fernando,
1908- , Bolivian; journalism
BL

DIEZ de TEJADA, Vicente, 1872-
1940?, Spanish; fiction SA
DIEZ del CORRAL, Luis, 1911- ,
Spanish; essays SA
DIEZ ECHARRI, Emiliano, 1901-63,
Spanish; nonfiction BL
DIEZ MEDINA, Fernando, 1908- ,
Bolivian; journalism, diary,
poetry MIN SA
DIEZE, Juan Dandres, 1729-85,
German; nonfiction BL
DIFOLO, fl. 300 B.C., Greek;
poetry SA
DIGBY, George see BRISTOL, George
D.
DIGBY, Sir Kenelm, 1603-65, Eng-
lish; nonfiction BRO KB
DIGBY, Kenelm Henry, 1800-80,
English; poetry, fiction, nonfic-
tion KBA
'DIGGES, Jeremiah' see BERGER,
Joseph
DIGGES, Sister Laurentia, 1910- ,
American; nonfiction CON
DIGGES, Leonard, 1588-1635, Eng-
lish; poetry, translations ST
DIGGINS, John Patrick, 1935- ,
American; nonfiction CON
DIGGINS, Julia E., American; juven-
iles WA
DIGGORY, James Clark, 1920- ,
American; nonfiction CON
DIGGS, Margaret Agneta, 1909- ,
American; nonfiction SCA
DI GIACOMO, Salvatore, 1860-1934,
Italian; fiction, poetry COL
FLE HAR SA ST
DIHATI, Muhammad-i Mas'ud,
-1947, Persian; fiction, jour-
nalism ST
DIHKHODA, Ali Akbar (Dakhow),
1880- , Persian; poetry ST
DIJKSTRA, Bram Abraham Jan,
1938- , American; nonfiction
CON
DIJKSTRA, Waling, 1821-1914,
Frisian; fiction ST
DIK, Victor, 1877-1931, Czech;
nonfiction SA
DIKTONIUS, Elmer Rafael, 1896-
1961, Swedish-Finnish; poetry,
fiction HAR ST
DIL, Zakhmi see HILTON, Richard
DI LELLA, Alexander A., 1929- ,
American; nonfiction CON
DI LEO, Joseph H., 1902- , Amer-
ican; nonfiction CON
DILKE, Annabel Mary, 1942- ,

American; fiction CON
DILKE, Charles Wentworth, 1789-
1864, English; criticism, es-
says BRO ST
DILKE, Sir Charles, Wentworth,
1843-1911, English; nonfiction
KBA
DILKE, Lady (Emilia Frances
Strong), 1840-1904, English;
criticism, nonfiction KBA
DILL, Alonzo Thomas, Jr.,
1914- , American; nonfiction
CON
DILL, George Marshall, Jr.,
1916- , American; nonfiction
CON
DILLARD, Dudley, 1913- ,
American; nonfiction CON
DILLARD, Polly Hargis, 1916- ,
American; nonfiction CON
DILLARD, Richard Henry Wilde,
1937- , American; poetry
CON
DILLEHAY, Ronald Clifford,
1935- , American; nonfiction
CON
DILLENBECK, Marsden K., Amer-
ican; nonfiction CON
DILLENBERGER, Jane, 1916- ,
American; nonfiction CON
DILLENBERGER, John, 1918- ,
American; nonfiction CON
DILLER, Angela, American; juven-
iles WA
DILLES, James, 1923- , Ameri-
can; fiction CON
DILLEY, Frank Brown, 1931- ,
American; nonfiction CON
DILLIARD, Irving Lee, 1904- ,
American; nonfiction CON
HOO
DILLINGHAM, William Byron,
1930- , American; nonfiction
CON
DILLISTONE, Frederick William,
1903- , English; nonfiction
CON
DILLON, Conley Hall, 1906- ,
American; nonfiction CON
DILLON, Eilis, 1920- , Irish;
juveniles COM CON WA
DILLON, George, 1906- , Amer-
ican; fiction, poetry HOO
KAT KT
DILLON, James Thomas, 1940- ,
American; nonfiction CON
DILLON, Merton L., 1924- ,
American; nonfiction CON

DILLON, Richard H., 1924- ,
American; nonfiction CON
DILLON, Wallace Neil, 1922- ,
American; nonfiction CON
DILLON, Wentworth see ROSCOM-
MON, Wentworth D.
DILLON, Wilton Sterling, 1923- ,
American; nonfiction CON
DILONG, Rudolf, 1905- , Slovak;
poetry ST
DILSON, Jesse, 1914- , American;
nonfiction CON
DILTHEY, Wilhelm, 1833-1911,
German; essays SA ST
DIMAN, Jeremiah Lewis, 1831-81,
American; nonfiction KAA
DIMICK, Kenneth M., 1937- ,
American; nonfiction CON
DIMITRI ROSTOVSKI, St. Tuptalo,
1651-1709, Russian; nonfiction,
plays HARK
DIMMETTE Celia Puhr, 1896- ,
American; poetry CON
DIMMITT, Richard Bertrand,
1925- , American; nonfiction
CON
DIMMOCK, Frederick Hayden,
1895- , English; juveniles DOY
DIMNET, Ernest, 1866- , French;
essays, nonfiction HOE KL KT
DIMOCK, Gladys Ogden, 1908- ,
American; nonfiction CON
DIMOCK, Hedley Gardiner, 1928- ,
American; nonfiction CON
DIMOCK, Marshall Edward, 1903- ,
American; nonfiction CON
DIMOND, Stanley Ellwood, 1905- ,
American; nonfiction CON
DIMOND, Stuart J., 1938- , Eng-
lish; nonfiction CON
DIMONDSTEIN, Geraldine, 1926- ,
American; nonfiction CON
DIMONT, Max I., 1912- , Lithua-
nian-American; nonfiction CON
DIMT, Christine see 'BUSTA,
Christine'
DINARCHUS, 360-292? B.C., Greek;
nonfiction ST
DINARCO de CORINTH, 360 B.C. - ,
Greek; nonfiction SA
'DINE S. S. Van' see WRIGHT,
Willard H.
DINEMANDY, Juan see DORAT, Juan
DINERMAN, Beatrice, 1933- ,
American; nonfiction CON
DINES, Glen, 1925- , American;
juveniles CON WA
'DINESEN, Isak' ('Tania B. Osceola';

'PIERRE Andrészel'; Baroness
Karen Blixen-Finecke), 1885-
1962, Danish; fiction FLE
HAR KT MAG RIC SA ST
DINESON, Jacob, 1856-1919,
Jewish; nonfiction ST
DINGELSTEDT, Franz von, 1814-
81, German; poetry, fiction,
plays AL HAR SA ST
DINGLE, Herbert, 1890- , Eng-
lish; nonfiction CON
DINGWALL, William Orr, 1934- ,
American; nonfiction CON
DINHOFER, Alfred ('Dino'),
1928- , American; nonfiction
CON
'DINIS, Júlio' (Joaquim Guilherme
Gomes Coelho), 1839-71,
Portuguese; fiction SA ST
DINITZ, Solomon, 1926- , Amer-
ican; nonfiction CON
DINIZ, 1261/79-1325, Portuguese;
poetry HAR ST
DINNERSTEIN, Leonard, 1934- ,
American; nonfiction CON
DINNIS, Enid, 1873-1942, English;
fiction HOE
'DINO' see DINHOFER, Alfred
DINOUART, Joseph Antoine
Toussaint, 1716-86, French;
nonfiction DIL
DINSDALE, Tim, 1924- , Amer-
ican; juveniles CON
DINSMOOR, Robert, 1757-1836,
American; poetry KAA
DINTENFASS, Mark, 1941- ,
American; fiction CON
DIO CASSIUS see CASSIUS Dio
Cocceianus
DIO CHRYSOSTOM, 50-115,
Roman; nonfiction ST
DIODORO de SICILY, 1st cent.
B.C., Greek; nonfiction SA
ST
DIOGENES ANTONIO, 1st cent.,
Greek; nonfiction SA
DIOGENES de APOLINIA, 5th
cent. B.C., Greek; nonfiction
SA
DIOGENES de SELEUCIA, 2nd
cent. B.C., Greek; nonfiction
SA
DIOGENES de SINOPE, 413-323
B.C., Greek; nonfiction SA
DIOGENES LAERTES, 2nd cent.,
Greek; nonfiction SA ST
DION CASIO, 155-240, Greek;
nonfiction SA

DION, Sister Raymond de Jesus, 1918- , American; nonfiction CON

DION CRISTOSTIMO, 40- , Greek; nonfiction SA

DIONIS, Don, 1261-1325, Portuguese; poetry SA

DIONISIO de SINOPE, 1st cent. B.C., Greek; poetry SA

DIONISO de THRACE, 2nd-1st cent. B.C., Greek; nonfiction SA

DIONISOPOULOS, Panagiotes Allan, 1921- , American; nonfiction CON

DIONYSIUS of HALICARNASSUS, 1st cent. B.C., Greek; nonfiction SA ST

DIONYSIUS the AREOPAGITE (Pseudo-Dionysius), 5th cent., Byzantine; nonfiction SA ST

DIONYSIUS the Carthusian, 1402-71, Flemish; nonfiction ST

DIONYSIUS THRAX, 150-90 B.C., Greek; nonfiction ST

DIOSCORIDES, 3rd cent. B.C., Greek; poetry ST

'DIOTEMA' see WYNNE-TYSON, Esme

DI PALMA, Raymond, 1943- , American; nonfiction CON

DIPPIETRO, Robert Joseph, 1932- , American; nonfiction CON

DIPHILUS, 4th-3rd cent. B.C., Greek; plays ST

DIPOKO, Mbella Sonne, 1936- , poetry MUR

DIPPLE, Elizabeth, 1937- , Canadian; fiction CON

DI PRIMA, Diane, 1934- , American; poetry, plays, fiction CON MUR

DIRICKSENS, J.J. see ZETTERNAM, Eugeen

DIRINGER, David, 1900- , English; nonfiction CON

DIRKSEN, Charles Joseph, 1912- , American; nonfiction CON

DE ROCCAFERRERA FERRERO, Giuseppe, M., 1912- , Italian-American; nonfiction CON

DIRRIM, Allen Wendell, 1929- , American; nonfiction CON

DIRVIN, Joseph I., 1917- , American; nonfiction CON

DISCEPOLO, Armando, 1887- , Argentinian; plays MIN

DISCH, Thomas M. ('Dobbin Thorpe'; 'Thom Demijohn'), 1940- ,

American; nonfiction CON

DISCHERL, Denis, 1934- , American; nonfiction CON

DISHER, Maurice Wilbron, 1893- , English; fiction CON

DISHMAN, Patricia L., 1939- , American; nonfiction CON

DISNEY, Doris Miles, 1907- , American; fiction CON

DISNEY, Walt, 1901-66, American; juveniles DOY

DISRAELI, Benjamin (Lord Beaconsfield), 1804-81, English; fiction KBA BRO MAG SA ST

D'ISRAELI, Isaac, 1766-1848, English; nonfiction, fiction, criticism BRO KBA SA ST

DISRAELI, Robert, 1903- , German; juvenile CON

DISTLER, Paul Francis, 1911- , American; nonfiction CON

DITHMAR, Edward Augustus, 1854-1917, American; criticism KAA

DITLEVSEN, Tove Irma Margit, 1918-42, Danish; poetry FLE ST

DITMARS, Raymond Lee, 1876-1942, American; juveniles KJU KT WA

DITZEN, Lowell Russell, 1913- , American; nonfiction CON

DITZEN, Rudolph see 'FALLADA, Hans'

DIVALE, William Tulio, 1942- , American; nonfiction CON

DI VALENTIN, Maria Messuri, 1911- , American; nonfiction CON

DIVER, Maud Marshal, 1867-1945, English; fiction BRO KT RIC

DIVERRES, Armel Hugh, 1914- , English; nonfiction CON

DIVETIA, Narsimharav, 1859-1937, Indian; poetry LAN

DIVINE, Arthur Durham ('David Rame'), 1904- , South African; fiction, journalism ST

DIVINE, Robert Alexander, 1929- , American; nonfiction CON

DIVINE, Thomas Francis, 1900- , American; nonfiction CON

DIVOKY, Diane, 1939- , American; nonfiction CON

DIX, Beulah Marie, 1876- , American; juveniles KJU

DIX, Dorothea Lynde, 1802-87, American; nonfiction KAA SA

DIX, Robert H., 1930- , American; nonfiction CON

DIXELIUS-BRETTNER, Hildur, 1879- , Swedish; fiction KT

'DIXON, Franklin W.' see ADAMS, Harriet S. and STRATEMEYER, Edward L.

'DIXON, Franklin W.' see SVENSON, Andrew E.

DIXON, Harry Vernor, 1908- , American; fiction CON

DIXON, Henry Hall ('The Druid'), 1822-70, English; nonfiction HIG KBA

DIXON, John Wesley, Jr., 1919- , American; nonfiction CON

DIXON, Marjorie Mack, 1887- , English; fiction CON WA

DIXON, Pierson John, 1904- , English; nonfiction CON

DIXON, Richard Watson, 1833-1900, English; poetry, nonfiction BRO KBA ST

'DIXON, Ruth' see BARROWS, Marjorie

DIXON, Thomas, 1864-1946, American; fiction JO KT

DIXON, William Hepworth, 1821-79, English; nonfiction BRO KBA ST

DIXON, Willia Scarth ('Wanderer'), 1848-1933, English; nonfiction HIG

DIXON, Wilmott ('Thormanby'), -1915, English; nonfiction HIG

DIZARD, Wilson Paul, 1922- , American; nonfiction CON

DIZENZO, Charles John, 1938- , American; plays CON

DIZNEY, Henry Franklin, 1926- , American; nonfiction CON

DJACENKO, Boris, 1917- , German; nonfiction AL

DJALSKI-BABIĆ, Ksaver Sandor, 1854- , Croatian; fiction ST

DJAMI, Abderramān, 1414-92, Persian; poetry SA

DJEDDAH, Eli, 1911- , English; nonfiction CON

DJELAI-ED-DIN-Abul-Fadl-Solluty, 1445-1505, Arab; nonfiction SA

DJELAI-ED-DIN, Mohamed Rumi, 1195-1274, Persian; poetry SA

DJORDJIC, Ignjat, 1675-1737, Dalmatian; poetry SA ST

DLUGOSZ, Jan ('Longinus'), 1415-80, Polish; nonfiction SA ST

DLUHOSCH, Eric, 1927- , Czech-American; nonfiction CON

DMITRIEV, Ivan Ivanovich, 1760-1837, Russian; poetry HARK SA ST

DMITRY, Rostovsky ('Demetrius of Rostov'), 1651-1709, Russian; nonfiction ST

DMOCHOWSKI, Franciszek Ksawery, 1762-1808, Polish; poetry, translations ST

DMOCHOWSKI, Franz von Sales, 1801-71, Polish; nonfiction SA

DMOCHOWSKI, Franz Xavier, 1762-1808, Polish; nonfiction SA

DMYTRYSHYN, Basil, 1925- , Polish-American; nonfiction CON

DOAN, Eleanor Lloyd, American; nonfiction, juvenile CON

DOANE, Gilbert Harry, 1897- , American; nonfiction CON

DOANE, Marion S. see WOODWARD, Grace S.

DOANE, Pelagie Hoffner, 1906- , American; juveniles CON FUL WA

DOBB, Maurice, 1900- , English; nonfiction CON

DOBBIN, John E., 1914- , American; nonfiction CON

DOBBINS, Charles Gordon, 1908- , American; nonfiction CON

DOBBINS, Gaines Stanley, 1886- , American; nonfiction CON

DOBBS, Rose, American; juveniles WA

DOBELL Bertram (Bertrand), 1842-1914, English; poetry KB SA

DOBELL, Isabel Marian Barclay, 1909- , American; juveniles CON

DOBELL, Sydney Thompson, 1824-74, English; poetry BRO KBA SA ST

DOBER, Richard P., American; nonfiction CON

DOBIE, Charles Caldwell, 1881- , American; fiction KT

DOBIE, Edith, 1894- , American; nonfiction CON

DOBIE, James Frank, 1888-1964, American; nonfiction CON KTS

DOBLER, Lavinia G., 1910- ,
American; nonfiction, juveniles
CON
DOBLES RODRIGUEZ, Fabián,
1918- , Costa Rican; poetry
MIN
DOBLES SEGREDO, Luis, 1890- ,
Costa Rican; poetry MIN
DOBNER, Maeva Park, 1918- ,
American; fiction CON
DOBRACZYNSKI, Jan ('Hozjusz';
'Eugeniusz Kurowski'), 1910- ,
Polish; nonfiction, fiction CON
DOBRANICH, Horacio, H., 1891- ,
Argentinian; essays MIN
DOBRE, Ion see 'CRIANEC, Nichifor'
DOBREE, Bonamy, 1891- , English;
nonfiction CON
DOBRENTEI, Gabor, 1786-1851,
Hungarian; poetry SA
DOBRIANSKY, Lev E., 1918- ,
American; nonfiction CON
DOBRIN, Arnold, 1928- , American;
juveniles CON
DOBROGEANU-GHEREA, Constantin,
1855-1920, Rumanian; criticism
COL SA ST
DOBROLYUBOV, Alexander Mikhaylo-
vich, 1876- , Russian; poetry
HARK
DOBROLYUBOV, Nikolay Aleksandro-
vich, 1836-61, Russian; criticism
essays HAR HARK KE SA ST
DOBROVOLSKY, Sergei Paulovich,
1908- , Russian-American; non-
fiction CON
DOBROVSKY, Josef, 1753-1829,
Czech; nonfiction HAR SA ST
DOBSON, E. Philip ('Philip Spring'),
1910- , English; nonfiction CON
DOBSON, Eric John, 1913- , Aus-
tralian; nonfiction CON
DOBSON, Henry Austin, 1840-1921,
English; poetry, criticism BRO
KBA ST
DOBSON, James Clayton, Jr.,
1936- , American; nonfiction
CON
DOBSON, John McCullough, 1940- ,
American; nonfiction CON
DOBSON, Richard Barrie, 1931- ,
English; nonfiction CON
DOBSON, Rosemary Bolton, 1920- ,
Australian; poetry MUR
DOBSON, William Arthur Charles
Harvey, 1913- , English; non-
fiction CON
DOBY, Tibor, 1914- , Hungarian-

American; nonfiction CON
DOBYNS, Henry Farmer, 1925- ,
American; nonfiction CON
DOBZHANSKY, Theodosius,
1900- , Russian-American;
nonfiction CON
DOBZYNSKI, Charles, 1929- ,
French; poetry DIF
DOCARANZA, Jeremías see
CARDENAS y RODRIGUEZ,
J. M. de
DOCKERELL, William Bryan,
1929- , English; nonfiction
CON
DOCKSTADER, Frederick J.,
1919- , American; nonfiction
CON
DODAT, François, 1908- ,
French; poetry SA
DODD, Arthur Edward, 1913- ,
English; poetry CON
DODD, Edward Benton, 1902- ,
American; juveniles CON
DODD, James Harvey, 1892- ,
American; nonfiction CON
DODD, Marguerite ('Marguerite
Braymer'), 1911- , American;
nonfiction CON
DODD, Wayne Donald ('Donald
Wayne'), 1930- , American;
nonfiction, juveniles CON
DODD, William, 1729-77, English;
nonfiction BRO KB ST
DODD, William E., 1869-1940,
American; nonfiction JO
DODDRIDGE, Joseph, 1769-1826,
American; nonfiction KAA
DODDRIDGE, Philip, 1702-51,
English; nonfiction BRO KB
DODDS, Gordon Barlow, 1932- ,
American; nonfiction CON
DODDS, John Wendell, 1902- ,
American; nonfiction CON
DODDS, Robert Clyde, 1918- ,
American; nonfiction CON
DODDS, Robert Hungerford,
1914- , American; nonfiction
CON
DODERER, Heimito von, 1896-
1966, Austrian; fiction, poetry,
essays AL FLE HAR KU
KUN LEN RIC
DODGE, Bertha Sanford, 1902- ,
American; juveniles CON WA
DODGE, Ernest Stanley, 1913- ,
American; nonfiction CON
DODGE, Harry Robert, 1929- ,
American; nonfiction CON

'DODGE, Langdon' see WOLFSON,
Victor
DODGE, Lowell, 1940- , American;
nonfiction CON
DODGE, Mabel see LUKAN, Mabel
G.D.
DODGE, Mary Abigail ('Gail Hamil-
ton'), 1833-96, American; es-
says KAA
DODGE, Mary Elizabeth Mapes ('Joel
Stacy'), 1831-1905, American;
juveniles DOY KAA WA
DODGE, Norton Townshend, 1927- ,
American; nonfiction CON
DODGE, Peter, 1926- , American;
nonfiction CON
DODGE, Richard Holmes, 1926- ,
American; nonfiction CON
'DODGE, Steve' see BECKER,
Stephen D.
DODGE, Theodore Ayrault, 1842-1909,
American; nonfiction, poetry
KAA
DODGSON, Charles Lutwidge see
'CARROLL, Lewis'
DODSLEY, Robert, 1703-64, English;
poetry, plays BRO KB ST
DODSLEY, Robert, 1703-64, English;
nonfiction SA
DODSON, Daniel B., 1918- , Amer-
ican; fiction CON
DODSON, Fitzhugh James, 1923- ,
American; nonfiction CON
DODSON, Kenneth MacKenzie,
1907- , American; juveniles
CON
DODSON, Oscar Henry, 1905- ,
American; nonfiction CON
DODSON, Richard Slicer, Jr.,
1896- , American; nonfiction
CON
DODSON, Tom, 1914- , American;
nonfiction CON
DODWELL, Peter Carpenter, 1930- ,
Canadian; nonfiction CON
DODWORTH, Dorothy L., American;
juveniles WA
'DOE, John' see THAYER, Tiffany
DOEBLER, Charles H., 1925- ,
American; nonfiction CON
DÖBLIN, Alfred ('Linke Poot'),
1878-1957, German; fiction, es-
says, plays AL COL FLE HAR
HO KAT KT KU KUN LEN SA ST
DOEBRENTEY, Gabriel, 1768-1851,
Hungarian; poetry, plays SA
DÖDERLIN, Karl Reinhold, 1917- ,
German; poetry, essays AL

DOEHRING, Donald Gene, 1927- ,
American; nonfiction CON
DOELL, Charles Edward, 1894- ,
American; nonfiction CON
DOELY, Sarah Bentley, 1946- ,
American; nonfiction CON
DÖPPE, Friedrich, 1922- , Ger-
man; nonfiction AL
DOERFFLER, Alfred ('Harris
Dunn'; 'Fred Ford'; 'Carl H.
Thomas'), 1884- , American;
nonfiction CON
DÖRFLER, Anton, 1890- , Ger-
man; nonfiction LEN
DÖRFLER, Peter, 1878- , Ger-
man; fiction COL KU LEN
DOERMANN, Humphrey, 1930- ,
American; nonfiction CON
DOERNENBURG, Emil, 1880-1933,
German-American; poetry ST
DOESBORCH, Jan van, fl. 1530- ,
Dutch; fiction ST
'DOESTICKS, Q.K., Philander'
see THOMSON, Mortimer N.
DOGAN, Matteis, 1920- , Ameri-
can; nonfiction CON
'DOGBERRY' see MULFORD,
Prentice
DOGGETT, Frank, 1906- , Amer-
ican; nonfiction CON
DOHEN, Dorothy, 1923- , Amer-
ican; fiction HO
DOHERTY, Charles Hugh, 1913- ,
English; juveniles CON
DOHERTY, Edward, 1890- ,
American; nonfiction, movies
HOE
DOHERTY, Herbert Joseph, Jr.,
1926- , American; nonfiction
CON
DOHERTY, Ivy R. Duffy, 1922- ,
Australian; nonfiction CON
DOHERTY, John Stephen, Ameri-
can; juveniles WA
DOHERTY, Martin W., 1899- ,
American; nonfiction HOE
DOHERTY, Robert W., 1935- ,
American; nonfiction CON
DOHRENWEND, Barbara Snell,
1927- , American; nonfiction
CON
DOIG, Jameson W., 1933- ,
American; nonfiction CON
DOISY, Pierre, -1760, French;
nonfiction DIL
DOIZ, Marco Antonio, 1889- ,
Cuban; nonfiction MIN
DOLAN, Albert Harold, 1892- ,

American; nonfiction HOE

DOLAN, Edward Francis, Jr.,
1924- , American; nonfiction
CON

DOLAN, John Patrick, 1923- ,
American; nonfiction CON

DOLAN, John Richard, 1893- ,
American; nonfiction CON

DOLAN, Paul, 1910- , American;
nonfiction CON

DOLBEN, Digby Mackworth, 1848-
67, English; poetry KBA

DOLBIER, Maurice, 1912- , American; juveniles FUL WA

DOLC y DOLC, Miguel, 1912- ,
Spanish; translations SA

DOLCE, Ludovico, 1508-68, Italian;
nonfiction ST

DOLCI, Danilo, 1924- , Italian;
essays RIC

DOLE, Jeremy Haskell, 1932- ,
American; fiction CON

DOLE, Nathan Haskell, 1852-1935,
American; fiction KT

DOLET, Etienne, 1509-46, French;
nonfiction, poetry HAR SA ST

DOLGOFF, Ralph L., 1932- ,
American; nonfiction CON

DOLGORUKOV, Natalia Borisovna,
1714-71, Russian; nonfiction ST

DOLIM, Mary Nuzum, 1925- ,
American; juveniles CON WA

DOLINER, Roy, 1932- , American;
fiction CON

DOLITSKY, Menachem Mendel,
1856-1931, Jewish; poetry, fiction ST

DOLL, Ronald C., 1913- , American; nonfiction CON

DOLLEN, Charles Joseph ('Joseph
Benedict'), 1926- , American;
nonfiction CON

DOLLIVER, Barbara Babcock, 1927- ,
American; nonfiction CON

DOLLOFF, Eugene Dinsmore, 1890- ,
American; nonfiction CON

DOLMATOVSKI, Yevgenii Aronovich,
1915- , Russian; poetry HARK

DOMETSCH, Carl Richard, Jr.,
1924- , American; nonfiction
CON

DOLPHIN, Robert, Jr., 1935- ,
American; nonfiction CON

DOLSON, Hildegarde, 1908- ,
American; nonfiction CON

DOMANSKA, Janina, Polish-American; juveniles CON WA

DOMASCHEVITSKY, Isaiah see

'BERSCHADSKY, Isaiah'

DOMECQ, Honorio Bustos see
BORGES, Jorge L.

DOMENCHINA, Juan José, 1898-
1960, Spanish; poetry, criticism, fiction BL COL SA

DOMENCICH, Thomas, A., American; nonfiction CON

DOMENGE, Jean, 1666-1735,
French; nonfiction DIL

DOMENICHI, Ludovico, 1515-64,
Italian; nonfiction ST

DOMERGUE, François Urbain,
1745-1810, French; nonfiction
DIL

DOMERGUE, Maurice ('Maurice
Dunoyer'), 1907- , French;
nonfiction CON

DOMETT, Alfred, 1811-87, English; poetry KBA ST

DOMINGO, Marcelino, 1884-1940?,
Spanish; journalism, fiction,
plays SA

DOMINGUEZ, Luis L. see LOPEZ
DOMINGUEZ, Luis

DOMINGUEZ, Manuel, 1866-1935,
Paraguayan; nonfiction SA

DOMINGUEZ, María Alicia,
1908- , Argentinian; poetry,
fiction, essays MIN SA

DOMINGUEZ BERRUETA, Juan,
1866-1958, Spanish; nonfiction
BL SA

DOMINGUEZ CAMARGO, Hernando,
-1656/59, Colombian; non-
fiction, poetry BL MIN

DOMINGUEZ CHARRO, Francisco,
1912-43, Spanish; poetry MIN
SA

'DOMINI, Jon' see LA RUSSO,
Dominic A.

'DOMINI, Rey' see LORDE, Audre

DOMINICI, Aníbal, 1837-97,
Venezuelan; nonfiction SA

DOMINICI, Giovanni, 1356-1419,
Italian; nonfiction ST

DOMINICI, Pedro César, 1872- ,
Venezuelan; fiction SA

DOMINIK, Hans, 1872- , German; nonfiction LEN

DOMINY, Eric Norman, 1918- ,
English; nonfiction CON

DOMJAN, Joseph, 1907- ,
Hungarian-American; juveniles
CON WA

DOMKE, Helmut George, 1914- ,
German; nonfiction CON

DOMKE, Martin, 1892- , German-

American; nonfiction CON
DOMMEN, Arthur John, 1934- ,
American; nonfiction CON
DOMMERMUTH, William P., 1925- ,
American; nonfiction CON
DOMMEYER, Frederick Charles,
1909- , American; nonfiction
CON
DOMPIERRE d'HORNOY, Alexandre
Marie François Paule de, 1742-
1828, French; nonfiction DIL
DOMSELAER, Tobia van, 1611-85,
Dutch; nonfiction ST
DON, Anton Francesco, 1513-74,
Italian; nonfiction HAR
DONAGAN, Alan Harry, 1925- ,
Australian; nonfiction CON
DONAGAN, Barbara Galley, 1927- ,
American; nonfiction CON
DONAGHY, Lyle, 1902-46, Irish;
poetry ST
DONAGHY, Thomas J., 1928- ,
American; nonfiction CON
DONAHEY, William, 1884-1970,
American; juveniles WA
DONAHOE, Barnard Francis, 1932- ,
American; nonfiction CON
DONAHOE, Edward, 1900- , Amer-
ican; fiction MAR
DONAHUE, Francis J., 1917- ,
American; nonfiction CON
DONAHUE, George T., 1911- ,
American; nonfiction CON
DONALD, Aida Di Pace, 1930- ,
American; nonfiction CON
DONALD, David Herbert, 1920- ,
American; nonfiction CON
'DONALD, Vivian' see MACKINNON,
Charles R.
'DONALDS, Gordon' see SHIRREFFS,
Gordon D.
DONALDSON, Elvin F., 1903- ,
American; nonfiction CON
DONALDSON, Gordon, 1913- ,
Scots; nonfiction CON
DONALDSON, Jean Chalmers, Amer-
ican; poetry PAC
DONALDSON, John William, 1811-61,
English; nonfiction KBA
DONALDSON, Malcolm, 1884- ,
American; nonfiction CON
DONALDSON, Norman, 1922- ,
English; nonfiction CON
DONALDSON, Scott, 1928- , Amer-
ican; nonfiction CON
DONALITIUS, Kristijonas see
DUONELAITIS, Kristijonas
DONART, Arthur Charles ('Anton

Donat'), 1936- , American;
nonfiction CON
DONAT, John Annesley, 1933- ,
English; nonfiction CON
DONATO, Anthony, 1909- ,
American; nonfiction CON
DONATO, Elfo, 4th cent.,
Roman; nonfiction SA
DONATO, Magda, 1903- , Spanish;
journalism, criticism, plays
SA
DONATO, Peitro see DI DONATO,
Pietro
DONATUS, Aelius, 4th cent.,
Roman; nonfiction ST
DONCEEL, Joseph F., 1906- ,
Belgian-American; nonfiction
CON
DONELSON, Irene Witmer,
1913- , American; nonfiction
CON
DONELSON, Kenneth Wilber,
1910- , American; nonfiction
CON
DONER, Mary Frances, 1893- ,
American; fiction CON WAF
DONEY, Willis Frederick, Jr.,
1925- , American; nonfiction
CON
DONHEISER, Alan D., 1936- ,
American; nonfiction CON
DONI, Anton Francesco, 1513-74,
Italian; nonfiction ST
DONICI, Alexandru, 1806-66,
Rumanian; fiction HAR SA
ST
DONINGTON, Robert, 1907- ,
English; nonfiction CON
DONIS, Miles, 1937- , American;
fiction CON
'DONKER, Anthonie' (Nicolaas
Anthonie Donkersloot), 1902- ,
Dutch; poetry ST
DONLEAVY, James Patrick,
1926- , American; fiction
CON MAT RIC
DONNA, Natalie, 1934- , Amer-
ican; juveniles CON WA
DONNAY, Maurice Charles,
1859-1945, French; plays
COL HAR MAT SA ST
DONN-BYRNE see BYRNE, Donn
DONNE, John, 1572-1631, English;
poetry BRO KB MAG SA SP
ST
DONNE, William Bodham, 1807-
82, English; essays KBA
DONNEAU de VISE, Jean, 1638-

1710, French; plays, journalism
DIF ST
DONNELLAN, Michael Thomas,
1931- , Irish-American; nonfiction CON
DONNELLY, Alton Stewart, 1920- ,
American; nonfiction CON
DONNELLY, Desmond Louis,
1920- , American; nonfiction
CON
DONNELLY, Dorothy Boillotat,
1903- , American; nonfiction
CON HOE
DONNELLY, Francis Patrick, 1869- ,
American; poetry HOE
DONNELLY, Sister Gertrude Joseph,
1920- , American; nonfiction
CON
DONNELLY, Ignatius, 1831-1901,
American; essays, fiction KAA
DONNELLY, James Howard, Jr.,
1941- , American; nonfiction
CON
DONNER, Jorn, 1933- , Finnish;
nonfiction, fiction CON
DONNISON, Frank Siegfried Vernon,
1898- , English; nonfiction
CON
DONNITHORNE, Audrey, 1922- ,
English; nonfiction CON
DONNO, Elizabeth Story, 1921- ,
American; nonfiction CON
DONOGHUE, Denis, 1928- , Irish;
nonfiction CON
DONOGHUE, Mildred Ransdorf,
American; nonfiction CON
DONOHUE, John K., 1909- , Amer-
ican; nonfiction CON
DONOHUE, John Waldron, 1917- ,
American; nonfiction CON
DONOSO, Armando, 1887-1946,
Chilean; essays, criticism BL
MIN SA
DONOSO, Francisco, 1894- ,
Chilean; poetry MIN
DONOS, Justo, 1800-68, Chilean;
journalism MIN
DONOSO, Ricardo, 1896- ,
Chilean; essays MIN
DONOS CORTES, Juan, 1809-53,
Spanish; nonfiction BL KE SA
ST
DONOUGHUE, Bernard, 1934- ,
English; nonfiction CON
DONOVAN, Edward Joseph, 1904- ,
Canadian; fiction CON
DONOVAN, Frank Robert, 1906- ,
American; juveniles CON WA

DONOVAN, James A., Jr.,
1917- , American; nonfiction
CON
DONOVAN, James Britt, 1916- ,
American; nonfiction CON
DONOVAN, Rev. John, 1861-1933,
Irish; nonfiction HO
DONOVAN, John, 1919- , Amer-
ican; nonfiction CON
DONOVAN, John Chauncey, 1920- ,
American; nonfiction CON
DONOVAN, Robert Alan, 1921- ,
American; nonfiction CON
DONOVAN, Robert John, 1912- ,
American; nonfiction CON
'DONOVAN, William' see BERKE-
BILE, Fred D.
DONS, Aage, 1903- , Danish;
fiction HAR ST
DONSON, Cyril ('Via Hartford';
'Russ Kidd'), 1919- , English;
fiction CON
DOOB, Anthony Newcomb, 1943- ,
American; nonfiction CON
DOOB, Leonard William, 1909- ,
American; nonfiction CON
DOODY, Francis Stephen, 1917- ,
American; nonfiction CON
'DOOG, K. Caj' see GOOD, Irving
J.
'DOOLEY, Mr.' see DUNNE,
Finley P.
DOOLEY, Arch Richard, 1925- ,
American; nonfiction CON
DOOLEY, David J., 1921- ,
American; nonfiction CON
DOOLEY, Roger Burke, 1920- ,
American; fiction CON HO
DOOLIN, Dennis James, 1933- ,
American; nonfiction CON
DOOLITTLE, Hilda ('H.D.'),
1886- , American; poetry
BRO FLE KL KT RIC SA ST
'DOONE, Jic' see MARSHALL,
James V.
DOORLY, Ruth K., 1919- , Amer-
ican; juveniles CON
'DOR, Ana' see CEDER, Georgiana
D.
'DORANT, Gene' see LENT, Dora
G.
DORAN, John, 1807-78, English;
nonfiction BRO KBA
DORAT, Claude Joseph, 1734-80,
French; poetry, plays DIL
DORAT, Jean (Daurat; Dinemandy),
1505-88, French; poetry
DIF SA

DORAY de LONGRAIS, Jean Paul,
1736-1800, French; translations
DIL

DORCHESTER, Lord, 1876- ,
English; nonfiction HIG

DORCY, Sister Mary Jean, 1914- ,
American; nonfiction, juveniles
CON

DORE, Anita, 1914- , American;
nonfiction CON

DORE, Claire Morin ('Claire France'),
1934- , Canadian; poetry, plays,
fiction CON

'DOREMUS, Thomas Edmund', 1922-
62, American; fiction CON

DORESTE, Ventura, 1922- , Spanish;
poetry, criticism SA

DOREY, Thomas Alan, 1921- ,
English; nonfiction CON

DORFLER, Peter, 1878- , German;
fiction SA

DORFMAN, Eugene, 1917- , American; nonfiction CON

DORFMAN, Robert, 1916- , American; nonfiction CON

'DORGELES, Roland' (Roland Leca-
velé), 1886- , French; fiction
COL DIF FLE HAR MAL SA ST

DORIAN, Edith McEwen, 1900- ,
American; fiction, juveniles CON

DORIAN, Frederick, 1902- , American; nonfiction CON

DORIAN, Marguerite, American;
poetry, juveniles CON

DORIGNY, Jean, -1731, French;
nonfiction DIL

DORIS, Lillian, 1899- , American;
nonfiction CON

DORLANT, Pieter (Petrus Dorlandus),
1454-1507, Dutch; nonfiction ST

DORLIAL, Peter Gondro, 1935- ,
Liberian; nonfiction CON

DORLING, Henry Taprell see 'TAF-
FRAIL'

DORMAN, Michael ('Jack Bishop'),
1932- , American; nonfiction
CON

DORMANDY, Clara, 1905- ,
Hungarian-English; fiction CON

DORMON, James Hunter, Jr.,
1936- , American; nonfiction
CON

DORN, Edward, 1929- , American;
poetry MUR

DORN, Frank, 1901- , American;
fiction CON

DORN, Jacob H., 1939- , American;
nonfiction CON

DORNBERG, John Robert, 1931- ,
German; nonfiction CON

DORNBUSCH, Charles Emil,
1907- , American; nonfiction
CON

DORNER, Peter Paul, 1925- ,
American; nonfiction CON

DORO, Edward, 1910- , American; poetry CON

DORONZO, Emmanuel, 1903- ,
Italian; nonfiction CON

DOROSHEVICH, Vlasi Mikhaylovich,
1864-1922, Russian; journalism
HARK ST

DOROSHKIN, Milton, 1914- ,
American; nonfiction CON

DORPALEN, Andreas, 1911- ,
American; nonfiction CON

DORR, Julia Caroline Ripley
('Caroline Thomas'), 1825-
1913, American; poetry, fiction
KAA

DORRIES, William Lyle, 1923- ,
American; nonfiction CON

DORRIS, Robert T., 1913- ,
American; nonfiction CON

D'ORS, Eugenio see ORS y ROVIRA,
Eugenio d'

DORSCH, Eduard, 1822-87, German-American; poetry ST

DORSEN, Norman, 1930- ,
American; nonfiction CON

DORSET, Catherine Ann Turner,
1750?-1817, English; poetry
KBA

DORSET, Earl of see SACKVILLE,
Thomas and Charles

DORSET, Phyllis Flanders,
1924- , American; nonfiction
CON

DORSETT, Lyle Wesley, 1938- ,
American; nonfiction CON

DORSEY, Anna Hanson McKinney,
1815-96, American; fiction
KAA

DORSEY, John Morris, 1900- ,
American; nonfiction CON

DORSEY, Sarah Anne Ellis, 1829-
79, American; fiction KAA

DORST, Jean Pierre ('Pierre
d'Urstelle'), 1924- , French;
nonfiction CON

DORST, Tankred, 1925- , German; plays MAT

DORVIGNY, Louis François
Archambault, 1742-1812,
French; plays DIL

DORWORTH, Alice Grey, 1907- ,

American; nonfiction CON
DOSHUN see HAYASHI RAZAN
DOSOFTEI, 1624-93, Rumanian;
poetry ST
DOS PASSOS, John, 1896-1970,
American; fiction, plays, poetry
BRO CON FLE HOO KL KT
MAG RIC SA ST WAF
DOSS, Helen Grigsby, 1915- ,
Anglo-American; juveniles CON
WA
DOSS, Margot Patterson, American;
nonfiction CON
'DOSSI, Carlo' (Alberto Pisani),
1849-1910, Italian; fiction COL
SA
DOSTER, William Clark, 1921- ,
American; nonfiction CON
DOSTOEVSKI, Fyodor Mikhailovich,
1821-81, Russian; fiction COL
KE HAR HARK SA ST MAG
DOTOR y MUNICIO, Angel, 1898- ,
Spanish; fiction, journalism,
criticism BL SA
DOTSON, Floyd, 1917- , American;
nonfiction CON
DOTSON, Lillian O., 1921- ,
American; nonfiction CON
DOTTIEVILLE, Jean Henri, 1716-
1807, French; nonfiction DIL
DOTTS, Maryann J., 1933- , Amer-
ican; nonfiction CON
DOTY, Brant Lee, 1921- , Ameri-
can; nonfiction CON
DOTY, James Edward, 1922- ,
American; nonfiction CON
DOTY, Rev. William Lodewick,
1919- , American; fiction,
nonfiction CON HO
DOUBLET, Jean, 1529-1604?,
French; poetry SA
DOUBLET, Marie Anne Legendre,
1677- , French; nonfiction DIL
DOUBTFIRE, Dianne Abrams,
1918- , American; nonfiction,
fiction CON
DOUCE, Francis, 1757-1834, Eng-
lish; nonfiction BRO
DOUCETTE, Leonard Eugene,
1936- , Canadian; nonfiction
CON
DOUGALL, Herbert Edward, 1902- ,
Canadian; nonfiction CON
DOUGHERTY, Ching-yi Hsu,
1915- , American; nonfiction
CON
DOUGHERTY, Joanna F. see
FOSTER, Joanna

DOUGHERTY, Richard, 1921- ,
American; fiction CON
DOUGHERTY, Richard M.,
1935- , American; nonfiction
CON
DOUGHTIE, Charles, American;
juveniles WA
DOUGHTY, Charles Montagu,
1843-1926, English; poetry,
nonfiction BRO FLE KAT
KBA MAG SP ST
DOUGHTY, Oswald, 1889- ,
English; nonfiction CON
'DOUGLAS, Albert' see ARM-
STRONG, Douglas A.
DOUGLAS, Lord Alfred Bruce,
1870-1945, English; poetry
BRO HOE
DOUGLAS, Amanda Minnie,
1831-1916, American; juveniles
KAA
DOUGLAS, Clarence B., 1864- ,
American; nonfiction MAR
DOUGLAS, Ellen see WILLIAM-
SON, Ellen D.
DOUGLAS, Gavin (Gawin), 1474-
1522, Scots; poetry BRO KB
SP ST
'DOUGLAS, George' see BROWN,
George D.
DOUGLAS, James Dixon, 1922- ,
Scots; nonfiction CON
'DOUGLAS, John' see STOKER,
Alan
DOUGLAS, John Scott, American;
juveniles WA
DOUGLAS, Leonard Marvin,
1910- , American; nonfiction
CON
DOUGLAS, Lloyd Carsel, 1877-
1951, American; fiction BRO
KAT KT MAG RIC SA WAF
DOUGLAS, Louis Hartwell, 1907- ,
American; nonfiction CON
DOUGLAS, Mack R., 1922- ,
American; nonfiction CON
DOUGLAS, Marjory Stoneman,
1890- , American; plays,
fiction, juveniles CON
DOUGLAS, Norman, 1868-1952,
Scots; fiction BRO KL KT
MAG RIC SA ST
'DOUGLAS, Olive' see BUCHAN,
Anna
'DOUGLAS, Robert' see ANDREWS,
Charles R. D. H.
'DOUGLAS, Shane' see WILKES-
HUNTER, Richard

DOUGLAS, William Orville, 1898- ,
American; nonfiction, juveniles
CON KTS PAC WA
DOUGLAS-HAMILTON, James,
1942- , Scots; nonfiction CON
DOUGLAS-HOME, Robin, 1932-68,
English; nonfiction, fiction CON
DOUGLAS-IRVINE, Helen, -1947,
Scots; fiction HOE
DOUGLASS, Donald McNutt, 1899- ,
American; fiction CON
DOUGLASS, Frances, 1913- ,
American; nonfiction SCA
DOUGLASS, Frederick, 1817?-95,
American; journalism, nonfiction
KAA
DOUGLASS, Harl Roy, 1892- ,
American; nonfiction CON
DOUGLASS, James W., 1937- ,
Canadian; nonfiction CON
DOUGLASS, Paul Franklin, 1904- ,
American; nonfiction CON
DOUGLASS, William ('William
Nadir'), 1691-1752, American;
nonfiction KAA
DOUGLAS-SCOTT-MONTAGU, Edward
John Barrington, 1926- , Eng-
lish; nonfiction CON
DOUIN, Firmin, 18th cent., French;
poetry DIL
DOULIS, Thomas, 1931- , American;
nonfiction CON
DOUMIC, René, 1860-1937, French;
criticism, essays COL SA
DOURADO, Autran, 1926- ,
Brazilian; fiction CON
DOUSA, Janus, 1545-1609, Dutch;
poetry ST
DOUSSOT, Joseph, -1752, French;
nonfiction DIL
DOUTY, Esther Morris, 1911- ,
American; nonfiction CON
DOUWES, DEKKER, Eduard see
'MULTATULI'
'DOVEGLION' see VILLA, Jose G.
DOVER, Clarence Joseph, 1919- ,
American; nonfiction CON
DOVER, Kenneth James, 1920- ,
English; nonfiction CON
D'OVIDIO, Francesco, 1849-1925,
Italian; criticism ST
DOVIZI, Bernardo ('Il Bibbiena'),
1470-1520, Italian; plays ST
DOW, Dorothy Minerva, 1903- ,
American; poetry HOO
DOW, Emily R., 1904- , American;
juveniles CON
DOW, Jose Kamal, 1936- , Colom-

bian-American; nonfiction
CON
DOW, Neal, 1906- , American;
nonfiction CON
DOW, Sterling, 1903- , Ameri-
can; nonfiction CON
DOWD, Douglas Fitzgerald,
1919- , American; nonfiction
CON
DOWD, Jerome, 1864- , Ameri-
can; nonfiction MAR
DOWD, Laurence Phillips,
1914- , American; nonfiction
CON
DOWDELL, Dorothy Karns,
1910- , American; juveniles
CON
DOWDEN, Anne Ophelia ('Anne
O. Todd'; Dowen), 1907- ,
American; juveniles CON
WA
DOWDEN, Edward, 1843-1913,
Irish; essays, criticism,
poetry, nonfiction BRO KBA ST
DOWDEY, Clifford Shirley, Jr.,
1904- , American; nonfiction,
fiction CON KT WAF
DOWDS, Gertrude, Irish-Canadian;
juveniles WA
DOWDY, Homer Earl, 1922- ,
American; nonfiction CON
'DOWDY, Mrs. Regera' see
GOREY, Edward St. J.
DOWELL, Coleman, 1925- ,
American; fiction, plays CON
DOWEN, Anne Ophelia Todd see
DOWDEN, Anne O.
'DOWERS, Penn' see PENDOWER,
Jacques
DOWLAND, John, 1563-1626?,
Irish; songs KB
DOWLER, James Ross, 1925- ,
American; nonfiction CON
'DOWLEY, D.M.' see MARRISON,
Leslie W.
DOWLING, Allen ('Jack King'),
1900- , American; nonfiction
CON
DOWLING, Basil Cairnes, 1910- ,
British; poetry MUR ST
DOWLING, Joseph Albert, 1926- ,
Scots; American; nonfiction
CON
DOWN, Goldie Malvern, 1918- ,
Australian; nonfiction CON
DOWNER, Alan Seymour, 1912-70,
American; nonfiction CON
DOWNER, Marion, -1971,

American; juveniles WA

DOWNES, Anne Miller, American; fiction WAF

DOWNES, Bryan Trevor, 1939- , Canadian; nonfiction CON

DOWNES, David Anthony, 1927- , American; nonfiction CON

DOWNES, Mollie P. see PANTER-DOWNES, Mollie P.

DOWNEY, Edmund Alan ('F.M. Allen'), 1889- , Irish; fiction, poetry HO

DOWNEY, Fairfax Davis, 1893- , American; juveniles, poetry, fiction CON WA

DOWNEY, Glanville, 1908- , American; nonfiction CON

DOWNEY, Harris, American; fiction CON

DOWNEY, Lawrence William Lorne, 1921- , Canadian; nonfiction CON

DOWNEY, Murray William, 1910- , Canadian; nonfiction CON

DOWNEY, Richard, 1881- , Irish; journalism, nonfiction HOE

DOWNIE, Mary Alice ('Dawe Hunter'), 1934- , American; poetry CON

DOWNIE, Norville M., 1910- , American; nonfiction CON

DOWNING, Andrew Jackson, 1815-52, American; nonfiction KAA

DOWNING, Arthur Benjamin, 1915- , English; nonfiction CON

'DOWNING, Major Jack' see SMITH, Seba

DOWNING, Lester N., 1914- , American; nonfiction CON

DOWNING, Todd, 1902- , American; fiction MAR

DOWNS, Hunton Leache, 1918- , American; nonfiction, plays CON

DOWNS, Jacques M., 1926- , American; nonfiction CON

DOWNS, Lenthiel Howell, 1915- , American; nonfiction CON

DOWNS, Norton, 1918- , American; nonfiction CON

DOWNS, Robert Bingham, 1903- , American; nonfiction CON

DOWSE, Robert E., 1933- , English; nonfiction CON

DOWSON, Ernest Christopher, 1867-1900, English; poetry BRO KBA SP ST

DOWST, Somerby Rohrer, 1926- , American; nonfiction CON

DOYLE, Sir Arthur Conan, 1859-

1930, English; juveniles, fiction BRO DOY KAT KT MAG RIC SA ST WA

DOYLE, Charles Desmond, 1928- , New Zealander; poetry CON MUR

DOYLE, Charles Hugo, 1904- , Canadian; juveniles HOE

DOYLE, Sir Francis Hastings Charles, 1810-88, English; poetry BRO HIG KBA

DOYLE, John Andrew, 1844-1907, English; nonfiction KBA

DOYLE, John Robert, 1910- , American; nonfiction CON

'DOYLE, Lynn' see MONTGOMERY, Leslie

DOYLE, Paul A., 1925- , American; nonfiction CON

DOYNO, Victor Anthony, 1937- , American; nonfiction CON

DOZER, Donald Marquand, 1905- , American; nonfiction CON

DOZY, Reniero, 1820-83, Dutch; nonfiction BL

DRABBLE, Margaret, 1939- , English; fiction CON RIC

DRACHKOVITCH, Milorad, 1921- , American; nonfiction CON

DRACHMAN, Edward Ralph, 1940- , American; nonfiction CON

DRACHMANN, Holger Hendrik, 1846-1908, Danish; poetry, fiction, plays COL HAR KE SA ST

DRACKETT, Philip ('Paul King'), 1922- , English; nonfiction CON

'DRACO, F.' see DAVIS, Julia

DRACONCIO, 5th cent., Greek; nonfiction SA

DRACONTIUS, Blossius Aemilius, 5th cent., Roman; poetry ST

DRAGE, Charles Hardinge, 1897- , English; fiction CON

DRAGOMIRESCU, Mihail, 1868- , Rumanian; nonfiction ST

'DRAGONET, Edward' see WILLIANSON, Thames R.

DRAGOUMES, Ion, 1878-1920, Greek; nonfiction ST

DRAKE, Albert, 1935- , American; poetry, nonfiction CON

DRAKE, Barbara Ann, 1939- , American; nonfiction CON

DRAKE, Benjamin, 1795-1841,
American; nonfiction KAA
DRAKE, Francis Samuel, 1828-85,
American; nonfiction KAA
DRAKE, Frank Donald, 1930- ,
American; nonfiction CON
DRAKE, Joan Howard, 1924- ,
English; juveniles CON
DRAKE, Joseph Rodman, 1795-1820,
American; poetry BRO KAA ST
'DRAKE, Lisl' see BEER, Eloise
C. S.
DRAKE, Michael, 1935- , English;
nonfiction CON
DRAKE, Richard Bryant, 1925- ,
American; nonfiction CON
DRAKE, Robert Young, Jr.,
1930- , American; fiction CON
DRAKE, Samuel Adams, 1833-1905,
American; nonfiction KAA
DRAKE, Samuel Gardner, 1798-1875,
American; nonfiction KAA
DRAKE, William A., 1899- ,
American; translations, poetry,
fiction, essays, criticism KL
DRAKE, William Donovan, 1922- ,
American; nonfiction CON
DRAKE, William Earle, 1903- ,
American; nonfiction CON
DRAKEFORD, John W., 1914- ,
Australian; nonfiction CON
DRALLE, Elizabeth Mary, 1910- ,
American; nonfiction CON
DRANE, James F., 1930- , Amer-
ican; nonfiction CON
'DRANEM' see MENARD
DRANGE, Theodore M., 1934- ,
American; nonfiction CON
DRANSFIELD, Michael John Pender
('Edward Tate'), 1948- ,
Australian; poetry CON
DRAPER, Alfred, 1924- , English;
nonfiction CON
DRAPER, Cena Christopher, 1907- ,
American; fiction CON
DRAPER, Edgar, 1926- , American;
nonfiction CON
DRAPER, Ellinor Elizabeth Nancy,
1915- , English; nonfiction CON
DRAPER, Hal, 1914- , American;
nonfiction CON
DRAPER, John William, 1811-82,
American; nonfiction BRO ST
DRAPER, John William, 1893- ,
American; poetry, nonfiction
CON
DRAPER, Lyman Copeland, 1815-91,
American; nonfiction KAA

DRAPER, Nancy, American;
juveniles WA
DRAPER, Theodore, 1912- ,
American; nonfiction CON
DRAPKIN, Frita, 1913- ,
American; juveniles HIL
DRAPKIN, Herbert, 1916- ,
American; nonfiction CON
DRAY, William Herbert, 1921- ,
Canadian; nonfiction CON
DRAYER, Adam Matthew, 1913- ,
American; nonfiction CON
DRAYTON, John, 1766-1822,
American; nonfiction KAA
DRAYTON, Michael, 1563-1631,
English; poetry, plays BRO
KB MAG SA SP ST
DRDA, Jan, 1915- , Czech;
fiction, plays ST
'DREETZ, Jochim' see BALL,
Kurt H.
DREIER, Frederik Henrik Hen-
nings, 1827-53, Danish; es-
says ST
DREIFUSS, Kurt, 1897- , Ger-
man-American; nonfiction CON
DREIKURS, Rudolf, 1897-1972,
Austrian-American; nonfiction
CON
DREISER, Theodore, 1871-1945,
American; fiction, plays, es-
says, poetry BRO FLE HOO
KL KT MAG MAT RIC SA ST
DREKMEIER, Charles, 1927- ,
American; nonfiction CON
DRENNAN, Donald Arthur,
1925- , American; nonfiction
CON
DRENNAN, William, 1754-1820,
Irish; poetry, nonfiction KBA
DREPANIO, Latino Pacato, 4th
cent., Roman; poetry SA
DRESBACH, Glenn Ward, 1889-
1968, American; poetry, non-
fiction CON HOO
DRESCHER, Martin, 1863-1920,
German-American; poetry ST
DRESCHER, Seymour, 1934- ,
American; nonfiction CON
DRESNER, Hal, 1937- , Ameri-
can; fiction CON
DRESNER, Samuel Hayim, 1923- ,
American; nonfiction CON
DRESSER, Julius A., 1838-93,
American; nonfiction KAA
DRESSL, Paul L., 1910- , Amer-
ican; nonfiction CON
DRETSKE, Frederick Irwin,

1932- , American; nonfiction
CON
DREUX, Albert ('Albert Maile'),
1887-1949, Canadian; nonfiction
SY
DREUX du RADIER, Jean François,
1714-80, French; nonfiction,
poetry, journalism, translations
DIL
DREW, Elizabeth, 1887-1965, Amer-
ican; nonfiction CON
DREW, Francis see BICKERSTAFFE-
DREW, Francis
DREW, Fraser Bragg Robert, 1913- ,
American; nonfiction CON
DREW, Katherine Fischer, 1923- ,
American; nonfiction CON
'DREW, Morgan' see PRICE, Robert
DREW-Bear, Robert, 1901- ,
English; nonfiction CON
DREWERY, Mary, 1918- , English;
juveniles CON
DREWRY, Guy Carleton, 1901- ,
American; poetry CON
'DREXEL Jay B.' see BIXBY,
Jerome L.
DREYER, Edward C., 1937- ,
American; nonfiction CON
DREYER, Max, 1862-1946, German;
plays, fiction COL MAT SA
DREYFUS, Edward Albert, 1937- ,
American; nonfiction CON
DREYFUS, Hubert Lederer, 1929- ,
American; nonfiction CON
DRIBBEN, Judith Strick, 1923- ,
Russian-American; nonfiction
CON
DRIEU la ROCHELLE, Pierre,
1893-1945, French; fiction, es-
says COL DIF FLE HAR MAL SA
ST
'DRINAN Adam' (Joseph Todd Gordon
Macleod), 1903- , Scots; poetry,
nonfiction MUR
DRINAN, Robert Frederick, 1920- ,
American; nonfiction CON
'DRING, Nathaniel' see McBROOM,
R. Curtis
DRINKALL, Gordon ('Don Demaine'),
1927- , English; nonfiction
CON
DRINKWATER, Francis Harold,
1886- , English; nonfiction
CON HO
DRINKWATER, John, 1882-1937,
English; poetry, plays BRO KL
KT MAT SA ST
DRINNON, Richard, 1925- , Amer-

ican; nonfiction CON
DRIVER, Charles Jonathan,
1939- , South African; poetry,
fiction CON MUR
DRIVER, Godfrey Rolles, 1892- ,
English; nonfiction CON
DRIVER, Harold Edson, 1907- ,
American; nonfiction CON
DRIVER, Samuel Rolles, 1846-
1914, English; nonfiction
KBA
DRIVER, Tom Faw, 1925- ,
American; nonfiction CON
DROESCHER, Vitus Bernward,
1925- , German-English;
nonfiction CON
DROIT, Michel, 1923- , Ameri-
can; nonfiction CON
DROOGENBROECK, Jan van ('Jan
Ferguut'), 1835-1902, Flemish;
poetry ST
DROPPERS, Carl Hyink, 1918- ,
American; nonfiction CON
DROR, Yehezkel (Deror), 1928- ,
Austrian; nonfiction CON
'DRORA, Bar' see LIEBERMANN,
Ahron S.
DROSSART LULOFS, Hendrik
Joan, 1906- , Dutch; nonfic-
tion CON
DROST, Aarnout, 1810-34, Dutch;
nonfiction ST
DROSTE, Coenraat, 1642-1734,
Dutch; nonfiction ST
DROSTE, Georg, 1866-1935,
German; nonfiction ST
DROSTE-HÜLSHOFF, Annette
Freiin von, 1797-1848,
German; poetry AL HAR KE
ST
DROTNING, Phillip Thomas ('Tom
Phillips'), 1920- , American;
nonfiction CON
DROVART ta VACHE, 13th cent.,
French; translations ST
DROUGHT, James William, 1931- ,
American; nonfiction, fiction
CON
DROUIN, Francis M., 1901- ,
Canadian; nonfiction CON
DROUOT, Paul, 1886-1915,
French; poetry DIF
DROWER, Ethel Stefana May
('E.S. Stevens'), 1879- ,
English; juveniles CON
DROWNE, Tatiana Balkoff, 1913- ,
American; nonfiction CON
DROZ, Antoine Gustave, 1832-95,

French; fiction SA

DROZ, François Xavier Joseph, 1773-1850, French; nonfictions SA

DROZE, Wilmon Henry, 1924- , American; nonfiction CON

DROZHZHIN, Spiridon Dmitrievich, 1848-1930, Russian; poetry HARK ST

'DRUCE, Christopher' see PULLING, Christopher R. D.

'DRUID, The' see DIXON, Henry H.

'DRUKKER J.' see PRESSER, Gerrit J.

DRUKS, Herbert, 1937- , Austrian-American; nonfiction CON

DRUM, Robert F., 1918- , American; nonfiction, fiction CON

DRUMMOND, Donald F., 1914- , American; nonfiction CON

DRUMMOND, Edith Marie Dulce Carman, 1883- , English; fiction CON

DRUMMOND, Ellen Lane, 1897- , American; nonfiction, fiction CON

DRUMMOND, Harold D., 1916- , American; nonfiction CON

DRUMMOND, Henry, 1851-97, Scots; nonfiction BRO KBA

DRUMMOND, Ian Macdonald, 1933- , Canadian; nonfiction CON

DRUMMOND, Jane, 1923- , South African; fiction CON

DRUMMOND, Kenneth Herbert, 1922- , American; nonfiction CON

DRUMMOND, Violet Hilda, 1911- , English; juveniles CON

'DRUMMOND, Walter' see SILVERBERG, Robert

DRUMMOND, William, 1585-1649, English; poetry BRO KB SP ST

DRUMMOND, William Henry, 1854-1907, Irish-Canadian; poetry BRO KT ST SY

DRUMMOND de ANDRADE, Carlos, 1902- , Brazilian; poetry FLE RIC SA

DRUMONT, Edouard Adolphe, 1844-1917, French; journalism DIF

DRUON, Maurice, 1918- , French; fiction, essays, plays CON DIC DIF FLE

DRURY, Allen, 1918- , American; fiction RIC

DRURY, Clifford Merrill, 1897- , American; nonfiction CON PAC

DRURY, James Westbrook, 1919- , American; nonfiction CON

DRURY, John, 1898-1972, American; poetry, nonfiction CON

DRURY, Maxine Cole ('Don Creighton'), 1914- , American; fiction CON

DRUYANOV, Alter ('Abgad Haedreyi'), 1870-1938, Jewish; essays ST

DRUZBACKA, Elzbieta Kowalska, 1695-1765, Polish; poetry ST

DRUZHININ, Alexander Vasilyevich, 1824-64, Russian; fiction, criticism, translations HARK ST

'DRYANDER' see ENZINAS, Francisco de

DRYDEN, Cecil Pearl, 1887- , American; nonfiction CON PAC

DRYDEN, John, 1631-1700, English; poetry, plays, essays BRO KB MAG SA SP ST

'DRYDEN, John' see ROWLAND, Donald S.

DRZAZGA, John, 1907- , American; nonfiction CON

DRZIC, Djordje, 1461-1501, Dalmatian; poetry ST

DRZIC, Marin, 1518-67, Dalmatian; poetry, plays SA ST

D'SOUZA, Rev. Jerome, 1897- , Indian; nonfiction HO

DUA, Ram Parkash, 1930- , American; nonfiction CON

'DUANE, Jim' see HURLEY, Vic

DUARTE, Don ('Elocuente'), 1391-1438, Portuguese; nonfiction SA ST

DUARTE, Juan Pablo, 1813-73/76, Dominican; nonfiction MIN

DUARTE, Mario, 1890-1934, Portuguese; plays SA

DUARTE, Urbano, 1855-1902, Brazilian; criticism SA

DUARTE de ALMEIDA, Manuel, 1844-1914, Portuguese; poetry SA

'DUAYEN, César' ('Emma de la Barra de Llanos'), -1932, Argentinian; fiction MIN

DUBARTAS, Guillaume de Salluste, 1544-90/1600, French; poetry DIF KE HAR MAL SA ST

DUBAY, Thomas Edward, 1921- , American; nonfiction CON

DU BAY, William H., 1934- ,

American; nonfiction CON

DUBE, Marcel, 1930- , Canadian;
fiction SY

DUBE, Rodolphe see HERTEL,
François

DU BELLAY, Guillaume, 1491-1543,
French; nonfiction ST

DU BELLAY, Joachim, 1522-60,
French; poetry, criticism DIF
KE HAR MAL SA ST

DUBIGNON, Abbe, 18th cent.,
French; nonfiction DIL

DUBILLARD, Roland, 1923- ,
French; plays MAT

DUBIN, Samuel Sanford, 1914- ,
American; nonfiction CON

DUBKIN, Lois Knudson, 1911- ,
American; nonfiction CON

'DU BLANC Daphne' see GROOM;
Arthur W.

DUBLE URRUTIA, Diego, 1877/
78- , Chilean; poetry MIN

DUBLIN, Jack, 1915- , American;
nonfiction CON

DU BOCAGE, Marie Ann Le Page,
1710-1802, French; nonfiction,
translations DIL

DUBOCAGE de BLEVILLE, Michel
Joseph, 1707-56, French; nonfiction DIL

DUBOIS Elfried Theresia Pichler,
1911- , Austrian-English; nonfiction CON

DU BOIS, Theodora McCormick,
1890- , American; juveniles
WA

DU BOIS, William Edward Burghardt,
1868- , American; fiction KAT
KT

DU BOIS, William Pène, 1916- ,
American; juveniles CON DOY
KJU WA

DUBOIS FONTANELLE, Jean Gaspard,
1737-1812, French; nonfiction
DIL

DUBOIS de JANCIGNY, Jean Baptiste,
1753-1808, French; nonfiction
DIL

DU BOS, Charles, 1882-1939/40,
French; nonfiction, essays,
criticism COL DIF HOE SA

DU BOS, Jean Baptiste, 1670-1742,
French; nonfiction DIF DIL SA

DU BOS, Jean Pierre, 1680-1755,
French; nonfiction DIL

DUBOS, Rene Jules, 1901- ,
French; nonfiction CON

DUBOSE, La Rocques Russ,

1926- , American; juveniles
COM CON

DU BOSE, Louise Jones ('Nancy
Telfair'), 1901- , American;
nonfiction CON

DU BOW, Fredric Lee, 1944- ,
American; nonfiction CON

DU BROFF, Sidney, 1929- ,
American; fiction CON

DUBRUCK, Alfred Joseph, 1922- ,
American; nonfiction CON

DU BRUCK, Edelgard Conradt,
1925- , German-American;
nonfiction CON

DUBS, Homer Hasenpflug, 1892- ,
American; nonfiction CON

DU BUAT-NANCAY, Louis
Gabriel, 1732-87, French;
nonfiction DIL

DUBUISSON, Pierre Ulric, 1746-
94, French; nonfiction DIL

DU BUS, Andre, 1936- , American; fiction CON

DU CAMP, Maxime, 1822-94,
French; journalism DIF

DU CANGE, Charles Du Fresne,
1610-88, French; nonfiction
DIF SA ST

DUCANGE, Victor Henri Joseph
Brahain, 1783-1833, French;
journalism, plays DIF

DUCAS, 15th cent., Byzantine;
nonfiction ST

DUCAS, Dorothy, 1905- , American; juveniles CON WA

DUCASSE, Curt John, 1881- ,
Franco-American; nonfiction
CON

DUCASSE, Isidore L. see
LAUTREAMONT, Le Comte de

DUCE, Robert, 1908- , English;
nonfiction CON

DU CERCEAU, Jean Antoine,
1670-1730, French; nonfiction
DIL

DUCHACEK, Ivo Duka, 1913- ,
Czech-American; nonfiction,
fiction CON

DU CHAILLU, Paul Belloni,
1835-1903, American; nonfiction KAA

DUCHAMP, Marcel, 1887- ,
French; nonfiction DIF

DUCHARME, Jacques, 1910- ,
American; nonfiction, fiction
HOE

DUCHE, Jacob, 1737/38-98,
American; nonfiction KAA

DUCHE, Jean, 1915- , French;
nonfiction CON
'DU CHESNE' see ENZINAS, Fran-
cisco de
DU CHESNE, André, 1584-1640,
French; nonfiction DIF SA
'DUCHESNE, Jacques' see SAINT
DENIS, Michel J.
DUCHESNE, Louis Marie Olivier,
1843-1922, French; nonfiction
DIF
DUCHESNE, Mathieu, -1752, French;
nonfiction DIL
DUCHESNE, Vincent, 1678-1724,
French; nonfiction DIL
'DUCHESS, The' see HUNGERFORD,
Margaret W.
DUCHOSAL, Louis Albert, 1862-1901,
Swiss; poetry ST
DUČIĆ, Jovan, 1871-1943, Serbian;
poetry COL FLE SA ST
DUCIS, Jean François, 1733-1816,
French; plays, poetry, transla-
tions DIF HAR SA ST
DUCKAT, Walter Benjamin, 1911- ,
American; nonfiction CON
DUCLOS, Charles Pinot, 1704-72,
French; fiction, nonfiction DIF
DIL HAR SA ST
DUCORNET, Erica, 1943- , Ameri-
can; nonfiction CON
DUCKWORTH, George Eckel, 1903-
72, American; nonfiction CON
DUCLOZ, Théodore Gourret, 1655-
1734, French; poetry DIL
DUDDEN, Arthur Power, 1921- ,
American; nonfiction CON
DU DEFFAND, Marie Anne Vichy de
Chamrond, 1697-1780, French;
letters DIF DIL
DUDEK, J.B. ('O.P. Iffle'), 1890- ,
American; nonfiction MAR
DUDEK, Louis, 1918- , Canadian;
poetry MUR SY
DUDESACK, Wendelin see FINDEISEN,
Kurt A.
DUDEVANT, Mme. see 'SAND,
George'
DUDGEON, Muriel Ann, American;
nonfiction PAC
DUDINTSEV, Vladimir, 1918- ,
Russian; fiction RIC
DUDLEY, Billy Joseph, 1931- ,
American; nonfiction CON
DUDLEY, Donald Reynolds, 1910- ,
English; nonfiction CON
DUDLEY, Ernest ('Ernest Vivian
Coltman'), 1908- , English;

fiction CON
DUDLEY, Geoffrey Arthur, 1917- ,
English; nonfiction CON
DUDLEY, Guilford, Jr., 1907- ,
American; nonfiction CON
'DUDLEY, Jay' see CHAPMAN,
J.D.
DUDLEY, Louise, 1884- , Amer-
ican; nonfiction CON
'DUDLEY, Nancy' see COLE,
Lois D.
DUDLEY, Owen Francis, 1882- ,
English; nonfiction HOE
DÜHRING, Eugen, 1833-1901,
German; nonfiction SA
'DUENDE de la COLEGATA, El'
see FERNANDEZ ARIAS,
Adelardo
DUEÑAS, Juan de, -1460,
Spanish; poetry BL SA
DÜRRENMATT, Friedrich, 1921- ,
Swiss; plays, fiction, essays
AL CON FLE HAR KU KUN
MAT RIC
DU FAIL, Noël, 1520-91, French;
fiction DIF ST
DUFAULT, Peter Kane, 1923- ,
American; poetry CON
DUFF, Charles St. Lawrence
('Cathal O Dubh'), 1894- ,
Irish; nonfiction CON
DUFF, Ernest Arthur, 1929- ,
American; nonfiction CON
DUFF, Douglas Valder, 1901- ,
English; nonfiction, fiction
HO
DUFF, Margaret K., American;
juveniles CON
DUFF, Sir Mountstuart E. see
GRANT DUFF, M.E.
DUFF, Raymond Stanley, 1923- ,
American; nonfiction CON
DUFFERIN, Lady (Helen Selina
Sheridan Blackwood), 1807-67,
English; songs, poetry BRO
KBA ST
DUFFERIN, Lord (Frederick
Temple Hamilton-Temple
Blackwood), 1826-1902, Eng-
lish; nonfiction KBA
DUFFET, Thomas, fl. 1678, Eng-
lish; plays ST
DUFF-GORDON, Lady Lucie, 1821-
69, English; nonfiction KBA
DUFFIELD, Anne Tate, 1893- ,
American; fiction CON
DUFFIELD, Samuel Augustus
Willoughby, 1843-87, Ameri-

can; hymns KAA

DUFFIN, Henry Charles, 1884- ,
English; nonfiction CON

DUFFUS, Robert Luther, 1888-1972,
American; fiction KT WAF

DUFFY, Sir Charles Gavan, 1816-
1903, Irish; poetry, journalism
BRO KBA ST

DUFFY, Elizabeth, 1904- , American; nonfiction CON

DUFFY, Helene Krainovich, 1926- ,
American; nonfiction CON

DUFFY, John, 1915- , English;
nonfiction CON

DUFFY, Maureen, 1933- , English;
fiction CON RIC

DUFFY, Thomas Gavan, 1888-1941,
Irish; nonfiction HOE

DUFORT, Joseph, 1685-1767,
French; nonfiction DIL

DUFOUR, Pierre Joseph,   -1786,
French; nonfiction DIL

DUFRENOY, Adelmide Gillete Billet,
1765-1825, French; nonfiction
SA

DU FRESNE de FRANCHEVILLE,
Joseph, 1704-81, French; nonfiction DIL

DUFRESNY, Charles Rivière, 1648-
1724, French; plays, poetry,
fiction DIF DIL SA ST

DUGAD, Louis, 1707-86, French;
nonfiction DIL

DUGAN, Alan, 1923- , American;
poetry MUR

DUGAN, James Thomas, 1912- ,
American; nonfiction CON

DUGANNE, Augustine Joseph Hickey,
1823-84, American; poetry, fiction KAA

DU GARD, Roger M. see MARTIN
DU GARD, Roger

DUGAS, Marcel, 1883-1947, Canadian;
nonfiction SY

DUGDALE, Sir William, 1605-86,
English; nonfiction BRO KB SA
ST

DUGGAL, Kartar Singh, 1917- ,
Indian; fiction LAN

DUGGAN, Alfred Leo, 1903-64,
English; fiction KTS RIC WA

DUGGAN, Eileen Mary, New Zealander;
poetry HOE MUR ST

DUGGAN, George Henry, 1912- ,
New Zealander; nonfiction CON

DUGGAN, Joseph John, 1938- ,
American; nonfiction CON

DUGGAN, Mary M., 1921- ,

American; juveniles CON

DUGGAN, Maurice, 1922- , New
Zealander; fiction ST

DUGGER, Ronnie, 1930- , American; nonfiction CON

DUGGER, Shepherd Monroe,
1854-1938, American; fiction
JO

DUGGINS, James Harry, Jr.,
1933- , American; nonfiction
CON

DUGHI, Nancy, American; fiction
CON

DUGMORE, Clifford William,
1909- , English; nonfiction
CON

DU GONE, French; nonfiction
DIL

DUGONICS, András, 1740-1818,
Hungarian; fiction, plays ST

DU GUET, Jacques Joseph, 1649-
1733, French; nonfiction DIL

DUGUID, Julian, 1902- , English;
essays, nonfiction KT

'DUGUID, Robert' see PRING-MILL,
Robert D. F.

DU GUILLET, Pernette, 1520-45,
French; poetry DIF KE ST

DU HALDE, Jean Baptiste, 1674-
1734, French; nonfiction DIL

DUHAMEL, George ('Denis
Thévenin'), 1884-1966, French;
poetry, fiction, plays, essays,
criticism COL DIF FLE HAR
KT MAL MAT RIC SA ST

DUHAMEL, Pierre Albert, 1920- ,
American; nonfiction CON

DUHAMEL, Roger, 1916- ,
Canadian; nonfiction ST SY

DUHL, Leonard J., 1926- ,
American; nonfiction CON

DUIGNAN, Peter, 1926- , American; nonfiction CON

DUIM, Frederik, 1674- , Dutch;
plays ST

DUJARDIN, Bénigne, 18th cent.,
French; nonfiction, plays,
fiction DIL

DUJARDIN, Edouard, 1861-1949,
French; fiction DIF

DU JARDIN, Rosamond Neal,
1902-63, American; juveniles,
fiction COM CON FUL HOO

DU JON, François see JUNIUS,
Franciscus

DUKE, Donald Norman ('Roger
Valentine'), 1929- , American; nonfiction CON

341   DUKE

'DUKE, John' see CHALMERS,
   Floyd S.
DUKE, Richard, 1658-1710/11,
   English; poetry ST
DUKELSKY, Vladimir ('Vernon Duke'),
   1903-69, American; fiction, non-
   fiction CON
DUKER, Sam, 1905- , American;
   nonfiction CON
DUKERT, Joseph Michael, 1929- ,
   American; juveniles CON WA
DUKES, Paul, 1934- , American;
   nonfiction CON
DUKORE, Bernard F. , 1931- ,
   American; nonfiction CON
DULAC, Edmund, 1882-1953,
   Franco-English; juveniles DOY
   KJU
DULACK, Thomas, 1935- , Ameri-
   can; fiction CON
DULANY, Daniel ('Antilon'), 1722-97,
   American; nonfiction KAA
DULANY, Harris, 1940- , Ameri-
   can; fiction CON
DU LAURA, Etienne,   -1706,
   French; nonfiction DIL
DULAURENS, Henri Joseph, 1719-
   97, French; nonfiction, poetry
   DIL
DULK, Albert Fredrich Benno, 1819-
   84, German; plays ST
DULLAART, Joan, 1629-81?, Dutch;
   plays, translations ST
DULLAERT, Heiman, 1636-84, Dutch;
   poetry ST
DULLES, Allen Welsh, 1893-1969,
   American; nonfiction CON
DULLES, Rev. Avery Robert,
   1918- , American; nonfiction
   CON HO
DULLES, Eleanor Lansing, 1895- ,
   American; nonfiction CON
DULLES, Foster Rhea, 1900-70,
   American; nonfiction CON KTS
DULLES, John Watson Foster,
   1913- , American; nonfiction
   CON
DULLIN, Charles, 1885- , French;
   nonfiction COL
DULSEY, Bernard M. , 1914- ,
   American; nonfiction CON
DUMARCHAIS, Pierre see MAC-
   ORLAN, Pierre
DUMAS, Adolphe, 1806-61, French;
   poetry, plays SA
DUMAS, Alexandre, 1802-70, French;
   juveniles, plays, fiction DIF
   DOY HAR KE MAG MAL SA ST

DUMAS, Alexandre, 1824-95,
   French; fiction, plays, poetry,
   essays DIF HAR KE MAG
   MAL SA ST
DUMAS, Gerald J. , 1930- ,
   American; juveniles CON
DU MAURIER, Daphne, 1907- ,
   English; fiction BRO CON
   KT MAG RIC SA
DU MAURIER, George Louis
   Palmella Buson, 1834-96,
   English; fiction BRO KBA
   MAG SA ST
DUMBLETON, William Albert,
   1927- , American; nonfiction
   CON
DUMITRIU, Petru, 1924- ,
   Rumanian; fiction RIC
DUMMER, Jeremiah, 1679-1739,
   American; nonfiction KAA
DUMONT, Pierre Etienne Louis,
   1759-1829, French; nonfiction
   HAR
DUMOULIN, Heinrich, 1905- ,
   German; nonfiction CON
DUMOURIEZ, Charles François
   Duperier, 1739-1823, French;
   nonfiction DIL
DUMPLETON, John La Fevre,
   1924- , English; nonfiction
   CON
'DUMPTY, Humpty S. ' see
   DENENBERG, Herbert S.
DUNAS, Joseph C. , 1900- ,
   American; nonfiction CON
DUNASH BEN LABRAT, 920-80?,
   Jewish; poetry, nonfiction ST
DUNBAR, Dorothy, 1923- ,
   American; fiction CON
DUNBAR, Ernest, 1927- , Amer-
   ican; nonfiction CON
DUNBAR, Janet, 1901- , English;
   nonfiction CON
DUNBAR, John Greenwall, 1930- ,
   English; nonfiction CON
DUNBAR, Paul Laurence, 1872-
   1906, American; poetry, fiction
   KAA ST
DUNBAR, Tony, 1949- , Ameri-
   can; nonfiction CON
DUNBAR, William, 1460/65-1521/
   30, Scots; poetry BRO KB
   SA SP ST
DUNBAR, Willis Frederick, 1902- ,
   American; nonfiction CON
DUNCAN, Anthony Douglas,
   1930- , English; poetry CON
DUNCAN, Ardinelle Bean, 1913- ,

American; juvenile CON

DUNCAN, Bowie, 1941- , American;
nonfiction CON

DUNCAN, Charles Thomas, 1914- ,
American; nonfiction CON

DUNCAN, Clyde H., 1903- ,
American; nonfiction CON

DUNCAN, Cyril John, 1916- ,
English; nonfiction CON

DUNCAN, David, 1913- , American;
fiction CON PAC WAF

DUNCAN, De Witt Clinton, 1829-
1909, American; poetry MAR

'DUNCAN, Gregory' see McCLINTOCK,
Marshall

DUNCAN, Hugh Dalziel, 1909- ,
Scots-American; nonfiction CON

'DUNCAN, Jane' see CAMERON,
Elizabeth J.

DUNCAN, Joseph Ellis, 1921- ,
American; nonfiction CON

'DUNCAN, Julia K.' see STRATE-
MEYER, Edward L.

DUNCAN, Kenneth Sandilands,
1912- , English; nonfiction
CON

DUNCAN, Kunigunde ('Flora Duncan
Isely'), 1886- , American;
juveniles, poetry CON

'DUNCAN, Lois' see ARQUETTE,
Lois S.

DUNCAN, Matthew, American;
journalism HOO

DUNCAN, Norman, 1871-1916,
American; juveniles, fiction
KJU SY

DUNCAN, Otis Dudley, 1921- ,
American; nonfiction CON

DUNCAN, Pam, 1938- , American;
nonfiction CON

DUNCAN, Pope Alexander, 1920- ,
American; nonfiction CON

DUNCAN, Robert Edward, 1919- ,
American; poetry, plays CON
MUR

DUNCAN, Ronald F.H., 1914- ,
British; poetry, plays BRO
CON MAT MUR RIC

DUNCAN, Sara Jeannette, 1862-
1922, Canadian; journalism,
nonfiction, fiction SY

DUNCAN, Thomas William, 1905- ,
American; fiction CON WAF

DUNCAN, William Murdoch ('John
Cassells'; 'Neill Graham';
'Martin Locke'; 'Peter Malloch';
'Lovat Marshall'), 1909- ,
Scots; fiction CON

DUNCOMBE, David Cameron,
1928- , American; nonfiction
CON

DUNCOMBE, Frances Riker,
1900- , American; juveniles
CON

'DUNDEE, Robert' see KIRSCH,
Robert R.

DUNDES, Alan, 1934- , American; nonfiction CON

DUNDONALD, Lord (Thomas
Cochrane), 1775-1860, Scots;
nonfiction KBA

DUNDY, Elaine, 1927- , American; fiction RIC

DUNHAM, Arthur, 1893- ,
American; nonfiction CON

DUNHAM, Barrows, 1905- ,
American; nonfiction CON

DUNHAM, Donald Carl, 1908- ,
American; nonfiction CON

DUNHAM, Henry Warren, 1906- ,
American; nonfiction CON

DUNHAM, John L., 1939- ,
American; juveniles CON

DUNHAM, Lowell, 1910- , American; nonfiction CON

DUNHAM, Mabel, 1881-1957,
Canadian; juveniles, fiction
SY

DUNHAM, Montrew Goetz, 1919- ,
American; nonfiction CON

DUNIN-MARTSINKEVICH, Vikenti,
1807-84, Russian; fiction
HARK

DUNIWAY, Abigail Jane Scott,
1834-1915, American; nonfiction
KAA

DUNKEL, Harold Baker, 1912- ,
American; nonfiction CON

DUNKERLEY, Roderic, 1884- ,
English; nonfiction CON

DUNKERLEY, William Arthur
('John Oxenham'), 1852-1941,
English; fiction, poetry BRO
KT

DUNKIN, Paul S., 1905- , American; nonfiction CON

DUNKMAN, William Edward,
1903- , American; nonfiction
CON

DUNLAP, Aurie Nichols, 1907- ,
American; nonfiction CON

'DUNLAP, Jane' see DAVIS,
Adelle

DUNLAP, Leslie Whittaker,
1911- , American; nonfiction
CON

'DUNLAP, Lon' see McCORMICK,
    Wilfred
DUNLAP, Orrin Elmer, Jr.,
    1896- , American; nonfiction
    CON
DUNLAP, William, 1766-1839,
    American; plays, nonfiction BRO
    KAA ST
DUNLEAVY, Gareth Winthrop, 1923- ,
    American; nonfiction CON
DUNLOP, Agnes Mary Robertson
    ('Elisabeth Kyle'; 'Jan Ralston'),
    Scots; juveniles CON DOY FUL
    WA
DUNLOP, Ian Geoffrey David, 1925- ,
    English; nonfiction CON
DUNLOP, John Colin, 1780?-1842,
    Scots; nonfiction BRO KBA
DUNLOP, John Thomas, 1914- ,
    American; nonfiction CON
DUNLOP, Richard, 1921- , Ameri-
    can; nonfiction CON
DUNLOP, William, 1792-1848,
    Canadian; journalism SY
DUNMORE, Spencer Sambrook,
    1928- , English; fiction CON
DUNN, Alan Cantwell, 1900- ,
    American; nonfiction, fiction
    CON
DUNN, Catherine Mary, 1930- ,
    American; nonfiction CON
DUNN, Delmer Delano, 1941- ,
    American; nonfiction CON
DUNN, Donald Harley, 1929- ,
    American; nonfiction CON
DUN, Douglas Eaglesham, 1942- ,
    Scots; poetry MUR
DUN, Edgar S., Jr., 1921- ,
    American; nonfiction CON
DUN, Ethel Deikman, 1932- ,
    American; nonfiction CON
DUN, Harold, 1929- , American;
    nonfiction CON
'DUNN, Harris' see DOERFFLER,
    Alfred
'DUNN, James' see WILKES-HUNTER,
    Richard
DUNN, James Taylor, 1912- ,
    American; nonfiction CON
DUNN, Jerry G., 1916- , Ameri-
    can; nonfiction CON
DUNN, Katherine Karen, 1945- ,
    American; nonfiction CON
DUNN, Marion Herndon, 1920- ,
    American; juveniles CON
DUNN, Patience Louise Ralli,
    1922- , English; juveniles
    CON

DUNN, Samuel Watson, 1918- ,
    American; nonfiction CON
DUNN, Stephen, 1939- , Ameri-
    can; poetry CON
DUNN, Waldo Hilary, 1882-1969,
    American; nonfiction CON
DUNN, William J., 1906- ,
    American; nonfiction CON
DUNN, William Lawrence, Jr.,
    1924- , American; nonfic-
    tion CON
DUNNE, Finley Peter ('Mr.
    Dooley'), 1867-1936, Ameri-
    can; fiction BRO HOE HOO
    KAT KT RIC
DUNNE, George Harold, 1905- ,
    American; nonfiction CON
DUNNE, John Gregory, 1930- ,
    American; fiction CON
DUNNE, John Scribner, 1929- ,
    American; nonfiction CON
DUNNE, John William, 1875-1949,
    English; nonfiction BRO
DUNNE, Peter Masten, 1889- ,
    American; nonfiction HOE
DUNNE, Philip, 1908- , Ameri-
    can; nonfiction CON
DUNNER, Joseph ('Germanicus';
    'Alexander Roth'), 1908- ,
    American; nonfiction CON
DUNNETT, Dorothy, 1923- ,
    Scots; fiction CON
DUNNING, Arthur Stephen, Jr.,
    1924- , American; nonfiction
    CON
DUNNING, Philip Hart, 1890-1968,
    American; plays MAT
DUNNINGTON, Hazel Brain, 1912- ,
    American; nonfiction CON
DU NOÜY, Pierre Lecomte,
    1883-1947, French; nonfiction
    HO
DUNOYER, Anne Marguerite Petit,
    1633/63-1720, French; non-
    fiction DIL SA
'DUNOYER, Maurice' see
    DOMERGUE, Maurice
DUNPHY, Jack, 1914- , Ameri-
    can; fiction CON
DUNS SCOTUS, Johannes, 1265?-
    1308?, English; nonfiction
    BRO KB SA ST
DUNSANY, Edward John Moreton
    Drax Plunkett, 1878-1957,
    English; poetry, plays BRO
    KL KT RIC MAT SA ST
DUNSHEATH, Joyce Houchen,
    1902- , English; nonfiction
    CON

DUNSON, Josh, 1941- , American;
nonfiction CON
'DUNSTAN, Andrew' see CHANDLER,
A. Bertram
DUNSTAN, Reginald Ernest, 1914- ,
English; nonfiction CON
DUNSTERVILLE, Galfrid C.K.,
1905- , English; nonfiction
CON
DUNTON, John, 1659-1733, English;
nonfiction KB
DUONELAITIS, Kristijonas (Donalitius),
1714-80, Lithuanian; poetry ST
DUPARC, Jacques Lenoir, 1702-89,
French; nonfiction, plays DIL
DUPATY, Charles Marguerite Mercier,
1746-88, French; nonfiction DIF
DUPEE, Frederick Wilcox, 1904- ,
American; nonfiction CON KTS
DU PERRIER, Charles,   -1692,
French; poetry ST
DU PERRON, Jacques Davy, 1556-1618,
French; nonfiction, poetry DIF
SA ST
DUPIN, Amantine A.L. see 'SAND,
George'
DUPLESSIS, Francois Xavier, 1694-
1771, Canadian-French; nonfiction
DIL
DU PLESSIS, Izak Dawid, 1900- ,
Afrikaans; poetry ST
DUPLESSIS, Stanslas, 1718-80,
French; poetry DIL
'DUBLESSIS, Yves' see JAURAND,
Yvonne
DUPLESSY de SAINTE, Hélène, Mere
French; letters DIL
DUPONCEAU, Pierre Etienne, 1760-
1844, Franco-American; nonfiction
KAA
'DUPONT, Paul' see FREWIN, Leslie
R.
DUPONT, Pierre, 1821-70, French;
poetry HAR
DUPRE, Catherine, English; fiction
CON
DUPRE, Claude, 1686-1736, French;
nonfiction DIL
DUPRE, Guy, 1928- , French;
fiction DIC
DUPRE, Louis Karel, 1925- ,
Belgian; nonfiction CON
DUPRE, Marie, 17th cent., French;
poetry SA
DUPRE d'AULNAY, Louis, 1670-
1758, French; nonfiction DIL
DUPRE de RICHEMONT, 18th cent.,
French; letters DIL

DUPRE de SAINT-MAUR, Nicolas
François, 1695-1774, French;
translations DIL
DUPREE, Anderson Hunter,
1921- , American; nonfiction
CON
'DUPRES, Henri' see FAWCETT,
Frank D.
DUPREY, Richard Allen, 1929- ,
American; nonfiction CON
DUPUIS, Adrian M. , 1919- ,
American; nonfiction CON
DUPUIS, Charles François, 1742-
1809, French; nonfiction DIL
DUPUY, Eliza Ann ('Annie Young'),
1814-81, American; fiction
KAA
DUPUY, Louis, 1709-95, French;
nonfiction DIL
DUPUY, Richard Ernest, 1887- ,
American; nonfiction CON
DUPUY, Trevor Nevitt, 1916- ,
American; nonfiction, juveniles
CON WA
DUQUE, Gonzaga, 1863-1911,
Brazilian; nonfiction, fiction
SA
DUQUE, Matiás, 1622?- ,
Spanish; poetry SA
DUQUE de ESTRADA, Diego,
1589-1647?, Spanish; poetry
BL SA
DUQUESNE José Domingo, 1747-
1822, Colombian; nonfiction
MIN
DURAN, Agustín, 1793-1862,
Spanish; nonfiction BL SA
DURAN, Manuel E. , 1925- ,
Spanish; poetry BL CON
DURAN Simeon Ben Zeham
('Rashbaz'), 1361-1444,
Spanish; poetry, nonfiction
ST
DURAN y TORTAJADA, Enrique,
1895- , Spanish; poetry SA
'DURAND, Alice' see GREVILLE,
Henry
DURAND, Loyal, Jr., 1902- ,
American; nonfiction CON
DURAND, François Jacques,
-1816, French; nonfiction
DIL
DURAND, Leópold, 1666-1749,
French; nonfiction DIL
DURAND, Luis, 1895/1902-54,
Chilean; journalism, fiction
MIN
DURAND, Ursin, 1682-1771,

French; nonfiction DIL

DURAND-BEDACIER, Catherine,
1670-1736, French; nonfiction
SA

DURAND de MAILLANE, 1729-1814,
French; nonfiction DIL

DURANDEAUX, Jacques, 1920- ,
French; nonfiction CON

DURANDO de SAINT Pourcain,
-1334, French; nonfiction
SA

DURANT, Ida Ariel K., 1898- ,
American; nonfiction CON

DURANT, John, 1902- , American;
juveniles CON WA

DURANT, William James, 1885- ,
American; nonfiction, fiction
BRO CON KAT KT

DURANT de la BERGERIE, Gilles,
1550-1615, French; fiction
DIF

DURANTY, Louis Emile Edmond,
1833-80, French; fiction DIF
HAR ST

DURANTY, Walter, 1884- ,
Anglo-American; journalism,
fiction KT

DURÃO, Jose de Santa Rita, 1722-
84, Brazilian; poetry SA ST

DURAS, Marguerite, 1914- ,
French; fiction CON DIC DIF
FLE HAR MAT PIN RIC

DURATSCHEK, Sister Mary Claudia,
1894- , Hungarian-American;
nonfiction CON

DURBAND, Alan, 1927- , English;
nonfiction CON

DURBIN, Mary Lou, 1927- , American; nonfiction CON

DURCAN, Paul, 1944- , Irish;
poetry MUR

DURDEN, Robert Franklin, 1925- ,
American; nonfiction CON

DUREAU de la MALLE, Jean Baptiste
Joseph René, 1742-1807, French;
translations DIL

DURELL, Ann, American; juveniles
WA

DURET, Edmond Jean Baptiste,
1671-1758, French; nonfiction
DIL

DUREY, d'HARNONCOURT, Pierre,
1690-1765, French; nonfiction
DIL

DUREY de NOINVILLE, Jacques
Bernard, 1682-1768, French;
nonfiction DIL

DURFEE David Arthur, 1929- ,

American; nonfiction CON

DURFEE, Job, 1790-1847, American; nonfiction KAA

D'URFEY, Thomas, 1653-1723,
English; poetry, plays BRO
KB

DURFORT-DURAS, Claire de
Kersaint, 1778-1829, French;
nonfiction SA

DURGNAT, Raymond Eric ('O. O.
Green'), 1932- , English;
nonfiction CON

DURHAM, John I., 1933- ,
American; nonfiction CON

DURHAM, Philip, 1912- ,
American; nonfiction CON

'DURIAN, Wolf' (Wolfgang Bechtle),
1892- , German; nonfiction
AL

DURIS de SAMOS, 370-281 B.C.,
Greek; nonfiction SA ST

DURIVAGE, Francis Alexander
('Old Un'), 1814-81, American; journalism, plays KAA

DURKEE, Mary C., 1921- ,
American; nonfiction CON

DURKHEIM, Emile, 1858-1917,
French; nonfiction COL DIF
SA

DURKIN, Joseph Thomas, 1903- ,
American; nonfiction CON

DURLACHER, Ed, American;
juveniles WA

DURNBAUGH, Donald F., 1927- ,
American; nonfiction CON

DUROCHE, Leonard Le Roy,
1933- , American; nonfiction
CON

DURON, Jacques, 1904- ,
French; poetry, essays DIF

DUROSELLE, Jean Baptiste Marie
Lucien Charles, 1917- ,
French; nonfiction CON

DUROSOI, Barnabé Farmian de
Rosoi, 1745-92, French;
fiction, plays DIL

DUROT, Augustin, fl. 1671-1756,
Belgian; nonfiction DIL

DURR, Fred, 1921- , American;
nonfiction CON

DURR, William Kirtley, 1924- ,
American; nonfiction CON

DURRANI, Mahmood Khan,
1914- , Pakistani; nonfiction
CON

DURRANT, Digby, 1926- , English; fiction CON

DURRELL, Donald De Witt,

1903- , American; nonfiction CON

DURRELL, Gerald Malcolm, 1925- , English; nonfiction CON RIC WA

DURRELL, Jacqueline Sonia Rasen, 1929- , English; nonfiction CON

DURRELL, Lawrence George ('Gaffer Peeslake'; 'Charles Norton'; 'Charles Norden'), 1912- , British; poetry, plays, fiction, criticism BRO CON FLE KTS MAT MUR RIC SP

DURRENBERGER, Robert Warren, 1918- , American; nonfiction CON

DURRETT, Reuben Thomas, 1824-1913, American; nonfiction KAA

DURRY, Marie Jeanne, 1901- , French; criticism, poetry DIF

DURST, Paul ('Peter Bannon'; 'John Chelton'; 'Jeff Cochran'; 'John Shane'), 1921- , American; fiction CON

DURUFLE, Louis Robert Parfait, 1742-93, French; poetry DIL

DURUY, Victor, 1811-91/94- , French; nonfiction DIF SA

DURYCH, Jaroslav, 1886-1962, Czech; poetry, fiction, plays COL FLE RIC SA ST

DU RYER, Pierre, 1600-58, French; plays, translations HAR KE ST

DUSAELX, Jean, 1728-99, French; nonfiction DIL

DU SAULT, Jean Paul, 1650- , French; nonfiction DIL

DU SAUTOY, Peter Francis De Courcy, 1921- , English; nonfiction CON

DUSENBERRY, William Howard, 1908- , American; nonfiction CON

DUSENBERY, Gail Sherrell, 1939- , American; poetry MUR

DUSENBURY, Winifred L. see FRAZER, Winifred D.

DUSHNITZKY-SHNER, Sara ('Sara Neshamith'), 1913- , Polish-Israeli; nonfiction CON

'DUŠIČ, Stanko' see BEGOVIČ, Milan

DU SOE, Robert C., 1892-1958, American; juveniles FUL

DU SOUHAIT, Le Seigneur, 16th cent., French; poetry, fiction SA

DUSTER, Troy, 1936- , American; nonfiction CON

DUTENS, Louis, 1730-1812, French; nonfiction, poetry DIL

DUTERTRE, Rodolphe, 1677-1762, French; nonfiction DIL

DUTHIE, Charles S., 1911- , American; nonfiction CON

DU TOIT, Jacob Daniel du see 'TOTIUS'

DUTOIT MEMBRINE, Jean Philippe, 1721-93, French; nonfiction DIL

DUTOURD, Jean, 1920- , French; fiction, essays DIC DIF KTS PIN

DUTT, Aksay-Kumar, 1820-86, Indian; nonfiction ST

DUTT, Michael Madhusudana, 1824-73, Indian; poetry, plays ST

DUTT, Rajani Palme, 1896- , English; nonfiction CON

DUTT, Ramesh Chandra, 1848-1909, Indian; nonfiction ST

DUTT, Toru, 1856-77, Indian; poetry ST

DUTTON, Geoffrey Piers Henry, 1922- , Australian; poetry, fiction, criticism MUR

DUTTON, Joan Parry, 1908- , American; nonfiction CON

DUTTON, Mary, 1922- , American; nonfiction CON

DUTTON, Ralph Stawell, 1898- , English; nonfiction CON

'DUTZ' see DAVIS, Mary O.

DUUN, Olav Julius, 1876-1939, Norwegian; fiction COL FLE HAR KAT KT MAG SA ST

DUUS, Peter, 1933- , American; nonfiction CON

DU VAIR, Guillaume, 1556-1621, French; nonfiction DIF ST

DU VAL, Francis Alan, 1916- , American; nonfiction CON

DUVAL, Paul Alexandre ('Jean Lorrain'), 1855-1906, French; fiction KE SA

DUVAL d'EPREMESNIL, Jean Jacques, 1714-65, French; nonfiction DIL

DUVALL, Evelyn Millis, 1906- , American; nonfiction CON

DUVALL, William Clyde, Jr., 1917- , American; nonfiction CON

DUVERDIER de la SORINIERE, Claude François, -1784, French; nonfiction DIL

DUVERNOIS, Henri Simon

Schevabacher, 1875-1937, French; fiction, journalism, plays DIF SA

DUVOISIN, Roger, 1904- , Swiss-American; juveniles COM CON DOY KJU WA

DUWEZ, Maurice see 'DEAUVILLE, Max'

DUYCKINCK, Evert Augustus, 1816-78, American; nonfiction KAA

DUYM, Jonkheer Jacob, 1547-1624, Dutch; poetry ST

DUYOS, Rafael, 1906- , Spanish; nonfiction, poetry BL SA

DUYSE, Prudens van, 1804-59, Flemish; poetry KE ST

DVIVEDI, Mahavir Prasad, 1870-1938, Indian; essays LAN

DVORETZKY, Edward, 1930- , American; nonfiction CON

DVORNIK, Francis, 1893- , Czech-American; nonfiction CON

DWECK, Susan, 1943- , American; nonfiction CON

DWIGGINS, Don, 1913- , American; nonfiction CON

'DWIGHT, Allan' see COLE, Lois D.

DWIGHT, John Sullivan, 1813-93, American; criticism KAA

DWIGHT, Marianne see ORVIS, Marianne D.

DWIGHT, Theodore, 1764-1846, American; editor KAA

DWIGHT, Theodore, 1796-1866, American; nonfiction KAA

DWIGHT, Theodore William, 1822-92, American; nonfiction KAA

DWIGHT, Timothy, 1752-1817, American; poetry BRO KAA ST

DWINGER, Edwin Erich ('Warner Beunelburg'; 'H. G. Konsalik'; 'Franz Schauwecker'; 'Heinz Stegeweit'; 'Heinrich Zerkaulen'), 1898- , German; fiction AL COL LEN SA

DWORKIN, Rita, 1928- , American; nonfiction CON

DYAL, James A., 1928- , American; nonfiction CON

DYAL, William M., Jr., 1928- , American; nonfiction CON

DYCE, Alexander, 1798-1869, Scots; nonfiction BRO KBA ST

DYCK, Anni, 1931- , German; nonfiction CON

DYCKMAN, John William, 1922- , American; nonfiction CON

DYCKMAN, Thomas Richard, 1932- , American; nonfiction CON

'DYE, Charles' see MacLEAN, Katherine

DYE, David L., 1925- , American; nonfiction CON

DYE, Harold Eldon, 1907- , American; nonfiction CON

DYE, James Wayne, 1934- , American; nonfiction CON

DYE, Thomas Roy, 1935- , American; nonfiction CON

DYER, Charles ('Raymond Dyer'; 'R. Kraselchik'; 'Charles Stretton'; Renshaw Stretton'), 1928- , English; plays, fiction CON

DYER, Sir Edward, 1543/45-1607, English; poetry BRO KB ST

DYER, Frederick C., 1918- , American; nonfiction CON

DYER, George, 1755-1841, English; poetry, criticism KB

DYER, George Edward, 1928- , American; nonfiction CON

DYER, John, 1699/1700-58, Welsh; poetry BRO KB SA ST

DYER, John M., 1920- , American; nonfiction CON

DYER, John Percy, 1902- , American; nonfiction CON

DYER, Louis, 1851-1908, American; nonfiction KAA

'DYER, Raymond' see DYER, Charles

DYGASINSKI, Tomaz, Adolf ('Dygas'), 1839-1902, Polish; fiction COL SA ST

DYGAT, Stanislaw, 1914- , Polish; fiction FLE

DYK, Viktor, 1877-1931, Czech; poetry, plays, essays, fiction COL FLE SA ST

DYKE, John, 1935- , English; juveniles CON

DYKEMA, Karl Washburn, 1906- , American; nonfiction CON

DYKEMAN, Wilma see STOKELY, Wilma D.

DYKES, Archie R., 1931- , American; nonfiction CON

'DYKES, Jack', 1929- , English; fiction CON

DYKES, Jefferson Chenoweth, 1900- , American; nonfiction CON

DYKSTRA, Robert R., 1930- ,
　　American; fiction CON
'DYLAN, Bob' (Robert Zimmerman),
　　1941- , American; poetry MUR
DYMENT, Clifford Henry, 1914-71,
　　English; fiction, poetry CON
　　MUR
DYMOV, Ossip (Joseph Pearlman),
　　1878-1959, Russian; plays MAT
DYNELY, James see MAYNE, William
DYNES, Russell Rowe, 1923- ,
　　Canadian; nonfiction CON
DYRNESS, William Arthur, 1943- ,
　　American; nonfiction CON
DYSON, Anne Jane, 1912- , Amer-
　　ican; nonfiction CON
DYSON, Edward, 1865-1931, Aus-
　　tralian; fiction, poetry RIC
DZHUBIN E. Georgievich see
　　'BAGRITZKY, Eduard'
DZHUGASHVILI, I.V. see 'STALIN,
　　Iosif V.'
DZIEWANOWSKI, Marian Kamil,
　　1913- , Russian-American;
　　nonfiction CON
DZYUBIN, Eduard see 'BAGRITSKY,
　　Eduard'

E

'E.D.M.' see MANSFIELD, Edward
　　D.
EADIE, Donald, 1919- , American;
　　nonfiction CON
EADIE, Thomas Michael, 1941- ,
　　Canadian; poetry MUR
'EADIE, W.P.R.' see GLASSCO,
　　John S.
EDMER (Edmer), 1060?-1124?,
　　English; nonfiction BRO KB ST
EAGER, Edward McMaken, -1964,
　　American; juveniles DOY FUL
　　WA
EAGLE, Dorothy, 1912- , English;
　　nonfiction CON
EAGLE, Joanna, 1934- , American;
　　nonfiction CON
EAGLE, Robert Harold, 1921- ,
　　American; nonfiction CON
EAKIN, Mary Katherine, 1917- ,
　　American; nonfiction CON
EALES, John Ray, 1910- ,
　　American; nonfiction CON
EALHWINE see ALCUIN
EALY, Lawrence Orr, 1915- ,
　　American; nonfiction CON
EAMES, Genevieve Torrey, Ameri-

can; juveniles WA
EANNES de AZURARA, Gomes
　　see ZURARA, Gomes E. de
EARDLEY-WILMOT, Sir John
　　Eardley, 1821-96, English;
　　nonfiction HIG
EARHART, Harry Byron, 1935- ,
　　American; nonfiction CON
EARL, David Margarey, 1911- ,
　　American; nonfiction CON
EARL, Lawrence, 1915- ,
　　Canadian; fiction CON
EARL of MARCH, 1876-1935,
　　English; nonfiction HIG
EARLE, John, 1601?-65, English;
　　essays, poetry BRO KB ST
EARLE, Mary Tracy, 1864- ,
　　American; fiction HOO
EARLE, Olive Lydia, English;
　　nonfiction, juveniles CON
　　FUL
EARLE, Peter G., 1923- ,
　　American; nonfiction CON
EARLE, Ralph, 1907- , Ameri-
　　can; nonfiction CON
'EARLEY, Martha' see WEST-
　　WATER, Sister Agnes Martha
EARLEY, Tom (Thomas Powell
　　Earley), 1911- , Welsh;
　　poetry CON MUR
EARLS, Michael, 1875-1937,
　　American; poetry, fiction
　　HOE
EARLY, Eleanor, American;
　　nonfiction HO KTS
EARNEST, Ernest Penney, 1901- ,
　　American; nonfiction CON
EARNSHAW, Brian, 1929- ,
　　Welsh; poetry CON
EARP, James William, American;
　　fiction MAR
EASSON, James, 1895- , Scots;
　　nonfiction CON
EAST, Ben, 1898- , American;
　　nonfiction CON
EAST, Charles, 1924- , Ameri-
　　can; nonfiction, fiction CON
EAST, John Marlborough, 1932- ,
　　English; nonfiction CON
EAST, John Porter, 1931- ,
　　American; nonfiction CON
'EAST Michael' see WEST, Morris
　　L.
EAST, P.D., 1921- , American;
　　nonfiction CON
'EASTAWAY, Edward' see THOM-
　　AS, Philip E.
EASTBURN, James Wallis, 1797-

1819, American; poetry KAA
EASTLAKE, Lady Elizabeth Rigby,
1809-93, English; nonfiction
BRO KBA
EASTLAKE, William Derry, 1917- ,
American; fiction CON
EASTMAN, Arthur Morse, 1918- ,
American; nonfiction CON
EASTMAN, Charles A., 1858-1939,
American; juvenile KJU
EASTMAN, Edward Roe, 1885- ,
American; nonfiction CON
EASTMAN, Elizabeth, 1905- ,
American; fiction WAF
EASTMAN, Frances Whittier,
1915- , American; nonfiction
CON
EASTMAN, Joel Webb, 1939- ,
American; nonfiction CON
EASTMAN, Max Forrester, 1883-
1969, American; nonfiction CON
KAT KT ST
EASTMAN, Philip D., American;
juveniles WA
EASTMAN, Richard Morse, 1916- ,
American; nonfiction CON
EASTON, David, 1917- , Canadian;
nonfiction CON
EASTON, Edward see MALERICH,
Edward P.
EASTON, Loyd David, 1915- ,
American; nonfiction CON
EASTON, Robert, 1915- , Ameri-
can; nonfiction CON
EASTON, Steward Copinger, 1907- ,
Anglo-American; nonfiction CON
EASTWICK, Ivy Ethel Olive, English;
juveniles, poetry CON WA
EASTWOOD, Charles Cyril ('Cyril
Eastwood'; 'Philip Hale'),
1916- , English; fiction CON
EATON, Charles Edward, 1916- ,
American; poetry, fiction CON
JO MUR
EATON, Clement, 1898- , Ameri-
can; nonfiction CON
EATON, Evelyn Sybil Mary, 1902- ,
Canadian-American; fiction KTS
SY WAF
'EATON, George L.' see VERRAL,
Charles S.
EATON, Jeanette, American; juveniles
KJU
EATON, John Herbert, 1927- ,
American; nonfiction CON
EATON, Joseph W., 1919- ,
American; nonfiction CON
EATON, Leonard K., 1922- ,

American; nonfiction CON
EATON, Trevor, 1934- , English;
nonfiction CON
EATON, Walter Prichard, 1878-1957,
American; criticism, essays,
poetry KAT KT
EAVES, James Clifton, 1912- ,
American; nonfiction CON
EAVEY, Charles Benton, 1889- ,
American; nonfiction CON
EAVEY, Louise Bone, 1900- ,
American; juveniles CON
EBEJER, Francis, 1925- ,
English; fiction, plays CON
EBELING, Gerhard, 1912- ,
German; nonfiction CON
EBELT, Alfred, 1904- , Ameri-
can; poetry HIL
EBENSTEIN, William, 1910- ,
American; nonfiction CON
EBER, Paul (Eberus), 1511-66,
German; poetry SA
EBERHARD, August Gottlob,
1769-1845, German; nonfiction,
poetry HAR
EBERHARD von CERSNE, fl.
1400, German; fiction ST
EVERHARD von GONDERSHEIM,
13th cent., German; poetry
ST
EBERHARDT, Newman Charles,
1912- , American; nonfiction
CON
EBERHART, Mignon, 1899- ,
American; fiction KT
EBERHART, Nell Richmond,
-1944, American; poetry
HOO
EBERHART, Richard, 1904- ,
American; poetry, plays CON
KTS MUR RIC SP
EBERHART, Wilfred Perry, 1924- ,
American; nonfiction CON
EBERLE, Irmengarde ('Allyn
Allen'; 'Phyllis Ann Carter'),
1898- , American; juveniles
COM CON KJU WA
EBERLE, Josef ('Sebastian Blau'),
1901- , German; poetry,
criticism, journalism FLE
EBERLIN von GÜNTZBURG,
Johann, 1465-1530, German;
fiction AL ST
EBERMAN, Gilbert Willis, 1917- ,
American; fiction, poetry
CON PAC
EBERMAYER, Erich, 1900- ,
German; nonfiction LEN

EBERS, Georg Moritz, 1837-98,
    German; fiction HAR KE SA ST
EBERSOLE, Alva Vernon, Jr.,
    1919- , American; nonfiction
    BL CON
EBERSTADT, Frederick, American;
    juveniles WA
EBERSTADT, Isabel Nash, 1934?- ,
    American; juveniles WA
EBERT, Arthur Frank ('Frank
    Arthur'), 1902- , English;
    fiction CON
EBERT, Johann Arnold, 1723-95,
    German; translations ST
EBERT, Karl Egon, 1801-82, Czech;
    poetry, plays HAR
EBERUS see EBER, Paul
EBLANA, Sister (Phyllis Margaret
    McEvoy), 1907- , American;
    nonfiction CON
EBLE II de VENTADORN, 1100-40,
    French; poetry ST
EBLE, Gui, 1190-1240, French;
    poetry ST
EBLE, Kenneth Eugene, 1923- ,
    American; nonfiction CON
EBLEN, Jack Ericson, 1936- ,
    American; nonfiction CON
'EBLIS, J. Philip' see PHILLIPS,
    James W.
EBNER, Ferdinand, 1882- , Ger-
    man; poetry KU
EBNER, Jeannie, 1918- , Swiss;
    nonfiction KU
EBNER, Margarethe, 1291-1351,
    German; nonfiction ST
EBNER-ESCHENBACH, Marie
    Dubsky, 1830-1916, Austrian;
    fiction, poetry, plays AL COL
    FLE HAR KE SA ST
EBON, Martin, 1917- , German-
    American; nonfiction CON
EBREO, Leone see ABARBANEL
    L.E.
EBSWORTH, George Arthur Raymond,
    1911- , Russian-English; non-
    fiction CON
EBY, Cecil DeGratte, 1927- , Amer-
    ican; nonfiction CON
EBY, Lois Christine ('Patrick Law-
    son'), 1908- , American;
    juveniles WA
ECA de QUEIROS, José Maria de,
    1845-1900, Portuguese; fiction
    COL HAR KE SA ST
ECBASIS CAPTIVI, 11th cent.,
    German; nonfiction AL
ECCART, Johannes see ECKHART,
    Meister

ECCIUS DEDOLATUS (Gehobette),
    16th cent., German; nonfiction
    AL
'ECCLES' see CHURCH, Richard
ECCLES, Henry E., 1898- ,
    American; nonfiction CON
ECCLES, William John, 1917- ,
    English; nonfiction CON
ECHAGÜE, Juan Pablo ('Jean
    Paul'), 1877-1950/51, Argen-
    tinian; journalism, criticism,
    essays MIN SA
ECHAGÜE, Pedro, 1800-75,
    Argentinian; fiction, plays
    SA
ECHAGÜE, Pedro, 1821-89,
    Argentinian; journalism MIN
ECHARD, Jacques, 1644-1724,
    French; nonfiction DIL
ECHARD, Laurence, 1670?-1730,
    English; nonfiction BRO
ECHARRI, Xavier de, 1913- ,
    Spanish; journalism SA
ECHEGARAY y EIZAGUIRRE,
    José, 1832/33-1916, Spanish;
    plays BL COL HAR KE MAG
    MAT RIC SA ST
ECHEGARAY y ELIZAGUIRRE,
    Miguel, 1848-1927, Spanish;
    plays BL SA
ECHERUO, Michael, 1937- ,
    Nigerian; poetry MUR
ECHEVARRIA, Aquílio, J.,
    1866-1900/09, Costa Rican;
    poetry, fiction MIN SA
ECHEVERRIA, Durand, 1913- ,
    American; nonfiction CON
ECHEVERRIA, Esteban Echevarria,
    1805-51, Argentinian; poetry
    BL MIN SA ST
ECHEVERRIA, José Antonio,
    1815-85, Cuban; poetry MIN
ECHEVARRIA BELLO de LLAR-
    RAIN, Ines, 1868- , Chilean;
    fiction MIN
ECHLIN, Edward P., 1930- ,
    American; nonfiction CON
ECHOLS, John Minor, 1913- ,
    American; nonfiction CON
ECKARDT, Alice Lyons,
    1923- , American; nonfiction
    CON
ECKARDT, Arthur Roy, 1918- ,
    American; nonfiction CON
ECKART, Dietrich see JOHST,
    Hanns
ECKART, Heinrich, 1260-1327,
    German; nonfiction SA
ECKBLAD, Edith Berven, 1923- ,

American; nonfiction CON
ECKBO, Garrett, 1910- ,
American; nonfiction CON
ECKE, Betty Tsend Yu-ho ('Tseng
Yu-ho'), 1923- , Chinese-
American; nonfiction CON
ECKELBERRY, Grace Kathryn,
1902- , American; nonfiction
CON
ECKER, Herman Paul, 1922- ,
American; nonfiction CON
ECKERMANN, Johann Peter,
1792-1854, German; poetry
HAR KE SA ST
ECKERSON, Olive Taylor, 1901- ,
Anglo-American; fiction CON
ECKERT, Allan W., 1931- , Amer-
ican; fiction CON
ECKERT, Horst ('Janosch'), 1931- ,
Polish-German; juveniles CON
ECKERT, Ruth Elizabeth, 1905- ,
American; nonfiction CON
ECKHART, Meister (Johannes
Eccard), 1260-1327, German;
nonfiction AL HAR KE ST
ECKHART, Johann George, 1664-
1730, German; nonfiction SA
ECKHOFF, Jean Henry, Dutch;
nonfiction DIL
ECKMAN, Frederick Willis, 1924- ,
American; nonfiction, poetry
CON
'ECKMAR, F.R.' see DE HARTOG,
Jan
ECKSTEIN, Alexander, 1915- ,
Yugoslav-American; nonfiction
CON
ECKSTEIN, Gustav, 1890- , Amer-
ican; nonfiction KTS
ECKSTEIN, Harry, American; non-
fiction CON
ECKSTEIN, Otto, 1927- , German-
American; nonfiction CON
'L'ECLAIREUR' see ALLUT, Jean
ECLOV, Shirley see PFOUTZ,
Shirley E.
ECONOMAKIS, Olga, American;
juveniles WA
ECONOMOU, George, 1934- ,
American; poetry CON MUR
ECROYD, Donald Howarth, 1923- ,
American; nonfiction CON
EDDINGTON, Sir Arthur Stanley,
1882-1944, English; nonfiction
BRO KT ST
EDDINS, Dwight, L., 1939- ,
American; nonfiction CON
EDDISON, Roger, 1916- , English;

nonfiction CON
EDDIUS, fl. 711-31, English;
poetry ST
EDDLEMAN, Henry Leo, 1911- ,
American; nonfiction CON
'EDDY, Albert' see GLASSCO,
John S.
EDDY, George Sherwood, 1871- ,
American; nonfiction KT
EDDY, Mary Morse Baker, 1821-
1910, American; nonfiction
KAA SA
EDDY, Roger Whittlesey, 1920- ,
American; nonfiction CON
EDDY, Samuel Kennedy, 1926- ,
American; nonfiction CON
EDEL, Abraham, 1908- ,
American; nonfiction CON
EDEL, Joseph Leon, 1907- ,
American; nonfiction CON
EDEL, Matthew David, 1941- ,
American; nonfiction CON
EDELL, Celeste, American;
fiction CON
EDELMAN, Lily, American;
juveniles WA
EDELMAN, Maurice, 1911- ,
English; fiction RIC
EDELMAN, Murray, 1919- ,
American; nonfiction CON
EDELMAN, Paul S., 1926- ,
American; nonfiction CON
EDELSON, Edward, 1932- ,
American; nonfiction CON
EDELSTADT, David, 1866-92,
Russian; poetry ST
EDEN, Helen Josephine Parry,
1885- , English; poetry HOE
EDEN, Richard, 1521?-76, Eng-
lish; translations KB
EDFELT, Johannes, 1904- ,
Swedish; poetry, criticism
FLE ST
EDGAR, John George, 1834-64,
English; juveniles BRO
EDGAR, Oscar Pelham, 1871-
1948, Canadian; criticism
ST SY
EDGARTON, Sarah Carter Mayo,
1819-48, American; poetry,
juveniles KAA
EDGE, Findley Bartow, 1916- ,
American; nonfiction CON
EDGERTON, Angie Rose, Ameri-
can; poetry HIL
EDGERTON, William Benbow,
1914- , American; nonfiction
CON

EDGEWORTH, Maria, 1767-1849,
English; juveniles, fiction BRO
DOY KBA MAG SA ST
EDGINGTON, Eugene Sinclair, 1924- ,
American; nonfiction CON
EDGLEY, Roy, 1925- , English;
nonfiction CON
EDGREN, Anne Charlotte Leffler,
1849-92, Swedish; plays HAR
SA ST
EDGREN, Harry Daniel, 1899- ,
American; nonfiction CON
EDIE, James M., 1927- , Ameri-
can; nonfiction CON
EDIGER, Peter J., 1926- , Amer-
ican; nonfiction CON
EDLIN, Rosabelle Alpern, 1914- ,
American; nonfiction CON
EDMAN, David, 1930- , American;
nonfiction CON
EDMAN, Irwin, 1896- , American;
nonfiction KT
EDMAN, Marion Louise, 1901- ,
American; juveniles CON
EDMAN, Victor Raymond, 1900- ,
American; nonfiction CON
EDMER see EADMER
EDMISTON, Helen Jean Mary,
1913- , English; fiction CON
EDMONDS, Cecil John, 1889- ,
English; nonfiction CON
'EDMONDS, Charles' see CARRING-
TON, Charles E.
EDMONDS, Helen Woods ('Anna
Kavan'), 1904-68, English; fic-
tion CON
EDMONDS, Ivy Gordon ('Gary
Gordon'), 1917- , American;
juveniles CON
EDMONDS, Richard W., American;
juveniles WA
EDMONDS, Vernon H., 1927- ,
American; nonfiction CON
EDMONDS, Walter Dumaux, 1903- ,
American; juveniles, fiction
COM CON FUL KAT KT MAG WA
WAF
EDMONSON, Munro Sterling, 1924- ,
American; nonfiction CON
EDMUNDS, Simeon, 1917- , English;
fiction CON
EDMUNDS, Thomas Murrell, 1898- ,
American; fiction, plays CON
EDOUARD de PARIS, 18th cent.,
French; nonfiction DIL
EDQVIST, Dagmar, 1903- ,
Swedish; fiction HAR ST
'EDSCHMID, Kasimir' (Eduard

Schmid), 1890-1966, German;
fiction COL FLE KU LEN
SA
EDSON, John Thomas ('Rod
Denver'; 'Chuck Nolan'),
1928- , English; nonfiction,
fiction CON
EDSON, Russell, American; non-
fiction CON
'EDUARDI, Guillermo' see ED-
WARDS, William B.
EDUARDO, Isaac G., 1861-1924,
Bolivian; poetry, plays, fic-
tion MIN
EDWARD, Second Duke of York,
1373-1415, English; nonfiction,
translations HIG ST
EDWARD, Agustín, 1876/78-1941,
Chilean; journalism, essays
MIN
'EDWARDS, Al' see NOURSE,
Alan E.
EDWARDS, Alejandro Alberto
('Miguel Fuenzelida'), 1874-
1932, Chilean; fiction MIN
EDWARDS, Allen Jack, 1926- ,
American; nonfiction CON
EDWARDS, Allen L., 1914- ,
American; nonfiction CON
EDWARDS, Amelia Ann Blandford,
1831-92, English; fiction,
poetry, nonfiction KBA SA
EDWARDS, Anthony David, 1936- ,
English; nonfiction CON
EDWARDS, Bertram see EDWARDS,
Herbert C.
EDWARDS, Cecile Pepin, 1916- ,
American; juveniles CON WA
EDWARDS, Charles, 1628-91,
Welsh; nonfiction ST
EDWARDS, Charles Edward,
1930- , American; nonfiction
CON
EDWARDS, Charlotte, American;
fiction CON
EDWARDS, Christine, 1902- ,
American; nonfiction CON
EDWARDS, Corwin D., 1901- ,
American; nonfiction CON
EDWARDS, David Lawrence,
1929- , English; nonfiction
CON
EDWARDS, Dorothy, English;
juveniles CON
EDWARDS, Edgar Owen, 1919- ,
American; nonfiction CON
EDWARDS, Rev. Edward J.,
1904- , American; nonfiction

fiction HO

EDWARDS, Frank Allyn, 1908- , American; nonfiction CON

EDWARDS, Gillian Mary, 1918- , English; nonfiction CON

EDWARDS, H. C. Ralph, 1894- , English; nonfiction CON

EDWARDS, Harvey, 1929- , American; nonfiction, juveniles CON

EDWARDS, Henry Harry, 1893- , English; nonfiction CON

EDWARDS, Herbert Charles ('Bertram Edwards'), 1912- , English; fiction CON

EDWARDS, Iorwerth Eiddon Stephen, 1909- , English; nonfiction CON

EDWARDS, James Donald, 1926- , American; nonfiction CON

EDWARDS, Jane Campbell, 1932- , American; fiction CON

EDWARDS, Jerome Earl, 1937- , American; nonfiction CON

EDWARDS, Jonathan, 1703-58, American; nonfiction BRO KAA MAG ST

EDWARDS, Josephine Cunnington, 1904- , American; nonfiction CON

EDWARDS, Julia Spalding, 1920- , American; nonfiction CON

'EDWARDS, Julie' see ANDREWS, Julie

'EDWARDS, Julie' see STRATE-MEYER, Edward L.

EDWARDS, Kenneth Morgan, 1912- , American; nonfiction CON

EDWARDS, Lee, 1932- , American; nonfiction CON

EDWARDS, Lionel, 1878- , English; nonfiction HIG

EDWARDS, Margaret Alexander, 1902- , American; fiction CON

EDWARDS, Marvin Louis, 1915- , American; nonfiction CON

EDWARDS, Matilda B. B. see BETHAM-EDWARDS, Matilda B.

'EDWARDS, Max' see BENJAMIN, Claude M. E. P.

EDWARDS, Monica le Doux Newton, 1912- , English; fiction, juveniles CON DOY

'EDWARDS, Norman' see WHITE, Theodore E.

EDWARDS, Sir Owen Morgan, 1858-1920, English; journalism, nonfiction KT ST

EDWARDS, Philip, 1923- , American; nonfiction CON

EDWARDS, Prior Maximilian Hemsley, 1914- , French-American; nonfiction CON

EDWARDS, Rem Blanchard, Jr., 1934- , American; nonfiction CON

EDWARDS, Richard, 1523?-66, English; poetry, plays BRO KB ST

EDWARDS, Roslyn ('Marge Alexander'), 1929- , American; juveniles CON

EDWARDS, Sally Cary, 1929- , American; fiction CON

'EDWARDS, Stephen' see PALES-TRANT, Simon S.

EDWARDS, Thomas, 1738/89-1810, Welsh; poetry ST

EDWARDS, Thomas Bentley, 1906- , English; nonfiction CON

EDWARDS, Thomas Robert, Jr., 1928- , American; nonfiction, poetry CON

EDWARDS, Verne Ervie, Jr., 1924- , American; nonfiction CON

EDWARDS, Ward, 1927- , American; nonfiction CON

EDWARDS, William, 1896- , English; nonfiction CON

EDWARDS, William Bennett ('Edouard Benet'; 'Harvey Brandt'; 'James L. Cranbrook'; 'Guillermo Eduardi'; 'Charles S. Johnson'; 'Capt. Wilbur Jones'; 'William C. L. Thompson'), 1927- , American; nonfiction CON

EDWARDS BELLO, Joaquín, 1888- , Chilean; fiction BL MIN SA ST

EDWIN, Brother B., 1912- , American; nonfiction CON

EE TIANG HONG, 1933- , Malaysian; poetry MUR

EEDEN, Frederik Willem van (Cornelis Paradijs), 1860-1932, Dutch; poetry, fiction, plays COL FLE SA ST

EEKHOUD, Georges, 1854-1927, Belgian; fiction, poetry COL DIF SA ST

EELES, Henry Swanston, 1897- , English; nonfiction HIG

EELLS, George, 1922- , American; nonfiction CON

EFEMEY, Raymond Frederick,

1928- , English; nonfiction
CON
EFFEN, Justus van, 1684-1735,
Dutch; nonfiction, essays SA ST
EFFINGER, George Alec, 1947- ,
American; nonfiction CON
EFIMIY see PATRIARCH TARNOVSKY,
Eftimiy
EFIRD, James Michael, 1932- ,
American; nonfiction CON
EFORO see EPHORUS
EFRATI, Jossef, 1770-1804, Jewish;
plays ST
EFRON, Alexander, 1897- , Amer-
ican; nonfiction CON
EFRON, Benjamin, 1908- , Russian-
American; nonfiction CON
EFROS, Israel Isaac ('Efrot'), 1891- ,
Polish-Israeli; nonfiction CON
ST
EFTIMIU, Victor, 1889- , Rumanian;
plays, fiction ST
EGAN, Edward Welstead ('Eamon
MacAedhagan'), 1922- , Ameri-
can; nonfiction CON
EGAN, Ferol, 1923- , American;
nonfiction CON
EGAN, Gerard, 1930- , American;
nonfiction CON
'EGAN, Lesley' see LININGTON,
Elizabeth
EGAN, Philip Sidney, 1920- ,
American; nonfiction CON
EGAN, Pierce, 1772-1849, English;
fiction, journalism BRO HIG
KBA MAG ST
EGAÑA, Juan, 1769-1836, Chilean;
plays MIN
EGBERT, Donald Drew, 1902-72,
American; nonfiction CON
EGBERT, Virginia Wylie, 1912- ,
American; nonfiction CON
EGBERTO de LIEJA, 11th cent.,
Flemish; poetry SA
EGBUNA, Obi B., 1938- ,
Nigerian; fiction, essays, plays
RIC
EGEN von BAMBERG, fl. 1320-40,
German; poetry ST
EGERMEIER, Elsie Emilie, 1890- ,
American; nonfiction CON
'EGERTON, George' see BRIGHT,
Mary C.
EGG, Mario, Hungarian-Swiss, non-
fiction CON
EGGE, Peter Andrias, 1869-1959,
Norwegian; poetry, fiction, plays
COL FLE KT SA ST

EGGELING, Hans Friedrich,
1878- , American; nonfiction
CON
EGGENBERGER, David, 1918- ,
American; nonfiction CON
EGGENSCHWILER, David, 1936- ,
American; nonfiction CON
EGGER, Rowland Andrews,
1908- , American; nonfiction
CON
EGGERATH, Werner, 1900- ,
German; nonfiction AL
EGGERS, Friedrich, 1819-72,
German; poetry ST
EGGERS, John Philip, 1940- ,
American; nonfiction CON
EGGERS, Karl, 1826-1900, Ger-
man; poetry ST
EGGERS, William T., 1912- ,
American; nonfiction CON
EGGERT, Gerald Gordon, 1926- ,
American; nonfiction CON
EGGLESTON, Edward, 1837-1902,
American; fiction BRO KAA
MAG ST
EGGLESTON, George Cary, 1839-
1911, American; fiction,
journalism, juveniles KAA
EGGLETON, Wilfrid, 1901- ,
English; nonfiction, fiction
CON
EGIDIO ROMANO, 1247- ,
Italian; nonfiction SA
EGILL, 10th cent., Icelandic;
poetry SA
EGINHARDO see EINHARD
EGLINGTON, Charles, 1918- ,
South African; poetry MUR
'EGLINTON, John' see MAGEE,
W. K.
EGLER, Frank Edwin, 1911- ,
American; nonfiction CON
EGNACIO, Giambattista Cipelli,
1473-1553, Italian; nonfiction
SA
EGUDU, Romanus N., 1940- ,
Nigerian; poetry MUR
EGUILAZ, Luis de, 1830-74,
Spanish; fiction, plays BL SA
EGUREN, José María, 1882-1942,
Peruvian; poetry, nonfiction
BL FLE SA ST
EHLE, John Marsden, Jr.,
1925- , American; nonfiction,
fiction CON
EHLERS, Henry James, 1907- ,
American; nonfiction CON
EHNINGER, Douglas Wagner,

1913- , American; nonfiction
CON

EHRE, Edward, 1905- , American;
fiction CON

EHRENBERG, Victor Leopold, 1891- ,
German-English; nonfiction CON

EHRENBURG, Ilya Grigorievich
(Erenburg), 1891-1967, Russian;
fiction, essays, poetry COL
FLE HAR HARK KAT KT RIC
SA ST

EHRENCRON-KIDDE, Astrid
Margarethe, 1871- , Danish;
fiction ST

EHRENKRANZ, Benjamin Wolf see
'ZBASHER, Velvel'

EHRENSTEIN, Albert, 1886-1950,
Austrian; poetry, criticism AL
FLE KU

EHRENSVÄRD, Carl August, 1745-
1800, Swedish; nonfiction ST

EHRENZWEIG, Albert Armin, 1906- ,
Austrian-American; nonfiction
CON

EHRESMANN, Julia M., 1939- ,
American; nonfiction CON

EHRET, Christopher, 1941- ,
American; nonfiction CON

EHRHARDT, Reinhold, 1900- ,
German; juveniles CON

EHRKE, Hans, 1898- , German;
poetry, fiction ST

EHRLICH, Amy, 1942- , American;
juveniles CON

EHRLICH, Arnold, 1923- , American; nonfiction CON

EHRLICH, Bettina Bauer ('Bettina'),
1903- , Austrian-American;
juveniles COM CON FUL WA

EHRLICH, Eugene H., 1922- ,
American; nonfiction CON

EHRLICH, Howard J., 1932- ,
American; nonfiction CON

EHRLICH, John Gunther, 1930- ,
American; fiction CON

EHRLICH, Leonard, 1905- , American; fiction KT

EHRLICH, Max, 1909- , American;
fiction CON

EHRLICH, Robert S., 1935- , nonfiction CON

EHRMAN, John Patrick William,
1920- , English; nonfiction CON

EHRMANN, Herbert Brutus, 1891- ,
American; nonfiction CON

EHRMANN, Marianne Brentano,
1755-95, Swiss; nonfiction SA

EIBL-EIBESFELDT, Irenaus,

1928- , Austrian; nonfiction
CON

EIBLING, Harold Henry, 1905- ,
American; nonfiction CON

EICH, Günter, 1907- , German;
poetry, radio AL FLE KU
KUN LEN RIC

EICHELBAUM, Samuel, 1894-1967,
Argentinian; fiction, plays
MAT MIN SA

EICHENBAUM, Boris Mikhaylovich,
1886- , Russian; criticism
ST

EICHENBERG, Fritz, 1901- ,
German-American; juveniles
FUL

EICHENDORF, Joseph Karl
Benedikt, 1788-1857, German;
poetry AL HAR KE SA ST

EICHENLAUB, John Ellis, 1922- ,
American; nonfiction CON

EICHENWALD, Yuly Isayevich
(Aikhenvald), 1872- , Russian;
criticism ST

EICHER, Ethel Elizabeth ('Edna
Temple Crane'; 'Emily Paul';
'William Paul'), American;
fiction CON

EICHHORN, David Max, 1906- ,
American; nonfiction CON

EICHHORN, Werner, 1899- ,
American; nonfiction CON

EICHHORN-NELSON, Wally,
1896- , German; nonfiction
AL

EICHNER, Alfred S., 1937- ,
American; nonfiction CON

EICHNER, Hans, 1921- , Austrian-
Canadian; nonfiction CON

EICHNER, James A., 1927- ,
American; nonfiction CON

EICKHOFF, Andrew Robert,
1924- , American; nonfiction
CON

EIDELBERG, Ludwig, 1898-1970,
Austrian-American; nonfiction
CON

EIDELBERG, Paul, 1928- ,
American; nonfiction CON

EIDOUS, Marc Antoine, 18th cent.,
French; translations DIL

EIDT, Robert C., 1923- , American; nonfiction CON

EIDUSON, Bernice Tabackman,
1921- , American; nonfiction
CON

EIFERT, Virginia Snider, 1911-66,
American; juveniles, nonfiction

COM CON WA
'EIFION WYN' (Eliseus Williams),
1867-1926, Welsh; poetry ST
EIGNER, Edwin Moss, 1931- ,
American; nonfiction CON
EIGNER, Laurence J., 1927- ,
American; poetry, essays, fic-
tion CON MUR
EIKE von REPKOW (Repgaw), 1180-
1233, German; nonfiction AL
ST
EIKER, Mathilde, 1893- , Ameri-
can; fiction KAT KT
EILHART von OBERG, 1170/80- ,
German; poetry ST
EILON, Samuel, 1923- , English;
nonfiction CON
EIMER, Dean Robert, 1927- ,
American; fiction CON
EIMERL, Sarel, 1925- , English;
nonfiction CON
EINAR, Alfden (Einarsen), 1732-85,
Icelandic; nonfiction SA
EINAR GILSSON, 14th cent., Ice-
landic; poetry SA
EINAR HAFLIDASON, 1307-93,
Icelandic; nonfiction SA
EINAR Helgason, 10th cent., Ice-
landic; poetry SA
EINAR Skulason, 1095-1160, Icelandic;
poetry SA
EINARSSON, Indridi, 1851-1939,
Icelandic; plays FLE HAR SA ST
EINBOND, Bernard Lionel, 1937- ,
American; nonfiction, poetry
CON
EINHARD (Einhart; Egenhardo),
770-840, French; nonfiction
AL SA ST
EINHORN, David, 1886- , Jewish;
poetry ST
EINSEL, Mary E., 1929- , Ameri-
can; nonfiction CON
EINSEL, Walter, American; juveniles
WA
EINSTEIN, Albert, 1879-1955, Ger-
man; nonfiction ST
EINSTEIN, Alfred, 1880-1952, Ger-
man; nonfiction KTS
EINSTEIN, Carl, 1885- , German;
nonfiction KU
EINZIG, Paul, 1897- , Hungarian-
English; nonfiction CON
EIPPER, Paul, 1891- , German;
juvenile KJU
EISELEY, Loren Corey, 1907- ,
American; nonfiction CON
EISENBERG, Azriel Louis, 1903- ,

American; juveniles WA
EISENBERG, Baron d', 18th cent.,
German; nonfiction DIL
EISENBERG, Dennis Harold,
1929- , South African; non-
fiction CON
EISENBERG, Larry, 1919- ,
American; nonfiction CON
EISENBERG, Ralph, 1930- ,
American; nonfiction CON
EISENHOWER, John Sheldon Doud,
1922- , American; nonfiction
CON
EISENLEN, Anne F. see 'PATER-
SON, Anne'
EISENMENGER, Robert Waltz,
1926- , American; nonfiction
CON
EISENREICH, Herbert, 1925- ,
German; nonfiction AL KU
EISENSCHIML, Otto, 1880-1963,
Austrian-American; nonfiction
CON
EISENSON, Jon, 1907- , Ameri-
can; nonfiction CON
EISENSTADT, Abraham S.,
1920- , American; nonfiction
CON
EISENSTADT, Shmuel Noah,
1923- , Polish-Israeli; non-
fiction CON
EISENSTAT, Jane Sperry,
1920- , American; nonfiction
CON
EISENSTEIN, Ira, 1906- , Amer-
ican; nonfiction CON
EISINGER, Chester Emanuel,
1915- , American; nonfiction
CON
EISMANN, Bernard Norman,
1933- , American; nonfiction
CON
EISNER, Betty Grover ('Rev. B.'),
1915- , American; nonfiction
CON
EISNER, Gisela Spanglet, 1925- ,
German-English; nonfiction
CON
EIST, Dietmar see DIETMAR von
EIST
EITEMAN, Wilford John, 1902- ,
American; nonfiction CON
EITNER, Lorenz E.A., 1919- ,
Czech-American; nonfiction
CON
EIXIMENIC, Francesc (Francisco
Eximenis), 1342?-1409?,
Spanish; nonfiction BL HAR

SA ST
EIZAGUIRRE, Jose I.V. see
   EYZAGUIRRE, Jose I.V.
'EJIMA, Kiseki' (Ejima Shigetomo),
   1667-1736, Japenese; fiction
   ST
EK, Karin, 1885-1926, Swedish;
   poetry ST
EKBLAW, Sidney Everette, 1903- ,
   American; nonfiction CON
EKEBLAD, Frederick Alfred,
   1917- , American; nonfiction
   CON
EKELÖF, Bengt Gunnar, 1907-68,
   Swedish; poetry, criticism FLE
   ST
EKELUND, Otto Vilhelm, 1880-1949,
   Swedish; poetry, essays COL
   FLE SA ST
EKIKEN see KAIBARA EKIKEN
EKIRCH, Arthur A., Jr., 1915- ,
   American; nonfiction CON
EKKEHART I (Gerald Waltharius),
   900/10-73, French; essays AL
   ST
EKKEHART IV, 930-1060, French;
   nonfiction ST
EKKER, Charles, 1930- , American;
   nonfiction CON
EKLUND, Gordon, 1945- , Ameri-
   can; nonfiction CON
EKLUND, Jane Mary see BALL,
   Jane E.
EKMAN, Paul, 1934- , American;
   nonfiction CON
EKMAN, Rosalind, 1933- , Ameri-
   can; nonfiction CON
EKNATH, 1548-1600/08, Indian;
   poetry LAN ST
EKOLA, Giles Chester, 1927- ,
   American; nonfiction CON
EKREM, Recâi-Zade Mahmud,
   1847-1914, Turkish; poetry, plays,
   fiction, criticism LAN
EKSTEIN, Rudolf, 1912- , Austrian-
   American; nonfiction CON
EKVALL, Robert Brainerd, 1898- ,
   American; nonfiction CON
EKWALL, Eldon Edward, 1933- ,
   American; nonfiction CON
EKWENSI, Cyprian, 1921- , Nigerian;
   fiction CON RIC
ELATH, Eliahu, 1903- , Russian;
   nonfiction CON
EL-AYOUTY, Yassin, 1928- ,
   Egyptian-American; fiction CON
ELAZAR, Daniel Judah, 1934- ,
   American; nonfiction CON

EL-BAZ, Farouk, 1938- ,
   Egyptian; nonfiction CON
ELBEE, 18th cent., French; plays
   DIL
ELBEE, Maurice Joseh Louis
   Gigot, 1752-74, French; non-
   fiction DIL
ELBERT, Edmund Joseph, 1923- ,
   American; nonfiction CON
ELBERT, Samuel Hoyt, 1907- ,
   American; nonfiction CON
ELBERTZHAGEN, Theodor Wallis,
   1888- , German; nonfiction
   LEN
ELBING, Alvar Oliver, Jr.,
   1928- , American; nonfiction
   CON
ELBING, Carol J., 1930- ,
   American; nonfiction CON
ELBOGEN, Paul, 1894- , Austrian-
   Danish; nonfiction CON
ELBRECHT, Paul G., 1921- ,
   American; nonfiction CON
ELCOCK, Howard James, 1942- ,
   English; nonfiction CON
ELDEFONSO, Edward, 1933- ,
   American; nonfiction CON
ELDER, Michael Aiken, 1931- ,
   English; nonfiction CON
ELDER, Robert Ellsworth, 1915- ,
   American; nonfiction CON
ELDER, Susan Blanchard
   ('Hermine'), 1835-1923,
   American; poetry KAA
'ELDERSHAW, Barnard'; Flora
   Eldershaw, 1897-1956, and
   Marjorie Barnard, 1897- ,
   Austrian; fiction RIC
ELDREDGE, Laurence Howard,
   1922- , American; nonfiction
   CON
EDLRIDGE, John E.T., 1936- ,
   English; nonfiction CON
ELDRIDGE, Paul, 1888- , Amer-
   ican; poetry, fiction CON
   MAR WAF
ELDRIDGE, Retha Hazel Giles,
   1910- , American; nonfiction
   CON
ELEANOR, Sister Joseph, Ameri-
   can; nonfiction CON
ELEGANT, Robert Sampson,
   1928- , American; nonfiction
   CON
'ELEUTER' see IWASZKIEWICZ,
   Jaroslav
ELEUTHEROPHILOS see LINSCH-
   OTEN, Paulus

ELEY, Lynn W., 1925- , American;
nonfiction CON
'ELFED' (Howel Elvet Lewis),
1860- , Welsh; poetry ST
ELFENBEIN, Julien, 1897- , Amer-
ican; nonfiction CON
ELFORD, Homer J.R., 1912- ,
American; nonfiction CON
ELGIN, Kathleen, 1923- , American;
juveniles CON
ELGSTRÖM, Per, 1781-1810,
Swedish; poetry ST
'ELIA' see LAMB, Charles
ELIADE, Mircea, 1907- , Rumanian;
fiction, essays FLE ST
ELIADE-RADULESCU, Ion see HELI-
ADE-RADULESCU, Ion
ELIANO, Claudio ('Sofista'), 260- ,
Italian; nonfiction SA
ELIANO el TACITURNO, 2nd cent.,
Greek; nonfiction SA
ELIAS, Father see PATER, Elias
ELIAS, Christopher, 1925- , Amer-
ican; nonfiction CON
ELIAS, Claude Edward, Jr., 1924- ,
American; nonfiction CON
'ELIAS, Eileen' see DAVIES, Eileen
W.
ELIAS, Taslim Olawale, 1914- ,
Nigerian; nonfiction CON
ELIAS, Willem ('Willem Vrancz'),
16th cent., Dutch; poetry ST
ELIAS de TEJADA, Francisco,
1917- , Spanish; essays SA
ELIASHIV, Isidore see 'MACHSHOVES
BAAL'
ELAIZ, Raphael, 1905- , Jewish;
poetry ST
ELIE, Robert, 1915- , Canadian;
fiction SY
ELIE de BEAUMONT, Jean Baptiste
Jacques, 1732-86, French; non-
fiction DIL
ELIE of WINCHESTER, 12th cent.,
Anglo-Norman; poetry ST
ELIGIUS, Franz J. see 'HALM,
Friedrich'
ELIJAH BEN Solomon ('Gaon of
Vilna'), 1720-97, Lithuanian-
Jewish; nonfiction KE ST
'ELIN Pelin' (Dimitur Ivanov Jotov),
1878-1949, Bulgarian; fiction
FLE ST
ELIOSEFF, Lee Andrew, 1933- ,
American; nonfiction CON
'ELIOT Alice' see JEWETT, Sarah
O.
'ELIOT, Anne' see COLE, Lois D.

ELIOT, Charles William, 1834-
1926, American; nonfiction
KAA
ELIOT, Ethel Augusta Cook,
1890- , American; fiction,
juveniles HOE
'ELIOT, George' (Mary Anne
Evans Cross), 1819-80,
English; fiction, poetry, essays,
BRO KBA MAG SA ST
ELIOT, George Fielding, 1894-
1971, American; nonfiction
KT
ELIOT, Jared, 1685-1763, Amer-
ican; nonfiction KAA
ELIOT, John, 1604-90, American;
nonfiction KAA
ELIOT, Samuel, 1821-98, Ameri-
can; nonfiction KAA
ELIOT, Thomas Stearns ('Charles
Augustus Conybeare'; 'Rev.
Charles James Grimble';
'Gus Krutzch'; 'Muriel A.
Schwartz'; 'J.A.D. Spence';
'Helen B. Trundlett'; 'Aged
Eagle'; 'Deliberate Pedant';
'Old Possum'), 1888-1964,
Anglo-American; poetry BRO
CON DOY FLE KL KT MAG
MAT RIC SA SP ST
ELIOVSON, Sima Benveniste,
1919- , South African; juven-
iles CON
ELIPANDO de TOLEDO, Spanish;
nonfiction SA
ELISABETH, Countess of Nassau-
Saarbrücken, 1397-1456, Ger-
man; fiction AL ST
ELISABETH, Queen of Rumania
('Carmen Sylva'), 1843-1916,
German; fiction, plays HAR
KE SA ST
ELISEE, Jean François Copel,
1726-83, French; nonfiction
DIL
'ELIZABETH' (May Annette
Beauchamp), 1906- , English;
fiction KAT
ELIZABETH I, 1533-1603, English;
translations, poetry BRO ST
ELIZABETH Marie, Sister, 1914- ,
American; nonfiction CON
ELKHOLLY, Abdo A., 1925- ,
Egyptian-American; nonfiction
CON
ELKIN, Benjamin, 1911- , Amer-
ican; juveniles CON WA
ELKIN, Stanley L., 1930- ,

American; fiction CON
ELKINS, Dov Peretz, 1937- , American; nonfiction, juveniles CON WA
ELKINS, Ella Ruth ('Ellarut Beddoe'; 'Ellaruth Wren'), 1929- , American; juveniles CON
ELKINS, William R., 1926- , American; nonfiction CON
ELLACOTT, Samuel Ernest, 1911- , English; juveniles CON
ELLARD, Gerald, 1894- , American; nonfiction HOE
ELLEDGE, Waymon Paul, 1938- , American; nonfiction CON
ELLEN, Barbara, 1938- , American; juveniles CON WA
ELLENBERGER, Henri Frederic, 1905- , Canadian; nonfiction CON
ELLER, Vermard Marion, 1927- , American; nonfiction CON
ELLERY, John Blaise, 1920- , American; nonfiction CON
ELLESMERE, Francis Egerton, 1800-57, English; nonfiction, poetry SA
ELLET, Charles, 1810-62, American; nonfiction KAA
ELLET, Elizabeth Fries Lummis, 1818-77, American; translations KAA
ELLETT, Marcella H., 1931- , American; nonfiction CON
ELLFELDT, Lois, 1910- , American; nonfiction CON
ELLIN, Elizabeth Muriel, 1905- , New Zealander; juveniles CON
ELLIN, Stanley Bernard, 1916- , American; fiction CON
ELLING, Karl A., 1935- , German-American; nonfiction CON
ELLING, Ray H., 1929- , American; nonfiction CON
ELLINGSWORTH, Huber W., 1928- , American; nonfiction CON
ELLINGTON, James Wesley, 1927- , American; nonfiction CON
ELLINWOOD, Leonard Webster, 1905- , American; nonfiction CON
ELLIOT, Edith Marie Farmer, 1912- , American; nonfiction, juveniles CON
ELLIOT, Elisabeth Howard, 1926- , American; fiction CON
ELLIOT, Henry Miers, 1808-53, English; essays SA

ELLIOT, Jean (Jane), 1727-1805, English; poetry BRO
ELLIOTT, Brian Robinson, 1910- , Australian; nonfiction CON
ELLIOTT, Clarence Orville, 1913- , American; nonfiction CON
ELLIOTT, Ebenezer, 1781-1849, English; poetry BRO KBA SA ST
ELLIOTT, Escalus Emmert III (Chip), 1945- , American; fiction CON
ELLIOTT, George Paul, 1918- , American; nonfiction, poetry, fiction, essays CON MUR
ELLIOTT, J.M.K., 1830- , English; nonfiction HIG
ELLIOTT, Jan Walter, 1939- , American; nonfiction CON
ELLIOTT, Janice, 1931- , English; fiction CON
ELLIOTT, John, 1938- , English; nonfiction CON
ELLIOTT, John Ed, 1931- , American; nonfiction CON
ELLIOTT, John Huxtable, 1930- , English; nonfiction CON
ELLIOTT, John R., Jr., 1937- , American; nonfiction CON
ELLIOTT, Jonathan, 1784-1846, American; editor KAA
ELLIOTT, Kit, 1936- , English; nonfiction CON
ELLIOTT, Lawrence, 1924- , American; nonfiction CON
ELLIOTT, Leonard M., 1902- , American; nonfiction CON
ELLIOTT, Margaret, American; poetry HIL
ELLIOTT, Neil, 1938- , American; nonfiction CON
ELLIOTT, Osborn, 1924- , American; nonfiction CON
ELLIOTT, Ralph H., 1925- , American; nonfiction CON
ELLIOTT, Raymond Pruitt, 1904- , American; nonfiction CON
ELLIOTT, Richard V., 1935- , American; nonfiction CON
'ELLIOTT, Robert' see GARFINKEL, Bernard
ELLIOTT, Robert Carl, 1914- , American; nonfiction CON
ELLIOTT, Sarah Barnwell, 1848-1928, American; fiction KAA
ELLIOTT, Spencer Hayward,

1883-   , Scots; nonfiction CON
ELLIOTT, Sumner Locke (Locke-
   Elliott), 1917-   , Australian-
   American; fiction, plays CON
ELLIOTT, William N., Jr., 1903-   ,
   American; nonfiction CON
ELLIS, Albert, 1913-   , American;
   nonfiction CON
ELLIS, Amanda M., 1898-   , Amer-
   ican; nonfiction CON
ELLIS, Charles Howard, 1895-   ,
   Australian; nonfiction CON
ELLIS, Christopher Royston George,
   1941-   , English; poetry, non-
   fiction CON
ELLIS, Clyde Taylor, 1908-   ,
   American; nonfiction CON
ELLIS, Cuthbert Hamilton, 1909-   ,
   English; nonfiction, fiction CON
ELLIS, David Maldwyn, 1914-   ,
   American; nonfiction CON
ELLIS, Edward Robb, 1911-   ,
   American; nonfiction CON
ELLIS, Edward Sylvester, 1840-1916,
   American; juveniles DOY KAA
ELLIS, Elmo Israel, 1918-   , Amer-
   ican; nonfiction, poetry CON
ELLIS, Frank K., 1933-   , Ameri-
   can; nonfiction CON
ELLIS, George, 1753-1815, English;
   fiction, nonfiction BRO KB ST
ELLIS, Harry Bearse, 1921-   ,
   American; juveniles, nonfiction
   CON WA
ELLIS, Henry Havelock, 1859-1939,
   English; nonfiction BRO KL KT
   SA ST
ELLIS, Hilda R. see DAVIDSON, Hilda
   R. E.
ELLIS, Howard Woodrow, 1914-   ,
   American; nonfiction CON
ELLIS, Humphrey Francis, 1907-   ,
   English; nonfiction CON
ELLIS, James, 1935-   , American;
   nonfiction CON
ELLIS, James Hervey Stewart,
   1893-   , American; nonfiction
   CON
ELLIS, John Breckenridge, 1870-   ,
   American; fiction MAR
ELLIS, Rev. John Tracy, 1905-   ,
   American; nonfiction CON HO
ELLIS, Leo Roy, 1909-   , American;
   fiction, juveniles CON
ELLIS, Lewis Ethan, 1898-   , Amer-
   ican; nonfiction CON
ELLIS, Marion Leroy, 1928-   ,
   American; nonfiction CON

ELLIS, Mary Jackson, 1916-   ,
   American; nonfiction, juveniles
   CON
ELLIS, Mary Leith, 1921-   ,
   American; nonfiction CON
'ELLIS, Maudie' see ELLIS,
   W. H. M.
ELLIS, Melvin Richard, 1912-   ,
   American; nonfiction CON
ELLIS, Norman R., 1924-   ,
   American; nonfiction CON
ELLIS, Olivia see WINTLE, Anne
ELLIS, Ray C., 1898-   , Ameri-
   can; nonfiction CON
ELLIS, Richard Nathaniel, 1939-   ,
   American; nonfiction CON
ELLIS, Richard White Bernard,
   1902-   , English; nonfiction
   CON
ELLIS, Robinson, 1834-1913,
   English; nonfiction, poetry
   KBA
ELLIS, W. H. M. ('Maudie Ellis'),
   1886-1942, English; nonfiction
   HIG
ELLISON, Alfred, 1916-   , Amer-
   ican; nonfiction CON
ELLISON, Gerald Alexander,
   1910-   , English; nonfiction
   CON
ELLISON, Harlan, 1934-   , Ameri-
   can; fiction CON
ELLISON, Henry, 1931-65, English;
   fiction CON
'ELLISON, Henry Leopold' (Henry
   Leopold Zeckhausen), 1903-   ,
   Austrian-English; nonfiction
   CON
ELLISON, Herbert Jay, 1929-   ,
   American; nonfiction CON
ELLISON, James E. ('Brother
   Flavius'), 1927-   , American;
   nonfiction CON
ELLISON, James Whitfield,
   1929-   , American; fiction
   CON
ELLISON, Jerome ('N. Emorey'),
   1907-   , American; fiction
   CON
ELLISON, John Malcus, 1889-   ,
   American; nonfiction CON
ELLISON, Ralph, 1914-   , Ameri-
   can; fiction CON FLE RIC
ELLISON, Reuben Young, 1907-   ,
   American; nonfiction CON
ELLISON, Virginia Howell
   ('Virginia Tier Howell'; 'Mary
   A. Mapes'; 'Virginia H. Mus-

sey'; 'V. H. Soskin'), 1910- ,
American; nonfiction, juveniles
CON

ELLISTON, Valerie Mae Walkinson,
1929- , Australian; fiction
CON

ELLMANN, Richard, 1918- ,
American; nonfiction CON

ELLSBERG, Edward, 1891- ,
American; juveniles, fiction
CON KJU WA WAF

'ELLSWORTH, Elmer' see THAYER,
Tiffany

ELLSWORTH, Paul Theodore,
1897- , American; nonfiction
CON

ELLSWORTH, Ralph Eugene,
1907- , American; nonfiction
CON

ELLSWORTH, Sallie Bingham,
1937- , American; nonfiction
CON

ELLWOOD, Gracia Fay ('Lucy-
Anne Linewood'), 1938- ,
American; nonfiction CON

ELLWOOD, Thomas, 1639-1713,
English; poetry BRO KB

ELMER, Irene Elizabeth, 1937- ,
American; juveniles, nonfiction
CON WA

ELMAN, Richard Martin ('Eric
Pearl'), 1934- , American;
fiction CON

EL-MELIGI, Abdel Moneim, 1923- ,
Egyptian-American; nonfiction
CON

ELMSLIE, Kenward, 1929- , American; poetry, translations CON
MUR

ELMSLIE, William Alexander Leslie,
1885- , English; nonfiction
CON

ELMSTROM, George P., 1925- ,
American; nonfiction CON

'ELOCUENTE' see DUARTE, Don

ELOLA y GUTIÉRREZ, José de,
1859-1935?, Spanish; nonfiction
SA

ELOY, François, 1748-1814, French;
nonfiction DIL

ELOY, Nicolas François Joseph,
1714-88, French; nonfiction DIL

'ELPHINSTONE, Francis' see
POWELL-SMITH, Vincent W. F.

ELPHINSTONE, Mountstuart, 1779-
1859, English; nonfiction BRO
KBA

ELPIDIO see HELPIDIO

'ELPIDON' see BALUCKI, Michael

ELSBREE, Langdon, 1929- ,
American; nonfiction CON

'ELLSCHOT, Willem' (Alfons de
Ridder), 1882-1960, Flemish;
fiction COL FLE ST

ELSEN, Albert Edward, 1927- ,
American; nonfiction CON

ELSENSOHN, Sister Mary Alfreda,
1897- , American; nonfiction
HO PAC

ELSKAMP, Max, 1862-1931,
Belgian; poetry, nonfiction
COL DIF FLE SA ST

ELSMERE, Jane Shaffer, 1932- ,
American; nonfiction CON

ELSNER, Gisela, 1937- , German; fiction CON RIC

ELSNER, Henry, Jr., 1930- ,
American; nonfiction CON

ELSON, Edward Lee Roy,
1906- , American; nonfiction
CON

ELSON, Louis Charles, 1848-
1920, American; criticism
KB

ELSON, Ruth Miller, 1917- ,
American; nonfiction CON

ELSTER, Kristian, 1881- ,
Norwegian; criticism SA

ELSTER, Kristian Mandrup,
1841-81, Norwegian; fiction
COL SA ST

ELSTOB, Elizabeth, 1663-1756,
English; nonfiction, translations
ST

ELSTOB, Peter, 1915- , Anglo-
American; nonfiction CON

ELSTON Allan Vaughan, 1887- ,
American; fiction CON

ELSTON, Gene, 1922- , American; nonfiction CON

ELTING, Mary ('Davis Cole';
'Campbell Tatham'; 'Benjamin
Brewster'), 1906- , American;
juveniles, fiction COM CON
FUL WA

ELTON, Geoffrey Rudolph, 1921- ,
English; nonfiction CON

'ELTON, John' see MARSH, John

ELTON, Oliver, 1861-1945, English; nonfiction BRO KT

'ELUARD, Paul' (Eugene Grindel),
1895-1952, French; poetry
COL DIC DIF FLE HAR KTS
MAL RIC SA ST

ELVIN, Anna Katharine Stevenson,
1933- , English; poetry CON

'ELVIN, Drake' see BEHA, Ernest

ELVIN, Harold, 1909- , English;
fiction CON

ELVIN, Herbert Lionel, 1905- ,
English; nonfiction CON

ELWARD, James Joseph, 1928- ,
American; plays CON

ELWART, Joan Potter, 1927- ,
American; juveniles COM CON

ELWELL, Fayette Herbert, 1885- ,
American; nonfiction CON

ELWELL, Felicia Rosemary, English; juveniles WA

ELWELL-SUTTON, Laurence Paul,
1912- , Irish; nonfiction CON

ELWEIN, Malcolm, 1903- , English;
nonfiction KTS

ELWIN, Whitwell, 1816-1900, English;
criticism BRO KBA

ELWOOD, Muriel, 1902- , English;
nonfiction CON

ELY, Donald Paul, 1930- , American; nonfiction CON

'ELY, Frederick' see KESSLER,
Jascha F.

ELY, George Herbert see 'STRANG,
Herbert'

ELY, Virginia Shackelford, 1899- ,
American; nonfiction CON

ELYOT, Sir Thomas, 1490?-1546,
English; nonfiction, translations
BRO KB ST

ELYS, Edmund, 1634?-1707, English;
poetry ST

ELYSIO, Filinto see NASCIMENTO,
Francisco M. do

ELZER, Anna E. M. see COURTHS-
MAHLER, Hedwig

EMADEDIN, Ismael see ABULFEDA

EMATS, Marcellus, 1848-1923,
Dutch; fiction, poetry, plays
COL SA

EMANUEL, James A., 1921- ,
American; poetry, nonfiction
CON

EMBERLEY, Barbara Anne, American; juveniles CON

EMBERLEY, Edward Randolph,
1931- , American; juveniles
CON WA

EMBEY, Philip see PHILIPP, Elliot
E.

EMBLEN, Donald Lewis ('Bart
Reynolds'), 1918- , American;
poetry CON

EMBREE, Ainslie Thomas, 1921- ,
American; nonfiction CON

EMBRY, Margaret Jacob, 1919- ,

American; juvenile CON

EMBURY, Emma Catherine, 1806-
63, American; poetry,
fiction KAA

EMENEAU, Murray Barnson,
1904- , American; nonfiction
CON

EMENHISER, Je Don Allen,
1933- , American; nonfiction
CON

'EMERENZER, Anton' see SCHNOG,
Karl

EMERSON, Alan David, 1900- ,
English; fiction CON

'EMERSON, Alice B.' see STRATE-
MEYER, Edward L.

EMERSON, Caroline Dwight,
1891- , American; juveniles
CON WA

EMERSON, Donald Conger,
1913- , Canadian; nonfiction
CON

EMERSON, Elizabeth Holaday,
1885- , American; plays,
fiction HOO

EMERSON, Everett Harvey,
1925- , American; nonfiction
CON

EMERSON, Henry Oliver ('Oliver
Gordon'), 1893- , English;
nonfiction CON

EMERSON, James Gordon, Jr.,
1926- , American; nonfiction
CON

EMERSON, Laura Salome, 1907- ,
American; nonfiction CON

EMERSON, O. B., 1922- , American; nonfiction CON

EMERSON, Ralph Waldo, 1803-82,
American; essays, poetry
BRO KAA MAG SA SP ST

'EMERSON, Ronald' see SCOTLAND,
James

EMERSON, Rupert, 1899- ,
American; nonfiction CON

EMERSON, Thomas Irwin, 1907- ,
American; nonfiction CON

EMERT, 18th cent., French;
fiction DIL

EMERY, Anne McGuigan, 1907- ,
American; juveniles COM
CON FUL WA

EMERY, David Amos, 1920- ,
American; nonfiction CON

EMERY, Russell Guy, 1908- ,
American; juveniles WA

'EMETH, Omer' see VAISSE,
Emilio

EMIE, Louis, 1900- , French;
poetry DIF
EMIN, Fyodor Alexandrovich, 1735?-
70, Russian; fiction HARK ST
'EMINESCU, Mihail' (Mihail Eminovici;
Iminovici), 1850-89, Rumanian;
poetry COL HAR KE SA ST
EMMA, Ronald David, 1920- ,
English; nonfiction CON
EMMANUEL, Philip D., 1909- ,
American; nonfiction CON
'EMMANUEL, Pierre' (Noel Mathieu),
1916- , French; poetry DIC
DIF FLE PIN SA
EMME, Eugene Morlock, 1919- ,
American; nonfiction CON
EMMERICH, Andre, 1924- ,
American; nonfiction CON
EMMERICK, Ronald Eric, 1937- ,
Australian; nonfiction CON
EMMERSON, Henry Russell, 1899- ,
American; nonfiction CON
EMMET, Dorothy Mary, 1904- ,
English; nonfiction CON
EMMETT, Daniel Decatur, 1815-1904,
American; songs KAA
EMMITT, Robert P., 1925- , Amer-
ican; nonfiction CON
EMMIUS, Ubbo, 1547-1626, Dutch;
nonfiction SA
EMMONS, Della Florence Gould,
1890- , American; fiction,
plays PAC
EMMRICH, Curt see 'BAMM, Peter'
EMO, 1175-1237, Frisian; nonfic-
tion ST
'EMOREY, N.' see ELLISON,
Jerome
EMPEDOCLES of ACRAGAS, 5th
cent. B.C., Greek; poetry
SA ST
EMPEY, LaMar T., 1923- , Amer-
ican; nonfiction CON
EMPIRICO, Sexto, 3rd cent., Roman;
nonfiction SA
EMPSON, William, 1906- , British;
poetry, criticism CON FLE KTS
MUR RIC SP
'EMRYS AP IWAN' (Robert Ambrose
Jones), 1851-1906, Welsh; criti-
cism ST
EMS, Rudold see RUDOLF von EMS
EMSLEY, Clare see PLUMMER,
Clare E.
EMSLIE M.C. see SIMPSON, Myrtle
L.
E'NAMI Kiemon see 'KI NO KAION'
ENBAQOM, 16th cent., Ethiopian;

nonfiction LAN
'ENCHO' (Debuchi Jirokichi;
Sanyutei), 1839-1900, Japanese;
fiction ST
ENCINA, Carlos, 1838-82, Argen-
tinian; poetry MIN
'ENCINA, Juan de la' see BLANCO,
Benjamín
ENCINA, Juan de la' see GUTIER-
REZ ABASCAL, Ricardo
ENCINA, Juan del (Enzina), 1468-
1529?, Spanish; plays, poetry
BL HAR KE SA ST
ENCINA ARMANET, Francisco
Antonio, 1874- , Chilean;
nonfiction MIN
ENCINAS, Francisco de, 1520-52,
Spanish; nonfiction SA
ENCINAS, Fray Pedro de, 1530-
95, Spanish; poetry BL SA
ENCISO, Diego see JIMENEZ de
ENCISE, Diego
ENCKELL, Rabbe Arnfinn,
1903- , Finnish; poetry,
plays, criticism FLE ST
ENDACOTT, George Beer, 1901- ,
English; nonfiction CON
ENDACOTT, Marie Violet, 1915- ,
English; nonfiction CON
ENDLER, Norman Solomon,
1931- , Canadian; nonfiction
CON
ENDO, Susaku, 1923- , Japanese;
fiction CON
ENDORE, Guy, 1900/01-70, Amer-
ican; fiction CON KAT WAF
ENDRIKAT, Fred, 1890- , Ger-
man; nonfiction LEN
ENEAN el TACTICO, 4th cent.
B.C., Greek; nonfiction SA
ENEAS de GAZA, 5th cent., Greek;
nonfiction SA
ENEHJELM, Helen Margaret
Mary af, 1909- , American;
fiction HO
ENELOW, Allen Jay, 1922- ,
American; nonfiction CON
ENERY, Robert Firestone,
1927- , American; nonfiction
CON
ENES, Antonio, 1848-1901,
Portuguese; plays, journalism
SA
ENESIDEMO, 1st cent. B.C.,
Greek; nonfiction SA
ENGBERG, Edward, 1928- ,
American; nonfiction CON
ENGBERG, Holger Laessoe,

1930- , Danish-American;
nonfiction CON
ENGDAHL, Sylvia Louise, 1933- ,
American; fiction CON
ENGEL, Alan Stuart, 1932- ,
American; nonfiction CON
ENGEL, Bernard F., 1921- ,
American; nonfiction CON
ENGEL, James F., 1934- ,
American; nonfiction CON
ENGEL, Johann Jakob, 1741-1802,
German; plays SA
ENGEL, Louis Henry, Jr., 1909- ,
American; nonfiction CON
ENGEL, Marian, 1933- , Canadian;
fiction CON
ENGEL, Monroe, 1921- , American;
fiction CON
ENGEL, Pauline Newton, 1918- ,
American; nonfiction CON
ENGEL, Salo, 1908- , Austrian-
American; nonfiction CON
ENGEL, Srul Morris, 1931- ,
Polish-Canadian; nonfiction CON
ENGELBERG, Edward, 1929- ,
German-American; nonfiction
CON
ENGELBRETSDATTER, Dorothe,
1634-1716, Norwegian; poetry
ST
ENGELEN, Adriaan Walraven ('H.
van Apeltern'), 1804-90, Dutch;
poetry ST
ENGELEN, Cornelis van, 1722-93,
Dutch; translations ST
ENGELHARDT, Zephyrin, 1851-1934,
American; nonfiction HOE
ENGELKE, Gerrit, 1890-1918, Ger-
man; poetry AL FLE KU
ENGELMANN, Siegfried E., 1931- ,
American; nonfiction CON
ENGELS, Friedrich, 1820-95, Ger-
man; nonfiction SA
ENGELS, John David, 1931- ,
American; poetry, criticism
CON MUR
ENGELS, Norbert Anthony, 1903- ,
American; fiction, poetry CON
ENGEMAN, John T., 1901- ,
American; juveniles WA
ENGER, Norman L., 1937- , Amer-
ican; nonfiction CON
ENGGASS, Robert, 1921- , Ameri-
can; nonfiction CON
ENGLAND, Barry, 1932- , English;
plays, fiction CON
ENGLAND, Martha Winburn, 1909- ,
American; nonfiction, transla-

tions CON
ENGLAND, Wilbur Birch, 1903- ,
American; nonfiction CON
ENGLANDER, Richard see
'ALTENBERG, Peter'
ENGLE, Eloise Hopper, 1923- ,
American; fiction CON
ENGLE, Paul Hamilton, 1908- ,
American; poetry, fiction
CON MUR
ENGLE, Thelburn LaRoy, 1901- ,
American; nonfiction CON
ENGLEBERT, Rev. Omer,
1893- , French; nonfiction
HO
ENGLEMAN, Finis Ewing,
1895- , American; nonfiction
CON
ENGLEKIRK, John E., 1905- ,
American; nonfiction BL
ENGLER, Richard Emil, Jr.,
1925- , American; nonfiction
CON
ENGLER, Robert, American; non-
fiction CON
ENGLERT, Clement Cyril,
1910- , American; nonfiction
CON
ENGLISH, Barbara Anne, 1933- ,
Scots; nonfiction CON
ENGLISH, Earl Franklin, 1905- ,
American; nonfiction CON
ENGLISH, Emma Jean Martin,
1937- , American; nonfiction
CON
ENGLISH, George Bethune, 1787-
1828, American; nonfiction
KAA
ENGLISH, James Wilson, 1915- ,
American; fiction CON
ENGLISH, Maurice, 1909- ,
American; poetry CON MUR
ENGLISH, Oliver Spurgeon, 1901- ,
American; nonfiction CON
ENGLISH, Ronald Frederick,
1913- , English; nonfiction
CON
ENGLISH, Thomas Dunn, 1819-
1902, American; poetry, plays
KAA
ENGLISH, Thomas Hopkins,
1895- , American; nonfiction
CON
ENGLIZIAN, H. Crosby, 1923- ,
American; nonfiction CON
ENGQUIST, Richard, 1933- ,
American; nonfiction CON
ENGSTRAND, Stuart David,

1904/05- , American; fiction
KTS WAF
ENGSTRÖM, Albert Laurentius
Johannes, 1869-1940, Swedish;
fiction COL FLE HAR SA ST
ENGUIDANOS, Miguel, 1924- ,
Spanish; nonfiction BL
ENIO, Quinto see ENNIUS, Quintus
ENKING, Ottomar, 1867-1945, Ger-
man; fiction ST
ENLOE, Cynthia Holden, 1938- ,
American; nonfiction CON
ENLOW, David Roland, 1916- ,
American; fiction CON
ENNETIERES, Marie ('Marie Deu-
tièrre'), 1500- , Belgian; poetry
SA
ENNIS, Robert Hugh, 1927- , Amer-
ican; nonfiction CON
ENNIUS, Quintus ('Quinto Enio'),
239-169 B.C., Roman; poetry
SA ST
ENNO, Ernst, 1875-1934, Estonian;
poetry, fiction FLE
ENNODIUS, Magnus Felix, 473-521,
Roman; poetry SA ST
ENOMIYA-LASSALLE, Hugo Makibi,
1898- , American; nonfiction
CON
ENOMOTO NO KIKAKU see KIKAKU
ENRICK, Norbert Lloyd, 1920- ,
German-American; nonfiction
CON
ENRIGHT, Dennis Joseph, 1920- ,
British; poetry, fiction, criticism
CON MUR RIC
ENRIGHT, Elizabeth, 1909-68,
American; juveniles KJU WA
ENRIQUEZ, Plinio, Chilean; fiction
MIN
ENRIQUEZ de ARMENDAREZ, 1548-
1628, Spanish; nonfiction MIN
ENRIQUEZ, del CASTILLO, Diego,
1433-1480/1504, Spanish; nonfic-
tion BL SA
ENRIQUEZ GOMEZ, Antonio, 1600-
60?, Spanish; poetry, plays,
fiction BL HAR SA ST
ENROTH, Clyde Adolph, 1926- ,
American; nonfiction CON
ENSCOE, Gerald Eugene, 1926- ,
American; nonfiction CON
ENSE, Varnhagen see VARNHAGEN
von ENSE, Karl A.
ENSLEY, Francis Gerald, 1907- ,
American; nonfiction CON
ENSLIN, Morton Scott, 1897- ,
American; nonfiction CON

ENSLIN, Theodore Vernon,
1925- , American; poetry
MUR
ENSOR, Alliston Rash, 1935- ,
American; nonfiction CON
ENSOR, Robert Charles Kirkwood,
1877- , English; nonfiction
ST
ENSTRAND, Stuart, 1905- ,
American; fiction HOO
ENTEMAN, Willard Finley,
1936- , American; nonfiction
CON
ENTHOVEN, Jacqueline, American;
nonfiction PAC
ENTIVE, Alan David, 1936- ,
American; nonfiction CON
ENTRAMBASGUAS y PEÑA,
Joaquín, 1904- , Spanish;
essays BL SA
ENTRECOLLES, François Xavier
d', 1662-1714, French; nonfic-
tion DIL
ENTWHISTLE, Harold, 1923- ,
English; nonfiction CON
ENTWISLE, Doris Roberts,
1924- , American; nonfiction
CON
ENTWISTLE, William James,
1896-1952, English; nonfiction
BL
ENVALLSON, Carl Magnus, 1756-
1806, Swedish; nonfiction ST
ENZENSBERGER, Hans Magnus,
1929- , German; poetry AL
FLE HAR KU KUN RIC
ENZINA, Juan del see ENCINA,
Juan del
ENZINAS, Francisco de ('Dryander';
'Du Chesne'), 1520-52, Spanish;
nonfiction BL ST
ENZO, 1220/25-72, Italian; poetry
ST
EÖTVÖS, József, 1813-71, Hun-
garian; fiction, poetry, essays
HAR SA ST
EON de BEAUMONT, Charles
Genevienve Louise, 1728-1810,
French; nonfiction DIL
'EPAFRONDITO' see WAGNER
Charles P.
'EPERNAY, Mark' see GALBRAITH,
John K.
EPHORUS (EFORO), 4th cent.
B.C., Greek; nonfiction SA
ST
EPHRAEM, 14th cent., Byzantine;
nonfiction ST

EPICHARMUS, 530-440 B.C.,
Greek; plays SA ST

EPICTETUS, 55-135, Greek; nonfiction SA ST

EPICURUS, 341-270 B.C., Greek;
nonfiction SA ST

EPIMENIDES, 600 B.C.- , Greek;
poetry SA

EPINAY, Louise Florence Pétronelle
d'Esclavelles d', 1726-83,
French; nonfiction DIF DIL HAR
SA

EPP, Eldon Jay, 1930- , American;
nonfiction CON

EPP, Frank Henry, 1929- , Canadian;
nonfiction CON

EPP, Margaret A. ('Agnes Goossen'),
Canadian; juveniles CON

EPPERSON, Gordon, 1921- , American; nonfiction CON

EPPINGA, Jacob D., 1917- , American; nonfiction CON

EPPLE, Anne Orth, 1927- , American; nonfiction CON

EPPS, Preston Herschel, 1888- ,
American; nonfiction CON

EPPS, Robert Lee, 1932- , American; nonfiction CON

EPSTEIN, Beryl Williams ('Adam
Allen'; 'Douglas Coe'; 'William
Beryl'), 1910- , American;
juveniles COM CON FUL WA

EPSTEIN, Cynthia Fuchs, 1922- ,
American; nonfiction CON

EPSTEIN, Edward Jay, 1935- ,
American; nonfiction CON

EPSTEIN, Edwin Michael, 1937- ,
American; nonfiction CON

EPSTEIN, Erwin Howard, 1939- ,
American; nonfiction CON

EPSTEIN, Howard Michael, 1927- ,
American; nonfiction CON

EPSTEIN, Leon D., 1919- , American; nonfiction CON

EPSTEIN, Morris, 1921- , American; nonfiction CON

EPSTEIN, Samuel ('Bruce Campbell';
'Martin Colt'; 'Charles Strong';
'Douglas Coe'), 1909- , Amer-
ican; juveniles, fiction COM
CON FUL WA

EPTON, Nina Consuelo, English;
fiction CON

EQUICOLA, Mario, 1470-1525,
Italian; nonfiction ST

ERAQI see IRAQI, Ibrahim

ERASMUS, Charles John, 1921- ,
American; nonfiction CON

ERASMUS, Desiderius, 1466/69-
1536, Dutch; essays AL BL
HAR KE MAG SA ST

'ERASMUS, M. Nott' see STUBER,
Stanley I.

ERATOSTHENES, 275-195 B.C.,
Greek; poetry SA ST

ERAUSO Catalina de ('La Monja
Alférez'), 1592-1625/50,
Spanish; nonfiction BL SA ST

ERB, Alta Mae, 1891- , American; nonfiction CON

ERB, Paul, 1894- , American;
nonfiction CON

ERBEN, Karel Jaromír, 1811-70,
Czech; poetry HAR KE SA ST

ERCELDOUNE, Thomas ('Thomas
the Rhymer'; Thomas Learmont),
1220?-97?, English; poetry
BRO KB ST

ERCILLA y ZUÑIGA, Alonso de,
1533-94, Spanish; poetry BL
HAR KE MIN SA ST

'ERCKMANN-CHATRIAN', Emile
Erckmann, 1822-99; Alexandre
Chatrian, 1826-90, French;
fiction DIF HAR KE SA ST

ERDMAN, Howard Loyd, 1935- ,
American; nonfiction CON

ERDMAN, Loula Grace, American;
juveniles, fiction COM CON
FUL WA WAF

ERDMAN, Nikolai Robertovich,
1902-70, Russian; plays MAT

ERDMAN, Vorse, 1911- , American; nonfiction CON

ERDÖS, Renee, 1879- , Hungarian;
fiction, poetry, plays ST

ERDOS, Paul Louis, 1914- ,
Hungarian-American; nonfiction
CON

ERENBURG, Ilya see EHRENBURG,
Ilya

'ERGE' see GREULICH, Emil R.

ERHARD Thomas A., 1923- ,
American; plays CON

'ERIC, Kenneth' see HENLEY,
Arthur

ERICCSON, Mary Kentra, 1910- ,
American; juveniles CON

ERICEIRA, Condessa de (Juana
Josefina de Menezes), 1651-
1709, Portuguese; poetry,
translations, plays SA

'ERICH, Otto' see HARTLEBEN,
Otto E.

ERICKSEN, Ephraim Gordon,
1917- , American; nonfiction
CON

ERICKSEN, Gerald Lawrence, 1931- ,
American; nonfiction CON
ERICKSEN, Kenneth Jerrold, 1939- ,
American; nonfiction CON
ERICKSON, Arvel Benjamin, 1905- ,
American; nonfiction CON
ERICKSON, Donald A., 1925- ,
Canadian; nonfiction CON
ERICKSON, Erling Arthur, 1934- ,
American; nonfiction CON
ERICKSON, Ernst Walfred, 1911- ,
American; nonfiction CON
ERICKSON, Keith V., 1943- ,
American; nonfiction CON
ERICKSON, Marion J., 1913- ,
American; nonfiction CON
ERICKSON, Melvin Eddy, 1918- ,
Canadian; nonfiction CON
ERICKSON, Phoebe, 1907- ,
American; juveniles CON WA
ERICKSON, Sabra Rollins ('Sabra
Holbrook'), 1912- , American;
juveniles CON
'ERICSON, Walter' see FAST,
Howard M.
ERIGENA, John (Scotus), 810-70?,
Irish; nonfiction BRO KBA SA
ERIKSON, Erik Homburger ('Erik
Homburger'), 1902- , Danish-
American; nonfiction CON
ERIKSON, Stanley, 1906- , Ameri-
can; nonfiction CON
ERIKSSON, Marguerite A., 1911- ,
American; nonfiction CON
ERINNA, 4th cent. B.C., Greek;
poetry SA ST
ERLANGER, Philippe, 1903- ,
French; fiction CON
ERLICH, Lillian Feldman, 1910- ,
American; juveniles CON WA
ERLICH, Victor, 1914- , Russian-
American; nonfiction CON
ERLINGSSON, Thorsteinn, 1858-1914,
Icelandic; poetry, journalism
COL FLE SA ST
ERMAN, Jean Pierre, 1733-1814,
German; nonfiction DIL
ERMENGEN, Franz van see
'HELLENS, Franz'
ERMOLDO, Nigellus, 9th cent.,
Italian; nonfiction SA
ERNECOURT, Alberte Barbara,
1608-60, French; nonfiction SA
ERNEST, Brother, American;
juveniles WA
ERNEST, Victor Hugo, 1911- ,
American; nonfiction CON
'ERNEST, William' see BERKEBILE,

Fred D.
ERNLE, Rowland Edmund Prothero,
1851-1937, English; nonfiction
KT
ERNO, Richard B., 1923- , Amer-
ican; nonfiction CON
ERNST, Alice Henson, American;
plays PAC
ERNST, Clara see BARNES,
Clara E.
ERNST, Earle, 1911- , Ameri-
can; nonfiction CON
ERNST, Margaret Samuels,
1894- , American; nonfiction
CON
ERNST, Margot Klabe, 1939- ,
American; nonfiction CON
ERNST, Morris, Leopold, 1888- ,
American; nonfiction CON
ERNST, Otto, 1862-1926, German;
plays, fiction MAT ST
ERNST, Paul Carl Friedrich,
1866-1933, German; plays,
fiction, essays AL COL FLE
HAR KU MAT SA ST
ERNST, Robert, 1915- , Ameri-
can; nonfiction CON
ERNSTING, Walter ('Clark Darl-
ton'), 1920- , German-Amer-
ican; nonfiction CON
ERP, Enriqueta van, 1466?-1548,
Dutch; nonfiction SA
ERPENBECK, Fritz, 1897- ,
German; nonfiction AL
'ERRATIC ENRIQUE' see LUKENS,
Henry C.
ERRAZURIZ, Crescente, 1839-
1931, Chilean; nonfiction MIN
ERRAZURIZ, Isidoro, 1835-98,
Chilean; poetry, nonfiction
MIN
ERRAZURIZ URMANETA, Rafael,
1861-1923, Chilean; poetry
MIN
ERRAZURIZ ZAÑARTU, Federico,
1825-77, Chilean; nonfiction
MIN
ERRO, Carlos Alberto, 1903- ,
Argentinian; essays MIN
ERSCH, Johann Samuel, 1766-
1828, German; nonfiction HAR
ERSHOV, Peter Pavlovich, 1815-
69, Russian; poetry ST
ERSKINE, Dorothy, 1906- ,
American; fiction WAF
ERSKINE, John, 1879- , Ameri-
can; poetry, essays KL KT
SA WAF

ERSKINE, Ralph, 1685-1752, English; poetry BRO

'ERSKINE, Rosalina' see LONGRIGG, Robert E.

ERSKINE, Thomas, 1788-1870, Scots; nonfiction BRO KBA

ERSKINE, Wilson Fiske, 1911- , American; nonfiction CON

ERSKINE, Lindop Audrey, English; fiction, plays RIC

ERTEL, Alexander Ivanovich, 1855-1908, Russian; nonfiction COL HARK SA ST

ERTEL, Richard James, 1922- , American; nonfiction CON

ERTER, Isaac, 1791-1851, Galician; nonfiction, translations ST

ERTZ, Susan, 1894?- , Anglo-American; fiction CON KL KT

ERVIN, Janet Halliday, 1923- , American; juveniles CON

ERVIN, Theodore Robert, 1928- , American; nonfiction CON

ERVINE, St. John Greer, 1883-1971, Irish; plays, criticism BRO KL KT MAT RIC SA ST

ERWIN, Edward James, 1937- , American; nonfiction CON

ERXLEBEN, Dorotea Cristiana Leporin, 1715-62, German; nonfiction SA

'ERYTHRAEUS, Ianus Nicius' (Gian Vittorio Rossi), 1577-1647, Italian; nonfiction ST

ESAD, Mehmed see 'GALIB SEYH'

ESCALADA, Miguel see VALBUENA y GUTIERREZ, Antonio

ESCALANTE, Eduardo, 1834-95, Spanish; poetry SA

ESCALANTO y PRIETO, Amós ('Juan García'), 1831-1902, Spanish; poetry, fiction BL SA

ESCALEGERO, Jula Cesare, 1484-1558, Italian; nonfiction SA

'ESCAMILLA, Pedro' (Julian Castellanos y Velasco), 1829?-1891, Spanish; fiction BL SA

ESCANDON, Ralph, 1928- , American; nonfiction CON

ESCARDO, Florencio, 1904- , Argentinian; poetry, criticism SA

ESCARPENTER, Claudio, 1922- , Cuban; nonfiction CON

ESCARRAZ, Donald Ray, 1932- , American; nonfiction CON

ESCHELBACH, Claire John, 1929- , American; nonfiction CON

ESCHENBACH, Wolfram see WOLFRAM von ESCHENBACH

ESCHENBURG, Johann Joachim, 1743-1823, German; nonfiction SA

ESCHENMAYER, Carl Adolph, 1768-1854, German; nonfiction SA

ESCHER, Franklin, Jr., 1915- , American; nonfiction CON

ESCHERICH, Elsa Falk, 1888- , American; fiction CON

ESCHERNY, François Louis, 1733-1815, French; letters, nonfiction DIL

ESCHHOLZ, Paul Anderson, 1942- , American; nonfiction CON

ESCHOLIER, Raymond, 1882- , French; fiction DIF

ESCLASANS, Agustín, 1895- , Spanish; poetry, essays, fiction SA

ESCOBAR, Antonio, 1854- , Cuban; journalism MIN

ESCOBAR, Emilio Antonio, 1857-85, Colombian; poetry, fiction MIN

ESCOBAR, Baltasar de, 16th cent., Spanish; poetry SA

ESCOBAR, Filiberto Julio, 1892- , Argentinian; criticism MIN

ESCOBAR, Julio, 1901- , Spanish; fiction SA

ESCOBAR, Luis, 1908- , Spanish; plays BL

ESCOBAR KIRKPATRICK, Luis, 1908- , Spanish; plays SA

ESCOBAR URIBE, Jorge, 20th cent., Colombian; poetry MIN

ESCOBAR y MENDOZA, Antonio de, 1589-1669, Spanish; poetry BL SA

ESCOBEDO, Nicolás Manuel, 1795-1837/40, Cuban; journalism MIN

ESCOHOTADO, Román, 1908- , Spanish; journalism SA

ESCOSURA, Patricio de la, 1807-78, Spanish; poetry, fiction, plays BL SA

ESCRIVA, Juan, -1520, Spanish; poetry SA ST

ESCRIVA DE ROMANI y ROCA DE TOGORES, Francisco, 1897-1956?, Spanish; poetry SA

ESCUDERO, Gonzalo, 1903- , Ecuadorian; poetry DI

'ESEK, Uncle' see SHAW, Henry W.
ESENIN, Sergey Alexandrovich
(Yesenin), 1895-1925, Russian;
poetry COL FLE HAR HARK
RIC SA ST
ESFANDIARY, Fereidoun M.,
1930- , Iranian; fiction CON
ESHELMAN, Byron Elias, 1915- ,
American; nonfiction CON
ESHLEMANN, Clayton, 1935- ,
American; poetry, translations
CON MUR
ESKELIN, Neil Joyner, 1938- ,
American; nonfiction CON
ESKELUND, Karl, 1918- , Danish;
nonfiction CON
ESKIN, Frada, 1936- , English;
nonfiction CON
ESKOW, Seymour, 1924- , Ameri-
can; nonfiction CON
ESLAVA, Antonio, de, 1570- ,
Spanish; fiction BL SA
ESLER, Anthony James, 1934- ,
American; fiction CON
ESMENARD, Joseph Alphonse, 1767-
1811, French; poetry, plays SA
ESON, Morris E., 1921- , Canadian-
American; nonfiction CON
ESPAGNAC, Jean Baptiste Joseph,
1713-83, French; nonfiction DIL
ESPANCA, Florbela, 1894-1930,
Portuguese; poetry SA
'ESPAÑOLITO' see SUAREZ FERNAN-
DEZ, Constantino
ESPARCIANO, Elio, 4th cent.,
Roman; nonfiction SA
ESPARZA, Eladio, 1885- , Spanish;
fiction, journalism SA
ESPEARD, François Bernard, 1639-
1743, French; nonfiction DIL
ESPEJO see SANTA CRUZ y ESPEJO
ESPEJO, Angel Custodio, 1866/69-
1930/32, Chilean; fiction MIN
ESPEJO, Eugenio Francisco Javier,
1747-95, Ecuadorian; nonfiction
DI SA
ESPEJO, Jerónimo, 1801-89, Argen-
tinian; nonfiction MIN
ESPEJO, Juan Nepomuceno, 1822- ,
Chilean; journalism MIN
ESPEÑEIRA, Antonio, 1855-1907,
Chilean; plays MIN
ESPENSHADE, Edward Bowman,
Jr., 1910- , American; nonfic-
tion CON
ESPER, Erwin, Allen, 1895- ,
American; nonfiction CON
ESPEY, John Jenkins, 1913- ,

American; nonfiction CON
ESPIC de LIROU, Jean François,
1740-1806, French; plays
DIL
ESPINA, Antonio, 1893/94- ,
Spanish; fiction, poetry BL
COL HAR ST
ESPINA Concha (Concepción
Espina de Serna), 1879-1955,
Spanish; poetry, fiction BL
COL FLE HAR KT SA ST
ESPINA GARCIA, Antonio, 1894- ,
Spanish; poetry, fiction, es-
says SA
ESPINAS, José María, 1927- ,
Spanish; nonfiction, fiction SA
ESPINEL, Vicente Martínez,
1550-1624, Spanish; poetry,
fiction BL KE SA ST
ESPINEL ADORNO, Jacinto,
1580?-1635, Spanish; nonfiction,
fiction SA
ESPINO, Federico Licsi, Jr.,
1939- , Filipino; poetry
MUR
ESPINOSA, Angel, 1889- ,
Spanish; poetry SA
'ESPINOSA, Enrique' see GLUS-
BERG, Samuel
ESPINOSA, Jose Edmundo, 1900-
67, American; nonfiction CON
ESPINOSA, Jose Modesto (Setosa),
1833-1916, Ecuadorian; non-
fiction DI
ESPINOSA, Juan Antonio, 1898- ,
Spanish; fiction, journalism
SA
ESPINOSA, Nicolás, 1520- ,
Spanish; poetry SA
ESPINOSA, Pedro, 1578-1650,
Spanish; editor, nonfiction
BL HAR SA ST
ESPINOSA MAESO, Ricardo,
1894- , Spanish; nonfiction
BL
ESPINOSA MEDRANO, Juan de,
1632-88, Peruvian; nonfiction,
poetry BL SA
ESPINOSA POLIT, Aurelio, 1894-
1961, Ecuadorian; criticism
DI
ESPINOSA y MALO, Félix de
Lucio ('El Lunarejo'), 1646-
91, Spanish; nonfiction SA
ESPINOZA, Januario, 1882-1946,
Chilean; journalism, fiction
MIN
ESPOSITO, John Cabrino, 1940- ,

American; nonfiction CON

ESPRIU, Salvador, 1913- , Spanish;
poetry, plays SA

ESPRONCEDA, José de, 1808-42,
Spanish; poetry BL HAR KE SA
ST

ESQUILACHE, Francisco de Borja y
Acevedo, 1582-1658, Spanish;
poetry BL ST

ESQUILO, 525-456 B.C., Greek;
poetry SA

ESQUINES, 389?-14 B.C., Greek;
nonfiction SA

ESQUIROS, Henri Alphonse, 1814-76,
French; fiction HAR

ESQUIU, Mamerto, 1826-82/83, Argentinian; nonfiction MIN

ESSER, Robin, 1933- , English;
fiction CON

ESSEX, Harry J., American; plays
CON

'ESSEX, Mary' see BLOOM, Ursula

ESSIG, Hermann, 1878-1918, German;
plays MAT

ESSOE, Gabe Attila, 1944- , Hungarian-American; nonfiction CON

ESSON, Thomas Louis Buvelot, 1879-
1943, Australian; plays MAT

ESTACIO, Cecilio, -168 B.C.,
Roman; poetry SA

ESTACIO, Publio Papinio, 61-96,
Roman; poetry SA

ESTAING, Charles Hector, 1729-98,
French; nonfiction DIL

ESTALA, Pedro, 1740-1820, Spanish;
nonfiction BL SA

'ESTANG, Luc' (Lucien Bastard),
1911- , French; poetry, fiction,
essays DIC DIF FLE

ESTANSINO, Greek; poetry SA

ESTAT, Baron d', -1800, French;
plays DIL

ESTAUNIE, Edouard, 1862-1943,
French; fiction COL FLE HAR
DIF SA ST

ESTCOURT, Richard, 1688-1712, English; plays KB

ESTEBAN SCARPA, Roque, 1914- ,
Chilean; poetry, nonfiction MIN
SA

ESTEBANEZ CALDERON, Serafin see
CALDERON, Serafín E.

ESTELLA, Diego de (Diego de San
Cristóbal), 1524-78, Spanish;
nonfiction BL HAR SA ST

ESTELLE, Sister Mary (Estelle
Casalandra), 1907- , American;

nonfiction CON

ESTELRICH, Juan, 1896-1958,
Spanish; nonfiction BL SA

ESTELRICH y PERELLO, Juan
Luis, 1856-1923, Spanish;
poetry, nonfiction BL SA

ESTENGER, Rafael, 1899- ,
Cuban; journalism, poetry,
criticism, essays MIN

ESTEP, Irene Compton, American; juveniles CON

ESTEP, William Roscoe, Jr.,
1920- , American; nonfiction
CON

ESTERGREEN, Marian Morgan,
1910- , American; nonfiction
CON

ESTERLY, Glenn, 1942- , American; nonfiction CON

ESTEROW, Milton, 1928- , American; nonfiction CON

ESTES, Eleanor Rosenfeldt,
1906- , American; fiction,
juveniles CON KJU WA WAF

ESTES, Rice, 1907- , American;
nonfiction CON

ESTES, Winston M., 1917- ,
American; fiction CON

ESTESICORO, Sículo, 640-555
B.C., Greek; poetry SA

ESTEY, George F., 1924- ,
Canadian; nonfiction CON

ESTHUS, Raymond, Arthur,
1925- , American; nonfiction
CON

ESTIENNE, Henri, 1531?-98,
French; nonfiction DIF HAR
KE SA ST

ESTIENNE, Robert, 1503-39,
French; nonfiction ST

ESTILPON Megarense, Greek;
nonfiction SA

ESTLANDER, Carl Gustaf, 1834-
1910, Finnish-Swedish; nonfiction ST

ESTOCK, Anne Martin, 1923- ,
American; fiction CON

'ESTORIL, Jean' see ALLAN,
Mabel E.

ESTRADA, Angel de, 1872-1923,
Argentinian; nonfiction MIN
SA

ESTRADA, Diego, 1589-1647?,
Spanish; nonfiction ST

ESTRADA, Doris Perkins,
1923- , American; plays
CON

ESTRADA, Genaro, 1887-1937,
Mexican; journalism, criticism
BL
ESTRADA, Ildefonso, -1911, Cuban;
journalism, poetry MIN
ESTRADA, Jacquelyn Ann, 1946- ,
American; nonfiction CON
ESTRADA, José Manuel, 1842-94/
97- , Argentinian; journalism,
essays MIN SA
ESTRADA, Jenaro, 1887-1937, Mexican;
poetry, criticism SA
ESTRADA, Rafael, 1901-34, Costa
Rican; poetry MIN
ESTRADA, Santiago, 1841-91, Argen-
tinian; poetry MIN
ESTRADA y AYALA, Aurora,
1902- , Ecuadorian; poetry DI
ESTRADA y SEGALERVA, José Luis,
1906- , Spanish; nonfiction SA
ESTRELLA GUTIERREZ, Fermín,
1900- , Argentinian; journalism,
poetry, fiction, criticism MIN
SA
ESTREMERA, Antonio, 1884- ,
Spanish; plays BL
ESTREMERA y CUENCA, José,
1852-95, Spanish; poetry, plays
SA
ESTRIN, Herman A., 1915- ,
American; nonfiction CON
ESTUÑIGA, Lope de see STUÑIGA,
Lope de
ETEROVICH, Francis Hyacinth,
1913- , American; nonfiction
CON
E'TESAMI, Parvin, 1906-41, Persian;
poetry LAN
ETHEREGE, Sir George (Etheredge),
1635?-91, English; plays, poetry
BRO KB MAG ST
ETHERIDGE, Eugene Wesley, 1925- ,
American; nonfiction CON
ETHERINGTON, Charles Leslie,
1903- , American; nonfiction
CON
ETHRIDGE, Willie Snow, 1900- ,
American; nonfiction CON
ETIEMBLE, René, 1910- , French;
criticism, fiction DIF
'ETIENNE' see KING-HALL, William
S. K.
ETIENNE, Charles Guillaume, 1777-
1845, French; journalism, plays
SA
ETIENNE de BOURBON, 1190-1261,
French; nonfiction ST
ETIENNE DE FOUGERES, -1178,

English; poetry ST
ETIENNE de ROUEN, fl. 1160,
French; poetry ST
ETLAR, Carit see 'BROSBALL,
Johan C. C.
ETMEKJIAN, James, 1916- ,
American; nonfiction CON
ETS, Marie Hall, 1895- , Amer-
ican; juveniles COM CON
KJU WA
ETSU see SUGIMOTO, Etsu I.
ETTELDORF, Raymond P.,
1911- , American; nonfiction
CON
ETTER, Dana, 1928- , Ameri-
can; poetry CON MUR
ETTER, Lester Frederick,
1904- , American; juveniles
CON
ETTINGER, Elzbieta, 1925- ,
Polish-American; fiction CON
ETTINGER, Robert Chester Wilson,
1918- , American; nonfiction
CON
ETTINGER, Salomon, 1799-1855,
Jewish; poetry, fiction, plays
ST
ETTLESON, Abraham, 1877- ,
American; nonfiction CON
'ETTRICK, SHEPHERD, The' see
HOGG, James
ETZIONI, Amitai Werner, 1929- ,
German-American; nonfiction
CON
ETZKOWITZ, Henry, 1940- ,
American; nonfiction CON
EUBANK, Weaver Keith, Jr.,
1920- , American; nonfiction
CON
EUBANKS, Ralph Travis, 1920- ,
American; nonfiction CON
EUBELIN, Charles, fl. 18th cent.,
French; nonfiction DIL
EUBUILIDES, 4th cent. B.C.,
Greek; nonfiction SA
EUBULUS, fl. 375-30 B.C.,
Greek; plays ST
EUCKEN, Rudolf Christoph, 1846-
1926, German; essays SA
EUCLID of ALEXANDRIA, fl.
300 B.C., Greek; nonfiction
ST
EUCLIF of MEGARA, 450-370/80
B.C., Greek; nonfiction SA
ST
EUDEMO de RHODES, 4th cent.
B.C., Greek; nonfiction SA
EUGENIS of TOLEDO, 600-58,

French; poetry SA ST

EUGENIUS VULGARIS, fl. 900,
Italian; nonfiction, poetry ST

EUGIPPIUS, fl. 500, African; nonfiction ST

EULENBERG, Herbert, 1876-1949,
German; plays, fiction COL
MAT SA AL

EULENSPIEGEL, Till, 16th cent.,
German; nonfiction AL

ELLER, John Elmer, 1926- , American; nonfiction CON

EULOGIO de CORDOBA, fl. 859,
Spanish; nonfiction SA

EUMATHE see EUSTADO

EUMENES, 250-313, Roman; nonfiction SA

EUNAPIUS, 345-420, Greek; nonfiction SA ST

EUNSON, Dale, 1904- , American;
fiction WAF

EUNSON, Robert Charles, 1912- ,
American; fiction CON

EUPHORION, 276 B.C., Greek;
poetry SA ST

EUPOLIS, 446-411 B.C., Greek;
poetry SA ST

EUQUERIA, 5th cent., Greek; poetry
SA

EURICH, Alvin Christophe, 1902- ,
American; nonfiction CON

EURINGER, Richard, 1891- , German; fiction, poetry COL SA

EURIPIDES, 485-06 B.C., Greek;
plays MAL SA ST

'EUROPEAN' see MOSLEY, Sir
Oswald W.

EUSDEN, Laurence, 1688-1730, English; poetry BRO KB

EUSEBIUS, 260/64-340, Greek; nonfiction SA ST

EUSKERKIN, Claus van,   -1520,
Dutch; nonfiction ST

EUSTACE, Cecil John, 1904- ,
English-Canadian; fiction HOE

EUSTACE, May Corcoran, 1904- ,
Irish; nonfiction CON

EUSTACHE, fl. 1170, French;
poetry ST

EUSTACHE d' AMIENS, 12th cent.,
French; poetry ST

EUSTADO (Eumathe), 12th cent.,
Greek; fiction SA

EUSTALHUIS,   -1192, Byzantine;
nonfiction ST

EUTROPIUS, 4th cent., Roman;
nonfiction SA ST

EVARGIUS of PONTUS, 345-99,

Egyptian; nonfiction SA ST

EVAGRIUS SCHOLASTICUS,
536- , Byzantine; nonfiction
SA ST

EVAN, William Martin, 1922- ,
American; nonfiction CON

EVANOFF, Vlad, 1916- , American; nonfiction CON

EVANS, Abbie Huston, 1881- ,
American; poetry MUR

EVANS, Abel, 1679-1737, English;
essays BRO

'EVANS, Alan' see STOKER, Alan

EVANS, Alfred Alexander,
1905- , English; nonfiction
CON

EVANS, Anne, 1820-70, English;
poetry KBA

EVANS, Sir Arthur John, 1851-
1941, English; nonfiction BRO

EVANS, Augusta Jane Wilson,
1835-1909, American; fiction
KAA

EVANS, Bergen Baldwin, 1904- ,
American; nonfiction CON

EVANS, Caradoc, 1878/83-1945,
Welsh; fiction BRO KAT KT
RIC ST

EVANS, Charles Stephen, 1948- ,
American; nonfiction CON

EVANS, Constance May ('Jane
Gray'; 'Mairi O'Nair'),
1890- , Canadian; fiction
CON

EVANS, David Ellis, 1930- ,
Welsh; nonfiction CON

EVANS, David Russell, 1937- ,
American; nonfiction CON

EVANS, Edna Hoffman, 1913- ,
American; juveniles WA

EVANS, Emyr Estyn, 1905- ,
English; nonfiction CON

EVANS, Eva Knox, 1905- ,
American; juveniles FUL WA

EVANS, Evan see 'IEUAN GLAN
GEIRIONYDD'

EVANS, Frances Monet Carter,
1923- , American; nonfiction
CON

EVANS, Francis Fallon, 1925- ,
American; nonfiction CON

EVANS, Gayle Edward, 1937- ,
American; nonfiction CON

EVANS, Geoffrey Charles, 1901- ,
English; nonfiction CON

EVANS, George, 1870-1915,
American; composer HOO

EVANS, George Bird ('Brandon

Bird'; 'Harris Evans'), 1906- ,
American; fiction CON
EVANS, George William II, 1920- ,
American; nonfiction CON
EVANS, Geraint Nantglyn Davies,
1935-71, Welsh; nonfiction CON
EVANS, Gordon Heyd, 1930- ,
American; nonfiction CON
'EVANS, Harris' see EVANS, George
B. and Evans, Kay Harris
EVANS, Hilary ('H. E. Agard'),
1929- , American; nonfiction
CON
EVANS, Howard Ensign, 1919- ,
American; poetry, nonfiction
CON
EVANS, Humphrey Marshall, Jr.,
1914- , American; nonfiction
CON
EVANS, Idella Marie Crowe,
1924- , American; nonfiction
CON
EVANS, Idrisyn Oliver, 1894- ,
South African; fiction CON
EVANS, Jack Naunton, 1920- ,
Welsh; nonfiction CON
EVANS, Jacob A., 1920- , Ameri-
can; nonfiction CON
EVANS, James Allan Stewart, 1931- ,
Canadian; nonfiction CON
EVANS, James Forrest, 1932- ,
American; nonfiction CON
EVANS, Jean Cherry Drummond,
1928- , English; fiction CON
EVANS, Joan, 1893- , English;
nonfiction CON
EVANS, John Walker, 1904- , Amer-
ican; nonfiction CON
EVANS, John Xavier, 1933- , Amer-
ican; nonfiction CON
EVANS, Joseph William, 1921- ,
American; nonfiction CON
EVANS, Julia Rendel ('Polly Hobson'),
1913- , English; fiction CON
WA
EVANS, Katherine Floyd, 1901-64,
American; juveniles CON WA
EVANS, Kathleen Marianne, 1911- ,
Welsh; nonfiction CON
EVANS, Kay Harris ('Harris Evans';
'Brandon Bird'), 1906- ,
American; fiction CON
EVANS, Laurence, 1923- , Amer-
ican; nonfiction CON
EVANS, Luther H., 1902- ,
American; nonfiction CON
EVANS, Margiad, 1909- , Welsh;
poetry ST

EVANS, Mary Anne see 'ELIOT,
George'
EVANS, Max, 1925- , American;
nonfiction, fiction CON
EVANS, Medford Bryan, 1907- ,
American; nonfiction CON
EVANS, Melbourne Griffith,
1912- , American; nonfiction
CON
'EVANS, Morgan' see DAVIES,
Leslie P.
EVANS, N. Dean, 1925- ,
American; nonfiction CON
EVANS, Nathaniel, 1742-67,
American; poetry KAA
EVANS, Oliver, 1915- , Ameri-
can; nonfiction CON
EVANS, Patricia Healy, 1920- ,
American; juveniles WA
EVANS, Paul, 1945- , British;
poetry MUR
EVANS, Richard Louis, 1906- ,
American; nonfiction CON
EVANS, Robert, Jr., 1932- ,
American; nonfiction CON
EVANS, Robert Franklin, 1930- ,
American; nonfiction CON
EVANS, Robert Henry, 1937- ,
English; nonfiction CON
EVANS, Robert Owen, 1919- ,
American; nonfiction CON
EVANS, Robert P., 1918- ,
American; nonfiction CON
EVANS, Rowland, Jr., 1921- ,
American; nonfiction CON
EVANS, Rupert N., 1921- ,
American; nonfiction CON
EVANS, Sebastian, 1830-1909,
English; poetry KBA
EVANS, Stanley George, 1912- ,
English; nonfiction CON
EVANS, Theophilus, 1693-1767,
Welsh; nonfiction ST
EVANS, Virginia Moran, 1909- ,
American; poetry, fiction
CON
EVANS, Warren Felt, 1817-89,
American; nonfiction KAA
EVANS, William McKee, 1923- ,
American; nonfiction CON
EVANS, William Howard, 1924- ,
American; nonfiction CON
EVANS DAVIES, Gloria, 1932- ,
British; poetry CON MUR
EVANSEN, Virginia Besaw,
1921- , American; fiction
CON
EVANS-JONES, Albert ('Cynan'),

1895- , Welsh; poetry, plays,
translations CON
EVANTUREL, Eudore, 1854-1919,
Canadian; nonfiction SY
'EVARISTOTELES' see ACEVEDO
GUERRA, Evaristo
EVARTS, Hal George, 1887-1934,
American; fiction KT
EVE, Joseph, 1760-1835, American;
poetry KAA
'EVELYN, Anthony' see WARD-
THOMAS, Evelyn B.
EVELYN, John, 1620-1706, English;
essays, diary BRO KB MAG ST
EVELYN, John Michael ('Michael
Underwood'), 1916- , English;
fiction CON
EVEMERO (Euhemero), 4th cent.
B. C., Greek; nonfiction SA
EVENNETT, Henry Outram, 1901- ,
English; nonfiction HO
EVENS, George Bramwell ('Romany'),
1884-1943, English; juveniles
DOY
EVERAERT, Cornelis, 1480-1556,
Dutch; poetry ST
EVERARD le MOINE, 12th cent.,
Anglo-Norman; poetry ST
EVERARDI, Joannes see SECUNDUS,
Joannes
EVERED, Philip, 1850- , English;
nonfiction HIG
EVEREST, Allan Seymour, 1913- ,
American; nonfiction CON
EVERETT, Alexander Hill, 1790-
1847, American; editor KAA
EVERETT, David, 1770-1813, Amer-
ican; poetry, journalism KAA
EVERETT, Donald E., 1920- ,
American; nonfiction CON
EVERETT, Edward, 1794-1865,
American; essays KAA
'EVERETT, Gail' see HALE, Arlene
EVERETT, Peter William, 1924- ,
American; nonfiction CON
EVERETT-GREEN, Evelyn ('Cecil
Adair'; 'Evelyn Ward'), 1856-
1932, English; juvenile DOY
EVER-HADANI, Aharon, 1899- ,
Jewish; fiction ST
EVERITT, Alan Milner, 1926- ,
English; nonfiction ST
EVERNDEN, Margery, 1916- ,
American; juveniles, plays CON
EVERS, Alf, 1905- , American;
juveniles WA
EVERSLEY, David Edward Charles
('William Small'), 1921- ,

German-English; nonfiction
CON
EVERSOLE, Finley T., 1933- ,
American; nonfiction CON
EVERSON, Dale Miller, 1928- ,
American; juveniles CON
EVERSON, Ida Gertrude, 1898- ,
American; nonfiction CON
EVERSON, Ronald Gilmour,
1903- , Canadian; poetry
CON MUR
EVERSON, William Keith,
1929- , American; juveniles
CON WA
EVERSON, William O. see
'ANTONINUS, Brother'
EVERTTS, Eldonna Louise,
1917- , American; nonfiction
CON
EVERY, George, 1909- , Ameri-
can; nonfiction CON
'EVERY, Philip Cochrane' see
BURNFORD, Sheila
EVLIYA CELEBI, 1611-82,
Turkish; nonfiction ST
'EVOE' see KNOX, Edmund G. V.
EVOY, John Joseph, 1911- ,
American; nonfiction CON
EVRA, 18th cent., French; plays
DIL
EVRARD the GERMAN, fl. 1280,
German; poetry ST
EVREINOV, Nikolai N. see
YEVREINOV, Nikolai N.
EVSLIN, Bernard, 1922- , Amer-
ican; nonfiction CON
EVTUSHENKO, Eugeny Alexandro-
vich (Yevtushenko), 1933- ,
Russian; poetry FLE HAR
RIC
EWALD, Carl, 1856-1908, Danish;
fiction, essays, journalism
HAR KE ST
EWALD, Herman Frederik, 1821-
1908, Danish; fiction HAR ST
EWALD, Johannes Jan, 1743-81,
Danish; poetry, plays HAR
KE SA ST
EWART, Andrew, 1911- , Scots;
nonfiction CON
EWART, Gavin Buchanan, 1916- ,
British; poetry MUR
EWBANK, Walter F., 1918- ,
English; nonfiction CON
EWEN, David, 1907- , American;
juvenile CON WA
EWEN, Frederic, 1899- , Aus-
trian-American; nonfiction
CON

EWEN, Robert B., 1940- ,
American; nonfiction CON
EWERS, John Canfield, 1909- ,
American; nonfiction CON
EWING, Alfred Cyril, 1899- ,
English; nonfiction CON
EWING, David Walkley, 1923- ,
American; nonfiction CON
EWING, John B., 1893- , Ameri-
can; nonfiction MAR
EWING, John Sinclair, 1916- ,
Canadian; nonfiction CON
EWING, Juliana Horatia, 1841-85,
English; juveniles BRO DOY
KBA ST
EWY, Donna, 1934- , American;
nonfiction CON
EWY, Rodger, 1931- , American;
nonfiction CON
'EX-R. S. M.' see LINDSAY, Harold
A.
'EXALL, Barry' see NUGENT, John
P.
EXELL, Frank Kingsley, 1902- ,
American; nonfiction CON
EXIMENIS, Francisco see EIMIMENIS,
Francesc
EXMAN, Eugene, 1900- , American;
nonfiction CON
EXPILLY, Jean Joseph, 1719-93,
French; nonfiction DIL
EYB, Albrecht see ALBRECHT VON
EYB
EYBERS, Elisabeth Francoise, 1915- ,
South African; poetry FLE ST
EYERLY, Jeannette Hyde ('Jeannette
Griffith'), 1908- , American;
fiction CON
EYCK, Frank, 1921- , German-
Canadian; nonfiction CON
EYEN, Tom ('Jerome Eyen';
'Roger Short, Jr.'), American;
plays CON
EYLES, Wilfred Charles, 1891- ,
Australian; nonfiction CON
EYRE, Katherine Wigmore, 1901- ,
American; juvenile FUL
EYRE, Samuel Robert, 1922- ,
English; nonfiction CON
EYSENCK, Hans Jurgen, 1916- ,
German-English; nonfiction
CON
EYSTEINN, Asgrímsson, 1310-61,
Icelandic; poetry KE ST
EYSTER, Charles William, 1917- ,
American; nonfiction CON
EYTH, Max von, 1836-1906, Ger-
man; fiction HAR ST

EYTINGE, Rose, 1835-1911,
American; nonfiction KAA
EYZAGUIRRE, Jaime de, 1908- ,
Chilean; essays MIN
EYZAGUIRRE, José Ignacio Víctor,
(Eizaguirre), -1880, Chilean;
nonfiction MIN
EZEKIEL, Nissim, 1924- , Indian;
poetry MUR
EZELL, Harry Eugene, 1918- ,
American; fiction, poetry CON
EZELL, John Samuel, 1917- ,
American; nonfiction CON
EZERA, Kalu, 1925- , Nigerian;
nonfiction CON
EZPONDA, Eduardo, 1815- ,
Cuban; poetry, fiction MIN
EZQUERRA ABADIA, Ramón,
1904- , Spanish; nonfiction
BL SA
EZRA, Abraham Ibn, 1092-1167,
Spanish; nonfiction SA
EZRA, Mosé Ibn, 1055/60- ,
Jewish; poetry SA
EZZO of BAMBERG, fl. 1060,
German; poetry AL HAR ST

F

'F. P. A.' see ADAMS, Franklin P.
FAAS, Larry Andrew, 1936- ,
American; nonfiction CON
FAASSEN, Pieter Jacobus Rosier,
1833-1907, Dutch; plays ST
FABA, Guido see FAVA, Guido
FABANI, Ana Teresa, 1922-49,
Argentinian; poetry, fiction
SA
FABBRI, Diego, 1911- , Italian;
plays FLE MAT
FABELL, Walter C., American;
juveniles WA
FABER, Charles Franklin, 1926- ,
American; nonfiction CON
FABER, Doris Greenberg, 1924- ,
American; juveniles CON WA
FABER, Frederich, William, 1814-
63, English; hymns, poetry
BRO KBA
FABER, Harold, 1919- , Ameri-
can; nonfiction, juveniles
CON WA
FABER, John Henry, 1918- ,
American; nonfiction CON
FABER, Melvyn Donald, 1936- ,
American; nonfiction CON
FABER, Nancy Weingarten,

1909- , American; juveniles
CON
FABE, Peter Christian Frederik,
1810-77, Danish; poetry ST
FABER, Walter ('Coronet'), 1857-
1928, English; nonfiction HIG
FABIAN, Donald Leroy, 1919- ,
American; nonfiction CON
FABIAN, Josephine Cunningham,
1903- , American; nonfiction
CON
'FABIAN, Vidal' see FAJARDO
FERNANDEZ, Enrique
FABIE ESCUDERA, Antonio María,
1834-99, Spanish; BL SA
FABILLI, Mary ('Aurora Bligh'),
1914- , American; poetry MUR
'FABIUS' see DICKINSON, John
FABIUS PICTOR, Quintus, 3rd cent.,
Roman; nonfiction SA ST
FABRA, Pompeu, 1869-1951, Catalan;
nonfiction ST
FABRE, Antone, 1710-93, French;
nonfiction DIL
FABRE, Emile, 1869-1955, French;
plays DIF
FABRE, Ferdinand, 1827/30-98,
French; fiction DIF HAR SA ST
FABRE, Jean Claude, 1668-1753,
French; nonfiction DIL
FABRE, Jean Henri, 1823-1915,
French; juveniles DIF KJU
FABRE, Lucien, 1889-1952, French;
nonfiction DIF
FABRE, Marie Joseph Victorin,
1785-1831, French; nonfiction
SA
FABRE de CHARRIN, 18th cent.,
French; nonfiction DIL
FABRE d'EGLANTINE, Philippe
François Nazaire, 1750-94,
French; plays, songs DIF DIL
HAR SA ST
FABRE d'OLIVET, Antoine, 1768-
1825, French; translations DIF
FABRI, Albrecht, 1911- , German;
nonfiction KU
FABRI, Gabriel, 1666-1711, French;
nonfiction DIL
FABRI, Pierre, -1520?, French;
nonfiction ST
FABRI, Ralph, 1894- , American;
nonfiction CON
FABRICIO, Georg, 1516-71, German;
nonfiction SA
FABRICIUS, Jan, 1871- , Dutch;
plays SA ST
FABRICIUS, Johan Albert, 1668-

1736, German; nonfiction HAR
KT SA
FABRICIUS, Johan Wigmore,
1899- , Dutch; fiction KT ST
FABRICIUS, Sara see 'SANDEL,
Cora'
FABRICY, Gabriel, -1800,
French; nonfiction DIL
FABRIZI, Cinzio Aloise, 16th
cent., Italian; poetry ST
FABRIZIO, Ray, 1930- , Ameri-
can; nonfiction CON
FABRY, Joseph Benedikt ('Peter
Fabrizius'), 1909- , Ameri-
can; nonfiction CON
FABRY, Rudolf, 1915- , Slovak;
poetry ST
FABRYCKY, Wolter Joseph,
1932- , American; nonfiction
CON
FABYAN, Robert, -1535, Eng-
lish; diary BRO KB
FACCIO, Rina see 'ALERAMO,
Sibilla'
FACIO, Justo A., 1859/61-1930/32,
Costa Rican; essays MIN SA
FACKENHEIM, Emil Ludwig,
1916- , German-Canadian;
nonfiction CON
FACKLAM, Margery Metz,
1927- , American; fiction
CON
FACKRE, Gabriel Joseph, 1926- ,
American; nonfiction CON
FADAYEV, Alexander Alexandro-
vich (A. A. Bulyga), 1901-56,
Russian; fiction FLE HAR
HARK RIC ST
FADER, Daniel, 1930- , Ameri-
can; nonfiction CON
FADERMAN, Lillian, 1940- ,
American; nonfiction CON
FADIMAN, Clifton, 1904- ,
American; criticism KT
FADIMAN, Edwin, Jr. ('Edwina
Mark'), 1925- , American;
fiction CON
FADIMAN, James, 1939- ,
American; nonfiction CON
FADNER, Frank Leslie, 1910- ,
American; nonfiction CON
FAERNE, Gabriel, 1520?-61,
Italian; poetry SA
FAESI, Robert, 1883- , Swiss;
poetry, fiction, plays FLE
HAR LEN
FAGAN, Barthélemy Christophe,
1702-55, French; plays DIL

FAGAN, Edward Richard, 1924- ,
American; nonfiction CON
FAGE, Durant, 1681-1750, French;
nonfiction DIL
FAGE, John Donnelly, 1921- ,
English; nonfiction CON
FAGEN, Richard R., 1933- ,
American; nonfiction CON
FAGER, Charles Eugene, 1942- ,
American; nonfiction CON
FAGLEY, Richard M., 1910- ,
American; nonfiction CON
FAGNAN, Marie Antoinette, 1710?-
70, French; fiction DIL SA
FAGOTHEY, Austin, 1901- , Amer-
ican; nonfiction CON
FAGUET, Emile, 1847-1916, French;
criticism, essays COL DIF HAR
KE SA ST
FAGUNDES VARELA, Luis Nicolás,
1841-75, Brazilian; poetry SA
FAGUNDO, Ana Maria, 1938- ,
Spanish-American; poetry CON
FAGUNWA, Daniel Olorunsemi,
1895-1963, Nigerian; fiction RIC
'FAGUS' (Georges Eugene Faillet),
1872-1933, French; poetry COL
DIF SA
FAGYAS, Maria ('Maria Helen Fay'),
Hungarian-American; plays, fic-
tion CON
FAHERTY, William Barnaby, 1914- ,
American; nonfiction CON
FAHEY, Rev. Denis, 1883- , Irish;
nonfiction HO
FAHEY, John, American; nonfiction
PAC
FA-HIEN, 399-454, Chinese; nonfic-
tion SA
FA-HSIEN, 420- , Chinese; nonfic-
tion ST
FAIDIT, Gaucelm, fl. 1190-1220,
French; poetry HAR
FAIGUET de VILLENEUVE, Joachim,
1703-80, French; nonfiction DIL
FAILLET, Georges Eugene see
'FAGUS'
FAIN, Haskell, 1926- , American;
nonfiction CON
FAINI, Diamante Medaglia, 1725-70,
Italian; poetry SA
FAINLIGHT, Harry, American; poetry
MUR
FAINLIGHT, Ruth Esther, 1931- ,
American; poetry CON MUR
FAINSOD, Merle, 1907-72, Ameri-
can; nonfiction CON
FAINZILBURG, Ilya A. see 'ILF,
Llya'

'FAIR, A. A.' see GARDNER,
Erle Stanley
'FAIR, C. A.' 1923- , English;
poetry MUR
FAIR, Charles M., 1916- ,
American; nonfiction CON
FAIR, James Rutherford, Jr.,
1920- , American; nonfiction
CON
FAIR, Ray Clarence, 1942- ,
American; nonfiction CON
FAIRBAIRN, Andrew Martin,
1838-1912, Scots; nonfiction
KBA
FAIRBAIRN, Arthur Rex Dugard,
1904-57, New Zealander;
poetry, essays RIC ST
FAIRBAIRN, Douglas, 1926- ,
American; fiction CON
FAIRBAIRNS, Zoe, 1948- , Eng-
lish; fiction CON
FAIRBANK, Alfred John, 1895- ,
English; nonfiction CON
FAIRBANK, Janet Ayer, American;
fiction HOO KT
FAIRBANK, John King, 1907- ,
American; nonfiction CON
FAIRBRIDGE, Dorothea, 1862-
1931, South African; fiction
ST
FAIRBRIDGE, Kingsley Ogilvie,
1885-1924, South African;
poetry ST
FAIRBROTHER, Nan, 1913-
71, English; nonfiction
CON
FAIRBURN, Arthur Rex Dugard
see FAIRBAIRN, Arthur
FAIRCHILD, Henry Pratt, 1880- ,
American; nonfiction KTS
FAIRCHILD, Hoxie Neale, 1894- ,
American; nonfiction CON
FAIRFAX, Edward, 1580-1635,
English; translations BRO KB
SA SP ST
FAIRFAX, John, 1930- , British;
poetry MUR
FAIRFAX-LUCY, Brian Fulke
Cameron Ramsay, 1898- ,
English; juveniles CON
FAIRFAX-BLAKEBOROUGH, John,
1883- , English; nonfiction
HIG
FAIRFIELD, Dame Cicily Isabel
see 'WEST, Rebecca'
'FAIRFIELD, John' see LIVING-
STONE, Harrison E.
FAIRFIELD, Roy Phillips, 1918- ,

American; nonfiction CON

FAIRFIELD, Sumner Lincoln, 1803-44, American; poetry KAA

'FAIRLESS, Michael' see BARBER, Margaret

FARILEY, Barker, 1887- , Anglo-Canadian; nonfiction CON

FAIRLEY, Michael Charles, 1937- , English; nonfiction CON

FAIRLEY, Peter, 1930- , English; nonfiction CON

FAIRMAN, Joan Alexandra, 1935- , American; nonfiction CON

FAIRMAN, Virgil B. see KLARMANN, Andrew F.

FAIRWEATHER, George W., 1921- , American; nonfiction CON

FAIRWEATHER, Virginia, 1922- , English; nonfiction CON

FAISSLER, Margareta, 1902- , American; nonfiction CON

FAIT, Hollis F., 1918- , American; nonfiction CON

FAITINELLI, Pietro de (Mugnone), 1290?-1349, Italian; poetry ST

FAJARDO FERNANDEZ, Enrique ('Fabián Vidal'), 1884-1946?, Spanish; journalism SA

FAKHR, Al-Din Jurjani, As'ad, 11th cent., Persian; poetry ST

FAKHR, Eddin, -1329, Arab; poetry SA

FAKHRY, Majid, 1923- , Lebanese; nonfiction CON

'FAKIR, Falstaff' see WALLENGREN, Axel

FALACORA, Luigi, 1890- , Italian; poetry SA

FALAGUERA, Ibn Shemtob (Palquiera), 1225-95, Spanish; nonfiction ST

FALAIZE, Carolina Filiberta Jacquemain, 1792-1852, French; nonfiction SA

FALCANDO, Hugo, 12th cent., Italian; nonfiction ST

FALCÃO, Cristovão, 1515-53, Portuguese; poetry SA ST

FALCO of BENEVENTO, fl. 1100-50, Italian; nonfiction ST

'FALCON, Samuel' see SHAPIRO, Samuel

FALCON, William Dyche, 1932- , American; nonfiction CON

FALCON-BARKER, Ted, 1923- , French; nonfiction CON

'FALCONER, James' see KIRKUP, James

'FALCONER, Lance' see HAWKER, Mary

FALCONER, William, 1732-69, Scots; poetry BRO KB SA ST

FALCONET, Ambroise, -1817, French; nonfiction DIL

FALCONET, Camille, 1671-1762, French; nonfiction DIL

FALCONET, Etienne Maurice, 1716-91, French; nonfiction DIL

FALCONET, Françoise Cécile de Chaumont, 1738-1819, French; plays DIL

FALCONET, de la BELLONIE, 18th cent., French; nonfiction DIL

FALCONIA, Proba, 4th cent., Roman; poetry SA

FALECO, 2nd cent. B.C., Greek; poetry SA

FALENSKI, Felicjan Medard ('Felicjan'), 1825-1910, Polish; poetry, plays, fiction ST

FALERO, Frank, Jr., 1937- , American; nonfiction CON

FALIH RIFKI ATAY, 1894- , Turkish; essays ST

FALK, Charles John, 1899- , American; nonfiction CON

FALK, Elsa see ESCHERICH, Elsa F.

FALK, Irving A., 1921- , American; nonfiction CON

FALK, Johan Daniel, 1768-1826, German; nonfiction SA

FALK, Leslie, A., 1915- , American; nonfiction CON

FALK, Richard Anderson, 1930- , American; nonfiction CON

FALK, Signi Lenea, 1906- , American; nonfiction CON

FALK, Stanley Lawrence, 1927- , American; nonfiction CON

FALK, Ze'ev Wilhelm, 1923- , German-Israeli; nonfiction CON

'FALKBERGET, Johan Petter' (J. P. Lillebakken), 1879-1967, Norwegian; fiction COL FLE SA ST

'FALKLAND, Samuel' see HEIJERMANS, Herman

FALKNER, John Meade, 1858-1932, English; juveniles BRO DOY

FALKNER, Leonard, 1900- , American; nonfiction CON

FALKNER, Murray Charles, 1899- , American; nonfiction CON

FALK-ROENNE, Arne, 1920- ,

Danish; nonfiction CON

FALL, Bernard B., 1926-67, Austrian-American; nonfiction CON

FALL, Thomas, American; juveniles WA

'FALLADA, Hans' (Rudolf Ditzen), 1893-1947, German; fiction AL FLE HAR KAT KT JKU LEN SA ST

FALLAV, Wesner, 1907- , American; nonfiction CON

FALLER, Kevin, 1920- , Irish; poetry, fiction MUR

FALLERS, Lloyd A., 1925- , American; nonfiction CON

FALLERSLEBEN, Hoffmann von see HOFFMANN von FALLERSLEBEN, August H.

FALLET, Nicolas, 1753-1801, French; poetry, plays DIL

FALLET, René, 1927- , French; fiction DIF

FALLON, Diego, 1834-1905, Colombian; poetry MIN SA

'FALLON, Martin' see PATTERSON, Henry

FALLON, Padraic, 1905- , Irish; poetry, plays MUR ST

FALLS, Dr. Arthur Grand Pré, 1901- , American; nonfiction SCA

FALLS, Charles Buckles, 1874- , American; juveniles KJU WA

FALLS, Cyril Bentham, 1888- , Irish; nonfiction CON

FALLSTRÖM, Daniel, 1858-1937, Swedish; poetry COL SA

FALSTER, Christian, 1690-1752, Danish; essays ST

FALUDY, George, 1913- , Hungarian-English; nonfiction, poetry CON

FAMIN Pierre Noel, 1740/44-1830, French; nonfiction DIL

FAMULARO, Joseph John, 1922- , American; nonfiction CON

FAN CH'ENG-TA, 1126-93, Chinese; poetry SA ST

FAN Chung-yen, 989-1052, Chinese; poetry ST

FAN, Kuang Huan, 1932- , Chinese-American; nonfiction CON

FANCUTT, Walter, 1911- , English; nonfiction CON

FANDLI, Juro, 1750-1811, Slovak; nonfiction ST

FANE, Julian Charles, 1927- , English; fiction CON

'FANE, Violet' see CURRIE, Lady Mary M.

FANG Hsiao-ju, 1357-1402, Chinese; nonfiction ST

FANG Pao, 1668-1749, Chinese; essays ST

FANGE, Augustin, 1709-84, French; nonfiction DIL

FANGEN, Ronald August, 1895-1946, Norwegian; fiction, plays, criticism FLE HAR SA ST

FANGER, Donald Lee, 1929- , American; nonfiction CON

FANNING, Leonard Multeken, 1888-1967, American; nonfiction CON

FANSHAWE, Anne Harrison, 1625-80, English; nonfiction, diary KB SA

FANSHAWE, Catherine Maria, 1765-1834, English; poetry BRO KBA

FANSHAWE, Sir Richard, 1608-66, English; translations, poetry BL BRO KB ST

FANT, Joseph Lewis III, 1928- , American; nonfiction CON

FANT, Louis Judson, Jr., 1931- , American; nonfiction CON

FANTA, J. Julius, 1907- , American; nonfiction CON

'FANTAZY' see GOMULICKI, Wiktor

FANTE, John Thomas, 1911- , American; fiction KT

FANTIN des ODOARDS, Antonio Esteban Nicolás, 1738-1820, French; nonfiction SA

FANTONI, Giovanni, 1755-1807, Italian; poetry HAR SA ST

FANU, Joseph Sheridan Lee see LE FANU, Joseph S.

FAQANI, Baba, -1519, Persian; poetry ST

FARABI (Alfarabi), 870-950, Arab; nonfiction SA ST

FARADAY, Michael, 1791-1867, English; nonfiction BRO KBA ST

FARADI, Abu-l-waled, 962-1013, Arab; nonfiction SA

'FARALLA, Dana' (Dorothy Wien), 1909- , American; fiction WAF

FARAZDAQ, -728/30, Arab; poetry LAN ST

FARB, Peter, 1929- , American; nonfiction CON

FARBER, Bernard, 1922- , Amer-

ican; nonfiction CON

FARBER, Donald C., American;
nonfiction CON

FARBER, Joseph C., 1903- ,
American; nonfiction CON

FARBEROW, Norman Louis, 1918- ,
American; nonfiction CON

FARCA, Marie C., 1935- , American; fiction CON

FARDEAU, Louis Gabriel, 1730-1806,
French; poetry, plays DIL

FARDIVEAU, René Marie Auguste
see BOYLESVE, René

'FAREL, Conrad' see BARDENS,
Dennis C.

FARER, Tom J., 1935- , American; nonfiction CON

FAREWELL, Nina see COOPER,
Mae K.

FARGIS, Paul McKenna, 1939- ,
American; nonfiction CON

'FARGO, Doone' see NORWOOD,
Victor G. C.

'FARGO, Joe' see RIKHOFF, James
C.

FARGO, Lucille Foster, 1880- ,
American; juveniles WA

FARGUE, León Paul, 1876-1947,
French; poetry COL DIF FLE
HAR MAL SA ST

FARGUS, Frederic, John ('Hugh
Conway'), 1847-85, English;
fiction KBA

FARIA, Manuel Severim de, 1583-
1653, Portuguese; nonfiction
SA

FARIA, Tomé de, 1558-1628,
Portuguese; nonfiction SA

FARIA y SOUZA, Manuel, 1590-
1640/49, Portuguese; nonfiction
SA ST

FARIAS BRITO, Raimundo de, 1863-
1917, Brazilian; nonfiction SA

FARICY, Robert Leo, 1926- ,
American; nonfiction CON

FARIDI, Shah Nasiruddin Mohammad,
1929- , Indian; fiction CON

FARIDU-DIN Atar see FERIO-EDDIN,
Mohammed

FARIES, Clyde J., 1928- , American; nonfiction CON

FARIGOULE, Louis see 'ROMAINS,
Jules'

FARIN de HAUTEMER, 18th cent.,
French; plays DIL

'FARINA, Abel' see RESTREPO,
Antonio M.

FARINA, Salvatore, 1846-1918,

Italian; fiction COL SA ST

FARIÑA NUÑEZ, Eloy, 1885-1929,
Paraguayan; poetry SA

FARINELLI, Arturo, 1867-1948,
Italian; nonfiction BL SA

FARIS, John T., 1871-1949,
American; nonfiction, journalism HOO

FARIS, Robert E. Lee, 1907- ,
American; nonfiction CON

FARISH, Margaret Kennedy,
1918- , American; nonfiction
CON

FARJEON, Benjamin Leopold,
1838-1903, English; fiction
KBA

FARJEON, Eleanor ('Chimaera';
'Tomfool'), 1881-1965, English;
juveniles COM CON DOY HO
KJU KT RIC WA

FARJEON, Herbert, 1887-1945/46,
English; criticism, plays BRO
RIC

FARJEON, Joseph J., 1883- ,
English; fiction KT

FARLEY, Eugene J., 1916- ,
American; nonfiction CON

FARLEY, Harriet ('Harriot Curtis),
1817-1907, American; nonfiction
KAA

FARLEY, James Aloysius, 1888- ,
American; nonfiction HO

FARLEY, Jean, 1928- , American; poetry CON

FARLEY, Robert (Farlie), fl.
1638, Scots; poetry ST

FARLEY, Walter, 1915- , American; juveniles COM CON KJU
WA

'FARMACEVTEN' see HOLM, Sven
A.

FARMER, Albert J., 1894- ,
Anglo-French; nonfiction CON

FARMER, Bernard James ('Owen
Fox'), 1902- , American;
fiction, nonfiction CON

FARMER, John, 1789-1838, American; nonfiction KAA

FARMER, Martha Louise, 1912- ,
American; nonfiction CON

FARMER, Penelope, 1939- ,
American; juveniles CON WA

'FARMER, Peter' see LLOYD,
John I.

FARMER, Philip Jose, 1918- ,
American; fiction CON

'FARMER, R. L.' see LAMONT,
Rosette C.

FARMER, Richard, 1735-97, English;
nonfiction BRO
FARMER, Richard Neil, 1928- ,
American; nonfiction CON
FARMER, Robert Allen, 1938- ,
American; nonfiction CON
'FARMER, Wendell' see DAVIS,
Lavinia R.
'FARNASH, Hugh' see LUFF,
Stanley G. A.
FARNBOROUGH, Baron see MAY,
Sir Thomas E.
FARNDALE, William Arthur James,
1916- , English; nonfiction
CON
'FARNHAM, Burt' see CLIFFORD,
Harold B.
FARNHAM, Eliza Woodson Burhans,
1815-64, American; nonfiction,
fiction, essays KAA
FARNHAM, Thomas Jefferson, 1804-
48, American; nonfiction KAA
FARNOL, John Jeffrey, 1878-1952,
English; fiction BRO KL KT RIC
FARNSWORTH, Edward Allan, 1928- ,
American; nonfiction CON
FARNSWORTH, Jerry, 1895- ,
American; nonfiction CON
FARNSWORTH, Lee Winfield,
1932- , American; nonfiction
CON
FARNSWORTH, Paul Randolph, 1899- ,
American; nonfiction CON
FARNUM, Mabel Adelaide, American;
nonfiction HOE
'FARNWALD' see STRUBBERG,
Friedrich
FARON, Louis C., 1923- , Ameri-
can; nonfiction CON
FARQUHAR, Francis Peloubet,
1887- , American; nonfiction
CON
FARQUHAR, George, 1678-1707,
English; plays BRO KB MAG
SA ST
FARQUHARSON, Martha see FINLEY,
Martha
FARR, David M. L., 1922- ,
Canadian; nonfiction CON
FARR, Diana Pullein-Thompson,
English; juveniles CON
'FARR, Douglas' see GILFORD,
Charles B.
FARR, Finis King, 1904- , Ameri-
can; nonfiction CON
FARR, Judith, 1936- , American;
nonfiction CON
FARR, Michael, 1924- , English;

nonfiction CON
FARR, Roger C., American;
nonfiction CON
FARRA, Madame E. see FAW-
CETT, Frank D.
FARRANT, Leda, 1927- , Italian;
fiction CON
FARRAR, Frederic William, 1831-
1903, English; juveniles, fic-
tion BRO DOY KBA ST
FARRAR Larston Dawn, 1915-70,
American; nonfiction CON
FARRAR, Ronald Truman, 1935- ,
American; nonfiction CON
FARRELL, Alan, 1920- , English;
nonfiction CON
FARRELL, Anne A., 1916- ,
American; juveniles CON
'FARRELL, Ben' see CEBULASH,
Mel
FARRELL, Catharine see O'CON-
NOR, Sister Mary C.
'FARRELL, David' see SMITH,
Frederick E.
'FARRELL, Desmond' see ORGAN,
John
FARRELL, James Thomas
('Jonathan Titulescu Fogarty,
Esq.'), 1904- , American;
fiction, essays BRO CON
FLE HOO KT MAG RIC ST
WAF
FARRELL, Kathleen Amy, 1912- ,
English; fiction CON
FARRELL, Kirby, 1942- , Amer-
ican; fiction CON
'FARRELL, M.J.' (Mrs. R. L.
Keane), 1905- , Irish; non-
fiction HIG
FARRELL, Melvin Lloyd, 1930- ,
American; nonfiction CON
FARRELL, Walter, 1902- , Amer-
ican; nonfiction HOE
FARRELLY, Mark John, 1927- ,
American; nonfiction CON
FARREN, Robert ('Roibeard
O'Farachain), 1909- , Irish;
poetry, criticism HOE MUR
ST
FARRER, Bryan David, 1906- ,
English; nonfiction CON
FARRER, Katharine Dorothy New-
man, 1911- , English; transla-
tions, fiction CON
'FARRERE, Claude' (Frédéric
Charles Pierre Edouard Bar-
gone), 1867-1957, French;
fiction, essays DIF FLE HAR
ST

FARRINGTON, Selwyn Kip, 1904- ,
American; juveniles WA

FARRIS, Martin Theodore, 1925- ,
American; nonfiction CON

FARRIS, Paul L., 1919- , American; nonfiction CON

FARRISON, William Edward,
1902- , American; nonfiction
CON

FARRISS, Nancy Marguerite,
1938- , American; nonfiction
CON

FARROW, George Edward, 1866-
1920?, English; juvenile DOY

FARROW, John Villiers, 1904- ,
Australian; nonfiction HOE

FARRUKHI, Abu'l Hasan, -1037/38,
Persian; poetry LAN SA ST

FARSON, Negley, 1890- , American;
journalism, fiction KT

FARUK NAFIZ CAMLIBEL, 1898- ,
Turkish; poetry ST

FARWELL, Byron E., 1921- ,
American; nonfiction CON

FARWELL, George Michell, 1911- ,
English; nonfiction CON

FARZAD, 1910- , Persian; poetry,
translations LAN ST

FASANA, Paul James, 1933- ,
American; nonfiction CON

FASEL, George William, 1938- ,
American; nonfiction CON

FASOLD, Ralph William August,
1940- , American; nonfiction
CON

FASOLO, Ugo, 1905- , Italian;
poetry SA

FAST, Howard Melvin ('Walter
Ericson'; 'E.V. Cunningham),
1914- , American; fiction CON
KTS RIC WA WAF

FAST, Julius ('Adam Barnett'),
1919- , American; nonfiction
CON

FASTENRATH, Juan, 1839-1908,
German; nonfiction BL

FASTOUL, Baude, 13th cent.,
French; poetry ST

FATCHEN, Max, 1920- , Australian;
juveniles CON

FATIO, Louise, 1904- , Swiss-American; juveniles CON FUL

FATONE, Vicente, 1903- , Argentinian; essays SA

FATOUROS, Arghyrios A., 1932- ,
Greek-American; nonfiction
CON

FATOUT, Paul, 1897- , American;

nonfiction CON

FAUCHARD de GRAND Ménil,
Jean B. see GRAND-MESNIL,
Jean B.

FAUCHER de SAINT, Maurier,
1844-97, Canadian; nonfiction
SY

FAUCHET, Claude, 1530-1601/02,
French; nonfiction DIF SA
ST

FAUCHET, Claude, 1744-93,
French; nonfiction DIL

FAUCHOIS, René, 1882-1962,
French; plays, poetry MAT

FAUCONNIER, Genoveva, French;
fiction SA

FAUCONNIER, Henri, 1879/85- ,
French; fiction DIF KT SA

FAUGERES, Marguerite Bleecher,
1771-1801, American; nonfiction SA

FAUJAS de SAINT FOND, Barthélemy, 1741-1819, French;
nonfiction DIL

FAULHABER, Martha, 1926- ,
American; nonfiction CON

FALHABER, Michael, 1869- ,
German; nonfiction HOE

FAULK, Odie B., 1933- , American; nonfiction CON

FAULKNER, Anne Irvin see
FAULKNER, Nancy I.

FAULKNER, Charles, H., 1937- ,
American; nonfiction CON

FAULKNER, Harold Underwood,
1890- , American; nonfiction
CON

FAULKNER, John, 1901-63, American; fiction CON

FAULKNER, Nancy Irvin (Anne),
1906- , American; juveniles
CON WA

FAULKNER, Peter, 1933- ,
English; nonfiction CON

FAULKNER, Ray Nelson, 1906- ,
American; nonfiction CON

FAULKNER, William, 1897-1962,
American; fiction, poetry BRO
FLE KL KT MAG MAT RIC
SA ST WAF

FAULKNOR, Clifford Vernon
('Pete Williams'), 1913- ,
Canadian; juveniles CON

FAUNCE, Roland Cleo, 1905- ,
American; nonfiction CON

FAUNCE, William Alden, 1928- ,
American; nonfiction CON

FAUPEL, John Francis, 1906- ,

English; nonfiction CON

FAUQUE, Henry, -1752, French; nonfiction DIL

FAUQUES, Marianne Agnès de, 1720-77/89, French; nonfiction DIL SA

FAUR, Louis François, 1746/55-1815, French; plays DIL

FAURE, Elie, 1873-1937, French; criticism, nonfiction COL DIF KAT KT SA

FAURE, Pierre Joseph Denis Guillaume, 1726-1818, French; nonfiction DIL

FAURE, Raoul Cohen, 1909- , Egyptian-American; fiction KTS WAF

FAURIEL, Claude Charles, 1772-1844, French; criticism SA

FAURIS de SAINT-VINCENS, Jules François Paul, 1718-98, French; nonfiction DIL

FAUROT, Jean Hiatt, 1911- , American; nonfiction CON

FAUSET, Arthur Huff, American; nonfiction CON

FAUSET, Jessie Redmon, 1884?- , American; fiction KT

FAUSOLD, Martin L., 1921- , American; nonfiction CON

FAUSSET, Hugh l'Anson, 1895- , English; criticism, poetry BRO KT

FAUST, Albert Bernhard, 1870-1951, German-American; poetry ST

FAUST, Frederick see 'BRAND, Max'

FAUST, Irvin, 1924- , American; fiction CON

FAUSTBUCH, 16th cent., German; nonfiction AL

FAUTH, Robert T., 1916- , American; nonfiction CON

FAVA, Guido (Faba), 1200-50, Italian; nonfiction ST

FAVART, Charles Nicolas Joseph Justin, 1749-1806, French; plays DIL

FAVART, Charles Simon, 1710-92, French; plays DIL HAR SA ST

FAVART, Marie Justine Benoite Cabaret du Ronceray, 1727-72, French; plays DIL

FAVART d'HERBIGNY, Christophe Elisú, 1727-93, French; nonfiction DIL

FAVETTI, Carlo, 1819-92, Raeto-Romansch; poetry ST

FAVIER, Jean Louis, 1720-84,

French; nonfiction DIL

FAVIER de BOULAT, Henri, 1670-1753, French; nonfiction DIL

FAVILLE, David Ernest, 1899- , American; nonfiction CON

FAVORINO, -137, Roman; nonfiction SA

FAVORINO (Varino; Guarino), 1460- , Italian; nonfiction SA

FAVRET, Andrew G., 1925- , American; nonfiction CON

FAWCETT, Clara Hallard, 1897- , English; nonfiction CON

FAWCETT, Edgar, 1847-1904, American; poetry, fiction, plays KAA

FAWCETT, Frank Dubrez ('Henri Dupres'; 'Madame E. Farra'; 'Eugene Glen'; 'Griff'; 'Coolidge McCann'; 'Elmer Eliot Saks'; 'Ben Sarto'; 'Simpson Stokes'), 1891- , English; nonfiction, fiction CON

FAWCETT, Henry, 1833-84, English; nonfiction BRO KBA ST

FAWCETT, Marion, 1931- , American; nonfiction CON

FAWCETT, William Claude, 1902-41, English; nonfiction HIG

FAWKES, Francis, 1721-77, English; poetry BRO ST

FAX, Elton Clay, 1909- , American; nonfiction CON

'FAXON, Lavinia' see RUSS, Lavinia

FAY, András, 1786-1864, Hungarian; fiction, essays HAR ST

FAY, Frederic Leighton, 1890- , American; nonfiction CON

FAY, Gerard Francis Arthur, 1913- , English; nonfiction CON

FAY, Leo Charles, 1920- , American; nonfiction CON

'FAY, Mary Helen' see FAGYAS, Maria

FAY, Sidney Bradshaw, 1876- , American; nonfiction KT

FAY, Stephen, 1938- , American; nonfiction CON

FAY, Theodore, Sedgwick, 1807-98, American; poetry KAA

FAY, Bernard, 1893- , French; nonfiction KT

FAYER, Mischa Harry, 1902- ,
American; nonfiction CON
FAYERWEATHER, John, 1922- ,
American; nonfiction CON
FAYZI, Abu'l Fayz, 1547-95,
Persian; poetry ST
FAZAKERLEY, George Raymond,
1921- , English; fiction CON
FAZIL Hüsnü Daglarca, 1912- ,
Turkish; poetry ST
FAZIO, Bartolomeo, 1400-57, Italian;
nonfiction SA ST
FAZIO degli UBERTI see UBERTI,
Fazio degli
FAZOL, Muhammad Abul, 1939- ,
Pakistani; nonfiction CON
FAZZANO, Joseph E. ('John Fitz-
gerald'), 1929- , American;
nonfiction CON
FEA, Henry Robert, 1914- ,
Canadian-American; nonfiction
PAC
FEAGIN Joe Richard, 1938- ,
American; nonfiction CON
FEAGLES, Anita MacRae ('Francis
MacRae'), 1926- , American;
fiction, juveniles CON WA
FEAGLES, Elizabeth see DAY, Beth
F.
FEAGUE, Mildred H., 1915- ,
American; juveniles CON
FEAL-DEIBE, Carlos, 1935- ,
Spanish-American; nonfiction
CON
FEARING, Kenneth Flexner, 1902/06-
61, American; fiction, poetry,
journalism HOO KT SA WAF
FEARON, George Edward, 1901- ,
English; nonfiction CON
FEARON, John Daniel, 1920- ,
American; nonfiction CON
FEARON, Peter Shaun, 1942- ,
English; nonfiction CON
FEATHERSTONE, Joseph Luke,
1940- , American; nonfiction
CON
'FEATHERSTONEHAUGH, Francis'
see Mac GREGOR, Alasdair A.
FEAVER, George Arthur, 1937- ,
Canadian; nonfiction CON
FEAVER, John Clayton, 1911- ,
American; nonfiction CON
FEBVRE, Lucien, 1878-1956,
French; nonfiction DIF
FECHNER, Gustav Theodor, 1801-
87, German; nonfiction, criticism
SA
FECHTER, Alyce Shinn, 1909- ,

American; juveniles CON
FECHTER, Paul, 1880- , Ger-
man; nonfiction LEN
FEDDE, Norman Andreas, 1914- ,
American; nonfiction CON
FEDDEN, Robin ('Henry Romilly'),
1908- , British; poetry fic-
tion CON MUR
FEDDER, Edwin Hersh, 1929- ,
American; nonfiction CON
FEDDER, Norman Joseph,
1934- , American; nonfiction,
plays CON
FEDDER, Ruth, 1907- , Ameri-
can; nonfiction CON
FEDELE, Alejandro Cassandra
Mapelli (Fidele), 1465-1558,
Italian; nonfiction SA
FEDELI, Aurelia, 12th cent.,
Italian; poetry SA
FEDER, Bernard, 1924- ,
American; nonfiction CON
FEDER, Ernest, 1913- , German-
American; nonfiction CON
FEDER, Karah Tal, 1920- ,
Dutch-English; juveniles CON
FEDERER, Heinrich, 1866-1928,
Swiss; fiction, essays AL
COL FLE LEN SA
FEDERMAN, Raymond, 1928- ,
Franco-American; nonfiction
CON
FEDIN, Konstantin Alexandrovich,
1892- , Russian; fiction COL
FLE HAR HARK RIC SA ST
FEDON, 4th cent. B.C., Greek;
nonfiction SA
FEDOROFF, Alexander, 1927- ,
American; nonfiction CON
FEDRO, 10-70, Roman; fiction
SA
FEDRO, 1st cent. B.C., Roman;
nonfiction SA
FEEHAN, Agnes M. see 'CLE-
MENTIA'
FEELEY, Kathleen, 1929- ,
American; nonfiction CON
FEENEY, Leonard, 1897- ,
American; poetry, fiction HOE
FEENEY, Rev. Thomas Butler,
American; fiction, poetry HO
FEENSTRA, Henry John, 1936- ,
Canadian; nonfiction CON
FEERICK, John David, 1936- ,
American; nonfiction CON
FEFFER, Itzik, 1900?-48, Jewish;
poetry LAN ST
FEGAN, Camilla, 1939- , English;

juveniles CON
FEHL, Philipp Pinhas, 1920- ,
    Austrian-American; nonfiction
    CON
FEHREN, Henry, 1920- ,
    American; nonfiction CON
FEHRENBACH, Theodore Reed, Jr.,
    1725- , American; nonfiction
    CON
FEHRENBACHER, Don E., 1920- ,
    American; nonfiction CON
FEHRS, Johann Hinrich, 1838-1916,
    German; poetry ST
FEIBLEMAN, James Kern, 1904- ,
    American; nonfiction CON KTS
FEIED, Frederick James, 1925- ,
    American; nonfiction CON
FEIFFER, Jules, 1929- , American;
    nonfiction CON
FEIGELSON, Naomi R., 1932- ,
    American; nonfiction CON
FEIGENBAUM, Lawrence H., 1918- ,
    American; nonfiction CON
FEIGL, Herbert, 1902- , American;
    nonfiction CON
FEIJO, Antonio Joquim de Castro,
    1862-1917, Portuguese; poetry
    COL HAR SA ST
FEIJOO y MONTENEGRO, Benito
    Jerónimo (Feyjóo), 1676-1764,
    Spanish; essays BL HAR KE
    SA ST
'FEIKEMA, Feike' see MANFRED,
    Frederick F.
FEIL, Hila, 1942- , American;
    juveniles CON
FEILDING, Charles Rudolph,
    1902- , Canadian; nonfiction
    CON
FEIN, Leonard J., 1934- , Ameri-
    can; nonfiction CON
FEINBERG, Abraham L., 1899- ,
    American; nonfiction CON
FEINBERG, Barry Vincent, 1938- ,
    South African; poetry CON
FEINBERG, Gerald, 1933- , Amer-
    ican; nonfiction CON
FEINBERG, Joel, 1926- , American;
    nonfiction CON
FEINBERG, Leonard, 1914- , Amer-
    ican; nonfiction CON
FEINGOLD, Eugene Neil, 1931- ,
    American; nonfiction CON
FEINGOLD, Henry Leo, 1931- ,
    German-American; nonfiction
    CON
FEINGOLD, Jessica, 1910- ,
    American; nonfiction CON

FEINGOLD, S. Norman, 1914- ,
    American; nonfiction CON
FEINSILVER, Alexander, 1910- ,
    American; nonfiction CON
FEINSILVER, Lillian Mermin,
    1917- , American; nonfiction
    CON
FEINSTEIN, Alan Shawn, 1931- ,
    American; nonfiction CON
FEINSTEIN, Moishe, 1897- ,
    Jewish; poetry ST
FEIRBERG, Mordechai Zeib,
    1874-99, Jewish; fiction ST
FEIS, Herbert, 1893-1973,
    American; nonfiction CON
FEIS, Ruth Stanley-Brown, 1892- ,
    American; nonfiction CON
FEISE, Ernst, 1884-1966, German-
    American; nonfiction CON
FEISILBER, Ilya see 'ILF, Ilya'
FEIT, Ewald Edward, 1924- ,
    Austrian-American; nonfiction
    CON
FEITAMA, Sijbrand (Feitcama),
    1694-1758, Dutch; criticism,
    translations SA ST
FEITELSON, Menachem Mendel,
    1870-1912, Jewish; nonfiction
    ST
FEITH, Herbert, 1930- , Aus-
    tralian; nonfiction CON
FEITH, Rhijnvis, 1753-1824,
    Dutch; poetry HAR KE SA
    ST
FEIWEL, George Richard, 1929- ,
    Polish-Canadian; nonfiction
    CON
FEJER, Jorge, 1766-1852,
    Hungarian; nonfiction SA
FEJES, Claire, 1920- , American;
    nonfiction CON
FEJES, Endre, 1923- , Hungar-
    ian-American; fiction CON
FEJTO François Philippe,
    1909- , Hungarian-French;
    nonfiction CON
FELD, Michael, 1938- , English;
    fiction CON
FELD, Ross, 1947- , American;
    poetry CON
FELD, Werner Joachim, 1910- ,
    German-American; nonfiction
    CON
FELDER, Raoul Lionel, 1934- ,
    American; nonfiction CON
FELDMAN, Burton, 1926- ,
    American; nonfiction CON
FELDMAN, Edmund Burke,

1924- , American; nonfiction
CON
FELDMAN, Edwin Barry, 1925- ,
American; nonfiction CON
FELDMAN, George Jay, 1904- ,
American; nonfiction CON
FELDMAN, Gerald Donald, 1937- ,
American; nonfiction CON
FELDMAN, Herbert H.S. ('Ross
McLeod'), 1910- , English;
nonfiction, fiction CON
FELDMAN, Irving Mordecai, 1928- ,
American; poetry CON MUR
FELDMAN, Kenneth A., 1937- ,
American; nonfiction CON
FELDMAN, Samuel Nathan, 1931- ,
American; nonfiction CON
FELDMAN, Solomon E., 1933- ,
American; nonfiction CON
FELDZAMEN, Alvin Norman,
1931- , American; nonfiction
CON
FELHEIM, Marvin, 1914- , Ameri-
can; nonfiction CON
FELIBIEN, André, 1619-95, French;
nonfiction SA
FELIBIEN, Jean François, 1658-1733,
French; nonfiction DIL
FELIBIEN D'AVAUX, Michel, 1665- ,
French; nonfiction DIL
FELICE, Fortuné Barthélemy, 1723-
89, French; nonfiction DIL
'FELICJAN' see FALENSKI, Felicjan
M.
FELINSKI, Alojzy, 1771-1820, Polish;
poetry, plays ST
FELIPE, Carlos, 1914- , Cuban;
fiction, plays SA
FELIPE, León, 1884- , Spanish;
poetry BL
FELIPE CAMINO, León, 1884- ,
Spanish; poetry SA
FELIPE TRIGO see TRIGO, Felipe
FELIU y CODINA, José, 1847-97,
Spanish; plays BL HAR SA ST
FELKER, Jere L., 1934- , Ameri-
can; nonfiction CON
FELKNOR, Bruce Lester, 1921- ,
American; nonfiction CON
FELL, Howard Barraclough, 1917- ,
American; nonfiction CON
FELL, Dr. John, 1625-96, English;
editor KB
FELL, Joseph Phineas III, 1931- ,
American; nonfiction CON
FELLER, François Xavier de,
1735-1802, French; nonfiction
DIL

FELLER, Robert William Andrew,
1918- , American; juveniles
WA
FELLNER, Rudolph, American;
juveniles WA
FELLNER, William John, 1905- ,
Hungarian-American; nonfiction
CON
'FELLOWES, Anne' see MANTLE,
Winifred L.
FELLOWES-GORDON, Ian Douglas
('Douglas Collier'; 'Ian
Gordon'), 1921- , English;
fiction CON
FELLOWS, Brian John, 1936- ,
English; nonfiction CON
FELLOWS, Sir Charles, 1799-
1860, English; nonfiction KBA
FELLOWS, Hugh P., 1915- ,
American; fiction CON
FELLOWS, Malcolm Stuart, 1924- ,
English; nonfiction CON
FELLOWS, Muriel H., American;
juveniles WA
FELLOWS, Otis Edward, 1908- ,
American; nonfiction CON
FELLTHAM, Owen, 1602?-68,
English; essays, poetry BRO
KB ST
FELS, Rendigs, 1917- , American;
nonfiction CON
FELSEN, Henry Gregor ('Angus
Vicker'), 1916- , American;
juveniles COM CON KJU WA
FELSHER, Howard D., 1927- ,
American; nonfiction CON
FELT, Jeremy Pollard, 1930- ,
American; nonfiction CON
FELT, Joseph Barlow, 1789-1869,
American; nonfiction KAA
FELT, Margaret Elley, 1917- ,
American; nonfiction CON PAC
FELTER, Emma K. Schroeder,
1896- , American; nonfiction
CON
FELTON, Cornelius Conway, 1807-
62, American; nonfiction KAA
FELTON, Harold William, 1902- ,
American; juveniles COM CON
FUL WA
FELTON, Mrs. Haleemon Shaik,
1913- , American; plays,
poetry SCA
FELTON, Ronald Oliver ('Ronald
Welch'), 1909- , Welsh;
fiction CON DOY
'FELTRE, Vittorino da' see
RAMBALDONI, Vittorino

FELTSKOG, Elmer N., 1935- ,
American; nonfiction CON
FELVER, Charles Stanley, 1916- ,
American; nonfiction CON
FEMIANO, Samuel D., 1932- ,
American; nonfiction CON
'FEMORA' see BRODEY, James M.
FENANDER, Elliot Watkins, 1938- ,
American; nonfiction CON
FENAROLI, Camila Solar de Asti,
18th cent., Italian; poetry SA
FENBY, Eric William, 1906- ,
English; nonfiction CON
FENEL, Charles Maurice,   -1720,
French; nonfiction DIL
FENEL, Jean Baptiste Pascal, 1695-
1753, French; nonfiction DIL
FENELON, François de Salignac de
Salignac de la Mothe, 1651-1715,
French; fiction DIF DIL HAR
KE MAL SA ST
FENELON, Gabriel Jacques de
Salignac, 1688- , French; non-
fiction DIL
FENEON, Félix, 1861-1944, French;
criticism DIF
FENESTELLA, 52-19 B.C., Roman;
nonfiction ST
FENESTRE de HOTOT, Pierre,
-1785, French; nonfiction
DIL
FENG, Meng-Lung, 1574-1645, Chi-
nese; nonfiction SA ST
FENG Fao, 882-954, Chinese; non-
fiction ST
FENIGER, Siegmund see 'NYANAPO-
NIKA'
FENIN, George Nicolaievich, 1916- ,
Russian-American; nonfiction
CON
FENLON, Paul Edward, 1921- ,
American; nonfiction CON
FENN, Charles Henry, 1907- ,
English; plays, fiction CON
FENN, Dan Huntington, Jr., 1923- ,
American; nonfiction CON
FENN, George Manville, 1831-1907/09,
English; juveniles BRO DOY KBA
FENNELL, James, 1766-1816, Amer-
ican; plays KAA
FENNELL, John L.I., 1918- , Eng-
lish; nonfiction CON
FENNELLY, Catherine, 1918- ,
American; nonfiction CON
FENNER, Carol Elizabeth, 1929- ,
American; juveniles CON
FENNER, Harry Wolcott, 1911-72,
American; nonfiction CON

FENNER, James, 1923- , Amer-
ican; nonfiction CON
FENNER, Kay Toy, American;
nonfiction CON
FENNER, Mildred Sandison, 1910- ,
American; nonfiction CON
FENNER, Phyllis Reid, 1899- ,
American; juveniles COM CON
WA
FENNER, Theodore Lincoln,
1919- , American; nonfiction
CON
FENNO, Richard Francis, Jr.,
1926- , American; nonfiction
CON
FENOLLOSA, Ernest Francisco,
1853-1908, American; poetry
KAA
FENOUILLOT de FALBAIRE de
Quincey, Charles Georges,
1727-1800, French; plays DIL
FENSCH, Edwin A., 1903- ,
American; nonfiction CON
FENSCH, Thomas ('Lander Moore'),
1943- , American; nonfiction
CON
FENSTERMAKER, Joseph Van,
1933- , American; nonfiction
CON
FENTEN, Donald X., 1932- ,
American; juveniles, fiction
CON
FENTON, Carroll Lane, 1900-69,
American; juveniles CON FUL
WA
FENTON, Edward, 1917- , Amer-
ican; fiction CON WA
FENTON, Elijah, 1682-1730, Eng-
lish; poetry, translations BRO
KB ST
'FENTON, Freda' see ROWLAND,
Donald S.
FENTON, Sir Geoffrey, 1539?-
1608, English; translations KB
FENTON, John Charles, 1921- ,
English; nonfiction CON
FENTON, John Harold, 1921- ,
American; nonfiction CON
FENTON, Joseph Clifford, 1906- ,
American; nonfiction CON HOE
FENTON, Mildred Adams, 1899- ,
American; juveniles FUL WA
FENTON, Sophia Harvati, 1914- ,
Greek-American; nonfiction
CON
'FENWICK, Kay' see BEAN, Keith
F.
FEOFAN PROKOPOVICH, 1681-

1736, Russian; nonfiction, poetry
HARK ST
FERAOUN, Mouloud, 1913-62,
French; fiction DIC
FERAUD, Jean François, 1725-1807,
French; nonfiction DIL
FERAVOLO, Rocco Vincent, 1922- ,
American; juveniles CON WA
FERBER, Edna, 1887-1968, Ameri-
can; fiction, plays BRO CON
FLE HOO KL KT MAT RIC SA
ST WAF
FERBER, Robert, 1922- , American;
nonfiction CON
FERDINAND, Theodore Nichols,
1929- , American; nonfiction
CON
FERDON Edwin Nelson, Jr., 1913- ,
American; nonfiction CON
FERDUSI Abul see FIRDUSI
FERECIDES,   -543, Greek; nonfic-
tion SA
FERECIDES, de ATHENS, 5th cent.
B.C., Greek; nonfiction SA
FERECRATES, 438-   B.C., Greek;
poetry SA
FEREY, François Placide Nicolas,
1735-1807, French; nonfiction
DIL
FERGUSON, Adam, 1723-1816,
English; nonfiction BRO SA ST
FERGUSON, Alfred R., 1915- ,
American; nonfiction CON
FERGUSON, Arthur Bowles,
1913- , Canadian; nonfiction
CON
FERGUSON, Charles Elmo, 1928- ,
American; nonfiction CON
FERGUSON, Charles W. ('Hilton
Gregory'), 1901- , American;
nonfiction CON
FERGUSON, Clarence Clyde, Jr.,
1924- , American; nonfiction
CON
FERGUSON, Donald Nivison, 1882- ,
American; nonfiction CON
FERGUSON, Elva Shartel, American;
nonfiction MAR
FERGUSON, Evelyn C. ('Evelyn C.
Nevin'), 1910- , American;
juveniles CON PAC
FERGUSON, Everett, 1933- ,
American; nonfiction CON
FERGUSON, Howard, 1908- , Irish;
nonfiction CON
FERGUSON, James Milton, 1936- ,
American; nonfiction CON
FERGUSON, John, 1921- , English;

nonfiction CON
FERGUSON, John Halcro, 1920- ,
English; nonfiction CON
FERGUSON, John Henry, 1907- ,
American; nonfiction CON
FERGUSON, Lucia Caroline
Loomis, 1887- , American;
nonfiction MAR
FERGUSON Marilyn ('Marilyn
Renzelman'), 1938- , Ameri-
can; nonfiction CON
FERGUSON, Mike, 1934- , Amer-
ican; nonfiction CON
FERGUSON, Oliver Watkins,
1924- , American; nonfiction
CON
FERGUSON, Peter Roderick Innes,
1933- , American; fiction,
poetry, translations CON
FERGUSON, Robert Douglas,
1921- , Canadian; nonfiction
CON
FERGUSON, Sir Samuel, 1810-86,
Scots; poetry BRO KBA ST
FERGUSON, Thompson, B., 1857-
1921, American; nonfiction
MAR
FERGUSSON, Sir Bernard Edward,
1911- , English; fiction CON
FERGUSSON, Erna, 1888-1964,
American; nonfiction CON
FERGUSSON, Francis, 1904- ,
American; criticism CON
KTS
FERGUSSON, Harvey, 1890-1971,
American; fiction KL WAF
FERGUSSON, Henry, 1890- ,
American; fiction KT
FERGUSSON, James, 1808-86,
English; nonfiction BRO
FERGUSSON, Robert, 1750-74,
Scots; poetry BRO KB ST
FERGUSSON HANNAY, Lady
('Doris Oppenheim Leslie'),
English; fiction CON KT
'FERGUUT, Jan' see DROOGEN-
BROECK
FERICHTAH, Mohamed Casem,
16th cent., Arab; nonfiction
SA
FERIENCIK, Mikulas Stefan, 1825-
81, Slovak; fiction ST
FERIO-EDDIN, Mohamed Ben
Ibraaim (Faridu-Din Atar),
1119- , Persian; poetry SA
FERKISS, Victor Christopher,
1925- , American; nonfiction
CON

FERLAND, Albert, 1872-1943,
Canadian; poetry SY

FERLAND, Jean Baptiste Antoine,
1808-65, French-Canadian; nonfiction ST

FERLIN, Nils Johan Einar, 1898-
1961, Swedish; poetry FLE ST

FERLINGHETTI, Lawrence ('Lawrence
Ferling'), 1919- , American;
poetry, fiction, plays CON MUR
RIC

FERLITA, Ernest Charles, 1927- ,
American; plays CON

FERLUS, François, 1748-1812, French;
nonfiction DIL

FERM, Betty, 1926- , American;
fiction CON

FERM, Deane William, 1927- ,
American; nonfiction CON

FERM, Robert Livingston, 1931- ,
American; nonfiction CON

FERM, Vergilius Ture Anselm, 1896- ,
American; nonfiction CON

FERMI, Laura Capon, 1907- , Italian-American; juveniles CON WA

FERMIN, Philippe,   -1778?, French;
nonfiction DIL

FERMOR, Patrick Leigh, 1915- ,
English; fiction RIC

FERN, Alan Maxwell, 1930- ,
American; nonfiction CON

'FERN, Edna' (Fernande Osthaus
Richter), 1861-1941, German-
American; fiction ST

FERN, Eugene A., 1919- , American; juveniles CON

'FERN, Fanny' see PARTON, Sarah
P. W.

FERNALD, John Bailey, 1905- ,
American; plays CON

'FERNAN, Caballero' see 'CABAL-
LERO, Fernán'

FERNANDES, Joaquim Teófilo see
BRAGA, Teófilo

FERNANDES COSTA, José, 1848-
1920, Portuguese; poetry SA

FERNANDEZ, Bachiller Sebastián,
16th cent., Spanish; plays SA

FERNANDEZ, Francisco,   -1922,
Argentinian; plays MIN

FERNANDEZ, Jorge, 1912- ,
Ecuadorian; fiction DI

FERNANDEZ, Joseph A., 1921- ,
American; nonfiction CON

FERNANDEZ, Juan Rómulo, 1884- ,
Argentinian; journalism, essays
MIN SA

FERNANDEZ, Julio A.; 1936- ,

American; nonfiction CON

FERNANDEZ, León, 1840-87,
Costa Rican; nonfiction MIN

FERNANDEZ, Lope, 15th cent.,
Spanish; nonfiction BL

FERNANDEZ, Luca, 1474?-1542,
Spanish; plays BL SA ST

FERNANDEZ, Macedonio, 1874-
1952, Argentinian; essays
MIN

FERNANDEZ, Sebastian, 16th cent.,
Spanish; plays BL

FERNANDEZ ALMAGRO, Melchor,
1895- , Spanish; criticism
BL COL SA

FERNANDEZ ARDAVIN, Luis,
1891-1962, Spanish; poetry,
plays BL SA

FERNANDEZ ARIAS, Adelardo
('El Duende de la Colegiata'),
1880-1951, Spanish; journalism,
fiction, plays SA

FERNANDEZ BESCHTEDT, Domingo,
1889-1954, Argentinian; poetry,
journalism, essay MIN

FERNANDEZ BREMON, José,
1839-1910, Spanish; journalism,
plays BL SA

FERNANDEZ COLLADO, Diego,
1912- , Spanish; poetry,
journalism, fiction SA

FERNANDEZ CORIA, José, 1877-
1942, Argentinian; nonfiction
MIN

FERNANDEZ CUENCA, Carlos,
1904- , Spanish; nonfiction
BL SA

FERNANDEZ da PONTE, Pedro
see PONTE, Pero de

FERNANDEZ de ALARCON,
Cristobalina, 1573-1646,
Spanish; poetry SA

FERNANDEZ de ANDRADA, Andrés,
1560- , Spanish; poetry BL
SA

FERNANDEZ de AVELLANEDA,
Licenciado Alonso, 18th cent.,
Spanish; plays BL SA ST

FERNANDEZ de CASTRO, José
Antonio, 1897- , Cuban;
journalism, nonfiction MIN

FERNANDEZ de CASTRO, Rafael,
1856-1920, Cuban; nonfiction
MIN

FERNANDEZ de CORDOBA,
Fernando, 1809-83, Argentinian;
nonfiction BL

FERNANDEZ de COSTANTINA,

Juan, -1520?, Spanish;
poetry SA
FERNANDEZ de HEREDIA, Juan,
1310?-96, Spanish; nonfiction
BL SA
FERNANDEZ de JERENA, Garci
(Ferrandos), Spanish; poetry
BL
FERNANDEZ del la CONCHA, Rafael,
1833- , Chilean; poetry, non-
fiction MIN
FERNANDEZ de la MORA, Gonzalo,
1924- , Spanish; essays, criti-
cism SA
FERNANDEZ de la REGUERE,
Ricardo, 1916- , Spanish; fic-
tion BL CON SA
FERNANDEZ de LIZARDI, José
Joaquín, 1776/78-1817/27,
Mexican; fiction, journalism
BL MAG SA ST
FERNANDEZ de LOS RIOS, Angel,
1821-80, Spanish; journalism
SA
FERNANDEZ de MADRID, Alonso,
1475-1559, Spanish; nonfiction
SA
FERNANDEZ de MINAYA, Lope,
1410-85, Spanish; nonfiction SA
FERNANDEZ de MORATIN, Leandro,
1760-1828, Spanish; plays, poetry
BL HAR KE SA ST
FERNANDEZ de MORATIN, Nicolás,
1737-80, Spanish; poetry, plays
BL HAR SA ST
FERNANDEZ de NAVARRETE, Martín,
1765-1844, Spanish; nonfiction
SA
FERNANDEZ de OVIEDO, Gonzalo
(Hernandez), 1478-1557, Spanish;
nonfiction SA BL
FERNANDEZ de PALENCIA, Alonso
see PALENCIA, Alonso F. de
FERNANDEZ de RIBERA, Rodrigo,
1579-1631, Spanish; poetry, non-
fiction BL SA
FERNANDEZ de ROJAS, Juan, 1750?-
1819, Spanish; poetry BL SA
FERNANDEZ de SAN Pedro, Diego
see SAN PEDRO, Diego de
FERNANDEZ de VELASCO, Bernardi-
no, 1701-69?, Spanish; poetry
SA
FERNANDEZ de VELASCO y PIMEN-
TAL, Bernardino (Duque de
Frias), 1783-1851, Spanish;
poetry BL HAR SA ST
FERNANDEZ del VILLAR, José,

1888-1945?, Spanish; plays
SA
FERNANDEZ de VILLEGAS,
Pedro, 1453-1536, Spanish;
poetry SA
FERNANDEZ ESPIRO, Diego,
1870/72-1912, Argentinian;
journalism MIN
FERNANDEZ ESPINO, José,
1809?-75, Spanish; poetry,
criticism, plays SA
FERNANDEZ FLORES, Darío,
1909- , Spanish; fiction BL
SA
FERNANDEZ FLORES, Isidoro
('Fernanflor'), 1840-1902,
Spanish; journalism BL SA
FERNANDEZ FLOREZ, Wenceslao,
1879/86-1964, Spanish; fic-
tion, criticism BL COL FLE
HAR SA ST
FERNANDEZ GRILO, Antonio,
1845-1926, Spanish; poetry,
journalism BL SA
FERNANDEZ GUARDIA, Ricardo,
1867-1950, Costa Rican; non-
fiction MIN SA
FERNANDEZ GÜELL, Rogelio,
1868-1918, Costa Rican; poetry,
essays MIN
FERNANDEZ GUERRA y ORBE,
Aureliano, 1816-91/94,
Spanish; criticism, plays,
journalism BL SA
FERNANDEZ GUERRA y ORBE,
Luis, 1818-90, Spanish; criti-
cism, plays SA
FERNANDEZ MADRID, José,
1789-1830, Colombian; poetry,
plays MIN SA
FERNANDEZ MARTIN, Cristóbal,
1892- , Spanish; nonfiction
SA
FERNANDEZ MONTALVA, Ricardo,
1866-99, Chilean; poetry MIN
FERNANDEZ MONTESINOS, José,
1897- , Spanish; nonfiction,
poetry, plays BL
FERNANDEZ MORENO, Baldomero,
1886-1950, Argentinian; nonfic-
tion, poetry MIN SA
FERNANDEZ MORENO, César,
1919- , Argentinian; poetry
MIN SA
FERNANDEZ MORENO, Manrique,
1928- , Argentinian; poetry
SA
FERNANDEZ NICOLAS, Severiano,

1920- , Spanish; fiction SA
FERNANDEZ NIETO, José María,
1920- , Spanish; poetry, journal-
ism SA
FERNANDEZ ORTELLANO, Manuel,
17th cent., Chilean; plays MIN
FERNANDEZ PEIDRAHITA, Lucas,
1624-88, Colombian; nonfiction
MIN
FERNANDEZ POUSA, Ramón, 1909- ,
Spanish; nonfiction BL
FERNANDEZ RAMIREZ, Salvador,
1896- , Spanish; nonfiction BL
SA
FERNANDEZ RUA, José Luis,
1916- , Spanish; nonfiction SA
FERNANDEZ SAAVEDRA, Manuel,
1796-1877, Colombian; nonfiction
MIN
FERNANDEZ SANTOS, Jesús, 1926- ,
Spanish; fiction BL SA
FERNANDEZ SANZ, Manuel, 1909- ,
Spanish; poetry SA
FERNANDEZ SHAW, Carlos, 1865-
1911, Spanish; poetry, plays
BL SA
FERNANDEZ SHAW, Guillermo,
1893- , Spanish; journalism,
plays SA
FERNANDEZ SPENCER, Antonio,
1922- , Dominican; poetry SA
FERNANDEZ VILLEGAS, Francisco
('Zeda'), 1856-1916, Spanish;
criticism, journalism, plays SA
FERNANDEZ y GONZALEZ, Fran-
cisco, 1833-1917, Spanish; non-
fiction SA
FERNANDEZ y GONZALEZ, Manuel,
1821-88, Spanish; fiction BL
COL SA ST
FERNANDO, Patrick, 1931- ,
Ceylonese; poetry MUR
'FERNANFLOR' see FERNANDEZ
FLORES, Isidoro
FERNEA, Elizabeth Warnock, 1927- ,
American; nonfiction CON
FERNEA, Robert Alan, 1932- ,
American; nonfiction CON
FERNOW, Berthold, 1837-1908,
American; nonfiction KAA
FERNS, Henry Stanley, 1913- ,
Canadian; nonfiction CON
FEROUX, Christophe Léon, 1730-
1803, French; nonfiction DIL
FERRACUTI, Franco, 1927- ,
Italian; nonfiction CON
FERRAN, Augusto, 1836-80,
Spanish; poetry BL SA

FERRAN, Jaime, 1928- , Spanish;
poetry BL SA
FERRAND de MONTHELON,
Antoine, 1686-1732, French;
nonfiction DIL
FERRANDES de JERENA, García,
14th cent., Spanish; poetry
SA ST
FERRAR, Nicholas, 1592-1637,
English; nonfiction KB
FERRARA, Il Cieco de see BELLO,
Francisco
FERRARA y MARINO, Dorestes,
1876- , Italian-Cuban; nonfic-
tion MIN
'FERRARI, Emilio' (Pérez Ferrari),
1850-1907, Spanish; poetry,
journalism BL SA
FERRARI, Giuseppe, 1811-76,
Italian; nonfiction ST
FERRARI, Paolo, 1822-89, Italian;
plays HAR SA
FERRARI, Severino, 1856-1905,
Italian; criticism, poetry COL
SA
FERRARI BILLOCH, Francisco,
1901-58, Spanish; nonfiction,
fiction SA
'FERRARS, E. X.' see BROWN,
Morna D.
'FERRARS, Elizabeth' see BROWN,
Morna D.
FERRATER-MORA, Jose, 1912- ,
Spanish-American; nonfiction
BL CON SA
FERRE, Frederic, 1933- , Amer-
ican; nonfiction CON
FERRE, Gustave A., 1918- ,
Swedish-American; nonfiction
CON
FERRE, Nels Fredrik Solomon,
1908-71, American; nonfiction
CON
FERREIRA, Antonio, 1528?-69,
Portuguese; plays, poetry
HAR KE MAG SA ST
FERREIRA Eduardo, 1869- ,
Spanish-Uruguayan; journalism
SA
FERREIRA de CASTRO, José
María, 1898- , Portuguese;
fiction, essays FLE HAR RIC
SA ST
FERREIRA de LACERDA, Bernarda,
1595-1644, Portuguese; poetry
SA
FERREIRA de VASCONCELLOS,
Jorge see VASCONCELLOS,

Jorge F. de

FERRELL, Mallory Hope, 1935- ,
American; nonfiction CON

FERRELL, Robert Hugh, 1921- ,
American; nonfiction CON

FERRELL, Robert Willingham,
1913- , American; nonfiction
CON

FERREOL, Marcel Auguste see
'ACHARD, Marcel'

FERRER, Aldo, 1927- , Argentinian;
nonfiction CON

FERRER, Olga P., 1912- , Spanish;
nonfiction BL

FERRER, Ventura Pascual, 1772-
1851, Cuban; journalism MIN

FERRER del RIO, Antonio, 1814-
72, Spanish; criticism BL SA
ST

FERRER VIDAL, Jorge, 1926- ,
Spanish; fiction BL SA

FERRERO, Guglielmo, 1871-1942,
Italian; nonfiction COL KT SA

FERRETIS, Jorge, 20th cent.,
Mexican; fiction SA

FERRI, Luigi, 1826-95, Italian;
nonfiction SA

FERRIAR, John, 1761-1815, English;
criticism BRO

FERRIER, James Frederick, 1808-
64, Scots; nonfiction BRO KBA

FERRIER, Janet Mackay, 1919- ,
Scots; nonfiction CON

FERRIER, Paul, 1843-1920, French;
plays HAR

FERRIER, Susan Edmounstone,
1782-1854, English; fiction BRO
KBA ST

FERRIERE, Claude de, 1639-1715,
French; nonfiction DIL

FERRIERE, Claude Joseph, 1748- ,
French; nonfiction DIL

FERRIERES, Charles Elie de, 1741- ,
French; nonfiction DIL

FERRIERES-MARSAT, Henriette
d' Monbielle, 1744-1837, French;
nonfiction DIL

FERRIL, Thomas Hornsby, 1896- ,
American; poetry, essays KTS
MUR

FERRIOL, Antoine, French; nonfiction DIL

FERRIS, Helen Josephine, 1890-
1969, American; juveniles KJU
WA

'FERRIS, James Cody' see STRATE-
MEYER, Edward L.

FERRIS, Paul Frederick, 1929- ,

Welsh; fiction CON

FERRISS, Abott Lamoyne,
1915- , American; nonfiction
CON

FERRO, Antonio, 1895- , Portuguese; journalism SA

FERRO, Robert Michael, 1941- ,
American; fiction CON

FERRON, Anselme, 1751-1816,
French; nonfiction DIL

FERRON, Jacques, 1921- ,
Canadian; fiction SY

FERRUS, Pero, Spanish; poetry
BL SA

FERRY, Anne Davidson, 1930- ,
American; nonfiction CON

FERRY, David Russell, 1924- ,
American; poetry, criticism
CON MUR

FERSH, Seymour H., 1926- ,
American; nonfiction CON

FERSTER, Marilyn Bender,
1926- , American; nonfiction
CON

FERTEL, Martin Dominique, 1672-
1752, French; nonfiction DIL

FERY, P. André, 1714-73, French;
poetry DIL

FESHBACH, Seymour, 1925- ,
American; nonfiction CON

FESLER, James William, 1911- ,
American; nonfiction CON

FESPERMAN, John Thomas, Jr.,
1925- , American; nonfiction
CON

FESS, Philip E., 1931- , American; nonfiction CON

FESSEL, Murray, 1927- , American; nonfiction CON

FESSENDEN, Seth Arthur, 1903- ,
American; nonfiction CON

FESSENDEN, Thomas Green
('Christopher Caustic'), 1771-
1837, American; journalism,
poetry KAA

FESSENKO, Tatiana Sviatenko,
1915- , Russian-American;
nonfiction CON

FESSIER, Michael, 1905- ,
American; fiction WAF

FESSLER, Loren W., 1923- ,
American; nonfiction CON

FEST, Thorrel Brooks, 1910- ,
American; nonfiction CON

FESTINGER, Leon, 1919- ,
American; nonfiction CON

FESTO, Sexto Pompeyo, 2nd-3rd
cent., Roman; nonfiction

SA ST
FET, Afanasy Afanasyvich ('Shenshin'),
1820-92, Russian; poetry HAR
HARK KE ST
FETLER, Andrew, 1925- , Latvian-
American; nonfiction CON
FETTER, Elizabeth Head ('Hannah
Lees'), 1904- , American;
fiction CON
FEUCHTERSLEBEN, Ernst von,
1806-40/49, Austrian; poetry,
essays HAR SA ST
FEUCHTWANGER, Lionel ('J.L.
Wetcheek'), 1884-1958, German-
American; fiction, poetry, plays
AL COL FLE HAR KL KT KU
LEN MAG MAT SA ST
FEUER, Lewis Samuel, 1912- ,
American; nonfiction CON
FEUERBACH, Ludwig, 1804-72,
German; nonfiction SA
FEUERLICHT, Ignace, Austrian-
American; nonfiction CON
FEUERLICHT, Roberta Strauss,
1931- , American; juveniles
CON
FEUERWERKER, Albert, 1927- ,
American; nonfiction CON
FEUILLET, Octave, 1821-90,
French; fiction, plays DIF HAR
KE SA ST
FEUTRY, Aime, 1720-89, French;
nonfiction, poetry DIL
FEVAL, Paul, 1860-1929, French;
fiction KT SA
FEVAL, Paul Henri Corentin, 1817-
87, French; fiction, plays DIF
HAR KE SA ST
'FEVERSTEIN, Emil' see HAMEIRI,
Avigdor
FEVRET de FONTETTE, Charles
Marie, 1710-72, French; nonfic-
tion DIL
FEY, Harold Edward, 1898- ,
American; nonfiction CON
FEYDEAU, Ernest Aimé, 1821-73,
French; fiction, nonfiction DIF
HAR SA ST
FEYDEAU, Georges, 1862-1921,
French; plays DIF HAR MAL
MAT RIC SA
FEYJOO, Benito J. see FEIJOO y
MONTENEGRO, Beniot J.
FEYLBRIEF, J.K. see 'OUDSHOORN
J. van'
FIALHO de ALMEIDA, José Valentim,
1857-1911, Portuguese; nonfiction
COL SA

FIALLO, Fabio, 1866-1942,
Dominican; poetry BL MIN
SA
FIARD, Jean Baptiste, 1736-1818,
French; nonfiction DIL
FICHET, Guillaume, 1433/40-80?,
French; nonfiction DIF ST
FICHMAN, Yaakov, 1881- ,
Jewish; poetry, criticism ST
FICHTE, Johan Gottleib, 1762-
1814, German; nonfiction HAR
SA
FICHTER, George S., 1922- ,
American; nonfiction CON
FICHTER, Joseph H., 1908- ,
American; nonfiction CON
HOE
FICHTER, William L., 1892- ,
American; nonfiction BL
FICINO, Marsilio, 1433-99,
Italian; nonfiction HAR KE SA
ST
FICKE, Arthur Davison, 1883- ,
American; poetry KT
FICKER, Victor B., 1937- ,
American; nonfiction CON
FICKERT, Kurt Joh, 1920- ,
German-American; nonfiction
CON
FICKETT, Harold L., Jr.,
1918- , American; nonfiction
CON
FICKETT, Lewis O., Jr., 1926- ,
American; nonfiction CON
FICKLING, Skip Forrest ('G.G.
Fickling'), 1925- , American;
fiction CON
FIDANZA, Giovanni di see
'BONAVENTURA'
FIDELE, Alejandro C.M. see
FEDEL, Alejandro C.M.
FIDELE de PAU, 17-18th cent.,
French; nonfiction DIL
FIDELIO, Edgar see HUNT, Edgar
H.
FIDLER, Kathleen Annie, English;
juveniles CON
FIEDLER, Fred Edward, 1922- ,
Austrian-American; nonfiction
CON
FIEDLER, Jean, American;
juveniles CON
FIEDLER, Jeannette Feldman,
American; juvenile CON
FIEDLER, Leslie Aaron, 1917- ,
American; nonfiction, poetry
CON
FIEDLER, Lois Wagner, 1928- ,

American; fiction CON
'FIELD, Andrew John' see WIEZELL, Richard J.
FIELD, Arthur Jordan, 1927- , American; nonfiction CON
FIELD, Barron, 1786-1846, English; poetry, essays KBA
FIELD, Ben, American; fiction WAF
'FIELD, Charles' see ROWLAND, Donald S.
FIELD, Edward, 1924- , American; poetry CON MUR
FIELD, Ernest R., 1925- , American; nonfiction CON
FIELD, Eugene, 1850-95, American; poetry, journalism, fiction BRO HOO KAA ST WA
FIELD, Frank, 1936- , English; nonfiction CON
'FIELD, Frank Chester' see ROBERTSON, Frank C.
FIELD, George Wallis, 1914- , Canadian; nonfiction CON
FIELD, Gordon Lawrence, 1939- , English; nonfiction CON
FIELD, Hazel Elizabeth, 1891- , American; nonfiction CON
FIELD, Irving Medcraft, 1934- , American; nonfiction CON
FIELD, James Alfred, Jr., 1916- , American; nonfiction CON
'FIELD, Joanna' see MILNER, Marion B.
FIELD, John Leslie, 1910- , American; fiction CON
FIELD, John Paul, 1936- , American; fiction CON
FIELD, Joyce Wolf, 1932- , American; nonfiction CON
FIELD, Leslie A., 1926- , American; nonfiction CON
FIELD, Mark George, 1923- , Swiss-American; nonfiction CON
FIELD, Maunsell Bradhurst, 1822-75, American; poetry KAA
'FIELD, Michael' see BRADLEY, Katherine H. and COOPER, Edith E.
FIELD, Minna Kagan, Polish-American; nonfiction CON
FIELD, Nathan, 1587-1620/33, English; plays BRO KB ST
FIELD, Rachel Lyman, 1894-1942, American; juveniles, fiction KJU KL KT RIC WA
FIELD, Roswell Martin, 1851-1919, American; journalism, fiction HOO KAA

FIELD, Sara Bard, 1882- , American; poetry KT
FIELD, Stanley, 1911- , Russian-American; nonfiction CON
FIELD, Thomas Parry, 1914- , American; nonfiction CON
FIELD, Thomas Warren, 1821-81, American; essays KAA
FIELD, Walter Taylor, 1861-1939, American; nonfiction HOO
FIELD, Rev. William Noé, 1915- , American; poetry HO
FIELDEN, Thomas Percival ('P. de Fletin'; 'E. De P. Flint'), 1882- , English; nonfiction CON
FIELDER, Mildred Craig, 1913- , American; poetry, nonfiction CON
FIELDING, A.E., 20th cent., English; fiction KT
'FIELDING, A.W.' see WALLACE, Alexander F.
FIELDING, Daphne Winifred Louise, 1904- , English; nonfiction CON
'FIELDING, Gabriel' see BARNSLEY, Alan G.
FIELDING, Henry, 1707-54, English; fiction, plays BRO KB MAG SA ST
FIELDING, Raymond E., 1931- , American; nonfiction CON
FIELDING, Sarah, 1710-68, English; fiction BRO KB SA ST
FIELDING, Temple Hornaday, 1913- , American; nonfiction CON
FIELDING, William John, 1886- , American; poetry, nonfiction CON
'FIELDING, Xan' see WALLACE, Alexander F.
FIELDS, Annie Adams, 1834-1915, American; poetry, diary KAA
FIELDS, James Thomas, 1817-81, American; nonfiction, poetry KAA
FIELDS, Joseph, 1895-1966, American; plays MAT
FIELDS, Maurice C., 1915- , American; poetry, plays SCA
FIELDS, Victor Alexander, 1901- , American; nonfiction CON
FIELDS, Wilbert J., 1917- , American; nonfiction CON
FIENE, Ernest, 1894- , Ameri-

can; nonfiction CON

FIENNES, Richard Nathaniel Twisleton-
Wykeham, 1909- , English; nonfiction CON

FIERRO, Humberto, 1890-1929,
Ecuadorian; poetry DI

FIESER, Max Eugene, 1930- ,
American; nonfiction CON

FIEVEE, Joseph, 1767-1839, French;
nonfiction SA

'FIFE, Duncan' (Mrs. Dean Atkinson),
1893- , English; nonfiction
HIG

FIFE, Robert Oldham, 1918- ,
American; nonfiction CON

FIFIELD, William, 1916- , American; fiction CON

FIGANIERE, Federico Francisco,
1827-1908, Portuguese; nonfiction SA

'FIGARO' see CLAPP, Henry Jr.

FIGGIS, Darrell ('Michael Ireland'),
1882-1925, Irish; poetry, fiction
ST

FIGH, Margaret Gillis, 1896- ,
American; nonfiction CON

'FIGHTER Pilot, A.' see JOHNSTON,
Hugh A.S.

FIGUEIREDO, Antonio Cándido de,
1846-1925, Portuguese; poetry SA

FIGUEIREDO, Fidelino de Sousa,
1888- , Portuguese; nonfiction
COL SA

FIGUEIREDO, Manuel de, 1725-1801,
Portuguese; plays ST

FIGUERA AYMERICH, Angela,
1902- , Spanish; poetry BL SA

FIGUEROA, Agustín de, 1909?- ,
Spanish; fiction SA

FIGUEROA, Francisco de, 1536-1617/
20, Spanish; nonfiction, poetry BL
SA

FIGUEROA, Francisco de, 1600-20,
Spanish; poetry ST

FIGUEROA, John Joseph Maria,
1920- , Jamaican; poetry MUR

FIGUEROA, Miguel, 1851-93, Cuban;
nonfiction MIN

FIGUEROA, Pedro Pablo, 1857-1909/
12, Chilean; journalism MIN

FIGUEROA y CORDOBA, Diego,
1619-73, Spanish; plays, poetry
BL SA ST

FIGUEROA y CORDOBA, José, 1625-
78, Spanish; plays, poetry BL
SA ST

FIGUEROA y TORRES, Alvaro, 1863-
1950, Spanish; nonfiction SA

FIGULI, Margita, 1910- , Slovak;
fiction ST

FIGURITO, Joseph, 1922- ,
Italian-American; nonfiction
CON

FIKRET, Tevfik, 1867-1915,
Turkish; journalism LAN ST

FIKSO, Eunice Cleland ('C. F.
Griffin'), 1927- , American;
fiction CON

FILAMON, 5th cent. B.C., Greek;
nonfiction SA

FILAS, Francis Lad, 1915- ,
American; nonfiction CON

FILASSIER, Jean Jacques, 1736-
1806, French; nonfiction DIL

FILBY, Percy William, 1911- ,
English; nonfiction CON

FILDEMO, 1st cent. B.C., Greek;
poetry SA

FILELFO, Francisco, 1398-1481,
Italian; nonfiction SA ST

FILEMON, 4th cent. B.C., Greek;
poetry SA

FILENE, Peter G., 1940- , American; nonfiction CON

'FILES, Manuel' see PHILE,
Manuel

FILIATRAULT, Jean, 1919- ,
Canadian; fiction SY

FILICAYA, Vicenzio de ('Filicaja;
Filicaia), 1642-1707, Italian;
poetry HAR SA ST

FILIMON, Neculai, 1819-65,
Rumanian; fiction ST

FILINTO ELYSIO see NASCIMENTO,
Francesco M. do

FILIPPO, Eduardo de, 1900- ,
Italian; plays FLE

FILISTO, 435- , Greek; nonfiction
SA

FILITAS, 3rd cent. B.C., Greek;
poetry SA

FILLER, Louis, 1912- , Russian-
American; nonfiction CON

FILLMER, Henry Thompson,
1932- , American; nonfiction
CON

FILLMORE, Lowell, 1880- , American; nonfiction CON

FILLMORE, Parker, 1878-1944,
American; juveniles KJU

FILLMORE, Roscoe Alfred, 1887- ,
American; nonfiction CON

FILLOY, Juan, 1894- , Argentinian; essays MIN

FILMER, Sir Robert, 1590?-1653,
English; nonfiction BRO

FILOCLES, 4th cent. B.C., Greek;
poetry SA
FILOLAO, 5th cent. B.C., Greek;
poetry SA
FILON de BIBLOS (Herenio), 70-101,
Greek; nonfiction SA
FILON de LARISA, 2nd-1st cent.
B.C., Greek; nonfiction SA
FILON el JUDIO, 20 B.C.-45 A.D.,
Jewish; nonfiction SA
FILOSTRATO, Flavio, 2nd cent.,
Greek; nonfiction SA
FILOXENES, 435-380 B.C., Greek;
poetry SA
FILSON, John, 1747-88, American;
nonfiction KAA
FINBERG, Herbert Patrick Reginald,
1900- , English; translations,
nonfiction CON
FINCH, Anne see WINCHILSEA,
Anne F.
FINCH, Francis Miles, 1827-1907,
American; poetry KAA
'FINCH, Matthew' see FINK, Merton
FINCH, Peter, 1947- , British;
poetry MUR
FINCH, Robert Duer Claydon, 1900- ,
Canadian; poetry, criticism
MUR ST SY
FINCK, Furman Joseph, 1900- ,
American; nonfiction CON
FINDEISEN, Kurt Arnold ('Wendelin
Dudesack'), 1883-1963, German;
nonfiction AL
FINDLAY, Bruce Allyn, 1895- ,
American; nonfiction CON
FINDLAY, David K., 1901- ,
Canadian; fiction CON
FINDLAY, John Niemeyer, 1903- ,
English; nonfiction CON
FINDLEY, Paul, 1921- , American;
nonfiction CON
FINDLEY, Timothy, 1930- ,
Canadian; fiction CON
FINE, Benjamin, 1905- , American;
nonfiction CON
FINE, Isadore V., 1918- , Ameri-
can; fiction CON
FINE, Ralph Adam, 1941- , Ameri-
can; nonfiction CON
FINE, Reuben, 1914- , American;
nonfiction CON
FINE, Sidney, 1920- , American;
nonfiction CON
FINE, Warren, 1943- , American;
fiction CON
FINE, William Michael, 1924- ,
American; nonfiction CON

FINEGAN, Jack, 1908- , Ameri-
can; nonfiction CON
FINEMAN, Irving ('Jonathan
Joseph'), 1893- , American;
nonfiction, plays CON KT
WAF
FINER, Leslie, 1921- , English;
nonfiction CON
FINET-DUVERGER, 18th cent.,
French; plays DIL
FINGER, Charles Joseph, 1871-
1941, Anglo-American; non-
fiction KL KT WA
FINGERIT, Julio Pablo, 1901- ,
Argentinian; fiction, essays,
criticism, translations MIN
FINGERIT, Marcos, 1903- ,
Argentinian; poetry, essays
MIN
FINGESTEN, Peter, 1916- ,
American; nonfiction CON
FINK, Arthur Emil, 1903- ,
American; nonfiction CON
FINK, Augusta, 1916- , Ameri-
can; nonfiction CON
'FINK, Brat' see DAVIS, Gwen
FINK, Merton ('Matthew Finch'),
1921- , English; fiction
CON
FINK, Zera Silver, 1902- ,
American; nonfiction CON
FINKEL, Donald, 1929- , Ameri-
can; poetry CON MUR
FINKEL, George Irvine, 1909- ,
English; nonfiction CON
FINKEL, Lawrence S., 1925- ,
American; nonfiction CON
FINKELSTEIN, Leonid Vladimiro-
vich, 1924- , Russian-English;
nonfiction CON
FINKELSTEIN, Louis, 1895- ,
American; nonfiction CON
FINKLE, Jason Leonard, 1926- ,
American; nonfiction CON
FINLAY, Campbell Kirkman,
1909- , American; fiction
CON
FINLAY, David James, 1934- ,
American; nonfiction CON
FINLAY, George, 1799-1875,
Scots; nonfiction BRO KBA
'FINLAY, Fiona' see STUART,
Vivian F.
FINLAY, Ian Hamilton, 1925- ,
Scots; poetry, plays, fiction
MUR
FINLAY, Matthew Henderson,
1916- , New Zealander;

nonfiction CON
FINLAY, Winifred Lindsay Crawford
McKissack, 1910- , English;
juveniles CON
FINLAYSON, Ann, 1925- , Ameri-
can; nonfiction CON
FINLAYSON, Roderick, 1904- ,
New Zealander; fiction ST
FINLEY, Harold Marshall, 1916- ,
American; nonfiction CON
FINLEY, Martha ('Martha Farquhar-
son'), 1828-1909, American;
juveniles, fiction DOY KAA
FINLEY, Moses I., 1912- , Amer-
ican; nonfiction CON
'FINN, Dorothy E.' see BORRELL,
Dorothy E.
FINN, Henry James William, 1787-
1840, American; plays KAA
FINN, Hugh Lauder, 1925- ,
Rhodesian; poetry, critics MUR
FINN, Ralph Leslie, 1912- , Eng-
lish; fiction CON
FINN, Reginald Patrick Arthur
Welldon ('R. Welldon Finn';
'Rex Welldon Finn'), 1900- ,
English; nonfiction CON
FINNEGAN, Ruth H. see MURRAY,
Ruth H.
FINNENBERG, Ezra, 1899-1946,
Jewish; poetry ST
FINNERAN, Richard John, 1943- ,
American; nonfiction CON
FINNEY, Charles Grandison, 1905- ,
American; fiction CON KT
FINNEY, Gertrude Elva Bridgeman,
American; juveniles, fiction
CON PAC WA
FINNEY, Gretchen Ludke, 1901- ,
American; nonfiction CON
'FINNEY, Mark' see MUIR, Kenneth
A.
FINNIGAN, Joan, 1925- , Canadian;
poetry CON MUR
FINNIN, Mary, Australian; poetry
MUR
FINOCHHIARO, Mary Bonomo,
1913- , American; nonfiction
CON
FINOT, Emilio, 1886-1915, Bolivian;
poetry, fiction MIN SA
FINOT, Enrique, 1891-1952, Bolivian;
essays, fiction, nonfiction MIN
SA
FINSTEIN, Max, American; poetry
MUR
FINZGAR, Franc Saleski, 1871-1962,
Slovene; poetry, fiction, plays
FLE

FIORE, Peter Amadeus, 1927- ,
American; nonfiction CON
FIORE, Silvestro, 1921- , Amer-
ican; nonfiction CON
FIORINO, A. John, 1926- , Amer-
ican; nonfiction CON
FIRBANK, Ronald, 1886-1926,
English; fiction FLE KAT
KT RIC SA ST
FIRCHOW, Peter Edgerley,
1937- , American; nonfiction
CON
FIRDUSI Abul Cassin Mansur
('Firdausi; Firdowsi; Ferdusi),
940-1019, Persian; poetry
LAN SA ST
FIREBRACE, Aylmer Newton
George, 1886- , English;
nonfiction CON
FIRENZUOLA, Agnolo Giovanni,
1493-1543, Italian; nonfiction
KE SA ST
FIRESIDE, Henry, 1929- ,
Austrian-American; nonfiction
CON
FIRESTONE, Shulamith, 1945- ,
American; nonfiction CON
FIREY, Walter Irving, Jr.,
1916- , American; nonfiction
CON
FIRISHTA, Mohammed Qazim,
1570-1611, Persian; nonfiction
ST
FIRKINS, Oscar W., 1864-1932,
American; criticism KT
FIRMAGE, George James, 1928- ,
American; nonfiction CON
FIRMICUS MATURNUS, Julius,
fl. 350, Roman; nonfiction
SA ST
FISCH, Gerald Grant, 1922- ,
Canadian; nonfiction CON
FISCH, Harold, 1923- , Israeli;
nonfiction CON
FISCH, Max Harold, 1900- ,
American; nonfiction CON
FISCHART, Johann Baptist
(Mentzer), 1546-89/90,
German; fiction, poetry AL
HAR KE SA ST
FISCHBACH, Julius, 1894- ,
American; juveniles CON
FISCHEL, Walter Joseph, 1902- ,
German-American; nonfiction
CON
FISCHER, Alex, 1882- , French;
nonfiction SA
FISCHER, Ann, 1919- , American;

nonfiction CON
FISCHER, Carl Hahn, 1903- ,
American; nonfiction CON
FISCHER, David Hackett, 1935- ,
American; nonfiction CON
FISCHER, Edward Adam, 1914- ,
American; nonfiction CON
FISCHER, Ernst, 1899-1972,
German; essays AL
FISCHER, George, 1932- , Amer-
ican; nonfiction CON
FISCHER, Gerald Charles, 1928- ,
American; nonfiction CON
FISCHER, Hans Erich, 1909-58,
Swiss; juveniles FUL
FISCHER, Johann Georg, 1816-97,
Swabian; poetry ST
FISCHER, John, 1910- , American;
nonfiction CON
FISCHER, John Lyle, 1923- ,
American; nonfiction CON
FISCHER, Leopold see BHARATI,
Agehananda
FISCHER, LeRoy Henry, 1917- ,
American; nonfiction CON
FISCHER, Louis, 1896-1970, Amer-
ican; journalism, nonfiction
CON KTS
FISCHER, Max, 1881- , German;
fiction SA
FISCHER Otokar, 1883-1938,
Czech; poetry, criticism COL
SA ST
FISCHER, Otto Peter Leck, 1904- ,
Danish; fiction, plays ST
FISCHER, Robert H., 1918- ,
American; nonfiction CON
FISCHER, Rudolf, 1901-57, German;
nonfiction AL
FISCHER, Vera Kistiakowsky,
1928- , American; nonfiction
CON
FISCHER, Wolfgang Georg, 1933- ,
Austrian-English; fiction CON
'FISCHL, Viktor' see DAGAN,
Avigdor
FISCHMAN, Leonard Lipman,
1919- , American; nonfiction
CON
FISH, Byron Morris, 1909- ,
American; journalism, nonfiction
PAC
'FISH, Julian' see CAMPBELL,
Blanche
FISH, Kenneth Lloyd, 1926- ,
American; nonfiction CON
FISH, Margery Towshend, 1892- ,
English; nonfiction CON

FISH, Robert L. ('Robert L.
Pike'), 1912- , American;
fiction CON
FISHBEIN, Morris, 1889- ,
American; nonfiction CON
FISHBURN, Hummel, 1901- ,
American; nonfiction CON
FISHEL, Leslie Henry, Jr.,
1921- , American; nonfiction
CON
FISHER, Aileen Lucia, 1906- ,
American; juveniles COM
CON FUL WA
FISHER, Alden Lowell, 1928- ,
American; nonfiction CON
FISHER, Allan George Barnard,
1895- , American; nonfiction
CON
FISHER, Anne Benson, 1898- ,
American; fiction WAF
FISHER, Charles William, 1916- ,
American; nonfiction CON
FISHER, David, Scots; juveniles
WA
FISHER, Dorothea Frances Can-
field, 1879-1958, American;
fiction KL KT WAF
FISHER, Edward, 1902- , Amer-
ican; fiction CON
FISHER, Ernest Arthur, 1887- ,
English; nonfiction CON
FISHER, Franklin Marvin,
1934- , American; nonfiction
CON
FISHER, Fred Lewis, 1911- ,
American; nonfiction CON
FISHER, George Park, 1827-1909,
American; nonfiction KAA
FISHER, Herbert Albert Laurens,
1865-1940, English; nonfiction
BRO KT SA
FISHER, Humphrey John, 1933- ,
New Zealander; nonfiction
CON
FISHER, John, 1469-1535, English;
nonfiction BRO KB ST
FISHER, John Hurt, 1919- ,
American; nonfiction CON
FISHER, Joseph Thomas, 1936- ,
American; nonfiction CON
'FISHER, Lane' see HOWARD,
James A.
FISHER, Laura Harrison, 1934- ,
American; fiction CON
FISHER, Lawrence V., 1923- ,
American; nonfiction CON
FISHER, Lee, 1908- , American;
nonfiction CON

FISHER, Leonard Everett, 1924- ,
American; juveniles, fiction
CON WA
FISHER, Lillian Estelle, 1891- ,
American; nonfiction CON MAR
FISHER, Lois Jeannette, 1909- ,
American; juveniles CON
FISHER, Louis, 1934- , American;
nonfiction CON
FISHER, Margaret Barrow, 1918- ,
American; nonfiction CON
FISHER, Margery Turner, 1913- ,
American; juveniles DOY WA
FISHER, Marvin, 1927- , Ameri-
can; nonfiction CON
FISHER, Mary L., 1928- , Ameri-
can; nonfiction CON
FISHER, Michael John, 1933- ,
Anglo-American; fiction CON
FISHER, Miles Mark, 1899- ,
American; nonfiction CON
FISHER, Miriam Louise Scharfe,
1939- , American; juveniles
CON
FISHER, Morris, 1922- , Ameri-
can; nonfiction CON
FISHER, Richard, 1936- , Ameri-
can; fiction CON
FISHER, Roger Dummer, 1922- ,
American; fiction CON
FISHER, Roy, 1930- , British;
poetry MUR
FISHER, Seymour, 1922- , Ameri-
can; nonfiction CON
FISHER, Thomas Henry see 'HENRY,
Thomas'
FISHER, Vardis, 1895-1968, Ameri-
can; fiction, poetry CON KAT
KT MAG WAF
'FISHER, Wade' see NORWOOD,
Victor G. C.
FISHER, Wallace, E., 1918- ,
American; nonfiction CON
FISHER, Walter R., 1931- , Amer-
ican; nonfiction CON
FISHER, Welthy Honsinger, 1880- ,
American; nonfiction CON
FISHLER, Mary Shiverick, 1920- ,
American; juveniles CON
FISHMAN, Betty Goldstein, 1918- ,
American; nonfiction CON
FISHMAN, George Samuel, 1937- ,
American; nonfiction CON
FISHMAN, Jack, 1920- , English;
nonfiction CON
FISHMAN, Leo, 1914- , American;
nonfiction CON
FISHWICK, Marshall William, 1923- ,

American; nonfiction CON
FISK, Ernest Kelvin, 1917- ,
Australian; nonfiction CON
FISK, McKee, 1900- , American;
nonfiction CON
FISKE, John ('Edmund Fisk
Green'), 1842-1901, American;
nonfiction BRO KAA SA ST
FISKE, Roger Elwyn, 1910- ,
English; nonfiction CON .
FISKE, Stephen Ryder, 1840-1916,
American; journalism KAA
FISKIN, Abram M.I., 1916- ,
Canadian; nonfiction CON
FISSON, Pierre, 1918- , French;
fiction, journalism DIC
FISTON, William see PHISTON,
William
FISZEL, Henryk, 1910- , Polish;
nonfiction CON
FITCH, Bob, 1938- , American;
nonfiction CON
'FITCH, Clarke' see SINCLAIR,
Upton
FITCH, Clyde see FITCH, William
C.
FITCH, Edwin Medbery, 1902- ,
American; nonfiction CON
FITCH, Florence Mary, 1875-1959,
American; juveniles FUL WA
FITCH, Sir Joshua Girling, 1824-
1903, English; nonfiction KBA
FITCH, Lyle Craig, 1913- , Amer-
ican; nonfiction CON
FITCH, Stanley K., 1920- ,
Canadian-American; nonfiction
CON
FITCH, William Clyde, 1865-1909,
American; plays KAA MAT ST
FITE, Gilbert Courtland, 1918- ,
American; nonfiction CON
'FITE, Mack' see SCHNECK,
Stephen
FITT, J. Nevill ('H.H.'), 1850- ,
English; nonfiction HIG
FITTING, Melvin Chris, 1942- ,
American; nonfiction CON
FITTS, Dudley, 1903-68, Ameri-
can; poetry KT
FITTS, William Howard, 1918- ,
American; nonfiction CON
FITZ, Jean De Witt, 1912- ,
American; nonfiction CON
'FITZALAN, Roger' see TREVOR,
Elleston
FITZELL, John, 1922- , Ameri-
can; nonfiction CON
FITZ-GEFFRY, Charles,   -1637/

38, English; poetry ST
FITZGERALD, Arlene J. ('Monica
Heath'), American; fiction CON
FITZGERALD, Barry Charles, 1939- ,
Australian; nonfiction CON
FITZGERALD, Cathleen, 1932- ,
Irish; nonfiction CON
FITZGERALD, Charles Patrick,
1902- , English; nonfiction
CON
FITZGERALD, Edward, 1809-83,
English; translations, letters
BRO KBA MAG SA SP ST
FITZGERALD, Edward E., 1919- ,
American; juveniles WA
FITZGERALD, Ernest A., 1925- ,
American; nonfiction CON
FITZGERALD, Francis Scott Key,
1896-1940, American; fiction
BRO FLE KL KT MAG RIC SA
ST
FITZGERALD, Gerald Edward,
1920- , American; nonfiction
CON
FITZGERALD, Gerald M., 1894- ,
American; nonfiction, poetry
HOE
FITZGERALD, Gerald Pierce, 1930- ,
American; poetry CON
'FITZGERALD, Hal' see JOHNSON,
Joseph E.
'FITZGERALD, Jack' see SHEA,
John G.
FITZGERALD, James Augustine,
American; nonfiction CON
'FITZGERALD, John' see FAZZANO,
Joseph E.
FITZGERALD, John D., 1873- ,
American; nonfiction SA
FITZGERALD, John Joseph, 1928- ,
American; nonfiction CON
FITZGERALD, Kevin, 1902- ,
Irish; nonfiction HO
FITZGERALD, Laurine Elisabeth,
1930- , American; nonfiction
CON
FITZGERALD, Lawrence Pennybaker
('Jack Lawrence'), 1906- ,
American; nonfiction CON
FITZGERALD, Patrick John, 1928- ,
English; nonfiction CON
FITZGERALD, Robert David, 1902- ,
Australian; poetry CON MUR
RIC ST
FITZGERALD, Robert Stuart, 1910- ,
American; nonfiction, poetry,
translations CON HO KTS
MUR

FITZGERALD, Thomas, 1819-91,
American; plays KAA
FITZGIBBON, Robert Louis
Constantine, 1919- , Ameri-
can; fiction, nonfiction CON
FITZGIBBON, Theodora Rosling,
1916- , English; nonfiction
CON
FITZHARDINGE, Joan Margaret
('Joan Phipson'), 1912- ,
English; juveniles COM CON
WA
FITZHUGH, Louise, 1928- ,
American; juveniles COM
CON WA
FITZLYON, Cecily April Mead,
1920- , English; translations,
nonfiction CON
FITZMAURICE, George, 1877-
1963, Irish; plays MAT ST
FITZMAURICE-KELLY, James,
1858-1923, English; nonfiction
BL KT SA
FITZMYER, Joseph Augustine,
1920- , English; nonfiction
CON
FITZNEAL, Richard, 1130-98,
English; nonfiction ST
FITZPATRICK, Sir James Percy,
1862-1931, English; juveniles,
fiction DOY ST
FITZPATRICK, Joseph Patrick,
1913- , American; nonfiction
CON
FITZPATRICK, Percy, 1862-1931,
South African; fiction RIC
FITZRALPH, Richard, -1360,
English; nonfiction KB
FITZSIMMONS, Cleo, 1900- ,
American; nonfiction CON
FITZSIMMONS, Mathew Anthony,
1912- , American; nonfiction
CON
FITZSIMMONS, Robert, American;
juveniles WA
FITZSIMMONS, Thomas, 1926- ,
American; nonfiction CON
FITZ-SIMONS, Foster, 1912- ,
American; fiction JO
FITZSIMONS, Neal, 1928- ,
American; nonfiction CON
FITZSIMONS, Raymund, English;
nonfiction CON
FITZSTEPHEN, William, -1190?,
English; nonfiction BRO KB
ST
FITZWILLIAM, William Wentworth
see MILTON, Viscount

FIXLER, Michael, 1927- , American; nonfiction CON

FJELDE, Rolf Gerhard, 1926- , American; plays, poetry CON

FLACIUS ILLYRICUS, Matthias, 1520-75, German; nonfiction ST

FLACK, Elmer Ellsworth, 1894- , American; nonfiction CON

FLACK, Marjorie, 1897-1958, American; juveniles KJU WA

FLAGG, Edmund, 1815-90, American; nonfiction KAA

FLAGG, Thomas Wilson, 1805-84, American; nonfiction KAA

FLAHERTY, David Harris, 1940- , Canadian; nonfiction CON

FLAHERTY, Douglas Ernest, 1939- , American; poetry CON MUR

FLAINVILLE, Jean François Augustin see JANVIER de FLAINVILLE, Jean

FLAKE, Chad John, 1927- , American; nonfiction CON

'FLAKE, Otto' (Leo F. Kotta), 1880-1963, German; fiction, essays, criticism, translations AL FLE KU LEN

FLAMANT, Guillaume, 1455-1540, French; nonfiction DIF

FLAMINIO, Marco Antonio, 1498-1550, Italian; poetry ST

FLAMM, Dudley, 1931- , American; fiction CON

FLAMMONDE, Paris, American; fiction CON

FLANAGAN, John Clemans, 1906- , American; nonfiction CON

FLANAGAN, John Theodore, 1906- , American; nonfiction CON

FLANAGAN, Rev. Joseph David see RAYMOND, Rev. M.

FLANAGAN, Neal M., 1920- , American; nonfiction CON

FLANAGAN, Robert James, 1941- , American; nonfiction CON

FLANDERS, Helen Hartness, 1890-1972, American; nonfiction CON

FLANDERS, Henry Jackson, Jr., 1921- , American; nonfiction CON

FLANDERS, Michael Henry, 1922- , English; juveniles CON WA

FLANDERS, Ned A., 1918- , American; nonfiction CON

FLANDERS, Ralph Edward, 1880- , American; nonfiction CON

FLANDRAU, Charles Macomb, 1871-1938, American; fiction, essays KT

FLANIGAN, Lloyd Allen, 1933- , American; nonfiction CON

FLANNERY, Edward Hugh, 1912- , American; nonfiction CON

FLANNERY, Harry W., 1900- , American; nonfiction CON

FLASCH, Jay, 1932- , American; nonfiction CON

FLATMAN, Thomas, 1637-88, English; poetry BRO KB ST

FLAUBERT, Gustave, 1821-80, French; fiction COL DIF HAR KE MAG MAL SA ST

FLAUGERGUES, Pauline de, 1799-1878, French; poetry SA

FLAVEL, John, 1627-91, English; nonfiction BRO

FLAVEL, John Hurley, 1928- , American; nonfiction CON

FLAVIN, Martin, 1883-1967, American; fiction, plays CON KT WAF

'FLAVIUS, Brother' see ELLISON, James E.

FLAVIUS Arrianus see ARRIAN

FLAXMAN, Traudl ('Traudl'), 1942- , German-American; juveniles CON

FLAYDERMAN, Philip Charles, 1930- , American; nonfiction CON

FLECHIER, Valentin Esprit, 1632-1710, French; nonfiction DIF SA

FLECK, Konrad, fl. 1220, German; poetry ST

FLECKER, James Elroy, 1884-1915, English; poetry, plays BRO KAT KT RIC SA SP ST

FLECKNOE, Richard, -1678?, English; poetry, plays BRO KB ST

FLEECE, Jeffrey Atkinson, 1920- , American; plays, nonfiction CON

FLEER, Jack David, 1937- , American; nonfiction CON

FLEG, Edmond, 1874- , French; poetry, essays, translations DIF

FLEGON, 2nd cent., Greek; nonfiction SA

FLEISCHBEIN, Sister M. Catherine Frederic, 1902- , American;

nonfiction CON

FLEISCHER, Manfred Paul, 1928- ,
German-American; nonfiction
CON

FLEISCHMAN, Albert Sidney,
1920- , American; juveniles,
fiction CON WA

FLEISCHMAN, Harry, 1914- ,
American; nonfiction CON

FLEISCHMANN, Glen Harvey,
1909- , American; nonfiction,
fiction CON

FLEISCHMANN, Harriet, 1904- ,
American; nonfiction CON

FLEISHER, Frederic, 1933- ,
Swedish; nonfiction CON

FLEISHER, Michael Lawrence,
1942- , American; nonfiction
CON

FLEISHMAN, Avron Hirsch, 1933- ,
American; nonfiction CON

FLEISHMAN, Edwin Alan, 1927- ,
American; nonfiction CON

FLEISSER, Marieluise, 1901- ,
German; nonfiction KU

FLEITMANN, Lida L., 1885- ,
English; nonfiction HIG

FLEMES, Christian, 1847-1926,
German; poetry ST

FLEIMING, Alice Mulcahey, 1928- ,
American; juveniles CON WA

FLEMING, Berry, 1899- , American; fiction, nonfiction CON
WAF

FLEMING, Charlotte Mary, 1894- ,
American; nonfiction CON

FLEMING, Denna Frank, 1893- ,
American; nonfiction CON

FLEMING, Elizabeth P., American;
juveniles WA

FLEMING, George Joseph, 1917- ,
American; nonfiction CON

FLEMING, Harold Manchester,
1900- , American; nonfiction
CON

FLEMING, Harold Lee, 1927- ,
American; fiction, poetry CON

FLEMING, Horace Kingston, 1901- ,
English; fiction CON

FLEMING, Ian Lancaster ('Atticus'),
1908-64, English; fiction CON
RIC WA

FLEMING, Margaret ('Pet Margery'),
1803-11, English; poetry, diary
BRO KBA

FLEMING, Miles, 1919- , English;
nonfiction CON

FLEMING, Paul, 1609-40, German;

poetry AL HAR KE ST

FLEMING, Peter, 1907- , English; nonfiction, fiction BRO
KT RIC

FLEMING, Sandford, 1888- ,
Australian; nonfiction CON

FLEMING, Thomas James
('Christopher Cain'; 'T. F.
James'; 'J. F. Thomas'),
1927- , American; fiction
CON

'FLEMING, Waldo' see WILLIAM-
SON, Thomas R.

FLEMING, William Coleman,
1909- , American; nonfiction
CON

FLEMMYNG, Robert, -1483,
English; poetry ST

FLERS, Robert de la Motte-Ango
de, 1872-1927, French; plays,
journalism COL DIF HAR
MAT SA

FLESCH, Rudolf, 1911- , Austrian-
American; nonfiction CON

FLESCHER, Irwin, 1926- , American; nonfiction CON

'FLETCHER, Adam' see FLEXNER,
Stuart B.

FLETCHER, Adele Whiteby
('Roberta Ormiston'), 1898- ,
American; nonfiction CON

FLETCHER, Andrew, 1655-1716,
English; nonfiction BRO

FLETCHER, Arnold Charles,
1917- , American; nonfiction
CON

FLETCHER, Beale, American;
juveniles WA

FLETCHER, Charlie M.H. see
SIMON, Charlie M.H. F.

FLETCHER, Colin, 1922- ,
Welsh; nonfiction CON

FLETCHER, Giles, 1549-1611,
English; poetry KB SP ST

FLETCHER, Giles, 1588?-1623,
English; poetry BRO KB SP
ST

FLETCHER, Grace Nies, 1895- ,
American; juveniles CON

FLETCHER, Harris Francis,
1892- , American; nonfiction
CON

FLETCHER, Larry Luft Verne
('John Garden'; 'John Hereford'),
1902- , English; fiction,
nonfiction CON

FLETCHER, Helen Jill ('Carol
Lee'; 'Charles Morey'),

1911- , American; juveniles, nonfiction CON WA

FLETCHER, Ian, 1920- , British; poetry MUR

FLETCHER, Inglis, 1888- , American; fiction HOO JO WAF CON

FLETCHER, Jesse C., 1931- , American; nonfiction CON

FLETCHER, John, 1579-1625, English; plays, poetry BRO KB MAG SA SP ST

FLETCHER, John Gould, 1886-1950, American; poetry BRO FLE KAT KT SA ST

FLETCHER, Joseph Francis III, 1905- , American; nonfiction CON

FLETCHER, Joseph Smith, 1863-1935, English; fiction BRO KT

FLETCHER, Phineas, 1582-1650, English; poetry BRO KB SP ST

FLETCHER, Robert Henry, 1885-1972, American; songs, poetry, fiction PAC

FLETCHER, Ronald, 1921- , English; nonfiction CON

FLETCHER, William Catherwood, 1932- , American; nonfiction CON

FLETIN, P. de see FIELDEN, Thomas P.

FLEURET, Fernand, 1884-1945, French; fiction DIF

FLEURIAU, Jean Joseph François, 1700-67, French; poetry DIL

FLEURIAU, P. Bertrand Gabriel, 1693-1773, French; nonfiction DIL

FLEURIAU, Thomas Charles, 18th cent., French; nonfiction DIL

'FLEURIDES, Ellie Rae' see SHERMAN, Eleanor R.

FLEURIEU, Charles Pierre Claret, 1738-1810, French; nonfiction DIL

FLEURON, Svend, 1874- , Danish; fiction HAR ST

FLEURY, 1705-46, French; poetry DIL

FLEURY, Amade, 1776-1820, French; nonfiction SA

FLEURY, Claude, 1640-1723, French; nonfiction SA

'FLEURY, Delphine' see AMATOR, Sister Mary

FLEURY, Jacques, 1730-73, French; nonfiction DIL

FLEURY, Jean Baptiste, 1698-1754,

French; nonfiction DIL

FLEURY, Julien, 1650-1725, French; nonfiction DIL

FLEURY-FERNAL, Charles, 1692-1768, French; nonfiction DIL

FLEX, Walter, 1887-1917, German; poetry, fiction, plays COL KU SA

FLEXER, Akim Lvovich ('A. Volynski'), 1863-1926, Russian; criticism HARK ST

FLEXNER, Abraham, 1866-1959, American; nonfiction KT

FLEXNER, James Thomas, 1908- , American; nonfiction CON

FLEXNER, Stuart Berg ('Adam Fletcher'; 'Steve Mees'; 'Collier Santee'), 1928- , American; nonfiction CON

FLEW, Antony Garrard Newton, 1923- , English; nonfiction CON

FLICK, Ella Maine, American; fiction HOE

FLICK, Lawrence Francis, 1856-1938, American; nonfiction HO

FLIEGEL, Hellmuth see 'HEYM, Stefan'

FLIEGER, Wilhelm, 1931- , German-American; nonfiction CON

FLIER, Michael Stephen, 1941- , American; nonfiction CON

FLIESS, Peter Joachim, 1915- , American; nonfiction CON

FLINDERS, Neil J., 1934- , American; nonfiction CON

FLINK, Salomon J., 1906- , American; nonfiction CON

FLINN, Michael Walter, 1917- , American; nonfiction CON

FLINS des OLIVIERS, Claude Marie Louis, 1757-1806, French; poetry, plays DIL

FLINT, Betty M., 1920- , Canadian; nonfiction CON

'FLINT, E. de P.' see FIELDEN, Thomas P.

FLINT, Frank Stewart, 1885- , English; poetry, translations BRO KT SA

FLINT, John Edgar, 1930- , Canadian; nonfiction CON

FLINT, Robert, 1838-1910, Scots; nonfiction KBA

FLINT, Timothy, 1780-1840,

American; fiction KAA

FLIPPO, Edwin Bly, 1925- , American; nonfiction CON

FLOAN, Howard Russell, 1918- , American; nonfiction CON

FLODOARDO (Frodoardo), 894-966, French; nonfiction SA

FLOETHE, Louise Lee, 1913- , American; juveniles CON WA

FLOETHE, Richard, 1901- , German-American; juveniles CON FUL

FLOHERTY, John Joseph, 1882-1964, American; juveniles KJU WA

FLONCEL, Albert François, 1697-1773, French; nonfiction DIL

FLONCEL, Albert Jerome, 1747- , French; nonfiction DIL

FLONCEL, Jeanne Françoise de Lavau, 1715-64, French; translation DIL

FLOOD, Kenneth Urban, 1925- , American; nonfiction CON

FLORA, Flether, 1914- , American; fiction CON

FLORA, James Royer, 1914- , American; juveniles, nonfiction COM CON

FLORA, Joseph Martin, 1934- , American; nonfiction CON

FLORANES VELEZ de ROBLES, Rafael, 1743-1801, Spanish; nonfiction BL SA

FLOREN, Lee ('Brett Austin'; 'Wade Hamilton'; 'Lew Smith'; 'Lee Thomas'; 'Len Turner'; 'Will Watson'; 'Claudia Hall'; 'Dave Wilson'; 'Sophia Nelson'; 'Marguerite Nelson'), 1910- , American; fiction CON PAC

'FLORENCE' see OSGOOD, Frances S. L.

FLORENCE, Harold, 1942- , American; nonfiction CON

FLORENCE of WORCESTER, -1118, English; diary BRO KB ST

FLORENSKI, Pavel Alexandrovich, 1882- , Russian; nonfiction HARK ST

FLORER, Warren Washburn, 1869- , American; criticism HOO

FLORES, Alfredo, 1900- , Bolivian; essays, criticism, fiction MIN

FLORES, Alonso, 1476-1520, Spanish; nonfiction BL SA

FLORES, Antonio, 1821-66, Spanish; journalism, fiction BL SA

FLORES, Ivan, 1923- , American; nonfiction CON

FLORES, Juan de, 1470?-1525, Spanish; fiction BL SA ST

FLORES, Luis B., 1860-1938, Costa Rican; poetry MIN

FLORES, Manuel María, 1840-85, Mexican; poetry SA

FLORES, Mario, 1892- , Bolivian; journalism MIN

FLORES ARENAS, Francisco, 1801-77, Spanish; poetry, plays BL SA

FLORES de OCARIZ, Juan, 17th cent., Colombian; nonfiction MIN

FLORES GARCIA, Francisco, 1846-1917, Spanish; journalism, plays SA

FLOREZ, Julio, 1867/69-1923, Colombian; poetry MIN SA ST

FLOREZ, Leónidas, 1839-92, Colombian; journalism, poetry MIN

FLOREZ de SETIEN, Enrique, 1702-73, Spanish; nonfiction BL SA ST

FLORIAN, Jean Pierre Claris de, 1755-94, French; fiction DIF DIL HAR KE SA ST

FLORIN, Lambert William, 1905- , American; nonfiction CON PAC

FLORINSKY, Michael T., 1894- , Russian-Swiss; nonfiction CON

FLORIO, John, 1553?-1625, English; translations BRO KB ST

FLORIT, Eugenio, 1903- , Spanish; poetry, essays BL MIN SA ST

FLORO, Lucio Anneo, 2nd cent., Roman; poetry SA

FLORUS, Lucius Annaeus, fl. 150, Roman; nonfiction ST

FLORY, Jane Trescott, 1917- , American; juveniles CON

FLORY, Julia McCune, 1882-1971, American; nonfiction CON

FLOWER, Dean S., 1938- , American; nonfiction CON

FLOWER, Desmond John Newman, 1907- , English; translations, nonfiction CON

FLOWER, Harry Alfred, 1901- , English; nonfiction CON

FLOWER, Harry John, 1936- , Canadian; fiction CON

FLOWER, Robin Ernest William, 1881-1946, English; poetry BRO

FLOWER, Sir William Henry, 1831-
99, English; nonfiction KBA
FLOWERS, Ann Moore, 1923- ,
American; nonfiction CON
FLOWERS, Charles, 1942- , Amer-
ican; fiction CON
FLOYD, Barry Neil, 1925- , Eng-
lish; nonfiction CON
FLOYD, Troy Smith, 1920- ,
American; nonfiction CON
FLOYD, William Anderson, 1928- ,
American; nonfiction CON
FLOYD, William Edward Gregory,
1939- , American; nonfiction
CON
FLUCK, Reginald Alan Paul,
1928- , Welsh; nonfiction CON
FLUDD, Robert (Flud), 1574-1633,
English; nonfiction KB
FLÜGEL, Heinz, 1907- , German;
nonfiction KU
FLUGI d'ASPERMONT, Conradin
('Fluock'), 1787-1874, Raeto-
Romansch; poetry ST
FLUMIANI, Carlo Maria, 1911- ,
Italian-American; nonfiction CON
FLUNO, Robert Younger, 1916- ,
American; nonfiction CON
FLYGARE-CARLEN, Emilie Smith,
1807-92, Swedish; fiction KE
ST
FLYGT, Sten G., 1911- , American;
nonfiction CON
FLYNN, Donald Robert, 1928- ,
American; plays CON
FLYNN, George Quitman, 1937- ,
American; nonfiction CON
FLYNN, James Joseph, 1911- ,
American; nonfiction CON
FLYNN, James R., 1934- , Amer-
ican; nonfiction CON
FLYNN, John Joseph, 1936- , Amer-
ican; nonfiction CON
FLYNN, John Thomas, 1882- ,
American; nonfiction, journalism
KT
FLYNN, Leslie Bruce, 1918- ,
American; nonfiction CON
FLYNN, Paul Patrick, 1942- ,
American; nonfiction CON
FLYNN, Robert Lopez, 1932- ,
American; fiction CON
'FLYNT, Josiah' see WILLARD:
Josiah F.
FLYNT, Wayne, 1940- , American;
nonfiction CON
FOA, Eugénie Rodrigues, 1789-1853,
French; nonfiction SA

FOAT FUGAY, Emine, 1897- ,
Turkish; nonfiction CON
FOCIUDES de MILETO, 580-20
B.C., Greek; poetry SA
FOCILLON, Henri, 1881-1943,
French; criticism DIF
'FOCK, Gorch' (Johann Kinau),
1880-1916, German; fiction,
plays ST
FOCKEES, Melchior, 17th cent.,
Dutch; plays ST
FOCQUENBROCH, Willem God-
schalk van, 1635-75, Dutch;
poetry, plays ST
FODA, Aun see FOXE, Arthur N.
FODOR, Eugene, 1905- ,
Hungarian-American; nonfiction
CON
FÖLDES, Jolán, 1903- , Hungarian;
fiction HAR KT ST
'FOERSTER, Eberhard' see
WEISENBORN, Gunther
FOERSTER, Norman, 1887- ,
Anglo-American; nonfiction,
criticism CON JO KT
FOFANOV, Konstantin Mikhaylovich,
1862-1911, Russian; poetry
COL HARK SA ST
FOFF, Arthur Raymond ('A.R.
Lawrence'; 'Karl Lawrence')
1925- , American; nonfiction,
fiction CON
'FOGARTY, Jonathan Titulescu,
Esq.' see FARRELL, James
T.
FOGARTY, Michael Patrick,
1916- , Irish; nonfiction CON
FOGAZZARO, Antonio, 1842-1911,
Italian; fiction, poetry, plays
COL HAR KT MAG SA ST
FOGEL, David, 1891- , Jewish;
poetry, fiction ST
FOGEL, Ruby, American; poetry
CON
FOGELQUIST, Donald F., 1916- ,
American; nonfiction BL
FOGELQVIST, Torsten, 1880-1941,
Swedish; criticism COL SA
FOGLE, French Rowe, 1912- ,
American; nonfiction CON
FOGLE, Richard Harter, 1911- ,
American; nonfiction CON
FOIK, Paul Joseph, 1880-1941,
Canadian; nonfiction HOE
FOINARD, Frédéric Maurice,
1683-1743, French; nonfiction
DIL
FOIX, J.V., 1894- , Spanish;

poetry, journalism, criticism
SA
FOKKE SIMONSZ, Arend, 1755-1812,
Dutch; poetry ST
FOKKEMA Douwe Wessel, 1931- ,
Dutch; poetry CON
FOLARD P. fr. M., 1683-1739,
French; plays DIL
FOLARD, Jean Charles de, 1669-
1752, French; nonfiction DIL
FOLDES, John, 1903- , Hungarian;
fiction SA
FOLEJEWSKI, Zbigniew, 1910- ,
American; nonfiction CON
FOLENGO, Teofilo, 1496?-1544,
Italian; poetry SA ST
FOLEY, Anna Bernice Williams,
1902- , American; juveniles
CON
FOLEY, Cedric John ('John Sawyer';
'Ian Sinclair'), 1917- , English;
fiction CON
FOLEY, Charles, 1908- , English;
nonfiction CON
FOLEY, Daniel Joseph, 1913- ,
American; juveniles CON WA
FOLEY, Helen see FOWLER, Helen
R. H.
FOLEY, Mary Louise Munro, 1933- ,
Canadian; fiction CON
FOLEY, William E., 1938- , Amer-
ican; nonfiction CON
FOLGER, Peter, 1617-90, American;
poetry KAA
FOLGORE da SAN Gimignano, 1270-
1330, Italian; poetry ST
FOGUERA, Joaquín, 1883-1919,
Spanish; poetry, criticism SA
FOLKARD, Charles James, 1878-
1963, English; juveniles DOY
FOLKERTSMA, Fellsje Boates,
1893- , Freisian; nonfiction ST
FOLKMAN, Jerome Daniel, 1907- ,
American; nonfiction CON
FOLLAIN, Jean, 1903-71, French;
poetry DIF MAL
FOLLEN, Eliza Lee Cabot, 1787-
1860, American; nonfiction
KAA
FOLLEN Karl Theodor Christian,
1796-1840, German-American;
poetry ST
FOLLETT, Helen Thomas, American;
juveniles WA
FOLLETT, Robert J.R., 1928- ,
American; nonfiction CON
FOLLEY, Terence T., 1931- ,
English; nonfiction CON

FOLLMANN, Joseph F., Jr.,
1908- , American; nonfiction
CON
FOLMSBEE, Stanley John,
1899- , American; nonfiction
CON
FOLQUET de MARSEILLE, 1160-
1231, French; poetry DIF
KE ST
FOLSOM, Elizabeth Irons,
1876- , American; fiction
HOO
FOLSOM, Franklin Brewster
('Benjamin Brewster'; 'Samuel
Cutler'; 'Michael Gorham';
'Lyman Hopkins'; 'Troy
Nesbit'), 1907- , American;
fiction, nonfiction CON WA
FOLSOM, Kenneth Everett, 1921- ,
American; nonfiction CON
FOLSOM, Marion Bayard, 1893- ,
American; nonfiction CON
FOLSOM, Michael Brewster,
1938- , American; juveniles
WA
FOLTA, Jeannette R., 1934- ,
American; nonfiction CON
FOLTIN, Lore Barbara, 1913- ,
Austrian-American; nonfiction
CON
FOLTZ, William Jay, 1936- ,
American; nonfiction CON
FOLZ, Hans, 1450-1515, German;
poetry AL ST
FOMBEURE, Maurice, 1906- ,
French; poetry DIF
FON EISEN, Anthony T., 1917- ,
American; juveniles CON
FONBLANQUE, Albany William,
1793-1872, English; journalism
BRO KBA ST
FONCEMAGNE, Etienne Larréault
de, 1694-1779, French; nonfic-
tion DIL
FONCK, Rev. John Christian
Leopold, 1865-1930, German;
nonfiction HO
FONDANE, Benjamin, 1898-1944,
French; poetry, essays DIF
FONER, Eric, 1943- , American;
nonfiction CON
FONER, Philip, 1910- , American;
nonfiction CON
FONSECA, Aloysius Joseph, 1915- ,
Indian; nonfiction CON
FONSECA, Antonio José Branquinho
da ('Antonio Madeira), 1905- ,
Portuguese; poetry, fiction,

plays, criticism FLE
FONSECA, Cristóbal, 1550?-1621,
Spanish; nonfiction BL HAR SA
ST
FONSECA, John R., 1925- , Amer-
ican; nonfiction CON
FONSEKA, Joseph Peter de, 1897- ,
Ceylonese; nonfiction HOE
FONTAINES, André, 1865-1948,
Franco-Belgian; poetry DIF HAR
ST
FONTAINE, Andre, 1921- , French;
nonfiction CON
FONTAINE, Alexis, 1705-71, French;
nonfiction DIL
FONTAINE, Charles, 1514-65,
French; poetry KE SA ST
FONTAINE, Jean Claude, 1715-1807,
French; nonfiction DIL
FONTAINE, Marie Pierre, 1712-
75, French; nonfiction DIL
FONTAINE de la ROCHE, Jacques,
1688-1761, French; nonfiction
DIL
FONTAINE-MALHERBE, Jean, 1740-
80, French; poetry, plays,
translations DIL
FONTAINES, Marie Louise Charlotte
de Pelard, -1730, French;
nonfiction DIL SA
FONTANA, Bernard Lee, 1931- ,
American; nonfiction CON
FONTANA, Gian, 1897-1935, Raeto-
Romansch; poetry, fiction ST
FONTANA, Oskar Maurus, 1889- ,
German; plays, fiction AL LEN
FONTANA, Vincent James, 1923- ,
American; nonfiction CON
FONTANE, Theodor, 1819-98, Ger-
man; criticism, poetry AL COL
HAR KE MAG SA ST
FONTANES, Louis, 1757-1821,
French; poetry ST
FONTANIEU, Gaspard Moise, 1693-
1767, French; nonfiction DIL
FONTENAI, Pierre Claude, 1663-
1742, French; nonfiction DIL
FONTENAY, Charles Louis, 1917- ,
Brazilian-American; fiction
CON
FONTENAY, Louis Abel, 1737-1806,
French; journalism, nonfiction
DIL
FONTENEAU, Leónard, -1780,
French; nonfiction DIL
FONTENELLE, Bernard le Bouvier
de, 1657-1757, French; poetry
DIF DIL HAR KE MAL SA ST

FONTENOT, Mary Alice, 1910- ,
American; juveniles CON
FONTENROSE, Joseph, 1903- ,
American; nonfiction CON
FONTENU, Louis François de,
1667-1759, French; nonfiction
DIL
FONTES, Hermes Martins, 1888-
1930, Brazilian; poetry SA
FONTETTE de SOMMERE, 18th
cent., French; fiction DIL
FONTEYN, Bernard, 1603-49?,
Dutch; plays ST
FONTEYN, Nicolaas, 1600-44?,
Dutch; plays ST
FONVIZIN, Denis Ivanovich,
1745-92, Russian; plays
HARK KE SA ST
FOORD, Archibald Smith, 1914- ,
American; nonfiction CON
FOOT, Hugh Mackintosh (Lord
Caradon), 1907- , English;
nonfiction CON
FOOT, Michael Richard Daniell,
1919- , English; nonfiction
CON
FOOT, Paul Mackintosh, 1937- ,
English; nonfiction CON
FOOTE, Dorothy Norris McBride,
1908- , American; nonfiction
CON
FOOTE, Samuel, 1720-77, Eng-
lish; plays BRO KB ST
FOOTE, Shelby, 1916- , Ameri-
can; fiction CON KTS
FORAN, Donald J., 1943- ,
American; nonfiction CON
FORBERG, Ati, American;
juveniles WA
FORBES, Allan, 1874- , English;
nonfiction HIG
FORBES, Archibald, 1838-1900,
Scots; nonfiction KBA
FORBES, Christopher Patrick,
1925- , English; nonfiction
CON
FORBES, De Loris Stanton ('De
Forbes'; 'Stanton Forbes';
'Forbes Rydell'), 1923- ,
American; fiction CON
FORBES, Edward, 1815-54, Eng-
lish; nonfiction KBA
FORBES, Elliot, 1917- , Ameri-
can; nonfiction CON
FORBES, Esther, 1891/94-1967,
American; juveniles, fiction
COM CON FUL HO KT WA
WAF

'FORBES, Graham B.' see STRATE-
MEYER, Edward L.
FORBES, Henry William, 1918- ,
Austrian-American; nonfiction
CON
FORBES, Jack D., 1934- , Ameri-
can; nonfiction CON
FORBES, James David, 1809-68,
Scots; nonfiction BRO KBA
FORBES, Joan Rosita, 1893- ,
English; nonfiction BRO
FORBES, Joanne R. Triebel,
1930- , American; nonfiction
CON
FORBES, John Van Gelder, 1916- ,
American; nonfiction CON
FORBES, Katherine Russell,   -1956,
American; juveniles WA
FORBES, Kathryn see McLEAN,
Kathryn A.
FORBES, Rosita Torr, 1893- ,
English; nonfiction KT
'FORBES, Stanton' see FORBES,
De Loris S.
FORBES, W. B. ('Maintop'),   -1928,
English; nonfiction HIG
FORBES-BOYD, Eric, 1897- ,
English; plays, fiction CON
FORBIN, Gaspard François Anne de,
1718- , French; nonfiction
DIL
FORBIS, William H., 1918- , Amer-
ican; nonfiction CON
FORBONNAIS, 1722-1800, French;
nonfiction DIL
FORBUS, Ina Bell, Scots-American;
fiction CON
FORCE, Peter, 1790-1868, American;
nonfiction KAA
FORCE, William M., 1916- ,
American; nonfiction CON
FORCEY, Charles Budd, 1925- ,
American; nonfiction CON
FORCIONE, Alban Keith, 1938- ,
American; nonfiction CON
FORD, Agnes Gibbs, 1902- ,
American; nonfiction CON
'FORD, Albert Lee' see STRATE-
MEYER, Edward L.
FORD, Alec George, 1926- ,
English; nonfiction CON
FORD, Alice, 1906- , American;
nonfiction CON
FORD, Amasa B., 1922- , Amer-
ican; nonfiction CON
FORD, Charles Henri, 1913- ,
American; nonfiction CON
FORD, Daniel Francis, 1931- ,

American; fiction CON
FORD, Donald Frank William,
1924- , English; nonfiction
CON
'FORD, Elbur' see HIBBERT,
Eleanor
FORD, Edsel, 1928-70, American;
poetry CON
FORD, Ford Madox ('Ford Madox
Hueffer'), 1873-1939, English;
fiction, criticism, poetry
BRO FLE KL KT MAG RIC
SA ST
FORD, Franklin Lewis, 1920- ,
American; nonfiction CON
'FORD, Fred' see DOERFFLER,
Alfred
FORD, George Harry, 1914- ,
Canadian-American; nonfiction
CON
FORD, George Lonnie, 1914- ,
American; nonfiction CON
FORD, Gordon Buell, Jr., 1937- ,
American; nonfiction CON
FORD, Guy Barrett, 1922- ,
American; nonfiction CON
FORD, Herbert Paul, 1927- ,
American; fiction CON
'FORD, Hildegarde' see MORRISON,
Velma F.
FORD, James Allen, 1920- ,
Scots; fiction CON
FORD, James Laurence Collier,
1907- , American; nonfiction
CON
FORD, Jeremiah Denis Mathias,
1873-1958, American; nonfiction
BL HOE
FORD, Jesse Hill, Jr., 1928- ,
American; fiction CON
FORD, John, 1586-1640?, English;
plays BRO KB MAG SA SP ST
FORD, Kathleen, 1932- , Ameri-
can; fiction CON
FORD, Lauren, 1891- , American;
juveniles WA
FORD, Lee, 1936- , American;
juveniles CON
FORD, Leighton F.S., 1931- ,
Canadian; nonfiction CON
FORD, Le Roy, 1922- , Ameri-
can; nonfiction CON
'FORD, Leslie' see BROWN, Z.J.
FORD, Lewis B. see PATTEN,
Lewis B.
'FORD, Marcia' see RADFORD,
Ruby L.
FORD, Margaret Patricia, 1925- ,

American; nonfiction CON

FORD, Mary Forker, 1905- , American; fiction CON

FORD, Nancy K., American; juvenile WA

FORD, Nick Aaron, 1904- , American; fiction CON

FORD, Norman Dennis, 1921- , Anglo-American; nonfiction CON

FORD, Patrick, 1835-1913, American; journalism KAA

FORD, Patrick, 1914- , Australian; nonfiction CON

FORD, Paul Leicester, 1865-1902, American; fiction, nonfiction BRO KAA

FORD, Phyllis Marjorie, 1928- , American; nonfiction CON

FORD, Richard, 1796-1858, English; nonfiction BL BRO KBA ST

FORD, Richard Brice, 1935- , American; nonfiction CON

FORD, Robert Arthur Douglass, 1915- , Canadian; poetry MUR SY

FORD, Robert E., American; fiction CON

FORD, Robert Nicholas, 1909- , American; nonfiction CON

FORD, Thomas Wellborn, 1924- , American; nonfiction CON

FORD, W. Herschel, 1900- , American; nonfiction CON

FORD, Worthington Chauncey, 1858-1941, American; nonfiction KT

FORDE, A.N., 1923- , West Indian; poetry, plays, fiction MUR

FORDE-JOHNSTON, James, 1927- , English; nonfiction CON

FORDNEY, John Wien, 1817-91, American; journalism, nonfiction KAA

FORDUN, John of, -1384, English; diary BRO ST

FORE, William Frank, 1928- , American; nonfiction CON

'FOREESTIER, Pauwels' see ALBERDINGK, Thijm J.A.

FORELL, George W., 1919- , German-American; nonfiction CON

FOREMAN, Carolyn Thomas, 1875- , American; nonfiction MAR

FOREMAN, Grant, 1869- , American; nonfiction MAR

FOREMAN, Harry, 1915- , Canadian-American; nonfiction CON

FOREMAN, Kenneth Joseph, 1891- ,

American; nonfiction CON

FOREMAN, Lawton Durant, 1913- , American; nonfiction CON

FOREMAN, Leonard London, 1901- , English; fiction CON

FOREMAN, Michael, 1938- , English; juvenile COM CON

FORER, Lois Goldstein, 1914- , American; nonfiction CON

FORER, Lucille Kremith, American; nonfiction CON

FORES, John, 1914- , English; fiction CON

'FOREST, Felix' see LINEBARGER, Paul M.A.

FOREST, Ilse, 1896- , American; nonfiction CON

FOREST, Jean, 18th cent., French; nonfiction DIL

FORESTER, Cecil Scott, 1899-1966, English; juveniles, fiction BRO DOY KT MAG RIC

'FORESTER, Mark' see HERBERT, Henry W.

FORESTIER, Pierre, 1654-1723, French; nonfiction DIL

FORETS, Louis René des, 1918- , French; fiction DIC DIF PIN

FOREZ see MAURIAC, François

FORGEOT, Nicolas Julien, 1738-78, French; plays DIL

'FORIO, Robert' see WEISS, Irving J.

FORMAGE, Jacques Charles César, 1749-1808, French; nonfiction DIL

FORMAN, Brenda Lu, 1936- , American; juveniles CON WA

FORMAN, Charles William, 1916- , American; nonfiction CON

FORMAN, Harrison, 1904- , American; juveniles CON WA

FORMAN, Harry Buxton (Henry), 1842-1917, English; nonfiction KBA

FORMAN, Henry James, 1879-1966, American; nonfiction CON

FORMAN, James Adam Sholto, 1915- , Scots; nonfiction CON

FORMAN, James Douglas, 1932- , American; nonfiction CON WA

FORMAN, Jonathan, 1887- , American; nonfiction CON

FORMAN, Leona S., 1940- , Amer-
ican; juveniles CON
FORMAN, Robert E., 1924- , Amer-
ican; nonfiction CON
FORMEY, Jean Henri Samuel, 1711-
97, French; nonfiction DIL
FORMICA, Mercedes, 1918?- ,
Spanish; fiction SA
FORNARI, Franco, 1921- , Italian;
nonfiction CON
FORNARIS, José, 1827-90, Cuban;
poetry, essays, fiction MIN SA
FORNELL, Earl Wesley, 1915- ,
American; nonfiction CON
FORNER, Juan Pablo, 1756-97,
Spanish; nonfiction BL SA ST
FORNERET, Xavier, 1809-84, French;
poetry DIF
FORNES, Maria Irene, 1930- ,
Cuban-American; plays CON
FORNIER, Henri Alain see 'ALAIN-
FORNIER'
FORNO, Lawrence Joseph, 1943- ,
American; nonfiction CON
'FORREST, Caleb' see TELFER,
Dariel
FORREST, Earle Robert, 1883- ,
American; nonfiction CON
FORREST, Felix C., 1913- ,
American; fiction WAF
'FORREST, Sybil' see MARKUN,
Patricia M.
FORREST, William, fl. 1581, Eng-
lish; poetry ST
FORREST, William George, 1925- ,
Scots; nonfiction CON
FORRESTER, Frank H., American;
juveniles WA
FORRESTER, Larry, 1924- , Scots;
nonfiction CON
FORRESTER, William Ray,
1911- , American; nonfiction
CON
FORSANZ, Hilaire, de, 1664-1737,
French; poetry DIL
FORSBERG, Malcolm I., 1908- ,
American; nonfiction CON
FORSEE, Frances Aylesa, Ameri-
can; juveniles COM CON
FORSH, Olga Dmitrievan ('A.
Terek'; Fors), 1873/75-1961,
Russian; fiction FLE HAR
HARK ST
FORSNÄS, V.A. see 'KOSKENNIEMI,
Veikko A.'
FORSSLUND, Karl Erik, 1872-1941,
Swedish; poetry, fiction COL
FORSTENREIM, Ana, 1846- ,

German; poetry SA
FORSTER, Arnold, 1912- , Amer-
ican; nonfiction CON
FORSTER, Edward Morgan, 1879-
1970, English; fiction BRO
CON FLE KL KT MAG RIC
SA ST
FORSTER, Johann George Adam,
1754-94, German; nonfiction
AL HAR KE ST
FORSTER, John, 1812-76, English;
nonfiction BRO KBA ST
FORSTER, Kurt, 1916- , Ameri-
can; nonfiction CON
FORSTMAN, Henry Jackson,
1929- , American; nonfiction
CON
FORSYTH, Anne, 1933- , Scots;
nonfiction CON
FORSYTH, David P., 1930- ,
American; nonfiction CON
FORSYTH, George Howard, Jr.,
1901- , American; nonfiction
CON
FORSYTH, Gloria, American;
juveniles WA
FORSYTH, Ilene Haering, 1928- ,
English; nonfiction CON
FORSYTH, James, 1913- ,
British; poetry, plays MAT
'FORSYTHE, Robert' see CRICHTON,
Kyle S.
FORT, Charles Hoy, 1874-1932,
American; criticism KT
'FORT, Paul' see STOCKTON,
Frank R.
FORT, Paul, 1872-1960, French;
poetry, criticism, plays COL
DIF FLE HAR MAL SA ST
FORT, William Edwards, Jr.,
1905- , American; nonfiction
CON
FORTEGUERRI, Escipión ('Cartero-
maco'), 1466-1515, Italian;
nonfiction SA
FORTEGUERRI, Nicolás, 1674-
1735, Italian; poetry SA
FORTESCUE, Sir John, 1394?-
1476?, English; nonfiction
BRO KB ST
FORTET, Jacques, 1698-1770,
French; nonfiction DIL
'FORTH, George' see FREDERIC,
Harold
'FORTINI, Franco' (Franco Lattes),
1917- , Italian; nonfiction
SA
FORTINI, Pietro, 1500-62, Italian;

fiction ST
FORTMAN, Edmund J., 1901- ,
American; nonfiction CON
'FORTUN, Elen' (Encarnación
Aragoneses Urquijo), 1886-1952,
Spanish; nonfiction, fiction BL
SA
FORTUN, Fernando, 1890-1914,
Spanish; poetry, criticism SA
FORTUNATUS, 1509- , German;
nonfiction AL
FORTUNATUS, Venantius Honorius,
540-600, Italian; nonfiction SA
ST
FORUGHI, -1943, Persian; nonfic-
tion LAN
'FORWARD, Luke' see PATRICK,
Johnstone G.
FORZANO, Gionacchino, 1883/84-
1970, Italian; plays COL MAT
SA
FOSCOLO, Ugo (Niccolo), 1778-1827,
Italian; poetry HAR KE SA ST
FOSCUE, Edwin Jay, 1899- , Amer-
ican; nonfiction CON
FOSDICK, Charles Austin ('Harry
Castlemon'), 1842-1915, Ameri-
can; juveniles KAA
FOSDICK, Harry Emerson, 1878-
1969, American; nonfiction KTS
WA
FOSDICK, William Whiteman, 1825-
1862, American; poetry, fiction
KAA
FOSKETT, Douglas John, 1918- ,
English; nonfiction CON
FOSKETT, Reginald, 1909- ,
English; nonfiction CON
FOSS, Philip Oliver, American;
nonfiction CON
FOSS, Sam Walter, 1858-1911,
American; poetry, journalism
BRO KAA
FOSS, Willia Otto, 1918- , Amer-
ican; juveniles CON WA
FOSSE, Giovanni Pietro delle see
'VALERIANO, Pierio'
FOSSUM, Robert M., 1923- ,
American; nonfiction CON
FOSTER, Charles Howell, 1913- ,
American; nonfiction CON
FOSTER, Charles Irving, 1898- ,
American; nonfiction CON
FOSTER, David William Anthony,
1940- , American; nonfiction
CON
FOSTER, Donn ('Dennis Saint-Eden'),
1948- , American; poetry

CON MUR
FOSTER, Doris Van Liew,
1899- , American; juveniles
CON
FOSTER, Elizabeth, 1905-63,
American; juveniles CON
FOSTER, Genevieve Stump,
1893- , American; juveniles
COM CON KJU WA
FOSTER, George Allen, 1907- ,
American; juveniles CON WA
FOSTER, H. Lincoln, 1906- ,
American; nonfiction CON
FOSTER, Hannah Webster, 1759-
1840, American; fiction, es-
says KAA
FOSTER, Henry Hubbard, Jr.,
1911- , American; nonfiction
CON
FOSTER, Jack Donald, 1930- ,
American; nonfiction CON
FOSTER, Joanna (Joanna Foster
Dougherty), 1928- , American;
juveniles CON
FOSTER, John, 1770-1843, English;
essays BRO KBA ST
FOSTER, John, 1915- , English;
nonfiction CON
FOSTER, John Thomas, 1925- ,
American; juveniles CON
FOSTER, Julian Francis Sherwood,
1926- , English; nonfiction
CON
FOSTER, Laura Louise James,
1918- , American; juveniles
CON
FOSTER, Lee Edwin, 1943- ,
American; fiction CON
FOSTER, Margery Somers, 1914- ,
American; nonfiction CON
FOSTER, Marguerite H., 1909- ,
American; nonfiction CON
FOSTER, Marian Curtis ('Mariana'),
1909- , American; juveniles
WA
FOSTER, Martha Standing, Amer-
ican; juveniles CON
FOSTER, Paul, 1931- , Ameri-
can; plays CON
'FOSTER, Richard' see CROSSEN,
Kendell F.
FOSTER, Ruel Elton, 1917- ,
American; nonfiction CON
FOSTER, Stephen Collins, 1826-
64, American; songs BRO
KAA
FOSTER, Virginia Ramos, 1936- ,
American; nonfiction CON

FOTHERGILL, Arthur Brian, 1921- ,
English; nonfiction CON
FOTHERGILL, George Algernon,
1868- , English; nonfiction
HIG
FOTHERGILL, Philip Gilbert,
1908- , English; nonfiction
CON
FOTTLER, Myron David, 1941- ,
American; nonfiction CON
FOUCAULT, Nicolas Joseph, 1643-
1721, French; nonfiction DIL
FOUCHER, 18th cent., French;
nonfiction DIL
FOUCHER, Paul, 1704-78, French;
nonfiction DIL
FOUCHER d'OBSONVILLE, 1734-
1802, French; nonfiction DIL
FOUCHET, Max-Pol, 1913- ,
French; poetry, essays DIC
DIF
FOUCHY, J. Paul, 1707-88, French;
nonfiction DIL
FOUCQUET, Jean François, 1663-
1740, French; nonfiction DIL
'FOUGASEE' see BIRD, Cyril K.
FOUGERAS, François Victor Chavaille,
1713-78, French; nonfiction DIL
FOUGERE, Jean, 1914- , French;
nonfiction DIF
FOUGERET de MONTBRON,
-1761, French; nonfiction
DIL
FOUGEROUX de BONDAROY, Auguste
Denis, 1732-89, French; nonfiction
DIL
FOUILLEE, Alfred Jules Emile, 1838-
1912, French; nonfiction DIF SA
FOUILLOU, Jacques, 1670-1736,
French; nonfiction DIL
FOULCHE-DELBOSC, Raimundo,
1684-1929, French; nonfiction
BL SA
FOULECHAT, Denis, 14th cent.,
French; translations ST
FOULKE, Roy Anderson, 1896- ,
American; nonfiction CON
FOULKES, Albert Peter, 1936- ,
English; nonfiction CON
FOULKES, Fred K., 1941- ,
American; nonfiction CON
FOULON, -1813, French; nonfic-
tion DIL
FOUNTAIN, Leatrice, 1924- ,
American; fiction CON
FOUQUE, Friedrich, H.K. see
LA MOTTE-FOUGUE, Friedrich
H.K.

FOUQUERE, Antoine Michel,
1641- , French; nonfiction
DIL
FOURAKER, Lawrence Edward,
1923- , American; nonfiction
CON
FOURCROY, Antoine François,
1755-1809, French; nonfiction
DIL
FOUREST, Georges, 1864-1945,
French; poetry DIF
'FOUREST, Michel' see WYNNE-
TYSON, Timothy J.L.
FOURIER, François Marie Charles,
1772-1837, French; nonfiction
DIF KE SA ST
FOURMONT, Claude Louis, 1703-
80, French; nonfiction DIL
FOURMONT, Etienne, 1683-1745,
French; nonfiction DIL
FOURMONT, Michel, 1690-1746,
French; nonfiction DIL
FOURNIE, 1738- , French; nonfic-
tion DIL
FOURNIER, Henry A.F. see
'ALAIN-FOURNIER'
FOURNIER, Jules, 1884-1918,
Canadian; poetry SY
FOURNIER, Pierre see 'GASCAR,
Pierre'
FOURNIER, Pierre Simon, 1712-
68, French; nonfiction DIL
FOURQUEVAUX, Jean Baptiste
Raymond (Pavie), 1693-1768,
French; nonfiction DIL
FOUSTE, Ethel Bonita Rutledge,
1926- , American; fiction,
juveniles CON
'FOURTH, Clifton' see MORSE, H.
Clifton
'FOURTH, Brother, The' see
AUNG, Maung H.
FOWKE, Edith Margaret, 1913- ,
Canadian; nonfiction, juveniles
CON
FOWLER, Alastair David Shaw,
1930- , Scots; nonfiction CON
FOWLER, Austin, 1928- , Ameri-
can; poetry, nonfiction CON
FOWLER, David Covington, 1921- ,
American; nonfiction CON PAC
FOWLER, Don D., 1936- ,
American; nonfiction CON
FOWLER, Francis George see
FOWLER, H.W.
FOWLER, Gene, 1890-1960,
American; journalism, fiction
HO KT

FOWLER, Gene, 1931- , American; poetry MUR

FOWLER, Helen Rosa Huxley ('Helen Foley'), 1917- , English; nonfiction CON

FOWLER, Henry Watson, 1858-1933, English; nonfiction BRO KT

FOWLER, Kenneth Abrams ('Clark Brooker'), 1900- , American; nonfiction CON

FOWLER, Mary Elizabeth, 1911- , American; nonfiction CON

FOWLER, Thomas, 1832-1904, English; nonfiction KBA

FOWLER, Wilfred, 1907- , English; nonfiction CON

FOWLER, Will, 1922- , American; nonfiction CON

FOWLER, William, fl. 1603- , Scots; poetry KB

FOWLES, John, 1927- , English; fiction CON RIC

FOWLIE, Wallace, 1908- , American; poetry, criticism CON KTS

FOX, Adam, 1883- , English; nonfiction CON

FOX, Aileen, 1907- , English; nonfiction CON

FOX, Alan John, English; nonfiction CON

FOX, Caroline, 1819-71, English; diary KBA

FOX, Charles Elliot, 1878- , English; nonfiction CON

FOX, Charles James, 1749-1806, English; nonfiction BRO ST

FOX, Charles John Frederick ('Yoi Over'), 1856- , English; nonfiction HIG

FOX, Charles Philip, 1913- , American; nonfiction CON

FOX, David Joseph, 1927- , American; nonfiction CON

FOX, Dorothy, American; juvenile WA

FOX, Douglas McMurray, 1940- , American; nonfiction CON

FOX, Edward Inman, 1933- , American; nonfiction BL CON

FOX, Edward Jackson, 1913- , Canadian-American; nonfiction CON

'FOX, Eleanor' see ST. JOHN, Wylly F.

FOX, Frederic Ewing, 1917- , American; nonfiction CON

FOX, Gardner Francis ('Jefferson Cooper'; 'Jeffrey Gardener'; 'James Kendricks'; 'Kevin Matthews'), 1911- , American; fiction CON

FOX, Geoffrey P., 1938- , American; nonfiction CON

FOX, George, 1624-91, English; nonfiction BRO KB

FOX, George Richard, 1934- , American; nonfiction CON

FOX, Grace Estelle, 1899- , American; nonfiction CON

FOX, Grace Imogene, 1907- , American; nonfiction CON

FOX, Henry Richard Vasall see HOLLAND, Lord

FOX, Hugh Bernard, Jr. ('Electra Magnetica'), 1930- , American; nonfiction CON

FOX, Jack Curtis, 1925- , American; nonfiction CON

FOX, John, 1862-1919, American; fiction BRO KAT KT RIC

FOX, John Howard, 1925- , American; nonfiction CON

FOX, Karl August, 1917- , American; nonfiction CON

FOX, Mary Virginia, 1919- , American; juveniles WA CON

'FOX, Owen' see FARMER, Bernard J.

FOX, Ralph Winston, 1900-37, Anglo-Canadian; fiction KT SA

FOX, Robert Barlow, 1930- , American; nonfiction CON

FOX, Ruth, 1895- , American; nonfiction CON

FOX, Samuel, 1905- , American; nonfiction CON

FOX, Stephen R., 1945- , American; nonfiction CON

FOX, Vernon Brittain, 1916- , American; nonfiction CON

FOX, Col. Victor J. see WINSTON, Robert A.

FOX, Willard, 1919- , American; nonfiction CON

FOX, William Lloyd, 1921- , American; nonfiction CON

FOX, William McNair, 1924- , American; nonfiction CON

FOX, William Price, Jr., 1926- , American; fiction CON

FOX, William Sherwood, 1878- , Canadian; nonfiction SY

FOX, William Wellington, 1909- , American; juveniles, nonfic-

tion CON WA
FOX MORCILLO, Sebastián, 1526?-
60, Spanish; nonfiction BL SA
FOXA, Agustín de, 1903-59, Spanish;
poetry, fiction, plays BL SA
FOXA, Francisco Javier, 1816-65,
Dominican; plays MIN
FOXA y LECANDA, Narciso, 1822-
83, Puerto Rican; poetry MIN
SA
FOXALL Raymond Jehoiada Campbell,
1916- , English; fiction CON
FOXE, Arthur Norman ('Aun Foda'),
1902- , American; nonfiction
CON
FOXE, John, 1516-87, English;
nonfiction BRO KB ST
FOY, Kenneth Russell ('Keith
Franklin'), 1922- , American;
fiction CON
FOY, Louis Etienne, -1778,
French; nonfiction DIL
FOZ, Braulio, 1791-1865, Spanish;
fiction, plays BL SA
'FRA ELBERTUS' see HUBBARD,
Elbert
FRACASTORO, Gerolamo, 1478-
1553, Italian; poetry SA ST
FRACCAROLI, Arnaldo, 1886- ,
Italian; fiction, plays, journalism
SA
FRACCHIA, Umberto, 1889-1930,
Italian; fiction HAR SA ST
FRACKENPOHL, Arthur Roland,
1924- , American; nonfiction
CON
FRAELICH, Richard Oddley, 1924- ,
American; nonfiction CON
FRAENKEL, Gerd, 1919- , German-
American; nonfiction CON
FRAENKEL, Heinrich ('Assiac';
'Caissa'; 'Cinna'), 1897- ,
German-English; nonfiction,
translations CON
FRAENKEL, Jack Runnels, 1932- ,
American; nonfiction CON
FRAENKEL, Osmond K., 1888- ,
American; nonfiction CON
FRAET, Frans, -1558, Dutch;
nonfiction ST
FRAGA IRIBARNE, Manuel, 1922- ,
Spanish; essays SA
FRAGA de LIS, Manuel, 1910- ,
Spanish; nonfiction SA
FRAGUEIRO, Mariano, 1795-1872,
Argentinian; nonfiction MIN
FRAGUIER, Claude François, 1666-
1728, French; nonfiction DIL

FRAHM, Anne B. Schwerdt,
1927- , American; nonfiction
CON
FRAHM, Ludwig, 1856-1936,
German; poetry ST
FRAIBERG, Louis Benjamin,
1913- , American; nonfiction
CON
FRAIGNEAU, André, 1907- ,
French; fiction, essays DIC
FRAILE RUIZ, Medardo, 1925- ,
Spanish; fiction, criticism
BL SA
FRAIN, Jean, 1641-1724, French;
nonfiction DIL
FRAINE, Harold George, 1900- ,
American; nonfiction CON
FRAISCHOT, Casimir see
FRESCHOT, Casimir
FRAKES, George Edward, 1932- ,
American; nonfiction CON
FRAM, David, 1903- , Jewish;
poetry ST
FRAM, Eugene Harry, 1929- ,
American; nonfiction CON
FRAME, Donald Murdoch, 1911- ,
American; nonfiction, transla-
tions CON
'FRAME, Janet' see CLUTHA,
Janet P. F.
FRAMERY, Nicolas Etienne,
1745-1810, French; poetry,
plays DIL
FRAMPTON, Merle Elbert,
1903- , American; nonfiction
CON
'FRANCE, Anatole' (Jacques
Anatole Thibault), 1844-1924,
French; fiction, essays COL
DIF FLE HAR KAT KT MAG
MAL RIC SA ST
'FRANCE, Claire' see DORE,
Claire M.
FRANCE, Malcolm, 1928- ,
English; nonfiction CON
FRANCE-HAYHURST, Evangeline
Chaworth-Musters, 1904- ,
English; juveniles CON
'FRANCES, Miss' see HORWICH,
Frances R.
FRANCES, Immanuel, 1618-1710,
Italian; nonfiction, poetry ST
FRANCES, José, 1883- , Spanish;
fiction, plays SA BL
FRANCESCHI, Juan Gustavo,
1881- , Argentinian; essays
MIN
FRANCESCO da BARBERINO,

1264-1348, Italian; poetry ST
FRANCHERE, Hoyt Catlin, American;
    nonfiction PAC
FRANCHERE, Ruth Myers, American;
    nonfiction PAC
FRANCHEVILLE, Joseph du Fresne,
    1704-81, French; nonfiction DIL
FRANCHI, Raffaello, 1899-1949,
    Italian; poetry, fiction, criticism
    SA
FRANCHY, Franz Karl, 1896- ,
    German; nonfiction LEN
FRANCIS, Alan David, 1900- ,
    English; nonfiction CON
'FRANCIS, Anne' see WINTLE, Anne
FRANCIS, Basil Haskins ('Austen
    Rhode'), 1906- , English; fiction
    CON
'FRANCIS, Daniel' see CRANNY,
    Titus
FRANCIS, David Noel, 1904- ,
    English; nonfiction CON
FRANCIS, Dick, 1920- , Welsh;
    fiction CON
'FRANCIS, Dee' see HAAS, Dorothy
    F.
FRANCIS, Dorothy Brenner, 1926- ,
    American; juveniles CON
FRANCIS, Francis, 1830- , English;
    nonfiction HIG
FRANCIS, Franz see JUNIUS,
    Franciscus
FRANCIS, Heln Dannefer, 1915- ,
    American; fiction CON
FRANCIS, Henry S., 1925- ,
    American; juveniles WA
FRANCIS, Herbert Edward, Jr.,
    1924- , American; nonfiction
    CON
FRANCIS, Marilyn, 1920- , Ameri-
    can; poetry, fiction CON
'FRANCIS, Michael' see CATTAUI,
    Georges
FRANCIS, Nelle Trew, 1914- ,
    American; nonfiction CON
FRANCIS, Pamela Mary, 1926- ,
    English; juveniles CON
'FRANCIS, Philip' see LOCKYEAR,
    Roger
FRANCIS, Sir Philip ('Junius'),
    1740-1818, Irish; nonfiction
    BRO KB ST
FRANCIS, Philip Sheridan, 1918- ,
    American; nonfiction CON
FRANCIS, R. Mabel, 1880- ,
    American; nonfiction CON
FRANCIS, Robert Churchill,
    1901- , American; poetry,

fiction CON MUR
FRANCIS, Roy G., 1919- ,
    American; nonfiction CON
FRANCIS of ASSISI (Giovanni
    Bernardone), 1182-1226,
    Italian; poetry HAR KE SA
    ST
FRANCK, Adolphe, 1809-93,
    French; nonfiction DIF
FRANCK, Frederick ('Frank
    Fredericks'), 1909- ,
    American; nonfiction CON
FRANCK, Hans, 1879-1964, Ger-
    man; fiction, plays, poetry
    AL FLE KU LEN MAT
FRANCK, Harry Alverson,
    1881- , American; nonfiction
    KT
FRANCK, Sebastian, 1499-1542/43,
    German; essays AL ST
FRANCK, Thomas M., 1931- ,
    American; nonfiction CON
FRANCKE, Kuno, 1855-1930,
    German-American; poetry ST
FRANCKFURTER, Philipp
    ('Pharrer von Kalenberg),
    15th cent., German; nonfiction
    AL
FRANC-NOHAIN, Maurice Etienne
    Legrand, 1873-1934, French;
    fiction DIF
FRANCO, Alberto, 1903- , Argen-
    tinian; poetry MIN SA
FRANCO, Dolores, 1916- ,
    Spanish; nonfiction BL
'FRANCO, Harry' see BRIGGS,
    Charles F.
FRANCO, Jean, 1914- , French;
    nonfiction CON
FRANCO, Jean, 1924- , English;
    nonfiction CON
FRANCO, Luis L., 1898- ,
    Argentinian; poetry MIN SA
FRANCO, Niccolò, 1515-70,
    Italian; poetry ST
FRANCO, Veronica, 1546/54-91,
    Italian; poetry SA ST
FRANCO BARRETO, Juan, 1600-
    69, Portuguese; poetry SA
FRANCOEUR, Robert Thomas,
    1931- , American; nonfiction
    CON
FRANCOIS, Jean, 1722- , French;
    nonfiction DIL
FRANCOIS, Laurent, 1698-1782,
    French; nonfiction DIL
FRANCOIS, Marie Louise von,
    1817-93, German; fiction

AL HAR ST
FRANCOIS, Pierre, 1932- , Franco-
American; nonfiction CON
FRANCOIS, William E., 1924- ,
American; nonfiction CON
FRANCOIS de SALES, Saint, 1567-
1622, French; nonfiction DIF
KE SA ST
FRANCOISE (Seignobosc), 1897-1961,
French; juveniles FUL
FRANCOIS-MARIE de COLSELS, fl.
1700, French; nonfiction DIL
FRANCOIS-MARIE de PARIS, 1634-
1714, French; nonfiction DIL
FRANCOIS-XAVIER de SAINT LÔ,
18th cent., French; nonfiction
DIL
FRANCO-MENDES, David, 1713-92,
Jewish; plays ST
FRANCOS RODRIGUEZ, José, 1862-
1931, Spanish; nonfiction, plays,
journalism BL SA
FRANCOVICH, Guillermo, 1901- ,
Bolivian; essays MIN SA
FRANDA, Marcus F., 1937- ,
American; nonfiction CON
FRANDSON, Arden N., 1902- ,
American; nonfiction CON
FRANHY, Franz Karl, 1896- ,
German; nonfiction KU
'FRANK' see WHITCHER, Frances
M. B.
FRANK, Andre Gunder, 1929- ,
German-Canadian; nonfiction
CON
FRANK, Anne, 1929-44, German-
Jewish; nonfiction RIC
FRANK, Benis M., 1925- , Amer-
ican; nonfiction CON
FRANK, Bernard, 1929- , French;
essays, journalism, essays
DIC DIF PIN
FRANK, Bruno, 1887-1945, German;
poetry, fiction, plays AL COL
FLE KL KT KU LEN MAT SA
FRANK, Charles Edward, 1911- ,
American; nonfiction CON
FRANK, Charles Raphael, Jr., 1937- ,
American; nonfiction CON
'FRANK, Elisabeth' see ZINNER,
Hedda
FRANK, Goldalie, 1908- , Ameri-
can; fiction CON
FRANK, Helmut Jack, 1922- ,
German-American; nonfiction
CON
FRANK, Irving, 1910- , American;
nonfiction CON

FRANK, Isaiah, 1917- ,
American; nonfiction CON
FRANK, Jeffrey, 1942- ,
American; fiction CON
FRANK, Jerome David, 1909- ,
American; nonfiction CON
FRANK, Joseph, 1916- , Ameri-
can; nonfiction CON
FRANK, Josette, 1893- , Ameri-
can; juveniles CON WA
FRANK, Lawrence Kelso, 1890- ,
American; nonfiction CON
FRANK, Leonhard 1882-1961,
German; fiction, plays AL
COL FLE KL KT KU KUN
LEN MAT SA
FRANK, May, American; poetry
MAR
FRANK, Murray, 1908- , Ameri-
can; nonfiction CON
FRANK, Nathalie D., 1918- ,
Russian-American; nonfiction
CON
FRANK, Pat ('Harry Hart'), 1907-
64, American; fiction CON
WAF
FRANK, Robert Worth, Jr.,
1914- , American; nonfiction
CON
FRANK, Ronald Edward, 1933- ,
American; nonfiction CON
FRANK, Semen Liudvigovich,
1877-1950, Russian; nonfiction
FLE HARK ST
FRANK, Stanley B., 1908- ,
American; nonfiction CON
FRANK, Waldo, 1889-1967, Ameri-
can; fiction, plays KL KT SA
WAF
FRANKAU, Gilbert, 1884-1952,
English; fiction BRO KT
FRANKAU, Mary Evelyn Atkinson
('M. E. Atkinson'), 1899- ,
English; fiction, juveniles CON
FRANKAU, Pamela, 1908-64,
English; fiction BRO HOE RIC
KT
FRANKE, Carl Wilfred, 1928- ,
American; nonfiction CON
FRANKEL, Charles, 1917- ,
American; nonfiction CON
FRANKEL, Edward, American;
juveniles WA
FRANKEL, Joseph, 1913- ,
Polish-English; nonfiction CON
FRANKEL, Sandor, 1943- , Amer-
ican; nonfiction CON
FRANKEN, Rose, 1898- , Amer-

ican; fiction, plays KT MAT
WAF
FRANKENA, William Klaas, 1908- ,
American; nonfiction CON
FRANKENBERG, Celestine Gilligan,
American; nonfiction CON
FRANKENBERG, Lloyd, 1907- ,
American; poetry, criticism,
fiction CON KTS SA
FRANKENSTEIN, Alfred Victor,
1906- , American; nonfiction
CON
FRANKENSTEIN, Carl, 1905- ,
German; nonfiction CON
FRANKFORT, Ellen, 1936- ,
American; nonfiction CON
FRANKFURTER, Philip, fl. 1400,
Austrian; poetry ST
'FRANKLIN, A.' see ARNOLD,
Adlai F.
FRANKLIN, Alexander John, 1921- ,
English; nonfiction CON
FRANKLIN, Benjamin, 1706-90, Amer-
ican; essays BRO KAA MAG ST
FRANKLIN, Billy Joe, 1940- ,
American; nonfiction CON
FRANKLIN, Burt, 1903- , Ameri-
can; nonfiction CON
'FRANKLIN, Charles' see USHER,
Frank
FRANKLIN, Denson Nauls, 1914- ,
American; nonfiction CON
FRANKLIN, Edward Herbert,
1930- , American; fiction CON
FRANKLIN, Elinor Anne, 1795-1825,
English; nonfiction SA
'FRANKLIN, Elizabeth' see CAMP-
BELL, Hannah
'FRANKLIN, Eugene' see BANDY,
Eugene F., Jr.
FRANKLIN, George Cory, 1872- ,
American; juveniles FUL
FRANKLIN, George E., 1890- ,
American; nonfiction CON
FRANKLIN, H. Bruce, 1934- ,
American; nonfiction CON
FRANKLIN, Harold, 1920- , Ameri-
can; juveniles CON
FRANKLIN, Harry, 1906- , English;
fiction CON
'FRANKLIN, Jay' see CARTER,
John F.
FRANKLIN, Sir John, 1786-1847,
English; nonfiction KBA
FRANKLIN, John Hope, 1915- ,
American; nonfiction CON
'FRANKLIN, Keith' see FOY,
Kenneth R.

FRANKLIN, Marc A., 1932- ,
American; nonfiction CON
'FRANKLIN, Max' see DEMING,
Richard
FRANKLIN, Miles ('Brent of Bin
Bin'), 1879-1954, Austrian;
fiction RIC ST
FRANKLIN, Ralph William, 1937- ,
American; nonfiction CON
FRANKLIN, Richard, 1918- ,
American; nonfiction CON
'FRANKLIN, Steve' see STEVENS,
Franklin
FRANKLIN da SILVEIRA TAVORA,
Juan, 1842-88, Brazilian;
fiction, criticism SA
FRANKLYN, Charles Aubrey
Hamilton, 1896- , English;
nonfiction CON
FRANKO, Ivan, 1856-1916, Russian;
fiction HARK SA
FRANKO, Lawrence G., 1942- ,
American; nonfiction CON
FRANKS, Cyril Maurice, 1923- ,
Welsh-American; nonfiction
CON
FRANKS, Robert Sleightholme,
1871-1963, English; nonfiction
CON
FRANSELLA, Fay, English; nonfic-
tion CON
FRANTZ, Charles, 1925- ,
American; nonfiction CON
FRANTZ, Joe B., 1917- , Amer-
ican; nonfiction CON
'FRANZ, Karl' see 'FREIS, Bruno'
FRANZ, Gottfried H., 1897- ,
Afrikaans; fiction ST
FRANZA, Jorge (Franzls), 401-
78, Byzantine; nonfiction SA
FRANZBLAU, Abraham Norman,
1901- , American; nonfiction
CON
FRANZBLAU, Rose Nadler,
1905- , Austrian-American;
nonfiction CON
FRANZEN, Franz Michael, 1772-
1847, Swedish; poetry SA ST
FRANZEN, Nils Olof, 1916- ,
Swedish; juveniles CON
FRANZERO, Carlo Maria, 1892- ,
Italian; nonfiction CON
FRANZWA, Gregory M., 1926- ,
American; nonfiction CON
FRANZIUS, Enno, 1901- , Amer-
ican; nonfiction CON
FRANZMANN, Martin H., Ameri-
can; nonfiction CON

FRANZOS, Karl Emil, 1848-1904,
Austrian; fiction, essays AL
HAR KE ST
FRAPIE, Léon, 1863-1949, French;
fiction DIF SA
FRAPPA, Jean Joseph, 1882- ,
French; journalism, fiction SA
FRASCONA, Joseph Lohengrin,
1910- , American; nonfiction
CON
FRASCONI, Antonio, 1919- ,
Uruguayan-American; juveniles
CON WA
'FRASCATORO, Gerald' see HORN-
BACK, Bert G.
FRASE, Robert William, 1912- ,
American; nonfiction CON
'FRASER, Alex' see BRINTON,
Henry
FRASER, Alexander Campbell, 1819-
1914, Scots; nonfiction KBA
FRASER, Arvonne S., 1925- , Amer-
ican; nonfiction CON
FRANSER, Beatrice, American;
juveniles WA
FRASER, Blair, 1909- , Canadian;
nonfiction CON
FRASER, Claud Lovat ('Richard
Honeywood'), 1890-1921, English;
juvenile KJU
FRASER, Colin, 1935- , English;
nonfiction CON
FRASER, Conan, 1930- , English;
fiction CON
FRASER, Douglas Ferrar, 1929- ,
American; nonfiction CON
FRASER, Edith Emily Rose Oram,
1903- , English; fiction CON
FRASER, Elise Parker, 1903- ,
American; fiction CON
FRASER, Ferrin, American; juveniles
WA
FRASER, George Sutherland, 1915- ,
Scots; criticism, translations
MUR
FRASER, Gordon Holmes, 1898- ,
Canadian; nonfiction CON
FRASER, John, 1931- , English;
nonfiction CON
FRASER, Kathleen, 1937- , Ameri-
can; poetry MUR
FRASER, Neil McCormick, 1902- ,
Scots; nonfiction CON
FRASER, Peter Shaw, 1932- ,
Scots; nonfiction CON
'FRASER, Ronald' see TILTMAN,
Ronald F.
FRASER, Russell Alfred, 1927- ,

American; nonfiction CON
FRASER, Stewart Erskine, 1929- ,
American; nonfiction CON
FRASER, W. Lionel, English;
nonfiction CON
FRASER, Waller Brown ('Brown
Waller'), 1905- , American;
nonfiction CON
FRASER HARRISON, Brian,
1918- , English; nonfiction
CON
FRASIER, James Edwin, 1923- ,
American; nonfiction CON
FRASNAY, Pierre de, 18th cent.,
French; poetry DIL
FRATCHER, William Franklin,
1913- , American; nonfiction
CON
'FRATER JOCUNDUS' see MÜLLER,
Wilhelm
FRATTI, Mario, 1927- , Italian-
American; plays MAT
FRAUNCE, Abraham, fl 1587-1633,
English; poetry KB ST
FRAUTSCH, Richard Lane,
1926- , American; nonfiction
CON
FRAUENLOB, Heinrich von Meissen,
1250-1318, German; poetry
AL KE ST
'FRAY, Candil' see BOBADILLA,
Emilio
'FRAY, Mocho' see ALVAREZ,
José S.
FRAYN, Michael, 1933- , English;
nonfiction, fiction CON
FRAZEE, Charles Aaron, 1929- ,
American; nonfiction CON
FRAZEE, Steve, 1909- , Ameri-
can; fiction CON
'FRAZER, Andrew' see MARLOWE,
Stephen
FRAZER, Sir James George,
1854-1941, Scots; nonfiction
BRO KT ST
FRAZER, Robert Walter, 1911- ,
American; nonfiction CON
FRAZER, William Johnson, Jr.,
1924- , American; nonfiction
CON
FRAZER, Winifred Dusenbruy
(Loesch), 1916- , American;
nonfiction CON
FRAZER-HURST, Douglas,
1883- , English; nonfiction
CON
FRAZIER, Claude Albee, Jr.,
1920- , American; nonfiction
CON

FRAZIER, George, 1911- , American; nonfiction CON
FRAZIER, Neta Lohnes, 1890- , American; juveniles, fiction CON PAC WA
FRAZIER, Thomas Richard, 1931- , American; nonfiction CON
'FREBONIUS, Justinus' see HONTHEIM, Jean N. de
FRECHETTE, Louis Honoré, 1839-1908, French-Canadian; poetry ST SY
FREDEGARIO, fl. 584-641, Roman; nonfiction SA
FREDEMAN, William Evan, 1928- , American; nonfiction CON
FREDEN, Gustaf, 1898- , Swedish; nonfiction BL
FREDENBURGH, Franz Alvah, 1906- , American; nonfiction CON
FREDERIC II (King of Prussia), 1712-86, French; poetry DIL ST
FREDERIC, Harold ('George Forth'), 1856-98, American; fiction BRO KAA MAG ST
FREDERICK II, 1194-1250, German-Norman; nonfiction ST
'FREDERIC, Dick' see DEMPEWOLFF, Richard F.
FREDERIC, John Hutchinson, 1896- , American; nonfiction CON
'FREDERICK, Oswald' see SNELLING, Oswald F.
'FREDERICKS, Arnold' see KUMMER, Frederic A.
'FREDERICKS, Frank' see FRANCK, Frederick
'FREDERICKS, Frohm' see KERNER, Fred
FREDERICKS, Pierce Griffin, 1920- , American; fiction CON
'FREDERICKS, Vic' see MAJESKI, William
FREDGE, Frederique, 1906- , Swiss; fiction CON
FREDMAN, Henry John, 1927- , English; fiction CON
FREDRICKS, Edgar John, 1942- , American; nonfiction CON
FREDRICKSON, George Marsh, 1934- , American; nonfiction CON
FREDRO, Alexander, 1793-1876, Polish; plays, poetry HAR KE SA ST
FREDRO, Andrezej Maksymilian,

1621-79, Polish; nonfiction ST
'FREE' see HOFFMAN, Abbie
FREE, Ann Cottrell, American; fiction CON
FREE, John (Phreas), -1465, English; nonfiction ST
FREE, Lloyd A., 1908- , American; nonfiction CON
FREE, William Joseph, 1933- , American; nonfiction CON
FREE, William Norris, 1933- , American; nonfiction CON
FREEBORN, Richard H., 1926- , American; nonfiction CON
FREED, Louis Franklin, 1903- , American; nonfiction CON
FREEDBERG, Sydney Joseph, 1914- , American; nonfiction CON
FREEDGOOD, Lillian Fischel, 1911- , American; nonfiction CON
FREEDLEY, George Reynolds, 1904-67, American; nonfiction CON
FREEDMAN, Benedict, 1919- , American; fiction WAF
FREEDMAN, David Noel, 1922- , American; nonfiction CON
FREEDMAN, Leonard, 1924- , Anglo-American; nonfiction CON
FREEMAN, Marcia Kohl, 1922- , American; nonfiction CON
FREEDMAN, Maurice, 1920- , English; nonfiction CON
FREEDMAN, Mervin B., 1920- , American; nonfiction CON
FREEDMAN, Morris, 1920- , American; nonfiction CON
FREEDMAN, Nancy, 1920- , American; fiction WAF
FREEDMAN, Robert Owen, 1941- , American; nonfiction CON
FREEDMAN, Ronald, 1917- , Canadian; nonfiction CON
FREEDMAN, Russell Bruce, 1929- , American; juveniles CON WA
FREEDMAN, Warren, 1921- , American; nonfiction CON
FREEHILL, Maurice Francis, 1915- , American; nonfiction CON
FREELAND, John Maxwell, 1920- , Austrian; nonfiction CON

FREELEY, Austin J., 1922- ,
American; nonfiction CON
FREELING, Nicolas, 1927- , English; fiction RIC
FREEMAN, Anne Frances ('Anne
Frances Huether'), 1936- ,
American; nonfiction CON
FREEMAN, Arthur, 1938- , American; nonfiction CON
'FREEMAN, Artur' see LIEBER-
MANN, Ahron S.
FREEMAN, Austin see FREEMAN,
Richard A.
FREEMAN, Clifford Wade, 1906- ,
American; nonfiction CON
FREEMAN, Darlene, 1934- , American; nonfiction CON
FREEMAN, David Hugh, 1924- ,
American; nonfiction CON
FREEMAN, Don, 1908- , American;
juveniles FUL WA
FREEMAN, Donald McKinley, 1931- ,
American; nonfiction CON
FREEMAN, Douglas Southall, 1886-
1953, American; nonfiction MAG
KT
FREEMAN, Edward Augustus, 1823-92,
English; nonfiction BRO KBA SA
ST
FREEMAN, Eugene, American;
juveniles WA
FREEMAN, Gillian, 1929- , American; fiction CON
FREEMAN, Godfrey, English; juveniles
WA
FREEMAN, Graydon La Verne ('Larry
Freeman'; 'James H. Thompson';
'Serry Wood'), 1904- , American;
fiction, nonfiction CON
FREEMAN, Harold Webber, 1899- ,
English; fiction KT
FREEMAN, Harrop Arthur, 1907- ,
American; nonfiction CON
FREEMAN, Howard Edgar, 1929- ,
American; nonfiction CON
FREEMAN, Ira Henry, 1906- ,
American; fiction CON
FREEMAN, Ira Maximilian, 1905- ,
American; juveniles FUL WA
FREEMAN, James Dillet ('D.J.
Mann'), 1912- , American;
nonfiction CON
FREEMAN, James Edwards, 1808-
84, American; nonfiction KAA
FREEMAN, Jean Todd, 1929- ,
American; juveniles CON
FREEMAN, John, 1880-1929, English; poetry, criticism, fiction

BRO KAT KT
FREEMAN, John Crosby ('Hugh
Guthrie'; 'Crosby MacDowell'),
1941- , American; nonfiction
CON
FREEMAN, Joseph, 1897- ,
American; fiction, poetry,
criticism KT WAF
'FREEMAN, Larry' see FREEMAN,
Graydon L.
FREEMAN, Lucy Greenbaum,
1916- , American; nonfiction
CON
FREEMAN, Lydia, 1907- ,
American; juveniles FUL
FREEMAN, Mae Blacker, 1907- ,
American; juveniles FUL WA
FREEMAN, Margaret Nadgwick,
1915- , American; nonfiction
CON
FREEMAN, Mary E. Wilkins,
1852-1930, American; fiction
KAT KT ST
FREEMAN, Sir Ralph, fl. 1610-
55, English; nonfiction ST
FREEMAN, Richard Austin, 1862-
1943, English; fiction KAT
KT BRO
FREEMAN, Richard Borden, 1908- ,
American; nonfiction CON
FREEMAN, Roger Adolf, 1904- , Austrian-American; nonfiction CON
FREEMAN, Ruth L. Sunderlin, 1907-,
American; nonfiction CON
FREEMAN, Serge Herbert, American; juveniles WA
FREEMAN, Thomas, fl. 1614,
English; essays BRO
FREEMAN, Thomas Walter, 1908- ,
American; nonfiction CON
FREEMAN, Walter Jackson, Jr.,
1895-1972, American; nonfiction
CON
FREEMAN, Warren Samuel, 1911- ,
American; nonfiction CON
FREEMAN-GRENVILLE, Greville
Stewart Parker, 1918- , English;
nonfiction CON
FREEMAN-ISHILL, Rose, 1895- ,
American; poetry, translations
CON
FREER, Harold Wiley, 1906- ,
American; nonfiction CON
FREER, Mrs. Otto see 'LEE, Agnes'
FREESTROM, Hubert J., 1928- ,
American; nonfiction CON
FREGAULT, Guy, 1918- ,
Canadian; nonfiction ST SY

'FREI, Bruno' ('Karl Franz'; 'Benedikt Freistadt'), 1897- , German; nonfiction AL

FREID, Jacob, 1913- , American; nonfiction CON

FREIDANK, fl. 1215-30, German; poetry AL ST

FREIDEL, Frank Burt, Jr., 1916- , American; nonfiction CON

FREIDIN, Seymour Kenneth, 1917- , American; nonfiction CON

FREIDSON, Eliot, 1923- , American; nonfiction CON

FREIHOFER, Lois Diane ('Lois Barth'), 1933- , American; juveniles CON

FREILICH, Morris, 1928- , Polish-American; nonfiction CON

FREILIGRATH, Ferdinand Hermann, 1810-76, German; poetry AL HAR KE SA ST

FREIRE, Francisco José, 1713-73, Portuguese; nonfiction SA

FREIRE, Gilberto, 1900- , Brazilian; nonfiction SA

FREIRE de ANDRADE, Jacinto, 1597-1657, Portuguese; nonfiction SA

FREIRE-MARIA, Newton, 1918- , Brazilian; nonfiction CON

FREISTADT, Benedikt see 'FREI, Bruno'

FREITAS BRANCO, João de, 1855-1910, Portuguese; nonfiction SA

FREITHEIM, Ference Erling, 1936- , American; nonfiction CON

FREIXEDO, Salvador, 1923- , Spanish; nonfiction CON

FREMANTLE, Anne Jackson, 1910- , English; fiction, journalism CON HO KTS

FREMERY, Barend de, 1750-1811, Dutch; poetry, translations ST

FREMGEN, James Morgan, 1933- , American; nonfiction CON

FREMINVILLE, Edme de la Poix de, 1680-1773, French; nonfiction DIL

FREMONT, Jessie Benton, 1824-1902, American; nonfiction KAA

FREMONT, John Charles, 1813-90, American; nonfiction KAA

FRENAIS, Joseph P., -1800, French; translations DIL

FRENAUD, André, 1907- , French; poetry DIF PIN

FRENCH, Alice ('Octave Thanet'), 1850-1934, American; fiction KAA

FRENCH, Allen, 1870-1946, American; juveniles KJU

FRENCH, Dorothy Kayser, 1926- , American; juveniles, fiction CON WA

FRENCH, Edward Livingstone, 1916- , Anglo-American; nonfiction CON

FRENCH, Fiona, 1944- , English; juveniles CON

FRENCH, Giles Leroy, 1894- , American; nonfiction PAC

FRENCH, Lucy Virginia Smith ('I. Inconnue'), 1825-81, American; poetry, fiction KAA

FRENCH, Marion Flood, 1920- , American; juveniles CON WA

'FRENCH, Paul' see ASIMOV, Isaac

FRENCH, Peter, 1918- , American; nonfiction CON

FRENCH, Robert Butler Digby, 1904- , American; nonfiction CON

FRENCH, Warren Graham, 1922- , American; nonfiction CON

FRENCH, William Marshall, 1907- , American; nonfiction CON

FREND, William Hugh Clifford, 1916- , English; nonfiction CON

FRENEAU, Philip Morin ('Robert Slender'), 1752-1832, American; poetry BRO KAA MAG SA ST

FRENKEL, Richard Eugene, 1924- , American; nonfiction CON

FRENSSEN, Gustav, 1863-1945, German; fiction, essays AL COL FLE HAR KL KT SA ST

FRENZ, Horst, 1912- , German-American; nonfiction CON

FRERE, James Arnold, 1920- , English; nonfiction CON

FRERE, John Hookham, 1769-1846, English; translations, nonfiction BL BRO KBA ST

FRERE, Paul, 1917- , French; nonfiction CON

FRERE, Sheppard Sunderland, 1916- , English; nonfiction CON

FRERET, Nicolas, 1688-1749,

French; nonfiction DIL SA

FRERICHS, Albert Christian, 1910- ,
American; nonfiction CON

FRERON, Elie Catherine, 1719-60/
76, French; criticism DIF

FRESCHET, Berniece Louise Speck,
1927- , American; juveniles
CON

FRESCHOT, Casimir (Fraischot),
1640-1720, French; nonfiction
CON

FRESCOBALDI, Dino, 1270-1316,
Italian; poetry KE ST

FRESCOBALDI, Leonardo, 1350?-
1420?, Italian; nonfiction HAR
ST

FRESCOBALDI, Matteo, 1297-1348,
Italian; poetry KE ST

FRESE, Dolores Warwick, 1936- ,
American; fiction CON

FRESE, Jacob, 1690-1729, Swedish;
poetry ST

FRESENUS, Fraitz see LOTTMANN,
Fritz

FRESNEDO y ZALDIVAR, María
Ascensión, Spanish; poetry SA

FREUCHEN, Lorentz Peter Elfred,
1886-1957, Danish; fiction, nonfiction HAR KT SA ST WA

FREUD, Sigmund, 1856-1939, Austrian; nonfiction KT KU KUN
MAG RIC SA ST

FREUDENBERGER, Herman, 1922- ,
German; nonfiction CON

FREUDENHEIM, Yehoshua, 1894- ,
Polish-Israeli; nonfiction CON

FREUDENTHAL, August, 1851-98,
German; poetry ST

FREUDENTHAL, Freidrich, 1849-
1929, German; poetry ST

FREUDENTHAL, Hans, 1905- ,
German; nonfiction CON

FREUND, Ernest Hans, 1905- ,
German-American; nonfiction
CON

FREUND, Gerald, 1930- , German-
American; nonfiction CON

FREUND, John Ernst, 1921- ,
German-American; nonfiction
CON

FREUND, Paul Abraham, 1908- ,
American; nonfiction CON

FREUND, Philip, 1909- , American;
fiction CON WAF

FREVAL, Claude François Guillemeau,
1745-70, French; nonfiction DIL

FREVIER, Charles Joseph, 1689-1770/
78, French; nonfiction DIL

FREWER, Glyn, 1931- , English;
juveniles CON WA

FREWIN, Leslie Ronald ('Paul
Dupont'), 1917- , English;
nonfiction CON

FREY, Friedrich Hermann see
'GREIF, Martin'

FREY, Henry A., 1923- , American; nonfiction CON

FREY, Jakob, 1520?-62?, German; plays AL ST

FREY, Leonard Hamilton, 1927- ,
American; nonfiction CON

FREY, Marlys, 1931- , American; nonfiction CON

FREY, Shaney, American; juveniles
WA

'FREYER, Frederic' see BALLIN-
GER, William S.

FREYER, Paul Herbert, 1920- ,
German; plays AL

FREYRE, Gilberto, 1900- ,
Brazilian; nonfiction RIC

FREYRE, Ricardo J. see JAIMES
FREYRE, Ricardo

FREYTAG, Gustave, 1816-95,
German; fiction, plays AL
COL HAR KE MAG SA ST

FREZZI, Federico, 1346-1416,
Italian; poetry ST

FRIAS Duque de see FERNANDEZ
de VELASCO y Pimental,
Bernardino

FRIAS, Francisco de, 1809-77,
Cuban; nonfiction MIN

FRIBOURG, Marjorie G., 1920- ,
American; juveniles CON WA

'FRICK, C.H.' see IRWIN, Constance F.

FRICK, Constance see IRWIN,
Constance F.

FRICK, George Frederick,
1925- , American; nonfiction
CON

FRICKE, Cedric V., 1928- ,
American; nonfiction CON

FRICKE, Vladimir Maximovich
(Fritsche), 1870-1929, Russian;
criticism ST

FRIDA, Emil see 'VRCHLICKY,
Jaroslav'

FRIDEGARD, Johan Jan Fridolf,
1897- , Swedish; fiction
FLE ST

FRIDJONSSON, Guomundur, 1869-
1944, Icelandic; fiction, essays,
poetry FLE

FRIDY, Wallace, 1910- , Ameri-

can; nonfiction CON
FRIED, Charles, 1935- , Czech-
American; nonfiction CON
FRIED, Eleanor L., 1913- ,
American; nonfiction CON
FRIED, Erich, 1921- , German;
nonfiction KU
FRIED, John James, 1940- , Amer-
ican; nonfiction CON
FRIED, Joseph P., 1939- , Amer-
ican; nonfiction CON
FRIED, Morton Herbert, 1923- ,
American; nonfiction CON
FRIEDBERG, Gertrude Tonkonogy,
American; plays, fiction CON
FRIEDBERG, Maurice, 1929- ,
Polish-American; nonfiction
CON
FRIEDELBAUM, Stanley Herman,
1927- , American; nonfiction
CON
FRIEDELL, Egon, 1878-1938,
Austrian; criticism, essays
AL FLE KU LEN
FRIEDEN, Bernard J., 1930- ,
American; nonfiction CON
FRIEDENTHAL, Richard, German;
nonfiction KU
FRIEDER, Emma, 1891- , Hungarian-
American; nonfiction CON
FRIEDERICH, Werner Paul, 1905- ,
American; nonfiction CON
FRIEDERICHSEN, Kathleen Hockman,
1910- , American; nonfiction
CON
FRIEDHEIM, Robert Lyle, 1934- ,
American; nonfiction CON
FRIEDL, Ernestine, 1920- ,
Hungarian-American; nonfiction
CON
FRIEDLAENDER, Ludwig, 1824-1909,
German; nonfiction SA
FRIEDLAENDER, Salomo, 1871- ,
German; nonfiction KU
FRIEDLAND, David Lionel, 1936- ,
South African; poetry MUR
FRIEDLAND, Hayim Abraham,
1891-1939, Jewish; poetry, fic-
tion ST
FRIEDLAND, Ronald Lloyd, 1937- ,
American; nonfiction CON
FRIEDLAND, Seymour, 1928- ,
American; nonfiction CON
FRIEDLAND, William H., 1923- ,
American; nonfiction CON
FRIEDLANDER, Albert Hoschander,
1927- , German-American;
nonfiction CON

FRIEDLANDER, Stanley Laurence,
1938- , American; nonfiction
CON
FRIEDLANDER, Walter Andreass
('Walter Andreas Kraft'),
1891- , German-American;
nonfiction CON
FRIEDMAN, Albert B., 1920- ,
American; nonfiction CON
FRIEDMAN, Alan Warren, 1939- ,
American; nonfiction CON
FRIEDMAN, Bernard Harper,
1926- , American; nonfiction,
fiction, poetry CON
FRIEDMAN, Bruce Jay, 1930- ,
American; fiction CON
FRIEDMAN, Edward Ludwig,
1903- , American; nonfiction
CON
FRIEDMAN, Estelle Ehrenwald,
1920- , American; juveniles
CON WA
FRIEDMAN, Eve Rosemary Tibber
('Robert Tibber'), 1929- ,
English; fiction CON
FRIEDMAN, John see PATER,
Elias
FRIEDMAN, Frieda, 1905- ,
American; juveniles FUL
FRIEDMAN, Isaac Kahn, 1870-
1931, American; journalism,
fiction HOO
FRIEDMAN, Kenneth, 1939- ,
American; plays CON
FRIEDMAN, Lawrence M.,
1930- , American; nonfiction
CON
FRIEDMAN, Maurice, 1921- ,
American; nonfiction CON
FRIEDMAN, Melvin Jack, 1928- ,
American; nonfiction CON
FRIEDMAN, Milton, 1912- ,
American; nonfiction CON
FRIEDMAN, Norman, 1925- ,
American; nonfiction, poetry
CON
FRIEDMAN, Roslyn Berger,
1924- , American; nonfiction
CON
FRIEDMAN, Stuart, 1913- ,
American; fiction CON
FRIEDMAN, Wolfgang G., 1907- ,
German-American; nonfiction
CON
FRIEDMANN, Yohanan, 1936- ,
Israeli; nonfiction CON
FRIEDRICH, Otto Alva, 1929- ,
American; fiction, juveniles
CON

FRIEDRICH, Paul, 1927- , American; nonfiction CON
FRIEDMAN, Roy, 1934- , American; fiction CON
FRIEDRICH von HAUSEN, 1150-90, German; poetry AL ST
FRIEL, Brian, 1929- , Irish; plays CON MAT
FRIELINK, Abraham Barend, 1917- , Dutch; nonfiction CON
FRIEND, Joseph Harold, 1909- , American; nonfiction CON
FRIEND, Robert, 1913- , American; poetry CON
FRIENDLICH, Richard J., 1909- , American; juveniles CON WA
FRIENDLY, Fred W., 1915- , American; nonfiction CON
FRIER, David A., 1931- , American, nonfiction CON
FRIERMOND, Elisabeth Hamilton, 1903- , American; juveniles CON FUL WA
FRIES, Adelaide Lisetta, 1871-1949, American; nonfiction JO
FRIES, Albert Charles, 1908- , American; nonfiction CON
FRIES, Fritz Rudolf, 1935- , German; nonfiction CON
FRIESEN, Gordon, American; fiction MAR
FRIIS MOLLER, Kai, 1888- , Danish; poetry, criticism ST
FRIIS-BAASTAD, Babbis Ellinor ('Babbis Friis Baastad'; 'Eleanor Babbis'; 'Babbis Friis'), 1921- , Norwegian-American; nonfiction CON
FRILLMANN, Paul W., 1911-72, American; nonfiction CON
FRIMANN, Claus, 1746-1826, Norwegian; poetry SA
FRIMMER, Steven, 1928- , American; nonfiction CON
FRIMOTH, Lenore Beck, 1927- , American; juveniles CON
FRINGS, Manfred S., 1925- , American; nonfiction CON
FRINICO, 5th cent. B.C., Greek; poetry SA
FRINICO ARRHABIO, 2nd cent., Greek; nonfiction SA
FRINK, Maurice, 1895- , American; nonfiction CON
FRINTA, Mojmir Svatopluk, 1922- , Czech-American; nonfiction CON
FRIOJONSSON, Guomundur, 1869-

1944, Icelandic; poetry, fiction, essays COL SA ST
FRIOJONSSON, Sigurjon, 1867- , Icelandic; poetry SA
FRISBEE, Lucy Post, American; juveniles WA
FRISBIE, Margery Rowbottom, 1929- , American; nonfiction CON
FRISBIE, Richard Patrick, 1926- , American; nonfiction CON
FRISCH, Max, 1911- , Swiss; plays, fiction AL FLE HAR KU KUN LEN MAT RIC
FRISCH, Morton J., 1923- , American; nonfiction CON
FRISCH, Otto Robert, 1904- , American; juveniles CON WA
FRISCHAUER, Willi, 1906- , Austrian-English; nonfiction CON
FRISCHLIN, Philipp Nicodemus, 1547-90, German; plays AL ST
FRISHMAN, David, 1862-1922, Jewish; fiction, translations LAN ST
FRISKEY, Margaret Richards ('Elizabeth Sherman'), 1901- , American; juveniles CON HOO WA
FRITSCHE Vladimir see FRICKE, Vladimir M.
FRITSCHLER, A. Lee, 1937- , American; nonfiction CON
FRITSCHUN, Gian Battista see FRIZZONI, Gian Battista
'FRITZ' see WHITEHALL, Harold
FRITZ, Henry Eugene, 1927- , American; nonfiction CON
FRITZ, Jean Guttery, 1915- , American; juveniles COM CON WA
FRITZ, Walter Helmut, 1929- , German; nonfiction KU
FRITZSCHE, Friedrich Wilhelm, 1825-1905, German; poetry AL
FRIZON, P. Nicolas, -1737, French; nonfiction DIL
FRIZZONI, Gian Battista (Fritschun), 1725-87?, Raeto-Romansch; poetry ST
FROBOESS, Harry August, 1899- , German-American; nonfiction CON
FRODOARDO see FLODOARDO
FRÖDING, Gustaf, 1860-1911

Swedish; poetry, journalism
COL HAR KE SA ST
FROES PEROEIM, Damián de, 18th
cent., Portuguese; nonfiction
SA
FROHMAN, Charles Eugene, 1901- ,
American; nonfiction CON
FROHOCK, Wilbur Merrill, 1908- ,
American; nonfiction CON
FROIDMONT, Helinand, 17th cent.,
French; poetry DIF
FROISSART, Sir Jea, 1338-1410?,
French; juveniles, poetry, non-
fiction DIF DOY HAR KE MAG
SA ST
FROLAND, Louis, -1746, French;
nonfiction DIL
FROMAGE, Pierre, 1678-1740,
French; nonfiction DIL
FROMAGET, Nicolas, -1759,
French; fiction, plays DIL
FROMAN, Elizabeth Hull, 1920- ,
American; juveniles CON
FROMAN, Lewis Acretius, Jr.,
1935- , American; nonfiction
CON
FROMAN, Robert Winslow, 1917- ,
American; juveniles, fiction
CON WA
FROMANT, 18th cent., French;
nonfiction DIL
'FROME, David' see BROWN,
Zenith J.
FROME, Michael, 1920- , Ameri-
can; nonfiction CON
FROMENTIN, Eugene, 1820-76,
French; fiction, criticism, non-
fiction DIF HAR KE MAG MAL
SA ST
FROMM, Erich, 1900- , German-
American; nonfiction KTS
FROMM, Erika, 1910- , German-
American; nonfiction CON
FROMM, Guy, 1933- , German-
American; nonfiction CON
FROMM, Harold, 1933- , Ameri-
can; nonfiction CON
FRONTAURA y VAZQUEZ, Carlos,
1834-1910, Spanish; fiction,
plays, journalism SA
'FRONTIER, Tex' see MILLER,
James P.
FRONTINUS, Sextus Julius, 30-
104, Roman; nonfiction SA
ST
FRONTO, Marcus Cornelius,
100-166, Roman; nonfiction
SA ST

FROOI, Ari see THORGILSSON,
Ari F.
FROOMKIN, Joseph, 1927- ,
American; nonfiction CON
FROSCHER, Wingate, 1918- ,
American; fiction CON
FROST, Elizabeth Hollister,
American; fiction WAF
FROST, Ernest, 1918- , English;
nonfiction, poetry, fiction
CON
FROST, Frances, 1905-59, Ameri-
can; juveniles, fiction FUL
WAF
FROST, Gerhard Emanuel, 1909- ,
American; nonfiction CON
FROST, Helen ('Dave Nichols'),
1898- , American; fiction
CON
FROST, James Arthur, 1918- ,
American; nonfiction CON
FROST, Joe L., 1933- , Ameri-
can; nonfiction CON
FROST, Lesley, American; fiction,
juveniles CON
FROST, Marjorie, 1914- ,
American; nonfiction CON
FROST, Max Gilbert, 1908- ,
American; fiction CON
FROST, Peter Kip, 1936- , Amer-
ican; nonfiction CON
FROST, Richard, 1929- , Ameri-
can; poetry CON
FROST, Richard H., 1930- ,
American; nonfiction CON
FROST, Richart T., 1926-72,
American; nonfiction CON
FROST, Robert Lee, 1874-1963,
American; poetry, plays BRO
FLE HIL KL KT MAG RIC
SA SP ST
FROST, S.E., Jr., 1899- ,
American; nonfiction CON
FROSTIC, Gwen, 1906- , Ameri-
can; nonfiction, poetry CON
HIL
FROSTICK, Michael, 1917- ,
English; nonfiction CON
FROTHINGHAM, Octavius Brooks,
1822-95, American; nonfiction
KAA
FROTHINGHAM, Richard, 1812-80,
American; nonfiction KAA
FROUDE, James Anthony, 1818-94,
English; nonfiction, essays
BRO KBA SA ST
FROUDE, Richard Hurrell, 1803-
36, English; poetry, essays
KBA

FROUMUND of TEGERNSEE, 960-
1008, German; poetry ST
'FROY, Herald' see DEGHY, Guy
FRUCHTER, Benjamin, 1914- ,
American; nonfiction CON
FRUCTUOSO, Gaspar, 1522-91,
Portuguese; nonfiction SA
FRUEHLING, Rosemary Therese,
1933- , American; nonfiction
CON
FRUG, Simon Samuel, 1860-1916,
Russian; poetry ST
FRUGONI, Carlo Innocenzo, 1692-
1768, Italian; poetry HAR ST
FRUGONI, Emilio, 1880- ,
Uruguayan; journalism, poetry
SA
FRUMAN, Norman, 1923- , Ameri-
can; nonfiction CON
FRUMKIN, Gene, 1928- , American;
nonfiction, poetry CON
FRUMKIN, Robert M. , 1928- ,
American; nonfiction CON
FRUYTIERS, Jan,   -1580,
Dutch; poetry ST
FRY, Barbarr ('Margaret Greco'),
1932- , American; fiction
CON
FRY, Carli, 1897- , Raeto-Romansch;
poetry, fiction, plays ST
FRY, Charles George, 1936- ,
American; nonfiction CON
FRY, Christopher, 1907- , English;
plays, translations BRO CON
FLE KTS MAG MAT MUR RIC SA
ST WA
'FRY, David' see ROPER, William L.
FRY, Donald Klein, Jr., 1937- ,
American; nonfiction CON
FRY, Edward Bernard, 1925- , Amer-
ican; nonfiction CON
FRY, Hilary G., 1922- , American;
nonfiction CON
FRY, Howard Tyrrell, 1919- , Aus-
tralian; nonfiction CON
FRY, Roger Elliot, 1866-1934, Eng-
lish; criticism KAT KT
FRY, Rosalie Kingsmill, 1911- ,
Canadian; juveniles CON WA
FRY, Theodore Penrose, 1892- ,
English; nonfiction HOE
FRY, William Finley, Jr., 1924- ,
American; nonfiction CON
FRYATT, Norma R., American;
juveniles WA
FRYBURGER, Vernon Ray, Jr.,
1918- , American; nonfiction
CON

FRYDMAN, Szajko (Zosa Szajkow-
ski), 1911- , Polish-Ameri-
can; nonfiction CON
FRYE, Charles Alton, 1936- ,
American; nonfiction CON
FRYE, Dean, American; juveniles
WA
FRYE, Northrop, 1912- , Canadian;
nonfiction CON SY
FRYE, Richard Nelson, 1920- ,
American; nonfiction CON
FRYE, Roland Mushat, 1921- ,
American; nonfiction CON
FRYER, Holly Claire, 1908- ,
American; nonfiction CON
FRYKENBERG, Robert Eric,
1930- , American; nonfiction
CON
FRYKLUND, Verne Charles,
1896- , American; nonfiction
CON
FRYKMAN, John Harvey, 1932- ,
American; nonfiction, poetry
CON
FRYMIER, Jack Rimmel, 1925- ,
American; nonfiction CON
FRYXELL, Andrés, 1795-1881,
Swedish; nonfiction SA
FUCHS, Abraham Moses, 1890- ,
Jewish; fiction ST
FUCHS, Daniel, 1934- , Ameri-
can; nonfiction CON
FUCHS, Erich, 1916- , German;
nonfiction CON
FUCHS, Günter Bruno, 1928- ,
German; nonfiction KU
FUCHS, Jacob, 1939- , American;
nonfiction CON
FUCHS, Josef, 1912- , German;
nonfiction CON
FUCHS, Lawrence H., 1927- ,
American; nonfiction CON
FUCHS, Rudolf, 1890-1942, Ger-
man; nonfiction AL
'FUCHS, Summer' see LISKY, I.
A.
FUCHS, Victor Robert, 1924- ,
American; nonfiction CON
FUCIK, Julius, 1904-43, Czech;
criticism, journalism ST
FUCILLA, Joseph G., 1897- ,
American; nonfiction BL
'FUCINI, Renato' (Neri Tanfucio),
1843-1921, Italian; poetry,
fiction COL SA ST
FÜERTRER, Ulrich, fl. 1450-
1500, German; poetry ST
FUEGI, John, 1936- , English;

nonfiction CON
FÜHMANN, Franz, 1922- , German;
poetry AL KU
FÜLÖP-MILLER, René, 1891- ,
Hungarian; nonfiction KL KT SA
FUENTE, Ricardo, 1866-1925,
Spanish; journalism SA
FUENTE, Vicente de la, 1817-89,
Spanish; nonfiction SA
FUENTES, Carlos, 1929- , Mexican;
fiction RIC
FUENZALIDA, Miguel see EDWARDS,
A. A.
FUENZALIDA GRANDOW, Alejandro,
1865-1942, Chilean; nonfiction
MIN
FÜRNBERG, Louis, 1909-57, German;
poetry, plays, fiction AL FLE
FUERTES, Gloria, 1920- , Spanish;
poetry SA
FUESS, Claude Moore, 1885- ,
American; nonfiction KT
FÜSSLI, Johann Heinrich, 1741-1825,
Swiss; translations KE ST
FÜST Milán, 1888- , Hungarian;
poetry, plays, fiction ST
FUET, Louis, 1681-1739, French;
nonfiction DIL
FUGARD, Athol, 1933- , South
African; plays RIC
FUGATE, Francis Lyle, 1915- ,
American; nonfiction CON
FUGATE, Joe K., 1931- , American;
nonfiction CON
FUGATE, Terence McCuddy, 1930- ,
American; fiction CON
FUHRO, Wilbur J., 1914- , Ameri-
can; nonfiction CON
FUJITA, Tamao, 1905- , Japanese;
nonfiction CON
FUJIWARA AKIHIRA, 989-1066,
Japanese; nonfiction ST
FUJIWARA NO IETAKA, 1158-1237,
Japanese; poetry ST
FUJIWARA NO KATAKO see 'DAINI
NO SAMMI'
FUJIWARA NO KINTO, 966-1041,
Japanese; poetry ST
FUJIWARA NO SADAIE (Teika), 1162-
1241, Japanese; poetry ST
FUJIWARA NO TOSHINGARI (Shunzei),
1114-1204, Japanese; poetry ST
FUJIWARA NO YOSHITSUNE, 1169-
1206, poetry, diary ST
'FUJIWARA SEIKA' (Fujiwara Shuku),
1561-1619, Japanese; nonfiction
ST
FUKEI, Gladys Arlene Harper,

1920- , American; nonfiction
CON
FUKUDA, Fsuneari, 1912- ,
Japanese; plays, criticism
MAT
FUKUDA, Tsutomu, 1905- ,
Japanese; poetry MUR
FUKUI, Haruhiro, 1935- ,
Japanese-American; nonfiction
CON
FUKUTAKE, Tadashi, 1917- ,
Japanese; nonfiction CON
FUKUZAWA YUKICHI, 1836-1901,
Japanese; nonfiction ST
FULBERT of CHARTRES, 975-1029,
French; poetry ST
FULBRIGHT, James William,
1905- , American; nonfiction
CON
FULCHER of CHARTRES, 1059-
1127, French; nonfiction ST
FULD, James J., 1916- , Amer-
ican; nonfiction CON
FULDA, Carl H., 1909- , Ameri-
can; nonfiction CON
FULDA, Ludwig, 1862-1932,
German; plays, translations
COL KU MAT SA
FULGENCIO, San, 463-533, Roman;
nonfiction SA
FULGENTIUS, Fabius Planciades,
fl. 500, Roman; nonfiction ST
FULL, Harold, 1919- , American;
nonfiction CON
FULLANA, Luis, 1871- , Spanish;
nonfiction SA
FULLER, Alice Cook, American;
juveniles WA
FULLER, Blair, 1927- , Ameri-
can; fiction CON
FULLER, Catherine Leuthold,
1916- , American; juveniles
CON
FULLER, Edmond, American;
juveniles WA
FULLER, Edwin Wiley, 1847-76,
American; poetry JO
FULLER, Frances see VICTOR,
Metta V. F.
FULLER, Henry Blake, 1857-1929,
American; fiction, criticism
HOO KT
FULLER, Iola, 1906- , American;
fiction WAF
FULLER, Jean Violet Overton,
1915- , English; nonfiction,
fiction CON
FULLER, John, English; nonfiction
CON

FULLER, John, 1937- , British;
   poetry CON MUR
FULLER, John Frederick Charles,
   1878- , English; nonfiction CON
FULLER, John Grant, Jr., 1913- ,
   American; nonfiction, fiction,
   plays CON
FULLER, Lois Hamilton, 1915- ,
   American; fiction CON
FULLER, Lon Luvois, 1902- ,
   American; nonfiction CON
FULLER, Margaret see FULLER,
   Sarah M.
FULLER, Miriam Morris, 1933- ,
   American; nonfiction CON
FULLER, Raymond Tifft, 1889- ,
   American; juveniles WA
FULLER, Reginald Horace, 1915- ,
   English; nonfiction CON
FULLER, Richard Buckminster,
   1895- , American; nonfiction
   CON
'FULLER, Roger' see TRACY, Donald
   F.
FULLER, Roy Broadbent, 1912- ,
   British; poetry, fiction, juveniles
   CON DOY KTS MUR RIC SP
FULLER, Sarah Margaret (Marchesa
   Ossoli), 1810-50, American;
   nonfiction BRO KAA SA ST WAF
FULLER, Thomas, 1608-61, English;
   nonfiction BRO KB
FULLER, Wayne Edison, 1919- ,
   American; nonfiction CON
FULLERTON, Alexander, 1924- ,
   English; juveniles CON
FULLERTON, Gail Putney, 1927- ,
   American; nonfiction CON
FULLERTON, Lady Georgiana
   Charlotte, 1812-85, English;
   fiction BRO KBA
FULLMER, Daniel Warren, 1922- ,
   American; nonfiction CON
FULLMER June Zimmerman, 1920- ,
   American; nonfiction CON
FULTON, Albert Rondthaler, 1902- ,
   American; nonfiction CON
FULTON, Norman, 1927- , Ameri-
   can; nonfiction CON
FULTON, Paul Cedric, 1901- ,
   American; nonfiction CON
FULTON, Robin, 1937- , Scots;
   poetry CON MUR
FULWELL, Ulpian, fl. 1586-72,
   English; poetry ST
FUMAGALLI, Angelo, 1728-1804,
   Italian; nonfiction SA
FUMEL, Jean Félix Henri de, 1717-

90, French; nonfiction DIL
FUMENTO, Rocco, 1923- ,
   American; nonfiction, fiction
   CON
FUMET, Stanislas, 1896- ,
   French; nonfiction DIF HOE
FUNDERBURK, Thomas Ray,
   1928- , American; nonfiction
   CON
FUNES, Gregorio, 1749-1829,
   Argentinian; nonfiction MIN
FUNK, Arthur Layton, 1914- ,
   American; nonfiction CON
FUNK, Peter Van Keuren, 1921- ,
   American; nonfiction CON
FUNK, Robert Walter, 1926- ,
   American; nonfiction CON
FUNYA NO YASUHIDE (Bunya),
   830-90, Japanese; poetry ST
FURAI SANJIN see HIRAGA GEN-
   NAI
FURBANK, Philip Nicholas,
   1920- , English; nonfiction
   CON
FURER, Howard Bernard, 1934- ,
   American; nonfiction CON
FURER-HAIMENDORF, Christoph
   von, 1909- , Austrian-
   British; nonfiction CON
FURETIERE, Abbé Antoine,
   1619-88, French; poetry,
   fiction DIF HAR KE ST
FURFEY, Paul Hanly, 1896- ,
   American; nonfiction CON
   HOE
FURGAULT, Nicolas, 1706-95,
   French; nonfiction DIL
FURGOLE, Jean Baptiste, 1690-
   1761, French; nonfiction DIL
FURIO, Marco Bibáculo, 1st cent.
   B.C., Roman; poetry SA
FURLONG CARDIFF, Guillermo,
   1889- , Argentinian; essays
   MIN SA
FURMANOV, Dmitry Andreyevich,
   1891-1926, Russian; fiction
   COL HAR HARK RIC SA ST
FURNAS, Marthedith, 1904- ,
   American; fiction WAF
FURNEAUX, Rupert, 1908- ,
   English; nonfiction CON
FURNESS, Edna Lue, 1906- ,
   American; nonfiction CON
FURNESS, William Henry, 1802-
   96, American; nonfiction KAA
FURNISH, Victor Paul, 1931- ,
   American; nonfiction CON
FURNISS, Harry, 1854-1925,

Irish; juveniles DOY
FURNISS, Norman Francis, 1922- ,
American; nonfiction CON
FURNIVALL, Frederick James,
1825-1910, English; nonfiction
BRO KBA
FURPHY, Joseph ('Tom Collins'),
1843-1912, English; fiction BRO
RIC ST
FURTADO, Celso, 1920- , Brazilian;
nonfiction CON
FURTADO, Francisco, 1740-1816,
Portuguese; poetry SA
FURUKAWA MOKUAMI see MOKUAMI
FURUQI, Muhammad Ali, 877-942,
Persian; fiction ST
FUSON, Benjamin Willis, 1911- ,
American; nonfiction CON
FUSS, Peter Lawrence, 1932- ,
German-American; nonfiction CON
FUSSELL, George Edwin, 1889- ,
English; nonfiction CON
FUSSELL, Paul, 1924- , American;
nonfiction CON
'FUSSENEGGER, Gertrud' (Gertrud
Dietz), 1912- , Austrian; fiction,
poetry, plays FLE KU LEN
FUSSNER, Frank Smith, 1920- ,
American; nonfiction CON
FUSTEL de COULANGES, Numa
Denys, 1830-89, French; non-
fiction DIF HAR KE SA ST
FU-SUNG-LING, 1622- , Chinese;
poetry SA
'FUTABATEI SHIMEI' (Hasegawa
Tatsunosuke), 1864-1909, Japanese;
fiction LAN ST
FUTRELLE, Jacques, 1875-1912,
American; journalism, fiction KT
FUZELIER, Louis, 1672-1752, French;
nonfiction, poetry DIL
'FUZULI' (Mehmed), 1494-1555, Turk-
ish; poetry LAN ST
FYFFE, Don, 1925- , American;
nonfiction CON
FYLEMAN, Rose, 1877-1957, English;
juveniles, poetry BRO DOY KJU
KL KT
FYODOROV, Innokenti Vasilievich
('Omulevski'), 1836-83, Russian;
fiction, poetry HARK
FYOT de la MARCHE, Claude
('Vaugimois'), 1630-1721, French;
nonfiction DIL
FYSH, Wilmot Hudson, 1895- ,
Australian; nonfiction CON
FYSON, Jenny Grace, 1904- , Eng-
lish; juveniles CON

G

'G.B.' see BOAS, Guy H. S.
'G.N.' see KLOOS, Willem J.T.
GAA, Charles John, 1911- ,
American; nonfiction CON
GAADAMBA, M., 1924- ,
Mongolian; fiction LAN
GAARD, David, 1945- , American;
nonfiction CON
GABE, Dora, 1886- , Bulgarian;
poetry ST
GABEL, Margaret, 1938- ,
American; nonfiction CON
GABIOT, Jean Louis, 1759-1811,
French; plays DIL
GABIROL, Solomon B.J. see
IBN GABIROL, Solomon B.J.
GABLEHOUSE, Charles, 1928- ,
American; nonfiction CON
GABLIK, Suzi, 1934- , American;
nonfiction CON
GABO, Naum, 1890- , Russian-
American; nonfiction CON
GABOR, Dennis, 1900- ,
Hungarian-English; nonfiction
CON
GABORIAU, Emile, 1835-73,
French; fiction DIF HAR KE
MAG SA ST
GABRIEL, Astrik L., 1907- ,
Hungarian-American; nonfiction
CON
GABRIEL, Gilbert Wolf, 1890- ,
American; fiction WAF
GABRIEL, José, 1896- , Argen-
tinian; fiction, criticism,
essays MIN
GABRIEL, Luci, 1597-1663,
Raeto-Romansch; nonfiction
ST
GABRIEL, Mari Cruz, 1926- ,
Indian; poetry, fiction MUR
GABRIEL, Ralph Henry, 1890- ,
American; nonfiction CON
GABRIEL, Steffan, 1565-1638,
Raeto Romansch; poetry ST
GABRIEL DE SAINTE CLAIRE,
18th cent., French; nonfiction
DIL
GABRIEL SIONITA, 1577-1648?,
nonfiction SA
GABRIEL y GALAN, José María,
1870-1905, Spanish; poetry
BL COL SA ST
GABRIELSON, Ira N., 1889- ,
American; nonfiction CON
GABRIELSON, James Brashear,

1917- , American; nonfiction
CON
'GABRYELLA' see ZMICHOWSKA,
Narcyza
GACE BRULE, -1214?, French;
poetry HAR ST
GACHE, Alberto I., 1854-1933,
Argentinian; journalism MIN
GACHE, Roberto, 1891- , Argen-
tinian; plays MIN SA
GACON, François, 1667-1725, French;
nonfiction DIL SA
GACON, Maria Armanda Juana, 1753-
1835, French; fiction SA
GADDA, Carlo Emilio, 1893-1973,
Italian; fiction FLE RIC SA
ST
GADDA, Conti Piero, 1902- , Italian;
fiction SA
'GADDES, Peter' see SHELDON,
Peter
GADDESDEN, John of, 1280-1361,
English; nonfiction ST
GADDIS, Peggy see DERN, Peggy G.
GADDIS, Thomas Eugene, 1908- ,
American; nonfiction CON
GADDIS, Vincent H., 1913- , Amer-
ican; nonfiction CON
GADDIS, William, 1922- , American;
nonfiction CON
GADGIL, Gangadhar Gopol, 1923- ,
Indian; fiction, criticism LAN
GADKAR, Ram Ganesa, 1885-1919,
Indian; poetry, plays LAN
GADOLA, Guglielm, 1902- , Raeto-
Romansch; fiction ST
GAEBELEIN, Frank Ely, 1899- ,
American; nonfiction CON
GAELAN TYL, Josef, 1808-56,
Czech; plays, poetry, fiction
SA
GAENG, Paul A., 1924- , Hungarian-
American; nonfiction CON
GAER, Joseph, 1897- , American;
juveniles, fiction CON FUL
WA
GAETA, Francesco, 1879-1927,
Italian; poetry COL SA
GAFFAREL, Jacques, 1601-81,
French; nonfiction SA
GAG, Flavia, 1907- , American;
juvenile CON FUL WA
GAG, Wanda, 1893-1946, American;
juveniles KJU KT WA
GAGE, Frances Dana Barker ('Aunt
Fanny'), 1808-84, American;
nonfiction KAA
GAGE, William, 1915- , American;

nonfiction CON
GAGE, William Whitney, 1925- ,
American; nonfiction CON
'GAGE, Wilson' see STEELE,
Mary Q. G.
GAGER, William, fl. 1580-1619,
English; plays KB ST
GAGINI, Carlos, 1865-1925, Costa
Rican; poetry, plays, fiction
MIN
GAGLIARDO, John Garver,
1933- , American; nonfiction
CON
GAGLIARDO, Ruth, American;
juveniles WA
GAGNIER, Jean, 1670-1740,
French; nonfiction DIL
GAGNON, Jean Louis, 1913- ,
Canadian; nonfiction CON
GAGNON, John Henry, 1931- ,
American; nonfiction CON
GAGUIN, Robert, 1425-1502,
French; nonfiction SA ST
GAICHIES, Jean, 1647-1731,
French; nonfiction DIL
GAIE, Jean Baptiste, 1755-1829,
French; nonfiction SA
GAIGNE, Alexis Toussaint,
-1817, French; plays DIL
GAILEY, James Herbert, Jr.,
1916- , American; nonfiction
CON
GAILLARD, André, 1894-1929,
French; poetry DIF
GAILLARD, Auger, 1530-94,
French; poetry ST
GAILLARD, Gabriel Henri, 1726-
1806, French; nonfiction DIL
GAILLARD de la BATAILLE,
Pierre Alexandre, 1708-79,
French; nonfiction DIL
GAIMAR, Geoffrey, fl. 1140?,
English; poetry, translations
BRO KB ST
GAINDE MONTAGNAC, Louis
Laurent Joseph, 1731-80,
French; nonfiction DIL
GAINBURG, Joseph Charles,
1894- , American; nonfiction
CON
GAINES, Diana, 1912- , American;
fiction CON
GAINES, Ernest J., 1933- ,
American; fiction CON
GAINES, Pierce Welch, 1905- ,
American; nonfiction CON
GAINSBRUGH, Glen M., 1949- ,
American; nonfiction CON

GAINSFORD, Thomas, -1624,
English; nonfiction ST
GAIO, Maestro see RIETI, Moses de
GAIO, Manuel da Silva, 1860-1934,
Portuguese; poetry, fiction,
criticism ST
GAIRDNER, James, 1828-1912,
Scots; nonfiction KBA
GAISER, Gerd, 1908- , German;
fiction AL FLE KU KUN RIC
LEN
'GAITE, Francis' see COLES, Cyrll
H.
GAITHER, Francis Ormond Jones,
1889- , American; fiction KTS
WAF
GAITHER, Gant, 1917- , American;
nonfiction CON
GAITSKELL, Charles Dudley, 1908- ,
English; nonfiction CON
GAJ, Ljudevit, 1809-72, Croatian;
nonfiction, poetry SA ST
GAJAMAN NONA, fl. 1800, Sinhalese;
poetry LAN
GAL, Hans, 1890- , Austrian-Scots;
nonfiction CON
GALA, Antonio, 1935- , Spanish;
poetry, essays, plays SA
'GALACION, Gala' (Grigore Pisculescu),
1879- , Rumanian; fiction ST
GALALU DIN RUMI, 1207- , Persian;
SA
GALAN, Angel María, 1836- ,
Colombian; nonfiction, journalism
MIN
GALAN, José M.G. see GABRIEL y
GALAN, José M.
GALANTE, Pierre, 1909- , French;
nonfiction CON
GALANTER, Eugene, 1924- , Ameri-
can; nonfiction CON
'GALATEO, Il' see DE FERRARIIS,
Antonio
GALAUP de CHASTEUIL, Pierre,
1643-1727, French; nonfiction
DIL
GALBRAITH, Clare Kearney, 1919- ,
American; nonfiction CON
GALBRAITH, Georgie Starbuck ('G.S.
Page'; 'Ann Patrice'; 'Penny Pen-
nington'; 'Stuart Pennington'),
1909- , American; fiction CON
GALBRAITH, Jean ('Correa'; 'Judith
Green'), 1906- , Australian;
nonfiction CON
GALBRAITH, John Kenneth ('Mark
Epernay'; 'Herschel McLandress'),
1908- , Canadian-American;

nonfiction CON
GALBRAITH, John S., 1916- ,
Scots-American; nonfiction
CON
GALBRAITH, Madlyn, 1897- ,
American; nonfiction CON
GALCZYNSKI, Konstanty Ildefons,
1906-53, Polish; plays, poetry
FLE
GALDAMES, Luis, 1865-1941,
Chilean; nonfiction MIN
GALDONE, Paul, Hungarian-
American; juveniles WA
GALDOS, Benito see PEREZ
GALDOS, Benito
GALE, Herbert Morrison, 1907- ,
American; nonfiction CON
'GALE, John' see GAZE, Richard
GALE, Norman Rowland, 1862-
1942, English; poetry BRO
GALE, Raymond Floyd, 1918- ,
American; nonfiction CON
GALE, Richard M., 1932- ,
American; nonfiction CON
GALE, Robert Lee, 1919- ,
American; nonfiction CON
GALE, Vi Hokenson, American;
poetry, fiction CON MUR
GALE, Zona, 1874-1938, American;
fiction, poetry BRO KL KT
MAT RIC ST
GALEANO, Eduardo Hughes,
1940- , Uruguayan; nonfiction
CON
GALECKI, Tadeusz see 'STRUG,
Andrzej'
GALEN, 129- , Greek; nonfiction
ST
GALENDO, Beatriz, 1475?-1534,
Spanish; nonfiction BL
'GALENO JUVENAL' (Juvenal
Galeno da Costa e Silva),
1836-1931, Brazilian; poetry
ST
GALENSON, Walter, 1914- ,
American; nonfiction CON
GALEOTA, Francesco, -1497,
Italian; poetry ST
GALES, Winifred Marshall, 1761-
1839, American; fiction JO
GALET, Jacques, -1726, French;
nonfiction DIL
GALFO, Armand J., 1924- ,
American; nonfiction CON
GALFRIDO de AVINESALE, 12th
cent., English; poetry SA
GALHARDO, Luiz, 1874-1929,
Portuguese; plays SA

GALHEGOS, Manuel, 1597-1665,
Portuguese; poetry SA
GALIANI, Ferdinando, 1728-87,
Italian; fiction DIL KE ST
'GALIB SEYH' (Mehmed Esad), 1757-
98, Turkish; poetry ST
GALIEN, Claude, 18th cent., French;
nonfiction DIL
GALIEN, Joseph, 1699-1782, French;
nonfiction DIL
GALILEI, Galileo, 1564-1642, Italian;
nonfiction HAR KE SA ST
GALINDO, Beatriz ('la Latina'),
1475-1534, Spanish; nonfiction
SA
GALINDO, Néstor, 1830-65, Bolivian;
poetry MIN SA
GALINDO HERRERO, Santiago, 1920- ,
Spanish; nonfiction SA
GALINSKY, Gotthard Karl, 1942- ,
German-American; nonfiction CON
GALION, Lucio Junio, 1st cent.,
Roman; nonfiction SA
GALITZIN, Dimitri, 1730-1803, Rus-
sian; nonfiction DIL
GALL, Alice Crew, American; juveniles
KJU WA
GALL, Sir William, 1777-1836, Eng-
lish; nonfiction KBA
'GALLAGER, Gale' see OURSLER,
William C.
GALLAGHER, John Fredrick, 1936- ,
American; nonfiction CON
GALLAGHER, Kent Grey, 1933- ,
American; nonfiction CON
GALLAGHER, Rev. Louis Joseph,
1885-1972, American; fiction,
nonfiction HO
GALLAGHER, Sister Mary Dominic,
1917- , American; nonfiction,
juveniles CON
GALLAGHER, Matthew Philip,
1919- , American; nonfiction
CON
GALLAGHER, Richard Fairington,
1926- , American; nonfiction
CON
GALLAGHER, Robert Emmett, 1922- ,
American; nonfiction CON
GALLAGHER, Thomas Michael, Amer-
ican; fiction, nonfiction CON
GALLAGHER, William Davis, 1808-94,
American; poetry KAA
GALLAHER, Art, Jr., 1925- , Amer-
ican; nonfiction CON
GALLAND, Antoine, 1646-1715,
French; nonfiction DIL SA
GALLANT, Roy Arthur, 1924- ,

American; juveniles CON
WA
GALLANT, Thomas Grady,
1920- , American; nonfiction
CON
GALLARDO y BLANCO, Bartolomé
José, 1776-1852, Spanish; non-
fiction BL SA ST
GALLATI, Mary Ernestine, Eng-
lish; nonfiction, poetry, fic-
tion CON
GALLATI, Robert R. J., 1913- ,
American; nonfiction CON
GALLEGLY, Joseph Stephen,
1898- , American; nonfiction
CON
GALLEGO, José Luis, 1913- ,
Spanish; poetry SA
GALLEGO, Juan Nicasio, 1777-
1853, Spanish; poetry BL
HAR SA ST
GALLEGO BURIN, Antonio, 1895-
1960, Spanish; nonfiction BL
GALLEGOS, Gerardo, 1905- ,
Ecuadorian; fiction DI
GALLEGOS, Rómulo, 1884-1969,
Venezuelan; fiction, plays BL
FLE MAG SA RIC ST
GALLER, David, 1929- , Ameri-
can; poetry, criticism CON
MUR
'GALLERITE, The' see BASON,
Frederick T.
GALLERY, Daniel, V., 1901- ,
American; fiction CON
GALLET, Paris, 1700-57, French;
plays DIL
GALLET, Sébastien, 1750- ,
French; plays DIL
GALLIAN, Marcello, 1902- ,
Italian; plays, criticism SA
GALLIANI, Fernando, 1728-1787,
Italian; nonfiction SA
GALLIANO CANCIO, Miguel,
1890- , Cuban; poetry MIN
GALLICO, Paul William, 1897- ,
American; fiction, journalism
BRO CON KTS RIC WAF
GALLIE, Minna Patricia Humph-
reys; 1920- , Welsh; fiction
CON
GALLIENNE, Eva see LE GAL-
LIENNE, Eva
GALLIFET, Joseph de, 1663-1749,
French; translations DIL
GALLIN, Mother Mary Alice, 1921- ,
American; nonfiction CON
GALLINA, Giacinto, 1852-97,

Italian; plays ST
GALLINGER, Osma Couch see TOD,
Osma G.
GALLIS, Joaquín Alfredo, 1859-1910,
Portuguese; nonfiction SA
GALLMAN, Waldemar John, 1899- ,
American; nonfiction CON
GALLOIS, Charles André Gustave
Leonard, 1789-1851, French;
nonfiction SA
GALLOIS, ·Jean, 1632-1707, French;
nonfiction DIL
GALLOWAY, Allan Douglas, 1920- ,
American; nonfiction CON
GALLOWAY, David Darryl, 1937- ,
American; nonfiction CON
GALLOWAY, George Barnes, 1898- ,
American; nonfiction CON
GALLOWAY, John C., 1915- ,
American; nonfiction CON
GALLOWAY, Joseph, 1731-1803,
American; nonfiction KAA
GALLOWAY, Margaret Cecilia, 1915- ,
English; nonfiction CON
GALLUP, Dick, 1941- , American;
poetry CON
GALLUP, Donald Clifford, 1913- ,
American; nonfiction CON
GALLUP, George Horace, 1901- ,
American; nonfiction CON
GALLUP, Richard John ('Harlan
Dangerfield'), 1941- , American;
poetry MUR
GALLUPI, Pascuale, 1770-1846,
Italian; nonfiction SA
GALLUS, Gaius Cornelius, 69-26 B. C.,
Roman; poetry ST SA
GALOUYE, Daniel Francis, 1920- ,
American; fiction CON
GALPIN, Barthélemy (Calpin),
-1790, French; nonfiction
DIL
GALSWORTHY, John ('John Sinjohn';
'A. R. P. -M.'), 1867-1933, English;
fiction, plays, criticism BRO
FLE KL KT MAG MAT RIC SA ST
GALT, John, 1779-1839, Scots; fiction
BRO KBA MAG SA ST SY
GALT, Thomas Franklin, Jr., 1908- ,
American; fiction CON FUL HIL
GALTIER, Jean Louis, 1720-82,
French; nonfiction DIL
GALTON, Sir Francis, 1822-1911,
English; nonfiction BRO KBA SA
GALUS, Henry Stanley, 1923- ,
American; nonfiction, fiction
CON
GALVAN, Manuel de Jesus, 1834-1910,

Spanish; fiction MIN SA ST
GALVÃO, Antonio, 1490?-1557,
Portuguese; nonfiction SA ST
GALVÃO, Duarte, 1435-1517,
Portuguese; nonfiction SA
GALVÃO, Henrique, 1895- ,
Portuguese; plays RIC
GALVARRIATO, Eulalia, 1905- ,
Spanish; essays, fiction BL
SA
GALVEZ, José, 1886- , Peruvian;
poetry ST
GALVEZ, José Ignacio, 1871/74-
1926, Colombian; journalism
MIN
GALVEZ, Manuel, 1882-1962,
Argentinian; fiction, poetry
BL FLE MIN RIC SA ST
GALVEZ, María Rosa de, 1768-
1806, Spanish; poetry, plays
SA
GALVEZ, Pedro Luis, 1882-1939,
Spanish; poetry SA
GALVEZ de Montalvo, Luis,
1549?-91?, Spanish; fiction,
poetry BL SA ST
'GALVEZ de MONTALVO, Luis'
see AVALLE-ARCE, Juan B.
GALVIN, John Rogers, 1929- ,
American; nonfiction CON
GALVIN, Patrick, 1927- , Irish;
poetry, plays MUR
GALVIN, Thomas John, 1932- ,
American; nonfiction CON
'GALWAY, Norman' see GENTRY,
Byron B.
GALZY, Jeanne, 1883- , French;
fiction DIF
GAMA, Duarte da, fl. 1490- ,
Portuguese; poetry ST
GAMA, Felipe José, 1713-42,
Portuguese; poetry SA
GAMA, José Basilio da, 1754-95,
Brazilian; poetry SA ST
GAMA, Juana, 1515?- , Portu-
guese; nonfiction SA
GAMACHE, Etienne Simon, 1672-
1756, French; nonfiction DIL
GAMALLO FIERROS, Dionisio,
1914- , Spanish; nonfiction,
poetry BL SA
GAMARRA, Abelardo, 1857-1924,
Peruvian; fiction, plays SA
GAMAS, 18th cent., French; plays
DIL
'GAMBADO, Geoffrey' see BUN-
BURY, Sir William H.
GAMBARA, Veronica, 1485-1550,

Italian; poetry SA ST

GAMBLE, Frederick, Irish; fiction
CON

GAMBLE, Sidney David, 1890- ,
American; nonfiction CON

GAMBOA, Federico, 1864-1939,
Mexican; fiction, nonfiction BL
SA ST

GAMBRELL, Herbert Pickens, 1898- ,
American; nonfiction CON

GAMBRILL, Richard V. N., 1890- ,
English; nonfiction HIG

GAMBS, John Sake, 1899- , American; nonfiction CON

GAMI, Mula Nurid Din Abdur, 15th
cent., Persian; poetry SA

GAMMAGE, Allen Z., 1917- , American; nonfiction CON

GAMORAN, Mamie Goldsmith, 1900- ,
American; nonfiction CON

GAMOW, George, 1904-68, Russian-
American; nonfiction KTS

GAM-PO-PA, 1079-1153, Tibetian;
nonfiction LAN

GAMSAKHURDIA, Konstantine, 1891- ,
Russian; fiction LAN

GAMSON, William A., 1934- , American; nonfiction CON

GAMST, Frederick Charles, 1936- ,
American; nonfiction CON

'GAN, Peter' (Richard Moering),
1894- , German; fiction KU

GANA, Federico, 1867/68-1926,
Chiles; nonfiction MIN

GAND, Michel Joseph, 1765-1802,
Belgian; nonfiction DIL

'GANDALAC, Lennard' see BERNE,
Eric L.

GANDARA, Carmen, Argentinian;
essays, fiction BL

GANDEE, Lee Rauss, 1917- ,
American; nonfiction CON

GANDELOT, L., 1720-85, French;
nonfiction DIL

GANDERSHEIM, Hrosvitha see
HROSVITHA von GANDERSHEIM

GANDHI, Mohandas Karamchand,
1869-1948, Indian; nonfiction ST

GANDIA, Enrique de, 1906- , Argentinian; nonfiction MIN

GANDO, Nicolas, -1767, French;
nonfiction DIL

GABDOLFI, Arístides see YUNQUE,
Alvaro

GANEA, Neculai, 1838-1916,
Rumanian; fiction, poetry ST

GANEAU, Pierre, 18th cent., French;
nonfiction DIL

GANGEL, Kenneth O., 1935- ,
American; nonfiction CON

GANGEMI, Kenneth, 1937- ,
American; fiction, poetry
CON

GANGERHOFER, Ludwig ('Rudolf
Herzog'; 'Friedrich Leinhard'),
1855-1920, German; nonfiction
AL

GANGES, Le Macon des see
LEMASSON, Daniel

GANGOTENA, Alfredo, 1904-44,
Ecuadorian; poetry ST

GANIVET, Angel, 1865-98,
Spanish; essays, fiction BL
COL HAR KE SA ST

GANLEY, Albert Charles, 1918- ,
American; nonfiction CON

'GANN, Ernest' (Ernest Kellogg),
1910- , American; fiction
CON PAC RIC WAF

GANNETT, Lewis, 1891- , American; criticism KT

'GANN, Lewis Henry' (Ludwig
Hermann Ganz), 1924- ,
German-American; nonfiction
CON

GANNETT, Ruth Chrisman,
1896- , American; juveniles
FUL

GANNETT, Stiles, 1923- ,
American; juveniles CON

GANNON, Rev. David, 1904- ,
American; nonfiction HO

GANNON, Rev. Robert, 1893- ,
American; nonfiction HO

GANNON, Robert Haines, 1931- ,
American; nonfiction CON

GANNON, Robert Ignatius, 1893- ,
American; nonfiction CON

GANOT, Robert, 1661-77, French;
nonfiction DIL

'GANPAT' see GOMPERTZ, Martin
L. A.

GANS, Eric L., 1941- , American; nonfiction CON

GANS, Herbert J., 1927- ,
German-American; nonfiction
CON

GANSFORT, Wessel, 1419-89,
Dutch; nonfiction ST

GANSHOFF, François Louis,
1895- , American; nonfiction
CON

'GANT, Jonathan' see ADAMS,
Clifton

GANTE, Jean de see JEAN of
JANDUN

GANTILLON, Simon, 1890- ,
French; plays HAR ST
GANTT, Fred, Jr., 1922- , Amer-
ican; nonfiction CON
GANZ, Ludwig Herman see 'GANN,
Lewis H.'
GANZEL, Dewey Alvin, Jr.,
1927- , American; nonfiction
CON
GANZGLASS, Martin Richard,
1941- , American; nonfiction
CON
GANZO, Robert, 1898- , French;
poetry DIF SA
GAON of VILNA see ELIJAH Ben
Solomon
GAOS, Alejandro, 1907-58, Spanish;
poetry BL SA
GAOS, José, 1902- , Spanish; non-
fiction BL
GAOS, Vicente, 1919- , Spanish;
poetry, nonfiction BL SA
GAOS y GONZALEZ-POLA, José,
1900- , Spanish; nonfiction SA
GARAGORRI, Paulino, 1916- ,
Spanish; nonfiction BL
GARARY, Blas, 1860-1910, Paraguayan;
nonfiction, journalism SA
GARAY, János, 1812-53, Hungarian;
poetry, plays, journalism ST
GARB, Solomon, 1920- , American;
nonfiction CON
GARBE, Robert, 1878-1927, German;
poetry ST
GARBER, Lee Orville, 1900- ,
American; nonfiction CON
GARBER, Otto, 1880-1949, German;
fiction ST
GARBETT, Colin Campbell, 1881- ,
English; nonfiction CON
GARBINI, Giovanni, 1931- , Italian;
nonfiction CON
GARBO, Norman, 1919- , American;
nonfiction CON
GARBORG, Arne (Aadne), 1851-1924,
Norwegian; fiction, poetry, essays,
plays COL KE SA ST
GARCÃO, Pedro Antonio Correia,
1724-72, Portuguese; poetry ST
GARCEAU, Oliver, 1911- , American;
nonfiction CON
GARCES, Enrique, 1906- , Ecuadorian;
fiction DI
GARCES, Jesús Juan, 1917- ,
Spanish; poetry, criticism BL
SA
GARCES, Julio, 1917- , Spanish;
poetry BL SA

GARCI SANCHEZ de BADAJOZ,
1460?-1526?, Spanish; poetry
BL SA ST
GARCIA, Antonio S., 1902- ,
Colombian; criticism, essays
MIN
GARCIA, Carlos, fl. 1575-1630,
Spanish; nonfiction, poetry
BL SA
GARCIA, Felix, 1897- , Spanish;
nonfiction BL
GARCIA, Fernandes de Jerena
see FERRANDES de JERENA,
Garci
GARCIA, José Gabriel, 1834/44-
1910, Diminican; nonfiction
MIN SA
'GARCIA, Juan' see ESCALANTE
Y PRIETO, Amós de
GARCIA, Juan Agustín, 1862-1923,
Argentinian; nonfiction MIN
SA
GARCIA, Manuel Adolfo, 1830-83,
Peruvian; poetry SA
GARCIA, Pantaleón, 1757-1827,
Argentinian; nonfiction MIN
GARCIA, Vicente ('Rectorde
Vallfogoná'), 1582-1623, Span-
ish; poetry SA
GARCIA ALVAREZ, Enrique,
1873-1931, Spanish; poetry
BL SA
GARCIA ARISTA y RIVERA,
Gregorio, 1876- , Spanish;
nonfiction SA
GARCIA AYUSO, Francisco,
1835-97, Spanish; nonfiction
SA
GARCIA BACCA, Juan David,
1901- , Spanish; nonfiction
BL SA
GARCIA BAENA, Pablo, 1923- ,
Spanish; nonfiction, journalism
BL SA
GARCIA BENAVENTE, Lorenzo,
1915- , Spanish; fiction,
plays SA
GARCIA BLANCO, Manuel, 1902- ,
Spanish; nonfiction BL
GARCIA CALDERON, Francisco,
1883-1953, Peruvian; essays
BL SA ST
GARCIA CALDERON, Ventura,
1886-1959, Peruvian; fiction,
poetry, criticism, essays,
journalism BL FLE SA ST
GARCIA CERECEDA, Martín,
1495?-1560?, Spanish;

nonfiction BL SA
GARCIA CHUECOS, Héctor, 1899- ,
Venezuelan; criticism SA
GARCIA DE DIEGO, Vicente, 1878- ,
Spanish; criticism BL SA
GARCIA de la BARGA, Andrés see
'CORPUS Barga'
GARCIA de la HUERTA y MUÑOZ,
Vicente Antonio, 1734-87, Spanish;
plays, poetry BL HAR KE SA ST
GARCIA de PRUNEDA, Salvador,
1912- , Spanish; fiction SA
GARCIA de QUEVEDO, José Heriberto,
1819-71, Venezuelan; poetry, non-
fiction BL SA ST
GARCIA de VALDEAVELLANO, Luis,
1904- , Spanish; nonfiction BL
GARCIA de VILLATTA, José, 1798?-
1850, Spanish; fiction, plays BL
SA
GARCIA ESCUDERO, José María,
1916- , Spanish; essays, criticism
SA
GARCIA FERREIRO, Alberto, 1862-
1902, Spanish; poetry, plays, jour-
nalism SA
GARCIA GODOY, Federico, 1857-1924,
Dominican; fiction, criticism MIN
SA
GARCIA GOMEZ, Aristides, 1863-1917,
Dominican; fiction MIN
GARCIA GOMEZ, Emilio, 1905- ,
Arab; nonfiction BL SA
GARCIA GOYENA y GASTELU, Rafael,
1776-1823, Guatemalan; fiction
SA ST
GARCIA GUTIERREZ, Antonio, 1813-
84, Spanish; plays BL HAR KE
SA ST
GARCIA HORTELANO, Juan, 1928- ,
Spanish; fiction RIC SA
GARCIA ICAZBALCETA, Joaquin,
1825-94, Mexican; nonfiction BL
SA
GARCIA KOLHY, Mario, 1866/71-
1935, Cuban; essays MIN
GARCIA LOPEZ, Juan Catalina ('Juan
Catalina'), 1845-1911, Spanish;
nonfiction SA
GARCIA LORCA, Federico, 1899-1936,
Spanish; poetry, plays BL COL
FLE HAR KT MAG MAT RIC SA
ST
GARCIA LORCA, Francisco, 1904- ,
Spanish; nonfiction BL SA
GARCIA LUENGO, Eusebio, 1905- ,
Spanish; fiction, plays BL SA
GARCIA MANSILLA, Daniel, 1868- ,

French-Argentinian; poetry,
plays, essays MIN
GARCIA MARQUEZ, Gabriel,
1928- , American; nonfiction
CON
GARCIA MARTI, Victoriano,
1881- , Spanish; journalism,
essays BL SA
GARCIA MATAMOROS, Alfonso,
1490?-1572, Spanish; nonfiction
SA
GARCIA MERCADAL, José,
1883- , Spanish; journalism
BL SA
GARCIA MEROU, Martín, 1862-
1905, Argentinian; journalism,
poetry MIN SA
GARCIA MONJE, Joaquín, 1881- ,
Costa Rican; nonfiction MIN
GARCIA MORENO, Gabriel, 1821-
75, Ecuadorian; poetry DI
GARCIA MORENTE, Manuel,
1888-1941/42, Spanish; non-
fiction BL COL SA
GARCIA NIETO, José, 1914- ,
Spanish; poetry BL SA
GARCIA PAVON, Francisco,
1919- , Spanish; plays BL
SA
GARCIA PELAYO, Manuel, 1909- ,
Spanish; essays BL
GARCIA SANCHIZ, Federico, 1884-
1964, Spanish; fiction BL SA
GARCIA SERRANO, Rafael,
1917- , Spanish; journalism,
fiction BL SA
GARCIA SOLALINDE, Antonio,
1892-1937, Spanish; nonfiction
BL SA
GARCIA SUELTO, Tomás, 1778-
1815, Spanish; poetry, nonfic-
tion SA
GARCIA TASARA, Gabriel, 1817-
75, Spanish; poetry BL SA
ST
GARCIA TEJADA, Juan Manuel,
1774-1845, Colombian; poetry
MIN
GARCIA VALDECASAS, Alfonso,
1904- , Spanish; nonfiction
BL SA
GARCIA VELA, Jose, 1885-1913,
Spanish; poetry BL
GARCIA VELLOSO, Enrique,
1880-1938, Argentinian;
journalism, fiction, plays
MIN SA
GARCIA VENERO, Maximiano,

1907- , Spanish; nonfiction SA
GARCIA VIELBA, Félix, 1897- ,
Spanish; nonfiction SA
GARCIA VIÑO, Manuel, 1928- ,
Spanish; nonfiction SA
GARCIASOL, Ramón de, 1913- ,
Spanish; poetry, fiction BL SA
GARCILASO de la VEGA ('El Inca'),
1539-1616, Spanish; nonfiction
BL HAR KE SA ST
GARCOLASO de la VEGA, 1503-36,
Spanish; poetry BL HAR KE SA
ST
GARCIN, Jean Laurent, 1735-61,
French; translations DIL
GARD, Joyce, English; juveniles WA
GARD, Richard Abbott, 1914- ,
Canadian; nonfiction CON
GARD, Robert Edward, American;
fiction, juveniles, plays WA
GARD, Sanford Wayne, 1899- ,
American; nonfiction CON
GARDEL, Maximilien Joseph Leópold
Philippe, 1741-87, French; non-
fiction DIL
GARDEN, Alexander, 1685-1756,
American; nonfiction KAA
GARDEN, Edward James Clarke,
1940- , Scots; nonfiction CON
'GARDEN, John' see FLETCHER,
Harry L. V.
GARDEN, Nancy, 1938- , American;
juveniles CON
GARDIN DUMESNIL, Jean Baptiste,
1720-1802, French; nonfiction
DIL
GARDINER, Alfred George ('Alpha of
the Plough'), 1865-1946, English;
journalism, essays BRO
GARDINER, Clinton Harry, 1913- ,
American; nonfiction CON
GARDINER, Glenn Lion, 1896-1962,
American; nonfiction, juvenile
CON
GARDINER, Judy, 1922- , English;
fiction CON
GARDINER, Marguerite Power Farmer
see BLESSINGTON, Lady
GARDINER, Patrick Lancaster, 1922- ,
English; nonfiction CON
GARDINER, Robert K. A., 1914- ,
English; nonfiction CON
GARDINER, Samuel Rawson, 1829-
1902, English; nonfiction BRO
KBA ST
GARDIZI, Abu Sa'id, 11th cent.,
Persian; nonfiction ST
GARDNER, Alan Harold, 1925- ,

English; nonfiction CON
GARDNER, Brian, 1931- , Eng-
lish; fiction CON
GARDNER, David P., 1933- ,
American; nonfiction CON
GARDNER, Dick see GARDNER,
Richard
GARDNER, Donald Robert Hugh,
1938- , British; poetry,
translations MUR
GARDNER, Dorothy E. M.,
1900- , English; nonfiction
CON
GARDNER, Edward Clinton,
1920- , American; nonfiction
CON
GARDNER, Erle Stanley ('A. A.
Fair'; 'Carleton Kendrake';
'Charles J. Kenny'), 1889- ,
American; fiction BRO CON
KT RIC SA
GARDNER, Gerald, 1929- ,
American; nonfiction CON
GARDNER, Isabella, 1895- ,
American; poetry SP
GARDNER, Isabella Stewart,
1915- , American; poetry
MUR
GARDNER, Jani, 1943- , Ameri-
can; nonfiction CON
GARDNER, Jeanne Le Monnier,
American; nonfiction CON
'GARDNER, Jeffrey' see FOX,
Gardner F.
GARDNER, John Edward, 1917- ,
American; nonfiction CON
GARDNER, John William, 1912- ,
American; nonfiction CON
GARDNER, Joseph L., 1933- ,
American; nonfiction CON
'GARDNER, Lawrence' see BRAN-
NON, William T.
GARDNER, Lilian Soskin, 1907- ,
American; juveniles WA
GARDNER, Lloyd Calvin, 1934- ,
American; nonfiction CON
GARDNER, Mary Adelaide,
1920- , American; nonfiction
CON
GARDNER, Nancy Bruff, 1915- ,
American; fiction, poetry
CON
GARDNER, Ralph David, 1923- ,
American; nonfiction CON
GARDNER, Richard ('Clifford
Anderson'; 'John Carver';
'Richard Cummings'; 'Richard
Orth'), 1931- , American;

fiction, nonfiction CON WA
GARDNER, Riley Wetherell, 1921- ,
American; nonfiction CON
GARDNER, Rufus Hallette, III,
1918- , American; nonfiction
CON
GARDNER, William Earl, 1928- ,
American; nonfiction CON
GARDNER, William Henry, 1902- ,
English; nonfiction CON
GARDNER-SMITH, Percival, 1888- ,
English; nonfiction CON
'GARDONS, S. S. see SNODGRASS,
William D.
GARDONYI, Géza, 1863-1925, Hun-
garian; fiction, poetry, plays
COL SA ST
GAREAU, Frederick Henry, 1923- ,
American; nonfiction CON
GARELICK, May, 1910- , American;
juveniles WA
GARESCHE, Edward Francis, 1876- ,
American; poetry, nonfiction
HOE
GARFIAS, Francisco, 1921- , Spanish;
poetry BL SA
GARFIAS, Pedro, 1884- , Spanish;
nonfiction SA
GARFIELD, Brian Wynne ('Bennett
Garland'; 'Frank O'Brian'; 'Brian
Wynne'; 'Frank Wynne'), 1939- ,
American; fiction CON
GARFIELD, Leon, 1921- , English;
juveniles, fiction COM CON DOY
GARFIELD, Sol Louis, 1918- ,
American; nonfiction CON
GARFIELD, Leon, 1921- , English;
juveniles, fiction COM CON DOY
GARFIELD, Sol Louis, 1918- , Amer-
ican; nonfiction CON
GARFIELD, Viola Edmundson, 1899- ,
American; nonfiction PAC
GARFINKEL, Bernard ('Robert Allan';
'Robert Elliott'), 1929- , Ameri-
can; juveniles CON
GARFINKEL, Herbert, 1920- ,
American; nonfiction CON
GARFITT, Roger, 1944- , English;
poetry CON
GARFORTH, Francis William, 1917- ,
English; nonfiction CON
GARGAZ, Pierre André, 18th cent.,
French; nonfiction DIL
GARIBAY y ZAMALLOA, Esteban de,
1525-99, Spanish; nonfiction BL
SA
GARIDEL, Pierre Joseph, 1658-1737,
French; nonfiction DIL

GARIGA, Pablo, 1853-93, Chilean;
poetry MIN
GARIN, François ('Guerin'), 1413-
60, French; poetry SA
'GARIN, N.' see MIKHAYLOVSKI,
N. G.
GARIOCH, Robert Sutherland,
1909- , Scots; poetry MUR
GARIS, Robert Erwin, 1925- ,
American; nonfiction CON
'GARLAND, Bennett' see GAR-
FIELD, Brian W.
'GARLAND, George' see ROARK,
Garland
GARLAND, Hamlin, 1860-1940,
American; fiction, poetry,
essays, plays BRO HOO KL
KT MAG ST
GARLAND, John, 1180-1258,
English; nonfiction, poetry
ST
GARLAND, Madge, 1900- ,
Australian; nonfiction CON
GARLANDE, John, 13th cent.,
English; poetry SA
GARLE, Hubert, 1856- , English;
nonfiction HIG
GARLEANU, Emil, 1878-1914,
Moldavian; fiction ST
GARLICK, Raymond, 1926- ,
British; poetry, criticism
MUR
GARLINGTON, Warren King,
1923- , American; nonfiction
CON
GARMENDIA, José Ignacio, 1841-
1925, Argentinian; nonfiction
SA
GARMON, William S., 1926- ,
American; nonfiction CON
GARNEAU, Alfred, 1836-1904,
Canadian; nonfiction, poetry
SY
GARNEAU, François Xavier,
1809-66, French-Canadian;
nonfiction ST SY
GARNEAU, René, 1907- ,
Canadian; nonfiction SY
GARNEAU, Saint Denys, 1912-
43, Canadian; nonfiction,
poetry ST SY
GARNEAU, Sylvain, 1930-53,
Canadian; poetry SY
GARNER, Alan, 20th cent.,
English; juveniles DOY
GARNER, Claud Wilton, 1891- ,
American; nonfiction CON
GARNER, Dwight L., 1913- ,

American; nonfiction CON

GARNER, Harry Hyman, 1910- ,
American; nonfiction CON

GARNER, Hugh, 1913- , Canadian;
fiction RIC SY

GARNER, Lafayette Ross, 1914- ,
American; nonfiction CON

GARNER, Samuel Paul, 1910- ,
American; nonfiction CON

GARNER, Wendell Richard, 1921- ,
American; nonfiction CON

GARNER, William, English; fiction
CON

GARNER, William Robin, 1936- ,
American; nonfiction CON

GARNETT, Arthur Campbell, 1894- ,
Australian-American; nonfiction
CON

GARNETT, David ('Leda Burke'),
1892- , English; fiction BRO
CON FLE KL KT MAG RIC SA ST

GARNETT, Edward, 1868-1937, English; criticism, essays, plays
KT ST

GARNETT, Eve R., 20th cent.,
English; juveniles CON DOY WA

GARNETT, Richard, 1835-1906, English; criticism, essays, poetry
BRO KBA ST

GARNETT, Richard Duncan Carey,
1923- , English; nonfiction
CON

GARNHAM, Nicholas, 1937- , English; nonfiction CON

GARNIER, Charles Georges Thomas,
1746-95, French; nonfiction DIL

GARNIER, Jean Jacques, 1729-1805,
French; nonfiction DIL SA

GARNIER, Julien, 1670- , French;
nonfiction DIL

'GARNIER, Pierre' see 'MAURRAS,
Charles M. P.'

GARNIER, Pierre Ignace, 1692-1763,
French; nonfiction DIL

GARNIER, Robert, 1545-90, French;
plays DIF HAR KE SA ST

GARNIER, Sébastien, 1551?-1607,
French; poetry SA

GAROIAN, Leon, 1925- , American;
nonfiction CON

GARRAGHAN, Gilbert Joseph, 1871-
1942, American; nonfiction HOE

GARRAN-COULON, Jean Philippe,
1747-1816, French; nonfiction
DIL

GARRARD, Lancelot Austin, 1904- ,
English; nonfiction CON

GARRATY, John A., 1920- , Amer-

ican; nonfiction CON

GARREAU, Jean Claude, 1715- ,
French; nonfiction DIL

GARRET, João Baptista da Silva,
1799-1854, Portuguese; fiction,
poetry, plays SA

GARRETSON, Robert L., 1920- ,
American; nonfiction CON

GARRETT, Alfred B., 1906- ,
American; nonfiction CON

GARRETT, Eileen Jeannette
('Jean Lyttle'), 1893-1970,
Irish; fiction CON

GARRETT, Garet, 1878- , American; fiction KT

GARRETT, George Palmer, 1929- ,
American; poetry, fiction
CON MUR

GARRETT, Helen, 1895- , American; juveniles WA

GARRETT, James Leo, Jr.,
1925- , American; nonfiction
CON

GARRETT, João B. da S. L. de
A. see ALMEIDA GARRETT,
João B. da S. L. de

GARRETT, John Allen, 1920- ,
American; nonfiction CON

GARRETT, Leonard Joseph,
1926- , American; nonfiction
CON

GARRETT, Leslie, 1931- ,
American; fiction CON

GARRETT, Lillian, 1914- ,
American; nonfiction CON

GARRETT, Peter K., 1940- ,
American; nonfiction CON

GARRETT, Romeo Benjamin,
1910- , American; nonfiction
CON

GARRETT, Thomas Michael,
1924- , American; nonfiction
CON

GARRETT, Thomas Samuel,
1913- , English; nonfiction
CON

'GARRETT, Truman' see JUDD,
Margaret H.

GARRETT, Wendell Douglas,
1929- , American; nonfiction
CON

GARRETT, William, 1890- ,
Scots; fiction CON

GARRICK, David, 1717-79, English; plays BRO KB SA ST

GARRIDO, Gilberto, 1887/96- ,
Colombian; translations MIN

GARRIDO, Luiz Guedes Coutinho,

1841-82, Portuguese; nonfiction
SA
GARRIDO, Miguel Angel, 1867-1908,
Dominican; journalism, essays
MIN
GARRIDO MERINO, Edgardo, 1894/
96- , Chilean; fiction, plays,
essays MIN
GARRIDO MERINO, Edgardo, 1906- ,
Chilean; fiction SA
GARRIGAN, Owen Walter, 1928- ,
American; nonfiction CON
GARRIGO SALIDO, Roque E.,
1876-1937, Cuban; journalism
MIN
GARRIGOU-LAGRANGE, Reginald
Marie, 1877- , French; nonfic-
tion HOE
GARRIGUE, Jean, 1914-72, American;
poetry, fiction CON KTS MUR
GARRIGUES de FROMENT, 18th cent.,
French; nonfiction DIL
GARRISON, Carl Claudius, 1900- ,
American; nonfiction CON
'GARRISON, Frederick' see SINCLAIR,
Upton B.
'GARRISON, Joan' see NEUBAUER,
William A.
GARRISON, Omar V., 1913- , Amer-
ican; nonfiction CON
GARRISON, R. Benjamin, 1926- ,
American; nonfiction CON
GARRISON, Webb Black ('Gary Web-
ster'), 1919- , American; non-
fiction CON
GARRISON, William Lloyd, 1805-79,
American; editor BRO KAA
GARRISON, Winfred Ernest, 1874- ,
American; nonfiction CON
GARSHIN, Vsevolod Mikhailovich,
1855-88, Russian; fiction COL
HAR HARK SA ST
GARSON, Barbara, American; plays
CON
GARSON, Noel George, 1931- , South
African; nonfiction CON
GARST, Doris Shannon ('Shannon
Garst'), 1894/99- , American;
juveniles COM CON KJU WA
GARSTANG, James Gordon, 1927- ,
English; nonfiction CON
GARSTEIN, Oskar Bernhard, 1924- ,
Norwegian; nonfiction CON
GART, Thiebold, 16th cent., German;
plays ST
GARTEN, Hugh Frederick, 1904- ,
English; nonfiction CON
GARTEN, Jan, American; juveniles
WA

GARTENAERE, Wernher de see
WERNHER du GARTENAERE
GARTENBERG, Leo, 1906- ,
Hungarian-American; nonfiction
CON
GARTER, Bernard ('Thomas'),
fl. 1565-79, English; poetry
ST
GARTH, Sir Samuel, 1661-1719,
English; poetry BRO DIL KB
ST
GARTHOFF, Raymond Leonard,
1929- , American; nonfiction
CON
'GARTHWAITE, Malaby' see
DENT, Anthony A.
GARTHWAITE, Marion Hook,
1893- , American; juveniles,
fiction CON WA
GARTLAND, Robert Aldrich,
1927- , American; juveniles
CON
GARTMAN, Louisa, 1920- ,
American; juvenile CON
GARTNER, Alan, 1935- , Ameri-
can; nonfiction CON
GARTNER, Chloe Maria, 1916- ,
American; fiction, plays CON
GARTNER, Lloyd P., 1927- ,
American; nonfiction CON
GARTON, Malinda Dean, American;
nonfiction CON
GARTON, Nancy Wells, 1908- ,
English; nonfiction CON
GARTON, Nina R., 1905- ,
American; nonfiction CON
'GARVE, Andrew' see WINTER-
TON, Paul
GARVER, Richard Bennett,
1934- , American; nonfiction
CON
GARVEY, Mona, 1934- , Ameri-
can; nonfiction CON
GARVIN, Hilda Katharine,
1904- , English; nonfiction,
poetry CON
GARVIN, Mrs. John see 'HALE,
Katherine'
GARVIN, Paul Lucian, 1919- ,
Austrian-American; nonfiction
CON
GARVIN, William, 1922- ,
American; nonfiction CON
GARWOOD, Darrell Nelson,
1909- , American; nonfiction
CON
'GARY, Romain' (Roman Kassef),
1914- , French; fiction DIC
DIF FLE RIC

GARZONI, Tommaso, 1549-89, Italian;
nonfiction ST
'GASCAR, Pierre' (Pierre Fournier),
1916- , French; fiction DIC
DIF FLE PIN
GASCO CONTELL, Emilio, 1898- ,
Spanish; nonfiction SA
GASCOIGNE, Bamber, 1935- , Eng-
lish; nonfiction CON
GASCOIGNE, George, 1525/35-77,
English; poetry, plays BRO KB
SA SP ST
GASCOIGNE, Rev. Noel Hamlyn,
1910- , New Zealander; nonfic-
tion HO
GASCOIGNE, Thomas, 1403/04-57/58,
English; nonfiction ST
'GASCON, The' see MILLER, Frederick
GASCON ADIKARAM, fl. 1707-39,
Sinhalese; poetry LAN
GASCOYNE, David Emery, 1916- ,
British; poetry, fiction, criticism
translations FLE MUR RIC SP
GASH, Norman, 1912- , Scots; non-
fiction CON
GASKELL, A. P., 1913- , New
Zealander; fiction ST
GASKELL, Elizabeth Cleghorn Steven-
son, 1810-65, English; fiction
BRO KBA MAG SA ST
GASKELL, Jane, 1941- , English;
fiction CON
GASKELL, John Philip Wellesley,
1926- , American; nonfiction
CON
GASKELL, Thomas F., 1916- ,
English; nonfiction CON
GASKIN, Catherine, 1929- , Aus-
tralian; fiction RIC
GASPAR, Enrique, 1842-1902, Spanish;
plays BL SA
GASPAR, Tido J., 1893- , Slovak;
fiction ST
GASPAR SIMOES, João, 1903- ,
Portuguese; criticism, fiction,
journalism SA
GASPAROTTI, Elizabeth Seifert see
SEIFERT, Elizabeth
GASPAROVIC, Pavel see 'HLBINA,
Pavel'
GASPE, Philippe Aubert de, 1786-
1871, French-Canadian; fiction
ST
GASPER, Louis, 1911- , American;
nonfiction CON
GASQUET, Francis Neil, 1846-1929,
English; nonfiction BRO
GASQUET, Joachim, 1873-1921,

French; poetry DIF
GASS, Irene, American; juveniles
WA
GASS, William Howard, 1924- ,
American; fiction CON
GASSENDI, Pierre, 1592-1655,
French; nonfiction DIF SA
ST
GASSERT, Robert George, 1921- ,
American; nonfiction CON
GASSET see ORTEGA y GASSET
GASSNER, Rev. Jerome Joseph,
1901- , Australian; nonfiction
HO
GASSNER, John Waldhorn, 1903-
67, American; nonfiction CON
GASSNER, Julius Stephen, 1915- ,
American; nonfiction CON
GASSOL, Buenaventura, 1893- ,
Spanish; poetry SA
GASTAUD, François, 1660-1732,
French; nonfiction DIL
GASTER, Theodor Herzl, 1906- ,
English; nonfiction CON
GASTEV, Alexey Kapitonovich,
1882- , Russian; poetry ST
GASTIL, Raymond Duncan,
1931- , American; nonfiction
CON
GASTON, Edwin Willmer, Jr.,
1925- , American; nonfiction
CON
GASTON, William, 1778-1844,
American; nonfiction JO
GASTON, Phoebus, 1331-91,
French; nonfiction ST
GAT, Dmitri Vsevolod, 1936- ,
American; nonfiction CON
GATELL, Angelina, 1926- ,
Spanish; nonfiction SA
GATCH, Milton McCormick, Jr.,
1932- , American; nonfiction
CON
GATELL, Frank Otto, 1931- ,
American; nonfiction CON
GATENBY, Rosemary, 1918- ,
American; fiction CON
GATES, Charles Marvin, 1904-63,
American; nonfiction PAC
GATES, Doris, 1901- , American;
juveniles COM CON KJU WA
GATES, Eunice Joiner, 1898- ,
American; nonfiction BL
GATES, Jean Key, 1911- , Amer-
ican; nonfiction CON
GATES, John Alexander, 1898- ,
American; nonfiction CON
GATES, John Floyd, 1915- ,

American; nonfiction CON

GATES, Lillian Francis, 1901- ,
English; nonfiction CON

GATES, Natalie, American; fiction
CON

GATES, Paul W., 1901- , American; nonfiction CON

GATES, Robbins Ladew, 1922- ,
American; nonfiction CON

GATEWOOD, Willard B., Jr.,
1931- , American; nonfiction
CON

GATICA MARTINEZ, Tomás, 1883/85-
1943, Chilean; journalism, plays
MIN

GATLIN, Douglas S., 1928- , American; nonfiction CON

GATNER, Elliott Sherman Mozian,
1914- , American; nonfiction
CON

GATON ARCE, Freddy, 1920- ,
Dominican; poetry MIN SA

GATTERER, Magdalena Felipina,
1756-1831, German; poetry SA

GATTEY, Charles Neilson, 1921- ,
English; plays CON

GATTI, Angelo, 1875- , Italian;
poetry, criticism, essays SA

'GATTI, Armand' (Dante Armando),
1924- , French; plays MAT

GATTI, Attilio, 1896- , Italian-
American; juveniles KJU WA

GATTI, Ellen Morgan, American;
juveniles WA

GATTI, Zoe de Gamond, 1812-54,
French; nonfiction SA

GATTO, Alfonso, 1909- , Italian;
poetry SA

GATTY, Margaret Scott, 1809-73,
English; juveniles BRO DOY ST

GATZKE, Hans Wilhelm, 1915- ,
German-American; nonfiction CON

GAUBIER de BARRAULD, Edme
Sulpice, -1773, French; plays
DIL

GAUBIL, Antoine, 1688- , French;
nonfiction DIL

GAUCELM, Faidit, 1185-1220, French;
poetry ST

GAUCHAT, Gabriel, 1709-79, French;
nonfiction DIL

GAUCHER, Charles Etienne, 1741-
1804, French; nonfiction DIL

GAUDEN, John, 1605-62, English;
nonfiction BRO KB

GAUDET, François Charles, 18th
cent., French; poetry DIL

GAUDET, Frederick Joseph, 1902- ,

Canadian; nonfiction CON

GAUDIN, Alexis, 1650-1707,
French; nonfiction DIL

GAUDIN, Jacques Maurice, 1740-
1810, French; nonfiction DIL

GAUDY, Franz, 1800-40, German;
nonfiction AL

GAUER, Harold, 1914- , American; nonfiction CON

GAUGERAN, Gabriel, 1677-1754,
French; nonfiction DIL

GAUL, Albro T., American;
juveniles WA

GAULD, Charles Anderson,
1911- , American; nonfiction
CON

GAULDEN, Ray ('Wesley Ray'),
1914- , American; fiction
CON

GAULDIE, William Sinclair,
1918- , American; nonfiction
CON

GAULLE, Charles de, 1890-1970,
French; nonfiction DIF

GAULLYER, Denis, 1688-1736,
French; nonfiction DIL

'GAULT, Mark' see COURNOS,
John

GAULT, William Campbell,
American; juveniles WA

'GAULTER, Bon' see MARTIN,
Sir Theodore

GAULTIER,   -1759, French;
plays DIL

GAULTIER, Jules de, 1858-1942,
French; nonfiction DIF

GAUNE, French; nonfiction DIF

GAUNE de CANGY, 18th cent.,
French; translations DIL

GAUNT, Leonard, 1921- , American; nonfiction CON

GAUNT, William, 1900- , English;
criticism CON KTS

GAUSTAD, Edwin Scott, 1923- ,
American; nonfiction CON

GAUTHIER, Mme, 18th cent.,
French; nonfiction DIL

GAUTHIER, François, 1660-1730,
French; poetry DIL

GAUTHIER, François Louis,
1696-1780, French; nonfiction
DIL

GAUTHIER BENITEZ, José, 1851-
80, Puerto Rican; poetry SA

GAUTHIER-VILLARS, Henri
('Willy'), 1859-1931, French;
nonfiction HAR

GAUTIER (Gualterius), French;

nonfiction SA
GAUTIER, Jean Baptiste (Gaulthier),
1685-1755, French; nonfiction DIL
GAUTIER, Jean Jacques, 1748-1829,
French; nonfiction DIL
GAUTIER, Judith, 1850-1917, French;
fiction DIF SA
GAUTIER, Théophile, 1811-72, French;
fiction, poetry, plays, criticism
DIF HAR KE MAG MAL SA ST
GAUTIER, Walter Mapes (Map), 12th
cent., Anglo-Norman; poetry SA
GAUTIER d'ARRAS, 17th cent.,
French; poetry DIF SA ST
GAUTIER de COINCY, 1177-1236,
French; nonfiction DIF SA ST
GAUTIER de DARGIES, fl. 1200,
French; poetry ST
GAUTIER d'EPINAL, fl. 1190- ,
French; poetry SA
GAUTIER de LILA, Philippe (De
Chatillon), 12th cent., French;
poetry SA
GAUTIER de METZ, 17th cent.,
French; poetry DIF SA
GAUTIER de MONTDORGE, Antoine,
1700-68, French; nonfiction DIL
GAUTIER de SIBERT, 1720-98,
French; nonfiction DIL
GAUTIER le LEU, 13th cent., French;
poetry ST
GAVER, Mary Virginia, 1906- ,
American; nonfiction CON
GAVETT, Joseph William, 1921- ,
American; nonfiction CON
GAVETT, Thomas William, 1932- ,
American; nonfiction CON
GAVIDIA, Francisco, 1864-1955,
Salvadorian; poetry BL SA
GAVIN, Catherine, Scots; fiction CON
GAVIN, James Maurice, 1907- ,
American; nonfiction CON
GAVIN BROWN, Wilfred Arthur,
1904- , English; nonfiction CON
GAVRILESCU, Alexandrina see
'CAZIMIR, Ottilia'
GAVRON, Daniel, 1935- , English;
fiction CON
GAVRONSKY, Serge, 1932- , Amer-
ican; poetry MUR
GAVSHON, Arthur Leslie, 1916- ,
South African; nonfiction CON
GAW, Walter A., 1904- , American;
nonfiction CON
'GAWSWORTH, John' see ARMSTRONG,
Terence I. F.
GAY, Delphine (Mme. Girardin), 1804-
55, French; poetry, fiction, plays

HAR SA ST
GAY, John, 1685-1732, English;
poetry, plays BRO KB MAG
SA SP ST
GAY, Kathlyn, 1930- , American;
juveniles CON
GAY, Laverne Kels, 1914- ,
American; fiction HO
GAY, Marie Françoise Sophie,
1776-1852, French; fiction
SA
'GAY, Penny' see ROAM, Pearl
L. S.
GAY, Peter Jack, 1923- ,
American; nonfiction CON
GAY, Sydney Howard, 1814-88,
American; journalism KAA
GAY, Zhenya, 1906- , American;
juvenile FUL WA
GAYA NUÑO, Juan Antonio,
1914- , Spanish; criticism
BL SA
GAYADEVA, 12th cent., Indian;
poetry SA
GAYANGOS y ARCE, Pascual,
1809-97, Spanish; nonfiction
BL SA ST
GAYARRE, Charles Etienne Arthur,
1805-95, American; nonfiction
KAA
GAYLE, Addison, 1932- , Amer-
ican; nonfiction CON
GAYLER, Charles, 1820-92,
American; plays, journalism
KAA
GAYLIN, Willard M., 1925- ,
American; nonfiction CON
GAYOT de PITAVEL, François,
1673-1743, French; nonfiction
DIL
GAYRE of GAYRE and NIGG,
Georg Robert, 1907- ,
Irish; nonfiction CON
GAZA, Teodoro de, 1400-78,
Byzantine; poetry SA
GAZAIGNES, Jean Antoine, 1717-
1802, French; nonfiction DIL
GAZAWAY, Rena, 1910- , Ameri-
can; nonfiction CON
GAZE, Richard ('John Gale'),
1917- , Anglo-American;
fiction CON
'GAZIEL' see 'CALVET, Agustín'
GAZON d'OURXIGNE, Sébastien
Marie Mathurin, -1784,
French; nonfiction DIL
GAZTELU, Angel, 1914- ,
Cuban; poetry MIN

GEACH, Christine ('Christine Wilson';
'Anne Lowing'), 1930- , English;
fiction CON
GEACH, Patricia Sullivan, 1916- ,
American; juveniles CON
GEANAKOPLOS, Deno John, 1916- ,
American; nonfiction CON
GEANEY, Dennis Joseph, 1914- ,
American; nonfiction CON
GEARHEART, Bill R., 1928- ,
American; nonfiction CON
GEARING, Frederick Osmond,
1922- , American; nonfiction
CON
'GEARING-THOMAS, G.' see NOR-
WOOD, Victor G.C.
GEARY, Douglas, 1931- , English;
nonfiction CON
GEARY, Hubert Valentine Rupert,
1894- , English; nonfiction CON
GEBHARD, Anna Laura Munro, 1914- ,
American; nonfiction CON
GEBHARD, Paul Henry, 1917- ,
American; nonfiction CON
GEBHART, Emile, 1839-1908, French;
fiction, nonfiction DIF SA
GABLER, Ernest, 1915- , American;
fiction, plays CON
GECK, Francis Joseph, 1900- ,
American; nonfiction CON
GECYS, Casimir C., 1904- , Ameri-
can; nonfiction CON
GEDDES, Alexander, 1737-1802, Irish;
nonfiction BRO
GEDDES, Sir Patrick, 1854-1932,
British; nonfiction KT
GEDDES, Virgil, 1897- , American;
plays, poetry KT
GEDOYN, Nicolas, 1667-1744, French;
nonfiction DIL
GEDULD, Harry M., 1931- , Ameri-
can; nonfiction CON
GEDYE, George Eric Rowe, 1890- ,
English; journalism KT
GEE, Ernest R., 1878- , English;
nonfiction HIG
GEE, Herbert Leslie, 1901- , Eng-
lish; fiction, juveniles CON
GEEL, Jacob, 1789-1862, Dutch;
criticism SA ST
GEERDTS, Hans Jürgen, 1922- ,
German; nonfiction AL
GEERTZ, Clifford, 1926- , American;
nonfiction CON
GEFAELL, Maria Luisa, 1918- ,
Spanish; nonfiction BL
GEFFEN, Roger, 1919- , American;
nonfiction CON

GEHMAN, Betsy Holland ('Anne
Klainikite'), 1932- , Ameri-
can; nonfiction CON
GEHMAN, Henry Snyder, 1888- ,
American; nonfiction CON
GEHMAN, Richard Boyd ('Frederick
Christian'; 'Martin Scott'),
1921-72, American; fiction,
nonfiction CON
GEHOBELTE, Eck see ECCIUS
DEDOTATUS
GEIB, August, 1842-79, German;
nonfiction AL
GEIBEL, Emanuel von, 1815-84,
German; poetry AL HAR KE
SA ST
GEIER, Arnold, 1926- , German-
American; nonfiction CON
GEIER, Woodrow A., 1914- ,
American; nonfiction CON
GEIFLER, Horst Wolfram,
1893- , German; nonfiction
LEN
GEIGER, Donald Jesse, 1923- ,
American; poetry, nonfiction
CON
GEIGER, Homer Kent, 1922- ,
American; nonfiction CON
GEIGER, Louis G., 1913- ,
American; nonfiction CON
GEIJER, Erik Gustaf (Geyer),
1783-1847, Swedish; poetry,
nonfiction KE SA ST
GEIJERSTAM, Gösta, 1888- ,
Swedish; fiction KT
GEIJERSTAM, Gustaf af, 1858-
1909, Swedish; fiction COL
HAR KE SA ST
GEIKIE, Sir Archibald, 1835-1924,
Scots; nonfiction KBA
'GEIL, E.C.L. van' see McGIL-
VREY, Laurence
GEILER von KAISERSBERG,
Johann, 1445-1510, German;
nonfiction AL ST
GEINOZ, Francois, 1696-1752,
Swiss; nonfiction DIL
GEIRINGER, Karl, 1899- ,
Austrian-American; nonfiction
CON
GEIS, Darlene Stern ('Ralph
Kelly'; 'Jane London'; 'Peter
Stevens'), American; juveniles
CON WA
GEIS, Gilbert, 1925- , American;
nonfiction CON
GEISEL, Theodor Seuss ('Dr.
Seuss'; 'Theo LeSieg'), 1904- ,

American; juveniles COM CON
DOY FUL KT WA
GEISLER, Norman Leo, 1932- ,
American; nonfiction CON
GEISMAR, Ludwig Leo, 1921- ,
German-American; nonfiction
CON
GEISMAR, Maxwell David, 1909- ,
American; criticism, essays
CON KTS
GEISSLER, Christian, 1928- , Ger-
man; nonfiction AL
GEIST, Harold, 1916- , American;
nonfiction CON
GEIWITZ, Peter James, 1938- ,
American; nonfiction CON
GELABERT, Francisco de Paula,
1834-94, Cuban; journalism, fic-
tion MIN
GELATT, Roland, 1920- , American;
nonfiction CON
GELB, Arthur, 1924- , American;
nonfiction CON
GELB, Barbara Stone, 1926- ,
American; nonfiction CON
GELB, Ignace Jay, 1907- , Polish-
American; nonfiction CON
GELBER, Harry G., 1926- , Austrian;
nonfiction CON
GELBER, Jack, 1932- , American;
plays CON MAT RIC
GELBER, Lionel Morris, 1907- ,
Canadian; nonfiction CON
GELD, Ellen Bromfield, 1932- ,
American; fiction CON
GELDENHAUER, Gerardus (Noviomagus),
1482-1542, Dutch; nonfiction ST
GELE, Jean, 17th cent., French;
nonfiction DIL
GELEE, Jacquemart, 18th cent.,
French; poetry DIF
GELEGBALSANG, 1846-1923,
Mongolian; poetry LAN
GELERNT, Jules, 1928- , American;
nonfiction CON
'GELERT', fl. 1800- , English;
nonfiction HIG
GELFAND, Lawrence Emerson,
1926- , American; nonfiction
CON
GELINAS, Gratien, 1909- , Canadian;
poetry, plays ST SY
GELLER, Allen, 1941- , American;
nonfiction CON
GELLERMAN, Saul William, 1929- ,
American; nonfiction CON
GELLERT, Christian Fürchtegott,
1715-69, German; poetry AL HAR

KE SA ST
GELLERT, Judith, 1925- ,
American; juveniles CON
GELLHORN, Ernst, 1893- ,
German-American; nonfiction
CON
GELLHORN, Martha, 1908- ,
American; fiction, journalism
KT WAF
GELLHORN, Walter, 1906- ,
American; nonfiction CON
GELLI, Giambattista, 1498-1563,
Italian; nonfiction HAR SA
ST
GELLINEK, Christian, 1930- ,
American; nonfiction CON
GELLIS, Roberta Leah Jacobs
1927- , American; fiction
CON
GELLIUO, Aulus, 123-65, Roman;
nonfiction ST
GELLNER, Ernest Andre, 1925- ,
English; nonfiction CON
GELLNER, John, 1907- , Aus-
trian-Canadian; nonfiction
CON
GELMAN, Steve, 1934- , Ameri-
can; juveniles CON
GELPI, Albert, 1931- , Ameri-
can; nonfiction CON
GELPI, Donald L., 1934- ,
American; nonfiction CON
GELSTAD, Einar Otto, 1888- ,
Danish; poetry, essays ST
GELVEN, Charles Michael,
1937- , American; nonfiction
CON
GELZER, Matthias, 1886- ,
Swiss; nonfiction CON
GEMA, Fray Eduardo, 1920- ,
Spanish; poetry SA
GEMELLI, Rev. Edoardo Agostino,
1878- , Italian; nonfiction
HO
GEMINA, 3rd cent., Roman; nonfic-
tion SA
GEMME, Francis Robert, 1934- ,
American; nonfiction CON
GEMMETT, Robert James,
1936- , American; nonfiction
CON
GEMMILL, Jane Brown, 1898- ,
American; juveniles CON
GENARD, François, 1722- ,
French; nonfiction DIL
GENDELL, Murray, 1924- ,
American; nonfiction CON
GENDIZER, Stephen Jules, 1930- ,

American; nonfiction CON

GENDLIN, Eugene T., 1926- ,
Austrian-American; nonfiction
CON

GENDZIER, Irene Lefel, 1936- ,
American; nonfiction CON

GENEBRARDO, Gilbert, 1537-97,
French; nonfiction SA

GENEBRIER, Claude, -1750,
French; nonfiction DIL

GENER, Pompeyo, 1848-1921,
Spanish; nonfiction BL SA

GENER CUADRADO, Eduardo, 1901- ,
Spanish; poetry SA

GENEST, Charles Claude, 1639-1717/
19, French; nonfiction SA ST

GENESTET, Petrus Augustus de, 1829-
61, Dutch; poetry SA ST

GENET, Edme Jacques, -1781,
French; nonfiction, translations
DIL

GENET, François, 1640-1707, French;
nonfiction DIL

GENET, Jean, 1910- , French; poetry,
plays, nonfiction CON DIC DIF
FLE HAR MAL MAT PIN RIC

GENEVE, C. F. de, 18th cent.,
French; nonfiction DIL

GENEVOIX, Maurice, 1890- ,
French; fiction DIF FLE HAR
MAL ST

GENGA, Leonora dei Conti della,
16th cent., Italian; poetry SA

GENGENBACH, Pamphilus, 1480-1524/
25, Swiss; poetry, plays AL ST

GENLIS, Stéphanie Félicité Ducrest
de St. Aubin de, 1746-1830,
French; nonfiction DIF HAR KE
SA

GENNADIOS SCHOLARIOS see GEORGE
SCHOLARIUS

GENNARI, Genevieve, 1920- , French;
fiction, essays DIC

GENNE, William H., 1910- , American; nonfiction CON

GENNEP, Jaspar von, 1515-80, German; plays ST

GENNES, Pierre de, 1701-59, French;
nonfiction DIL

GENSICKE, Guillerma Herz, 1779-
1882, German; nonfiction SA

GENTHE, Charles Vincent, 1937- ,
American; nonfiction CON

GENTIL, Andre Antoine Pierre,
1725-1800, French; nonfiction
DIL

GENTIL, Jean Baptiste Joseph, 1726-
99, French; nonfiction DIL

GENTIL BERNARD, Pierre Joseph
Justin, 1710- , French; nonfiction DIL

GENTILE, Giovanni, 1875-1944,
Italian; nonfiction COL HAR
SA ST

GENTLEMAN, David William,
1930- , English; juveniles
CON

GENTLES, Frederick Ray,
1912- , Canadian; nonfiction
CON

GENTRY, Byron B. ('Norman
Galway'), 1913- , American;
poetry CON

GENTRY, Curt, 1931- , American; nonfiction CON

GENTRY, Dwight L., 1919- ,
American; nonfiction CON

GENTY, Louis, 1743-1817,
French; nonfiction DIL

'GEOFFREY, Theodate' see WAY-
MAN, Dorothy G.

GEOFFREY of MONMOUTH,
1100?-54, English; diary
BRO KB SA ST

GEOFFREY of VENDOME, 1070-
1132, French; nonfiction ST

GEOFFREY of VINSAUF, fl.
1210- , English; nonfiction
ST

GEOFFRIN, Marie Thérèse Rodit
de, 1699-1777, French; nonfiction DIL SA

GEOFFROY, Etienne François,
1672-1731, French; nonfiction
DIL

GEOFFROY, Jean Baptiste,
1706- , French; nonfiction,
plays DIL

GEOFFROY, Julien François,
1743-1814, French; nonfiction
DIL SA

GEOGHEGAN, Sister Barbara,
1902- , American; nonfiction
CON

GEORGAKAS, Dan, 1938- ,
American; poetry HIL

GEORGE, Alexander Lawrence,
1920- , American; nonfiction
CON

GEORGE, Charles, -1731,
French; nonfiction DIL

GEORGE, Charles Hilles, 1922- ,
American; nonfiction CON

GEORGE, Claude Swanson, Jr.,
1920- , American; nonfiction
CON

GEORGE, Edgar Madison, 1907- ,
American; nonfiction CON
GEORGE, Francois, 1717-84, French;
nonfiction DIL
GEORGE, Henry, 1839-97, American;
nonfiction BRO KAA
GEORGE, Jean Craighead, 1919- ,
American; juveniles, fiction
COM CON FUL WA
GEORGE, John Lothar, 1916- ,
American; juveniles CON CON
WA
'GEORGE, Marion E.' see BENJAMIN,
Claude M. E. P.
GEORGE, Mary Dorothy, English;
nonfiction CON
GEORGE, Mary Yanaga, 1940- ,
American; nonfiction CON
GEORGE, Norvil Lester, 1902- ,
American; nonfiction CON
'GEORGE, Orson' see LARNER,
Jeremy
GEORGE, Robert Esmonde Gordon
('Robert Sencourt'), 1890/94- ,
English; nonfiction CON HOE
GEORGE, Roy Edwin, 1923- , Eng-
lish; nonfiction CON
GEORGE, Stefan Anton, 1868-1933,
German; poetry, criticism AL
COL FLE HAR KT KU KUN LEN
MAG RIC SA ST
GEORGE, Walter Lionel, 1882-1926,
English; fiction KAT KT
'GEORGE, Wilma' see CROWTHER,
Wilma
GEORGE ACROPDITES, 1217-82,
Byzantine; nonfiction ST
GEORGE CEDRENUS, 11th cent.,
Byzantine; nonfiction ST
GEORGE CODINUS CUROPALATES,
14th cent., Byzantine; nonfiction
ST
GEORGE GEMISTUS PLETHON,
1350/55-1450/52, Byzantine;
nonfiction SA ST
GEORGE MONACHUS (Hamartholus),
9th cent., Byzantine; nonfiction
ST
GEORGE of TREBIZOND, 1395-1484,
Greek; nonfiction ST
GEORGE PACHYMERES, 1242-1310,
Byzantine; nonfiction ST
GEORGE PHRANTZES, 1401- ,
Byzantine; nonfiction ST
GEORGE PISIDES, 7th cent., Byzantine;
poetry ST
GEORGE SCHOLARIUS (Gennadius),
-1468, Byzantine; nonfiction
ST

GEORGE the Syncellus, fl. 750-
810, Byzantine; nonfiction
ST
GEORGESCU-ROEGEN, Nicholas,
1906- , Rumanian-American;
nonfiction CON
'GEORGI' see HOERNLE, Edwin
GEORGI, Charlotte, American;
nonfiction CON
GEORGIOU, Constantine, 1927- ,
American; nonfiction CON
GERALD see EKKEHART I
GERALD, Alexander, 1728-95,
Scots; nonfiction BRO
GERALD, James Edward, 1906- ,
American; nonfiction CON
GERALD, John Bart, 1940- ,
American; nonfiction CON
GERALD, Ziggy see ZEIGERMAN,
Gerald
GERALDINI, Alessandro, 1455-
1525, Italian; nonfiction ST
'GERALDY, Paul' (Paul Le Fevre),
1885- , French; poetry,
plays COL DIF MAT SA
GERANDO, Joseph Marie, 1772-
1842, French; nonfiction SA
GERARD, Albert Stanislas, 1920- ,
Belgian; nonfiction CON
GERARD, Charles Franklin,
1914- , American; fiction
CON
'GERARD, Gaston' see OSTER-
GAARD, Geoffrey N.
GERARD, Jane, American; fiction
CON
GERARD, John, 1545-1612, Eng-
lish; nonfiction KB
GERARD, Louis Philippe, 1737-
1813, French; nonfiction DIL
GERARD de NERVAL see NERVAL,
Gérard de
GERARD DESRIVIERES, Jean
Alexandre, 1745-1814?, French;
nonfiction, poetry DIL
GERARD-LIBOIS, Jules C. ('G.
Heinz'), 1923- , Belgian;
nonfiction CON
GERASSI, John, 1931- , Ameri-
can; nonfiction CON
GERBER, Albert Benjamin,
1913- , American; nonfiction
CON
GERBER, Dan, 1940- , American;
nonfiction CON
GERBER, Douglas Earl, 1933- ,
Canadian; nonfiction CON
GERBER, Helmut E., 1920- ,

German-American; nonfiction
CON

GERBER, Merrill Joan, 1938- ,
American; fiction CON

GERBER, William, 1908- ,
American; nonfiction CON

GERBERT of AURILLAC (Pope
Silvester II), 940-1003, French;
letters ST

GERBERT de MONTREUIL (Gilbert),
fl. 1228- , French; poetry
DIF HAR ST

GERBIER de la MASSILAYE, Pierre
Jean Baptiste, 1725-88, French;
nonfiction DIL

GERBILLON, Jean François, 1654-
1707, French; nonfiction DIL

GERBOTH, Walter W., 1925- ,
American; nonfiction CON

GERCHUNOFF, Alberto, 1884-1950,
Argentinian; journalism, fiction
MIN SA

GERDIL, Hyacinthe Sigismond, 1718-
1802, French; nonfiction DIL

GERDES, Florence Marie, 1919- ,
American; nonfiction CON

GERDTS, William H., 1929- , American; nonfiction CON

GERGEN, Kenneth Jay, 1934- ,
American; nonfiction CON

GERHARD von MINDEN, 14th cent.,
German; fiction ST

GERHARDI, William Alexander,
1895- , English; fiction CON
KL KT RIC

GERHARDT, Paul, 1607-66, German;
hymns, poetry AL HAR KE SA
ST

GERHOH of REICHERSBERG, 1093-
1169, French; nonfiction ST

GERIN, Winifred, English; nonfiction
CON

GERIN-LAJOIE, Antoine, 1824-82,
French-Canadian; poetry, fiction
ST SY

GERLACH, Don Ralph, 1932- ,
American; nonfiction CON

GERLACH, Jens, 1926- , German;
poetry AL

GERLACHE, Etienne Constantin,
1785-1871, Belgian; nonfiction
SA

GERLAN, Legaux de see LEGOOZ,
Bénigne

GERMAN, Yuri see HERMAN, Yuri
P.

GERMANE, Gayton E., 1920- ,
American; nonfiction CON

'GERMANICUS' see DUNNER,
Joseph

GERMANN, Albert Carl, 1921- ,
American; nonfiction CON

GERMANUS see BACHUR, Elijah

GERMAR, William Herbert,
1911- , American; nonfiction
CON

GERMEZ, Adam C. van, 1610-67,
Dutch; plays ST

GERMON, Barthélemi, 1663-1718,
French; nonfiction DIL

GERNERT, Eleanor Towles,
1928- , American; nonfiction
CON

GERNEVALDE, 18th cent., French;
plays DIL

GERNSHEIM, Helmut, 1913- ,
American; nonfiction CON

GEROK, Friedrich Karl von,
1815-90, German; poetry
HAR ST

GEROLD, William, 1932- ,
American; nonfiction CON

GEROU, Guillaume, 1701-67,
French; nonfiction DIL

GEROULD, Daniel C., 1928- ,
American; nonfiction, plays
CON

GEROULD, Katharine Fullerton,
1879- , American; fiction,
essays KT

GEROV, Nayden, 1823-1900,
Bulgarian; poetry, nonfiction
ST

GERRING, Ray H., 1926- ,
American; nonfiction CON

GERRISH, Brian Albert, 1931- ,
English; nonfiction CON

GERRITY, David James ('Callt
Goran'; 'Mitch Hardin'),
1923- , American; fiction
CON

GERSAINT, Edme François,
-1750, French; nonfiction
DIL

GERSDORF, Enriqueta Catalina,
1648-1726, German; poetry
SA

GERSH, Harry, 1912- , American;
nonfiction CON

GERSHEN, Martin, 1924- ,
American; nonfiction CON

GERSHENSON, Daniel Enoch,
1935- , American; nonfiction
CON

GERSHENZON, Mikhail Osipovich,
1869-1925, Russian; nonfiction,

essays COL HARK SA ST

GERSHMAN, Herbert S., 1926-71,
American; nonfiction CON

GERSHOM BEN JUDAH, 960-1028,
German; poetry ST

GERSHON, Karen Tripp, 1923- ,
British; poetry MUR

GERSHOY, Leo, 1897- , Russian-
American; nonfiction CON

GERSON, Jean Charlier de, 1363-
1429, French; nonfiction DIF
HAR SA ST

GERSON, Louis Leib, 1921- ,
Polish; American; nonfiction CON

GERSON, Noel B., 1914- , American; juveniles WA

GERSON, Wolfgang, 1916- , American; nonfiction CON

GERSONIDES, Levi Ben ('Ralbag'),
1288-1344, French; nonfiction ST

GERSTÄCKER, Freidrich, 1816-72,
German; fiction AL HAR KE ST

GERSTENBERG, Alice, American;
fiction, plays HOO

GERSTENBERG, Heinrich Wilhelm von,
1737-1823, German; plays, criticism AL HAR KE ST

GERSTENBERGER, Donna Lorine,
1929- , American; nonfiction
CON

GERSTER, Georg Anton, 1928- ,
Swiss; nonfiction CON

GERSTINE, John, 1915- , American;
fiction CON

GERSTL, Joel E., 1932- , Czech-
American; nonfiction CON

GERSTNER, Edna Suckau, 1914- ,
American; fiction CON

GERSTNER, John Henry, 1914- ,
American; nonfiction CON

GERT, Bernard, 1934- , American;
nonfiction CON

GERTEINY, Alfred Georges, 1930- ,
American; nonfiction CON

GERTLER, Menard M., 1919- ,
American; nonfiction CON

GERTMAN, Samuel, 1915- , American; nonfiction CON

GERTRUDE, Saint, 1256-1334, German?; nonfiction SA

GERTSEN, Alexander I. see HERZEN,
Alexander I.

GERTZ, Elmer, 1906- , American;
nonfiction CON

GERTZOG, Irwin Norman, 1933- ,
American; nonfiction CON

GERVAISE, François Armand, 1660-
1751, French; nonfiction DIL

GERVAISE de LATOUCHE, Jean
Charles, 1715-82, French;
nonfiction DIL

GERVASE of CANTERBURY, 1141-
1210, English; nonfiction SA
ST

GERVASE of TILBURY, 1150-
1235, English; nonfiction SA
ST

GERVASI, Frank Henry, 1908- ,
American; nonfiction CON

GERWIG, Anna Mary, 1907- ,
American; nonfiction CON

GERWIN, Donald, 1937- , American; nonfiction CON

GERY, André Guillaume de, 1727-
86, French; nonfiction DIL

GESCH, Dorothy K., 1923- ,
American; nonfiction CON

GESCH, Roy George, 1920- ,
American; nonfiction CON

GESNEL, Mathieu, 1714- ,
French; nonfiction DIL

GESNER, Carol, 1922- , American; nonfiction CON

GESNER, Elsie Miller, 1919- ,
American; fiction CON

GESSNER, Lynne ('Merle Clark'),
1919- , American; juveniles
CON

GESSNER, Salomon, 1730-88,
Swiss; poetry AL HAR SA ST

GESVRES, François, 17th cent.,
French; nonfiction DIL

GETHIN, Lady Grace, 1676-97,
English; nonfiction SA

GETINO, Luis G. Alonso, 1877-
1947, Spanish; nonfiction BL
SA

GETLEIN, Dorothy Woolen, 1921- ,
American; nonfiction CON

GETLEIN, Frank, 1921- , American; nonfiction CON

GETTLEMAN, Marvin E., 1933- ,
American; nonfiction CON

GETZ, Gene Arnold, 1932- ,
American; nonfiction CON

GEULINCZ, Arnold, 1625-69,
Belgian; nonfiction SA

GEVERS, Marie, 1883- , Belgian;
fiction, poetry ST

GEVIGNEY, Jean Baptiste Guillaume, 18th cent., French;
nonfiction DIL

GEWECKE, Clifford George, Jr.,
1930- , American; nonfiction
CON

GEWIRTZ, Leonard Benjamin,

1918-   , American; nonfiction
CON
GEYER, Alan, 1931-   , American;
nonfiction CON
GEYER, Erico Gustave see GEIJER,
Erik G.
'GEYER, Francis' see HARWOOD,
Gwendoline, N. F.
GEYER, Georgie Anne, 1935-   ,
American; nonfiction CON
GEYMAN, John P., 1931-   , Ameri-
can; nonfiction CON
GEYTER, Julius de, 1830-1905,
Flemish; poetry SA ST
GEZELLE, Guido, 1830-99, Flemish;
poetry COL HAR KE SA ST
GEZI, Kalil I. ('Kal'), 1930-   ,
Iraqi-American; nonfiction CON
GHA'ANI see QA'ANI, Habib A.
GHAI, Dharam P., 1936-   , Kenyan;
nonfiction CON
GHALIB, 1797-1869, Indian; poetry
LAN ST
GHAZZALI (Qazali; Algazel), 1059-
1111, Arab; nonfiction LAN SA
ST
GHELDERODE, Michel de, 1898-1962,
French; plays DIC DIF FLE MAL
MAT RIC
'GHEON, Henri' (Henri Leon Vaugeon;
Vangeon), 1875-1944, French;
plays, fiction, essays COL DIF
FLE HAR HOE MAT SA ST
GHEORGHIU, C. Virgil, 1905-   ,
Rumanian; fiction RIC ST
GHEORGHIU, Constantin Virgil,
1916-   , Rumanian; fiction, essays
CON FLE
GHERARDI, Giovanni (Giovanni da
Prato), 1367-1442/46, Italian;
poetry ST
GHERARDI del TESTA, Tommaso,
1818-81, Italian; fiction, plays
ST
GHEREA, Ion see DOBROGEANU-
GHEREA, Constantin
GHERITY, James Arthur, 1929-   ,
American; nonfiction CON
GHERMAN, Yury Pavlovich, 1910-   ,
Russian; fiction ST
GHICA, Ion, 1816-97, Rumanian;
nonfiction ST
GHIL, René, 1862-1925, French;
poetry COL DIF HAR SA ST
GHIRALDO, Alberto, 1874/75-1946,
Argentinian; journalism, plays,
essays BL MIN SA
GHISELIN, Brewster, 1903-   ,

American; poetry CON MUR
GHISELLI, Edwin Ernest, 1907-   ,
American; nonfiction CON
GHISELLI, Luca, 1910-   , Italian;
nonfiction SA
GHISTELE, Cornelis van ('Talpa';
'de Mol'), 1520?-70?, Dutch;
poetry ST
GHOSE, Sudhindra Nath, 1899-   ,
Indian; nonfiction CON
GHOSE, Zulfirkar, 1935-   ,
Pakistani; poetry, fiction
MUR
GHOSH, Cerun Kumar, 1930-   ,
Indian; nonfiction CON
GHURYE, Govind Sadashiv, 1893-   ,
American; nonfiction CON
GIACOMETTI, Paolo, 1816-82,
Italian; plays HAR ST
GIACOMINO da VERONA, 13th
cent., Italian; poetry ST
GIACOMINO PUGLIESE, fl. 1200-
50, Italian; poetry ST
GIACOMO, Salvatore de see
DI GIACOMO, Salvatori
GIACOMO da LENTINI see JACOPO
da LENTINI
GIACONI, Luisa, 1870-   , Italian;
poetry SA
GIACOSA, Giuseppe, 1847-1906,
Italian; fiction, plays COL
HAR MAT SA ST
GIAFAR Bin Muhammed, Abu
Abdallah (Rudagi), 875?-954,
Persian; poetry SA
GIAMBONI, Bono, 1230-1300,
Florentine; nonfiction ST
GIAMBULLARI, Pier Francesco,
1495-1555, Italian; nonfiction
ST
GIANAKARIS, Constantine John,
1934-   , American; nonfiction
CON
GIANAKOULIS, Theodore, Greek-
American; juveniles, poetry,
journalism WA
GIANNETTI, Louis D., 1937-   ,
American; nonfiction CON
GIANNI dei RICEVUTI, Lapo see
LAPO, Gianni
GIANNONE, Pietro, 1676-1748,
Italian; nonfiction SA ST
GIANNONE, Richard, 1934-   ,
American; nonfiction CON
GIANNOTTI, Donato, 1492-1573,
Italian; nonfiction ST
GIAT see ISAAC IBN GAYYAT
GIBB, Hamilton Alexander

Rossheen, 1895-1971, English;
nonfiction CON
GIBB, Jack Rex, 1914- , American;
nonfiction CON
'GIBB, Lee' see DEGHY, Guy
'GIBB, Lee' see WATERHOUSE, Keith
S.
GIBBI, Alonzo Lawrence, 1915- ,
American; juveniles WA
GIBBINGS, Robert, 1889-1958, Irish;
nonfiction BRO KTS
GIBBON, Edward, 1737-94, English;
criticism, nonfiction BRO KB
MAG SA ST
'GIBBON, Lewis Grassic' see MITCH-
ELL, James L.
GIBBON, Monk, 1896- , Irish; poetry
MUR ST
GIBBON, Percevial, 1879-1926,
South African; poetry, fiction ST
GIBBONS, Brian, 1938- , English;
nonfiction CON
GIBBONS, Euell Theophilus, 1911- ,
American; nonfiction CON
GIBBONS, Floyd Phillips, 1887-1939,
American; nonfiction HOE KT
GIBBONS, Helen Bay, 1921- , Amer-
ican; nonfiction CON
GIBBONS, James Sloan, 1810-92,
American; nonfiction KAA
GIBBONS, John Stephen Reynolds,
1882- , English; nonfiction HOE
GIBBONS, Robert, 1915- , American;
fiction WAF
GIBBONS, Stella Dorothea, 1902- ,
English; fiction, poetry BRO CON
KT RIC
GIBBS, Alonzo Lawrence, 1915- ,
American; poetry, fiction CON
GIBBS, Anthony, 1902- , English;
fiction CON
GIBBS, Anthony Matthews, 1933- ,
Australian; nonfiction CON
GIBBS, Arthur Hamilton, 1888- ,
English; fiction KL KT
GIBBS, Atwood James, 1922- ,
American; nonfiction CON
GIBBS, Barbara Golffing, 1912- ,
American; poetry, criticism
CON MUR
GIBBS, Henry St. John Clair ('Simon
Harvester'), Anglo-American;
fiction CON
GIBBS, James Atwood, Jr., Ameri-
can; nonfiction PAC
GIBBS, Mark, 1920- , English;
nonfiction CON
GIBBS, Paul T., 1897- , American;

nonfiction CON
GIBBS, Peter Bawtree, 1903- ,
English; nonfiction CON
GIBBS, Sir Philip Hamilton, 1877-
1962, English; journalism, fic-
tion BRO HOE KL KT RIC
GIBBS, Raphael Sanford, 1912- ,
American; nonfiction CON
PAC
GIBBS, Willa, 1917- , American;
fiction WAF
GIBBS, William E., 1936- ,
American; nonfiction CON
GIBBS-SMITH, Charles Harvard
('Charles Harvard'), 1909- ,
English; nonfiction CON
GIBBY, Robert Gwyn, 1916- ,
American; nonfiction CON
GIBELIN, Esprit Antoine, 1739-
1814, French; nonfiction
DIL
GIBERGA, Elíseo, 1854-1916,
Cuban; poetry MIN SA
GIBERSON, Dorothy Dodds, Amer-
ican; fiction CON
GILBERT, Balthazar, 1662-1741,
French; nonfiction DIL
GIBERT, Jean Pierre, 1660-1736,
French; nonfiction DIL
GIBERT, Joseph Balthazar, 1711-
71, French; nonfiction DIL
GIBERT de MONTREUIL see
GERBERT de MONTREUIL
GIBIAN, George, 1924- , Czech-
American; nonfiction CON
GIBRAN, Kahlil (Jubrian), 1883-
1931, Syrian-American; fiction,
poetry KT ST
GIBSON, Charles, 1920- ,
American; nonfiction CON
GIBSON, Charles Edmund, 1916- ,
American; nonfiction CON
GIBSON, Derlyne, 1936- , Amer-
ican; nonfiction CON
GIBSON, Donald B., 1933- ,
American; nonfiction CON
GIBSON, Ernest Dana, 1906- ,
American; nonfiction CON
GIBSON, Frank K., 1924- ,
American; nonfiction CON
GIBSON, Gertrude Hevenr,
1906- , American; nonfiction
CON
'GIBSON, Harry Clark' see HUB-
LER, Richard G.
GIBSON, James Lawrence,
1935- , American; nonfiction
CON

GIBSON, John, 1907- , American;
nonfiction CON

GIBSON, John Mendinghall, 1899- ,
American; nonfiction CON

'GIBSON, Josephine' see JOSLIN,
Sesyle

GIBSON, Katharine, 1893- , American; juveniles KJU

GIBSON, Morgan, 1929- , American;
plays, poetry CON

GIBSON, Raymond Eugene, 1924- ,
American; nonfiction CON

GIBSON, Reginald Walter, 1901- ,
English; nonfiction CON

GIBSON, Walker, 1919- , American;
nonfiction CON

GIBSON, Wilfred Wilson, 1878- ,
English; poetry, plays BRO KL
KT SA

GIBSON, William, 1914- , American;
plays, fiction, poetry CON MAT

GIBSON, William Carleton, 1913- ,
American; nonfiction CON

GIBSON, William Edward, 1944- ,
American; nonfiction CON

GIBSON, William Hamilton, 1850-96,
American; nonfiction KAA

GIBSON PARRA, Percy, 1908- ,
Peruvian; poetry, essays, plays
SA

GICOVATE, Bernard, 1922- , American; nonfiction CON

GIDAL, Sonia Epstein, 1922- ,
German-English; juveniles COM
CON WA

GIDAL, Tim Nahum, 1909- , German-American; juveniles COM
CON WA

GIDDINGS, James Louis, 1909- ,
American; nonfiction CON

GIDDINGS, Robert Lindsay, 1935- ,
American; nonfiction CON

GIDE, André, 1869-1951, French;
fiction, plays, poetry, nonfiction
COL DIF FLE HAR KL KT MAG
MAL MAT RIC SA ST

GIDE, Charles, 1847-1932, French;
nonfiction DIF

GIEDION, Siegfried, 1893- , Swiss;
nonfiction KTS

GIEGLING, John Allen, 1935- ,
Anglo-American; fiction CON

GIELGUD, Val Henry, 1900- ,
English; nonfiction, plays CON

GIERGIELEWICZ, Mieczyslaw ('Feliks
Bielski'; 'M.G.'), Polish-American; nonfiction CON

GIEROW, Karl Ragnar Kunt, 1904- ,

Swedish; poetry, plays MAT
ST

'GIERSCH, Julius' see ARNADE,
Charles W.

GIERTZ, Bo Harald, 1905- ,
Swedish; nonfiction CON

GIES, Frances, 1915- , American; nonfiction CON

GIES, Joseph Cornelius, 1916- ,
American; fiction CON

GIES, Thomas George, 1921- ,
American; nonfiction CON

GIESE, Franz, 1845-1901, German; fiction ST

GIESEY, Ralph Edwin, 1923- ,
American; nonfiction CON

GIESLER-ANNEKE, Mathilde
Franziska, 1817-84, German-
American; nonfiction ST

GIFFORD, Charles Henry, 1913- ,
English; nonfiction CON

GIFFORD, Edward Stewart, Jr.,
1907- , American; nonfiction
CON

GIFFORD, Humfrey, fl. 1580- ,
English; poetry, translations
ST

GIFFORD, Richard, 1725-1807,
English; poetry BRO

GIFFORD, William, 1756-1826,
English; poetry, criticism
BRO KBA SA ST

'GIFFORD-JONES, W.' see
WALKER, Kenneth F.

GIGAS, Emil, 1849-1931, Danish;
nonfiction BL

GIGLI, Girolamo, 1660-1722,
Italian; plays ST

GIGLIO, Ernest David, 1931- ,
American; nonfiction CON

GIGUERE, Diane, 1937- ,
Canadian; fiction CON

GIGUERE, Roland, 1929- ,
Canadian; poetry SY

GIH, Andrew, 1901- , American;
nonfiction CON

'GIJSEN, Marnix' (Jan Albert
Goris), 1899- , Flemish;
poetry, fiction, essays COL
FLE SA ST

GIL, Augusto, 1873-1929, Portuguese; poetry COL SA ST

GIL, David Georg, 1924- ,
American; nonfiction CON

GIL, Federico Guillermo, 1915- ,
Cuban-American; nonfiction
CON

GIL, Ildefonso Manuel, 1912- ,

Spanish; poetry BL
GIL, Pedro E., 19th cent., Chilean;
  journalism MIN
GIL, Ricardo, 1855-1908, Spanish;
  poetry BL COL SA
GIL, Rodolfo, 1872-1939, Spanish; non-
  fiction BL SA
GIL-ALBERT, Juan, 1911- , Spanish;
  nonfiction BL SA
GIL FORTOUL, José, 1862-1943,
  Venezuelan; fiction SA
GIL GILBERT, Enrique, 1912- ,
  Ecuadorian; fiction DI
GIL LOPEZ, Ildefonso Manuel,
  1912- , Spanish; nonfiction SA
GIL POLO, Gaspar, 1529?-85/91,
  Spanish; poetry BL SA ST
GIL VICENTE see VICENTE, Gil
GIL y CARRASCO, Enrique, 1815-46,
  Spanish; fiction, poetry BL HAR
  KE SA ST
GIL y ZARATE, Antonio, 1793-1861,
  Spanish; plays BL SA ST
GILANI, Abd al Qadir, 1077?-1166?,
  Arab; nonfiction ST
GILB, Corinne Lathrop, 1925- ,
  Canadian; nonfiction CON
GILBERT, Agnes Joan Sewell, 1931- ,
  American; fiction CON
GILBERT, Allan H., 1888- , Amer-
  ican; nonfiction, translations
  CON
GILBERT, Arthur, 1926- , American;
  nonfiction CON
GILBERT, Benjamin Franklin, 1918- ,
  American; nonfiction CON
GILBERT, Bentley Brinkerhoff,
  1924- , American; nonfiction
  CON
GILBERT, Creighton Eddy, 1924- ,
  American; nonfiction CON
GILBERT, Doris Wilcox, American;
  nonfiction CON
GILBERT, Douglas L., 1925- ,
  American; nonfiction CON
GILBERT, François Hilaire, 1757-
  1800, French; nonfiction DIL
GILBERT, G.R., 1917- , New
  Zealander; fiction ST
GILBERT, Gabriel, 1610-80, French;
  plays, poetry SA ST
GILBERT, Glenn Gordon, 1936- ,
  American; nonfiction CON
GILBERT, Helen Earle, American;
  juveniles WA
GILBERT, Herman Cromwell, 1923- ,
  American; fiction CON
GILBERT, Sir Humfrey, 1578/79- ,

English; nonfiction ST
GILBERT, Jack Glenn, 1925/34- ,
  American; poetry CON MUR
GILBERT, James, 1935- , Eng-
  lish; nonfiction CON
GILBERT, Jarvey, 1917- , Amer-
  ican; nonfiction CON
GILBERT, Sir John Thomas, 1829-
  98, Irish; nonfiction KBA
GILBERT, Kenneth, 1889- ,
  American; juveniles, fiction
  PAC
GILBERT, Martin, 1936- , Eng-
  lish; nonfiction CON
GILBERT, Sister Mary see DE
  FREES, Mary M.
GILBERT, Michael Francis,
  1912- , English; fiction CON
'GILBERT, Miriam' see PRES-
  BERG, Miriam G.
'GILBERT, Nan' see GILBERTSON,
  Mildred
GILBERT, Nicolas Joseph Laurent,
  1751-80, French; poetry DIF
  DIL HAR KE SA ST
GILBERT, Ruth see MACKAY,
  Florence R.
GILBERT, Ruth Gallard (Ains-
  worth), 1908- , English;
  poetry, juveniles CON DOY
GILBERT, Stephen, 1912- , Eng-
  lish; fiction CON
GILBERT, William, 1540-1603,
  English; nonfiction KB
GILBERT, Sir William Schwenck,
  1836-1911, English; poetry,
  plays BRO KBA MAG MAT
  SP ST
GILBERT de MONS, 1160-1225,
  Flemish; nonfiction SA
GILBERT de VOISINS, Auguste,
  1877-1939, French; fiction
  DIF
GILBERT de VOISINS, Pierre,
  1684-1769, French; nonfiction
  DIL
GILBERTO de la PORREE, 1070-
  1154, French; nonfiction SA
GILBERTS, Helen, 1909- , Amer-
  ican; fiction CON
GILBERTSON, Merrill Thomas,
  1911- , American; nonfiction
  CON
GILBERTSON, Mildred Geiger
  ('Nan Gilbert'), 1908- ,
  American; juveniles COM
  CON
GILBEY, Tresham, 1862- ,

English; nonfiction HIG
GILBEY, Sir Walter, 1831-1914,
English; nonfiction HIG
GILBOA, Yehoshua A., 1918- ,
Israeli; nonfiction CON
GILBREATH, Alice, 1921- , American; nonfiction CON
GILBRETH, Frank B., Jr., 1911- ,
American; juveniles, nonfiction
COM CON
GILCHER, Edwin L., 1909- , American; nonfiction CON
GILCHRIST, Alan W. ('Alan Cowan'),
1913- , American; nonfiction
CON
GILCHRIST, John Thomas, 1927- ,
English; nonfiction CON
GILDAS (Sapiens; Badonicus), 516?-
70?, Welsh; nonfiction BRO KB
ST
GILDEN, Bert ('K.B. Gilden'),
-1971, American; fiction CON
GILDEN, Katya ('K.B. Gilden'),
American; fiction CON
GILDER, George F., 1939- , American; fiction CON
GILDER, Richard Watson, 1844-1909,
American; poetry, journalism
BRO KAA
GILDER, Rosamond de Kay, American;
nonfiction CON
GILDERSLEEVE, Basil Lanneau, 1831-
1924, American; nonfiction KAA
GILDERSLEEVE, Thomas Robert,
1927- , American; nonfiction
CON
GILDNER, Gary, 1938- , American;
poetry CON
GILDON, Charles, 1665-1724, English; criticism, plays BRO ST
GILES, Carl Howard, 1935- , American; nonfiction CON
'GILES, Gordon A.' see BINDER,
Otto O.
GILES, Janice Holt, American; fiction
CON
'GILES, Kris' see NIELSEN, Helen
B.
'GILES, Norman' (Norman Robert
McKeown), 1879-1947, South
African; fiction ST
'GILES, Raymond' see HOLT, John
R.
GILES of ROME, 1246/47-1316,
Italian; nonfiction ST
GILFILLAN, George, 1813-78, Scots;
nonfiction, criticism BRO KBA
GILFILLAN, Robert, 1798-1850,

Scots; poetry BRO KBA
GILFOND, Henry, American;
juveniles COM CON
GILFORD, Charles Bernard
('Donald Campbell'; 'Douglas
Farr'; 'Elizabeth Gregory'),
1920- , American; plays,
fiction CON
GILGEN, Albert Rudolph, 1930- ,
American; nonfiction CON
GILHOOLEY, Leonard, 1921- ,
American; nonfiction CON
GILI GAYA, Samuel, 1892- ,
Spanish; nonfiction BL SA
GILKES, Antony Newcombe, 1900- ,
English; nonfiction CON
GILKEY, Langdon Brown, 1919- ,
American; nonfiction CON
GILKIN, Iwan, 1858-1923/24,
Belgian; poetry, plays COL
HAR SA ST
GILL, Bob, 1931- , American;
nonfiction CON
GILL, Brendan, 1914- , American; fiction KTS
GILL, Charles, 1871-1918, Canadian; poetry SY
GILL, David Lawrence William,
1934- , British; poetry,
criticism CON MUR
GILL, Eric Rowland, 1882-1940,
English; nonfiction HOE KTS
GILL, Evan Robertson, 1892- ,
English; nonfiction CON
GILL, Frederick Cyril, 1898- ,
English; nonfiction CON
GILL, Jerry H., 1933- , American; nonfiction CON
GILL, Joseph, 1901- , American;
nonfiction CON
GILL, M. Lakshmi, 1943- ,
Indian-Canadian; poetry MUR
GILL, Richard Cochran, 1901- ,
American; juveniles WA
GILL, Richard Thomas, 1927- ,
American; nonfiction CON
GILL, Ronald Crispin, 1916- ,
English; nonfiction CON
GILL, Traviss ('Gill Odell'),
1891- , English; plays,
juveniles CON
GILLARD, John Thomas, 1900-42,
American; nonfiction HOE
GILLCHREST, Muriel Noyes,
1905- , American; nonfiction
CON
GILLE, Valère, 1867- , Belgian;
poetry COL SA

GILLELAN, George Howard, 1917- ,
American; juveniles CON WA
GILLENSON, Lewis William, 1918- ,
American; nonfiction CON
GILLES de PARIS, fl. 1200, French;
poetry ST
GILLES de VINIER,   -1252, French;
poetry ST
GILLESE, John Patrick ('Dale O'Hara';
'John A. Starr'), 1920- , Cana-
dian; nonfiction, fiction CON
GILLESPIE, George, 1613-48, Scots;
nonfiction BRO
GILLESPIE, Gerald, 1933- , Ameri-
can; nonfiction CON
GILLESPIE, Janet Wicks, 1913- ,
American; nonfiction CON
GILLESPIE, John E., 1921- , Ameri-
can; nonfiction CON
GILLESPIE, Neal Cephas, 1933- ,
American; nonfiction CON
GILLESPIE, Susan, 1906- , Ameri-
can; nonfiction, fiction CON
GILLET, François Pierre, 1648-1720,
French; nonfiction DIL
GILLET, Joseph Eugene, 1888-1958,
Belgian; nonfiction BL
GILLET, Louis, 1876-1943, French;
nonfiction DIF
GILLET, Louis Joachim, 1680-1753,
French; nonfiction DIL
GILLET, Rev. Martin, 1875-1951,
French; nonfiction HO
GILLET de MOIVRE, 18th cent.,
French; nonfiction DIL
GILLETT, Charlie, 1942- , English;
nonfiction CON
GILLETT, Eric Walkey, 1893- ,
English; nonfiction CON
GILLETT, Henry Martin, 1902- ,
English; nonfiction HO
GILLETT, Margaret, 1930- ,
Australian-Canadian; nonfiction,
fiction CON
GILLETT, Mary Bledsoe, American;
juveniles CON
GILLETTE, Arnold Simpson, 1904- ,
American; nonfiction CON
GILLETTE, Henry Sampson, 1915- ,
American; juveniles CON
GILLETTE, William, 1855-1937,
American; plays MAT
GILLHAM, Charles Edward, 1898- ,
American; fiction HOO
GILLHAM, D.G., 1921- , South
African; nonfiction CON
GILLIAMS, Maurice, 1900- ,
Flemish; poetry, essays FLE

GILLIARD, Edmond, 1875- ,
Swiss; essays, criticism ST
GILLIATT, Penelope, 1932- ,
English; fiction CON
GILLIES, John, 1747-1836, Scots;
nonfiction BRO
GILLIES, Mary Davis, 1900- ,
American; nonfiction CON
GILLIGAN, Edmund, 1899-1973,
American; fiction, journalism
KTS
GILLIN, Donald George, 1930- ,
American; nonfiction CON
GILLIS, James Martin, 1876- ,
American; nonfiction HOE
GILLIS, John R., 1939- , Ameri-
can; nonfiction CON
GILLISPIE, Charles Coulston,
1918- , American; nonfiction
CON
GILLMAN, Olga Marjorie, 1894- ,
American; fiction CON
GILLMAN, Richard, 1929- ,
American; poetry CON
GILLMOR, Frances, 1903- ,
American; fiction CON
GILLMORE, David, 1934- , Eng-
lish; fiction CON
GILLON, Adam, 1921- , Ameri-
can; nonfiction CON
GILLON, Diana Pleasance Case,
1915- , English; fiction CON
GILLON, Meir Selig, 1907- ,
English; fiction CON
GILLOT, Jacques, 1550-1619,
French; nonfiction SA
GILLQUIST, Peter E., 1938- ,
American; nonfiction CON
GILLSTRAP, Robert Lawrence,
1933- , American; nonfiction
CON
GILM, Hermann von, 1812-64,
Austrian; poetry HAR ST
GILMAN, Dorothy see BUTTERS,
Dorothy G.
GILMAN, Lawrence, 1878-1939,
American; journalism KT
GILMAN, Stephen, 1917- , Amer-
ican; nonfiction BL
GILMAN, William, 1909- , Amer-
ican; nonfiction CON
GILMER, Beverly Von Haller,
1909- , American; nonfiction
CON
GILMER, Frank Walker, 1935- ,
American; nonfiction CON
GILMORE, Charles Lee, Ameri-
can; nonfiction CON

GILMORE, Don ('Gil Davis'), 1930- ,
American; nonfiction CON
GILMORE, Eddy Lanier King, 1907- ,
American; nonfiction CON
GILMORE, Edith Spacil, 1920- ,
American; translations, juveniles
CON
GILMORE, Gene, 1920- , American;
nonfiction CON
GILMORE, Horace Herman, 1903- ,
American; juveniles WA
GILMORE, Iris, American; juveniles
WA
GILMORE J. Herbert, Jr., 1925- ,
American; nonfiction CON
GILMORE, Jene Carlton, 1933- ,
American; nonfiction CON
GILMORE, John, 1937- , American;
fiction CON
GILMORE, Mary Jean, 1865- , Aus-
tralian; poetry, fiction RIC ST
GILMOUR, Garth Hamilton, 1925- ,
New Zealander; nonfiction CON
GILPATRIC, Guy, 1896- , American;
fiction KT
GILPATRICK, Eleanor Gottesfacht,
1930- , American; nonfiction
CON
GILPATRICK, Naomi, 1918- ,
American; fiction, poetry HOE
GILPIN, Alan, 1924- , Australian;
nonfiction CON
GILPIN, Robert G., 1930- , Ameri-
can; nonfiction CON
GILPIN, William, 1724-1804, English;
nonfiction KB ST
GILPIN, William, 1813?-94, Ameri-
can; nonfiction KAA
GILROY, Frank D., 1925- , Ameri-
can; plays MAT
GILSON, Charles, 1878-1943, English;
juveniles DOY
GILSON, Etienne Henri, 1884- ,
French; nonfiction DIF HOE KT
SA
GILSON, Goodwin Woodrow, 1918- ,
American; nonfiction CON
GILSON, Paul, 1906- , French;
poetry DIF
GILSON, Thomas Quinleven, 1916- ,
American; nonfiction CON
GILTINAN, Caroline, 1884- , Ameri-
can; poetry HOE
GILZEAN, Elizabeth Houghton Blanchet
('Elizabeth Houghton'; 'Mary Hunton'),
1913- , Canadian; fiction CON
GIMAT de BONNEVAL, Jean Baptiste,
18th cent., French; fiction DIL

GIMBEL, John, 1922- , Ameri-
can; nonfiction CON
GIMBUTAS, Marija Alseika,
1920- , Lithuanian-American;
nonfiction CON
GIMENEZ ARNAU, José Antonio,
1912- , Spanish; journalism,
fiction, plays BL SA
GIMENEZ CABALLERO, Ernesto,
1899- , Spanish; nonfiction,
essays, journalism BL COL
HAR SA ST
GIMENEZ PASTOR, Arturo
(Jiménez), 1872-1947?, Ar-
gentinian; poetry, essays,
plays MIN
GIMPEL, Herbert J., 1915- ,
American; nonfiction CON
GIMSON, Alfred Charles, 1917- ,
English; nonfiction CON
'GIN and BEER' see ANDREWS,
Tom
GINARD de la ROSA, Rafael,
1848-1918, Spanish; nonfiction
SA
GINDIN, James, 1926- , Ameri-
can; nonfiction CON
GINER de los RIOS, Francisco,
1839-1915, Spanish; journalism
BL COL HAR SA ST
GINER de los RIOS, Francisco,
1917- , Spanish; poetry, es-
says, criticism SA
GINER de los RIOS, Hermengildo,
1847-1923, Spanish; nonfiction
BL SA
GINGERICH, Melvin, 1902- ,
American; nonfiction CON
GINGELL, Benjamin Broughton,
1924- , British; poetry MUR
GINGER, Helen, 1916- , Ameri-
can; nonfiction CON
GINGER, John, 1933- , English;
fiction CON
GINGLEND, David R., 1913- ,
American; nonfiction CON
GINGOLD, Hermione Ferdinanda,
English; nonfiction CON
GINGRICH, Arnold, 1903- ,
American; nonfiction CON
GINGRICH, Felix Wilbur, 1901- ,
American; nonfiction CON
GINGUENE, Pierre Louis, 1748-
1816, French; nonfiction SA
DIF
GINIGER, Kenneth Seeman, 1919- ,
American; nonfiction CON
GINISTY, Paul, 1855-1932, French;

nonfiction SA
GINNS, Ronald, 1896- , American;
nonfiction CON
GINSBERG, Allen, 1926- , Ameri-
can; poetry CON FLE MUR RIC
GINSBERG, Asher see AHAD HA'AM
GINSBERG, Louis, 1895- , American;
poetry CON MUR
GINSBERG, Mordechai Aharon, 1795-
1846, Jewish; essays ST
GINSBERG, Robert, 1937- , Ameri-
can; nonfiction CON
GINSBURG, Christina David, 1831-
1914, Polish-English; nonfiction
KBA
GINSBURG, Mirra, American; nonfic-
tion CON
GINSBURG, Seymour, 1927- , Ameri-
can; nonfiction CON
GINSBURGH, Robert Neville, 1923- ,
American; nonfiction CON
GINSBURY, Norman, 1902- , English;
translations, plays CON
GINZBURG, Asher see 'AHAD HA-
AM'
GINZBURG, Eli, 1911- , American;
nonfiction CON
GINZBURG, Ralph, 1929- , Ameri-
can; nonfiction CON
GINZBURG, Simeon, 1890-1948,
Jewish; poetry ST
GINZKEY, Franz Karl, 1871- ,
German; nonfiction LEN
GIOBERTI, Vincenzo, 1801-52,
Italian; nonfiction KE SA ST
GIONO, Jean, 1895-1970, French;
fiction, essays, plays COL DIC
DIF FLE HAR KT MAG MAL
MAT RIC SA ST
GIORDANI, Igino, 1894- , Italian;
nonfiction HOE
GIORDANI, Pietro, 1774-1842,
Italian; nonfiction ST
GIORDANO da PISA (da Rivalto),
1260-1311, Italian; nonfiction ST
GIORNO, John, 1936- , American;
poetry CON MUR
GIOTTI, Virgilio, 1885- , Italian;
poetry SA
GIOVANE, Juliana, 1753- , German;
nonfiction SA
GIOVANE, Juliane de, 1805- ,
French; nonfiction DIL
GIOVANN FIORENTINO, 14th cent.,
Florentine; nonfiction HAR ST
GIOVANNETTI, Alberto, 1913- ,
Italian; nonfiction CON
GIOVANNI, Nikki, 1943- , American;

nonfiction CON
GIOVANNI da PRATO see
GHERARDI, Giovanni
GIOVANNITTI, Arturo, 1884- ,
Italian-American; poetry KT
GIOVANNITTI, Len, 1920- ,
American; fiction, nonfiction
CON
GIOVIO, Paolo, 1483-1552,
Italian; nonfiction SA ST
GIPPIUS see HIPPIUS, Zinaida N.
GIPSON, Frederick B., 1908- ,
American; juveniles COM
CON WA
GIPSON, Lawrence Henry, 1890-
1971, American; nonfiction
CON
GIRALDI Giglio Gregorio, 1479-
1552, Italian; poetry SA ST
GIRALDI, Giovanni Battista
(Cinthio; Cintio; Cinzio),
1504-73, Italian; fiction, poetry,
plays HAR KE SA ST
GIRALDUS de BARRI (Cambrensis),
1146?-1220, English; nonfiction
BRO KB ST
GIRARD, Gabriel, 1677-1748,
French; nonfiction DIL SA
GIRARD, Pierre, 1892- , Swiss;
fiction ST
GIRARD, Rene Noel, 1923- ,
Franco-American; nonfiction
CON
GIRARD d' AMIENS, 13th cent.,
French; poetry ST
GIRARD RAIGNE, 18th cent.,
French; poetry DIL
GIRARDET, P. Alexis, 1723-89,
French; nonfiction DIL
GIRARDET, Philibert, 1694-1754,
French; nonfiction DIL
GIRARDIN, Mme. see GAY,
Delphine
GIRARDIN, Emile de, 1806-81,
French; journalism, fiction
HAR
GIRARDIN, Jean Baptiste, -1783,
French; nonfiction DIL
GIRARDIN, Jean Jacques Félix,
1678-1753, French; nonfiction
DIL
GIRARDIN, René Louis, 1735-
1808, French; nonfiction DIL
GIRARDON, Emile, 1806-81,
French; essays, journalism
SA
GIRARDOT P., 18th cent.,
French; nonfiction DIL

'GIRAUD, Albert' (Albert Kayenbergh),
1860-1929, Belgian; poetry COL
HAR SA ST
GIRAUD, Claude Marie, 1711-80,
French; nonfiction DIL
GIRAUD, Jean Baptiste, 1701-76,
French; translations DIL
GIRAUDEAU, Bonaventure, 1697- ,
French; nonfiction DIL
GIRAUDOUX, Jean, 1882-1944,
French; poetry, fiction, plays
COL DIF FLE HAR KAT KT MAG
MAL MAT RIC SA ST
GIRAUT de BORNELH (Borneil),
1165-1220, French; poetry KE
GIRDLESTONE, Cuthbert Morton,
1895- , English; nonfiction CON
GIRO, Valentín, 1883-1949,
Dominican; poetry MIN SA
GIROD, Gordon H., 1920- , Ameri-
can; nonfiction CON
GIRON, Diego, 1530-90, Spanish;
poetry BL SA
GIRON de REBOLLEDO, Ana, 16th
cent., Spanish; nonfiction SA
GIRONDO, Oliverio, 1891- ,
Argentinian; poetry MIN
GIRONELLA, José María (Pous),
1917- , Spanish; fiction BL
FLE KTS RIC SA
GIROUX, André, 1916- , Canadian;
nonfiction SY
GIRSON, Rochelle, American; non-
fiction CON
GIRTIN, Thomas, 1913- , English;
nonfiction CON
'GIRUN, Gian' (Ursina Clauvotgeer),
1898- , Raeto-Romansch; fiction
ST
GIRVAN, Helen Masterman, 1891- ,
American; juveniles FUL WA
'GISANDER' see SCHNABEL, Johann
G.
GISBERT, Blaise, 1637-1731, French;
nonfiction DIL
GISEKE, Nikolaus Dietrich, 1724-65,
German; poetry ST
GISH, Arthur G., 1939- , American;
nonfiction CON
GISOLFI, Anthony M., 1909- ,
Italian-American; nonfiction CON
GISSING, George Robert, 1857-1903,
English; fiction, criticism BRO
KBA MAG SA ST
GIST, Noel Pitts, 1899- , American;
nonfiction CON
GIST, Ronald R., 1932- , American;
nonfiction CON

GITLIN, Murray, 1903- , Ameri-
can; fiction CON
GITLIN, Todd, 1943- , American;
nonfiction CON
GITLOW, Abraham Leo, 1918- ,
American; nonfiction CON
GITMAN, William Henry, 1911- ,
American; nonfiction CON
GITTELL, Marilyn, 1931- ,
American; nonfiction CON
GITTELSOHN, Roland Bertram,
1910- , American; nonfiction
CON
GITTINGER, Roy, 1878- , Ameri-
can; nonfiction MAR
GITTINGS, Jo Grenville Manton,
1919- , English; fiction,
nonfiction, juveniles CON WA
GITTINGS, John, 1938- , English;
nonfiction CON
GITTINGS, Robert William Victor,
1911- , English; nonfiction,
poetry CON MUR
GITTLEMAN, Edwin, 1929- ,
American; nonfiction CON
GITTLER, Joseph Bertram,
1914- , American; nonfiction
CON
GIULIOTTI, Domenico, 1877- ,
Italian; poetry, nonfiction
COL HO SA
GIURLANI, Aldo see 'PALAZ-
ZESCHI, Aldo'
GIUSEPPI, John Anthony, 1900- ,
English; nonfiction CON
GIUSTI, Giuseppe, 1809-50,
Italian; poetry HAR SA ST
GIUSTI, Roberto Fernando,
1887- , Argentinian; criti-
cism, essays MIN SA
GIUSTINIAN, Leonardo, 1388-
1446, Italian; poetry ST
GIUTTARI, Theodore Richard,
1931- , American; nonfiction
CON
GIVANEL y MAS, Juan, 1868- ,
Spanish; nonfiction SA
'GJALLANDI, Thorgils' (Jón
Stefansson), 1851-1915, Ice-
landic; fiction SA ST
'GJALSKI, Ksaver Sandor' (Ljubo
Babic), 1854-1935/36,
Croatian; fiction COL SA
GJELLERUP, Karl Adolph, 1857-
1919, Danish; fiction, plays
COL FLE HAR KE RIC SA
ST
GJÖRWELL, Carl Christoffer,

1731-1811, Swedish; journalism ST

GLAAB, Charles Nelson, 1927- , American; nonfiction CON

GLAD, Betty, 1929- , American; nonfiction CON

GLAD, Donald, 1915- , American; nonfiction CON

GLADDEN, Edgar Norman ('Norman Mansfield'), 1897- , English; nonfiction CON

GLADKOV, Fedor Vasilievich, 1883-1958, Russian; fiction, plays, poetry COL FLE HAR HARK KT RIC SA ST

GLADSTONE, Gary, 1935- , American; juveniles CON

GLADSTONE, William Ewart, 1809-98, English; nonfiction BRO ST

'GLADWIN, William Zachary' see ZOLLINGER, Gulielma

GLADYCH, B. Michael, 1910- , Polish-American; nonfiction CON

GLAESER, Ernst, 1902-63, German; fiction AL KT KU LEN SA

GLAETTLI, Walter Eric, 1920- , Swiss-American; nonfiction CON

GLAHE, Fred Rufus, 1934- , American; nonfiction CON

GLANVILL, Joseph, 1636-80, English; nonfiction BRO KB

GLANVILL, Ranulf de, -1190, English; nonfiction ST

GLANVILLE Bartholomew de see BARTHOLOMAEUS ANGELICUS

GLANVILLE, Brian Lester, 1931- , English; fiction CON

GLANVILLE, Ernest, 1856-1925, South African; fiction ST

GLANZ, Aaron see 'LEYELES, A.'

GLANZ, Edward Coleman, 1924- , American; nonfiction CON

GLAPTHORNE, Henry, 1610-44?, English; plays, poetry BRO KB ST

GLASCOCK, William Nugent, 1787?-1847, English; fiction BRO KBA

GLASER, Edward, 1918-72, American; nonfiction BL

'GLASER, Eleanor Dorothy' see ZONIK, Eleanor D.

GLASER, Eric Michael, 1913- , Czech-English; nonfiction CON

GLASER, Kurt, 1914- , American; nonfiction CON

GLASER, Lynn, 1943- , American; nonfiction CON

GLASER, Milton ('Max Catz'),

1929- , American; fiction CON

GLASER, Robert, 1921- , American; nonfiction CON

GLASER, Rollin Oliver, 1932- , American; nonfiction CON

GLASER, William Arnold, 1925- , American; nonfiction CON

GLASGOW, Ellen Anderson Gholson, 1874-1945, American; fiction, poetry BRO FLE KL KT MAG RIC SA ST

GLASGOW, George, 1891- , English; nonfiction HO

GLASGOW, Gordon Henry Harper, 1926- , English; nonfiction CON

GLASHEEN, Patrick, 1897- , Irish; nonfiction CON

GLASKOWSKY, Nicholas A. Alexander, Jr., 1928- , American; nonfiction CON

GLASPELL, Susan, 1882-1948, American; fiction, plays KL KT MAT ST WAF

GLASS, Justine C. see CORRALL, Alice E.

GLASS, Sister M. Fides, 1889- , American; nonfiction HO

GLASS, Montague Marsden, 1877-1934, American; plays, fiction KT

GLASS, Stanley Thomas, 1932- , English; nonfiction CON

GLASSBRENNER, Adolf ('Brennglas'), 1810-76, German; nonfiction AL HAR

GLASSBERG, Bertrand Younker, 1902- , American; nonfiction CON

GLASSBURNER, Bruce, 1920- , American; nonfiction CON

GLASSCO, John Stinson ('George Colman'; 'Grace Davignon'; 'W. P. R. Eadie'; 'Silas N. Gooch'; 'George Henderson'; 'S. Colson Haig'; 'Nordyk Nudleman'; 'Jean de Saint-Luc'; 'Miles Underwood'; 'Hideki Okada'), 1909- , Canadian; poetry, fiction CON MUR

GLASSCOCK, Anne Bonner ('Michael Bonner'), 1924- , American; fiction CON

GLASSE, Robert Marshall, 1929- , American; nonfiction CON

GLASSER, Allen, 1918- ,

American; nonfiction CON
GLASSER, Paul Harold, 1929- ,
American; nonfiction CON
GLASSMAN, Michael, 1899- ,
American; nonfiction CON
GLASSON, Thomas Francis, 1906- ,
English; nonfiction CON
GLASSOP, Jack Lawson, 1913- ,
Australian; nonfiction CON
GLATIGNY, Gabriel De, 1690-1755,
French; nonfiction DIL
GLATIGNY, Joseph Albert Alexandre,
1839-73, French; poetry DIF
HAR KE ST
GLATSTEIN, Yaacov (Jacob), 1896-
1971, Jewish; poetry LAN ST
GLATTHORN, Allan A., 1924- ,
American; nonfiction, juveniles
CON
GLATZER, Nahum Norbert, 1903- ,
Austrian-American; nonfiction
CON
GLAUBER, Uta Heil, 1936- , Ger-
man; nonfiction CON
GLAUS, Marlene, 1933- , American;
nonfiction CON
GLAZAROVA, Jarmila Polivinská,
1901- , Czech; fiction RIC ST
GLAZE, Andrew Louis, III, 1920- ,
American; juveniles, poetry CON
GLAZE, Thomas Edward, 1914- ,
American; nonfiction CON
GLAZEBROOK, Philip, 1937- , Eng-
lish; fiction CON
GLAZENER, Mary Underwood, 1921- ,
American; plays CON
GLAZER, Nathan, 1923- , American;
nonfiction CON
GLAZER, Nona Y. see GLAZER-
MALBIN, Nona
GLAZER, Sidney, 1905- , American;
nonfiction CON
GLAZER-MALBIN, Nona, 1932- ,
American; nonfiction CON
GLAZIER, Kenneth MacLean, 1912- ,
Canadian; nonfiction CON
GLAZIER, Lyle Edward, 1911- ,
American; poetry CON
GLEADOW, Rupert Seeley ('Justin
Case'), 1909- , English; nonfic-
tion CON
GLEASON, Eugene Franklin ('Gene
Gleason'), 1914- , American;
fiction CON
GLEASON, Harold, 1892- , Ameri-
can; nonfiction CON
GLEASON, Madeline, 1913- , Ameri-
can; poetry MUR

GLEASON, Robert Walter,
1917- , American; nonfiction
CON
GLEAVES, Suzanne, 1904- ,
American; nonfiction CON
GLEBOV, Anatoli Glebovich,
1899- , Russian; plays MAT
GLECKNER, Robert Francis,
1925- , American; nonfiction
CON
GLEDHILL, Alan, 1895- , Eng-
lish; nonfiction CON
GLEESON, Ruth Ryall, 1925- ,
American; nonfiction CON
GLEICK, Beth Youman, American;
juveniles WA
GLEIG, George Robert, 1796-1888,
Scots; fiction, nonfiction BRO
KBA
GLEIM, Johann Wilhelm Ludwig,
1719-1803, German; poetry
AL HAR KE ST
GLEIN, Johan Wilhelm, 1719-1803,
German; poetry SA
GLEISSER, Marcus David, 1923- ,
American; nonfiction CON
GLEN, Duncan Munro, 1933- ,
English; nonfiction CON
'GLEN, Eugene' see FAWCETT,
Frank D.
GLEN, Isa, American; fiction KL
GLEN, John Stanley, Canadian;
nonfiction CON
GLEN, Robert S., 1925- , Scots;
nonfiction CON
GLEN, William, 1789-1826, Scots;
poetry BRO KBA
GLENDINNING, Richard, 1917- ,
American; fiction CON
GLENN, Harold Theodore, 1910- ,
American; nonfiction CON
GLENN, Isa, 1888- , American;
fiction KT
GLENN, Jacob B., 1905- , Amer-
ican; nonfiction CON
GLENN, Norval Dwight, 1933- ,
American; nonfiction CON
GLENN, Paul Joseph, 1893- ,
American; nonfiction HOE
GLENNON, James, 1900- , Aus-
tralian; nonfiction CON
GLENNON, Maurade, 1926- ,
Irish; fiction CON
GLENNY, Lyman A., 1918- ,
American; nonfiction CON
GLEON, Genevieve Savalette de,
1732-95, French; nonfiction
DIL SA

GLESENER, Edmond, 1874- ,
Belgian; fiction COL SA
GLESER, Goldene Cohnberg, 1915- ,
American; nonfiction CON
GLESSING, Robert John, 1930- ,
American; nonfiction CON
GLIAUDA, Jurgis, 1906- , Russian-
American; fiction CON
GLICA, Miguel (Ghycas), 12th cent.,
Byzantine; nonfiction SA
GLICHEZAERE see HEINRICH der
GLEISSNER
GLICK, Carl Cannon ('Capt. Frank
Cunningham'; 'Peter Holbrook'),
1890- , American; fiction,
juveniles, plays CON
GLICK, Edward Bernard, 1929- ,
American; nonfiction CON
GLICK, Garland Wayne, 1921- ,
American; nonfiction CON
GLICK, Henry Robert, 1942- , Amer-
ican; nonfiction CON
GLICK, Paul Charles, 1910- , Amer-
ican; nonfiction CON
GLICK, Thomas Frederick, 1939- ,
American; nonfiction CON
GLICK, Virginia Kirkus, 1893- ,
American; nonfiction CON
GLICKEL von HAMELN, 1645-1724,
Jewish; nonfiction ST
GLICKSBERG, Charles Irving, 1900- ,
American; nonfiction CON
GLICKSMAN, Abraham Morton, 1911- ,
American; nonfiction CON
GLIDDEN, Frederick Dilley ('Luke
Short'), 1908- , American; fic-
tion CON
GLIDDEN, Horace Knight, 1901- ,
American; nonfiction CON
GLIDEWELL, John Calvin, 1919- ,
American; nonfiction CON
GLIEWE, Unada Grace, 1927- ,
American; juveniles CON
GLIKES, Erwin, 1937- , Belgian-
American; nonfiction CON
GLIKBERG, Alex N. see GLÜCK-
BERG, Alex N.
GLINES, Carroll Vance, Jr.,
1920- , American; nonfiction
CON
GLINKA, Fyodor Nikolayevich, 1786-
1880, Russian; poetry HARK ST
GLINSKI, Kazimierz, 1850-1920,
Polish; poetry ST
GLISIC, Milovan, 1847-1908, Serbian;
journalism, plays, translations
ST
GLISSANT, Edouard, 1928- , French;

poetry DIF PIN
GLOCK, Marvin D., 1912- ,
American; nonfiction CON
GLOGER, Gotthold, 1924- , Ger-
man; nonfiction AL
GLOS, Raymond Eugene, 1903- ,
American; nonfiction CON
GLOTZ, Gustave, 1862-1935,
French; nonfiction DIF
GLOUX, Olivier see 'AIMARD,
Gustave'
GLOVACH, Linda, 1947- , Amer-
ican; juveniles CON
GLOVER, Archibald F., 1902- ,
American; nonfiction SCA
GLOVER, David Tony ('Little Sun'),
1939- , American; nonfiction
CON
GLOVER, Denis James Matthews,
1912- , New Zealander;
poetry MUR RIC ST
GLOVER, Janice, 1919- , Ameri-
can; nonfiction CON
GLOVER, John Desmond, 1915- ,
Australian-American; nonfic-
tion CON
GLOVER, Leland Ellis, 1917- ,
American; nonfiction CON
GLOVER, Michael, 1922- , Eng-
lish; nonfiction CON
GLOVER, Richard, 1712-85, Eng-
lish; poetry, plays BRO KB
SA
GLOWACKI, Alexander see 'PRUS,
Boleslaw'
GLUBB, John Bagot, 1897- ,
English; nonfiction CON
GLUBOK, Shirley Astor, Ameri-
can; juveniles CON WA
GLUCK, Jay, 1927- , American;
nonfiction CON
GLUCK, Louise, 1943- , Ameri-
can; poetry CON
GLUCKMAN, Max, 1911- , Eng-
lish; nonfiction CON
GLÜCK, Barbara E. see 'PAOLI,
Betty'
GLUECK, Eleanor Touroff, 1898-
1972, American; nonfiction
CON
GLÜCK, Louise Elisabeth, 1943- ,
American; poetry MUR
GLUECK, Nelson, 1900- , Ameri-
can; nonfiction CON
GLUECK, Sheldon, 1896- , Amer-
ican; nonfiction CON
GLUECK, William Frank, 1934- ,
American; nonfiction CON

GLÜCKBERG, Alexander Mikhaylovich
('Sasha Cherney'; Glikberg), 1880-
1933, Russian; poetry HARK ST
GLÜCKEL, von HAMELN, 1645-1724,
Jewish; nonfiction HAR
GLUSBERG, Samuel ('Enrique Espino-
sa'), 1898- , Argentinian; journal-
ism, essays, criticism MIN
GLUSTROM, Simon W., 1924- ,
American; nonfiction CON
GLUT, Donald Frank ('Don Grant';
'Johnny Jason'; 'Victor Morrison';
'Rod Richmond'; 'Mick Rogers';
'Dr. Spektor'; 'Dale Steele';'Bradley
D. Thorne'), 1944- , American;
fiction CON
GLUTH, Oskar, 1887- , German;
poetry LEN
GLYN, Caroline, 1947- , English;
poetry, fiction CON
GLYN, Elinor, 1864-1943, English;
fiction BRO KT RIC SA
GLYNN, Jeanne Davis, 1932- ,
American; fiction CON
GLYNNE-JONES, William, 1907- ,
American; juveniles fiction
CON
GMELIN, Otto see KOLBENHEYER,
Erwin G.
GNAROWSKI, Michael, 1934- ,
Canadian; poetry MUR
GNAPHEUS, Guilhelmsu (Wilhelm
de Volder), 1493-1568, Dutch;
nonfiction ST
GNATHAENA, Greek; poetry SA
GNEDICH, Nikolay Ivanovich, 1784-
1833, Russian; poetry, translations
HARK SA ST
GNESSIN, Uri-Nissan, 1879-1913,
Jewish; fiction ST
GNOLF, Domenico ('Giulio Orsini'),
1838-1915, Italian; poetry, criti-
cism COL SA ST
GO, Puan Seng, 1904- , Chinese;
nonfiction CON
GOBET, Nicolas, 1735-81, French;
nonfiction DIL
GOBETTI, Piero, 1901-26, Italian;
criticism COL SA
GOBIN, Robert, fl. 1507, French;
poetry ST
GOBINEAU, Arthur, 1816-82, French;
fiction COL MAL SA ST
GOBINEAU, Joseph Arthur, 1816-82,
French; nonfiction DIF HAR KE
GOBIND SINGH, 1666-1708, Indian;
poetry LAN
GOBLE, Lloyd Neil, 1933- , Ameri-

can; nonfiction, fiction CON
GOBLOT, Edmond, 1858-1935,
French; nonfiction SA
GOCKEL, Herman W., 1906- ,
American; nonfiction CON
GODARD d'AUCOUR, Claude,
1716-95, French; nonfiction
DIL
GODBERT, Geoffrey Harold,
1937- , British; poetry MUR
GODBOLD, Edward Stanley, Jr.,
1942- , American; nonfiction
CON
GODBOUT, Jacques, 1933- ,
Canadian; poetry SY
GODEBSKI Cyprian, 1765-1809,
Polish; poetry ST
GODDARD, Burton Leslie, 1910- ,
American; nonfiction CON
GODDARD, Donald, 1934- , Ameri-
can; nonfiction CON
GODDARD, Jack R., 1930- ,
American; fiction CON
GODDARD, William, fl. 1615- ,
English; fiction ST
GODDEN, Rumer, 1907- , English;
juveniles CON DOY FUL KT
RIC WA
GODE van AESCH, Alex Gottfried
Freidrich ('Alex Gode'),
1906- , German-American;
nonfiction, translations CON
GODEFROI de LEIGNI, fl. 1170- ,
French; poetry ST
GODEFROY, Denis, 1549-1621,
French; nonfiction SA
GODEFROY, Denis, 1615-81,
French; nonfiction SA
GODEFROY, Thomas, 1580-1649,
French; nonfiction SA
GODESCALC, 805-69, Saxon;
poetry ST
GODESCARD, Jean François, 1728-
1800, French; translations DIL
GODET, Philippe, 1850-1922,
Swiss; criticism, journalism,
poetry ST
GODEWYCK, Pieter van, 1593-
1660, Dutch; poetry ST
GODEY, Louis Antoine, 1804-78,
American; nonfiction KAA
GODFREY, Cuthbert John, English;
nonfiction CON
GODFREY, Frederick M., 1901- ,
German-English; nonfiction
CON
GODFREY, Henry F., 1906- ,
American; nonfiction CON

GODFREY, Thomas, 1736-63, American; poetry, plays BRO JO KAA ST

GODFREY of VITERBO, 1120-91, German; poetry ST

GODINEZ, Felipe, 1588-1639?, Spanish; nonfiction BL SA ST

GODKIN, Daniel, 1612-86/87, American; nonfiction KAA

GODKIN, Edwin Lawrence, 1831-1902, American; nonfiction, editor BRO KBA

GODLEY, Alfred Denis, 1856-1925, Irish; nonfiction, poetry BRO

'GODLEY, John' see KILBRACKEN, John R. G.

'GODOLPHIN, Mary' see AIKIN, Lucy

GODOLPHIN, Sidney, 1609/10-43, English; poetry ST

GODOY, Armand, Cuban; poetry, essays MIN

GODOY, Juan, 1911- , Chilean; fiction MIN

GODOY, Juan Guadberto, 1793-1864, Argentinian; poetry MIN

GODOY, Lucila see 'MISTRAL, Gabriela'

GODOY y SALA, Ramón de, 1867-1917, Spanish; poetry, plays SA

GODSEY, John Drew, 1922- , American; nonfiction CON

GODWIN, Francis, 1562?-1633, English; nonfiction ST

GODWIN, Gail, 1937- , American; fiction CON

GODWIN, George Stanley, 1889- , English; fiction, nonfiction CON

GODWIN, John ('John Stark'), 1928- , Australian-American; fiction CON

GODWIN, Mary Wollstonecraft, 1759-97, English; nonfiction BRO KB SA ST

GODWIN, Parke, 1816-1904, American; nonfiction KAA

GODWIN, William, 1756-1836, English; fiction, nonfiction BRO KBA MAG SA ST

GOEBEL, Julius, 1857-1931, German-American; nonfiction ST

GOECKINGK, Leopold Freidrich Günther, 1748-1828, German; nonfiction AL

GOEDECKE, Walter Robert, 1928- , American; nonfiction CON

GOEDERTIER, Joseph M., 1907- , Belgian; nonfiction CON

GOEDICKE, Patricia McKenna, 1931- , American; poetry CON MUR

GOEDICKE, Victor Alfred, 1912- , American; nonfiction CON

GOELLER, Carl, 1930- , American; nonfiction CON

GOEN, Clarence Curtis, Jr., 1924- , American; nonfiction CON

GOENAGA, Florentino, 1859- , Colombian; fiction, journalism MIN

GOENEY, William Morton, 1914- , American; fiction CON

GOENS, Rijklof Michael, 1748-1810, Dutch; essays, translations ST

GOERCH, Carl, 1891- , American; nonfiction JO

GOERING, Reinhard, 1887-1936, German; plays KU MAT

GÖRLICH, Günter, 1928- , German; nonfiction AL

GÖRLING, Lars, 1931-66, Swedish; fiction CON

GÖRRES, Jakob Joseph von, 1776-1848, German; nonfiction AL HAR ST

GÖRTZ, Adolf, 1920- , German; nonfiction AL

GOERTZ, Arthémise, 1905- , American; fiction WAF

GOES, Damião de, 1502-74, Portuguese; nonfiction SA

GOES, Albrecht, 1908- , German; poetry, criticism AL FLE KU LEN

GOES, Johannes Antonides van der, 1647-84, Dutch; poetry ST

GOETEL, Ferdynand, 1890-1960, Polish; fiction COL HAR KT RIC SA ST

GOETHALS, George W., 1920- , American; nonfiction CON

GOETHE, Johann Wolfgang von, 1749-1832, German; plays, fiction, poetry AL HAR KE MAG SA ST

GÖTT, Emil, 1864-1908, German; plays COL SA ST

GOETTEL, Elinor, 1930- , American; nonfiction CON

GOETZ, Billy E., 1904- , American; nonfiction CON

'GOETZ, Curt' (Kurt Götz), 1888-1960, German; nonfiction AL KU LEN

GOETZ, Delia, 1898- , American; juveniles, translations WA

GOETZ, George see CLAVERTON,
Victor F.
GÖTZ, Johann Nikolaus, 1721-81,
German; poetry AL HAR ST
GOETZ, Ignacio L., 1933- ,
Venezuelan-American; nonfiction
CON
GOETZ, Lee Garrett, 1932- ,
American; nonfiction CON
GOETZ, Wolfgang, 1885-1955, Ger-
man; plays, essays, criticism
KU LEN MAT
GOETZMANN, William H., 1930- ,
American; nonfiction CON
GOEVERNEUR, Jan Jacob Antony
('Jan de Rijmer'), 1809-89,
Dutch; poetry, translations,
juveniles ST
GOFF, Frederick Richmond, 1916- ,
American; nonfiction CON
GOFF, Martyn, 1923- , English;
fiction CON
GOFFART, Walter Andre, 1934- ,
German-Canadian; nonfiction CON
GOFFE, Thomas, 1591-1629, English;
poetry ST
GOFFIN, Robert, 1898- , French;
poetry, essays, fiction DIC DIF
GOFFMAN, Erving, 1922- , Canadian;
nonfiction CON
GOFFSTEIN, Marilyn Brooke, 1940- ,
American; nonfiction CON
GOFMAN, Modest Lyudvigovich (Hof-
man), 1887- , Russian; essays
ST
GOFMAN, Viktor see HOFFMAN,
Viktor V.
GOGA, Octavian, 1881-1938, Rumanian;
poetry, essays FLE ST
GOGAN, Liam, 1891- , Irish; non-
fiction HO
GOGARTY, Oliver St. John, 1878-
1957, Irish; poetry BRO HOE
KT RIC SA ST
GOGGAN, John Patrick see 'PATRICK,
John'
GOGAL, Nikolai Vasilyevich, 1809-52,
Russian; fiction, plays HAR HARK
KE MAG SA ST
GOHDES, Clarence Louis Frank,
1901- , American; nonfiction
CON
GOHMAN, Fred Joseph ('Spider Webb'),
1918- , American; fiction CON
GOICOECHEA, Ramón Eugenio de,
1922- , Spanish; poetry, fiction
SA
GOINS, Ellen Haynes, 1927- , Amer-

ican; nonfiction CON
GOIS, Damião de, 1502-74,
Portuguese; nonfiction ST
GOIST, Park Dixon, 1936- ,
American; nonfiction CON
GOJAWICZYNSKA, Pola (Apolonia),
1896- , Polish; fiction,
plays COL ST SA
'GOKALP, Ziya' (Mehmed Ziya),
1875-1924, Turkish; poetry
SA ST
GOKHALE, Bolkrishna Govind,
1919- , Indian-American;
nonfiction CON
GOLANN, Cecil Paige, 1921- ,
American; juveniles CON
'GOLAU, Salomon von' see LOGAU,
Friedrich von
GOLAY, Frank Hendman, 1915- ,
American; nonfiction CON
GOLBURGH, Stephen J., 1935- ,
American; nonfiction CON
GOLD, Doris B., 1919- , Ameri-
can; nonfiction, poetry CON
GOLD, Douglas, 1894- , Ameri-
can; nonfiction CON
GOLD, Herbert, 1924- , Ameri-
can; fiction CON RIC
GOLD, Ivan, 1932- , American;
translations, fiction CON
GOLD, Joseph, 1933- , English;
nonfiction CON
GOLD, Martin, 1931- , Ameri-
can; nonfiction CON
'GOLD, Michael' (Irving Granich),
1894-1967, American; fiction,
journalism, plays CON KL
KT MAT
GOLD, Milton J., 1917- , Ameri-
can; nonfiction CON
GOLDBERG, Barney, 1918- ,
American; fiction CON
GOLDBERG, Herbert S., 1926- ,
American; nonfiction CON
GOLDBERG, Herman Raphael,
1915- , American; nonfiction
CON
GOLDBERG, Isaac, 1887-1938,
American; nonfiction KT
GOLDBERG, Joseph Philip,
1918- , American; nonfiction
CON
GOLDBERG, Louis, 1908- ,
Australian; nonfiction CON
GOLDBERG, Martha, 1907- ,
American; juveniles WA
GOLDBERG, Menahem see
BORAISCHE, Menahem

GOLDBERG, Milton Allan, 1919- ,
American; nonfiction CON
GOLDBERG, Percy Selvin, 1917- ,
English; nonfiction CON
GOLDBERG, Reuben Lucius, 1883- ,
American; nonfiction CON
GOLDBERGER, Arthur Stanley,
1930- , American; nonfiction
CON
GOLDE, Peggy, 1930- , American;
nonfiction CON
GOLDEN, Arthur, 1924- , American;
nonfiction CON
GOLDEN, Harry Lewis, 1903- ,
American; nonfiction CON
GOLDEN, Jeffrey S., 1950- , Amer-
ican; fiction CON
GOLDEN, Leon, 1930- , American;
nonfiction CON
GOLDEN, Louis Lawrence Lionel,
Canadian; nonfiction CON
GOLDEN, Morris, 1926- , American;
nonfiction CON
GOLDEN, Ruth Isbell, 1910- , Ameri-
can; nonfiction CON
'GOLDEN, Gorse', 20th cent., English;
juveniles DOY
GOLDENBERG, Heather see SPEARS,
Heather
GOLDENSON, Daniel R., 1944- ,
American; nonfiction CON
GOLDENSON, Robert Myar, 1908- ,
American; nonfiction CON
GOLDENTHAL, Allan Benarria,
1920- , American; nonfiction
CON
GOLDFADEN, Avraham, 1840-1908,
Jewish; plays, poetry LAN MAT
ST
GOLDFADER, Edward H., 1930- ,
American; nonfiction CON
GOLDFARB, Nathan, 1913- , Ameri-
can; nonfiction CON
GOLDFARB, Ronald L., 1933- ,
American; nonfiction CON
GOLDFARB, Russell M., 1934- ,
American; nonfiction CON
GOLDFRANK, Helen Colodny ('Helen
Kay'), 1912- , American; juveniles
CON WA
GOLDFRIED, Marvin Robert, 1936- ,
American; nonfiction CON
GOLDHURST, William, 1929- ,
American; nonfiction CON
GOLDIN, Augusta, 1906- , American;
juveniles CON
GOLDIN, Judah, 1914- , American;
nonfiction CON

GOLDING, Arthur, 1536-1605/06- ,
English; translations BRO
KB SP ST
GOLDING, Louis, 1895-1958,
English; fiction BRO KL KT
RIC SA
GOLDING, Louis, 1907- , Eng-
lish; nonfiction CON
GOLDING, Morton Jay ('Stephanie
Lloyd'; 'Jay Martin'; 'M. M.
Michaeles'; 'Patricia Morton'),
1925- , American; fiction
CON
GOLDING, William Gerald, 1911- ,
English; fiction, plays CON
FLE RIC MAT
GOLDMAN, Albert, 1927- ,
American; nonfiction CON
GOLDMAN, Arnold Melvyn, 1936- ,
American; nonfiction CON
GOLDMAN, Eric Frederick,
1915- , American; nonfiction
CON
GOLDMAN, Irving, 1911- ,
American; nonfiction CON
GOLDMAN, Lee A., 1946- ,
American; plays CON
GOLDMAN, Marshall, 1930- ,
American; nonfiction CON
GOLDMAN, Merle, 1931- ,
American; nonfiction CON
GOLDMAN, Michael Paul, 1936- ,
American; poetry, criticism
CON MUR
GOLDMAN, Peter Louis, 1933- ,
American; nonfiction CON
GOLDMAN, Phyllis W., 1927- ,
American; nonfiction CON
GOLDMAN, Richard Franko,
1910- , American; nonfiction
CON
GOLDMAN, Ronald, English; non-
fiction CON
GOLDMAN, Sheldon, 1939- ,
American; nonfiction CON
GOLDMAN, Sherli Evens, 1930- ,
American; nonfiction CON
GOLDMAN, William W., 1931- ,
American; fiction CON
GOLDMANN, Lucien, 1913-70,
Rumanian-French; nonfiction
CON
GOLDNER, Bernard Burton,
1919- , American; nonfiction
CON
GOLDNER, Jack, 1900- , Austrian-
American; nonfiction CON
GOLDONI, Carlo, 1707-93, Italian;

plays HAR KE MAG SA ST
GOLDRING, Douglas, 1887-1960, English; fiction BRO KT
GOLDRING, Patrick Thomas Zachary, 1921- , Irish; nonfiction CON
GOLDSCHEIDER, Ludwig, 1896- , Austrian; nonfiction CON
GOLDSCHMIDT, Meir (Aaron Meyer), 1819-87, Danish; fiction, plays, journalism HAR KE SA ST
GOLDSCHMIDT, Walter, 1913- , American; nonfiction CON
GOLDSCHMIDT, Yaaqov, 1927- , German; nonfiction CON
GOLDSEN, Rose Kohn, 1918- , American; nonfiction CON
GOLDSMITH, Arthur A., Jr., 1926- , American; nonfiction CON
GOLDSMITH, Carol Evan, 1930- , American; fiction CON
GOLDSMITH, Ilse Sondra Weinberg, 1933- , German-American; juveniles CON
GOLDSMITH, Oliver, 1728-74, Irish; fiction, plays, poetry, essays BRO KB MAG SA SP ST SY
'GOLDSMITH, Peter' see PRIESTLEY, J. B.
GOLDSON, Rae Lillian Sigalowitz, 1893- , American; nonfiction CON
GOLDSTEIN, Abraham Samuel, 1925- , American; nonfiction CON
GOLDSTEIN, David, 1870- , English; nonfiction HOE
GOLDSTEIN, David, 1933- , English; nonfiction CON
GOLDSTEIN, E. Ernest, 1918- , American; nonfiction CON
GOLDSTEIN, Edward, 1923- , American; nonfiction CON
GOLDSTEIN, Jonathan Amos, 1929- , American; nonfiction CON
GOLDSTEIN, Joseph, 1923- , American; nonfiction CON
GOLDSTEIN, Kenneth Michael, 1940- , American; nonfiction CON
GOLDSTEIN, Leo S., 1924- , American; nonfiction CON
GOLDSTEIN, Richard, 1944- , American; nonfiction CON
GOLDSTEIN, Roberta Butterfield, 1917- , American; fiction, poetry CON
GOLDSTEIN, Sidney, 1927- , American; nonfiction CON

GOLDSTEIN, William Isaac ('Solomon Bolo'; 'Rex Lode'), 1932- , American; nonfiction CON
GOLDSTRON, Robert Conroy ('James Stark'), 1927- , American; juveniles, fiction CON
GOLDSTONE, Richard H., 1921- , American; nonfiction CON
GOLDSWORTHY, David, 1938- , Australian; nonfiction CON
GOLDTHWAITE, Eaton K., 1907- , American; fiction CON
GOLEIN, Jean, 1320?-1403, French; translations ST
GOLEMBIEWSKI, Robert Thomas, 1932- , American; nonfiction CON
GOLENISHCHEV-KUTUZOV, Count Arseni Arkadievich; 1848-1912/13, Russian; poetry HARK ST
GOLF, Loyal Eugene, 1926- , American; nonfiction CON
GOLFFING, Barbara see GIBBS, Barbara
GOLFFING, Francis Charles, 1910- , American; poetry, fiction, translations CON
GOLIGHTLY, Bonnie Helen, 1919- , American; fiction CON
GOLITSYN, Prince Dmitri Petrovich ('Muravlin'), 1860-1919, Russian; fiction, poetry HARK
GOLL, Iwan (Yvan; Isaac Lang; 'Iwan Lassang'; 'Tristan Torsi'; 'Johannes Thor'; 'Tristan Thor'), 1891-1950, German; poetry, fiction, essays, plays AL DIF FLE KU KUN MAT
GOLL, Reinhold Weimar, 1897- , American; juveniles, fiction CON WA
GOLLAN, Robin, 1917- , Australian; nonfiction CON
GOLLANCZ, Sir Israel, 1864-1930, English; nonfiction BRO
GOLLER, Celia Fremlin, 1914- , English; fiction CON
GOLLINGS, Franklin O.A., 1919- , American; nonfiction CON
GOLLOMB, Joseph, 1881-1950, Russian-American; juveniles KJU KT WA

GOLLWITZER, Heinz, 1917- , German; nonfiction CON
GOLOBIE, John, -1927, American; nonfiction MAR
'GOLON, Sergeanne', Serge Golon, 1903-72, and Anne Golon, 1921- , French; fiction RIC
GOLOVINE, Michael Nicholas, 1903-65, American; nonfiction CON
GOLSSENAU see VIETH von GOLSSENAU
GOLZ, Reinhardt Lud, 1936- , Canadian; nonfiction CON
GOMARA, Francisco Lopez de see LOPEZ de GOMARA, Francisco
GOMBERG, Adeline Wishengard, 1915- , American; nonfiction CON
GOMBERG, Vladimir Germanovich ('Vladimir Lidin'), 1894- , Russian; fiction COL HAR HARK KT SA ST
GOMBERG, William, 1911- , American; nonfiction CON
GOMBERVILLE, Marin Le Roy, 1600-74, French; fiction DIF SA ST
GOMBOULD, Jean Ogier de, 1570-1666, French; poetry SA ST
GOMBROWICZ, Witold, 1904/05-69, Polish-Argentinian; fiction, plays CON FLE MAT RIC
GOMERSAL, Robert, 1602-46, English; plays ST
GOMERSALL, William, 1850- , English; nonfiction HIG
GOMES, Francisco Luiz, 1829-69, Portuguese; journalism SA
GOMES, Manuel Teixeira, 1862-1941, Portuguese; fiction ST
GOMES de AMORIM, Francisco, 1827-91, Portuguese; poetry, plays SA
GOMES LEAL, Antonio Duarte, 1848-1921, Portuguese; poetry SA ST
GOMEZ, Francisco, 1873/76-1938, Colombian; fiction MIN
GOMEZ, Juan Gualberto, 1854-1933, Cuban; journalism MIN
GOMEZ, Laureano, 1889- , Colombian; journalism MIN
GOMEZ, Madeleine Angélique Poisson, 1684-1770, French; plays DIL SA
GOMEZ, Manrique, 1412?-90, Spanish; poetry BL SA ST
GOMEZ, Pedro Alcántara, 20th cent., Colombian; poetry MIN
GOMEZ, Ruperto S., 1837-1910,

Colombian; poetry MIN
GOMEZ, Valentín, 1843-1907, Spanish; plays BL SA
'GOMEZ CARRILLO, Enrique' (Enrique Gómez Tible), 1873-1927/30, Guatemalan; nonfiction BL SA
GOMEZ CORNEJO, Carlos, 1904- , Bolivian; poetry, essays MIN
GOMEZ de AVELLANEDA, Gertrudis, 1814-73, Spanish; poetry, fiction, plays BL MIN SA ST
GOMEZ de BAQUERO Eduardo ('Andrenio'), 1866-1929, Spanish; journalism, criticism BL COL SA
GOMEZ de CASTRO, Alvar, 1523-90, Spanish; nonfiction SA
GOMEZ de CIUDAD REAL, Alvar, 1488-1538, Spanish; poetry SA
GOMEZ de CIUDAD REAL, Fernando, 1408?-57, Spanish; nonfiction SA
GOMEZ de HERRERA, Rodrigo, 1580-1641, Spanish; poetry, plays SA
GOMEZ de la MUERTA, Jerónimo, 1568?-1643, Spanish; poetry SA
GOMEZ de la MATA, Jacinto Germán, 1888- , Spanish; fiction SA
GOMEZ de la SERNA, Gaspar, 1918- , Spanish; nonfiction BL SA
GOMEZ de la SERNA, Julio, 1896- , Spanish; journalism BL SA
GOMEZ de la SERNA, Ramón ('Greguería'), 1888- , Spanish; fiction, plays, essays BL COL FLE KAT KT SA ST
GOMEZ de QUEVEDO VILLEGAS see QUEVEDO VILLEGAS, Francisco
GOMEZ de VIDAURRE, Felipe, 18th cent., Chilean; nonfiction MIN
GOMEZ DOMINGO, Manuel ('Rienzi'), 1891- , Spanish; nonfiction SA
GOMEZ HERMOSILLA, José Mamerto, 1771-1837, Spanish; nonfiction BL
GOMEZ JAUME, Alfredo, 1878-1946, Colombian; journalism,

poetry MIN

GOMEZ KEMP, Vicente, 1914/15- ,
Cuban; poetry MIN

GOMEZ LEDO, Avelino, 1895- ,
Spanish; nonfiction SA

GOMEZ MESA, Luis, 1902- ,
Spanish; criticism BL SA

GOMEZ MORENO, Manuel, 1870- ,
Spanish; nonfiction BL

GOMEZ NISA, Pío, 1925- , Spanish;
poetry SA

GOMEZ PEREIRA, Antonio, 1500-60,
Spanish; nonfiction BL SA

GOMEZ RESTREPO, Antonio, 1869-
1947, Colombian; nonfiction BL
MIN SA

GOMEZ ROJAS, Domingo (Daniel
Vazquez), 1896-1920, Chilean;
poetry MIN

GOMEZ y HERMOSILLA, José
Mamerto, 1771-1837, Spanish;
nonfiction SA

GOMICOURT, Augustin Pierre Damiens
de, 1723-90, French; nonfiction
DIL

GOMIS, Lorenzo, 1924- , Spanish;
poetry BL SA

GOMMERSZ, Job, -1543, Dutch;
poetry ST

GOMORI, George, 1934- , Hungarian-
English; poetry CON

GOMPERTZ, Martin Louis Alan ('Ganpat'), 1886- , English; fiction
HOE

GOMPERZ, Heinrich, 1873-1944,
Austrian; criticism SA

GOMPERZ, Theodor, 1832-1912,
Austrian; criticism SA

GOMULICKI, Wiktor ('Fantazy'),
1851-1919, Polish; poetry, fiction
ST

GONCALVES CRESPO, Antonio Cándido,
1847-83, Brazilian; poetry SA

GONCALVES DIAS, Antonio, 1823-64,
Portuguese; poetry SA

GONCALVES de MAGALHAES, Domingo
Jose, 1811-82, Brazilian; poetry,
essays, plays SA ST

GONCALVES DIAS, Antonio, 1823-64,
Brazilian; poetry ST

GONCALVES TEIXEIRA y SOUZA,
Antonio, 1812-61, Brazilian;
poetry, fiction SA

GONCHAROV, Ivan Alexandrovich,
1812-91, Russian; fiction HAR
HARK KE MAG SA ST

GONCOURT, Edmond Louis Antoine
Huot de, 1822-96, French; fiction,

nonfiction COL DIF HAR KE
MAG MAL SA ST

CONCOURT, Jules Alfred Huot
de, 1830-70, French; fiction,
nonfiction COL DIF HAR KE
MAL MAG SA ST

GONDI, Paul de see 'RETZ'

GONDOT, Pierre Thomas (Gondeau),
18th cent., French; plays DIL

GONDOU, Bernard, 18th cent.,
French; nonfiction DIL

GONDRA, Manuel, 1850?- ,
Paraguayan; nonfiction SA

GONELLA, Guido, 1905- , Italian;
nonfiction HO

GONGORA, Manuel de, 1889- ,
Spanish; poetry, plays, journalism SA

GONGORA y ARGOTE, Luis de,
1561-1627, Spanish; poetry
BL HAR KE SA ST

GONGORA y MARMOLEJO,
Alonso de, 1520-76, Chilean;
nonfiction MIN

GONZAGA, Lucrecia, 1522-76,
Italian; nonfiction SA

GONZAGA, Tomás Antonio, 1744-
1808/10, Brazilian; poetry
SA ST

GONZALES MARTINEZ, Enrique,
1871-1952, Mexican; poetry
FLE

GONZALES, Angel Custodio,
1918- , Chilean; nonfiction
MIN

GONZALEZ, Arturo F. Jr.,
1928- , American; nonfiction
CON

GONZALEZ, Diego, 1731/32-94,
Spanish; poetry BL SA ST

GONZALEZ, Eugenio, 1902- ,
Chilean; fiction MIN

GONZALEZ, Federico, Chilean;
poetry MIN

GONZALEZ, Fernando, 1896- ,
Colombian; fiction MIN

GONZALEZ, Fernando, 1901- ,
Spanish; poetry BL SA

GONZALEZ, Florentino, 1805/06-
74/75, Colombian; nonfiction
MIN

GONZALEZ, Joaquín V., 1863-
1923, Argentinian; nonfiction
MIN

GONZALEZ, Juan Natalicio,
1897- , Paraguayan; poetry
BL SA

GONZALEZ, Juan Vicente, 1808-

66, Venezuelan; nonfiction, poetry
SA ST
GONZALEZ, Justo Luis, 1937- ,
Cuban-American; nonfiction CON
GONZALEZ, Luis Felipe, 1882- ,
Costa Rican; essays, nonfiction
MIN
GONZALEZ, Manuel Dionisio, 1815-
83, Cuban; poetry, plays MIN
GONZALEZ, Nestor Vicente Madali,
1915- , Filipino; nonfiction,
fiction CON
GONZALEZ, Pedro Antonio, 1863-
1903/05, Chilean; poetry MIN
SA
GONZALEZ ANAYA, Salvador, 1879-
1955, Spanish; poetry BL SA
GONZALEZ, ARINTERO, Juan, 1860-
1928, Spanish; nonfiction SA
GONZALEZ ARRILL, Bernardo, 1892- ,
Argentinian; journalism, essays,
fiction, plays MIN SA
GONZALEZ BASTIAS, Jorge, 1879-
1954, Chilean; poetry BL MIN
GONZALEZ BLANCO, Andrés, 1888-
1924, Spanish; poetry, fiction BL
SA
GONZALEZ BLANCO, Edmundo, 1879-
1938, Spanish; nonfiction BL SA
GONZALEZ BLANCO, Pedro, 1880?- ,
Spanish; nonfiction BL SA
GONZALEZ CALDERON, Luciano,
20th cent., Argentinian; poetry,
essays MIN
GONZALEZ CAMARGO, Joaquín,
1865-86, Colombian; poetry MIN
GONZALEZ CARBALHO, José,
1901- , Argentinian; journalism,
poetry MIN SA
GONZALEZ CARVAJAL, Tomás,
1747-1834, Spanish; poetry SA
GONZALEZ CASTILLO, José, 1885-
1937, Argentinian; plays MIN
GONZALEZ CASTRO, Augusto, 1897- ,
Argentinian; journalism, poetry
MIN
GONZALEZ DAVILA, Gil, 1578-1658,
Spanish; nonfiction SA
GONZALEZ de AMEZUA, Agustín,
1881-1956, Spanish; nonfiction
BL SA
GONZALEZ de CANDAMO, Bernardo,
1881- , Spanish; fiction BL SA
GONZALEZ de CLAVIJO, Ruy,
-1412, Spanish; nonfiction BL
SA ST
GONZALEZ de ESLAVA, Fernán,
1534?-1601?, Mexican; plays ST

GONZALEZ de la PEZUELA y
CEBALLOS-ESCALERA, Juan
(Conde de Chestes), 1809-
1906, Spanish; nonfiction,
plays BL SA
GONZALEZ de SALAS, José
Antonio, 1588-1654, Spanish;
nonfiction BL SA
GONZALEZ del CASTILLO, Juan
Ignacio, 1763-1800, Spanish;
nonfiction, plays BL SA ST
GONZALEZ del VALLE, José
Zacarías, 1820-51, Cuban;
nonfiction MIN
GONZALEZ LANUZA, Eduardo,
1900- , Argentinian; poetry
MIN SA
GONZALEZ LOPEZ, Luis, 1889- ,
Spanish; fiction, plays, essays
SA
GONZALEZ MARTINEZ, Enrique,
1871-1952, Mexican; nonfiction
BL SA ST
GONZALEZ MAS, Ezequiel, 1919- ,
Spanish; nonfiction SA
GONZALEZ OLMEDILLA, Juan,
1893- , Spanish; poetry, fic-
tion SA
GONZALEZ PALENCIA, Angel,
1889-1949, Spanish; nonfiction
BL SA
GONZALEZ PEÑA, Carlos, 1885-
1955, Mexican; fiction, criti-
cism SA
GONZALEZ PRADA, Manuel, 1848-
1918, Peruvian; poetry, criti-
cism, essays BL FLE SA ST
GONZALEZ ROJO, Enrique, 1899-
1939, Mexican; poetry SA
GONZALEZ RUANO, César,
1903- , Spanish; poetry, fic-
tion BL SA
GONZALEZ RUCAVADO, Claudio,
1868/78-1928/29, Costa Rican;
fiction, essay MIN
GONZALEZ RUIZ, Nicolás, 1897- ,
Spanish; journalism, plays
BL SA
GONZALEZ SERRANO, Urbano,
1848-1904, Spanish; nonfiction
BL SA
GONZALEZ SUAREZ, Federico,
1844-1917, Ecuadorian; essays,
nonfiction DI
GONZALEZ TRILLO, E. (Luis
Ortiz Beheti), 1906- , Argen-
tinian; poetry, translations
MIN

GONZALEZ TUÑON, Enrique, 1901-
43, Argentinian; fiction MIN

GONZALEZ TUÑON, Raúl, 1905- ,
Argentinian; poetry MIN SA

GONZALEZ VERA, José Santos,
1897- , Chilean; journalism
MIN

GONZALEZ VIQUEZ, Cleto, 1858-
1937, Costa Rican; essays MIN

GONZALEZ ZELEDON, Manue (Magon),
1864-1936, Costa Rican; nonfiction BL MIN

GONZALO DE BERCEO, 1195/98-
1265/70, Spanish; poetry HAR
KE

GOOCH, Briso Dowling, 1925- ,
American; nonfiction CON

GOOCH, George Peabody, 1873-1968,
English; nonfiction CON KTS

'GOOCH, Silas N.' see GLASSCO,
John S.

GOOD, Carter Victor, 1897- ,
American; nonfiction CON

'GOOD, Edward' see OVED, Mosheh

GOOD, Edwin Marshall, 1928- ,
American; nonfiction CON

GOOD, Harry Gehman, 1880- ,
American; nonfiction CON

GOOD, Irving John ('K. Caj Doog'),
1916- , English; nonfiction
CON

GOOD, Lawrence R., 1924- , American; nonfiction CON

GOODALL, John Strickland, 1908- ,
English; juveniles CON

GOODALL, Marcus Campbell, 1914- ,
English; nonfiction CON

GOODALL, Walter, 1706?-66, Scots;
nonfiction BRO

GOODAVAGE, Joseph F., 1925- ,
American; nonfiction CON

GOODE, Richard Benjamin, 1916- ,
American; nonfiction CON

GOODENOUGH, Erwin Ramsdell,
1893-1965, American; nonfiction
CON

GOODENOUGH, Ward Hunt, 1919- ,
American; nonfiction CON

GOODFIELD, Gwyneth June, 1927- ,
English; nonfiction CON

GOODFRIEND, Arthur, 1907- ,
American; nonfiction CON

GOODGOLD, Edwin, 1944- , American; nonfiction CON

GOODHEART, Barbara, 1934- ,
American; nonfiction, juveniles
CON

GOODHEART, Eugene, 1931- ,

American; nonfiction CON

GOODIER, Alban, 1869-1939,
English; juveniles, fiction
HOE

GOODIN, Gayle, 1938- , American; nonfiction CON

GOODIN, Peggy, 1923- , American; fiction WAF

GOODING, Cynthia, 1924- ,
American; nonfiction, fiction
CON

GOODING, John Ervine, 1940- ,
English; nonfiction CON

GOODIS, David, 1917-67, American; fiction CON WAF

GOODLAD, John I., 1920- ,
American; nonfiction CON

GOODMAN, Charles Schaffner,
1916- , American; nonfiction
CON

GOODMAN, David Michael,
1936- , American; nonfiction
CON

GOODMAN, David S., 1917- ,
American; nonfiction CON

GOODMAN, Denise see LEVERTOV,
Denise

GOODMAN, Elaine, 1930- ,
American; nonfiction CON

GOODMAN, Elizabeth R., 1912- ,
American; nonfiction CON

GOODMAN, Elliot Raymond,
1923- , American; nonfiction
CON

GOODMAN, George J. W. ('Adam
Smith'), 1930- , American;
nonfiction CON

GOODMAN, Jay J., 1940- ,
American; nonfiction CON

GOODMAN, Jonathan, 1931- ,
English; poetry, fiction CON

GOODMAN, Kenneth S., 1927- ,
American; nonfiction CON

GOODMAN, Louis Wolf, 1942- ,
American; nonfiction CON

GOODMAN, Mitchell, 1923- ,
American; fiction CON

GOODMAN, Paul, 1911-72, American; fiction, plays, poetry
CON KTS MUR WAF

GOODMAN, Percival, 1904- ,
American; nonfiction CON

GOODMAN, Philip, 1911- ,
American; nonfiction CON

GOODMAN, Randolph, 1908- ,
American; nonfiction, plays
CON

GOODMAN, Roger B., 1919- ,

American; nonfiction CON
GOODMAN, Walter, 1927- , American; nonfiction CON
GOODNOW, Henry Frank, 1917- , American; nonfiction CON
GOODNOW, Jacqueline Jarrett, 1924- , Australian; nonfiction CON
GOODOVITCH, Israel Meir, 1934- , Israeli; nonfiction CON
GOODREAU, William Joseph, Jr., 1931- , American; nonfiction, poetry CON
GOODRICH, Arthur Frederic, 1878- , American; nonfiction SA
GOODRICH, Charles Augustus, 1790-1862, American; nonfiction KAA
GOODRICH, Frances C., 1933- , American; nonfiction CON
GOODRICH, Frank Boott ('Dick Tinto'), 1826-94, American; plays KAA
GOODRICH, Luther Carrington, 1894- , American; nonfiction CON
GOODRICH, Robert Edward, 1909- , American; nonfiction CON
GOODRICH, Samuel Griswold ('Peter Parley'), 1793-1860, English; juveniles DOY KAA SA
GOODRUM, Charles Alvin, 1923- , American; nonfiction CON
GOODSALL, Robert Harold, 1891- , English; nonfiction CON
GOODSELL, Fred Field, 1880- , American; nonfiction CON
GOODSELL, Jane Neubergen, American; juveniles PAC
GOODSPEED, Donald James, 1919- , Canadian; nonfiction CON
GOODSPEED, Edgar Johnson, 1871- , American; nonfiction HOO KTS
GOODSTEIN, Leonard David, 1927- , American; nonfiction CON
GOODWIN, Albert, 1906- , English; nonfiction CON
GOODWIN, Crawfurd David Wycliffe, 1934- , Canadian; nonfiction CON
GOODWIN, Harold Leland ('John Blaine'; 'Hal Goodwin'; 'Blake Savage'), 1914- , American; fiction, nonfiction CON
'GOODWIN, Mark' see MATTHEWS, Stanley G.
GOODWIN, Richard Murphey, 1913- , American; nonfiction CON
GOODWIN, Thomas, 1600-80, English; nonfiction BRO
GOODWYN, Lawrence, 1928- , American; nonfiction CON
GOODY, Joan Edelman, 1935- , American; nonfiction CON
GOODYEAR, Robert Arthur Hanson, 1877-1948, English; juveniles DOY
GOODYEAR, William Henry, 1846-1923, American; nonfiction KAA
GOOGE, Barnabe, 1540-94, English; poetry, translations BRO KB ST
GOOLD-ADAMS, Richard, 1916- , Australian; nonfiction CON
GOONERATNE, Malini Yasmine, 1935- , Ceylonese; nonfiction CON
GOONERATNE, Yasmine (Dias Bandaranaike), 1936- , Ceylonese; poetry MUR
'GOOSSEN, Agnes' see EPP, Margaret A.
GOOSSEN, Irvy W., 1924- , American; nonfiction CON
'GORA' see GORNICKI, Lukasz
'GORALCZYK, Kazimierz' see ANCZYC, Wladyslaw
'GORAN, Callt' see GERRITY, David S.
GORAN, Morris, 1918- , American; nonfiction CON
GORBATOV, Boris Leontyevish, 1908-54, Russian; fiction HAR HARK RIC ST
GORBEA LEMMI, Eusebio, 1881-1945, Spanish; fiction, essays, plays SA
GORBUNOV, Ivan Fyodorovich, 1831-95, Russian; fiction HAR HARK ST
GORDAN, Cyrus Herzl, 1908- , American; nonfiction CON
GORDENKER, Leon, 1923- , American; nonfiction CON
GORDH, George Rudolph, 1912- , American; nonfiction CON
GORDIMER, Nadine, 1923- , South African; fiction CON RIC
GORDIN, Jacob, 1853-1909, American; plays KAA MAT ST
GORDIS, Robert, 1908- , American; nonfiction CON
GORDON, Adam Lindsay, 1833-70, Australian; poetry BRO HIG KBA ST

GORDON, Ahron David, 1856-1902,
Jewish; essays ST
GORDON, Albert L., 1903- , Ameri-
can; nonfiction CON
'GORDON, Alex' see COTLER, Gordon
GORDON, Albin J., 1912- , Ameri-
can; nonfiction CON
GORDON, Ambrose, Jr., 1920- ,
American; nonfiction CON
GORDON, Angelique, 1791-1839,
French; nonfiction SA
GORDON, Arthur, 1912- , American;
fiction CON
GORDON, Bernard de, fl. 1250,
French; nonfiction ST
GORDON, Bernard Ludwig, 1931- ,
American; nonfiction CON
GORDON, Caroline, 1895- , Ameri-
can; fiction CON HO KT MAG
WAF
GORDON, Charles William ('Ralph
Connor'), 1860-1937, Canadian;
fiction BRO KT RIC ST SY
GORDON, Dane R., 1925- , Ameri-
can; nonfiction, plays CON
GORDON, David Cole, 1922- , Ameri-
can; nonfiction CON
'GORDON, Donald' see PAYNE,
Donald G.
GORDON, Donald Craigie, 1911- ,
American; nonfiction CON
GORDON, Donald Ramsey, 1929- ,
Canadian; nonfiction CON
GORDON, Dorothy Lerner, 1893- ,
American; juvenile WA
GORDON, Edmund Wyatt, 1921- ,
American; nonfiction CON
GORDON, Edwin, 1927- , American;
nonfiction CON
GORDON, Ernest, 1916- , Scots-
American; nonfiction CON
'GORDON, Frederick' see STRATE-
MEYER, Edward L.
'GORDON, Fritz' see JARVIS,
Frederick G., Jr.
'GORDON, Gary' see EDMONDS, Ivy
G.
GORDON, George Byron, 1911- ,
American; nonfiction CON
GORDON, George Newton, 1926- ,
American; nonfiction CON
GORDON, Gerald, 1909- , South
African; nonfiction CON
GORDON, Giles Alexander Esme,
1940- , British; poetry, fiction
MUR
GORDON, Gordon ('The Gordons'),
1912- , American; fiction CON

GORDON, Guanetta Stewart,
American; poetry CON
GORDON, Harold Jackson, Jr.,
1919- , American; nonfiction
CON
'GORDON, Ian' see FELLOWES-
GORDON, Ian D.
GORDON, Ian Alistair, 1908- ,
Scots; nonfiction CON
GORDON, Ida L., 1904- , Eng-
lish; nonfiction CON
'GORDON, Janet' see WOODHAM-
SMITH, Cecil B. F.
GORDON, John, 1925- , Ameri-
can; juveniles CON
GORDON, Judah Loeb ('Yehudah
Leib'), 1830-92, Jewish; poetry
KE
GORDON, Leonard A., 1938- ,
American; nonfiction CON
GORDON, Leonard Herman David,
1928- , American; nonfiction
CON
'GORDON, Lew' see BALDWIN,
Gordon C.
GORDON, Lillian L., 1925- ,
American; nonfiction CON
GORDON, Lois G., 1938- ,
American; nonfiction CON
GORDON, Mildred ('The Gordons'),
1912- , American; fiction
CON
GORDON, Mitchell, 1925- , Amer-
ican; nonfiction CON
GORDON, Myron Jules, 1920- ,
American; nonfiction CON
GORDON, Neil see MacDONELL,
Archibald
GORDON, Noah, 1926- , Ameri-
can; fiction CON
'GORDON, Oliver' see EMERSON,
Henry O.
GORDON, Patricia, 1909- ,
English; fiction CON
'GORDON, Peter' see WILKES-
HUNTER, Richard
'GORDON, Rex' see HOUGH, Stanley
B.
GORDON, Richard, 1921- , Eng-
lish; fiction RIC
GORDON, Richard Lewis, 1934- ,
American; nonfiction CON
GORDON, Robert Aaron, 1908- ,
American; nonfiction CON
GORDON, Robert Coningsby,
1921- , Australian; nonfiction
CON
GORDON, Sanford Daniel, 1924- ,

American; nonfiction CON
GORDON, Selma see LANES, Selma
    G.
'GORDON, Stewart' see SHIRREFFS,
    Gordon D.
GORDON, Sydney, 1914- , English;
    nonfiction CON
GORDON, Theodore J., 1930- ,
    American; nonfiction CON
GORDON, Thomas, 1918- , Ameri-
    can; nonfiction CON
'GORDON, Tom' see THOMAS, Gordon
'GORDON, Uncle' see ROE, Frederic
    G.
GORDON, Walter Kelly, 1930- ,
    American; nonfiction CON
GORDON, Wendell Chaffee, 1916- ,
    American; nonfiction CON
GORDON, Yehuda Leib, 1830-92,
    Jewish; fiction, poetry, essays
    LAN ST
GORDON WALKER, Patrick Christien,
    1907- , English; nonfiction CON
GORE, Catherine Grace Frances,
    1799-1861, English; fiction, plays
    BRO KBA SA
GORE, Charles, 1853-1932, English;
    nonfiction BRO
GORE, William Jay, 1924- , Ameri-
    can; nonfiction CON
GORE-BOOTH, Eva Selena, 1870-
    1926, English; poetry BRO ST
GORELICK, Molly C., 1920- , Amer-
    ican; juveniles CON
GORELIK, Mordecai, 1899- , Ameri-
    can; nonfiction CON
GORELL, Ronald Gorell Barnes,
    1885- , English; poetry, fiction
    BRO
GORENKO, Anna A. see 'AKHAMA-
    TOVA A.'
GORER, Geoffrey, Edgar, 1905- ,
    British; nonfiction KTS
GORES, Joseph N., 1931- , Ameri-
    can; fiction CON
GOREY, Edward St. John ('Eduard
    Blutig'; 'Mrs. Regera Dowdy';
    'Redway Grode'; 'O. Mude';
    'Ogdred Weary'; 'Dreary Wodge'),
    1925- , American; fiction CON
GORGIAS, 485-380 B.C., Greek;
    nonfiction SA ST
GORGO, 7th cent. B.C., Greek;
    poetry SA
GORHAM, Charles Orson, 1911- ,
    American; fiction CON WAF
GORHAM, Maurice Anthony Coneys
    ('Walter Rault'), 1902- , English;

nonfiction CON HO
'GORHAM, Michael' see FOLSOM,
    Franklin
'GORION, Micha Yoseph Bin' see
    BERDICHEWSKI, Micah J.
GORIS, Jan Albert see 'GIJSEN,
    Marnix'
'GORKY, Maxim' (Aleksei
    Maksimovich Peshkov; Gorki),
    1868-1936, Russian; fiction,
    plays COL FLE HAR HARK
    KL KT MAG MAT RIC SA ST
GORMAN, Burton William, 1907- ,
    American; nonfiction CON
'GORMAN, Ginny' see KANTO,
    Peter
GORMAN, Herbert Sherman,
    1893- , American; fiction,
    essays KT WAF
GORMAN, Katherine, American;
    poetry CON
GORNALL, Thomas, 1912- ,
    English; nonfiction CON
GORNFIELD, Arkady Georgievich,
    1867- , Russian; criticism
    ST
GORNICKI, Lukasz (Góra), 1527-
    1603, Polish; nonfiction ST
GORODETSKI, Sergey Mitrofano-
    vich, 1884- , Russian;
    poetry HARK ST
GOROSCH, Max, 1912- , Swedish;
    nonfiction BL
GOROSITO HEREDIA, Luis,
    1902- , Argentinian; poetry
    SA
GOROSTIZA, Celestino, 1904- ,
    Mexican; plays, fiction SA
GOROSTIZA, José, 1901- ,
    Mexican; poetry BL SA
GOROSTIZA, Manuel Eduardo,
    1789-1851, Mexican; fiction,
    plays BL SA ST
GORRELL, Robert Mark, 1914- ,
    American; nonfiction CON
'GORRI, Tobia' see BOITO,
    Arrigo
GORRISH, Walter, 1909- , Ger-
    man; nonfiction AL
GORRITI, Juan Ignacio de, 1766/68-
    1841/42- , Argentinian; non-
    fiction MIN SA
GORRITI, Juana Manuela, 1818/19-
    74/92, Argentinian; fiction
    MIN SA
GORSKI, Artur ('Quadimodo'),
    1870- , Polish; poetry, trans-
    lations ST

GORTER, Herman, 1864-1927, Dutch;
poetry COL SA ST
GORTER, Simon, 1838-71, Dutch;
nonfiction ST
GORTNER, Ross Aiken, Jr., 1912- ,
American; nonfiction CON
'GORYAN, Sirak' see SAROYAN,
William
GOSCELIN of CANTERBURY, -1099,
English; nonfiction ST
GOSE, Elliott Beckley, Jr., 1926- ,
Canadian; nonfiction CON
GOSHAY, Robert C., 1931- , Ameri-
can; nonfiction CON
GOSHEN, Charles Ernest, 1916- ,
American; nonfiction CON
GOSLICKI, Wawrzyniec Grzymala
('Goslicius; Laurentius Grimalius),
1530-1607, Polish; nonfiction ST
GOSLIN, David A., 1936- , Ameri-
can; nonfiction CON
GOSLING, John Neville, 1905- ,
English; fiction CON
GOSLING, William Flower, 1901- ,
English; nonfiction CON
'GOSLOVICH, Marianne' see BROWN,
Morris C.
GOSNELL, Elizabeth Duke Tucker,
1921- , American; nonfiction,
poetry CON
GOSS, Fred, 1873- , English; non-
fiction HIG
GOSSART, Jean Baptiste, French;
poetry DIL
GOSSE, Sir Edmund William, 1849-
1928, English; criticism BRO
KAT KT RIC SA ST
GOSSETT, Margaret, American;
juveniles WA
GOSSETT, Thomas F., 1916- , Amer-
ican; nonfiction CON
GOSSMAN, Lionel, 1929- , Scots-
American; nonfiction CON
GOSSON, Stephen, 1555-1624, English;
poetry BRO KB ST
GOSSOUIN de METZ, 13th cent.,
French; poetry ST
GOSZCZYNSKI, Seweryn, 1801-76,
Polish; poetry ST
GOTLIEB, Phyllis Fay Bloom, 1926- ,
Canadian; poetry, fiction CON
MUR
GOTOBA, 1180-1239, Japanese; poetry
ST
GOTSCHE, Otto, 1904- , German;
nonfiction AL
GOTSHALK, Dilman Walter, 1901- ,
American; nonfiction CON

GOTTA, Salvator, 1887- ,
Italian; fiction HAR ST
GOTTEHRER, Barry H., 1935- ,
American; nonfiction CON
GOTTER, Freidrich Wilhelm,
1746-97, German; plays,
poetry HARK SA ST
GOTTERER, Malcolm Harold,
1924- , American; nonfiction
CON
GOTTESMAN, Irving Isadore,
1935- , American; nonfiction
CON
GOTTESMAN, Ronald, 1933- ,
American; nonfiction CON
GOTTFRIED, Alexander, 1919- ,
Hungarian-American; nonfiction
CON
GOTTFRIED, Martin, 1933- ,
American; nonfiction CON
GOTTFRIED, Theodore Mark
('Leslie Behan'; 'Harry
Gregory'; 'Ted Mark'; 'Kathe-
rine Tobias'), 1928- , Amer-
ican; fiction CON
GOTTFRIED von NEIFEN, fl.
1234-55, Swabian; poetry ST
GOTTFRIED von STRASSBURG,
12th cent., German; poetry
AL HAR KE MAG SA ST
'GOTTHELF, Jeremias' (Albert
Bitzius), 1797-1854, Swiss;
fiction AL HAR KE SA ST
GOTTIFREDI, Bartolomeo, 16th
cent., Italian; poetry ST
GOTTLIEB, Bernhardt Stanley,
1898- , American; nonfiction
CON
GOTTLIEB, Gerald, 1923- ,
American; juveniles CON WA
GOTTLIEB, Lois Davidson,
1926- , American; nonfiction
CON
GOTTLIEB, Robin Grossman,
1928- , American; juveniles,
translations CON WA
GOTTLIEB, William P., Ameri-
can; juveniles WA
GOTTLOBER, Abraham Baer
('Abag'; 'Mahalel'), 1811-99,
Jewish; poetry, fiction ST
GOTTSCHALK, Louis Reichenthal,
1899- , American; nonfiction
KTS CON
GOTTSHCALL, Franklin Henry
('H. Borneman'), 1902- ,
American; nonfiction CON
GOTTSCHALL, Rudolf von, 1823-

1909, German; poetry, plays HAR
GOTTSCHED, Johann Christoph, 1700-
66, German; criticism AL HAR KE
SA ST
GOTTSCHEDIN, Luise Adelgunta
Viktorie Kulmus, 1713-62, German;
nonfiction AL SA ST
GOTTVALS, Vernon Detwiler, Jr.,
1924- , American; nonfiction
CON
GOUDAR, Ange, 1720-91, French;
nonfiction DIL
GOUDEY, Alice E., 1898- , Ameri-
can; juveniles WA
GOUDGE, Elizabeth, 1900- , English;
fiction, juveniles COM CON DOY
KT RIC SA WA
GOUDY, Frederic, 1865-1947, Ameri-
can; nonfiction HOO
GOUFFE, Armand, 1775-1845, French;
poetry, plays SA
GOUGAUD, Louis, 1877-1941, French;
nonfiction HOE
GOUGE, William M., 1796-1863,
American; nonfiction KAA
GOUGE de CESSIERES, François
Etienne, 1724-82, French; poetry
DIL
GOUGES, Marie Olympe, 1748-93,
French; nonfiction, plays DIL SA
GOUGH, Catherine, 1931- , English;
juveniles CON
GOUGH, John Bartholomew, 1817-86,
American; nonfiction KAA
GOUGH, John Wiedhofft, 1900- ,
Welsh; nonfiction CON
GOUGH, Richard, 1735-1809, English;
nonfiction BRO ST
GOUGH, Vera, English; nonfiction
CON
GOUJET, Abbé Claude Pierre, 1697-
1767, French; nonfiction DIF
DIL
GOULARD, Matilde, Spanish; nonfiction
BL
GOULART, Ronald Joseph, 1933- ,
American; nonfiction, fiction CON
GOULBURN, Edward, fl. 1765-1822,
English; poetry HIG
GOULD, Alfred Ernest, 1909- , Eng-
lish; nonfiction CON
GOULD, Beatrice Blackmar, 1898- ,
American; nonfiction CON
GOULD, Cecil Hilton Monk, 1918- ,
English; nonfiction CON
GOULD, Charles Newton, 1868- ,
American; nonfiction MAR
GOULD, Douglas Parsons, 1919- ,

American; nonfiction CON
GOULD, Edward Sherman, 1805-
85, American; nonfiction
KAA
GOULD, Felix, American; fiction
CON
GOULD, Gerald, 1885-1936, Eng-
lish; journalism, poetry BRO
GOULD, Hannah Flagg, 1789-1865,
American; poetry KAA
GOULD, James Adams, 1922- ,
American; nonfiction CON
GOULD, James Warren, 1924- ,
American; nonfiction CON
GOULD, Jean Rosalind, 1909/19- ,
American; juveniles CON WA
GOULD, John Thomas, 1908- ,
American; essays KTS
GOULD, Joseph Edmund, 1912- ,
American; nonfiction CON
'GOULD, Lettie' see PAXSON,
Ethel
GOULD, Mary Earle, 1885- ,
American; nonfiction CON
GOULD, Maurice M., 1909- ,
American; nonfiction CON
'GOULD, Michael' see AYRTON,
Michael
GOULD, Nathaniel, 1857-1919,
English; fiction, nonfiction
BRO HIG
GOULD, Peter Robin, 1932- ,
American; nonfiction CON
GOULD, Wesley Larson, 1917- ,
American; nonfiction CON
GOULDEN, Joseph C., Jr.,
1934- , American; nonfiction
CON
GOULDER, Grace, 1893- , Amer-
ican; nonfiction CON
GOULDNER, Alvin W., 1920- ,
American; nonfiction CON
GOULDSBURY, Henry Cullen,
1881-1916, Rhodesian; poetry,
fiction ST
GOULET, Robert Joseph, 1924- ,
Canadian; fiction CON
GOULETT, Harlan Mador, 1927- ,
American; nonfiction CON
GOULIN, Jean, 1728-99, French;
nonfiction DIL
GOULLART, Peter, 1902- ,
Russian-English; nonfiction
CON
GOURCY, François Antoine Etienne,
18th cent., French; nonfiction
DIL
GOURDIE, Thomas, 1913- , Scots;

nonfiction CON

GOURDIN, François Philippe, 1739-1825, French; nonfiction DIL

GOURDIN, Michel, -1708, French; nonfiction DIL

GOUREVITCH, Doris Jeanne, American; nonfiction CON

GOURLEY, Gerald Douglas, 1911- , American; nonfiction CON

GOURLIE, Norah Dundas, Scots; nonfiction CON

GOURLIN, Pierre Sébastien, 1695-1775, French; nonfiction DIL

GOURMEAU, Jean, -1761, French; nonfiction DIL

GOURMONT, Remy de, 1858-1915, French; fiction, plays, poetry, essays COL DIF FLE KAT KT MAG SA ST

GOURNAY, Marie Le Jars de, 1566-1645, French; nonfiction SA

GOURNE, Pierre Mathias de, 1702-70, French; nonfiction DIL

GOURREGES, J. B., -1780, French; poetry DIL

GOUSSELIN, Jean Claude, 18th cent., French; nonfiction DIL

GOUTTES, Jean Louis, 1740-94, French; nonfiction DIL

GOUVEIA, Frei Antonio de, 1757-1628, Portuguese; nonfiction SA

GOUYE de LONGUEMARE, 1715-63, French; nonfiction DIL

GOVAW, Christine Noble ('Mary Allerton'; 'J. N. Darby'), 1898- , American; juveniles, fiction CON WA WAF

GOVE, Philip Babcock, 1902-72, American; nonfiction CON

GOVE, Samuel Kimball, 1923- , American; nonfiction CON

GOVEIA, Elsa Vesta, 1925- , English; nonfiction CON

GOVER, John Robert, 1929- , American; fiction CON

GOVINDA, Laura Anagarika, 1898- , American; nonfiction CON

GOVONI, Corrado, 1884- , Italian; fiction, poetry SA ST

GOVONI, Laura E., 1914- , American; nonfiction CON

GOVORCHIN, Gerald Gilbert, 1912- , Yugoslav-American; nonfiction CON

GOVY, Georges, 1910- , French; fiction DIF

GOW, Ronald, 1897- , English; plays CON

GOWAN, John Curtis, 1912- , American; nonfiction CON

GOWANS, Alan, 1923- , Canadian; nonfiction CON

GOWEN, James Anthony, 1928- , American; nonfiction CON

GOWEN, Samuel Emmett, 1902- , American; fiction CON

GOWER, Herschel, 1919- , American; nonfiction CON

GOWER, John, 1330?-1408, English; poetry BRO KB SA SP ST

GOWING, Lawrence Burnett, 1918- , English; nonfiction CON

GOWLAND, Mariano Ezequiel, 1933- , American; nonfiction CON

GOY de SILVA, Ramón, 1888-1962, Spanish; poetry, plays BL SA

GOYAU, Georges Pierre Louis Theophile, 1869-1939, French; nonfiction HOE

GOYCOECHEA MENENDEZ, Martín ('Lucio Stella'), 1877-1906, Argentinian; journalism, plays MIN

GOYEN, Charles William, 1915- , American; fiction CON

GOYENA, Pedro, 1843-92, Argentinian; journalism MIN

'GOYENECHE, Gabriel' see AVALLE-ARCE, Juan B.

GOYON d'ARSAC, Guillaume Henri Charles, 1740-1805, French; nonfiction DIL

GOYON de la PLOMBANIE, Henri de, -1808, French; nonfiction DIL

GOYRI de MENENDEZ PIDAL, María, 1873-1954, Spanish; nonfiction BL SA

GOYTISOLO, Juan, 1931- , Spanish; fiction BL RIC SA

GOYTISOLO GOY, José Agustín, 1928- , Spanish; poetry SA

GOZLAN, León, 1803-66, French; journalism, fiction DIF

GOZZANO, Guido Gustavo, 1883-1916, Italian; poetry COL FLE KE SA ST

GOZZI, Carlo, 1720-1806, Italian; poetry, plays HAR KE SA ST

GOZZI, Gaspare, 1713-86, Italian; poetry, journalism, criticism HAR SA ST

GRAA, Thomas François, 1713-98/99- , French; nonfiction DIL
GRABBE, Christian Deitrich, 1801-36, German; plays AL HAR KE ST
GRABER, Alexander ('Alexander Cordell'), 1914- , English; fiction CON
GRABER, Doris A., 1923- , American; nonfiction CON
GRABERG de HEMSOE, Jakob, 1776-1847, Swedish; nonfiction SA
GRABILL, Joseph L., 1931- , American; nonfiction CON
GRABMANN, Rev. Martin, 1875-1949, German; nonfiction HO
GRABNER, Hasso, 1911- , German; poetry AL
GRABO, Norman Stanley, 1930- , American; nonfiction CON
GRABOWSKI, Zbigniew Anthony ('Axel Heyst'), 1903- , Polish-English; nonfiction CON
GRACA ARANHA, José Pereira de, 1868-1931, Brazilian; nonfiction SA ST
'GRACE, Joseph' see HORNBY, John
GRACE, William Joseph, 1910- , American; poetry, nonfiction CON HO
GRACIAN see ARIAS, Augusto
GRACIAN, Baltasar, 1601-58, Spanish; fiction BL
GRACIAN, Jerónimo, 1545-1614, Spanish; nonfiction BL SA
GRACIAN DANTISCO, Lucas, 1557?-1615?, Spanish; nonfiction BL SA
GRACIAN de ALDERETE, Diego, 1510?-1600?, Spanish; nonfiction BL SA
GRACIAN y MORALES, Baltasar, 1601-58, Spanish; nonfiction HAR KE SA ST
GRACIO FALISCO, Roman; poetry SA
'GRACQ, Julien' (Louis Poirier), 1910- , French; fiction, essays, plays, translations DIC DIF FLE KTS MAL PIN
GRACY, David Bergen, II, 1941- , American; nonfiction CON
GRACZA, Margaret Young, 1928- , American; nonfiction CON
GRAD, Frank P., 1924- , Austrian-American; nonfiction CON
GRADE, Arnold Edward, 1928- , American; poetry CON
GRADNIK, Alojz, 1882- , Slovene;

poetry FLE ST
GRADY, Henry Woodfin, 1850-89, American; journalism KAA
GRAEBNER, Norman A., 1915- , American; nonfiction CON
GRAEBNER, Walter, 1909- , American; nonfiction CON
GRAEF, Hilda Charlotte, 1907- , German-American; nonfiction, translations CON HO
GRAEFE, Julius see MEIER-GRAEFE, Julius
GRAEFF, Grace M., 1918- , American; nonfiction CON
GRAEME, Sheila, 1944- , English; fiction CON
GRAEVIUS, Johan George, 1622-1703, German; criticism SA
GRAF, Arturo, 1848-1913, Italian; poetry, criticism COL SA ST
GRAF, Ernest, 1879- , English; nonfiction HOE
GRAF, Oscar Maria, 1894-1967, German; fiction, poetry AL FLE KT KU LEN SA
GRAF, Rudolf F., 1926- , Austrian-American; nonfiction CON
GRAFENBERG, Wirnt see WIRNT von GRAFENBERG
GRAFF, Gerald Edward, 1937- , American; nonfiction CON
GRAFF, Henry Franklin, 1921- , American; nonfiction CON
GRAFF, Sigmund, 1898- , German; plays MAT
GRAFF, Stewart, American; juveniles WA
GRAFFIGNY, Françoise d' Issembourg, 1695-1758, French; letters DIF DIL SA
GRAFTON, Richard, -1572, English; diary, translations BRO ST
GRAGS-PA RGYAL-MTSHAN, 1147-1216, Tibetan; nonfiction LAN
GRAHAM, Rev. Aelred, 1907- , English; nonfiction CON HO
GRAHAM Ada, 1931- , American; juveniles CON
GRAHAM, Al, 1897- , American; juvenile WA
GRAHAM, Alberta Powell, American; juveniles WA
GRAHAM, Alexander John, 1930- , English; nonfiction CON

GRAHAM, Alice Walworth, 1905- ,
American; fiction CON
GRAHAM, Angus Charles, 1919- ,
Welsh; nonfiction CON
GRAHAM, Billy see GRAHAM,
William F.
GRAHAM, Clarence Reginald, 1907- ,
American; juveniles WA
GRAHAM, Cunninghame see CUNNING-
HAME, Robert B.C.
GRAHAM, Donald Wilkinson, 1900- ,
Canadian; nonfiction CON
GRAHAM, Dorothy, 1893- ,
American; fiction KT WAF
GRAHAM, Eleanor, 1896- , English;
juveniles DOY
'GRAHAM, Ennis' see MOLESWORTH,
Mary L.
GRAHAM, Frank, Jr., 1925- ,
American; juveniles CON WA
GRAHAM, Fred Patterson, 1931- ,
American; nonfiction CON
GRAHAM, George Rex, 1813-94,
American; editor KAA
GRAHAM, Grace, 1910- , American;
nonfiction CON
GRAHAM, Gwethalyn, 1913- ,
Canadian; fiction ST SY
GRAHAM, Harry Edward, 1940- ,
American; nonfiction CON
GRAHAM, Harry Jocelyn Clive, 1874-
1936, English; juveniles, poetry
BRO DOY
GRAHAM, Helen Holland, American;
juveniles WA
GRAHAM, Henry, 1930- , English;
poetry MUR
GRAHAM, Howard Jay, 1905- ,
American; nonfiction CON
'GRAHAM, Hugh' see BARROWS,
Marjorie
GRAHAM, Hugh Davis, 1936- ,
American; nonfiction CON
'GRAHAM, James' see MONTROSE,
James G.
GRAHAM, James Walter, 1906- ,
Canadian; nonfiction CON
GRAHAM, John, 1926- , American;
nonfiction, juveniles CON
GRAHAM, John Alexander, 1941- ,
American; fiction CON
GRAHAM, John Remington, 1940- ,
American; nonfiction CON
GRAHAM, Jory, American; nonfiction
CON
GRAHAM, Loren R., 1933- , Amer-
ican; nonfiction CON
GRAHAM, Lorenz Bell, 1902- ,

American; juveniles COM
CON
GRAHAM, Margaret Althea, 1924- ,
American; nonfiction CON
GRAHAM, Margaret Bloy, 1920- ,
Canadian; juveniles FUL
GRAHAM, Maude Fitzgerald Susan
('Susan'), 1912- , American;
juveniles CON
'GRAHAM, Neill' see DUNCAN,
William M.
GRAHAM, Otis, L., Jr., 1935- ,
American; nonfiction CON
GRAHAM, Patricia Albjerg,
1935- , American; nonfiction
CON
GRAHAM, Rachel Metcalf, 1895- ,
American; poetry CON
GRAHAM, Ramona see COOK,
Ramona G.
GRAHAM, Sir Reginald, 1835-
1920, English; nonfiction HIG
GRAHAM, Richard, 1934- ,
American; nonfiction CON
GRAHAM, Robert, 1735?-97?,
Scots; songs BRO
GRAHAM, Robert Bontine Cunning-
hame, 1852-1936, English;
nonfiction BRO KAT KT SA
ST
GRAHAM, Robert G., 1925- ,
American; nonfiction CON
GRAHAM, Sean, 1920- , German-
English; fiction CON
GRAHAM, Shirley, 1907- , Amer-
ican; nonfiction, juveniles,
plays FUL KTS WA
GRAHAM, Stephen, 1884- , Eng-
lish; nonfiction BRO KT
GRAHAM, Thomas Francis,
1923- , American; nonfiction
CON
GRAHAM, William Franklin (Billy),
1918- , American; nonfiction
CON
GRAHAM, William Fred, 1930- ,
American; nonfiction CON
GRAHAM, William Sydney, 1918- ,
Scots; poetry MUR
GRAHAM, Winston M., 1911- ,
English; fiction RIC
GRAHAME, James, 1765-1811,
Scots; poetry BRO KBA ST
GRAHAME, Kenneth, 1859-1932,
English; juveniles, fiction,
essays BRO DOY KAT KT
MAG RIC ST WA
GRAHAME, Simon (Simion), 1570-

1614, Scots; nonfiction BRO
GRAINDOR de BRIE, -1189?,
    French; poetry ST
GRAINDOR de DOUAI, fl. 1200,
    French; poetry ST
GRAINGER, Anthony John, 1929- ,
    English; nonfiction CON
GRAINGER, James, 1721-66, English;
    poetry BRO KB ST
GRAINVILLE, Jean Baptiste Christophe,
    1760-1805, French; fiction, poetry,
    translations DIL
GRAINVILLE, Pierre de, 1642-1720,
    French; nonfiction DIL
GRALAPP, Leland Wilson, 1921- ,
    American; nonfiction, fiction CON
GRAM, Harold Albert, 1927- ,
    Canadian; nonfiction CON
GRAMATKY, Hardie, 1907- , Ameri-
    can; juvenile KJU COM CON WA
GRAMBS, Jean Dresden, 1919- ,
    American; nonfiction CON
GRAMET, Charles, American; juveniles
    CON WA
'GRAMMATICUS' see BLAIKLOCK,
    Edward M.
GRAMMATICUS, Aelfric see AELFRIC
GRAMPP, William Dyer, 1914- ,
    American; nonfiction CON
GRAMSBERGEN, Matthys, 17th cent.,
    Dutch; fiction ST
GRAN, Gerhard von der Lippe,
    1866-1925, Norwegian; criticism
    ST
GRANADA, Luis de (Conde de Tendilla),
    1504-88, Spanish; nonfiction BL
    HAR KE SA ST
GRANADO, Félix Antonio del, 1873- ,
    Bolivian; poetry, essays, criticism
    MIN
GRANAT, Robert, 1925- , Cuban-
    American; nonfiction CON
GRANATA, María, 1920/23- , Ar-
    gentinian; poetry MIN
GRANATSTEIN, Jack Lawrence,
    1939- , Canadian; nonfiction
    CON
GRANBERG, Wilbur John, 1906- ,
    American; juveniles CON PAC
GRANBERRY, Edwin, 1897- , Amer-
    ican; fiction CON KL KT
GRANCOLAS, Jean, -1732, French;
    nonfiction DIL
GRAND, Anselme, -1766, French;
    nonfiction DIL
GRAND, Elliott Mansfield, 1895- ,
    American; nonfiction CON
GRAND, Flurin, 1847-1926, Raeto-

Romansch; poetry ST
GRAND, Gordon, 1883- , English;
    nonfiction HIG
'GRAND, Sarah' (Frances Eliza-
    beth Clark McFall), 1862- ,
    English; fiction KT
GRANDA, Nicolás, 1840-1915,
    Argentinian; journalism, plays
    MIN SA
GRANDBOIS, Alain, 1900- ,
    Canadian; poetry, fiction ST
    SY
GRANDCHAMP, fl. 1702, French;
    nonfiction DIL
GRANDE, Adriano, 1897- ,
    Italian; poetry SA
GRANDE, Luke M., 1922- ,
    American; nonfiction CON
'GRANDE VITESSE' see WALKER-
    LEY, Rodney L.
GRANDIDIER, Claude, -1776,
    French; nonfiction DIL
GRANDIDIER, Philippe André,
    1752-87, French; nonfiction
    DIL
GRANDJEAN de FOUCY, Jean
    Paul, 1707-88, French; nonfic-
    tion DIL
GRANDMESNIL, Jean Baptiste
    Fauchard de, 1737-1816,
    French; plays DIL
GRANDMONT, Eloi de, 1921- ,
    Canadian; poetry SY
GRANDMONTAGNE, Francisco,
    1866-1936, Spanish; essays,
    poetry BL COL SA ST
GRANDPRE, François Joseph
    Darut, 1726-92, French; non-
    fiction DIL
GRANDSEN, Karl Watts, 1925- ,
    British; poetry, criticism
    MUR
GRANDVAL, Charles Francois
    Racot de, 1710-84, French;
    plays DIL
GRANDVAL, Nicolas Racot de,
    1676-1753, French; plays DIL
GRANDVOINET de VERRIERE,
    -1745, French; translations
    DIL
GRANGE, Cyril ('Onlooker';
    'Quill'), 1900- , English;
    nonfiction CON
GRANELL, Manuel ('Manuel
    Cristóbal'), 1906- , Spanish;
    nonfiction BL SA
GRANET, François, 1692-1741,
    French; nonfiction DIL

GRANET, Jean Joseph, 1685-1759,
French; nonfiction DIL

GRANGE, John, fl. 1577- , English;
poetry ST

GRANGER, Bruce Ingham, 1920- ,
American; nonfiction CON

GRANGER, Clive William John,
1934- , Welsh; nonfiction CON

GRANGER, James, 1723-76, English;
nonfiction BRO ST

GRANICH, Irving see 'GOLD, Michael'

GRANICK, David, 1926- , American;
nonfiction CON

GRANITE, Harvey R., 1927- , American; nonfiction CON

'GRANITE, Tony' see POLITELLA,
Dario

GRANJEL, Luis S., 1920- ,
Spanish; nonfiction SA

GRANOVSKI, Timofey Nikolayevich,
1813-55, Russian; nonfiction
HARK ST

GRANOWSKY, Alvin, 1936- , American; fiction CON

GRANSON, Oton de, 1345?-97, French;
poetry ST

'GRANT, Allen' see WILSON, James
G.

GRANT, Anne ('of Laggan'), 1755-
1838, Scots; poetry, essays,
nonfiction BRO KBA SA

GRANT, Bruce, 1893- , American;
juveniles CON WA

'GRANT, Don' see GLUT, Donald F.

GRANT, Dorothy Fremont, 1900- ,
American; fiction CON HOE WAF

GRANT, Frederik Clifton, 1891- ,
American; nonfiction CON

GRANT, Hilda Kay ('Jan Hilliard'),
Canadian; fiction CON

GRANT, James, 1822-87, Scots;
fiction BRO KBA

GRANT, James Augustus, 1827-92,
Scots; nonfiction BRO

GRANT, Jane Cole, 1895-1972,
American; nonfiction CON

'GRANT, Joan' see KELSEY, Joan M.

GRANT, Joan, 1907- , English;
fiction RIC

GRANT, John Webster, 1919- , American; nonfiction CON

GRANT, Judith, 1929- , American;
nonfiction CON

GRANT, Madeleine Parker, 1895- ,
American; juveniles WA

GRANT, Mary Amelia, 1890- ,
American; nonfiction CON

GRANT, Michael, 1914- , English;

nonfiction CON

GRANT, Neil, 1938- , American;
juveniles CON

GRANT, Nigel Duncan Cameron,
1932- , Scots; nonfiction CON

GRANT, Ozro F., 1908- , American; nonfiction CON

GRANT, Richard Babson, 1925- ,
American; nonfiction CON

GRANT, Robert, 1852-1940,
American; fiction KT

GRANT, Ulysses Simpson, 1822-
85, American; nonfiction HOO

GRANT, Vernon Wesley, 1904- ,
American; nonfiction CON

GRANT, William Leonard, 1914- ,
American; nonfiction CON

GRANT DUFF, Sir Mountstuart
Elphinstone, 1829-1906, Scots;
essays BRO KBA

GRANTHAM, Alexander William
George Herder, 1899- ,
English; nonfiction CON

GRANTHAM, Dewey Wesley, Jr.,
1921- , American; nonfiction
CON

'GRANTLAND, Keith' see BEAU-
MONT, Charles

GRANVILLE, George (Lord Lans-
downe), 1667-1734/35, English; poetry, plays ST

GRANVILLE, W. Wilfred, 1905- ,
English; nonfiction CON

GRANVILLE-BARKER, Harley,
1877-1946, English; plays,
essays, criticism BRO KL
KT MAG MAT RIC SA ST

'GRAPHO' see OAKLEY, Eric G.

GRAPPIN, Herménegilde Pierre
Philippe, 1738- , French;
nonfiction DIL

GRAS, Félix, 1844-1901, French;
poetry, fiction COL SA

GRASLIN, Jean Joseph Louis,
1727-90, French; nonfiction
DIL

GRASS, Günter, 1927- , German;
poetry, plays, fiction AL
CON FLE HAR KU KUN MAT
RIC

GRASSET, François, 18th cent.,
French; translations DIL

GRATIEN, Jean Baptiste Guillaume,
1747-99, French; nonfiction DIL

GRATRY, Auguste Alphonse, 1805-
72, French; nonfiction DIF SA

GRATTAN, Clinton Hartley, 1902- ,
American; criticism CON KT

GRATTAN, Henry, 1746-1820, Irish;
nonfiction ST
GRATTAN, Thomas Colley, 1792-1864,
Irish; fiction, nonfiction BRO
KBA ST
GRATTIUS, fl. 8 A.D., Roman;
poetry ST
GRAU, Shirley Ann, 1929- , Ameri-
can; fiction CON
GRAU DELGADO, Jacinto, 1877-
1958, Spanish; plays BL COL
FLE MAT SA ST
GRAUBARD, Mark A., 1904- ,
American; nonfiction CON
GRAUMAN, Lawrence, Jr., 1935- ,
American; nonfiction CON
GRAVE, Jean Hyacinthe, 18th
cent., French; plays, poetry
DIL
GRAVE, Juan José, 1872-1934,
Portuguese; nonfiction SA
GRAVE, Selwyn Alfred, 1916- ,
New Zealander; nonfiction CON
GRAVELOT, Hubert François Bourguig-
non, 1689-1773, French; nonfiction
DIL
GRAVER, Lawrence, 1931- , Ameri-
can; nonfiction CON
GRAVERELLE, 18th cent., French;
nonfiction DIL
GRAVEROL, Jean, 1647-1718/30,
French; nonfiction DIL
GRAVES, Alfred Percival, 1846-1931,
Irish; poetry BRO KBA ST
GRAVES, Allen Willis, 1915- ,
American; nonfiction CON
GRAVES, Charles Parlin ('John Parlin'),
1911-72, American; nonfiction,
juveniles CON WA
GRAVES, Clotilde see 'DEHAN, Richard'
GRAVES, John Alexander, 1920- ,
American; fiction CON
GRAVES, Leon Bernúl, 1946- ,
American; nonfiction CON
GRAVES, Richard, 1715-1804,
English; fiction, poetry KB
GRAVES, Robert Ranke, 1895- ,
English; poetry, fiction, essays,
translations BRO CON FLE KL
KT MAG MUR RIC SA SP ST WA
GRAVES, Wallace, 1922- , Ameri-
can; nonfiction CON
GRAVES, William Brooke, 1899- ,
American; nonfiction CON
GRAVES, William Whites, 1871- ,
American; nonfiction HOE
GRAVESON, Igance Hyacinthe Amat
de, 1670-1733, French; nonfic-

tion DIL
GRAVIER, 18th cent., French;
nonfiction DIL
GRAVIER, Laurent, 1654-1717,
French; nonfiction DIL
GRAVIERE de RAULOY, Antoine
Gabriel, 18th cent., French;
nonfiction DIL
GRAVILLE, Barthélemy Claude
Graillard de, 1727-64, French;
journalism DIL
GRAVINA, Gian Vincenzo, 1664-
1718, Italian; criticism,
poetry, plays HAR ST
GRAVLUND, Thorkild Thastum,
1879-1939, Danish; fiction ST
GRAVOIS, Jean, 1650-1733,
French; nonfiction DIL
GRAY, Alexander, 1882-1968,
Scots; nonfiction, poetry CON
ST
GRAY, Alfred Orren, 1914- ,
American; nonfiction CON
GRAY, Alice, American; juveniles
WA
GRAY, Asa, 1810-88, American;
nonfiction KAA
GRAY, Basil, 1904- , English;
nonfiction CON
GRAY, Charles Augustus, 1938- ,
American; nonfiction CON
GRAY, Clifford F., 1930- ,
American; nonfiction CON
GRAY, David, 1838-61, Scots;
poetry BRO KBA
GRAY, David, 1870- , American;
nonfiction HIG
GRAY, Dulcie, English; plays,
fiction CON
GRAY, Dwight Elder, 1903- ,
American; nonfiction CON
GRAY, Elizabeth Janet (Vining),
1902- , American; juveniles,
fiction, nonfiction CON JO
KJU WA
GRAY, Floyd Francis, 1926- ,
American; nonfiction CON
GRAY, Genevieve Stuck (Jenny),
1920- , American; nonfiction
CON
GRAY, George Hugh ('Tony Gray'),
1922- , Irish; fiction CON
GRAY, Gibson, 1922- , American;
nonfiction CON
GRAY, Giles Wilkeson, 1889- ,
American; nonfiction CON
GRAY, James, 1899- , American;
fiction, criticism CON KT
WAF

GRAY, James Robert, 1921- ,
American; nonfiction CON
'GRAY, Jane' see EVANS, Constance
M.
GRAY, Jenny see GRAY, Genevieve
S.
GRAY, Jesse Glenn, 1913- , Ameri-
can; nonfiction CON
GRAY, John, 1913- , Scots; nonfiction
CON
GRAY, John Richard, 1929- , Ameri-
can; nonfiction CON
GRAY, John Stanley, 1894- , Ameri-
can; nonfiction CON
GRAY, John Wylie, 1935- , Ameri-
can; nonfiction CON
GRAY, Mary Agatha, 1868- , Ameri-
can; fiction, juveniles HOE
GRAY, Nicholas Stuart, 1922- ,
Scots; plays, fiction CON
GRAY, Oscar Shalom, 1926- , Amer-
ican; nonfiction CON
GRAY, Patricia Clark ('Virginia Clark'),
American; juveniles WA CON
GRAY, Ralph Dale, 1933- , American;
nonfiction CON
GRAY, Richard Butler, 1922- , Amer-
ican; nonfiction CON
GRAY, Robert Fred, 1912- , Ameri-
can; nonfiction CON
GRAY, Robert Keith, 1923- , Ameri-
can; nonfiction CON
GRAY, Robert Mack, 1922- , Ameri-
can; nonfiction CON
GRAY, Ronald Douglas, 1919- ,
English; nonfiction CON
GRAY, Ronald Francis, 1918- ,
American; nonfiction CON
GRAY, Simon ('James Holliday';
'Hamish Reade'), 1936- , Eng-
lish; plays, fiction CON
GRAY, Thomas, 1716-71, English;
poetry BRO KB MAG SA SP ST
'GRAY, Tony' see GRAY, George H.
'GRAY, Walter' see MATTHAEI,
Clara
GRAY, Wellington B., 1919- ,
American; nonfiction CON
GRAY, William Bittles, 1891- ,
American; nonfiction CON
GRAY of HETON, Sir Thomas ('Grey'),
-1369?, English; nonfiction
ST
GRAYBEAL, David McConnell, 1921- ,
American; nonfiction CON
GRAYBILL, Ronald D., 1944- ,
American; nonfiction CON
GRAYLAND, Eugene Charles, New

Zealander; nonfiction CON
GRAYLAND, Valerie Merle Span-
ner, New Zealander; fiction,
juveniles CON
GRAYSON, Cecil, 1920- , Eng-
lish; nonfiction CON
GRAYSON, Cary Travers, Jr.,
1919- , American; nonfiction
CON
'GRAYSON, David' see BAKER,
Ray S.
GRAYSON, Marion Forbourg,
1906- , American; juveniles
CON WA
GRAYSON, Robert A., 1927- ,
American; nonfiction CON
GRAYZEL, Solomon, 1896- ,
American; nonfiction CON
GRAZZINI, Anto Francesco ('Il
Lasca'), 1503-84, Italian;
plays, fiction SA ST
GRCIC, Jovan Milenko, 1846-75,
Serbian; poetry, translations
ST
GREAN, Stanley, 1920- , Amer-
ican; nonfiction CON
'GREAT COMTE, The' see
HAWKESWORTH, Eric
'GREAT MERLIN' see RAWSON,
Clayton
GREATOREX, Elizabeth R. see
RIDDELL, Elizabeth R.
GREAVES, Harold Richard Goring,
1907- , American; nonfiction
CON
GREAVES, Margaret, 1914- ,
English; nonfiction CON
GREAVES, Ralph C. J., 1889- ,
English; nonfiction HIG
GREAVES, Richard Lee, 1938- ,
American; nonfiction CON
GREBAN, Arnoul, 1420-71?,
French; plays DIF HAR ST
GREBAN, Simon, -1473, French;
plays, poetry ST
GREHANIER, Bernard, 1903- ,
American; nonfiction CON
GREBE, Maria Ester, 1928- ,
Chilean; nonfiction CON
GREBENSHCHIKOV, Grigory Dmit-
rievich, 1882- , Russian; fic-
tion ST
GREBSTEIN, Lawrence Charles,
1937- , American; nonfiction
CON
GREBSTEIN, Sheldon Norman,
1928- , American; nonfiction
CON

GRECA, Alcides, 1889- , Argentinian; fiction, essays MIN

GRECH, Nikolay Ivanovich, 1787-1867, Russian; journalism, nonfiction HARK ST

'GRECO, Margaret' see FRY, Barbara

GRECOURT, Jean Baptiste Joseph Willart, 1683-1743, French; nonfiction DIL

GREELEY, Andrew Moran, 1928- , American; nonfiction CON

GREELEY, Horace, 1811-72, American; journalism BRO KAA ST

'GREEN, A. S. ' see GRINEVSKI, Alexander S.

'GREEN, Adam' see WEISGARD, Leonard

GREEN, Adwin Wigfall, 1900- , American; nonfiction CON

GREEN, Rev. Andrew, 1865-1950, American; poetry HO

GREEN, Anna Katharine, 1846-1935, American; fiction KL KT

GREEN, Anne, 1891- , American; fiction WAF

GREEN, Anne, 1899- , American; fiction HO KL KT

GREEN, Anne M. , 1922- , American; fiction CON

GREEN, Arnold Wilfred, 1914- , American; nonfiction CON

GREEN, Arthur Samuel, 1927- , American; nonfiction CON

GREEN, Asa, 1789-1839, American; fiction KAA

GREEN, Bernard, 1927- , English; nonfiction CON

'GREEN, Bryan' see DAVIS, Horace B.

GREEN, Bryan Stuart Westmacott, 1901- , English; nonfiction CON

GREEN, Charlotte Hilton, 1889- , American; nonfiction JO

GREEN, Constance McLaughlin, 1897- , American; nonfiction CON

'GREEN, D. ' see CASEWITT, Curtis

GREEN, David Bronte, 1910- , English; juveniles CON

GREEN, David E. , 1942- , American; nonfiction CON

GREEN, Donald Ross, 1924- , American; nonfiction CON

GREEN, Dorothy see AUCHTERLONIE, Dorothy

GREEN, Edmund Fisk see FISKE, John

GREEN, Edward, 1920- , American; nonfiction CON

GREEN, Eleanor, 1911- , American; fiction WAF

GREEN, Elizabeth Adine Herkimer, 1906- , American; nonfiction CON

GREEN, Fletcher Melvin, 1895- , American; nonfiction CON

GREEN, Frances Harriet Whipple, 1805-78, American; nonfiction KAA

GREEN, Frederick Lawrence, 1902-53, British; fiction KTS

GREEN, Frederick Pratt, 1903- , British; poetry MUR

GREEN, George, 1793-1841, English; nonfiction KBA

GREEN, Gerald, 1922- , American; fiction CON

GREEN, Harold Paul, 1922- , American; nonfiction CON

'GREEN, Henry' (Henry Vincent Yorke), 1905- , English; fiction BRO FLE MAG RIC KTS ST

GREEN, James Leroy, 1919- , American; nonfiction CON

GREEN, John Alden, 1925- , Canadian; nonfiction CON

GREEN, John Richard, 1837-83, English; nonfiction BRO KBA ST

GREEN, Joseph, 1706-80, American; poetry KAA

GREEN, Joseph, 1931- , American; nonfiction, fiction CON

GREEN, Joseph Franklin, Jr. , 1924- , American; nonfiction CON

'GREEN, Judith' see GALBRAITH, Jean

GREEN, Julien Hartridge (Julian), ('Theophile Delaporte'; 'David Irland'), 1900- , American-French; fiction, plays BRO COL DIC DIF FLE HAR HO KL KT CON MAG MAT MAL RIC SA ST

GREEN, Leslie Claude, 1920- , English; nonfiction CON

GREEN, Margaret Murphy, 1926- , American; nonfiction CON WA

GREEN, Martin, 1927- , English; nonfiction CON

GREEN, Mary Ann Everett Wood, 1818-95, English; nonfiction KBA

GREEN, Mary McBurney, 1896- ,

American; juveniles CON WA
GREEN, Mary Moore, 1906- ,
American; nonfiction CON
GREEN, Matthew, 1696-1737, English;
poetry BRO KB ST
GREEN, Maurice Richard, 1922- ,
American; nonfiction CON
GREEN, Maury, 1916- , American;
nonfiction CON
GREEN, Nathanael, 1935- , Ameri-
can; nonfiction CON
'GREEN, O.O.' see DURGNAT, Ray-
mond E.
GREEN, Otis Howard, 1898- , Amer-
ican; nonfiction BL CON
GREEN, Paul Eliot, 1894- , Ameri-
can; plays, fiction, movies CON
FLE JO KL KT MAT SA
GREEN, Peter Morris ('Denis
Delaney'; 'Artifax'), 1924- ,
English; translations, nonfiction
CON
GREEN, Reginald Herbold, 1935- ,
American; nonfiction CON
GREEN, Roger Lancelyn, 1918- ,
English; poetry, fiction, plays
CON COM DOY WA
GREEN, Rosalie Beth, 1917- ,
American; nonfiction CON
'GREEN, Sheila Ellen' (Sheila Green-
wald), 1934- , American; fiction
CON
GREEN, Stanley, 1923- , American;
nonfiction CON
GREEN, Thomas Hill, 1836-82, Eng-
lish; nonfiction BRO KBA ST
GREEN, Vivian Hubert Howard, 1915- ,
English; nonfiction CON
GREEN, William Henry, 1825-1900,
American; nonfiction KAA
GREENACRE, Phyllis, 1894- , Amer-
ican; nonfiction CON
GREENAWALT, Robert Kent, 1936- ,
American; nonfiction CON
GREENAWAY, Kate, 1846-1901, Eng-
lish; juveniles DOY KJU WA
GREENBAUM, Fred, 1930- , Ameri-
can; nonfiction CON
GREENBAUM, Leonard, 1930- ,
American; nonfiction CON
GREENBAUM, Sidney, 1929- , Eng-
lish; nonfiction CON
GREENBERG, Alvin David, 1932- ,
American; nonfiction CON
GREENBERG, Clement, 1909- ,
American; criticism CON KTS
GREENBERG, Daniel A., 1934- ,
American; nonfiction CON

GREENBERG, Daniel S., 1931- ,
American; nonfiction CON
GREENBERG, Harvey R.,
1935- , American; nonfiction
CON
GREENBERG, Herbert, 1935- ,
American; nonfiction CON
GREENBERG, Joanne Goldenberg,
1932- , American; nonfiction,
fiction CON
GREENBERG, Milton, 1927- ,
American; nonfiction CON
GREENBERG, Morris S., 1924- ,
Polish-American; nonfiction
CON
GREENBERG, Moshe, 1928- ,
American; nonfiction CON
GREENBERG, Robert Arthur,
1930- , American; nonfiction
CON
GREENBERG, Selma, 1930- ,
American; nonfiction CON
GREENBERG, Sidney, 1917- ,
American; nonfiction CON
GREENBLATT, Manuel Harry,
1922- , American; nonfiction
CON
GREENBLATT, Robert Benjamin,
1906- , Canadian; nonfiction
CON
GREENBLUM, Joseph, 1925- ,
American; nonfiction CON
GREENBURG, Dan, 1936- ,
American; fiction CON
'GREENE, Adam' see SCOTT,
Peter D.
GREENE, Albert Gorton, 1802-68,
American; poetry BRO KAA
GREENE, Alvin Carl ('Arthur C.
Randolph'; 'Mateman Weaver'),
1923- , American; nonfiction
CON
GREENE, Anne Bosworth, 1878- ,
Anglo-American; juveniles,
nonfiction KT
GREENE, Carla, 1916- , Ameri-
can; juveniles COM CON WA
GREENE, David H., 1913- ,
American; nonfiction CON
GREENE, Donald Johnson, 1916- ,
Canadian-American; nonfiction
CON
GREENE, Edward Lee, 1843-1915,
American; nonfiction KAA
GREENE, Felix, 1909- , English;
nonfiction CON
GREENE, Francis Vinton, 1850-
1921, American; nonfiction
KAA

GREENE, Gael, American; nonfiction
CON
GREENE, George Washington, 1811-
83, American; nonfiction KAA
GREENE, Graham, 1904- , English;
juveniles, plays, essays, poetry
BRO CON DOY FLE KL KT MAG
MAT HOE RIC SA ST
GREENE, Harris, 1921- , Ameri-
can; fiction CON
GREENE, Harry A., 1889- , Ameri-
can; nonfiction CON
GREENE, Herbert, 1898- , English;
fiction CON
GREENE, Jack Phillip, 1931- ,
American; nonfiction CON
GREENE, James H., 1915- , Ameri-
can; nonfiction CON
GREENE, Janet Churchill, 1917- ,
American; nonfiction CON
GREENE, Jay E., 1914- , American;
nonfiction CON
GREENE, Jonathan Edward, 1943- ,
American; poetry CON MUR
GREENE, Josiah E., 1911- , Ameri-
can; fiction WAF
GREENE, Lee Seifert, 1905- , Ameri-
can; nonfiction CON
GREENE, Mark R., 1923- , American;
nonfiction CON
GREENE, Maxine, 1917- , American;
nonfiction CON
GREENE, Reynolds William, Jr.,
1924- , American; nonfiction
CON
GREENE, Richard Leighton, 1904- ,
American; nonfiction CON
'GREENE, Robert' see DEINDORFER,
Robert G.
GREENE, Robert, 1558-92, English;
plays, fiction BRO KB MAG SA
SP ST
GREENE, Shirley Edward, 1911- ,
American; nonfiction CON
GREENE, Thomas McLernon, 1926- ,
American; nonfiction CON
GREENE, Victor Robert, 1933- ,
American; nonfiction CON
GREENE, Walter E., 1929- , Ameri-
can; nonfiction CON
GREENE, Ward, 1892-1956, American;
fiction KT WAF
GREENE, Wilda, 1911- , American;
nonfiction CON
GREENE, William C., 1933- , Amer-
ican; nonfiction CON
GREENER, Leslie, 1900- , South
African; nonfiction CON

GREENER, Michael John, 1931- ,
American; nonfiction CON
GREENEWALT, Crawford Hallock,
1902- , American; nonfiction
CON
GREENFIELD, Irving A., 1928- ,
American; nonfiction CON
GREENFIELD, Jeff, 1943- ,
American; nonfiction CON
GREENFIELD, Jerome, 1923- ,
American; fiction CON
GREENFIELD, Patricia Marks,
1940- , American; nonfiction
CON
GREENFIELD, Sidney Martin,
1932- , American; nonfiction
CON
GREENFIELD, Stanley B.,
1922- , American; nonfiction
CON
GREENFIELD, Thelma N., 1922- ,
American; nonfiction CON
GREENHAW, Harold Wayne,
1940- , American; fiction
CON
GREENHILL, Basil Jack, 1920- ,
English; nonfiction CON
GREENHOOD, Clarence David
('Mark Sawyer'), 1895- ,
American; poetry, nonfiction
CON
GREENHOW, Robert, 1800-54,
American; nonfiction KAA
GREENHUT, Melvin L., 1921- ,
American; nonfiction CON
GREENLAW, Paul Stephen, 1930- ,
American; nonfiction CON
GREENLEAF, Barbara Kaye,
1942- , American; nonfiction
CON
GREENLEAF, Moses, 1777-1834,
American; nonfiction KAA
GREENLEAF, Richard Edward,
1930- , American; nonfiction
CON
GREENLEAF, William, 1917- ,
American; nonfiction CON
GREENLEE, Jacob Harold, 1918- ,
American; nonfiction CON
GREENOUGH, Horatio, 1805-52,
American; nonfiction KAA
GREENOUGH, William Croan,
1914- , American; nonfiction
CON
GREEN-PRICE, Sir Richard Dansey
('Borderer'), 1872-1909, Eng-
lish; nonfiction HIG
GREENSPAN, Charlotte L.,

1921- , American; nonfiction CON
GREENSPUN, Herman Milton (Hank),
1909- , American; nonfiction CON
GREENSTOCK, David Lionel, 1912- ,
Irish; nonfiction CON
GREENSTONE, J. David, 1937- ,
American; nonfiction CON
GREENWALD, Harold, 1910- ,
American; nonfiction CON
GREENWALD, Sheila see 'GREEN,
Sheila E.'
GREEN-WANSTALL, Kenneth (Ken
Wanstall), 1918- , English,
fiction CON
'GREENWAY, Granfather' see CANNON,
Charles J.
GREENWAY, John, 1919- , Ameri-
can; nonfiction CON
GREENWOOD, Duncan, 1919- ,
English; plays CON
GREENWOOD, Edward Alister (Ted),
1930- , American; juveniles
CON
GREENWOOD, Frank, 1924- ,
American; nonfiction CON
GREENWOOD, Gordon, 1913- ,
Australian; nonfiction CON
GREENWOOD, Gordon Edward,
1935- , American; nonfiction
CON
'GREENWOOD, Grace' see LIPPIN-
COTT, Sara J.C.
GREENWOOD, Julia Eileen Courtenay
('Francis Askham'), 1910- ,
English; fiction CON
GREENWOOD, Marianne Hederstrom,
1926- , Swedish; nonfiction
CON
GREENWOOD, Theresa, 1936- ,
American; nonfiction CON
GREENWOOD, Walter, 1903- ,
English; fiction, plays BRO KT
RIC
GREER, Carlotta C., 1879- ,
American; nonfiction CON
GREER, Herb, 1929- , American;
fiction CON
GREER, Louise, 1899- , American;
nonfiction CON
GREER, Thomas Hoag, 1914- ,
American; nonfiction CON
GREET, Kenneth Gerald, 1918- ,
English; nonfiction CON
GREET, Thomas Young, 1923- ,
American; nonfiction CON
GREEVER, William St. Clair, 1916- ,
American; nonfiction CON PAC
GREFFEUILLE, Charles De, 1668-

1743, French; nonfiction DIL
GREFFLINGER, Georg, 1620-77,
German; poetry ST
GREG, William Rathbone, 1809-
81, English; fiction BRO
KBA ST
GREGG, Andrew K. ('Tom Vine-
gar'), 1929- , American;
fiction, nonfiction CON
GREGG, Davis Weinert, 1918- ,
American; nonfiction CON
GREGG, James Erwin, 1927- ,
American; nonfiction CON
GREGG, James R., 1914- ,
American; nonfiction CON
GREGG, Josiah, 1806-50, Ameri-
can; nonfiction KAA
'GREGG, Martin' see McNEILLY,
Wilfred G.
GREGG, Pauline, English; nonfic-
tion CON
GREGG, Richard Alexander,
1927- , American; nonfiction
CON
GREGH, Fernand, 1873-1960,
French; poetry DIF
GREGOIRE, Gaspard, French;
nonfiction DIL
GREGOIRE de LYON, 18th cent.,
French; nonfiction DIL
GREGOIRE de ROSTRENEN, 18th
cent., French; nonfiction
DIL
GREGOIRE de TOURS, 528-94,
French; nonfiction DIF
GREGOR, Arthur, 1923- , Amer-
ican; poetry, juveniles, plays
CON MUR
GREGOR, Howard Frank, 1920- ,
American; nonfiction CON
GREGOR, Rex H., 1922- ,
American; nonfiction CON
GREGORAS, Nicephorus, 1295-
1360, Byzantine; nonfiction
KE SA ST
GREGORCIC, Simon, 1844-1906,
Slovene; poetry ST
GREGOR-DELLIN, Martin,
1926- , German; nonfiction
KU
GREGORIA, Francisca de Santa
Teresa, 1653-1736, Spanish;
nonfiction SA
GREGORIAN, Vartan ('V. Herian'),
1935- , Iranian-American;
nonfiction CON
GREGORIVIUS, Ferdinand Adolf,
1821-91, German; fiction,

translations, poetry, plays KE ST
GREGOR-TAJOVSKY, Josef, 1874-1940,
Slovak; fiction, plays ST
GREGORY, Saint, -270, Roman; non-
fiction SA
'GREGORY, Elizabeth' see GILFORD,
Charles B.
'GREGORY, Harry' see GOTTFRIED,
Theodore M.
'GREGORY, Hilton' see FERGUSON,
Charles W.
GREGORY, Horace Victor, 1898- ,
American; poetry, criticism CON
KAT KT MUR SA
GREGORY, Isabella Augusta Persu,
1852-1932, Irish; plays KAT KT
MAG MAT RIC ST
GREGORY, Jackson, 1882- , Ameri-
can; fiction KT
GREGORY, Langlon Richard, 1923- ,
English; nonfiction CON
GREGORY, Padraic, 1886- , Irish;
poetry, plays HOE ST
GREGORY, Robert Lloyd, 1892- ,
American; nonfiction CON
GREGORY, Ross, 1933- , American;
nonfiction CON
GREGORY, Roy, 1935- , English;
nonfiction CON
'GREGORY, Sean' see HOSSENT,
Harry
GREGORY, Stephen see PENDLETON,
Donald E.
GREGORY, Theophilus Stephen, 1897- ,
English; nonfiction HOE
GREGORY I, the GREAT, 540-604,
Italian; nonfiction SA ST
GREGORY ACINDYNUS, 14th cent.,
Byzantine; nonfiction ST
GREGORY of NAZIANZUS, 329-90,
Greek; nonfiction SA ST
GREGORY of NYSSA, 331-95/97,
Greek; nonfiction SA ST
GREGORY of TOURS, 538-94, Gallo-
Roman; nonfiction SA ST
GREGORY PALAMAS, 14th cent.,
Byzantine; nonfiction ST
'GREGSON, Paul' see OAKLEY, Eric
G.
'GREGUERIA' see GOMEZ de la
SERNA, Ramón
GREIF see GRYPHIUS, Andreas
GREIF, Edwin Charles, 1915- ,
American; nonfiction CON
'GREIF, Martin' (Friedrich Hermann
Frey), 1839-1911, German;
poetry, plays AL HAR ST
GREIFF, León de (Bogislao), 1895- ,

Colombian; nonfiction, poetry
MIN SA
GREK, Maxim see MAXIM GREK
GRENAN, Bénigne, 1681-1723,
French; nonfiction DIL
GRENAN, Pierre, 1660-1722,
French; poetry DIL
GRENDHAL, Jay Spencer, 1943- ,
American; nonfiction CON
'GRENDON, Edward' see LE SHAN,
Lawrence L.
'GRENDON, Stephen' see DERLETH,
August W.
GRENE, Marjorie Glicksman,
1910- , American; nonfiction
CON
'GRENELLE, Lisa' see MUNROE,
Elizabeth L.
GRENET, 18th cent., French; non-
fiction DIL
GRENFELL, Julian, 1888-1915,
English; poetry KT
GRENFELL, Sir Wilfred Thomason,
1865-1940, English; nonfiction
fiction BRO KT
GRENIER, 18th cent., French;
plays DIL
GRENIER, Jacques Raymond,
1736-1803, French; nonfiction
DIL
GRENIER, Jean, 1898- , French;
nonfiction DIF
GRENIER, Mildred, 1917- ,
American; nonfiction, juvenile
CON
GRENIER, Pierre Nicolas, 1725-
89, French; nonfiction DIL
GRENNAN, Margaret Rose, Amer-
ican; nonfiction HOE
GRENVILLE, John A.S., 1928- ,
American; nonfiction CON
GREPPO, Jean Baptiste, 1712-67,
French; nonfiction DIL
GRESBAN, Arnold (Greban), 15th
cent., French; poetry SA
GRESBAN, Simon (Greban), 15th
cent., French; poetry SA
GRESHAM, Claude Hamilton, Jr.
('Grits Gresham'), 1922- ,
American; nonfiction CON
GRESHAM, William Lindsay,
1909- , American; fiction
KTS
GRESLAN Pierre, 1702-68,
French; nonfiction DIL
GRESNICK, Antoine Frédéric,
1752-99, French; plays DIL
GRESSER, Seymour (Sy), 1926- ,

American; poetry CON

GRESSET, Jean Baptiste Louis, 1709-77, French; poetry DIF DIL SA ST

GRESSLEY, Gene Maurice, 1931- , American; nonfiction CON

GRETSER, Jakob, 1562-1625, German; plays ST

GRETZ, Susanna, 1937- , American; juveniles CON

GREULICH, Emil Rudolf ('Erge'), 1909- , German; nonfiction AL

GREVENIUS, Herbert, 1901- , Swedish; plays MAT

GREVILLE, Charles Cavendish Fulke, 1794-1865, English; diary BRO KBA SP ST

GREVILLE, Fulke see BROOKE, Fulke G.

GREVILLE, Henry ('Alice Durand'), 1842-1902, French; fiction HAR

GREVIN, Jacques, 1538-70, French; poetry, plays DIF SA ST

GREW, Raymond, 1930- , American; nonfiction CON

GREWER, Eira Mary, 1931- , English; nonfiction CON

GREY, Anthony, 1938- , English; nonfiction, fiction CON

GREY, Sir Edward see GREY of FALLODON, E. G.

'GREY, Elizabeth' see HOGG, Beth T.

GREY, Sir George, 1812-98, New Zealander; nonfiction ST

GREY, Ian, 1918- , New Zealander; nonfiction CON

GREY, Jane, 1537-54, English; nonfiction SA

GREY, Vivian Hoffman, American; juveniles CON

GREY, Zane, 1872-1939, American; fiction BRO KT RIC SA ST

GREY of FALLODON, Edward, 1862-1933, English; nonfiction BRO KT

'GREY OWL' (Archie Belaney), 1885- , English; juvenile DOY

'GREY OWL' see BELANEY, George S.

GREYSER, Stephen A., 1935- , American; nonfiction CON

GREZ, Vicente, 1847-1909, Chilean; journalism, poetry MIN

GRIBBIN, Lenore S. ('Petunia Worble-fister'), 1922- , American; fiction CON

GRIBBLE, James, 1938- , American;

nonfiction CON

GRIBBONS, Warren David, 1921- , American; nonfiction CON

GRIBEAUVAL, Jean Baptiste Vaquette, 1713-89, French; nonfiction DIL

GRIBOYEDOV, Alexander Sergeyevich, 1795-1829, Russian; plays HAR HARK SA ST

GRICE, Frederick, 1910- , English; nonfiction CON

GRIEB, Kenneth J., 1939- , American; nonfiction CON

GRIECHEN-MÜLLER see MÜLLER, Wilhelm

GRIECK, Claude de, 1625-70, English; plays ST

GRIEG, Johan Nordahl Bruun, 1902-43, Norwegian; fiction, plays COL FLE HAR MAT RIC SA ST

GRIEG, Michael, 1922- , American; nonfiction CON

GRIEN, Raúl, 1924- , Spanish; journalism BL SA

GRIER, B. R., 1913- , Welsh; nonfiction CON

GRIER, Eldon, 1917- , Canadian; poetry MUR

GRIERSON, Constancia, 1706-33, Irish; poetry SA

GRIERSON, Edward, 1914- , English; fiction CON

GRIERSON, Elizabeth W., Scots; juveniles KJU

GRIERSON, Francis (Benjamin H. J. F. Shepard), 1848-1929, American; essays KT

GRIERSON, Sir Herbert John Clifford, 1866-1960, Scots; nonfiction BRO KT ST

GRIERSON, John, 1909- , English; nonfiction CON

GRIERSON, Monica Linden, 1914- , English; fiction CON

GRIESE, Freidrich, 1890- , German; fiction AL COL KU MAT SA

GRIETHUYSEN, Sibille van, 1620-44, Dutch; poetry ST

GRIEVE, Andrew W., 1925- , American; nonfiction CON

GRIEVE, Christopher Murray ('Hugh MacDiarmid'; 'Isobel Guthrie'; 'A. K. Laidlaw'; 'James MacLaren'; 'Pteleon'), 1892- , Scots; poetry, criti-

cism BRO CON FLE KT MUR
RIC SP ST

GRIFALCONI, Ann, 1929- , American; juveniles COM CON

'GRIFF' see FAWCETT, Frank D.

'GRIFF' see McKEAG, Ernest L.

GRIFFEN, Gerald, 1803-40, Irish;
poetry, fiction ST

GRIFFEN, Glen C., 1934- , Franco-
American; nonfiction CON

GRIFFEN, James Jeffers, 1923- ,
American; fiction CON

GRIFFET, Henri, 1698-1771, French;
nonfiction DIL

GRIFFET de la BEAUME, Antoine
Gilbert, 1756-1805, French;
translations, plays DIL

GRIFFIN, Al, 1919- , American;
nonfiction CON

GRIFFIN, Arthur Harold, 1911- ,
English; nonfiction CON

GRIFFIN, Bartholomew, -1602,
English; poetry BRO KB

'GRIFFIN, C.F.' see FIKSO, Eunice
C.

GRIFFIN, Charles Henry, 1922- ,
American; nonfiction CON

GRIFFIN, Donald Redfield, 1915- ,
American; nonfiction CON

GRIFFIN, Ella, American; juveniles
WA

GRIFFIN, Ernest George, 1916- ,
English; nonfiction CON

GRIFFIN, Gerald, 1803-40, Irish;
fiction, plays, poetry BRO
KBA MAG

GRIFFIN, Gillett Good, 1928- ,
American; juveniles WA

GRIFFIN, Jacqueline P., 1927- ,
American; nonfiction CON

GRIFFIN, James A., 1934- ,
American; nonfiction CON

GRIFFIN, John Howard, 1920- ,
American; fiction, journalism
CON

GRIFFIN, Mary Claire, 1924- ,
American; nonfiction CON

GRIFFIN, Stuart, 1917- , American;
nonfiction CON

GRIFFIN, Velma, American; juveniles
WA

GRIFFIN, William Lloyd, 1938- ,
American; poetry, fiction CON

GRIFFIS, William Elliott, 1843-
1928, American; nonfiction KAA

GRIFFITH, A. Kinney, 1897- ,
American; nonfiction CON

GRIFFITH, A. Leonard, 1920- ,

English; nonfiction CON

GRIFFITH, Albert Joseph, Jr.,
1932- , American; nonfiction
CON

GRIFFITH, Benjamin Woodward,
Jr., 1922- , American; nonfiction CON

GRIFFITH, Elisabeth, 1730?-93,
English; fiction SA

GRIFFITH, Ernest Stacey, 1896- ,
American; nonfiction CON

'GRIFFITH, Jeannette' see
EVEYERLY, Jeannette H.

GRIFFITH, Leon Odell, 1921- ,
American; fiction CON

GRIFFITH, Lucille Blanche,
1905- , American; nonfiction
CON

GRIFFITH, Paul, 1921- , American; nonfiction CON

GRIFFITH, Richard Edward, 1912- ,
American; nonfiction CON

GRIFFITH, T.A., 1821- , English;
nonfiction HIG

GRIFFITH, Thomas, 1915- ,
American; nonfiction CON

GRIFFITH, Will, 1889-1950,
American; journalism HOO

GRIFFITH, Winthrop, 1931- ,
American; nonfiction CON

GRIFFITHS, Alan Bede, 1906- ,
English; nonfiction CON

GRIFFITHS, Ann Thomas, 1776-
1805, Welsh; hymns ST

GRIFFITHS, Brynly David,
1933- , Welsh; poetry MUR

GRIFFITHS, Daniel Edward,
1917- , American; nonfiction
CON

GRIFFITHS, Gordon Douglas,
1910- , English; nonfiction
CON

GRIFFITHS, Helen, 1939- ,
English; juveniles CON

GRIFFITHS, Louise Benckenstein,
1907- , American; nonfiction
CON

GRIFFITHS, Michael Compton,
1928- , Welsh; nonfiction
CON

GRIFFITHS, Reginald, 1912- ,
South African; poetry, fiction
MUR

GRIFFITHS, Richard Mathias,
1935- , Welsh; nonfiction
CON

GRIFFITHS, Sally, 1934- , Welsh;
fiction CON

GRIFFY de JUVIGNAC, 18th cent.,
French; nonfiction DIL

GRIGG, Charles M., 1918- ,
American; nonfiction CON

GRIGGS, Charles Irwin, 1902- ,
American; nonfiction CON

GRIGNAN, Françoise Marguerite de
Sévigne, 1648-1705, French;
nonfiction SA

GRIGNION de MONTFORT, Louis
Marie, 1673-1716, French;
nonfiction DIL

GRIGNON, Claude Henri, 1894- ,
Canadian; fiction ST SY

GRIGORIEV, Apollon Alexandrovich,
1822-64, Russian; criticism,
poetry HARK KE ST

GRIGOROVICH, Dmitry Vasilyevich,
1822-99, Russian; fiction HAR
HARK ST

GRIGSBY, Hugh Blair, 1806-81,
American; nonfiction KAA

GRIGSON, Geoffrey Edward Harvey,
1905- , English; poetry, criticism BRO CON KTS MUR WA

GRILLET, Jean Louis, 1756-1812,
French; nonfiction DIL

GRILLO, Emilio, 1940- , American;
nonfiction SCA

GRILLO, Maximiliano, 1868-1949,
Colombian; nonfiction MIN

GRILLOT, Jean Joseph, 1708-65,
French; nonfiction DIL

GRILLPARZER, Franz, 1791-1872,
Austrian; plays, poetry AL BL
HAR KE MAG SA ST

GRILO, Antonio F. see FERNANDEZ
GRILO, Antonio

GRIMAL, Pierre Antoine, 1912- ,
French; nonfiction CON

GRIMALD, Nicholas (Grimsald;
Grimvald; Grimoald), 1519-62,
English; poetry BRO KB ST

GRIMALDI, John V., 1916- , American; nonfiction CON

GRIMALIUS LAURENTIUS see GOSLICKI,
Warwrzyniec G.

GRIMAULT, Berthe, 1940- , French;
fiction CON

GRIMBLE, Rev. Charles James see
ELIOT, Thomas S.

GRIMBLE, Ian, 1921- , American;
nonfiction CON

GRIMELLI see ASSING, Ludmila

GRIMES, Alan P., 1919- , American;
nonfiction CON

GRIMES, James Stanley, 1807-1903,
American; nonfiction KAA

GRIMES, Joseph Evans, 1928- ,
American; nonfiction CON

GRIMES, Lewis Howard, 1915- ,
American; nonfiction CON

GRIMLEY, Mildred Hess, 1919- ,
American; juveniles CON

GRIMM, August Heinrich, 1873- ,
German; fiction ST

GRIMM, Frederic Melchior von,
1723-1807, German-French;
criticism DIF DIL ST

GRIMM, Hans, 1875-1959, German;
fiction, essays AL COL KU
SA

GRIMM, Harold John, 1901- ,
American; nonfiction CON

GRIMM, Jacob Ludwig Karl, 1785-
1863, German; juveniles, nonfiction AL DOY HAR KE SA
ST WA

GRIMM, Wilhelm Karl, 1786-1859,
German; juveniles, nonfiction
AL DOY HAR KE SA ST
WA

GRIMME, Freidrich Wilhelm,
1827-87, German; fiction
ST

GRIMMELSHAUSEN, Hans Jakob
Christoffel von, 1622-76, Ger-
man; fiction AL KE MAG SA
ST

GRIMOALD, Nicholas see GRIMALD,
Nicholas

GRIMOARD, Philippe Henri, 1750-
1815, French; nonfiction DIL

GRIMOD de la REYNIERE,
Alexandre Balthasar Laurent,
1758-1838, French; nonfiction
DIF

GRIMSHAW, Beatrice Ethel, 1871-
1953, Irish; fiction BRO HOE

'GRIMSHAW, Mark' see McKEAG,
Ernest L.

'GRIMSLEY, Gordon' see GROOM,
Arthur W.

GRIMSLEY, Ronald, 1915- ,
English; nonfiction CON

GRIMSLEY, Will Henry, 1914- ,
American; nonfiction CON

GRIMSTED, David Allen, 1935- ,
American; nonfiction CON

GRIMVALD, Nicholas see
GRIMALD, Nicholas

'GRIN, A.' see GRINEVSKI, A. S.

GRINDEA, Miron, 1909- ,
Rumanian-English; nonfiction
CON

GRINDEL, Eugene see 'ELUARD,
Paul'

GRINDELL, Robert Maclean, 1933- ,
American; nonfiction CON
GRINDLEY, John Thomas Ellam,
1926- , American; fiction CON
GRINDROD, Muriel Kathleen, 1902- ,
English; nonfiction CON
'GRINEVICH' see YAKUBOVICH,
Pyotr F.
GRINEVSKI, Alexander Stepanovich
('A. Grin'; 'A. S. Green'), 1880-
1932, Russian; fiction HAR
HARK RIC ST
GRINGHUIS, Richard H., 1918- ,
American; juveniles CON WA
'GRINGO, Harry' see WISE, Henry A.
GRINGORE, Pierre, 1475-1538,
French; poetry, plays DIF ST
'GRINNEL, David' see WOLLHEIM,
Donald A.
GRINNELL, George Bird, 1849-1538,
American; juveniles KJU
GRINSELL, Leslie Valentine, 1907- ,
English; nonfiction CON
GRINSTEAD, Jesse Edward, 1866- ,
American; fiction SCA
GRINSTEIN, Alexander, 1918- ,
American; nonfiction CON
GRIPARI, Pierre, 1925- , French;
juveniles, plays CON
GRIPE, Maria Kristina, 1923- ,
Swedish; juveniles COM CON
GRIPENBERG, Bertel, 1878- ,
Finnish; poetry COL SA ST
GRIPT, Charles, 18th cent., French;
nonfiction DIL
GRISAR, Hartmann, 1845-1932, Ger-
man; nonfiction HOE
GRISEL, Joseph, 1703-87, French;
nonfiction DIL
GRISEWOOD, Harman Joseph Gerard,
1906- , English; nonfiction
CON
GRISEZ, Germain G., 1929- , Amer-
ican; nonfiction CON
GRISHAM, Noel, 1916- , American;
nonfiction CON
GRISOT, Jean Urbain (Grizot), 1710-
72, French; nonfiction DIL
GRISPINO, Joseph Aloysius, 1922- ,
American; nonfiction CON
GRISWOLD, Erwin Nathaniel, 1904- ,
American; nonfiction CON
GRISWOLD, Francis, 1902- , Amer-
ican; fiction KT
GRISWOLD, Frank Gray, 1854-1937,
American; nonfiction HIG
GRISWOLD, Rufus Wilmot ('Ludwig'),
1815-57, American; editor KAA
ST

GRISWOLD, Wesley Southmayd,
1909- , American; nonfiction
CON
GRISWOLD, William McCrillis,
1853-99, American; nonfiction
KAA
GRITSCH, Eric W., 1931- ,
American; nonfiction CON
GRIVAS, Theodore, 1922- ,
American; nonfiction CON
GRIVEL, Guillaume, 1735-1810,
French; nonfiction DIL
GRIZOT, Jean Urbain see GRISOT,
Jean U.
GROB, Gerald N., 1931- ,
American; nonfiction CON
GROB, Johann, 1643-97, Swiss;
poetry ST
GROCH, Judith Goldstein, 1929- ,
American; juveniles CON WA
'GRODE, Redway' see GOREY,
Edward St. J.
GROEN van PRINSTERER,
Guillaume, 1801-76, Dutch;
journalism ST
GRÖNDAL, Benedikt Sveinbjarnar-
son, 1826-1907, Icelandic;
poetry, fiction COL HAR KE
ST SA
GROENE, Janet, 1936- , Ameri-
can; nonfiction CON
GROENINGEN, August Pieter
Van ('Willem van Oevere'),
1865-94, Dutch; fiction ST
GROETHUYSEN, Bernard, 1887-
1946, French; essays, criticism
DIF
GROGGER, Paula, 1892- , Ger-
man; nonfiction LEN
GROHSKOPF, Bernice, 1921- ,
American; nonfiction CON
GROLLMAN, Earl A., 1925- ,
American; nonfiction CON
GROLLMES, Eugene E., 1931- ,
American; nonfiction CON
GRO-LUNG-PA Blo-Gros Byung-
Gnas, 11th cent., Tibetan;
nonfiction LAN
GROMAN, George L., 1928- ,
American; nonfiction CON
GRONBACH, Vilhelm Peter, 1873-
1948, Danish; criticism ST
GRONEMAN, Chris Harold,
1906- , American; nonfiction
CON
GRONOVIUS, Jakob, 1642-1716,
Dutch; nonfiction SA
GRONOVIUS, Johannes Fredericus,
1611-71, Dutch; nonfiction

SA ST

GRONOWICZ, Antoni, 1913- , Polish;
poetry, fiction, juveniles CON
WA

GRONVOLD, Magnus, 1887-1960,
Norwegian; nonfiction BL

GROOM, Arthur William ('Graham
Anderson'; 'George Anderson';
'Daphne du Blane'; 'Gordon
Grimsley'; 'Bill Pembury'; 'John
Stanstead'; 'Maurice Templar';
'Martin Toonder'), 1898-1964,
English; juveniles, fiction, nonfic-
tion CON

GROOM, Bernard, 1892- , English;
poetry CON

GROOME, Francis Hindes, 1851-1902,
English; nonfiction BRO KBA ST

GROOT, Hugo de see GROTIUS, Hugo

GROOT, José Manuel, 1800-78,
Colombian; nonfiction MIN

GROOT, Pieter de, 1615-78, Dutch;
poetry ST

GROOTE, Geert, 1340-84, Dutch;
nonfiction ST

GROS, Léon Gabriel, 1901- , French;
criticism, poetry DIF

GROS de BESPLAS, Joseph Marie Anne,
1734-83, French; nonfiction DIL

GROS de BOZE, Claude see BOZE,
Claude G.

GROSART, Alexander Balloch, 1827-
99, Scots; editor BRO

GROSBARD, Ulu, 1929- , American;
nonfiction CON

GROSE, Francis, 1731?-91, English;
nonfiction BRO KB

GROSECLOSE, Elgin, 1899- , American; fiction, nonfiction CON MAR
WAF

GROSIER, Jean Baptiste, 1743- ,
French; nonfiction DIL

GROSJEAN, Jean, 1912- , French;
poetry, translations DIC DIF
PIN

GROSLEY, Louis François, 1760- ,
French; plays DIL

GROSLEY, Pierre Jean, 1716-85,
French; nonfiction DIL

GROSOFSKY, Leslie see 'GROSS,
Leslie'

GROSS, Bertram Myron, 1912- ,
American; nonfiction CON

GROSS, Beverly, 1938- , American;
nonfiction CON

GROSS, Carl H., 1911- , American;
nonfiction CON

GROSS, Ernest Arnold, 1906- ,

American; nonfiction CON

GROSS, Feliks, 1906- , Polish-
American; nonfiction CON

GROSS, Franz Bruno, 1919- ,
Austrian-American; nonfiction
CON

GROSS, Gerald, 1932- , American; nonfiction CON

GROSS, Harvey S., 1922- ,
American; nonfiction CON

GROSS, Irma Hannah, 1892- ,
American; nonfiction CON

GROSS, Joel, 1949- , American;
fiction CON

GROSS, Johannes, Heinrich,
1916- , German; nonfiction
CON

GROSS, John, 1935- , English;
nonfiction CON

GROSS, John J., 1912-70, American; nonfiction CON

GROSS, John Owen, 1894- ,
American; nonfiction CON

GROSS, Kenneth G., 1938- ,
American; nonfiction CON

'GROSS, Leslie' (Leslie Grosofsky),
1927- , American; fiction
CON

GROSS, Llewellyn Zwicker,
1914- , American; nonfiction
CON

GROSS, Martin Arnold, 1934- ,
American; nonfiction CON

GROSS, Martin L., 1925- ,
American; nonfiction CON

GROSS, Richard Edmund, 1920- ,
American; nonfiction CON

GROSS, Ronald, 1935- , American;
nonfiction CON

GROSS, Seymour L., 1926- ,
American; nonfiction CON

GROSS, Shelley, 1938- , American; nonfiction, poetry CON

GROSS, Suzanne, 1933- , American; poetry CON

GROSS, Walter, 1923- , American; nonfiction CON

GROSS, William Joseph, 1894- ,
American; nonfiction, juveniles
CON

GROSSACK, Martin Myer, 1928- ,
American; nonfiction CON

GROSSBACH, Robert, 1941- ,
American; nonfiction CON

GROSSETESTE, Robert ('Robert of
Lincoln'), 1175-1253, English;
nonfiction BRO ST

GROSSHANS, Henry, 1921- ,

American; nonfiction CON
GROSSHOLTZ, Jean, 1929- , American; nonfiction CON
GROSSI, Tommaso, 1790-1853, Italian; poetry, fiction ST
GROSSKOPF, Johannes Friedrich Wilhelm, 1885-1948, Afrikaans; plays ST
GROSSKURTH, Phyllis, 1924- , Canadian; nonfiction CON
GROSSMAN, Alfred, 1927- , American; fiction CON
GROSSMAN, Allen R., 1932- , American; fiction, poetry CON
GROSSMAN, Edith Howitt Searle, 1863-1931, New Zealander; fiction RIC ST
GROSSMAN, Herbert, 1934- , American; nonfiction CON
GROSSMAN, Leonid Petrovich, 1888-1966, Russian; fiction HAR ST
GROSSMAN, Morton Charles, 1719- , American; nonfiction CON
GROSSMAN, Reuben see 'AVINOAM'
GROSSMAN, Ronald Philip, 1934- , American; nonfiction CON
GROSSMAN, Sebastian P., 1934- , German-American; nonfiction CON
GROSSMAN, Vasily Semyonovich, 1905-64, Russian; fiction HAR HARK ST
GROSSMAN, William Leonard, 1906- , American; nonfiction CON
GROSSMANN, Gustav Friedrich Wilhelm, 1746-96, German; plays DIL SA
GROSSMANN, Reinhardt S., 1931- , American; nonfiction CON
GROSSMITH, George, 1847-1912, English; fiction, plays BRO ST
GROSSO, Alfonso, 1928- , Spanish; fiction SA
GROSSON, Jean Baptiste Bernard, 1733-1800, French; nonfiction DIL
GROSSVOGEL, David I., 1925- , American; nonfiction CON
GROSSWIRTH, Marvin, 1931- , American; nonfiction CON
GROTE, George, 1794-1871, English; nonfiction BRO KBA SA
GROTE, John, 1813-86, English; nonfiction KBA
GROTH, Klaus, 1819-99, German; poetry AL KE ST
GROTIUS, Hugo ('Hugo de Groot'),

1583-1645, Dutch; nonfiction HAR KE ST
GROTIUS, Jan Hugo de Groot, 1583-1645, Dutch; nonfiction SA
GROU, Jean Nicolas, 1731- , French; nonfiction DIL
GROUVENTALL, Grouber de, 19th cent., German; nonfiction DIL
GROULT, Pierre, Belgian; nonfiction BL
GROULZ, Leonel Adolphe, 1878- , Canadian; nonfiction ST SY
'GROUPE, Darryl R.' see BUNCH, David R.
GROUSSAC, Paul, 1848-1929, French-Argentinian; nonfiction BL MIN SA ST
GROUSSARD, Serge, 1920- , French; fiction, juveniles DIC DIF
GROUSSET, René, 1885-1952, French; nonfiction DIF
GROUT, Ruth Ellen, 1901- , American; nonfiction CON
GROUVELLE, Philippe Antoine, 1757-1806, French; nonfiction DIL
GROVE, Frederick, 1913- , American; fiction CON
GROVE, Frederick Philip, 1872-1942/48, Canadian; fiction, essays RIC ST SY
GROVE, Jack William, 1920- , English; nonfiction CON
GROVE, Matthew, English; poetry ST
'GROVE, Will O.' see BRISTER, Richard
GROVER, David Hubert, 1925- , American; nonfiction CON
GROVER, Eulalie Osgood, 1873- , American; juveniles WA
GROVER, Henry Montague, 1791-1866, English; plays, poetry KBA
GROVER, Linda, 1934- , American; fiction CON
GROVES, Francis Richard, 1889- , English; nonfiction CON
GROVES, Harold Martin, 1897- , American; nonfiction CON
GROVES, Harry Edward, 1921- , American; nonfiction CON
GROVES, Reginald, 1908- , Eng-

lish; nonfiction CON
GROVES, Ruth Clouse, 1902- , American; nonfiction CON
GROVES-RAINES, Ralph Gore Antony, 1913- , American; juveniles WA
GROZELLIER, Nicolas, 1692-1778, French; nonfiction DIL
GRUB, Geore, 1812-93, Scots; nonfiction BRO
GRUB, Phillip D., 1932- , American; nonfiction CON
GRUBAR, Francis Stanley, 1924- , American; nonfiction CON
GRUBB, Davis Alexander, 1919- , American; fiction CON
GRUBB, Frederick Crichton-Stuart, 1930- , British; poetry MUR
GRUBB, Kenneth George, 1900- , English; nonfiction CON
GRUBB, Norman Percy, 1895- , English; nonfiction CON
GRUBBS, Frank Leslie, Jr., 1931- , American; nonfiction CON
GRUBBS, Robert Lowell, 1919- , American; nonfiction CON
GRUBE, George Max Antony, 1899- , Belgian-Canadian; nonfiction CON
GRUBE, John Dun, 1930- , Canadian; poetry MUR
GRUBEL, Herbert G., 1934- , German-American; nonfiction CON
GRUBER, Frank ('Stephen Acre'; 'Charles K. Boston'; 'John K. Vedder'), 1904-69, American; fiction CON
GRUBER, Jacob William, 1921- , American; nonfiction CON
GRUBER, Joseph John, Jr., 1930- , American; nonfiction CON
GRUBER, Ruth Michaels, American; nonfiction CON
GRUBERG, Martin, 1935- , American; nonfiction CON
GRUBINSKI, Waclaw, 1883- , Polish; plays, criticism COL ST
GRUDIN, Louis, 1898- , American; nonfiction CON
GRUEL, Guillaume, 1410?-75?, French; nonfiction ST
'GRÜN, Anastasius' (Anton Alexander von Auersperg), 1806-76, Austrian; poetry AL HAR ST
GRUEN, John, Franco-American; nonfiction CON
GRUEN, Victor David, 1903- , Austrian-American; nonfiction CON

GRUENBAUM, Adolf, 1923- , German-American; nonfiction CON
GRUENBERG, Benjamin Charles, 1875- , Rumanian-American; nonfiction CON
GRÜNBERG, Carlos M., 1903- , Argentinian; poetry, essays MIN
GRÜNBERG, Karl ('Schlark'; 'Schnafte'; 'Kage'; 'Atta Troll'; 'Herbert Wendt'), 1891- , German; nonfiction AL
GRUENBERG, Sidonie Matsner, 1881- , Austrian-American; juveniles COM CON WA
GRUENHAGEN, Robert W., 1932- , American; nonfiction CON
GRUENING, Ernest Henry, 1887- , American; journalism KT
GRUFFYDD, Peter, 1935- , British; poetry MUR
GRUFFYDD, William John, 1881- , Welsh; poetry ST
GRUHN, Carrie Myers, 1907- , American; fiction CON
GRULIOW, Leo, 1913- , American; nonfiction CON
GRUMBACH, Doris Isaac, 1918- , American; fiction CON
GRUMBINE, E. Evalyn McNally, 1900- , American; juveniles WA
GRUMLEY, Michael, 1941- , American; nonfiction CON
GRUMELLI, Antonio, 1928- , Italian; nonfiction CON
GRUMME, Marguerite Evelyn, American; nonfiction CON
GRUNDSTEIN, Nathan David, 1913- , American; nonfiction CON
GRUNDTVIG, Nikolai Frederik Severin, 1783-1872, Danish; poetry HAR KE SA ST
GRUNDTVIG, Svend Hersleb, 1824-83, Danish; nonfiction ST
GRUNDY, Sydney, 1848-1914, English; plays KBA
GRUNWALD, Constantine see de GRUNWALD, Constantine
GRUNWALD, Stefan ('Eric Ludwig'; 'Frederic Ludwig'), 1933- , American; fiction, nonfiction CON
GRUSD, Edward Elihu, 1904- ,

American; nonfiction CON

GRUSHEVSKY, Mikhail Sergeyevich (Hrushevsky), 1866-1934, Ukrainian; fiction ST

GRUSKIN, Alan Daniel, 1904-70, American; nonfiction CON

GRUTER, Jean (Gruterus), 1560-1627, Belgian; nonfiction SA

GRUTZMACHER, Harold Martin, Jr., 1930- , American; nonfiction CON

GRYNBERG, Henryk, 1936- , Polish-American; fiction CON

GRYPHIUS, Andreas (Greif), 1616-64, German; poetry, plays AL HAR KE SA ST

GRYST, Edward George, 1911- , Australian; nonfiction CON

GUADAGNOLO, Joseph Francis, 1912- , American; nonfiction CON

GUAIFERIUS of SALERNO, fl. 1050- , Italian; poetry ST

GUAL, Adrián, 1872-1943, Spanish; nonfiction SA

GUALTERIUS see GAUTIER

GUANABARA, Alcindo, 1865-1918, Brazilian; journalism SA

GUANDOLO, John, 1919- , American; nonfiction CON

GUANES, Alejandro, 1872-1925, Paraguayan; nonfiction, plays BL SA

'GUARD, Theodore de la' see WARD, Nathaniel

GUARDINI, Romano, 1885- , Italian-German; nonfiction HOE KU KUN

GUARESCHI, Giovanni, 1908-68, Italian; fiction, journalism FLE HO KTS RIC SA

GUARIN, José David, 1830-90, Colombian; poetry, fiction, journalism MIN

GUARIN, Pierre, 1678- , French; nonfiction DIL

GUARINI, Giovanni Battista, 1537/38-1612, Italian; poetry, plays HAR KE SA ST

GUARINI, Guarino ('Guarino da Verona'), 1374-1460, Italian; nonfiction SA ST

GUARINO see FAVORINO

GUARINO, Battista, 1434-1503, Italian; nonfiction ST

GUARNER, Luis, 1902- , Spanish; poetry BL SA

GUASCO, Octavien de, 1715-83, French; nonfiction DIL

GUBACK, Thomas Henry, 1937- , American; nonfiction CON

GUBERLET, Muriel Lewin, 1889- , American; nonfiction PAC

GUBSER, Nicholas, J., 1938- , American; nonfiction CON

GUDDE, Erwin Gustav, 1889- , German-American; nonfiction CON

GUDEN de la BRENELLERIE, Paul Philippe, 1738-1812, French; nonfiction DIL

GUDER, Eileen Likens, 1919- , American; nonfiction CON

GUDJONSSON, Halldór Kiljan see 'LAXNESS, Halldór K.'

GUDMUNDSON, Shirley M., Anglo-American; juveniles WA

GUDMUNDSSON, Kristmann, 1902- , Icelandic; fiction FLE SA

GUDRUN (Kudrun), 13th cent., German; nonfiction AL

GUDSCHINSKY, Sarah Caroline, 1919- , American; nonfiction CON

GUDZIY, Nikolay Kalinnikovich (Gudzy), 1887- , Russian; nonfiction ST

GUEDALLA, Philip, 1889-1944, English; nonfiction, poetry BRO KL KT RIC SA

GUEDE, Norina Maria Esterina Lami, 1913- , Italian-American; nonfiction CON

GUEDIER de SAINT AUBIN, Henri Michel, 1695-1742, French; nonfiction DIL

GÜELL y RENTE, José, 1818-84, Cuban; poetry, fiction, plays MIN

GUEHENNO, Marcel Jean, 1890- , French; fiction, essays DIF FLE ST

GÜIRALDES, Ricardo, 1886-1927, Argentinian; fiction, poetry FLE BL MAG MIN RIC SA ST

GUELBENZU y AYALA, Juan, 1912- , Spanish; journalism SA

GUENARD, Antoine, 1726-1806, French; nonfiction DIL

GUENARD, Isabell, 1751-1829, French; fiction SA

GÜNDERODE, Karoline von, 1780-1806, German; poetry SA ST

GUENEAU de MONTBEILLARD, Philibert, 1720-85, French; nonfiction DIL

GUENEE, Antoine, 1717-1803, French; nonfiction DIL

GUENETTE, Robert, 1935- , American; plays CON

GUENIN, Marc Claude, 1730-1807, French; nonfiction DIL

GUENON, René Jean Marie Joseph, 1886-1951, French; nonfiction DIF

GÜNTEER, 12th cent., German; poetry SA

GÜNTHER, Agnes Breuning, 1863-1911, German; fiction COL ST

GUENTHER, Charles John, 1920- , American; nonfiction CON

GÜNTHER, Egon, 1927- , German; nonfiction AL

GÜNTHER, Herbert, 1906- , German; nonfiction KU

GÜNTHER, Johann Christian, 1695-1723, German; poetry AL HAR KE ST

GUENTHER, John Lewis, American; poetry, nonfiction CON

GUER, Jean Antoine, -1764, French; nonfiction DIL

'GUERAN de LIOST' (Jaume Bofill i Mates), 1877-1933, Catalan; poetry ST

GUERARD, Albert Joseph, 1914- , American; fiction, criticism CON KT KTS WAF

GUERARD, Robert, 1641-1715, French; nonfiction DIL

GUERET, Jean Louis Gabriel, 1687-1739, French; nonfiction DIL

GUERIN, Charles Louis Augustin, 1873-1907, poetry DIF HAR KE ST

GUERIN, Eugénie de, 1805-48, French; nonfiction SA

GUERIN, François see GARIN, François

GUERIN, François, 1681-1751, French; nonfiction DIL

GUERIN, Georges Maurice de, 1810-39, French; poetry DIF HAR KE MAL ST

GUERIN, Nicolas François, 1711-82, French; nonfiction DIL

GUERIN, Wilfred Louis, 1929- , American; nonfiction CON

GUERIN de FREMICOURT, Jean Nicolas, 18th cent., French; plays DIL

GUERIN du ROCHER, Pierre Marie Stanislas, 1731- , French; nonfiction DIL

GUERIN du ROCHER, Robert François, 1736-92, French; nonfiction DIL

GUERNES de PONT-SAINTE-MAXENCE, 12th cent., French; poetry ST

GUERNSEY, James Lee, 1923- , American; nonfiction CON

GUEROULT, Louis Nicolas, -1774, French; poetry DIL

GUERRA, José Eduardo, 1893-1943, Bolivian; poetry, essays, fiction, criticism MIN SA

GUERRA, José Joaquín de, 1873-1933, Colombian; nonfiction MIN

GURERRA, Misael see PARRA-GUEZ, Ismael

GUERRA, Rosa, -1840, Argentinian; journalism, poetry MIN

GUERRA JUNQUEIRO, Abilio, 1850-1923, Portuguese; poetry COL HAR SA ST

GUERRA NAVARRO, Francisco, 1909- , Spanish; journalism SA

GUERRA y SANCHEZ, Ramiro, 1880- , Cuban; journalism nonfiction MIN

GUERRANT, Edward Owings, 1911- , American; nonfiction CON

GUERRAZZI, Francesco Domenico, 1804-73, Italian; nonfiction ST

GUERRERO, Teodoro, 1824-1904/05, Cuban; journalism, fiction MIN

GUERRERO RUIZ, Juan, 1893-1955, Spanish; poetry BL

GUERRERO ZAMORA, Juan, 1927- , Spanish; poetry, fiction, plays BL SA

GUERRIER, Dennis, 1923- , English; nonfiction CON

GUERRINI, Olindo see 'STECCHET-TI, Lorenzo'

GUESNIE, Claude, 1647-1722, French; nonfiction DIL

GUEST, Anthony Gordon, 1930- , English; nonfiction CON

GUEST, Barbara Pinson, 1920- , American; poetry CON MUR

GUEST, Lady Charlotte see SCHREIBER, Lady Charlotte G.

GUEST, Edgar Albert, 1881-1959, American; poetry HIL SP

GUEST, Edwin, 1800-80, English;
nonfiction KBA

GUEST, Harry (Genry Bayly Guest),
1932- , British; poetry, translations MUR

GUEST, Ivor Forbes, 1920- , English; nonfiction CON

'GÜTERSLOH, Albert Paris' (Albert
Konrad Kiehtreiber), 1887- ,
Austrian; fiction, poetry FLE
KU KUN

GUETTARD, Jean Etienne, 1715-86,
French; nonfiction DIL

GUEULETTE, Thomas Simon, 1683-
1766, French; nonfiction, fiction,
plays DIL

GUEVARA, Antonio de, 1480?-1545,
Spanish; nonfiction BL HAR KE SA
ST

GUEVARA, José, 1719-1806, Argentinian; nonfiction MIN

GUEVARA, Luis V. de see VELEZ de
GUEVARA y DUEÑAS, Luis

GUEVARA, Miguel de, Spanish; nonfiction BL

GUEVARA, Tomás, 1865-1935, Chilean;
nonfiction MIN

GUEVREMONT, Germaine, 1900- ,
Canadian; fiction ST SY

GUFFIN, Gibert L., 1906- , American; fiction CON

GUFFROY, Armand Benoît Joseph,
1743-1801, French; nonfiction
DIL

GUGLIELMINETTI, Amalia, 1885?- ,
Italian; poetry, fiction COL SA

GUI de CAMBRAI, 12th cent.,
French; poetry ST

GUI II, 17th cent., French; poetry
DIF

GUIARD de SERVIGNE, Jean Baptiste,
18th cent., French; poetry, fiction DIL

GUIART, Antonio see GUYARD,
Antonio

GUIART, Guillaume, 1280?-1316?,
French; nonfiction ST

GUIBAUD, P. Eustache, 1711-94,
French; nonfiction DIL

GUIBERT, Mme., 1725-87, French;
poetry, plays DIL

GUIBERT, Alexandrine Louise
Boutinon de, 1765-1826, French;
nonfiction DIL

GUIBERT, Jacques Antoine Hippolyte,
1743-90, French; nonfiction DIL

GUIBERT, Michel Claude, 1697-1784,
French; nonfiction DIL

GUIBERT de NOGENT, 1053-
1124?, French; nonfiction
DIF ST

GUIBOURG, Edmundo, 1893- ,
Argentinian; journalism, criticism, plays MIN

GUICCIARDINI, Francesco, 1483-
1540, Italian; nonfiction HAR
KE SA ST

GUICHARD, Eleánore, 1719-47/50,
French; fiction DIL

GUICHARD, Henry, fl. 1703- ,
French; plays DIL

GUICHARD, Jean François, 1731-
1811, French; nonfiction, plays
DIL

GUICHARD, P. Louis Anastase,
-1737, French; nonfiction
DIL

GUIDACCI, Marghirita, 1921- ,
Italian; poetry SA

GUIDEO, Manoello see IMMANUEL
ben Solomon

GUIDI, Alessandro, 1650-1712,
Italian; poetry ST

GUIDI, Louis, 1710-80, French;
nonfiction DIL

GUIDICCIONI, Giovanni, 1500-41,
Italian; poetry ST

'GUIDO' see KLOOS, Willem J.T.

GUIDO, Angel, 1896- , Argentinian;
criticism, nonfiction MIN

GUIDO da PISA, 14th cent., Italian;
nonfiction ST

GUIDO delle COLONNE, 13th cent.,
Italian; poetry SA

GUIDO y SPANO, Carlos, 1827-
1918, Argentinian; poetry, fiction BL MIN SA ST

GUIDON, Jon, 1892- , Raeto-
Romansch; poetry ST

GUIGNES, Joseph de, 1721-1800,
French; nonfiction DIL

GUIGO I, 1083/84-1136, French;
nonfiction ST

GUIGOUD-PIGALE, Pierre, 1748-
1816, French; plays DIL

GUILBERT, Pierre, 1697-1759,
French; nonfiction DIL

GUILBERTO de NOGENT, 1053-
1124, French; nonfiction SA

GUILD, Lurelle Van Arsdale,
1898- , American; nonfiction
CON

GUILDAY, Peter, 1884-1947,
American; nonfiction HOE

GUILES, Fred Lawrence, 1922- ,
American; nonfiction CON

GUILET, Pernette du see DU GUILLET,
Pernette
GUILFORD, Joan S., 1928- , Ameri-
can; nonfiction CON
GUILFORD, Joy Paul, 1897- , Ameri-
can; nonfiction CON
GUILHADE, João Garcia de, fl.
1250- , Portuguese; poetry ST
GUILHEM IX, Duke of Aquitaine, 1076-
1126, French; poetry KE ST HAR
GUILHEM, Adémar, 1165-1217, French;
poetry ST
GUILHEM di BERGUEDAN, 1170-1200,
French; poetry ST
GUILHEM de CABESTANH, 12th cent.,
French; poetry ST
GUILHEM FIGUEIRA, 1215-50, French;
poetry ST
GUILHEM MONTANHAGOL, fl. 1244-58,
French; poetry ST
GUILLARD de BEAURIEU, 1728-95,
French; plays DIL
GUILLAUME, Alfred, 1888- , Eng-
lish; nonfiction CON
GUILLAUME, Charles, -1778,
French; nonfiction DIL
GUILLAUME, Jean Baptiste, 1728-
96, French; nonfiction DIL
GUILLAUME, Jeanette G. Flierl,
1899- , American; fiction CON
GUILLAUME de DEGUILLEVILLE,
1295-1358, French; poetry ST
GUILLAUME de FERRIERES, fl.
1202, French; poetry ST
GUILLAUME de LORRIS, 1215?-40?,
French; poetry DIF HAR KE MAG
SA ST
GUILLAUME de MACHAUT, 1300-77,
French; poetry DIF HAR KE MAL
ST
GUILLAUME de SAINT THIERRY,
1085-1148, French; nonfiction
DIF
GUILLAUME le BRETON, fl. 1225,
French; poetry SA ST
GUILLAUME le CLERC, 13th cent.,
French; poetry DIF SA ST
GUILLAUME le VINIER, -1245,
French; poetry ST
GUILLAUME IX, 1071-1127, French;
poetry DIF
GUILLAUMIN, Emile, 1873-1951,
French; fiction DIF
GUILLEMAIN, Charles Jacob, 1750-
99, French; plays DIL
GUILLEMAID, Louis Nicolas, 1729- ,
French; nonfiction, plays DIL
GUILLEMIN, Pierre, 1721-47, French;

nonfiction DIL
GUILLEN, Alberto, 1900- ,
Spanish; poetry, fiction SA
GUILLEN, Jorge, 1893- , Spanish;
poetry, criticism BL COL
FLE HAR RIC SA ST
GUILLEN, Nicolás, 1902/04- ,
Cuban; poetry BL FLE MIN
SA ST
'GUILLEN, Pascual' (Manuel
Desco), 1891- , Spanish;
plays SA
GUILLEN, Rafael, 1933- ,
Spanish; poetry, plays SA
GUILLEN de CASTRO see CASTRO
Y BELLVIS, Guillén de
GUILLEN de SEGOVIA, Pero,
1413-74, Spanish; poetry BL
SA ST
GUILLEN SALAYA, Francisco,
1899- , Spanish; journalism,
essays SA
GUILLERMO de AUVERGNE,
-1249, French; nonfiction
SA
GUILLERMO de CONCHES, 1080-
1154, French; nonfiction SA
GUILLERMO de CHARTERS, 1225-
80, French; nonfiction SA
GUILLERMO de CHAMPEAUX,
1070-1127, French; nonfiction
SA
GUILLERMO de JUMIEGES, 11th
cent., French; nonfiction SA
GUILLERMO de MACHAU, 1284-
1370, French; poetry SA
GUILLERMO de NANGIS, -1302,
French; nonfiction SA
GUILLERMO de POITERS, 1020- ,
French; nonfiction SA
GUILLERMO de PULLA, 10th cent.,
Italian; nonfiction SA
GUILLET de BLARU, Philippe,
1671-1757, French; nonfiction
DIL
GUILLEVIC, Eugène, 1907- ,
French; poetry DIC DIF
GUILLO, Constance, -1730,
French; nonfiction DIL
GUILLON de LOISE, 18th cent.,
French; plays DIL
GUILLON de MONTLEON, Amade,
1758-1842, French; nonfiction
SA
GUILLOT, René, 1900- , French;
juveniles DOY FUL WA
GUILLOT, Victor Juan, 1886-1940,
Argentinian; fiction MIN

GUILLOT de la CHASSAGNE, Ignace Vincent, 1705-50, French; fiction, plays DIL

GUILLOT du HAMEL, Pierre Jean François, 1730-1816, French; nonfiction DIL

GUILLOUX, Louis, 1889- , French; fiction COL DIF FLE HAR KT MAL SA ST

GUILPIN, Edward, 16th cent., English; poetry ST

GUIMARA, Angel, 1849- , Spanish; poetry, plays SA

GUIMARD, Marie Madeleine, 1743-1816, French; nonfiction DIL

GUIMARAENS, Afonso, 1870-1921, Brazilian; poetry SA

GUIMERA, Angel (Guimara), 1849-1924, Spanish; plays, poetry BL COL ST

GUIMOND, James, 1936- , American; nonfiction CON

GUIMOND de la TOUCHE, Claude, 1723-60, French; plays DIL

GUINAGH, Kevin Joseph, 1897- , American; nonfiction CON

GUINEY, Louise Imogen, 1861-1920, American; poetry, essays BRO KT

GUINIZELLI, Guido (Guinicelli), 1230-76, Italian; poetry KE SA ST

GUINN, Paul Spencer, Jr., 1928- , American; nonfiction CON

GUION, Robert Morgan, 1924- , American; nonfiction CON

GUIOT, François Joseph André, 1739-1807, French; nonfiction DIL

GUIOT de DIJON (Jocelin), 18th cent., French; poetry DIF ST

GUIOT de PROVINS, 12th-13th cent., French; poetry DIF ST

GUIRAO, Ramón, 1908-49, Cuban; poetry MIN

GUIRAUD, Pierre Marie Thérèse, 1788-1848, French; poetry, plays SA

GUIRAUDET, Charles Philippe Toussaint, 1754-1804, French; nonfiction, poetry DIL

GUIRAUT de BORNELH (Borneil), 1165-1220, French; poetry ST

GUIRAUT RIQUIER, 1254-92, French; poetry ST

GUIS, 18th cent., French; plays DIL

GUISCHARDT, Charles Theophile, 1724/29-75, French; nonfiction DIL

GUITERAS, Eusebio, 1823-89?, Cuban; fiction MIN

GUITERAS, Pedro José, 1814-90, Cuban; nonfiction MIN

GUITERMAN, Arthur, 1871-1943, American; poetry BRO KL KT

GUITHER, Harold D., 1927- , American; nonfiction CON

'GUITRY, Sacha' (Alexander Pierre Georges), 1885-1957, French; plays COL DIF HAR KT MAT SA ST

GUITTON, d' AREZZO, 1225?-93?, Italian; poetry KE ST

GUIZOT, François Pierre Guillaume, 1787-1874, French; nonfiction DIF HAR SA

GUIZOT, Pauline Elisa Meulan, 1773- , French; nonfiction, fiction SA

GULBRANNSEN, Trygve, 1894- , Norwegian; fiction KT

GULICK, Grover C. ('Bill Gulick'), 1916- , American; nonfiction CON PAC

GULICK, Peggy, 1918- , American; juveniles WA

GULLAHORN, Genevieve, Lithuanian-American; juveniles WA

GULLANS, Charles Bennett, 1929- , American; poetry CON MUR

GULLASON, Thomas Arthur, 1924- , American; nonfiction CON

GULLBERG, Hjalmar Robert, 1898-1961, Swedish; poetry, criticism COL FLE SA ST

GULLEY, Halbert Edison, 1919- , American; nonfiction CON

GULLEY, Norman, 1920- , English; nonfiction CON

GULLICK, Charles Francis William Rowley, 1907- , American; nonfiction CON

GULLICK, John Michael, 1916- , English; nonfiction CON

GULLIFORD, Ronald, 1920- , English; nonfiction CON

GULLON, Ricardo, 1908- , Spanish; nonfiction BL SA

GUMILLA, José, 1686/90-1750/58, Colombian; nonfiction MIN

GUMILYOV, Nikolay Stepanovich (Gumilev), 1886-1921, Russian; poetry COL FLE HAR HARK KE RIC SA ST

GUMMERE, Francis Barton, 1855-1919,
American; nonfiction KT
GUMP, Richard Benjamin, 1906- ,
American; nonfiction CON
GUMPERT, Martin, 1897- , Ger-
man; nonfiction KU LEN
GUNDERS, Henry, 1924- , German-
American; nonfiction CON
GUNDERSON, Doris V., American;
nonfiction CON
GUNDERSON, Keith, 1935- , Ameri-
can; poetry CON
GUNDERSON, Robert Gray, 1915- ,
American; nonfiction CON
GUNDOLF, Friedrich, 1880- ,
German; nonfiction KU
GUNDREY, Elizabeth, 1924- , Eng-
lish; nonfiction CON
GUNDRY, Robert Horton, 1932- ,
American; nonfiction CON
GUNDULIC, Ivan Dzivo ('Giovanni
Gondola'), 1589-1638, Dalmatian;
poetry SA ST
GUNJI, Masakatsu, 1913- , Japanese;
nonfiction CON
GUNN, Aneas, 1870-1961, Australian;
fiction RIC
GUNN, James E. ('Edwin James'),
1923- , American; fiction CON
GUNN, John Alexander Wilson, 1937- ,
American; nonfiction CON
GUNN, Sister Mary Agnes David,
1928- , American; nonfiction
CON
GUNN, Neil Miller, 1891-1973,
Scots; fiction BRO KT SA ST
GUNN, Peter Nicholson, 1914- ,
Australian; nonfiction CON
GUNN, Thomson William, 1924/29- ,
British; poetry CON MUR RIC
SP
GUNN, William Harrison, 1934- ,
American; fiction CON
GUNNARSSON, Gunnar, 1889- ,
Icelandic; fiction, plays, poetry
COL FLE HAR KT MAG RIC SA
ST
GUNNELL, John C., 1933- , Ameri-
can; nonfiction CON
GUNNING, Robert, 1908- , American;
nonfiction CON
GUNNING, Susannah Minifie, 1740?-
1800, English; fiction KB
GUNTER, Archibald Clavering, 1847-
1907, American; fiction KAA
GUNTER, J. Bradley Hunt, 1940- ,
American; nonfiction CON
GUNTER, Peter Addison Yancey,

1936- , American; nonfiction
CON
GUNTHER, fl. 1180- , German;
poetry ST
GUNTHER, Albert Everard,
1903- , English; nonfiction
CON
GUNTHER, Erna, 1896- ,
American; nonfiction PAC
GUNTHER, Gerald, 1927- ,
German-American; nonfiction
CON
GUNTHER, John, 1901-70, Ameri-
can; nonfiction, fiction,
juveniles BRO COM CON HOO
KT ST WA WAF
GUNTHER, Max, 1927- , Anglo-
American; nonfiction CON
GUNTHER, Peter F., 1920- ,
American; nonfiction CON
GUNTHORPE, John, -1498,
English; nonfiction ST
GUNTRIP, Henry James Samuel,
1901- , English; nonfiction
CON
GUOLAUGSSON, Jónas, 1887-1916,
Icelandic; poetry, fiction ST
GUOMUNDSSON, Gudmundur, 1874-
1919, Icelandic; poetry ST
GUOMUNDSSON, Kristmann
Borgfjörd, 1902- , Icelandic;
fiction COL HAR SA ST
GUOMUNDSSON, Tómas, 1901- ,
Icelandic; poetry ST
GUPPY, Nicholas Gareth Lech-
mere, 1925- , English;
nonfiction CON
GUPTA, Sulekh Chandra, 1928- ,
Indian; nonfiction CON
GUPTA, Ram Chandra ('Rama'),
1927- , Indian; nonfiction
CON
GURIAN, Waldemar, 1902- , Rus-
sian; nonfiction HOE
GURK, Paul, 1880-1953, German;
nonfiction KU LEN
GURKO, Leo, 1914- , Polish-
American; nonfiction CON
GURKO, Miriam, American; nonfic-
tion CON
GURNEY, Edmund, 1847-88,
English; nonfiction KBA
GURNEY, Gene, 1924- , Ameri-
can; fiction CON
GURNEY, J. Eric, 1910- ,
Canadian-American; juveniles
CON WA
GURNEY, Nancy Jack, Canadian;

juveniles WA
GURNEY, Thomas, 1705-70, English;
nonfiction KB
GURO, Elena, -1913, Russian;
poetry ST
GURR, Andrew John, 1936- , Eng-
lish; nonfiction CON
GURULUGOMI, fl. 1200- , Sinhalese;
nonfiction LAN
GURUITSCH, Aron, 1901- , Russian-
American; nonfiction CON
'GUS, Uncle' see REY, Hans A.
GUSEV, Sergey Ivanovich, 1867-1963
('Gusev-Orenburgski'), Russian;
fiction HAR HARK KT SA ST
GUSMAO, Alejandro de, 1629-1724,
Brazilian; nonfiction SA
GUSMAO, Bartolomé Lorenzo de,
1685-1724, Brazilian; nonfiction
SA
GUSS, Donald Leroy, 1929- , Ameri-
can; nonfiction CON
GUSS, Leonard M., 1926- , Ameri-
can; nonfiction CON
GUSSMAN, Boris William, 1914- ,
English; nonfiction CON
GUSSOW, Joan Dye, 1928- , Ameri-
can; nonfiction CON
GUSTAF-JANSON Gösta, 1902- ,
Swedish; fiction HAR ST
GUSTAFSON, Alrik, 1903- , Amer-
ican; nonfiction CON
GUSTAFSON, Donald F., 1934- ,
American; nonfiction CON
GUSTAFSON, Elton T., American;
juveniles WA
GUSTAFSON, James Moody, 1925- ,
American; nonfiction CON
GUSTAFSON, Ralph Barker, 1909- ,
Canadian; poetry, fiction, plays
CON KTS MUR SY
GUSTAFSON, Richard Folke, 1934- ,
American; nonfiction CON
'GUSTAFSON, Sarah R.' see RIED-
MAN, Sarah R.
GUSTAITIS, Rasa, 1934- , Lithuanian-
American; nonfiction CON
GUSTAV III, 1746-92, Swedish; plays
ST
GUSTAVINO, Enrique, 1898- ,
Argentinian; criticism, plays
MIN
GUSTAVINO, Juan Esteban, 1868- ,
Argentinian; nonfiction MIN
GUSTAVSON, Carl Gustav, 1915- ,
American; nonfiction CON
GUSTEAU, François, 1699-1761,
French; plays DIL

GUTENBERG, Arthur William,
1920- , German-American;
nonfiction CON
GUTERMAN, Stanley Sanford,
1934- , American; nonfiction
CON
GUTH, Paul, 1910- , French;
nonfiction DIF
GUTHEIM, Frederick, 1908- ,
American; nonfiction CON
GUTHMAN, Edwin, 1919- ,
American; nonfiction CON
GUTHMANN, Harry G., 1896- ,
American; nonfiction CON
GUTHRIE, Alfred Bertram, Jr.,
1901- , American; fiction
KTS MAG PAC WAF
GUTHRIE, Anne, 1890- , Ameri-
can; juveniles CON WA
GUTHRIE, Donald, 1916- , Eng-
lish; nonfiction CON
GUTHRIE, Harvey Henry, Jr.,
1924- , American; nonfiction
CON
'GUTHRIE, Hugh' see FREEMAN,
John C.
'GUTHRIE, Isobel' see GRIEVE,
Christopher M.
GUTHRIE, James Shields ('David
Creed'), 1931- , American;
fiction CON
'GUTHRIE, John' see BRODIE,
John
GUTHRIE, John Alexander, 1907- ,
Scots-American; nonfiction
CON
GUTHRIE, Ramon, 1896-1973,
American; poetry, fiction
CON MUR
GUTHRIE, Thomas, 1803-73,
Scots; nonfiction BRO KBA
GUTHRIE, Thomas Anstey ('F.
Anstey'), 1856-1934, English;
fiction BRO DOY KT SA
GUTHRIE-SMITH, William Herbert,
1861-1940/46, New Zealander;
fiction RIC ST
GUTIERRE de CETINA, 1520-57?,
Spanish; poetry BL SA ST
GUTIERREZ, Alberto, 1863/73-
1928, Bolivian; nonfiction
MIN
GUTIERREZ, Eduardo, 1851-89,
Argentinian; criticism MIN
GUTIERREZ, Ernesto, 1920- ,
Nicaraguan; poetry SA
GUTIERREZ, Federico A., 20th
cent., Argentinian; poetry
MIN

GUTIERREZ, Fernando, 1911- ,
Spanish; poetry BL SA
GUTIERREZ, Francisco Antonio,
1848- , Colombian; poetry MIN
GUTIERREZ, Joaquín, 1918- , Costa
Rican; poetry, fiction, essays
MIN
GUTIERREZ, José Rosendo, 1840- ,
Bolivian; poetry MIN SA
GUTIERREZ, Juan María, 1809-78,
Argentinian; poetry BL MIN SA
ST
GUTIERREZ MOISES see 'VALLE,
Rosamel del'
GUTIERREZ, Ricardo, 1836-96,
Argentinian; poetry BL MIN SA
GUTIERREZ, Ricardo, 1877/79- ,
Argentinian; journalism, criticism,
poetry MIN
GUTIERREZ ABASCAL, Ricardo ('Juan
de la Encina'), 1890-1963, Spanish;
nonfiction BL SA
GUTIERREZ ALBELO, Emetario,
1905- , Spanish; poetry SA
GUTIERREZ de MIGUEL, Valentín,
1891- , Spanish; journalism
SA
GUTIERREZ de PIÑERES, Germán
(Piñerez), 1816-72, Colombian;
fiction, poetry MIN
GUTIERREZ GAMERO, Emilio, 1844-
1935, Spanish; nonfiction BL SA
GUTIERREZ GONZALEZ, Gregorio,
1826-72, Colombian; nonfiction
BL MIN SA ST
GUTIERREZ NAJERA, Manuel ('Puck';
'Recamier'), 1859-95, Mexican;
journalism, poetry BL SA ST
GUTIERREZ SOLANO, José, 1886-
1945, Spanish; fiction BL SA
GUTKIND, Erwin Anton, American;
nonfiction CON
GUTMAN, Judith Mara, 1928- ,
American; nonfiction CON
GUTMAN, Robert W., 1925- , Amer-
ican; nonfiction CON
GUTMANN, James, 1897- , Ameri-
can; nonfiction CON
GUTMANN, Simcha Alter see 'BEN-
ZION Sh'
GUTSCHE, Thelma, 1915- , South
African; nonfiction CON
GUTTELING, Henricus Zacharias,
Alexander, 1884-1910, Dutch;
poetry ST
GUTTENBRUNNER, Michael, 1919- ,
German; poetry AL
GUTTERIDGE, Bernard, 1916- ,

British; poetry, fiction MUR
GUTTERIDGE, William Frank,
1919- , English; nonfiction
CON
GUTTERSON, Herbert Lindsley,
Jr., 1915- , American; fic-
tion CON
GUTTMACHER, Alan F., 1898-1974,
American; nonfiction CON
GUTTMACHER, Manfred Schan-
farber, 1898- , American;
nonfiction CON
GUTTMANN, Alexander, Hungarian-
American; nonfiction CON
GUTTMANN, Allen, 1932- ,
American; nonfiction CON
GUTTSMAN, Wilhelm Leo,
1920- , English; nonfiction
CON
GUTZKE, Manford George, 1896- ,
American; nonfiction CON
GUTZKOW, Karl Ferdinand, 1811-
78, German; plays, fiction
AL HAR KE SA ST
GUY, Anne Welsh, American;
juveniles CON
GUY, Harold A., 1904- , English;
nonfiction CON
GUY, Rosa Cuthbert, 1925- ,
American; fiction CON
GUY de BAZOCHES, 1146-1203,
French; poetry ST
GUYARD, Antonio (Guiart), 1692-
1760, French; nonfiction
DIL
GUYARD de BERVILLE, N.,
1697-1770/78, French;
nonfiction DIL
GUYAU, Jean Marie, 1854-88,
French; poetry, nonfiction
DIF SA
GUYON, Claude Marie, 1699-
1771, French; nonfiction
DIL
GUYON, Jeanne Marie Bouvier,
1648-1717, French; letters,
nonfiction DIF DIL SA
GUYOT, Alexis Toussaint,
-1734, French; nonfiction
DIL
GUYOT, Edme Gilles, 1706-86,
French; nonfiction DIL
GUYOT, Germain Antoine, 1694-
1756, French; nonfiction
DIL
GUYOT, Guillaume Germain,
1724-1800, French; nonfiction
DIL

GUYOT de MERVILLE, Michel,
1696-1755, French; nonfiction
DIL SA
GUYOT de PROVINS, 12th cent.,
French; poetry SA
GUYOT DESFONTAINES, Pierre
F. see DESFONTAINES, Pierre
F.G.
GUYOT-GRANDMAISON, Pierre Jean
Jacques, 1719-84, French; non-
fiction DIL
GUYS, Pierre Augustin, 1721-99,
French; nonfiction DIL
GUYTON, Arthur Clifton, 1919- ,
American; nonfiction CON
GUYTON de MORVEAU, Louis
Bernard, 1737-1816, French;
nonfiction DIL
GUZIE, Tad Walter, 1934- , Ameri-
can; nonfiction CON
GUZMAN, Alcibíades, 1859-1919,
Bolivian; nonfiction SA
GUZMAN, Augusto, 20th cent.,
Bolivian; journalism, fiction
MIN SA
GUZMAN, Diego Rafael de, 1848-
1920, Colombian; journalism,
fiction MIN
GUZMAN, Ernesto A., 1877- ,
Chilean; poetry MIN
GUZMAN, Martín Luis, 1887- ,
Mexican; journalism BL ST
'GUZMAN, Nicomedes' (Oscar
Vázquez), 1914- , Chilean;
fiction MIN
GUZMAN CHUCHAGA, Juan, 1895/96- ,
Chilean; poetry MIN SA
GUZMAN y FRANCO, Martín Luis,
1887- , Mexican; journalism,
fiction SA
GUZMAN y la CERDA, María Isidra,
1768-1803, Spanish; poetry SA
GUZZWELL, John, 1930- , English;
nonfiction CON
GVADANYI, József, 1725-1801,
Hungarian; poetry ST
GWALTNEY, Francis Irby, 1921- ,
American; fiction CON
GWALTNEY, John Langston, 1928- ,
American; nonfiction CON
GWERDER, Alexander Xaver, 1923- ,
German; nonfiction KU
GWILLIAM, Kenneth Mason, 1937- ,
English; nonfiction CON
GWIRTZMAN, Milton S., 1933- ,
American; nonfiction CON
GWYN, Richard, 1934- , English;
nonfiction CON

GWYN, William Brent, 1927- ,
American; nonfiction CON
GWYNN, Denis Rolleston, 1893- ,
English; nonfiction CON HOE
GWYNN, Stephen Lucius, 1864-
1950, Irish; poetry, criticism
BRO KT
GWYNNE, John Harold, 1899- ,
American; juveniles WA
GYAL-TSHAB-RJE, 1364-1432,
Tibetan; nonfiction LAN
GYLDENVAND, Lily M., 1917- ,
American; nonfiction CON
GYLLEMBOURGH-EHRENSVÄRD,
Thomasine Christine Buntzen,
1773-1856, Danish; fiction ST
GYLLENBORG, Carl, 1679-1746,
Swedish; plays ST
GYLLENBORG, Gustaf Fredrik,
1731-1808, Swedish; poetry
ST
GYÖNGYÖSI, István, 1629?-1704,
Hungarian; poetry ST
GYP (Sybille Gabreille Marie
Antoinette Riquetti de Mirabeau),
'Martel de Janville', 1849-
1923/32- , French; fiction
DIF HAR SA
GYULAI, Pal, 1826-1909,
Hungarian; criticism, poetry,
fiction COL KE SA ST

H

'H.D.' see DOOLITTLE, Hilda
'H.H.' see FITT, J. Nevill
'H.H.' see JACKSON, Helen
M. F.H.
'H.M.W.' see WANG, Hui-Ming
HAABY, Lawrence O., 1915- ,
American; nonfiction CON
HAAC, Oscar Alfred, 1918- ,
American; nonfiction CON
HAAFNER, Jacob Godfried
(Haffner), 1755-1809, Dutch;
nonfiction ST
HAAG, Jessie Helen, 1917- ,
American; nonfiction CON
HAAKER, Ann M., American;
nonfiction CON
HAAN, Aubrey Edwin, 1908- ,
American; nonfiction CON
HAAN, Fonger de, 1855- , Dutch;
nonfiction SA
HAAN, Jakob Israel van, 1881-
1924, Dutch; poetry, fiction
SA

HAAR, Bernard Ter, 1806-80,
Dutch; poetry ST
HAAR, Charles Monroe, 1920- ,
Belgian-American; nonfiction
CON
HAAR, Franklin B., 1906- , Ameri-
can; nonfiction CON
HAAR, James, 1929- , American;
nonfiction CON
HAARER, Alec Ernest ('Shanwat'),
1894- , English; nonfiction
CON
HAARHOFF, Theodore Johannes,
1882- , South African; nonfic-
tion CON
HA-ARI see LURIA, Isaac B. S.
HAAS, Albert E., 1917- , American;
nonfiction CON
HAAS, Benjamin Leopold, 1926- ,
American; fiction CON
HAAS, Dorothy F. ('Dee Francis'),
American; juveniles CON
HAAS, Francis Joseph, 1889- ,
American; nonfiction HOE
HAAS, Harold Irwin, 1925- , Ameri-
can; nonfiction CON
HAAS, Mary Odin, 1910- , Ameri-
can; nonfiction CON
HAAS, Mary Rosamond, 1910- ,
American; nonfiction CON
HAAS, Michael, 1938- , American;
nonfiction CON
HAAS, Raymond Michael, 1935- ,
American; nonfiction CON
HAAS, Rosamond Edwards, 1908- ,
American; poetry HOE
HAAS, Willy, 1891- , German; non-
fiction KU
HAASE, Ann Marie Bernazza, 1942- ,
American; nonfiction CON
HAASE, John, 1923- , German-
American; fiction CON
HABBEMA, Koos see HEIJERMANS,
Herman
HABBERTON, John, 1842-1921,
American; juveniles, editor BRO
DOY KAA
HABBERTON, William, American;
juveniles WA
'HABE, Hans' (Jean Bekessy), 1911- ,
German-American; fiction,
journalism KTS
HABECK, Fritz, 1916- , German;
nonfiction AL KU
HABEL, Norman C., 1932- ,
Australian; nonfiction CON
HABENSTREIT, Barbara, 1937- ,
American; nonfiction CON

HABER, Audrey, 1940- , Ameri-
can; nonfiction CON
HABER, Heinz, 1913- , German-
American; juveniles WA
HABER, Louis, 1910- , American;
nonfiction CON
HABER, Ralph Norman, 1932- ,
American; nonfiction CON
HABER, Samuel, 1928- , Ameri-
can; nonfiction CON
HABER, Tom Burns, 1900- ,
American; nonfiction CON
HABER, William, 1899- , Ameri-
can; nonfiction CON
HABERMAN, Donald Charles,
1933- , American; nonfiction
CON
HABERT, François, 1508-61,
French; poetry SA
HABERT, Louis, 1636-1718,
French; nonfiction DIL
HABGOOD, John Stapylton, 1927- ,
English; nonfiction CON
HABIG, Marion Alphonse, 1901- ,
American; nonfiction CON
HOE
HABINGTON, Thomas, 1560-1647,
English; nonfiction, translations
ST
HABINGTON, William, 1605-54,
English; poetry BRO KB ST
HABLUTZEL, Philip, 1935- ,
American; nonfiction CON
HACH, Clarence Woodrow,
1917- , American; nonfiction
CON
HACHARD de SAINT STANISLAS,
18th cent., French; nonfiction
DIL
HACHETT, Albert, 1900- ,
American; plays, jouvenile
MAT WA
HACHETTE de PORTES, Henri,
1712-95, French; nonfiction
DIL
HACHEY, Thomas Eugene,
1938- , American; nonfiction
CON
HACHIMONJIYA, Jisho see ANDO
JISHO
HACIKYAN, Agop J., 1931- ,
Turkish-Canadian; nonfiction
CON
HACK, Maria Barton, 1777-1844,
English; juveniles KBA
HACK, Walter G., 1925- , Amer-
ican; nonfiction CON
HACKER, Andrew, 1929- ,

American; nonfiction CON

HACKER, Louis Morton, 1899- ,
American; nonfiction CON KT

HACKER, Mary Louise, 1908- ,
English; fiction CON

HACKER, Rose Goldbloom, 1906- ,
English; nonfiction CON

HACKETT, Cecil Arthur, 1908- ,
English; nonfiction CON

HACKETT, Donald F., 1918- ,
American; nonfiction CON

HACKETT, Francis Goodrich, 1883-1962,
American; nonfiction, fiction,
criticism, juveniles HOO KL KT
SA ST WA

HACKETT, Herbert Lewis, 1917-64,
American; nonfiction CON

HACKETT, John W., 1924- , English; nonfiction CON

HACKETT, Laura Lyman, 1916- ,
American; nonfiction CON

HACKETT, Marie G., 1923- ,
American; nonfiction CON

HACKETT, Paul, 1920- , American;
fiction CON

HACKFORTH-JONES, Frank Gilbert,
1900- , English; fiction CON

HACKLÄNDER, Friedrich Wilhelm
von, 1816-77, German; nonfiction
AL HAR

HACKMAN, Martha L., 1912- ,
American; nonfiction CON

HACKNEY, Alan, 1924- , English;
fiction CON

HACKNEY, Vivian, 1914- , American; nonfiction CON

HACKS, Peter, 1928- , German;
plays AL KU MAT

HADAMAR von LABER, fl. 1335-40,
Bavarian; fiction ST

HADAS, Moses, 1900-66, American; nonfiction CON

HADATH, Gunby ('John Mowbray'),
1880-1954, American; juveniles
DOY

HADAWI, Sami, 1904- , Israeli-
American; nonfiction CON

HADDAD, George M., 1910- ,
American; nonfiction CON

HADDEN, Maude Miner, 1880- ,
American; nonfiction CON

'HADDO, Oliver' see PUECHNER,
Ray

HADDO, Walter, 1516-171/72- ,
English; nonfiction ST

HADER, Berta Hoerner, American;
juveniles KJU WA

HADER, Elmer, 1889- , American;

juveniles KJU WA

HADEWYCH, Sor, 13th cent.,
Flemish; nonfiction SA ST

HADFIELD, Ellis Charles Raymond
('Charles Alexander'), 1909- ,
English; nonfiction, juveniles
CON

HADFIELD, Miles Heywood,
1903- , English; nonfiction
CON

HADJI-KHALFAH (Kalib Tscheleld),
1600- , Turkish; nonfiction
SA

HADLAUB, Johannes, fl. 1300,
Swiss; poetry ST

HADLEY, Eleanor Martha,
1916- , American; nonfiction
CON

'HADLEY, Franklin' see WINTHER-
BOTHAM, Russell R.

HADLEY, Hamilton, 1896- ,
American; nonfiction CON

HADLEY, Thomas E., American;
poetry HIL

HADLOW, Leonard Harold, 1908- ,
English; nonfiction CON

HADOUX, 18th cent., French; nonfiction DIL

HADRIAN, Publius Aelius, 76-
183, Roman; poetry ST

HADWIGER, Don F., 1930- ,
American; nonfiction CON

HAEBERLE, Erwin Jakob,
1936- , American; nonfiction
CON

HAEBICH, Kathryn A., 1899- ,
American; nonfiction CON

HAECHT, Willem van, 1530-85?,
Dutch; poetry ST

HAECKEL, Ernst, 1834-1919,
German; nonfiction SA

HAECKER, Theodor, 1879-1945,
German; nonfiction HO KU
KUN

'HAEDREYI, Abgad' see DRUYA-
NOV, Alter

HAEFTLE, John William, 1913- ,
American; nonfiction CON

HÄGERSTROM, Axel, 1865- ,
Swedish; essays SA

HAEGGLUND, Bengt, 1920- ,
Swedish; nonfiction CON

'HAEMSTEDE, Witte van' see
WITTE, Jacob E. de

HAENICKE, Diether H., 1935- ,
American; nonfiction CON

HAENSEL, Carl, 1889- , German; nonfiction LEN

HAENTZSCHEL, Adolph Theodore,
1881- , American; nonfiction
CON
HAERING, Bernard, 1912- , German; nonfiction CON
HÄRING, George Wilhelm see
'ALEXIS, Willibald'
HÄRTLING, Peter, 1933- , German;
nonfiction KU
HÄTZERLIN, Clara, fl. 1452-76,
German; poetry ST
'HAFIZ' (Shams ud-din Mohammed),
1320/24-88/89, Persian; poetry
LAN MAG SA ST
HAFIZ IBRAHIM, Muhammad, 1871-
1932, Egyptian; poetry ST
HAFLEY, James, 1928- , American;
nonfiction CON
HAFNER, Lawrence E., 1924- ,
American; nonfiction CON
HAFNER, Philip, 1731-64, Austrian;
plays ST
HAFSA, Arab; poetry SA
HAFSTEIN, Hannes, 1861-1922,
Icelandic; poetry ST
HAGA, Enoch, 1931- , American;
nonfiction CON
HAGALIN, Guomundur Geslason,
1898-1927, Icelandic; fiction,
poetry, plays COL FLE SA ST
HAGAN, Charles Banner, 1905- ,
American; nonfiction CON
HAGAN, John Thomas, 1926- ,
American; nonfiction CON
HAGAN, Willia Thomas, 1918- ,
American; nonfiction CON
'HAGAR, George' see MARIA del
RAY, Sister
HAGBERG, Carl August, 1810-64,
Swedish; translation ST
'HAGE, J. van den' see OLTMANS,
Jan F.
HAGE, Jerald, 1932- , American;
nonfiction CON
HAGEDORN, Friedrich von, 1708-54,
German; poetry HAR KE ST
HAGEDORN, Hermann, 1882- ,
American; poetry, fiction KT
HAGELMAN, Charles William Jr.,
1920- , American; nonfiction
CON
HAGELSTANGE, Rudolf, 1912- ,
German; poetry, fiction, essays
AL FLE KU KUN LEN
HAGEMAN, Howard Garberich,
1921- , American; nonfiction
CON
HAGEN, Clifford Warren, Jr.,

1943- , American; fiction
CON
HAGEN, Elizabeth Pauline, 1915- ,
American; nonfiction CON
HAGEN, Everett E., 1906- ,
American; nonfiction CON
HAGEN, Friedrich Heinrich,
1780-1856, German; nonfic-
tion SA
HAGENAU, Reinmar see REINMAR
von HAGENAU
HAGIER, Alice Rogers, 1894- ,
American; juveniles, fiction
CON WA
HAGER, Henry B., 1926- ,
American; fiction CON
HAGERTY, Nancy K., 1935- ,
American; nonfiction CON
HAGGARD, Sir Henry Rider,
1856-1925, English; juveniles,
fiction BRO DOY KAT KT
MAG SA
'HAGGARD, Paul' see LONGSTRET,
Stephen
'HAGGARD, William' see CLAY-
TON, Richard H. M.
HAGIWARA SAKUTARO, 1887-
1942, Japanese; poetry LAN
'HAGON, Priscilla' see ALLAN,
Mabel E.
HAGSTROM, Warren Olaf,
1930- , American; nonfiction
CON
HAGSTRUM, Jean Howard,
1913- , American; nonfiction
CON
HAGTHORPE, John, fl. 1627- ,
English; poetry ST
HAHN, Emily, 1905- , American;
nonfiction, fiction, juveniles
CON KTS WA
HAHN, Hannelore, 1926- , Ger-
man-American; fiction CON
HAHN, Harlan, 1939- , Ameri-
can; nonfiction CON
HAHN, Roger, 1932- , Franco-
American; nonfiction CON
HAHN, Yelena Andreyevna
('Zeneida R-va'), 1814-42,
Russian; fiction HARK
HAHN-HAHN, Ide, 1805- , Ger-
man; nonfiction SA
HANHER, Jane Edith, 1940- ,
American; nonfiction CON
HAI GAON (Hai Ben Sherira),
939-1038, Iraqi; poetry ST
HAIDU, Peter, 1931- , Franco-
American; nonfiction CON

HAIG, Irvine Reid Sterling, 1936- ,
American; nonfiction CON
HAIG-BROWN, Roderick Langmere,
1908- , Canadian; nonfiction
CON ST SY
HAIGERTY, Leo James, 1924- ,
American; nonfiction CON
HAIGHT, Anne Lyon, 1895- , Ameri-
can; nonfiction CON
HAIGHT, Gordon Sherman, 1901- ,
American; nonfiction CON
HAIGHT, John McVickar, Jr.,
1917- , American; nonfiction
CON
HAIGHT, Mabel V. Jackson, 1912- ,
South African; nonfiction CON
HAIL, Marshall, 1905- , American;
nonfiction CON
HAILES, Sir David Dalrymple, 1726-
92, Scots; nonfiction BRO ST
HAILEY, Arthur, 1920- , Canadian;
fiction, plays CON SY
HAILLAN, Bernard de Girard, 1535-
1610, French; poetry SA
HAILLET de COURONNE, Jean
Baptiste, Guillaume, 1728-1810,
French; nonfiction DIL
HAILPERIN, Herman, 1899- , Amer-
ican; nonfiction CON
HAIMAN, Franklyn Saul, 1929- ,
American; nonfiction CON
HAIMANN Miecislaus Albin Francis
Joseph, 1888- , Polish-American;
nonfiction HOE
HAIMANN, Theo, 1911- , German-
American; nonfiction CON
HAIME, Agnes Irvine Constance
Adasm, ('Persis'), 1884- , Eng-
lish; fiction CON
HAIMOWITZ, Morris Loeb, 1918- ,
American; nonfiction CON
HAINES, Aubrey Leon, 1914- ,
American; nonfiction PAC
HAINES, Donal Hamilton, 1886- ,
American; fiction HIL
HAINES, Francis, 1899- , American;
nonfiction CON
HAINES, Francis D., Jr., 1923- ,
American; nonfiction PAC
HAINES, Gail Kay, 1943- , Ameri-
can; juveniles CON
HAINES, George Henry, Jr., 1937- ,
American; nonfiction CON
HAINES, John M., 1924- , Ameri-
can; nonfiction, poetry CON MUR
HAINES, Perry Franklin, 1889- ,
American; nonfiction CON
HAINES, Walter Wells, 1918- ,

American; nonfiction CON
HAINES, William Wister, 1908- ,
American; fiction, plays
CON KTS MAT
HAIR, Paul Edward Hedley,
1926- , English; nonfiction
CON
HAIR, William Ivy, 1930- ,
American; nonfiction CON
HAISLIP, Harvey Shadle, 1889- ,
American; fiction CON
HAISLIP, John, 1925- , Ameri-
can; poetry CON
HAITHCOX, John Patrick, 1933- ,
American; nonfiction CON
HAITON, 1306- , Italian; nonfic-
tion SA
HAITZE, Pierre Joseph, 1648-
1736, French; nonfiction DIL
HAJ, Fareed, 1935- , American;
nonfiction CON
HAJEK Z LIBOCAN, Václav,
1553- , Czech; nonfiction
ST
HAKE, Thomas Gordon, 1809-95,
English; poetry BRO KBA
HAKES, Joseph Edward, 1916- ,
American; nonfiction CON
HAKIM, Tewfik, 1902- , Egyptian;
plays, fiction, essays ST
HAKLUYT, Richard, 1552-1616,
English; nonfiction BRO KB
MAG ST
HAKUSEKI see ARAI HAKUSEKI
HALACY, Daniel Stephen, 1919- ,
American; juveniles CON WA
HALAS, Frantisek, 1901-49/50,
Czech; poetry FLE HAR ST
HALASZ, Nicholas, 1895- , Amer-
ican; nonfiction CON
HALBE, Max, 1865-1944/45,
German; plays, fiction AL
COL FLE MAT SA
HALBERSTADT, William Harold,
1930- , American; nonfiction
CON
HALBERTSMA, Eeltje, 1797-1858,
Frisian; nonfiction ST
HALCON, Manuel, 1902- ,
Spanish; fiction BL SA
HALCROW, Harold Graham,
1911- , American; nonfiction
CON
HALDANE, John Burdon Sanderson,
1892-1964, English; nonfiction
BRO KT
HALDEMAN, Charles Heuss,
1931- , American; fiction
CON

HALE, Allean Lemmon, 1914- ,
American; nonfiction, plays CON
HALE, Arlene ('Louise Christopher';
'Gail Everett'; 'Mary Anne Tate'),
1924- , American; fiction, juven-
iles CON WA
HALE, Charles Adams, 1930- , Amer-
ican; nonfiction CON
HALE, Charles Leslie, 1902- ,
English; nonfiction CON
HALE, Dennis, 1944- , American;
nonfiction CON
HALE, Edward Everett ('Col. Frederic
Ingham'), 1822-1909, American;
fiction BRO KAA MAG
'HALE, Garth' (Albert Benjamin Cun-
ningham), 1888- , American;
fiction WAF
'HALE, Helen' see MULCAHY, Lucille
B.
HALE, Katherine (Mrs. John Garvin),
1878- , Canadian; poetry, essays
ST
HALE, Kathleen, 20th cent., English;
juveniles DOY
HALE, Leon, 1921- , American;
nonfiction CON
HALE, Linda Howe, 1929- , Ameri-
can; juveniles CON
HALE, Lucretia Peabody, 1820-1900,
American; juveniles DOY KAA
HALE, Sir Matthew, 1609-76, Eng-
lish; nonfiction BRO KB ST
'HALE, Michael' see BULLOCK,
Michael
HALE, Nancy, 1908- , American;
fiction CON KTS
HALE, Oron James, 1902- , Amer-
ican; nonfiction CON
'HALE, Philip' see EASTWOOD,
Charles C.
HALE, Sarah Josepha Buell, 1788-
1879, American; editor, fiction
BRO KAA
HALE, Susan, 1833-1910, American;
nonfiction KAA
HALECKI, Oscar, 1891- , Australian;
nonfiction HOE SA
HALEK, Vítézslav, 1835-74, Czech;
poetry, fiction, plays COL KE
SA ST
HALES, John, 1584-1656, English;
nonfiction BRO KB ST
HA-LEVI, Judah see JUDAH BEN
SAMUEL
HALEVY, Daniel, 1872- , French;
nonfiction DIF
HALEVY, Ludowic, 1834-1908,

French; fiction, plays DIF
HAR KE MAG MAT SA ST
HALEY, Andrew Gallagher,
1904- , American; nonfiction
CON
HALEY, Gail E., 1939- , Ameri-
can; juveniles CON
HALEY, Jay, 1923- , American;
nonfiction CON
HALEY, Joseph E., 1915- ,
American; nonfiction CON
HALEY, Kenneth Harold Dobson,
1920- , English; nonfiction
CON
HALI, Altaf Husain, 1837-1914,
Arab; nonfiction ST
HALIBURTON, Thomas Chandler,
1796-1865, Canadian; nonfic-
tion, fiction BRO KBA SA
ST SY
HALID ZIYA USAKLIGIL, 1865-
1945, Turkish; fiction, essays
SA ST
HALIDE EDIB ADIVAR, 1883/85-
1964, Turkish; fiction SA ST
HALIFAX, Marquis of see
SAVILE, Sir George
HALIFAX, Charles Montagu, Earl
of, 1661-1715, English; fiction
BRO ST
HALIO, Jay Leon, 1928- ,
American; nonfiction CON
HALKET, Lady Anna, 1632-99,
English; nonfiction SA
HALL, A. Rupert, 1920- , Eng-
lish; nonfiction CON
'HALL, Adam' see TREVOR, El-
leston
HALL, Adele, 1910- , American;
juveniles, fiction CON WA
HALL, Andrew, 1935- , English;
fiction CON
HALL, Angus, 1932- , English;
fiction CON
HALL, Anna Gertrude, 1882- ,
American; nonfiction CON
HALL, Anna Maria Fielding ('S.C.
Hall'), 1800-81, Irish; fiction
poetry BRO KBA SA ST
HALL, Arlene Stevens, 1923- ,
American; nonfiction CON
HALL, Arthur Vine, 1862- ,
South African; poetry ST
HALL, Asa Zadel, 1875- ,
American; nonfiction CON
HALL, Basil, 1788-1844, Scots;
nonfiction, fiction BRO KBA
HALL, Bennie Caroline Humble

('Hall Bennett'; 'Emily Marshall'),
American; fiction CON
HALL, Calvin Springer, 1909- ,
American; nonfiction CON
HALL, Challis Alva, Jr., 1917- ,
American; nonfiction CON
'HALL, Claudia' see FLOREN, Lee
HALL, Clifton L., 1898- , Ameri-
can; nonfiction CON
HALL, Donald Andrew, Jr., 1928- ,
American; poetry CON MUR SP
WA
HALL, Donald John, 1903- , English;
nonfiction, fiction CON
HALL, Donald Ray, 1933- , Ameri-
can; nonfiction CON
HALL, Edward (Halle), 1499?-1547,
English; nonfiction BRO KB ST
HALL, Douglas Kent, 1938- , Amer-
ican; nonfiction CON
HALL, Elizabeth Corneilia, 1898- ,
American; nonfiction CON
HALL, Elizabeth Wason ('Betty Wason'),
1912- , American; nonfiction
CON
HALL, Elvajean, 1910- , American;
juveniles CON WA
HALL, Esther Greenacre, American;
juveniles WA
'HALL, Evan' see HALLERAN,
Eugene E.
HALL, Fitzedward, 1825-1901,
Anglo-American; nonfiction KAA
HALL, Geoffrey Fowler, 1888- ,
English; fiction CON
HALL, George Riley, 1865- , Amer-
ican; poetry MAR
HALL, Geraldine Marion, 1935- ,
American; nonfiction CON
HALL, Gimone, 1940- , American;
nonfiction CON
HALL, Gordon Langley, Anglo-Amer-
ican; juveniles, fiction, nonfiction,
plays CON WA
'HALL, Gordon Langley' see SIMMONS,
Dawn L.
HALL, Granville Stanley, 1844-1924,
American; nonfiction KT
HALL, Henry Marion, 1877- ,
American; nonfiction CON
HALL, Hessel Duncan, 1891- ,
Australian; nonfiction CON
'HALL, Holworthy' see PORTER,
Harold E.
'HALL, J. de P.' see McKELWAY,
St. Clair
HALL, J. Tilman, 1916- , Ameri-
can; nonfiction CON

HALL, James, 1793-1868, Ameri-
can; nonfiction HOO KAA ST
HALL, James Byron, 1918- ,
American; fiction CON
HALL, James Norman, 1887-1951,
American; fiction KAT KT
MAG WA WAF
HALL, Jerome, 1901- , Ameri-
can; nonfiction CON
'HALL, Jesse' see BAESEN, Victor
'HALL, John' see STEVENSON,
John H.
HALL, John, 1627-56, English;
poetry ST
HALL, John Clive, 1920- ,
British; poetry, criticism
MUR
HALL, John F., 1919- , Ameri-
can; nonfiction CON
HALL, John O.P., 1911- , Amer-
ican; nonfiction CON
HALL, John Whitney, 1916- ,
American; nonfiction CON
HALL, Josef Washington ('Upton
Close'), 1894-1960, American;
journalism, fiction BRO KT
HALL, Joseph, 1574-1656, Eng-
lish; fiction BRO KB ST
HALL, Kathleen Mary, 1924- ,
English; nonfiction CON
HALL, Kenneth Franklin, 1926- ,
American; nonfiction CON
HALL, Lawrence Sargent, 1915- ,
American; nonfiction CON
HALL, Leland, 1883- , Ameri-
can; nonfiction KT
HALL, Livingston, 1903- ,
American; nonfiction CON
HALL, Lynn, 1937- , American;
juveniles COM CON
HALL, Marie Boas, 1919- ,
English; nonfiction CON
HALL, Marguerite Radclyffe,
1886?-1943, English; fiction,
poetry BRO
HALL, Marjorie see YEAKLEY,
Marjory H.
HALL, Mark W., 1943- , Amer-
ican; nonfiction CON
HALL, Martin Hardwick, 1925- ,
American; nonfiction CON
HALL, Mary Anne, 1934- ,
American; nonfiction CON
HALL, Maurits Cornilis van
('Frank Floriszoon van Arkel'),
1768-1858, Dutch; poetry, non-
fiction ST
HALL, Michael Garibaldi, 1926- ,

American; nonfiction CON

HALL, Natalie Watson, 1923- , American; nonfiction CON

HALL, Oakley Maxwell ('Jason Manor'), 1920- , American; fiction CON

HALL, Patrick, 1932- , English; fiction CON

HALL, Peter Geoffrey, 1932- , English; nonfiction CON

HALL, Radclyffe, 1886-1943, English; fiction, poetry RIC KL KT

HALL, Richard, 1925- , English; nonfiction CON

HALL, Robert, 1764-1831, English; nonfiction BRO KBA

HALL, Robert Anderson, Jr., 1911- , American; nonfiction CON

HALL, Robert E., 1924- , American; nonfiction CON

HALL, Rodney, 1935- , Australian; poetry MUR

HALL, Roger Wolcott, 1919- , American; fiction CON

HALL, Rosalys Haskell, 1914- , American; juveniles CON FUL WA

HALL, Rubylia Ray, 1910- , American; fiction CON

HALL, S. C. see HALL, Anne Maria

HALL, Samuel Carter, 1800-89, Irish; nonfiction ST

HALL, Sarah Ewing, 1761-1830, American; nonfiction KAA

HALL, Ted Byron, 1902- , American; nonfiction CON

HALL, Thomas, 1610-65, English; nonfiction ST

HALL, Thor, 1927- , Norwegian-American; nonfiction CON

HALL, Tord Erik Martin, 1910- , Swedish; nonfiction CON

HALL, Trevor Henry, 1910- , English; nonfiction CON

HALL, Vernon, Jr., 1913- , American; nonfiction CON

HALL, Wade H., 1934- , American; nonfiction CON

HALL, Walter Earl, Jr., 1940- , American; poetry CON

HALL, William Norman, 1915- , American; juveniles WA

HALL, Willis, 1929- , English; plays MAT

HALLACK, Cecily, 1898-1938, English; fiction HOE

HALLAJ, Husain Ben Mansur, 858-922, Persian; nonfiction ST

HALLAM, A., 18th cent., French; translations DIL

HALLAM, Arthur Henry, 1811-33, English; poetry, essays KBA

HALLAM, Henry, 1777-1859, English; nonfiction BRO KBA SA ST

HALLAM, Herbert Enoch, 1923- , English; nonfiction CON

HALLAM, John Harvey, 1917- , English; nonfiction CON

HALLAM, Samuel Benoni Atlantis, 1915- , American; fiction CON

HALLBERG, Charles William, 1899- , American; nonfiction CON

HALLE, Edward see HALL, Edward

HALLE, Louis Joseph, 1910- , American; nonfiction CON

HALLECK, Titz-Greene, 1790-1867, American; poetry BRO KAA ST

HALLECK, Seymour Leon, 1929- , American; nonfiction CON

HALLER, Adolf, 1897- , Swiss; juveniles WA

HALLER, Albrecht Von, 1708-77, Swiss; poetry AL HAR KE ST

HALLER, Amédée Emmanuel de, 1735-86, Swiss; nonfiction DIL

HALLER, Charles Louis, 1768-1854, Swiss; nonfiction SA

HALLER, Mark Hughlin, 1928- , American; nonfiction CON

HALLER, Robert Spencer, 1933- , American; nonfiction CON

HALLERAN, Eugene Edward ('Donn Broward'; 'Evan Hall'), 1905- , American; fiction CON

HALLET, Jean Pierre, 1927- , Belgian-American; nonfiction CON

HALLETT, Ellen Kathleen, 1899- , English; nonfiction CON

HALLETT, Graham, 1929- , English; nonfiction CON

HALLFREDR, Otarsson, 967- , Icelandic; poetry SA

HALLGARTEN, Siegfried Fritz, 1902- , German-English; nonfiction CON

HALLGREN, Mauritz Alfred, 1899- , American; journalism,

essays KT
HALLGRIMSON, Jansson see 'KAMBAN,
Guomundur'
HALLGRIMSSON, Jónas, 1807-45, Ice-
landic; poetry, fiction KE SA ST
HALLIBURTON, Maurine, 1889- ,
American; poetry MAR
HALLIBURTON, Richard, 1900-39,
American; nonfiction BRO KAT KT
HALLIBURTON, Thomas C. see
'SLICK, Sam'
HALLIBURTON, Warren J., 1924- ,
American; nonfiction CON
HALLIDAY, Ernest Milton, 1913- ,
American; nonfiction CON
HALLIDAY, Frank Ernest, 1903- ,
American; nonfiction CON
'HALLIDAY, James' see SYMINGTON,
David
'HALLIDAY, Michael' see CREASEY,
John
HALLIDAY, William Ross, 1926- ,
American; nonfiction PAC
HALLIE, Philip P., 1922- , Ameri-
can; nonfiction CON
HALLIGAN, Nicholas, 1917- , Ameri-
can; nonfiction CON
HALLIN, Emily Watson, 1919- ,
American; juveniles CON
HALLINAN, Nancy, 1921- , English;
fiction CON
HALLINAN, Vincent, 1896- , Ameri-
can; fiction CON
HALLIWELL-PHILLIPS, James
Orchard, 1820-89, English; non-
fiction BRO
HALLMAN, Ralph Jefferson, 1911- ,
American; nonfiction CON
HALLMANN, Johann Christian,
1647?-1704, German; plays ST
HALLO, William W., 1928- , Ger-
man-American; nonfiction CON
HALLOCK, Charles, 1834-1917,
American; nonfiction KAA
HALLORAN, Richard Colby, 1930- ,
American; nonfiction CON
HALLOWELL, Alfred Irving, 1892- ,
American; nonfiction CON
HALLOWELL, John Hamilton, 1913- ,
American; nonfiction CON
HALL-QUEST, Edna Olga Wilbour,
1899- , American; juveniles
CON WA
HALLS, Wilfred Douglas, 1918- ,
American; nonfiction CON
HALLSTEAD, William Finn, III,
1924- , American; juveniles
CON

HALL-STEVENSON, John see
STEVENSON, John H.
HALLSTRÖM, Per August Leonard,
1866-1960, Swedish; poetry,
plays COL FLE HAR MAT
SA ST
HALM, George Nikolaus, 1901- ,
German-American; nonfiction
CON
'HALM, Friedrich' (E. F. J. von
Münch-Bellinghausen; Franz J.
Eligius), 1806-71, Austrian;
poetry, plays, fiction AL
HAR KE ST
HALMAEL, Hendrik van, 1654-
1718, Dutch; plays ST
HALMAR, Augusto d' see
D'HALMAR, Augusto
HALMOS, Paul, 1911- , Hungar-
ian-English; nonfiction CON
HALPE, Ashley, 1933- , Cey-
lonese; poetry MUR
HALPER, Albert, 1904- , Amer-
ican; fiction CON HOO KT
WAF
HALPERIN, Irving, 1922- , Amer-
ican; nonfiction CON
HALPERIN, Morton H., 1938- ,
American; nonfiction CON
HALPERIN, Samuel, 1930- ,
American; nonfiction CON
HALPERN, Abraham Meyer,
1914- , American; nonfiction
CON
HALPERN, Daniel, 1945- ,
American; nonfiction CON
HALPERN, Joel M., 1929- ,
American; nonfiction CON
HALPERN, Manfred, 1924- ,
American; nonfiction CON
HALPERN, Martin, 1929- , Amer-
ican; poetry, nonfiction CON
HALPERN, Moishe Leib, 1886-
1932, Jewish; poetry ST
HALPERT, Inge D., 1926- ,
German-American; nonfiction
CON
HALPERT, Stephen, 1941- ,
American; nonfiction CON
HALPIN, Andrew Williams,
1911- , American; nonfiction
CON
HALPINE, Charles Graham
('Miles O'Reilly'), 1829-68,
American; poetry, journalism
KAA
HALS, Ronald M., 1926- ,
American; nonfiction CON

HALSALL, Elizabeth, 1916- , American; nonfiction CON

HALSBAND, Robert, 1914- , American; nonfiction CON

HALSELL, Grace, 1923- , American; nonfiction CON WA

HALSEY, Albert Henry, 1923- , American; nonfiction CON

HALSEY, Elizabeth, 1890- , American; nonfiction CON

HALSEY, George Dawson, 1889- , American; nonfiction CON

HALSEY, Martha T., 1932- , American; nonfiction CON

HALSMAN, Philippe, 1906- , Latvian-American; nonfiction CON WA

HALSTEAD, Murat, 1829-1908, American; journalism KAA

HALT, 1837-1914, Indian; poetry LAN

HALTER, Carl, 1915- , American; nonfiction CON

HALTRECHT, Montague, 1932- , English; fiction CON

HALVERSON, Richard C., 1916- , American; nonfiction CON

HALVERSON, William Hagen, 1930- , American; nonfiction CON

'HALVID, Einar' see HELWIG, Werner

HALVORSON, Arndt Leroy, 1915- , American; nonfiction CON

HAM, Wayne, 1938- , Canadian; nonfiction CON

HAMACHEK, Don E., 1933- , American; nonfiction CON

HAMADHANI (Badi 'Az-Zaman), 968-1008, Persian; poetry, letters LAN ST

HAMALIAN, Leo, 1920- , American; nonfiction CON

HAMANN, Johann Georg, 1730-88, German; nonfiction AL HAR KE ST

HAMBERG, Daniel, 1924- , American; nonfiction CON

HAMBLETON, Jack, American; juveniles WA

HAMBLETON, Ronald, 1917- , Canadian; poetry, fiction MUR SY

HAMBLIN, Charles Leonard, 1922- , Australian; nonfiction CON

HAMBLIN, Dora Jane, 1920- , American; nonfiction CON WA

HAMBURG, Carl Heinz, 1915- , German-American; nonfiction CON

HAMBURGER, Anne Ellen File see 'BERESFORD, Anne'

HAMBURGER, Kaete, 1896- , German; nonfiction CON

HAMBURGER, Max, 1897- , German-American; nonfiction CON

HAMBURGER, Michael Peter Leopold, 1924- , British; translations, poetry, criticism CON MUR

HAMBURGER, Philip, 1914- , American; fiction CON

HAMBY, Alonzo L., 1940- , American; nonfiction CON

HAMD ALLAH-i MUSTOWFI, 1281/82- , Persian; nonfiction ST

'HAMEIRI, Avigdor' (Emil Feuerstein), 1886-1970, Jewish; poetry LAN

HAMELIN, Octave, 1856-1907, French; nonfiction DIF SA

HAMELL, Patrick Joseph, 1910- , Irish; nonfiction CON

HAMERLING, Robert (Rupert Johann Hammerling), 1830-89, Austrian; poetry, fiction AL HAR SA ST

HAMERMESH, Morton, 1915- , American; translations CON

HAMERTON, Philip Gilbert, 1834-94, English; criticism, essays BRO KBA

HAMES, Alice Inez, 1892- , New Zealander; nonfiction CON

HAMID al-Din, Abu Bakr Omar, -1164, Persian; essays ST

HAMIL, Thomas Arthur, 1928- , American; juveniles WA

'HAMILL, Ethel' see WEBB, Jean Francis

HAMILL, Pete, 1935- , American; nonfiction CON

HAMILL, Robert Hoffman, 1912- , American; nonfiction CON

HAMILTON, Dr. Alexander ('Loquacious Scribbe, Esq.'), 1712-56, American; diary, essays KAA

HAMILTON, Alexander, 1755/57-1804, American; nonfiction BRO KAA MAG ST

HAMILTON, Alfred Starr, American; poetry MUR

HAMILTON, Anthony, 1646?-1720,

English; fiction KB ST

HAMILTON, Antoine, 1646- , Irish; nonfiction DIL

HAMILTON, Bertram Lawson St. John, 1914- , English; nonfiction CON

HAMILTON, Charles ('Ralph Redway'; 'Frank Richards'; 'Hilda Richards'), 1913- , American; fiction CON

HAMILTON, Charles Harold St. John, 1876-1961, English; juveniles DOY

HAMILTON, Charles Walter, 1890- , American; nonfiction CON

HAMILTON, Clayton, 1881- , American; plays, criticism KT

'HAMILTON, Clive' see LEWIS, Clive S.

HAMILTON, Cosmo, 187?-1942, English; fiction, plays KT

HAMILTON, David Boyce, Jr., 1918- , American; nonfiction CON

HAMILTON, Donald Bengtsson, 1916- , American; fiction CON

HAMILTON, Dorothy, 1906- , American; juveniles CON

HAMILTON, Earl Jefferson, 1899- , American; nonfiction CON

HAMILTON, Edith, 1869- , American; nonfiction KT

HAMILTON, Edmond, 1904- , American; fiction CON

HAMILTON, Edward G., 1897- , American; nonfiction CON

HAMILTON, Edward John, 1834-1918, American; nonfiction KAA

HAMILTON, Eleanor Poorman, 1909- , American; nonfiction CON

HAMILTON, Elizabeth, 1758-1816, Scots; poetry, fiction BRO KBA

HAMILTON, Elizabeth, 18th cent., English; nonfiction SA

HAMILTON, Elizabeth, 1906- , Irish; nonfiction CON

'HAMILTON, Ernest' see MERRILL, Judith

HAMILTON, Franklin Willard, 1923- , American; poetry, nonfiction CON

'HAMILTON, Gail' see DODGE, Mary A.

HAMILTON, Sir George Rostrevor, 1888-1967, English; poetry SP

HAMILTON, Harry, 1896- , American; fiction, movies HOO

HAMILTON, Henry W., 1898- , American; nonfiction CON

HAMILTON, Holman, 1910- , American; nonfiction CON

HAMILTON, Horace Ernst, 1911- , American; nonfiction, poetry CON

HAMILTON, Howard Devon, 1920- , American; nonfiction CON

HAMILTON, Ian, 1938- , American; poetry MUR

HAMILTON, J. Wallace, 1900- , Canadian; nonfiction CON

'HAMILTON, Jack' see BRANNON, William T.

HAMILTON, Jean Tyree, 1909- , American; nonfiction CON

HAMILTON, Colonel John Potter, fl. 1781, English; nonfiction HIG

HAMILTON, Joseph Grégoire de Roulhac, 1878- , American; nonfiction JO

'HAMILTON, Kay' see DE LEEUW, Cateau

HAMILTON, Kenneth Morrison, 1917- , English; nonfiction CON

HAMILTON, Marshall Lee, 1937- , American; nonfiction CON

HAMILTON, Mary Agnes Adamson ('Iconoclast'), 1883- , Scots; fiction BRO KT

'HAMILTON, Michael' see CHETHAM-STRODE, Warren

HAMILTON, Michael Pollock, 1927- , English; nonfiction CON

HAMILTON, Milton Wheaton, 1901- , American; nonfiction CON

HAMILTON, Patrick, 1904-62, English; fiction, plays KTS MAT RIC

HAMILTON, Raphael Noteware, 1892- , American; nonfiction CON

HAMILTON, Robert, 1908- , English; nonfiction HO

'HAMILTON, Robert W.' see STRATEMEYER, Edward L.

HAMILTON, Ronald, 1909- , English; nonfiction CON

HAMILTON, Russel, American; juveniles WA

HAMILTON, Seena M., 1926- , American; nonfiction CON

HAMILTON, Thomas, 1789-1842, Scots; fiction BRO KBA

HAMILTON, Virginia, 1936- ,

American; juveniles CON WA
'HAMILTON, Wade' see FLOREN, Lee
HAMILTON, William (of Gilbertfield),
1665?-1751, Scots; nonfiction,
poetry BRO KE ST
HAMILTON, William (of Bangour),
1704-54, Scots; poetry BRO KB
ST
HAMILTON, Sir William, 1788-1856,
Scots; nonfiction BRO KBA SA
ST
HAMILTON, William Baskerville,
1908-72, American; nonfiction
CON
HAMILTON-EDWARDS, Gerald Kenneth
Savery, 1906- , English; nonfic-
tion CON
HAMIT, Abdulhak Tarhan, 1852-1937,
Turkish; poetry, plays LAN SA
HAMLIN, Gladys Eva, American;
nonfiction CON
HAMLIN, Griffith Askew, 1919- ,
American; nonfiction CON
HAMM, Jack, 1916- , American;
nonfiction CON
HAMM, Russell Leroy, 1926- ,
American; fiction, nonfiction,
poetry CON
HAMMARSKÖLD, Lars, 1785-1827,
Swedish; nonfiction ST
HAMMEL, Faye, 1929- , Ameri-
can; nonfiction CON
HAMMEN, Oscar John, 1907- ,
American; nonfiction CON
HAMMENHÖG, Waldemar, 1902- ,
Swedish; fiction ST
HAMMER, Emanuel Frederick,
1926- , American; nonfiction
CON
HAMMER, Franz, 1908- , German;
nonfiction AL
'HAMMER, Jacob' see OPPENHEIMER,
Joel L.
HAMMER, Jeanne Ruth, 1912- ,
Russian; nonfiction CON
HAMMER, Richard, 1928- , Ameri-
can; nonfiction CON
HAMMERKEN, Thomas see THOMAS
à KEMPIS
HAMMERMAN, Donald R., 1925- ,
American; nonfiction CON
HAMMERMAN, Gay Morenus, 1926- ,
American; nonfiction CON
HAMMER-PURGSTALL, Jósef, 1774-
1856, Austrian; nonfiction SA
HAMMERSTEIN, Oscar II, 1895-1961,
American; plays MAT
HAMMERTON, Sir John Alexander,

1871-1949, Scots; criticism
BRO
HAMMES, John Anthony, 1924- ,
American; nonfiction CON
HAMMETT, Dashiell, 1894-1961,
American; fiction BRO KT
MAG RIC SA ST
HAMMETT, Samuel Adams
('Philip Paxton'), 1816-65,
American; fiction KAA
HAMMON, Jupiter, 1720-1800,
American; poetry KAA
HAMMOND, Albert Lanphier,
1892- , American; nonfittion
CON
HAMMOND, Edwin Hughes, 1919- ,
American; nonfiction CON
HAMMOND, Dr. Francis M.,
1911- , Canadian-American;
nonfiction SCA
HAMMOND, Guyton Bowers,
1930- , American; nonfiction
CON
HAMMOND, Henry, 1605-60,
English; nonfiction KB
HAMMOND, Jabez Delano, 1778-
1855, American; nonfiction
KAA
HAMMOND, MacSawyer, 1926- ,
American; nonfiction, poetry
CON MUR
HAMMOND, Nicholas Geoffrey
Lempriere, 1907- , English;
nonfiction CON
HAMMOND, Paul Young, 1929- ,
American; nonfiction CON
HAMMOND, Percy, 1873-1936,
American; journalism, criti-
cism KT
HAMMOND, Philip C., 1924- ,
American; nonfiction CON
HAMMOND, Phillip Everett,
1931- , American; nonfiction
CON
HAMMOND, Ralph see HAMMOND-
INNES, Ralph
HAMMOND, Ross William, 1918- ,
American; nonfiction CON
HAMMOND, Thomas Taylor,
1920- , American; nonfiction
CON
HAMMOND, William, 1614- ,
English; poetry ST
HAMMOND, Innes Ralph ('Ham-
mond Innes'; 'Ralph Hammond'),
1913- , American; fiction
CON RIC WA
HAMMONTREE, Marie Gertrude,

1913- , American; nonfiction
CON
HAMOIRE, 18th cent., French; plays
DIL
HAMORI, Laszlo Dezso, 1911- , Hun-
garian-American; nonfiction CON
HAMP, Eric Pratt, 1920- , English;
nonfiction CON
'HAMP, Pierre' (Pierre Bourillon),
1876- , French; fiction COL
DIF HAR SA ST
HAMPDEN-TURNER, Charles M.,
1934- , American; nonfiction
CON
HAMPEL, Fritz see 'SLANG'
HAMPSCH, Harold George, 1927- ,
American; nonfiction CON
HAMPSON, Norman, 1922- , Eng-
lish; nonfiction CON
HAMPTON, Christopher James,
1946- , English; fiction, plays
CON
HAMPTON, Harold Duane, 1932- ,
American; nonfiction CON
HAMPTON, Kathleen, 1923- ,
American; fiction CON
'HAMPTON, Mark' see NORWOOD,
Victor G. C.
HAMPTON, Robert E., 1924- ,
American; nonfiction CON
HAMPTON, William Albert, 1929- ,
English; nonfiction CON
HAMRE, Leif, 1924- , Norwegian;
fiction CON
'HAMSUN, Knut' (Knud Pedersen
Hamsund), 1859-1952, Norwegian;
fiction, plays COL FLE HAR KL
KT MAG RIC SA ST
'HAN Suyin' (Elizabeth K. Chow Com-
ber), 1917- , Chinese; fiction
CON RIC
HAN YONGUN, 1879-1944, Korean;
poetry LAN
HAN YÜ, 768-824, Chinese; essays,
poetry LAN ST
HANCARVILLE, Pierre François
Hugues, 1719-1805, French; non-
fiction DIL
HANCE, William A., 1916- , Ameri-
can; nonfiction CON
HANCHETT, William, 1922- , Amer-
ican; nonfiction CON
HANCOCK, Alice Van Fossen, 1890- ,
American; juveniles CON
'HANCOCK, Keith' see HANCOCK,
William K.
HANCOCK, Leslie, 1941- , American;
nonfiction CON

HANCOCK, M. Donald, 1939- ,
American; nonfiction CON
HANCOCK, Malcolm ('Mal'),
1936- , American; nonfiction
CON
HANCOCK, Mary A., 1923- ,
American; juveniles CON
HANCOCK, Ralph Lowell, 1903- ,
American; juveniles, nonfic-
tion CON
HANCOCK, William Keith ('Keith
Hancock'), 1898- , Australian;
nonfiction CON
HAND, Geoffrey Joseph Philip
Mccaulay ('Barry Sweeney'),
1931- , Irish; nonfiction
CON
HAND, Thomas Alypius, 1915- ,
Irish; nonfiction CON
HANDEL, Gerald, 1924- , Amer-
ican; nonfiction CON
HANDEL-MAZZETTI, Enrica von,
1871-1955, Austrian; fiction,
poetry AL COL HOE FLE
LEN KU SA
HANDFORTH, Thomas Schofield,
1897-1948, American; juveniles
KJU WA
HANDLER, Julian Harris, 1922- ,
American; nonfiction CON
HANDLER, Philip, 1917- ,
American; nonfiction CON
HANDLEY-TAYLOR, Geoffrey,
1920- , American; nonfiction
CON
HANDLIN, Mary Flug, 1913- ,
American; nonfiction CON
HANDLIN, Oscar, 1915- , Amer-
ican; nonfiction CON KTS
HANDOVER, Phyllis Margaret,
English; nonfiction CON
HANDSCOMBE, Richard, 1935- ,
English; juveniles CON
HANDY, Robert Theodore,
1918- , American; nonfiction
CON
HANDY, Rollo, 1927- , Ameri-
can; nonfiction CON
HANES, Elizabeth Sill, Ameri-
can; nonfiction CON
HANES, Frank Borden, 1920- ,
American; fiction CON JO
HANEY, John B., 1931- , Amer-
ican; nonfiction CON
HANEY, Thomas K., 1936- ,
American; nonfiction CON
HANEY, William V., 1925- ,
American; nonfiction CON

HAN-FEI-TZU,   -233 B. C., Chinese;
 nonfiction ST
HANFF, Helene, American; nonfiction
 CON
HANFORD, Lloyd David, 1901- ,
 American; nonfiction CON
HANGEN, Putnam Welles, 1930- ,
 American; nonfiction CON
HANH, Nhat, Vietnamese; poetry
 MUR
HANKA, Vaclav, 1791-1861, Czech;
 poetry SA ST
HANKE, Enriqueta Guillermina,
 1885- , German; nonfiction SA
HANKE, Howard August, 1911- ,
 American; nonfiction CON
HANKE, Lewis U., 1905- , Ameri-
 can; nonfiction BL
HANKEY, Cyril Patrick, 1886- ,
 English; nonfiction CON
'HANKIN, St. John' (Emile Clavering),
 1869-1909, English; plays MAT
'HANKINS, Clabe' see McDONALD,
 Erwin L.
HANKINSON, Cyril Francis James,
 1895- , English; nonfiction CON
HANKS, Lucien Mason, 1910- ,
 American; nonfiction CON
HANLE, Dorothea Zack, 1917- ,
 American; nonfiction, juveniles
 CON
HANLEY, Boniface Francis, 1924- ,
 American; nonfiction CON
HANLEY, Clifford ('Henry Calvin'),
 1922- , American; fiction, plays
 CON
HANLEY, Gerald Anthony, 1916- ,
 English; fiction CON KTS RIC
HANLEY, Hope Anthony, 1926- ,
 American; nonfiction CON
HANLEY, James, 1901- , Irish;
 fiction BRO KT RIC SA
HANLEY, Katharine Ross, 1932- ,
 American; nonfiction CON
HANLEY, Theodore Dean, 1917- ,
 American; nonfiction CON
HANLEY, Thomas O'Brien, 1918- ,
 American; nonfiction CON
HANLEY, William, 1931- , Ameri-
 can; plays MAT
HANNA, Geneva R., American;
 juveniles WA
HANNA, J. Marshall, 1907- ,
 American; nonfiction CON
HANNA, Lavone Agnes, 1896- ,
 American; nonfiction CON
HANNA, Thomas, 1928- , American;
 nonfiction CON

HANNA, William, 1808-82, Eng-
 lish; nonfiction BRO
HANNAK, Johann Jacques,
 1892- , Austrian; nonfiction
 CON
HANNAN, Joseph Francis, 1923- ,
 American; fiction CON
HANNAU, Hans Walter, 1904- ,
 Austrian-American; nonfiction
 CON
HANNAY, James, 1827-73, Scots;
 criticism, fiction, journalism
 BRO KBA ST
HANNAY, James ('George A.
 Birmingham'), 1865-1950,
 Anglo-Irish; fiction BRO KAT
 KT RIC ST
HANNAY, Patrick,   -1629?,
 English; poetry KB ST
HANNEMAN, Audre Louise,
 1926- , American; fiction,
 nonfiction CON
HANNETAIRE, Jean Nicolas
 Servandoni, 1718-80, French;
 plays DIL
HANNIBAL, Edward, 1936- ,
 American; fiction CON
HANNING, Hugh, 1925- , English;
 nonfiction CON
HANNUM, Alberta Pierson,
 1906- , American; fiction
 JO WAF
HANNUM, Sara, American;
 juveniles WA
HANO, Arnold, 1922- , American;
 juveniles, fiction CON WA
HANOTAUX, Albert August Gabriel,
 1853- , French; nonfiction
 SA
HANRIEDER, Wolfram F.,
 1931- , American; nonfiction
 CON
HANSEN, Alfred Earl, 1927- ,
 American; nonfiction CON
HANSEN, Anton see 'TAMMSARRE,
 A. H. '
HANSBERRY, Lorraine, 1930-65,
 American; plays MAT
HANSEN, Alvin Harvey, 1887- ,
 American; nonfiction CON
HANSEN, Bertrand Lyle,
 1922- , American; nonfiction
 CON
HANSEN, Carl Francis, 1906- ,
 American; nonfiction CON
HANSEN, Chadwick Clarke,
 1926- , American; nonfiction
 CON

HANSEN, Donald Charles, 1935- ,
American; nonfiction CON
HANSEN, Gary Barker, 1935- ,
American; nonfiction CON
HANSEN, Harry, 1884- , American;
nonfiction HOO KAT KT WA
HANSEN, Joseph ('Rose Brock';
'James Colton'; 'James Coulton'),
1923- , American; fiction CON
HANSEN, Kenneth Harvey, 1917- ,
American; nonfiction CON
HANSEN, Klaus Juergen, 1931- ,
American; nonfiction CON
HANSEN, Marcus Lee, 1892-1938,
American; nonfiction KT
HANSEN, Martin Alfred, 1909-55,
Danish; fiction, essays FLE ST
HANSEN, Mary Lewis Patterson,
1933- , American; fiction CON
HANSEN, Mauritz Christopher, 1794-
1842, Norwegian; fiction ST
HANSEN, Niles Maurice, 1937- ,
American; nonfiction CON
HANSEN, Norman J., 1918- ,
American; nonfiction CON
HANSEN, Richard Herbert, 1929- ,
American; nonfiction CON
HANSEN, Terrence Leslie, 1920- ,
American; nonfiction CON
HANSEN, William Lee, 1928- ,
American; nonfiction CON
HANSER, Richard Frederick, 1909- ,
American; fiction, translations,
nonfiction CON
HANSJAKOB, Heinrich, 1837-1916,
German; nonfiction AL
HANSON, Albert Henry, 1913- ,
English; nonfiction CON
HANSON, Anne Coffin, 1921- ,
American; nonfiction CON
HANSON, Anthony Tyrrell, 1916- ,
English; nonfiction CON
HANSON, Eugene Kenneth, 1930- ,
American; nonfiction, juveniles
CON
HANSON, Howard Gordon, 1931- ,
American; poetry CON
HANSON, Joan, 1938- , American;
juveniles CON
HANSON, Kenneth O., 1922- ,
American; poetry MUR
HANSON, Norwood Russell, 1924- ,
American; nonfiction CON
HANSON, Pauline, 1950- , American;
poetry MUR
HANSON, Peggy, 1934- , American;
nonfiction CON
HANSON, Richard Patrick Crosland,

1916- , English; nonfiction
CON
HANSON, Richard Simon, 1931- ,
American; nonfiction CON
HANSON, Robert Carl, 1926- ,
American; nonfiction CON
HANSON, Robert P., American;
nonfiction CON
HANSON, Ruth Katie, 1900- ,
American; juveniles CON
HANSSON, Ola, 1860-1925,
Swedish; poetry, essays, fic-
tion COL FLE SA ST
HANSTEN, Philip D., 1943- ,
American; nonfiction CON
HAPGOOD, Charles Hutchins,
1904- , American; nonfiction
CON
HAPGOOD, David, 1926- , Amer-
ican; nonfiction CON
HAPGOOD, Hutchins, 1869-1944,
American; journalism, fiction,
essays HOO KT
HAPGOOD, Mrs. Hutchins (Neith
Boyce), 1872-1951, American;
fiction HOO
HAPGOOD, Norman, 1868-1937,
American; nonfiction, journal-
ism HOO KT
HAPPEL, Eberhard Werner, 1648-
90, German; fiction ST
HAPPEL, Robert A., 1916- ,
American; nonfiction CON
HAQ, Mahbub ul, 1934- ,
Pakistani; nonfiction CON
'HARALD, Eric' see BOESEN,
Victor
HARAMBASIC, August, 1861-1911,
Croatian; poetry ST
HARBAGE, Alfred Bennett ('Thomas
Kyd'), 1901- , American;
nonfiction, fiction CON KTS
HARBAOUGH, Henry, 1817-67,
American; nonfiction KAA ST
HARBAUGH, William Henry,
1920- , American; nonfiction
CON
HARBERGER, Arnold C., 1924- ,
American; nonfiction CON
HARBERT, Earl Norman, 1934- ,
American; nonfiction CON
HARBESON, Gladys Evans,
American; nonfiction CON
HARBIN, Calvin Edward, 1916- ,
American; nonfiction CON
HARBIN, Robert, 1909- , South
African; juveniles CON
'HARBINSON, Robert' see BRYANS,

Robert H.

HARBOTTLE, Michael Neale,
1917- , English; nonfiction
CON

HARBRON, John Davison, 1924- ,
Canadian; nonfiction CON

HARCAVE, Sidney Samuel, 1916- ,
American; nonfiction CON

HARCHEROAD, Fred Farley,
1918- , American; nonfiction
CON

HARCOUET de LONGEVILLE see
LONGEVILLE

HARCOURT, Geoffrey Colin,
1931- , Australian; nonfiction
CON

HARCOURT, Melville ('Criticus'),
1909- , English; nonfiction
CON

HARD, Frederick, 1897- , American; nonfiction CON

HARDCASTLE, Michael, 1933- ,
English; fiction CON

HARDEN, Donald Benjamin, 1901- ,
Irish; nonfiction CON

HARDEN, John, American; nonfiction
JO

HARDEN, Oleta Elizabeth McWhorter,
1935- , American; nonfiction
CON

HARDENBERG, Friedrich Leopold
('Novalis'), 1772-1801, German;
poetry AL HAR KE SA ST

HARDER, Eleanor Loraine, 1925- ,
American; juveniles CON

HARDER, Irma Lankow, 1915- ,
German; nonfiction AL

HARDGRAVE, Robert Lewis, Jr.,
1939- , American; nonfiction
CON

HARDIE, Frank, 1911- , English;
nonfiction CON

HARDIMAN, James W., 1919- ,
English; nonfiction CON

'HARDIN, Clement' see NEWTON,
Dwight B.

HARDIN, Garrett James, 1915- ,
American; nonfiction CON

'HARDIN, Mitch' see GERRITY,
David J.

HARDIN, Paul III, 1931- , American; nonfiction CON

'HARDIN, Peter' see VACZEK,
Louis

'HARDIN, Tom' see BAUER, Erwin
A.

HARDING, Bertita Leonarz, 1907- ,
German-American; nonfiction

CON KT

'HARDING, Carl B.' see BARKER
Elver A.

HARDING, Denys Clement Wyatt,
1906- , English; nonfiction
CON

HARDING, Harold Friend, 1903- ,
American; nonfiction CON

HARDING, Jack, 1914- , American; nonfiction CON

HARDING, James, 1929- ,
American; nonfiction CON

HARDING, Thomas Grayson,
1937- , American; nonfiction
CON

HARDING, Walter, 1917- , American; nonfiction CON

'HARDING, Wes' see KEEVILL,
Henry J.

HARDINGE, Helen Mary Cecil,
1901- , English; fiction
CON

HARDINGHAM, John Frederick
Watson, 1916- , New Zea-
lander; nonfiction CON

HARDION, Jacques, 1686-1766,
French; nonfiction DIL

HARDISON, Osborne Bennett, Jr.,
1928- , American; nonfiction
CON

HARDMAN, Richards Lynden
('Bronson Howitzer'), 1924- ,
American; fiction CON

HARDON, John Anthony, 1914- ,
American; nonfiction CON

HARDOY, Jorge Enrique, 1926- ,
Argentinian; nonfiction CON

HARDT, Ernst, 1876-1947, German; plays, fiction COL
MAT SA

HARDT, John Pearce, 1922- ,
American; nonfiction CON

HARDUIN, Alexandre Xavier,
1718-85, French; nonfiction
DIL

HARDUYN, Justus de, 1582-1641,
Flemish; poetry ST

'HARDWICK, Adam' see CONNOR,
John A.

HARDWICK, Clyde Thomas,
1915- , American; nonfiction
CON

HARDWICK, Elizabeth, 1916- ,
American; fiction CON

HARDWICK, Richard Holmes, Jr.
('Rick Holmes'), 1923- ,
American; nonfiction, fiction
CON

HARDY, Alexandre, 1570/75-1632, French; plays DIF KE ST

'HARDY, Alice Dale' see STRATE-MEYER, Edward L.

HARDY, Arthur Sherburne, 1847-1930, American; fiction, poetry KT

'HARDY, Douglas' see ANDREWS, Charles R. D. H.

HARDY, Edward Rochie, 1908- , American; nonfiction CON

HARDY, Evelyn, 1902- , American; nonfiction CON

HARDY, Frank, 1917- , Australian; fiction RIC

HARDY, John Edward, 1922- , American; nonfiction, fiction CON

HARDY, John Philips, 1933- , Australian; nonfiction CON

HARDY, Leroy Clyde, 1927- , American; nonfiction CON

HARDY, Michael James Langley, 1933- , English; nonfiction CON

HARDY, Pierre, 1720-68, French; nonfiction DIL

HARDY, Richard Earl, 1938- , American; nonfiction CON

HARDY, Ronald Harold, 1919- , English; nonfiction CON

HARDY, Siméon Prosper, 1729-1806, French; nonfiction DIL

HARDY, Thomas, 1840-1928, English; juveniles, poetry, plays, fiction BRO DOY FLE KAT KBA MAG MAT RIC SA SP ST

HARDY, William George, 1896- , Canadian; nonfiction, fiction CON SY

HARDY, William Marion, 1922- , American; fiction CON

HARDYCK, Curtis Dale, 1929- , American; nonfiction CON

HARDYNG, John, 1378-1465?, English; nonfiction ST

HARE, Alexander Paul, 1923- , American; nonfiction CON

HARE, Augustus John Cuthbert, 1834-1903, English; nonfiction BRO KBA ST

HARE, Augustus William, 1792-1834, English; nonfiction BRO

HARE, C. E., 1893- , English; nonfiction HIG

HARE, Eric B., 1894- , American; juveniles CON

HARE, Frederick Kenneth, 1919- , English; nonfiction CON

HARE, John, 1935- , English; nonfiction CON

HARE, Julius Charles, 1795-1855, English; nonfiction BRO KBA

HARE, Peter H., 1935- , American; nonfiction CON

HARE, Richard Gilbert, 1907- , English; nonfiction CON

HARE, Richard Mervyn, 1919- , English; nonfiction CON

HARE, Van Court, Jr., 1929- , American; nonfiction CON

HAREL, Marie Maximilien, 1749-1823, French; nonfiction DIL

HAREN, Jhr. Willem van, 1710-68, Dutch; poetry ST

HAREN, Onno Zweir van, 1713-79, Dutch; plays, poetry HAR ST

HARESNAPE, Geoffrey Laurence, 1939- , South African; poetry, fiction, criticism MUR

HAREVEN, Tamara K., 1937- , Rumanian-American; nonfiction CON

HARGRAVE, O. T., 1936- , American; nonfiction CON

HARGRAVE, Rowena, 1906- , American; nonfiction CON

HARGREAVES, Harry, 1922- , English; nonfiction CON

HARGREAVES, John D., 1924- , English; nonfiction CON

HARGREAVES, Mary Wilma Massey, 1914- , American; nonfiction CON

HARGREAVES, Reginald Charles ('Aiguillette'), 1888- , English; nonfiction CON

HARGREAVES-MAWDSLEY, William Norman ('Norman Mawdsley'), 1921- , English; nonfiction, poetry CON

HARGROVE, Barbara Watts, 1924- , American; nonfiction CON

HARGROVE, Katharine T., American; nonfiction CON

HARGROVE, Marion Lawton, Jr., 1919- , American; fiction, nonfiction JO KTS

HARGROVE, Merwin Matthew, 1910- , American; nonfiction CON

HARIK, Iliya F., 1934- , American; nonfiction CON

HARING, Firth, 1937- , American; fiction CON

HARING, Joseph Emerick,

1931- , American; nonfiction
CON
HARING, Norris G., 1923- , American; nonfiction CON
HARING, Philip Smyth, 1915- , American; nonfiction CON
HARINGER, Johann Jakob, 1898- , German; nonfiction KU
HARINGTON, Donald, 1935- , American; fiction CON
HARINGTON, James see HARRINGTON, James
HARINGTON, John, fl. 1550- , English; translations ST
HARINGTON, Sir John, 1561-1612, English; translations BRO KB ST
HARIOT, Thomas see HARRIOT, Thomas
HARIRI, 1054-1122, Arab; nonfiction, poetry LAN SA ST
HARISCANDRA, Bharatendu, 1846-84, Indian; plays, poetry LAN
HARIZI, Judah Ben Solomon, 1165-1235?, Spanish-Jewish; poetry ST
HARK, Mildred see McQUEEN, Mildred H.
'HARKAWAY, Hal' see STRATEMEYER, Edward L.
HARKER, Lizzie Allen Watson, 1863-1933, English; fiction, plays BRO KT
HARKEY, William G., 1914- , American; nonfiction CON
HARKINS, Philip ('John Blaine'), 1912- , American; juveniles CON FUL WA
HARKINS, William E., 1921- , American; nonfiction CON
HARKNESS, Bruce, 1923- , American; nonfiction CON
HARKNESS, David James, 1913- , American; nonfiction CON
HARKNESS, David William, 1937- , English; nonfiction CON
HARKNESS, Georgia, American; nonfiction CON
HARKNESS, Marjory Gane, 1880- , American; nonfiction CON
'HARLAN, Glen' see CEBULASH, Mel
HARLAN, Louis Rudolph, 1922- , American; nonfiction CON
HARLAND, Henry ('Sidney Luska'), 1861-1905, American; fiction BRO KAA
'HARLE, Elizabeth' see ROBERTS, Irene
'HARLEQUIN' see REED,

Alexander W.
'HARLEY, John' see MARSH, John
HARLOW, Alvin Tay, 1875- , American; juveniles WA
HARLOW, Lewis Augustus, 1901- , American; nonfiction CON
HARLOW, Rex Francis, 1892- , American; nonfiction MAR
HARLOW, Samuel Ralph, 1885-1972, American; nonfiction CON
HARLOW, Victor E., 1876- , American; nonfiction MAR
HARLOW, William M., 1900- , American; nonfiction CON
HARMAN, Richard Alexander, 1917- , English; nonfiction CON
HARMAN, Thomas, fl. 1567- , English; nonfiction ST
HARMAN, Willis Walter, 1918- , American; nonfiction CON
HARMER, Mabel, 1894- , American; nonfiction CON
HARMER, Ruth Mulvey, 1919- , American; nonfiction CON
HARMON, Allen Jackson, 1926- , American; nonfiction CON
HARMON, Gary L., 1935- , American; nonfiction CON
HARMON, James Judson, 1933- , American; fiction CON
HARMON, Lyn S., 1930- , American; juveniles CON
HARMON, Maurice, 1930- , Irish; nonfiction CON
HARMON, Robert Bartlett, 1932- , American; nonfiction CON
HARMON, William, 1938- , American; nonfiction, poetry CON
HARMS, Ernest, 1895- , German-American; nonfiction CON
HARMS, John, 1900- , German-American; nonfiction CON
HARMS, Robert Thomas, 1932- , American; nonfiction CON
HARNACK, Curtis Arthur, 1927- , American; nonfiction CON
HARNACK, Robert Victor, 1927- , Italian-American; nonfiction CON
HARNETT, Cynthia Mary, 1893- , English; juveniles CON DOY WA

HARNETTY, Peter, 1927- , English;
nonfiction CON
HARNEY, Edgar P. , American; non-
fiction SCA
HARNY de GUERVILLE, 18th cent.,
French; plays DIL
HARO DELAGE, Eduardo, 1889- ,
Spanish; nonfiction SA
HARO, Robert Peter, 1936- ,
American; nonfiction CON
HARO TEGGLEN, Eduardo, 1924- ,
Spanish; plays SA
HARPER, George McLean, 1863-1947,
American; nonfiction KT
HARPER, Heinrich, 1912- , Aus-
trian; nonfiction CON
HARPER, Howard, 1904- , Ameri-
can; nonfiction CON
HARPER, Howard M. , Jr., 1930- ,
American; nonfiction CON
HARPER, John Russell, 1914- ,
Canadian; nonfiction CON
HARPER, Michael S. , 1938- ,
American; nonfiction, poetry CON
HARPER, Robert Alexander, 1924- ,
American; nonfiction CON
HARPER, Robert Johnston Craig,
1927- , Scots; nonfiction CON
HARPER, Wilhelmina, 1884- ,
American; juveniles CON WA
HARPESTRAENG, Henrik,   -1244,
Danish; nonfiction ST
HARPOLE, Patricia Chayne, 1933- ,
American; nonfiction CON
HARPSFIELD, Nicolas, 1519-75,
English; nonfiction ST
HARPUR, Charles, 1813-68, Aus-
tralian; poetry ST
HARR, Wilber C. , 1908- , Ameri-
can; nonfiction CON
HARRADEN, Beatrice, 1864-1936,
English; fiction BRO KT RIC SA
HARRAH, David, 1926- , American;
nonfiction CON
HARRAL, Stewart, 1906-64, American;
nonfiction CON
HARRAR, Ellwood Scott, 1905- ,
American; nonfiction CON
HARRE, Horace Romano, 1927- ,
New Zealander; nonfiction CON
HARRE, John, 1931- , New Zealander;
nonfiction CON
HARRELL, Allen Waylan, 1922- ,
American; nonfiction CON
HARRELL, Costen Jordan, 1885- ,
American; nonfiction CON
HARRELL, David Edwin, Jr.,
1930- , American; nonfiction
CON

HARRELL, Irene Burk ('Amos
Amor'; 'Mildred Wyalan'),
1927- , American; nonfiction
CON
HARRELL, John G. , 1922- ,
American; nonfiction CON
HARRELL, Thomas Willard,
1911- , American; nonfiction
CON
HARRELSON, Walter Joseph,
1919- , American; nonfiction
CON
HARRIES, Karsten, 1937- ,
German-American; nonfiction
CON
HARRIGAN, Anthony Hart,
1925- , American; nonfiction
CON
HARRIGAN, Edward (Ned), 1845-
1911, American; plays, fiction
KAA MAT
HARRIMAN, John, 1904- , Amer-
can; fiction KT WAF
HARRIMAN, Margaret, 1928- ,
English; fiction CON
HARRIMAN, Richard Levett,
1944- , American; nonfiction
CON
HARRINGTON, Donald Szantho,
1914- , American; nonfiction
CON
HARRINGTON, Elbert Willington,
1901- , American; nonfiction
CON
'HARRINGTON, George F. ' see
BAKER, William M.
HARRINGTON, Harold David,
1903- , American; nonfiction
CON
HARRINGTON, James (Harington),
1611-77, English; nonfiction
BRO KB SA
'HARRINGTON, K.' see BEAN,
Keith F.
HARRINGTON, Lyn Evelyn Davis,
1911- , Canadian; juveniles
CON WA
HARRINGTON, Mark Raymond
('Ramon de la Cuevas';
'Jiskogo'; 'Tonashi'), 1882- ,
American; nonfiction CON
HARRINGTON, Michael, 1928- ,
American; nonfiction CON
HARRINGTON, Thelma, 1896- ,
American; juveniles JO
HARRINGTON, William, 1931- ,
American; nonfiction CON
HARRIOT, Thomas (Hariot;
Heriot), 1560-1621, English;

nonfiction JO
HARRIS, Alan, 1928- , English;
nonfiction CON
HARRIS, Albert Josiah, 1908-
American; nonfiction CON
HARRIS, Alice Kessler, 1941- ,
English; nonfiction CON
'HARRIS, Andrew' see POOLE,
Frederick K.
HARRIS, Benjamin, fl. 1673-
1716, American; journalism
KAA
HARRIS, Benjamin Maxawell, 1923- ,
American; nonfiction CON
HARRIS, Bernice Kelly, 1892/94- ,
American; fiction, plays CON
JO WAF
HARRIS, Bertha, 1937- , American;
fiction CON
HARRIS, Charles Houston III, 1937- ,
American; nonfiction CON
HARRIS, Chauncy Dennison, 1914- ,
American; nonfiction CON
HARRIS, Chester W., 1910- , Amer-
ican; nonfiction CON
HARRIS, Christie Lucy Irwin, 1907- ,
American; fiction CON
HARRIS, Clyde E., Jr., American;
nonfiction CON
HARRIS, Cyril, 1891- , Canadian;
fiction CON
HARRIS, Dale Benner, 1914- , Amer-
ican; nonfiction CON
HARRIS, Douglas Herschel, Jr.,
1930- , American; nonfiction
CON
HARRIS, Elliot, 1932- , American;
nonfiction CON
HARRIS, Ernest Edward, 1914- ,
American; nonfiction CON
HARRIS, Foster, 1903- , American;
fiction MAR
HARRIS, Frank, 1856-1931, Welsh;
journalism, nonfiction, fiction
BRO KL KT RIC SA
HARRIS, Frank Brayton ('Kirkpatrick
West'), 1932- , American; non-
fiction CON
HARRIS, Gene Gray, 1929- , Ameri-
can; juveniles CON
HARRIS, George Washington, 1814-69,
American; fiction KAA
HARRIS, Irving David, 1914- ,
American; nonfiction CON
HARRIS, James, 1709-80, English;
nonfiction BRO
HARRIS, Jane Allen, 1918- , Ameri-
can; nonfiction CON

HARRIS, Janet, 1932- , Ameri-
can; juveniles CON
HARRIS, Jessica Lee, 1939- ,
American; nonfiction CON
HARRIS, Joel Chandler ('Obediah
Skinflint'), 1848-1908, Ameri-
can; fiction, juveniles BRO
DOY KAA MAG ST WA
HARRIS, John Beynon see 'WYND-
HAM, John'
HARRIS, John Roy, 1915- ,
American; poetry CON
HARRIS, John Sharp, 1917- ,
American; nonfiction CON
HARRIS, Joseph, 1650-1715,
English; plays ST
HARRIS, Joseph Pratt, 1896- ,
American; nonfiction CON
HARRIS, Julian Earle, 1896- ,
American; nonfiction CON
'HARRIS, Kathleen' see HUMPH-
RIES, Adelaide M.
'HARRIS, Larry M.' see JANIFER,
Laurence M.
HARRIS, Leon A., Jr., 1926- ,
American; juveniles CON WA
HARRIS, Louis, 1921- , Ameri-
can; nonfiction CON
HARRIS, Louise, 1903- , Ameri-
can; nonfiction CON
'HARRIS, Macdonald' see HEINEY,
Donald W.
HARRIS, Marguerite Schmous,
1899- , American; poetry
MUR
HARRIS, Marilyn see SPRINGER,
Marilyn H.
HARRIS, Marion Rose Young,
1925- , Welsh; nonfiction
CON
HARRIS, Marjorie Silliman,
1890- , American; fiction
CON
HARRIS, Mark ('Jack Atkins';
'Willis J. Ingram'; 'Henry
Martha'; 'Alex Washington';
'Henry J. Wiggen'; 'Jack R.
Wright'), 1922- , American;
fiction CON
HARRIS, Marshall Dees, 1903- ,
American; nonfiction CON
HARRIS, Mary, 1905- , English;
fiction HO
HARRIS, Mary K., 1905- ,
English; juveniles, fiction
CON
HARRIS, Max, 1931- , Australian;
poetry, fiction MUR RIC

HARRIS, Michael Richard, 1936- ,
American; nonfiction CON
HARRIS, Miles Fitzgerald, 1913- ,
American; nonfiction CON
HARRIS, Miriam Coles, 1834-1925,
American; fiction KAA
HARRIS, Philip Robert, 1926- ,
American; nonfiction CON
HARRIS, Robert Jennings, 1907- ,
American; nonfiction CON
HARRIS, Robert Laird, 1911- ,
American; nonfiction CON
HARRIS, Robert Taylor, 1912- ,
American; nonfiction CON
HARRIS, Robin Sutton, 1919- ,
Canadian; nonfiction CON
'HARRIS, Roger' see WILSON, Roger
H. L.
HARRIS, Ronald Walter, 1916- ,
English; nonfiction CON
HARRIS, Rosemary Jeanne, English;
fiction, juveniles CON
HARRIS, Seymour Edwin, 1897- ,
American; nonfiction KTS
HARRIS, Sheldon Howard, 1928- ,
American; nonfiction CON
HARRIS, Stephen LeRoy, 1937- ,
American; nonfiction CON
HARRIS, Theodore Wilson, 1921- ,
British; poetry, fiction, criticism
MUR
HARRIS, Thomas Lake, 1823-1906,
American; poetry KAA
HARRIS, Walter A., 1929- , Ameri-
can; nonfiction CON
HARRIS, William C., 1933- , Ameri-
can; nonfiction CON
HARRIS, William Torrey, 1835-1909,
American; nonfiction KAA
HARRISON, Barbara, 1941- , Ameri-
can; fiction CON
HARRISON, Brian, 1909- , Irish;
nonfiction CON
HARRISON, C. William, 1913- ,
American; juveniles WA
HARRISON, Charles Yale, 1898- ,
American; fiction WAF
HARRISON, Chip, 1952- , American;
fiction CON
HARRISON, Constance Gary ('Refugitta'),
1843-1920, American; fiction KAA
HARRISON, Edith Ogden, American;
juveniles HOO
HARRISON, Everett Falconer, 1902- ,
American; nonfiction CON
HARRISON, Francis Burton, 1873-1957,
American; nonfiction HO
HARRISON, Fred, 1917- , American;

nonfiction CON
HARRISON, Frederic, 1831-1923,
English; criticism, essays
KBA
HARRISON, George Bagshawe,
1894- , English; nonfiction
CON HO KTS
HARRISON, George Russell,
1893- , American; nonfiction
CON
HARRISON, Gessner, 1807-62,
American; nonfiction KAA
HARRISON, Harry Max, 1925- ,
American; fiction CON
HARRISON, Henry Sydnor, 1880-
1930, American; fiction KT
HARRISON, Howard, 1930- ,
American; nonfiction CON
HARRISON, James, 1937- ,
American; poetry CON
HARRISON, James Albert, 1848-
1911, American; nonfiction
KAA
HARRISON, Jane Ellen, 1850-1928,
English; nonfiction BRO
HARRISON, Jim, 1937- , Ameri-
can; poetry MUR
HARRISON, John Baughman,
1907- , American; nonfiction
CON
HARRISON, John Fletcher Clews,
1921- , English; nonfiction
CON
HARRISON, John Marshall,
1914- , American; nonfiction
CON
HARRISON, Keith Edward, 1932- ,
Australian; poetry MUR
HARRISON, Kenneth Cecil,
1915- , English; nonfiction
CON
HARRISON, Louise Collbran,
1908- , American; nonfiction
CON
HARRISON, Lowell Hayes, 1922- ,
American; nonfiction CON
HARRISON, Mary St. Leger
Kingsley ('Lucas Malet'),
1852-1931, English; fiction
HOE KT
HARRISON, Raymond H., 1911- ,
American; nonfiction CON
HARRISON, Robert, 1932- ,
American; nonfiction CON
HARRISON, Royden John, 1927- ,
English; nonfiction CON
HARRISON, Saul I., 1925- ,
American; nonfiction CON

HARRISON, Sydney Gerald, 1924- ,
English; nonfiction CON
HARRISON, Walter Munford, 1888- ,
American; nonfiction MAR
'HARRISON, Whit' see WHITTINGTON,
Harry
HARRISON, Wilfrid, 1909- , Scots;
nonfiction CON
HARRISON, William, 1534-93, English;
nonfiction KB
HARRISON, Willia, 1933- , American;
fiction CON
HARRISON, William C., 1919- , Amer-
ican; juveniles CON
HARRISON CHURCH, Ronald James,
1915- , English; nonfiction CON
HARRISS, Clement Lowell, 1912- ,
American; nonfiction CON
HARROD, Leonard Montague, 1905- ,
English; nonfiction CON
HARROD, Roy Forbes, 1900- ,
English; nonfiction CON
HARROWER, Molly, 1906- , South
African; nonfiction CON
HARRY, Blind see HENRY the MIN-
STREL
HARRY, Myriam, 1880- , German;
nonfiction SA
HARSA, 606-47, Indian; plays LAN
HARSDÖRFFER, Georg Philip, 1607-
58, German; poetry AL KE ST
HARSENT, David, 1942- , English;
poetry MUR
HARSH, Wayne C., 1924- , Ameri-
can; nonfiction CON
HARSHA (Harshavardhana), 7th cent.,
Indian; poetry ST
HARSHAW, Ruth Hetzel, American;
juveniles WA
HARSS, Luis, 1936- , Chilean; fic-
tion CON
HARSTAD, Peter Tjernagel, 1935- ,
American; nonfiction CON
HART, Albert Bushnell, 1854-1943,
American; nonfiction KT
HART, Albert Gailord, 1909- ,
American; nonfiction CON
HART, Arthur Tindal, 1908- ,
English; nonfiction CON
HART, Carolyn Gimpel, 1936- ,
American; juveniles CON
HART, Donald John, 1917- ,
American; nonfiction CON
HART, Edward L., 1916- , Ameri-
can; nonfiction CON
HART, Frances Newbold Noyes, 1890-
1943, American; fiction KT
'HART, Harry' see FRANK, Pat

HART, Heinrich, 1855-1906, Ger-
man; criticism, plays, poetry
AL COL SA ST
HART, Herbert Michael, 1928- ,
American; nonfiction CON
HART, Hubert Lionel, Adolphus,
1907- , English; nonfiction
CON
HART, Henry Cowles, 1916- ,
American; nonfiction CON
HART, Henry Hersch, 1886- ,
American; translations, non-
fiction CON
HART, James David, 1911- ,
American; nonfiction CON
HART, Jim Allee, 1914- , Amer-
ican; nonfiction CON
HART, John Edward, 1917- ,
American; nonfiction CON
HART, John Fraser, 1924- ,
American; nonfiction CON
HART, Julius, 1859-1930, German;
criticism, plays, poetry AL
COL SA
HART, Larry, 1920- , American;
nonfiction CON
HART, Moss, 1904-61, American;
plays KT MAT ST
HART, Liddell, Basil see LID-
DELL HART, Basil H.
HART, Ray Lee, 1929- , Ameri-
can; nonfiction CON
HART, Richard, 1908- , Ameri-
can; nonfiction CON
HART, Vorhis Donn, 1918- ,
American; nonfiction CON
HARTCUP, Guy, 1919- , English;
nonfiction CON
HART-DAVIS, Duff, 1936- ,
English; nonfiction CON
HARTE, Francis Brett, 1836-1902,
American; fiction, poetry
BRO KAA MAG SA ST WA
HARTE, Marjorie see McEVOY,
Marjorie H.
HARTENBUSCH, Juan Eugenio
see HARTZENBUSCH, Juan
E.
HARTENDORP, Abram Van
Heyningen, 1893- , Dutch-
American; nonfiction CON
HARTER, Helen O'Connor, 1905- ,
American; juveniles CON
HARTER, Lafayette George, Jr.,
1918- , American; nonfiction
CON
HARTFORD, Ellis Ford, 1905- ,
American; nonfiction CON

HARTFORD, Claire, 1913- , American; nonfiction CON

HARTFORD, George Huntington, 1911- , American; nonfiction CON

'HARTFORD, Via' see DONSON, Cyril

HARTH, Robert, 1940- , American; nonfiction CON

HARTICH, Alice, 1888- , American; juveniles, poetry CON

HARTIG, François de Paule, 1758-97, Austrian; nonfiction DIL

HARTJE, Robert George, 1922- , American; nonfiction CON

HARTKE, Vance, 1919- , American; nonfiction CON

'HARTLAND, Marion' see TERHUNE, Mary V. H.

HARTLAUB, Felix, 1913-45, German; fiction, plays, essays AL FLE KU

HARTLAUD, Genoveva, 1915- , German; nonfiction KU

HARTLEBEN, Otto Erich ('Otto Erich'), 1864-1905, German; plays, poetry AL COL HAR MAT SA ST

HARTLEY, David, 1705-57, English; nonfiction BRO KB ST

HARTLEY, Ellen Raphael, 1915- , American; nonfiction CON

HARTLEY, John Irvin, 1921- , American; nonfiction CON

HARTLEY, Leslie Poles, 1895-1972, English; fiction BRO FLE KTS RIC

HARTLEY, Lodwick Charles, 1906- , American; nonfiction CON JO

HARTLEY, Marie, 1905- , American; nonfiction CON

HARTLEY, Rachel M., 1895- , American; nonfiction CON

HARTLEY, William Brown, 1913- , American; fiction CON

HARTLIB, Samuel, 1596/1600-62, Polish; nonfiction ST

HARTLIEB, Johannes, fl. 1439-63, German; translations ST

HARTMAN, David N., 1921- , American; nonfiction CON

HARTMAN, Gertrude, 1905- , American; juveniles KJU

HARTMAN, Louis Francis, 1901- , American; nonfiction CON

HARTMAN, Olov, 1906- , Swedish; nonfiction CON

'HARTMAN, Patience' see ZAWOD-SKY, Patience

HARTMAN, Rachel Frieda, 1920-72, American; fiction CON

HARTMAN, Robert S., 1910- , German-American; nonfiction CON

'HARTMAN, Roger' see MEHTA, Rustam J.

HARTMANN, Carl Robert Edward von, 1842-1906, German; nonfiction HAR SA

HARTMANN, Ernest, 1934- , Austrian-American; nonfiction CON

HARTMANN, Frederick Howard, 1922- , American; nonfiction CON

HARTMANN, Klaus, 1925- , American; nonfiction CON

HARTMANN, Moritz, 1821-72, Austrian; journalism, fiction AL HAR ST

HARTMANN, Nicolai, 1882- , German; nonfiction SA

HARTMANN von AUE, 1170-1210/20- , German; poetry AL HAR KE MAG SA ST

HARTNETT, Michael, 1941- , Irish; poetry MUR

'HARTNY, Tsishka' (D. Zhilunovich), 1887- , Russian; fiction HARK

HARTOG, Henri, 1869-1904, Dutch; fiction ST

'HARTOG, Jan de' (F. R. Eckmar), 1914- , Dutch; fiction, essays, plays FLE KTS SA ST

HARTSHORNE, Charles, 1897- , American; nonfiction CON

HARTSHORNE, Richard, 1899- , American; nonfiction CON

HARTSHORNE, Thomas Llewellyn, 1935- , American; nonfiction CON

HART-SMITH, William, 1911- , Australian; poetry CON MUR

HARTUNG, Hugo, 1902- , German; nonfiction KU

HARTUP, Willard Wert, 1927- , American; nonfiction CON

HARTWELL, Dickson Jay, 1906- , American; nonfiction CON

'HARTWELL, Nancy' see CALLAHAN, Claire W.

HARTWELL, Ronald Max, 1921- , Australian; nonfiction CON

HARTWIG, Marie Dorothy, 1906- , American; nonfiction CON

HARTZENBUSCH, Juan Eugenio, 1806-80, Spanish; plays, poetry BL HAR KE SA ST

HARTZHEIM, Joseph, 1694-1763, German; nonfiction SA

'HARVARD, Charles' see GIBBS-SMITH, Charles H.

HARVEY, Charles John Derrick, 1922- , South African; poetry CON MUR

HARVEY, Christopher, 1597?-1663, English; poetry ST

HARVEY, F. W., 1888- , English; nonfiction HOE

HARVEY, Frank Laird, 1913- , American; fiction CON

HARVEY, Gabriel, 1545?-1630, English; poetry, criticism BRO KB ST

HARVEY, Ian Douglas, 1914- , English; nonfiction CON

HARVEY, James O., 1926- , American; nonfiction CON

HARVEY, Jean Charles, 1891- , Canadian; fiction SY

HARVEY, John Frederick, 1921- , American; nonfiction CON

HARVEY, John Hooper, 1911- , English; nonfiction CON

HARVEY, Lashley Grey, 1900- , American; nonfiction CON

HARVEY, O. J., 1927- , American; nonfiction CON

'HARVEY, Rachel' see BLOOM, Ursula

HARVEY, Robert, 1884- , English; nonfiction CON

HARVEY, Ruth Charlotte, 1918- , American; nonfiction CON

HARVEY, Van Austin, 1926- , American; nonfiction CON

HARVEY, William, 1578-1657, English; nonfiction KB

HARWARD, Timothy Blake, 1932- , English; nonfiction CON

HARWELL, Richard Barksdale, 1915- , American; nonfiction CON

'HARWIN, Brian' see HENDERSON, Le Grand

HARWOOD, Alice Mary, English; nonfiction, poetry CON

HARWOOD, Edwin, 1939- , Ameri-

can; nonfiction CON

'HARWOOD, Gina' see BATTIS-COMBE, Esther G. H.

HARWOOD, Gwendoline Nessie Foster ('Walter Lehmann'; 'Francis Geyer'; 'Miriam Stone'), 1920- , Australian; poetry MUR

HARWOOD, Isabella ('Ross Neil'), 1840?-88, English; plays, fiction KBA

HARWOOD, Lee, 1939- , English; nonfiction CON MUR

HARWOOD, Pearl Augusta Bragdon, 1903- , American; juveniles CON

HARWOOD, Ronald, 1934- , American; fiction, plays CON

HARYCH, Theo, 1903-58, German; nonfiction AL

HASDEU, Bogdan Petruceiu, 1836/38-1907, Rumanian; nonfiction, poetry, plays ST

HASEBROEK, Johannes Petrus ('Jonathan'), 1812-96, Dutch; poetry, essays ST

'HASEGAWA, Nyozekan' (Hasegawa Manjiro), 1874- , Japanese; fiction ST

HASEGAWA TATSUNOSUKE see 'FUTABATEI SHIMEI'

HASEK, Jaroslav, 1883-1923, Czech; fiction COL FLE HAR KT RIC SA ST

HASELDEN, Kyle Emerson, 1913-68, American; nonfiction CON

HASENCLEVER, Walter, 1890-1940, German; plays, poetry AL COL FLE KU KUN MAT SA

HASENCLEVER, Wilhelm, 1837-89, German; nonfiction AL

HASENKAMP, Gottfried, 1902- , German; nonfiction KU

HASHIM, Ahmet, 1889-1933, Turkish; poetry, essays SA

HASKELL, Arnold Lionel, 1903- , English; nonfiction CON

HASKELL, Francis, 1928- , English; nonfiction CON

HASKELL, Helen Eggleston, American; juveniles KJU

HASKETT, Edythe Rance, 1915- , American; fiction CON

HASKIN, Dorothy Clark ('Howard Clark'), 1905- , American; nonfiction, juveniles CON

HASKINS, George Lee, 1915- ,
American; nonfiction CON
HASKINS, James, 1941- , American;
juveniles CON
HASKINS, Minnie Louise, 1875-1957,
English; poetry BRO
HASLAM, Gerald W., 1937- , Ameri-
can; nonfiction CON
HASLER, Joan, 1931- , English;
nonfiction CON
HASLEY, Louis Leonard, 1906- ,
American; nonfiction CON
HASLEY, Lucile, 1909- , American;
nonfiction CON HO
HASLING, John, 1928- , American;
nonfiction CON
HASS, Charles Glen, 1915- , Amer-
ican; nonfiction CON
HASSALL, Christopher, 1912-63,
English; poetry, plays RIC
HASSALL, William Owen, 1912- ,
English; nonfiction CON
HASSAN, Ihab Habib, 1925- , Egyp-
tian-American; nonfiction CON
HASSAN, William Ephraim, Jr.,
1923- , American; nonfiction
CON
HASSAN ibn Thabit, -674, Arab;
poetry ST
HASSAUREK, Friedrich, 1831-85,
German-American; poetry ST
HASSELROT, Bengt, 1910- ,
Swedish; nonfiction BL
HASSELS, Adela Florence Cory see
'HOPE, Laurence'
HASSELT, André Henri Constant van,
1806-74, Belgian; poetry HAR
KE ST
HASSENGER, Robert Leo, 1937- ,
American; nonfiction CON
HASSING, Per, 1916- , Swedish-
American; nonfiction CON
HASSLER, Hans, Leo see SCHEIN,
Johann H.
HASSLER, Warren W., Jr., 1926- ,
American; nonfiction CON
HASTE, Gwendolen, 1889- , Ameri-
can; poetry, juveniles HOO
HASTINGS, Adrian, 1929- , Ameri-
can; nonfiction CON
'HASTINGS, Alan' see WILLIAMSON,
Geoffrey
HASTINGS, Arthur Claude, 1935- ,
American; nonfiction CON
HASTINGS, Cecily Mary Eleanor,
1924- , American; nonfiction
CON
'HASTINGS, Harrington' see MARSH,
John

HASTINGS, Lewis Macdonald,
1882- , Rhodesian; poetry
ST
HASTINGS, Paul Giuler, 1914- ,
American; nonfiction CON
HASTINGS, Phyllis Dora Hodge
('John Bedford'; 'E. Chatterton
Hodge'; 'Rosina Land'; 'Julia
Mayfield'), English; fiction
CON
HASTINGS, William Thomson,
1881- , American; nonfiction
CON
'HATAI' (Shah Ismail), 1486-1524,
Turkish; poetry ST
HATCH, Alden, 1898- , Ameri-
can; juveniles WA
HATCH, Alden Denison, 1935- ,
American; nonfiction CON
HATCH, Eric, 1901-73, American;
fiction KT WAF
HATCH, John, 1917- , English;
nonfiction CON
HATCH, Preble Delloss Kellogg,
1898- , American; fiction
CON
HATCH, Raymond Norris, 1911- ,
American; nonfiction CON
HATCH, Richard Allen, 1940- ,
American; nonfiction CON
HATCH, Richard W., 1898- ,
American; juveniles DOY
HATCHER, Harlan Henthorne,
1898- , American; criticism
fiction CON KT
HATCHER, John, 1942- , Eng-
lish; nonfiction CON
HATCHER, Nathan Brazzell,
1897- , American; nonfiction,
fiction CON
HATEF, 1903-51, Persian; nonfic-
tion LAN
HATFIELD, Walter Wilbur,
1882- , American; juveniles,
nonfiction HOO
HATHAWAY, Baxter L., 1909- ,
American; nonfiction CON
HATHAWAY, Dale Ernest, 1925- ,
American; nonfiction CON
'HATHAWAY, Jan' see NEUBAUER,
William A.
HATHAWAY, Lulu Bailey, 1903- ,
English; nonfiction CON
HATHAWAY, Sibyl Collings,
1884- , American; nonfiction
CON
HATHAWAY, Starke Rosecrans,
1903- , American; nonfiction
CON

HATHCOCK, Louise, American; non-
fiction CON
HATHORN, Richmond Yancey,
1917- , American; nonfiction
CON
HATIF of ISFAHAN, Sayd Ahmed,
-1784, Persian; poetry ST
HATIM al TA'I, fl. 600- , Arab;
poetry ST
HATT, Harold Ernest, 1932- ,
Canadian-American; nonfiction
CON
HATTERY, Lowell Harold, 1916- ,
American; nonfiction CON
HATTON, Joseph, 1841-1907, Eng-
lish; fiction, plays, journalism
KBA
HATTON, Ragnhild Marie, 1913- ,
Norwegian-English; nonfiction
CON
HATTON, Robert Wayland, 1934- ,
American; nonfiction CON
HATTORI Ransetsu see 'RANSETSU'
'HATURIM, Ba'al' see JACOB BEN
ASHER
HATZFELD, 18th cent., French;
nonfiction DIL
HATZFELD, Adolf von, 1892- ,
German; nonfiction KU
HATZFELD, Helmut A., 1892- ,
German; nonfiction BL
HAUBERG, Clifford Alvin, 1906- ,
American; nonfiction CON
HAUCH, Johannes Carsten, 1790-
1872, Danish; poetry, plays,
fiction HAR KE ST
HAUCK, Allan, 1925- , American;
nonfiction CON
HAUDIQUIER, Jean Baptiste (Haudi-
quer), 1715-75, French; nonfic-
tion DIL
HAUENSCHILD, Richard G.S. see
'WALDAU, Max'
HAUFF, Wilhelm, 1802-27, German;
juveniles, fiction, poetry AL
DOY HAR KE SA ST WA
HAUGAARD, Erik Christian, 1923- ,
Danish; juveniles CON WA
HAUGAARD, William Paul, 1929- ,
American; nonfiction CON
HAUGEN, Edmund Bennett, 1913- ,
American; nonfiction CON
HAUGEN, Einar Ingvald, 1906- ,
American; nonfiction CON
HAUGH, Irene, 1906- , Irish;
criticism, poetry HO
HAUGHTON, Rosemary Luling,
1927- , English; juveniles,

fiction, nonfiction CON
HAUGHTON, William, fl. 1598- ,
English; plays KBA ST
HAUGWITZ, August Adolf von,
1645-1706, German; plays
ST
'HAUK, Maung' see HOBBS, Cecil
C.
HAUKLAND, Andreas, 1873- ,
Norwegian; fiction SA
HAULLEVILLE, Eric de, 1900-41,
Belgian; poetry, fiction, es-
says COL DIF SA
HAUN, Paul, 1906- , American;
nonfiction CON
HAUPOLD GAY, Augusto, 1915- ,
Spanish; poetry SA
HAUPTMANN, Carl, 1855-1921,
German; plays, fiction AL
COL FLE HAR KU MAT SA
ST
HAUPTMANN, Gerhart, 1862-1946,
German; plays, fiction AL
COL FLE HAR KL KT KU
KUN LEN MAG MAT RIC SA
ST
HAUPTMANN, Helmut, 1928- ,
German; nonfiction AL
HAUSEN, Freidrich see FRIED-
RICH von HAUSEN
HAUSENTSTEIN, Wilhelm
('Johann Armbruster'), 1882-
1957, German; nonfiction KU
HAUSER, Arnold, 1892- , Hun-
garian; nonfiction KTS
HAUSER, Harald, 1912- , Ger-
man; nonfiction AL
HAUSER, Heinrich, 1901- , Ger-
man; fiction KT LEN SA
'HAUSER, Kaspar' see TUCHOL-
SKY, Kurt
HAUSER, Margaret Louise ('Gay
Head'), 1909- , American;
fiction CON
HAUSER, Marianne, 1910- ,
American; fiction, nonfiction
CON
HAUSER, Phillip Morris, 1909- ,
American; nonfiction CON
HAUSHOFRER, Albrecht, 1903-
45, German; poetry, plays
AL KU LEN
HAUSKNECHT, Murray, 1925- ,
American; nonfiction CON
HAUSMAN, Warren H., 1939- ,
American; nonfiction CON
HAUSMANN, Bernard A., 1899- ,
American; nonfiction CON

HAUSMANN, Manfred, 1898- , German; nonfiction AL KU LEN
HAUSSING, Hans Wilhelm, 1916- , German; nonfiction CON
HAUTEFEUILLE, Jean de, 1647-1724, French; nonfiction DIL
HAUTEMER, Farn de see FARIN de HAUTEMER
HAUTETERRE, 18th cent., French; plays DIL
HAUTEVILLE, Juan de, 12th cent., French; poetry SA
HAUTPOUL, Anne Marie de Montegeroult, 1763- , French; plays SA
HAUTZIG, Esther Rudomin, 1930- , Polish-American; juveniles CON WA
HAVARD, William Clyde, Jr., 1923- , American; nonfiction CON
HAVE, Adrien Joseph, 1739-1817, French; nonfiction DIL
HAVEL, Václav, 1936- , Czech; essays, poetry, plays MAT
HAVELOCK, Eric A., 1903- , English; nonfiction CON
HAVEMAN, Robert H., 1936- , American; nonfiction CON
HAVEMANN, Ernest Carl, 1912- , American; nonfiction CON
HAVEN, Emily Bradley Neal ('Alice G. Lee'; 'Cousin Alice'; 'Clara Cushman'; 'Alice B. Haven'), 1827-63, American; juveniles, fiction KAA
HAVEN, Richard, 1924- , American; nonfiction CON
'HAVENHAND, John' see COX, John Roberts
HAVENS, George Remington, 1890- , American; nonfiction CON
HAVERGAL, Frances Ridley, 1836-79, English; poetry, juveniles KBA
HAVERKAMP-BERGEMANN, Egbert, 1923- , American; nonfiction CON
HAVERKORN, Willem, 1753-1826, Dutch; plays, poetry ST
HAVERSCHMIDT, François ('Piet Paaltjens'), 1835-94, Dutch; poetry HAR ST
HAVERSTICK, John Mitchell, 1919- , American; nonfiction CON
HAVESTADT, Bernardo, 1715- , Chilean; nonfiction MIN
HAVIGHURST, Alfred Freeman, 1904- , American; nonfiction CON

HAVIGHURST, Marion Boyd, American; juveniles, poetry, fiction CON FUL WA
HAVIGHURST, Robert James, 1900- , American; nonfiction CON
HAVIGHURST, Walter, 1901- , American; nonfiction, juveniles, fiction COM CON FUL HOO KTS WA WAF
HAVILAND, Virginia, 1911- , American; nonfiction CON
HAVILL, Edward, 1907- , American; fiction WAF
HAVIUS, Jacobus, 1637-80, Dutch; plays ST
HAVLICE, Patricia Pate, 1943- , American; nonfiction CON
HAVLICEK BOROVSKY, Karel, 1821-56, Czech; criticism, poetry, journalism KE SA ST
HAVRAN, Martin J., 1929- , American; nonfiction CON
HAW, Richard Claude, 1913- , South African; nonfiction CON
HAWES, Evelyn Johnson, American; nonfiction, fiction CON
HAWES, Frances Cooper Richmond, 1897- , American; nonfiction CON
HAWES, Gene Robert, 1922- , American; nonfiction CON
HAWES, Judy, 1913- , American; juveniles CON
HAWES, Stephen, 1475-1530, English; poetry SA ST
HAWES, Charles Boardman, 1889-1923, American; fiction KAT KT WA
HAWES, Stephen, 1475?-1523, English; poetry BRO KB
'HAWK EYE' see CARLISLE, R. H.
HAWKEN, William R., 1917- , American; nonfiction CON
HAWKER, Mary Elizabeth ('Lanoe Falconer'; Lance?), 1848-1908, Scots; fiction KBA
HAWKER, Robert Stephen, 1803-75, English; poetry BRO KBA SP ST
HAWKES, Glenn Rogers, 1917- , American; nonfiction CON
HAWKES, Hester, 1900- , American; juveniles WA
HAWKES, Jacquetta Hopkins, 1910- , English; nonfiction KTS

HAWKES, John, fl. 1790- , English;
nonfiction HIG
HAWKES, John ('Clendennen Burne,
Jr.'), 1925- , American; fiction
CON FLE
HAWKES, Terence, 1932- , English;
nonfiction CON
HAWKESWORTH, Eric ('The Great
Comte'), 1921- , Welsh; non-
fiction CON
HAWKESWORTH, John, 1715?-73,
English; nonfiction, plays, transla-
tions KB ST
HAWKINS, Sir Anthony Hope see
'HOPE, Anthony'
HAWKINS, Arthur, 1903- , American;
nonfiction CON
HAWKINS, Brett William, 1937- ,
American; nonfiction CON
HAWKINS, Rev. Denis J.B., 1906- ,
English; nonfiction HO
HAWKINS, Gerald Stanley, 1928- ,
English; nonfiction CON
HAWKINS, Helena Ann Quail, 1905- ,
American; juveniles CON
HAWKINS, Henry, 1572-1646, English;
translations ST
HAWKINS, Hugh Dodge, 1929- , Amer-
ican; nonfiction CON
HAWKINS, Quail, American; juveniles
WA
HAWKINS, Robert, 1923- , American;
nonfiction CON
HAWKINS, William, 1605-37, English;
plays, poetry ST
HAWKINS, William Waller, 1912- ,
American; fiction CON
HAWKINSON, John, 1912- , Ameri-
can; nonfiction CON
HAWKINSON, John Samuel, 1912- ,
American; juveniles CON WA
HAWKINSON, Lucy Ozone, 1924- ,
American; juveniles WA
HAWKS, Edward, 1878- , English;
nonfiction HOE
HAWKS, Francis Lester, 1798-1866,
American; nonfiction KAA
HAWLEY, Amos Henry, 1910- ,
American; nonfiction CON
HAWLEY, Cameron, 1905-69, Amer-
ican; fiction CON
HAWLEY, Ellis W., 1929- , Ameri-
can; nonfiction CON
HAWLEY, Jane Stouder, 1936- ,
American; nonfiction CON
'HAWLEY, Mabel C.' see STRATE-
MEYER, Edward L.
HAWORTH, Lawrence, 1926- ,

American; nonfiction CON
HAWORTH-BOOTH, Michael,
1896- , American; nonfiction
CON
HAWTHORNE, Hildegarde, Ameri-
can; juvenile KJU WA
HAWTHORNE, Ivy Ellen Jennie
Crawley, 1916- , English;
juveniles CON
HAWTHORNE, Julian, 1846-1934,
American; fiction KT
HAWTHORNE, Nathaniel, 1804-64,
American; juveniles, fiction,
essays BRO DOY KAA MAG
SA ST
HAWTON, Hector ('Virginia Cur-
zon'), 1901- , English;
fiction CON
HAY, Eloise Knapp, 1926- ,
American; nonfiction CON
HAY, George Campbell ('Mac
Iain Dheòrsa'), 1915- , Scots;
poetry MUR
HAY, Gyula, 1900- , Hungarian;
plays MAT
'HAY, Ian' see BEITH, Sir John
H.
HAY, Jacob ('Hilary Terme'),
1920- , American; nonfiction
CON
HAY, John Milton, 1835/38-1905,
American; nonfiction, poetry
BRO HOO KAA ST
HAY, Leon Edwards, American;
nonfiction CON
HAY, Peter, 1935- , German-
American; nonfiction CON
HAY, Sara Henderson, 1906- ,
American; poetry CON
HAY, Stephen Northup, 1925- ,
American; nonfiction CON
HAY, William Gosse, 1875-1945,
Australian; fiction ST
HAYAKAWA, Samuel Ichiyé,
1906- , American; nonfiction
CON KTS
'HAYASHI, Razan' (Hayashi
Tadashi; Doshun), 1583-1657,
Japanese; nonfiction ST
'HAYASHI SHUNSAI' (Hayashi Jo),
1618-1680, Japanese; nonfic-
tion ST
HAYASHI SUMINORI see KAGAWA
KAGEKI
HAYASHI, Tetsumaro, 1929- , Japa-
nese-American; nonfiction CON
HAYCOX, Ernest, 1899-1950,
American; fiction KTS

HAYCRAFT, Howard, 1905- ,
American; juveniles CON WA
HAYCRAFT, Molly Costain, 1911- ,
American; nonfiction CON
HAYDEN, Albert Arthur, 1923- ,
American; nonfiction CON
HAYDEN, Donald Eugene, 1915- ,
American; nonfiction CON
HAYDEN, Eric William ('Cire'), 1919- ,
American; nonfiction CON
HAYDEN, Howard K., 1930- ,
American; juveniles CON
HAYDEN, John Olin, 1932- , Amer-
ican; nonfiction CON
HAYDEN, Katharine Shepard, Ameri-
can; poetry MAR
HAYDEN, Robert E., 1913- , Ameri-
can; poetry MUR
HAYDN, Hiram Collins, 1907- ,
American; fiction, criticism CON
KTS WAF
HAYDON, Benjamin Robert, 1786-1846,
English; nonfiction KBA ST
HAYDON, Glen, 1896- , American;
nonfiction CON
HAYEK, Friedrich August von, 1899- ,
Austrian-English; nonfiction KTS
HAYER, Jean Nicolas Hubert, 1708-
80, French; nonfiction DIL
HAYES, Alfred, 1911- , American;
fiction, plays, poetry KTS WAF
HAYES, Ann Louise, 1924- , Amer-
ican; nonfiction CON
HAYES, Anna Hansen, 1886- ,
American; fiction, nonfiction
CON PAC
HAYES, Carlton Joseph Huntley,
1882-1964, American; nonfiction
CON HOE KTS
HAYES, Dorsha, American; fiction
WAF
HAYES, Douglas Anderson, 1918- ,
American; nonfiction CON
HAYES, Eugene Nelson, 1920- ,
American; nonfiction CON
'HAYES, Evelyn' see BETHELL, Mary
U.
HAYES, Florence Sooy, 1895- ,
American; juveniles WA
HAYES, Francis Clement, 1904- ,
American; nonfiction CON
HAYES, Grace Person, 1919- ,
American; nonfiction CON
'HAYES, Henry' see KIRK, John F.
HAYES, John F. ('Frederick J.
Terrence'), 1904- , Canadian;
juveniles CON
HAYES, Joseph ('Joseph H. Arnold'),

1918- , American; fiction,
plays CON
HAYES, Louis D., 1940- ,
American; nonfiction CON
HAYES, Captain M. Horace,
1840- , English; nonfiction
HIG
HAYES, Margaret, 1925- , Eng-
lish; nonfiction CON
HAYES, Nelson Taylor, 1903-71,
American; nonfiction CON
HAYES, Ralph Eugene, 1927- ,
American; fiction CON
HAYES, Robert Mayo, 1926- ,
American; nonfiction CON
HAYES, Samuel Perkins, 1910- ,
American; nonfiction CON
HAYES, Wayland Jackson, 1893- ,
American; nonfiction CON
HAYES, Will, American; juveniles
CON
HAYES, William Dimitt, 1913- ,
American; juveniles CON WA
HAYLEY, William, 1745-1820,
English; poetry BRO KBA SA
ST
HAYLEY BELL, Mary, English;
plays CON
HAYMAN, David, 1927- , Ameri-
can; nonfiction CON
HAYMAN, Hazel see PEEL, Hazel
M.
HAYMAN, John Luther, Jr.,
1929- , American; nonfiction
CON
HAYMAN, Max, 1908- , Canadian-
American; nonfiction CON
HAYMAN, Ronald, 1932- , Eng-
lish; nonfiction CON
HAYMES, Robert C., 1931- ,
American; nonfiction CON
HAYNE, Paul Hamilton, 1830-86,
American; poetry BRO KAA
ST
HAYNES, Alfred Henry ('Keith
Christie'), 1910- , American;
nonfiction CON
'HAYNES, Anna' see MADLEE,
Dorothy H.
'HAYNES, Linda' see SWINFORD,
Betty J. W.
HAYNES, Maria Schnee, 1912- ,
Austrian-American; nonfiction
CON
'HAYNES, Pat' see McKEAG,
Ernest L.
HAYNES, Robert Talmadge, Jr.,
1926- , American; nonfiction
CON

HAYNES, William Warren, 1921- ,
American; nonfiction CON
HAYS, Brooks, 1898- , American;
nonfiction CON
HAYS, David Glenn, 1928- , Ameri-
can; nonfiction CON
HAYS, Denys, 1915- , English; non-
fiction CON
HAYS, Elinor Rice, American; fiction
CON
HAYS, Hobe, American; juveniles WA
HAYS, Hoffman Reynolds, 1904- ,
American; fiction, criticism, plays
KTS MUR
HAYS, Paul R., 1903- , American;
nonfiction CON
HAYS, Peter L., 1938- , German-
American; nonfiction CON
HAYS, Richard D., 1942- , Ameri-
can; nonfiction CON
HAYS, William Shakespeare, 1837-
1907, American; journalism,
poetry KAA
HAYS, Wilma Pitchford, 1909- ,
American; juveniles COM CON
WA
HAYTER, Alethea, 1911- , English;
nonfiction CON
HAYTER, William Goodenough,
1906- , English; nonfiction CON
HAYWARD, Abraham, 1801-84, Eng-
lish; essays BRO KBA
HAYWARD, Charles Harold, 1898- ,
English; nonfiction CON
HAYWARD, Sir John, 1564?-1627,
English; nonfiction BRO KB
HAYWARD, John Forrest, 1916- ,
English; nonfiction CON
HAYWARD, John Frank, 1918- ,
American; nonfiction CON
HAYWARD, Richard, 1893- , Irish;
nonfiction CON
'HAYWARD, Richard' see COZZENS,
Frederick S.
'HAYWARD, Richard' see KENDRICK,
Baynard H.
HAYWARD, Rev. William, 1870-1945,
American; nonfiction HO
HAYWOOD, Carolyn, 1898- , Amer-
ican; juveniles COM CON KJU
WA
HAYWOOD, Charles, 1904- , Russian-
American; nonfiction CON
HAYWOOD, Eliza, 1693-1756, English;
fiction BRO KB ST
HAYWOOD, John Alfred, 1913- ,
English; nonfiction CON
HAYWOOD, Richard Mansfield,

1905- , American; nonfiction
CON
HAYWOOD, Richard Mowbray,
1933- , American; nonfiction
CON
HAZAÑAS y la RUA, Joaquín,
1862-1934, Spanish; nonfiction
BL SA
'HAZARD, Jack' see BOOTH,
Edwin
HAZARD, John Newbold, 1909- ,
American; nonfiction CON
'HAZARD, Laurence' see BARR,
Patricia M.
HAZARD, Leland, 1893- , Amer-
ican; nonfiction CON
HAZARD, Patrick D., 1927- ,
American; nonfiction CON
HAZARD, Paul, 1878-1944, French;
criticism COL DIF SA
HAZAZ, Chayim, 1898- , Jewish;
fiction ST
HAZELRIGG, Meredith Kent,
1942- , American; nonfiction
CON
HAZELTINE, Alice Isabel, 1878- ,
American; juveniles WA
'HAZELTON, Alexander' see ARM-
STRONG, William A.
HAZELTON, Roger, 1909- , Amer-
ican; nonfiction CON
HAZEN, Allen Tracy, 1904- ,
American; nonfiction CON
HAZLETT, Edward Everett,
1892- , American; juveniles
WA
HAZLITT, Henry, 1894- , Amer-
ican; criticism CON KAT
HAZLITT, William, 1778-1830,
English; essays, criticism
BRO KBA MAG SA ST
HAZLITT, William Carew, 1834-
1913, English; nonfiction SA
HAZO, Robert G., 1931- ,
American; nonfiction CON
HAZO, Samuel John, 1928- ,
American; poetry CON MUR
HAZON, Jacques Albert, 1708-79,
French; nonfiction DIL
HAZZARD, Shirley, 1931- ,
Australian; fiction CON
'HEAD, Ann' see MORSE, Anne C.
HEAD, Bessie, 1937- , English;
fiction CON
HEAD, Constance, 1939- , Amer-
ican; nonfiction CON
HEAD, Sir Edmund Walker, 1805-
68, English; nonfiction KBA

HEAD, Sir Francis Bond, 1793-1875, English; nonfiction BRO KBA ST

'HEAD, Gay' see HAUSER, Margaret L.

'HEAD, Matthew' see CANADAY, John E.

HEAD, Richard, 1637-87, English; nonfiction ST

HEAD, Timothy E., 1934- , American; nonfiction CON

HEADINGS, Mildred J., 1908- , American; nonfiction CON

HEADLAM, Walter George, 1866-1908, English; nonfiction, poetry BRO KT

'HEADLEY, Elizabeth' see CAVANNA, Betty

HEADLEY, Joel Tyler, 1813-97, American; nonfiction KAA

HEADLEY, Phineas Camp, 1819-1903, American; nonfiction KAA

HEADSTROM, Birger Richard, 1902- , American; juveniles CON WA

HEADY, Earl Orel, 1916- , American; nonfiction CON

HEAGNEY, Anne, 1901- , American; fiction CON

HEAGNEY, Harold J., 1890- , American; fiction, juvenile HOE

HEAL, Edith ('Berrien'; 'Eileen Page'; 'Margaret Powers'), 1903- , American; nonfiction, fiction, juveniles CON

HEAL, Jeanne Bennett, 1917- , English; nonfiction CON

HEALD, Edward Thornton, 1885- , American; nonfiction CON

HEALD, Henry, 1779- , American; letters KAA

HEALEY, Francis George, 1903- , English; nonfiction CON

HEALEY, John, -1610, English; translations ST

HEALY, David Frank, 1926- , American; nonfiction CON

HEALY, Fleming, 1911- , American; nonfiction CON

HEALY, George Robert, 1923- , American; nonfiction CON

HEALY, Paul Francis, 1915- , American; nonfiction CON

HEALY, Richard J., 1916- , American; nonfiction CON

HEALY, Sean Desmond, 1927- , English; fiction CON

HEANEY, John S., 1925- , Irish-American; nonfiction CON

HEANEY, Seamus, 1939- , Irish; poetry MUR

HEAP, Desmond, English; nonfiction CON

HEAPS, Willard Allison, 1909- , American; juveniles WA

HEARD, George Alexander, 1917- , American; nonfiction CON

HEARD, Henry Fitz Gerald, 1889-1971, English; essays, nonfiction CON KT

HEARD, Joseph Norman ('Joe Norman'), 1920- , American; nonfiction CON

HEARDER, Harry, 1924- , English; nonfiction CON

HEARN, Lafcadio ('Koizumi Yakumo'), 1850-1904, English; fiction, translations BRO KAA MAG SA ST

HEARNE, Thomas, 1678-1735, English; nonfiction BRO KB ST

HEARON, Shelby, 1931- , American; fiction CON

HEARSEY, John Edward Nicholl, 1928- , English; nonfiction CON

'HEARTMAN, Harold' see MEBANE, John H.

HEASMAN, Kathleen Joan, 1913- , English; nonfiction CON

HEATH, Charles Monroe, 1899- , American; nonfiction CON

HEATH, Douglas Hamilton, 1925- , American; nonfiction CON

HEATH, Dwight Braley, 1930- , American; nonfiction CON

HEATH, Edward Richard George, 1916- , English; nonfiction CON

HEATH, Ernest James, 1920- , English; nonfiction CON

HEATH, G. Louis, 1944- , American; nonfiction CON

HEATH, James Ewell, 1792-1862, American; nonfiction KAA

HEATH, Jim Frank, 1931- , American; nonfiction CON

'HEATH, Monica' see FITZGERALD, Arlene J.

HEATH, Robert W., 1931- , American; nonfiction CON

HEATH, Roy, 1917- , American; nonfiction CON

HEATH, Royton Edward, 1907- ,

English; nonfiction CON

HEATH, William Webster, 1929- ,
American; nonfiction CON

HEATHCOTT, Mary see KEEGAN,
Mary H.

HEATH-STUBBS, John Francis
Alexander, 1918- , British;
poetry, translations, plays,
criticism CON MUR KTS RIC

HEATON, Charles Huddleston,
1928- , American; nonfiction
CON

HEATON, Herbert, 1890- , English;
nonfiction CON

HEAVEY, Jean, American; fiction
CON

HEAVYSEGE, Charles, 1816-76,
Canadian; plays, fiction, poetry
ST SY

HEBARD, Edna Laura Henriksen,
1913- , American; nonfiction
CON

HEBB, Donald Oldings, 1904- ,
Canadian; nonfiction CON

HEBBEL, Christian Friedrich, 1831-
63, German; plays, poetry AL
HAR KE MAG SA ST

HEBEL, Johann Peter, 1760-1826,
German; poetry AL HAR ST

HEBER, Reginald, 1783-1826, English;
hymns, poetry BRO KBA ST

HEBERT, French; nonfiction DIL

HEBERT, Anne, 1916- , Canadian;
poetry, fiction ST SY

HEBERT, Arthur Gabriel, 1886-1963,
English; nonfiction CON

HEBERT, Artigues, 18th cent., French;
plays DIL

HEBERT, Jacques, 1923- , Canadian;
nonfiction CON

HEBERT, Jacques René, 1757-97,
French; nonfiction DIL

HEBERT, Maurice, 1888-1960,
Canadian; nonfiction SA

HEBRAIL, Jacques, 1716- , French;
nonfiction DIL

HEBREO, León see ABARBANEL,
Juda

HEBSON, Ann Hellebusch, 1925- ,
American; fiction CON

HECATAEUS, 525 B.C., Greek; nonfiction ST

HECATEO de ABDERA, Greek; nonfiction SA

HECATEO de MILETO, fl. 500 B.C.,
Greek; nonfiction SA

HECHT, Anthony Evan, 1923- ,
American; poetry CON MUR SP

HECHT, Ben, 1894-1964, American; fiction, plays HOO KL
KT MAT SA

HECHT, Henri Joseph ('Henri
Maik'), 1922- , French;
fiction CON

HECHT, James Lee, 1926- ,
American; nonfiction CON

HECHT, Joseph C., 1924- ,
American; nonfiction CON

HECHT, Marie Bergenfeld,
1918- , American; nonfiction
CON

HECHT, Roger, 1926- , American; poetry CON

HECHTLINGER, Adelaide, 1914- ,
American; nonfiction CON

HECK, Bessie Holland, 1911- ,
American; juveniles CON

HECKEL, Robert V., 1925- ,
American; nonfiction CON

HECKER, Willem, 1817-1909,
Dutch; poetry ST

HECKERT, Josiah Brooks, 1893- ,
American; nonfiction CON

HECKMAN, Hazel Melissa Price,
1904- , American; nonfiction
CON PAC

HECKMAN, William Oscar,
1921- , American; nonfiction
CON

HECKMANN, Herbert, 1930- ,
German; nonfiction KU

HECKSCHER, August, 1913- ,
American; nonfiction CON

HECQUET, Mme., 18th cent.,
French; nonfiction DIL

HECQUET, Adrian, 1510-80,
French; poetry SA

HECQUET, Philippe, 1661-1737,
French; nonfiction DIL

HECQUET, Robert, 1693-1775,
French; nonfiction DIL

HEDAYAT, Sadiq see HIDAYAT,
Sadiq

HEDBERG, Carl Olof Olle,
1899- , Swedish; fiction FLE
HAR

HEDBERG, Frans, 1828-1908,
Swedish; plays, poetry ST

HEDBERG, Nils, 1903- , Swedish;
nonfiction BL

HEDBERG, Olle, 1899- , Swedish;
fiction ST

HEDBERG, Tor Harald, 1862-1931,
Swedish; plays, fiction, poetry
COL MAT SA ST

HEDBORN, Samuel, 1783-1849,

Swedish; poetry ST
'HEDBROOKE, Andrew' see SILL,
Edward R.
HEDDE, Wilhelmina Genevava, 1895- ,
American; nonfiction CON
HEDDEN, Worth Tuttle ('Winifred
Woodley'), 1896- , American;
fiction CON JO WAF
HEDENVIND-ERIKSSON, Gustav,
1880- , Swedish; fiction ST
HEDERRA, Francisco, 1863-1944,
Chilean; fiction, plays MIN
HEDGE, Frederick Henry, 1805-90,
American; nonfiction KAA
HEDGE, Leslie Joseph, 1922- ,
English; fiction CON
HEDGE, Levi, 1766-1844, American;
nonfiction KAA
HEDGEMAN, Anna Arnold, 1899- ,
American; nonfiction CON
HEDGES, Sidney George, 1897- ,
American; nonfiction CON
HEDGES, Trimble Raymond, 1906- ,
American; nonfiction CON
HEDGES, Ursula M., 1940- , New
Zealander; juveniles CON
HEDGES, William Leonard, 1923- ,
American; nonfiction CON
HEDIN, Sven Anders, 1865-1952,
Swedish; nonfiction KT SA
HEDLEY, George Percy, 1899- ,
American; nonfiction CON
HEDLUND, Ronald David, 1941- ,
American; nonfiction CON
HEDOUIN, Jean Baptiste, 1749-1802,
French; nonfiction DIL
HEDRICH, Freidrich see MEISSNER,
Alfred von
HEDRICK, Addie M., 1903- ,
American; fiction, poetry CON
HEDRICK, Basil Calvin, 1932- ,
American; nonfiction CON
HEDRICK, Floyd Dudley, 1927- ,
American; nonfiction CON
HEEK, Van see HEGIUS, Alexander
HEELU, Jan van ('Jan van Leeuwe'),
13th cent., Dutch; poetry ST
HEEMSKERK, Johan van, 1597-1656,
Dutch; poetry ST
HEENAN, Rev. John Carmel, 1905- ,
English; nonfiction HO
HEER, David MacAlpine, 1930- ,
American; nonfiction CON
HEER, Friedrich, 1916- , German;
nonfiction KU
HEER, Nancy Whittier, American;
nonfiction CON
HEERE, Lucas de, 1534-84, Dutch;

poetry ST
HEEREN, Arnold Hermann Ludwig,
1760-1842, German; nonfiction
SA
HEERESMA, Heere, 1932- ,
Dutch; nonfiction, fiction CON
HEERMANCE, J. Noel, 1939- ,
American; nonfiction CON
HEERWAGEN, Paul K., 1895- ,
American; juveniles CON
HEFFERNAN, James Anthony
Walsh, 1939- , American;
nonfiction CON
HEFFERNAN, William A.,
1937- , American; nonfiction
CON
HEFFLEY, Wayne, 1927- , Amer-
ican; nonfiction CON
HEFLEY, James Carl, 1930- ,
American; nonfiction CON
HEGARTY, Edward J., 1891- ,
American; nonfiction CON
HEGARTY, Sister Mary Loyala,
1918- , Irish-American;
nonfiction CON
HEGARTY, Reginald Beaton,
1906- , American; juveniles
CON WA
HEGEL, Georg Wilhelm Friedrich,
1770-1831, German; nonfiction
HAR KE SA ST
HEGEMON of Thasos, 5th cent.
B.C., Greek; fiction SA ST
HEGER, Theodore Ernest, 1907- ,
American; nonfiction CON
HEGESANDRO, 2nd cent. B.C.,
Greek; nonfiction SA
HEGESIAS, Greek; nonfiction SA
HEGESINO, 2nd cent., Greek; non-
fiction SA
HEGESIPO, 4th cent. B.C., Greek;
nonfiction SA
HEGESIPPUS see JOSEPHUS,
Flavius
'HEGESIPPUS' see SCHONFIELD,
Hugh J.
HEGGEN, Thomas Orlo, 1919-49,
American; fiction MAG KTS
HEGGOY, Alf Andrew, 1938- ,
American; nonfiction CON
HEGIAS, 5th cent., Greek; non-
fiction SA
HEGIUS, Alexander (Van Heek),
1430-98, German; nonfiction
ST
HEIBERG, Gunnar Edvard Rode,
1857-1929, Norwegian; plays,
criticism COL FLE MAT

SA ST

HEIBERG, Johan Ludvig, 1791-1860,
Danish; criticism, plays, poetry
HAR KE SA ST

HEIBERG, Johanne Luise Pätges,
1812-90, Danish; plays ST

HEIBERG, Peter Andreas, 1758-1841,
Danish; poetry, plays KE ST

HEIBY, Walter Albert, 1918- , American; nonfiction CON

HEICHER, Merlo K. W., 1882- ,
American; nonfiction CON

HEIDBREDER, Margaret Ann,
1933- , American; nonfiction
CON

HEIDE, Heinrich, 1895- , German-
American; poetry ST

HEIDEGGER, Martin, 1889- ,
German; nonfiction KTS KU KUN
RIC SA

HEIDENREICH, Charles Albert, 1917- ,
American; nonfiction CON

HEIDERSTADT, Dorothy, 1907- ,
American; juveniles CON WA

HEIDENSTAM, Carl Gustav Verner
von, 1859-1940, Swedish; poetry
COL FLE HAR KAT KT MAG SA
ST

HEIDINGSFIELD, Myron S., 1914- ,
American; nonfiction CON

HEIFETZ, Harold, 1919- , American;
plays, fiction CON

HEIGES, P. Myers, 1887- , American; nonfiction CON

HEIJERMANS, Herman ('Iwan Jelako-
witch'; 'Samuel Falkland'; 'Koos
Habbema'; Heyermans), 1864-1924,
Dutch; plays, fiction COL FLE
HAR KE MAT SA ST

HEIJKE, John, 1927- , Dutch; nonfiction CON

HEIKEL, Karin Alice see 'VALA,
Katri W.'

HEILBRONER, Joan Knapp, 1922- ,
American; juveniles CON

HEILBRONNER, Robert Louis,
1919- , American; nonfiction
CON

HEILBRONNER, Walter Leo, 1924- ,
German-American; nonfiction
CON

HEILBRUNN, Otto, 1906- , German-
English; nonfiction CON

HEILIG, Matthias R., 1881- , American; nonfiction CON

HEILIGER, Edward Martin, 1909- ,
American; nonfiction CON

HEILMAN, Arthur William, 1914- ,

American; nonfiction CON

HEILMAN, Robert Bechtold, 1906- ,
American; nonfiction CON
PAC

HEILPRIN, Angelo, 1853-1907,
American; nonfiction KAA

HEIM, Alice Winifred, 1913- ,
English; nonfiction CON

HEIM, Ralph Daniel, 1895- ,
American; nonfiction CON

HEIMAN, Grover George, 1920- ,
American; fiction CON

HEIMAN, Judith, 1935- , American; fiction CON

HEIMANN, Moritz, 1868- ,
German; nonfiction KU

HEIMANN, Susan, 1940- , American; nonfiction CON

HEIMARCK, Theodore, 1906- ,
American; nonfiction CON

HEIMART, Alan Edward, 1928- ,
American; nonfiction CON

HEIMBECK, Raeburne Seeley,
1930- , American; nonfiction
CON

HEIMER, Melvin Lytton, 1915-71,
American; fiction CON

HEIMLER, Eugene, 1922- ,
Hungarian-English; poetry
CON

HEIMS, Daniel see HEINSIUS,
Daniel

HEIMSATH, Charles H., 1928- ,
American; nonfiction CON

HEIN, Lucille Eleanor, 1915- ,
American; nonfiction CON

HEINE, Heinrich, 1797-1856,
German; poetry, essays AL
HAR MAG KE SA ST

HEINESEN, Andreas William,
1900- , Danish; fiction,
poetry ST

HEINEY, Donald William ('Mac-
donald Harris'), 1921- ,
American; nonfiction, fiction
CON

HEINISCH, Rev. Paul, 1878- ,
Austrian; nonfiction HO

HEINL, Robert Debs, Jr.,
1916- , American; nonfiction
CON

HEINLEIN, Robert Anson ('Lyle
Monroe'; 'John Riverside';
'Caleb Sanders'; 'Anson Mac-
Donald'), 1907- , American;
juveniles, fiction CON FUL
KTS RIC WA

HEINRICH JULIUS, Duke of

Brunswick, 1564-1613, German;
plays AL ST
HEINRICH der GLEISSNER (Gleche-
zaere), 12th cent., German; non-
fiction AL SA ST
HEINRICH von dem TÜRLIN, fl. 1215-
20, Austrian; poetry ST
HEINRICH von FREIBERG, fl. 1290,
German; poetry ST
HEINRICH von LAUXENBERG, fl. 1415-
58, German; hymns ST
HEINRICH von MELK, fl. 1160, Aus-
trian; poetry, fiction AL HAR ST
HEINRICH von MORUNGEN (Sanger-
hausen), 1200-22, German; poetry
AL KE ST
HEINRICH von MÜGELN, 1320-72,
German; poetry ST
HEINRICH von NEUSTADT, fl. 1312,
Austrian; poetry ST
HEINRICH von NÖRDLINGEN, fl.
1332, Swiss; translations ST
HEINRICH von RUGGE, fl. 1175-91,
Swabian; poetry ST
HEINRICH von VELDEKE, fl. 1170-85,
Flemish; poetry AL KE SA ST
HEINS, Arthur James, 1931- , Amer-
ican; nonfiction CON
HEINSE, Johann Jakob Wilhelm, 1749-
1803, German; fiction HAR ST
HEINSIUS, Daniel (Heims), 1580-1655,
Dutch; poetry KE SA ST
HEINSIUS, Nicolás, 1620-81, Dutch;
nonfiction SA
HEINSIUS, Nicolaes, Jr., 1656-1718,
Dutch; fiction ST
HEINSOHN, Augereau Gray, Jr.,
1896- , American; nonfiction
CON
'HEINZ, G.' see GERARD-LIBOIS,
Jules C.
HEINZ, Wilfred Charles, 1915- ,
American; nonfiction CON
HEINZE, Kurt see 'NELL, Peter'
HEINZELIN von KONSTANZ, fl. 1300,
Swiss; poetry ST
HEINZEN, Karl, 1809-80, German-
American; poetry ST
HEINZMANN, George Melville,
1916- , American; fiction CON
HEIRICH, Max, 1931- , American;
nonfiction CON
HEISE, Edward Tyler, 1912- , Amer-
ican; nonfiction CON
HEISELER, Bernt von, 1907- , Ger-
man; plays KU LEN MAT
HEISELER, Henry von, 1875-1928,
German; poetry, plays, criticism

COL KU MAT SA
HEISERMAN, Arthur Ray, 1929- ,
American; fiction, nonfiction
CON
HEISSENBÜTTEL, Helmut, 1921- ,
German; nonfiction AL KU
KUN
HEITLER, Walter Heinrich,
1904- , German; nonfiction
CON
HEITMAN, Sidney, 1924- , Amer-
ican; nonfiction CON
HEITMANN, Hans, 1904- , Ger-
man; fiction, plays ST
HEITNER, Robert R., 1920- ,
American; nonfiction CON
HEJAZI, Muhammad see HIJAZI,
Muhammad
HEKMAT, Ali Asqar, 1893- ,
Persian; nonfiction ST
HEKTOR, Enno, 1820-74, Frisian;
plays ST
HEKTOROVIC, Petar, 1487-1572,
Dalmatian; translations, poetry
ST
HELAINE, Abbe, 18th cent.,
French; translations DIL
HELCK, C. Peter, 1893- , Amer-
ican; nonfiction CON
HELD, Jack Preston, 1926- ,
American; nonfiction CON
'HELD, Kurt' see KLÄBER, Kurt
HELD, Royer Burnell, 1921- ,
American; nonfiction CON
HELD, Virginia Potter, 1929- ,
American; nonfiction CON
HELE, Thomas d', 1740-80,
French; plays DIL
HELFERT, Erich Anton, 1931- ,
Czech-American; nonfiction
CON
HELFMAN, Elizabeth Seaver,
1911- , American; juveniles
CON WA
HELFMAN, Harry, 1910- , Amer-
ican; juveniles CON WA
HELGAND (Helgad), 11th cent.,
French; nonfiction SA
HELGESEN, Poul, 1485-1535,
Danish; nonfiction ST
'HELIADE-RADULESCU, Ion'
(Eliad Ion), 1802-72, Rumanian;
translations, poetry ST
HELIAND, 830- , German; poetry
AL
HELIE, Paulus see HELGESEN,
Poul
HELINAND de FROIDMONT, 17th

cent., French; poetry DIF
HELINANDO, Dans, 1170-1237, French; poetry SA
HELIODORUS, 3rd cent., Greek; poetry SA ST
HELITZER, Florence Saperstein, 1928- , American; fiction CON
HELLAAKOSKI, Aaro Antti, 1893-1952, Finish; poetry FLE
HELLANICUS, 480- B.C., Greek; nonfiction ST
'HELLENS, Franz' (Frédéric van Ermengem), 1881- , Belgian; fiction, poetry COL DIF SA ST
HELLER, Binem, 1908- , Jewish; poetry ST
HELLER, Celia Stopnicka, Polish-American; nonfiction CON
HELLER, David, 1922- , American; nonfiction CON
HELLER, Deane, 1924- , American; nonfiction CON
HELLER, Erich, 1911- , American; nonfiction CON
HELLER, Francis Howard, 1917- , Austrian-American; nonfiction CON
HELLER, Herbert L., 1908- , American; nonfiction CON
HELLER, Joseph, 1923- , American; fiction CON RIC
HELLER, Robert William, 1933- , American; nonfiction CON
HELLER, Walter Wolfgang, 1915- , American; nonfiction CON
HELLER, Yomtob Lipmann, 1579-1654, Jewish; poetry ST
HELLERSTEIN, Jerome R., 1907- , American; nonfiction CON
HELLIE, Richard, 1937- , American; nonfiction CON
HELLMAN, Harold (Hal), 1927- , American; juveniles CON
HELLMAN, Hugo E., 1908- , American; nonfiction CON
HELLMAN, Lillian, 1905- , American; poetry, plays CON MAG MAT KT ST
HELLMAN, Robert, 1919- , American; poetry, plays CON
HELLMUTH, Jerome, 1911- , American; nonfiction CON
HELLMUTH, William Frederick, Jr., 1920- , American; nonfiction CON
HELLO, Ernest, 1828-85, French; nonfiction DIF
HELLOT, Jean, 1685-1766, French;

nonfiction DIL
HELLREIGEL, Rev. Martin B., 1890- , German; nonfiction HO
HELLSTRÖM, Gustaf, 1882-1953, Swedish; fiction, essays COL SA ST
HELLSTROM, Ward, 1930- , American; nonfiction CON
HELLVIG, Amélie, 1776-1831, German; nonfiction SA
HELLWIG, Monika Konrad ('Mary Cuthbert'), 1929- , German-American; nonfiction CON
HELLYER, Arthur George Lee, 1902- , English; nonfiction CON
HELLYER, David Tirrell, 1913- , American; nonfiction CON
HELM, Bertrand P., 1929- , American; nonfiction CON
HELM, Ernest Eugene, 1928- , American; nonfiction CON
HELM, Peter James, 1916- , English; fiction CON
HELM, Robert Meredith, 1917- , American; nonfiction CON
HELM, Thomas William, 1919- , American; juveniles, fiction CON
HELMAN, Edith F., American; nonfiction BL
HELMER, William F., 1926- , American; nonfiction CON
HELLMERICKS, Constance Chittenden, 1918- , American; nonfiction CON
HELMERICKS, Harmon R. (Bud), 1917- , American; nonfiction CON
HELMERS, Jan Frederik, 1767-1813, Dutch; poetry ST
'HELMI, Jack' see SANDS, Leo G.
HELMING, Ann, American; nonfiction CON
HELMKER, Judith Anne, 1940- , American; nonfiction CON
HELMOLD, 1108-77, German; nonfiction SA
HELMOLD of BOSAU, 1125-77, German; nonfiction ST
HELMORE, Geoffrey Anthony, 1922- , English; nonfiction CON
HELMREICH, Ernst Christian, 1902- , American; nonfiction CON

HELMSTADTER, Gerald C., 1925- , American; nonfiction CON

'HELOISE' see CRUSE, Heloise

HELOISE, 1101-64, French; letters DIF

HELPER, Hinton Rowan, 1829-1909, American; nonfiction JO KAA

HELPIDIO (Elpidio), 5th cent., Roman; poetry SA

HELPS, Sir Arthur, 1813-75, English; essays, fiction, nonfiction BRO KBA ST

HELPS, Racey, 1913-71, English; juveniles COM CON

HELSON, Harry, 1898- , American; nonfiction CON

HELTAI, Jenő, 1871- , Hungarian; fiction ST

HELTON, David Kirby, 1940- , American; fiction CON

HELTON, Tinsley, 1915- , American; nonfiction CON

HELVETIUS, Catherine, 1719-1800, French; nonfiction SA

HELVETIUS, Claude Adrien, 1715-71, French; nonfiction DIF DIL HAR KE SA ST

HELVETIUS, Jean Adrien, 1661-1727, German; translations DIL

HELVETIUS, Jean Claude Adrien, 1685-1755, French; nonfiction DIL

HELWIG, David Gordon, 1938- , Canadian; poetry CON MUR

HELWIG, Werner ('Einar Halvid'), 1905- , German; nonfiction KU LEN

HELYOT, Pierre, 1660-1716, French; nonfiction DIL

HEMACANDRA, 1089-1173, Indian; nonfiction LAN ST

HEMANS, Felicia Dorothea Browne, 1793-1835, English; poetry BRO KBA SA ST

HEMBREE, Charles R., 1938- , American; nonfiction CON

HEMDAHL, Reuel Gustaf, 1903- , American; nonfiction CON

HEMELDONCK, Emil van, 1897- , Flemish; fiction ST

HEMENWAY, Robert, 1921- , American; fiction CON

HEMERY, 18th cent., French; nonfiction DIL

HEMING, Arthur, 1870-1940, Canadian; fiction SY

HEMING, William (Hemminge), 1602-51, English; poetry, plays ST

HEMINGBURGH, Walter de, fl. 1300, English; nonfiction ST

HEMINGWAY, Ernest Miller, 1899-1961, American; fiction BRO FLE HIL HOO KL KT MAG MAT RIC SA ST WAF

HEMINGWAY, John H., Jr., 1944- , American; fiction CON

'HEMINGWAY, Taylor' see RYWELL, Martin

HEMLEBEN, Sylvester John, 1902- , American; nonfiction CON

HEMLEY, Cecil Herbert, 1914-66, American; nonfiction, poetry CON

HEMLOW, Joyce, 1906- , Canadian; nonfiction CON

HEMMER, Jarl Robert, 1893-1944, Finnish; poetry, fiction COL SA ST

HEMMING, John Henry, 1935- , Canadian; nonfiction CON

HEMMINGE, William see HEMING, William

HEMMINGSEN, Niels, 1513-1600, Danish; nonfiction ST

HEMON, Louis, 1880-1913, French-Canadian; fiction COL DIF KAT KT MAG SA ST

HEMPHILL, George, 1922- , American; nonfiction CON

HEMPHILL, Martha Loche, 1904- , American; nonfiction CON

HEMPHILL, William Edwin, 1912- , American; nonfiction CON

HEMPSTONE, Smith, 1929- , American; nonfiction CON

HEMSTERHUIS, François, 1721-90, Dutch; nonfiction DIL HAR SA ST

HEMSTERHUIS, Tiberio, 1685-1766, Dutch; nonfiction SA

HEMYNG, Bracebridge, 1841-1901, English; juveniles DOY

HENAO, José Jesús María, 1868/70-1944, Colombian; nonfiction MIN

HENAULT, Charles Jean François, 1685-1770, French; poetry DIL SA

HENAULT, Gilles, 1920- , Canadian; poetry SY

HENAULT, Marie Josephine, 1921- , American; nonfiction CON

HENCKELL, Karl, 1864-1929, German; nonfiction AL

HENDEL, Charles William, 1890- , American; nonfiction CON

HENDEL, Samuel, 1909- , American; nonfiction CON

'HENDERLEY, Brooks' see STRATEMEYER, Edward L.

HENDERLITE, Rachel, 1905- , American; nonfiction CON

HENDERSON, Alexander John, 1910- , English; nonfiction CON

HENDERSON, Algo Donmyer, 1897- , American; nonfiction CON

HENDERSON, Alma Estella, American; fiction MAR

HENDERSON, Archibald, 1877-1963, American; criticism JO KT

HENDERSON, Bert C., 1904- , American; poetry CON

HENDERSON, Bill ('Luke Walton'), 1941- , American; nonfiction CON

HENDERSON, Dan Fenno, 1921- , American; nonfiction CON

HENDERSON, Daniel McIntyre, 1851-1906, American; poetry KAA

HENDERSON, David, 1942- , American; nonfiction CON MUR

'HENDERSON, George' see GLASSCO, John S.

HENDERSON, George, 1931- , Scots; nonfiction CON

HENDERSON, George Patrick, 1915- , Scots; nonfiction CON

HENDERSON, George Poland, 1920- , English; nonfiction CON

HENDERSON, Hamish, 1919- , Scots; poetry MUR

HENDERSON, Ian, 1910- , Scots; nonfiction CON

HENDERSON, Isabel, 1933- , Scots; nonfiction CON

HENDERSON, James, 1934- , American; nonfiction CON

HENDERSON, John, 1915- , American; plays, nonfiction CON

HENDERSON, John Steele, 1919- , American; nonfiction CON

HENDERSON, John William, 1910- , American; nonfiction CON

HENDERSON, Keith M., 1934- , American; nonfiction CON

HENDERSON, Kenneth David Druitt, 1903- , English; nonfiction CON

HENDERSON, Le Grand ('Brian Harwin'), 1901- , American; juveniles CON KJU WA

HENDERSON, Nola, 1896- , American; fiction MAR

HENDERSON, Philip Prichard, 1906- , English; poetry, nonfiction CON

HENDERSON, Randall, 1888- , American; nonfiction CON

HENDERSON, Richard, 1924- , American; nonfiction CON

HENDERSON, Robert see HENRYSON, Robert

HENDERSON, Robert M., 1926- , American; nonfiction CON

HENDERSON, Robert Waugh, 1920- , American; nonfiction CON

HENDERSON, Shirley Prudence Ann, 1929- , English; nonfiction CON

HENDERSON, Stephen E., 1925- , American; nonfiction CON

HENDERSON, William, 1922- , American; nonfiction CON

HENDERSON, William James, 1855-1937, American; criticism KT

HENDERSON, William Leroy, 1927- , American; nonfiction CON

HENDERSON, William Otto, 1904- , English; nonfiction CON

HENDERSON, Winslow, 1921- , American; fiction CON

HENDERSON, Zenna Chlarson, 1917- , American; juveniles fiction CON

HENDRICK, Burton Jesse, 1870-1949, American; nonfiction, journalism KT

HENDRICK, George, 1929- , American; nonfiction CON

HENDRICK, Ives, 1898-1972, American; nonfiction CON

HENDRICK, Paula Griffith, 1928- , American; juveniles CON

HENDRICKS, Frances Wade Kellam, 1900- , American; nonfiction CON

HENDRICKS, George D., 1913- , American; fiction CON

HENDRICKSON, James E., 1932- , American; nonfiction CON

HENDRICKSON, Robert Augustus,
1923- , American; nonfiction
CON
HENDRICKSON, Walter Brookfield,
Jr., 1936- , American; nonfic-
tion CON
HENDRIK VAN GENT, 1217-93, Dutch;
nonfiction ST
HENDRIKS, Arthur Lemière, 1922- ,
Jamaican; poetry MUR
HENDRIKSEN, Eldon Sende, 1917- ,
American; nonfiction CON
HENDRY, James Findlay, 1912- ,
Scots; nonfiction CON
HENEMAN, Herbert Gerhard, Jr.,
1916- , American; nonfiction
CON
HENFREY, Colin Vere Fleetwood,
1941- , English; nonfiction CON
HENFREY, Norman, 1929- , English;
nonfiction CON
HENINGER, Simeon Kahn, Jr.,
1922- , American; nonfiction
CON
HENISSART, Paul, 1923- , Ameri-
can; nonfiction CON
'HENJO' (Yoshimene No Munesada;
Sojo), 1816-90, Japanese; poetry
ST
HENKE, Emerson Overbeck, 1916- ,
American; nonfiction CON
HENKEL, Stephen C., 1933- ,
American; nonfiction CON
HENKES, Robert, 1922- , American;
nonfiction CON
HENKIN, Louis, 1917- , Russian-
American; nonfiction CON
HENLE, Mary, 1913- , American;
nonfiction CON
HENLE, Theda O., 1918- , Ameri-
can; fiction CON
HENLEY, Arthur ('Kenneth Eric';
'Webb Jones'), 1921- , American;
nonfiction CON
HENLEY, John, 1692-1756, English;
nonfiction KB
HENLEY, Norman, 1915- , American;
nonfiction CON
HENLEY, William Ernest, 1849-1903,
English; poetry, criticism BRO
KBA SA SP ST
HENN, Thomas Rice, 1901- , Irish;
nonfiction CON
HENNEBERT, Jean Baptiste François,
1726-95, French; nonfiction DIL
HENNEBO, Robert, 1685-1737, Dutch;
poetry ST
HENNEQUE, Leon, 1851-1935, French;

fiction DIF
HENNEQUIN, Charles Maurice,
1863-1926, French; plays
SA
HENNEQUIN, Claude, 1654-1738,
French; nonfiction DIL
HENNESSEY, James J., 1926- ,
American; nonfiction CON
HENNESSEY, Roger Anthony Sean,
1937- , English; nonfiction
CON
HENNESSY, Bernard C., 1924- ,
American; nonfiction CON
HENNESSY, Jossleyn, 1903- ,
English; nonfiction CON
HENNESSY, Mary L., 1927- ,
American; nonfiction CON
HENNIN, Pierre Michel, 1728-
1807, French; nonfiction DIL
HENNING, Charles Nathanial,
1915- , American; nonfiction
CON
HENNING, Edward B., 1922- ,
American; nonfiction CON
HENNINGS, Emmy see BALL-
HENNINGS, Emmy
HENNINGSEN, Agnes Kathinka
Malling, 1868- , Danish; fic-
tion, plays ST
HENNINGSEN, Charles Frederick,
1815-77, American; nonfiction
KAA
HENREY, Madeleine, 1906- ,
French; nonfiction CON
HENRI, Adrian Maurice, 1932- ,
British; poetry, plays CON
MUR
'HENRI, G.' see CLEMENT,
George H.
HENRI d'ANDELY, 13th cent.,
French; poetry ST
HENRI de MONDEVILLE, fl.
1300, French; nonfiction ST
HENRIAU, Jean Marie, 1661-1738,
French; nonfiction DIL
HENRION, fl. 1772-79, French;
plays DIL
HENRION, Nicolas, 1663-1720,
French; nonfiction DIL
'HENRIOT, Emile' (Emile Maigrot),
1889-1961, French; fiction,
criticism DIF HAR ST
HENRIQUE de GANTE, 13th cent.,
French; nonfiction SA
HENRIQUES, Robert David Quixano,
1905-67, British; fiction KTS
HENRIQUEZ, Camilo, 1769-1825,
Spanish; journalism BL MIN
SA

HENRIQUEZ, Enrique, 1859-1940,
Dominican; poetry MIN

HENRIQUEZ, Luis, 16th cent.,
Portuguese; poetry SA

HENRIQUEZ, Rafael Américo,
1899- , Dominican; poetry MIN
SA

HENRIQUEZ CARVAJAL, Federico,
1848-1952, Dominican; nonfiction
MIN

HENRIQUEZ PEREZ, Honorio,
1879- , Chilean; journalism,
fiction, poetry MIN

HENRIQUEZ URENA, Max, 1885- ,
Dominican; nonfiction, poetry
MIN SA

HENRIQUEZ UREÑA, Pedro, 1884-
1946, Dominican; nonfiction BL
MIN SA

HENRY VIII of England, 1491-1547,
English; poetry BRO ST

HENRY, Bessie Walker, 1921- ,
English; nonfiction CON

HENRY, Carl F.H., 1913- , American; nonfiction CON

'HENRY, Daniel' see KAHNWEILER,
Daniel H.

HENRY, Harold Wilkinson, 1926- ,
American; nonfiction CON

HENRY, Hugh Thomas, 1862-1946,
American; nonfiction HOE

HENRY, Joanne Landers, 1927- ,
American; juveniles CON

HENRY, Joseph B., 1901- , American; nonfiction CON

HENRY, Laurin Luther, 1921- ,
American; nonfiction CON

HENRY, Marguerite, 1902- , American; juveniles CON HOO KJU WA

HENRY, Matthew, 1662-1714, English;
nonfiction BRO ST

'HENRY, O.' see PORTER, William
S.

HENRY, Patrick, 1736-99, American;
nonfiction KAA

HENRY, Ralph Chester ('Eric Thane';
'John Paris'), 1912- , American;
fiction PAC

HENRY, Robert, 1718-90, English;
nonfiction BRO

HENRY, Robert Selph, 1889- , American; nonfiction CON

HENRY, Samuel J., 1879- , American; nonfiction HIG

'HENRY, Thomas' (Thomas Henry
Fisher), 1879-1962, English;
juveniles DOY

HENRY, Vera, Canadian; fiction CON

HENRY, W.P., 1929- , American; nonfiction CON

HENRY, William Wirt, 1831-1900,
American; nonfiction KAA

HENRY of AVRANCHES, -1262,
English; poetry ST

HENRY of HUNTINGDON, 1084?-
1155, English; nonfiction BRO
KB ST

HENRY of SETTIMELLO, 12th
cent., Italian; poetry ST

HENRY the MINSTREL ('Blind
Harry'), -1492, English;
poetry BRO KB ST

HENRYSON, Robert (Henderson),
1430?-1506, Scots; poetry
BRO KB SP ST

HENSCHKE, Alfred see KLABUND

'HENSEN, Herwig' (Florent Constant Albert Mielants),
1917- , Belgian; poetry,
plays MAT

HENSHALL, Audrey Shore,
1927- , English; nonfiction
CON

HENSHAW, James Ene, 1924- ,
Nigerian; plays RIC

HENSLEY, Joe L., 1926- ,
American; fiction CON

HENSON, Clyde Eugene, 1914- ,
American; nonfiction CON

HENSON, Josiah, 1789-1883,
American; nonfiction KAA

HENTOFF, Nat, 1925- , American; juveniles, fiction, nonfiction CON WA

HENTY, George Alfred, 1832-1902,
English; juveniles, fiction
BRO DOY KBA ST

HENTZ, Caroline Lee Whiting,
1800-56, American; nonfiction,
fiction JO KAA

HENWOOD, James N.J., 1932- ,
American; nonfiction CON

HENZ, Rudolf ('R. Miles'), 1897- ,
German; nonfiction KU

HENZE, Donald Frank, 1928- ,
American; nonfiction CON

HENZI, Rodolphe, 1731-1803,
French; nonfiction DIL

HEPBURN, Ronald William,
1927- , Scots; nonfiction
CON

HEPNER, Harry Walker, 1893- ,
American; nonfiction CON

HEPPENSTALL, John Rayner,
1911- , British; poetry,
fiction CON MUR

HEPPENSTALL, Margit Strom,
1913- , American; nonfiction
CON
HEPPLE, Bob Alexander, 1934- ,
South African; nonfiction CON
HEPPNER, Samuel, 1913- ,
English; nonfiction CON
HEPWORTH, Charles Philip, 1912- ,
English; nonfiction CON
HEPWORTH, James B., 1910- ,
American; nonfiction CON
HERAUD, John Abraham, 1799-1887,
English; poetry, plays, criticism
BRO KBA
HERACLIDES, Alexandrine; nonfiction
SA
HERACLIDES of LESBOS, 2nd cent.
B.C., Greek; nonfiction SA
HERACLIDES PONTICUS, 390-10 B.C.,
Greek; nonfiction SA ST
HERACLITUS of EPHUSUS, 500 B.C.,
Greek; nonfiction SA ST
HERAUD, John Abraham, 1799-1887,
English; poetry, plays ST
HERAULT de SECHELLES, Marie
Jean, 1759-94, French; nonfiction
DIL
'HERAUT BERRY, Le' see LE
BOUVIER, Gilles
HERAVI, Mehdi, 1940- , Irani-
American; nonfiction CON
HERBART, Johan Friedrich, 1776-
1841, German; nonfiction SA
HERBEN, Jan, 1857-1936, Czech;
fiction ST
HERBER, Bernard P., 1929- ,
American; nonfiction CON
HERBER, Lewis, 1921- , American;
nonfiction CON
HERBERS, John N., 1923- , Ameri-
can; nonfiction CON
HERBERT, Sir Alan Patrick, 1890-
1971, English; poetry, fiction
BRO KL KT RIC
'HERBERT, Arthur' see SHAPPIRO,
Herbert A.
HERBERT, Cecil L., English; poetry
MUR
HERBERT, Claude Jacques, 1700-58,
French; nonfiction DIL
HERBERT, Don ('Mr. Wizard'),
1917- , American; juveniles
COM CON WA
HERBERT, Lord Edward of Cherbury,
1583-1648, English; poetry KB
SA SP ST BRO
HERBERT, Frederick Hugh, 1897- ,
Austrian; plays, fiction, movies
KTS

HERBERT, George, 1593-1633,
English; poetry BRO KB MAG
SP ST
HERBERT, Henry William ('Frank
Forester'), 1807-58, American;
nonfiction, poetry HIG KAA ST
HERBERT, Jean Daniel Fernand,
1897- , French; nonfiction
CON
HERBERT, John, 1924- , Eng-
lish; nonfiction CON
HERBERT, Kevin Barry John,
1921- , American; nonfiction
CON
HERBERT, Mary see PEMBROKE,
Mary Herbert, Countess of
HERBERT, Reginald, 1841- ,
English; nonfiction HIG
HERBERT, Robert Louis, 1929- ,
American; nonfiction CON
HERBERT, Sir Thomas, 1606-82,
English; nonfiction BRO
HERBERT, Xavier, 1911- ,
Australian; fiction RIC
HERBERT, Zbigniew, 1924- ,
Polish; poetry, plays MAT
HERBERT le DUC de DAMMARTIN,
fl. 1180-87, French; poetry
ST
HERBERTSON, Gary J., 1938- ,
American; nonfiction CON
HERBES (Hebert), 13th cent.,
French; poetry SA
HERBIN, Auguste François Julien,
1783-1806, French; nonfiction
DIL
HERBORT von FRITZLAR, fl.
1210-17, Hessian; poetry ST
HERBST, Josephine Frey, 1897-
1969, American; fiction CON
KAT KT WAF
HERBST, Jurgen F.H., 1928- ,
German-American; nonfiction
CON
HERBST, Winfrid, 1891- ,
American; juveniles HOE
HERCKMANS, Elias, 1596-1644,
Dutch; poetry ST
HERCULANO de CARVALHO e
ARAUJO, Alexandre, 1810-77,
Portuguese; fiction, poetry
HAR SA ST
HERCULES, Frank E.M., 1917- ,
American; nonfiction CON
HERCZEG, Ferenc, 1863- ,
Hungarian; plays, fiction
COL SA ST
HERD, David, 1732-1810, Scots;
nonfiction BRO

HERDAL, Harald, 1900- , Danish;
poetry, fiction FLE ST
HERDAN, Gustav, 1897- , Czech-
English; nonfiction CON
HERDER, Johann Gottfried, 1744-1803,
German; criticism AL HAR KE
SA ST
HEREDIA, José María de, 1803-39,
Cuban; poetry BL MIN SA ST
HEREDIA, José María de, 1842-1905,
Cuban; poetry COL DIF HAR KE
MAL MIN SA ST
HEREDIA, Marie Louise A. de see
'HOUVILLE, Gerard d'
HEREDIA, Nicolás, 1852/55-1901/05,
Dominican; fiction, essays MIN
HEREDIA y MOTA, Nicolás, 1855-1901,
Cuban; nonfiction, fiction MIN
'HEREFORD, John' see FLETCHER,
Harry L. V.
HEREFORD, Robert A., 1902- ,
American; juveniles WA
HEREN, Louis P., 1919- , English;
nonfiction CON
HERFORD, Charles Harold, 1853-1931,
English; criticism KT
HERFORD, Oliver, 1863-1935, English;
fiction, poetry BRO KT
HERGENROTHER, Joseph von, 1824-90,
German; nonfiction SA
HERGER see SPERVOGEL
HERGESHEIMER, Joseph, 1880-1954,
American; fiction BRO KL KT
MAG RIC SA ST
HERGOT, Hans Johann, 1527- ,
German; nonfiction AL
'HERIAN, V.' see GREGORIAN,
Vartan
'HERIAT, Philippe' (R. G. Payelle),
1898-1971, French; plays, fiction
HAR SA ST
HERIAT, Raymond Gerard Payelle,
1898- , French; fiction, plays
DIF
HERICOURT du VATIER, Louis d',
1687-1752, French; nonfiction
DIL
HERINGTON, C. John, 1924- ,
English; nonfiction CON
HERIOT, Angus, 1927- , American;
nonfiction, fiction CON
HERIOT, Thomas see HARRIOT,
Thomas
HERISSANT, Louis Antoine Prosper,
1745-69, French; nonfiction DIL
HERISSANT, Louis Théodore, 1743-
1811, French; nonfiction DIL
HERISSANT des CARRIERES, Jean

Thomas, 1742-1820, French;
nonfiction DIL
HERLICIO, David, 1558-1636,
German; nonfiction SA
HERLIHY, Rev. Francis, 1912- ,
New Zealander; nonfiction
HO
HERLIHY, James Leo, 1927- ,
American; fiction CON
HERMAGORAS de TEMNOS,
230-160, Greek; nonfiction
SA
HERMAN, George Richard,
1925- , American; nonfiction,
poetry, fiction CON
HERMAN, Simon Nathan, 1912- ,
South African; nonfiction CON
HERMAN, Sondra Renee, 1932- ,
American; nonfiction CON
HERMAN, Stanley M., 1928- ,
American; nonfiction CON
HERMAN, Yuri Pavlovich (German),
1910- , Russian; fiction HAR
HARK
HERMAN the LAME, 1013-54,
German; nonfiction, poetry
ST
HERMANN, Edward Julius,
1919- , American; nonfiction
CON
'HERMANN, Georg' (George Her-
man Borchardt), 1871-1943,
German; nonfiction AL
HERMANN, Gerhart see 'MOSTAR,
Gerhart H.'
HERMANN, Johann Gottfried Jakob,
1772-1848, German; nonfiction
SA
HERMANN, Karl Freidrich, 1804-
55, German; nonfiction SA
HERMANN, Theodore Placid,
1909- , American; nonfiction
CON
HERMANN von SACHSENHEIM,
1365-1458, German; poetry
AL
HERMANN-NEISSE, Max, 1886-
1941, German; poetry, fiction,
plays AL COL FLE KU SA
'HERMANNS, Peter' see BRAN-
NON, William T.
HERMANNS, William, 1895- ,
German-American; nonfiction
CON
HERMANS, Willem Fredrik,
1921- , Dutch; poetry, fic-
tion CON
HERMANT, Abel, 1862-1950,

French; fiction COL DIF HAR
SA ST
HERMANT, Jean, 1650-1725, French;
nonfiction DIL
HERMENEGILDO, Alfredo, 1936- ,
Spanish; nonfiction BL
HERMENS, Ferdinand Aloysius,
1906- , German; nonfiction
HO
HERMES, Abbe, fl. 1781-91, French;
nonfiction DIL
HERMES, Johann Timotheus, 1738-
1821, German; fiction AL HAR
ST
HERMES TRISMEGISTUS, 3rd cent.,
Greek; nonfiction ST
HERMESIANAX, fl. 336 B.C., Greek;
poetry SA
HERMIAS, 2nd cent., Greek; nonfic-
tion SA
HERMILLY, 1710-78, French; transla-
tions DIL
'HERMINE' see ELDER, Susan B.
'HERMLIN, Stephan' (Rudolf Leder),
1915- , German; nonfiction,
essays, poetry AL KU KUN
HERMOGENES, Greek; nonfiction SA
HERMOSILLA, José G. see GOMEZ
HERMOSILLA, José M.
HERN, George Anthony ('Andrew Hope';
'Potiphar'), 1916- , English;
nonfiction CON
HERNANDEZ, Al, 1929- , Filipino-
American; nonfiction CON
HERNANDEZ, Alonso, 1460?-1516,
Spanish; poetry SA
HERNANDEZ, Alonso, 16th cent.,
Spanish; nonfiction BL
HERNANDEZ, Frances, 1926- ,
American; nonfiction CON
HERNANDEZ, José, 1834-86/94,
Argentinian; poetry BL MAG SA
ST
HERNANDEZ, Lope, 1896- , Spanish;
fiction SA
HERNANDEZ, Luisa Josefina, Mexican;
plays SA
HERNANDEZ, Máximo, 1890-1951,
Spanish; fiction, essays, journalism
SA
HERNANDEZ, Miguel, 1910-42, Spanish;
poetry BL FLE HAR SA ST RIC
HERNANDEZ AQUINO, Luis, 1907- ,
Puerto Rican; poetry SA
HERNANDEZ CATA, Alfonso, 1885-
1942, Cuban; fiction, poetry,
plays BL MIN SA ST
HERNANDEZ de GONCER, Federico,

1918- , Spanish; nonfiction
SA
HERNANDEZ de OVIEDO, Gonzalo
see FERNANDEZ de OVIEDO
Gonzalo
HERNANDEZ FRANCO, Tomás,
1904- , Spanish; poetry SA
HERNANDEZ GIRBAL, Florentino,
1908- , Spanish; nonfiction
SA
HERNANDEZ GONZALEZ, Luis,
1896- , Spanish; poetry SA
HERNANDEZ MIR, Guillermo,
1884-1955, Spanish; fiction,
plays SA
HERNANDEZ MUJARES, Enrique,
1859-1914, Cuban; journalism,
essays, poetry MIN
HERNANDEZ PUEYRREDON, Jose,
1834-86, Argentinian; poetry
MIN
HERNDL, George, C., 1927- ,
American; nonfiction CON
HERNDON, Booton, 1915- ,
American; fiction, nonfiction
CON
HERNDON, William Henry, 1818-
91, American; nonfiction HOO
HERNE, James A. ('James Ahern'),
1839-1901, American; plays
KAA MAT ST
HERNER, Charles H., 1930- ,
American; nonfiction CON
HERNTON, Calvin C., 1932- ,
American; poetry CON
HERO, 2nd cent. B.C., Greek;
nonfiction ST
HERO, Alfred Olivier, Jr.,
1924- , American; nonfiction
CON
HERODAS, 3rd cent. B.C.,
Greek; poetry ST
HERODES, Claudio Atico, 101-77
B.C., Greek; nonfiction SA
HERODIAN, Aelius Herodianus,
2nd cent., Greek; nonfiction
SA ST
HERODIANO de ALEXANDRIA,
3rd cent., Greek; nonfiction
SA
HERODORO PONTICO, 1st cent.
B.C., Greek; nonfiction SA
HERODOTUS, 484-25 B.C., Greek;
nonfiction MAG SA ST
HEROËT, Antoine, 1492-1568,
French; poetry DIF KE ST
HEROLD, André Ferdinand, 1865-
1940, French; poetry, plays
COL SA

HEROLD, Brenda, 1948- , American;
poetry CON
HEROLD, Jean Christopher, 1919- ,
Czech-American; nonfiction CON
HERONDAS, 3rd cent. B.C., Greek;
poetry SA
HEROUVILLE, Abbe, fl. 1768-79,
French; nonfiction DIL
HEROUVILLE DE CLAYE, Antoine de,
1713-82, French; nonfiction DIL
HERP, Henricus,   -1478, Dutch;
nonfiction ST
HERR, Daniel J., 1917- , American;
nonfiction CON
HERR, Edwin L., 1933- , American;
nonfiction CON
HERR, Lucien, 1869-1926, French;
nonfiction DIF
HERR, Richard, 1922- , American;
nonfiction CON
HERRADA de LANDSBERG, 1195- ,
German; nonfiction SA
HERRENGET, 18th cent., French;
nonfiction DIL
HERRERA, Antonio de, 1549-1625,
Spanish; nonfiction, poetry BL
HERRERA, Ataliva, 1888-1954, Ar-
gentinian; poetry, criticism, es-
says MIN
HERRERA, Darío, 1870-1914,
Panamanian; poetry SA
HERRERA, Ernesto, 1886-1917,
Uruguayan; plays MAT SA
HERRERA, Fernando de, 1534-97,
Spanish; poetry BL HAR KE SA ST
HERRERA, Flavio, 1895- , Guatema-
lan; nonfiction SA
HERRERA, Gabriel Alonso de, 1474?-
1534/39, Spanish; nonfiction BL
SA ST
HERRERA, Hernando Alonso de, 1460-
1527, Spanish; nonfiction SA
HERRERA, Marta de Warnken see
'MORGAN, Patricia'
HERRERA OBES, Julio, 1846- ,
Uruguayan; nonfiction SA
HERRERA PETERE, José, 1910- ,
Spanish; fiction SA
HERRERA y MALDONADO, Francisco
de, 16th cent., Spanish; poetry SA
HERRERA y REISSIG, Julio, 1875-
1910, Uruguayan; poetry BL
FLE SA ST
HERRERA y RIVERA, Rodrigo,
1592-1657, Spanish; poetry,
plays BL SA
HERRERA y TORDESILLAS, Antonio
de, 1559-1625, Spanish; nonfic-

tion SA ST
HERRERO GARCIA, Miguel,
1885-1962, Spanish; nonfiction
BL SA
HERRESHOFF, David, 1921- ,
American; nonfiction CON
HERRESHOFF, Lewis Francis,
1890-1972, American; nonfic-
tion CON
HERRICK, Bruce Hale, 1936- ,
American; nonfiction CON
HERRICK, Marvin Theodore
('John Smith'), 1899-1966,
American; nonfiction CON
HERRICK, Robert, 1591-1674,
English; poetry BRO KB MAG
SP ST
HERRICK, Robert, 1868-1938,
American; fiction BRO HOO
KAT KT RIC
HERRICK, Walter Russell, Jr.,
1918- , American; nonfiction
CON
HERRICK, William, 1915- ,
American; fiction CON
HERRING, Ralph Alderman,
1901- , American; nonfiction
CON
HERRING, Reuben, 1922- , Amer-
ican; nonfiction CON
HERRIOT, Edouard, 1872-1957,
French; nonfiction DIF SA
HERRIOT, Peter, 1939- , Eng-
lish; nonfiction CON
HERRIOTT, Robert E., 1929- ,
American; nonfiction CON
HERRMANN, Frank, 1927- ,
English; nonfiction CON
HERRMANN, Ignát, 1854-1935,
Czech; fiction ST
HERRMANN, Klaus Jacob, 1929- ,
German-Canadian; nonfiction
CON
HERRMANNS, Ralph, 1933- ,
German-Swedish; nonfiction
CON
HERRNSTADT, Richard L.,
1926- , American; nonfiction
CON
HERRON, Edward Albert, 1912- ,
American; fiction CON
HERRAN, Ima Honaker, 1899- ,
American; nonfiction CON
HERRON, Lowell William,
1916- , American; nonfiction
CON
HERRON, Orley R., Jr., 1933- ,
American; nonfiction CON

HERRON, Shaun, 1912- , Irish;
   fiction CON
HERRON, William George, 1933- ,
   American; nonfiction CON
HERSAN, Marc Antoine, 1652-1724,
   French; nonfiction DIL
HERSCH, Virginia, 1896- , Ameri-
   can; fiction WAF
HERSCHBERGER, Ruth Margaret
   ('Josephine Langstaff'), 1917- ,
   American; nonfiction, fiction,
   plays CON KTS MUR
HERSCHEL, Sir John Frederick
   William, 1792-1871, English;
   nonfiction BRO KBA ST
HERSEY, Jean, 1902- , American;
   nonfiction CON
HERSEY, John Richard, 1914- ,
   American; fiction CON KTS
   MAG SA ST WAF
HERSEY, William Dearborn, 1910- ,
   American; nonfiction CON
HERSHAN, Stella K., 1915- , Aus-
   trian-American; fiction CON
HERSHBERGER, Hazel Kuhns ('Hazel
   Allen'), American; juveniles CON
HERSHEY, Burnet, 1896-1971,
   Rumanian-American; fiction,
   plays CON
HERSHKOWITZ, Leo, 1924- , Amer-
   ican; nonfiction CON
HERSHON, Robert, 1936- , American;
   poetry CON
HERSHOWITZ, Herbert Bennett, 1925- ,
   American; nonfiction CON
HERSKOVITS, Melville Jean, 1895-1963,
   American; nonfiction KTS
HERST, Herman Jr., 1909- , Amer-
   ican; nonfiction CON
HERTEL, François (Rodolphe Dube),
   1905- , Canadian; fiction SY
HERTOG, Ary Den, 1889- , Dutch;
   fiction, plays ST
HERTSENS, Marcel, 1918- , English;
   nonfiction CON
HERTZ, Henrik (Heyman), 1798-1870,
   Danish; plays, fiction, poetry HAR
   KE SA ST
HERTZ, Kenneth Victor, 1945- ,
   Canadian; poetry MUR
HERTZ, Peter Donald, 1933- , Ger-
   man-American; nonfiction CON
HERTZ, Richard Cornell, 1916- ,
   American; nonfiction CON
HERTZ, Solange Strong, 1920- ,
   American; nonfiction CON
HERTZ, Wilhelm, 1835-1902, Ger-
   man; poetry ST
HERTZBERG, Arthur, 1921- ,

Polish-American; nonfiction
   CON
HERTZBERG, Ewald F. de, 1725-
   95, German; nonfiction DIL
HERTZBERG, Nancy see KEESING,
   Nancy
HERTZLER, Joyce O., 1895- ,
   American; nonfiction CON
HERTZMAN, Lewis, 1927- ,
   Canadian; nonfiction CON
HERVAS y COBO de la TORRE,
   José Gerardo de ('Don Hugo
   Herrera de Jaspedós'; 'Jorge
   Pitillas'), -1742, Spanish;
   fiction BL SA ST
HERVAS y PANDURO, Lorenzo,
   1735-1809, Spanish; nonfiction
   BL SA ST
HERVE, P. François Marie,
   1722- , French; nonfiction
   DIL
HERVEY, Harry, 1900-51, Amer-
   ican; fiction WAF
HERVEY, James, 1714-58, English;
   nonfiction BRO KB ST
'HERVEY, Jane' see McGaw,
   Naomi B.T.
HERVEY, Lord John, 1696-1743,
   English; diary BRO KB ST
HERVEY, Michael, 1920- , Eng-
   lish; fiction CON
HERVIEU, Julien Placide, 1671-
   1746, French; nonfiction DIL
HERVIEU, Paul Ernest, 1857-
   1915, French; fiction, plays
   COL DIF HAR KE MAT SA
   ST
HERVIEU de la BOISSIERE, Abbe,
   18th cent., French; nonfiction
   DIL
HERVIN, Jean, 1703-64, French;
   nonfiction DIL
HERWEGEN, Ildefons, 1874-1946,
   German; nonfiction HOE
HERWEGH, Georg, 1817-75, Ger-
   man; poetry AL HAR ST
HERWIG, Franz, 1880- , Ger-
   man; nonfiction KU
HERXEN, Dirc van, 1381-1457,
   Dutch; poetry ST
HERZ, Martin Florian, 1917- ,
   American; nonfiction CON
HERZEL, Catherine William,
   1908- , American; nonfiction
   CON
HERZEN, Alexander Ivanovich
   (Gertsen), 1812-70, Russian;
   journalism HAR HARK KE
   SA ST

HERZFELDE, Wieland, 1896- , German; nonfiction AL

HERZKA, Heinz Stefan, 1935- , Austrain; nonfiction CON

HERZL, Theodor, 1860-1904, Jewish; plays, journalism KE

HERZMANOVSKY-ORLANDO, Fritz von, 1877-1954, Austrian; fiction FLE KU

HERZOG, Arthur III, 1927- , American; nonfiction CON

HERZOG, Emile see 'MAUROIS, André'

HERZOG, John Phillip, 1931- , American; nonfiction CON

HERZOG, Rudolf see GANGERHOFER, Ludwig

HERZOG, Stephen Joel, 1938- , American; nonfiction CON

'HERZOG, Wilhelm' see REHFISCH, Hans J.

HERZOG, Ernst, 12th cent., German; nonfiction AL

HESBURGH, Theodore Martin, 1917- , American; nonfiction CON

HESCHEL, Abraham Joshua, 1907-72, Polish-American; nonfiction, poetry CON

HESDIN, Jean see ACART de HESDIN, Jean

HESELTINE, George Coulehan, 1895- , English; essays, translations HOE

HESELTINE, Nigel, 1916- , Irish; poetry, fiction CON MUR

HESIOD, 735 B.C. - , Greek; poetry MAG SA ST

HESIQUIO, Greek; nonfiction SA

HESIQUIO de MILETO, 6th cent., Greek; nonfiction SA

HESKETH, Phoebe Rayner, 1909- , English; poetry CON

HESKETT, J. L., 1933- , American; nonfiction CON

HESKY, Olga, English; fiction CON

HESLA, David Heimarck, 1929- , American; nonfiction CON

HESLEP, Robert Durham, 1930- , American; nonfiction CON

HESLIN, Richard, 1936- , American; nonfiction CON

HESLOP, J. Malam, 1923- , American; nonfiction CON

HESPELLE, Auguste, 1731- , French; nonfiction DIL

HESS, Albert Gunter, 1929- , German-American; nonfiction CON

HESS, Anthony see 'CUTHBERT, Fr.'

HESS, Fjeril, 1893- , American; juveniles KJU

HESS, Gary Ray, 1937- , American; nonfiction CON

HESS, John Milton, 1929- , American; nonfiction CON

HESS, Lilo, 1916- , German-American; juveniles CON

HESS, Robert Daniel, 1920- , American; nonfiction CON

HESS, Robert L., 1932- , American; nonfiction CON

HESS, Stephen, 1933- , American; nonfiction CON

HESS, William N., 1925- , American; nonfiction CON

HESSE, Everet W., American; nonfiction BL

HESSE, Hermann ('Hermann Lauscher'; 'Emil Sinclair'), 1877-1962, German; fiction, poetry AL COL CON FLE HAR KAT KT KU LEN KUN MAG RIC SA ST

HESSE, Mary Brenda, 1924- , English; nonfiction CON

HESSE, Max René, 1885- , German; nonfiction KU LEN

HESSELN, Mathieu Robert De, 1733- , French; nonfiction DIL

HESSELTINE, William Best, 1902-63, American; nonfiction CON

HESSERT, Paul, 1925- , American; nonfiction CON

HESSION, Charles Henry, 1911- , American; nonfiction CON

HESSLINK, George K., 1940- , American; nonfiction CON

HESSUS, Helius Eobanus ('Koch'), 1488-1540, German; poetry AL ST

HESTEAU, Loys, 1560-1624, French; poetry ST

HESTER, Hubert Inman, 1895- , American; nonfiction CON

HESTER, James J., 1931- , American; nonfiction CON

HESTER, Kathleen B., 1905- , American; nonfiction CON

HESTER, Marcus B., 1937- , American; nonfiction CON

HETH, Edward Harris, 1909- , American; fiction WAF

HETH, Meir, 1932- , Israeli; nonfiction CON

HETHERINGTON, George, 1916- , Irish; poetry ST

HETHERINGTON, Hugh William,

1903- , American; nonfiction CON
HETHMON, Robert Henry, 1925- ,
American; nonfiction CON
HETTICH, David William, 1932- ,
American; nonfiction CON
HETTLINGER, Richard Frederick,
1920- , Anglo-American; non-
fiction CON
HETZLER, Stanley Arthur, 1919- ,
American; nonfiction CON
HETZRON, Robert, 1937- , Hungar-
ian-American; nonfiction CON
HEUMAN, William ('George Kramer'),
1912- , American; fiction CON
WA
HEUSCHELE, Otto Hermann, 1900- ,
German; essays KU LEN
HEUSCHER, Julius E., 1918- ,
American; nonfiction CON
HEUSS, John, 1908- , American;
nonfiction CON
HEUSS, Theodor, 1884- , German;
nonfiction KU
HEUSSLER, Robert, 1924- , Amer-
ican; nonfiction CON
HEUZET, Jean, 1660-1728, French;
nonfiction DIL
HEWES, Anges Danforth, American;
juveniles KJU WA
HEWES, Dorothy, 1922- , American;
nonfiction CON
HEWES, Henry, 1917- , American;
nonfiction CON
HEWES, Ralph Anthony, 1909- ,
English; nonfiction CON
HEWETT, Anita, 1918- , American;
juveniles CON WA
HEWETT, Dorothy Coade, 1923- ,
Australian; poetry, plays, fiction
MUR
HEWETT, Harold Pease, 1882- ,
English; nonfiction HIG
HEWETT, William S., 1924- ,
American; nonfiction CON
HEWINS, Geoffrey Shaw, 1889- ,
English; nonfiction CON
HEWITSON, John Nelson, 1917- ,
English; nonfiction CON
HEWITT, Andrew, 1913- , Ameri-
can; fiction JO
HEWITT, Barnard Wolcott, 1906- ,
American; nonfiction CON
HEWITT, Geof George F., 1943- ,
American; poetry CON MUR
HEWITT, Herbert James, 1890- ,
English; nonfiction CON
HEWITT, John Harold, 1907- ,
British; poetry MUR ST

HEWITT, John Hill, 1801-90,
American; journalism, poetry
KAA
HEWITT, William Henry, 1936- ,
American; nonfiction CON
HEWLETT, John, 1905- ,
American; fiction WAF
HEWLETT, Maurice Henry, 1861-
1923, English; fiction, poetry
BRO KAT KT RIC
HEWLETT, Richard Greening,
1923- , American; nonfiction
CON
HEWSON, John, 1930- , English;
nonfiction CON
HEXHAM, John of, fl. 1180,
English; nonfiction ST
HEXNER, Ervin Paul, 1893- ,
Czech-American; nonfiction
CON
'HEXT, Harrington' see PHILL-
POTTS, Eden
'HEXTALL, David' see PHILLIPS-
BIRT, Douglas
HEXTER, Jack H., 1910- ,
American; nonfiction CON
HEY, Nigel Stewart, 1936- ,
English; juveniles CON
HEYDON, Peter Richard, 1913- ,
Australian; nonfiction CON
HEYDUK, Adolf, 1835-1923,
Czech; poetry ST
HEYE, Jan Pieter, 1809-76,
Dutch; poetry ST
HEYEL, Carl, 1908- , American;
nonfiction CON
HEYEN, William, 1940- , Ameri-
can; nonfiction CON
HEYER, Georgette, 1902- , Eng-
lish; fiction KT RIC
HEYERDAHL, Thor, 1914- ,
Norwegian; juveniles, nonfic-
tion COM CON KTS RIC
HEYERMANS, Herman see HEIJER-
MANS, Herman
HEYLIGER, William, 1884- ,
American; juveniles HOE KJU
WA
HEYLIN, Peter (Heylyn), 1600-62,
English; nonfiction BRO KB
ST
HEYM, George, 1887-1912, Ger-
man; poetry AL COL FLE KU
KUN SA ST
'HEYM, Stefan' (Hellmuth Fliegel),
1913- , German-American;
fiction AL CON KTS KU WAF
HEYMANS, Gerardus, 1857-1930,

Dutch; nonfiction SA

HEYNE, Christian Gottlob, 1729-1812,
German; nonfiction SA

HEYNICKE, Kurt, 1891- , German;
plays, poetry KU MAT

HEYNLIN, J. see JOHANNES A
LAPIDE

HEYNS, Maria, 1621- , Dutch;
poetry, fiction ST

HEYNS, Zacharias, 1566-1638?,
Dutch; translations ST

HEYRICK, Thomas, 1650?-94, English; poetry ST

HEYSE, Paul Johann Ludwig von,
1830-1914, German; fiction, poetry
AL COL HAR KE SA ST

HEYSHAM, W. Nuñez ('Aesop'),
1825-1905, English; nonfiction
HIG

'HEYST, Axel' see GRABOWSKI,
Zbigniew A.

HEYWARD, Dorothy, 1890-1961,
American; fiction, plays MAT

HEYWARD, DuBose, 1885-1940,
American; fiction, poetry, plays
BRO KL KT MAG MAT RIC

HEYWOOD, Elisa, 1693-1756, English;
fiction SA

HEYWOOD, Jasper, 1535-97/98, English; poetry, translations ST

HEYWOOD, John, 1497?-1580?, English; plays BRO KB ST

HEYWOOD, Terence, South African;
poetry CON MUR

HEYWOOD, Thomas, 1573/74-1641/
50, English; plays BRO KB MAG
ST

HIAT, Elchik see KATZ, Menke

HIBBEN, Frank Cummings, 1910- ,
American; nonfiction CON

HIBBERT, Christopher, 1924- ,
English; nonfiction CON

HIBBERT, Eleanor Burford ('Elbur
Ford'; 'Victoria Holt'; 'Kathleen
Kellow'; 'Jean Plaidy'; 'Ellalice
Tate'), 1906- , English; juveniles,
fiction COM CON RIC

HIBBERT, Ray Eldon, 1932- , American; nonfiction CON

HIBBS, Paul, 1906- , American;
nonfiction CON

HIBDON, James Edward, 1924- ,
American; nonfiction CON

HICHENS, Robert Smythe, 1864-1950,
English; fiction BRO KAT KT
RIC

HICK, John, 1922- , English; nonfiction CON

HICKEN, Ricardo,   -1940,
Argentinian; plays MIN

HICKEN, Victor, 1921- , American; nonfiction CON

HICKERSON, John Melancthon,
1897- , American; nonfiction
CON

HICKES, George, 1642-1715,
English; nonfiction ST

HICKEY, Neil, 1931- , American; nonfiction CON

HICKEY PELLIZZONI, Margarita,
1753-93?, Spanish; poetry
SA

HICKMAN, Martha Whitmore,
1925- , American; nonfiction
CON

HICKOK, Laurens Perseus, 1798-
1888, American; nonfiction
KAA

HICKOK, Lorena A., American;
juveniles WA

HICKS, Charles Balch, 1916- ,
American; nonfiction CON

HICKS, Clifford B., 1920- ,
American; juveniles CON
WA

HICKS, David E., 1931- , American; nonfiction CON

'HICKS, Eleanor B.' see COERR,
Eleanor

HICKS, Granville, 1901- , American; fiction CON KT WAF

'HICKS, Harvey' see STRATE-
MEYER, Edward L.

HICKS, John D., 1890- , American; nonfiction CON

HICKS, John Kenneth, 1918- ,
American; fiction CON

HICKS, Mary A., 1911- , American; nonfiction JO

HICKS, Warren Braukman, 1921- ,
American; nonfiction CON

HICKS, William, 17th cent., English; fiction ST

HICKY, Daniel Whitehead, 1902- ,
American; poetry HOE

HIDALGO, Alberto, 1897- ,
Peruvian; poetry SA

HIDALGO, Bartolomé José, 1788-
1822, Uruguayan; poetry SA
ST

HIDALGO, Gaspar Lucas, 1560-
1617?, Spanish; nonfiction
SA

HIDALGO, José Luis, 1919-47,
Spanish; poetry BL FLE
SA

HIDAYAT, Riza Quli Khan, 1800-71,
Persian; poetry ST
HIDAYAT, Sadiq (Hedayat), 1903-51,
Persian; fiction ST
HIDDEN, Norman Frederick, British;
poetry MUR
'HIDEKI OKADA' see GLASSCO, John
S.
HIDY, Ralph Willard, 1905- , Amer-
ican; nonfiction CON
HIEATT, Allen Kent, 1921- , Amer-
ican; nonfiction CON
HIEATT, Constance Bartlett, 1928- ,
American; nonfiction CON
HIEBERT, David Edmond, 1910- ,
American; nonfiction CON
HIEBERT, Paul Gerhardt ('Sarah
Binks'), 1892- , Canadian;
fiction, nonfiction CON RIC SY
HIEL, Emmanuel, 1834-99, Flemish;
poetry ST
HIEROCLES, 4th cent., Roman;
nonfiction SA
HIEROCLES de ALEXANDRIA, Greek;
nonfiction SA
HIERRO, José, 1922- , Spanish;
journalism, poetry, fiction BL
SA
HIERTA, Lars Johan, 1801-72,
Swedish; nonfiction ST
HIFLER, Joyce, 1925- , American;
nonfiction CON
HIFNI NASIF, Malak (Bahithat-al-
Badiyah), 1886-1918, Egyptian;
poetry, essays ST
HIGBEE, Edward Counselman,
1910- , American; nonfiction
CON
HIGBY, Mary Jane, American; nonfic-
tion CON
HIGDEN, Ranulf (Ralph), -1364,
English; nonfiction BRO KB ST
HIGDON, Hal ('Lafayette Smith'),
1931- , American; nonfiction
CON
HIGENBOTTAM, Frank, 1910- ,
English; nonfiction CON
HIGGENS, Paul Lambourne, 1916- ,
American; nonfiction CON
HIGGIE, Lincoln William, 1938- ,
American; nonfiction CON
HIGGINBOTHAM, John E., 1933- ,
English; nonfiction CON
HIGGINBOTHAM, Robert Don, 1931- ,
American; nonfiction CON
HIGGINS, Aidan, 1927- , Irish;
fiction CON
HIGGINS, Albert Corbin, 1930- ,

American; nonfiction CON
HIGGINS, Angus John Brockhurst,
1911- , Welsh; nonfiction
CON
HIGGINS, Colin, 1941- , Ameri-
can; nonfiction CON
HIGGINS, Don, 1928- , American;
juveniles CON
HIGGINS, Frederick Robert,
1896-1941, Irish; poetry ST
HIGGINS, Jean C., 1932- ,
American; poetry CON
HIGGINS, Marguerite, 1920-66,
American; nonfiction CON
HIGGINS, Reynold Alleyne,
1916- , English; nonfiction
CON
HIGGINS, Richard C., 1938- ,
English; nonfiction, plays
CON
HIGGINS, Rosalyn Cohen, 1937- ,
English; nonfiction CON
HIGGINS, Thomas Joseph, 1899- ,
American; nonfiction CON
HIGGINS, Trumbull, 1919- ,
American; nonfiction CON
HIGGINS, William Robert, 1938- ,
American; nonfiction CON
HIGGINSON, Alexander Henry,
1876- , American; nonfiction
HIG
HIGGINSON, Fred Hall, 1921- ,
American; nonfiction CON
HIGGINSON, John, 1616-1708,
American; nonfiction KAA
HIGGINSON, Thomas Wentworth,
1823-1911, American; nonfic-
tion, essays, letters KAA
HIGGS, Eric Sidney, 1908- ,
English; nonfiction CON
HIGH, Dallas M., 1931- , Amer-
ican; nonfiction CON
HIGHAM, Charles, 1931- ,
British; poetry CON MUR
HIGHAM, David, 1895- , English;
nonfiction CON
HIGHAM, John, 1920- , Ameri-
can; nonfiction CON
HIGHAM, Robin David Stewart,
1925- , Anglo-American;
nonfiction CON
HIGHAM, Roger, 1935- , English;
nonfiction CON
HIGHET, Gilbert, 1906- , Scots-
American; nonfiction CON
KTS
HIGHSMITH, Patricia, 1921- ,
American; fiction CON

HIGHSMITH, Richard Morgan, Jr.,
1920- , American; nonfiction
CON PAC
HIGHTOWER, Florence Cole,
1916- , American; juveniles,
fiction CON WA
HIGINIO, Gayo Julio, 170-110 B.C.,
Roman; nonfiction SA
HIGMAN, Francis Montgomery,
1935- , English; nonfiction CON
HIGSON, Kit, 20th cent., English;
juveniles DOY
'HIGUCHI Ichiyo' (Higuchi Natsuko),
1872-96, Japanese; fiction LAN
ST
HIJAZI Muhammad (Hejazi), 1899/
1900- , Persian; fiction LAN
ST
HIKMET, Nazim, 1902-63, Turkish;
poetry, plays RIC SA
HILAIRE, Saint, 306-67, French;
nonfiction SA
HILARION see ILARION
HILARY, fl. 1125, English; poetry
ST
HILBERG, Raul, 1926- , Austrian-
American; nonfiction CON
HILLIARD, d'AUBERTEUIL, Michel
René, 1750-89, French; nonfic-
tion DIL
HILBERRY, Conrad Arthur, 1928- ,
American; nonfiction CON
HILBERT, Jaroslav, 1871-1936,
Czech; plays COL SA ST
HILBORN, Harry Warren, 1900- ,
Canadian; nonfiction BL CON
HILD, August, 1894- , German;
fiction AL
HILDEBERT, 1056-1133, French;
poetry ST
'HILDEBRAND' see BEETS, Nicolaas
HILDEBRAND, Dietrich von, 1889- ,
German; nonfiction HOE
HILDEBRAND, George Herbert,
1913- , American; nonfiction
CON
HILDEBRAND, Joel Henry, 1881- ,
American; nonfiction CON
HILDEBRAND, Verna, 1924- ,
American; nonfiction CON
HILDEBRANDSLIED, 9th cent.,
German; poetry AL
HILDEGAERSBERCH, Wiliem van,
1350-1409, Dutch; poetry ST
HILDEGARDE, Saint, 1100-80?,
nonfiction SA
HILDEGARD OF BINGEN, 1098-1179,
German; nonfiction ST

HILDER, Rowland, 1905- ,
English; juveniles DOY
HILDESHEIMER, Wolfgang,
1916- , German; nonfiction,
plays KU KUN MAT
HILDGARD, Ferdinand Heinrich
Gustav see 'VILLARD, Henry'
HILDICK, Edmund Wallace,
1925- , English; juveniles
COM CON DOY
HILDRETH, Richard, 1807-65,
American; nonfiction KAA
HILDUM, Donald Clayton,
1930- , American; nonfiction
CON
HILENDARSKY, Paissiy (Otets
Paissiy), 1722-93, Belgian;
nonfiction HAR ST
HILGER, Sister Mary Inez,
1891- , American; nonfiction
CON
HILL, Aaron, 1685-1750, English;
poetry, plays BRO KB ST
HILL, Alfred Tuxbury, 1908- ,
American; nonfiction CON
HILL, Barrington Julian Warren,
1915- , American; nonfiction
CON
HILL, Brian ('Marcus Magill'),
1896- , English; nonfiction
CON
HILL, Claude, 1911- , German-
American; nonfiction CON
HILL, Clifford S., 1927- ,
English; nonfiction CON
HILL, David Charles, 1936- ,
American; juveniles CON
'HILL, Dee' see ZUCKER, Dolores
M. B.
HILL, Donna Marie, 1921- ,
American; fiction, juveniles
CON
HILL, Douglas, 1935- , Canadian;
poetry MUR
HILL, Earle, 1941- , American;
fiction CON
HILL, Elizabeth Starr, 1925- ,
American; nonfiction CON
HILL, Evan, 1919- , American;
nonfiction CON
HILL, Frank Ernest, 1888- ,
American; nonfiction KT WA
HILL, Frederic Stanhope, 1805-51,
American; plays KAA
HILL, Geoffrey, 1932- , British;
poetry MUR SP
HILL, George Birkbeck Norman,
1835-1903, English; nonfiction
KBA

HILL, George Edward, 1907- ,
American; nonfiction CON
HILL, Gladwin, 1914- , American;
nonfiction CON
'HILL, Grace Brooks' see STRATE-
MEYER, Edward L.
HILL, Grace Livingston, 1865-1947,
American; fiction KT
HILL, Hamlin, 1931- , American;
nonfiction CON
HILL, Henry Bertram, 1907- ,
American; nonfiction CON
'HILL, Hyacinthe' see ANDERSON,
Virginia R. C.
HILL, James Newlin, 1934- , Amer-
ican; nonfiction CON
HILL, Jim Dan, 1897- , American;
nonfiction CON
HILL, John Campbell, 1888- , Scots;
nonfiction CON
HILL, John Edward Christopher,
1912- , English; nonfiction CON
HILL, John Hugh, 1905- , American;
nonfiction CON
HILL, John M., 1887- , American;
nonfiction BL
HILL, John Paul, 1936- , American;
nonfiction CON
HILL, John Stanley ('Stan Wiley'),
1929- , American; nonfiction
CON
HILL, Kathleen Louise ('Kay'),
1917- , Canadian; plays, fiction
CON
'HILL, King' see ROBERTSON, Frank
C.
HILL, Knox Calvin, 1910- , Ameri-
can; nonfiction CON
HILL, Lee Halsey, 1899- , Ameri-
can; nonfiction CON
HILL, Leroy Draper, Jr., 1935- ,
American; nonfiction CON
HILL, Leslie Alexander, 1918- ,
English; nonfiction CON
HILL, Lorna, 1902- , English;
juveniles CON WA
HILL, Margaret Ohler ('Rachel
Bennett²; 'Andrea Thomas'),
1915- , American; fiction,
juveniles CON WA
'HILL, Monica' see WATSON, Jane W.
HILL, Norman Llewellyn, 1895- ,
American; nonfiction CON
HILL, Peter Proal, 1926- , Ameri-
can; nonfiction CON
HILL, Philip George, 1934- , Amer-
ican; nonfiction CON
'HILL, Poll' see HUMPHREYS, Mary
E. H.

HILL, Ralph Nading, 1917- ,
American; juveniles CON WA
HILL, Richard, 1901- , Anglo-
American; nonfiction CON
HILL, Richard Desmond, 1920- ,
English; nonfiction CON
HILL, Richard E., 1920- ,
American; nonfiction CON
HILL, Richard Fontaine, 1941- ,
American; fiction CON
HILL, Richard Johnson, 1925- ,
American; nonfiction CON
HILL, Robert White, 1919- ,
American; nonfiction, juveniles
CON WA
HILL, Rosalind Mary Theodosia,
1908- , English; nonfiction
CON
HILL, Roscoe Earl, 1936- ,
American; nonfiction CON
HILL, Rudolph Nelson, 1903- ,
American; poetry MAR
HILL, Ruth Livingston see MUNCE,
Ruth H.
HILL, Samuel Ervin, 1913- ,
American; nonfiction CON
HILL, Samuel Smythe, 1927- ,
American; nonfiction CON
HILL, Susan, 1942- , American;
fiction CON
HILL, Thomas, -1599?, Eng-
lish; nonfiction, translations
ST
HILL, Thomas English, 1929- ,
American; nonfiction CON
HILL, West Thompson, Jr.,
1915- , American; nonfiction
CON
HILL, William Joseph, 1924- ,
American; nonfiction CON
HILL, Winifred Farrington,
1929- , American; nonfiction
CON
HILLARD, George Stillman,
1808-79, American; nonfiction
KAA
'HILLARD, Gustav' (Gustav Stein-
bömer), 1881- , German;
nonfiction KU
HILLARY, Richard Hope, 1919-43,
English; nonfiction KTS
'HILLAS, Julian' see DASHWOOD,
Robert J.
HILLCOURT, William, 1900- ,
American; juvenile WA
HILLE, Peter, 1854-1904, Ger-
man; poetry, fiction, plays
AL COL SA ST
HILLEGAS, Mark Robert, 1926- ,

American; nonfiction CON

HILLER, Lejaren Arthur, Jr.,
1924- , American; nonfiction
CON

HILLERMAN, Tony, 1925- , American; fiction CON

HILLERT, Margaret, 1920- , American; poetry HIL

HILLERY, George Anthony, Jr.,
1927- , American; nonfiction
CON

HILLES, Frederick Whiley, 1900- ,
American; nonfiction CON

HILLES, Helen Train, 1905- ,
American; juveniles WA

HILLGARTH, Jocelyn Nigel, 1929- ,
American; nonfiction CON

HILLHOUSE, James Abraham, 1789-
1841, American; poetry KAA

'HILLIARD, Jan' see GRANT, Hilda
K.

HILLIARD, Noel Harvey, 1929- ,
New Zealander; fiction CON

HILLIER, Bevis, 1940- , English;
nonfiction CON

HILLIER, Jack Ronald, 1912- ,
English; nonfiction CON

HILLIKER, Grant, 1921- , American; nonfiction CON

HILLING, David, 1935- , English;
nonfiction CON

HILLIS, Charles Richard, 1913- ,
Canadian; nonfiction CON

'HILLMAN, May' see HIPSHMAN,
May

HILL-RIED, William Scott, 1890- ,
American; nonfiction CON

HILLS, George, 1918- , English;
nonfiction CON

HILLS, Lawrence Rust, 1924- ,
American; nonfiction CON

HILLS, Stuart Lee, 1932- , American; nonfiction CON

HILLSE, Theodore Lewis, 1925- ,
New Zealander; nonfiction CON

HILLSON, Maurice, 1925- , American; nonfiction CON

HILLWAY, Tyrus, 1912- , American;
nonfiction CON

HILLYER, Robert Silliman, 1895-1961,
American; poetry KAT KT SP

HILLYER, Virgil Mores, 1875-1931,
American; juveniles KJU WA

HILMAN, Johannes, 1802-81, Dutch;
plays, poetry ST

HILSDALE, Eric Paul, 1922- ,
American; nonfiction CON

HILSMAN, Roger, 1919- , Ameri-

can; nonfiction CON

HILTNER, Seward, 1909- ,
American; nonfiction CON

HILTON, Alice Mary, 1924- ,
American; nonfiction CON

HILTON, Arthur Clement, 1851-
77, English; poetry KBA

HILTON, Bruce, 1930- , American; nonfiction CON

HILTON, Earl Raymond, 1914- ,
American; nonfiction CON

HILTON, George Woodman,
1925- , American; nonfiction
CON

HILTON, Irene Pothus, 1912- ,
Anglo-American; fiction CON

HILTON, James, 1900-54, English;
fiction BRO KT MAG RIC SA

HILTON, Ralph, 1907- , American; nonfiction CON

HILTON, Richard (Zakhmi Dil),
1894- , Pakistani; nonfiction
CON

HILTON, Ronald, 1911- , American; nonfiction BL CON

HILTON, Suzanne, 1922- , American; juveniles CON

HILTON, Thomas Leonard, 1924- ,
American; nonfiction CON

HILTON, Walter, -1396, English; nonfiction ST

HIMELICK, James Raymond,
1910- , American; nonfiction
CON

HIMELSTEIN, Morgan Yale,
1926- , American; nonfiction
CON

HIMERIUS, 310-85, Greek;
nonfiction SA ST

HIMES, Chester Bomar, 1909- ,
American; fiction CON WAF

HIMES, Joseph Sandy, 1908- ,
American; nonfiction CON

HIMMELHEBER, Diana Martin,
1938- , American; fiction
CON

HIMSTREET, William Charles,
1923- , American; nonfiction
CON

HINDE, Richard Standish Elphinstone, 1912- , Irish; nonfiction CON

'HINDE, Thomas' see CHITTY,
Sir Thomas W.

HINDLE, Brooke, 1918- , American; nonfiction CON

HINDLE, Wilfred Hope, 1903-67,
American; nonfiction CON

HINDMAN, Jane Ferguson, 1905- ,
American; juveniles CON
HINDREY, Karl August, 1875-1947,
Estonian; fiction FLE
HINDS, Evelyn Margery, English;
juveniles CON
HINDS, John, fl. 1780, English; non-
fiction HIG
HINDUS, Maurice Gershon, 1891-1969,
American; fiction KT WAF
HINDUS, Milton Henry, 1916- ,
American; nonfiction CON
HINE, Al, 1915- , American; juveniles,
fiction CON WA
HINE, Frederick R., 1925- , Ameri-
can; nonfiction CON
HINE, Sesyle Joslin see JOSLIN,
Sesyle H.
HINE, William Daryl, 1936- ,
Canadian-American; poetry, fic-
tion CON MUR
HINE, Robert Van Norden, Jr.,
1921- , American; nonfiction
CON
HINES, Neal Oldfield, 1908- , Amer-
ican; nonfiction CON
HINES, Paul David, 1934- , Ameri-
can; nonfiction CON
HINES, Robert Stephan, 1926- ,
American; nonfiction CON
HINGLEY, Ronald Francis, 1920- ,
Scots; nonfiction, translations
CON
HINGORANI, Rup C., 1925- ,
Indian; nonfiction CON
HINKINS, Virginia, American;
juvenile WA
HINKLE, Olin Ethmer, 1902- ,
American; nonfiction CON
HINKLE, Thomas Clark, 1876-1949,
American; juveniles WA
HINKSON, Katharine see TYNAN,
Katharine
HINKSON, Pamela, Irish; nonfiction,
juveniles HOE
HINMAN, Charlton J.K., 1911- ,
American; nonfiction CON
HINMAN, Robert Benedict, 1920- ,
American; nonfiction CON
HINNEBUSCH, William Aquinas,
1908- , American; nonfiction
CON
'HINO ASHIHEI' (Tamai Katsunori),
1907- , Japanese; nonfiction
ST
HINOJOSA y NAVEROS, Eduard de,
1852-1919, Spanish; nonfiction
BL SA

HINRICHS, August, 1879- ,
German; plays ST
HINRICHSEN, Ludwig, 1872- ,
German; plays, fiction ST
HINRICHSEN, Max Henry, 1901- ,
German-English; nonfiction
CON
HINSHAW, Cecil Eugene, 1911- ,
American; nonfiction CON
HINSLEY, Francis Harry,
1918- , English; nonfiction
CON
HINSON, Edward Glenn, 1931- ,
American; nonfiction CON
HINTERHOFF, Eugene, 1895- ,
English; nonfiction CON
HINTIKKA, Kaarlo Jaakko Juhani,
1929- , Finnish; nonfiction
CON
HINTON, Bernard L., 1937- ,
American; nonfiction CON
HINTON, Harold Clendenin,
1924- , American; nonfiction
CON
HINTON, James, 1822-75, Eng-
lish; nonfiction BRO KBA ST
'HINTON, Richard W.' see ANGOFF,
Charles
HINTON, William H., 1919- ,
American; nonfiction CON
HINTZE, Guenther, 1906- ,
American; nonfiction CON
'HIOVER, Harry' see BINDLEY,
Charles
HIPARQUIA, 4th cent. B.C.,
Greek; nonfiction SA
HIPATIA, 370/80-415, Greek; non-
fiction SA
HIPERIDES, 359-22 B.C., Greek;
nonfiction SA
HIPIAS de ELIS, Greek; nonfiction
SA
HIPON, 5th-4th cent. B.C.,
Greek; nonfiction
SA
HIPONACTE de EPHESUS,
540 B.C.- , Greek; poetry
SA
HIPONAX, 4th cent. B.C., Greek;
poetry SA
HIPPARCHUS of NICAEA, 2nd
cent. B.C., Greek; nonfiction
ST
HIPPEL, Theodor Gottlieb von,
1741-96, German; fiction,
plays AL HAR ST
HIPPEL, Ursula von, German-
American; juveniles WA

HIPPIAS of ELIS, 5th cent. B.C.,
Greek; nonfiction ST
HIPPIUS, Zinaida Nikolayevna (Gippius;
Anton Krayni), 1867-1945, Rus-
sian; poetry COL HARK ST SA
HIPPOLYTUS, Saint, 160-235, Greek;
nonfiction SA
HIPPOCRATES, 460 B.C., Greek;
nonfiction ST
HIPPONAX, 6th cent. B.C., Greek;
poetry SA ST
HIPPOPOTAMUS, Eugene H., see
KRAUS, Robert
HIPSHMAN, May ('Hay Hillman'),
1919- , American; juveniles
WA
HIPSKIND, Verne Kenneth, 1925- ,
American; nonfiction CON
'HIRAGA, Gennai' ('Hiraga Kunitomo';
'Furai Sanjin'), 1729-80,
Japanese; plays ST
HIRAOKA KIMITAKE see 'MISHIMA,
Yukio'
HIRATA, Atsutane, 1776-1843,
Japanese; poetry ST
HIRAZAWA TSUNETOMI see 'KISANJI'
HIRCIO, Aulo, 90-43 B.C., Roman;
nonfiction SA
HIRN, Irjo, 1870-1952, Finnish; non-
fiction SA ST
HIRSCH, Eric Donald, Jr., 1928- ,
American; nonfiction CON
HIRSCH, Ernest Albert, 1924- ,
German-American; nonfiction
CON
HIRSCH, Fred, 1931- , Austrian-
American; nonfiction CON
HIRSCH, Lester M., 1925- , Amer-
ican; nonfiction CON
HIRSCH, S. Carl, 1913- , American;
juveniles COM CON
HIRSCH, Seev, 1931- , German-
Israeli; nonfiction CON
HIRSCH, Walter, 1919- , German-
American; nonfiction CON
HIRSCH, Werner Z., 1920- , German-
American; nonfiction CON
'HIRSCH, William R.' see LINGEMAN,
Richard R.
HIRSCH, William Randolph see NAVA-
SKY, Victor S.
HIRSCHBEIN, Peretz, 1880-1948,
Jewish-American; plays, fiction
FLE ST MAT
HIRSCHBERG, Cornelius, 1901- ,
American; fiction CON
HIRSCHFELD, Albert, 1903- , Amer-
ican; nonfiction CON

HIRSCHFELD, George, 1873-1942,
German; fiction, plays MAT
HIRSCHFIELD, Herman, 1905- ,
American; nonfiction CON
HIRSCHMAN, Albert O., 1915- ,
German-American; nonfiction
CON
HIRSCHMAN, Jack, 1933- ,
American; poetry MUR
HIRSCHMEIER, Johannes, 1921- ,
German; nonfiction CON
HIRSHBERG, Albert S., 1909-72,
American; juveniles CON WA
HIRSHFIELD, Daniel S., 1942- ,
American; nonfiction CON
HIRSHSON, Stanley Philip,
1928- , American; nonfiction
CON
HIRST, David Wayne, 1920- ,
American; nonfiction CON
HIRST, Henry Beck, 1813-74,
American; poetry KAA
HIRST, Rodney Julian, 1920- ,
English; nonfiction CON
HIRST, Wilma Ellis, 1914- ,
American; nonfiction CON
HIRT, Michael Leonard, 1934- ,
Polish-American; nonfiction
CON
HIRTIUS, Aulus,   -43 B.C.,
Roman; nonfiction ST
HISER, Iona Seibert, 1901- ,
American; nonfiction CON
'HISLOP, Andrew' see CLARKE,
Marcus
HISLOP, Codman, 1906- , Amer-
ican; nonfiction CON
'HISPANO, Cornelio' (Ismael
López), 1880/82- , Colombian;
journalism, nonfiction, poetry
MIN
HISS, Alger, 1904- , American;
nonfiction CON
HITA, Arcipreste see RUIZ, Juan
HITA, Ginés P. see PEREZ de
HITA, Ginés
HITCHCOCK, Ethan Allen, 1798-
1870, American; nonfiction
KAA
HITCHCOCK, George P., 1914- ,
American; poetry CON MUR
HITCHCOCK, James, 1938- ,
American; nonfiction CON
'HITCHCOCK, W.' see MURDOCH,
Frank H.
HITCHIN, Martin Newburn ('Martin
Mewburn'), 1917- , English;
nonfiction, fiction CON

HITCHMAN, James H., 1932- ,
American; nonfiction CON
HITCHMAN, Janet, 1916- , English;
nonfiction CON
HITOMARO see KAKINOMOTO NO
HITOMARO
HITREC, Joseph George, 1912- ,
Yugoslav-American; fiction
CON WAF
HITSMAN, John Mackay, 1917- ,
Canadian; nonfiction CON
HITT, Russell Trovillo, 1905- ,
American; juveniles CON
HITTE, Kathryn, American; juveniles
CON WA
HITTELL, John Shertzer, 1825-1901,
American; journalism KAA
HITTELL, Theodore Henry, 1830-
1917, American; nonfiction KAA
HITTI, Philip Khuri, 1886- ,
Lebanese-American; nonfiction
CON
HIXSON, Richard F., 1932- , Amer-
ican; nonfiction CON
HIXSON, William Butler, Jr., 1940- ,
American; nonfiction CON
HJÄRNE, Urban, 1641-1724, Swedish;
poetry ST
HJELTE, George, 1893- , American;
nonfiction CON
HJORLEIFSSON KWRAN, Einar,
1859- , Icelandic; poetry, essays
SA
HJORTO, Knud, 1869-1931, Danish;
fiction FLE ST
HJORTSBERG, William Reinhold,
1941- , American; fiction CON
HLADIK, Vaclav, 1868-1913, Czech;
fiction SA
HLAING, Princess of, 1833-75,
Burmese; poetry LAN
HLASKO, Marek, 1934-69, Polish;
fiction FLE RIC
HLAVACEK, Karel, 1874-98, Czech;
poetry COL SA ST
'HLBINA, Pavel' (Pavel Gasparovic),
1908- , Slovak; poetry ST
HO, Alfred Kuo-liang, 1919- ,
Chinese-American; nonfiction
CON
HO, Ping-ti, 1917- , Chinese-
American; nonfiction CON
HOADLEY, Irene Braden, 1938- ,
American; nonfiction CON
HOADLY, Benjamin, 1676-1761,
English; nonfiction BRO ST
HOAG, Edwin, 1926- , American;
nonfiction, juveniles CON WA

HOAGLAND, Edward, 1932- ,
American; fiction CON
HOAGLAND, Everett III, 1942- ,
American; poetry CON
HOAGLAND, Kathleen Mary Dooher,
Irish; fiction CON
HOANG VAN CHI, 1915- ,
Vietnamese; nonfiction CON
HOARE, Robert John, 1921- ,
English; juveniles CON
HOBAN, Lillian, American;
juveniles CON
HOBAN, Russell Conwell, 1925- ,
American; juveniles COM
CON WA
HOBART, Alice Nourse Tisdale,
1882-1967, American; fiction
CON KT WAF
'HOBART, Black' see SANDERS,
Ed
HOBART, Lois Elaine, American;
juveniles CON WA
'HOBBES, John Oliver' see
CRAIGIE, Pearl M. T.
HOBBES, Thomas, 1588-1679,
English; essays BRO KB
MAG SA ST
HOBBS, Cecil Carlton ('Maung
Hauk'), 1907- , American;
nonfiction CON
HOBBS, Charles Rene, 1931- ,
American; nonfiction CON
HOBBS, Herschel Harold, 1907- ,
American; nonfiction CON
HOBBS, John Leslie, 1916-64,
American; nonfiction CON
HOBBS, William Beresford,
1939- , English; nonfiction
CON
HOBEN, John B., 1908- , Amer-
ican; nonfiction CON
HOBERECHT, Earnest, 1918- ,
American; nonfiction CON
HOBHOUSE, Christina, 1941- ,
English; fiction CON
HOBHOUSE, John Cam see
BROUGHTON, John C. H.
HOBLEY, Leonard Frank, 1903- ,
English; nonfiction, juveniles
CON
HOBSBAUM, Philip Dennis,
1932- , English; nonfiction,
poetry CON MUR
HOBSBAWM, Eric John Ernest
('Francis Newton'), 1917- ,
English; nonfiction CON
HOBSON, Anthony Robert Alwyn,
1921- , Welsh; nonfiction
CON

HOBSON, Burton Harold, 1933- ,
American; nonfiction CON
HOBSON, E. S. C., 1850- , English;
nonfiction HIG
HOBSON, George Carey, 1890-1945,
Afrikaans; nonfiction ST
HOBSON, Harry ('Hank'; 'Hank Janson'),
1908- , English; fiction CON
'HOBSON, Laura Z.' (Laura Keane
Zametkin; 'Felice Quist'), 1900- ,
American; fiction CON KTS
WAF
'HOBSON, Polly' see EVANS, Julia R.
HOBSON, Samuel Bonnin, 1888- ,
Afrikaans; fiction ST
HOBY, Sir Thomas, 1530-66, English;
translations BRO KB ST
HOCCLEVE, Thomas see OCCLEVE,
Thomas
HOCH, Edward D. ('Irwin Booth';
'Stephen Dentinger'; 'Pat McMahon';
'Mister X'; 'R. L. Stephens'),
1930- , American; fiction CON
HOCHFIELD, George, 1926- , Ameri-
can; nonfiction CON
HOCHHUTH, Rolf, 1931- , German;
plays CON MAT RIC
HOCHMAN, Sandra, 1936- , Ameri-
can; poetry CON MUR
HOCHWÄLDER, Fritz, 1911- , Aus-
trian; plays AL CON FLE KU
MAT RIC
HOCHWALD, Werner, 1910- , Ger-
man; nonfiction CON
'HOCKABY, Stephen' see MITCHELL,
Gladys
HOCKETT, Charles Francis, 1916- ,
American; nonfiction CON
HOCKING, Brian, 1914- , English;
nonfiction CON
HOCKING, Joseph, 1860-1937, Eng-
lish; fiction BRO KT
HOCKING, Silas Kitto, 1850-1935,
English; fiction BRO
HOCKING, William Ernest, 1873-1966,
American; nonfiction CON KTS
HOCKLEY, Graham Charles, 1931- ,
American; nonfiction CON
HODDER-WILLIAMS, Christopher,
1927- , English; nonfiction,
fiction CON
'HODDIS, Jakob van' (Hans Davidsohn),
1887- , German; nonfiction
KU
HODES, Aubrey, 1927- , South
African; nonfiction CON
HODGART, Matthew John Caldwell,
1916- , Scots; nonfiction CON

HODGE, Charles, 1797-1878,
American; nonfiction KAA
'HODGE, E. Chatterton' see
HASTINGS, Phyllis D. H.
HODGE, Francis Richard, 1915- ,
American; nonfiction CON
HODGE, Jane Aiken, 1917- ,
American; juveniles CON WA
HODGE, Marshall Bryant, 1925- ,
American; nonfiction CON
HODGE, Paul William, 1934- ,
American; nonfiction CON
HODGES, Barbara K. Webber
('Elizabeth Cambridge'),
1893- , English; fiction
KT
HODGES, Carl G., 1902-64, Amer-
ican; juveniles, fiction CON
WA
HODGES, Cyril ('Cyril Hughes'),
1915- , Welsh; poetry MUR
HODGES, Cyril Walter, 1909- ,
English; juveniles COM CON
DOY WA
HODGES, Doris Marjorie ('Char-
lotte Hunt'), 1915- , English;
fiction CON
HODGES, Elizabeth Jamison,
American; juveniles COM
CON WA
HODGES, Graham Rushing,
1915- , American; juveniles
CON
HODGES, Harold Mellor, 1922- ,
American; nonfiction CON
HODGES, Henry G., 1888- ,
American; nonfiction CON
HODGES, Henry Woolmington
MacKenzie, 1920- , English;
nonfiction CON
HODGES, John Cunyus, 1892- ,
American; nonfiction CON
HODGES, Margaret Moore,
1911- , American; juveniles
COM CON
'HODGES, Turner' see MORE-
HEAD, Albert H.
HODGETTS, John Edwin, 1917- ,
Canadian; nonfiction CON
HODGINS, Bruce Willard, 1931- ,
Canadian; nonfiction CON
HODGKIN, Thomas, 1831-1913,
English; nonfiction KBA
HODGSON, David Hargraves,
1939- , Australian; nonfiction
CON
HODGSON, Godfrey Michael
Talbot, 1934- , English;

nonfiction CON
HODGSON, Leonard, 1889- , English; nonfiction CON
HODGSON, Marshall G.S., 1922- , American; nonfiction CON
'HODGSON, Norma' see RUSSELL Norman H.L.
HODGSON, Peter Crafts, 1934- , American; nonfiction CON
HODGSON, Peter E., 1928- , English; nonfiction CON
HODGSON, Phyllis, 1909- , English; nonfiction CON
HODGSON, Ralph, 1871-1962, English; poetry BRO KAT KT SP
HODGSON, Richard Sargeant, 1924- , American; nonfiction CON
HODGSON, Robert David, 1923- , American; nonfiction CON
HODGSON, Shadworth, 1832-1912, English; nonfiction KBA
HODIN, Félix, 1698-1755, French; nonfiction DIL
HODNETT, Edward, 1901- , American; nonfiction CON
HODSON, Henry Vincent, 1906- , American; nonfiction CON
HODZA, Michal Miloslav, 1811-70, Slovak; poetry ST
HOEBEL, Edward Adamson, 1906- , American; nonfiction CON
HOECK, Theobald, 1573-1618, German; poetry ST
HOEFLICH, Eugen see BEN GAVRIEL, Moscheh Y.
HÖGBERG, Olof, 1855-1932, Swedish; fiction COL FLE
HOEHLING, Adolph A., 1915- , American; nonfiction CON
HOEHLING, Mary Duprey, 1914- , American; juveniles WA
HOEHNER, Harold W., 1935- , American; nonfiction CON
HÖIJER, Benjamin, 1767-1812, Swedish; nonfiction ST
HOEKEMA, Anthony Andrew, 1913- , American; nonfiction CON
HOEL, Sigurd, 1890-1960, Norwegian; fiction COL FLE HAR SA ST
HÖLDERLIN, Johann Christian Friedrich, 1770-1843, German; poetry AL HAR KE ST
HÖLLERER, Walter, 1922- , German; nonfiction AL KU
HÖLTY, Ludwig Heinrich Christoph, 1748-76, German; poetry AL HAR KE ST
HOEN, Pieter ('A. Contraduc'; 'A.

Produc'; 'Martinus Scribe'; 'Ierus de Jonge'; 'A. Schasz'), 1744-1818, Dutch; poetry ST
HOENIG, Julius, 1916- , Czech-Canadian; nonfiction CON
HOENIGSWALD, Henry M., 1915- , German-American; nonfiction CON
HOERNLE, Edwin ('Georgi'), 1883-1952, German; poetry AL
HOETINK, Harmannus, 1931- , American; nonfiction CON
HOEVEN, Willem van der, 18th cent., Dutch; plays, poetry ST
HOFDIJK, Willem Jakobszoon, 1816-88, Dutch; poetry ST
HOFF, Carol, 1900- , American; juveniles, nonfiction CON
'HOFF, Gertrud' see MATTHAEI, Clara
HOFF, Harry Summerfield ('William Cooper'), 1910- , English; fiction CON RIC
HOFF, Marilyn, 1942- , American; fiction CON
HOFF, Sydney, 1912- , American; juveniles CON WA
HOFFBAUER, Johan Christoph, 1766-1827, German; nonfiction SA
HOFFECKER, John Savin, 1908- , American; nonfiction CON
HOFFELD, Donald Raymond, 1933- , American; nonfiction CON
HOFFENSTEIN, Samuel, 1890- , American; poetry KL KT
HOFFER, Charles Russell, 1929- , American; nonfiction CON
HOFFER, Eric, 1902- , American; nonfiction CON
HOFFERBERT, Richard Ira, 1937- , American; nonfiction CON
HOFFHAM, Otto Christiaan Frederik, 1744-99, Dutch; poetry, plays ST
HOFFINE, Lyla, American; juveniles CON
HOFFMAN, Abbie J. ('Free'; 'Spiro Igloo'; 'George Metesky'), 1936- , American; nonfiction CON
HOFFMAN, Adeline Mildred, 1908- , American; nonfiction CON

HOFFMAN, Arthur S., 1926- ,
American; nonfiction CON
HOFFMAN, Arthur Wolf, 1921- ,
American; nonfiction CON
HOFFMAN, Betty Hannah, 1918- ,
American; nonfiction CON
HOFFMAN, Charles Fenno, 1806-84,
American; poetry, fiction BRO
KAA ST
HOFFMAN, Daniel Gerard, 1923- ,
American; poetry, nonfiction
CON MUR
HOFFMAN, Frederick John, 1909- ,
American; nonfiction CON
HOFFMAN, Gail, 1896- , American;
nonfiction CON
HOFFMAN, George W., 1914- ,
Austrian-American; nonfiction
CON
HOFFMAN, Gloria, American;
juveniles WA
HOFFMAN, Helmut, 1912- , Ger-
man; nonfiction CON
HOFFMAN, Hester Rosalyn, 1895- ,
American; nonfiction CON
HOFFMAN, L. Richard, 1930- ,
American; nonfiction CON
HOFFMAN, Lee, 1932- , American;
fiction CON
HOFFMAN, Lisa ('Candida'), 1919- ,
German-American; nonfiction
CON
HOFFMAN, Lois Wladis, 1929- ,
American; nonfiction CON
HOFFMAN, Michael Jerome, 1939- ,
American; fiction CON
HOFFMAN, Phyllis Miriam, 1944- ,
American; juveniles
CON
HOFFMAN, Richard Lester, 1937- ,
American; nonfiction
CON
HOFFMAN, Robert L., 1937- ,
American; nonfiction
CON
HOFFMAN, Ross John Swartz,
1902- , American; nonfiction
HOE
HOFFMAN, Viktor Viktorovich
(Gofman), 1884-1911, Russian;
poetry HARK ST
HOFFMAN, William, 1925- ,
American; plays, fiction CON
HOFFMANN, Ann Marie, 1930- ,
English; nonfiction CON
HOFFMANN, Banesh, 1906- , Eng-
lish; nonfiction CON
HOFFMANN, Charles G., 1921- ,

American; nonfiction
CON
HOFFMANN, Donald, 1933- ,
American; nonfiction
CON
HOFFMANN, Eleanor, 1895- ,
American; juveniles
CON
HOFFMANN, Elizabeth see
'LANGGÄSSER, Elizabeth'
HOFFMANN, Erik Peter, 1939- ,
American; nonfiction CON
HOFFMANN, Ernst Theodor
Amadeus, 1776-1822, German;
juveniles, fiction AL DOY
HAR KE MAG SA ST
HOFFMANN, Felix, 1911- ,
Swiss; juveniles CON
HOFFMANN, François Benite,
1760-1828, French; plays,
criticism SA
HOFFMANN, Heinrich, 1809-94,
German; juveniles DOY HAR
HOFFMANN, Hilde, 1927- ,
German-American; juveniles
CON
HOFFMANN, Kai Anton Carl
Nyholm, 1874-1949, Danish;
poetry ST
HOFFMANN, Margaret Jones,
1910- , American; nonfiction,
fiction CON WA
HOFMANN, Melita Cecelia,
American; nonfiction CON
HOFFMANN, Ruth, 1893- ,
German; nonfiction KU LEN
HOFFMANN, Stanley, 1928- ,
Austrian-American; nonfiction
CON
HOFFMANN, Walter see 'KOLBEN-
HOFF, Walter'
HOFFMANN VON FALLERSLEBEN,
August Heinrich, 1798-1874,
German; poetry AL HAR KE ST
HOFFMANOVIA, Klementyna
Tánska, 1798-1845, Polish;
fiction, nonfiction SA ST
HOFFNER, Pelagie D. see DOANE,
Pelagie H.
HOFINGER, Johannes, 1905- ,
Austrian; nonfiction CON
HOFLAND, Barbara Wreaks,
1770-1844, English; fiction,
juveniles KBA SA
HOFMAN, Anton see HOLLO,
Anselm
HOFMAN, Jan Baptist, 1758-1835,
Flemish; poetry, plays ST

HOFMANN, Hans, 1923- , Swiss-
American; nonfiction CON
HOFMANN VON HOFMANNSWALDAU,
Christian, 1617-79, German;
poetry AL KE HAR ST
HOFMANNSTHAL, Hugo van, 1874-
1929, Austrian; poetry, plays
AL COL FLE HAR KAT KT KU
KUN LEN MAT RIC SA ST
HOFMILLER, Josef, 1872- , German;
essays KU
HOFSINDE, Robert, 1902- , Danish-
American; juveniles WA
HOFSTADTER, Albert, 1910- ,
American; nonfiction CON
HOFSTADTER, Richard, 1916-70,
American; nonfiction CON
HOFSTEIN, David, 1889- , Jewish;
poetry ST
HOGAN, Bernice Harris, 1929- ,
American; nonfiction CON
HOGAN, Inez, 1895- , American;
fiction, juveniles COM CON
FUL WA
HOGAN, James, 1898- , Irish;
nonfiction HO
HOGAN, John, 1805-92, American;
nonfiction KAA
HOGAN, John Charles, 1919- ,
American; nonfiction CON
HOGAN, Robert Goode, 1930- ,
American; nonfiction CON
HOGAN, Robert Ray, 1908- , Amer-
ican; fiction CON
HOGAN, Ursula, 1899- , American;
nonfiction CON
HOGAN, Willard Newton, 1909- ,
American; nonfiction CON
HOGAN, William Francis, 1930- ,
American; nonfiction CON
'HOGARTH, Jr.' see KENT, Rockwell
'HOGARTH, Douglas' see PHILLIPS-
BIRT, Douglas
HOGAS, Calistrat, 1847-1917, Ru-
manian; nonfiction ST
HOGBEN, Lancelot Thomas, 1895- ,
English; nonfiction BRO KT
HOGBERA, Olof, 1835-1932,
Swedish; fiction SA
HOGBIN, Herbert Ian, 1904- , Eng-
lish; nonfiction CON
HOGEBOOM, Amy, 1891- , Ameri-
can; juveniles WA
HOGENDORN, Jan Stafford, 1937- ,
American; nonfiction CON
HOGG, Beth Tootill ('Elizabeth Grey'),
1917- , English; juveniles CON
WA

HOGG, Garry, 1902- , English; ju-
veniles COM CON DOY
HOGG, Ian Vernon, 1926- ,
English; nonfiction CON
HOGG, James ('The Ettrick
Shepherd'), 1770-1835, Scots;
poetry, fiction BRO KBA SA
ST
HOGG, Quintin McGarel, 1907- ,
English; nonfiction CON
HOGG, Robert Lawrence, 1942- ,
Canadian; poetry MUR
HOGG, Thomas Jefferson, 1792-
1862, English; nonfiction BRO
ST
HOGG, William Richey, 1921- ,
American; nonfiction CON
HOGGART, Richard, 1918- ,
English; nonfiction CON
HOGHENDORP, Gijsbrecht van,
1589-1639, Dutch; plays ST
HOGNER, Dorothy Childs, Ameri-
can; juveniles CON KJU WA
HOGNER, Nils, 1893-1970, Ameri-
can; juveniles KJU WA
HOGREFE, Pearl, American;
nonfiction CON
HOGROGIAN, Nonny, American;
juveniles WA
HOGUE, Arthur Reed, 1906- ,
American; nonfiction CON
HOHBERG, Wolfgang Helmhard
van, 1612-88, Austrian;
poetry ST
HOHENBERG, John, 1906- ,
American; nonfiction CON
HOHENBERG, Paul Marcel,
1933- , French; nonfiction
CON
HOHENHAUSEN, Isabel Filipina
Amalia, 1789- , German;
nonfiction SA
HOHENHEIM, Philippus A.T.B.
von see 'PARACELSUS'
'HOHENTHAL, Karl' see MAY,
Karl F.
'HOHLBAUM, Robert' see
KOLBENHEYER, Erwin G.
HOHN, Hazel Stamper, American;
nonfiction CON
HOHNEN, David, 1925- , Danish;
nonfiction CON
HOHOFF, Curt, 1913- , German;
nonfiction KU
HOIG, Stanley Warlick, 1924- ,
American; nonfiction CON
HOJEDA, Diego de (Ojeda), 1571-
1615, Spanish; poetry BL

HAR SA ST

HOKE, Helen L. ('Helen Sterling'),
1903- , American; juveniles
WA

HOLADAY, Allan Gibson, 1916- ,
American; nonfiction CON

HOLBACH, Paul Henri Thiry, 1723-89,
French; nonfiction DIF DIL HAR
KE SA ST

HOLBECHE, Philippa Jack ('Philippa
Shore'), 1919- , English; fiction
CON

HOLBERG, Ludvig, 1684-1754, Nor-
wegian-Danish; plays, essays,
poetry HAR KE SA ST

HOLBERT, Richard A., 1889-1942,
American; juveniles KJU WA

HOLBERG, Ruth Langland, 1889/91- ,
American; juveniles, fiction,
poetry COM CON KJU WA

HOLBIK, Karel, 1920- , Czech-
American; nonfiction CON

HOLBO, Paul Sothe, 1929- , American; nonfiction CON

HOLBORN, Hajo, 1902-69, German-
American; nonfiction CON

HOLBORN, Louise W., 1898- ,
German; nonfiction CON

HOLBROOK, David Kenneth, 1923- ,
British; poetry, fiction, criticism
CON MUR

HOLBROOK, John, 1788-1854, American; nonfiction KAA

'HOLBROOK, Peter' see GLICK, Carl
C.

'HOLBROOK, Sabra' see ERICKSON,
Sabra P.

HOLBROOK, Stewart Hall, 1893-1964,
American; juveniles COM CON
KTS PAC WA

HOLCK, Manfred, Jr., 1930- ,
American; nonfiction CON

HOLCOMB, Jerry Leona, 1927- ,
American; nonfiction CON

HOLCOMBE, Arthur Norman, 1884- ,
English; nonfiction CON

HOLCROFT, Montague Henry, 1902- ,
New Zealander; fiction RIC ST

HOLCROFT, Thomas, 1745-1809,
English; plays, fiction BRO KB
ST

HOLDEN, Beatrice Paget, 1873- ,
English; nonfiction HIG

HOLDEN, Molly Gilbert, 1927- ,
British; poetry, fiction CON MUR

HOLDEN, Raymond Peckham ('Richard
Peckham'), 1894-1972, American;
poetry, juveniles CON KT WA

HOLDEN, Willis Sprague, 1909- ,
American; nonfiction CON

HOLDER, William G., 1937- ,
American; juveniles CON

HOLDERLIN, Johan Christian
Friedrich, 1770-1843, German;
poetry SA

HOLDHEIM, William Wolfgang,
1926- , German-American;
nonfiction CON

HOLDING, Charles H., 1897- ,
American; fiction CON

HOLDING, James Clark Carlisle,
Jr. ('Clark Carlisle'; 'Ellery
Queen, Jr.'), 1907- , Amer-
ican; juveniles CON WA

HOLDREN, Bob R., 1922- ,
American; nonfiction CON

HOLDREN, John Paul, 1944- ,
American; nonfiction CON

HOLDSWORTH, Irene, English;
fiction CON

HOLDSWORTH, Mary Zvegintzov,
1908- , Russian-English;
nonfiction CON

HOLECEK, Josef, 1853-1929,
Czech; fiction COL FLE SA
ST

HOLGERSEN, Alma, 1903- ,
German; nonfiction LEN

HOLGUIN, Carlos, 1832-94,
Colombian; nonfiction MIN

HOLGUIN y CARO, Hernando,
1870-1921, Colombian; nonfiction, poetry MIN

HOLIDAY, Frederick William,
1921- , English; nonfiction
CON

HOLINSHED, Raphael (Hollingshead), -1530?, English;
diary BRO KB ST

HOLISHER, Desider, 1901-72,
Hungarian-American; nonfiction
CON

HOLL, Adelaide Hinkle, 1910- ,
American; juveniles CON

HOLLAND, Lord (Henry Richard
Vasall Fox), 1773-1840, English; nonfiction KBA SA

HOLLAND, Abraham, -1625/26,
English; poetry, translations
ST

HOLLAND, Alma Boice, American; nonfiction CON

HOLLAND, Cecilia Anastasia,
1943- , American; fiction
CON

HOLLAND, Claudia Emmerson,

1903- , American; fiction WAF
HOLLAND, Edwin Clifford ('Orlando'),
1794-1824, American; poetry KAA
HOLLAND, Francis Ross, Jr., 1927- ,
American; nonfiction CON
HOLLAND, Glen A., 1920- , Ameri-
can; nonfiction CON
HOLLAND, Isabelle, 1920- , Ameri-
can; juveniles CON
HOLLAND, James Gordon, 1927- ,
American; nonfiction CON
HOLLAND, James R. ('J. H. Rand'),
1944- , American; nonfiction
CON
'HOLLAND, Jan' see VITRINGA,
Annes J.
HOLLAND, John Lewis, 1919- ,
American; nonfiction CON
HOLLAND, Josiah Gilbert ('Timothy
Titcomb'), 1819-81, American;
editor, poetry, fiction BRO KAA
HOLLAND, Joyce Flint, 1921- ,
American; juveniles CON
'HOLLAND, Katrin' see 'ALBRAND,
Martha'
'HOLLAND, Kel' see WHITTINGTON,
Harry
HOLLAND, Kenneth John, 1918- ,
American; nonfiction CON
HOLLAND, Laurence Bedwell,
1920- , American; nonfiction
CON
HOLLAND, Marion, 1908- , Ameri-
can; juveniles WA
HOLLAND, Norman Norwood, 1927- ,
American; nonfiction CON
HOLLAND, Philemon, 1552-1637, Eng-
lish; translations BRO KB ST
HOLLAND, Sir Richard, fl. 1450,
English; poetry BRO KB ST
HOLLAND, Robert, 1940- , Ameri-
can; nonfiction CON
HOLLAND, Robert Emmet, 1892-1946,
American; nonfiction HOE
HOLLAND, Rupert Sargent, 1878- ,
American; juveniles KJU
HOLLANDER, Arie Nicolaas Jan den,
1906- , Dutch; nonfiction CON
HOLLANDER, John, 1929- , Ameri-
can; poetry, criticism CON MUR
WA
HOLLANDER, Lee M., 1880- ,
American; translations, nonfiction
CON
HOLLANDER, Paul, 1932- , Ameri-
can; nonfiction CON WA
HOLLANDER, Robert, 1933- , Ameri-
can; nonfiction CON

HOLLANDER, Sophie Smith,
1911- , American; nonfiction
CON
HOLLANDER, Stanley Charles,
1919- , American; nonfiction
CON
HOLLANDER, Wather von,
1892- , German; essays
LEN
HOLLES, Robert Owen, 1926- ,
English; fiction CON
HOLLEY, Edward Gailon, 1927- ,
American; nonfiction CON
HOLLEY, Bobbie Lee, 1927- ,
American; nonfiction CON
HOLLEY, Irving Brinton, Jr.,
1919- , American; nonfiction
CON
HOLLEY, Marietta ('Josiah Allen's
Wife'), 1836-1926, American;
essays KAA
HOLLEY, Mary Austin, 1784-
1846, American; nonfiction
KAA
HOLLI, Melvin George, 1933- ,
American; nonfiction CON
'HOLLIDAY, James' see GRAY,
Simon
HOLLIDAY, Joseph ('Jack Bosco';
'Jack Dale'), 1910- ,
Canadian; juveniles CON
HOLLIDAY, Robert Cortes,
1880- , American; essays
KT
HOLLIER, Claude, 1761-94,
French; nonfiction, poetry
DIL
HOLLING, Holling Clancy, 1900- ,
American; juveniles KJU WA
HOLLINGSHEAD, August de Bel-
mont, 1907- , American;
nonfiction CON
HOLLINGSHEAD, Raphael see
HOLINSHED, Raphael
HOLLINGSHEAD, Ronald Kyle,
1941- , American; fiction
CON
HOLLINGSWORTH, Jesse, 1893- ,
American; nonfiction, poetry
JO
HOLLINGSWORTH, Joseph Rogers,
1932- , American; nonfiction
CON
HOLLINGSWORTH, Paul M.,
1932- , American; nonfiction
CON
HOLLIS, Christopher, 1902- ,
English; nonfiction HOE

HOLLIS, Daniel Walker, 1922- ,
American; nonfiction CON
'HOLLIS, Jim' see SUMMERS,
Hollis S. Jr.,
HOLLIS, Joseph William, 1922- ,
American; nonfiction CON
HOLLIS, Lucile Ussery, 1921- ,
American; nonfiction CON
HOLLIS, Maurice Christopher,
1902- , English; nonfiction BRO
HOLLISTER, C. Warren, 1930- ,
American; nonfiction CON
HOLLISTER, Charles Ammon, 1918- ,
American; nonfiction CON
HOLLISTER, George Erwin, 1905- ,
American; nonfiction CON
HOLLISTER, Gideon Hiram, 1817-81,
American; nonfiction KAA
HOLLISTER, Leo E., 1920- , Amer-
ican; nonfiction CON
HOLLMANN, Clide John, 1896-1966,
American; nonfiction CON
HOLLO, Anselm ('Sergei Bielyi';
'Anton Hofman'), 1934- , Fin-
nish-English; fiction, poetry,
nonfiction CON MUR
HOLLOM, Philip Arthur Dominic,
1912- , English; nonfiction CON
HOLLON, W. Eugene, 1913- , Ameri-
can; nonfiction CON
HOLLONIUS, Ludwig ('Holle'), fl.
1605, German; plays ST
HOLLOWAY, Brenda Wilmar ('Sarah
Verney'), 1908- , English; non-
fiction CON
HOLLOWAY, Emory, 1885- , Ameri-
can; nonfiction KT
HOLLOWAY, George Edward Talbot,
1921- , English; nonfiction CON
HOLLOWAY, Harry, 1925- , Ameri-
can; nonfiction CON
HOLLOWAY, John, 1920- , British;
poetry, criticism CON MUR
HOLLOWAY, Mark, 1917- , English;
nonfiction CON
HOLLOWAY, Maurice, 1920- ,
American; nonfiction CON
HOLLOWAY, Robert J., 1921- ,
American; nonfiction CON
HOLLOWAY, Teresa Bragunier
('Elizabeth Beatty'; 'Margaret
Vail McLeod'), 1906- , Ameri-
can; fiction CON
HOLLOWAY, William Vernon, 1903- ,
American; nonfiction CON
HOLLOWOOD, Albert Bernard, 1910- ,
English; nonfiction CON
HOLLY, Jan, 1785-1849, Slovak;

poetry ST
HOLLY, Joan Carol ('J. Hunter
Holly'), 1932- , American;
nonfiction CON
HOLLY, John Fred, 1915- ,
American; nonfiction CON
HOLM, Donald Raymond ('Peter
Denali'), 1918- , American;
nonfiction, fiction CON
HOLM, Else Anne Lise, 1922- ,
Danish; juveniles COM CON
HOOM, Hannebo, Norwegian;
juveniles WA
HOLM, John Cecil, 1904- ,
American; plays MAT
HOLM, Marilyn D. Franzen,
1944- , American; nonfiction
CON
HOLM, Oscar William, American;
nonfiction PAC
'HOLM, Saxe' see JACKSON,
Helen M. F. H.
HOLM, Sven Aage ('Farmacevten'),
1902- , Danish; fiction CON
HOLM, Torfhildur Thorsteinsdottir,
1845-1918, Icelandic; fiction
KE ST
HOLMAN, Alan Edward, 1934- ,
English; nonfiction CON
HOLMAN, Clarence Hugh, 1914- ,
American; nonfiction, fiction
CON
HOLMAN, Dennis Idris, 1915- ,
American; nonfiction CON
HOLMAN, Felice, 1919- , Amer-
ican; juveniles, poetry CON
WA
HOLMAN, Harriet R., 1912- ,
American; nonfiction CON
HOLMAN, Hugh, 1914- , Ameri-
can; fiction JO
HOLMEBERG, Eduardo Ladislao,
1852-1939, Argentinian; fic-
tion MIN
HOLME, Bryan, 1913- , Ameri-
can; juveniles WA
HOLME, Constance, 1881-1955,
English; fiction BRO
HOLMELUND, Paul, 1890- ,
Norwegian-American; nonfic-
tion CON
HOLMER, Paul Leroy, 1916- ,
American; nonfiction CON
HOLMES, Abiel ('Myron'), 1763-
1837, American; nonfiction
KAA
HOLMES, Arthur F., 1924- ,
English; nonfiction CON

HOLMES, Charles Mason, 1923- ,
American; nonfiction CON
HOLMES, Colin, 1938- , American;
nonfiction CON
HOLMES, Constance, English; fiction
KT
HOLMES, Daniel Henry, 1851-1908,
American; poetry KAA
HOLMES, David Charles ('David
Charlson'), 1919- , American;
juveniles CON
HOLMES, David Morton, 1929- ,
Canadian; nonfiction CON
HOLMES, Edward Morris, 1910- ,
American; nonfiction CON
HOLMES, Geoffrey Shorter, 1928- ,
English; nonfiction CON
'HOLMES, H. H.' see BOUCHER,
Anthony
'HOLMES, Jay' see HOLMES, Joseph
E.
HOLMES, John Clellon, 1926- ,
American; fiction CON
HOLMES, John Haynes, 1879- ,
American; nonfiction KTS
HOLMES, John Michael Aleister,
1931- , English; fiction, poetry
CON
HOLMES, Joseph Everett ('Jay
Holmes'), 1922- , American;
nonfiction CON
HOLMES, Kenneth Lloyd, 1915- ,
American; nonfiction CON PAC
HOLMES, Lowell Don, 1925- ,
American; nonfiction CON
HOLMES, Marjorie Rose, 1910- ,
American; juveniles, fiction
CON WA WAF
HOLMES, Mary Jane Hawes, 1825-
1907, American; fiction KAA
HOLMES, Oliver Wendell, 1809-94,
American; poetry, fiction, es-
says BRO KAA MAG SA ST
HOLMES, Parker Manfred, 1895- ,
American; nonfiction CON
HOLMES, Paul Allen, 1901- , Amer-
ican; nonfiction CON
HOLMES, Paul Carter, 1931- ,
American; nonfiction CON
'HOLMES, Rick' see HARDWICK,
Richard H., Jr.
HOLMES, Theodore, 1928- , Amer-
ican; poetry MUR
HOLMES, Urban Tigner, 1900- ,
American; nonfiction CON
HOLMES, Wilfred Jay ('Alec Hudson'),
1900- , American; nonfiction
CON

HOLMES, William Kersley (F.O.O.
Serrifile), 1882- , English;
nonfiction CON
HOLMQUIST, Anders ('Ostrowsky'),
1933- , Swedish; nonfiction
CON
'HOLMSEN, Bjarne P.' see
HOLZ, Arno
HOLSTEIN, Ludvig Detlef, 1864-
1943, Danish; poetry ST
HOLMSTRAND, Marie Juline
Gunderson, 1908- , Ameri-
can; juveniles CON
HOLMSTRÖM, Israel, 1660-1708,
Swedish; poetry ST
HOLMSTROM, John Edwin,
1898- , English; nonfiction
CON
HOLMSTROM, Lynda Lytle,
1939- , American; nonfiction
CON
HOLMVIK, Oyvind ('Oy-vik';
'Paprika'; 'Sepia'), 1914- ,
Norwegian; nonfiction CON
HOLSAERT, Eunice, American;
juveniles WA
HOLSAPPLE, Lloyd B., 1884- ,
American; nonfiction HOE
HOLSINGER, Jane Lumley, Amer-
ican; juveniles CON WA
HOLST, Johan Joergen, 1937- ,
Norwegian-American; nonfiction
CON
HOLSTEIN, Ludvig Greve, 1864-
1943, Danish; poetry COL
SA
HOLSTI, Kalevi Jacque, 1935- ,
American; nonfiction CON
HOLSTI, Ole Rudolf, 1933- ,
Swiss-American; nonfiction
CON
HOLT, Edgar Crawshaw, 1900- ,
American; fiction, nonfiction
CON
'HOLT, Gavin' see RODDA,
Charles
HOLT, John Agee, 1920- , Amer-
ican; nonfiction CON
HOLT, John Robert ('John Arre';
'Raymond Giles'), 1926- ,
American; fiction CON
HOLT, Laurence James, 1939- ,
New Zealander; nonfiction
CON
HOLT, Lee Elbert, 1912- ,
American; nonfiction CON
HOLT, Margaret see PARISH,
Margaret H.

HOLT, Robert T., 1928- , American;
nonfiction CON

'HOLT, Stephen' see THOMPSON,
Harlan H.

'HOLT, Tex' see JOSCELYN, Archie
L.

HOLT, Thelma Tewett, 1913- ,
American; juveniles CON

'HOLT, Victoria' see HIBBERT,
Eleanor

HOLT, William, 1897- , English;
fiction CON

HOLTAN, Orley I., 1933- , American; nonfiction CON

HOLTBY, Winifred, 1898-1935, English; fiction BRO KT RIC ST

HOLTEI, Karl von, 1798-1880, German; plays, poetry, fiction AL
HAR ST

HOLTER, Don W., 1905- , American;
nonfiction CON

HOLTHUSEN, Hans Egon, 1913- ,
German; poetry, criticism AL
HAR KU LEN RIC ST

HOLTON, Gerald James, 1922- ,
German-American; nonfiction CON

'HOLTON, Leonard' see WIBBERLEY,
Leonard

HOLTZ, Avraham, 1934- , American;
nonfiction CON

HOLTZ-BAUMERT, Gerhard, 1927- ,
German; nonfiction AL

HOLTZMAN, Abraham, 1921- ,
American; nonfiction CON

HOLTZMAN, Paul Douglas, 1918- ,
American; nonfiction CON

HOLTZMAN, Wayne Harold, 1923- ,
American; nonfiction CON

HOLUB, Miroslav, 1923- , Czech;
poetry, fiction CON

HOLYDAY, Barten (Holiday), 1593-
1661, English; plays, translations
ST

HOLYER, Erna Maria, 1925- , German-American; juveniles CON

HOLYOAKE, George Jacob, 1817-1906,
English; nonfiction KBA

HOLZ, Arno ('Bjarne P. Holmsen'),
1863-1929, German; nonfiction,
poetry, play COL FLE HAR KU
KUN MAT SA ST

'HOLZ, Detlev' see BENJAMIN,
Walter

HOLZAPFEL, Rudi ('Rooan Hurkey';
'R. Patrick Ward'), 1938- ,
American; poetry, nonfiction CON
MUR

HOLZER, Hans, 1920- , Austrian;
nonfiction CON

HOLZMAN, Philip Seidman,
1922- , American; nonfiction
CON

HOLZMAN, Robert Stuart, 1907- ,
American; nonfiction CON

HOLZNER, Rev. Joseph, 1875-
1947, German; nonfiction HO

HOMAN, Helen Walker, American;
nonfiction HOE

HOMAN, Robert Anthony, 1929- ,
English; fiction CON

HOMANS, Peter, 1930- , American; nonfiction CON

HOMBERGER, Conrad P., 1900- ,
German-American; nonfiction
CON

'HOMBURGER, Erik' see ERIKSON,
Erik H.

HOME, Alexander see HUME,
Alexander

'HOME, Cecil' see WEBSTER,
Julia

HOME, Henry (Lord Kames),
1696-1782, Scots; criticism
BRO KB SA ST

HOME, John, 1722-1808, Scots;
plays BRO KB SA ST

HOME, William Douglas, 1912- ,
Scots; plays MAT

HOMEM CRISTO, Francisco Manuel,
1892-1928, Portuguese; nonfiction SA

HOMEM de MELO, Pedro, 1904- ,
Portuguese; poetry SA

HOMER, 9th cent. B.C., Greek;
poetry MAG SA ST

HOMER, William Innes, 1929- ,
American; nonfiction CON

HOMMIUS, Festus, 1567-1642,
Dutch; translations ST

'HOMORAS' see NUTTALL, Jeff

HOMSHER, Lola Mae, 1913- ,
American; nonfiction CON

'HOMUNCULUS' see RADECKI,
Sigismond van

HOMZE, Alma C., 1932- ,
American; juveniles CON

HOMZE, Edward L., 1930- ,
American; nonfiction CON

HONDERICH, Ted, 1933- ,
Canadian; nonfiction CON

HONDIUS, Petrus, 1578-1621,
Dutch; poetry ST

HONE, Joseph, 1882- , Irish;
nonfiction ST

HONE, Ralph Emerson, 1913- ,
American; nonfiction CON

HONE, William, 1780-1842, English;
nonfiction BRO KBA ST
HONEY, Patrick James, 1922- ,
Irish; nonfiction CON
HONEY, William Houghton, 1910- ,
Australian; nonfiction CON
'HONEYWOOD, Richard' see FRASER,
Claud L.
HONG, Edna H., 1913- , American;
nonfiction, juveniles CON
HONG, Howard Vincent, 1912- ,
American; nonfiction CON
HONGNANT, P. Claude René, 1671-
1745, French; nonfiction DIL
HONIG, Donald, 1931- , American;
nonfiction, fiction CON
HONIG, Edwin, 1919- , American;
poetry, criticism MUR ST
HONIGH, Cornelis, 1845-96, Dutch;
poetry ST
HONIGMANN, Ernest Anselm Joachim,
1927- , American; nonfiction
CON
HONIGMANN, John Joseph, 1914- ,
American; nonfiction CON
HONNESS, Elizabeth Hoffman, 1904- ,
American; juveniles COM CON
WA
HONNOLD, John Otis, Jr., 1915- ,
American; nonfiction CON
HONORE, Antony Maurice, 1921- ,
English; nonfiction CON
HONORE de SAINTE-MARIE, Blaise,
1651-1729, French; nonfiction
DIL
HONORIUS, Augustodunensis, 1090-
1150, ?, nonfiction ST
HONTHEIM, Jean Nicolas de ('Justinus
Frebonius'), 1701-90, French;
nonfiction DIL
HOOD, David Crockett, 1937- , Amer-
ican; nonfiction CON
HOOD, Donald Wilbur, 1918- , Amer-
ican; nonfiction CON
HOOD, Dora Ridout, 1885- , Canadian;
fiction CON
HOOD, Flora Mae, 1898- , Ameri-
can; fiction CON
HOOD, Francis Campbell, 1895- ,
Scots; nonfiction CON
HOOD, Joseph F., 1925- , Ameri-
can; juveniles CON
HOOD, Margaret Page, 1892- ,
American; fiction CON
HOOD, Martin Sinclair Frankland,
1917- , Irish; nonfiction CON
HOOD, Robert E., 1926- , American;
nonfiction CON

HOOD, Thomas, 1799-1845,
English; poetry BRO HIG KBA
SA SP ST
HOOD, Tom, 1835-74, English;
nonfiction, poetry BRO KBA
HOOFMAN, Elisabeth Koolaart,
1664-1736, Dutch; poetry ST
HOOFNAGLE, Keith Lundy,
1941- , American; juveniles
CON
HOOFT, Peter Cornelisz, 1581-
1647, Dutch; poetry HAR KE
SA ST
HOOFT, William Dirckszy, 1594-
1658, Dutch; plays ST
HOOGASIAN-VILLA, Susie, 1921- ,
American; fiction CON
HOOGE, Romeyn de, 1645-1708,
Dutch; nonfiction ST
HOOGENBOOM, Olive, 1927- ,
American; nonfiction CON
HOOGESTRAAT, Wayne E., Amer-
ican; nonfiction CON
HOOGSTRATEN, David Franszoon
van, 1658-1724, Dutch; trans-
lations, poetry ST
HOOGSTRATEN, Frans van, 1632-
96, Dutch; poetry, translations
ST
HOOGSTRATEN, Jan van, 1662-
1756, Dutch; nonfiction ST
HOOGSTRATEN, Samuel Van,
1627-78, Dutch; poetry ST
HOOGVLIET, Arnold, 1687-1763,
Dutch; poetry ST
HOOK, Frank Scott, 1922- ,
American; nonfiction CON
HOOK, James, 1772-1828, English;
fiction KBA
HOOK, Julius Nicholas, 1913- ,
American; nonfiction CON
HOOK, Luce Joseph (Hooke),
1716-96, French; nonfiction
DIL
HOOK, Sidney, 1902- , Ameri-
can; nonfiction CON KTS
HOOK, Theodore Edward, 1788-
1841, English; fiction, plays,
journalism BRO KBA SA ST
HOOK, Walter Farquhar, 1798-
1875, English; nonfiction BRO
KBA ST
HOOKE, Nina Warner, 1907- ,
American; nonfiction CON
HOOKER, James Ralph, 1929- ,
American; nonfiction CON
HOOKER, Sir Joseph Dalton,
1817-1911, English; nonfiction
KBA

HOOKER, Richard, 1554-1600, English; nonfiction BRO KB ST

HOOKER, Thomas, 1586-1647, American; nonfiction KAA

HOOKER, Sir William Jackson, 1785-1865, English; nonfiction KBA

HOOKES, Nicholas, 1628-1712, English; poetry ST

HOOKHAM, Hilda Kenriette Kuttner, 1915- , English; nonfiction CON

HOOKS, Arah, 1906- , American; nonfiction JO

HOOKS, Gaylor Eugene (Gene), 1927- , American; nonfiction CON

HOOLE, Daryl Van Dam, 1934- , American; nonfiction CON

HOOLE, Willam Stanley, 1903- , American; nonfiction CON

HOOP, Adriaan van der, 1802-41, Dutch; poetry ST

'HOOPER, Byrd' see ST. CLAIR, Byrd H.

HOOPER, Douglas, 1927- , English; nonfiction CON

HOOPER, Ellen H. Sturgis, 1812?-48, American; poetry KAA

HOOPER, John William, 1926- , American; nonfiction CON

HOOPER, Johnson Jones, 1815-62, American; fiction JO KAA

HOOPER, Lucy Hamilton James, 1835-93, American; poetry, journalism KAA

HOOPER, Walter McGehee, 1931- , American; nonfiction CON

HOOPER, William Loyd, 1931- , American; nonfiction CON

HOOPES, Clement R., 1906- , American; fiction CON

HOOPES, Donelson Farquhar, 1932- , American; nonfiction CON

HOOPES, Ned Edward, 1932- , American; nonfiction CON

HOOPES, Robert Griffith, 1920- , American; nonfiction CON

HOOPES, Roy, 1922- , American; nonfiction CON

HOOS, Ida Russakoff, 1912- , American; nonfiction CON

'HOOSIER, Poet' see RILEY, James W.

HOOSON, David J.M., 1926- , English; nonfiction CON

HOOSON, Isaac Daniel, 1880-1948, Welsh; poetry ST

'HOOTON, Charles' see ROWE, Vivian C.

HOOTON, Earnest Albert, 1887- , American; nonfiction KT

HOOVER, Calvin Bryce, 1897- , American; nonfiction CON

HOOVER, Dwight W., 1926- , American; nonfiction CON

HOOVER, Edgar M., 1907- , American; nonfiction CON

HOOVER, Hardy, 1901- , American; nonfiction CON

HOOVER, Helen Drusella Blackburn ('Jennifer Price'), 1910- , American; juveniles CON

HOOVER, John Edgar, 1895-1972, American; nonfiction CON

HOPCRAFT, Arthur, 1932- , English; nonfiction CON

HOPE, Alec, Derwent, 1907- , Australian; poetry CON MUR RIC

'HOPE, Andrew' see HERN, George A.

'HOPE, Anthony' (Sir Anthony Hope Hawkins), 1863-1933, English; juveniles, fiction BRO DOY KAT KT MAG RIC SA ST

HOPE, Ashley, Gay, 1914- , American; nonfiction CON

HOPE, Charles Evelyn Graham, 1900- , English; fiction, juveniles CON

'HOPE, Felix' see WILLIAMSON, Claude C. H.

HOPE, Francis, 1938- , British; poetry MUR

HOPE, James Barron, 1829-89, American; journalism, poetry KAA

'HOPE, Laura Lee' see ADAMS, Harriet S. and STRATEMEYER, Edward L.

'HOPE, Laurence' (Adela Florence Cory Hassels), 1865-1904, English; poetry BRO KT

HOPE, Marjorie Cecelia, 1923- , American; nonfiction CON

HOPE, Quentin Manning, 1923- , American; nonfiction CON

HOPE, Ronald Sidney, 1921- , English; nonfiction CON

HOPE, Thomas, 1770-1831, English; fiction BRO KBA ST

HOPE, Welborn, 1903- , American; poetry CON MAR

HOPE SIMPSON, Jacynth, 1930- ,
English; juveniles, fiction CON

HOPEWELL, Sydney, 1924- , German-English; poetry CON

HOPF, Alice Lightner ('A. M. Lightner'), 1904- , American;
juveniles CON

HOPKE, William E., 1918- , American; nonfiction CON

'HOPKINS, A.T.' see TURNGREN,
Annette

HOPKINS, Bill, 1928- , Welsh; fiction CON

HOPKINS, Charles, 1664-1700, English; poetry, plays ST

HOPKINS, Clark ('Roy Lee'),
1895- , American; juveniles
WA

HOPKINS, George Emil, 1937- ,
American; nonfiction CON

HOPKINS, Gerard Manley, 1844-89,
English; poetry BRO KBA MAG
SP ST

HOPKINS, Harry, 1913- , Anglo-
American; nonfiction CON

HOPKINS, Jack Walker, 1930- ,
American; nonfiction CON

HOPKINS, James Franklin, 1909- ,
American; nonfiction CON

HOPKINS, Jasper Stephen, Jr.,
1936- , American; nonfiction
CON

HOPKINS, Jeremiah see NOTT, Henry
J.

HOPKINS, Jerry, 1935- , American;
nonfiction CON

HOPKINS, John, -1570, English;
poetry BRO ST

HOPKINS, John, 1674/75- , English;
poetry ST

HOPKINS, John Henry, 1792-1868,
American; nonfiction KAA

HOPKINS, Joseph Gerard Edward,
1909- , American; nonfiction,
juveniles CON

HOPKINS, Kenneth ('Christopher
Adams'; 'Anton Burney'; 'Warwick
Mannon'; 'Paul Marsh'; 'Edmund
Marshall'; 'Arnold Meredith'),
1914- , American; fiction, poetry,
juveniles CON

HOPKINS, Lee Bennett, 1938- ,
American; nonfiction CON

HOPKINS, Lemuel, 1750-1801,
American; fiction KAA

'HOPKINS, Lyman' see FOLSOM,
Franklin

HOPKINS, Marjorie, 1911- ,
American; juveniles CON

HOPKINS, Mark, 1802-87, American; nonfiction KAA

HOPKINS, Mark Wyatt, 1931- ,
American; nonfiction CON

HOPKINS, Matthew, -1647,
English; nonfiction KB

HOPKINS, Prynce C., 1885- ,
American; nonfiction CON

HOPKINS, Samuel, 1721-1803,
American; nonfiction KAA

HOPKINS, Terence Kilbourne,
1928- , American; nonfiction
CON

HOPKINS, Thomas Johns, 1930- ,
American; nonfiction CON

HOPKINS, Vivian C., 1907- ,
American; nonfiction CON

HOPKINSON, Clement Allan Slade,
1934- , Guyanese; poetry
MUR

HOPKINSON, Diana, 1912- , English; nonfiction CON

HOPKINSON, Francis, 1737-91,
American; poetry, essays,
fiction BRO KAA ST

HOPKINSON, Henry Thomas,
1905- , English; fiction CON

HOPKINSON, Joseph, 1770-1842,
American; songs BRO

HOPLEY-WOOLRICH, Cornell
George ('George Hopley'; 'William Irish'; 'Cornell Woolrich'),
1903/06- , American; fiction
CON KTS

HOPPE, Arthur Watterson, 1925- ,
American; fiction CON

HOPPE, Emil Otho, 1878- ,
German-English; nonfiction
CON

HOPPENSTEDT, Elbert M.,
1917- , American; fiction
CON

HOPPER, Columbus Burwell,
1931- , American; nonfiction
CON

HOPPER, David H., 1927- ,
American; nonfiction CON

HOPPER, John, 1934- , American; poetry CON

HOPPER, Nora, 1871-1906, Irish;
poetry ST

HOPPER, Vincent Foster, 1906- ,
American; nonfiction CON

HOPPOCK, Robert, 1901- ,
American; nonfiction CON

HOPREKSTAD, Olav Ragnvaldsson,

1875- , Norwegian; plays ST
HOPSON, Dan, Jr., 1930- , American; nonfiction CON
HOPWOOD, Avery, 1882-1928, American; journalism, plays MAT
HOPWOOD, Robert R., 1910- , English; nonfiction CON
HORA, Josef, 1891-1945, Czech; poetry COL FLE HAR SA ST
HORACE (Quintus Horatius Flaccus), 65-27 B.C., Roman; poetry MAG SA ST
HORAK, M. Stephen, 1920- , American; nonfiction CON
HORAN, James David, 1914- , American; nonfiction CON
HORAN, Kenneth O'Donnell, 1890- , American; fiction HOO WAF
HORAN, William D., 1933- , American; nonfiction CON
HORAPOLO (Horus Apollo), 5th cent., Greek; nonfiction SA
'HORATIO, Jane' see CUDLIPP, Edythe
HORBACH, Michael, 1924- , German; fiction CON
HORCHLER, Richard Thomas, 1925- , American; nonfiction CON
HORDER, John Pearson Peter, 1936- , British; poetry MUR
HORDERN, William Edward, 1920- , Canadian; nonfiction CON
HORE, J.P., 19th cent., English; nonfiction HIG
HORE, María Gertrudis, 1742-1801, Spanish; poetry SA
HORECKY, Paul Louis, 1913- , Czech-American; nonfiction CON
HORELICK, Arnold Lawrence, 1928- , American; nonfiction CON
HORGAN, John Joseph, 1881- , Irish; nonfiction HOE
HORGAN, Paul, 1903- , American; fiction CON HOE KT WA WAF
HORI, Ichiro, 1910- , Japanese; nonfiction CON
HORIA, Vintila, 1910- , Russian-French; fiction RIC
HORIE, Shigeo, 1903- , Japanese; nonfiction CON
HORKA-FOLLICK, Lorayne Ann, 1940- , American; nonfiction CON
HORLER, Sydney, 1888-1954, English; fiction BRO
HORLOCK, J.K.W. ('Scurtator'), fl. 1800, English; nonfiction HIG

HORMAN, Richard E., 1945- , American; nonfiction CON
HORMAN, William, 1450-1535, English; nonfiction KB ST
HORN, Alfred Aloysisu ('Trader Horn'; 'Alfred A. Smith'), 1861?-1931, English; nonfiction KT
HORN, Daniel, 1934- , Austrian; nonfiction CON
HORN, David Bayne, 1901- , Scots; nonfiction CON
HORN, Franz Christoph, 1781-1837, German; nonfiction SA
HORN, George Francis, 1917- , American; nonfiction CON
HORN, Henry Eyster, 1913- , American; nonfiction CON
HORN, Jeanne P., 1925- , American; nonfiction CON
HORN, John Leonard, 1928- , American; nonfiction CON
HORN, John Stephen, 1931- , American; nonfiction CON
HORN, Robert M., 1933- , American; nonfiction CON
HORN, Siegfried Herbert, 1908- , American; nonfiction CON
HORN, Stefan F., 1900- , Austrian-American; nonfiction CON
HORN, Thomas D., 1918- , American; nonfiction CON
HORN, Walter William, 1908- , German-American; nonfiction CON
HORNADAY, William Temple, 1854-1937, American; nonfiction KT
HORNBACK, Bert Gerald ('Gerald Frascatoro'), 1935- , American; nonfiction CON
HORNBEIN, Thomas F., American; nonfiction PAC
HORNBERGER, Theodore, 1906- , American; nonfiction CON
HORNBLOW, Leonora, Schinasi, American; juveniles WA
HORNBY, John ('Joseph Grace'; 'Gordon Summers'), 1913- , English; nonfiction, juveniles CON
HORNE, Alistair Allan, 1925- , English; nonfiction CON
HORNE, Cynthia Miriam ('Cynthia Pilkington'), 1939- , English; juveniles CON
HORNE, Geoffrey ('Gil North'),

1916-   , English; fiction CON
'HORNE, Howard' see PAYNE, Pierre
   S. R.
HORNE, Hugh Robert ('Jane Madison'),
   1915-   , American; nonfiction
   CON
HORNE, Richard, Henry, 1803-84,
   English; poetry, fiction, essays,
   juveniles, criticism BRO KBA
   ST
HORNE, Thomas Hartwell, 1780-1862,
   English; nonfiction BRO ST
HORNECK, Otocar de, 1250-1310,
   German; nonfiction SA
HORNER, Dave, 1934-   , American;
   nonfiction CON
HORNER, George Frederick, 1899-   ,
   American; nonfiction CON
HORNER, Thomas Marland, 1927-   ,
   American; nonfiction CON
HORNEY, Karen Danielsen, 1885-
   1952, German-American; nonfic-
   tion KTS
HORNIG, Heinrich, 1876-   , German;
   poetry ST
HORNOS, Axel, 1907-   , American;
   nonfiction CON
HORNOT, Antoine ('Dejean'), 18th
   cent., French; nonfiction DIL
HORNSBY, Alton, Jr., 1940-   ,
   American; nonfiction CON
HORNSBY, Roger A., 1926-   , Amer-
   ican; nonfiction CON
HORNUNG, Clarence Pearson, 1899-   ,
   American; nonfiction CON
HORNUNG, Ernest William, 1866-1921,
   English; fiction BRO KT RIC SA
HOROVITZ, Frances Margaret Hooker,
   1938-   , British; poetry MUR
HOROVITZ, Israel, 1939-   , Ameri-
   can; plays CON
HOROVITZ, Michael, 1935-   , British;
   poetry MUR
HOROVITZ, Yaakov, 1901-   , Jewish;
   nonfiction ST
HOROWITZ, David Joel, 1939-   ,
   American; nonfiction CON
HOROWITZ, Edward, 1904-   , Amer-
   ican; nonfiction CON
HOROWITZ, Leonard Martin, 1937-   ,
   American; nonfiction CON
HOROWITZ, Mardi John, 1934-   ,
   American; nonfiction CON
HOROWITZ, Robert S., 1924-   ,
   American; nonfiction CON
HOROZCO, Sebastián de, 1510-80,
   Spanish; nonfiction BL SA
HOROZCO y COVARRUBIAS see

COVARRUBIAS y OROZCO,
   Juan and Sebastian
HORRABIN, James Francis,
   1884-1962, English; juveniles
   DOY
HORRENT, Jules, Belgian; non-
   fiction BL
HORROCKS, Edna M., 1908-   ,
   American; nonfiction, juveniles
   CON
HORROCKS, John Edwin, 1913-   ,
   American; nonfiction CON
HORSBURGH, Howard John Neate,
   1918-   , Canadian; nonfiction
   CON
HORSEFIELD, John Keith,
   1901-   , English; nonfiction
   CON
'HORSELY, Ramsbottom' see
   BERNE, Eric L.
HORSEMAN, Elaine Hall, 1925-   ,
   English; juveniles CON
HORSMAN, Reginald, 1931-   ,
   Anglo-American; nonfiction
   CON
HORST, Karl Auguste, 1913-   ,
   German; nonfiction KU
HORST, Samuel Levi, 1919-   ,
   American; nonfiction CON
HORT, Fenton John Anthony,
   1828-92, Irish; nonfiction
   KBA
HORTENSIA de CASTRO, Púbila,
   1548-95, Portuguese; poetry
   SA
HORTENSIUS, Quintus H. Hortalus,
   114-50 B.C., Roman; nonfic-
   tion SA ST
HORTON, Frank E., 1939-   ,
   American; nonfiction CON
HORTON, George Moses, 1797-
   1883, American; poetry JO
HORTON, John William, 1905-   ,
   English; nonfiction CON
HORTON, Paul Burleigh, 1916-   ,
   American; nonfiction CON
HORUS APOLLO see HORAPOLO
HORVATH, Betty, 1927-   , Amer-
   ican; juveniles CON
HORVATH, Ödön von, 1901-38,
   Austrian; fiction, plays FLE
   KT KU KUN MAT SA
HORVATH, Violet M., 1924-   ,
   American; nonfiction CON
HORWICH, Frances Rappoport
   ('Miss Frances'), 1908-   ,
   American; juveniles CON
HORWITZ, Bela ('Bela Chasan'),

18th cent., Jewish; nonfiction
ST
HORWITZ, Julius, 1920- , American; nonfiction CON
HORWOOD, Harold, 1923- , American; fiction CON
HOSAIN, Waez, -1514, Persian; poetry SA
HOSEIN BEN Ali, 15th cent., Persian; nonfiction SA
HOSELITZ, Bert Frank, 1913- , Austrian-American; nonfiction CON
HOSFORD, Dorothy, 1900-52, American; juveniles FUL
HOSIE, Stanley William, 1922- , Australian; nonfiction CON
HOSKINS, John, 1566-1638, English; poetry ST
HOSKINS, Katherine de Montalant Lackey, 1909- , American; poetry CON MUR
HOSKINS, Robert ('Grace Corren'), 1933- , American; fiction, juveniles CON
HOSKINS, William George, 1908- , English; nonfiction CON
HOSKYN-ABRAHALL, Clare Constance Drury, English; juveniles CON
HOSLEY, Richard, 1921- , American; nonfiction CON
HOSMER, Charles Bridgham, Jr., 1932- , American; nonfiction CON
HOSMER, Hezekiah Lord, 1814-93, American; nonfiction KAA
HOSMER, James Kendall, 1834-1927, American; nonfiction KAA
HOSMER, William Howe Cuyler, 1814-77, American; poetry KAA
HOSOKAWA, William K., 1915- , American; nonfiction CON
HOSPERS, John, Jr., 1918- , American; nonfiction CON
HOSS, Marvin Allen, 1929- , American; nonfiction CON
HOSSENT, Harry ('Sean Gregory'; 'Kevin O'Malley'), 1916- , English; fiction CON
HOSTETTER, Benjamin Charles, 1916- , American; nonfiction CON
HOSTLER, Charles Warren, 1919- , American; nonfiction CON
HOSTOS, Eugenio María de, 1839-1903, Spanish; nonfiction BL SA ST
HOSTOVSKY, Egon, 1908- , Czech;

fiction FLE HAR RIC ST
HOSTROP, Richard Winfred, 1925- , American; nonfiction CON
HOSTRUP, Jens Christian, 1818-92, Danish; poetry ST
HOTCHKISS, Jeanette, 1901- , American; nonfiction CON
HOTCHKISS, Ralf D., 1947- , American; nonfiction CON
HOTSON, John Hargrove, 1930- , American; nonfiction CON
HOTSON, John Leslie, 1897- , Canadian; nonfiction KTS
HOTTINGER, Jean Henri, 1620-67, Swiss; nonfiction SA
HOTTINGER, Jean Jacques, 1750-1819, Swiss; nonfiction SA
HOTTINGER, Jean Jacques, 1783-1869, Swiss; nonfiction SA
HOU, Chi-ming, 1924- , Chinese-American; nonfiction CON
HOU, Fang-Mū, 1618-55, Chinese; essays ST
HOUARD, David, 1725-1802, French; nonfiction DIL
HOUBRAKEN, Arnold, 1660-1719, Dutch; nonfiction ST
HOUBIGANT, P. Charles François, 1686-1783, French; nonfiction DIL
HOUCK, John William, 1931- , American; nonfiction CON
HOUDAR de LA MOTTE, Antoine, 1672-1731, French; plays, poetry ST
HOUEDARD, Dom Pierre Sylvester, 1924- , British; poetry MUR
HOUEL, Jean Pierre Louis Laurent, 1735-1813, French; nonfiction DIL
HOUGH, Emerson, 1857-1923, American; fiction KAT KT
HOUGH, Graham Goulder, 1908- , British; poetry MUR
HOUGH, Helen Charlotte, 1924- , English; juveniles CON
HOUGH, Henry Beetle, 1896- , American; fiction, nonfiction CON KTS WAF
HOUGH, Henry Wade, 1906- , American; nonfiction CON
HOUGH, John T., Jr., 1946- , American; nonfiction CON
HOUGH, Joseph Carl, Jr., 1933- , American; nonfiction CON

HOUGH, Louis, 1914- , American;
nonfiction CON
HOUGH, Richard Alexander ('Bruce
Carter'), 1922- , American;
English; juveniles CON WA
HOUGH, Stanley Bennett ('Rex
Gordon'; 'Bennett Stanley'),
1917- , English; fiction CON
HOUGHTELING, James Lawrence,
Jr., 1920- , American; nonfic-
tion CON
HOUGHTON, Lord (Richard Monckton
Milnes), 1809-85, English; poetry,
nonfiction BRO KBA ST
HOUGHTON, Charles Norris, 1909- ,
American; nonfiction CON
'HOUGHTON, Claude' see OLDFIELD,
Claude H.
'HOUGHTON, Elizabeth' see GILZEAN,
Elizabeth H. B.
HOUGHTON, Eric, 1930- , English;
juveniles CON WA
HOUGHTON, George Willam, 1905- ,
Scots; nonfiction CON
HOUGHTON, Neal Doyle, 1895- ,
American; nonfiction CON
HOUGHTON, Walter Edwards, 1904- ,
American; nonfiction CON
HOUGHTON, William Stanley, 1881-
1913, English; plays BRO KT
MAT RIC
HOUGRON, Jean, 1923- , French;
fiction DIC
HOULE, Cyril Owen, 1913- , Amer-
ican; nonfiction CON
HOULT, Norah, 1901- , Irish; fic-
tion KT ST
HOUN, Franklin Wu, 1920- ,
Chinese-American; nonfiction
CON
'HOUSE, Anne W.' see McCAULEY,
Elfrieda B.
HOUSE, Charles Albert, 1916- ,
American; fiction, juveniles CON
HOUSE, Edward Howard, 1836-1901,
American; journalism KAA
HOUSE, Jay Elmer, 1872-1936, Amer-
ican; journalism KT
HOUSE, Robert Burton, 1892- ,
American; nonfiction CON
HOUSE, Roy Temple, 1878- , Amer-
ican; nonfiction MAR
HOUSEHOLD, Geoffrey, 1900/03- ,
English; juveniles, fiction DOY
KT
HOUSELANDER, Caryll, English;
fiction HOE
HOUSEPIAN, Marjorie, 1923- ,

American; fiction CON
HOUSMAN, Alfred Edward, 1859-
1936, English; poetry, criti-
cism BRO FLE KL KT MAG
RIC SA SP ST
HOUSMAN, Laurence, 1865-1959,
English; plays, fiction BRO
KT KAT MAT SA
HOUSSAYE, Arsène Houset, 1815-
96, French; fiction DIF HAR
SA
HOUSSAYE, Henri, 1848-1911,
French; nonfiction SA
HOUSSEAU, Etienne, -1763,
French; nonfiction DIL
HOUSTON, James D., 1933- ,
American; nonfiction CON
HOUSTON, James Mackintosh,
1922- , Scots; nonfiction
CON
HOUSTON, Joan, 1928- , Ameri-
can; juveniles CON WA
HOUSTON, John Porter, 1933- ,
American; nonfiction CON
HOUSTON, Noel, 1909- , Ameri-
can; play JO
HOUSTON, Robert, 1935- ,
American; nonfiction CON
HOUSTON, William Robert, Jr.,
1928- , American; nonfiction
CON
HOUT, Jan van, 1542-1609,
Dutch; poetry ST
HOUTART, François, 1925- ,
Belgian; nonfiction CON
HOUTHAKKER, Hendrik Samuel,
1924- , American; nonfiction
CON
HOUTS, Marshall Wilson, 1919- ,
American; nonfiction CON
HOUTTEVILLE, Alexandre Claude
François, 1686-1742, French;
nonfiction DIL
'HOUVILLE, Gérard d'' (Marie
Louise A. de Heredia),
1875- , French; poetry COL
SA
HOVDE, Christian Arneson, 1922- ,
American; nonfiction CON
HOVELL, Lucy A. Peterson,
1916- , American; poetry,
juveniles CON WA
HOVERSTEN, Chester E.,
1922- , American; nonfiction
CON
HOVEY, Richard, 1864-1900,
American; poetry HOO KAA
'HOWADJI' see CURTIS, George
W.

HOUWAERT, Jan Baptist, 1533-99, Dutch; plays ST

HOVANNISIAN, Richard G., 1932- , American; nonfiction CON

HOVDA, Robert Walker, 1920- , American; nonfiction CON

HOVDE, Howard, 1928- , American; nonfiction CON

HOVDEN, Anders, 1860-1943, Norwegian; poetry, fiction ST

HOVEDEN, John and Roger see HOWDEN, John of

HOVEY, Elwyn Paul, 1908- , American; plays, nonfiction CON

HOVEY, Richard Bennett, 1917- , American; nonfiction CON

HOWARD, Alan, 1934- , American; nonfiction CON

HOWARD, Alvin Wendell, 1922- , American; nonfiction CON

HOWARD, Arthur Ellsworth Dick, 1933- , American; nonfiction CON

HOWARD, Bion B., 1912- , American; nonfiction CON

HOWARD, Blanche Willis (Baroness von Teuffel), 1898- , American; fiction KAA

HOWARD, Bronson Crocker, 1842-1908, American; plays BRO KAA MAT

HOWARD, C. Jeriel, 1939- , American; nonfiction CON

HOWARD, Charles Frederick, 1904- , Canadian; nonfiction CON

HOWARD, Christopher, 1913- , English; nonfiction CON

HOWARD, Rev. Clarence J., 1907- , American; nonfiction SCA

'HOWARD, Coralie' see COGSWELL, Coralie N.

HOWARD, David Morris, 1928- , American; nonfiction CON

HOWARD, Derek Lionel, 1930- , English; nonfiction CON

HOWARD, Donald Roy, 1927- , American; nonfiction CON

HOWARD, Edward, 1624- , English; essays, poetry, plays ST

HOWARD, Edward, -1841, English; fiction, juveniles BRO DOY KBA ST

HOWARD, Edwin Johnston, 1901- , American; nonfiction CON

HOWARD, Elizabeth (Mizner), 1907- , American; juveniles CON FUL WA

HOWARD, Elizabeth Jane, 1923- ,

English; fiction CON RIC

HOWARD, Elizabeth Metzger, American; fiction WAF

HOWARD, Esme William, 1863-1939, English; nonfiction HOE

HOWARD, Florence Ruth, American; fiction WAF

HOWARD, Fred David, 1919- , American; nonfiction CON

'HOWARD, Frederich' see CARLISLE, Frederich H.

'HOWARD, H.L.' see WELLS, Charles J.

HOWARD, Harold P., 1905- , American; nonfiction CON

'HOWARD, Hartley' see OGNALL, Leopold H.

HOWARD, Helen Addison, 1904- , American; nonfiction CON PAC

HOWARD, Henry see SURREY, Henry H., Earl of

HOWARD, Ian P., 1927- , English; nonfiction CON

HOWARD, J. Woodford, Jr., 1931- , American; nonfiction CON

HOWARD, James Arch ('Laine Fisher'), 1922- , American; fiction CON

HOWARD, Jane Temple, 1935- , American; nonfiction CON

HOWARD, John Tasker, 1890- , American; nonfiction KTS

HOWARD, Joseph Kinsey, 1906-51, American; nonfiction KTS

HOWARD, Joseph Leon, 1917- , American; nonfiction CON

HOWARD, Joyce, 1922- , English; fiction, plays CON

HOWARD, Kenneth Samuel, 1882- , American; nonfiction CON

HOWARD, Lowell Bennett, 1925- , American; nonfiction CON

'HOWARD, Mark' see RIGSBY, Howard

HOWARD, Michael Eliot, 1922- , English; nonfiction CON

HOWARD, Munroe ('Philip St. Clair'), 1913- , American; nonfiction CON

HOWARD, Patricia Lowe, 1937- , English; nonfiction CON

HOWARD, Peter Dunsmore ('Cato'), 1908-65, English; plays, nonfiction CON

HOWARD, Richard, 1929- , American; poetry MUR

HOWARD, Sir Robert, 1626-98, English; plays BRO KB ST

HOWARD, Robert West ('Michael Case'), 1908- , American; nonfiction CON

HOWARD, Sidney Coe, 1891-1939, American; plays, fiction KL KT MAT ST

HOWARD, Thomas, 1930- , American; nonfiction CON

'HOWARD, Vechel' see RIGSBY, Howard

HOWARD, Vernon Linwood, 1918- , American; juveniles, plays WA

HOWARD, Warren Starkie, 1930- , American; nonfiction CON

HOWARTH, David, 1912- , English; fiction CON

HOWARTH, Donald, 1931- , English; plays CON

HOWARTH, William Louis, 1940- , American; nonfiction CON

HOWDEN, John of (Hoveden), -1275, English; poetry ST

HOWDEN, Roger of (Hoveden), -1201, English; nonfiction ST

HOWE, Carrol Bruce, 1910- , American; nonfiction PAC

HOWE, Charles L., 1932- , American; fiction CON

HOWE, Daniel Walker, 1937- , American; nonfiction CON

HOWE, Edgar Watson, 1853-1937, American; essays, fiction KAT KT MAG

HOWE, Ellic, 1910- , English; nonfiction CON

HOWE, George, 1898- , American; fiction WAF

HOWE, Helen Huntington, 1905- , American; fiction CON KTS

HOWE, Henry, 1816-93, American; nonfiction KAA

HOWE, Irving, 1920- , American; criticism CON KTS

HOWE, John, 1630-1705, English; nonfiction BRO ST

HOWE, Jonathan Trumbull, 1935- , American; nonfiction CON

HOWE, Joseph, 1804-73, Canadian; nonfiction KBA SY

HOWE, Julia Ward, 1819-1910, American; poetry BRO KAA

HOWE, Mark Antony de Wolfe, 1864- , American; nonfiction KT

HOWE, Muriel ('Barbara Redmayne'), English; fiction CON

HOWE, Nelson, 1935- , American; nonfiction, poetry CON

HOWE, Reuel Lanphier, 1905- , American; nonfiction CON

HOWE, Samuel Gridley, 1801-76, American; nonfiction KAA

HOWE, Warren Asquith, 1910- , American; nonfiction CON

HOWELL, Anthony, 1945- , British; poetry MUR

HOWELL, Clinton T., 1913- , American; nonfiction CON

HOWELL, James, 1594?-1666, English; letters BL BRO KB ST

HOWELL, John Christian, 1924- , American; nonfiction CON

HOWELL, James Edwin, 1928- , American; nonfiction CON

HOWELL, John Michael, 1933- , American; nonfiction CON

HOWELL, Leon, 1936- , American; nonfiction CON

HOWELL, Robert Lee, 1928- , American; nonfiction CON

HOWELL, Roger, Jr., 1936- , American; nonfiction CON

'HOWELL, S.' see STYLES, Frank S.

HOWELL, Thomas, fl. 1567-81, English; poetry ST

HOWELL, Virginia Tier see ELLISON, Virginia H.

HOWELL, Wilbur Samuel, 1904- , American; nonfiction CON

HOWELLS, John Gwilym, 1918- , American; nonfiction CON

HOWELLS, William Dean, 1837-1920, American; fiction, plays, essays, poetry BL BRO KAA MAG MAT SA ST

HOWELLS, William White, 1908- , American; nonfiction CON

HOWER, Ralph Merle, 1903- , American; nonfiction CON

HOWES, Barbara, 1914- , American; poetry CON MUR

HOWES, Paul Griswold, 1892- , American; nonfiction CON

HOWES, Raymond Floyd, 1903- , American; nonfiction CON

HOWES, Robert Gerard, 1919- , American; nonfiction CON

HOWES, Royce Bucknam, 1901- , American; fiction CON

HOWICK, William Henry, 1924- , Canadian; nonfiction CON

HOWIE, Carl Gordon, 1920- ,

American; nonfiction CON

HOWIE, John, 1735-93, English; nonfiction BRO

HOWITH, Harry ('Marc Wyman'), 1934- , Canadian; poetry CON MUR

HOWITT, Mary, 1799-1888, English; nonfiction, juveniles BRO KBA ST

HOWITT, Samuel, 1750-1823, English; nonfiction HIG

HOWITT, William, 1792-1879, English; nonfiction, juveniles, poetry BRO KBA ST

'HOWITZER, Bronson' see HARDMAN, Richards, L.

'HOWORTH, M. K.' see BLACK, Margaret K.

HOWORTH, Muriel, English; juveniles CON

HOWTON, Frank William, 1925- , American; nonfiction CON

HOY, Cyrus H., 1926- , American; nonfiction CON

HOY, David, 1930- , American; nonfiction CON

HOY, John C., 1933- , American; nonfiction CON

HOY, Thomas, 1659-1718, English; translations ST

HOYE, Anna Scott, 1915- , American; nonfiction CON

HOYEM, Andrew, 1935- , American; poetry CON MUR

HOYER, George W., 1919- , American; nonfiction CON

HOYER, Harvey Conrad, 1907- , American; nonfiction CON

HOYLAND, Michael, 1925- , English; nonfiction CON

HOYLE, Edmund, 1672-1769, English; nonfiction KB

HOYLE, Fred, 1915- , English; fiction, plays CON RIC

HOYLE, Martha Byrd, 1930- , American; nonfiction CON

HOYLEMAN, Merle, American; poetry MAR

HOYLES, James Arthur, 1908- , English; nonfiction CON

HOYO MARTINEZ, Arturo del, 1917- , Spanish; criticism, fiction SA

HOYOS y VINENT, Antionio de, 1886-1940, Spanish; fiction SA

HOYT, Charles Alva, 1931- , American; nonfiction CON

HOYT, Charles Hale, 1860-1900,

American; plays KAA MAT

HOYT, Edwin Palmer, 1923- , American; juveniles CON WA

HOYT, Elizabeth Ellis, 1893- , American; nonfiction CON

HOYT, Herman Arthur, 1909- , American; nonfiction CON

HOYT, Homer, 1896- , American; nonfiction CON

HOYT, Jo Wasson, 1927- , American; nonfiction CON

HOYT, Joseph Bixby, 1913- , American; nonfiction CON

HOYT, Mary Finch, American; juveniles WA

HOYT, Murray, 1904- , American; nonfiction CON

HOYT, Olga Gruhzit, 1922- , American; juveniles CON

HOYT, Vance Joseph, 1889- , American; fiction MAR

HOZ y MOTA, Juan Claudio de, 1622-1714?, Spanish; plays, fiction BL SA ST

HOZIER, Louis Pierre, 1685-1767, French; nonfiction DIL

'HOZJUSZ' see DOBRACZYNSKI, Jan

HRABAN see RABANUS MAURUS

HRISTOV, Kiril, 1875-1945, Bulgarian; nonfiction ST

HROMADKA, Josef L., 1889- , Czech; nonfiction CON

HRONSKY, Jozef C., 1896- , Slovak; fiction ST

HORTSVITHA, fl. 960, German; plays AL SA ST

HRUSOVSKY, Jàn, 1892- , Slovak; fiction ST

HSI K'ANG, 223-62, Chinese; poetry ST

HSIA, Chih Tsing, 1921- , Chinese-American; nonfiction CON

HSIA, Tsi-An, 1916-65, Chinese-American; nonfiction CON

HSIAO CH'IEN, 1911- , Chinese; journalism ST

HSIAO, Kung-Chuan, 1897- , Chinese-American; nonfiction CON

HSIAO, Tso-Liang, 1910- , Chinese; nonfiction CON

HSIAO, T'ung, 501-31, Chinese; poetry ST

HSIEH, Ling-Yün, 385-433, Chinese; poetry ST

HSIEH, Ping-Ying, 1908- , Chinese; nonfiction ST

HSIEH, T'iao, 464-99, Chinese;
poetry ST
HSIEH WAN-YING see 'PING HSIN'
HSIN Chi'i-Chi, 1140-1207, Chinese;
poetry LAN
HSIUNG FU-HSI, 1900- , Chinese;
plays ST
HSIUNG, James Chieh, 1935- ,
American; nonfiction CON
HSU, Cho-Yun, 1930- , Chinese;
nonfiction CON
HSU, Francis Lang Kwang, 1909- ,
Chinese-American; nonfiction
CON
HSU, Immanuel C.Y., 1923- ,
Chinese-American; nonfiction
CON
HSU, Kai-Yu, 1922- , Chinese-
American; nonfiction CON
HSÜ Chih-mo, 1899?-1931, Chinese;
poetry LAN ST
HSÜ kuang ch-i, 1562-1633, Chinese;
nonfiction ST
HSÜ LING, 507-83, Chinese; poetry
ST
HSÜ SHEN, 1st cent., Chinese; non-
fiction ST
'HSÜAN CHU' see SHEN YEN-PING
HSÜAN-TSANG, 602-54, Chinese; non-
fiction ST
HSÜN-TZU, 300 B.C., Chinese; non-
fiction ST
HU SHIH, 1891-1962, Chinese; fiction
LAN ST
HU TS'ENG, 9th cent., Chinese;
poetry ST
HUACO, George A., 1927- , Ameri-
can; nonfiction CON
HUAMAN POMA de AYALA, Felipe,
1534-1615?, Peruvian; nonfiction
BL SA
HUANG CHING-JEN, 1749-83, Chinese;
poetry ST
HUANG, David Shih-Li, 1931- ,
Chinese-American; nonfiction CON
HUANG, T'ing Chien, 1045-1105, Chi-
nese; poetry ST
HUANG, Tsung-Hsi, 1610-95, Chinese;
nonfiction ST
HUARTE de SAN JUAN, Juan, 1530-
91, Spanish; nonfiction BL SA ST
HUBACH, Robert Rogers, 1916- ,
American; poetry, nonfiction CON
HUBALEK, Claus, 1926- , German;
plays MAT
HUBARTT, Paul Leroy, 1919- , Amer-
ican; juveniles CON
HUBBARD, Bernard Rosecrans, 1888- ,

American; juveniles HOE
HUBBARD, David Allan, 1928- ,
Canadian; nonfiction CON
HUBBARD, David Graham, 1920- ,
American; nonfiction CON
HUBBARD, Donald Lee, 1929- ,
American; juveniles CON
HUBBARD, Elbert ('Fra Elbertus'),
1856-1915, American; fiction,
essays, journalism BRO KT
HOO
HOBBARD, Frank McKinney ('Kin
Hubbard'; 'Abe Martin'),
1868-1930, American; fiction,
journalism KT
HUBBARD, Freeman Henry,
1894- , American; nonfiction
CON
'HUBBARD, Margaret Ann' see
PRILEY, Margaret H.
HUBBARD, Preston John, 1918- ,
American; nonfiction CON
HUBBARD, Robert Hamilton,
1916- , Canadian; nonfiction
CON
HUBBARD, Thomas Leslie Wallan,
1905- , English; poetry
CON
HUBBARD, William, 1621-1704,
American; nonfiction KAA
HUBBELL, Harriet Weed, 1909- ,
American; juveniles CON
WA
HUBBELL, Jay Broadus, 1885- ,
American; nonfiction CON
HUBBELL, Lindley Williams,
1901- , American; poetry
CON
HUBBELL, Patricia, 1928- ,
American; juveniles CON
HUBBELL, Richard Whittaker,
1914- , American; nonfiction
CON
HUBER, Jack Travis, 1918- ,
American; nonfiction CON
HUBER, Marie, 1695-1753, Ger-
man; nonfiction SA
HUBER, Michel, 1727-1804, Ger-
man; translations DIL
HUBER, Morton Wesley, 1923- ,
American; nonfiction CON
HUBER, Richard Miller, 1922- ,
American; nonfiction CON
HUBER, Thomas, 1937- , Amer-
ican; nonfiction CON
HUBERMAN, Edward, 1910- ,
American; nonfiction CON
HUBERMAN, Elizabeth Duncan

Lyle, 1915- , American; nonfic-
tion CON
HUBERMAN, Leo, 1903- , American;
nonfiction CON
HUBERT, Antonis de, 1590-1636,
Dutch; poetry ST
HUBERT, Marie, 1695-1753, French;
nonfiction DIL
HUBIN, Allen J., 1936- , American;
nonfiction CON
HUBKA, Betty Josephine Morgan,
1924- , American; juveniles
CON
HUBLER, Edward Lorenzo, 1902- ,
American; nonfiction CON
HUBLER, Richard Gibson ('Harry
Clark Gibson'), 1912- , Ameri-
can; nonfiction, fiction CON WAF
HUBNER, Charles William, 1835-
1929, American; poetry KAA
HUBNER, Manuel Eduardo, 1903- ,
Chilean; fiction, poetry, essays
MIN
HUBNER BEZANILLA Jorge,
1892- , Chilean; poetry MIN
HUBY, Pamela Margaret Clark,
1922- , American; nonfiction
CON
HUC, Evariste Regis, 1813-60,
French; nonfiction ST
HUC, Philippe see 'DEREME, Tristan'
HUCH, Fredrich, 1873-1913, Ger-
man; fiction AL COL FLE HAR
SA ST
HUCH, Ricarda ('Richard Hugo'), 1864-
1947, German; poetry, fiction,
essays AL COL FLE HAR KAT
KT KU KUN LEN SA ST
HUCHEL, Peter, 1903- , German;
poetry, radio, nonfiction AL
FLE KU KUN
HUCHOUN (Huchown; Hucheon), 14th
cent., English; poetry BRO KB
ST
HUCKABY, Gerald, 1933- , Ameri-
can; poetry CON
HUCKINS, Wesley C., 1918- ,
American; nonfiction CON
HUDDLE, Frank, Jr., 1943- ,
American; nonfiction CON
HUDDLESTON, Lee Eldridge,
1935- , American; nonfiction
CON
HUDDLESTON, Rodney Desmond,
1937- , English; nonfiction CON
HUDDY, Delia, 1934- , English;
juveniles CON
HUDGINS, Herbert Cornelius, Jr.,

1932- , American; nonfiction
CON
HUDNUT, Robert K., 1934- ,
American; nonfiction CON
HUDON, Edward Gerard, 1915- ,
American; nonfiction CON
'HUDSON, Alice' see HOLMES,
Wilfred J.
HUDSON, Arthur Palmer,
1892- , American; nonfiction
CON
HUDSON, Charles, 1795-1881,
American; journalism KAA
HUDSON, Charles Melvin, Jr.,
1932- , American; nonfiction
CON
HUDSON, Derek, 1911- , English;
nonfiction CON
HUDSON, Gladys Watts, 1926- ,
American; nonfiction CON
HUDSON, Henry Norman, 1814-
86, American; nonfiction
KAA
HUDSON, James Albert, 1924- ,
American; nonfiction CON
HUDSON, James Jackson, 1919- ,
American; nonfiction CON
HUDSON, Jay William, 1874- ,
American; fiction KT
'HUDSON, Jeffrey' see CRICHTON,
Michael
HUDSON, John Allen, 1927- ,
American; nonfiction CON
HUDSON, Liam, 1933- , Ameri-
can; nonfiction CON
HUDSON, Lois Phillips, 1927- ,
American; fiction CON
HUDSON, Michael Craig, 1938- ,
American; nonfiction CON
HUDSON, Michael Huckleberry,
1939- , American; nonfiction
CON
HUDSON, Peggy, 1936- ,
American; nonfiction CON
HUDSON, Randolph Hoyt, 1927- ,
American; nonfiction CON
HUDSON, Robert Lofton, 1910- ,
American; nonfiction CON
'HUDSON, Stephen' (Sydney Schiff),
English; fiction KL KT
HUDSON, Thomas, fl. 1610,
Scots; poetry KB
HUDSON, Thomson Jay, 1834-
1903, American; journalism
KAA
HUDSON, William Henry, 1841-
1922, English; essays, fiction
BRO KAT KT MAG RIC

HUDSON, William Henry, 1862-1918,
Anglo-American; nonfiction KT
ST
HUDSON, Wilma Jones, 1916- ,
American; juveniles CON
HUDSON, Winthrop Still, 1911- ,
American; nonfiction CON
HUE de ROTELANTDE, 12th cent.,
Anglo-Norman; poetry ST
HUECK, Catherine de, 1900- ,
Russian; nonfiction HO
HUEFFER, Ford Madox see FORD,
Ford M.
HUEGLI, Albert George, 1913- ,
American; nonfiction CON
HUELSENBECK, Richard, 1892- ,
German; fiction, poetry AL FLE
HÜLSHOFF, Annette D. see DROSTE-
HÜLSHOFF, Annette F.
HUERNE de la MOTHE, François
Charles, 18th cent., French;
nonfiction DIL
HUERTA, Vicente G. de la see
GARCIA de la HUERTA, Vicente
HUERTA y VEGA, Francisco Manuel
de la, 1697-1752, Spanish; nonfic-
tion SA
HÜSEYIN, Rahmin Gürpinar, 1864-1944,
Turkish; fiction ST
HUESSY, Hans R., 1921- , German-
American; nonfiction CON
HUESTON, Ethel, 1887- , American;
fiction WAF
HUET, Coenraad Busken (Thrasybulus),
1826-86, Dutch; nonfiction COL
HAR KE SA ST
HUET, Pierre Daniel, 1630-1721,
French; nonfiction DIF SA ST
HUET de FROBERVILLE, Claude
Jean Baptiste, 18th cent., French;
nonfiction DIL
HUETE, Jaime de, -1530?, Spanish;
poetry, plays SA
'HUETHER, Anne F.' see FREEMAN,
Anne F.
HUFANA, Alejandrino G., 1926- ,
Filipino; poetry, plays MUR
HUFF, Betty Tracy, Welsh; nonfiction
CON
HUFF, Darrell, 1913- , American;
nonfiction CON
HUFF, Robert, 1924- , American;
poetry CON MUR
HUFF, Vaughn Edward, 1935- ,
Canadian; nonfiction CON
HUFFARD, Grace Thompson, 1892- ,
American; juveniles CON
HUFFERT, Anton M., 1912- ,

Rumanian-American; nonfiction
CON
HUFFMAN, Franklin Eugene,
1934- , American; nonfiction
CON
HUFTON, Olwen H., 1938- ,
English; nonfiction CON
HUGGETT, Frank Edward, 1924- ,
English; nonfiction CON
HUGGINS, Alice Margaret,
1891- , American; juveniles
CON
HUGGINS, Nathan Irvin, 1927- ,
American; nonfiction CON
HUGH of ST. VICTOR, 1096-
1141, Saxon; nonfiction ST
HUGH PRIMAS of ORLEANS, fl.
1136, French; poetry ST
HUGHES, Anthony John, 1933- ,
English; nonfiction CON
HUGHES, Arthur, 1832-1915, Eng-
lish; juveniles DOY
HUGHES, Arthur Joseph, 1928- ,
American; nonfiction CON
HUGHES, Charles James Penne-
thorne, 1907-67, English;
nonfiction CON
HUGHES, Charles Lloyd, 1933- ,
American; nonfiction CON
HUGHES, Christopher John, 1918- ,
English; nonfiction CON
HUGHES, Colin Anfield, 1930- ,
Australian; nonfiction CON
'HUGHES, Cyril' see HODGES,
Cyril
HUGHES, Daniel, 1929- , Amer-
ican; poetry CON
HUGHES, Dorothy Belle Flanagan,
1904- , American; fiction
KTS
HUGHES, Dorothy Berry, 1910- ,
American; nonfiction CON
HUGHES, Douglas Allan, 1938- ,
American; nonfiction CON
HUGHES, Felicity, 1938- , Eng-
lish; nonfiction CON
HUGHES, George Edward, 1918- ,
American; nonfiction CON
HUGHES, Gervase, 1905- ,
English; nonfiction CON
HUGHES, Glenn Arthur, 1894-
1964, American; plays,
poetry PAC
HUGHES, Glyn, 1935- , English;
poetry CON
HUGHES, Harold Kenneth, 1911- ,
American; nonfiction CON
HUGHES, Hatcher, 1886?-1945,

American; plays JO KT MAT
HUGHES, Helen Gintz, 1928- , Czech-
Australian; nonfiction CON
HUGHES, Henry Stuart, 1916- ,
American; nonfiction CON
HUGHES, James, 1890- , American;
nonfiction CON
HUGHES, James Quentin, 1920- ,
English; nonfiction CON
HUGHES, John, 1677-1720, English;
essays, plays, translation BRO
ST
HUGHES, John Ceiriog see 'CEIRIOG'
HUGHES, John Cledwyn, 1920- ,
Welsh; nonfiction, juveniles CON
HUGHES, John Paul, 1920- , Ameri-
can; nonfiction CON
HUGHES, Judith Markham, 1941- ,
American; nonfiction CON
HUGHES, Kenneth, 1922- , English;
fiction CON
HUGHES, Langston, 1902-67, Ameri-
can; poetry, fiction, juveniles
CON FLE KL KT MAT SA ST
WA
HUGHES, Mary Louise, 1910- ,
American; nonfiction CON
HUGHES, Merrit Yerkes, 1893- ,
American; nonfiction CON
HUGHES, Nathaniel Cheairs, Jr.,
1930- , American; nonfiction
CON
HUGHES, Owain Gardner Collingwood,
1943- , English; fiction CON
HUGHES, Paul Lester, 1915- ,
American; nonfiction CON
HUGHES, Philip, 1895- , English;
nonfiction CON HOE
HUGHES, Philip Edgecumbe, 1915- ,
Australian; nonfiction CON
HUGHES, Richard Arthur Warren,
1900- , English; juveniles, fic-
tion, plays, poetry BRO CON
DOY FLE KL KT MAG RIC ST
HUGHES, Richard Edward, 1927- ,
American; nonfiction CON
HUGHES, Robert John, 1930- ,
American; nonfiction CON
HUGHES, Robert William, 1821-1901,
American; editor KAA
HUGHES, Rupert, 1872-1956, American;
fiction, plays, essays KL KT
HUGHES, Ted, 1930- , British;
poetry, juveniles CON MUR RIC
SP
HUGHES, Thomas, fl. 1587, English;
plays ST
HUGHES, Thomas, 1822-96, English;

juveniles, fiction BRO DOY
KBA MAG SA ST
HUGHES, Thomas Parke,
1923- , American; nonfiction
CON
HUGHES, Thomas Rowland,
1903-49, Welsh; fiction ST
HUGHES, Walter Llewellyn,
1910- , English; nonfiction
CON
HUGHEY, Ruth Willard, 1899- ,
American; nonfiction CON
HUGILL, Stanley James, 1906- ,
English; nonfiction CON
HUGO, Count of Montfort, 1357-
1425, German; poetry ST
HUGO, Charles Louis, 1667-1739,
French; nonfiction DIL
'HUGO, Richard' see HUCH,
Ricarda
HUGO, Richard Franklin, 1923- ,
American; poetry MUR PAC
HUGO, Victor, 1802-85, French;
fiction, poetry, plays DIF
HAR KE MAG MAL SA ST
HUGO de ORLEANS, 1098-1160,
French; poetry SA
HUGO de SAINT VICTOR, 1096-
1141, German; nonfiction SA
DIF
HUGO von TRIMBERG, 1230-1313,
German; nonfiction AL ST
HUGUENIN, Jean René, 1936-
62, French; fiction DIC
HUGUES de BERZE, 1150?-1219,
French; poetry ST
HUGUES d'OISY, 1150-90?,
French; poetry ST
HUHN, Kurt, 1902- , German;
nonfiction AL
HUHTA, James Kenneth, 1937- ,
American; nonfiction CON
HUI SHIH, -310 B.C., Chinese;
nonfiction ST
HUI TUNG, 1697-1758, Chinese;
nonfiction ST
HUIDOBRO, Maria Teresa de,
1922- , Spanish; poetry SA
HUIDOBRO, Vicente García,
1893-1948, Chilean; poetry,
fiction BL FLE KT MIN RIC
SA ST
HUIE, William Bradford, 1910- ,
American; fiction, journalism
CON KTS
HUIE, William Orr, 1911- ,
American; nonfiction CON
HUISINGA BAKKER, Pieter,

1713-1801, Dutch; poetry ST
HUISSER des ESSARTS, 18th cent.,
French; plays DIL
HUITFELDT, Arild, 1546-1609,
Danish; nonfiction ST
HUIZINGA, Johan, 1872-1945, Dutch;
nonfiction KTS
HULA, Harold, L., 1930- , American; nonfiction CON
'HULDA' (Unnur Benediktsdóttir
Bjarkland), 1881-1946, Icelandic;
poetry, fiction ST
HULICKA, Irene Mackintosh, 1927- ,
Canadian; nonfiction CON
HULL, David Stewart, 1938- , American; nonfiction CON
HULL, Denison Bingham, 1897- ,
American; nonfiction CON
HULL, Edith Maude, English; fiction
BRO KT
HULL, Eleanor Means, 1913- , American; juveniles CON
HULL, Eugene Leslie, 1928- ,
American; nonfiction CON
'HULL, H. Braxton' see JACOBS,
Helen H.
HULL, Helen Rose, -1971, American; nonfiction, fiction CON
KAT KT WAF
HULL, John Howarth Eric, 1923- ,
English; nonfiction CON
HULL, Katherine, 1921- , American;
nonfiction, juveniles CON
HULL, Oswald, 1919- , English;
nonfiction CON
HULL, Raymond, 1919- , English;
plays, nonfiction CON
'HULL, Richard' see SAMPSON, R.H.
HULL, Rev. Robert, 1886-1932, English; nonfiction HO
HULL, Roger H., 1942- , American;
nonfiction CON
HULL, William Doyle, 1918- , American; poetry CON
HULL, William Edward, 1930- ,
American; nonfiction CON
HULME, Kathryn, 1900- , American;
fiction CON
HULME, Thomas Ernest, 1883-1917,
English; nonfiction KAT KT
HULME, William Edward, 1920- ,
American; nonfiction CON
HULSE, Herman La Wayne,
1922- , American; nonfiction
CON
HULSE, James Warren, 1930- ,
American; nonfiction CON
HULSE, Stewart Harding, Jr.,

1931- , American; nonfiction
CON
HULTGREN, Thor, 1902- , American; nonfiction CON
HULTENG, John L., 1921- ,
American; nonfiction CON
HULTMAN, Charles William,
1930- , American; nonfiction
CON
HULTS, Dorothy Niebrugge, 1898- ,
American; nonfiction CON
HUMBERT, Pierre Hubert, 1685/
86-1779, French; nonfiction
DIL
HUMBERT de MONTMORET,
-1525, French; poetry ST
HUMBLE, William Frank, 1948- ,
English; fiction CON
HUMBOLDT, Friedrich Heinrich
Alexander von, 1769-1859,
German; nonfiction AL HAR
KE SA ST
HUMBOLDT, Karl Wilhelm von,
1867-1835, German; nonfiction
AL BL HAR KE SA ST
HUME, Alexander (Home), 1560-
1609, English; poetry BRO
HUME, Alexander, 1811-59, Scots;
poetry KBA
HUME, Cyril, 1900- , American;
fiction KAT KT
HUME, David, 1711-76, English;
essays BRO KB MAG SA ST
HUME, Ferguson Wright ('Fergus
Hume'), 1859-1932, English;
fiction BRO KT SA
HUME, Lotta Carsevell, American; nonfiction CON
HUME, Martin Andrew Sharp,
1843-1910, English; nonfiction
KBA
HUME, Robert D., 1944- ,
American; nonfiction CON
HUME, Ruth Fox, 1922- , American; juveniles WA
HUMES, Dollena Joy, 1921- ,
American; nonfiction CON
HUMES, Harold L., 1926- ,
American; fiction CON
HUMES, Samuel, 1930- , American; nonfiction CON
'HUMFREY, C.' see OSBORNE,
Charles H.C.
HUMFREY, Laurence, 1527-89/90,
English; nonfiction ST
HUMMEL, Charles E., 1923- ,
American; nonfiction CON
HUMMEL, George Frederick,

1882- , American; fiction KT
HUMMEL, Ray Orvin, Jr., 1909- ,
American; nonfiction CON
HUMMEL, Ruth Stevenson, 1929- ,
American; juveniles CON
HUMPHREVILLE, Frances Tibbetts,
1909- , American; nonfiction
CON
HUMPHREY, Grace, 1882- , Ameri-
can; juveniles HOO
HUMPHREY, Michael Edward, 1926- ,
English; nonfiction CON
HUMPHREYS, Alexander Jeremiah,
1913- , American; nonfiction
CON
HUMPHREYS, Alice Lee, 1893- ,
American; fiction CON
HUMPHREYS, Cecil Frances see
ALEXANDER, Cecil F.
HUMPHREYS, David, 1752-1818,
American; poetry KAA
HUMPHREYS, Eliza Margaret ('Rita'),
-1938, English; fiction BRO
HUMPHREYS, Emyr Lowen, 1919- ,
Welsh; juveniles CON
HUMPHREYS, John Richard Adams,
1918- , American; fiction CON
HUMPHREYS, Mary Eglantyne Hill
('Poll Hill'), 1914- , English;
nonfiction CON
HUMPHREYS, Robert Allan Laud,
1930- , American; nonfiction
CON
HUMPHREYVILLE, Theresa R.,
1918- , American; nonfiction
CON
HUMPHRIES, Adelaide M. ('Kathleen
Harris'; 'Wayne Way'; 'Token
West'), 1898- , American; fiction
CON
HUMPHRIES, George Rolfe, 1894-1969,
American; nonfiction CON
'HUMPHRIES, Jack' see KELLY,
Jonathan F.
HUMPHRIES, Helen Speirs Dickie,
1915- , Scots; fiction CON
HUMPHRIES, Rolfe, 1894- , Amer-
ican; poetry KT
HUNDLEY, Norris Cecil, Jr.,
1935- , American; nonfiction
CON
HUNEEUS GANA, Antonio, 1870-1950,
Chilean; nonfiction MIN
HUNEKER, James Gibbons, 1860-
1921, American; criticism KAT
KT ST
HUNERYAGER, Sherwood George,
1933- , American; nonfiction
CON

HUNG SHENG, 1646-1704, Chinese;
plays ST
HUNGERFORD, Edward Buell,
1900- , American; juvenile
CON WA
HUNGERFORD, Harold Ralph,
1928- , American; nonfiction
CON
HUNGERFORD, Margaret Wolfe
('The Duchess'), 1850-97,
Irish; fiction KBA
'HUNGERFORD, Pixie' see
BRINSMEAD, Hesba F.
HUNKER, Henry L., 1924- ,
American; nonfiction CON
HUNNEX, Milton De Verne,
1917- , American; nonfic-
tion CON
HUNNINGS, Neville March,
1929- , English; nonfiction
CON
HUNNIS, William, -1597, Eng-
lish; poetry BRO ST
HUNSAKER, David Malcolm,
1944- , American; nonfiction
CON
HUNSINGER, Paul, 1919- ,
American; nonfiction CON
HUNT, Barbara, 1907- , Ameri-
can; fiction CON
'HUNT, Charlotte' see HODGES,
Doris M.
HUNT, Chester L., 1912- ,
American; nonfiction CON
HUNT, Clara Whitehill, 1871- ,
American; juveniles KJU
HUNT, David, 1942- , American;
nonfiction CON
HUNT, Douglas, 1918- , Ameri-
can; nonfiction CON
HUNT, Edgar Huberg Fidelio,
1909- , English; nonfiction
CON
HUNT, Elgin Fraser, 1895- ,
American; nonfiction CON
HUNT, Florine Elizabeth, 1928- ,
American; nonfiction CON
'HUNT, Francis' see STRATE-
MEYER, Edward L.
HUNT, Frazier, 1885-1967, Ameri-
can; juveniles, fiction HOO
HUNT, George Pinney, 1918- ,
American; juveniles WA
HUNT, Gladys M., 1926- ,
American; nonfiction CON
'HUNT, Harrison' see BALLARD
Willis T.
HUNT, Harry Draper, 1935- ,
American; nonfiction CON

HUNT, Helen M. see JACKSON,
Helen M. F. H.

HUNT, Howard, 1918- , American;
fiction WAF

HUNT, Hugh, 1911- , English; nonfiction, plays CON

HUNT, Ignatius, 1920- , American;
nonfiction CON

HUNT, Inez Whitaker, 1899- ,
American; nonfiction, poetry CON

HUNT, Irene, 1907- , American;
juveniles, fiction COM CON WA

HUNT, Isaac, 1742-1809, American;
nonfiction KAA

HUNT, James Henry Leigh, 1784-1859,
Engish; poetry, criticism, essays,
plays BRO KBA SA SP ST

HUNT, John J., 1929- , American;
nonfiction CON

HUNT, John P., 1915- , American;
nonfiction CON

HUNT, John Wesley, 1927- , American; nonfiction CON

HUNT, Joseph McVicker, 1906- ,
American; nonfiction CON

HUNT, Kari, American; juveniles
WA

HUNT, Kellogg Wesley, 1912- ,
American; nonfiction CON

'HUNT, Kyle' see CREASEY, John

HUNT, Lawrence J., 1920- ,
American; fiction CON

HUNT, Leslie Gordon, 1906-70,
American; nonfiction CON

HUNT, Mabel Leigh, 1892- ,
American; juveniles COM CON
JO KJU WA

HUNT, Marigold, 1905- , English;
juveniles HO

HUNT, Maurice, P., 1915- , American; nonfiction CON

HUNT, Morton Magill, 1920- ,
American; nonfiction CON

'HUNT, Penelope' see NAPIER,
Priscilla

HUNT, Peter, 1922- , English;
fiction CON

HUNT, Raymond G., 1928- ,
American; nonfiction CON

HUNT, Richard Norman, 1931- ,
American; nonfiction CON

HUNT, Robert Cushman, 1934- ,
American; nonfiction CON

HUNT, Todd T., 1938- , American; nonfiction CON

HUNT, Violet, 1866-1942, English;
fiction BRO KAT KT RIC

HUNT, Vere D., fl. 1825, English;

nonfiction HIG

HUNT, William Dudley, Jr.,
1922- , American; nonfiction
CON

HUNTER, Alan James Herbert,
1922- , English; nonfiction
CON

HUNTER, Allan Armstrong,
1893- , Canadian; juveniles,
nonfiction CON

'HUNTER, Anole' see CRAWFORD,
Everett

'HUNTER, Anson' see ORRMONT,
Arthur

HUNTER, Archibald Macbride,
1906- , Scots; nonfiction
CON

HUNTER, Beatrice Trum, 1918- ,
American; nonfiction CON

HUNTER, Bonnie Bonham, American; fiction MAR

'HUNTER, Christine' see HUNTER,
Maud L.

HUNTER, Dard, 1883-1966, American; nonfiction CON

'HUNTER, Dawe' see DOWNIE,
Mary A.

HUNTER, Doris A., 1929- ,
American; nonfiction CON

HUNTER, Edward, 1902- ,
American; nonfiction CON

HUNTER, Evan ('Hunt Collins';
'Richard Marsten'; 'Ed
McBain'), 1926- , American;
fiction CON RIC WA

HUNTER, Frederick James,
1916- , American; nonfiction
CON

HUNTER, Geoffrey Basil Bailey,
1925- , English; nonfiction
CON

'HUNTER, Hall' see MARSHALL,
Edison

HUNTER, Jack Dayton, 1921- ,
American; fiction CON

HUNTER, James Alston Hope,
1902- , English; nonfiction
CON

HUNTER, James Paul, 1934- ,
American; nonfiction CON

HUNTER, Jim, 1939- , English;
fiction CON

'HUNTER, John' see BALLARD,
Willis T.

'HUNTER, John' see HUNTER,
Maud L.

HUNTER, John Fletcher Mac-
Gregor, 1924- , Canadian;

nonfiction CON

HUNTER, John M., 1921- ,
American; nonfiction CON

HUNTER, Kermit, 1910- , American; plays JO MAT

HUNTER, Kristin Eggleston, 1931- ,
American; juveniles, fiction
CON WA

HUNTER, Leslie Stannard, 1890- ,
Scots; nonfiction CON

HUNTER, Maud Lily ('Christine
Hunter'; 'John Hunter'; 'Charlotte
Steer'), 1910- , English; fiction
CON

'HUNTER, Mollie' see McILWRAITH,
Maureen

HUNTER, Norman Charles, 1899-1971,
English; fiction DOY

'HUNTER, Paul' see WEAVER,
Bertrand

HUNTER, Sam, 1923- , American;
nonfiction CON

HUNTER, Victoria Alberta, 1929- ,
American; nonfiction CON

HUNTER, William Albert, 1908- ,
American; nonfiction CON

HUNTER, William C., 1812-91,
American; nonfiction KAA

HUNTER, William Randolph see
'BRADFORD, Joseph'

HUNTER, Sir William Wilson, 1840-
1900, Scots; nonfiction KBA

HUNTER BLAIR, Sir David Oswald,
1853-1939, Scots; nonfiction
HOE

HUNTER BLAIR, Pauline Clarke
('Helen Clare'), 1921- , English;
juveniles CON DOY WA

HUNTINGTON, Archer Milton, 1870-
1955, American; nonfiction BL

HUNTINGTON, E. Gale, 1902- ,
American; nonfiction CON

HUNTINGTON, Harriet Elizabeth,
1909- , American; juveniles
COM CON FUL WA

HUNTINGTON, Jedediah Vincent,
1815-62, American; fiction KAA

HUNTINGTON, Samuel Phillips, 1927- ,
American; nonfiction CON

HUNTINGTON, Virginia, 1889- ,
American; fiction CON

HUNTINGTON, William Clarence,
1876- , American; nonfiction
PAC

HUNTLEY, Frank Livingstone, 1902- ,
American; nonfiction CON

HUNTLEY, Herbert Edwin, 1892- ,
English; nonfiction CON

HUNTLEY, James Robert,
1923- , American; nonfiction
CON

HUNTLEY, Lydia H. see SIGOUR-
NEY, Lydia H. H.

HUNTLY, Francis E. see MAYNE,
Ethel C.

'HUNTON, Mary' see GILZEAN,
Elizabeth H. B.

HUNTON, Richard Edwin,
1924- , American; nonfiction
CON

HUNTRESS, Keith Gibson, 1913- ,
American; nonfiction CON

HUNTSBERGER, John Paul,
1931- , American; nonfiction
CON

HUNTSBERRY, William Emery,
1916- , American; fiction
CON

HUNZICKER, Beatrice Plumb,
1886- , Anglo-American;
juveniles, nonfiction CON

HUON de MERY, 13th cent.,
French; poetry DIF ST

HUONDER, Gion Antoni, 1824-67,
Raeto Romansch; poetry ST

HUON le ROI de CAMBRAI, 13th
cent., French; poetry ST

HUPPE, Bernard E., 1911- ,
American; nonfiction CON

HUPPERT, George, 1934- ,
Czech-American; nonfiction
CON

HUPPERT, Hugo, 1902- , German; poetry, essays AL

HURBAN, Jozef Ludovit Miloslav,
1836-88, Slovak; poetry, fiction, criticism ST

HURBAN VAJANSKY, Svetozár,
1847-1916, Slovak; poetry,
fiction COL KE SA ST

HURD, Charles Wesley Bolick,
1903- , American; nonfiction
CON

HURD, Clement, 1908- , American; juveniles COM CON
FUL WA

HURD, Douglas, 1930- , English;
nonfiction CON

HURD, Edith Thacher ('Juniper
Sage'), 1910- , American;
juveniles COM CON FUL WA

HURD, John Coolidge, Jr.,
1928- , American; nonfiction
CON

HURD, Richard, 1720-1808, English; nonfiction BRO KB

HURE, Anne, 1918- , French; nonfic-
tion CON
HUREWITZ, Jacob Coleman, 1914- ,
American; nonfiction CON
'HURKEY, Rooan' see HOLZAPFEL,
Rudi
HURLBERT, William Henry, 1827-
95, American; journalism KAA
HURLBUT, Cornelius Searlee Jr.,
1906- , American; nonfiction
CON
HURLBUT, Jesse Lyman, 1843-1930,
American; nonfiction KT
HURLBUTT, Robert Harris, III,
1924- , American; nonfiction
CON
HURLEY, Doran, 1906-64, American;
fiction CON HOE
HURLEY, Jane Hezel, 1928- , Amer-
ican; nonfiction CON
HURLEY, John, 1928- , American;
nonfiction CON
HURLEY, Leslie, American; juveniles
WA
HURLEY, Neil, 1925- , American;
nonfiction CON
HURLEY, Vic ('Jim Duane'; 'Duane
Richards'), 1898- , American;
nonfiction CON
HURLEY, Wilfred Geoffrey, 1895- ,
American; nonfiction CON
HURLEY, William James, Jr.,
1924- , American; juvenile
CON
HURLEY, William Maurice, 1916- ,
American; nonfiction CON
HURNE, Ralph, 1932- , English;
nonfiction CON
HURST, Alexander Anthony, 1917- ,
English; fiction CON
HURST, Charles G., Jr., 1928- ,
American; nonfiction CON
HURST, Fannie, 1889-1968, American;
fiction BRO CON KL KT RIC WAF
HURST, James Marshall, 1924- ,
American; nonfiction CON
HURST, Michael Charles, 1931- ,
English; nonfiction CON
HURSTON, Zora Neale, 1903- ,
American; fiction KT SA
WAF
HURTADO, Antonio, 1825-78,
Spanish; nonfiction BL
'HURTADO de la VERA, Pedro'
(Pedro Faria), 1545?-1600,
Spanish; poetry BL SA
HURTADO de MENDOZA, Diego,
1503?-75, Spanish; poetry BL

KE SA ST
HURTADO de MENDOZA y LAR-
REA, Antonio, 1586-1644,
Spanish; poetry BL SA ST
HURTADO de TOLEDO, Luis,
1523?-90, Spanish; plays BL
SA
HURTADO de VELARDE, Alfonso,
Spanish; plays BL
HURTADO y J. de la SERNA,
Juan, 1875-1944, Spanish;
nonfiction BL SA
HURTADO y VALHONDO, Antonio,
1825-78, Spanish; poetry,
plays, fiction, journalism
SA
HURTADO y VELARDE, Alfonso,
1582?-1638, Spanish; poetry,
plays SA
HURTAULT, Pierre Thomas
Nicolas, 1719-91, French;
nonfiction DIL
HURTER AMMAN, Freidrich
Manuel, 1787-1865, Austrian;
nonfiction SA
HURWITZ, Abraham B., 1905- ,
American; nonfiction CON
HURWITZ, Howard Lawrence,
1916- , American; nonfiction
CON
HURWITZ, Ken, 1948- , Ameri-
can; fiction CON
HURWITZ, Moshe, 1844-1910,
Jewish; plays MAT
HURWITZ, Samuel J., 1912- ,
American; nonfiction CON
HURWOOD, Bernhardt J. ('Mallory
T. Knight'; 'D. Gunther
Wilde'), 1926- , American;
fiction CON
HUS, Françoise Necelle, fl. 1760,
French; plays DIL
HUS, Jan, 1369/71-1415, Bohemi-
an; nonfiction HAR KE ST SA
HUSAIN, Adrain (Syed Akbar Hu-
sain), 1942- , British;
poetry MUR
HUSEN, Torsten, 1916- ,
Swedish; nonfiction CON
HUSEYIN, Rahmi Gürpinar, 1864-
1944, Turkish; fiction SA
HUSON, Paul Anthony, 1942- ,
American; fiction CON
HUSS, Roy, 1927- , American;
nonfiction CON
HUSSEIN, Nadir, 1939- ,
Pakistani; poetry MUR
HUSSERL, Edmund, 1859-1938,

German; nonfiction SA KU

HUSSEY, Maurice Percival, 1925- ,
American; nonfiction CON

HUSSLEIN, Joseph, 1873- , American;
nonfiction HOE

HUSSON, Jules F. F. see CHAMPFLEU-
RY, Jules F. F. H.

HUSSOVIUS, Mikolaj (Hussowski),
1475/85-1533, Polish; poetry
ST

HUSTON, Luther A., 1888- ,
American; nonfiction CON

HUSTVEDT, Lloyd Merlyn, 1922- ,
American; nonfiction CON

HUSZAR, George B. de, 1919- ,
Swiss; nonfiction CON

HUTCHENS, Eleanor Newman, 1919- ,
American; nonfiction CON

HUTCHENS, John Kennedy, 1905- ,
American; nonfiction PAC

HUTCHESON, Francis, 1694-1746,
Irish; nonfiction BRO KB SA ST

HUTCHINGS, Alan Eric, 1910- ,
English; nonfiction CON

HUTCHINGS, Arthur James Bramwell,
1906- , English; nonfiction CON

HUTCHINGS, Margaret Joscelyne,
1918- , English; nonfiction CON

HUTCHINGS, Monica Mary, 1917- ,
English; nonfiction CON

HUTCHINGS, Raymond, 1924- ,
English; nonfiction CON

HUTCHINS, Carleen Maby, 1911- ,
American; nonfiction CON

HUTCHINS, Francis Gilman ('Frank
Madison'), 1939- , American;
nonfiction CON

HUTCHINS, Robert Maynard, 1899- ,
American; nonfiction HOO

HUTCHINS, Ross Elliott, 1906- ,
American; nonfiction, juveniles
CON WA

HUTCHINSON, Alfred, 1924- ,
South African; plays RIC

HUTCHINSON, Arthur Stuart Menteth,
1879/80-1971, English; fiction
BRO KT MAG RIC

HUTCHINSON, Cecil Alan, 1914- ,
Anglo-American; nonfiction CON

HUTCHINSON, G. T., 1880- , English; nonfiction HIG

HUTCHINSON, George Evelyn, 1903- ,
English; fiction CON

HUTCHINSON, Hugh Lester, 1904- ,
English; nonfiction CON

HUTCHINSON, Lucy Apsley, 1620-76?,
English; nonfiction, translations
BRO KB ST

HUTCHINSON, Margaret Massey,
1904- , English; nonfiction
CON

HUTCHINSON, Michael E.,
1925- , English; nonfiction
CON

HUTCHINSON, Pearse, 1927- ,
Irish; poetry MUR

HUTCHINSON, Ray Coryton,
1907- , English; fiction
CON KT RIC

HUTCHINSON, Richard Wyatt,
1894- , American; nonfiction
CON

HUTCHINSON, Robert, 1924- ,
American; poetry, fiction
CON

HUTCHINSON, Thomas, 1711-80,
American; nonfiction KAA

HUTCHISON, Bruce, 1901- ,
Canadian; fiction ST SY

HUTCHISON, Chester Smith,
1901- , American; nonfiction
CON

HUTCHISON, Earl R., 1926- ,
American; nonfiction CON

HUTCHISON, Harold F., 1900- ,
English; nonfiction CON

HUTCHISON, Jane Campbell,
1932- , American; nonfiction
CON

HUTCHISON, Sidney Charles,
1912- , English; nonfiction
CON

HUTCHISON, William Robert,
1930- , American; nonfiction
CON

HUTH, Alfred Henry, 1850-1910,
English; nonfiction ST

'HUTH, Ernst' see SCHNOG,
Karl

HUTH, Henry, 1815-78, English;
nonfiction ST

HUTHMACHER, J. Joseph,
1929- , American; nonfiction
CON

HUTMAN, Norma Louise, 1935- ,
American; nonfiction CON

HUTT, Maurice George, 1928- ,
English; nonfiction CON

HUTTEN, Ulrich von, 1488-1523,
German; nonfiction AL HAR
KE SA ST

HUTTENBACH, Robert A., 1928- ,
German-American; nonfiction
CON

HUTTON, Nelson Allen, 1904- ,
American; fiction CON

HUTTON, Catherine, 1756-1846, English; fiction, nonfiction KBA
HUTTON, Edward, 1875- , English; nonfiction HOE
HUTTON, John Henry, 1885- , English; nonfiction CON
HUTTON, Joseph Bernard, 1911- , Bohemian-English; nonfiction CON
HUTTON, Laurence, 1843-1904, American; essays KAA
HUTTON, Maurice, 1856-1940, Canadian; nonfiction SY
HUTTON, Richard Holt, 1826-97, English; nonfiction BRO KBA ST
HUUS, Helen, 1913- , American; nonfiction CON
HUXLEY, Aldous Leonard, 1894-1963, English; fiction, essays, poetry, plays BRO FLE KT MAG RIC SA ST
HUXLEY, Anthony Julian, 1920- , English; nonfiction CON
HUXLEY, Elspeth, 1907- , English; fiction RIC
HUXLEY, George, 1932- , English; nonfiction CON
HUXLEY, Herbert Henry ('Stenus'), 1916- , English; nonfiction CON
HUXLEY, Sir Julian Sorrell ('Balbus'), 1887- , English; nonfiction CON KT RIC SA
HUXLEY, Laura Archer, Italian-American; nonfiction CON
HUXLEY, Thomas Henry, 1825-95, English; nonfiction BRO KBA MAG SA ST
HUXLEY-BLYTHE, Peter James, 1925- , English; nonfiction CON
HUXTABLE, William John Fairchild, 1912- , English; nonfiction CON
HUYBERT, Petrus Antonious de, 1693-1780, Dutch; poetry ST
HUYDECOPER, Balthazar, 1695-1778, Dutch; poetry, plays ST
HUYGENS, Constantýn, 1596-1687, Dutch; poetry KE SA ST
'HUYSMANS, Joris Karl' (Charles Marie Georges Huysmans), 1848-1907 COL DIF FLE HAR KE MAG MAL SA ST
HUYSMANS, Roelof see AGRICOLA, Rudolf
'HVIEZDOSLAV' (Pavol Országh), 1849-1921, Slovak; poetry COL FLE KE SA ST
HYAMS, Barry, 1911- , American;

nonfiction CON
HYAMS, Edward Solomon, 1910- , English; nonfiction, fiction, translations CON RIC
HYAMS, Joe, 1923- , American; nonfiction CON
HYATT, James Philip, 1909- , American; nonfiction CON
HYATT, Stanley Portal, 1877-1914, Rhodesia; fiction ST
HYDE, Dayton Odgen, American; nonfiction CON
HYDE, Douglas, 1860-1949, Irish; poetry, fiction, plays BRO KT MAT ST
HYDE, Douglas, 1911- , English; nonfiction HO
HYDE, Edward see CLARENDON, Edward H.
HYDE, George E., 1882- , American; nonfiction CON
HYDE, Harford Montgomery, 1907- , Irish-American; nonfiction CON
HYDE, Laurence, 1914- , English; fiction, juveniles CON
HYDE, Louise Kepler, Jr., 1901- , American; nonfiction CON
HYDE, Margaret Oldroyd, 1917- , American; juveniles COM CON WA
'HYDE, Robin' (Irish Wilkinson), 1906-39, New Zealander; poetry, fiction, journalism RIC ST
HYDE, Simeon Jr., 1919- , American; nonfiction CON
HYDE, Thomas, 1636-1703, English; nonfiction SA
HYDE, Wayne Frederick, 1922- , American; nonfiction CON
HYDER, Clyde Kenneth, 1902- , American; nonfiction CON
HYERS, M. Conrad, 1933- , American; nonfiction CON
HYGEN, John Bernitz, 1911- , Norwegian; nonfiction CON
HYGINUS, Roman; nonfiction ST
HYLAND, Henry Stanley, 1914- , English; nonfiction CON
HYLAND, James A., 1888- , Irish; fiction HOE
HYLANDER, Clarence John, 1897-1964, American; nonfiction, juveniles CON WA
HYLTON, Delmer Paul, 1920- , American; nonfiction CON

HYMAN, Dick, 1904- , American;
nonfiction CON
HYMAN, Frieda Clark, 1913- ,
American; nonfiction CON
HYMAN, Harold Melvin, 1924- ,
American; nonfiction CON
HYMAN, Herbert Hiram, 1918- ,
American; nonfiction CON
HYMAN, Ronald T., 1933- , Ameri-
can; nonfiction CON
HYMAN, Stella Blount, American;
poetry, fiction JO
HYMANS, Louis, 1829-84, Belgian;
journalism, nonfiction SA
HYME, Albert, 1893- , American;
nonfiction CON
HYMES, Dell Hathaway, 1927- ,
American; nonfiction CON
HYMES, Lucia Manley, 1907- ,
American; juveniles CON
HYMOFF, Edward, 1924- , American;
nonfiction CON
HYND, John, fl. 1606- , English;
fiction ST
HYNDMAN, Jane Andrews ('Lee
Wyndham'), 1912- , Russian-
American; juveniles COM CON
FUL WA
HYNE, Charles John Cutcliffe Wright,
1865-1944, English; fiction BRO
KT
HYNEMAN, Charles S., 1900- ,
American; nonfiction CON
HYON CHIN 'GON, 1900-41, Korean;
fiction LAN
HYPERIDES, 389-23 B.C., Greek;
nonfiction ST
HYSLOP, James, 1798-1827, Scots;
poetry KBA

I

'I.H.G.', 1860- , English; nonfiction
HIG
'I.S.' see SCHNEIDER, Isidor
IAMBLICHUS, 250-325, Greek; nonfic-
tion ST
IAMS, Jack, 1910- , American;
fiction WAF
IANNIELLO, Lynne Young, 1925- ,
American; nonfiction CON
IATRIDES, John Orestes, 1932- ,
Greek-American; nonfiction CON
IBAÑEZ, Vicente see BLASCO
IBAÑEZ, Vicente
IBAÑEZ, Jaime, 1919- , Colombian;
poetry, fiction MIN

IBAÑEZ, Pedro Maria, 1854-1919,
Colombian; nonfiction MIN
IBAÑEZ, Victor M., 20th cent.,
Bolivian; fiction MIN
IBAÑEZ de SEGOVIA, Gaspar
('Marqués de Mondéjar'),
1628-1708, Spanish; nonfiction
BL SA
IBARA SAIKAKU (Ihara), 1642-93,
Japanese; fiction, poetry
LAN MAG ST
IBARBOUROU, Juana Fernández
de' (J. Fernández Morales;
'Jeanette d' Ibar'; 'Juana de
América), 1895- , Uruguayan;
poetry BL FLE SA ST
IBARGÜENGOITIA, Jorge, 1928- ,
Mexican; plays SA
IBARGUREN, Carlos, 1879-1956,
Argentinian; essays, nonfiction
MIN
IBARZABAL y PLA, Federico,
1894- , Cuban; journalism,
poetry, fiction MIN
IBBETSON, Agnes Thompson,
1757-1828, English; nonfiction
SA
IBBOTSON, M. Christine, 1930- ,
English; juveniles CON
IBEAS, Bruno, 1879- , Spanish;
essays SA
IBICO, 6th cent. B.C., Greek;
poetry SA
IBN 'ABBAD (as-Sahib), 938-95,
Persian; nonfiction, letters
LAN
IBN ABD RABBIHI, 860-940,
Arab; poetry ST
IBN ABDUN, -1134, Arab;
poetry ST
IBN AL ARABI, Muhyiddin, 1165-
1240, Arab; nonfiction ST
IBN AL ATHIR, 1160-1233, Arab;
nonfiction ST
IBN AL FARID see IBNUL FARID
IBN al-Jatib see ABENNALJATIB
IBN AL-KHATIB (Lisan ad-Din),
1313-74, Arab; nonfiction,
poetry LAN ST
IBN AL-MUQAFFA, 721-57, Arab;
nonfiction LAN ST
IBN AL MU'TAZZ, 861-908, Arab;
poetry LAN ST
IBN ARABSAH, 1389-1440, Arab;
nonfiction SA
IBN AR-RUMI, 836-96, Arab;
poetry LAN ST
IBN BAJJA (Abu Bakr Muhammad;

IGGERS, Wilma Abeles, 1921- ,
Czech-American; nonfiction CON
IGGULDEN, John Manners, 1917- ,
American; fiction CON
IGLESIA PARGA, Ramón, 1905-48,
Spanish; essays SA
IGLESIA y SANTOS, Alvaro de la,
1859-1940, Cuban; journalism
MIN
IGLESIAS, Ignacio, 1871-1928,
Spanish; poetry, plays SA ST
IGLESIAD de la CASA, José, 1748-91,
Spanish; poetry BL HAR SA ST
IGLESIAS HERMEDIA, Prudencio,
1884-1919, Spanish; journalism
SA
IGLESEAS HOGAN, Rubén see
YGLESIAS HOGAN, Rubén
IGLESIAS PAZ, César, 1881/82-1922,
Argentinian; plays MIN
IGLESIES, Ignasi, 1871-1928, Spanish;
plays COL
'IGLOO, Spiro' see HOFFMAN, Abbie
IGNACE, Dom, 18th cent., French;
nonfiction DIL
IGNACIO de LOYOLA see LOYOLA,
Ignatius
IGNATOFF, David (Ignatofski),
1885- , Jewish; poetry ST
IGNATOW, David, 1914- , American;
poetry CON MUR
IGNJATOVIC, Jakov, 1824-88, Serbian;
poetry, fiction ST
'IGNOTUS' (Hugo Veigelsberg), 1869- ,
Hungarian; criticism, poetry COL
ST
IGNOTUS, Paul, 1901- , Hungarian-
English; nonfiction CON
IGO, John H., Jr., 1927- , Ameri-
can; poetry CON
IHARA, Saikaku see IBARA SAIKAKU
IHDE, Don, 1934- , American; non-
fiction CON
IHLENFELD, Kurt, 1901- , German;
nonfiction KU
IHRE, Jan, 1707-80, Swedish; nonfic-
tion SA
IIAMS, Thomas M., Jr., 1928- ,
American; nonfiction CON
IIDA see 'SOGI'
IK, Kim Yong, Korean; juveniles WA
IKE, Nobutaka, 1916- , American;
nonfiction CON
IKEJIANI, Okechukwa, 1917- , Ni-
gerian; nonfiction CON
IKERMAN, Ruth C. Percival, 1910- ,
American; nonfiction CON
IKOR, Roger, 1912- , French; fic-

tion DIF FLE
ILANKOVATIKAL, 2nd cent.,
Indian; poetry LAN
ILARDI, Vincent, 1925- , Amer-
ican; nonfiction CON
ILARION (Hilarion), fl. 1051-55,
Russian; nonfiction HARK ST
ILBERG, Werner, 1896- , Ger-
man; fiction, essays, criticism
AL
ILCHMAN, Warren Frederick,
1934- , American; nonfiction
CON
ILDEBERTO de LAVARDIN,
1056-1133, French; nonfiction
SA
ILDEFONSO de TOLEDO, San,
1607-67, Spanish; nonfiction
SA
ILENKOV, Vasili Pavlovich,
1897- , Russian; fiction,
plays MAT
'ILES, Bert' see ROSS, Zola H.
'ILES, Francis' see COX, A.B.
'ILF, Ilya' (Ilya Arnoldovich
Fainzilburg; Feisilber), 1897-
1937, Russian; fiction COL
HAR HARK KT RIC SA ST
ILGEN, Pedro Reinhold, 1869-
1920, German-American;
poetry ST
ILIC, Vojislav J., 1862-94,
Serbian; poetry COL SA ST
ILIE, Paul, 1932- , American;
nonfiction CON
'ILIN, M.' see MARSHAK, Ilia
A.
ILINGWORTH, Frank M.B.,
1908- , English; nonfiction
CON
ILLAKOWICZ, Kozimiera,
1892- , Polish; poetry COL
SA ST
ILLESCAS, Gonzalo, 1565?- ,
Spanish; nonfiction SA
ILLICK, Joseph E., 1934- ,
American; nonfiction CON
ILLINGWORTH, Neil, 1934- ,
English; nonfiction CON
ILLINGWORTH, Ronald Stanley,
1909- , English; nonfiction
CON
ILLWITZER, Elinor G., 1934- ,
American; nonfiction CON
ILLYES, Gyula, 1902- , Hungarian;
poetry, fiction, essays, plays,
translations RIC ST FLE
ILSLEY, Velma, 1918- , Ameri-

can; juveniles CON

ILYIN, Mikhail Andreyevich ('Mikhail Osorgin'), 1878-1942, Russian; fiction COL HAR HARK RIC SA ST

IMAZ ECHEVERRIA, Eugenio, 1900-51?, Spanish; essays, criticism, journalism SA

IMBER, Naphtali Herz, 1856-1909, Jewish; poetry ST

IMBERT, Barthélemy, 1747-90, French; plays, poetry DIL SA

IMBERT de BOUDEAUX, Guillaume, 1744-1803, French; nonfiction DIL

IMBS, Bravig, 1904- , American; fiction, poetry KT

IMERTI, Arthur D., 1915- , American; nonfiction CON

IMINOVICI, Mihail see EMINESCU, Mihail

IMLAY, Gilbert, 1754-1828?, American; fiction KAA

IMMANUEL BEN SOLOMON (Manoello Guideo), 1270?-1331?, Italian-Jewish; poetry HAR KE ST

IMMANUEL FRANCES see FRANCES, Immanuel

IMMEL, Mary Blair, 1930- , American; juveniles CON WA

IMMERMANN, Karl Lebrecht, 1796-1840, German; fiction, plays, poetry AL HAR KE SA ST

IMMERZUL, Johannes Jr., 1776-1841, Dutch; nonfiction ST

IMMROTH, John Phillip, 1936- , American; nonfiction CON

IMPERIAL, Micer Francisco, 15th cent., Spanish; poetry SA ST

IMRU 'AL QAYS,   -540, Arab; poetry LAN ST

INADA, Lawson Fusao, 1938- , American; poetry, nonfiction CON

INBAU, Fred E., 1909- , American; nonfiction CON

INBER, Vera Mikhailovna, 1890/93- , Russian; poetry HARK RIC ST

'INCA, El' see GARCILASO de la VEGA

INCARVILLE, Pierre, 1706-57, French; nonfiction CON

INCH, Morris Alton, 1925- , American; nonfiction CON

INCHAUSTEGUI, Cabral, Héctor, 1912- , Dominican; poetry MIN SA

INCHBALD, Elizabeth Simpson,

1753-1821, English; fiction, plays BRO KB SA ST

INCLAN, Ramon M. del see VALLE INCLAN, Ramon M. del

'INCONNUE, L.' see FRENCH, Lucy V.S.

IND, Allison ('Phil Stanley'; 'Richard Wallace'), 1903- , American; fiction CON

INDIK, Bernard Paul, 1932- , American; nonfiction CON

INDO, Claudio (Jorge Jovet), Chilean; poetry, essays MIN

INEZ, Colette, 1931- , Belgian-American; poetry CON

INFIELD, Glenn Berton ('George Powers'; 'Frank Rodgers'; 'Arthur Tolby'), 1920- , American; nonfiction CON

INGALLS, Daniel Henry Holmes, 1916- , American; nonfiction CON

INGALLS, Jeremy, 1911- , American; nonfiction, translations, poetry CON

INGALLS, Leonard, American; juveniles WA

INGAMELLS, Rex, 1913-55, Australian; poetry RIC

INGARD, Karl Uno, 1921- , Swedish-American; nonfiction CON

INGE, Milton Thomas, 1936- , American; nonfiction CON

INGE, William Motter, 1913-73, American; plays CON KTS MAT RIC

INGE, William Ralph, 1860-1954, English; nonfiction BRO KT

INGELAND, Thomas, 1560- , English; plays ST

INGELGREN, Georg, 1782-1813, Swedish; poetry ST

INGELO, Nathaniel, 1621?-83, English; poetry ST

INGELOW, Jean, 1820-97, English; poetry, fiction, juveniles BRO DOY KBA ST

INGELS, Simon van (Ingen), 1618-60?, Dutch; poetry ST

INGEMANN, Bernhard Severin, 1789-1862, Danish; fiction, poetry, plays HAR KE SA ST

INGENIEROS, José, 1877-1925, Argentinian; nonfiction MIN SA

INGERSOLL, Charles Jared, 1782-

1862, American; plays KAA
INGERSOLL, Ralph McAllister,
1900-   , American; nonfiction
CON KTS
INGERSOLL, Robert Green, 1833-
99, American; nonfiction HOO
KAA
'INGHAM, Col. Frederic' see HALE,
Edward E.
INGILBY, Joan Alicia, 1911-   ,
English; nonfiction CON
INGLE, Clifford, 1915-   , Ameri-
can; nonfiction CON
INGLE, Dwight Joyce, 1907-   , Amer-
ican; nonfiction CON
INGLES, Glenn Lloyd, 1901-   , Amer-
ican; nonfiction CON
INGLIN, Meinrad, 1893-   , Swiss;
fiction FLE LEN KU
INGLIS, Brian St. John, 1916-   ,
Irish; nonfiction CON
INGLIS, David Rittenhouse, 1905-   ,
American; nonfiction CON
INGLIS, James, 1927-   , American;
nonfiction CON
INGLIS, Robert Morton Gall, 1910-   ,
Scots; nonfiction CON
INGOULT, Nicolas Louis, 1689-   ,
French; nonfiction DIL
INGRAHAM, Joseph Holt, 1809-60,
American; nonfiction, fiction
KAA
INGRAHAM, Leonard William,
1913-   , American; nonfiction
CON
INGRAHAM, Vernon L., 1924-   ,
American; nonfiction CON
INGRAM, Archibald Kenneth,
1882-   , English; nonfiction CON
INGRAM, Derek Thynne, 1925-   ,
English; nonfiction CON
INGRAM, James Carlton, 1922-   ,
American; nonfiction CON
INGRAM, John Kells, 1823-1907,
Irish; poetry KBA
INGRAM, Mildred Prewett Bowen,
American; fiction CON
'INGRAM, Willis J.' see HARRIS,
Mark
INGRAMS, Doreen, 1906-   , English;
nonfiction CON
INGULFO, 1030-1109, English; nonfic-
tion SA
INJANASHI, 1837-91, Mongolian; es-
says, poetry, nonfiction LAN
INKELES, Alex, 1920-   , American;
nonfiction CON
INLOW, Gail Maurice, 1910-   , Amer-

ican; nonfiction CON
INMAN, Billie Jo Andrew, 1929-   ,
American; nonfiction CON
INMAN, Henry, 1837-99, Ameri-
can; nonfiction KAA
INMAN, Jack Ingles, 1919-   ,
American; nonfiction CON
INMAN, Robert Anthony, 1931-   ,
American; fiction CON
'INMAN, Will' see McGIRT,
William A.
INNES, Brian, 1928-   , English;
nonfiction CON
INNES, Cosmo, 1798-1874, Scots;
nonfiction BRO KBA ST
'INNES, Hammond' see HAMMOND
INNES, Ralph
'INNES, Michael' (John Innes
Mackintosh Stewart), 1906-   ,
English; fiction BRO KT RIC
INNES, Rosemary Elizabeth Jack-
son ('R. E. Jackson'), Scots;
juveniles CON
INNES, Thomas, 1662-1744, Scots;
nonfiction CON ST
INNIS, Harold A., 1894-1952,
Canadian; nonfiction SY
INNIS, Pauline B. Coleman,
1918-   , English; nonfiction
CON
INOUE, Tetsujiro, 1856-1944,
Japanese; poetry ST
INOUE YASUSHI, 1907-   , Japa-
nese; fiction LAN
INOUE, Yukitoshi ('Yuki'),
1945-   , Japanese; poetry
CON
INOUYE, Daniel Ken, 1924-   ,
American; nonfiction CON
'INSIGHT, James' see COLEMAN,
Robert W. A.
'INYART, Gene' see NAMOVICZ,
Gene I.
INSUA, Alberto, 1885-1963,
Cuban; fiction BL MIN SA
INSUA, Waldo de, 1858-1916,
Spanish; fiction, journalism
SA
INTERIAN de AYALA, Fray Juan,
1656-1730, Spanish; poetry
SA
²IOLO MORGANWG' (Edward
Williams), 1747-1826, Welsh;
poetry ST
ION, 484/81-424/21 B.C., Greek;
poetry SA ST
IONESCO, Eugene, 1912-   ,
Rumanian-French; plays

CON DIC DIF FLE HAR MAL
MAT PIN RIC
IOOR, William, fl. 1780-1830, Ameri-
can; plays KAA
IORGA, Nicolae, 1871-1940, Rumanian;
nonfiction, essays, poetry, plays
COL FLE SA ST
IOSIF, Stefan Octavian, 1875-1913,
Rumanian; poetry HAR ST
IPARRAGUIRRE, José María de,
1820-81, Spanish; poetry SA
IPCAR, Dahlov Zorach, 1917- ,
American; juveniles COM CON
WA
IPSEN, David Carl, 1921- , Ameri-
can; juveniles CON
IPUCHE, Pedro Leandro, 1889- ,
Uruguayan; poetry, fiction,
journalism SA
IPUCHE, Riva Rolina, 1920?- ,
Uruguayan; fiction SA
IQBAL, Sir Muhammad, 1873-1938,
Indian; poetry, nonfiction FLE
LAN SA ST
'IQUA' see BORCHARD, Ruth B.
IRAILH, Augustin Simon, 1719-94,
French; nonfiction DIL SA
IRAJ JALAL al-MAMALIK, Mirza,
1874-1925, Persian; poetry LAN
ST
IRANZO, Miguel Lucas de, 15th cent.,
Spanish; nonfiction SA
IRAQI, Ibrahim (Eraqio),   -1289,
Persian; poetry ST
IRBY, Kenneth, 1936- , American;
poetry MUR
IRELAND, Alan Stuart, 1940- ,
British; poetry MUR
IRELAND, David, 1927- , Australian;
plays, fiction CON
IRELAND, Earl Crowell, 1928- ,
American; nonfiction CON
IRELAND, Joseph Norton, 1817-98,
American; nonfiction KAA
IRELAND, Kevin Mark, 1933- ,
New Zealander; poetry MUR
'IRELAND, Michael' see FIGGIS,
Darrell
IRELAND, Norman Olin, 1907- ,
American; nonfiction CON
IRELAND, William Henry, 1777-1835,
English; fiction BRO ST
IREMONGER, Lucille d'Oyen, Eng-
lish; nonfiction CON
IREMONGER, Valentin, 1918- , Irish;
poetry MUR ST
IRENAEUS, 2nd cent., Roman; nonfic-
tion ST

IRESON, Barbara Francis,
1927- , English; poetry,
juveniles CON
IRIARTE, Juan De, 1702-71,
Spanish; nonfiction BL
IRIARTE, Tomás de, 1750-91,
Spanish; poetry, plays SA
IRIARTE, Tomás de, 1794/95-
1876, Argentinian; nonfiction
MIN BL
IRIARTE y CISNEROS, Juan,
1702-71, Spanish; poetry SA
IRIARTE y OROPESA, Tomás de
(Yriarte), 1750-91, Spanish;
poetry, plays HAR KE ST
IRIBARREN, José María, 1906- ,
Spanish; essays, fiction BL
SA
IRIBARREN, Manuel, 1903- ,
Spanish; fiction, poetry, plays
SA
IRION, Mary Jean, 1922- ,
American; nonfiction CON
IRION, Paul Ernst, 1922- ,
American; nonfiction CON
IRISARRI, Antonio José (Dionisio
Terraza y Rejón), 1786-1868,
Guatemalan; nonfiction BL
SA
IRISARRI, Hermógenes, 1819-
86, Chilean; journalism, poetry
MIN
IRISH, Marian D., 1909- ,
American; nonfiction CON
'IRISH, William' see HOPLEY-
WOOLRICH, Cornell G.
IRIYE, Akira, 1934- , Ameri-
can; nonfiction CON
'IRLAND, David' see GREEN,
Julien
'IRON, Ralph' see SCHREINER,
Olive
'IRONMASTER, Maximus' see
WILKINSON, John D.
'IRONQUILL' see WARE, Eugene
F.
IRVIN, Eric, 1908- , Australian;
poetry MUR
IRVIN, Margaret Elizabeth Con-
nolly, 1916- , Australian;
poetry, criticism MUR
IRVINE, Demar Buel, 1908- ,
American; nonfiction CON
IRVINE, Helen Douglas see
DOUGLAS-IRVINE, Helen
IRVINE, Keith, 1924- , Ameri-
can; nonfiction CON
IRVINE, William, 1906- ,

American; nonfiction KTS

IRVING, Clifford Michael, 1930- ,
American; nonfiction CON

IRVING, David John Caldwell,
1938- , English; nonfiction
CON

IRVING, Edward, 1792-1834, English;
nonfiction BRO KBA

IRVING, Gordon, 1918- , American;
fiction CON

IRVING, John Treat ('John Quod'),
1812-1906, American; fiction,
essays KAA

IRVING, John Winslow, 1942- ,
American; fiction CON

IRVING, Nancy see SEVERN,
William I.

IRVING, Peter, 1771-1838, American;
nonfiction KAA

'IRVING, Robert' see ADLER, Irving

IRVING, Robert Lock Graham,
1877- , English; nonfiction CON

IRVING, Thomas Ballantine, 1914- ,
Canadian-American; nonfiction
CON

IRVING, Washington ('Diedrich
Knickerbocker'), 1783-1859,
American; juveniles, fiction,
essays BL BRO DOY KAA MAG
SA ST

IRVING, William, 1766-1821, American; poetry KAA

'IRVING, William' see SEVERN,
William I.

IRWIN, Constance Freick ('C. H.
Freick'; 'Constance Frick'),
1913- , American; nonfiction
CON

IRWIN, Grace, American; juvenile
WA

IRWIN, Grace Lilian, 1907- ,
Canadian; fiction CON

IRWIN, Inez Haynes, 1873- ,
American; fiction KT

IRWIN, Keith Gordon, 1885-1964,
American; nonfiction CON

IRWIN, Margaret, 1889-1967, English; nonfiction KTS RIC

IRWIN, Patricia K. see PAGE,
Patricia K.

IRWIN, Raymond, 1902- , English;
nonfiction CON

IRWIN, Ruth Beckey, 1906- ,
American; nonfiction CON

IRWIN, Thomas Caulfield, 1823-92,
Irish; poetry, essays ST

IRWIN, Vera Rushforth, 1913- ,
American; nonfiction CON

IRWIN, Wallace Admah, 1876- ,
American; fiction KT

IRWIN, William Henry, 1873- ,
American; fiction KT

IRZYKOWSKI, Karol, 1873-1944,
Polish; criticism ST

ISAAC, Joanne, 1934- , American; juveniles CON

ISAAC, Paul Edward, 1926- ,
American; nonfiction CON

ISAAC, Rael Jean Isaacs, 1933- ,
American; nonfiction CON

ISAAC, Stephen, 1925- , American; nonfiction CON

ISAAC IBN GAYYAT (Giat;
Ghayyath), 1038-89, Spanish-
Jewish; poetry ST

ISAACS, Alan, 1925- , English;
nonfiction CON

ISAACS, E. Elizabeth, 1917- ,
American; nonfiction CON

ISAACS, Harold Robert, 1910- ,
nonfiction CON

ISAACS, Jorge, 1837-95, Colombian; poetry, fiction BL MIN
SA ST

ISAACS, Neil D., 1931- , American; nonfiction CON

ISAACS, Stan, 1929- , American;
nonfiction CON

ISAACSON, Robert L., 1928- ,
American; nonfiction CON

'ISABEL' see MOWATT, Anna
C. O. R.

ISABEL de JESUS, 1586-1648,
Spanish; nonfiction SA

ISABEL of SCHNAUGE, Saint,
1138-65, German; nonfiction
SA

ISCAR PEREYRA, Fernando,
1886- , Spanish; essays,
fiction, journalism SA

ISAEUS, 420-350 B. C., Greek;
nonfiction ST

ISAIS, Juan M., 1926- , American; nonfiction CON

ISAKOWSKI, Mijail, 1900- ,
Russian; poetry SA ST

ISAURA, Clemencia, 15th cent.,
French; nonfiction SA

ISBISTER, Clair, 1915- , Australian; nonfiction CON

ISCANO, Josephus, 1170-1224,
English; poetry SA

ISCHYIUS, Christiaen (Sterck;
Van Vrijaldenhoven), 16th cent.,
Dutch; poetry ST

ISE, John, 1885- , American;

nonfiction CON
ISELI, Beny J., Swiss; nonfiction
SA
'ISELY, Flora Duncan' see DUNCAN,
Kunigunde
ISELY, Helen Sue Pearson, 1917- ,
American; poetry CON
ISEMINGER, Gary, 1937- , Ameri-
can; nonfiction CON
ISENBERG, Irwin M., 1931- , Amer-
ican; nonfiction CON
ISENBERG, Seymour, 1930- , Amer-
ican; nonfiction CON
ISH, Florence Ross, American; non-
fiction SCA
ISHING, Iwao, 1921- , American;
nonfiction CON
ISHQI, Muhammad-Reza, 1893-1923,
Persian; poetry ST
ISHEE, John A., 1934- , American;
nonfiction CON
ISHERWOOD, Christopher William
Bradshaw, 1904- , Anglo-Ameri-
can; fiction, plays BRO CON FLE
KT MAT RIC
ISHIDANZANGWANGJIL, 1854?- ,
Mongolian; poetry LAN
ISHIKAWA, Masomochi ('Ishikawa Gabo'),
1754-1830, Japanese; fiction,
poetry ST
ISHIKAWA TAKUBOKU, 1886-1912,
Japanese; poetry, diary, criticism
FLE LAN ST
ISHISANGBO, 1848- , Mongolian;
fiction LAN
ISH-KISHOR, Judith, 1892- , Ameri-
can; nonfiction CON
ISH-KISHOR, Sulasmith, English;
juveniles, poetry WA
ISHLON, Deborah, 1925- , Lithuanian-
American; fiction CON
ISIDOR, 8th cent., German; nonfiction
AL
ISIDORE de NIORT, 18th cent., French;
nonfiction DIL
ISIDORE of SEVILLE, 570-636, Roman;
nonfiction SA ST
ISILO, 348-280 B.C., Greek; poetry
SA
'ISIS' see TORBETT, Harvey D.L.
'ISIS COPIA' see MAYY
ISLA y LOSADA, María Francisca de,
1735- , Spanish; nonfiction SA
ISLA y ROJO, José Francisco de,
1703-81, Spanish; fiction, transla-
tion BL HAR KE SA ST
ISLE, Walter Whitfield, 1933- ,
American; nonfiction CON

'ISLWYN' (William Thomas),
1832-78, Welsh; poetry ST
ISMAIL, A.H., 1923- , American;
nonfiction CON
ISMAIL, Shah see HATAI
ISNARD, Achille Nicolas,   -1802,
French; nonfiction DIL
ISOCRATES, 436-338 B.C., Greek;
nonfiction ST
ISPIRESCU, Petre, 1830-87,
Rumanian; fiction ST
ISRAEL, Charles Edward, 1920- ,
American; nonfiction CON SY
ISRAEL, Fred L., 1934- , Amer-
ican; nonfiction CON
ISRAEL, Jerry Michael, 1941- ,
American; nonfiction CON
ISRAEL, John Warren, 1935- ,
American; nonfiction CON
ISRAEL, Marion Louise, 1882- ,
American; juveniles CON
ISRAEL, Saul, 1910- , American;
nonfiction CON
ISSA see KOBAYASHI, Issa
'ISSACHAR' see STANFORD, John
K.
ISSAKAKIAN, Avetik, 1875-1957,
Armenian; poetry LAN
ISSAWI, Charles Philip, 1916- ,
American; nonfiction CON
ISSERLES, Moses ('Ramaa'),
1525-72, Polish-Jewish; non-
fiction ST
ISTOMIN, Karion,   -1717, Rus-
sian; poetry HARK
ISTRATI, Panait, 1884-1935,
Rumanian; fiction DIF FLE
HAR KT RIC SA ST
ISWOLSKY, Helen, 1896- ,
Russian-French; nonfiction
CON HOE
ITALIAANDER, Rolf Bruno Maxi-
milian; 1913- , German-
American; nonfiction CON
ITAPARICA, J. Manuel de Santa
Maria, 1704-69, Brazilian;
poetry SA
'ITHACUS' see SHAW, John
'ITO JINSAI' (Ito Koresada),
1627-1705, Japanese; nonfic-
tion ST
'ITO TOGAI' (Ito Nagatane),
1670-1736, Japanese; nonfic-
tion ST
ITURRONDO, Francisco ('Delio'),
1800-68, Spanish-Cuban;
poetry MIN SA
ITZKOFF, Seymour William,

1928- , American; nonfiction
CON
IVIE, Robert M., 1930- , American;
nonfiction CON
IVAN IV the TERRIBLE, 1530-84,
Russian; letters ST
IVAN, Gustave ('Gus Tavo'), Ameri-
can; juveniles WA
IVAN, Martha Miller Pfaff ('Martha
Miller'; 'Gus Tavo'), 1909- ,
American; juveniles CON WA
IVANCEVICH, John M., 1939- ,
American; nonfiction CON
IVANOV, Georgyi Vladimirovich,
1894-1958, Russian; poetry, fic-
tion FLE
IVANOV, Svsevolod Vyacheslavovich,
1895-1963, Russian; fiction COL
FLE HAR HARK MAT RIC SA ST
IVANOV, Vyacheslav Ivanovich, 1866-
1945/49, Russian; fiction, non-
fiction, poetry COL FLE HARK
SA ST
'IVANOV-RAZUMNI' ('Razumnik';
Vasilyevich Ivanov), 1882- ,
Russian; nonfiction ST
IVASK, Ivar Vidrih, 1927- ,
Latvian-American; nonfiction
CON
IVENS, Michael, 1924- , British;
poetry CON MUR
IVES, Burl, 1909- , American;
nonfiction HOO
IVES, Edward Dawson (Sandy), 1925- ,
American; nonfiction CON
'IVES, Lawrence' see WOODS,
Frederich
IVES, Sumner, 1911- , American;
nonfiction CON
'IVNEV, Ryurik' (Mikhail Alexandro-
vich Kovalëv), 1893- , Russian;
poetry, fiction ST
IVO, Lêdo, 1924- , Brazilian; poetry,
fiction RIC
'IVO, Pedro' (Carlos Lopes), 1849-
1909, Portuguese; nonfiction SA
IVO of CHARTRES, Saint, 1040-1116,
French; nonfiction ST
IVOI, Paul Deleutre, 1856-1915,
French; fiction DIF
IVRY, Jean d', fl. 1508-30, French;
nonfiction, translations ST
IWAMATSU, Jun ('Taro Yashima'),
1908- , Japanese-American;
juveniles WA
IWASE SEI see 'SANTO, Kyden'
IWASCKIEWICZ, Jaroslav ('Eleuter'),
1894- , Polish; poetry, fiction,
plays COL FLE MAT SA ST

IWATA, Masakazu, 1917- ,
American; nonfiction CON
'IWAYA, Sazanami' (Iwaya Sueo),
1870-1933, Japanese; juvenile
ST
IXART, José see YXART y
MORAGAS, José
IYENGAR, K. R. Srinivasa, 1908- ,
Indian; nonfiction CON
IYENGAR, S. Kesava, 1894- ,
American; nonfiction CON
IZA ZAMACOLA, Juan Antonio
de, 1756-1826, Spanish; fic-
tion BL SA
IZARD, Barbara, 1926- , Amer-
ican; nonfiction CON
IZMAYLOV, Alexander Yefimovich,
1779-1831, Russian; fiction
HARK ST
'IZUMI KYOKA' (Izumi Kyotaro),
1873-1939, Japanese; fiction
ST
IZUMI, Shikibu, 947-1030,
Japanese; poetry, diary, fic-
tion SA ST

J

JABAVU, Noni, 1921- , South
African; fiction RIC
JABAY, Earl, 1925- , American;
nonfiction CON
JABINEAU, Henri, -1792,
French; nonfiction DIL
JABLONSKI, Edward, 1922- ,
American; juveniles CON
WA
JABLONSKY, Boleslav, 1813-81,
Czech; poetry SA
JABLONSKY, Paul Ernest, 1693-
1757, German; nonfiction SA
JABOATAO, Antonio de Santa
María, 1695-1768, Brazilian;
nonfiction SA
JACCOTTET, Philippe, 1925- ,
French; poetry PIN
JACK, Donald Lamont, 1924- ,
English; fiction CON
'JACK the RIPPER' see CAMPOS,
Jose An.
JACKER, Corinne Litvin, 1933- ,
American; juvenile CON WA
JACKMAN, Edwin Russell, 1894-
1967, American; nonfiction
CON PAC
JACKMAN, Leslie Arthur James,
1919- , English; nonfiction
CON

JACKMAN, Sydney Wayne, 1925- ,
American; nonfiction CON
JACKS, Lawrence Pearsall, 1860-
1955, English; nonfiction BRO
KT RIC
JACKS, Leo Vincent, 1896- , Ameri-
can; fiction HO
JACKSON, Alan, 1938- , Scots; poetry
MUR
JACKSON, Berkley R., 1937- , Amer-
ican; nonfiction CON
JACKSON, C. Paul, American; fiction
HIL
JACKSON, Caary Paul ('Colin
Lochlons'; 'Jack Paulson'),
1902- , American; juveniles
CON WA
JACKSON, Carlton, 1933- , Ameri-
can; nonfiction CON
JACKSON, Carol ('Peter Michaels'),
1911- , American; nonfiction
HO
JACKSON, Charles Reginald, 1903- ,
American; fiction KTS MAG WAF
JACKSON, Chester Oscar, 1901- ,
American; nonfiction CON
JACKSON, Donald Dean, 1919- ,
American; nonfiction CON
JACKSON, Donald De Avila, 1920- ,
American; nonfiction CON
JACKSON, Dorothy Virginia Steinhauer,
1924- , American; fiction CON
JACKSON, Douglas N., 1929- , Amer-
ican; nonfiction CON
JACKSON, Esther Merle, 1922- ,
American; nonfiction CON
JACKSON, Gabriel, 1921- ,
American; nonfiction CON
JACKSON, Gabriele, Bernhard,
1934- , German-American;
nonfiction CON
JACKSON, George Stuyvesant, 1906- ,
American; nonfiction CON
JACKSON, H.C.L., 1894-1954,
American; journalism HIL
JACKSON, Helen Maria Fiske Hunt
('H. H.'; 'Saxe Holm'), 1830-
85, American; poetry, fiction,
essays BRO KAA SA ST
JACKSON, Henry Martin, 1912- ,
American; nonfiction PAC
JACKSON, Henry Rootes, 1820-98,
American; poetry KAA
JACKSON, Hubert Cross, 1917- ,
American; nonfiction CON
JACKSON, Herbert G., Jr.,
1928- , American; nonfiction
CON

JACKSON, Holbrook, 1874-1948,
English; nonfiction BRO KAT
KT
JACKSON, Jacquelyne Johnson,
1932- , American; nonfiction
CON
JACKSON, Jesse, 1908- , Ameri-
can; juveniles CON COM WA
JACKSON, John Arthur, 1929- ,
English; nonfiction CON
JACKSON, John Nicholas, 1925- ,
English; nonfiction CON
JACKSON, Joseph, 1924- , Eng-
lish; nonfiction CON
JACKSON, Joseph Henry, 1894- ,
American; criticism KT
JACKSON, Joy Juanita, 1928- ,
American; nonfiction CON
JACKSON, Kenneth T., 1939- ,
American; nonfiction CON
JACKSON, Laura see RIDING,
Laura
JACKSON, Mary Coleman, Ameri-
can; juveniles WA
JACKSON, Nora see TENNANT,
Nora J.
JACKSON, Norman, 1932- ,
English; poetry CON MUR
JACKSON, Orpha Cook ('O. B.
Jackson'), American; juveniles
WA
JACKSON, Paul R., 1905- ,
American; nonfiction CON
JACKSON, Percival Ephrates,
1891- , American; nonfiction
CON
JACKSON, Peter, 1928- , South
African; poetry MUR
JACKSON, Philip Wesley, 1928- ,
American; nonfiction CON
'JACKSON, R. E.' see INNES,
Rosemary E. J.
JACKSON, Robert, 1911- , Eng-
lish; nonfiction CON
JACKSON, Robert Blake, 1926- ,
American; juveniles CON
WA
JACKSON, Robert J., 1936- ,
Canadian; nonfiction CON
JACKSON, Robert Sumner,
1926- , American; nonfiction
CON
JACKSON, S. Wesley, 1936- ,
American; nonfiction CON
'JACKSON, Sally' see KELLOGG,
Jean
'JACKSON, Sam' see TRUMBO,
Dalton

JACKSON, Shirley, 1919-65, American; juveniles, fiction COM CON KTS WAF

JACKSON, William Godfrey Fothergill, 1917- , English; fiction CON

JACKSON, William Thomas Hobdell, 1915- , English; nonfiction CON

JACKSON, William Turrentine, 1915- , American; nonfiction CON

JACKSON, William Vernon, 1926- , American; nonfiction CON

JACKSON VEYAN, José, 1852-1935, Spanish; poetry, plays SA

JACO, Egbert Gartly, 1923- , American; nonfiction CON

JACOB, Alaric, 1909- , Scots; nonfiction CON

JACOB, Charles E., 1931- , American; nonfiction CON

JACOB, Ernest Fraser, 1894- , English; nonfiction CON

JACOB, Heinrich Eduard, 1889- , German; nonfiction KU

JACOB, Max, 1876-1944, French; poetry COL DIF FLE HAR MAL SA ST

JACOB, Nancy Louise, 1943- , American; nonfiction CON

JACOB, Naomi Ellington, 1884/89-1964, English; fiction BRO HOE KT RIC

JACOB, Paul, 1940- , Indian; poetry MUR

JACOB, Pierre, 18th cent., French; nonfiction DIL

JACOB, Piers Anthony Dillingham ('Piers Anthony'), 1934- , English; nonfiction CON

JACOB, Violet Kennedy-Erskine, 1863-1946, English; poetry, fiction BRO ST

JACOB BEN ASHER ('Ba'al Haturim'; 'Ribah'), 1269-1343, Spanish-Jewish; nonfiction ST

JACOBI, Carl Richard, 1908- , American; fiction CON

JACOBI, Friedrich Heinrich, 1743-1819, German; fiction AL HAR SA ST

JACOBI, Johan Georg, 1740-1814, German; poetry AL SA ST

JACOBI, Jolande Szekacs, 1890- , Hungarian-Swiss; nonfiction CON

JACOBS, Arthur David, 1922- , English; nonfiction CON

JACOBS, Beth, American; juveniles WA

JACOBS, Christian Friedrich Wilhelm, 1764-1847, German; nonfiction SA

JACOBS, Clyde Edward, 1925- , American; nonfiction CON

JACOBS, Daniel Norman, 1925- , American; nonfiction CON

JACOBS, Flora Gill, 1918- , American; juveniles CON WA

JACOBS, Frank, 1929- , American; juveniles, fiction CON WA

JACOBS, Glenn, 1940- , American; nonfiction CON

JACOBS, Harvey, 1915- , American; nonfiction CON

JACOBS, Harvey, 1930- , American; fiction CON

JACOBS, Hayes Benjamin, 1919- , American; fiction, poetry CON

JACOBS, Helen Hull ('H. Braxton Hull'), 1908- , American; nonfiction, juveniles CON WA

JACOBS, Herbert A., 1903- , American; nonfiction CON

JACOBS, Jane, 1916- , American; nonfiction CON

JACOBS, Jerry, 1932- , American; nonfiction CON

JACOBS, John Kedzie, 1918- , American; nonfiction CON

JACOBS, Joseph, 1854-1916, American; juveniles, nonfiction DOY KBA

JACOBS, Leah see GELLIS, Roberta L. J.

JACOBS, Leland B., American; juveniles WA

JACOBS, Louis, 1920- , English; nonfiction CON

JACOBS, Louis Jr., 1921- , American; juveniles COM CON

JACOBS, Melville, 1902- , American; nonfiction CON

JACOBS, Milton, 1920- , American; nonfiction CON

JACOBS, Paul, 1918- , American; nonfiction CON

JACOBS, Pepita Jimenez, 1932- , American; nonfiction CON

JACOBS, Roderick Arnold, 1934- , English; nonfiction CON

'JACOBS, Thomas C. H.' see PENDOWER, Jacques

JACOBS, Walter Darnell ('Peter Oboe'), 1922- , American; nonfiction CON

JACOBS, Wilbur Ripley, 1918- ,
American; nonfiction CON
JACOBS, William Wymark, 1863-
1943, English; fiction BRO KAT
KT RIC ST
JACOBSEN, Jens Peter, 1847-85,
Danish; fiction, poetry COL HAR
KE MAG SA ST
JACOBSEN, Jorgen Frantz, 1900-38,
Danish; fiction HAR ST
JACOBSEN, Josephine, 1908- ,
Canadian; poetry CON
JACOBSEN, Lyle E., 1929- , Amer-
ican; nonfiction CON
JACOBSEN, Ole Irving, 1896- ,
American; poetry CON
JACOBSOHN, Siegfried see OSSIETZKY,
Carl von
JACOBSOHN-LASK, B. see 'LASK,
Berta'
JACOBSON, Dan, 1929- , South
African; fiction CON RIC
JACOBSON, Edmund, 1888- , Ameri-
can; nonfiction CON
JACOBSON, Ethel, American; poetry
CON
JACOBSON, Harold Karan, 1929- ,
American; nonfiction CON
JACOBSON, Howard Boone, 1925- ,
American; nonfiction CON
JACOBSON, Nolan Pliny, 1909- ,
American; nonfiction CON
JACOBSON, Sheldon Albert, 1903- ,
American; nonfiction CON
JACOBSON, 'Spider', 1890- , English;
nonfiction HIG
JACOBUS, Donald Lines, 1887- ,
American; poetry, nonfiction CON
JACOBUS, Elaine Wegener, 1908- ,
American; nonfiction, juveniles
CON
JACOBUS, Lee A., 1935- , Ameri-
can; nonfiction CON
JACOBUS de VORAGINE (Jacopo da
Varazzo; Jaragine), 1228/30-98,
Italian; nonfiction HAR KE SA
ST
JACOBY, Leopold, 1840-95, German;
nonfiction AL
JACOBY, Neil Herman, 1909- ,
American; nonfiction CON
JACOPO da LENTINI (Giacomo),
1185-1240?, Italian; poetry
HAR KE ST
JACOPONE de TODI, Jacopo de
Benedetti, 1250-1306, Italian;
nonfiction, poetry HAR KE SA
ST

JACOT de BOINOD, Bernard Louis
(B. L. Jacot), 1898- , Eng-
lish; fiction CON
JACQUEMART, Gelée, 13th cent.,
French; poetry ST
JACQUEMART, Nicolas François,
1735-99, French; nonfiction
DIL
JACQUEMIN, Nicolas, 1727-1819,
French; nonfiction DIL
JACQUES, Mathieu Joseph, 1736-
1821, French; nonfiction DIL
JACQUES, Robin, 1920- , Eng-
lish; juveniles DOY
JACQUES de VITRY, 1180-1240,
French; nonfiction HAR
JACQUET, Louis, 1732-93,
French; nonfiction DIL
JACQUET, Pierre,   -1766,
French; nonfiction DIL
JACQUIER, P. François, 1711-
88, French; nonfiction DIL
JACQUIER, Maurice,   -1753,
French; nonfiction DIL
JACQUIN, Armand Pierre (Jaquin),
1721-80, French; nonfiction
DIL
JADELOT, Nicolas, 1738-93,
French; nonfiction DIL
JADOS, Stanley S., 1912- ,
Polish-American; nonfiction
CON
JAECK, Gordon Sloan, 1916- ,
American; nonfiction CON
JAEGER, Cyril Karel Stuart,
English; fiction CON
JAEGER, Edmund Carroll, 1887- ,
American; nonfiction CON
JAEGER, Hans, Hendrik, 1854-
1910, Norwegian; fiction,
plays KE ST
JÄGER, Johann see CROTUS,
Rubeanus
JAEGER, Werner Wilhelm,
1888- , German; nonfiction
KU
JAEGHER, Rev. Paul de, 1880- ,
Belgian; nonfiction HO
JAEN, Didier Tisdel, 1933- ,
American; nonfiction CON
JÄNDEL, Ragnar, 1895-1939,
Swedish; poetry COL SA
JÄRNFELT, Arvid (Hilja Kahila),
1861-1932, Finnish; fiction,
plays ST
JAFFA, Harry Victor, 1918- ,
American; nonfiction CON
JAFFE, Abram J., 1912- ,

American; nonfiction CON

JAFFE, Bernard, 1896- , American; nonfiction CON

JAFFE, Dan, 1933- , American; poetry CON MUR

JAFFE, Elsa see BARTLETT, Elsa J.

JAFFE, Eugene D., 1937- , American; nonfiction CON

JAFFE, Frederich, S., 1925- , American; nonfiction CON

JAFFE, Gabriel Vivian ('Vivian Poole'), 1923- , English; nonfiction CON

JAFFE, Harold, 1938- , American; nonfiction CON

JAFFE, Louis Leventhal, 1905- , American; nonfiction CON

JAFFE, Michael, 1923- , English; nonfiction CON

JAGANNATH, Das, 16th cent., Indian; poetry LAN

JAGENDORF, Moritz Adolf, 1888- , Austrian-American; juveniles, plays COM CON FUL WA

JAGGARD, Geoffrey William, 1902- , English; nonfiction CON

JAGGER, John Hubert, 1880- , English; nonfiction CON

JAGO, Richard, 1715-81, English; poetry KB

JAHER, Frederic Cople, 1934- , American; nonfiction CON

JAHIER, Piero, 1884- , Italian; poetry COL SA

JAHIZ, 776?-869, Arab; essays, nonfiction LAN SA

JAHN, Fernand Heinrich, 1789-1828, Danish; nonfiction SA

JAHN, Friedrich Ludwig, 1778-1852, German; nonfiction SA

JAHN, Johan, 1750-1816, German; nonfiction SA

JAHN, Melvin Edward, 1938- , American; nonfiction CON

JAHN, Moritz, 1884- , German; poetry, fiction ST

JAHNN, Hans Henry, 1894-1959, German; fiction, plays AL FLE KU KUN LEN MAT

JAHODA, Gloria ('Adelaide Love'), 1926- , American; nonfiction CON

JAILLOT, Claude Hubert, 1690-1749, French; nonfiction DIL

JAILLOT, Jean Baptiste Michel, 1710-80, French; nonfiction DIL

JAIMES, Julio Lucas, 1840-1910,

Bolivian; poetry MIN SA

JAIMES FREYRE, Raúl, 1887- , Bolivian; poetry MIN

JAIMES FREYRE, Ricardo, 1868/72-1933, Bolivian; poetry, nonfiction, criticism BL MIN FLE SA ST

JAIN, Girilal, 1922- , Indian; nonfiction CON

JAIN, Ravindra Kumar, 1937- , American; nonfiction CON

JAIN, Sagar C., 1930- , American; nonfiction CON

JAIN, Sharad Chandra, 1933- , Indian; nonfiction CON

JAKEMES, 13th cent., French; poetry HAR ST

JAKOBOVITS, Leon Alex, 1938- , American; nonfiction CON

JAKOBS, Karl Heinz, 1929- , German; nonfiction AL

JAKSCH, Wenzel, 1896- , German; nonfiction CON

JAKSHIC, Dura, 1832-78, Serbian; poetry SA ST

JALAL al DIN RUMI see MOWLAVI

JALLABERT, Nicolas, 1700-70, French; nonfiction DIL

JALOUX, Edmond, 1878-1949, French; criticism, fiction COL DIF FK FLE HAR SA ST

JAMAL ZADEH, Siyyid Muhammad Ali, 1897- , Persian; fiction LAN ST

JAMBLICO (Yamblico), 2nd cent., Greek; fiction SA

JAMET, Pierre Charles, -1770, French; nonfiction DIL

JAMES I of SPAIN, 1208-76, Spanish; nonfiction ST

JAMES I, King of Scotland, 1394-1437, English; poetry BRO KB SP ST

JAMES VI, of Scotland and I of England, 1566-1625, English; essays BRO KB ST

'JAMES, Allen' see ALLEN, James L. Jr.

'JAMES, Andrew' see KIRKUP, James

JAMES, Arthur Walter, 1912- , American; nonfiction CON

'JAMES, Brian' see THOMAS, Gordon and TIERNEY, John L.

JAMES, Bruno Scott, 1906- , English; translations,

nonfiction CON
JAMES, Cary Amory, 1935- ,
American; nonfiction CON
JAMES, Charles Lyman, 1934- ,
American; nonfiction CON
JAMES, David Burnett Stephen
('Stephen Vizard'), 1919- , Eng-
lish; nonfiction, fiction CON
JAMES, David Gwilym, 1905- , Eng-
lish; nonfiction CON
JAMES, Denise, American; nonfiction
CON
JAMES, Donald H., 1905- , Ameri-
can; nonfiction CON
JAMES, Dorris Clayton, 1931- ,
American; nonfiction CON
JAMES, Edgar C., 1933- , Ameri-
can; nonfiction CON
JAMES, Edward Topping, 1917- ,
American; nonfiction CON
'JAMES, Edwin' see GUNN, James E.
JAMES, Edwin Oliver, 1889- , Eng-
lish; nonfiction CON
JAMES, Eric Arthur, 1925- , Eng-
lish; nonfiction CON
JAMES, Estelle, 1935- , American;
nonfiction CON
JAMES, Fleming, Jr., 1904- ,
American; nonfiction CON
JAMES, George Payne Rainsford,
1801-60, English; fiction, non-
fiction BRO KBA ST
JAMES, Harry Clebourne, 1896- ,
Canadian; nonfiction CON
JAMES, Henry, 1811-82, American;
nonfiction KAA
JAMES, Henry, 1843-1916, American;
fiction, criticism BRO FLE
KAA KAT MAG MAT RIC SA ST
JAMES, Henry, 1879-1947, American;
nonfiction KT
JAMES, Henry Thomas, 1915- ,
American; nonfiction CON
JAMES, Joseph B., 1912- , Ameri-
can; nonfiction CON
'JAMES, Josephine' see STERNE,
Emma G.
JAMES, Judith see JENNINGS, Leslie
N.
JAMES, Marquis, 1891-1955, Ameri-
can; journalism, nonfiction KT
MAR
'JAMES, Matthew' see LUCEY, James
D.
JAMES, Montague Rhodes, 1862-1936,
English; nonfiction BRO KT RIC
JAMES, Norah Cordner, 1900- ,
English; fiction CON KT

JAMES, Norma Wood, American;
juveniles WA
'JAMES, Paul' see WARBURG,
James P.
JAMES, Philip Seaforth, 1914- ,
English; nonfiction CON
JAMES, Phyllis Dorothy, 1920- ,
English; fiction CON
JAMES, Robert Clarke, 1918- ,
American; nonfiction CON
JAMES, Robert Vidal Rhodes,
1933- , American; nonfiction
CON
'JAMES, Ronald' see PRESTON,
James
'JAMES, Simon' see KUNEN,
James S.
JAMES, Stanley Bloomfield,
1869- , English; nonfiction
HOE
JAMES, Sydney Vincent, Jr.,
1929- , American; nonfiction
CON
JAMES, Thelma Gray, 1899- ,
American; juveniles CON
'JAMES, T. F.' see FLEMING,
Thomas J.
JAMES, Theodore, Jr., 1934- ,
American; nonfiction CON
JAMES, Weldon Bernard, 1912- ,
American; nonfiction CON
JAMES, Will, 1892-1942, Ameri-
can; juveniles, fiction KJU
KT WA
JAMES, William, 1842-1910,
American; nonfiction BRO
KAA MAG SA ST
JAMES, William Louis Gabriel,
English; nonfiction CON
JAMES, William Milbourne,
1881- , English; nonfiction
CON
JAMES, William Roderick, 1892- ,
American; fiction KL
JAMESON, Anna Brownell, 1794-
1860, Irish; criticism BRO
KBA ST SY
JAMESON, Anne Murphy, 1797- ,
Irish; nonfiction SA
'JAMESON, Eric' see TRIMMER,
Eric J.
JAMESON, Malcolm, 1891-1945,
American; juveniles WA
JAMESON, Margaret Storm,
1897- , English; fiction BRO
KL KT RIC
JAMESON, Victor Loyd, 1924- ,
American; fiction CON

JAMET, François Louis, 1713-78,
    French; nonfiction DIL
JAMI, Nur al Din Abd, 1414-92,
    Persian; poetry LAN ST
JAMIESON, John, 1759-1838, Scots;
    nonfiction BRO
JAMIESON, Leland, 1904- , Amer-
    ican; fiction MAR
JAMIESON, Paul Fletcher, 1903- ,
    American; nonfiction CON
JAMIESON, Peter ('Shalder'), British;
    poetry MUR
JAMIL, 660-701, Arab; poetry LAN
JAMIN, Nicolas, 1711-82, French;
    nonfiction DIL
JAMISON, Andrew, 1948- , Ameri-
    can; nonfiction CON
JAMISON, Cecilia Viets Dakin,
    1837?-1909, American; fiction
    KAA
JAMISON, David Flavel, 1810-64,
    American; nonfiction KAA
JAMME, Albert, Joseph, 1916- ,
    Belgian-American; nonfiction
    CON
JAMMES, Francis, 1868-1938,
    French; poetry, fiction COL DIF
    FLE HAR HOE KT MAL SA ST
JAMYN, Amadis, 1540-93?, French;
    poetry DIF SA ST
JAN, George Pokung, 1925- ,
    Chinese-American; nonfiction
    CON
JAN van RUUSBROEC see RUUSBROEC,
    Jan van
JANDA, Kenneth Frank, 1935- ,
    American; nonfiction CON
JANE, Mary Childs, 1909- ,
    American; juveniles, fiction
    CON WA
JANELLE, Pierre, 1891- , French;
    nonfiction HO
JANES, Edward C., 1908- , Ameri-
    can; juveniles WA
JANES, Lewis George, 1844-1901,
    American; nonfiction KAA
JANES OLIVE, José, 1913-56?,
    Spanish; journalism, poetry SA
JANEWAY, Elizabeth Hall, 1913- ,
    American; fiction, nonfiction KTS
    WA WAF
JANGER, Allen Robert, 1932- , Amer-
    ican; nonfiction CON
'JANICE' see BRUSTLEIN, Janice T.
JANICIUS, Lemens (Janicki), 1516-43,
    Polish; poetry HAR ST
JANIFER, Lawrence Mark ('Andrew
    Blake'; 'Larry M. Harris'; 'Mark

Phillips'), 1933- , American;
    fiction CON
JANIN, Jules Gabriel, 1804-74,
    French; fiction, criticism
    HAR SA
JANIN de COMBE BLANCHE,
    Jean, 1731-1811, French;
    nonfiction DIL
JANIS, Irving Lester, 1918- ,
    American; nonfiction CON
JANIS, Jack Harold, 1910- ,
    American; nonfiction CON
JANKELEVITCH, Vladimir,
    1903- , French; nonfiction
    DIF
JANKOWSKY, Kurt Robert,
    1928- , American; nonfiction
    CON
JANNER, Greville Ewan ('Ewan
    Mitchell'), 1928- , Welsh;
    nonfiction CON
JANNEY, Russell, 1884- , Amer-
    ican; fiction WAF
JANNEY, Samuel McPherson,
    1801-80, American; nonfiction
    KAA
JANNSEN, Lydia see 'KOIDULA'
JANNY, Amelia, 1840-1914,
    Portuguese; poetry SA
'JANOSCH' see ECKERT, Horst
JANOWITZ, Morris, 1919- ,
    American; nonfiction CON
JANOWKSY, Oscar Isaiah, 1900- ,
    Polish-American; nonfiction
    CON
'JANS, Emerson' see BIXBY,
    Jerome L.
JANSEN, Clifford J., 1935- ,
    South African; nonfiction CON
'JANSEN, Jared' see CEBULASH,
    Mel
JANSEN, John Frederich, 1918- ,
    American; nonfiction CON
JANSENIO, Cornelius Jansen,
    1585-1638, Dutch; nonfiction
    SA
JANSEVSKIS, Jekabs, 1865-1931,
    Latvian; fiction, poetry, plays
    ST
JANSON, Donald, 1921- ,
    American; nonfiction CON
JANSON, Dora Jane Heineberg,
    American; juveniles WA
'JANSON, Hank' see HOBSON,
    Harry and NORWOOD, Victor
    G. C.
JANSON, Horst Woldemar,
    1913- , American; juveniles

nonfiction CON WA

JANSON, Kristofer Nagel, 1841-1917,
Norwegian; fiction COL HAR SA
ST

JANSON, Ture, 1886- , Finnish; fiction SA

JANSSEN, Lawrence Harm, 1921- ,
American; nonfiction CON

JANSSON, Tove Marika, 1914- ,
Finnish; juveniles CON DOY

JANSZ, Louris, 16th cent., Dutch;
poetry ST

JANTO (Xantus), 6th-5th cent. B.C.,
Greek; nonfiction SA

JANUNCEY, James H., 1916- ,
English; nonfiction CON

JANUS PANNONIUS see CSEZMICZEY,
János

JANVIER, Margaret Thomson ('Margaret Vandegrift'), 1844-1913,
American; fiction, poetry KAA

JANVIER, Thomas Allibone ('Black
Ivory'), 1849-1913, American;
journalism KAA

JANVIER de FLAINVILLE, Jean
François Augustin, 1717-
French; nonfiction DIL

JAPICX, Gysbert, 1603-66, Frisian;
poetry SA ST

JAQUES, Elliott, 1917- , English;
nonfiction CON

JARA, Max, 1886- , Chilean; poetry
MIN

JARA, Ramón Angel, 1852-1917,
Chilean; journalism MIN

JARA CARRILLO, Pedro, 1878-1927,
Spanish; poetry, journalism SA

JARAMILLO ALVARADO, Pio ('Petro-
nio'), 1889- , Ecuadorian; essays,
nonfiction DI

JARD, François, 1675-1768, French;
nonfiction DIL

JARDIEL PONCELA, Enrique, 1901-
52, Spanish; fiction, plays,
journalism BL MAT SA

JARDINE, Jack ('Larry Maddock';
'Howard L. Cory'), 1931- ,
American; fiction, nonfiction
CON

JARES, Joe, 1937- , American;
nonfiction CON

JARIR,   -730, Arab; poetry LAN
ST

JARMAIN, W. Edwin, 1938- ,
Canadian; nonfiction CON

JARMAN, Cosette C., 1909- , New
Zealander; nonfiction CON

JARMAN, Geraint, 1950- , Welsh;

poetry MUR

JARMAN, Jesse E., Jr., 1917- ,
American; nonfiction SCA

JARMAN, Thomas Leckie, 1907- ,
English; nonfiction CON

JARMUTH, Sylvia L., 1922- ,
American; nonfiction CON

JARNEFELT, Arvid, 1861- ,
Finnish; fiction SA

JARNES, Benjamin, 1888-1949,
Spanish; fiction, criticism
BL COL FLE HAR SA ST

JAROMIR ERBEN, Karel, 1811-70,
Czech; poetry SA

JARRELL, Randall, 1914-65,
American; poetry CON FLE
JO KTS RIC SA SP WA

JARRETT, Bede, English; nonfiction HOE

JARRETT, Cora Hardy ('Faraday
Keene'), 1877- , American;
fiction KT

JARRETT, Harold Reginald,
1916- , English; nonfiction
CON

JARRY, Alfred Henri, 1873-1907,
French; poetry, plays, fiction
COL DIF FLE HAR KE MAL
MAT SA ST

JARS, Gabriel, 1732-69, French;
nonfiction DIL

JARVES, James Jackson, 1818-88,
American; nonfiction KAA

JARVIS, Charles, English; translations BL

JARVIS, Frank Washington, 1939- ,
American; nonfiction CON

JARVIS, Frederick Gordon, Jr.
('Fritz Gordon'), 1930- ,
American; fiction CON

JARVIS, Jennifer Mary, 1935- ,
English; nonfiction CON

JARVIS, William Donald, 1913- ,
American; nonfiction CON

JASEN, David Alan, 1937- ,
American; nonfiction CON

JASHEMSKI, Wilhelmina Feemster,
1910- , American; nonfiction
CON

'JASMIN' (Jacques Boé), 1798-1864,
French; poetry HAR ST

JASNORZEWSKA, Marja ('Pawli-
kowska'), 1899-1945, Polish;
poetry, plays COL SA ST

JASNY, Naum, 1883- , Russian-
American; nonfiction CON

'JASON, Johnny' see GLUT,
Donald F.

JASPEDOS, Don Hugo Herrera de
see HERVAS y COBO de la
TORRE, Jose G.

JASPERS, Karl, 1883-1969, German;
nonfiction KTS KU KUN RIC SA

JASTAK, Joseph Florian, 1901- ,
Polish-American; nonfiction CON

JASTROW, Joseph, 1863-1944, American;
nonfiction KT

JASTROW, Robert, 1925- , American;
nonfiction CON

'JASTRUN, Mieczyslaw' (Mieczyslaw
Agatstein), 1903- , Polish; fiction, poetry FLE

JASZI, Jean Yourd, American;
juveniles WA

JAUBERT, Pierre, 1715-80, French;
nonfiction DIL

JAUCOURT, Louis de, 1704-79,
French; nonfiction DIL

JAUFRE, Rudel de Blaya, 12th cent.,
French; poetry DIF HAR KE ST

JAULT, Auguste François, 1700-37,
French; nonfiction DIL

JAURAND, Yvonne ('Yves Duplessis'),
1912- , French; nonfiction CON

JAUREGUI y AGUILAR, Juan de,
1583-1641, Spanish; poetry BL
SA ST

JAUREGUI ROSQUELLAS, Alfredo,
1879- , Bolivian; essays MIN

JAURES, Jean, 1859-1914, French; nonfiction SA

JAUSS, Anne Marie, 1907- , German-
American; juveniles CON WA

JAUSSIN, Louis Amant, -1767,
French; nonfiction DIL

JAVITS, Eric Moses, 1931- , American; nonfiction CON

JAVITS, Jacob Koppel, 1904- , American; nonfiction CON

JAVOROV, Pejo (Kracolov), 1878-1914,
Bulgarian; poetry FLE

JAWORSKI, Irene D., American;
juveniles WA

JAWORSKI, Leon, 1905- , American;
nonfiction CON

JAY, Antoine, 1770-1854, French;
nonfiction SA

JAY, Antony Rupert, 1930- , English;
nonfiction CON

JAY, Eric George, 1907- , English;
nonfiction CON

JAY, John, 1745-1829, American;
essays MAG

JAY, Mae Foster, 1881- , American;
juveniles, fiction HOO

JAY, Peter Antony Charles, 1945- ,

English; poetry MUR

'JAY, Simon' see ALEXANDER,
Colin J.

JAY, William, 1789-1858, American; nonfiction KAA

'JAY BEE' see BRADFORD,
Joseph

JAYABAHU DEVARAKSITA, 14th
cent., Indian; nonfiction LAN

JAYADEVA, 12th cent., Indian;
poetry LAN ST

JAYASI, Malik Muhammad, fl.
1540, Indian; poetry LAN

JAYME, William North, 1925- ,
American; nonfiction CON

JAYNE, Sears, 1920- , American; nonfiction CON

'JAYNES, Clare' (Jane Rothschild
Mayer), 1903- , and Clara
Gatzert Spiegel, 1904- ,
American; fiction CON WA

JAYNES, Ruth, 1899- , American;
juveniles CON

JAZAYERY, Mohammad Ali,
1924- , Irani-American; nonfiction CON

'JEAKE, Samuel, Jr.' see AIKEN,
Conrad P.

JEAL, Tim, 1945- , English;
fiction CON

JEAN, Gabrielle Lucille ('Sister
Jean de Milan'), 1924- ,
American; nonfiction CON

JEAN, Marcel, 1900- , French;
nonfiction CON

JEAN BURIDAN, 1288-1359?,
French; nonfiction SA

JEAN CLOPINEL de MEUNG see
MEUNG, Jean de

JEAN d' ARRAS, 14th cent.,
French; nonfiction DIF HAR
ST

JEAN de JANDUN, -1328,
French; nonfiction ST SA

JEAN DE MEUNG see MEUNG,
Jean de

JEAN de VIGNAI, 14th cent.,
French; nonfiction ST

JEAN FRANCOIS de Dieppe,
18th cent., French; nonfiction
DIL

JEAN le COURT (Brisebarre),
-1340?, French; poetry
ST

'JEAN PAUL' see RICHTER,
Johann P. F.

JEAN RENART, 13th cent., French;
poetry ST

JEANNERAT, Pierre Gabriel, 1902- ,
  French-English; nonfiction CON
JEANNERET-GRIS, Charles Edouard
  see 'LE CORBUSSIER'
JEANS, Sir James Hopwood, 1877-
  1946, English; nonfiction BRO
  KT ST
JEAURAT, Edme Sébastien, 1724-1803,
  French; nonfiction DIL
JEBAVY, Václav Ignac see 'BREZINA,
  Otokar'
JEBB, Hubert Miles, Gladwyn,
  1900- , English; nonfiction CON
JEBB, Sir Richard Claverhouse, 1841-
  1905, English; nonfiction BRO
  KBA
JEDAIAH, ha-Penini Bedersi, 1270?-
  1345?, French-Jewish; poetry
  HAR ST
JEDAMUS, Paul, 1925- , American;
  nonfiction CON
JEDRZEJEWICZ, Waclaw, 1893- ,
  American; nonfiction CON
JEEVES, Malcolm Alexander, 1926- ,
  English; nonfiction CON
JEFFCOTT, Percival Robert,
  1876- , American; nonfiction
  PAC
JEFFERIES, Richard, 1848-87,
  English; juveniles, fiction, es-
  says BRO DOY KBA ST
JEFFERIES, Susan Herring, 1903- ,
  American; fiction CON
JEFFERS, Harry Paul, 1934- ,
  American; juveniles WA
JEFFERS, Jo Johnson, 1931- ,
  American; juveniles, fiction
  CON
JEFFERS, Robinson, 1887-1962, Amer-
  ican; poetry, plays BRO FLE KL
  KT MAG MAT RIC SA SP ST
JEFFERSON, Alan, 1921- , English;
  nonfiction CON
JEFFERSON, Blanche Waugaman,
  1909- , American; nonfiction
  CON
JEFFERSON, Carter Alfred, 1927- ,
  American; nonfiction CON
'JEFFERSON, Ian' see DAVIES,
  Leslie P.
JEFFERSON, Thomas, 1743-1826,
  American; essays BRO MAG
  ST
JEFFERY, Grant ('Peter Paul
  Turner'), 1924- , Canadian;
  nonfiction CON
JEFFERY, Lilian Hamilton, 1915- ,
  English; nonfiction CON

JEFFERY, Ransom, 1943- ,
  American; plays, fiction CON
JEFFREY, Adi-Kent Thomas,
  1916- , American; nonfiction
  CON
JEFFREY, Francis, 1773-1850,
  English; criticism BRO KBA
  ST
JEFFREY, Lloyd Nicholas,
  1918- , American; nonfiction
  CON
JEFFREY, Mildred Mesurac,
  American; fiction, poetry
  CON
JEFFREY, Rosa Griffith Vernter
  Johnson ('Rosa'), 1828-94,
  American; poetry, fiction
  KAA
'JEFFREY, Ruth' see BELL,
  Louise P.
JEFFREY, William, 1896-1946,
  Scots; poetry, journalism BRO
JEFFREYS, Montagu Vaughan
  Castelman, 1900- , American;
  nonfiction CON
JEFFRIES, Charles Joseph,
  1896- , English; nonfiction
  CON
JEFFRIES, Roderic Graeme
  ('Jeffrey Ashford'), 1926- ,
  English; juveniles CON WA
JEFFRIES, Virginia Murrill,
  1911- , American; fiction
  CON
JEFFS, Julian, 1931- , English;
  nonfiction CON
JEFFS, Rae, 1921- , English;
  nonfiction CON
JEFKINS, Frank William, 1920- ,
  English; nonfiction CON
JEGE see NADASI, Ladislav
'JELAKOMITH, Iwan' see HEIJER-
  MANS, Herman
JELF, Wilfrid, -1935, English;
  nonfiction HIG
JELLICOE, Ann, 1928- , English;
  plays MAT RIC
JELLICOE, Geoffrey Alan, 1900- ,
  English; nonfiction CON
JELLICOE, Sidney, 1906- , Eng-
  lish; nonfiction CON
JELLINEK, Oskar, 1886- , Ger-
  man; nonfiction KU
JELLINEK, Paul, 1897- , Aus-
  trian; nonfiction CON
JELLISON, Charles Albert, Jr.,
  1924- , American; nonfiction
  CON

'JELUSICH, Mirko' see KOLBENHEYER, Erwin G.

JENISON, Don P., 1897- , American; fiction CON

JENKINS, Clive, 1926- , Welsh; nonfiction CON

JENKINS, Frances Briggs, 1905- , American; nonfiction CON

JENKINS, Gladys Gardner, 1901- , English; nonfiction CON

JENKINS, Geoffrey, 1920- , South African; fiction CON

JENKINS, Gwyn, 1919- , Welsh; fiction CON

JENKINS, John Geraint, 1929- , Welsh; nonfiction CON

JENKINS, John Robin, 1912- , American; nonfiction CON

JENKINS, Harold, 1909- , English; nonfiction CON

JENKINS, Holt M., 1920- , American; juveniles CON

JENKINS, James Jerome, 1923- , American; nonfiction CON

JENKINS, John Stilwell, 1818-52, American; nonfiction KAA

JENKINS, Michael Romilly Heald, 1936- , American; nonfiction CON

JENKINS, Romilly James Heald, 1907- , English; nonfiction CON

JENKINS, Roy Harris, 1920- , Welsh; nonfiction CON

JENKINS, William Fitzgerald ('Murray Leinster'), 1896- , American; fiction CON

JENKINSON, Edward Bernard, 1930- , American; nonfiction CON

JENKINSON, Michael, 1938- , English; nonfiction CON

JENKS, Almet, 1892- , American; nonfiction CON

JENKS, Clarence Wilfred, 1909- , English; nonfiction CON

JENKS, Randolph, 1913- , American; nonfiction CON

JENNER, Delia, 1944- , English; nonfiction CON

JENNER, William John Francis, 1940- , English; nonfiction CON

JENNESS, Aylette, 1934- , American; juveniles CON

JENNETT, Sean, 1912/16- , Irish; poetry MUR ST

JENNINGS, Edward Morton, III, 1936- , American; nonfiction CON

JENNINGS, Elizabeth Joan, 1926- , British; poetry MUR RIC

JENNINGS, Garry Gayne, 1928- , American; juveniles, fiction CON WA

JENNINGS, James Murray, 1924- , American; nonfiction CON

JENNINGS, Jesse David, 1909- , American; nonfiction CON

JENNINGS, John Edward, Jr. ('Bates Baldwin'; 'Joel Williams'), 1906- , American; fiction CON KTS WA WAF

JENNINGS, Leslie Nelson ('A.B. Brooke'; 'Cyril Cafagne'; 'James McGregor Cartwright'; 'Baroness Julie Desplaines'; 'Judith James'; 'Paul Rayson'), 1890- , American; poetry, essays CON

JENNINGS, Paul Francis, 1918- , English; nonfiction CON

JENNINGS, Richard Wormington, 1907- , American; nonfiction CON

'JENNINGS, S.M.' see MEYER, Jerome S.

JENNINGS, William Dale, 1917- , American; plays, fiction CON

JENNINGS, William Ivor, 1930-65, English; nonfiction CON

'JENNISON, C.S.' see STARBIRD, Kaye

JENNISON, Keith Warren, Canadian; juveniles WA

JENNISON, Peter Saxe, 1922- , American; nonfiction CON

JENOCRATES, 394-14 B.C., Greek; nonfiction SA

JENOFANES, 600-520 B.C., Greek; nonfiction SA

JENOFONTE, 430-355 B.C., Greek; nonfiction SA

JENOFANTE de EPHESUS, 3rd cent., Greek; nonfiction SA

JENS, Walter, 1923- , German; fiction, essays, criticism FLE KU LEN

JENSEN, Adolph E., 1899- , American; nonfiction CON

JENSEN, Ann, American; nonfiction CON

JENSEN, Arthur Robert, 1923- , American; nonfiction CON

JENSEN, Clayne R., 1930- , American; nonfiction CON

JENSEN, David E., American;
juveniles WA
JENSEN, De Lamar, 1925- , American; nonfiction CON
JENSEN, Fritz, 1903-55, German; nonfiction AL
JENSEN, H. James, 1933- , American; nonfiction CON
JENSEN, Irving L., 1920- , American; nonfiction CON
JENSEN, Johannes Vilhelm, 1873-1950, Danish; fiction, poetry, essays COL FLE HAR KAT KT MAG RIC SA ST
JENSEN, John Hjalmar, 1929- , American; nonfiction CON
JENSEN, John Martin, 1893- , American; nonfiction CON
'JENSEN, Julie' see McDONALD, Julie
JENSEN, Lawrence Neil, 1924- , American; nonfiction CON
JENSEN, Mary ten Eyck Bard, 1904-70, American; fiction, juveniles CON
JENSEN, Oliver Ormerod, 1914- , American; nonfiction CON
JENSEN, Paul K., 1916- , Canadian; nonfiction CON
JENSEN, Pauline Marie Long, 1900- , American; nonfiction CON
JENSEN, Richard J., 1941- , American; nonfiction CON
JENSEN, Rolf Arthur, 1912- , English; nonfiction CON
JENSEN, Thit Maria Kirstine Dorothea, 1876- , Danish; fiction ST
JENSEN, Wilhelm, 1837-1911, German; fiction HAR ST
JENSON, Robert William, 1930- , American; nonfiction CON
JENT, John William, 1877- , American; nonfiction MAR
JENTZ, Gaylord A., 1931- , American; nonfiction CON
JENYNS, Soame, 1704-87, English; nonfiction KB
JEPSON, Edgar Alfred, 1863-1938, English; fiction BRO
JEREMIAS, Joachim, 1900- , German; nonfiction CON
JEREMY, Sister Mary, American; poetry CON HO
JERENA, Garci F. see FERRANDES de JERENA, Garcí
JEREZ, Francisco de, 1504-39, Spanish; nonfiction BL

JERICA, Pablo de, 1781-1883?, Spanish; poetry, fiction SA
'JERMAN, Sylvia Paul' see COOPER, Sylvia
JEROME, Saint, 346-420, Greek; nonfiction SA ST
JERONE, Jerome Klapka, 1859-1927, English; fiction, plays BRO KAT KT MAG MAT RIC SA ST
JEROME, Judson, 1927- , American; poetry CON MUR
'JEROME, Mark' see APPLEMAN, Mark J.
JEROME, Stephen, fl. 1604-50, English; nonfiction KB
JEROME de CARDEA, 3rd cent. B.C., Greek; nonfiction SA
JERONIMA de la ASUNCION, fl. 1620, Spanish; nonfiction SA
JERR, William A., American; juveniles WA
JERROLD, Douglas, 1893- , English; nonfiction, fiction BRO HOE
JERROLD, Douglas William, 1803-57, English; plays BRO KBA SA
JERROLD, William Blanchard, 1826-84, English; journalism KBA
JERSILD, Arthur Thomas, 1902- , American; nonfiction CON
JERSILD, Paul Thomas, 1931- , American; nonfiction CON
JESENSKY, Janko, 1874-1945, Slovak; poetry, fiction FLE RIC ST
JESSE, Edward, 1780-1868, English; nonfiction BRO
JESSE, Friniwyd Tennyson, 1889-1958, English; fiction BRO KT
JESSE, John Heneage, 1815-74, English; nonfiction BRO
'JESSE, Michael' see BALDWIN, Michael
JESSEN, Juliana Maria, 1760-1832, Danish; poetry SA
'JESSEY, Cornelia' see SUSSMAN, Cornelia S.
JESSEY, Cornelia, 1910- , American; fiction WAF
JESSOP, Thomas Edmund, 1896- , English; nonfiction CON
JESSOPP, Augustus, 1823-1914, English; nonfiction KBA
JESUS, Sor Ana, 1545- , Spanish; nonfiction SA

JESUS, Carolina Maria de, 1921- ,
   Brazilian; diary, fiction RIC
JESUS, Frei Tomé de, 1529-82,
   Portuguese; nonfiction ST
JETER, Jacquelyn I., 1935- , Amer-
   ican; juveniles CON
JETT, Stephen Clinton, 1938- , Amer-
   ican; nonfiction CON
JETTE, Fernand, 1921- , American;
   nonfiction CON
JEUNE, P. Claude Mansuel,   -1788,
   French; nonfiction DIL
JEVONS, William Stanley, 1835-82,
   English; nonfiction BRO KBA
JEWELL, Derek, 1927- , English;
   nonfiction CON
JEWELL, Edward Alden, 1888- ,
   American; nonfiction, criticism
   KT
JEWELL, Malcolm Edwin, 1928- ,
   American; nonfiction CON
JEWETT, Alyce Lowrie Williams,
   1928- , American; nonfiction
   CON
JEWETT, Eleanore Myers, 1890- ,
   American; fiction, juveniles
   CON FUL
JEWETT, Sarah Orne ('Alice Eliot'),
   1849-1909, American; fiction
   BRO KAA MAG ST WA
JEWSBURY, Geraldine Endsor, 1812-
   80, English; fiction BRO KBA
'JEZ, Thodor Tomasz' (Zygmunt
   Fortunat Milkowski), 1824-1915,
   Polish; fiction ST
JEZARD, Alison, 1919- , English;
   fiction CON
JEZE, 18th cent., French; nonfiction
   DIL
JEZEWSKI, Bohdan Olgierd, 1900- ,
   Polish-English; nonfiction CON
JHABVALA, Ruth Prawer, 1927- ,
   Polish-Indian; fiction CON RIC
JIANOU, Ionel, 1905- , Rumanian-
   French; nonfiction CON
JIDEJIAN, Nina, 1921- , American;
   nonfiction CON
JIJENA SANCHEZ, Rafael, 1904- ,
   Argentinian; poetry MIN SA
JILEMNICKY, Peter, 1901- , Slovak;
   fiction ST
'JIM, Lord' see SUBERCASAUX,
   Benjamín
JIMENEZ, Alberto, Spanish; nonfiction
   BL
JIMENEZ, Auristela Castro de, 1886- ,
   Costa Rican; poetry MIN
JIMENEZ, Juan Ramón, 1881-1958,

Spanish; poetry BL COL FLE
   HAR MAG RIC SA ST
JIMENEZ, Max, 1908-42, Costa
   Rican; poetry MIN
JIMENEZ, Ramón Emilio, 1886- ,
   Dominican; nonfiction, poetry
   MIN SA
JIMENEZ, Salvador, 1922- ,
   Spanish; poetry SA
JIMENEZ de CISNEROS, Francisco
   (Cardenal Cisneros), 1436-
   1517, Spanish; nonfiction BL
JIMENEZ de ENCISO, Diego
   (Ximenez), 1585-1634, Spanish;
   nonfiction, plays BL SA ST
JIMENEZ de PATON, Bartolomé,
   1569-1640, Spanish; nonfiction
   BL SA
JIMENEZ de QUESADA, Gonzalo,
   1502-79, Spanish; fiction SA
JIMENEZ de QUESADA, Gonzalo,
   1496/1502-79, Colombian; non-
   fiction BL MIN
JIMENEZ de RADA, Rodrigo see
   XIMENEZ de RADA, Rodrigo
JIMENEZ de URREA see URREA,
   Jerónimo J. de
JIMENEZ de URREA, Jerónimo,
   1505?-65, Spanish; poetry SA
JIMENEZ de URREA, Pedro Manuel
   (Ximenez), 1486?-1536?,
   Spanish; poetry, fiction BL
   SA ST
JIMENEZ MARTOS, Luis, 1926- ,
   Spanish; poetry, journalism
   SA
JIMENEZ PASTOR, Arturo see
   GIMENEZ PASTOR, Arturo
JIMENEZ RUEDA, Julio, 1896- ,
   Mexican; criticism, plays,
   fiction SA
JINSAI see ITO JINSAI
JIPPENSHA, Ikku, 1865-1831,
   Japanese; fiction, plays LAN
   MAG SA ST
JIRASEK, Lalois, 1851-1930,
   Czech; poetry, fiction, plays
   COL SA ST
JIROKICHI, Debuchi see 'ENCHO'
JISHO see ANDO JISHO
'JISKOGO' see HARRINGTON,
   Mark R.
JNANESVAR, fl. 1290, Indian;
   poetry LAN ST
JOACHIM of FIORE, 1145-1205,
   Italian; nonfiction ST
JOAD, Cyril Edwin Mitchinson,
   1891-1953, English; nonfiction

BRO KT
JOANNET, Claude, 1716-89, French;
nonfiction DIL
JOBAL, François, 1661- , French;
nonfiction DIL
JOBERT, L. P. Louis, 1637-1719,
French; nonfiction DIL
JOBES, Gertrude Blumenthal, 1907- ,
American; nonfiction, fiction CON
JOBIT, Pierre, French; nonfiction BL
JOBST, Clarence F., 1894- , Amer-
ican; play ST
JOCELIN see GUIOT de DIJON
'JOCELYN, Richard' see CLUTTER-
BUCK, Richard
JOCHUMSSON, Matthias, 1835-1920,
Icelandic; plays, translations COL
KE SA ST
JOCKERS, Ernst, 1887- , German-
American; poetry ST
JODELLE, Etienne, 1832-73, French;
plays, poetry DIF HAR KE SA
ST
JOEDICKE, Juergen, 1925- , German;
nonfiction CON
JOEL, 13th cent., Byzantine; nonfic-
tion SA ST
JOELS, Merrill E., American; nonfic-
tion CON
JÖRGENSEN, Johannes, 1866- , Dan-
ish; nonfiction HOE SA
JOFEN, Jean, 1922- , Austrian-Amer-
ican; nonfiction CON
JOFRE, Hermogene, 19th cent.,
Bolivian; plays MIN
'JOHANN, Reinhart d' see MERCK,
Johann H.
JOHANN VON NEUMARKT, 1310-80,
German; translations ST
JOHANN von TEPL, 1350?-1415?,
Bohemian; nonfiction HAR KE ST
JOHANN von WURZBERG, fl. 1314,
German; fiction ST
'JOHANNES a LAPIDE' (J. Heynlin),
1430-96, Swiss; nonfiction ST
JOHANNES de ALTA SILVA, fl. 1184,
German; nonfiction ST
JOHANNES MAGNUS, 1488-1544,
Swedish; nonfiction ST
JOHANNES von SAAZ, 1350-1414,
German; poetry AL
JOHANNESEN, Richard Lee, 1937- ,
American; nonfiction CON
'JOHANNESSON, Olof' see ALFVEN,
Hannes O. G.
JOHANNIS, Theodore Benjamin, Jr.,
1914- , American; nonfiction
CON

JOHANNSEN, Hano D., 1933- ,
German-English; nonfiction
CON
JOHANNSEN, Robert Walter,
1925- , American; nonfiction
CON
JOHANSEN, Dorothy O., 1904- ,
American; nonfiction, juveniles
CON PAC
JOHANSEN, Margaret Alison,
1896- , American; juveniles
WA
JOHANSON, Klara, 1875-1948,
Swedish; criticism, journalism,
essays ST
JOHANSSEN, Ernst, 1898- ,
German; fiction SA
JOHANSSON, Lars (Lucidor),
1638-74, Swedish; poetry HAR
ST
JOHN VI CANTACUZENUS, 1292-
1383, Byzantine; nonfiction
KE ST
JOHN, Elizabeth (Betty) Beaman,
'B. John', Betty John; 'Beth
St. John'), 1907- , Ameri-
can; nonfiction, juveniles CON
JOHN, Errol, 1925?- , West
Indian; plays MAT
'JOHN, Eugenie' see 'MARLITT,
Eugenie'
JOHN, Robert, American; nonfic-
tion CON
JOHN APOSTLE, Saint, 1st cent.,
Jewish; nonfiction SA
JOHN BECCUS, -1293, Byzan-
tine; nonfiction ST
JOHN CHRYSOSTOM, Saint, 344-
407, Greek; nonfiction SA
JOHN CINNAMUS, 1143-95,
Byzantine; nonfiction ST
JOHN, Climax, Saint (Climacus),
525-605, Jewish; nonfiction
SA ST
JOHN CYPARISSIOTES, 14th cent.,
Byzantine; nonfiction ST
JOHN DAMASCUS, Saint, 676-
760?, nonfiction SA
JOHN DOXOPATRES, 11th cent.,
Byzantine; nonfiction ST
JOHN GEOMETRES (Kyriotes),
10th cent., Byzantine; poetry
SA ST
JOHN ITALUS, 11th cent., Byzan-
tine; nonfiction ST
JOHN KYRIOTES see JOHN
GEOMETRES

JOHN MALALAS, 491?-578?, Byzan-
tine; nonfiction ST
JOHN MAUROPOUS, 11th cent.,
Byzantine; nonfiction ST
JOHN MOSCHUS, -1619, Greek;
nonfiction ST
JOHN of ARDERNE, 1307-80, English;
nonfiction ST
JOHN of DAMASCUS, 675-749, Byzan-
tine; nonfiction ST
JOHN of FECAMP, 990-1078, Italian;
nonfiction ST
JOHN of SALISBURY, 1120?-80, Eng-
lish; nonfiction BRO KB SA ST
JOHN of the CROSS see JUAN de la
CRUZ
JOHN of TREVISA, 1326-1402/12,
English; translations BRO KB
ST
JOHN PECHA (Peckham), 1230-92,
English; nonfiction SA ST
JOHN PHILOPONUS, 6th cent.,
Greek; nonfiction ST
JOHN SCYLITZES, 11th cent.,
Byzantine; nonfiction ST
JOHN the LYDIAN, 490- , Byzan-
tine; nonfiction ST
JOHN TZETZES, 1110-80, Byzantine;
poetry ST
JOHN XIPHILINUS, 1010/13-75, Byzan-
tine; nonfiction ST
JOHN ZONARUS, 12th cent., Byzan-
tine; nonfiction ST
JOHNES, Thomas, 1748-1816, Anglo-
Welsh; translations ST
JOHNPOLL, Bernard Keith, 1926- ,
American; nonfiction CON
'JOHNS, Avery' see COUSINS,
Margaret
'JOHNS, Foster' see SELDES, Gilbert
V.
'JOHNS, Geoffrey' see WARNER,
George G. J.
JOHNS, John Edwin, 1921- , Ameri-
can; nonfiction CON
'JOHNS, Kenneth' see BULMER,
Henry K.
JOHNS, Orrick, 1887- , American;
poetry KT
JOHNS, Richard Alton, 1929- , Amer-
ican; nonfiction CON
JOHNS, Warren L., 1929- , American;
nonfiction CON
JOHNS, Captain William Earl, 1893-
1968, English; juveniles DOY
JOHNSON, A. see JOHNSON, Anna-
bell J. and JOHNSON, Edgar
R.

'JOHNSON, A. E.' see JOHNSON,
Annabell and JOHNSON, Edgar
JOHNSON, Alan Packard, 1929- ,
American; nonfiction CON
JOHNSON, Albert, 1904- , Amer-
ican; nonfiction, plays CON
JOHNSON, Alvin, 1874-1971,
American; nonfiction KTS
JOHNSON, Anna see 'DARING,
Hope'
JOHNSON, Annabell Jones ('A.
Johnson'; 'A. E. Johnson'),
1921- , American; fiction
COM CON
JOHNSON, Arnold Waldemar,
1900- , American; nonfiction
CON
JOHNSON, Arthur Menzies,
1921- , American; nonfiction
CON
JOHNSON, B. Pauline, 1905- ,
American; nonfiction PAC
JOHNSON, B. S., 1933- ,
British; poetry, fiction CON
MUR RIC
JOHNSON, Barry Lynn, 1934- ,
American; nonfiction CON
JOHNSON, Benjamin A., 1937- ,
American; nonfiction CON
'JOHNSON, Benjamin F.' see
RILEY, James W.
JOHNSON, Bernard, 1933- ,
English; nonfiction CON
JOHNSON, Bruce, 1933- , Ameri-
can; nonfiction CON
JOHNSON, Byron Lindberg,
1917- , American; nonfiction
CON
JOHNSON, Carl Edward, 1937- ,
American; nonfiction CON
JOHNSON, Carol Virginia, 1928- ,
American; nonfiction CON
JOHNSON, Cecil Edward, 1927- ,
American; nonfiction CON
JOHNSON, Chalmers Ashby,
1931- , American; nonfiction
CON
JOHNSON, Charles Benjamin,
1928- , English; translations,
nonfiction CON
JOHNSON, Charles Ellicott, 1920- ,
American; nonfiction CON
JOHNSON, Charles Frederick,
American; juveniles WA
'JOHNSON, Charles S.' see ED-
WARDS, William B.
JOHNSON, Christopher ('Louis
McIntosh'), 1931- , English;

nonfiction CON
JOHNSON, Claudius Osborne, 1894- ,
American; nonfiction PAC
JOHNSON, Clive White, Jr., 1930- ,
American; nonfiction CON
'JOHNSON, Crockett' see LEISK,
David J.
JOHNSON, Curtis Lee ('Lee Wallek';
'Walter Whiz'), 1928- , American; nonfiction CON
JOHNSON, Dale Arthur, 1936- ,
American; nonfiction CON
JOHNSON, David, 1927- , English;
nonfiction CON
JOHNSON, David Gale, 1916- ,
American; nonfiction CON
JOHNSON, David George, 1906- ,
English; nonfiction CON
JOHNSON, Donald Barton, 1933- ,
American; nonfiction CON
JOHNSON, Donald Bruce, 1921- ,
American; nonfiction CON
JOHNSON, Donald McEwen, 1909- ,
American; nonfiction CON
JOHNSON, Donald McIntosh ('Guy de
Montfort'), 1903- , English;
fiction, nonfiction CON
JOHNSON, Donovan Albert, 1910- ,
American; nonfiction CON
JOHNSON, Dorothy Marie, 1905- ,
American; fiction, juveniles CON
PAC
JOHNSON, Early Ashby, 1917- , American; nonfiction CON
JOHNSON, Edgar, 1901- , American;
nonfiction CON KTS WA
JOHNSON, Edgar Augustus Jerome,
1900- , American; nonfiction
CON
JOHNSON, Edgar Andrew, 1915- ,
American; nonfiction CON
JOHNSON, Edgar Raymond ('A. E.
Johnson'), 1912- , American;
juveniles COM CON
JOHNSON, Edith C., American; nonfiction MAR
JOHNSON, Edward, 1598-1672, American; nonfiction KAA
JOHNSON, Edward Stowers, English;
poetry, fiction CON
JOHNSON, Edward Warren, 1941- ,
American; fiction CON
JOHNSON, Electa Search, 1909- ,
American; nonfiction CON
JOHNSON, Elizabeth, 1911- , American; juveniles CON
JOHNSON, Ellen H., 1910- , American; nonfiction CON

JOHNSON, Elmer Douglas,
1915- , American; nonfiction
CON
JOHNSON, Elmer Hubert, 1917- ,
American; nonfiction CON
JOHNSON, Emily Pauline, 1862-
1913, Canadian; poetry KBA
ST
JOHNSON, Enid, 1892- , American; juveniles WA
JOHNSON, Eric Warner, 1918- ,
American; nonfiction CON
JOHNSON, Eyvind Olof Verner,
1900- , Swedish; fiction
FLE HAR ST
JOHNSON, Falk Simmons, 1913- ,
American; nonfiction CON
JOHNSON, Franklyn Arthur,
1921- , American; nonfiction
CON
JOHNSON, Gaylord, 1884- ,
American; nonfiction CON
JOHNSON, Geoffrey, 1893- ,
English; poetry, translations,
nonfiction CON
JOHNSON, George, 1917- , American; nonfiction CON
JOHNSON, George Orville,
1915- , American; nonfiction
CON
JOHNSON, Gerald White, 1890- ,
American; journalism, fiction
JO KTS WA
JOHNSON, Halvard, 1936- ,
American; poetry CON
JOHNSON, Harold Benjamin, Jr.,
1931- , American; nonfiction
CON
JOHNSON, Harold L., 1924- ,
American; nonfiction CON
JOHNSON, Harold Scholl, 1929- ,
American; nonfiction CON
JOHNSON, Harold V., 1897- ,
American; nonfiction CON
JOHNSON, Harry Gordon, 1923- ,
English; nonfiction CON
JOHNSON, Harry L., 1929- ,
American; nonfiction CON
JOHNSON, Harry Morton, 1917- ,
American; nonfiction CON
JOHNSON, Harvey Leroy, 1904- ,
American; nonfiction CON BL
JOHNSON, Haynes Bonner, 1931- ,
American; fiction CON
JOHNSON, Helen Louise Kendrick,
1844-1917, American; nonfiction KAA
JOHNSON, Herbert Alan, 1934- ,

American; nonfiction CON
JOHNSON, Herbert J., 1933- ,
American; nonfiction CON
JOHNSON, Herbert Webster, 1906- ,
American; nonfiction CON
JOHNSON, Hildegard Binder, 1908- ,
German-American; nonfiction
CON
JOHNSON, Howard Albert, 1915- ,
American; nonfiction CON
JOHNSON, Irma Bolan, 1903- ,
American; juveniles CON
JOHNSON, Irving McClure, 1905- ,
American; nonfiction CON
JOHNSON, Jalmar Edwin, 1905- ,
American; nonfiction CON
JOHNSON, James, -1811, Scots;
nonfiction KBA
JOHNSON, James Henry, 1930- ,
Irish; nonfiction CON
JOHNSON, James Jay, 1939- ,
American; nonfiction CON
JOHNSON, James L., 1927- ,
American; fiction CON
JOHNSON, James Ralph, 1922- ,
American; juveniles COM CON WA
JOHNSON, James Rosser, 1916- ,
American; nonfiction CON
JOHNSON, James Weldon, 1871-1938,
American; poetry, essays, fiction
KL KT
JOHNSON, Jean Dye, 1920- , Amer-
ican; nonfiction CON
JOHNSON, Jinna see JOHNSON,
Virginia
JOHNSON, John J., 1912- , Ameri-
can; nonfiction CON
JOHNSON, Johnni, 1922- , Ameri-
can; nonfiction CON
JOHNSON, Joseph Earl ('Hal Fitz-
gerald'), 1946- , American; non-
fiction CON
JOHNSON, Josephine Winslow, 1910- ,
American; fiction, poetry CON
KT WAF
JOHNSON, Kathryn, 1929- , Amer-
ican; nonfiction CON
JOHNSON, Keith Barnard, 1933- ,
American; nonfiction CON
JOHNSON, Kenneth Mitchell, 1903- ,
American; nonfiction CON
JOHNSON, L.D., 1916- , American;
nonfiction CON
JOHNSON, Lewis Kerr, 1904- ,
American; nonfiction CON
JOHNSON, Lionel Pigot, 1867-1902,
English; poetry, criticism BRO
KBA ST

JOHNSON, Lois Smith, 1894- ,
American; juveniles CON
JOHNSON, Louis, 1924- , New
Zealander; poetry MUR RIC
ST
JOHNSON, Lucius Henry, 1863-
1940, American; plays HOO
JOHNSON, Margaret, 1926- ,
American; nonfiction CON
JOHNSON, Margaret Sweet, 1893- ,
American; juveniles KJU WA
JOHNSON, Marion Georgina Wikeley
('Georgina Masson'), 1912- ,
English; nonfiction CON
JOHNSON, Marshall D., 1935- ,
American; nonfiction CON
'JOHNSON, Martha' see LANSING,
Elizabeth C.
'JOHNSON, Mary Louise' see
KING, Mary L.
JOHNSON, Mary Ritz, 1904- ,
Hungarian-American; nonfic-
tion CON
JOHNSON, Maryanna, 1925- ,
Belgian-American; nonfiction
CON
JOHNSON, Maurice O., 1913- ,
American; nonfiction CON
JOHNSON, Merle Alleson ('Pastor
X.'), 1934- , American;
nonfiction CON
JOHNSON, Nicholas, 1934- ,
American; nonfiction CON
JOHNSON, Olga Weydemeyer,
1901- , American; nonfiction
CON
JOHNSON, Oliver Adolph, 1923- ,
American; nonfiction CON
JOHNSON, Osa Helen Leighty,
1894-1953, American;
juveniles WA
JOHNSON, Owen McMahon,
1878-1952, American;
fiction KL KT
JOHNSON, Pamela Hansford
('Nap Lombard'), 1912- ,
English; fiction BRO CON
KTS RIC
JOHNSON, Patrick Spencer,
1938- , American; nonfiction
CON
JOHNSON, Paul Bede, 1928- ,
English; nonfiction CON
JOHNSON, Paul Emanuel, 1898- ,
American; nonfiction CON
JOHNSON, Paul Victor, 1920- ,
American; nonfiction CON
JOHNSON, Pauline, 1862-1913,

Canadian; poetry SY
JOHNSON, Pauline B., American;
nonfiction CON
JOHNSON, Philip Arthur, 1915- ,
American; nonfiction CON
JOHNSON, Quentin G., 1930- ,
American; nonfiction CON
JOHNSON, Raymond Edward,
1927- , American; fiction
CON
JOHNSON, Richard, 1573-1659?,
English; nonfiction, poetry, fic-
tion BRO KB ST
JOHNSON, Richard August, 1937- ,
American; nonfiction CON
JOHNSON, Richard C., 1919- ,
American; nonfiction CON
JOHNSON, Richard M., 1934- ,
American; nonfiction CON
JOHNSON, Robbin Sinclair, 1946- ,
American; nonfiction CON
JOHNSON, Robert Clyde, 1919- ,
American; nonfiction CON
JOHNSON, Robert E., American;
juveniles WA
JOHNSON, Robert Erwin, 1923- ,
American; nonfiction CON
JOHNSON, Robert J., 1933- ,
American; nonfiction CON
JOHNSON, Robert L., 1919- ,
American; nonfiction CON
JOHNSON, Robert Leon, Jr., 1930- ,
American; nonfiction CON
JOHNSON, Robert Owen, 1926- ,
American; nonfiction CON
JOHNSON, Robert Underwood, 1853-
1937, American; poetry KT
JOHNSON, Robert Willard, 1921- ,
American; nonfiction CON
JOHNSON, Ronald ('Theodore Chamber-
lain'), 1935- , American;
nonfiction, poetry CON MUR
JOHNSON, Ruby Kelley, 1928- ,
American; nonfiction CON
JOHNSON, Russell James, 1917- ,
American; nonfiction CON
JOHNSON, Samuel, 1649-1703, English;
nonfiction BRO
JOHNSON, Samuel, 1696-1772, Amer-
ican; nonfiction KAA
JOHNSON, Samuel, 1709-84, English;
poetry, fiction, essays BRO
KB MAG SA SP ST
JOHNSON, Samuel, 1822-82, American;
hymns KAA
JOHNSON, Samuel Augustus, 1895- ,
American; nonfiction CON
JOHNSON, Samuel Lawrence, 1909- ,

American; nonfiction CON
JOHNSON, Shirley King, 1927- ,
American; juveniles CON
JOHNSON, Siddie Joe, 1905- ,
American; juveniles KJU WA
JOHNSON, Stanley Lewis, 1920- ,
American; nonfiction CON
JOHNSON, Stanley Patrick, 1940- ,
English; fiction CON
JOHNSON, Thomas Burglad,
-1840, English; nonfiction
HIG
JOHNSON, Thomas Frank, 1920- ,
American; nonfiction CON
JOHNSON, Uwe, 1934- , German;
fiction CON FLE KU KUN
RIC
JOHNSON, Van Loran, 1908- ,
American; nonfiction CON
JOHNSON, Vernon Cecil, 1886- ,
English; nonfiction HOE
JOHNSON, Virginia (Jinna),
1914- , American; poetry
CON
JOHNSON, Virginia E., 1925- ,
American; nonfiction CON
JOHNSON, Virginia Wales,
1849-1916, American; juveniles
KAA
JOHNSON, Virginia Weisel ('Vir-
ginia Cousin'), 1910- ,
American; nonfiction CON
PAC
'JOHNSON, W. Bolingbroke' see
BISHOP, Morris
JOHNSON, Walter Frank, Jr.,
1914- , American; nonfiction
CON
JOHNSON, Walter Ryerson,
1901- , American; nonfiction,
fiction, juveniles CON
JOHNSON, Warren Arthur,
1937- , American; nonfiction
CON
JOHNSON, Wendell Story, 1927- ,
American; nonfiction CON
JOHNSON, Wendell Andrew Leroy,
1906-65, American; nonfiction
CON
JOHNSON, William Alexander,
1932- , American; nonfiction
CON
JOHNSON, William Branch,
1893- , English; nonfiction
CON
JOHNSON, William R., American;
nonfiction CON
JOHNSON, William Weber,

1909- , American; juveniles
CON WA
JOHNSON, Winifred MacNally,
1905- , American; nonfiction
CON
JOHNSON-MARSHALL, Percy E. A.,
1915- , English; nonfiction CON
JOHNSSON, Ulrika Vilhelmina see
CANTH, Minna
JOHNSTON, Aaron Montgomery,
1915- , American; nonfiction
CON
JOHNSTON, Agnes C. see DAZEY,
Agnes J.
JOHNSTON, Alexander, 1849-89,
American; nonfiction KAA
JOHNSTON, Angus James, II, 1916- ,
American; nonfiction CON
JOHNSTON, Anna see 'CARBERY,
Eithne'
JOHNSTON, Annie Fellows, 1863-1931,
American; juveniles KT
JOHNSTON, Arthur, 1587-1641, Eng-
lish; poetry BRO ST
JOHNSTON, Arthur, 1924- , English;
nonfiction CON
JOHNSTON, Avin Harry, 1906- ,
American; nonfiction CON
JOHNSTON, Bernard, 1934- , Amer-
ican; nonfiction CON
JOHNSTON, Bernice Houle, 1914- ,
American; nonfiction CON
JOHNSTON, Charles Hepburn, 1912- ,
English; fiction CON
JOHNSTON, Denis, 1901- , Irish;
plays KTS ST
JOHNSTON, Dorothy Greenbock,
1915- , American; juveniles
CON
JOHNSTON, Frances Jonsson, 1925- ,
American; fiction CON
JOHNSTON, George Benson, 1913- ,
Canadian; poetry, translations
CON MUR SY
JOHNSTON, George Burke, 1907- ,
American; nonfiction CON
JOHNSTON, Sir Harry Hamilton,
1858-1927, English; fiction BRO
KT
JOHNSTON, Henry (Hank), 1922- ,
American; nonfiction CON
JOHNSTON, Herbert Leo, 1912- ,
Canadian; nonfiction CON
JOHNSTON, Johanna, American;
juvenile WA
JOHNSTON, John Hubert, 1921- ,
American; nonfiction CON
JOHNSTON, Hugh Anthony Stephen

('A Fighter Pilot'; 'Hugh
Sturton'), 1913-67, English;
nonfiction CON
JOHNSTON, Laurie, American;
juveniles WA
JOHNSTON, Leonard, 1920- ,
English; nonfiction CON
JOHNSTON, Louisa Mae, Ameri-
can; juveniles WA
JOHNSTON, M. Francis, 1900- ,
American; juveniles HOE
JOHNSTON, Mary, 1870-1936,
American; fiction, plays KL
KT MAG
JOHNSTON, Minton Coyne, 1900- ,
Canadian; nonfiction CON
JOHNSTON, Myrtle, 1909- ,
Irish; fiction KT
JOHNSTON, Ralph E., 1902- ,
American; juveniles WA
JOHNSTON, Richard Malcolm,
1822-98, American; fiction
KAA
JOHNSTON, Ronald, 1926- ,
Scots; fiction CON
JOHNSTON, Thomas E., 1931- ,
American; nonfiction CON
JOHNSTON, William, 1925- ,
English; nonfiction CON
JOHNSTON, William Denis,
1901- , Irish; plays CON
MAT
JOHNSTON, William Murray,
1936- , American; nonfiction
CON
JOHNSTON, William Preston,
1831-99, American; nonfiction
KAA
JOHNSTON, Winifred, American;
nonfiction MAR
JOHNSTONE, Charles, 1719?-
1800?, Irish; fiction BRO ST
JOHNSTONE, Henry Webb, Jr.,
1920- , American; nonfiction
CON
JOHNSTONE, Kathleen Yerger,
1906- , American; juveniles
CON
'JOHNSTONE, Ted' see McDANIEL,
David E.
JOHO, Wolfgang, 1908- , German;
nonfiction AL
JOHST, Hanns ('Dietrich Eckart';
'Gerhart Schumann'), 1890- ,
German; plays, poetry, essays
AL COL KU MAT SA
JOINER, Charles Wycliffe,
1916- , American; nonfiction
CON

JOINER, Verna Jones, 1896- ,
American; nonfiction CON
JOINVILLE, Jean de, 1224-1317,
French; nonfiction DIF HAR KE
SA ST
JOKAI, Maurus (Moricz; Mor), 1825-
1904, Hungarian; fiction COL
HAR KE MAG SA ST
JOKOSTRA, Peter, 1912- , German;
nonfiction KU
JOLINON, Joseph, 1887- , French;
fiction DIF
JOLIVEAU, Nicolas René, 1790- ,
French; plays DIL
JOLIVEAU de SEGRAIS, Marie
Madeleine Gehur, 1756-1830,
French; poetry SA
JOLIVET, Regis, 1891- , French;
nonfiction CON
JOLL, Edna Casler, -1963, Ameri-
can; poetry PAC
JOLL, James Bysse, 1918- , English;
nonfiction CON
JOLLIFFE, Harold Richard, 1904- ,
Canadian; nonfiction CON
JOLLIFFE, John Edward Austin,
1891-1964, American; nonfiction
CON
JOLLY, Cyril Arthur, 1910- , Eng-
lish; nonfiction CON
JOLLY, François Antoine, 1672-1753,
French; plays DIL
JOLSEN, Ragnhild Theodora, 1875-
1908, Norwegian; fiction SA ST
JOLY, Cyril Bencraft, 1918- ,
English; fiction CON
JOLY, Jean Pierre, 1697-1774,
French; nonfiction DIL
JOLY, Philippe Louis, 1680-1755,
French; nonfiction DIL
JOLY, R. P. Joseph Romain, 1715-
1805, French; nonfiction DIL
JOLY de FLEURY, Guillaume
François, 1675-1756, French;
nonfiction DIL
JOLY de FLEURY, Jean Omer, 1700-
55, French; nonfiction DIL
JOLY de MAIZEROY, Paul Gidéon,
1719-80, French; nonfiction DIL
JOMART, Norbert, 1671-1738,
French; nonfiction DIL
JOMBERT, Charles Antoine, 1712-84,
French; nonfiction DIL
JONAS, Arthur, 1930- , American;
nonfiction CON
JONAS, Carl, 1913- , American;
fiction CON KTS
JONAS, George, 1935- , Hungarian-

Canadian; plays, poetry CON
MUR
JONAS, Ilsedore B., German-
American; nonfiction CON
JONAS, Klaus Werner, 1920- ,
German-American; nonfiction
CON
JONAS, Manfred, 1927- , Ameri-
can; nonfiction CON
'JONATHAN' see HASEBROEK,
Johannes P.
JONCICH, Geraldine, 1931- ,
American; nonfiction CON
JONCKBLOET, Willem Jozef
Andries, 1817-85, Dutch; non-
fiction ST
JONCOURT, Elie de, 1700-70,
French; translations DIL
JONCOURT, Pierre de, 1650-1725,
French; nonfiction DIL
JONCOUX, Françoise Marguerite
de, 1660-1715, French;
translations DIL
JONCTIJS, Daniel Ewoutsz, 1611-
54, Dutch; poetry ST
JONES, Adrienne, 1915- , Amer-
ican; fiction, juveniles CON
JONES, Alexander, 1906- , Eng-
lish; nonfiction CON
JONES, Amanda Theodosia, 1835-
1914, American; poetry KAA
JONES, Archer, 1926- , Ameri-
can; nonfiction CON
JONES, Archie Neff, 1900- ,
American; nonfiction CON
JONES, Arthur Morris, 1899- ,
English; nonfiction CON
JONES, Barbara, English; nonfic-
tion CON
JONES, Billy Mac, 1925- ,
American; nonfiction CON
JONES, Bob Jr., 1911- , Ameri-
can; nonfiction CON
JONES, Brian, 1938- , British;
poetry MUR
JONES, Carolyn Sue, 1932- ,
American; fiction CON
JONES, Charles, 1910- , Welsh;
nonfiction, fiction CON
JONES, Charles Colcock, Jr.,
1831-93, American; nonfiction
KAA
JONES, Charles Oscar, 1931- ,
American; nonfiction CON
JONES, Charles Victor, 1919- ,
English; fiction, plays CON
JONES, Charles William, 1905- ,
American; nonfiction CON

JONES, Christopher William, 1937- ,
American; poetry CON
JONES, Clifford Merton, 1902- ,
English; nonfiction CON
'JONES, Cork Leg' see JONES,
Thomas
JONES, Cranston E., 1918- , Amer-
ican; nonfiction CON
JONES, Cyril Meredith, 1904- ,
Welsh; nonfiction CON
JONES, Daisy Marvel, 1906- ,
American; nonfiction CON
JONES, Daniel, 1881-1967, English;
nonfiction CON
JONES, David, 1895- , Welsh;
poetry CON MUR RIC SP
JONES, David Gwenallt, 1899- ,
Welsh; poetry ST
JONES, David Mervyn, 1922- ,
English; nonfiction CON
JONES, Donald Lawrence, 1938- ,
American; poetry CON
JONES, Donald Lewis, 1925- ,
English; nonfiction CON
JONES, Dorothy Holder ('Duane
Jones'), 1925- , American;
fiction CON
JONES, Douglas C., 1924- , Amer-
ican; nonfiction CON
JONES, Douglas Gordan, 1929- ,
Canadian; poetry CON MUR SY
'JONES, Duane' see JONES, Dorothy
H.
JONES, Du Pre Anderson, 1937- ,
American; fiction CON
JONES, Ebenezer, 1820-60, English;
poetry BRO KBA ST
JONES, Edward Allen, 1903- ,
American; nonfiction CON
JONES, Edward Ellsworth, 1926- ,
American; nonfiction CON
JONES, Edward Harral, Jr., 1922- ,
American; nonfiction CON
JONES, Elbert Winston, 1911- ,
American; nonfiction CON
JONES, Eli Stanley, 1884- , Ameri-
can; nonfiction KTS
JONES, Elizabeth Orton, 1910- ,
American; juveniles HOO KJU
WA
JONES, Emlyn David, 1912- ,
American; nonfiction CON
JONES, Emrys, 1920- , Welsh;
nonfiction CON
JONES, Endsley Terrence, 1941- ,
American; nonfiction CON
JONES, Ernest Charles, 1819-68,
English; poetry, fiction BRO

KBA ST
JONES, Evan, 1915- , American;
nonfiction CON
JONES, Evan, 1927- , Jamaican;
poetry MUR
JONES, Evan Lloyd, 1931- ,
Australian; poetry MUR
JONES, Eve Spiro-John, 1924- ,
American; nonfiction CON
JONES, Everett Lee, 1915- ,
American; nonfiction CON
JONES, Felix Edward Aylmer
('Felix Aylmer'), 1889- ,
English; nonfiction CON
JONES, Frances Price, 1890- ,
American; nonfiction CON
JONES, Frank Edward, 1917- ,
Canadian; nonfiction CON
JONES, Frank Lancaster, 1937- ,
American; nonfiction CON
JONES, Gary Martin, 1925- ,
Welsh; nonfiction CON
JONES, Gene, 1928- , American;
fiction CON
JONES, George Curtis, 1911- ,
American; nonfiction CON
JONES, George Fenwick, 1916- ,
American; nonfiction CON
JONES, George Hilton, 1924- ,
American; nonfiction CON
JONES, George William, 1931- ,
American; nonfiction CON
JONES, Glyn, 1905/07- , Welsh;
poetry, fiction CON MUR ST
JONES, Goronwy John, 1915- ,
Welsh; nonfiction CON
JONES, Gwendolyn, American;
nonfiction CON
JONES, Gwyn Owain, 1917- ,
Welsh; nonfiction CON
JONES, Harold, 1904- , English;
juveniles DOY
JONES, Helen Hinckley, 1903- ,
American; fiction CON WA
JONES, Henry Arthur, 1851-1929,
English; plays, essays BRO
KAT KBA MAG MAT SA ST
JONES, Henry John Franklin,
1924- , English; nonfiction
CON
JONES, Houston Gwynne, 1924- ,
American; nonfiction CON
JONES, Howard Mumford, 1892- ,
American; poetry, criticism
KTS
JONES, Hugh, 1670-1760, Ameri-
can; nonfiction KAA
JONES, Idwal, 1891- , American;

fiction WAF
JONES, Jack, 1884- , Anglo-Welsh;
fiction, plays ST
JONES, James, 1921- , American;
fiction CON FLE HOO KTS RIC
JONES, Jenkin Lloyd, 1911- ,
American; nonfiction CON
JONES, Jo, English; nonfiction CON
'JONES, Joanna' see BURKE, John F.
JONES, John Beauchamp, 1810-66,
American; fiction KAA
JONES, John Bush, 1940- , American;
nonfiction CON
JONES, John Idris, 1938- , Welsh;
poetry MUR
JONES, John Ithel, 1911- , Welsh;
nonfiction CON
JONES, Joseph Jay, 1907/08- ,
American; nonfiction HIG CON
JONES, Joseph Stevens, 1809-77,
American; plays KAA
JONES, Juanita Nuttall, 1912- ,
American; juveniles WA
JONES, Katharine Macbeth, 1900- ,
American; nonfiction CON
JONES, Kenneth S., 1919- , Ameri-
can; nonfiction CON
JONES, LeRoi, 1934- , American;
poetry, plays, fiction CON
MAT MUR
JONES, Lloid, 1908- , American;
juveniles WA
JONES, Lloyd Scott, 1931- , Ameri-
can; nonfiction CON
JONES, Louis Clark, 1908- ,
American; nonfiction CON
JONES, Madeline Adams, 1913- ,
American; juveniles CON
JONES, Madison Percy, Jr., 1925- ,
American; fiction CON
'JONES, Major' see THOMPSON,
William T.
JONES, Major J., American; non-
fiction CON
JONES, Maldwyn Allen, 1922- ,
American; nonfiction CON
JONES, Marc Edmund, 1888- ,
American; nonfiction CON
JONES, Margaret Boone, 1924- ,
American; juveniles CON
JONES, Margaret E.W., 1938- ,
American; nonfiction CON
JONES, Mary Alice, 1898- ,
American; juvenile CON FUL
WA
JONES, Mary Brush, 1925- ,
American; nonfiction CON
JONES, Mary Voell, 1933- , Amer-

ican; juveniles CON
JONES, Maxwell Shaw, 1907- ,
South African-American; non-
fiction CON
JONES, Morris Val, 1914- ,
American; nonfiction CON
JONES, Nard, 1904- , American;
nonfiction PAC
JONES, Oakah L., Jr., 1930- ,
American; nonfiction CON
'JONES, Orlando' see LOOKER,
Antonina H.
JONES, Owen Rogers, 1922- ,
English; nonfiction CON
'JONES, Pat' see JONES, Virgil
C.
JONES, Peter, 1921- , English;
juveniles CON
JONES, Peter d'Alroy, 1931- ,
English; nonfiction CON
JONES, Pirkle, 1914- , Ameri-
can; nonfiction CON
JONES, R.O., 1925- , English;
nonfiction BL
JONES, Richard, 1790-1855, Eng-
lish; nonfiction KBA
JONES, Richard Benjamin, 1933- ,
English; nonfiction CON
JONES, Richard Lloyd, 1873- ,
American; nonfiction MAR
JONES, Robert Ambrose see
'EMRYS ap IWAN'
JONES, Robert Emmet, 1928- ,
American; nonfiction CON
JONES, Robert Epes, 1908- ,
American; nonfiction CON
JONES, Robert Huhn, 1927- ,
American; nonfiction CON
JONES, Robert Owen, 1928- ,
American; nonfiction CON
JONES, Ruby A. Hiday, 1908- ,
American; poetry CON
JONES, Rufus Matthew, 1863-
1948, American; nonfiction
KTS
JONES, Russell Bradley, 1894- ,
American; nonfiction CON
JONES, Scott N., 1929- , Ameri-
can; nonfiction CON
JONES, Stacy Vanderhoff, 1894- ,
American; nonfiction CON
JONES, Stanley Llewellyn, 1918- ,
American; nonfiction CON
JONES, Thomas ('Cork Leg Jones'),
fl. 1750, English; nonfiction
HIG
JONES, Thomas B., 1929- ,
American; nonfiction CON

JONES, Thomas C., American;
nonfiction, fiction SCA
JONES, Thomas Gwynn, 1871-1949,
Welsh; poetry ST
JONES, Thomas Martin, 1916- ,
American; nonfiction CON
JONES, Vane A., 1917- , American;
nonfiction CON
JONES, Virgil Carrington ('Pat Jones'),
1906- , American; nonfiction
CON
JONES, Walter Benton, 1893- ,
American; nonfiction CON
JONES, Walter Paul, 1891- , Amer-
ican; nonfiction CON
JONES, Ward, 1904- , American;
fiction WAF
'JONES, Webb' see HENLEY, Arthur
JONES, Weyman, 1928- , American;
juveniles CON WA
'JONES, Capt. Wilbur' see EDWARDS,
William B.
JONES, Wilbur Devereux, 1916- ,
American; nonfiction CON
JONES, Sir William, 1746-94, English;
nonfiction BRO KB ST
JONES, William Alfred, 1817-1900,
American; criticism, essays KAA
JONES, William McKendrey, 1927- ,
American; nonfiction CON
JONES, William Powell, 1901- , Amer-
ican; nonfiction CON
JONES, William Thomas, 1910- ,
American; nonfiction CON
JONES, Willis Knapp, 1895- , Ameri-
can; nonfiction CON
JONES-EVANS, Eric, 1898- , Ameri-
can; plays CON
JONG see DE JONG
JONG, Adrianus Michael de, 1888-
1943, Dutch; fiction ST
'JONGE, Ierus de' see HOEN,
Pieter
JONGHE, Adriaen de see JUNIUS,
Hadrianus
JONK, Clarence, 1906- , American;
nonfiction, poetry, juveniles,
fiction CON
JONKLAAS, David, 1932- , Ceylonese;
poetry MUR
JONSEN, Albert Rupert, 1931- ,
American; nonfiction CON
JONSON, Ben, 1572?-1637, Scots; plays,
poetry BRO KB MAG SA SP ST
JONSSON, Finnur, 1858- , Finnish;
nonfiction SA
JONSSON, Hjalmar ('Bólu-Hjálmar),
1796-1875, Icelandic; poetry

SA ST
JONSSON, Karl, 1134-1213,
Icelandic; fiction ST
JOOS, Martin George, 1907- ,
American; nonfiction CON
JOOST, Nicholas Teynac, 1916- ,
American; nonfiction CON
JORAVSKY, David, 1925- ,
American; nonfiction CON
JORDA y CALBO, Evaldo C.,
1891- , Spanish; nonfiction
SA
JORDAN, Alma Theodora, 1929- ,
West Indian; nonfiction CON
JORDAN, Amos Azariah, 1922- ,
American; nonfiction CON
JORDAN, Charles Etienne, 1700-
45, French; nonfiction DIL
JORDAN, Clarence Leonard,
1912- , American; nonfiction
CON
JORDAN, David Malcolm, 1935- ,
American; nonfiction CON
JORDAN, Elizabeth, 1868-1947,
American; fiction, plays,
essays HOE
'JORDAN, Gail' see DERN, Peggy
G.
JORDAN, Gerald Ray, 1896-1964,
American; nonfiction CON
JORDAN, Grace Edgington, Amer-
ican; journalism, fiction
CON PAC
JORDAN, Helen R.A. see ASHTON,
Helen R.J.
JORDAN, John Emory, 1919- ,
American; nonfiction CON
JORDAN, Jorgu, Rumanian; nonfic-
tion BL
JORDAN, June ('June Meyer'),
1936- , American; fiction
CON
JORDAN, Luis María, 1883-1926/
33, Argentinian; poetry, fiction
MIN
JORDAN, Max, 1895- , American;
nonfiction HOE
JORDAN, Mildred, 1901- ,
American; fiction CON KTS
WAF
JORDAN, Norman, 1938- ,
American; poetry CON
JORDAN, Patrick M., 1941- ,
American; nonfiction CON
JORDAN, Philip Dillon, 1903- ,
American; juveniles CON
WA
JORDAN, Robert Paul, 1921- ,

American; nonfiction CON
JORDAN, Stello, 1914- , American;
nonfiction CON
JORDAN, Terry Gilbert, 1938- ,
American; nonfiction CON
JORDAN, Thomas, 1612-85, English;
plays, poetry ST
JORDAN, Thurston C., Jr., 1940- ,
American; nonfiction CON
JORDAN, Weymouth Tyree, 1912- ,
American; nonfiction CON
JORDAN, Wilbur Kitchener, 1902- ,
American; nonfiction CON
JORDAN, Wilhelm, 1819-1904, Ger-
man; poetry AL HAR ST
JORDAN, William A., 1928- , Amer-
ican; nonfiction CON
JORDAN, William Stone, Jr., 1917- ,
American; nonfiction CON
JORDAN, Winthrop Donaldson,
1931- , American; nonfiction
CON
JORDAN, Zbigniew A., 1911- ,
Polish-Canadian; nonfiction CON
JORDANES, fl. 550, Goth; nonfiction
ST
JORDEN, Eleanor Harz, American;
nonfiction CON
JORDI de SANT JORDI, 14th cent.,
Spanish; poetry SA
JORDY, William Henry, 1917- , Amer-
ican; nonfiction CON
JORE, Claude François, 1699-1775,
French; nonfiction DIL
JORGE PISIDIO, 12th cent., Byzantine;
poetry SA
JORGE de TREBISONDA, 1396-1485,
Byzantine; translations SA
'JORGE PITILLAS' see HERVAS y
COBO de la TORRE, Jose G.
JORGENSEN, Jens Johannes, 1866-
1956, Danish; poetry, fiction,
essays COL FLE ST
JORGENSEN, Mary V. see VENN,
Mary E.
'JORGENSON, Ivar' see SILVERBERG,
Robert
JORISZ, David, 1501-56, Dutch;
poetry ST
JORRIN, José Silverio, 1816-97,
Cuban; nonfiction MIN
JORSTAD, Erling Theofore, 1930- ,
American; nonfiction CON
JORTIN, John, 1698-1770, English;
nonfiction BRO ST
JOSCELYN, Archie L. ('A.A. Archer';
'Al Cody'; 'Tex Holt'; 'Evelyn
McKenna'; 'Lynn Westland'),

1899- , American; fiction
CON PAC
JOSE, James Robert, 1939- ,
American; nonfiction CON
JOSE ben JOSE see YOSE BEN
YOSE
JOSE BONIFACIO see ANDRADE
y SILVA, José B.
JOSEPH, Alexander, 1907- ,
American; juveniles CON
WA
JOSEPH, Bertram Leon, 1915- ,
Welsh-American; nonfiction
CON
JOSEPH, David I., 1941- ,
American; nonfiction CON
JOSEPH, Donald, 1898- , Amer-
ican; fiction WAF
JOSEPH, James Herz ('Lowell
Adams'), 1924- , American;
nonfiction CON
JOSEPH, Joan Levy, 1939- ,
Israeli; juveniles CON
JOSEPH, John, 1923- , Ameri-
can; nonfiction CON
'JOSEPH, Jonathan' see FINEMAN,
Irving
JOSEPH, Joseph Maron, 1903- ,
American; nonfiction CON
JOSEPH, Marie de Besancon,
1719-90, French; nonfiction
DIL
JOSEPH, Michael Kennedy,
1914- , New Zealander;
poetry, fiction CON MUR RIC
ST
JOSEPH, Richard, 1910- ,
American; nonfiction CON
JOSEPH, Stephen, 1921- , Eng-
lish; nonfiction CON
JOSEPH, Stephen M. ('Bic Water-
man'), 1938- , American;
nonfiction CON
JOSEPH GENESIUS, 10th cent.,
Byzantine; nonfiction ST
JOSEPH of EXETER, -1210,
English; poetry ST
JOSEPH of SICILY, 9th cent.,
Byzantine; nonfiction ST
JOSEPH VOLOTSKY, 15th cent.,
Russian; nonfiction ST
JOSEPHS, Ray ('Jay Raphael'),
1912- , American; nonfiction
CON
JOSEPHSON, Clifford A., 1922- ,
American; nonfiction CON
JOSEPHSON, Hannah, 1900- ,
American; nonfiction CON

JOSEPHSON, Matthew, 1899- ,
American; criticism, nonfic-
tion KL KT
JOSEPHSON, Ragnar, 1891- ,
Swedish; poetry, plays MAT ST
JOSEPHUS, Flavius (Hegesippus),
37-100, Jewish; nonfiction SA ST
JOSEPHY, Alvin M., Jr., 1915- ,
American; nonfiction CON
JOSEY, Elonnie Junius, 1924- ,
American; nonfiction CON
JOSHUA, Wynfred, 1930- , Ameri-
can; nonfiction CON
JOSI, Gaurisankar Govardhanram,
1892- , Indian; fiction LAN
JOSI, Umasankar Jethalal, 1917- ,
Indian; poetry, criticism LAN
'JOSIAH Allen's Wife' see HOLLEY,
Marietta
JOSIKA, Miklós, 1794-1865, Hungarian;
fiction HAR ST
JOSIPOVICI, Gabriel, 1940- ,
French; nonfiction, fiction CON
JOSLIN, Sesyle Hene ('Josephine
Gibson'; 'G.B. Kirtland'), 1929- ,
American; juveniles COM CON
WA
JOSSE, 18th cent., French; plays
DIL
JOTOV, Dimitur Ivanov see 'ELIN
PELIN'
JOTUNI, Maria Kustaava Hagrén,
1890- , Finnish; fiction, plays
ST
JOUBERT, François, 1689-1763,
French; nonfiction DIL
JOUBERT, Joseph, 1754-1824, French;
nonfiction DIF MAL SA
JOUBERT, Pierre, 18th cent., French;
nonfiction DIL
JOUFFROY, Théodore Simon, 1796-
1842, French; nonfiction DIF
SA
'JOUHANDEAU, Marcel' (Marcel
Provence), 1888- , French;
fiction COL DIF FLE HAR MAL
SA ST
JOUIN, Nicolas, 1684-1757, French;
nonfiction DIL
JOUKOVSKI, Vasili Andrevich, 1783-
1852, Russian; plays SA
JOULLAIN, F.C., 18th cent., French;
nonfiction DIL
JOURDAIN, François Claude Maur,
1721-82, French; nonfiction DIL
JOURDAN, Jean Baptiste, 1711-93,
French; plays DIL
JOUVANCY, Joseph de (Jouvency),

1643-1719, French; nonfiction
DIL
JOUVE, Joseph, 1701-58, French;
nonfiction DIL
JOUVE, Pierre Jean, 1887- ,
French; poetry, essays, fic-
tion COL DIC DIF FLE HAR
MAL SA ST
JOUVENEL des URSINS, Jean,
1388-1473, French; nonfiction
ST
JOUVET, Louis Jules Eugene Louis,
1887-1951, French; criticism
COL FLE
JOUY, Victor Joseph Etienne,
1764-1846, French; nonfiction
DIF SA
JOVANOVIC, Jovan Zmaj, 1833-
1904, Serbian; poetry SA ST
JOVE, José María, 1920- ,
Spanish; fiction SA
JOVELLANOS, Gaspar Melchor de,
1744-1811, Spanish; nonfiction,
poetry, plays BL HAR KE
SA ST
JOVET, Jorge see 'INDO, Claudio'
JOVINE, Francesco, 1902-50,
Italian; fiction, plays FLE
HAR SA ST
JOWETT, Benjamin, 1817-93/98,
English; nonfiction, translations
BRO KBA ST
JOWIARD, Sidney Marshall,
1926- , Canadian; nonfiction
CON
JOY, Barbara Ellen, 1898- ,
American; nonfiction CON
JOY, Charles Rhind, 1885- ,
American; juveniles WA
JOY, Donald Martin, 1928- ,
American; nonfiction CON
JOY, Edward Thomas, 1909- ,
English; nonfiction CON
JOY, Kenneth Ernest, 1908- ,
American; nonfiction CON
JOYCE, Ernest, 1899- , Ameri-
can; nonfiction CON
JOYCE, George Hayward, 1864-
1943, English; nonfiction
HOE
JOYCE, James Augustin Aloysius,
1882-1941, Irish; fiction,
poetry, plays BRO FLE KL
KT MAG MAT RIC SA ST
JOYCE, James Daniel, 1921- ,
American; nonfiction CON
JOYCE, John Alexander, 1842- ,
American; poetry, essays KAA

JUDY, Marvin Thornton, 1911- ,
American; nonfiction CON
JUDY, William Lewis ('Wymar Port'),
1891- , American; nonfiction
CON
JÜNGER, Ernst, 1895- , German;
fiction, essays AL COL FLE
HAR KTS KU KUN LEN RIC ST
JÜNGER, Friedrich Georg, 1898- ,
German; poetry, essays, fiction
AL FLE KU LEN
JUENIN, Gaspard, 1650-1713, French;
nonfiction DIL
JUENIN, Pierre, 1668-1747, French;
nonfiction DIL
JUERGENSEN, Hans, 1919- , Ger-
man-American; nonfiction, poetry
CON
JUFRE de AGUILA, Melchor, Chilean;
nonfiction MIN
JUHANI, Aho, 1861-1921, Finnish;
fiction SA
JUHASZ, Leslie A. see SHEPARD,
Leslie A.
JUILLARD, Laurent, 1658-1730,
French; poetry DIL
JUILLY, Bernard Joseph, 1728- ,
French; nonfiction, poetry DIL
JUKES, John Thomas Geoffrey,
1928- , Australian; nonfiction
CON
JUKOVSKI, Vassili A., 1786-1852,
Russian; poetry SA
JULES-BOIS, Henri Antoine, 1869-
1943, French; plays, fiction,
essays, poetry, nonfiction HOE
JULIA MARTINEZ, Eduardo, 1887- ,
Spanish; nonfiction BL SA
JULIAN, Constance, 1863- , Aus-
tralian; nonfiction HO
JULIAN, Flavius Claudius ('Julian
the Apostate'), 331-63, Roman;
nonfiction ST
JULIAN, Nancy R., American;
juveniles WA
JULIAN de TOLEDO, San, -690,
Spanish; nonfiction SA
JULIANA of NORWICH (Julian),
1342?-1413, English; nonfiction
BRO ST
'JULIE, Sister', 1868-1947, English;
nonfiction HOE
JULIER, Virginia Cheatham, 1918- ,
American; juveniles CON
JULIN, Joseph R., 1926- , Ameri-
can; nonfiction CON
JULINE, Ruth Bishop, 1900- ,
American; fiction CON

JULITTE, Pierre Gaston Louis,
1910- , French; nonfiction
CON
JULIUS, Flavius Claudius, 331-66,
Roman; nonfiction SA
JULLAIN, Philippe, 1919- ,
French; fiction DIC
JULLIAN, Camille, 1859-1933,
French; nonfiction DIF
JULLIEN, Jean Thomas Edouard,
1854-1919, French; plays
MAT
JUMPER, Andrew Albert,
1927- , American; nonfiction
CON
'JUMPP, Hugo' see MacPEEK,
Walter G.
JUNCO, Alfonso, 1896- , Mexican;
journalism, essays, poetry
SA
'JUNE, Jennie' see CROLY, Jane
C.
JUNG, Carl Gustav, 1875- ,
Swiss; nonfiction KT KU
KUN SA
JUNG, Franz, 1888- , German;
nonfiction KU
JUNG, Hwa Yol, 1932- , Ameri-
can; nonfiction CON
JUNG, John A., 1937- , Ameri-
can; nonfiction CON
JUNGER, Ernst, 1895- ,
German; fiction, essays SA
'JUNGLE DOCTOR' see WHITE,
Paul H. H.
JUNGMANN, Josef Jakub, 1773-
1847, Czech; nonfiction, criti-
cism, poetry KE SA ST
JUNGMANN, Rev. Joseph Andrew,
1889- , German; nonfiction
HO
JUNG-STILLING, Johann Heinrich
('Heinrich Stilling'), 1740-1817,
German; nonfiction AL HAR
ST
'JUNIUS', fl. 1769-71, English;
letters BRO ST
'JUNIUS' see also FRANCIS, Sir
Philip
JUNIUS, Franciscus (Francis;
Franz; Du Jon; Francois),
1589-1677, English; nonfiction
KB ST
JUNIUS, Hadrianus (Adriaen de
Johghe), 1511-75, Dutch;
poetry ST
JUNKER, Georges Adam, 1720-
1805, French; nonfiction DIL

JUNKER, Karen Stensland, 1916- ,
Swedish; fiction CON
JUNKINS, Donald, 1931- , Ameri-
can; poetry CON
JUNQUEIRA FREIRE, Luis José,
1832-55, Brazilian; poetry SA
JUNQUEIRO, Abílio M.G. see
GUERRA JUNQUEIRO, Abílio
JUNQUIERIS, Jean Baptiste de, 1713-
86, French; nonfiction DIL
JUPO, Frank J., 1904- , German-
American; juveniles, fiction CON
WA
JUPP, James, 1932- , English; nonfic-
tion CON
JUPTNER, Joseph Paul, 1913- ,
American; nonfiction CON
JURADO de la PARRA, José, 1856-
1915, Spanish; poetry, plays SA
JURADO MORALES, José, 1900- ,
Spanish; poetry, plays SA
JURAIN, Henri, 18th cent., French;
nonfiction DIL
JURCIC, Josip, 1844-81, Slovene;
poetry, fiction ST
JURGENSEN, Barbara Bitting,
1928- , American; fiction CON
JURIEU, Pierre, 1637-1713, French;
nonfiction DIL
JURJANI (Abd al-Qahir), -1078,
Arab; nonfiction LAN
JURJEVICH Ratibor-Ray Momchilo,
1915- , Yugoslav-American;
nonfiction CON
JURJI, Edward J., 1907- , Syrian-
American; nonfiction CON
JURKOVIC, Janko, 1827-89, Croatian;
fiction, plays ST
JUSSAWALLA, Adil Jehangir, 1940- ,
Indian; poetry MUR
JUSSERAND, Jean Adrien Antoine
Jules, 1855-1932, French; non-
fiction KT
JUST, Belá, 1906-54, Hungarian;
fiction FLE
JUST, Ward Swift, 1935- , Ameri-
can; nonfiction CON
JUSTER, Norton, 20th cent., Ameri-
can; juveniles CON DOY
JUSTICE, Donald Rodney, 1925- ,
American; poetry CON MUR
'JUSTICIAR' see POWELL-SMITH,
Vincent W. F.
JUSTIN, Saint, 2nd cent., Roman;
nonfiction SA
JUSTIN MARTYR, 100-65, Greek;
nonfiction ST
JUSTINUS, Marcus Junianus, 2nd-

3rd cent., Roman; nonfiction
SA ST
JUSTIZ y de VALLE, Tomás
Juan de, 1872- , Cuban;
fiction, plays, essays MIN
JUSTO, Jaan Bautista, 1865-1928,
Argentinian; nonfiction MIN
JUSTUS, May, 1898- , American;
juveniles COM CON KJU WA
JUTIKKALA, Eino Kaarlo Ilmari,
1907- , Finnish; nonfiction
CON
JUVENAL (Decimus Junius
Juvenalis), 55-135, Roman;
poetry MAG SA ST
JUVENCUS, Gaius Vettius, 4th
cent., Spanish; nonfiction SA
ST
JUVENAL de CARLENCAS, Félix
de, 1679-1760, French; non-
fiction DIL
JUVENTIN, Jean Jacques, 1741-
1801, French; nonfiction DIL

K

'K. R.' see ROMANOV, Konstantin
R.
KAAB, Ben Zohaih, Arab; poetry
SA
KAALUND, Hans Vilhelm, 1818-
85, Danish; poetry ST
KA'B IBN ZUHAYR, 17th cent.,
Arab; poetry ST
KABAK, Abraham Aba, 1880-1944,
Jewish; fiction, criticism ST
KABIR, 1430-1518?, Indian;
poetry LAN SA ST
KABRAJI, Fredoon, 1897- ,
Indian; nonfiction, poetry CON
KACIC-MEOSIC, Andrija, 1704-60,
Dalmatian; poetry ST
KACZER, Illes, 1887- , Hungarian;
fiction, plays CON
KACZKOWSKI, Zygmunt, 1825-96,
Polish; fiction ST
KADA AZUMAMARO, 1669-1736,
Japanese; nonfiction ST
KADAI, Heino Olavi, 1931- ,
Estonian-American; nonfiction
CON
KADARI, Shraga, 1907- , Jewish;
fiction ST
KADE BANDROWSKI, Juliusz,
1885-1944, Polish; nonfiction
HAR
KADEN, Juljusz see BANDROWSKI,

Juljusz
KADLER, Henry Eric, 1922- ,
Czech-American; nonfiction CON
KADLUBEK, Vicente, 1161-1223,
Polish; nonfiction SA ST
KADRI, Yakup, 1888- , Turkish;
fiction SA
KADUSHIN, Alfred, 1916- , Ameri-
can; nonfiction CON
KADUSHIN, Charles, 1932- , Ameri-
can; nonfiction CON
KAEGI, Walter Emil, Jr., 1937- ,
American; nonfiction CON
KAELBLING, Rudolf, 1928- , Ger-
man-American; nonfiction CON
KÄMPCHEN, Heinrich, 1847-1912,
German; nonfiction AL
KÄSTNER, Abraham Gotthelf, 1719-
1800, German; nonfiction AL
KÄSTNER, Erhart, 1904- , German;
essays, fiction FLE KU
KÄSTNER, Erich, 1899- , English;
juvenile, fiction, poetry, plays
AL COL DOY FLE HAR KU KUN
LEN MAT SA ST
KAFFKA, Margit, 1880-1918, Hun-
garian; poetry, fiction COL SA ST
KAFKA, Franz, 1883-1924, Czech;
fiction AL COL FLE HAR KAT
KT KU KUN LEN MAG RIC SA
ST
KAFKA, John, 1905- , Austrian-
American; fiction WAF
KAFKA, Sherry, 1937- , American;
fiction CON
KAFKER, Frank A., 1931- , Ameri-
can; nonfiction CON
'KAGA NO CHIYO' (Chiyoni; Kukuzoya
Chiyo), 1703-75, Japanese; poetry
ST
KAGAN, Benjamin, 1914- , Polish-
Israeli; fiction CON
KAGAN, Donald, 1932- , Lithuanian-
American; nonfiction CON
KAGAN, Jerome, 1929- , American;
nonfiction CON
KAGANOWSKI, Ephraim, 1893- ,
Jewish; fiction ST
KAGAWA KAGEKI (Hayashi Suminori),
1768-1843, Japanese; poetry ST
KAGAWA, Toyohiko, 1888- ,
Japanese; fiction, essays KT SA
ST
'KAGE' see GRÜNBERG, Karl
KAGY, Frederich David, 1917- ,
American; nonfiction CON
KAHALE, Ludwig M., 1712-75,
German; nonfiction SA

KAHAN, Gerald, 1923- , Ameri-
can; nonfiction CON
KAHAN, Stanley, 1931- , Ameri-
can; nonfiction CON
KAHANE, Henry R., 1902- ,
American; nonfiction BL
KAHILA, Hilja see JÄRNEFELT,
Arvid
KAHL, Ann Hammel, 1929- ,
American; juveniles CON
KAHL, Virginia, 1919- , Ameri-
can; juveniles FUL WA
KAHLAU, Heinz, 1931- , Ger-
man; poetry AL
KAHLE, Roger Raymond, 1943- ,
American; nonfiction CON
KAHLER, Erich Gabriel, 1885-
1970, Czech-American; non-
fiction CON KU
KAHLER, Woodland, 1895- ,
American; nonfiction CON
KAHN, Alfred J., 1919- , Ameri-
can; nonfiction CON
KAHN, David, 1930- , American;
nonfiction CON
KAHN, Ely Jacques, Jr., 1916-
72, American; journalism
KTS
KAHN, Frank Jules, 1938- ,
American; nonfiction CON
KAHN, Gilbert, 1912- , Ameri-
can; nonfiction CON
KAHN, Gustave, 1859-1936,
French; poetry, fiction, essays
COL HAR SA ST
KAHN, Lothar, 1922- , American;
nonfiction CON
KAHN, Maximo José, 1897- ,
Spanish; fiction, essays,
journalism SA
KAHN, Robert Irving, 1910- ,
American; nonfiction CON
KAHN, Robert Louis, 1918- ,
American; nonfiction CON
KAHN, Roger, 1927- , Ameri-
can; nonfiction CON WA
KAHN, Simon, 1944- , American;
nonfiction CON
KAHN, Stephen, 1940- , Ameri-
can; nonfiction CON
KAHN, Sy M., 1924- , Ameri-
can; nonfiction CON
KAHN, Theodore Charles, 1912- ,
American; nonfiction CON
KAHNWEILER, Daniel Henry
('Daniel Henry'), 1884- ,
German-French; nonfiction
CON

KAHRL, Stanley J., 1931- , American; nonfiction CON
'KAIBARA EKIKEN' (Kaibara Atsunobu), 1630-1714, Japanese; essays ST
KAIKAVUS ibn-i Iskander, 11th cent., Persian; nonfiction ST
KAIM-CAUDLE, Peter Robert, 1916- , German-English; nonfiction CON
KAIN, Franz, 1922- , German; nonfiction AL
KAIN, John Forrest, 1935- , American; nonfiction CON
KAIN, Richard Morgan, 1908- , American; nonfiction CON
KAIN, Richard Yerkes, 1936- , American; nonfiction CON
KAISER, Georg, 1878-1945, German; plays, fiction AL COL FLE HAR KAT KT KU KUN MAT SA ST
KAISER, Karl, 1868- , German; nonfiction AL
KAISER, Robert Blair, 1930- , American; nonfiction CON
KAISER, Walter Jacob, 1931- , American; nonfiction CON
KAISERSBERG, Geiler see GEILER von KAISERSBERG
KAITZ, Edward M., 1928- , American; nonfiction CON
KAKACEK, Gen, American; juveniles WA
KAKAPO, Leilani, 1939- , American; fiction CON
KAKAR, Sudhir, 1938- , Indian; nonfiction, fiction CON
KAKINOMOTO NO HITAMARO, 655-710, Japanese; poetry LAN ST
'KALA' see GEZI, Kalil I.
KALA U (Maung), 1678?-1738?, Burmese; nonfiction LAN
KALASHNIKOFF, Nicholas, 1888-1961, Russian-American; juveniles FUL
KALB, Marvin L., 1930- , American; nonfiction CON
KALB, Sam William, 1897- , American; nonfiction CON
KALENBERG, Pfarrer von see FRANKFURTER, Philipp
KALER, James O. see 'OTIS, James'
KALES, Emily Fox, 1944- , American; nonfiction CON
KALEVALA see LÖNNROT, Elias
KALFOV, Damyan, 1887- , Bulgarian; fiction ST
KALHANA, 13th cent., Indian; poetry ST
KALIDASA (Calidasa), 5th cent., Indian; plays, poetry LAN MAG

SA ST
KALIJARVI, Thorsten Valentine, 1897- , American; nonfiction CON
KALIM of HAMADAN, Abu Talib, -1652, Persian; poetry ST
KALINCIAK, Ján, 1822-71, Slovak; fiction, poetry ST
KALINS, Dorothy G., 1942- , American; nonfiction CON
KALIR, Eleazar (Killir; Kiklir), 6th-8th cent., Jewish; poetry ST
KALISH, Donald, 1919- , American; nonfiction CON
KALISH, Richard Allan, 1930- , American; nonfiction CON
KALISHER, Simpson, 1926- , American; nonfiction CON
'KALKI' see KRSNAMURTTI, R.
KALKOWSKA, Eleanore, 1883-1937, German; nonfiction AL
KALL, Abraham, 1743-1821, Danish; nonfiction SA
KALLAS, Aino Julia Maria Krohn, 1878- , Finnish-Estonian; fiction KT SA
KALLAS, James Gus, 1928- , American; nonfiction CON
KALLAUS, Norman F., 1924- , American; nonfiction CON
KALLEN, Horace Meyer, 1882- , American; nonfiction KTS
KALLENBACH, William Warren, 1926- , American; nonfiction CON
KALLICH, Martin, 1918- , American; nonfiction CON
KALLMAN, Chester Simon, 1921- , American; poetry MUR
KALLSEN, Theodore John, 1915- , American; nonfiction CON
KALMA, Douwe, 1896- , Frisian; poetry ST
'KALMAS, Ain' see MAND, Ewald
KALMIJN, Jo, 1905- , Dutch; juveniles CON
KALNAY, Francis, Hungarian-American; juveniles WA
KALONYMOS (Meshullam), Jewish; nonfiction ST
KALOW, Gert, 1921- , German; nonfiction CON
KALT, Bryson R., 1934- , American; nonfiction CON
KALUGER, George, 1921- , American; nonfiction CON

KALUSKY, Rebecca, American; juveniles WA
KALVOS, Andreas Ivannides, 1792-1869, Greek; poetry ST
KALYANARAMAN, Aiyaswamy, 1903- , Indian; nonfiction CON
KAMARCK, Andrew Martin, 1914- , American; nonfiction CON
'KAMBAN, Guimundur' (Jansson Hallgrimson), 1888-1945, Icelandic; plays, fiction COL HAR FLE SA ST
'KAMBU, Joseph' see AMAMOO, Joseph G.
KAMEN, Henry Arthur, 1936- , English; nonfiction CON
KAMENETSKY, Ihor, 1927- , Ukrainian-American; nonfiction CON
KAMENEV, Gavriil Petrovich, 1772-1803, Russian; poetry HARK ST
KAMENKA, Eugene, 1928- , German; nonfiction CON
KAMENOVA, Anna, 1894- , Bulgarian; fiction ST
KAMENSKI, Anatoli Pavlovich, 1877- , Russian; fiction, poetry, plays HARK SA
KAMENSKI, Vasili, 1884- , Russian; poetry, fiction, plays COL ST
'KAMERMAN, Sylvia E.' see BURACK Sylvia
KAMES, Lord see HOME, Henry
'KAMIN, Nick' see ANTONICK, Robert J.
KAMINS, Jeanette, American; fiction, plays CON
KAMINSKY, Alice R., American; nonfiction CON
KAMINSKY, Jack, 1922- , American; nonfiction CON
KAMINSKY, Peretz, 1916- , American; poetry CON
KAMM, Jacob Oswald, 1918- , American; nonfiction CON
KAMM, Jan Dorinda, 1952- , American; fiction CON
KAMM, Josephine Hart, 1905- , English; juveniles, fiction CON
KAMMAN, William, 1930- , American; nonfiction CON
KAMMEN, Michael Gedalich, 1936- , American; nonfiction CON
KAMMERER, Gladys M., 1909- , American; nonfiction CON
KAMMEYER, Kenneth Carl William, 1931- , American; nonfiction CON

KAMO CHOMEI, 1153-1216, Japanese; poetry, essays LAN SA ST
KAMO MABUCHI, 1697-1769, Japanese; nonfiction SA ST
KAMPAN, 9th cent., Indian; poetry LAN
KAMPEN, Irene Trepel, 1922- , American; nonfiction CON
KAMPEN, Nicolas Godofred, 1776-1839, Dutch; nonfiction SA
KAMPF, Abraham, 1920- , American; nonfiction CON
KAMPF, Louis, 1929- , Austrian-American; nonfiction CON
KAMPOV, Boris Nikolayevich ('Boris Polevoy'), 1908- , Russian; fiction, journalism HARK ST
KAMRANY, Nake M., 1934- , Afghani-American; nonfiction
KAN PAO, 4th cent., Chinese; nonfiction ST
'KANAGAKI ROBUN' (Nozaki Bunyo), 1829-94, Japanese; fiction ST
'KAN 'AMI KIYOTSUGU' (Yusaki S. Kiyotsugu), 1333-84, Japanese; plays SA ST
KANAZAWA, Masakota, 1934- , Japanese; nonfiction CON
KANDAOUROFF, Berice, 1912- , English; nonfiction CON
KANDEL, Denise Bystryn, 1933- , Franco-American; nonfiction CON
KANDEL, Isaac Leon, 1881- , Russian-American; nonfiction CON
KANDEL, Lenore, American; poetry MUR
KANDELL, Alice S., 1938- , American; nonfiction, juveniles CON
KANE, Elisha Kent, 1820-57, American; nonfiction KAA
KANE, Frank ('Frank Boyd'), 1912-68, American; fiction CON
KANE, H. Victor, 1906- , Irish; nonfiction CON
KANE, Harnett Thomas, 1910- , American; fiction, nonfiction, journalism HO KTS WAF
KANE, Henry Bugbee, 1902- , American; juveniles WA
KANE, John Joseph, 1909- ,

American; nonfiction CON
KANE, Robert S., 1925- , Ameri-
  can; nonfiction CON
KANET, Roger Edward, 1936- ,
  American; nonfiction CON
K'ANG HSI, 1654-1722, Chinese;
  nonfiction ST
KANG, Shin T., 1935- , Korean-
  American; nonfiction CON
KANG, Younghill, 1903- , Korean-
  American; nonfiction, fiction KT
K'ANG YU-WEI, 1858-1927, Chinese;
  nonfiction ST
KANIN, Garson, 1912- , American;
  plays, fiction CON MAT
KANNER, Leo, 1894- , American;
  nonfiction CON
KANOF, Abram, 1903- , Russian-
  American; nonfiction CON
KANOVSKY, Eliyahu, 1922- ,
  Canadian; nonfiction CON
KANT, Immanuel, 1724-1804, German;
  essays HAR KE MAG SA ST
KANTEMIR, Antiokh Dmitrievich
  (Cantemir), 1708-44, Russian;
  poetry HARK KE ST
KANTEMIR, Dimitrie (Cantemir),
  1673-1723, Moldavian; nonfiction
  KE SA ST
KANTERS, Robert, 1910- , French;
  criticism DIF
KANTO, Peter ('John Dexter'; 'Ginny
  Gorman'; 'Deral Pilgrim'; 'E. R.
  Rangely'; 'Olivia Rangely'), 1932- ,
  American; fiction CON
KANTONEN, Taito Almar, 1900- ,
  Finnish-American; nonfiction
  CON
KANTOR, Harry, 1911- , American;
  nonfiction CON
KANTOR, James, 1927- , South
  African; nonfiction CON
KANTOR, Mackinley, 1904- , Ameri-
  can; fiction KT RIC WA WAF
KANTOR-BERG, Friedrich see 'TOR-
  BERG, Friedrich'
KANWAR, Mahfooz A., 1939- ,
  Pakistani-Canadian; nonfiction
  CON
KANY, Charles Emil, 1895- ,
  American; nonfiction CON
KANYA-FORSTNER, Alexander Sydney,
  1940- , Hungarian-English; non-
  fiction CON
KANZE MOTOKIYO see SE'AMI
  MOTOKIYO
KANZER, Mark, 1908- , American;
  nonfiction CON

KAO CH'I, 1336-74, Chinese;
  poetry ST
KAO-IUNG-KIA, 15th cent.,
  Chinese; plays SA
KAO MING, 14th cent., Chinese;
  plays ST
KAO SHIH, 700?-65, Chinese;
  poetry ST
KAO TSE-CH'ENG (Kao Ming),
  1305-68, Chinese; plays MAG
KAPELNER, Alan, American;
  nonfiction CON
KAPFER, Miriam Bierbaum,
  1935- , American; nonfiction
  CON
KAPFER, Philip Gordon, 1936- ,
  American; nonfiction CON
KAPLAN, Abraham, 1918- ,
  Russian-American; nonfiction
KAPLAN, Albert A., American;
  juveniles WA
KAPLAN, Allan, 1932- , Ameri-
  can; poetry CON
KAPLAN, Anne Bernays, 1930- ,
  American; fiction CON
KAPLAN, Arthur, 1925- , Amer-
  ican; fiction CON
KAPLAN, Benjamin, 1911- ,
  American; nonfiction CON
KAPLAN, Boche ('A. K. Roche'),
  1926- , American; nonfiction
  CON
KAPLAN, Charles, 1919- ,
  American; nonfiction CON
KAPLAN, Frederich Israel,
  1920- , American; nonfiction
  CON
KAPLAN, Harold, 1916- , Ameri-
  can; nonfiction CON
KAPLAN, Harold J., 1918- ,
  American; fiction KTS
KAPLAN, Irma, 1900- , Swedish;
  juveniles CON
KAPLAN, Jacob J., 1920- ,
  American; nonfiction CON
KAPLAN, Jean Caryl Korn ('Jean
  Caryl'), 1926- , American;
  juveniles CON WA
KAPLAN, Justin, 1925- , Ameri-
  can; nonfiction CON
KAPLAN, Lawrence Jay, 1915- ,
  American; nonfiction CON
KAPLAN, Lawrence Samuel,
  1924- , American; nonfiction
  CON
KAPLAN, Margaret de Mille,
  American; juveniles WA

KAPLAN, Max, 1911- , American; nonfiction CON

KAPLAN, Morton A., 1921- , American; nonfiction CON

KAPLAN, Philip, 1916- , American; nonfiction CON

KAPLAN, Robert B., 1928- , American; nonfiction CON

KAPLAN, Samuel, 1935- , American; nonfiction CON

KAPLAN, Saul Howard, 1938- , American; juveniles CON

KAPLON, Morton Fischel, 1921- , American; nonfiction CON

KAPLOW, Jeffry, 1937- , American; nonfiction CON

KAPNIST, Vasili Vasilyevich, 1757-1823, Russian; poetry HARK ST

KAPP, Friedrich, 1824-84, German-American; nonfiction ST

KAPP, Johann Gottfried, 1897- , German; nonfiction KU

KAPP, Karl William, 1910- , American; nonfiction CON

KAPP, Paul, American; juveniles WA

KAPP, Reginald Otto, 1885-1966, English; nonfiction CON

KAPPEL, Philip, 1901- , American; nonfiction CON

KAPPEN, Charles Vaughan, 1910- , American; nonfiction CON

'KARA GIORG' (Gustav Brühl), 1826-1903, German-American; poetry ST

KARACAOGLAN, 17th cent., Turkish; poetry ST

KARADZIC, Vuk Stefanovic, 1787-1864, Serbian; nonfiction KE SA ST

'KARAI, Senryu' (Karai Hachiemon), 1718-90, Japanese; poetry ST

KARALIYCHEV, Angel, 1902- , Bulgarian; fiction ST

KARAMZIN, Nikolay Mikhaylovich, 1765/66-1826, Russian; fiction, journalism HAR HARK KE SA ST

KARANIKAS, Alexander, 1916- , American; nonfiction CON

KARANTH, Kota Sivaram, 1902- , Indian; poetry, fiction LAN

'KARASEK ZE LVOVIC, Jiri' (Josif Jiri Antonín Karásek), 1871- , Czech; fiction, poetry, plays SA ST

KARAVELOV, Liuben, 1837-79, Bulgarian; poetry SA ST

KARDOUCHE, George Khalil, 1935- , Arab; nonfiction CON

KAREL HAVLICEK see HAVLICEK BOROVSKY, Karel

KAREN, Ruth, 1922- , German-American; juveniles CON WA

KAREYEV, Nikolay Ivanovich, 1850-1931, Russian; nonfiction HARK

KARG, Elissa Jane, 1951- , American; nonfiction CON

KARGER, Delmar William, 1913- , American; nonfiction CON

KARIEL, Henry S., 1924- , German-American; nonfiction CON

KARIG, Walter, 1898- , American; fiction, journalism KTS WAF

KARINTHY, Frigyes, 1887-1938, Hungarian; fiction, plays, poetry, essays FLE HAR ST

KARIUKI, Josiah Mwangi, 1931- , Kenyan; poetry MUR

KARIV, Abraham (Krivoruz'ka), 1890- , Jewish; poetry, essays ST

KARK, Nina Mary Mabey ('Nina Bawden'), 1925- , English; fiction, juveniles CON

KARL, Frederick Robert, 1927- , American; nonfiction CON

KARL, Jean Edna, 1927- , American; nonfiction CON

KARLAN, Richard, 1919- , American; fiction CON

KARLEN, Arno Milner, 1937- , American; fiction, translations CON

KARLEN, Delmar, 1912- , American; nonfiction CON

KARLFELDT, Erik Axel, 1864-1931, Swedish; poetry COL FLE HAR KT RIC SA ST

KARLGREN, Klas Bernhard Johannes, 1889- , Swedish; nonfiction CON

KARLIN, Jules, 1899- , Russian-American; nonfiction CON

KARLIN, Robert, 1918- , American; nonfiction CON

KARLINS, Marvin, 1941- , American; fiction CON

KARLOVEVITZ, Robert F., 1922- , American; nonfiction CON

KARLSSON, Elis Viktor, 1905- , Finnish; nonfiction CON

KARMEL, Alex, 1931- , American;
fiction CON
KARNES, Thomas Lindas, 1914- ,
American; nonfiction CON
KARNEY, Beulah Mullen, American;
juveniles CON
KARO, Joseph see CARO, Joseph
'KAROL, K. S.' see KEWES, Karol
KAROLIDES, Nicholas James, 1928- ,
American; nonfiction CON
'KARONIN' (Nikolay E. Petropavlovsky),
1857-92, Russian; fiction ST
'KAROV, Rabbi' see LEVINSKI,
Elchanan L.
KARP, Abraham J., 1921- , Polish-
American; nonfiction CON
KARP, David, 1922- , American;
fiction CON
KARP, Ivan C., 1926- , American;
fiction CON
KARP, Lila, 1933- , American;
fiction CON
KARP, Mark, 1922- , American;
nonfiction CON
KARP, Stephen Arnold, 1928- ,
American; nonfiction CON
KARPAT, Kemal Hasim, 1925- ,
Rumanian-American; nonfiction
CON
KARPELES, Maud, 1885- , American;
nonfiction CON
KARPF, Holly W., 1946- , American;
nonfiction CON
KARPIN, Fred Leon, 1913- , Ameri-
can; nonfiction CON
KARPIUSKI, Franz (Karpinski), 1741-
1825, Polish; poetry, diary SA
ST
KARPLUS, Walter J., 1927- , Aus-
trian-American; nonfiction CON
KARR, Earl Ralph, 1918- , American;
nonfiction CON
KARR, Jean Baptiste Alphonse, 1808-
90, French; nonfiction DIF HAR
SA ST
KARRER, Rev. Otto, 1888- , Ger-
man; nonfiction HO
KARSAVIN, Lev Platonovich, 1882- ,
Russian; nonfiction ST
KARSCH, Anna Luise, 1722-91, Ger-
man; poetry AL SA
KARSH, Yousuf, 1908- , Turkish-
Canadian; nonfiction CON
KARSHNER, Roger, 1928- , Ameri-
can; nonfiction CON
KARSTEN, Peter, 1938- , American;
nonfiction CON
'KARTA, Nat' see NORWOOD, Victor

G. C.
KARVE, Dinaker Dhondo, 1899- ,
Indian; nonfiction CON
KARVE, Irawati, 1905- ,
Burmesen; nonfiction CON
KASACK, Herman, 1896- , Ger-
man; poetry, plays, fiction
AL FLE KU LEN
KASCHNITZ-WEINBERG, Marie
Luise von, 1901- , German;
poetry, fiction, radio AL
FLE KU KUN LEN
KASDAN, Sara Moskovitz, 1911- ,
American; fiction CON
KASE, Francis Joseph, 1910- ,
Czech-American; nonfiction
CON
KASENKINA, Oksana Stepanovna,
1896- , Russian; nonfiction,
fiction HO
KASER, David, 1924- , Ameri-
can; nonfiction CON
KASER, Michael Charles, 1926- ,
English; nonfiction CON
KASH, Don Eldon, 1934- , Amer-
ican; nonfiction CON
KASHIFI, Husain Va'iz, -1505,
Persian; nonfiction ST
KASIM MANSUR, Abul see
FIRDUSI, Abul C. M.
KASIRAM DAS, fl. 1600, Indian;
poetry LAN
KASPER, Sydney H., 1911- ,
American; nonfiction CON
KASPERSON, Roger E., 1938- ,
American; nonfiction CON
KASPROWICZ, Jan, 1860-1926,
Polish; poetry, plays, transla-
tion COL FLE HAR MAT RIC
SA ST
KASRAVI, -1946, Persian; non-
fiction LAN
KASRILS, Ronald, 1938- , Amer-
ican; nonfiction CON
KASS, Norman, 1934- , American;
nonfiction CON
KASSAK, Lajos, 1887- , Hun-
garian; poetry, fiction FLE
ST
KASSAM, Yusuf O., 1943- ,
Tanzanian; poetry MUR
KASSEBAUM, Gene Girard,
1929- , American; nonfiction
CON
KASSEF, Roman see 'GARY,
Romain'
KASSIL, Lev, 1905- , Russian;
fiction RIC

KASSIRER, Norman, American;
juveniles WA
KASSNER, Rudolf, 1873-1959, Austrian; essays, fiction FLE KU
KUN
KASSOF, Allen, 1930- , American;
nonfiction CON
KAST, Fremont E., 1926- , American; nonfiction CON
'KAST, Peter' (Carl Preissner),
1894-1959, German; nonfiction
AL
KASTEELE, Pieter Leonard van de,
1748-1810, Dutch; poetry, translations ST
KASTEN, Lloyd, 1905- , American;
nonfiction BL
KASTENBAUM, Robert Jay, 1932- ,
American; nonfiction CON
KASTER, Joseph, 1912- , American;
nonfiction CON
KASTLE, Herbert David, 1924- ,
American; nonfiction CON
KASTNER, Jonathan, 1937- , American; nonfiction CON
KASTNER, L. E., 1868?- , English;
nonfiction SA
KASTNER, Marianna, 1940- , American; nonfiction CON
'KASTOS, Emiro' see RESTREPO,
Juan de D.
KATALINIC, Rikard Jeretov, 1861- ,
Dalmatian; poetry ST
KATAYEV, Valentin Petrovich
(Kataev), 1897- , Russian; fiction, plays COL FLE HAR HARK
KT MAT RIC SA ST
KAYAYEV, Yevgeni see 'PETROV,
Yevgeni'
KATCHADOURIAN, Vahe ('Vahe
Katcha'), 1928- , French; nonfiction, fiction CON
KATCHMER, George Andrew, 1916- ,
American; nonfiction CON
KATE, Jan Jakob, 1819-89, Dutch;
translations ST
KATENEN, Pavel Alexandrovich,
1792-1853, Russian; poetry,
plays, translations HARK KE ST
'KATERLA, Józef' see ZEROMSKI,
Stefan
KATES, Robert W., 1929- , American; nonfiction CON
'KATHRYN' see SEARL, Kathryn A.
KATIB CELEBI, Mustafa ('Hadji
Khalifa'), 1608-57, Turkish; nonfiction ST
KATICIC, Radoslav, 1930- , Croatian;

nonfiction CON
KATKOV, Mikhail Nikoforovich,
1818-87, Russian; nonfiction,
journalism HAR HARK ST
KATKOV, Norman, 1918- ,
American; fiction CON WAF
KATO, Shuichi, 1919- , Japanese;
nonfiction CON
KATONA, József, 1791-1830,
Hungarian; plays HAR ST
KATOPE, Christopher G.,
1918- , American; nonfiction
CON
KATRAK, Kersy Dady, 1936- ,
Indian; poetry, criticism MUR
KATSH, Abraham Isaac, 1908- ,
Polish-American; nonfiction
CON
KATYRYOV-ROSTOVKSKI, Prince
Ivan M., 17th cent., Russian;
poetry HARK ST
KATZ, Bobbi, 1933- , American; fiction CON
KATZ, Elias, 1912- , American; nonfiction CON
KATZ, Ellis, 1938- , American;
nonfiction CON
KATZ, H. W., 1906- , German;
fiction KT SA
KATZ, Irving I., 1907- , American; nonfiction CON
KATZ, Jacob, 1904- , Hungarian;
nonfiction CON
KATZ, John Stuart, 1938- ,
American; nonfiction CON
KATZ, Joseph, 1910- , Canadian;
nonfiction CON
KATZ, Leo, 1892-1954, German;
nonfiction AL
KATZ, Leonard, 1926- , American; nonfiction CON
KATZ, Martin, 1929- , American; nonfiction CON
KATZ, Marvin Charles, 1930- ,
American; nonfiction CON
KATZ, Menke (Elchik Hiat),
1906- , Lithuanian-American;
poetry CON
KATZ, Michael Barry, 1939- ,
American; nonfiction CON
KATZ, Milton, 1907- , American;
nonfiction CON
KATZ, Robert, 1933- , American;
nonfiction CON
KATZ, Robert L., 1917- ,
American; nonfiction CON
KATZ, Samuel, 1914- , South
African; nonfiction CON

KATZ, Sanford N., 1933- , American; nonfiction CON
KATZ, Stanley Nider, 1934- , American; nonfiction CON
KATZ, Steven, 1935- , American; fiction, poetry CON
KATZ, William A., 1924- , American; nonfiction CON
KATZ, William Loren, 1927- , American; nonfiction CON
'KA-TZETNIK 135633', Polish; fiction CON
KATZMAN, Allen, 1937- , American; poetry CON
'KATZNELSON, Jehuda Loeb' (Bukki ben Yogli), 1847-1917, Jewish; nonfiction LAN
KATZNER, Kenneth, 1930- , American; nonfiction CON
KAUDER, Emil, 1901- , German-American; nonfiction CON
KAUDZITE, Matiss, 1848-1926, Latvian; fiction ST
KAUDZITE, Reinis, 1839-1920, Latvian; fiction ST
KAUFFMAN, Christmas Carol, 1902- , American; nonfiction, fiction CON
KAUFFMAN, Donald Thomas, 1920- , American; nonfiction CON
KAUFFMAN, Dorotha Strayer, 1925- , American; juveniles CON
KAUFFMAN, George Bernard, 1930- , American; nonfiction CON
KAUFFMAN, Henry J., 1908- , American; nonfiction CON
KAUFFMANN, 18th cent., French; nonfiction DIL
KAUFFMANN, Fritz Alexander, 1891- , German; nonfiction KU
KAUFFMANN, Lane, 1921- , American; fiction CON
KAUFFMANN, Stanley ('Spranger Barry'), 1916- , American; nonfiction, play CON WAF
KAUFMAN, Arnold S., 1927- , American; nonfiction CON
KAUFMAN, Bel, American; fiction CON
KAUFMAN, Bob, 1925- , American; poetry, fiction MUR
KAUFMAN, Burton I., 1940- , American; nonfiction CON
KAUFMAN, Donald David, 1933- , American; nonfiction CON
KAUFMAN, Edmund George, 1891- , American; nonfiction CON

KAUFMAN, George Simon, 1889-1961, American; plays BRO KL KT MAT RIC SA ST
KAUFMAN, Gerald Bernard, 1930- , English; nonfiction CON
KAUFMAN, Gordon Dester, 1925- , American; nonfiction CON
KAUFMAN, Irving, 1920- , American; nonfiction CON
KAUFMAN, Kenneth Carlyle, 1887- , American; poetry MAR
KAUFMAN, Lenard, 1913- , American; fiction KTS WAF
KAUFMAN, Mervyn D., 1932- , American; nonfiction CON
KAUFMAN, Robert, 1931- , American; fiction CON
KAUFMAN, Rosamond V.P., 1923- , American; nonfiction CON
KAUFMAN, Sherwin A., 1920- , Russian-American; nonfiction CON
KAUFMAN, Sue see BARONDESS, Sue K.
KAUFMAN, Wallace ('Vickers'), 1939- , American; nonfiction CON
KAUFMAN, William Irving, 1922- , American; nonfiction CON
KAUFMANN, Helen Loeb, 1887- , American; nonfiction CON
KAUFMANN, Myron S., 1921- , American; fiction CON
KAUFMANN, Ralph James, 1924- , American; nonfiction CON
KAUFMANN, Walter, 1921- , German-American; nonfiction AL CON
KAUFMANN, Ulrich George, 1920- , German-American; nonfiction CON
KAUFMANN, William W., 1918- , American; nonfiction CON
KAUL, Karl Friedrich, 1906- , German; fiction AL
KAUL, Zinda, 1884- , Indian; poetry LAN
KAULA, Edna Mason, 1906- , American; juveniles CON WA
KAUP, Elizabeth Dewing, 1885- , American; fiction WAF
KAUPER, Paul Gerhardt, 1907- , American; nonfiction CON
KAUSLER, Donald Harvey, 1927- ,

American; nonfiction CON
KAUTH, Benjamin, 1914- , American;
 nonfiction CON
KAUTILYA, fl. 322-298 B.C., Indian;
 poetry LAN ST
KAUTSKY, Minna, 1837-1912, German;
 nonfiction AL
KAVALER, Lucy, American; juveniles
 WA
'KAVAN, Anna' see EDMONDS, Helen
 W.
KAVAN, Josef see 'NOR, A.C.'
KAVANAGH, Julia, 1824-77, English;
 fiction BRO KBA
KAVANAGH, Patrick, 1905-67, Irish;
 poetry RIC ST
KAVANAGH, Patrick Joseph Gregory,
 1931-67, British; poetry MUR
KAVANAUGH, James Joseph, 1929- ,
 American; nonfiction CON
KAVANAUGH, Kiernan, 1928- , Amer-
 ican; nonfiction CON
KAVANAUGH, Robert E., 1926- ,
 American; nonfiction CON
KAVELIN, Konstantin Dmitrievich,
 1818-85, Russian; nonfiction
 HARK ST
KAVENGH, William Keith, 1926- ,
 American; nonfiction CON
'KAVERIN, Venyamin' (Venyamin
 Alexandrovich Zilberg), 1902- ,
 Russian; fiction COL FLE HAR
 HARK RIC SA ST
KAVESH, Robert Allyn, 1927- ,
 American; nonfiction CON
KAVET, Robert, 1924- , American;
 fiction CON
KAVIRAJ CAKRAVARTI, fl. 1696-
 1714, Indian; poetry, translations
 LAN
KAVLI, Guthorm, 1917- , Norwegian;
 nonfiction CON
KAVOLIS, Vytautas, 1930- , Lithua-
 nian-American; nonfiction CON
KAWABATA, Yasunari, 1899-1972,
 Japanese; fiction FLE LAN
KAWAHITO, Kiyoshi, 1939- ,
 Japanese-American; nonfiction
 CON
KAWAI, Kazuo, 1904-63, Japanese-
 American; nonfiction CON
KAWAJIMA ONITSURA, 1661-1738,
 Japanese; poetry ST
'KAWAKAMI, Bizan' (Kawakami
 Akira), 1869-1908, Japanese;
 fiction ST
KAWAKAMI, Toyo Suyemoto, 1916- ,
 American; nonfiction CON

KAWATAKE MOKUAMI see
 MOKUAMI
KAWIN, Bruce F., 1945- ,
 American; nonfiction CON
KAWIN, Ethel, American; nonfic-
 tion CON
KAY, Albert William, 1930- ,
 English; nonfiction CON
KAY, Barbara Ann, 1929- ,
 American; nonfiction CON
KAY, Brian Ross, 1924- , New
 Zealander-American; nonfiction
 CON
KAY, Ernest ('George Ludlow';
 'Alan Random'), 1915- , Eng-
 lish; nonfiction CON
'KAY, George' see LAMBERT,
 Eric
KAY, George, 1924- , British;
 poetry MUR
KAY, George, 1936- , American;
 nonfiction CON
KAY, Harry, 1919- , English;
 nonfiction CON
'KAY, Helen' see GOLDFRANK,
 Helen C.
KAY, Kenneth Edmond, 1915- ,
 American; fiction CON
KAY, Mara, American; nonfiction
 CON
KAY, Terence, 1918- , English;
 fiction CON
KAY, Thomas O., 1932- , Amer-
 ican; nonfiction CON
'KAYE, Barbara' see MUIR,
 Barbara K.
KAYE, Sir John William, 1814-76,
 English; nonfiction BRO KBA
 ST
KAYE, Geraldine Hughesdon,
 1925- , English; juveniles
 CON
KAYE, Julian Bertram, 1925- ,
 American; nonfiction CON
KAYE, Philip A., 1920- , Amer-
 ican; nonfiction CON
KAYENBERGH, Albert see
 'GERAUD, Albert'
KAYE-SMITH, Sheila, 1887-1956,
 English; fiction, poetry BRO
 HOE KL KT MAG RIC
KAYIRA, Legson Didimu, 1940- ,
 Malawian; fiction CON
KAYSEN, Carl, 1920- , American;
 nonfiction CON
KAYSER, Elmer Louis, 1896- ,
 American; nonfiction CON
KAYSING, Bill, 1922- , Ameri-

can; nonfiction CON
KAYYHAM, Omar see OMAR KAYYHAM
KAZAKOV, Yuri Pavlovich, 1927- ,
  Russian; fiction CON RIC
KAZAMIAS, Andreas M., 1927- ,
  American; nonfiction CON
KAZAN, Elia, 1929- , American;
  fiction CON
KAZANTZAKIS, Nikos, 1882-1957,
  Greek; poetry, fiction, essays,
  plays FLE KTS RIC
KAZEMZADEH, Firuz, 1924- ,
  Russian-American; nonfiction
  CON
KAZIMIROVICH, Yuri see 'BATTRU-
  SHAITIS, Jurgis'
KAZIN, Alfred, 1915- , American;
  criticism CON KTS
KAZIN, Vasili Vasilievich, 1898- ,
  Russian; poetry COL HARK ST
KAZINCZY, Ferenc, 1759-1831,
  Hungarian; poetry ST
KEABLE, Robert, 1887-1927, English;
  fiction BRO KT
KEALY, Edward Joseph, 1936- ,
  American; nonfiction CON
KEAN, Charles Duell, 1910-63, Amer-
  ican; nonfiction CON
KEANE, Bil, 1922- , American;
  nonfiction CON
KEANE, Ellsworth McGranahan
  ('Shake Keane'), 1927- , British;
  poetry, criticism MUR
KEANE, John B., 1928- , English;
  nonfiction, plays CON
KEANE, Mrs. R. L. see 'FARRELL,
  M. J.'
'KEANE, Shake' see KEANE, Ells-
  worth MC.
KEARNEY, Hugh Francis, 1924- ,
  English; nonfiction CON
KEARNEY, James Robert III, 1929- ,
  American; nonfiction CON
KEARNEY, John, 1865-1941, Irish;
  nonfiction HOE
KEARNS, Francis Edward, 1931- ,
  American; nonfiction CON
KEARNS, Jame Aloysius III, 1949- ,
  American; nonfiction CON
KEARNS, Lionel John, 1937- ,
  Canadian; poetry CON MUR
KEARNY, Edward N. III, 1936- ,
  American; nonfiction CON
KEARY, Annie, 1825-79, English;
  fiction BRO KBA ST
KEAST, James D., 1930- , Ameri-
  can; nonfiction CON
KEAST, William Rea, 1914- ,

American; nonfiction CON
KEATING, Charlotte Matthews,
  1927- , American; nonfiction
  CON
KEATING, Edward M., 1925- ,
  American; nonfiction CON
KEATING, Henry Raymond Fitz-
  walter, 1926- , English;
  fiction CON
KEATING, John McLeod, 1830-
  1906, American; nonfiction
  KAA
KEATING, Joseph, 1865-1939,
  Scots; nonfiction HOE
KEATING, Lawrence Alfred
  ('John Keith Bassett'; 'H. C.
  Thomas'), 1903-66, American;
  juveniles, fiction CON WA
KEATING, Leo Bernard, 1915- ,
  Canadian; fiction, juveniles
  CON
KEATING, Louis Clark, 1907- ,
  American; nonfiction CON
KEATING, Norma, American;
  juveniles, poetry WA
KEATS, Charles B., 1905- ,
  American; nonfiction CON
KEATS, Ezra Jack, 1916- ,
  American; juveniles FUL WA
KEATS, John, 1795-1821, English;
  poetry BRO KBA MAG SA SP
  ST
KEAY, Frederick, 1915- , Eng-
  lish; nonfiction CON
KEBLE, John, 1792-1866, English;
  poetry, essays BRO KBA ST
KEBLE, Thomas, 1793-1875,
  English; nonfiction KBA
KEDDELL, Georgina Murray,
  1913- , Canadian; nonfiction
  CON
KEDDIE, Nikki Ragozin, 1930- ,
  American; nonfiction CON
KEDOURIE, Elie, 1926- , Iraqi-
  English; nonfiction CON
KEDZIE, Daniel Peter, 1930- ,
  American; nonfiction CON
KEE, Howard Clark, 1920- ,
  American; nonfiction CON
KEEBLE, John, 1944- , Canadian;
  fiction CON
KEECH, William John, 1904- ,
  American; nonfiction CON
KEECH, William Robertson, 1939- ,
  American; nonfiction CON
KEEFE, Donald Joseph, 1924- ,
  American; nonfiction CON
KEEFER, Truman Frederick,

1930- , American; nonfiction CON
KEEGAN, Mary Heathcott ('Mary Raymond'), 1914- , American; fiction CON
'KEEL, Laura' see BERGE, Carol
KEELE, Kenneth David ('Peter Cassils'), 1909- , English; nonfiction CON
KEELER, Harry Stephen, 1894- , American; fiction HOO
KEELER, Sister Jerome, 1895- , American; nonfiction HOE
KEELER, Katherine Southwick, 1887- , American; juveniles WA
KEELEY, Edmund Leroy, 1928- , American; nonfiction CON
KEELEY, Joseph Charles, 1907- , American; nonfiction CON
'KEELING, Clinton Harry, 1932- , English; nonfiction CON
'KEELING, E. B.' see CURL, James S.
KEELING, Jill Annette Shaw, 1923- , English; nonfiction CON
'KEELIVINE, Christopher' see PICKEN, Andrew
KEEN, John Ernest, 1937- , American; nonfiction CON
KEEN, Martin L., 1913- , American; juveniles CON
KEENAN, Rev. Alan, 1920- , Irish; nonfiction HO
KEENAN, Boyd Raymond, 1928- , American; nonfiction CON
'KEENE, Carolyn' see ADAMS, Harriet S. and STRATEMEYER, Edward L.
KEENEY, Charles James, 1912- , American; nonfiction CON
KEENE, Donald, 1922- , American; nonfiction, translations CON
'KEENE, Faraday' see JARRETT, Cora H.
KEENE, Foxhall P., 1867-1941, English; nonfiction HIG
KEENE, James Calvin, 1908- , American; nonfiction CON
KEENLEYSIDE, Hugh Llewellyn, 1898- , American; nonfiction CON
KEEP, John L. H., 1926- , English; nonfiction CON
KEEPING, Charles, 1924- , English; juveniles CON
KEESECKER, William Francis, 1918- , American; nonfiction CON

KEESHAN, Robert J., 1927- , American; fiction CON
KEESING, Nancy Florence Hertzberg, 1923- , Australian; poetry, criticism CON MUR RIC
KEESLAR, Oreon, 1907- , American; fiction CON
KEETON, Elizabeth Baker, 1919- , American; juveniles CON
KEETON, George Williams, 1902- , English; nonfiction CON
KEETON, Morris Teuton, 1917- , American; nonfiction CON
KEETON, Robert Ernest, 1919- , American; nonfiction CON
KEEVIL, Henry John ('Clay Allison'; 'Bill Bonney'; 'Wes Hardin'; 'Frank McLowery'; 'Johnny Ringo'), 1914- , English; fiction CON
KEEZER, Dexter Merriam, 1895- , American; nonfiction CON
KEGEL, Charles H., 1924- , American; nonfiction CON
KEGEL, Max, 1850-1902, German; nonfiction AL
KEGLEY, Charles William, 1912- , American; nonfiction CON
KEHL, Delmar George, 1936- , American; nonfiction CON
KEHM, Freda Irma Samuels, American; nonfiction CON
KEHOE, Constance De Muzio, 1933- , American; nonfiction CON
KEHOE, Monika, 1909- , American; nonfiction CON
KEHOE, William E., 1933- , American; nonfiction CON
KEIGHTLEY, Thomas, 1789-1872, Irish; nonfiction BRO KBA ST
KEIM, Charles J., 1922- , American; nonfiction CON
KEIMER, Samuel, 1688-1739, American; nonfiction KAA
'KEIR, Christine' see POPESCU, Christine
KEIR, David Edwin, 1906- , Scots; poetry, nonfiction CON
KEIR, David Lindsay, 1895- , English; nonfiction CON
KEIRSTEAD, Burton Seely, 1907-, American; nonfiction CON
KEISER, Norman Fred, 1930- , American; nonfiction CON
KEISLAR, Evan Rollo, 1913- ,

American; nonfiction CON
KEISMAN, Michael Edward, 1932- ,
American; nonfiction CON
KEITH, Agnes Newton, 1901- ,
American; nonfiction CON KTS
KEITH, Sir Arthur, 1866-1955, Scots;
nonfiction KTS
'KEITH, Carlton' see ROBERTSON,
Keith
'KEITH, David' see STEEGMULLER,
Francis
'KEITH, Donald' see MONROE, Keith
KEITH, Harold Verne, 1903- ,
American; juveniles COM CON
FUL WA
KEITH, Herbert F., 1895- , Ameri-
can; nonfiction CON
KEITH, K. Wymand, 1924- , Ameri-
can; nonfiction CON
KEITH, Robert, 1681-1757, Scots;
nonfiction BRO
KEITH, William John, 1934- , Eng-
lish; nonfiction CON
KEITHLEY, Erwin M., 1905- ,
American; nonfiction CON
KEITHLEY, George, 1935- , Ameri-
can; poetry CON
KEITH-LUCAS, Alan, 1910- , Eng-
lish; nonfiction CON
KELBER, Magda, 1908- , German;
nonfiction CON
KELDER, Diane, 1934- , American;
nonfiction CON
KELEN, Emery, 1896- , Hungarian-
American; nonfiction CON
'KELL, Joseph' see BURGESS,
Anthony
KELL, Richard Alexander, 1927- ,
British; poetry, fiction, essays
CON MUR
KELLAND, Clarence Buddington,
1881-1964, American; fiction
HIL KT WAF
KELLAWAY, Frank Gerald, 1922- ,
English; fiction CON
KELLAWAY, George Percival, 1909- ,
English; nonfiction CON
KELLEHER, Daniel Lawrence, 1883- ,
Irish; poetry, plays HO
KELLER, Albert Galloway, 1874-1956,
American; nonfiction KT
KELLER, Allan, 1904- , American;
nonfiction CON
KELLER, Frances Ruth, 1911- ,
American; juveniles WA
KELLER, Gerard, 1829-99, Dutch;
fiction, essays ST
KELLER, Gottfried, 1819-90, Swiss;

fiction, poetry AL COL HAR
KE MAG SA ST
KELLER, Rev. James Gregory,
1900- , American; nonfiction
HO
KELLER, John Esten, 1917- ,
American; nonfiction BL
KELLER, Morton, 1929- , Amer-
ican; nonfiction CON
KELLER, Thomas Franklin,
1931- , American; nonfiction
CON
KELLER, Werner Rudolf August
Wolfgang, 1909- , German-
Swiss; nonfiction CON
KELLERMANN, Bernhard, 1879-
1951, German; essays AL KU
LEN SA
KELLETT, Ernest Edward, 1864-
1950, English; criticism, es-
says BRO
KELLEY, Alden Drew, 1903- ,
American; nonfiction CON
KELLEY, Donald Reed, 1931- ,
American; nonfiction CON
KELLEY, Earl Clarence, 1895- ,
American; nonfiction CON
KELLEY, Eugene John, 1922- ,
American; nonfiction CON
KELLEY, Francis Clement,
1870- , American; nonfiction
HOE MAR
KELLEY, Hubert Williams, Jr.,
1926- , American; nonfiction
CON
KELLEY, James Douglas Jerrold,
1847-1922, American; nonfic-
tion KAA
KELLEY, Joanna Elizabeth, 1910- ,
English; nonfiction CON
KELLEY, Page Hutto, 1924- ,
American; nonfiction CON
KELLEY, Robert, 1925- , Amer-
ican; nonfiction CON
KELLEY, Stanley, Jr., 1926- ,
American; nonfiction CON
KELLEY, William, 1929- ,
American; fiction CON
KELLEY, William Thomas, 1917- ,
American; nonfiction CON
KELLGREN, Johan Henrik, 1751-
95, Swedish; poetry, plays
HAR KE SA ST
KELLING, Furn L., 1914- ,
American; juveniles CON
KELLING, Hans Wilhelm, 1932- ,
German-American; nonfiction
CON

KELLNER, Bruce, 1930- , American; fiction CON
KELLNER, Esther ('Esther Cooper'), American; fiction CON
KELLNER, John William, 1918- , American; nonfiction CON
KELLNER, L., 1904- , German-English; nonfiction CON
KELLOGG, Charles Flint, 1929- , American; nonfiction CON
KELLOGG, Edward, 1790-1858, American; nonfiction KAA
KELLOGG, Elijah, 1813-1901, American; juveniles KAA
KELLOGG, Ernest see 'GANN, Ernest'
KELLOGG, Jean ('Sally Jackson'), 1916- , American; juveniles CON WA
KELLOGG, Winthrop Niles, 1898- , American; nonfiction CON
'KELLOW, Kathleen' see HIBBERT, Eleanor
KELLOW, Norman B., 1914- , American; nonfiction CON
KELLY, Alfred H., 1907- , American; nonfiction CON
KELLY, Averill Alison, 1913- , English; nonfiction CON
KELLY, Balmer Hancock, 1914- , American; nonfiction CON
KELLY, Rev. Bernard J., 1910- , Irish; nonfiction HO
KELLY, Bernard W., 1872- , English; nonfiction HOE
KELLY, Blanche Mary, 1881- , American; nonfiction HOE
KELLY, David Michael, 1938- , American; poetry CON
KELLY, Edward Hanford, 1930- , American; nonfiction CON
KELLY, Eleanor Mercien, 1880- , American; fiction KAT KT
KELLY, Eric Philbrook, 1884- , American; juveniles KJU KL WA
KELLY, Faye Lucius, 1914- , American; nonfiction CON
KELLY, Florence Finch, 1858-1939, American; fiction, journalism HOO
KELLY, Frank K., 1914- , American; nonfiction CON
KELLY, George A., 1916- , American; nonfiction CON
KELLY, George Edward, 1887- , American; plays KAT KT MAT
KELLY, Gerald Ray, 1930- , American; fiction CON
KELLY, Henry Ansgar, 1934- , American; nonfiction CON

KELLY, Hugh, 1739-77, Irish; plays BRO KB ST
KELLY, James F. see FITZ-MAURICE-KELLY, James
KELLY, John, 1913- , American; fiction WAF
KELLY, John Bernard, 1888- , American; nonfiction HOE
KELLY, John M., Jr., 1919- , American; nonfiction CON
KELLY, John Norman Davidson, 1909- , Scots; nonfiction CON
KELLY, Jonathan Falconbridge ('Cerro Gordo'; 'Jack Humphries'; 'O. K.'), 1817-55?, American; fiction KAA
KELLY, Judith, 1908- , American; fiction WAF
KELLY, Lawrence Charles, 1932- , American; nonfiction CON
KELLY, Mary Coolican, 1927- , English; nonfiction CON
KELLY, Maurice N., 1919- , Australian; nonfiction CON
KELLY, Philip John, 1896-1972, American; nonfiction CON
'KELLY, Ralph' see GEIS, Darlene S.
KELLY, Regina Z., American; nonfiction CON
KELLY, Robert, 1935- , American; poetry, fiction CON MUR
KELLY, Robert Glynn, 1920- , American; fiction CON
KELLY, Thomas, 1909- , English; nonfiction CON
KELLY, Tim, 1935- , American; plays, fiction CON
KELLY, William Leo, 1924- , American; nonfiction CON
KELLY, William Watkins, 1928- , American; nonfiction CON
KELMAN, Herbert Chanoch, 1927- , Austrian-American; nonfiction CON
KELMAN, Steven, 1948- , American; nonfiction CON
KELPIUS, Johann, 1673-1708, German-American; poetry ST
KELSEY, Alice Geer, 1896- , American; juveniles COM CON FUL WA
KELSEY, Joan Marshall ('Joan Grant'), 1907- , English; fiction CON
KELSEY, Morton Trippe, 1917- ,

American; nonfiction CON
KELSO, Louis O., 1913- , American;
nonfiction CON
KELTON, Elmer, 1926- , American;
fiction CON
KELVIN, Lord (Sir William Thomson),
1824-1907, Irish; nonfiction KBA
KEMAL, Namik, 1840-88, Turkish;
poetry SA ST
KEMAL, Yashar, 1922- , Turkish;
fiction RIC
KEMBLE, Frances Anne Butler
(Fanny), 1809-93, English; poetry,
plays, diary KAA KBA
KEMBLE, James, Australian; nonfic-
tion CON
KEMBLE, John Mitchell, 1807-57,
English; nonfiction KBA
KEMELMAN, Harry, 1908- ,
American; fiction CON
KEMENY, John George, 1926- ,
Hungarian-American; nonfiction
CON
KEMENY, Zsigmond, 1814-75, Hun-
garian; fiction SA ST
KEMMERER, Donald Lorenzo,
1905- , American; nonfiction
CON
KEMP, Abraham, 17th cent., Dutch;
nonfiction, plays ST
KEMP, Betty, 1916- , English;
nonfiction CON
KEMP, Charles F., 1912- ,
American; nonfiction CON
KEMP, Diana Mayle, 1919- ,
English; fiction CON
KEMP, Peter Mant Macintyre, 1915- ,
American; nonfiction CON
KEMP, Robert, 1885-1959, French;
criticism DIF
KEMP, Robert, 1908- , Scots; plays,
fiction CON
KEMP, Roy Zell, 1910- , American;
poetry CON
KEMP, Tom, 1921- , English; non-
fiction CON
KEMP, William, fl. 1600, English;
plays ST
KEMPE, Margery, 1373-1440, English;
nonfiction ST
KEMPER, Donald J., 1929- , Ameri-
can; nonfiction CON
KEMPER, Inez, 1906- , American;
nonfiction CON
KEMPF, Joseh George, 1893- ,
American; nonfiction, translations
HOE
KEMPHER, Ruth Moon, 1934- ,

American; poetry CON
KEMPIS, Thomas à see THOMAS
à KEMPIS
KEMPNER, Alfred see 'KERR,
Alfred'
KEMPNER, Mary Jean, 1913-69,
American; nonfiction CON
KEMPSON, F. Claude, 1860- ,
English; nonfiction HIG
KEMPSTER, Mary Yates, 1911- ,
English; juveniles CON
KEN, Thomas (Kenn), 1637-1711,
English; nonfiction, hymns
BRO KB ST
KENDALL, Carol Seeger, 1917- ,
American; juveniles CON WA
KENDALL, David Evan, 1944- ,
American; nonfiction CON
KENDALL, Edith Lorna, 1921- ,
English; nonfiction CON
KENDALL, Elaine Becker,
1929- , American; nonfiction
CON
KENDALL, George Wilkins, 1809-
67, American; nonfiction KAA
KENDALL, Henry Clarence, 1841-
82, Australian; poetry BRO
KBA
KENDALL, Henry Madison, 1901-
66, American; nonfiction CON
'KENDALL, Lace' see STOUTEN-
BERG, Adrien P.
KENDALL, Lyle Harris, Jr.,
1919- , American; nonfiction
CON
KENDALL, Paul Murray, 1911- ,
American; nonfiction CON
KENDALL, Robert, 1934- , Amer-
ican; nonfiction CON
KENDALL, Thomas Henry, 1839-
82, Australian; poetry ST
KENDALL, Timothy, fl. 1577,
English; translations ST
KENDALL, Willmoore ('Alan
Monk'), 1909- , American;
nonfiction CON
KENDLER, Howard Harvard,
1919- , American; nonfiction
CON
'KENDRAKE, Carleton' see
GARDNER, Erle S.
KENDRICK, Baynard Hardwick
('Richard Hayward'), 1894- ,
American; nonfiction, fiction
CON WAF
KENDRICK, Daniel see KENRICK,
Daniel
KENDRICK, David Andrew, 1937- ,

American; nonfiction CON
'KENDRICKS, James' see FOX,
Gardner F.
KENDRIS, Christopher, 1923- ,
American; nonfiction CON
'KENEAN, Paul Roger' see CLIFFORD,
Martin
KENELLY, John William, Jr.,
1935- , American; nonfiction
CON
KENEN, Peter Bain, 1932- , Amer-
ican; nonfiction CON
KENEZ, Peter, 1937- , Hungarian;
nonfiction CON
KENISTON, Kenneth, 1930- , Amer-
ican; nonfiction CON
KENISTON, R. Hayward, 1883- ,
American; nonfiction BL
KENKO see YOSHIDA, Kenko
KENN, Thomas see KEN, Thomas
KENNAMER, Lorrin, Jr., 1924- ,
American; nonfiction CON
KENNAN, George Frost, 1904- ,
American; nonfiction CON
KENNAN, Kent Wheeler, 1913- ,
American; nonfiction CON
KENNARD, Mrs. Edward, 1850-1914,
English; nonfiction HIG
KENNARD, Marietta Conway, Ameri-
can; poetry HOO
KENNARD-DAVIS, Arthur, 1910- ,
English; juveniles, fiction CON
KENNEDIE, John see KENNEDY,
John
KENNEDY, Charles Rann, 1808-67,
English; poetry KBA
KENNEDY, Charles, 1871-1950,
Anglo-American; plays KT
KENNEDY, David M., 1941- ,
American; nonfiction CON
KENNEDY, Eugene Cullen, 1928- ,
American; nonfiction CON
KENNEDY, George Alexander, 1928- ,
American; nonfiction CON
KENNEDY, Gerald Hamilton ('G.
Hobab Kish'), 1907- , American;
nonfiction CON
KENNEDY, James Hardee, 1915- ,
American; nonfiction CON
KENNEDY, James William, 1905- ,
American; nonfiction CON
KENNEDY, John (Kennedie), fl. 1626,
Scots; poetry ST
KENNEDY, John Fitzgerald, 1917-63,
American; nonfiction CON
KENNEDY, John Pendelton ('Mark
Littleton'), 1795-1870, American;
fiction BRO KAA MAG ST

KENNEDY, Joseph Charles see
KENNEDY, X. J.'
KENNEDY, Kieran A., 1935- ,
Irish; nonfiction CON
KENNEDY, Leo, 1907- , Canadian;
poetry SY
KENNEDY, Leonard Anthony,
1922- , English; nonfiction
CON
KENNEDY, Malcolm Duncan,
1895- , Scots; nonfiction CON
KENNEDY, Margaret, 1896-1967,
English; fiction, plays KL
KT BRO MAT RIC SA
KENNEDY, Michael, 1926- ,
American; nonfiction CON
KENNEDY, Patrick, 1901-73,
Irish; fiction KBA
KENNEDY, Ralph Dale, 1897-1965,
American; nonfiction CON
KENNEDY, Raymond A., 1934- ,
American; fiction, plays CON
KENNEDY, Richard Sylvester,
1920- , American; nonfiction
CON
KENNEDY, Robert Emmet, Jr.,
1937- , American; nonfiction
CON
KENNEDY, Robert Francis, 1925-
68, American; nonfiction CON
KENNEDY, Ruth Lee, 1895- ,
American; nonfiction BL
KENNEDY, Stetson, 1916- ,
American; nonfiction CON
KENNEDY, Walter, 1460?-1508?,
Scots; poetry BRO KB
'KENNEDY, X. J.' (Joseph Charles
Kennedy), 1929- , American;
poetry CON MUR
'KENNEGGY, Richard' see NET-
TALL, Richard G.
KENNELL, Ruth Epperson, 1893- ,
American; juveniles CON
KENNELLY, Brendan, 1936- ,
Irish; poetry, fiction CON
MUR
KENNER, Charles Leroy, 1933- ,
American; nonfiction CON
KENNER, William Hugh, 1923- ,
Canadian; nonfiction CON
KENNERLY, Karen, 1940- ,
American; nonfiction CON
'KENNETH, Mr.' see MARLOWE,
Kenneth
KENNETT, Lee, 1931- , Ameri-
can; nonfiction CON
KENNEY, Alice Patricia, 1937- ,
American; nonfiction CON

KENNEY, George Churchill, 1889- ,
    Canadian; nonfiction CON
KENNEY, James Francis, 1884- ,
    Canadian; nonfiction HOE
KENNEY, John Paul, 1920- ,
    American; nonfiction CON
KENNEY, Sylvia W., 1922- , Amer-
    ican; nonfiction CON
KENNICK, William Elmer, 1923- ,
    American; nonfiction CON
'KENNY, Charles J.' see GARDNER,
    Erle S.
KENNY, Ellsworth Newcomb, 1909- ,
    American; juvenile CON WA
KENNY, Hugh, American; juveniles
    WA
KENNY, John P., 1909- , American;
    nonfiction CON
'KENNY, Kathryn' see STACK, Nicolett
KENNY, Michael, 1863-1946, Irish-
    American; nonfiction HOE
KENNY, Michael, 1923- , English;
    nonfiction CON
KENNY, W. Henry, 1918- , Amer-
    ican; nonfiction CON
KENOYER, Natlee Peoples, 1907- ,
    American; juveniles CON
KENRICK, Daniel (Kendrick), 1652-
    85, English; poetry ST
'KENT, Alexander' see METHOLD,
    Kenneth W.
KENT, Allen, 1921- , American;
    nonfiction CON
KENT, Donald P., 1916- , Amer-
    ican; nonfiction CON
KENT, George Otto, 1919- , Aus-
    trian-American; nonfiction CON
KENT, George W., 1928- , Ameri-
    can; nonfiction CON
KENT, Homer Austin, Jr., 1926- ,
    American; nonfiction CON
KENT, James, 1763-1847, Ameri-
    can; nonfiction KAA
KENT, John, 1820- , English; non-
    fiction HIG
KENT, John Henry Somerset, 1923- ,
    English; nonfiction CON
KENT, Louise Andrews ('Theresa
    Tempest'), 1886-1969, American;
    juveniles, fiction CON KJU KTS
    WA WAF
KENT, Margaret, 1894- , English;
    juveniles COM CON
'KENT, Michael' see BROWN,
    Beatrice B.
KENT, Nora, 1899- , English; fic-
    tion CON
'KENT, Philip' see BULMER, Henry
    K.

KENT, Rockwell ('Hogarth, Jr.'),
    1882-1971, American; nonfic-
    tion CON KL KT
'KENT, Tony' see CRECHALES,
    Anthony G.
KENTFIELD, Calvin, 1924- ,
    American; nonfiction CON
'KENTON, Maxwell' see SOUTHERN,
    Terry
KENTON, Warren, 1933- , Amer-
    ican; nonfiction CON
KENWARD, James Macara,
    1908- , English; nonfiction,
    fiction CON
KENWORTHY, Leonard S., 1912- ,
    American; nonfiction CON
KENYON, Frank Wilson, 1912- ,
    English; fiction CON
KENYON, James William, 1910- ,
    English; nonfiction, fiction,
    juveniles CON
KENYON, John Philipps, 1927- ,
    English; nonfiction CON
KENYON, Kathleen Mary, 1906- ,
    English; nonfiction CON
KENYON, Ley, 1913- , English;
    nonfiction CON
KENYON, Michael, 1931- , Eng-
    lish; fiction CON
KENYON, Raymond G., 1922- ,
    American; juveniles WA
KENYON, Theda, American; fic-
    tion WAF
KEOGH, Lilian Gilmore ('Lilian
    Patrick'), 1927- , American;
    nonfiction CON
KEPES, Juliet, 1919- , Anglo-
    American; juveniles WA
KEPHART, Horace, 1862-1931,
    American; nonfiction JO
KEPHART, Newell C., 1911- ,
    American; nonfiction CON
KEPLER, Thomas Samuel, 1897-
    1963, American; nonfiction
    CON
KEPPEL, George Thomas see
    ALBERMARLE, Lord
KEPPLE, Ella Huff, 1902- ,
    American; nonfiction CON
KEPPLER, Carl Francis, 1909- ,
    American; nonfiction CON
KER, Patrick, fl. 1691, Scots;
    poetry ST
KER, William Paton, 1855-1923,
    Scots; nonfiction BRO KT ST
KER WILSON, Barbara, 1929- ,
    English; fiction, juveniles
    CON
KERALIO, Louis Félix, 1731-93,

French; nonfiction, translations
DIL
KERALIO, Louise de Guynenment,
1758-1821, French; nonfiction DIL
KERANFLECH, Charles Hercule,
1730- , French; nonfiction DIL
KERBER, August Frank, 1917- ,
American; nonfiction CON
KERBY, William J., 1870-1936,
American; nonfiction HOE
KERCKHOVEN, Peter Frans, van,
1818-57, Flemish; fiction, poetry,
plays ST
KEREKES, Tibor ('Rotarius'), 1893- ,
Hungarian-American; nonfiction
CON
KERENSKY, Oleg, 1930- , English;
nonfiction CON
KERENYI, Karl, 1897- , German;
nonfiction KU
KERESZTY, Roch Andrew, 1933- ,
Hungarian-American; nonfiction
CON
KERGUELIN-FREMAREC, Yves Joseph
de, 1745-97, French; nonfiction
DIL
KERIGAN, Florence ('Frances Kerry'),
1896- , American; juveniles CON
KERLAN, Irvin, 1912-63, American;
nonfiction CON
KERMAN, Gertrude Lerner, 1909- ,
Canadian; nonfiction CON
KERMANI, Taghi Thomas, 1929- ,
Iraqi-American; nonfiction CON
KERMODE, John Frank, 1919- ,
English; nonfiction CON
KERN, Alfred, 1919- , French;
fiction DIC DIF PIN
KERN, Alfred, 1924- , American;
fiction CON
'KERN, E. R.' see KERNER, Fred
KERN, Janet Rosalie, 1924- , Amer-
ican; fiction CON
KERNAN, Jerome Bernard, 1932- ,
American; nonfiction CON
KERNAN, Thomas Dickenson, 1903- ,
American; nonfiction HOE
KERNAN, William Fergus, 1892- ,
American; nonfiction HOE
KERNER, Ben, American; juveniles
WA
KERNER, Fred ('Frohm Fredricks';
'E. R. Kern'; 'Frederick Kerr'),
1921- , Canadian; nonfiction CON
KERNER, Justinus Andreas Christian,
1786-1862, German; poetry AL
HAR KE ST
KEROUAC, Jack (Jean Louis Lebris de

Kerouac), 1922- , American;
poetry, fiction CON FLE MUR
RIC
KERPELMAN, Larry Cyril, 1939- ,
American; nonfiction CON
'KERR, Alfred' (Alfred Kempner),
1867-1948, German; essays,
criticism FLE KU
KERR, Lady Anne, 1883-1941,
English; nonfiction HOE
'KERR, Ben' see ARD, William T.
KERR, Donald Gordon Grady,
1913- , Canadian; nonfiction
CON
KERR, Elizabeth M., 1905- ,
American; nonfiction CON
'KERR, Frederich' see KERNER,
Fred
KERR, Harry Price, 1928- ,
American; nonfiction CON
KERR, James Stolee, 1928- ,
Canadian; juveniles CON
KERR, Jean, 1923- , American;
plays CON
KERR, Jessica, 1901- , Irish-
American; nonfiction CON
KERR, Kathel Austin, 1938- ,
American; nonfiction CON
KERR, Laura Nowak, 1904- ,
American; juveniles WA
'KERR, Norman D.' see SIEBER,
Sam D.
'KERR, Orpheus C.' see NEWELL,
Robert H.
KERR, Rose Netzorg, 1892- ,
American; nonfiction CON
KERR, Sophie, 1880-1965, Amer-
ican; fiction KT WAF
KERR, Walter Francis, 1913- ,
American; nonfiction CON
'KERRY, Frances' see KERIGAN,
Florence
'KERRY, Lois' see ARQUETTE,
Lois S.
KERSAINT, Armand Guy Simon de,
1742-93, French; nonfiction
DIL
KERSH, Gerald, 1909-68, English;
journalism, nonfiction KTS
KERSHAW, Alister Nasmyth,
1921- , Australian; fiction,
nonfiction CON
KERSHNER, Howard Eldred, 1891- ,
American; nonfiction CON
KERSNIK, Janko, 1852-97,
Slovene; fiction ST
KERTESZ, Stephen Denis, 1924- ,
Hungarian-American; non-

KEYES, Nelson Beecher, 1894- ,
American; juveniles WA
KEYES, Sidney Arthur Kilworth,
1922-43, English; poetry BRO
RIC ST
KEYFITZ, Nathan, 1913- , Canadian;
nonfiction CON
KEYNES, John Maynard, 1883-1946,
English; nonfiction BRO KT ST
KEYS, John D., 1938- , American;
nonfiction CON
KEYS, Thomas Edward, 1908- ,
American; nonfiction CON
KEYSERLING, Eduard von, 1855-1918,
German; fiction AL COL FLE
HAR SA
KEYSERLING, Count Hermann Alex-
ander, 1880-1946, German; non-
fiction KAT KT SA
KEYSERLING, Robert Wendelin,
1905- , Russian; nonfiction HO
KEYT, David Alan, 1930- , Ameri-
can; nonfiction CON
KEYT, George, 1901- , Ceylonese;
poetry MUR
KHADDURI, Majid, 1909- , Iraqi;
nonfiction CON
KHADILKAR, Krsnaj Prabhakar,
1872-1948, Indian; plays LAN
KHAN KHANA, 1556-1613, Indian;
poetry LAN
KHANLARI, Parviz Natel, 1914- ,
Persian; poetry ST
KHANNA, Jaswant Lal, 1925- ,
Pakistani-American; nonfiction
CON
KHANSA, 17th cent., Arab; poetry
KHAQANI, Afzal, 1126-98, Persian;
poetry LAN ST
KHARE, Narayan Bhaskar ('Bapu'),
1882- , Indian; nonfiction CON
KHAS-GRUB-RJE, 1385-1438,
Tibetan; nonfiction LAN
KHAYYAN, Omav see OMAR KHAYYAM
KHAZZOOM, J. Daniel, 1932- ,
American; nonfiction CON
KHEMNITSER, Ivan Ivanovich (Chem-
nitzer), 1745-84, Russian; fiction
HARK ST
KHERA, Sucha Singh, 1903- , Indian;
nonfiction CON
KHERASAKOV, Mikhail Matveyevich,
1733-1807, Russian; poetry HARK
ST
KHERDIAN, David, 1931- , American;
nonfiction CON
KHIAN-LUNG (Kien-Lung), 1709-99,

Chinese; fiction, poetry SA
'KHLEBNIKOV, Velimér' (Viktor
Vladimirovich Khlebnikov),
1885-1922, Russian; poetry,
fiction COL FLE HARK SA
ST
KHMELNITSKI, Nikolay Ivanovich,
1789-1846, Russian; fiction
HARK
KHODASEVICH, Vladislav Felilsya-
novich, 1886-1939, Russian;
poetry, criticism COL FLE
HARK SA ST
KHOMYAKOV, Alexey Stepanovich,
1804-60, Russian; nonfiction,
poetry HAR HARK KE ST
KHOND MIR, Qiyas, 1475-1535/37,
Persian; nonfiction ST
KHONDEMYR, Gaiatheddin
Mohamed, 15th-16th cent.,
Persian; nonfiction SA
KHOURI, Fred John, 1916- ,
American; nonfiction CON
KHUSHAL KNAN KHATAK, 1613-
87, Persian; poetry ST
KHUSROW DIHALAVI, Abu'l
('Amir Khurrow'), 1253-1325,
Persian; poetry ST
KHVOROSTININ, Prince Ivan
Andreyevich, -1625, Rus-
sian; poetry HARK
KHVYLYOVY, Mykola, 1893-1933,
Russian; nonfiction HARK
KHWARIZMI, Abu, 10th cent.,
Arab; nonfiction ST
'KI NO KAION' (E'nami Kiemon),
1663-1742, Japanese; plays
ST
KI NO TOMONORI, -906?,
Japanese; poetry ST
KI TSURAYUKI, 870-946, Japanese;
poetry, diary LAN ST
KIANG, Ying-Cheng, American;
nonfiction CON
KIBLER, Robert Joseph, 1934- ,
American; nonfiction CON
KIBLER, William W., 1942- ,
American; nonfiction CON
KICKHAM, Charles Joseph, 1826-
82, Irish; fiction, poetry BRO
ST
KID, Thomas see KYD, Thomas
KIDD, Aline Halstead, 1922- ,
American; nonfiction CON
KIDD, Benjamin, 1858-1916,
English; nonfiction KT
KIDD, David Lundy, 1926- ,
American; nonfiction CON

KIDD, Harry, 1917- , Scots; nonfiction CON
KIDD, James Robbins, 1915- , Canadian; nonfiction CON
'KIDD, Russ' see DONSON, Cyril
KIDD, Walter E. ('Conrad Pendleton'), 1917- , American; poetry, fiction CON
KIDDE, Harald Henrik Sager, 1878-1918, Danish; fiction SA ST
KIDDELL, John, 1922- , American; fiction CON
KIDDELL-MONROE, Joan, 1908- , English; juveniles CON DOY
KIDDER, Frederic, 1804-85, American; nonfiction KAA
KIDDLE, Lawrence Bayard, 1907- , American; nonfiction BL CON
KIDNER, Elaine see 'LANE, Jane'
KIDNEY, Dorothy Boone, 1919- , American; nonfiction CON
KIDRON, Hedva B. see BEN-ISRAEL-KIDRON, Hedva
KIEFER, Tillman W., 1898- , American; nonfiction CON
KIEFER, William Joseph, 1925- , American; nonfiction CON
KIEHTREIBER, Albert Konrad see 'GÜTERSLOH, Albert P.
KIELL, Norman, 1916- , American; nonfiction CON
KIELLAND, Alexander Lange (Kyelland), 1849-1906, Norwegian; fiction, plays COL HAR KE SA ST
KIELTY, Bernardine, -1973, American; juveniles WA
KIELY, Benedict, 1919- , Irish-American; nonfiction, fiction CON HO
KIELY, Jerome, 1925- , Irish; poetry MUR
KIELY, Mary Frances, American; juveniles HOE
KIENBERGER, Vincent Ferrer, 1893- , American; nonfiction HOE
KIENE, Julia, American; juveniles WA
KIENIEWICZ, Stefan, 1907- , Polish; nonfiction CON
KIEN-LUNG see KHIAN-LUNG
KIERAN, John Francis, 1892- , American; nonfiction HOE
KIERKEGAARD, Soren, 1813-55, Danish; essays HAR KE MAG SA ST
KIERNAN, Victor Gordon, 1913- ,

English; nonfiction CON
KIES, Johann, 1713-81, German; nonfiction DIL
KIESCHNER, Sidney see 'KINGSLEY, Sidney'
KIESLER, Charles Adolphus, 1934- , American; nonfiction CON
KIESLER, Sara Beth, 1940- , American; nonfiction CON
KIESLING, Christopher Gerald, 1925- , American; nonfiction CON
KIEV, Ari, 1933- , American; nonfiction CON
KIGIN see KITAMURA KIGIN
'KIKAKU' (Takemoto, Enomoto No Kikaku), 1661-1707, Japanese; poetry ST
KIKLIR, Eleazar see KALIR, Eleazar
KIKUCHI HIROSHI KAN, 1888-1948, Japanese; plays, fiction MAT ST
KILANDER, Holger Frederich, 1900- , American; nonfiction CON
KILBOURN, William Morley, 1926- , Canadian; nonfiction CON
KILBRACKEN, John Raymond Godley ('John Godley'), 1920- , English; fiction CON
'KILBURN, Henry' see RIGG, Henry K.
KILBURN, Robert Edward, 1931- , American; juveniles CON
KILBY, Clyde Samuel, 1902- , American; nonfiction CON
KILBY, Peter, 1935- , American; nonfiction CON
KILDAHL, Phillip A., 1912- , American; nonfiction CON
KILDUFF, Mary Dorrell, 1901- , American; nonfiction CON
KILEY, Frederick, 1932- , American; nonfiction CON
KILGORE, James Columbus, 1928- , American; nonfiction CON
KILGOUR, Raymond Lincoln, 1903- , American; nonfiction CON
KILLANIN, Lord (Michael Morris), 1914- , English; nonfiction CON
KILLE, Mary F., 1948- , American; nonfiction CON

KILLIAN, Lewis Martin, 1919- ,
American; nonfiction CON
KILLIAN, Ray A., 1922- ,
American; nonfiction CON
KILLIGREW, Anna, 1660-85, English;
poetry SA
KILLIGREW, Henry, 1613-1700,
English; plays KB
KILLIGREW, Thomas, 1612-83,
English; plays BRO KB ST
KILLIGREW, Thomas, 1657-1719,
English; plays KB
KILLIGREW, Sir William, 1606-95,
English; plays ST
KILLILEA, Marie Lyons, 1913- ,
American; juveniles COM CON
KILLION, Katheryn L., 1936- ,
American; fiction CON
KILLIR, Eleazar see KALIR, Eleazar
'KILLREYNARD, Earl of' see BELL,
Charles W.
KILMARTIN, Edward John, 1923- ,
American; nonfiction CON
KILMER, Alfred Joyce, 1886-1918,
American; poetry, journalism,
BRO KAT KT
KILMER, Aline, 1888-1941, American;
poetry HOE
KILMER, Kenton, 1909- , American;
nonfiction CON
KILPATRICK, Franklin Peirce,
1920- , American; nonfiction
CON
KILPATRICK, James Jackson,
1920- , American; nonfiction
CON
KILPI, Volter Adalbert, 1874-1939,
Finnish; fiction FLE
KILREON, Beth see WALKER,
Barbara K.
KILSON, Marion, 1936- , American;
nonfiction CON
KILTY, William, 1757-1821, Ameri-
can; nonfiction KAA
KILVERT, Margaret Cameron, 1867-
1947, American; nonfiction HOO
KIM, Chin W., 1936- , Korean-
American; nonfiction CON
KIM, Chong ik Eugene, 1930- ,
Korean-American; nonfiction CON
KIM CH'ONT'AEK, 17th cent., Korean;
poetry LAN
KIM, Helen, 1899- , Korean; nonfic-
tion CON
KIM, Kwan Bong, 1936- , Korean;
nonfiction CON
KIM, Kwan Ho, 1936- , Korean;
nonfiction CON

KIM, Kyung-Won, 1936- ,
Korean; nonfiction CON
KIM MANJUNG, 1637-92, Korean;
nonfiction, fiction ST
KIM, Richard Chong Chin, 1923- ,
American; nonfiction CON
KIM, Richard E., 1932- ,
Korean; fiction CON
KIM SAKKAT, 1807-63, Korean;
poetry LAN
KIM, Seung Hee, 1936- ,
Korean; nonfiction CON
KIM SUJANG, 1691- , Korean;
poetry LAN
KIM TONGIN, 1900-51, Korean;
fiction LAN
KIM, Yong-ik, 1920- , Korean-
American; fiction CON
KIM, Yoon Hough, 1934- ,
Korean-American; nonfiction
CON
KIM, Young Hum, 1920- , Korean-
American; nonfiction CON
KIMBALL, Richard Burleigh,
1816-92, American; nonfiction
KAA
KIMBALL, Solon Toothaker,
1909- , American; nonfiction
CON
KIMBALL, Spencer Levan, 1918- ,
American; nonfiction CON
KIMBALL, Stanley Buchholz,
1926- , American; nonfiction
CON
KIMBALL, Warren F., 1935- ,
American; nonfiction CON
KIMBLE, David, 1921- , English;
nonfiction CON
KIMBLE, Gregory Adams, 1917- ,
American; nonfiction CON
KIMBRELL, Grady, 1933- ,
American; nonfiction CON
KIMBROUGH, Edward, 1918- ,
American; fiction WAF
KIMBROUGH, Emily, 1899- ,
American; juveniles, nonfic-
tion COM CON
KIMBROUGH, Robert Alexander
III, 1929- , American; non-
fiction CON
KIMCHE, Dov, 1889- , Jewish;
fiction ST
KIMCHI, David, 1160-1235,
French-Jewish; nonfiction ST
KIMMEL, Melvin, 1930- , Amer-
ican; nonfiction CON
KIMPEL, Ben Franklin, 1905- ,
American; nonfiction CON

KINASTON, Sir Francis see KYNASTON, Sir Francis
KINAU, Johann see 'FOCK, Gorch'
KINAU, Rudolf, 1887- , German; fiction ST
'KINCAID, Alan' see RIKHOFF, James C.
KINCAID, Suzanne Moss, 1936- , American; nonfiction CON
KINCK, Hans Ernst, 1865-1926, Norwegian; fiction, plays, essays COL SA ST
KINDALL, Alva Frederick, 1906- , American; nonfiction CON
KINDER, Faye, 1902- , American; nonfiction CON
KINDER, James S., 1895- , American; nonfiction CON
KINDI, -870, Arab; nonfiction ST
KINDRED, Wendy Good, 1937- , American; juveniles CON
KINDREGAN, Charles Peter, 1935- , American; nonfiction CON
KINERT, Reed Charles, 1912- , American; juveniles WA
KINES, Thomas Alvin, 1922- , Canadian; nonfiction CON
KING, Adele Cockshoot, 1932- , American; nonfiction CON
KING, Alfred M., 1933- , American; nonfiction CON
KING, Alvy Leon, 1932- , American; nonfiction CON
KING, Annette, 1941- , American; fiction CON
KING, Anthony Stephen, 1934- , Canadian; nonfiction CON
KING, Archdale Arthur, 1890- , English; nonfiction CON
'KING, Arthur' see CAIN, Arthur H.
KING, Basil, 1859-1928, American-Canadian; fiction KT SY
KING, Betty Patterson, 1925- , American; nonfiction CON
KING, Blanche Black Busey, 1893- , American; nonfiction HOO
KING, Clarence, 1842-1901, American; nonfiction KAA
KING, Clyde Stuart, 1919- , American; nonfiction CON
KING, Coretta Scott, 1927- , American; nonfiction CON
KING, Cynthia, 1925- , American; juveniles CON
KING, Donald B., 1913- , American; nonfiction CON
KING, Edith Weiss, 1930- , American; nonfiction CON

KING, Edmund James, 1914- , English; nonfiction CON
KING, Edmund Ludwig, 1914- , American; nonfiction BL CON
KING, Edward Smith, 1848-96, American; journalism, poetry KAA
KING, Francis Henry ('Frank Cauldwell'), 1923- , American; nonfiction, fiction, poetry CON MUR RIC
KING, Francis Paul, 1922- , American; nonfiction CON
KING, Frederick Murl, 1916- , American; nonfiction CON
KING, Glen D., 1925- , American; nonfiction CON
KING, Harold, 1874- , American; journalism, fiction HOO
KING, Helen Hayes, 1937- , American; juveniles CON
KING, Henry, 1592-1669, English; poetry BRO KB SP ST
KING, Homer W., 1907- , American; nonfiction CON
'KING, Jack' see DOWLING, Allen
KING, James Terrell, 1933- , American; nonfiction CON
KING, James W., 1920- , American; nonfiction CON
KING, Jere Clemens, 1910- , American; nonfiction CON
'KING, John' see McKEAG, Ernest L.
KING, John Q. Taylor, 1921- , American; nonfiction CON
KING, K. De Wayne Dewey, 1925- , American; nonfiction CON
'KING, Kennedy' see BROWN, George D.
KING, Larry L., 1929- , American; fiction CON
KING, Lester Snow, 1908- , American; nonfiction CON
KING, Louise Wooster, American; nonfiction CON
KING, Marcet Alice Hines, 1922- , American; nonfiction CON
KING, Marian, American; nonfiction CON
KING, Marjorie Cameron (Peggy), 1909- , Canadian; fiction CON
KING, Martha Bennett, American; juveniles, plays WA
'KING, Martin' see MARKS, Stanley

KING, Martin Luther, Jr., 1929-68,
American; nonfiction CON
KING, Mary Louise ('Mary Louise
Johnson'), 1911- , American;
nonfiction CON
KING, Noel Quixote, 1922- , Eng-
lish; nonfiction CON
'KING, Norman A.' see TRALINS,
S. Robert
KING, O. H. P., 1902- , American;
nonfiction CON
KING, Patricia ('Kathey White'),
1930- , American; juveniles
CON
'KING, Paul' see DRACKETT, Philip
KING, Preston Thedore, 1936- ,
American; nonfiction CON
KING, Ray Aiken, 1933- , Ameri-
can; nonfiction CON
KING, Richard Austin, 1929- ,
American; nonfiction CON
KING, Richard G., 1922- , Ameri-
can; nonfiction CON
KING, Robert Charles, 1928- ,
American; nonfiction CON
KING, Robert G., 1929- , American;
nonfiction CON
KING, Robin, 1919- , American;
juveniles CON
KING, Roma Alvah, Jr., 1914- ,
American; nonfiction CON
KING, Rufus, 1917- , American;
nonfiction CON
KING, Seth S., American; juveniles
WA
KING, Spencer Bidwell, Jr., 1904- ,
American; nonfiction CON
KING, Terry Johnson, 1929- ,
American; fiction CON
KING, Thomas James, 1925- , Amer-
ican; nonfiction CON
KING, Willard L., 1893- , American;
nonfiction CON
KING, William, 1650-1729, Irish;
nonfiction KB
KING, William, 1663-1712, English;
fiction KB ST
KING, William Richard, 1938- ,
American; nonfiction CON
KINGDON, John Wells, 1940- ,
American; nonfiction CON
KINGDON, Robert McCune, 1927- ,
American; nonfiction CON
KINGERY, Robert Ernest, 1913- ,
American; nonfiction CON
KING-HALL, Magdalen, 1904-71,
English; fiction CON
KING-HALL, William Stephen Richard

('Etienne'), 1893-1966, English;
poetry, nonfiction, plays CON
KING-HELE, Desmond George,
1927- , English; nonfiction
CON
KINGLAKE, Alexander William,
1809-91, English; nonfiction
BRO KBA ST
KINGMAN, Mary Lee, 1919- ,
American; juveniles COM
CON FUL WA
KINGO, Thomas Hansen, 1634-
1703, Danish; poetry, hymns
HAR SA ST
KINGSBURY, Arthur, 1939- ,
American; nonfiction CON
KINGSBURY, Jack Dean, 1934- ,
American; nonfiction CON
KINGSBURY, John Merriam,
1928- , American; nonfiction
CON
KINGSBURY, Robert C., 1924- ,
American; nonfiction CON
'KINGSBURY, Vernon L.' see
LUKENS, Henry C.
KINGSFORD, William, 1819-98,
Canadian; nonfiction BRO KBA
ST
KINGSLEY, Charles, 1819-75,
English; juveniles, plays, fic-
tion, poetry BRO DOY HIG
KBA MAG SA ST WA
KINGSLEY, George Henry, 1827-
92, English; nonfiction KBA
KINGSLEY, Henry, 1830-76, Eng-
lish; fiction BRO KBA MAG
ST
KINGSLEY, Mary Henrietta, 1862-
1900, English; nonfiction BRO
KBA ST
'KINGSLEY, Robert' see CLARKE,
John C.
'KINGSLEY, Sidney' (Sidney
Kieschner'), 1906- , Ameri-
can; plays KT MAT
'KINGSMILL, Hugh' see LUNN,
Hugh K.
KINGSNORTH, George William,
1924- , English; nonfiction
CON
KINGSTON, Albert James, 1907- ,
American; nonfiction CON
KINGSTON, Elizabeth Chudleigh,
1720- , English; nonfiction
SA
KINGSTON, Frederick Temple,
1925- , American; nonfiction
CON

KINGSTON, William Henry Giles,
1814-80, English; juveniles BRO
DOY KBA ST
KINKADE, Richard Paisley, 1939- ,
American; nonfiction CON
'KINKAID, Matt' see ADAMS, Clifton
KINKEAD, Eugene Francis, 1906- ,
American; nonfiction CON
KINKEL, Gottfried, 1815-82, German;
poetry AL HAR KE ST
KINKER, Johannes, 1764-1845, Dutch;
nonfiction KE ST
KINLEY, Phyllis Gillespie, 1930- ,
American; juveniles CON
KINNAMON, Keneth, 1932- , Ameri-
can; nonfiction CON
KINNEAR, Elizabeth K., 1902- ,
American; nonfiction CON
KINNEAR, Michael, 1937- ,
Canadian; nonfiction CON
KINNELL, Galway, 1927- , Ameri-
can; poetry CON MUR
KINNEY, Arthur Frederick, 1933- ,
American; nonfiction CON
KINNEY, C. Cleland, 1915- ,
Canadian; juveniles CON
KINNEY, Elizabeth Clementine Dodge
Stedman, 1810-89, American;
essays, poetry KAA
KINNEY, Harrison, 1921- , Ameri-
can; juveniles CON
KINNEY, Jean Brown, 1912- ,
American; juveniles CON
KINNEY, Lucien Blair, 1895- ,
American; nonfiction CON
KINNESON, William Andrew, 1932- ,
American; nonfiction CON
KINNOSUKE NATSUME see 'NATSUME
SOSEKI'
KINOSHITA JUNJI, 1914- , Japanese;
plays LAN MAT
KINOSHITA NAOE, 1869-1937,
Japanese; fiction LAN ST
KINO TSURAIUKI, 883-946, Japanese;
poetry, criticism SA
KINROSS, Lord Patrick ('Patrick
Balfour'), 1904- , Scots; fiction
CON
KINSBRUNER, Jay, 1939- , Ameri-
can; nonfiction CON
KINSCHOT, A. C. de, 18th cent.,
French; plays DIL
KINSELLA, Paul L., 1923- ,
American; nonfiction CON
KINSELLA, Thomas, 1928- , Irish;
poetry CON MUR RIC
KINSEY, Barry Allen, 1931- , Amer-
ican; nonfiction CON

'KINSEY-JONES, Brian' see BALL,
Brian N.
KINSLEY, James, 1922- , Scots;
nonfiction CON
KINSMAN, Frederic Joseph,
1868-1944, American; nonfic-
tion HOE
KINSOLVING, Sally Bruce, 1876- ,
American; poetry HOE
KINSTLER, Everett Raymond,
1926- , American; nonfiction
CON
KINTNER, William Roscoe,
1915- , American; nonfiction
CON
KINTO see FUJIWARA NO KINTO
KINTSCH, Walter, 1932- , Amer-
ican; nonfiction CON
KINWELMERSH, Francis, fl. 1570,
English; poetry ST
KIN-WUN MIN-GYI, 1821-1908,
Burmese; nonfiction LAN
KINZER, Betty, 1922- , Ameri-
can; nonfiction CON
KIORCHEV, Dimo, 1882-1929,
Bulgarian; nonfiction ST
KIPARSKY, Valentin Julius
Alexander, 1904- , Russian-
Finnish; nonfiction CON
'KIPENGA, Ernestine' see
STORSVE, La Vaughn
KIPLING, Joseph Rudyard, 1865-
1936, English; juveniles, fic-
tion, poetry BRO DOY FLE
KL KT MAG RIC SA SP ST
WA
KIPPHARDT, Heinar, 1922- ,
German; plays MAT
KIPPLEY, John Francis, 1930- ,
American; nonfiction CON
KIRBY, David Peter, 1936- ,
English; nonfiction CON
KIRBY, Douglas J., 1929- ,
English; juveniles CON
KIRBY, Edward Stuart, 1909- ,
English; nonfiction CON
KIRBY, Jack Temple, 1938- ,
American; nonfiction CON
'KIRBY, Jean' see McDONNELL,
Virginia B.
'KIRBY, Jean' see ROBINSON,
Chaille P.
KIRBY, Mary Sheelah Flanagan,
1916- , Irish; nonfiction
CON
KIRBY, Thomas Austin, 1904- ,
American; nonfiction CON
KIRBY, William, 1817-1906,

Canadian; fiction ST SY
KIRCHENER, Glenn, 1930- , American; nonfiction CON
KIRCHER, Athanasius, 1602- , German; nonfiction SA
KIRCHMAIR, Thomas see 'NOOGEORGUS, Thomas'
KIRCHNER, Walther, 1905- , German-American; nonfiction CON
KIRCHOFF, Theodor, 1828-99, German-American; nonfiction ST
KIRDAR, Uner, 1933- , Turkish; nonfiction CON
KIREYEVSKY, Ivan Vasilyevich, 1806-56, Russian; criticism HARK ST
KIREYEVSKY, Peter Vasilyevich, 1808-56, Russian; poetry ST
KIRILL, Turovski, 12th cent., Russian; nonfiction HARK
KIRILLOV, Vladimir Timofeyevich, 1889- , Russian; poetry HARK
KIRILOV, Ivan, 1876-1936, Bulgarian; fiction ST
KIRK, Clara Marburg, 1898- , American; nonfiction CON
KIRK, David, 1935- , American; nonfiction CON
KIRK, Donald, 1938- , American; nonfiction CON
KIRK, Geoffrey Stephen, 1921- , English; nonfiction CON
KIRK, George Eden, 1911- , English; nonfiction CON
KIRK, H. David, 1918- , German-Canadian; nonfiction CON
KIRK, Hans Rudolf, 1898- , Danish; fiction FLE ST
KIRK, Irene (Irina), 1926- , American; nonfiction CON
KIRK, James Albert, 1929- , American; nonfiction CON
KIRK, John Foster ('Henry Hayes'), 1824-1904, American; nonfiction KAA
KIRK, Richard Edmund ('Jeffrey Church'), 1931- , American; nonfiction CON
KIRK, Robert Warner, American; nonfiction CON
KIRK, Russell Amos, 1918- , American; nonfiction CON
KIRK, Ruth Eleanor, American; nonfiction PAC
KIRK, Ruth Kratz, 1925- , American; juveniles CON WA
KIRK, Thomas Hobson ('K. H. Thomas'), 1899- , American; fiction CON

KIRKBRIDGE, Ronald, 1912- , American; fiction CON WAF
KIRKCONNELL, Watson, 1895- , Canadian; poetry, translations MUR ST SY
KIRKE, Edward, 1553-1613, English; criticism KB
KIRKENDALL, Lester Allen, 1903- , American; nonfiction CON
KIRK-GREENE, Christopher Walter Edward, 1926- , English; nonfiction CON
KIRKHAM, E. Bruce, 1938- , American; nonfiction CON
KIRKHAM, Michael, 1934- , English; nonfiction CON
KIRKLAND, Bryant Mays, 1914- , American; nonfiction CON
KIRKLAND, Caroline Matilda Stansbury ('Mary Clavers'), 1801-64, American; nonfiction KAA
KIRKLAND, Edward Chase, 1894- , American; nonfiction CON
KIRKLAND, Jack M., 1902-69, American; plays MAT
KIRKLAND, Joseph, 1830-94, American; fiction, journalism BRO HOO KAA ST
KIRKLAND, Winifred Margaretta, 1872-1943, American; fiction, essays, journalism JO
KIRKMAN, Francis, 1632?-74, English; translations ST
KIRKPATRICK, Dow Napier, 1917- , American; nonfiction CON
KIRKPATRICK, Ivone Augustine, 1897- , English; nonfiction CON
KIRKPATRICK, Lyman Beckford, Jr., 1916- , American; nonfiction CON
KIRKUP, James ('Terahata Jun'; 'Tsuyuki Shigeru'; 'Andrew James'; 'James Falconer'; 'Ivy B. Summerforest'), 1923- , British; poetry, plays CON MUR
KIRKUS, Virginia see GLICK, Virginia K.
KIRKWOOD, Ellen Swan, 1904- , American; juveniles CON
KIRKWOOD, James, 1930- , American; plays, fiction CON
KIRKWOOD, Kenneth P., 1899-1968, American; nonfiction CON

KIRN, Ann, American; juveniles WA
KIROUAC, Joseph Louis Conrad see
  'MARIE-VICTORIN, Frere'
KIRSCH, Arthur Clifford, 1932- ,
  American; nonfiction CON
KIRSCH, Felix Marie, 1884-1945,
  American; nonfiction HOE
KIRSCH, Leonard Joel, 1934- ,
  American; nonfiction CON
KIRSCH, Robert R. ('Robert Bancroft';
  'Robert Dundee'), 1922- , Ameri-
  can; fiction CON
KIRSCHENBAUM, Aaron, 1926- ,
  American; nonfiction CON
KIRSCHENER, Linda Rae, 1939- ,
  American; nonfiction CON
KIRSCHNER, Allen, 1930- , Ameri-
  can; nonfiction CON
KIRSCHTEN, Ernest, 1902- , Ameri-
  can; nonfiction CON
KIRSHON, Vladimir Mikhaylovich,
  1902-38, Russian; plays COL HAR
  HARK MAT SA ST
KIRSNER, Robert, 1921- , Lithuanian-
  American; nonfiction CON
KIRST, Hans Hellmut, 1914- , Ger-
  man; fiction AL RIC
'KIRTLAND, G. B.' see JOSLIN, Sesyle
KIRVAN, John J., 1932- , Canadian;
  nonfiction CON
KIRWAN, Albert Dennis, 1904- ,
  American; fiction CON
KIRWAN, Laurence Patrick, 1907- ,
  English; nonfiction CON
KIRWAN, Molly Morrow ('Charlotte
  Morrow'), 1906- , English;
  fiction CON
KIRWIN, Harry Wynne, 1911-63,
  American; nonfiction CON
KIRZNER, Israel Mayer, 1930- ,
  Anglo-American; nonfiction CON
KISAMORE, Norman Dale, 1928- ,
  American; nonfiction CON
'KISANJI' (Hirazawa; Meiseido;
  Tsunetomi), 1735-1813, Japanese;
  poetry ST
KISCH, Egon Erwin, 1885-1948,
  German; nonfiction AL
KISEKI see EJIMA KISEKI
KISER, Clyde Vernon, 1904- ,
  American; nonfiction CON
KISER, Martha Gwinn, American;
  juveniles WA
KISFALUDY, Károly (Charles),
  1788-1830, Hungarian; plays,
  poetry KE SA ST
KISFALUDY, Sándor, 1772-1844,
  Hungarian; poetry, plays KE SA
  ST

'KISH, G. Hobab' see KENNEDY,
  Gerald H.
KISH, George, 1914- , Hungarian-
  American; nonfiction CON
KISH, Leslie, 1910- , Hungarian-
  American; nonfiction CON
KISIELEWSKI, Jan August, 1876-
  1918, Polish; plays ST
KISINGER, Grace Gelvin Maze,
  1913- , American; juveniles
  CON WA
KISKER, George W., 1912- ,
  American; nonfiction CON
KISMARIC, Carole, 1942- ,
  American; juveniles CON
KISS, József, 1843-1921, Hungarian;
  poetry COL SA
KISSANE, Leedice McAnelly,
  1905- , American; nonfiction
  CON
KISSEN, Fanny, 1904- , Ameri-
  can; juveniles CON
KISSIN, Eva H., 1923- , Ameri-
  can; juveniles CON
KISSINGER, Henry Alfred, 1923- ,
  German-American; nonfiction
  CON
KISSLING, Fred R., Jr., 1930- ,
  American; nonfiction CON
KIST, Willem, 1758-1841, Dutch;
  fiction ST
KISTEMAECKERS, Henry Hubert
  A., 1872- , Belgian; plays,
  fiction COL SA
KISTER, Kenneth F., 1935- ,
  American; nonfiction CON
KISTENER, Kunz, fl. 1350, Ger-
  man; poetry ST
KITABATAKE CHIKAFUSA, 1292-
  1354, Japanese; nonfiction
  ST
KITAGAWA, Daisuke, 1910- ,
  Japanese-American; nonfiction
  CON
KITAGAWA, Joseph M., 1915- ,
  Japanese-American; nonfiction
  CON
'KITAMURA KIGIN' (Kitamura
  Kyunosuke), 1625-1705, Japa-
  nese; poetry ST
KITANO, Harry H. L., 1926- ,
  American; nonfiction CON
KITCHEN, Helen Angell, 1920- ,
  American; nonfiction CON
KITCHEN, Herminie Broedel,
  1901- , American; nonfiction
  CON
KITCHEN, Paddy, 1934- , Eng-
  lish; nonfiction, fiction CON

KITE, Elizabeth, 1864- , American;
nonfiction HOE
'KITE, Larry' see SCHNECK, Stephen
KITOWICZ, Jedrzej, 1728-1804,
Polish; diary ST
KITSON, Clark George Sydney Robert,
1900- , English; nonfiction
CON
KITSON, Jack William, 1940- , Amer-
ican; nonfiction CON
KITTO, H. D. F., 1897- , English;
nonfiction CON
KITTO, John, 1804-54, English;
nonfiction BRO ST
KITTREDGE, George Lyman, 1860-
1941, American; nonfiction KT
KITZBERG, August, 1856-1927,
Estonian; plays, fiction ST
KITZINGER, Sheila, 1929- , Eng-
lish; nonfiction CON
KITZINGER, Uwe Webster, 1928- ,
English; nonfiction CON
'KIVI, Aleksis' (Aleksis Stenvall),
1834-72, Finnish; fiction KE SA
ST
KIZER, Carolyn, 1925- , American;
poetry MUR
KJAER, Nils, 1870-1924, Norwegian;
essays, plays SA ST
KJELGAARD, James Arthur, 1910-
59, American; juveniles KJU
WA
KJELLGREN, Josef, 1907-48,
Swedish; fiction ST
KJOME, June Creola, 1920- ,
American; fiction CON
KLAAR, Ernst, 1861-1920, German;
nonfiction AL
KLAAS, Joe, 1920- , American;
fiction CON
KLAASSEN, Leo Hendrik, 1920- ,
Dutch; nonfiction CON
'KLABUND' (Alfred Henschke),
1890-1928, German; poetry,
fiction, plays AL COL FLE
HAR KU MAT SA ST
KLÄBER, Kurt ('Kurt Held'; 'Lisa
Tetzner'), 1897-1959, German;
fiction AL
KLAFS, Carl E., 1911- , Ameri-
can; nonfiction CON
KLAGSBRUN, Francine Lifton,
American; nonfiction CON
'KLAHIFA, Hadji' see KABIT CELEBI,
Mustafa
'KLAINIKITE, Anne' see GEHMAN,
Betsy H.
KLAIRWAL, T. de, 18th cent.,

French; plays DIL
KLAJ, Johann, 1616-56, German;
poetry ST AL
KLAPERMAN, Libby Mindlin,
1921- , Russian-American;
juveniles CON
KLAPP, Orrin E., 1915- ,
American; nonfiction CON
KLAPPER, Charles Frederich,
1905- , English; nonfiction
CON
KLAPPER, Marvin, 1922- ,
American; nonfiction CON
KLAPPERT, Peter, 1942- ,
American; poetry CON
KLARE, George Roger, 1922- ,
American; nonfiction CON
KLARMANN, Andrew F. ('Virgil
B. Fairman'), 1866-1931,
German-American; fiction
HOE
KLASS, Morton, 1927- , Ameri-
can; nonfiction CON
KLASS, Philip J., 1919- ,
American; nonfiction CON
KLASS, Sheila Solomon, 1927- ,
American; fiction CON
KLASS, Sholom, 1916- , Ameri-
can; nonfiction CON
KLASSEN, William, 1930- ,
American; nonfiction CON
KLAUE, Lola Shelton, 1903- ,
American; juveniles CON
KLAUSLER, Alfred Paul, 1910- ,
American; nonfiction CON
KLAUSMEIER, Herbert J., 1915- ,
American; nonfiction CON
KLAUSNER, Joseph, 1874- ,
Jewish; essays ST
KLAUSNER, Samuel Zundel,
1923- , American; nonfiction
CON
KLAW, Spencer, 1920- , Ameri-
can; nonfiction CON
KLAYMAN, Maxwell Irving,
1917- , American; nonfiction
CON
KLDIASHVILI, David, 1862-1931,
Russian; fiction LAN
KLEBE, Charles Eugene, 1907- ,
American; nonfiction CON
KLEES, Fredric Spang, 1901- ,
American; nonfiction CON
KLEIMAN, Robert, 1918- ,
American; nonfiction CON
KLEIN, Aaron E., 1930- ,
American; nonfiction CON
KLEIN, Abraham Moses, 1909-72,

Canadian; poetry, fiction MUR
KTS SY ST
KLEIN, Alexander, 1918- , Hungarian-
American; nonfiction CON
KLEIN, Bernard, 1921- , American;
nonfiction CON
KLEIN, Arnold William, 1945- ,
American; nonfiction CON
KLEIN, David, 1919- , American;
juveniles CON WA
KLEIN, Donald Charles, 1923- ,
American; nonfiction CON
KLEIN, Eduard, 1923- , German;
nonfiction AL
KLEIN, Ernest, 1899- , Hungarian-
Canadian; nonfiction CON
KLEIN, Felix, 1862- , French;
nonfiction HOE
KLEIN, Frederic Shriver, 1904- ,
American; nonfiction CON
KLEIN, H. Arthur, American; juven-
iles, nonfiction CON WA
KLEIN, John Jacob, 1929- , Ameri-
can; nonfiction CON
KLEIN, Josephine F. H., 1926- ,
German-English; nonfiction CON
KLEIN, Leonore Glotzer, 1916- ,
American; juveniles CON WA
KLEIN, Marcus, 1928- , American;
nonfiction CON
KLEIN, Martin A., 1934- , Ameri-
can; nonfiction CON
KLEIN, Maury, 1939- , American;
nonfiction CON
KLEIN, Mina Cooper, English; non-
fiction CON
KLEIN, Muriel Walzer, 1920- ,
American; nonfiction CON
KLEIN, Philip Alexander, 1927- ,
American; nonfiction CON
KLEIN, Philip Shriver, 1909- ,
American; nonfiction CON
KLEIN, Rose Schweitzer, 1918- ,
American; nonfiction CON
KLEIN, Ted U., 1926- , Ameri-
can; nonfiction CON
KLEIN, Woody, 1929- , American;
fiction CON
KLEINBAUER, Walter Eugene, 1937- ,
American; nonfiction CON
KLEINE-AHLBRANDT, William Laird,
1932- , American; nonfiction
CON
KLEINFELD, Vincent A., 1907- ,
American; nonfiction CON
KLEINHANS, Theodore John,
1924- , American; nonfiction
CON

KLEINMANN, Jack Henry, 1932- ,
American; nonfiction CON
KLEINMUNTZ, Benjamin, 1930- ,
American; nonfiction CON
KLEIST, Bernd Wilhelm Heinrich
von, 1777-1811, German; non-
fiction AL HAR KE MAG SA
ST
KLEIST, Ewald Christian von,
1715-59, German; poetry AL
HAR ST
KLEMENT, Frank Ludwig, 1908- ,
American; nonfiction CON
KLEMER, Richard Hudson, 1918-
72, American; nonfiction CON
KLEMKE, Elmer D., 1926- ,
American; nonfiction CON
KLEMM, Wilhelm ('Felix Brazil'),
1881- , German; nonfiction
KU
KLEMPNER, John, 1898-1972,
American; fiction WAF
KLENK, Robert William, 1934- ,
American; nonfiction CON
KLENZ, William, 1915- , Ameri-
can; nonfiction CON
KLENZE, Camillo van, 1865-1943,
German-American; nonfiction
ST
KLEPPER, Jochen, 1903-42, Ger-
man; poetry, fiction, essays
AL FLE KU LEN
KLERER, Melvin, 1926- , Ameri-
can; nonfiction CON
KLETT, Guy Soulliard, 1897- ,
American; nonfiction CON
KLEWIN, William Thomas ('Tom
Matthews'), 1921- , Ameri-
can; nonfiction CON
KLEYN, Johannes Petrus, 1760-
1805, Dutch; poetry ST
KLICPERA, Václav Kliment, 1792-
1859, Czech; plays ST
KLIEVER, Lonnie Dena, 1931- ,
American; nonfiction CON
KLIJN, Barend, 1774-1829, Dutch;
poetry ST
KLIJN, Hendrik Harmsen, 1773-
1856, Dutch; plays, poetry
ST
'KLIKSPAAN' see KNEPPELHOUT,
Johannes
KLIMA, Ivan, 1931- , Czech;
nonfiction CON
KLIMENT OHRIDSKY, 840-916,
Bulgarian; nonfiction ST
KLIMENT, Smolyatich (Clement),
fl. 1147, Russian; nonfic-

tion HARK
KLIMISCH, Sister Mary Jane, 1920- ,
American; nonfiction CON
KLIMOWICZ, Barbara, 1927- , American; juveniles CON
KLINCK, Carl Frederick, 1908- ,
Canadian; nonfiction CON
KLINCK, George Alfred, 1903- ,
Canadian; nonfiction CON
KLINDT-JENSEN, Ole, 1918- ,
Danish; nonfiction CON
KLINE, George Louis, 1921- , American; nonfiction CON
KLINE, Lloyd W., 1931- , American;
nonfiction CON
KLINE, Morris, 1908- , American;
nonfiction CON
KLINE, Norman, 1935- , American;
nonfiction CON
KLINE, Peter, 1936- American;
nonfiction CON
KLINEFELTER, Walter, 1899- ,
American; nonfiction CON
KLING, Robert Edward, Jr., 1925- ,
American; nonfiction CON
KLING, Simcha, 1922- , American;
nonfiction CON
KLINGER, Eric, 1933- , American;
nonfiction CON
KLINGER, Friedrich Maxmilian von,
1752-1831, German; plays, fiction AL HAR KE SA ST
KLINGER, Kurt, 1914- , German;
nonfiction CON
KLINGSOR, Tristan, 1874- , French;
poetry DIF
KLINKHAMER, Govert, 1702-74,
Dutch; poetry ST
KLINKNER, Ferdinand, 1880- ,
American; poetry HOE
KLIPSTEIN, Editha, 1880- ,
German; nonfiction LEN
KLIPSTEIN, Louis Frederick, 1813-78, American; nonfiction KAA
KLISE, Eugene Storm, 1908- , American; nonfiction CON
KLITGAARD, Mogens, 1906-45,
Danish; fiction FLE ST
KLOETZLI, Walter, Jr., 1921- ,
American; nonfiction CON
KLONG-CHEN-RAB-BYAMS-PA,
1308-63, Tibetan; nonfiction LAN
KLONG-RDOL BLA-MA, 1729- ,
Tibetan; nonfiction LAN
KLONOWICZ, Sebastian Fabian, 1545-1602, Polish; poetry ST
KLOOS, Willem Johan Theodro ('G. N.'; 'Sebastian Sr.'; 'Guido'),

1859-1938, Dutch; poetry,
criticism COL SA ST
KLOOSTER, Fred H., 1922- ,
American; nonfiction CON
KLOOSTERMAN, Simke, 1878-1938, Prisian; fiction, poetry
ST
KLOPSTOCK, Friedrich Gottlieb,
1724-1803, German; poetry
AL HAR KE SA ST
KLOS, Frank William Jr., 1924- ,
American; nonfiction CON
KLOSE, Norma Cline, 1936- ,
American; juveniles CON
KLOSS, Phillips, 1902- ,
American; poetry CON
KLUBERTANZ, George Peter,
1912- , American; nonfiction
CON
KLUCKHOHN, Clyde, 1905- ,
American; nonfiction KTS
KLUCKHOHN, Frank L., 1907-70,
American; nonfiction CON
KLUGE, Kurt, 1886-1940, German; fiction AL HAR KU
LEN ST
KLUGER, James R., 1939- ,
American; nonfiction CON
KLUGER, Richard, 1934- , American; fiction CON
KLUWE, Mary Jean, 1925- ,
American; nonfiction CON
'KLYCHKOV, Sergey' see LESHEN-KOV, S. A.
KLYUCHEVSKY, Vasily Osipovich,
1842-1911, Russian; nonfiction
ST
KLYUSHNIKOV, Ivan Pavlovich,
1811-95, Russian; poetry ST
KLYUSHNIKOV, Victor Petrovich,
1841-92, Russian; fiction ST
KLYUYEV, Nikolai Alekseyevich,
1885/87-1937, Russian; poetry
FLE HAR HARK RIC ST
KNACHEL, Philip Atherton, 1926- ,
American; nonfiction CON
KNAPLUND, Paul, 1885- , American; nonfiction CON
KNAPP, Albert, 1798-1864, German; poetry ST
KNAPP, Bettina Liebowitz,
American; nonfiction CON
KNAPP, Joseph Grant, 1900- ,
American; nonfiction CON
KNAPP, Lewis Mansfield, 1894- ,
American; nonfiction CON
KNAPP, Robert Hampden, 1915- ,
American; nonfiction CON

KNAPP, Samuel Lorenzo ('Ignatius L.
Robertson'; 'Shahcoolen'; 'Marshall
Soult'), 1783-1838, American; non-
fiction KAA SA
KNAPP, William Ireland, 1835-1908,
American; nonfiction BL SA
KNAPPER, Christopher Kay, 1940- ,
American; nonfiction CON
KNAPTON, Ernest John, 1902- ,
English; nonfiction CON
KNATCHBULL-HUGESSEN, Edward
Hugessen (Lord Brabourne), 1829-
93, English; juveniles DOY
KNAUTH, Joachim, 1931- , German;
plays AL
KNEBEL, Fletcher, 1911- , Ameri-
can; fiction ST
KNECHT, Robert Jean, 1926- ,
English; nonfiction CON
KNEEBONE, Geoffrey Thomas,
1918- , English; nonfiction
CON
KNEESE, Allen Victor, 1930- , Amer-
ican; nonfiction CON
KNEIP, Jakob, 1881- , German;
poetry KU LEN
KNELLER, John William, 1916- ,
English; nonfiction CON
KNEPLER, Henry William, 1922- ,
American; nonfiction CON
KNEPPELHOUT, Johannes ('Klikspaan'),
1814-85, Dutch; nonfiction HAR
KE ST
KNEVET, Ralph, 1600-71, English;
poetry ST
KNEZEVICH, Stephen Joseph,
1920- , American; nonfiction
CON
KNIAZNIN, Franciszek Dionizy,
1750-1807, Polish; poetry, plays
HAR ST
KNIBBS, Harry (Henry), Herbert,
1874-1945, Canadian; poetry,
fiction KT
KNICKERBOCKER, Charles Herrick,
1922- , American; fiction
'KNICKERBOCKER, Diedrich' see
IRVING, Washington
KNICKERBOCKER, Kenneth Leslie,
1905- , American; nonfiction
CON
'KNIFESMITH' see CUTLER, Ivor
KNIFFEN, Fred Bowerman, 1900- ,
American; nonfiction CON
KNIGGE, Adolf Franz Friedrich von,
1752-96, German; nonfiction
AL HAR ST
'KNIGHT, Adam' see LARIAR,

Lawrence
KNIGHT, Charles, 1791-1873,
English; nonfiction BRO KBA
ST
KNIGHT, Charles W., 1891- ,
American; fiction CON
KNIGHT, Clayton, 1891- ,
American; juveniles CON
WA
'KNIGHT, David' see PRATHER,
Richard S.
KNIGHT, David C., American;
juveniles WA
KNIGHT, Edgar W., 1886- ,
American; nonfiction JO
KNIGHT, Eric, 1897-1943, Eng-
lish; juveniles, fiction DOY
KT MAG WA
KNIGHT, Etheridge, 1931/33- ,
American; poetry CON MUR
KNIGHT, Everett, 1919- , Amer-
ican; nonfiction CON
KNIGHT, Captain Frank, 1905-72,
English; juveniles DOY
KNIGHT, G. Norman, 1891- ,
English; nonfiction CON
KNIGHT, George Angus Fulton,
1909- , Scots; nonfiction
CON
KNIGHT, George Wilson, 1897- ,
Anglo-Canadian; criticism
CON KT
KNIGHT, Graham, 1921- , Eng-
lish; nonfiction CON
KNIGHT, Harold Vincent, 1907- ,
American; nonfiction CON
KNIGHT, Hattie M., 1908- ,
American; nonfiction CON
KNIGHT, Henry Cogswell ('Arthur
Singleton, Esq.'), 1789-1835,
American; poetry KAA
KNIGHT, Henry Gally, 1786-1846,
English; nonfiction, poetry
BRO ST
KNIGHT, Herbert Ralph, 1895- ,
American; nonfiction CON
KNIGHT, Hilary, American;
juveniles WA
KNIGHT, Hugh McCown, 1905- ,
American; nonfiction CON
KNIGHT, Ione Kemp, 1922- ,
American; nonfiction CON
KNIGHT, Isabel Frances, 1930- ,
American; nonfiction CON
'KNIGHT, James' see SCHNECK,
Stephen
KNIGHT, James A., 1918- ,
American; nonfiction CON
KNIGHT, Joseph, 1829-1907, Eng-

lish; criticism, nonfiction KBA
KNIGHT, Karl F., 1930- , American; nonfiction CON
'KNIGHT, Mallory T.' see HURWOOD, Bernhardt J.
KNIGHT, Margaret Kennedy Horsey, 1903- , English; nonfiction CON
KNIGHT, Maxwell, 1900- , English; nonfiction, juveniles CON
KNIGHT, Norman Louis, 1895- , American; fiction CON
KNIGHT, Oliver Holmes, 1919- , American; nonfiction CON
KNIGHT, Paul Emerson, 1925- , American; nonfiction CON
KNIGHT, Peter, English; juveniles WA
KNIGHT, Richard Payne, 1749-1824, English; poetry ST
KNIGHT, Roy Clement, 1907- , English; nonfiction CON
KNIGHT, Ruth Adams, 1898- , American; juveniles CON WA FUL
KNIGHT, Sarah Kemble, 1666-1727, American; diary BRO KAA
KNIGHT, Thomas Stanley, Jr., 1921- , American; nonfiction CON
KNIGHT, William Nicholas, 1939- , American; nonfiction, plays CON
KNIGHT, Walker Leigh, 1924- , American; nonfiction CON
KNIGHTLEY, Phillip, 1929- , American; nonfiction CON
'KNIGHT-PATTERSON, W. M.' see KULSKI, Wladslaw W.
KNIGHTS, Lionel Charles, 1906- , English; criticism CON KTS
KNIGHTS, Peter Roger, 1938- , American; nonfiction CON
KNIPE, Alden Arthur, 1870-1950, American; juveniles KJU
KNIPE, Emilie Benson, 1870- , American; juveniles KJU
KNIPE, Humphry, 1941- , South African; nonfiction CON
KNIPSCHIELD, Donald Harold, 1940- , American; nonfiction CON
KNISTER, Raymond, 1900-32, Canadian; poetry, fiction SY
KNITTEL, John Hermann, 1891- , Swiss; fiction, nonfiction AL KT LEN
KNOBLAUGH, H. Edward, 1904- , American; nonfiction HOE
KNOBLER, Nathan, 1926- , American; nonfiction CON
KNOBLOCK, Edward, 1874-1945,

American; plays, fiction BRO MAT
KNOEBL, Kuno, 1936- , Austrian; nonfiction CON
KNOEPFLE, John, 1923- , American; poetry CON MUR
KNOEPFLMACHER, Ulrich Camillus, 1931- , German; nonfiction CON
KNOLES, George Harmon, 1907- , American; nonfiction CON
KNOLL, Gerald M., 1942- , American; nonfiction CON
KNOLL, Robert Edwin, 1922- , American; nonfiction CON
KNOLLENBERG, Bernhard, 1892- , American; nonfiction CON
KNOLLES, Richard, 1550?-1610, English; nonfiction BRO KB ST
KNOPF, Terry Ann, American; nonfiction CON
KNORR, Albert Scofield, 1929- , American; poetry CON
KNORRING, Sofia Margareta Zelow, 1797-1848, Swedish; fiction HAR KE ST
KNORTZ, Karl, 1841-1918, German-American; nonfiction ST
KNOTT, Middleton O'Malley, 1876- , Irish; nonfiction HIG
KNOTT, William Cecil, Jr. ('Bill J. Carol'), 1927- , American; fiction CON
KNOTT, William Kilborn ('Bill Knott'), American; poetry MUR
KNOWLES, Alison, 1933- , American; nonfiction CON
KNOWLES, Asa Smallidge, 1909- , American; nonfiction CON
KNOWLES, Dorothy, 1906- , South African; nonfiction CON
KNOWLES, Herbert, 1798-1817, English; poetry BRO
KNOWLES, James Sheridan, 1784-1862, Irish; plays BRO KBA SA ST
KNOWLES, John, 1926- , American; fiction CON
KNOWLES, Joseph William, 1922- , American; nonfiction CON
KNOWLES, Louis Leonard, 1947- , American; nonfiction CON
KNOWLES, Malcolm Shepherd, 1913- , American; nonfiction CON
KNOWLES, Michael Clive David,

1896- , English; nonfiction CON
KNOWLTON, Robert Almy, 1914- ,
American; nonfiction CON
KNOWLTON, William H., 1927- ,
American; juveniles CON
KNOX, Alexander, 1757-1831, Irish;
nonfiction KBA
'KNOX, Calvin M.' see SILVERBERG,
Robert
KNOX, Edmund George Valpy ('Evoe'),
1881-1971, English; fiction, poetry
BRO KT
KNOX, Henry Macdonald, 1916- ,
Scots; nonfiction CON
KNOX, Isa see CRAIG, Isa
KNOX, John, 1505/13-72, Scots;
nonfiction BRO KB ST
KNOX, John, 1900- , American;
nonfiction CON
KNOX, John Ballenger, 1909- ,
American; nonfiction CON
KNOX, Robert Buick, 1918- ,
American; nonfiction CON
KNOX, Ronald Arbuthnot, 1888-1957,
English; nonfiction BRO HOE
RIC KT
KNOX, Rose B., 1879- , American;
juveniles JO KJU
KNOX, Thomas Wallace, 1835-96,
American; journalism KAA
KNOX, Vera Huntingdon, Canadian;
nonfiction CON
KNOX, Vicesimus, 1752-1821, English;
essays BRO ST
KNOX, Willia, 1789-1825, English;
poetry BRO
KNOX, William ('Robert MacLeod'),
1928- , Scots; fiction CON
KNOX-JOHNSTON, Robin, 1939- ,
American; nonfiction CON
KNUDSEN, Jacob Christian Lindberg,
1858-1917, Danish; fiction COL
FLE KE SA ST
KNUDSEN, Knud, 1812-95, Norwegian;
nonfiction SA
KNUDSON, Harry R. Jr., American;
nonfiction PAC
KNUDSON, Rozanne ('R.R.'), 1932- ,
American; nonfiction CON
KNUSEL, Jack Leonard, 1923- ,
American; nonfiction CON
KNUTSON, Kent Siguart, 1924- ,
American; nonfiction CON
KNYAZHNIN, Yakov Borisovich, 1742-
91, Russian; plays HARK ST
KO HUNG, 253?-333?, Chinese; nonfic-
tion ST
'KOBAYASHI ISSA' (Kobayashi Nobuyuki),

1763-1828, Japanese; poetry
ST
'KOBAYASHI, Masako M.' see
MATSUNO, Masako
KOBAYASHI TAKIJI, 1903-33,
Japanese; fiction LAN ST
KOBER, Arthur, 1900- , Ameri-
can; nonfiction, plays CON
KT MAT
KOBLER, Arthur Leon, 1920- ,
American; nonfiction CON
PAC
KOBLER, Mary Turner S.,
1930- , American; nonfiction
CON
'KOBO DAISHI' (Saiki Mana; Kukai),
774-835, Japanese; nonfiction
ST
KOCH, Christian Guillaume de,
1737-1813, French; nonfiction
DIL
KOCH, Christine Wüllner, 1869-
1951, German; poetry ST
KOCH, Claude Francis, 1918- ,
American; poetry, fiction
CON HO
KOCH, Dorothy Clarke, 1924- ,
American; juveniles CON WA
KOCH, Frederich Henry, 1877-
1944, American; plays JO
KOCH, Hans Gerhard, 1913- ,
German; nonfiction CON
KOCH, Helen Lois, 1895- ,
American; nonfiction CON
KOCH, Kenneth, 1925- , Ameri-
can; poetry, plays, fiction
CON MUR
KOCH, Martin, 1882-1940, Swedish;
journalism COL SA ST
KOCH, Richard, 1921- , Ameri-
can; nonfiction CON
KOCH, Robert, 1918- , American;
nonfiction CON
KOCH, Thilo, 1920- , German;
nonfiction, poetry, fiction
CON
KOCH, Thomas Walter, 1933- ,
American; nonfiction CON
KOCH, Vivienne, 1914- , Ameri-
can; criticism KTS
KOCH, William H., Jr., 1923- ,
American; nonfiction CON
KOCHANOWSKI, Jan, 1530-84,
Polish; poetry, plays HAR
KE SA ST
KOCHANOWSKI, Piotr, 1566-1620,
Polish; poetry ST
KOCHEN, Manfred, 1928- ,

American; nonfiction CON
KOCHKUROV, Nikolay Ivanovich
('Artyom Vesyoly'; Vesely),
1899- , Russian; fiction HARK
ST
KOCHMAN, Thomas, 1936- , German-American; nonfiction CON
KOCHOWSKI, Wespazjan, 1633-1700,
Polish; poetry ST
KOCIC, Petar, 1877-1916, Serbian;
fiction ST
KOCK, Charles Paul de, 1793-1871,
French; fiction DIF HAR KE
SA ST
KOCK, Johan O., -1955, Danish;
nonfiction BL
'KODA ROHAN' (Koda Shigeyuki),
1867-1947, Japanese; fiction ST
KODANDA RAO, Pandurangi, 1889- ,
Indian; nonfiction CON
KOEHLER, Alan Robert, 1928- ,
American; nonfiction CON
KOEHLER, George E., 1930- ,
American; nonfiction CON
KOEHLER, George Stanley, 1915- ,
American; nonfiction CON
KOEHLER, Nikki, 1951- , American;
nonfiction CON
KOEHLER, W. R., 1914- , American; nonfiction CON
KÖHLER, Wolfgang, 1887- ,
German-American; nonfiction KTS
KÖLSCSEY, Ferenc, 1790-1838,
Hungarian; poetry, criticism ST
KÖLWEL, Gottfried, 1889- , German;
nonfiction KU
KOEMAN, Jacob, 17th cent., Dutch;
poetry ST
KOEN, Ross Y., 1918- , American;
nonfiction CON
KÖNEMANN von JERXHEIM, -1316,
German; poetry ST
KOENEN, Hendrik Jacob, 1809-74,
Dutch; poetry ST
KOENERDINGH, Jan, 1632-1705,
Dutch; plays ST
KOENIG, Allen Edward, 1939- ,
American; nonfiction CON
KOENIG, Clyde Eldo, 1919- , American; nonfiction CON
KOENIG, Duane Walter, 1918- , American; nonfiction CON
KÖNIG, Johann Ulrich, 1688-1744,
German; poetry ST
KOENIG, Laird, American; fiction,
plays CON
KOENIG, Leo, 1889- , Jewish;
essays, criticism ST

KOENIG, Louis William, 1916- ,
American; nonfiction CON
KÖNIG, Rother, 12th cent., German; nonfiction AL
KOENIG, Samuel, 1899-1972,
American; nonfiction CON
KOENIGSBERGER, Helmut George,
1918- , American; nonfiction
CON
KOENIGSHOVEN, James Twinger,
1346-1420, German; nonfiction
SA
KOENIGSMARK, Maria Aurora,
1673- , German; nonfiction
SA
KOEPPEN, Wolfgang, 1906- ,
German; fiction AL FLE KU
KUN LEN
KÖPRÜLÜ, Mehmed Fuad, 1890- ,
Turkish; nonfiction ST
'KOERBER, Lenka von' (Helene
von der Leyen), 1888-1958,
German; fiction AL
KOERING, Ursula, 1921- , American; juveniles FUL
KÖRMENDI, Ferenc, 1900- ,
Hungarian-American; fiction
WAF
KÖRNER, Gustav Philipp, 1809-96,
German-American; nonfiction
ST
KOERNER, James D., 1923- ,
American; nonfiction CON
KÖRNER, Karl Theodor, 1791-
1813, German; poetry, plays
AL HAR KE ST
KOERNER, Stephan, 1913- ,
Czech-English; nonfiction CON
'KÖRNER-SCHRADER, Paul' (Karl
Schrader), 1900-62, German;
nonfiction AL
KOESIS, Robert, 1935- , American; plays CON
KOESTENBAUM, Peter, American;
translations CON
KOESTLER, Arthur, 1905- ,
Hungarian; fiction, essays
CON FLE KTS MAG RIC ST
KOETSVELD, Cornelis Eliza van,
1807-93, Dutch; essays, juveniles ST
KOFOED, John C., 1894- ,
American; nonfiction CON
KOFFLER, Camilla see 'YLLA'
KOGALNICEANU, Mihail, 1817-
91, Moldavian; nonfiction ST
KOGAN, Bernard Robert, 1920- ,
American; nonfiction CON

KOGAN, Herman, 1914- , American;
nonfiction CON
KOGAN, Peter Siměnovich, 1872-1931,
Russian; nonfiction ST
KOGAWA, Joy Nozomi Nakayama,
1935- , Canadian; poetry MUR
KOGIKU, Kiichiro Chris, 1927- ,
Japanese-American; nonfiction
CON
KOGINOS, Manny T., 1933- , Amer-
ican; nonfiction CON
KOGOS, Frederick, 1907- , Russian-
American; nonfiction CON
KOH, Byung Chul, 1936- , Korean-
American; nonfiction CON
KOH, Sung Jae, 1917- , Korean-
American; nonfiction CON
KOHAK, Erazim V., 1933- , Czech-
American; nonfiction CON
'KOHAVI, Y.' see STERN, Jay B.
KOHEN-RAZ, Reuven, 1921- , Czech-
Israeli; nonfiction CON
KOHL, Marguerite, American; juveniles
WA
KOHLER, Foy David, 1908- , Ameri-
can; nonfiction CON
KOHLER, Heinz, 1934- , German-
American; nonfiction CON
KOHLER, Sister Mary Hortense,
1892- , American; nonfiction
CON
KOHLHAASE, Wolfgang, 1931- ,
German; nonfiction AL
KOHN, Bernice Herstein, 1920- ,
American; juveniles CON WA
KOHN, Hans, 1891-1971, Czech-
American; nonfiction CON KTS
KOHN, Jacob, 1881- , American;
nonfiction CON
KOHNER, Frederick, 1905- , Czech-
American; plays, fiction CON
RIC
KOHT, Halvdan, 1873- , Norwegian;
criticism ST
'KOIDULA' (Lydia Emilie F. Janssen),
1843-86, Estonian; poetry ST
'KOIKAWA, Harumachi' (Kurahashi
Kiwame), 1744-89, Japanese; fic-
tion, poetry ST
KOINER, Richard B., 1929- , Amer-
ican; fiction CON
'KOIZUMI, Yakumo' see HEARN,
Lafcadio
KOJIMA, Takashi, 1902- , Japanese;
fiction CON
KOJUHAROV, Todor ('Feyda Chorny';
'Capt. Kopeykin'), 1894-1945,
Bulgarian; journalism ST

'KOKHANOVSKAYA' see
SOKHANSKAYA, Naaezhda S.
KOKOSCHKA, Oscar, 1886- ,
Austrian; plays, fiction FLE
KU HAR MAT
KOLAJA, Jiri Thomas, 1919- ,
Czech-American; nonfiction
CON
KOLAR, Slavko, 1891- , Croatian;
fiction ST
KOLARS, Frank, 1899-1972, Amer-
ican; juveniles, fiction CON
'KOLAS, Yakub' (K. Mitskevich),
1882- , Russian; fiction
HARK
KOLASKY, John, 1915- , Canadian;
nonfiction CON
KOLB, Annette, 1875-1967, Ger-
man; fiction, essays AL FLE
HAR KU LEN ST
KOLB, Erwin John, 1924- ,
American; nonfiction CON
KOLB, Gwin Jackson, 1919- ,
American; nonfiction CON
KOLB, Harold Hutchinson, Jr.,
1933- , American; nonfiction
CON
KOLB, Kenneth, 1926- , Ameri-
can; fiction, plays CON
KOLBE, Henry Eugene, 1907- ,
American; nonfiction CON
KOLBENHEYER, Erwin Guido
('Hjalmar Kutzleb'; 'Otto
Gmelin'; 'Robert Hohlbaum';
'Mirko Jelusich'), 1878-1962,
German; fiction, plays AL
COL FLE HAR KU MAT SA ST
'KOLBENHOFF, Walter' (Walter
Hoffmann), 1908- , German;
nonfiction KU LEN
KOLBREK, Loyal, 1914- , Amer-
ican; nonfiction CON
KOLENDA, Konstantin, 1923- ,
American; nonfiction CON
KOLESNIK, Walter Bernard,
1923- , American; nonfiction
CON
KOLINSKI, Charles James, 1916-,
American; nonfiction CON
KOLJEVIC, Svetozar, 1930- ,
American; nonfiction CON
KOLKO, Gabriel, 1932- , Ameri-
can; nonfiction CON
KOLLAR, Jan, 1793-1852, Slovak;
poetry KE SA ST
KOLLATAJ, Hugo, 1750-1812,
Polish; nonfiction ST
KOLLBRUNNER, Oskar, 1895-

1932, Swiss-American; poetry ST
KOLLEK, Theodore, 1911- , Austrian-
Israeli; nonfiction CON
KOLLER, James, 1936- , American;
poetry MUR
KOLLER, John M., 1938- , Ameri-
can; nonfiction CON
KOLLER, Lawrence Robert, 1912- ,
American; nonfiction CON
KOLLER, Marvin Robert, 1919- ,
American; nonfiction CON
KOLLOCK, William Raymond, 1940- ,
American; poetry CON
KOLLONTAI, Alexandra Mikhaylovna
(Kollontay), 1872-1951, Russian;
nonfiction ST
KOLMAN-CASSIUS, Jaroslav, 1883- ,
Czech; poetry ST
'KOLMAR, Gertrud' (Gertrud Chod-
ziesner), 1894-1943, German;
poetry AL FLE KU
KOLMODIN, Olof, 1690-1753, Swedish;
poetry ST
KOLSON, John Clifford, 1920- ,
American; nonfiction CON
KOLSTOE, Oliver Paul, 1920- ,
American; nonfiction CON
KOLTSOV, Alexey Vasilyevich, 1809-
42, Russian; poetry HARK KE
SA ST
KOLTUN, Frances Lang, American;
nonfiction CON
KOMACHI see ONO NO KOMACHI
KOMARNICKI, Titus, 1896- , Polish-
English; nonfiction CON
KOMAROV, Matvey, 18th cent., Rus-
sian; fiction ST
KOMAROVSKY, Mirra, Russian-Ameri-
can; nonfiction CON
KOMENSKY, Jan Amos see COMENIUS,
Jan A.
KOMEY, Ellis Ayitey, 1927- ,
Ghanaian; poetry MUR
KOMISAR, Lucy, 1942- , American;
nonfiction, juveniles CON
KOMMERELL, Max, 1902-44, German;
criticism, essays, plays, poetry
FLE KU LEN
KOMROFF, Manuel, 1890- , American;
fiction, juveniles COM CON KL
KT WA WAF
KONADU, Samuel Asare ('K. A. Bediako'),
1932- , Ghanaian; nonfiction
CON
KONARSKI, Hieronim Stanislaw, 1700-
73, Polish; nonfiction, plays ST
KONCZACKI, Zbigniew Andrzej,
1917- , Polish-Canadian; nonfic-

tion CON
KONDRATOWIEZ, Ludwik see
'SYROKOMLA, Wladyslaw'
'KONEVSKOY, Ivan Ivanovich' (I. I.
Oraeus), 1877-1901, Russian;
poetry ST
KONI, Anatoly Fedorovich, 1844-
1927, Russian; nonfiction ST
KONICK, Marcus, 1914- ,
American; nonfiction, plays
CON
KONINGH, Abraham de, 1587-
1619, Dutch; poetry ST
KONIGSBERG, Conrad Isidore,
1916- , English; nonfiction
CON
KONIGSBURG, Elaine Lobl,
1930- , American; nonfiction,
juveniles CON WA
KONINGSBERGER, Hans, 1921- ,
Dutch-American; fiction, plays
CON
'KONISH, Raizan (Konishi Iemon),
1654-1716, Japanese; poetry
ST
KONKLE, Janet Everest, 1917- ,
American; nonfiction CON
KONNYRE, Leslie, 1914- ,
Hungarian-American; nonfiction
CON
KONOPKA, Gisela, 1910- , Ger-
man-American; nonfiction
CON
KONOPNICKA, Maria Wasilowska,
1842-1910, Polish; poetry,
fiction COL KE SA ST
KONRAD, Evelyn, 1930- ,
Austrian-American; nonfiction
CON
KONRAD see ROLANDSLIED
KONRAD, Pfaffe, 1130-70,
Bavarian; nonfiction ST
KONRAD von AMMENHAUSEN,
fl. 1337, Swiss; nonfiction ST
KONRAD von FUSSESBRUNN, fl.
1180-1210, Austrian; poetry
ST
KONRAD von HEIMESFURT, fl.
1225-30, German; nonfiction
ST
KONRAD von MEGENBURG, 1309-
74, German; nonfiction ST
KONRAD von WÜRZBERG, 1220?-
87, German; poetry AL HAR
ST
'KONSALIK, H. G.' see DWINGER,
Edwin E.
KONSTANTINOV, Aleko, 1863-97,

Bulgarian; fiction, journalism ST
KONSTANTINOV, Konstantin, 1890- ,
Bulgarian; fiction ST
KONTOS, Peter George, 1935- ,
American; nonfiction CON
KONVITZ, Milton Ridvas, 1908- ,
American; nonfiction CON
KOOB, Derry Delos, 1933- , American; nonfiction CON
KOOB, Theodora J. Foth, 1918- ,
American; juveniles CON WA
KOONCE, Ray F., 1913- , American; nonfiction CON
KOOP, Katherine C. ('Katherine C.
LaMancusa'), 1923- , American;
nonfiction CON
KOOSER, Theodore, 1939- , American; poetry CON
KOPERNIK, Mikolaj see COPERNICUS,
Nicolaus
KOPEYKIN, Capt. see KOJUHAROV,
Todor
KOPISCH, August, 1799-1853, German;
poetry AL ST
KOPIT, Arthur, 1938- , American;
plays MAT
KOPKIND, Andrew David, 1935- ,
American; nonfiction CON
KOPLIN, Harry Thomas, 1923- ,
American; nonfiction CON
KOPLITZ, Eugene De Vere, 1928- ,
American; nonfiction CON
KOPLOWITZ, Jan, 1909- , German;
nonfiction AL
KOPP, Anatole, 1915- , Russian-French; nonfiction CON
KOPP, Oswald W., 1918- , American; nonfiction CON
KOPP, Richard L., 1934- , American; nonfiction CON
KOPP, Sheldon Bernard, 1929- ,
American; nonfiction CON
KOPPETT, Leonard, 1923- , Russian-American; nonfiction CON
KOPPITZ, Elizabeth Munsterberg,
1919- , German-American; nonfiction CON
KOPPMAN, Lionel, 1920- , American; nonfiction CON
KOPS, Bernard, 1926- , British;
poetry, fiction, plays CON MAT
MUR RIC
KOPTA, Josef, 1894- , Czech;
fiction ST
KOPYCINSKI, Joseph Valentine,
1923- , American; nonfiction
CON
KORAËS, Adamtios (Coraes; Coray),

1748-1833, Greek; nonfiction
KE SA ST
KORBEL, John, 1918- , American; nonfiction CON
KORBEL, Josef, 1909- , Czech-American; nonfiction CON
KORBONSKI, Andrezej, 1927- ,
Polish-American; nonfiction
CON
KORBONSKI, Stefan, 1903- ,
Polish-American; nonfiction
CON
KOREN, Edward, 1935- , American; juveniles CON
KOREN, Henry J., 1912- ,
Dutch-American; nonfiction
CON
KORENIOWSKI, Józef, 1797-1863,
Polish; poetry, plays, fiction
ST
KORG, Jacob, 1922- , American;
nonfiction CON
KORGES, James ('Peter J.
Longleigh, Jr.'), 1930- ,
American; nonfiction CON
KORINFSKY, Apollon Apollonovich,
1868- , Russian; poetry ST
KORIYAMA, Naoshi, 1926- ,
Japanese; poetry, criticism
MUR
KORKFER, Dana, 1908- , American; nonfiction, juveniles
CON
KORMONDY, Edward John, 1926- ,
American; nonfiction CON
KORN, Alejandro, 1860-1936,
Argentinian; essays, criticism
MIN SA
KORN, Bertram, Wallace, 1918- ,
American; nonfiction CON
KORNAI, Janos, 1928- , Hungarian; nonfiction CON
KORNAROS, Vitzentzos, 17th
cent., Creatan; poetry, plays
ST
KORNBLUTH, Jesse, 1946- ,
American; nonfiction CON
KORNEICHUK, Alexander Yevdokimovich, 1910-72, Ukranian;
plays COL SA ST HAR
KORNER, Karl T., 1791-1813,
German; poetry SA
KORNFELD, Paul, 1889-1942,
German; plays, fiction FLE
KORNIYCHUK, Alexander, 1905- ,
Russian; fiction, plays HARK
MAT
KORNFELD, Paul, 1889-1942,

German; plays, fiction FLE
KORNIYCHUK, Alexander, 1905- ,
Russian; fiction, plays HARK
MAT
KORNFELD, Paul, 1889-1942, German; plays KU MAT
KORNHAUSER, William, 1925- ,
American; nonfiction CON
KORNRICH, Milton, 1933- , American; nonfiction CON
'KORNSCHLAG' see SCHNOG, Karl
KOROL, Alexander G., 1900- ,
Russian-American; nonfiction
CON
KOROLENKO, Vladimir Galaktionovich,
1853-1921, Russian; fiction COL
FLE KE HAR HARK SA ST
KORSI, Demetrio (Coorsi), 1899- ,
Greek-Panamanian; nonfiction
BL
KORT, Wesley Albert, 1935- ,
American; nonfiction CON
KORTH, Francis Nicholas, 1912- ,
American; nonfiction CON
KORTNER, Peter, 1924- , American;
fiction CON
KORTUM, Karl Arnold, 1745-1824, German; fiction AL ST
KORWIN-PIOTROWSKA, Gabriela see
ZAPOLSKA, Gabriela
KORZENIOWSKI, Jézel, 1797-1863,
Polish; poetry, plays SA
KORZENIOWSKI, Jozef Teodor Konrad
Nalicz see CONRAD, Joseph
KORZYBSKI, Alfred, 1879-1950,
Polish-American; nonfiction KTS
KOSA, John, 1914- , American;
nonfiction CON
'KOSACH, L.' see UKRAINKA, Lesya
KOSCHADE, Alfred, 1928- , American; nonfiction CON
KOSCHWITZ, Otto, 1902-44, German-American; fiction ST
KOSHI, George M., 1911- , American; nonfiction CON
KOSHLAND, Ellen, 1947- , American; poetry CON
KOSINSKI, Jerzy Nikodem ('Joseph
Novak'), 1933- , Polish-American; fiction CON
KOSINSKI, Leonard V., 1923- ,
American; nonfiction CON
'KOSKENNIEMI, Veikko Antero' (V.A.
Forsnäs), 1885- , Finnish;
poetry, fiction ST
KOSLOW, Jules, 1916- , American;
nonfiction CON
KOSOR, Josip, 1879-1961, Serbian;

plays, poetry HAR ST
KOSS, Stephen Edward, 1940- ,
American; nonfiction CON
KOSSMANN, Rudolf Richard,
1934- , American; nonfiction
CON
KOSSAK-SZCZUCKA, Zofia,
1890- , Polish; fiction COL
HAR HO KTS SA ST
KOST, Robert John, 1913- ,
American; juveniles CON
KOSTELANETZ, Richard Cory,
1940- , American; nonfiction
CON
KOSTEN, Andrew, 1921- ,
American; nonfiction CON
KOSTER, Richard Morton, 1934- ,
American; fiction CON
KOSTIA, Conde see VALDIVIA,
Aniceto
KOSTIC, Laza, 1841-1910,
Serbian; poetry, plays, criticism ST
KOSTICH, Dragos D., 1921- ,
Yugoslav-American; juveniles
CON WA
KOSTKA, Edmund Karl, 1915- ,
German-American; nonfiction
CON
KOSTOMAROV, Nikolai Ivanovich,
1817-85, Russian; nonfiction
SA ST
KOSTOV, Stefan, 1879-1939,
Bulgarian; plays ST
KOSTROV, Efim Ivanovich, 1752-96, Russian; poetry, translations ST
KOSTROWITSKI, Wilhelm Appolinaris de see 'APOLLINAIREE,
Guillaume'
KOSTYLYEV, Valentin Ivanovich,
1888-1950, Russian; fiction
HAR HARK ST
'KOSUGI TENGAI' (Kosugi Tamezo),
1865- , Japanese; fiction ST
KOSZTOLANYI, Dezsö, 1885-1936,
Hungarian; fiction, poetry COL
FLE SA ST
KOTHARI, Rajni, 1928- , Indian;
nonfiction CON
KOTHEN, Rev. Robert, 1900- ,
Belgian; nonfiction HO
KOTKER, Norman, 1931- , American; nonfiction CON
KOTLER, Milton, 1935- , American; nonfiction CON
KOTLER, Philip, 1931- , American; nonfiction CON

KOTLOWITZ, Robert, 1924- , American; fiction CON
KOTLYAREVSKY, Ivan, 1769-1838, Ukranian; fiction HARK SA ST
KOTLYAREVSKY, Nestor Alexandrovich, 1863-1925, Russian; nonfiction ST
KOT-MURLYKA see WAGNER, Nikolay P.
KOTOSHIKHIN, Grigory Karpovich, 17th cent., Russian; nonfiction ST
KOTSCHEVAR, Lendal Henry, 1908- , American; nonfiction CON
KOTSUJI, Abraham Setsuzau, 1899- , Japanese; nonfiction CON
KOTT, Jan, 1914- , Polish; nonfiction CON
KOTTA, Leo F. see 'FLAKE, Otto'
KOTSYUBINSKY, Mykhaylo, 1864-1913, Ukranian; fiction HARK ST
KOTTMAN, Richard Norman, 1932- , American; nonfiction CON
KOTZ, Nick, 1932- , American; nonfiction CON
KOTZ, Samuel, 1930- , Canadian; nonfiction CON
KOTZEBUE, August Friedrich Ferdinand von, 1761-1819, German; plays AL HAR KE SA ST
KOTZIN, Michael Charles, 1941- , American; nonfiction CON
KOUSOULAS, Dimitrios George, 1923- , American; nonfiction CON
KOUTS, Anne, 1945- , American; juveniles CON
KOUTS, Hertha Pretorius, 1922- , American; fiction CON
KOUWENHOVEN, John Atlee, 1909- , American; nonfiction CON
KOUYOUMDJIAN, Dikran see 'ARLEN, Michael'
KOVAČIĆ, Ante, 1854-89, Croatian; poetry ST
KOVAČIĆ, Ivan Goran, 1913-43, Croatian; poetry ST
KOVACS, Imre, 1913- , Hungarian-American; nonfiction CON
KOVALËV, Mikhail A. see 'IVNEV, Ryurik'
KOVALEVSKAYA, Sonya (Kovalevsky), 1850-91, Russian; nonfiction ST
KOVALIK, Nada, 1926- , Canadian; nonfiction CON WA
KOVALIK, Vladimir, 1928- , Czech-American; nonfiction CON
KOVARSKY, Irving, 1918- , Ameri-

can; nonfiction CON
KOVEL, Joel S., 1936- , American; nonfiction CON
KOVEL, Ralph, 1920- , American; nonfiction CON
KOVEL, Terry, 1928- , American; nonfiction CON
KOVRIG, Bennett, 1940- , Hungarian-Canadian; nonfiction CON
KOWALSKI, Frank, 1907- , American; nonfiction CON
KOWITZ, Gerald Thomas, 1928- , American; nonfiction CON
KOZAKOV, Mikhail Emanuelovich, 1897- , Russian; fiction HARK ST
KOZARAC, Josip, 1858-1906, Croatian; fiction, poetry ST
KOZELKA, Paul, 1909- , American; nonfiction CON
KOZIK, Frantisek, 1909- , Czech; fiction RIC
KOZLOV, Ivan Ivanovich, 1779-1840, Russian; poetry HARK ST
KOZLOWSKI, Theodore T., 1917- , American; nonfiction CON
KOZMA, Presbyter (Cosmas), 10th cent., Bulgarian; nonfiction ST
KOZMIAN, Kajetan, 1771-1856, Polish; poetry HAR ST
KRACHOLOV see YAVOROV
KRACK, Hans Günter, 1921- , German; nonfiction AL
KRACMAR, John Z., 1916- , Czech-English; nonfiction CON
KRACOLOV see JAVOROV, Pejo
KRADER, Lawrence, 1919- , American; nonfiction CON
KRADITOR, Aileen S., 1928- , American; nonfiction CON
KRAEHE, Enno E., 1921- , American; nonfiction CON
KRÄMER-BADONI, Rudolf, 1913- , German; nonfiction KU LEN
KRAENZEL, Carl Frederich, 1906- , American; nonfiction PAC
KRAENZEL, Margaret Powell ('Wallace Blue'), 1899- , American; juveniles, poetry CON
KRAFT, Joseph, 1924- , American; nonfiction CON
KRAFT, Kenneth, 1907- , American; fiction CON

KRAFT, Leonard Edward, 1923- ,
American; nonfiction CON
KRAFT, Robert Alan, 1934- , Ameri-
can; nonfiction CON
KRAFT, Ruth Bussenius, 1920- ,
German; nonfiction AL
KRAFT, Virginia, 1932- , American;
nonfiction CON
'KRAFT, Walter Andreas' see FRIED-
LANDER, Walter A.
KRAFT, Werner, 1896- , German;
nonfiction KU
KRAFT, William F., 1938- , Ameri-
can; nonfiction CON
KRAG, Thomas, 1868-1913, Norwegian;
fiction COL SA ST
KRAG, Vilhelm Andreas Wexels, 1871-
1933, Norwegian; poetry, fiction,
plays COL SA ST
KRAHN, Fernando, American; juveniles
WA
KRAILSHEIMER, Alban John, 1921- ,
English; nonfiction CON
KRAINS, Hubert, 1862-1934, Belgian;
fiction COL SA
KRAJENKE, Robert William, 1939- ,
American; nonfiction CON
KRAL, Frano, 1903- , Slovak;
poetry, fiction ST
KRAL, Janko, 1822-76, Slovak;
poetry ST
KRAMARZ, Joachim, 1931- , Polish-
German; nonfiction CON
KRAMER, Aaron, 1921- , American;
poetry, nonfiction CON
KRAMER, Alfred Theodore, 1892- ,
American; nonfiction CON
KRAMER, Edith, 1916- , Austrian-
American; nonfiction CON
KRAMER, Eugene Francis, 1921- ,
American; nonfiction CON
KRAMER, Frank Raymond, 1908- ,
American; nonfiction CON
'KRAMER, George' see HEUMAN,
William
KRAMER, George, American;
juveniles WA
KRAMER, Judith Rita, 1933- ,
American; nonfiction CON
KRAMER, Nora, American; juveniles
WA
KRAMER, Roland Laird, 1898- ,
American; nonfiction CON
KRAMER, Samuel Noah, 1897- ,
Russian-American; nonfiction
CON
KRAMER, Simon Paul, 1914- ,
American; nonfiction CON

KRAMER, Theodor, 1897-1958,
Austrian; poetry AL FLE KU
ST
KRAMISH, Arnold ('J. Lincoln
Paine'), 1923- , American;
nonfiction CON
KRAMM, Joseph, 1907- , Amer-
ican; plays KTS MAT
KRAMON, Florence, 1920- ,
American; juveniles CON
KRAMP, Willy, 1902- , German;
nonfiction KU LEN
KRAMRISCH, Stella, 1898- ,
American; nonfiction CON
KRANJEC, Misko, 1908- ,
Slovene; fiction ST
KRANIDAS, Kathleen Collins,
1931- , American; fiction
CON
KRANJCEVIC, Silvije Strahimir,
1865-1908, Croatian; poetry
COL SA ST
KRATZ, Hazel Newman, 1920- ,
American; fiction CON
KRANZ, Edwin Kirker, 1949- ,
American; nonfiction CON
KRANZBERG, Melvin, 1917- ,
American; nonfiction CON
KRAPP, George Philip, 1872-
1934, American; nonfiction KT
'KRAPP, R. M.' see ADAMS,
Robert M.
'KRASELCHIK, R.' see DYER,
Charles
KRASECKI, Ignacy, 1735-1801,
Polish; poetry, criticism SA
ST HAR KE
KRA-SHIS RGYAL-MTSHAN,
-1925?, Tibetan; nonfiction
LAN
KRASILOVSKY, Phyllis, 1926- ,
American; juvenile COM CON
FUL WA
KRASINSKI, Zygmunt, 1812-59,
Polish; poetry, plays, fiction
HAR KE SA ST
'KRASKO, Ivan' see BOTTO, Ján
KRASLOW, David, 1926- , Amer-
ican; nonfiction CON
KRASNER, Leonard, 1924- ,
American; nonfiction CON
KRASNER, William, 1917- ,
American; nonfiction CON
KRASNEY, Samuel A. ('Sam
Curzon'), 1922- , American;
fiction CON
KRASNOHORSKA, Elíska Pechová,
1847-1926, Czech; poetry HAR
ST

KRASNOV, Peter Nikalayevich (Krass-
noff), 1869-1947, Russian; fiction
HAR KT SA
KRASNOV, Peter Nikolayevich, 1882- ,
Russian; fiction ST
KRASSNER, Paul, 1932- , American;
nonfiction CON
KRASTEV, Krastyu, 1866-1919,
Bulgarian; criticism ST
KRASZEWSKI, Jozef Ignacy ('K. F.
Pasternak'; 'B. Boleslawita'),
1812-87, Polish; fiction HAR
KE SA ST
KRATOCHVIL, Paul, 1932- , Czech-
English; nonfiction CON
KRATOVIL, Robert, 1910- , Ameri-
can; nonfiction CON
KRATZENSTEIN, Jossef Jr., 1904- ,
American; nonfiction CON
KRAUCH, Velma, 1916- , American;
fiction CON
KRAUS, George, 1930- , American;
nonfiction CON
KRAUS, Hans Peter, 1907- , Austrian-
American; nonfiction CON
KRAUS, Karl, 1874-1936, German;
essays, plays AL COL FLE KU
KUN MAT SA ST
KRAUS, Michael, 1901- , American;
nonfiction CON
KRAUS, Richard Gordon, 1923- ,
American; nonfiction CON
KRAUS, Robert, 1925- , American;
juveniles CON WA
KRAUS, Sidney, 1927- , American;
nonfiction CON
KRAUS, W. Keith, 1934- , Ameri-
can; nonfiction CON
KRAUSE, Hanns, 1916- , German;
nonfiction AL
KRAUSE, Harry Dieter, 1932- ,
German-American; nonfiction
CON
KRAUSE, Herbert, 1905- , Ameri-
can; fiction WAF
KRAUSE, Karl Christian Friedrich,
1781-1832, German; nonfiction
SA
KRAUSE, Sydney Joseph, 1925- ,
American; nonfiction CON
KRAUSE, Walter, 1917- , Ameri-
can; nonfiction CON
KRAUSHAAR, Otto Frederich, 1901- ,
American; nonfiction CON
KRAUSS, Paul Gerhardt, 1905- ,
American; nonfiction CON
KRAUSS, Robert G., 1924- , Amer-
ican; nonfiction CON

KRAUSS, Robert M., 1931- ,
American; nonfiction CON
KRAUSS, Ruth, 1901- , American;
juveniles, poetry COM CON
FUL WA
KRAUSS, Werner, 1900- , Ger-
man; nonfiction KU
KRAUTTER, Elisa see BIALK,
Elisa
KRAVCHINSKI, Sergey Mikhaylo-
vich ('S. Stepnyak'), 1851-95,
Russian; fiction HAR HARK
ST
KRAVETZ, Nathan, 1921- ,
American; juveniles CON
KRAVIS, Irving Bernard, 1916- ,
American; nonfiction CON
KRAWIEC, Theophile Stanley,
1913- , American; nonfiction
CON
KRAWITZ, Ruth Lifshitz, 1929- ,
American; nonfiction CON
KRAYNI, Anton see HIPPIUS,
Zinaida N.
KRAZE, Hanna Heide, 1920- ,
German; poetry AL
KRCMERY, Stefan, 1892- ,
Slovak; poetry ST
KREBS, Alfred H., 1920- ,
American; nonfiction CON
KREBS, Nikolas see CUSA,
Nicolás de
KREBS, Richard Julius Herman
see 'VALTIN, Jean'
KREDEL, Fritz, 1900- , Ger-
man-American; juveniles FUL
KREDENSER, Gail, 1936- ,
American; juveniles CON
KREFETZ, Gerald, 1932- ,
American; nonfiction CON
KREIDER, Carl, 1914- , Ameri-
can; nonfiction CON
KREIG, Margaret B. Baltzell
('Peggy Craig'), 1922- ,
American; nonfiction CON
KREIMBORG, Alfred, 1883- ,
American; poetry, plays SA
KREINDLER, Lee Stanley, 1924- ,
American; nonfiction CON
KREININ, Mordechai, 1930- ,
American; nonfiction CON
KREISEL, Henry, 1922- ,
Canadian; fiction SY
KREISMAN, Leonard Theodore,
1925- , American; nonfiction
CON
KREJCI see TAYLOR, Jerome
KRELL, Max, 1887- , German;

nonfiction KU
KREML, Anne Lee, 1930- , American; nonfiction CON
KREMPEL, Daniel Spartacus, 1926- , American; nonfiction CON
KRENKEL, John Henry, 1906- , American; nonfiction CON
KRENTEL, Mildred White ('Mrs. Miggy'), 1921- , American; nonfiction CON
KRENTS, Harold Eliot, 1943- , American; fiction CON
KRENTZ, Edgar Martin, 1928- , American; nonfiction CON
KREPPS, Robert Wilson, 1919- , American; fiction CON
KRESH, Paul, 1919- , American; nonfiction CON
KRESS, Paul Frederich, 1935- , American; nonfiction CON
KRESTOVSKY, Vsevolod Vladimerovich, 1840-95, Russian; fiction HAR HARK ST
KRETZER, Max, 1854-1941, German; nonfiction AL COL HAR SA
KRETZMANN, Adalbert Raphael, 1903- , American; nonfiction CON
KREUDER, Ernst, 1903- , German; nonfiction AL KU LEN
KREUTER, Kent, 1932- , American; nonfiction CON
KREUTZWALD, Friedrich Reinhold, 1803-82, Estonian; poetry ST
KREUZER, James R., 1913- , American; nonfiction CON
KREVE-MICKIEVICIUS, Vincas, 1882- , Lithuanian; poetry, plays, fiction ST
KREVITSKY, Nathan I., 1914- , American; nonfiction CON
KREY, Laura Lettie Smith, 1890- , American; fiction KT
KREYCHE, Gerald F., 1927- , American; nonfiction CON
KREYCHE, Robert J., 1920- , American; nonfiction CON
KREYMBORG, Alfred, 1883-1966, American; poetry, plays KL KT
KREZ, Konrad, 1828-52, German-American; poetry ST
KRIEGEL, Leonard, 1933- , American; nonfiction CON
KRIEGER, Arnold, 1904- , German; nonfiction LEN
KRIEGER, Leonard, 1918- , American; nonfiction CON

KRIEGER, Murray, 1923- , American; nonfiction CON
KRIEGHBAUM, Hillier Hiram, 1902- , American; nonfiction CON
KRIEGMAN, Oscar Marvin, 1930- , American; nonfiction CON
KRIESBERG, Louis, 1926- , American; nonfiction CON
KRIGE, Uys, 1910- , South African; poetry, plays, essays, translations RIC ST
KRILLE, Otto, 1878-1954, German; nonfiction AL
KRIM, Seymour M., 1922- , American; fiction, essay CON
KRIMERMAN, Leonard Isaiah, 1934- , American; nonfiction CON
KRINSKY, Carol Herselle, 1937- , American; nonfiction CON
KRIPKE, Dorothy Karp, American; juveniles CON
KRISLOV, Samuel, 1929- , American; nonfiction CON
KRISPYN, Egbert, 1930- , Dutch-American; nonfiction CON
KRISTEIN, Marvin Michael, 1926- , American; nonfiction CON
KRISTELLER, Paul Oskar, 1905- , German-American; nonfiction CON
KRISTENSEN, Tom, 1893- , Danish; poetry, fiction, criticism FLE ST
KRISTOF, Jane, 1932- , American; juveniles CON
KRISTOFFERSEN, Eva M., 1901- , Danish-American; juveniles WA
KRISTOL, Irving, 1920- , American; nonfiction CON
KRITTIVASA, fl. 1370- , Indian; poetry ST
KRITZECK, James, 1930- , American; nonfiction CON
KRIVORUZ'KA see KARIV, Abraham
KRIZHANICH, Yury, 17th cent., Croatian; nonfiction ST
KRLEZA, Miroslav, 1893- , Croatian; poetry, fiction, plays COL FLE MAT RIC SA ST
KROCHMAL, Abraham, 1817/23-95, Jewish; criticism ST
KROCHLMAL, Nahman ('Renaq'),

1785-1840, Jewish; nonfiction
ST
KROCK, Arthur, 1887-1974, American;
nonfiction CON
KROEBER, Theodora Kracaw,
1897- , American; juveniles
CON COM
KROEGER, Arthur, 1908- ,
American; nonfiction CON
KROEGER, Frederick Paul, 1921- ,
American; nonfiction CON
KROEGER, Paul, 1907- , American;
poetry MAR
KROETSCH, Robert, 1927- , Canadian;
fiction, poetry CON
KRÖGER, Theodor, 1897- , German;
nonfiction LEN
KROG, Helge, 1889-1962, Norwegian;
plays HAR MAT RIC ST
KROGER, William S., 1906- , Amer-
ican; nonfiction CON
KORHN, Ernst Christopher, 1888- ,
American; nonfiction CON
KROKANN, Inge, 1893- , Norwegian;
fiction, poetry ST
'KROLL, Burt' see ROWLAND,
Donald S.
KROLL, Francis Lynde, 1904- ,
American; juveniles CON
KROLL, Harry Harrison, 1888- ,
American; fiction KTS WAF
KROLOW, Karl Gustav Heinrich,
1915- , German; poetry, essays
AL FLE HAR KU KUN LEN
KROMER, Marcin, 1512-89, Polish;
nonfiction ST
KORNEGGER, Maria Elisabeth,
1932- , Austrian-American;
nonfiction CON
KRONENBERG, Henry Harold,
1902- , American; nonfiction
CON
KRONENBERGER, Louis, 1904- ,
American; criticism, fiction CON
KTS
KRONER, Richard, 1884- , German-
American; nonfiction CON
KRONHAUSEN, Eberhard Wilhelm,
1915- , German-American; nonfic-
tion CON
KRONHAUSEN, Phyllis Carmen,
1929- , American; nonfiction
CON
KRONICK, David A., 1917- , Ameri-
can; nonfiction CON
KRONINGER, Robert Henry, 1923- ,
American; nonfiction CON
KROOK, Enoch, 18th cent., Dutch;

poetry, plays ST
KROOSS, Herman E., 1912- ,
American; nonfiction CON
KROPINSKI, Ludwik, 1767-1844,
Polish; fiction, plays HAR
ST
KROPOTKIN, Peter Alexeyevich,
1842-1921, Russian; nonfic-
tion COL HARK KE SA ST
KROPP, Lloyd, American; fiction
CON
KROSNEY, Mary Stewart, 1939- ,
American; nonfiction CON
KRSNA DAS, fl. 1581, Indian;
nonfiction LAN
KRSNAMURTTI, R. ('Kalki'),
1899-1954, Indian; fiction
LAN
KRTTIBAS OJHA, 15th cent.,
Indian; poetry LAN
KRUCHONYKH, Alexey Yeleseye-
vich, 1886- , Russian; poetry
HARK ST
KRUCZKOWSKI, Leon, 1900- ,
Polish; fiction, plays COL
MAT ST
KRUDY, Gyula, 1878-1933, Hun-
garian; nonfiction ST
KRÜDENER, Valeria Barbara Julia
de Wietinghoff, 1766-1824,
German; nonfiction SA
KRUEGER, Anne O., 1934- ,
American; nonfiction CON
KRÜGER, Bartholomäus, fl. 1580-
87, German; plays ST
KRUEGER, Christoph (Kruger),
1937- , German; nonfiction
CON
KRÜGER, Ferdinand, 1843-1915,
German; fiction ST
KRUEGER, John Richard, 1927- ,
American; nonfiction CON
KRÜGER, Thomas A., 1936- ,
American; nonfiction CON
KRÜSS, James, German; juveniles
WA
KRUG, Edward August, 1911- ,
American; nonfiction CON
KRUG, Wilhelm Trangott, 1770-
1842, German; nonfiction
SA
KRUGER, Arthur Newman,
1916- , American; nonfiction
CON
KRUGER, Charles Rayne, South
African; fiction CON
KRUGER, Christoph see KRUEGER,
Christoph

KRUGER, Daniel H., 1922- , American; nonfiction CON
'KRUGER, Paul' see SEBENTHALL, Roberta E.
KRUL, Jan H., 1602-46, Dutch; poetry ST
KRULIK, Stephen, 1933- , American; nonfiction CON
'KRULL, Felix' see WHITE, James D.
KRUM, Charlotte, 1886- , American; juveniles WA
KRUMGOLD, Joseph, 1908- , American; juveniles COM CON FUL WA
KRUPP, Nate, 1935- , American; nonfiction CON
KRUPP, Sherman Roy, 1926- , American; nonfiction CON
KRUSCH, Werner E., 1927- , German-Canadian; juveniles CON WA
KRUSENSTJERNA, Agnes von, 1894-1940, Swedish; fiction COL FLE SA ST
KRUSH, Beth, American; juveniles FUL
KRUSH, Joe, American; juveniles FUL
KRUSKAL, William Henry, 1919- , American; nonfiction CON
KRUTCH, Joseph Wood, 1893-1970, American; criticism BRO CON KL KT
KRUTILLA, John Vasil, 1922- , American; nonfiction CON
'KRUTZCH, Gus' see ELIOT, Thomas S.
KRUZAS, Anthony Thomas, 1914- , American; nonfiction CON
KRYLOV, Ivan Andreyevich, 1768/69-1844, Russian; fiction HAR HARK KE SA ST
KRYMOV, Vladimir Pimenovich, 1878- , Russian; fiction RIC
'KRYMOV, Yuri' see BEKLEMISHEV, Yuri S.
KRYTHE, Maymie Richardson, American; nonfiction CON
KRZESINSKI, Andrew John, 1884- , Polish; nonfiction HOE
KRZYCKI, Andrzej see CRICIUS
KRZYZANIAK, Marian, 1911- , American; nonfiction CON
KRZYZANOWSKI, Jerzy Roman, 1922- , Polish-American; nonfiction CON
KSHEMENDRA, fl. 1037, Indian;

fiction ST
KU YEN-WU, 1613-82, Chinese; nonfiction ST
KUAN, Han-Ch'ing, 1241?-1322?, Chinese; plays LAN ST
KUAN-TZU, 7th cent., Chinese; nonfiction ST
'KUBA' (Kurt Barthel), 1914- , German; poetry AL
KUBALA, Ludwik, 1839-1918, Polish; nonfiction ST
'KUBASCH, Maria' (Marja Kubasec), 1890- , German; nonfiction AL
KUBECK, James Ernest, 1920- , American; fiction CON
KUBIAK, William J., 1929- , American; nonfiction CON
KUBICEK, Robert Vincent, 1935- , Canadian; nonfiction CON
KUBIE, Nora Gottheil Benjamin, 1899- , American; juveniles CON WA
KUBIN, Alfred, 1877-1959, Austrian; fiction, essays FLE KU
KUBIS, Pat ('Casey Scott'), 1928- , American; fiction CON
KUBLER, George Alexander, 1912- , American; nonfiction CON
KUBLIN, Hyman, 1919- , American; nonfiction CON
KUBLY, Herbert Oswald Nicholas, 1915- , American; fiction, plays, nonfiction CON
KUBOTA, Akira, 1932- , American; nonfiction CON
KUBOTA, Mantaro, 1899, Japanese; plays, fiction ST
KUBSCH, Hermann Werner, 1911- , German; plays AL
KUBY, Erich, 1910- , German; nonfiction AL
KUCERA, Henry, 1925- , American; nonfiction CON
KUCKHOFF, Adam, 1887-1943, German; nonfiction AL
KUDLICH, Hans, 1823-1917, German-American; nonfiction ST
KUDRUN see GUDRUN
KUDZOLKO, M. see 'CHAROT, Mikhas'
KÜCHELBECKER, Wilhelm Karlovich, 1797-1846, German-Russian; nonfiction HAR

HARK ST
'KÜFER, Bruno' see SCHEERBART,
Paul
KÜGELGEN, Wilhelm, von, 1802-67,
German; nonfiction AL
KUEHL, John, 1928- , American;
nonfiction CON
KUEHL, Warren Frederich, 1924- ,
American; nonfiction CON
KÜHN, Christoffel Hermanus see
MIKRO
KUEHN, Dorothy Dalton, 1915- ,
American; poetry CON
KUEHNELT-LEDDIHN, Erik
('Francis Stuart Campbell';
'Chester F. O'Leary'; 'Tomislav
Vitezovic'), 1909- , Austrian-
American; nonfiction CON HOE
KUEI-KU-TZU, 4th cent., Chinese;
nonfiction ST
KUEI YU-KUANG, 1506-71, Chinese;
nonfiction ST
KÜKELHAUS, Heinz, 1902- , Ger-
man; nonfiction LEN
KÜLLER, Johannes see AMMERS-
KÜLLER, Johanna Von
KÜLPE, Oswald, 1852-1915, German;
nonfiction SA
KUENNE, Robert Eugene, 1924- ,
American; nonfiction CON
KUENZLI, Alfred Eugene, 1923- ,
American; nonfiction CON
KÜRENBERG, Joachim, 1892- ,
German; nonfiction LEN
KÜRENBERGER, fl. 1150-70, Ger-
man; poetry AL ST
KÜRNBERGER, Ferdinand, 1821-79,
German; nonfiction AL
KUERSTEINER, Alberto Federico,
1865-1917, American; nonfiction
BL
KUFELDT, George, 1923- , Ameri-
can; nonfiction CON
KUFNER, Herbert Leopold, 1927- ,
German-American; nonfiction
CON
KUGEL, James, 1945- , American;
nonfiction CON
KUGELMASS, Joseph Alvin, 1910-72,
American; juveniles CON WA
KUGLER, Franz Theodor, 1808-58,
German; poetry HAR ST
KUH, Edwin, 1925- , American;
nonfiction CON
KUH, Katharine W., 1904- , Amer-
ican; nonfiction CON
KUH, Richard H., 1921- , Ameri-
can; nonfiction CON
KUHAR, Lovro see 'VORANC,

Prezihov'
KUHLMAN, John Melville, 1923- ,
American; nonfiction CON
KUHLMANN, Quirinus, 1651-89,
German; poetry AL KE ST
KUHN, Alfred, 1914- , American;
nonfiction CON
KUHN, Ferdinand, 1905- , Amer-
ican; nonfiction CON
KUHN, Irene Corbally, American;
nonfiction CON
KUHN, Martin A., 1924- ,
German-American; nonfiction
CON
KUHN, Rene Leilani, 1923- ,
American; fiction WAF
KUHN, Thomas Samuel, 1922- ,
American; nonfiction CON
KUHN, Tillo E., 1919- , Ameri-
can; nonfiction CON
KUHN, William Ernst, 1922- ,
Swiss-American; nonfiction
CON
KUHN, Wolfgang Erasmus, 1914- ,
German; nonfiction CON
KUHNER, Herbert, 1935- ,
Austrian-American; fiction,
plays CON
KUHNS, Grant Wilson, 1929- ,
American; nonfiction CON
KUHNS, Richard Francis, Jr.,
1924- , American; nonfiction
CON
KUHNS, William, 1943- , Ameri-
can; nonfiction CON
KUIC, Vukan, 1923- , Yugoslav-
American; nonfiction CON
KUIPER, Gerard Peter, 1905- ,
American; nonfiction CON
KUISEL, Richard Francis, 1935- ,
American; nonfiction CON
KUITERT, Harminus Martinus,
1924- , Dutch; nonfiction
CON
KUJAWA, Duane, 1938- , Ameri-
can; nonfiction CON
KUJOTH, Jean Spealman, 1935- ,
American; nonfiction CON
KUKAI see KOBO DAISHI
KUKOLNIK, Nestor Vasilyevich,
1809-68, Russian; plays HARK
ST
'KUKUCIN, Marten' (Matej Benodr),
1860-1928, Slovak; fiction
FLE ST
KUKUZOYA, Chiyo see 'KAGA NO
CHIYO'
KULENOVIC, Skender, 1910- ,
Croatian; poetry ST

KULISH, Mykola, 1892- , Ukranian;
fiction HARK
KULISH, Panko, 1819-97, Ukranian;
fiction HARK
KULKA, Georg Christoph, 1897- ,
German; nonfiction KU
KULKARNI, Ramchandra Ganesh,
1931- , American; nonfiction
CON
KULMANN, Elisabeth, 1808-25, German; poetry SA ST
KULSKI, Julian Eugene, 1929- ,
Polish-American; nonfiction CON
KULSKI, Wladslaw Wszebor ('W. W.
Coole'; 'W. M. Knight-Patterson';
'Politicus'), 1903- , American;
nonfiction CON
KULSTEIN, David J., 1916- , American; nonfiction CON
KULUKUNDIS, Elias, 1937- , English;
nonfiction CON
'KUMALO, Peter' see CLARKE, Peter
KUMAR, Shiv Kulmar, 1921- , Indian;
nonfiction CON
KUMARADASA, fl. 450, Indian;
poetry ST
KUMARAVYAS, 15th cent., Indian;
poetry LAN
KUMAZAWA BANZAN, 1619-91,
Japanese; nonfiction ST
KUME, Masao, 1891-1952, Japanese;
nonfiction ST
KUMICIC, Eveenij, 1850-1904,
Croatian; fiction, plays ST
KUMIN, Maxine Winokur, 1925- ,
American; juveniles, poetry
CON WA
KUMMEL, Bernhard, 1919- , American; nonfiction CON
KUMMER, Frederic Arnold ('Arnold
Fredericks'), 1873-1943, American; juveniles, plays WA
KUNCEWICZOWA, Marja Szczepánska,
1897- , Polish; fiction COL
CON HAR ST
KUNCZ, Aladár, 1886-1931, Hungarian;
fiction HAR ST
KUN-DGA Bzang-po, 1832-1444,
Tibetan; nonfiction LAN
KUN-DGA Rgval Mtshan, 1182-1251,
Tibetan; nonfiction LAN
KUN-DGA Snying-po, 1092-1158,
Tibetan; nonfiction LAN
KUNEN, James Simon ('Simon James'),
1948- , American; nonfiction
CON
KUNENE, Mazisi, 1930- , South
African; poetry MUR

KUNERT, Günter, 1929- , German; poetry AL KU
KUNEV, Trifon, 1880-1951,
Bulgarian; poetry HAR ST
K'UNG An-Kuo, 130-90 B. C.,
Chinese; nonfiction ST
K'UNG CHI, -420 B. C., Chinese;
nonfiction ST
K'UNG CH'iu see CONFUCIUS
K'UNG, Shang-Jen, 1648-1718,
Chinese; plays ST
KUNG, Shien Woo, 1905- ,
Chinese-American; nonfiction
CON
K'UNG, Ying-Ta, 574-648, Chinese;
nonfiction ST
KUNIKIDA, Doppo, 1871-1908,
Japanese; fiction, essays,
poetry ST
KUNITOMO see HIRAGA, Gennai
KUNITZ, Stanley Jasspon, 1905- ,
American; poetry MUR SP
KUNNES, Richard, 1941- , American; nonfiction CON
KUNREUTHER, Howard, 1938- ,
American; nonfiction CON
KUNST, Hermann see SMITH,
Walter C.
KUNSTLER, William M., 1919- ,
American; nonfiction CON
KUNTZ, John Kenneth, 1934- ,
American; nonfiction CON
KUNTZ, Kenneth A., 1916- ,
American; nonfiction CON
KUNTZ, Paul G., 1915- , American; nonfiction CON
KUNZ, Phillip Ray, 1936- ,
American; nonfiction CON
KUNZ, Virginia Brainard, 1921- ,
American; nonfiction CON
KUNZE, Reiner, 1933- , German;
poetry AL
KUO HSIANG, -312, Chinese;
nonfiction ST
KUO Mo-Jo, 1893- , Chinese;
poetry, essays, plays LAN
ST
KUO, Ping-Chia, 1908- , Chinese-
American; nonfiction CON
KUP, Alexander Peter, 1924- ,
English; nonfiction CON
'KUPALA, Yanka' (I. Lutsevich),
1882-1942, Russian; fiction
HARK SA
KUPER, Hilda, Beemer, 1911- ,
American; nonfiction CON
KUPER, Jack, 1932- , Polish-
Canadian; nonfiction CON

KUPER, Leo, 1908-　, South African-
American; nonfiction CON
KUPFERBERG, Herbert, 1918-　,
American; nonfiction CON
KUPFERBERG, Naphtali (Tuli), 1923-　,
American; nonfiction CON
KUPPERMAN, Joel J., 1936-　,
American; nonfiction CON
KUPRIN, Aleksandr Ivanovich, 1870-
1938, Russian; fiction COL
FLE HAR HARK KAT KT RIC
SA ST
KUPSCH, Joachim, 1926-　, German;
nonfiction AL
KURCHASHI KIWAME see 'KOIKAWA
HARUMACHI'
KURATA, Hyakuzo, 1891-1943, Japa-
nese; plays, essays ST
KURATH, Gertrude Prokosch, 1903-　,
American; nonfiction CON
KURATH, Hans, 1891-　, Austrian-
American; nonfiction CON
KURATOMI, Chizuko, 1939-　,
Japanese; juveniles CON
KURBSKI, Prince Andrey, 1528-83,
Russian; nonfiction HARK ST
KURELLA, Alfred ('B. Ziegler';
'Viktor Röbig'; 'A. Bernard'),
1895-　, German; fiction AL
KURIEN, Christopher, Thomas,
1931-　, Indian; nonfiction CON
KURIHARA, Kenneth Kinkichi, 1910-
72, Japanese-American; nonfiction
CON
KURKUL, Edward, 1916-　, American;
juveniles CON
KURLAND, Philip B., 1921-　, Amer-
ican; nonfiction CON
KUROCHKIN, Vasili Stepanovich, 1831-
75, Russian; poetry HARK ST
KURONUSHI see OTOMO NO KURONUSHI
'KUROWSKI, Eugeniusz' see DOBRA-
CZYNSKI, Jan
KURSH, Charlotte Olmsted, 1912-　,
American; nonfiction CON
KURSH, Harry, 1919-　, American;
nonfiction CON
KURTEN, Bjorn Olof, 1924-　, Fin-
nish; nonfiction CON
KURTIS, Arlene Harris, 1927-　,
American; nonfiction CON
KURTZ, Harold, 1913-　, American;
nonfiction CON
KURTZ, Katherine, 1944-　, Ameri-
can; nonfiction CON
KURTZ, Kenneth Hassett, 1928-　,
American; nonfiction CON
KURTZ, Paul, 1925-　, American;

nonfiction CON
KURTZ, Stephen G., 1926-　,
American; nonfiction CON
KURTZMAN, Joel, 1947-　, Amer-
ican; fiction CON
'KURZ, Artur R.' see SCORTIA,
Thomas N.
KURZ, Carmen, 1920-　, Spanish;
fiction SA
KURZ, Hermann, 1813-73, Ger-
man; nonfiction AL HAR ST
KURZ, Isolde, 1853-1944, Ger-
man; poetry, fiction AL COL
FLE KU LEN SA
KURZ, Mordecai, 1934-　, Israeli;
nonfiction CON
KURZ, Paul Konrad, 1927-　,
German; nonfiction CON
KURZMAN, Paul Alfred, 1938-　,
American; nonfiction CON
KURZWEG, Bernhard F., 1926-　,
American; nonfiction CON
KURZWEIL, Zvi Erich, 1911-　,
Czech; nonfiction CON
KUSAN, Ivan, 1933-　, Yugoslav,
juveniles CON WA
KUSCHE, Lothar ('Felix Mantel'),
1929-　, German; nonfiction
AL
KUSENBERG, Kurt ('Hans Ohl und
Simplex'), 1904-　, German;
fiction AL KU LEN
KUSHCHEVSKI, Ivan Afanasievich,
1847-76, Russian; fiction
HARK ST
KUSHEL, Gerald, 1930-　, Amer-
ican; nonfiction CON
KUSIN, Vladimir Victor, 1929-　,
Czech-English; nonfiction CON
KUSKIN, Karla Seidman, 1932-　,
American; juveniles COM
CON WA
KUTASH, Samuel Benjamin, 1912-　,
American; nonfiction CON
KUTLER, Stanley I., 1934-　,
American; nonfiction CON
KUTNER, Nanette, 1906?-62,
American; nonfiction CON
KUTZ, LeRoy M., 1922-　, Amer-
ican; nonfiction CON
KUTZLEB, Hjalmar see KOLBEN-
HEYER, Erwin G.
KUYKENDALL, Ralph Simpson,
1885-1963, American; nonfiction
CON
KUZMA, Greg, 1944-　, American;
poetry CON
KUZMANY, Karol, 1806-66, Slovak;

poetry, fiction ST
KUZMIN, Mikhail Alekseyevich,
1875-1936, Russian; fiction,
poetry FLE HARK ST
KVALE, Velma Ruth, 1898- , Amer-
ican; juveniles CON
KVAPIL, Jaroslav, 1868- , Czech;
poetry, plays SA ST
KVARAN, Einar Hjörleifsson, 1859-
1938, Icelandic; fiction, plays,
poetry COL SA ST
KVITKA-OSNOVYANEKO, Grigory,
1779-1843, Ukrania; fiction ST
KVITKO, Leib, 1893- , Russian;
poetry ST
KWAN, Kian Moon, 1929- , Chinese-
American; nonfiction CON
KWANT, Remy C. , 1918- , Dutch;
nonfiction CON
KWEDER, Adele, 1910- , American;
nonfiction CON
KWEDER, David James, 1905- ,
American; nonfiction CON
KWOLEK, Constance see PORCARI,
Constance K.
KYBERG, Henry E. Jr., 1928- ,
American; nonfiction CON
'KYD, Thomas' see HARBAGE,
Alfred B.
KYD, Thomas (Kid), 1557/58-94/95,
English; plays BRO KB MAG
SP ST
KYELLAND, Alexander L. see
KIELLAND, Alexander L.
KYFFIN, Maurice,   -1599, Welsh;
poetry, translations ST
KYGER, Joanne, 1934- , American;
poetry MUR
KYLE, Anne D., 1896- , American;
juveniles KJU
'KYLE, Elisabeth' see DUNLOP,
Agnes M.R.
KYNASTON, Sir Francis (Kinaston),
1587-1642, English; poetry KB
ST
KYNE, Peter Bernard, 1880- ,
American; fiction KT SA
KYOKUTEI BAKIN see BAKIN,
Kyokutei
'KYORAI' (Mukai Kanetoki), 1651-1704,
Japanese; poetry ST
KYPRIANOS, Iossif see SAMARAKIS,
Antonis
KYRE, Joan Randolph, 1935- , Amer-
ican; nonfiction CON
KYRE, Martin Theodore, Jr., 1928- ,
American; nonfiction CON
KYTLE, Raymond, 1941- , American;

nonfiction CON
KYUSO see 'MURO KYUSO'

Jul 39.8